US GOVERNMENT

UNITED STATES CODE

With official Annotations

2018-2019

TITLE 11 BANKRUPTCY

Revised November 12, 2018

NAK PUBLISHING

TITLE 11—BANKRUPTCY

Table of Contents

CHAPTER 1—GENERAL PROVISIONS *20*
CHAPTER 3—CASE ADMINISTRATION *36*
    SUBCHAPTER I—COMMENCEMENT OF A CASE 37
    SUBCHAPTER II—OFFICERS 40
    SUBCHAPTER III—ADMINISTRATION 44
    SUBCHAPTER IV—ADMINISTRATIVE POWERS 48
CHAPTER 5—CREDITORS, THE DEBTOR, AND THE ESTATE *60*
    SUBCHAPTER I—CREDITORS AND CLAIMS 61
    SUBCHAPTER II—DEBTOR'S DUTIES AND BENEFITS 72
    SUBCHAPTER III—THE ESTATE 86
CHAPTER 7—LIQUIDATION *98*
    SUBCHAPTER I—OFFICERS AND ADMINISTRATION 99
    SUBCHAPTER II—COLLECTION, LIQUIDATION, AND DISTRIBUTION OF THE ESTATE 103
    SUBCHAPTER III—STOCKBROKER LIQUIDATION 107
    SUBCHAPTER IV—COMMODITY BROKER LIQUIDATION 110
    SUBCHAPTER V—CLEARING BANK LIQUIDATION 114
CHAPTER 9—ADJUSTMENT OF DEBTS OF A MUNICIPALITY *114*
    SUBCHAPTER I—GENERAL PROVISIONS 115
    SUBCHAPTER II—ADMINISTRATION 116
    SUBCHAPTER III—THE PLAN 118
CHAPTER 11—REORGANIZATION *119*
    SUBCHAPTER I—OFFICERS AND ADMINISTRATION 121
    SUBCHAPTER II—THE PLAN 128
    SUBCHAPTER III—POSTCONFIRMATION MATTERS 136

SUBCHAPTER IV—RAILROAD REORGANIZATION..139

CHAPTER 12—ADJUSTMENT OF DEBTS OF A FAMILY FARMER OR FISHERMAN WITH REGULAR ANNUAL INCOME 142

SUBCHAPTER I—OFFICERS, ADMINISTRATION, AND THE ESTATE..143

SUBCHAPTER II—THE PLAN..145

CHAPTER 13—ADJUSTMENT OF DEBTS OF AN INDIVIDUAL WITH REGULAR INCOME..149

SUBCHAPTER I—OFFICERS, ADMINISTRATION, AND THE ESTATE..149

SUBCHAPTER II—THE PLAN..152

CHAPTER 13 contemplates the filing of a plan only by the debtor.............................152

CHAPTER 15—ANCILLARY AND OTHER CROSS-BORDER CASES..............................156

SUBCHAPTER I—GENERAL PROVISIONS...157

SUBCHAPTER II—ACCESS OF FOREIGN REPRESENTATIVES AND CREDITORS TO THE COURT..............157

SUBCHAPTER III—RECOGNITION OF A FOREIGN PROCEEDING AND RELIEF....................................158

SUBCHAPTER IV—COOPERATION WITH FOREIGN COURTS AND FOREIGN REPRESENTATIVES..........159

SUBCHAPTER V—CONCURRENT PROCEEDINGS 159

This title was enacted by Pub. L. 95–598, title I, §101, Nov. 6, 1978, 92 Stat. 2549
Chap.
Sec.
1.
General Provisions
101
3.
Case Administration
301
5.
Creditors, the Debtor, and the Estate
501
7.
Liquidation
701
9.
Adjustment of Debts of a Municipality
901
11.
Reorganization
1101
12.
Adjustments of Debts of a Family Farmer or Family Fisherman with Regular Annual Income [1]
1201

13.
Adjustment of Debts of an Individual With Regular Income
1301
15.
Ancillary and Other Cross-Border Cases
1501

Amendments

2005—Pub. L. 109–8, title VIII, §801(b), title X, §1007(d), Apr. 20, 2005, 119 Stat. 145, 188, substituted "Adjustments of Debts of a Family Farmer or Family Fisherman with Regular Annual Income" for "Adjustment of Debts of Family Farmers with Regular Annual Income" in item for chapter 12 and added item for chapter 15.

1994—Pub. L. 103–394, title V, §501(d)(39), Oct. 22, 1994, 108 Stat. 4147, struck out item for chapter 15, "United States Trustees".

1986—Pub. L. 99–554, title II, §257(a), Oct. 27, 1986, 100 Stat. 3114, added item for chapter 12.

Table I

This Table lists the sections of former Title 11, Bankruptcy, and indicates the sections of Title 11, as revised by Pub. L. 95–598 which cover similar and related subject matter.

Title 11 Former Sections	Title 11 New Sections
1(1)–(3)	Rep.
1(4)	101(12)
1(5)–(7)	Rep.
1(8)	101(8)
1(9), (10)	Rep.
1(11)	101(9)
1(12), (13)	Rep.
1(14)	101(11)
1(15), (16)	Rep.
1(17)	101(17), (18)
1(18)	Rep.
1(19)	101(26)
1(20)–(22)	Rep.
1(23)	101(30)
1(24)	101(31)
1(25), (26)	Rep.
1(27)	101(34)
1(28), (29)	Rep.
1(29a)	101(38)
1(30)	101(40)
1(31)	Rep.
1(32)	101(24)
1(33), (34)	Rep.
1(35)	102(7)
11(a)(1)	109(a)
11(a)(2)	502(j)
11(a)(2A)	505(a), (b)
11(a)(3), (4)	Rep.
11(a)(5)	721
11(a)(6)	Rep.
11(a)(7)	363
11(a)(8)	350
11(a)(9)–(14)	Rep.
11(a)(15)	105
11(a)(16)	Rep.
11(a)(17)	324
11(a)(18)	303(i)
11(a)(19), (20)	Rep.
11(a)(21)	543(b), (c)
11(a)(22)	305(a)(2)
11(b)	Rep.
21	303(h)
22	109(b)
22(a)	301
22(b)	303(a)
23(a)	Rep.
23(b)	303(b)
23(c)–(f)	Rep.
23(g)	723
23(h)–(k)	Rep.
24	522
25(a)(1)	343, 521(4)
25(a)(2)	Rep.
25(a)(3)	521(2)
25(a)(4)	521(3)
25(a)(5)	521(3)
25(a)(6)	521(2)
25(a)(7)	521(2)
25(a)(8), (9)	521(1)
25(a)(10)	343, 344
25(a)(11)	521(3)
25(b)	Rep.
26	541(a)
27, 28	Rep.
29(a)	362

29(b)–(d)	Rep.
29(e)	108(a), (b)
29(f)	108(c)
30, 31	(See former 501–1103)
32(a)	727(a)(10), 1141(d)(4)
32(b)	727(c)
32(c)(1)	727(a)(2), (4)
32(c)(2)	727(a)(3)
32(c)(3)	727(a)(4)
32(c)(4)	727(a)(2)
32(c)(5)	727(a)(8), (9)
32(c)(6)	727(a)(6)
32(c)(7)	727(a)(5)
32(c)(8)	Rep.
32(d), (e)	Rep.
32(f)	524(a)
32(g), (h)	Rep.
33	727(d), (e), 1328(e)
34	524(e)
35(a)(1)	523(a)(1)
35(a)(2)	523(a)(2)
35(a)(3)	523(a)(3)
35(a)(4)	523(a)(4)
35(a)(5), (6)	Rep.
35(a)(7)	523(a)(5)
35(a)(8)	523(a)(6)
35(b)	523(b), 349(a)
35(c)	523(c)
35(c)(4)	362
41(a)	Rep.
41(b)	303(d)
41(c)–(e)	Rep.
41(f)	301
42	T. 28 §1480
43	Rep.
44(a)	343
44(b)–(f)	Rep.
44(g)	549(c)
44(h)–(l)	Rep.
45–51	Rep.
52, 53	Rep.
54	Rep.
55	T. 28 §1475
61–71	Rep.
72(a)	702
72(b)	705
72(c)	327(c)
73	321
74	325, 703(a)
75(a)(1)	704(1)
75(a)(2)	345
75(a)(3)	704(2)
75(a)(4)	Rep.
75(a)(5)	704(2)
75(a)(6)	Rep.
75(a)(7)	704(3)
75(a)(8)	704(4)
75(a)(9)	704(5)
75(a)(10)	704(6)
75(a)(11), (12)	Rep.
75(a)(13)	704(8)
75(a)(14)	Rep.
75(b), (c)	Rep.
76(a), (b)	Rep.
76(c)	326(a), 330
76(d)	Rep.
76(e)	326(d)
76(f), (g)	Rep.
76a	330
77	107
78(a)	Rep.
78(b)	322(a)
78(c)	322(b)(1)
78(d)	322(b)(2)
78(e)	Rep.

78(f), (g)	322(b)(2)
78(h)	Rep.
78(i)	322(c)
78(j)–(l)	Rep.
78(m)	322(d)
78(n)	Rep.
79–82	Rep.
91, 92	341
93(a)–(c)	Rep.
93(d)	502(a), (c)
93(e)	Rep.
93(f)	502(b)
93(g)	502(d)
93(h)	506(a), (b)
93(i)	501(b), 509
93(j)	724(a)
93(k)	502(j)
93(l), (m)	Rep.
93(n)	501(a), 726(a)(3)
93a	Rep.
94	342
95(a)	301
95(b)	303(b)
95(c), (d)	Rep.
95(e)	303(b)
95(f)	303(c)
95(g)	303(j), 707
95(h)	Rep.
96	547
96(a)(4)	547(e)(1)(B)
96(b)	550, 551
96(c)	547(c)(4), 553
96(d)	329
96(e)(1)	741
96(e)(2)	745, 751, 752
96(e)(3)	753
96(e)(5)	749
101	345
101a	Rep.
102(a)(1)	503(b)(2)
102(a)(2)–(4)	Rep.
102(b)	Rep.
102(c)	504
102(d)	Rep.
103	101(4)
103(a)(9)	502(b)(7)
103(c)	365
103a	Rep.
104(a)	507
104(a)(1)	503(b)
104(a)(2)	507(a)(3)
104(a)(4)	502(b)(4), 505(a), (b)
104(b)	Rep.
105(a)–(c)	Rep.
105(d)	508
105(e)	Rep.
106(a)	347(a)
106(b)	Rep.
107(a)	349(b), 547(b), (d), 551
107(b), (c)	545
107(c)(1)(A)	545(1)
107(c)(1)(B)	545(2), 546(b)
107(c)(1)(C)	545(3), (4)
107(c)(2)	551
107(c)(3)	724(b)
107(d)(1)(a)–(c)	Rep.
107(d)(1)(d)	101(26)
107(d)(1)(e)	Rep.
107(d)(2)	548(a)
107(d)(3)	550
107(d)(4)	548(b)
107(d)(5)	548(d)(1)
107(d)(6)	548(c), 550, 551
107(d)(7)	Rep.
107(e), (f)	Rep.

108	502(b)(3), 553
109(a)	303(e)
109(b)	303(i)
109(c)	Rep.
109(d)	303(g), 543(b), (c)
110(a)	541(a)
110(a)(3)	541(b)
110(a)(5)	522(d)(7), (8)
110(b)	365
110(c)	541(e), 544(a)
110(d)(1)	549(a)
110(d)(2), (3)	542(c)
110(d)(4), (5)	Rep.
110(e)	544(b)
110(f)	363
110(g)–(i)	Rep.
111, 112	Rep.
201, 202	(See former 501–1103)
202a–204	Rep.
205(a)	Rep.
205(b)	1171(b), 1172
205(c)(1)	1163
205(c)(2)	1166
205(c)(3)–(5)	Rep.
205(c)(6)	1169
205(c)(7)–(13)	Rep.
205(d)	Rep.
205(e)	1173
205(f)–(i)	Rep.
205(j)	1168
205(k), (*l*)	Rep.
205(m)	101(33)
205(n)	1167, 1171(a)
205(*o*)	1170
205(p)–(s)	Rep.
205a	Rep.
206, 207	(See former 501–1103)
208	Rep.
301–303	Rep.
401(1)	101(4)
401(2)	Rep.
401(3)	101(9)
401(4)	Rep.
401(5)	101(11)
401(6)	101(28)
401(7)	101(30)
401(8)	101(12)
401(9)	Rep.
401(10)	902(2)
401(11)	903(3)
402(a)	Rep.
402(b)(1), (2)	901
402(b)(3)	Rep.
402(c)	904
402(d)	921(b)
403	903
404	101(29), 109(c)
405(a)	921(a), (c)–(f)
405(b)	901, 924
405(c)	Rep.
405(d)	923
405(e)	901
405(e)(1)	922(a)
405(f), (g)	Rep.
405(h)	901, 926
406, 407	Rep.
408(a)	925
408(b)	901
408(c)	Rep.
409	901
410(a)	941, 942
410(b)	942
411, 412	901
413	901, 943(a)
414(a)	901

414(b)(1)	943(b)(5), (6)
414(b)(2)	943(b)(2)
414(b)(3)	Rep.
414(b)(4)	943(b)(3)
414(b)(5)	Rep.
414(b)(6)	943(b)(4)
415(a)	944(a)
415(b)(1)	944(b)
415(b)(2)	944(c)
416(a)	Rep.
416(b)	901
416(c)	Rep.
416(d)	347(b), 901
416(e)	945(a)
416(f)	Rep.
417	946
418	927
501, 502	Rep.
506(1)	101(4)
506(2), (3)	Rep.
506(4)	101(9)
506(5)	101(12)
506(6)	101(11)
506(7)	Rep.
506(8)	101(23)
506(9)	101(31)
506(10)	Rep.
506(11)	101(35)
506(12), (13)	Rep.
507	1124
511, 512	Rep.
513	362
514, 515	Rep.
516(1)	365
516(2)	364
516(3)	363
516(4)	362
516(5), (6)	1110
517–521	Rep.
526	303(b)
527	Rep.
528	T. 28 §1472
529–533	Rep.
536, 537	303(d)
541–549	Rep.
556	1104(a)
557	327
558	101(13)
559	1105
560	324, 1104(c)
561, 562	Rep.
563	1107(a)
564	1106(a)(2)
565	Rep.
566	107
567(1)	1106(a)(3)
567(2)	Rep.
567(3)	1106(a)(4)(A)
567(4)	Rep.
567(5)	1106(a)(4)
567(6)	Rep.
568	1104(b), 1106(b)
569	1106(a)(5)
570	1121
571–574	Rep.
575	1125(d)
576	1125(b)
577, 578	Rep.
579	1126, 1128(a)
580	1128(b)
586	541(a)
587	1106
588	1107(a)
589	1108
590	Rep.

591	327
596	501(a), 1111
597	1122
598	501(a)
599	1126(a)
600, 601	Rep.
602	502(b)(7)
603	1126(e)
604	1143
605	347(b)
606	1109(b)
607	1109
608	1109(a)
609–613	Rep.
616(1)	1123(b)(1)
616(2)	1123(a)(5), (b)(4)
616(3)	Rep.
616(4)	1123(b)(2)
616(5)	1123(a)(3)
616(6)	1123(a)(2)
616(7)–(9)	Rep.
616(10)	1123(a)(5)
616(11)	1123(a)(7)
616(12)(a)	1123(a)(6)
616(12)(b)	Rep.
616(13)	1123(b)(3)
616(14)	1123(b)(5)
621(1)	1129(a)(1)
621(2)	1129(a)(7), (11)
621(3)	1129(a)(3)
621(4)	1129(a)(4)
621(5)	1129(a)(5)
622	1127
623	1127(d)
624(1)	1141(a)
624(2)	1129(a)(6), 1142(a)
624(3), (4)	Rep.
625	Rep.
626	1141(c)
627	1142(b)
628(1)	1141(d)(1)–(3)
628(2)–(4)	Rep.
629(a)	1101(2)
629(b)	Rep.
629(c)	1127(b)
636	1112(b)
637	Rep.
638	348
641(1), (2)	Rep.
641(3), (4)	330
641(5)	503(b)(4)
642(1)	503(b)(3), (5)
642(2)	Rep.
642(3)	503(b)(4)
643	503(b)(3), (4)
644(1)	330
644(2)	503(b)(4)
644(3)	330
644(4)	503(b)(3), (4)
645–650	Rep.
656–659	Rep.
661	108(c)
662	Rep.
663	362
664(a)	1145(a)
664(b)	1145(b)
665, 666	Rep.
667	1146(c)
668	346(j)(1)
669	1129(d)
670	346(j)(5)
671, 672	Rep.
676	Rep.
701, 702	Rep.
706(1), (2)	Rep.

706(3)	101(12), 109(d)
706(4)	Rep.
706(5)	101(31)
707(1)	101(9)
707(2)	101(4), (11)
708	1124
711, 712	Rep.
713(1)	365
713(2)	363
713(3)	Rep.
714	362
715, 716	Rep.
721–728	Rep.
731–733	Rep.
734	341
735	341
735(3)	1128(a)
736	341
736(2)	501(a)
736(3)	343
737(1)	Rep.
737(2)	1129(a)(9)
737(3)	1128(a)
738	1102
739(1)(a)	1103(c)(2)
739(1)(b)–(e)	1103(c)(3)
739(1)(f)	1104(c)(5)
739(2)	503(b)(4), 1103(a)
741	Rep.
742	1107(a)
743	1108
744	364
751	1122
752	Rep.
753	502(b)(7)
754, 755	Rep.
755a	501(a)
756	Rep.
757(1)	Rep.
757(2)	1123(b)(2)
757(3)–(7)	Rep.
757(8)	1123(b)(5)
761	1129(a)(3)
762	Rep.
763	1127
764	1127(d)
765	1127(c)
766(1)	1129(a)(1)
766(2)	1129(a)(7), (11)
766(3)	1129(a)(2)
766(4)	1129(a)(3)
767(1)	1141(a)
767(2)–(4)	Rep.
768–770	Rep.
771	1141(d)(1)–(3)
772	Rep.
776, 777	1112(b)
778	348
779–781	Rep.
786	1144
787(1)	1127(b)
787(2)	1127(c)
787(3)	1127(d)
787(4)	Rep.
791	108(c)
792	Rep.
793(a)	1145(a)
793(b)	1145(b)
794	Rep.
795	346(j)(1)
796	346(j)(5)
797	Rep.
799	Rep.
801, 802	Rep.
806(1)	Rep.

806(2)	101(4)
806(3), (4)	Rep.
806(5)	101(9)
806(6)	101(12), 109(d)
806(7)	101(11)
806(8)	101(23)
806(9)	101(31)
807	1124
811, 812	Rep.
813(1)	365
813(2)	363
813(3)	Rep.
814	362
815, 816	Rep.
821–827	Rep.
828	362
831	Rep.
832	1104(a)
833	Rep.
834	341
835	341, 1128(a)
836	341
836(2)	501(a)
836(3)	343
837(1)	1104(a)
837(2)	Rep.
837(3)	1128(a)
841	Rep.
842	1106
843	348
844	1107(a)
845	1108
846	364
851	501(a), 1111
852	1122
853	Rep.
854	501(a)
855–857	Rep.
858	502(b)(7)
859	Rep.
861(1)–(3)	Rep.
861(4)	1123(b)(2)
861(5), (6)	Rep.
861(7)	1123(b)(4)
861(8)	Rep.
861(9)	1123(a)(3)
861(10)	1123(a)(2)
861(11)	Rep.
861(12)	1123(a)(5)
861(13)	1123(b)(5)
866	Rep.
867	1129(a)(3)
868	Rep.
869	1127(a), (b)
870	1127(d)
871	1127(c)
872(1)	1129(a)(1)
872(2)	1129(a)(7), (11)
872(3)	1129(a)(2)
872(4)	1129(a)(3)
872(5)	1129(a)(4)
873(1)	1141(a)
873(2)	1142(a)
873(3)	Rep.
874	1141(c)
875	1142(b)
876	1141(d)(1)–(3)
877	Rep.
881, 882	1112(b)
883	348
884–886	Rep.
891(1)	Rep.
891(2), (3)	330
892(1)	503(b)(3)
892(2)	Rep.

892(3)	503(b)(4)
893(1)	Rep.
893(2)	503(b)(4)
893(3)	330
893(4)	503(b)(4)
894–898	Rep.
906–909	Rep.
911	1144
916	108(c)
917	362
918(a)	1145(a)
918(b)	1145(b)
919	Rep.
920	346(j)(1)
921	1129(d)
922	346(j)(5)
923	Rep.
926	Rep.
1001, 1002	Rep.
1006(1)	101(4)
1006(2)	101(9)
1006(3)	101(12), 109(e)
1006(4)	101(11)
1006(5)	Rep.
1006(6)	101(31)
1006(7)	Rep.
1006(8)	101(24), 109(e)
1007	Rep.
1011, 1012	Rep.
1013(1)	365
1013(2)	Rep.
1014	362
1015, 1016	Rep.
1021–1026	Rep.
1031	341
1032, 1033	343, 501(a)
1033(1)	1321
1033(2)	1324
1033(5)	1303
1036	Rep.
1037	Rep.
1041–1044	1322(b)(1)
1046(1)	1322(b)(2)
1046(2)	1322(a)(2)
1046(3)	1322(a)(1)
1046(4)	1329(a)
1046(5)	1322(b)(7)
1046(6)	1322(b)(10)
1046(7)	1325(a)(3)
1051	Rep.
1052	1323(a)
1053	1323(c)
1054	Rep.
1055	1325(a)(1)
1056(a)(1)	1325(a)(6)
1056(a)(2)	Rep.
1056(a)(3)	1325(a)(3)
1056(a)(4)	502(b)
1056(b)	1327(a)
1057	Rep.
1058	1326(a)
1059	1328(a), (c), (d)
1060	1328(b)
1061	Rep.
1062	348, 1307
1066	348
1067	Rep.
1068, 1069	1330
1071	108(c)
1076	Rep.
1077–1079	1305(a)(1)
1080	Rep.
1086	Rep.
1101–1103	Rep.
1200–1255	

Table II
This Table lists the sections of revised Title 11, Bankruptcy, and indicates the sections of former Title 11, which covered similar and related subject matter.

Title 11 New Sections	Title 11 Former Sections
101(1)–(3)	
101(4)	103, 401(1), 506(1), 707(2), 806(2), 1006(1)
101(5)–(7)	
101(8)	1(8)
101(9)	1(11), 401(3), 506(4), 707(1), 806(5), 1062(2)
101(10)	
101(11)	1(14), 401(5), 506(6), 707(2), 806(7), 1006(4)
101(12)	1(4), 401(8), 506(5), 706(3), 806(6), 1006(3)
101(13)	558
101(14)–(16)	
101(17), (18)	1(17)
101(19)–(21)	
101(22)	T. 15 §77ccc(7)
101(23)	506(8), 806(8)
101(24)	1(32), 1006(8)
101(25)	
101(26)	1(19), 107(d)(1)(d)
101(27)	
101(28)	401(6)
101(29)	404
101(30)	1(23), 401(7)
101(31)	1(24), 506(9), 706(5), 806(9), 1006(6)
101(32)	
101(33)	205(m)
101(34)	1(27)
101(35)	506(11)
101(36), (37)	
101(38)	1(29a)
101(39)	T. 15 §78c(a)(4), (5)
101(40)	1(30)
102(1)–(6)	
102(7)	1(35)
102(8)	
103, 104	
105	11(a)(15)
106	
107	77, 566
108(a), (b)	29(e)
108(c)	29(f), 661, 791, 1076
109(a)	11(a)(1)
109(b)	22
109(c)	404
109(d)	706(3), 806(6)
109(e)	1006(3), (8)
301	22(a), 41(f), 95(a)
302	
303(a)	22(b)
303(b)	23(b), 95(b), (e), 526
303(c)	95(f)
303(d)	41(b), 536, 537
303(e)	109(a)
303(f)	
303(g)	109(d)
303(h)	21
303(i)	11(a)(18), 19(b)
303(j)	95(g)
303(k)	
304	
305(a)(1)	
305(a)(2)	11(a)(22)
305(b), (c)	
306	
321	73
322(a)	78(b)
322(b)(1)	78(c)
322(b)(2)	78(d), (f), (g)
322(c)	78(i)
322(d)	78(m)

323	11(a)(17), 560
324	74
325	76(c)
326(a)	
326(b), (c)	
326(d)	76(e)
327	557, 591
327(c)	72(c)
328	
329	96(d)
330	76(c), 76a, 641(3), (4), 644(1), (3), 891(2), (3), 893(3)
331	
341	91, 92, 734–736, 834–836, 1032, 1033
342	94
343	44(a), 25(a)(1), (10), 736(3), 836(3), 1033(1)
344	25(a)(10)
345	101, 75(a)(2)
346(a)–(i)	
346(j)(1)	668, 795, 920
346(j)(2)–(4)	
346(j)(5)	670, 796, 922
346(j)(6), (7)	
347(a)	106(a)
347(b)	416(d), 605
348	638, 778, 843, 1066, 1067
349(a)	35(b)
349(b)	107(a)
350	11(a)(8)
361	
362	29(a), 35(c)(4), 513, 516(4), 663, 714, 814, 828, 917, 1014
363	11(a)(7), 110(f), 516(3), 713(2), 813(2)
364	516(2), 744, 846
365	103(c), 110(b), 516(1), 713(1), 813(1), 1013(1)
366	
501(a)	93(n), 596, 598, 736(2), 755a, 836(2), 851, 854, 1033(1)
501(b)	93(i)
501(c), (d)	
502(a)	93(d)
502(b)	93(f), 1056(b)
502(b)(3)	108
502(b)(4)	104(a)(4)
502(b)(7)	103(a)(9), 602, 753, 858
502(c)	93(d)
502(d)	93(g)
502(e)–(i)	
502(j)	93(k), 11(a)(2)
503(a)	
503(b)	104(a)(1)
503(b)(2)	102(a)(1)
503(b)(3)	642(1), 643, 644(4), 892(1)
503(b)(4)	641(5), 642(3), 643, 644(2), (4), 739(2), 892(3), 893(2), (4)
503(b)(5)	642(1)
504	102(c)
505(a), (b)	11(a)(2A), 104(a)(4)
505(c)	
506(a), (b)	93(h)
506(c), (d)	
507	104(a)
507(a)(3)	104(a)(2)
508	105(d)
509	93(i)
510	
521(1)	25(a)(8), (9)
521(2)	25(a)(3), (6), (7)
521(3)	25(a)(4), (5), (11)
521(4)	25(a)(1)
522	24
523(a)(1)	35(a)(1)
523(a)(2)	35(a)(2)
523(a)(3)	35(a)(3)
523(a)(4)	35(a)(4)
523(a)(5)	35(a)(7)

523(a)(6)	35(a)(8)
523(a)(7)–(9)	
523(b)	35(b)
523(c)	35(c)
523(d)	
524(a)	32(f)
524(b)–(d)	
524(e)	34
525	
541(a)	26, 110(a), 586
541(b)	110(a)(3)
541(c), (d)	
541(e)	110(c)
542(a), (b)	
542(c)	110(d)(2), (3)
542(d), (e)	
543(a)	
543(b), (c)	11(a)(21), 109(d)
543(d)	
544(a)	110(c)
544(b)	110(e)
545	107(b), (c)
545(1)	107(c)(1)(A)
545(2)	107(c)(1)(B)
545(3), (4)	107(c)(1)(C)
546(a)	
546(b)	107(c)(1)(B)
546(c)	
547	96
547(b)	107(a)
547(c)(4)	96(c)
547(d)	107(a)
547(e)(1)(B)	96(a)(4)
548(a)	107(d)(2)
548(b)	107(d)(4)
548(c)	107(d)(6)
548(d)(1)	107(d)(5)
548(d)(2)	
549(a)	110(d)(1)
549(b)	
549(c)	44(g)
549(d)	
550	96(b), 107(d)(3), (6)
551	96(b), 107(a)(3), (c)(2), (d)(6), 110(e)(2)
552	
553	96(c), 108
554	
701	
702	72(a)
703(a)	74
703(b), (c)	
704(1)	75(a)(1)
704(2)	75(a)(3), (5)
704(3)	75(a)(7)
704(4)	75(a)(8)
704(5)	75(a)(9)
704(6)	75(a)(10)
704(7)	
704(8)	75(a)(13)
705	72(b)
706	
707	95(g)
721	11(a)(5)
722	
723	23(g)
724(a)	93(j)
724(b)	107(c)(3)
724(c), (d)	
725	
726(a)(1), (2)	
726(a)(3)	93(n)
726(a)(4)–(6), (b), (c)	
727(a)(1)	
727(a)(2)	32(c)(1), (4)
727(a)(3)	32(c)(2)

727(a)(4)	32(c)(1), (3)
727(a)(5)	32(c)(7)
727(a)(6)	32(c)(6)
727(a)(7)	
727(a)(8), (9)	32(c)(5)
727(a)(10)	32(a)
727(b)	
727(c)	32(b)
727(d), (e)	33
728	
741	96(e)(1)
742–744	
745	96(e)(2)
746–748	
749	96(e)(5)
750	
751	96(e)(2)
752	96(e)(2), (3)
761–766	
901	402(b)(1), (2), 405(b), (e), (h), 408(b), 409, 411, 412, 413, 414(a), 416(b), (d)
902(1)	
902(2)	401(10)
902(3)	401(11)
902(4)	
903	403
904	402(c)
921(a)	405(a)
921(b)	402(d)
921(c)–(f)	405(a)
922(a)	405(e)(1)
922(b)	
923	405(d)
924	405(b)
925	408(a)
926	405(h)
927	418
941	410(a)
942	410(a), (b)
943(a)	413
943(b)(1)	
943(b)(2)	414(b)(2)
943(b)(3)	414(b)(4)
943(b)(4)	414(b)(6)
943(b)(5), (6)	414(b)(1)
944(a)	415(a)
944(b)	415(b)(1)
944(c)	415(b)(2)
945(a)	416(e)
945(b)	
946	417
1101(1)	
1101(2)	629(a)
1102	738
1103(a)	739(2)
1103(b), (c)(1)	
1103(c)(2)	739(1)(a)
1103(c)(3)	739(1)(b)–(e)
1103(c)(4)	
1103(c)(5)	739(1)(f)
1103(d)	
1104(a)	556, 832, 837(1)
1104(b)	568
1104(c)	560
1105	559
1106	587, 842
1106(a)(2)	564
1106(a)(3)	567(1)
1106(a)(4)	567(5)
1106(a)(4)(A)	567(3)
1106(a)(5)	569
1106(b)	568
1107(a)	563, 588, 742, 844
1107(b)	
1108	589, 743, 845

1109	607
1109(a)	608
1109(b)	606
1110	516(5), (6)
1111	596, 851
1112(a)	
1112(b)	636, 776, 777, 881, 882
1112(c)–(e)	
1121	570
1122	597, 751, 852
1123(a)(1)	
1123(a)(2)	616(6), 861(10)
1123(a)(3)	616(5), 861(9)
1123(a)(4)	
1123(a)(5)	616(2), (10), 861(12)
1123(a)(6)	616(12)(a)
1123(a)(7)	616(11)
1123(b)(1)	616(1)
1123(b)(2)	616(4), 757(2), 861(4)
1123(b)(3)	616(13)
1123(b)(4)	616(2), 861(7)
1123(b)(5)	616(14), 757(8), 861(13)
1123(c)	
1124	507, 708, 807
1125(a)	
1125(b)	576
1125(c)	
1125(d)	575
1125(e)	
1126	579
1126(a)	599
1126(e)	603
1127	622, 763
1127(a)	869
1127(b)	629(c), 787(1), 869
1127(c)	765, 787(2), (3), 871
1127(d)	623, 764, 870
1128(a)	579, 735(3), 737(3), 835, 837(3)
1128(b)	580
1129(a)(1)	621(1), 766(1), 872(1)
1129(a)(2)	766(3), 872(3)
1129(a)(3)	621(3), 761, 766(4), 867, 872(4)
1129(a)(4)	621(4), 872(5)
1129(a)(5)	621(5)
1129(a)(6)	624(2)
1129(a)(7)	621(2), 766(2), 872(2)
1129(a)(8)	
1129(a)(9)	737(2)
1129(a)(10)	
1129(a)(11)	621(2), 766(2), 872(2)
1129(b), (c)	
1129(d)	669, 921
1141(a)	624(1), 767(1), 873(1)
1141(b)	
1141(c)	626, 874
1141(d)(1)–(3)	628(1), 771, 876
1141(d)(4)	32(a)
1142(a)	624(2), 873(2)
1142(b)	627, 875
1143	604
1144	786, 911
1145(a)	664(a), 793(a), 918(a)
1145(b)	664(b), 793(b), 918(b)
1145(c), (d)	
1146(a), (b)	
1146(c)	667
1146(d)	
1161, 1162	
1163	205(c)(1)
1164, 1165	
1166	205(c)(2)
1167	205(n)
1168	205(j)
1169	205(c)(6)
1170	205(o)

1171(a)	205(n)
1171(b)	205(b)
1172	205(b)
1173	205(e)
1174	
1301, 1302	
1303	1036
1304	
1305(a)(1)	1080
1305(a)(2), (b), (c)	
1306	
1307	1066
1321	1033(2)
1322(a)(1)	1046(4)
1322(a)(2)	1046(3)
1322(a)(3)	
1322(b)(1)	1046(1)
1322(b)(2)	1046(2)
1322(b)(3)–(6)	
1322(b)(7)	1046(6)
1322(b)(8), (9)	
1322(b)(10)	1046(7)
1322(c)	
1323(a)	1053
1323(b)	
1323(c)	1054
1324	1033(5)
1325(a)(1)	1056(a)(1)
1325(a)(2)	
1325(a)(3)	1051, 1056(a)(4)
1325(a)(4), (5)	
1325(a)(6)	1056(a)(2)
1325(b)	
1326(a)	1059
1326(b)	
1327(a)	1057
1327(b), (c)	
1328(a)	1060
1328(b)	1061
1328(c), (d)	1060
1328(e)	33
1329(a)	1046(5)
1329(b), (c)	
1330	1071
1501–151326	

Enacting Clause

Pub. L. 95–598, title I, §101, Nov. 6, 1978, 92 Stat. 2549, provided in part: "The law relating to bankruptcy is codified and enacted as title 11 of the United States Code, entitled 'Bankruptcy', and may be cited as 11 U.S.C. §—."

Repeals

Pub. L. 95–598, title IV, §401(a), Nov. 6, 1978, 92 Stat. 2682, provided that: "The Bankruptcy Act [act July 1, 1898, ch. 541, 30 Stat. 544, as amended] is repealed."

Effective Date

Pub. L. 95–598, title IV, §402, Nov. 6, 1978, 92 Stat. 2682, as amended by Pub. L. 98–249, §1(a), Mar. 31, 1984, 98 Stat. 116; Pub. L. 98–271, §1(a), Apr. 30, 1984, 98 Stat. 163; Pub. L. 98–299, §1(a), May 25, 1984, 98 Stat. 214; Pub. L. 98–325, §1(a), June 20, 1984, 98 Stat. 268; Pub. L. 98–353, title I, §§113, 121(a), July 10, 1984, 98 Stat. 343, 345; Pub. L. 98–454, title X, §1001, Oct. 5, 1984, 98 Stat. 1745, provided that:

"(a) Except as otherwise provided in this title [sections 401 to 411], this Act [for classification to the Code, see Tables] shall take effect on October 1, 1979.

"(b) Except as provided in subsections (c) and (d) of this section, the amendments made by title II [sections 201 to 252] of this Act shall not be effective.

"(c) The amendments made by sections 210, 214, 219, 220, 222, 224, 225, 228, 229, 235, 244, 245, 246, 249, and 251 of this Act shall take effect on October 1, 1979.

"(d) The amendments made by sections 217, 218, 230, 247, 302, 314(j), 317, 327, 328, 338, and 411 of this Act shall take effect on the date of enactment of this Act [Nov. 6, 1978].

"(e) [Repealed. Pub. L. 98–454, title X, §1001, Oct. 5, 1984, 98 Stat. 1745]."

[Amendment of section 402(b) of Pub. L. 95–598, set out above, by section 113 of Pub. L. 98–353 effective June 27, 1984, see section 122(c) of Pub. L. 98–353, set out as an Effective Date note under section 151 of Title 28, Judiciary and Judicial Procedure.]

Savings Provision

Pub. L. 95–598, title IV, §403, Nov. 6, 1978, 92 Stat. 2683, as amended by Pub. L. 98–353, title III, §382, July 10, 1984, 98 Stat. 364, provided that:

"(a) A case commenced under the Bankruptcy Act, [act July 1, 1898, ch. 541, 30 Stat. 544, as amended], and all matters and proceedings in or relating to any such case, shall be conducted and determined under such Act as if this Act had not been enacted, and the substantive rights of parties in connection with any such bankruptcy case, matter, or proceeding shall continue to be governed by the law applicable to such case, matter, or proceeding as if the [this] Act had not been enacted.

"(b) Notwithstanding subsection (a) of this section, sections 1165, 1167, 1168, 1169, and 1171 of title 11 of the United States Code, as enacted by section 101 of this Act, apply to cases pending under section 77 of the Bankruptcy Act ([former] 11 U.S.C. 205) on the date of enactment of this Act [Nov. 6, 1978] in which the trustee has not filed a plan of reorganization.

"(c) The repeal [of the Bankruptcy Act] made by section 401(a) of this Act does not affect any right of a referee in bankruptcy, United States bankruptcy judge, or survivor of a referee in bankruptcy or United States bankruptcy judge to receive any annuity or other payment under the civil service retirement laws.

"(d) The amendments made by section 314 of this Act [for classification to the Code, see Tables] do not affect the application of chapter 9, chapter 96, section 2516, section 3057, or section 3284 of title 18 of the United States Code to any act of any person—

"(1) committed before October 1, 1979; or

"(2) committed after October 1, 1979, in connection with a case commenced before such date.

"(e) Notwithstanding subsection (a) of this section—

"(1) a fee may not be charged under section 40c(2)(a) of the Bankruptcy Act [former 11 U.S.C. 68(c)(2)(a)] in a case pending under such Act after September 30, 1979, to the extent that such fee exceeds $200,000;

"(2) a fee may not be charged under section 40c(2)(b) of the Bankruptcy Act in a case in which the plan is confirmed after September 30, 1978, or in which the final determination as to the amount of such fee is made after September 30, 1979, notwithstanding an earlier confirmation date, to the extent that such fee exceeds $100,000;

"(3) after September 30, 1979, all moneys collected for payment into the referees' salary and expense fund in cases filed under the Bankruptcy Act shall be collected and paid into the general fund of the Treasury; and

"(4) any balance in the referees' salary and expense fund in the Treasury on October 1, 1979, shall be transferred to the general fund of the Treasury and the referees' salary and expense fund account shall be closed."

Pub. L. 98–353, title III, §381, July 10, 1984, 98 Stat. 364, provided that: "This subtitle [(§§381, 382) amending section 403(e) of Pub. L. 95–598, set out above] may be cited as the 'Referees Salary and Expense Fund Act of 1984'."

History of Bankruptcy Acts

The bankruptcy laws were revised generally and enacted as Title 11, Bankruptcy, by Pub. L. 95–598, Nov. 6, 1978, 92 Stat. 2549.

Earlier bankruptcy laws included the following acts:

Apr. 4, 1800, ch. 19, 2 Stat. 19, repealed Dec. 19, 1803, ch. 6, 2 Stat. 248.

Aug. 19, 1841, ch. 9, 5 Stat. 440, repealed Mar. 3, 1843, ch. 82, 5 Stat. 614.

Mar. 2, 1867, ch. 176, 14 Stat. 517, the provisions of which were incorporated in Rev. Stat. Title LXI, §§4972 to 5132, were materially amended June 22, 1874, ch. 390, 18 Stat. 178, and were repealed June 7, 1878, ch. 160, 20 Stat. 99.

The Bankruptcy Act of July 1, 1898, ch. 541, 30 Stat. 544, as amended, sometimes called the Nelson Act, repealed by Pub. L. 95–598.

The Chandler Act of July 22, 1938, ch. 575, 52 Stat. 883, which revised the Bankruptcy Act generally and materially amended the provisions covering corporate reorganizations, repealed by Pub. L. 95–598.

National Bankruptcy Review Commission

Pub. L. 103–394, title VI, Oct. 22, 1994, 108 Stat. 4147, established the National Bankruptcy Review Commission to (1) investigate and study issues and problems relating to title 11, United States Code, (2) evaluate the advisability of proposals and current arrangements with respect to such issues and problems, (3) solicit divergent views of all parties concerned with the operation of the bankruptcy system, and (4) prepare and submit to the Congress, the Chief Justice, and the President a report not later than 2 years after the date of its first meeting, and provided for termination of the Commission 30 days after submission of the report which was submitted on Oct. 20, 1997.

Commission on the Bankruptcy Laws of the United States

Pub. L. 91–354, §§1–6, July 24, 1970, 84 Stat. 468, as amended by Pub. L. 92–251, Mar. 17, 1972, 86 Stat. 63; Pub. L. 93–56, §1, July 1, 1973, 87 Stat. 140, established the Commission on the Bankruptcy Laws of the United States, to study and recommend changes to this title, which ceased to exist 30 days after the date of submission of its final report which was required prior to July 31, 1973.

[1] So in original. Does not conform to chapter heading.

CHAPTER 1—GENERAL PROVISIONS

Sec.
101.
Definitions.
102.
Rules of construction.
103.
Applicability of chapters.
104.
Adjustment of dollar amounts.
105.
Power of court.
106.
Waiver of sovereign immunity.
107.
Public access to papers.
108.
Extension of time.
109.
Who may be a debtor.
110.
Penalty for persons who negligently or fraudulently prepare bankruptcy petitions.
111.
Nonprofit budget and credit counseling agencies; financial management instructional courses.
112.
Prohibition on disclosure of name of minor children.

AMENDMENTS

2005—Pub. L. 109–8, title I, §106(e)(2), title II, §233(b), Apr. 20, 2005, 119 Stat. 41, 74, added items 111 and 112.

1994—Pub. L. 103–394, title III, §308(b), Oct. 22, 1994, 108 Stat. 4137, added item 110.

§101. Definitions

In this title the following definitions shall apply:

(1) The term "accountant" means accountant authorized under applicable law to practice public accounting, and includes professional accounting association, corporation, or partnership, if so authorized.

(2) The term "affiliate" means—

(A) entity that directly or indirectly owns, controls, or holds with power to vote, 20 percent or more of the outstanding voting securities of the debtor, other than an entity that holds such securities—

(i) in a fiduciary or agency capacity without sole discretionary power to vote such securities; or

(ii) solely to secure a debt, if such entity has not in fact exercised such power to vote;

(B) corporation 20 percent or more of whose outstanding voting securities are directly or indirectly owned, controlled, or held with power to vote, by the debtor, or by an entity that directly or indirectly owns, controls, or holds with power to vote, 20 percent or more of the outstanding voting securities of the debtor, other than an entity that holds such securities—

(i) in a fiduciary or agency capacity without sole discretionary power to vote such securities; or

(ii) solely to secure a debt, if such entity has not in fact exercised such power to vote;

(C) person whose business is operated under a lease or operating agreement by a debtor, or person substantially all of whose property is operated under an operating agreement with the debtor; or

(D) entity that operates the business or substantially all of the property of the debtor under a lease or operating agreement.

(3) The term "assisted person" means any person whose debts consist primarily of consumer debts and the value of whose nonexempt property is less than $150,000.[1]

(4) The term "attorney" means attorney, professional law association, corporation, or partnership, authorized under applicable law to practice law.

(4A) The term "bankruptcy assistance" means any goods or services sold or otherwise provided to an assisted person with the express or implied purpose of providing information, advice, counsel, document preparation, or filing, or attendance at a creditors' meeting or appearing in a case or proceeding on behalf of another or providing legal representation with respect to a case or proceeding under this title.

(5) The term "claim" means—

(A) right to payment, whether or not such right is reduced to judgment, liquidated, unliquidated, fixed, contingent, matured, unmatured, disputed, undisputed, legal, equitable, secured, or unsecured; or

(B) right to an equitable remedy for breach of performance if such breach gives rise to a right to payment, whether or not such right to an equitable remedy is reduced to judgment, fixed, contingent, matured, unmatured, disputed, undisputed, secured, or unsecured.

(6) The term "commodity broker" means futures commission merchant, foreign futures commission merchant, clearing organization, leverage transaction merchant, or commodity options dealer, as defined in section 761 of this title, with respect to which there is a customer, as defined in section 761 of this title.

(7) The term "community claim" means claim that arose before the commencement of the case concerning the debtor for which property of the kind specified in section 541(a)(2) of this title is liable, whether or not there is any such property at the time of the commencement of the case.

(7A) The term "commercial fishing operation" means—

(A) the catching or harvesting of fish, shrimp, lobsters, urchins, seaweed, shellfish, or other aquatic species or products of such species; or

(B) for purposes of section 109 and chapter 12, aquaculture activities consisting of raising for market any species or product described in subparagraph (A).

(7B) The term "commercial fishing vessel" means a vessel used by a family fisherman to carry out a commercial fishing operation.

(8) The term "consumer debt" means debt incurred by an individual primarily for a personal, family, or household purpose.

(9) The term "corporation"—

(A) includes—

(i) association having a power or privilege that a private corporation, but not an individual or a partnership, possesses;

(ii) partnership association organized under a law that makes only the capital subscribed responsible for the debts of such association;

(iii) joint-stock company;

(iv) unincorporated company or association; or

(v) business trust; but

(B) does not include limited partnership.

(10) The term "creditor" means—

(A) entity that has a claim against the debtor that arose at the time of or before the order for relief concerning the debtor;

(B) entity that has a claim against the estate of a kind specified in section 348(d), 502(f), 502(g), 502(h) or 502(i) of this title; or

(C) entity that has a community claim.

(10A) The term "current monthly income"—

(A) means the average monthly income from all sources that the debtor receives (or in a joint case the debtor and the debtor's spouse receive) without regard to whether such income is taxable income, derived during the 6-month period ending on—

(i) the last day of the calendar month immediately preceding the date of the commencement of the case if the debtor files the schedule of current income required by section 521(a)(1)(B)(ii); or

(ii) the date on which current income is determined by the court for purposes of this title if the debtor does not file the schedule of current income required by section 521(a)(1)(B)(ii); and

(B) includes any amount paid by any entity other than the debtor (or in a joint case the debtor and the debtor's spouse), on a regular basis for the household expenses of the debtor or the debtor's dependents (and in a joint case the debtor's spouse if not otherwise a dependent), but excludes benefits received under the Social Security Act, payments to victims of war crimes or crimes against humanity on account of their status as victims of such crimes, and payments to victims of international terrorism (as defined in section 2331 of title 18) or domestic terrorism (as defined in section 2331 of title 18) on account of their status as victims of such terrorism.

(11) The term "custodian" means—

(A) receiver or trustee of any of the property of the debtor, appointed in a case or proceeding not under this title;

(B) assignee under a general assignment for the benefit of the debtor's creditors; or

(C) trustee, receiver, or agent under applicable law, or under a contract, that is appointed or authorized to take charge of property of the debtor for the purpose of enforcing a lien against such property, or for the purpose of general administration of such property for the benefit of the debtor's creditors.

(12) The term "debt" means liability on a claim.

(12A) The term "debt relief agency" means any person who provides any bankruptcy assistance to an assisted person in return for the payment of money or other valuable consideration, or who is a bankruptcy petition preparer under section 110, but does not include—

(A) any person who is an officer, director, employee, or agent of a person who provides such assistance or of the bankruptcy petition preparer;

(B) a nonprofit organization that is exempt from taxation under section 501(c)(3) of the Internal Revenue Code of 1986;

(C) a creditor of such assisted person, to the extent that the creditor is assisting such assisted person to restructure any debt owed by such assisted person to the creditor;

(D) a depository institution (as defined in section 3 of the Federal Deposit Insurance Act) or any Federal credit union or State credit union (as those terms are defined in section 101 of the Federal Credit Union Act), or any affiliate or subsidiary of such depository institution or credit union; or

(E) an author, publisher, distributor, or seller of works subject to copyright protection under title 17, when acting in such capacity.

(13) The term "debtor" means person or municipality concerning which a case under this title has been commenced.

(13A) The term "debtor's principal residence"—

(A) means a residential structure if used as the principal residence by the debtor, including incidental property, without regard to whether that structure is attached to real property; and

(B) includes an individual condominium or cooperative unit, a mobile or manufactured home, or trailer if used as the principal residence by the debtor.

(14) The term "disinterested person" means a person that—
(A) is not a creditor, an equity security holder, or an insider;
(B) is not and was not, within 2 years before the date of the filing of the petition, a director, officer, or employee of the debtor; and
(C) does not have an interest materially adverse to the interest of the estate or of any class of creditors or equity security holders, by reason of any direct or indirect relationship to, connection with, or interest in, the debtor, or for any other reason.

(14A) The term "domestic support obligation" means a debt that accrues before, on, or after the date of the order for relief in a case under this title, including interest that accrues on that debt as provided under applicable nonbankruptcy law notwithstanding any other provision of this title, that is—
(A) owed to or recoverable by—
(i) a spouse, former spouse, or child of the debtor or such child's parent, legal guardian, or responsible relative; or
(ii) a governmental unit;

(B) in the nature of alimony, maintenance, or support (including assistance provided by a governmental unit) of such spouse, former spouse, or child of the debtor or such child's parent, without regard to whether such debt is expressly so designated;
(C) established or subject to establishment before, on, or after the date of the order for relief in a case under this title, by reason of applicable provisions of—
(i) a separation agreement, divorce decree, or property settlement agreement;
(ii) an order of a court of record; or
(iii) a determination made in accordance with applicable nonbankruptcy law by a governmental unit; and

(D) not assigned to a nongovernmental entity, unless that obligation is assigned voluntarily by the spouse, former spouse, child of the debtor, or such child's parent, legal guardian, or responsible relative for the purpose of collecting the debt.

(15) The term "entity" includes person, estate, trust, governmental unit, and United States trustee.
(16) The term "equity security" means—
(A) share in a corporation, whether or not transferable or denominated "stock", or similar security;
(B) interest of a limited partner in a limited partnership; or
(C) warrant or right, other than a right to convert, to purchase, sell, or subscribe to a share, security, or interest of a kind specified in subparagraph (A) or (B) of this paragraph.

(17) The term "equity security holder" means holder of an equity security of the debtor.
(18) The term "family farmer" means—
(A) individual or individual and spouse engaged in a farming operation whose aggregate debts do not exceed $3,237,000 [1] and not less than 50 percent of whose aggregate noncontingent, liquidated debts (excluding a debt for the principal residence of such individual or such individual and spouse unless such debt arises out of a farming operation), on the date the case is filed, arise out of a farming operation owned or operated by such individual or such individual and spouse, and such individual or such individual and spouse receive from such farming operation more than 50 percent of such individual's or such individual and spouse's gross income for—
(i) the taxable year preceding; or
(ii) each of the 2d and 3d taxable years preceding;

the taxable year in which the case concerning such individual or such individual and spouse was filed; or
(B) corporation or partnership in which more than 50 percent of the outstanding stock or equity is held by one family, or by one family and the relatives of the members of such family, and such family or such relatives conduct the farming operation, and
(i) more than 80 percent of the value of its assets consists of assets related to the farming operation;
(ii) its aggregate debts do not exceed $3,237,000 [1] and not less than 50 percent of its aggregate noncontingent, liquidated debts (excluding a debt for one dwelling which is owned by such corporation or partnership and which a shareholder or partner maintains as a principal residence, unless such debt arises out of a farming operation), on the date the case is filed, arise out of the farming operation owned or operated by such corporation or such partnership; and
(iii) if such corporation issues stock, such stock is not publicly traded.

(19) The term "family farmer with regular annual income" means family farmer whose annual income is sufficiently stable and regular to enable such family farmer to make payments under a plan under chapter 12 of this title.
(19A) The term "family fisherman" means—
(A) an individual or individual and spouse engaged in a commercial fishing operation—
(i) whose aggregate debts do not exceed $1,500,000 [1] and not less than 80 percent of whose aggregate noncontingent, liquidated debts (excluding a debt for the principal residence of such individual or such individual and spouse, unless such debt arises out of a commercial fishing operation), on the date the case is filed, arise out of a commercial fishing operation owned or operated by such individual or such individual and spouse; and
(ii) who receive from such commercial fishing operation more than 50 percent of such individual's or such individual's and spouse's gross income for the taxable year preceding the taxable year in which the case concerning such individual or such individual and spouse was filed; or

(B) a corporation or partnership—
(i) in which more than 50 percent of the outstanding stock or equity is held by—
(I) 1 family that conducts the commercial fishing operation; or
(II) 1 family and the relatives of the members of such family, and such family or such relatives conduct the commercial fishing operation; and

(ii)(I) more than 80 percent of the value of its assets consists of assets related to the commercial fishing operation;
(II) its aggregate debts do not exceed $1,500,000 [1] and not less than 80 percent of its aggregate noncontingent, liquidated debts (excluding a debt for 1 dwelling which is owned by such corporation or partnership and which a shareholder or partner maintains as a principal residence, unless such debt arises out of a commercial fishing operation), on the date the case is filed, arise out of a commercial fishing operation owned or operated by such corporation or such partnership; and
(III) if such corporation issues stock, such stock is not publicly traded.

(19B) The term "family fisherman with regular annual income" means a family fisherman whose annual income is sufficiently stable and regular to enable such family fisherman to make payments under a plan under chapter 12 of this title.

(20) The term "farmer" means (except when such term appears in the term "family farmer") person that received more than 80 percent of such person's gross income during the taxable year of such person immediately preceding the taxable year of such person during which the case under this title concerning such person was commenced from a farming operation owned or operated by such person.
(21) The term "farming operation" includes farming, tillage of the soil, dairy farming, ranching, production or raising of crops, poultry, or livestock, and production of poultry or livestock products in an unmanufactured state.
(21A) The term "farmout agreement" means a written agreement in which—
(A) the owner of a right to drill, produce, or operate liquid or gaseous hydrocarbons on property agrees or has agreed to transfer or assign all or a part of such right to another entity; and
(B) such other entity (either directly or through its agents or its assigns), as consideration, agrees to perform drilling, reworking, recompleting, testing, or similar or related operations, to develop or produce liquid or gaseous hydrocarbons on the property.

(21B) The term "Federal depository institutions regulatory agency" means—
(A) with respect to an insured depository institution (as defined in section 3(c)(2) of the Federal Deposit Insurance Act) for which no conservator or receiver has been appointed, the appropriate Federal banking agency (as defined in section 3(q) of such Act);
(B) with respect to an insured credit union (including an insured credit union for which the National Credit Union Administration has been appointed conservator or liquidating agent), the National Credit Union Administration;
(C) with respect to any insured depository institution for which the Resolution Trust Corporation has been appointed conservator or receiver, the Resolution Trust Corporation; and
(D) with respect to any insured depository institution for which the Federal Deposit Insurance Corporation has been appointed conservator or receiver, the Federal Deposit Insurance Corporation.

(22) The term "financial institution" means—
(A) a Federal reserve bank, or an entity that is a commercial or savings bank, industrial savings bank, savings and loan association, trust company, federally-insured credit union, or receiver, liquidating agent, or conservator for such entity and, when any such Federal reserve bank, receiver, liquidating agent, conservator or entity is acting as agent or custodian for a customer (whether or not a "customer", as defined in section 741) in connection with a securities contract (as defined in section 741) such customer; or
(B) in connection with a securities contract (as defined in section 741) an investment company registered under the Investment Company Act of 1940.

(22A) The term "financial participant" means—
(A) an entity that, at the time it enters into a securities contract, commodity contract, swap agreement, repurchase agreement, or forward contract, or at the time of the date of the filing of the petition, has one or more agreements or transactions described in paragraph (1), (2), (3), (4), (5), or (6) of section 561(a) with the debtor or any other entity (other than an affiliate) of a total gross dollar value of not less than $1,000,000,000 in notional or actual principal amount outstanding (aggregated across counterparties) at such time or on any day during the 15-month period preceding the date of the filing of the petition, or has gross mark-to-market positions of not less than $100,000,000 (aggregated across counterparties) in one or more such agreements or transactions with the debtor or any other entity (other than an affiliate) at such time or on any day during the 15-month period preceding the date of the filing of the petition; or
(B) a clearing organization (as defined in section 402 of the Federal Deposit Insurance Corporation Improvement Act of 1991).

(23) The term "foreign proceeding" means a collective judicial or administrative proceeding in a foreign country, including an interim proceeding, under a law relating to insolvency or adjustment of debt in which proceeding the assets and affairs of the debtor are subject to control or supervision by a foreign court, for the purpose of reorganization or liquidation.
(24) The term "foreign representative" means a person or body, including a person or body appointed on an interim basis, authorized in a foreign proceeding to administer the reorganization or the liquidation of the debtor's assets or affairs or to act as a representative of such foreign proceeding.
(25) The term "forward contract" means—
(A) a contract (other than a commodity contract, as defined in section 761) for the purchase, sale, or transfer of a commodity, as defined in section 761(8) of this title, or any similar good, article, service, right, or interest which is presently or in the future becomes the subject of dealing in the forward contract trade, or product or byproduct thereof, with a maturity date more than two days after the date the contract is entered into, including, but not limited to, a repurchase or reverse repurchase transaction (whether or not such repurchase or reverse repurchase transaction is a "repurchase agreement", as defined in this section) [2] consignment, lease, swap, hedge transaction, deposit, loan, option, allocated transaction, unallocated transaction, or any other similar agreement;
(B) any combination of agreements or transactions referred to in subparagraphs (A) and (C);
(C) any option to enter into an agreement or transaction referred to in subparagraph (A) or (B);
(D) a master agreement that provides for an agreement or transaction referred to in subparagraph (A), (B), or (C), together with all supplements to any such master agreement, without regard to whether such master agreement provides for an agreement or transaction that is not a forward contract under this paragraph, except that such master agreement shall be considered to be a forward contract under this paragraph only with respect to each agreement or transaction under such master agreement that is referred to in subparagraph (A), (B), or (C); or
(E) any security agreement or arrangement, or other credit enhancement related to any agreement or transaction referred to in subparagraph (A), (B), (C), or (D), including any guarantee or reimbursement obligation by or to a forward contract merchant or financial participant in connection with any agreement or transaction referred to in any such subparagraph, but not to exceed the damages in connection with any such agreement or transaction, measured in accordance with section 562.

(26) The term "forward contract merchant" means a Federal reserve bank, or an entity the business of which consists in whole or in part of entering into forward contracts as or with merchants in a commodity (as defined in section 761) or any similar good, article, service, right, or interest which is presently or in the future becomes the subject of dealing in the forward contract trade.
(27) The term "governmental unit" means United States; State; Commonwealth; District; Territory; municipality; foreign state; department, agency, or instrumentality of the United States (but not a United States trustee while serving as a trustee in a case under this title), a State, a Commonwealth, a District, a Territory, a municipality, or a foreign state; or other foreign or domestic government.
(27A) The term "health care business"—
(A) means any public or private entity (without regard to whether that entity is organized for profit or not for profit) that is primarily engaged in offering to the general public facilities and services for—
(i) the diagnosis or treatment of injury, deformity, or disease; and
(ii) surgical, drug treatment, psychiatric, or obstetric care; and

(B) includes—
(i) any—
(I) general or specialized hospital;
(II) ancillary ambulatory, emergency, or surgical treatment facility;
(III) hospice;
(IV) home health agency; and
(V) other health care institution that is similar to an entity referred to in subclause (I), (II), (III), or (IV); and

(ii) any long-term care facility, including any—
(I) skilled nursing facility;
(II) intermediate care facility;
(III) assisted living facility;
(IV) home for the aged;
(V) domiciliary care facility; and
(VI) health care institution that is related to a facility referred to in subclause (I), (II), (III), (IV), or (V), if that institution is primarily engaged in offering room, board, laundry, or personal assistance with activities of daily living and incidentals to activities of daily living.

(27B) The term "incidental property" means, with respect to a debtor's principal residence—
(A) property commonly conveyed with a principal residence in the area where the real property is located;
(B) all easements, rights, appurtenances, fixtures, rents, royalties, mineral rights, oil or gas rights or profits, water rights, escrow funds, or insurance proceeds; and
(C) all replacements or additions.

(28) The term "indenture" means mortgage, deed of trust, or indenture, under which there is outstanding a security, other than a voting-trust certificate, constituting a claim against the debtor, a claim secured by a lien on any of the debtor's property, or an equity security of the debtor.
(29) The term "indenture trustee" means trustee under an indenture.
(30) The term "individual with regular income" means individual whose income is sufficiently stable and regular to enable such individual to make payments under a plan under chapter 13 of this title, other than a stockbroker or a commodity broker.
(31) The term "insider" includes—
(A) if the debtor is an individual—
(i) relative of the debtor or of a general partner of the debtor;
(ii) partnership in which the debtor is a general partner;
(iii) general partner of the debtor; or
(iv) corporation of which the debtor is a director, officer, or person in control;

(B) if the debtor is a corporation—
(i) director of the debtor;
(ii) officer of the debtor;
(iii) person in control of the debtor;
(iv) partnership in which the debtor is a general partner;
(v) general partner of the debtor; or
(vi) relative of a general partner, director, officer, or person in control of the debtor;

(C) if the debtor is a partnership—
(i) general partner in the debtor;
(ii) relative of a general partner in, general partner of, or person in control of the debtor;
(iii) partnership in which the debtor is a general partner;
(iv) general partner of the debtor; or
(v) person in control of the debtor;

(D) if the debtor is a municipality, elected official of the debtor or relative of an elected official of the debtor;
(E) affiliate, or insider of an affiliate as if such affiliate were the debtor; and
(F) managing agent of the debtor.

(32) The term "insolvent" means—
(A) with reference to an entity other than a partnership and a municipality, financial condition such that the sum of such entity's debts is greater than all of such entity's property, at a fair valuation, exclusive of—
(i) property transferred, concealed, or removed with intent to hinder, delay, or defraud such entity's creditors; and
(ii) property that may be exempted from property of the estate under section 522 of this title;

(B) with reference to a partnership, financial condition such that the sum of such partnership's debts is greater than the aggregate of, at a fair valuation—
(i) all of such partnership's property, exclusive of property of the kind specified in subparagraph (A)(i) of this paragraph; and
(ii) the sum of the excess of the value of each general partner's nonpartnership property, exclusive of property of the kind specified in subparagraph (A) of this paragraph, over such partner's nonpartnership debts; and

(C) with reference to a municipality, financial condition such that the municipality is—
(i) generally not paying its debts as they become due unless such debts are the subject of a bona fide dispute; or
(ii) unable to pay its debts as they become due.

(33) The term "institution-affiliated party"—
(A) with respect to an insured depository institution (as defined in section 3(c)(2) of the Federal Deposit Insurance Act), has the meaning given it in section 3(u) of the Federal Deposit Insurance Act; and
(B) with respect to an insured credit union, has the meaning given it in section 206(r) of the Federal Credit Union Act.

(34) The term "insured credit union" has the meaning given it in section 101(7) of the Federal Credit Union Act.
(35) The term "insured depository institution"—
(A) has the meaning given it in section 3(c)(2) of the Federal Deposit Insurance Act; and
(B) includes an insured credit union (except in the case of paragraphs (21B) and (33)(A) of this subsection).

(35A) The term "intellectual property" means—
(A) trade secret;
(B) invention, process, design, or plant protected under title 35;
(C) patent application;
(D) plant variety;
(E) work of authorship protected under title 17; or
(F) mask work protected under chapter 9 of title 17;

to the extent protected by applicable nonbankruptcy law.
(36) The term "judicial lien" means lien obtained by judgment, levy, sequestration, or other legal or equitable process or proceeding.
(37) The term "lien" means charge against or interest in property to secure payment of a debt or performance of an obligation.
(38) The term "margin payment" means, for purposes of the forward contract provisions of this title, payment or deposit of cash, a security or other property, that is commonly known in the forward contract trade as original margin, initial margin, maintenance margin, or variation margin, including mark-to-market payments, or variation payments.
(38A) The term "master netting agreement"—
(A) means an agreement providing for the exercise of rights, including rights of netting, setoff, liquidation, termination, acceleration, or close out, under or in connection with one or more contracts that are described in any one or more of paragraphs (1) through (5) of section 561(a), or any security agreement or arrangement or other credit enhancement related to one or more of the foregoing, including any guarantee or reimbursement obligation related to 1 or more of the foregoing; and
(B) if the agreement contains provisions relating to agreements or transactions that are not contracts described in paragraphs (1) through (5) of section 561(a), shall be deemed to be a master netting agreement only with respect to those agreements or transactions that are described in any one or more of paragraphs (1) through (5) of section 561(a).

(38B) The term "master netting agreement participant" means an entity that, at any time before the date of the filing of the petition, is a party to an outstanding master netting agreement with the debtor.
(39) The term "mask work" has the meaning given it in section 901(a)(2) of title 17.
(39A) The term "median family income" means for any year—
(A) the median family income both calculated and reported by the Bureau of the Census in the then most recent year; and
(B) if not so calculated and reported in the then current year, adjusted annually after such most recent year until the next year in which median family income is both calculated and reported by the Bureau of the Census, to reflect the percentage change in the Consumer Price Index for All Urban Consumers during the period of years occurring after such most recent year and before such current year.

(40) The term "municipality" means political subdivision or public agency or instrumentality of a State.
(40A) The term "patient" means any individual who obtains or receives services from a health care business.
(40B) The term "patient records" means any record relating to a patient, including a written document or a record recorded in a magnetic, optical, or other form of electronic medium.
(41) The term "person" includes individual, partnership, and corporation, but does not include governmental unit, except that a governmental unit that—
(A) acquires an asset from a person—
(i) as a result of the operation of a loan guarantee agreement; or
(ii) as receiver or liquidating agent of a person;

(B) is a guarantor of a pension benefit payable by or on behalf of the debtor or an affiliate of the debtor; or
(C) is the legal or beneficial owner of an asset of—
(i) an employee pension benefit plan that is a governmental plan, as defined in section 414(d) of the Internal Revenue Code of 1986; or
(ii) an eligible deferred compensation plan, as defined in section 457(b) of the Internal Revenue Code of 1986;

shall be considered, for purposes of section 1102 of this title, to be a person with respect to such asset or such benefit.
(41A) The term "personally identifiable information" means—
(A) if provided by an individual to the debtor in connection with obtaining a product or a service from the debtor primarily for personal, family, or household purposes—
(i) the first name (or initial) and last name of such individual, whether given at birth or time of adoption, or resulting from a lawful change of name;
(ii) the geographical address of a physical place of residence of such individual;
(iii) an electronic address (including an e-mail address) of such individual;
(iv) a telephone number dedicated to contacting such individual at such physical place of residence;
(v) a social security account number issued to such individual; or
(vi) the account number of a credit card issued to such individual; or

(B) if identified in connection with 1 or more of the items of information specified in subparagraph (A)—
(i) a birth date, the number of a certificate of birth or adoption, or a place of birth; or
(ii) any other information concerning an identified individual that, if disclosed, will result in contacting or identifying such individual physically or electronically.

(42) The term "petition" means petition filed under section 301, 302, 303 and [3] 1504 of this title, as the case may be, commencing a case under this title.
(42A) The term "production payment" means a term overriding royalty satisfiable in cash or in kind—
(A) contingent on the production of a liquid or gaseous hydrocarbon from particular real property; and
(B) from a specified volume, or a specified value, from the liquid or gaseous hydrocarbon produced from such property, and determined without regard to production costs.

(43) The term "purchaser" means transferee of a voluntary transfer, and includes immediate or mediate transferee of such a transferee.
(44) The term "railroad" means common carrier by railroad engaged in the transportation of individuals or property or owner of trackage facilities leased by such a common carrier.
(45) The term "relative" means individual related by affinity or consanguinity within the third degree as determined by the common law, or individual in a step or adoptive relationship within such third degree.
(46) The term "repo participant" means an entity that, at any time before the filing of the petition, has an outstanding repurchase agreement with the debtor.
(47) The term "repurchase agreement" (which definition also applies to a reverse repurchase agreement)—

(A) means—
(i) an agreement, including related terms, which provides for the transfer of one or more certificates of deposit, mortgage related securities (as defined in section 3 of the Securities Exchange Act of 1934), mortgage loans, interests in mortgage related securities or mortgage loans, eligible bankers' acceptances, qualified foreign government securities (defined as a security that is a direct obligation of, or that is fully guaranteed by, the central government of a member of the Organization for Economic Cooperation and Development), or securities that are direct obligations of, or that are fully guaranteed by, the United States or any agency of the United States against the transfer of funds by the transferee of such certificates of deposit, eligible bankers' acceptances, securities, mortgage loans, or interests, with a simultaneous agreement by such transferee to transfer to the transferor thereof certificates of deposit, eligible bankers' acceptance, securities, mortgage loans, or interests of the kind described in this clause, at a date certain not later than 1 year after such transfer or on demand, against the transfer of funds;

(ii) any combination of agreements or transactions referred to in clauses (i) and (iii);

(iii) an option to enter into an agreement or transaction referred to in clause (i) or (ii);

(iv) a master agreement that provides for an agreement or transaction referred to in clause (i), (ii), or (iii), together with all supplements to any such master agreement, without regard to whether such master agreement provides for an agreement or transaction that is not a repurchase agreement under this paragraph, except that such master agreement shall be considered to be a repurchase agreement under this paragraph only with respect to each agreement or transaction under the master agreement that is referred to in clause (i), (ii), or (iii); or

(v) any security agreement or arrangement or other credit enhancement related to any agreement or transaction referred to in clause (i), (ii), (iii), or (iv), including any guarantee or reimbursement obligation by or to a repo participant or financial participant in connection with any agreement or transaction referred to in any such clause, but not to exceed the damages in connection with any such agreement or transaction, measured in accordance with section 562 of this title; and

(B) does not include a repurchase obligation under a participation in a commercial mortgage loan.

(48) The term "securities clearing agency" means person that is registered as a clearing agency under section 17A of the Securities Exchange Act of 1934, or exempt from such registration under such section pursuant to an order of the Securities and Exchange Commission, or whose business is confined to the performance of functions of a clearing agency with respect to exempted securities, as defined in section 3(a)(12) of such Act for the purposes of such section 17A.

(48A) The term "securities self regulatory organization" means either a securities association registered with the Securities and Exchange Commission under section 15A of the Securities Exchange Act of 1934 or a national securities exchange registered with the Securities and Exchange Commission under section 6 of the Securities Exchange Act of 1934.

(49) The term "security"—
(A) includes—
(i) note;
(ii) stock;
(iii) treasury stock;
(iv) bond;
(v) debenture;
(vi) collateral trust certificate;
(vii) pre-organization certificate or subscription;
(viii) transferable share;
(ix) voting-trust certificate;
(x) certificate of deposit;
(xi) certificate of deposit for security;
(xii) investment contract or certificate of interest or participation in a profit-sharing agreement or in an oil, gas, or mineral royalty or lease, if such contract or interest is required to be the subject of a registration statement filed with the Securities and Exchange Commission under the provisions of the Securities Act of 1933, or is exempt under section 3(b) of such Act from the requirement to file such a statement;
(xiii) interest of a limited partner in a limited partnership;
(xiv) other claim or interest commonly known as "security"; and
(xv) certificate of interest or participation in, temporary or interim certificate for, receipt for, or warrant or right to subscribe to or purchase or sell, a security; but

(B) does not include—
(i) currency, check, draft, bill of exchange, or bank letter of credit;
(ii) leverage transaction, as defined in section 761 of this title;
(iii) commodity futures contract or forward contract;
(iv) option, warrant, or right to subscribe to or purchase or sell a commodity futures contract;
(v) option to purchase or sell a commodity;
(vi) contract or certificate of a kind specified in subparagraph (A)(xii) of this paragraph that is not required to be the subject of a registration statement filed with the Securities and Exchange Commission and is not exempt under section 3(b) of the Securities Act of 1933 from the requirement to file such a statement; or
(vii) debt or evidence of indebtedness for goods sold and delivered or services rendered.

(50) The term "security agreement" means agreement that creates or provides for a security interest.

(51) The term "security interest" means lien created by an agreement.

(51A) The term "settlement payment" means, for purposes of the forward contract provisions of this title, a preliminary settlement payment, a partial settlement payment, an interim settlement payment, a settlement payment on account, a final settlement payment, a net settlement payment, or any other similar payment commonly used in the forward contract trade.

(51B) The term "single asset real estate" means real property constituting a single property or project, other than residential real property with fewer than 4 residential units, which generates substantially all of the gross income of a debtor who is not a family farmer and on which no substantial business is being conducted by a debtor other than the business of operating the real property and activities incidental thereto.

(51C) The term "small business case" means a case filed under chapter 11 of this title in which the debtor is a small business debtor.

(51D) The term "small business debtor"—
(A) subject to subparagraph (B), means a person engaged in commercial or business activities (including any affiliate of such person that is also a debtor under this title and excluding a person whose primary activity is the business of owning or operating real property or activities incidental thereto) that has aggregate noncontingent liquidated secured and unsecured debts as of the date of the filing of the petition or the date of the order for relief in an amount not more than $2,000,000 [1] (excluding debts owed to 1 or more affiliates or insiders) for a case in which the United States trustee has not appointed under section 1102(a)(1) a committee of unsecured creditors or where the court has determined that the committee of unsecured creditors is not sufficiently active and representative to provide effective oversight of the debtor; and

(B) does not include any member of a group of affiliated debtors that has aggregate noncontingent liquidated secured and unsecured debts in an amount greater than $2,000,000 [1] (excluding debt owed to 1 or more affiliates or insiders).

(52) The term "State" includes the District of Columbia and Puerto Rico, except for the purpose of defining who may be a debtor under chapter 9 of this title.

(53) The term "statutory lien" means lien arising solely by force of a statute on specified circumstances or conditions, or lien of distress for rent, whether or not statutory, but does not include security interest or judicial lien, whether or not such interest or lien is provided by or is dependent on a statute and whether or not such interest or lien is made fully effective by statute.

(53A) The term "stockbroker" means person—
(A) with respect to which there is a customer, as defined in section 741 of this title; and
(B) that is engaged in the business of effecting transactions in securities—
(i) for the account of others; or
(ii) with members of the general public, from or for such person's own account.

(53B) The term "swap agreement"—
(A) means—
(i) any agreement, including the terms and conditions incorporated by reference in such agreement, which is—
(I) an interest rate swap, option, future, or forward agreement, including a rate floor, rate cap, rate collar, cross-currency rate swap, and basis swap;
(II) a spot, same day-tomorrow, tomorrow-next, forward, or other foreign exchange, precious metals, or other commodity agreement;
(III) a currency swap, option, future, or forward agreement;
(IV) an equity index or equity swap, option, future, or forward agreement;
(V) a debt index or debt swap, option, future, or forward agreement;
(VI) a total return, credit spread or credit swap, option, future, or forward agreement;
(VII) a commodity index or a commodity swap, option, future, or forward agreement;
(VIII) a weather swap, option, future, or forward agreement;
(IX) an emissions swap, option, future, or forward agreement; or
(X) an inflation swap, option, future, or forward agreement;

(ii) any agreement or transaction that is similar to any other agreement or transaction referred to in this paragraph and that—
(I) is of a type that has been, is presently, or in the future becomes, the subject of recurrent dealings in the swap or other derivatives markets (including terms and conditions incorporated by reference therein); and
(II) is a forward, swap, future, option, or spot transaction on one or more rates, currencies, commodities, equity securities, or other equity instruments, debt securities or other debt instruments, quantitative measures associated with an occurrence, extent of an occurrence, or contingency associated with a financial, commercial, or economic consequence, or economic or financial indices or measures of economic or financial risk or value;

(iii) any combination of agreements or transactions referred to in this subparagraph;

(iv) any option to enter into an agreement or transaction referred to in this subparagraph;

(v) a master agreement that provides for an agreement or transaction referred to in clause (i), (ii), (iii), or (iv), together with all supplements to any such master agreement, and without regard to whether the master agreement contains an agreement or transaction that is not a swap agreement under this paragraph, except that the master agreement shall be considered to be a swap agreement under this paragraph only with respect to each agreement or transaction under the master agreement that is referred to in clause (i), (ii), (iii), or (iv); or

(vi) any security agreement or arrangement or other credit enhancement related to any agreements or transactions referred to in clause (i) through (v), including any guarantee or reimbursement obligation by or to a swap participant or financial participant in connection with any agreement or transaction referred to in any such clause, but not to exceed the damages in connection with any such agreement or transaction, measured in accordance with section 562; and

(B) is applicable for purposes of this title only, and shall not be construed or applied so as to challenge or affect the characterization, definition, or treatment of any swap agreement under any other statute, regulation, or rule, including the Gramm-Leach-Bliley Act, the Legal Certainty for Bank Products Act of 2000, the securities laws (as such term is defined in section 3(a)(47) of the Securities Exchange Act of 1934) and the Commodity Exchange Act.

(53C) The term "swap participant" means an entity that, at any time before the filing of the petition, has an outstanding swap agreement with the debtor.

(56A) [4] The term "term overriding royalty" means an interest in liquid or gaseous hydrocarbons in place or to be produced from particular real property that entitles the owner thereof to a share of production, or the value thereof, for a term limited by time, quantity, or value realized.

(53D) The term "timeshare plan" means and shall include that interest purchased in any arrangement, plan, scheme, or similar device, but not including exchange programs, whether by membership, agreement, tenancy in common, sale, lease, deed, rental agreement, license, right to use agreement, or by any other means, whereby a purchaser, in exchange for consideration, receives a right to use accommodations, facilities, or recreational sites, whether improved or unimproved, for a specific period of time less than a full year during any given year, but not necessarily for consecutive years, and which extends for a period of more than three years. A "timeshare interest" is that interest purchased in a timeshare plan which grants the purchaser the right to use and occupy accommodations, facilities, or recreational sites, whether improved or unimproved, pursuant to a timeshare plan.

(54) The term "transfer" means—
(A) the creation of a lien;
(B) the retention of title as a security interest;
(C) the foreclosure of a debtor's equity of redemption; or
(D) each mode, direct or indirect, absolute or conditional, voluntary or involuntary, of disposing of or parting with—
(i) property; or
(ii) an interest in property.

(54A) The term "uninsured State member bank" means a State member bank (as defined in section 3 of the Federal Deposit Insurance Act) the deposits of which are not insured by the Federal Deposit Insurance Corporation.

(55) The term "United States", when used in a geographical sense, includes all locations where the judicial jurisdiction of the United States extends, including territories and possessions of the United States.

(Pub. L. 95–598, Nov. 6, 1978, 92 Stat. 2549; Pub. L. 97–222, §1, July 27, 1982, 96 Stat. 235; Pub. L. 98–353, title III, §§391, 401, 421, July 10, 1984, 98 Stat.

364, 366, 367; Pub. L. 99–554, title II, §§201, 251, 283(a), Oct. 27, 1986, 100 Stat. 3097, 3104, 3116; Pub. L. 100–506, §1(a), Oct. 18, 1988, 102 Stat. 2538; Pub. L. 100–597, §1, Nov. 3, 1988, 102 Stat. 3028; Pub. L. 101–311, title I, §101, title II, §201, June 25, 1990, 104 Stat. 267, 268; Pub. L. 101–647, title XXV, §2522(e), Nov. 29, 1990, 104 Stat. 4867; Pub. L. 102–486, title XXX, §3017(a), Oct. 24, 1992, 106 Stat. 3130; Pub. L. 103–394, title I, §106, title II, §§208(a), 215, 217(a), 218(a), title III, §304(a), title V, §501(a), (b)(1), (d)(1), Oct. 22, 1994, 108 Stat. 4111, 4124, 4126–4128, 4132, 4141–4143; Pub. L. 106–554, §1(a)(5) [title I, §112(c)(3), (4)], Dec. 21, 2000, 114 Stat. 2763, 2763A–393, 2763A–394; Pub. L. 109–8, title I, §102(b), (k), title II, §§211, 226(a), 231(b), title III, §306(c), title IV, §§401(a), 414, 432(a), title VIII, §802(b), title IX, §907(a)(1), (b), (c), title X, §§1004, 1005, 1007(a), title XI, §1101(a), (b), title XII, §1201, Apr. 20, 2005, 119 Stat. 32, 35, 50, 66, 73, 80, 104, 107, 110, 145, 170, 175, 186, 187, 189, 192; Pub. L. 109–390, §5(a)(1), Dec. 12, 2006, 120 Stat. 2695; Pub. L. 111–327, §2(a)(1), Dec. 22, 2010, 124 Stat. 3557.)

Historical and Revision Notes
legislative statements

Section 101(2) defines "affiliate." The House amendment contains a provision that is a compromise between the definition in the House-passed version of H.R. 8200 and the Senate amendment in the nature of a substitute to H.R. 8200. Subparagraphs (A) and (B) are derived from the Senate amendment and subparagraph (D) is taken from the House bill, while subparagraph (C) represents a compromise, taking the House position with respect to a person whose business is operated under a lease or an operating agreement by the debtor and with respect to a person substantially all of whose property is operated under an operating agreement by the debtor and with respect to a person substantially all of whose property is operated under an operating agreement by the debtor and the Senate position on leased property. Thus, the definition of "affiliate" excludes persons substantially all of whose property is operated under a lease agreement by a debtor, such as a small company which owns equipment all of which is leased to a larger nonrelated company.

Section 101(4)(B) represents a modification of the House-passed bill to include the definition of "claim" a right to an equitable remedy for breach of performance if such breach gives rise to a right to payment. This is intended to cause the liquidation or estimation of contingent rights of payment for which there may be an alternative equitable remedy with the result that the equitable remedy will be susceptible to being discharged in bankruptcy. For example, in some States, a judgment for specific performance may be satisfied by an alternative right to payment, in the event performance is refused; in that event, the creditor entitled to specific performance would have a "claim" for purposes of a proceeding under title 11.

On the other hand, rights to an equitable remedy for a breach of performance with respect to which such breach does not give rise to a right to payment are not "claims" and would therefore not be susceptible to discharge in bankruptcy.

In a case under chapter 9 to title 11, "claim" does not include a right to payment under an industrial development bond issued by a municipality as a matter of convenience for a third party.

Municipalities are authorized, under section 103(c) of the Internal Revenue Code of 1954, as amended [title 26], to issue tax-exempt industrial development revenue bonds to provide for the financing of certain projects for privately owned companies. The bonds are sold on the basis of the credit of the company on whose behalf they are issued, and the principal, interest, and premium, if any, are payable solely from payments made by the company to the trustee under the bond indenture and do not constitute claims on the tax revenues or other funds of the issuing municipalities. The municipality merely acts as the vehicle to enable the bonds to be issued on a tax-exempt basis. Claims that arise by virtue of these bonds are not among the claims defined by this paragraph and amounts owed by private companies to the holders of industrial development revenue bonds are not to be included among the assets of the municipality that would be affected by the plan.

Section 101(6) defines "community claim" as provided by the Senate amendment in order to indicate that a community claim exists whether or not there is community property in the estate as of the commencement of the case.

Section 101(7) of the House amendment contains a definition of consumer debt identical to the definition in the House bill and Senate amendment. A consumer debt does not include a debt to any extent the debt is secured by real property.

Section 101(9) of the Senate amendment contained a definition of "court". The House amendment deletes the provision as unnecessary in light of the pervasive jurisdiction of a bankruptcy court under all chapters of title 11 as indicated in title II of the House amendment to H.R. 8200.

Section 101(11) defines "debt" to mean liability on a claim, as was contained in the House-passed version of H.R. 8200. The Senate amendment contained language indicating that "debt" does not include a policy loan made by a life insurance company to the debtor. That language is deleted in the House amendment as unnecessary since a life insurance company clearly has no right to have a policy loan repaid by the debtor, although such company does have a right of offset with respect to such policy loan. Clearly, then, a "debt" does not include a policy loan made by a life insurance company. Inclusion of the language contained in the Senate amendment would have required elaboration of other legal relationships not arising by a liability on a claim. Further the language would have required clarification that interest on a policy loan made by a life insurance company is a debt, and that the insurance company does have right to payment to that interest.

Section 101(14) adopts the definition of "entity" contained in the Senate-passed version of H.R. 8200. Since the Senate amendment to H.R. 8200 deleted the U.S. trustee, a corresponding definitional change is made in chapter 15 of the House amendment for U.S. trustees under the pilot program. Adoption by the House amendment of a pilot program for U.S. trustees under chapter 15 requires insertion of "United States trustee" in many sections. Several provisions in chapter 15 of the House amendment that relate to the U.S. trustee were not contained in the Senate amendment in the nature of a substitute.

Section 101(17) defines "farmer", as in the Senate amendment with an income limitation percentage of 80 percent instead of 75 percent.

Section 101(18) contains a new definition of "farming operation" derived from present law and the definition of "farmer" in the Senate amendment. This definition gives a broad construction to the term "farming operation".

Section 101(20) contains a definition of "foreign representative". It clarifies the House bill and Senate amendment by indicating that a foreign representative must be duly selected in a foreign proceeding.

Section 101(35) defines "security" as contained in the Senate amendment. H.R. 8200 as adopted by the House excluded certain commercial notes from the definition of "security", and that exclusion is deleted.

Section 101(40) defines "transfer" as in the Senate amendment. The definition contained in H.R. 8200 as passed by the House included "setoff" in the definition of "transfer". Inclusion of "setoff" is deleted. The effect is that a "setoff" is not subject to being set aside as a preferential "transfer" but will be subject to special rules.

senate report no. 95–989

Section 101 of title 11 contains 40 definitions:

Paragraph (1) defines "accountant" as an accountant authorized under applicable law to practice accounting. The term includes a professional accounting association, corporation, or partnership if applicable law authorizes such a unit to practice accounting.

Paragraph (2) defines "affiliate." An affiliate is an entity with a close relationship to the debtor. It includes a 20 percent parent or subsidiary of the debtor, whether a corporate, partnership, individual, or estate parent.

The use of "directly or indirectly" in subparagraphs (A) and (B) is intended to cover situations in which there is an opportunity to control, and where the existence of that opportunity operates as indirect control.

"Affiliate" is defined primarily for use in the definition of insider, infra, and for use in the chapter 11 reorganization cases. The definition of "affiliate" does not include an entity acting in a fiduciary or agency capacity if the entity does not have the sole discretionary power to vote 20 percent of the voting securities but hold them solely as security and have not exercised the power to vote. This restriction applies to a corporate affiliate under subparagraph (B) of paragraph (2).

Subsections (C) and (D) of paragraph (2) define affiliate also as those persons and entities whose business or substantially all of whose property is operated under a lease or operating agreement by a debtor and whose business or property is more than 50 percent under the control of the debtor.

The definition of "attorney" in paragraph (3) is similar to the definition of accountant.

Paragraph (4) defines "claim." The effect of the definition is a significant departure from present law. Under present law, "claim" is not defined in straight bankruptcy. Instead it is simply used, along with the concept of provability in section 63 of the Bankruptcy Act [section 103 of former title 11], to limit the kinds of obligations that are payable in a bankruptcy case. The term is defined in the debtor rehabilitation chapters of present law far more broadly. The definition in paragraph (4) adopts an even broader definition of claim than is found in the present debtor rehabilitation chapters. The definition is any right to payment, whether or not reduced to judgment, liquidated, unliquidated, fixed, contingent, matured, unmatured, disputed, undisputed, legal, equitable, secured, or unsecured. The definition also includes as a claim an equitable right to performance that does not give rise to a right to payment. By this broadest possible definition and by the use of the term throughout the title 11, especially in subchapter I of chapter 5, the bill contemplates that all legal obligations of the debtor, no matter how remote or contingent, will be able to be dealt with in the bankruptcy case. It permits the broadest possible relief in the bankruptcy court.

Paragraph (5) defines "commodity broker" by reference to various terms used and defined in subchapter IV of chapter 7, Commodity Broker Liquidation. The terms are described in connection with section 761, infra.

Paragraph (6) defines "community claim" for those eight States that have community property laws. The definition is keyed to the liability of the debtor's property for a claim against either the debtor or the debtor's spouse. If the debtor's property is liable for a claim against either, that claim is a community claim.

Paragraph (7) defines "consumer debt". The definition is adapted from the definition used in various consumer protection laws. It encompasses only a debt incurred by an individual primarily for a personal, family, or household purpose.

The definition of "corporation" in paragraph (8) is similar to the definition in current law, section 1(8) [section 1(8) of former title 11]. The term encompasses any association having the power or privilege that a private corporation, but not an individual or partnership, has; partnership associations organized under a law that makes only the capital subscribed responsible for the debts of the partnership; joint-stock company; unincorporated company or association; and business trust. "Unincorporated association" is intended specifically to include a labor union, as well as other bodies that come under that phrase as used under current law. The exclusion of limited partnerships is explicit, and not left to the case law.

Paragraph (9) defines "court" as the bankruptcy judge in the district in which the case is pending except in municipal adjustment and railroad reorganization cases, where "court" means the Federal district judge.

Paragraph (10) [enacted as (9)] defines "creditor" to include holders of prepetition claims against the debtor. However, it also encompasses certain holders of claims that are deemed to arise before the date of the filing of the petition, such as those injured by the rejection of an executory contract or unexpired lease, certain investment tax credit recapture claim holders, "involuntary gap" creditors, and certain holders of the right of setoff. The term also includes the holder of a prepetition community claim. A guarantor of or surety for a claim against the debtor is also a creditor, because he holds a contingent claim against the debtor that becomes fixed when he pays the creditor whose claim he has guaranteed or insured.

Paragraph (11) [enacted as (10)] defines "custodian." There is no similar definition in current law. It is defined to facilitate drafting, and means a prepetition liquidator of the debtor's property, such as an assignee for the benefit of creditors, a receiver of the debtor's property, or administrator of the debtor's property. The definition of custodian to include a receiver or trustee is descriptive, and not meant to be limited to court officers with those titles. The definition is intended to include other officers of the court if their functions are substantially similar to those of a receiver or trustee.

"Debt" is defined in paragraph (12) [enacted as (11)] as a liability on a claim. The terms "debt" and "claim" are coextensive: a creditor has a "claim" against the debtor; the debtor owes a "debt" to the creditor. This definition of "debt" and the definition of "claim" on which it is based, proposed 11 U.S.C. 101(4), does not include a transaction such as a policy loan on an insurance policy. Under that kind of transaction, the debtor is not liable to the insurance company for repayment; the amount owed is merely available to the company for setoff against any benefits that become payable under the policy. As such, the loan is not a claim (it is not a right to payment) that the company can assert against the estate; nor is the debtor's obligation a debt (a liability on a claim) that will be discharged under proposed 11 U.S.C. 523 or 524.

Paragraph (13) [enacted as (12)] defines "debtor." Debtor means person or municipality concerning which a case under title II has been commenced. This is a change in terminology from present law, which identifies the person by or against whom a petition is filed in a straight bankruptcy liquidation case as the "bankrupt," and a person or municipality that is proceeding under a debtor rehabilitation chapter (chapters VIII through XIII of the Bankruptcy Act) [chapters 8 through 13 of former title 11] as a "debtor." The term "debtor" is used for both kinds of cases in this bill, for ease of reference in chapters 1, 3, and 5 (which apply to straight bankruptcy and reorganization cases).

Paragraph (14) [enacted as (13)] defines "disinterested person." The definition is adapted from section 158 of chapter X of current law [section 558 of former title 11], though it is expanded and modified in some respects. A person is a disinterested person if the person is not a creditor, equity security holder, or insider; is not and was not an investment banker of the debtor for any outstanding security of the debtor (the change from underwriter in current law to investment banker is to make the term more descriptive and to avoid conflict with the definition of underwriter in section 2(11) of the Securities Act of 1933 (15 U.S.C. 77b(11)); has not been an investment banker for a security of the debtor within 3 years before the date of the filing of the petition (the change from five years to three years here conforms the definition with the statute of limitations in the Securities Act of 1933) [15 U.S.C. 77m], or an attorney for such an investment banker; is not an insider of the debtor or of such an investment banker; and does not have an interest materially adverse to the estate.

"Entity" is defined, for convenience, in paragraph (15) [enacted as (14)], to include person, estate, trust, and governmental unit. It is the most inclusive of the various defined terms relating to bodies or units.

Paragraph (16) defines "equity security." The term includes a share or stock in a corporation, a limited partner's interest in a limited partnership, and a warrant or right to subscribe to an equity security. The term does not include a security, such as a convertible debenture, that is convertible into equity security, but has not been converted.

Paragraph (17) [enacted as (15)] defines "equity security holder" for convenience as the holder of an equity securing of the debtor.

Paragraph (18) [enacted as (17)] defines "farmer". It encompasses only those persons for whom farming operations contribute 75 percent or more of their total income.

Paragraphs (19) and (20) define "foreign proceeding" and "foreign representative". A foreign proceeding is a proceeding in another country in which the debtor has some substantial connection for the purpose of liquidating the estate of the debtor or the purpose of financial rehabilitation of the debtor. A foreign representative is the representative of the estate in a foreign proceeding, such as a trustee or administrator.

Paragraph (21) defines "governmental unit" in the broadest sense. The definition encompasses the United States, a State, Commonwealth, District, Territory, municipality, or foreign state, and a department, agency, or instrumentality of any of those entities. "Department, agency, or instrumentality" does not include an entity that owes its existence to State action, such as the granting of a charter or a license but that has no other connection with a State or local government or the Federal Government. The relationship must be an active one in which the department, agency, or instrumentality is actually carrying out some governmental function.

Paragraph (22) defines "indenture." It is similar to the definition of indenture in the Trust Indenture Act of 1939 [15 U.S.C. 77ccc(7)]. An indenture is the instrument under which securities, either debt or equity, of the debtor are outstanding.

Paragraph (23) defines "indenture trustee" as the trustee under an indenture.

Paragraph (24) defines "individual with regular income." The effect of this definition, and of its use in section 109(e), is to expand substantially the kinds of individuals that are eligible for relief under chapter 13, Adjustment of Debts of an Individual with Regular Income. Chapter XIII [chapter 13 of former title 11] is now available only for wage earners. The definition encompasses all individuals with incomes that are sufficiently stable and regular to enable them to make payments under a chapter 13 plan. Thus, individuals on welfare, social security, fixed pension incomes, or who live on investment incomes, will be able to work out repayment plans with their creditors rather than being forced into straight bankruptcy. Also, self-employed individuals will be eligible to use chapter 13 if they have regular incomes.

However, the definition excludes certain stockbrokers and commodity brokers, in order to prohibit them from proceeding under chapter 13 and avoiding the customer protection provisions of chapter 7.

"Insider", defined in paragraph (25), is a new term. An insider is one who has a sufficiently close relationship with the debtor that his conduct is made subject to closer scrutiny than those dealing at arms length with the debtor. If the debtor is an individual, then a relative of the debtor, a partnership in which the debtor is a general partner, a general partner of the debtor, and a corporation controlled by the debtor are all insiders. If the debtor is a corporation, then a controlling person, a relative of a controlling person, a partnership in which the debtor is a general partner, and a general partner of the debtor are all insiders. If the debtor is a partnership, then a general partner of or in the debtor, a relative of a general partner in the debtor, and a person in control are all insiders. If the debtor is a municipality, then an elected official of the debtor is an insider. In addition, affiliates of the debtor and managing agents are insiders.

The definition of "insolvent" in paragraph (26) is adopted from section 1(19) of current law [section 1(19) of former title 11]. An entity is insolvent if its debts are greater than its assets, at a fair valuation, exclusive of property exempted or fraudulently transferred. It is the traditional bankruptcy balance sheet test of insolvency. For a partnership, the definition is modified to account for the liability of a general partner for the partnership's debts. The difference in this definition from that in current law is in the exclusion of exempt property for all purposes in the definition of insolvent.

Paragraph (27) defines "judicial lien." It is one of three kinds of liens defined in this section. A judicial lien is a lien obtained by judgment, levy, sequestration, or other legal or equitable process or proceeding.

Paragraph (28) defines "lien." The definition is new and is very broad. A lien is defined as a charge against or interest in property to secure payment of a debt or performance of an obligation. It includes inchoate liens. In general, the concept of lien is divided into three kinds of liens: judicial liens, security interests, and statutory liens. Those three categories are mutually exclusive and are exhaustive except for certain common law liens.

Paragraph (29) defines "municipality." The definition is adapted from the terms used in the chapter IX (municipal bankruptcy) [chapter 9 of former title 11] amendment to the Bankruptcy Act enacted in 1976 (Pub. L. 94–260). That amendment spoke in terms of "political subdivision or public agency or instrumentality of a State". Bankruptcy Act Sec. 84 [section 404 of former title 11]. The term municipality is defined by those three terms for convenience. It does not include the District of Columbia or any territories of the United States.

"Person" is defined in paragraph (30). The definition is a change in wording, but not in substance, from the definition in section 1(23) of the Bankruptcy Act [section 1(23) of former title 11]. The definition is also similar to the one contained in 1 U.S.C. sec. 1, but is repeated here for convenience and ease of reference. Person includes individual partnership, and corporation. The exclusion of governmental units is made explicit in order to avoid any confusion that may arise if, for example, a municipality is incorporated and thus is legally a corporation as well as governmental unit. The definition does not include an estate or a trust, which are included only in the definition of "entity" in proposed 11 U.S.C. 101(14).

"Petition" is defined for convenience in paragraph (31). Petition is a petition under section 301, 302, 303, or 304 of the bankruptcy code—that is, a petition that commences a case under title 11.

Paragraph (32) defines purchaser as a transferee of a voluntary transfer, such as a sale or gift, and includes an immediate or mediate transferee of a purchaser.

The definition of "railroad" in paragraph (33) is derived from section 77 of the Bankruptcy Act [section 205 of former title 11]. A railroad is a common carrier by railroad engaged in the transportation of individuals or property, or an owner of trackage facilities leased by such a common carrier. The effect of the definition and the use of the term in section 109(d) is to eliminate the limitation now found in section 77 of the Bankruptcy Act that only railroads engaged in interstate commerce may proceed under the railroad reorganization provisions. The limitation may have been inserted because of a doubt that the commerce power could not reach intrastate railroads. Be that as it may, this bill is enacted under the bankruptcy power.

Paragraph (34) defines "relative" as an individual related by affinity or consanguinity within the third degree as determined by the common law, and includes individuals in a step or adoptive relationship. The definition is similar to current law, but adds the latter phrase. This definition should be applied as of the time when the transaction that it concerns took place. Thus, a former spouse is not a relative, but if, for example, for purposes of the preference section, proposed 11 U.S.C. 547(b)(4)(B), the transferee was a spouse of the debtor at the time of the transfer sought to be avoided, then the transferee would be relative and subject to the insider rules, even if the transferee was no longer married to the debtor at the time of the commencement of the case or at the time of the commencement of the preference recovery proceeding.

Paragraph (35) defines "security." The definition is new and is modeled on the most recent draft of the American Law Institute's proposed securities code, with some exceptions. The interest of a limited partner in a limited partnership is included in order to make sure that everything that is defined as an equity security is also a "security." The definition, as with the definition of "entity", "insider", and "person", is open-ended because the term is not susceptible of precise specification. Thus the courts will be able to use the characterization provided in this definition to treat with new kinds of documents on a flexible basis.

Paragraphs (36) and (37) defined "security agreement" and "security interest." A security interest is one of the kinds of liens. It is a lien created by an agreement. Security agreement is defined as the agreement creating the security interest. Though these terms are similar to the same terms in the Uniform Commercial Code, article IX, they are broader. For example, the U.C.C. does not cover real property mortgages. Under this definition, such a mortgage is included, as are all other liens created by agreement, even though not covered by the U.C.C. All U.C.C. security interests and security agreements are, however, security interests and security agreements under this definition. Whether a consignment or a lease constitutes a security interest under the bankruptcy code will depend on whether it constitutes a security interest under applicable State or local law.

Paragraph (38) defines another kind of lien, "statutory lien." The definition, derived from current law, states that a statutory lien is a lien arising solely by force of statute on specified circumstances or conditions and includes a lien of distress for rent (whether statutory, common law, or otherwise). The definition excludes judicial liens and security interests, whether or not they are provided for or are dependent on a statute, and whether or not they are made fully effective by statute. A statutory lien is only one that arises automatically, and is not based on an agreement to give a lien or on judicial action. Mechanics', materialmen's, and warehousemen's liens are examples. Tax liens are also included in the definition of statutory lien.

"Stockbroker" is defined in paragraph (39) as a person engaged in the business of effecting transactions in securities for the account of others or with members of the general public from or for such person's own account, if the person has a customer, as defined. Thus, the definition, derived from a combination of the definitions of "broker" and "dealer" in the Securities Exchange Act of 1934 [15 U.S.C. 78c], encompasses both brokers and dealers. The definition is used in section 109 and in subchapter III of chapter 7, Stockholder Liquidation. The term does not encompass an employee who acts for a principal that "effects" transaction or deals with the public, because such an employee will not have a "customer".

Paragraph (40) defines "transfer." It is derived and adapted, with stylistic changes, from section 1(30) of the Bankruptcy Act [section 1(30) of former title 11]. A transfer is a disposition of an interest in property. The definition of transfer is as broad as possible. Many of the potentially limiting words in current law are deleted, and the language is simplified. Under this definition, any transfer of an interest in property is a transfer, including a transfer of possession, custody, or control even if there is no transfer of title, because possession, custody, and control are interests in property. A deposit in a bank account or similar account is a transfer.

References in Text

The Social Security Act, referred to in par. (10A)(B), is act Aug. 14, 1935, ch. 531, 49 Stat. 620, which is classified generally to chapter 7 (§301 et seq.) of Title 42, The Public Health and Welfare. For complete classification of this Act to the Code, see section 1305 of Title 42 and Tables.

The Internal Revenue Code of 1986, referred to in pars. (12A)(B) and (41)(C), is classified generally to Title 26, Internal Revenue Code.

Section 3 of the Federal Deposit Insurance Act, referred to in pars. (12A)(D), (21B)(A), (33)(A), (35)(A), and (54A), is classified to section 1813 of Title 12, Banks and Banking.

Sections 101 and 206(r) of the Federal Credit Union Act, referred to in pars. (12A)(D), (33)(B), and (34), are classified to sections 1752 and 1786(r), respectively, of Title 12, Banks and Banking.

The Investment Company Act of 1940, referred to in par. (22)(B), is title I of act Aug. 22, 1940, ch. 686, 54 Stat. 789, which is classified generally to subchapter I (§80a–1 et seq.) of chapter 2D of Title 15, Commerce and Trade. For complete classification of this Act to the Code, see section 80a–51 of Title 15 and Tables.

Section 402 of the Federal Deposit Insurance Corporation Improvement Act of 1991, referred to in par. (22A)(B), is classified to section 4402 of Title 12, Banks and Banking.

The Securities Exchange Act of 1934, referred to in pars. (47)(A)(i), (48), (48A), and (53B)(B), is act June 6, 1934, ch. 404, 48 Stat. 881, which is classified principally to chapter 2B (§78a et seq.) of Title 15, Commerce and Trade. Sections 3, 6, 15A, and 17A of the Act are classified to sections 78c, 78f, 78o–3 and 78q–1, respectively, of Title 15. For complete classification of this Act to the Code, see section 78a of Title 15 and Tables.

The Securities Act of 1933, referred to in par. (49)(A)(xii), is act May 27, 1933, ch. 38, title I, 48 Stat. 74, which is classified generally to subchapter I (§77a et seq.) of chapter 2A of Title 15, Commerce and Trade. Section 3(b) of the Act is classified to section 77c(b) of Title 15. For complete classification of this Act to the Code, see section 77a of Title 15 and Tables.

The Gramm-Leach-Bliley Act, referred to in par. (53B)(B), is Pub. L. 106–102, Nov. 12, 1999, 113 Stat. 1338. For complete classification of this Act to the Code, see Short Title of 1999 Amendment note set out under section 1811 of Title 12, Banks and Banking, and Tables.

The Legal Certainty for Bank Products Act of 2000, referred to in par. (53B)(B), is title IV of H.R. 5660, as enacted by Pub. L. 106–554, §1(a)(5), Dec. 21, 2000, 114 Stat. 2763, 2763A-457, which is classified to sections 27 to 27f of Title 7, Agriculture. For complete classification of this Act to the Code, see Short Title of 2000 Amendment note set out under section 1 of Title 7 and Tables.

The Commodity Exchange Act, referred to in par. (53B)(B), is act Sept. 21, 1922, ch. 369, 42 Stat. 998, which is classified generally to chapter 1 (§1 et seq.) of Title 7, Agriculture. For complete classification of this Act to the Code, see section 1 of Title 7 and Tables.

Amendments

2010—Par. (13A)(A). Pub. L. 111–327, §2(a)(1)(A)(i), inserted "if used as the principal residence by the debtor" after "a residential structure".

Par. (13A)(B). Pub. L. 111–327, §2(a)(1)(A)(ii), inserted "if used as the principal residence by the debtor" before period at end.

Par. (35)(B). Pub. L. 111–327, §2(a)(1)(B), substituted "paragraphs (21B) and (33)(A)" for "paragraphs (23) and (35)".

Par. (40B). Pub. L. 111–327, §2(a)(1)(C), substituted "record relating to a patient, including a written document or a" for "written document relating to a patient or a".

Par. (42). Pub. L. 111–327, §2(a)(1)(D), which directed substitution of "303 and 1504" for "303, and 304", was executed by making the substitution for "303, or 304" to reflect the probable intent of Congress.

Par. (51B). Pub. L. 111–327, §2(a)(1)(E), inserted "thereto" before period at end.

Par. (51D)(A). Pub. L. 111–327, §2(a)(1)(F), inserted "of the filing" after "as of the date".

2006—Par. (22)(A). Pub. L. 109–390, §5(a)(1)(A), struck out "(domestic or foreign)" after "an entity" and inserted "(whether or not a 'customer', as defined in section 741)" after "custodian for a customer".

Par. (22A)(A). Pub. L. 109–390, §5(a)(1)(B), inserted "(aggregated across counterparties)" after "principal amount outstanding" and substituted "at such time or on any day during the 15-month period preceding the date of the filing of the petition" for "on any day during the previous 15-month period" in two places.

Par. (25)(A). Pub. L. 109–390, §5(a)(1)(C), inserted ", as defined in section 761" after "commodity contract" and substituted "repurchase or reverse repurchase transaction (whether or not such repurchase or reverse repurchase transaction is a 'repurchase agreement', as defined in this section)" for "repurchase transaction, reverse repurchase transaction,".

Par. (53B)(A)(i)(II). Pub. L. 109–390, §5(a)(1)(D)(i)(I), substituted ", precious metals, or other commodity" for "or precious metals".

Par. (53B)(A)(i)(VIII). Pub. L. 109–390, §5(a)(1)(D)(i)(III), substituted "option, future, or forward agreement" for "weather derivative, or weather option".

Par. (53B)(A)(i)(IX), (X). Pub. L. 109–390, §5(a)(1)(D)(i)(II), (IV), added subcls. (IX) and (X).

Par. (53B)(A)(ii). Pub. L. 109–390, §5(a)(1)(D)(ii), inserted "or other derivatives" after "dealings in the swap" in subcl. (I) and substituted "future, option, or spot transaction" for "future, or option" in subcl. (II).

Par. (53B)(B). Pub. L. 109–390, §5(a)(1)(E), substituted "the Gramm-Leach-Bliley Act, the Legal Certainty for Bank Products Act of 2000, the securities laws (as such term is defined in section 3(a)(47) of the Securities Exchange Act of 1934) and the Commodity Exchange Act" for "the Securities Act of 1933, the Securities Exchange Act of 1934, the Public Utility Holding Company Act of 1935, the Trust Indenture Act of 1939, the Investment Company Act of 1940, the Investment Advisers Act of 1940, the Securities Investor Protection Act of 1970, the Commodity Exchange Act, the Gramm-Leach-Bliley Act, and the Legal Certainty for Bank Products Act of 2000".

2005—Pub. L. 109–8, §1201(1), substituted "In this title the following definitions shall apply:" for "In this title—" in introductory provisions.

Pars. (1), (2). Pub. L. 109–8, §1201(2), (8), inserted "The term" after par. designation and substituted a period for semicolon at end.

Par. (3). Pub. L. 109–8, §1201(2), (8), inserted "The term" after par. designation and substituted a period for semicolon at end.

Pub. L. 109–8, §226(a)(1), added par. (3).

Par. (4). Pub. L. 109–8, §1201(2), (8), inserted "The term" after par. designation and substituted a period for semicolon at end.

Par. (4A). Pub. L. 109–8, §1201(2), (8), inserted "The term" after par. designation and substituted a period for semicolon at end.

Pub. L. 109–8, §226(a)(2), added par. (4A).

Pars. (5) to (7). Pub. L. 109–8, §1201(2), (8), inserted "The term" after par. designation and substituted a period for semicolon at end.

Pars. (7A), (7B). Pub. L. 109–8, §1201(2), (8), inserted "The term" after par. designation and substituted a period for semicolon at end.

Pub. L. 109–8, §1007(a)(1), added pars. (7A) and (7B).

Pars. (8) to (10). Pub. L. 109–8, §1201(2), (8), inserted "The term" after par. designation and substituted a period for semicolon at end.

Par. (10A). Pub. L. 109–8, §1201(2), (8), inserted "The term" after par. designation and substituted a period for semicolon at end.

Pub. L. 109–8, §102(b), added par. (10A).

Pars. (11), (12). Pub. L. 109–8, §1201(2), (8), inserted "The term" after par. designation and substituted a period for semicolon at end.

Par. (12A). Pub. L. 109–8, §1201(8), which directed the substitution of a period for a semicolon at end, could not be executed because par. (12A) ended in a period after amendment by Pub. L. 109–8, §226(a)(3). See below.

Pub. L. 109–8, §1201(2), inserted "The term" after par. designation.

Pub. L. 109–8, §§211(1), 226(a)(3), added par. (12A) and struck out former par. (12A) which read as follows: " 'debt for child support' means a debt of a kind specified in section 523(a)(5) of this title for maintenance or support of a child of the debtor;".

Par. (13). Pub. L. 109–8, §1201(2), (8), inserted "The term" after par. designation and substituted a period for semicolon at end.

Par. (13A). Pub. L. 109–8, §1201(2), (8), inserted "The term" after par. designation and substituted a period for semicolon at end.

Pub. L. 109–8, §306(c)(1), added par. (13A).

Par. (14). Pub. L. 109–8, §1201(2), (8), inserted "The term" after par. designation and substituted a period for semicolon at end.

Pub. L. 109–8, §414, amended par. (14) generally. Prior to amendment, par. (14) consisted of subpars. (A) to (E) defining "disinterested person".

Par. (14A). Pub. L. 109–8, §1201(2), (8), inserted "The term" after par. designation and substituted a period for semicolon at end.

Pub. L. 109–8, §211(2), added par. (14A).

Pars. (15) to (17). Pub. L. 109–8, §1201(2), (8), inserted "The term" after par. designation and substituted a period for semicolon at end.

Par. (18). Pub. L. 109–8, §1201(2), (8), inserted "The term" after par. designation and substituted a period for semicolon at end.

Par. (18)(A). Pub. L. 109–8, §1005, substituted "for—
"(i) the taxable year preceding; or
"(ii) each of the 2d and 3d taxable years preceding;
the taxable year" for "for the taxable year preceding the taxable year".

Pub. L. 109–8, §1004(1), substituted "$3,237,000" for "$1,500,000" and "not less than 50 percent" for "not less than 80 percent".

Par. (18)(B)(ii). Pub. L. 109–8, §1004(2), substituted "$3,237,000" for "$1,500,000" and "50 percent" for "80 percent".

Par. (19). Pub. L. 109–8, §1201(2), (8), inserted "The term" after par. designation and substituted a period for semicolon at end.

Pars. (19A), (19B). Pub. L. 109–8, §1201(2), (8), inserted "The term" after par. designation and substituted a period for semicolon at end.

Pub. L. 109–8, §1007(a)(2), added pars. (19A) and (19B).

Pars. (20) to (21B). Pub. L. 109–8, §1201(2), (8), inserted "The term" after par. designation and substituted a period for semicolon at end.

Par. (22). Pub. L. 109–8, §1201(2), (8), inserted "The term" after par. designation and substituted a period for semicolon at end.

Pub. L. 109–8, §907(b)(1), added par. (22) and struck out former par. (22) which consisted of introductory provisions and subpars. (A) and (B) defining "financial institution".

Par. (22A). Pub. L. 109–8, §1201(2), (8), inserted "The term" after par. designation and substituted a period for semicolon at end.

Pub. L. 109–8, §907(b)(2), added par. (22A).

Pars. (23), (24). Pub. L. 109–8, §1201(2), (8), inserted "The term" after par. designation and substituted a period for semicolon at end.

Pub. L. 109–8, §802(b), added pars. (23) and (24) and struck out former pars. (23) and (24) which read as follows:

"(23) 'foreign proceeding' means proceeding, whether judicial or administrative and whether or not under bankruptcy law, in a foreign country in which the debtor's domicile, residence, principal place of business, or principal assets were located at the commencement of such proceeding, for the purpose of liquidating an estate, adjusting debts by composition, extension, or discharge, or effecting a reorganization;

"(24) 'foreign representative' means duly selected trustee, administrator, or other representative of an estate in a foreign proceeding;".

Par. (25). Pub. L. 109–8, §1201(2), (8), inserted "The term" after par. designation and substituted a period for semicolon at end.

Pub. L. 109–8, §907(a)(1)(A), substituted "means—" for "means", designated subsequent provisions as subpar. (A), substituted ", or any other similar agreement" for ", or any combination thereof or option thereon", and added subpars. (B) to (E).

Par. (26). Pub. L. 109–8, §1201(2), (8), inserted "The term" after par. designation and substituted a period for semicolon at end.

Pub. L. 109–8, §907(b)(3), added par. (26) and struck out former par. (26) which read as follows: " 'forward contract merchant' means a person whose business consists in whole or in part of entering into forward contracts as or with merchants in a commodity, as defined in section 761(8) of this title, or any similar good, article, service, right, or interest which is presently or in the future becomes the subject of dealing in the forward contract trade;".

Par. (27). Pub. L. 109–8, §1201(2), (8), inserted "The term" after par. designation and substituted a period for semicolon at end.

Par. (27A). Pub. L. 109–8, §1201(2), (8), inserted "The term" after par. designation and substituted a period for semicolon at end.

Pub. L. 109–8, §1101(a)(2), added par. (27A). Former par. (27A) redesignated (27B).

Pub. L. 109–8, §306(c)(2), added par. (27A).

Par. (27B). Pub. L. 109–8, §1201(2), (8), inserted "The term" after par. designation and substituted a period for semicolon at end.

Pub. L. 109–8, §1101(a)(1), redesignated par. (27A) as (27B).

Pars. (28) to (34). Pub. L. 109–8, §1201(2), (8), inserted "The term" after par. designation and substituted a period for semicolon at end.

Par. (35). Pub. L. 109–8, §1201(2), (8), inserted "The term" after par. designation and substituted a period for semicolon at end.

Par. (35)(B). Pub. L. 109–8, §1201(3), substituted "paragraphs (23) and (35)" for "paragraphs (21B) and (33)(A)".

Par. (35A). Pub. L. 109–8, §1201(2), (4), inserted "The term" after par. designation and substituted a period for "; and" at end.

Pars. (36), (37). Pub. L. 109–8, §1201(2), (8), inserted "The term" after par. designation and substituted a period for semicolon at end.

Par. (38). Pub. L. 109–8, §1201(2), (4), inserted "The term" after par. designation and substituted a period for "; and" at end.

Pars. (38A), (38B). Pub. L. 109–8, §1201(2), (8), inserted "The term" after par. designation and substituted a period for semicolon at end.

Pub. L. 109–8, §907(c), added pars. (38A) and (38B).

Par. (39). Pub. L. 109–8, §1201(2), inserted "The term" after par. designation.

Par. (39A). Pub. L. 109–8, §1201(2), (8), inserted "The term" after par. designation and substituted a period for semicolon at end.

Pub. L. 109–8, §102(k), added par. (39A).

Par. (40). Pub. L. 109–8, §1201(2), (8), inserted "The term" after par. designation and substituted a period for semicolon at end.

Pars. (40A), (40B). Pub. L. 109–8, §1201(2), (8), inserted "The term" after par. designation and substituted a period for semicolon at end.

Pub. L. 109–8, §1101(b), added pars. (40A) and (40B).

Par. (41). Pub. L. 109–8, §1201(2), (8), inserted "The term" after par. designation and substituted a period for semicolon at end.

Par. (41A). Pub. L. 109–8, §1201(2), (8), inserted "The term" after par. designation and substituted a period for semicolon at end.

Pub. L. 109–8, §231(b), added par. (41A).

Pars. (42) to (45). Pub. L. 109–8, §1201(2), (8), inserted "The term" after par. designation and substituted a period for semicolon at end.

Par. (46). Pub. L. 109–8, §1201(2), (8), inserted "The term" after par. designation and substituted a period for semicolon at end.

Pub. L. 109–8, §907(a)(1)(B), substituted "at any time before" for "on any day during the period beginning 90 days before the date of".

Par. (47). Pub. L. 109–8, §1201(2), (8), inserted "The term" after par. designation and substituted a period for semicolon at end.

Pub. L. 109–8, §907(a)(1)(C), amended par. (47) generally. Prior to amendment, par. (47) read as follows: " 'repurchase agreement' (which definition also applies to a reverse repurchase agreement) means an agreement, including related terms, which provides for the transfer of certificates of deposit, eligible bankers' acceptances, or securities that are direct obligations of, or that are fully guaranteed as to principal and interest by, the United States or any agency of the United States against the transfer of funds by the transferee of such certificates of deposit, eligible bankers' acceptances, or securities with a simultaneous agreement by such transferee to transfer to the transferor thereof certificates of deposit, eligible bankers' acceptances, or securities as described above, at a date certain not later than one year after such transfers or on demand, against the transfer of funds;".

Par. (48). Pub. L. 109–8, §1201(2), (8), inserted "The term" after par. designation and substituted a period for semicolon at end.

Pub. L. 109–8, §907(a)(1)(D), inserted ", or exempt from such registration under such section pursuant to an order of the Securities and Exchange Commission," after "1934".

Par. (48A). Pub. L. 109–8, §1201(2), (8), inserted "The term" after par. designation and substituted a period for semicolon at end.

Pub. L. 109–8, §401(a), added par. (48A).

Pars. (49) to (51A). Pub. L. 109–8, §1201(2), (8), inserted "The term" after par. designation and substituted a period for semicolon at end.

Par. (51B). Pub. L. 109–8, §1201(2), (5), (8), inserted "The term" after par. designation and "who is not a family farmer" after "income of a debtor" and substituted a period for "thereto having aggregate noncontingent, liquidated secured debts in an amount no more than $4,000,000;".

Pars. (51C), (51D). Pub. L. 109–8, §1201(2), (8), inserted "The term" after par. designation and substituted a period for semicolon at end.

Pub. L. 109–8, §432(a), added pars. (51C) and (51D) and struck out former par. (51C) which read as follows: " 'small business' means a person engaged in commercial or business activities (but does not include a person whose primary activity is the business of owning or operating real property and activities incidental thereto) whose aggregate noncontingent liquidated secured and unsecured debts as of the date of the petition do not exceed $2,000,000;".

Pars. (52) to (53A). Pub. L. 109–8, §1201(2), (8), inserted "The term" after par. designation and substituted a period for semicolon at end.

Par. (53B). Pub. L. 109–8, §1201(2), (8), inserted "The term" after par. designation and substituted a period for semicolon at end.

Pub. L. 109–8, §907(a)(1)(E), amended par. (53B) generally. Prior to amendment, par. (53B) consisted of introductory provisions and subpars. (A) to (C) defining "swap agreement".

Par. (53C). Pub. L. 109–8, §1201(2), (8), inserted "The term" after par. designation and substituted a period for semicolon at end.

Par. (53D). Pub. L. 109–8, §1201(2), (8), inserted "The term" after par. designation and substituted a period for semicolon at end.

Par. (54). Pub. L. 109–8, §1201(8), substituted a period for semicolon at end.

Pub. L. 109–8, §1201(6), added par. (54) and struck out former par. (54) which read as follows: "The term 'transfer' means every mode, direct or indirect, absolute or conditional, voluntary or involuntary, of disposing of or parting with property or with an interest in property, including retention of title as a security interest and foreclosure of the debtor's equity of redemption;".

Pub. L. 109–8, §1201(2), inserted "The term" after par. designation.

Par. (54A). Pub. L. 109–8, §1201(8), which directed the substitution of a period for semicolon at end, could not be executed because par. (54A) ended in a period after amendment by Pub. L. 109–8, §1201(4). See below.

Pub. L. 109–8, §1201(4), (7), substituted "The term" for "the term", realigned left margin, and substituted a period for "; and" at end.

Par. (55). Pub. L. 109–8, §1201(2), (8), inserted "The term" after par. designation and substituted a period for semicolon at end.

Par. (56A). Pub. L. 109–8, §1201(8), which directed the substitution of a period for semicolon "in each of paragraphs (40) through (55)" at end, was executed to par. (56A), to reflect the probable intent of Congress, because par. (56A) follows par. (53C) in text.

Pub. L. 109–8, §1201(2), inserted "The term" after par. designation.

2000—Par. (22). Pub. L. 106–554, §1(a)(5) [title I, §112(c)(3)], amended par. (22) generally. Prior to amendment par. (22) read as follows: " 'financial institution' means a person that is a commercial or savings bank, industrial savings bank, savings and loan association, or trust company and, when any such person is acting as agent or custodian for a customer in connection with a securities contract, as defined in section 741 of this title, such customer;".

Par. (54A). Pub. L. 106–554, §1(a)(5) [title I, §112(c)(4)], added par. (54A).

1994—Par. (3). Pub. L. 103–394, §501(a)(1), redesignated par. (3) as (21B) and inserted it after par. (21A).

Par. (6). Pub. L. 103–394, §501(b)(1)(A), substituted "section 761" for "section 761(9)" after "customer, as defined in".

Par. (12A). Pub. L. 103–394, §304(a), added par. (12A).

Par. (21B). Pub. L. 103–394, §501(a)(1), redesignated par. (3) as (21B).

Par. (22). Pub. L. 103–394, §501(b)(1)(B), substituted "section 741" for "section 741(7)".

Par. (33)(A). Pub. L. 103–394, §501(d)(1)(A)(i), struck out "(12 U.S.C. 1813(u))" after "section 3(u) of the Federal Deposit Insurance Act".

Par. (33)(B). Pub. L. 103–394, §501(d)(1)(A)(ii), struck out "(12 U.S.C. 1786(r))" after "Act".

Par. (34). Pub. L. 103–394, §501(d)(1)(B), struck out "(12 U.S.C. 1752(7))" after "Act".

Par. (35). Pub. L. 103–394, §501(b)(1)(C), (d)(1)(C), struck out "(12 U.S.C. 1813(c)(2))" after "Act" in subpar. (A) and substituted "paragraphs (21B)" for "paragraphs (3)" in subpar. (B).

Par. (35A). Pub. L. 103–394, §501(a)(4), redesignated par. (56) defining "intellectual property" as (35A) and inserted it after par. (35).

Par. (39). Pub. L. 103–394, §501(a)(5), redesignated par. (57) defining "mask work" as (39) and inserted it after par. (38). Former par. (39) redesignated (51A).

Par. (41). Pub. L. 103–394, §106, amended par. (41) generally. Prior to amendment, par. (41) read as follows: " 'person' includes individual, partnership, and corporation, but does not include governmental unit, *Provided, however*, That any governmental unit that acquires an asset from a person as a result of operation of a loan guarantee agreement, or as receiver or liquidating agent of a person, will be considered a person for purposes of section 1102 of this title."

Par. (42A). Pub. L. 103–394, §208(a)(1), added par. (42A).

Par. (48). Pub. L. 103–394, §501(d)(1)(D), struck out "(15 U.S.C. 78q–1)" after "Act of 1934" and "(15 U.S.C. 78c(12))" after "such Act".

Par. (49)(A)(xii). Pub. L. 103–394, §501(d)(1)(E)(i), struck out "(15 U.S.C. 77a et seq.)" after "Act of 1933" and "(15 U.S.C. 77c(b))" after "such Act".

Par. (49)(B). Pub. L. 103–394, §501(b)(1)(D), (d)(1)(E)(ii), substituted "section 761" for "section 761(13)" in cl. (ii) and struck out "(15 U.S.C. 77c(b))" after "Act of 1933" in cl. (vi).

Par. (51A). Pub. L. 103–394, §501(a)(2), redesignated par. (39) as (51A) and inserted it after par. (51).

Par. (51B). Pub. L. 103–394, §218(a), added par. (51B).

Par. (51C). Pub. L. 103–394, §217(a), added par. (51C).

Par. (53A). Pub. L. 103–394, §501(a)(3), (b)(1)(E), redesignated par. (54) defining "stockbroker" as (53A) and substituted "section 741" for "section 741(2)" in subpar. (A).

Par. (53B). Pub. L. 103–394, §501(a)(3), redesignated par. (55) defining "swap agreement" as (53B).

Par. (53C). Pub. L. 103–394, §501(a)(3), redesignated par. (56) defining "swap participant" as (53C).

Par. (53D). Pub. L. 103–394, §501(a)(3), (d)(1)(F), redesignated par. (57) defining "timeshare plan" as (53D) and substituted semicolon for period at end.

Par. (54). Pub. L. 103–394, §501(a)(3), redesignated par. (54) defining "stockbroker" as (53A).

Par. (55). Pub. L. 103–394, §501(a)(3), redesignated par. (55) defining "swap agreement" as (53B).

Pub. L. 103–394, §215, inserted "spot foreign exchange agreement," after "forward foreign exchange agreement,".

Par. (56). Pub. L. 103–394, §501(a)(3), redesignated par. (56) defining "swap participant" as (53C).

Pub. L. 103–394, §501(a)(4), redesignated par. (56) defining "intellectual property" as (35A) and inserted it after par. (35).

Par. (56A). Pub. L. 103–394, §208(a)(2), added par. (56A) and inserted it after par. defining "swap participant".

Par. (57). Pub. L. 103–394, §501(a)(3), redesignated par. (57) defining "timeshare plan" as (53D).

Pub. L. 103–394, §501(a)(5), redesignated par. (57) defining "mask work" as (39) and inserted it after par. (38).

1992—Par. (21A). Pub. L. 102–486 added par. (21A).

1990—Par. (3). Pub. L. 101–647, §2522(e)(4), added par. (3). Former par. (3) redesignated (4).

Pars. (4) to (23). Pub. L. 101–647, §2522(e)(3), redesignated pars. (3) to (22) as (4) to (23), respectively. Former par. (23) redesignated (24).

Par. (24). Pub. L. 101–647, §2522(e)(3), redesignated par. (23) as (24). Former par. (24) redesignated (25).

Pub. L. 101–311, §201(1), inserted "as defined in section 761(8) of this title, or any similar good, article, service, right, or interest which is presently or in the future becomes the subject of dealing in the forward contract trade," after "transfer of commodity," and ", including, but not limited to, a repurchase transaction, reverse repurchase transaction, consignment, lease, swap, hedge transaction, deposit, loan, option, allocated transaction, unallocated transaction, or any combination thereof or option thereon" after "entered into".

Par. (25). Pub. L. 101–647, §2522(e)(3), redesignated par. (24) as (25). Former par. (25) redesignated (26).

Pub. L. 101–311, §201(2), substituted "a commodity, as defined in section 761(8) of this title, or any similar good, article, service, right, or interest which is presently or in the future becomes the subject of dealing in the forward contract trade" for "commodities".

Pars. (26) to (32). Pub. L. 101–647, §2522(e)(3), redesignated pars. (25) to (31) as (26) to (32), respectively. Former par. (32) redesignated (36).

Par. (33). Pub. L. 101–647, §2522(e)(2), added par. (33). Former par. (33) redesignated (37).

Par. (34). Pub. L. 101–647, §2522(e)(2), added par. (34). Former par. (34) redesignated (38).

Pub. L. 101–311, §201(4), added par. (34). Former par. (34) redesignated (36).

Par. (35). Pub. L. 101–647, §2522(e)(2), added par. (35). Former par. (35) redesignated (39).

Pub. L. 101–311, §201(4), added par. (35). Former par. (35) redesignated (37).

Par. (36). Pub. L. 101–647, §2522(e)(1), redesignated par. (32) as (36). Former par. (36) redesignated (40).

Pub. L. 101–311, §201(3), redesignated par. (34) as (36). Former par. (36) redesignated (38).

Pars. (37) to (48). Pub. L. 101–647, §2522(e)(1), redesignated pars. (33) to (44) as (37) to (48), respectively. Former pars. (45) to (48) redesignated (49) to (52), respectively.

Pub. L. 101–311, §201(3), redesignated pars. (35) to (46) as (37) to (48), respectively. Former pars. (47) and (48) redesignated (49) and (50), respectively.

Pars. (49), (50). Pub. L. 101–647, §2522(e)(1), redesignated pars. (45) and (46) as (49) and (50), respectively. Former pars. (49) and (50) redesignated (53) and (54) defining "stockbroker", respectively.

Pub. L. 101–311, §201(3), redesignated pars. (47) and (48) as (49) and (50), respectively. Former pars. (49) and (50) redesignated (51) and (52), respectively.

Pub. L. 101–311, §101(2), added pars. (49) and (50). Former pars. (49) and (50) redesignated (51) and (52), respectively.

Par. (51). Pub. L. 101–647, §2522(e)(1), redesignated par. (47) as (51). Former par. (51) redesignated (55) defining "swap agreement".

Pub. L. 101–311, §201(3), redesignated par. (49) as (51). Former par. (51) redesignated (53).

Pub. L. 101–311, §101(1), redesignated par. (49) as (51). Former par. (51) redesignated (53).

Par. (52). Pub. L. 101–647, §2522(e)(1), redesignated par. (48) as (52). Former par. (52) redesignated (56) defining "swap participant".

Pub. L. 101–311, §201(3), redesignated par. (50) as (52). Former par. (52) redesignated (54) defining "transfer".

Pub. L. 101–311, §101(1), redesignated par. (50) as (52). Former par. (52) redesignated (54).

Par. (53). Pub. L. 101–647, §2522(e)(1), redesignated par. (49) as (53). Former par. (53) redesignated (57) defining "timeshare plan".

Pub. L. 101–311, §201(3), redesignated par. (51) as (53). Former par. (53) redesignated (55) defining "United States".

Pub. L. 101–311, §101(1), redesignated par. (51) as (53). Former par. (53) redesignated (55).

Par. (54). Pub. L. 101–647, §2522(e)(1), redesignated par. (50) as (54) defining "stockbroker".

Pub. L. 101–311, §201(3), redesignated par. (52) as (54) defining "transfer". Former par. (54) redesignated (56) defining "intellectual property".

Pub. L. 101–311, §101(1), redesignated par. (52) as (54).

Par. (55). Pub. L. 101–647, §2522(e)(1), redesignated par. (51) as (55) defining "swap agreement".

Pub. L. 101–311, §201(3), redesignated par. (53) as (55) defining "United States". Former par. (55) redesignated (57) defining "mask work".

Pub. L. 101–311, §101(1), redesignated par. (53) as (55).

Par. (56). Pub. L. 101–647, §2522(e)(1), redesignated par. (52) as (56) defining "swap participant".

Pub. L. 101–311, §201(3), redesignated par. (54) as (56) defining "intellectual property".

Par. (57). Pub. L. 101–647, §2522(e)(1), redesignated par. (53) as (57) defining "timeshare plan".

Pub. L. 101–311, §201(3), redesignated par. (55) as (57) defining "mask work".

1988—Par. (31). Pub. L. 100–597 inserted "and a municipality" after "partnership" in subpar. (A) and added subpar. (C).

Pars. (52), (53). Pub. L. 100–506 added pars. (52) and (53).

1986—Par. (14). Pub. L. 99–554, §201(1), substituted "governmental unit, and United States trustee" for "and governmental unit".

Pars. (17), (18). Pub. L. 99–554, §251(2), (3), added pars. (17) and (18) and redesignated former pars. (17) and (18) as (19) and (20), respectively.

Par. (19). Pub. L. 99–554, §251(1), (2), redesignated former par. (17) as (19) and inserted "(except when such term appears in the term 'family farmer')". Former par. (19) redesignated (21).

Pars. (20) to (25). Pub. L. 99–554, §251(2), redesignated former pars. (18) to (23) as (20) to (25), respectively. Former pars. (24) and (25) redesignated (26) and (27), respectively.

Par. (26). Pub. L. 99–554, §201(2), inserted "(but not a United States trustee while serving as a trustee in a case under this title)".

Pub. L. 99–554, §251(2), redesignated former par. (24) as (26). Former par. (26) redesignated (28).

Pars. (27) to (42). Pub. L. 99–554, §251(2), redesignated former pars. (25) to (40) as (27) to (42), respectively. Former pars. (41) and (42) redesignated (43) and (44), respectively.

Par. (43). Pub. L. 99–554, §251(2), redesignated former par. (41) as (43). Former par. (43) redesignated (45).

Par. (43)(A)(xv). Pub. L. 99–554, §283(a)(1), substituted "security" for "secuity".

Pars. (44) to (50). Pub. L. 99–554, §251(2), redesignated former pars. (42) to (48) as (44) to (50), respectively. Former par. (49) redesignated (51).

Par. (51). Pub. L. 99–554, §283(a)(2), substituted a period for the semicolon at the end thereof.

Pub. L. 99–554, §251(2), redesignated former par. (49) as (51).

1984—Par. (2)(D). Pub. L. 98–353, §421(a), struck out "or all" after "business".

Par. (8)(B). Pub. L. 98–353, §421(b), substituted a semicolon for the colon at end of subpar. (B).

Par. (9)(B). Pub. L. 98–353, §421(c), inserted reference to section 348(d).

Par. (14). Pub. L. 98–353, §421(d), inserted "and" after "trust,".

Pars. (19) to (21). Pub. L. 98–353, §421(j)(3), (4), added par. (19) and redesignated former pars. (19), (20), and (21) as (20), (21), and (24), respectively.

Pars. (22), (23). Pub. L. 98–353, §421(j)(2), (5), added pars. (22) and (23) and redesignated former pars. (22) and (23) as (25) and (26), respectively.

Pars. (24) to (26). Pub. L. 98–353, §421(j)(2), redesignated former pars. (21) to (23) as (24) to (26), respectively. Former pars. (24) to (26) redesignated (27) to (29), respectively.

Par. (27). Pub. L. 98–353, §421(e), (j)(2), redesignated former par. (24) as (27) and substituted "stockbroker" for "stock broker". Former par. (27) redesignated (30).

Par. (28). Pub. L. 98–353, §421(j)(2), redesignated former par. (25) as (28). Former par. (28) redesignated (31).

Par. (29). Pub. L. 98–353, §421(f), (j)(2), redesignated former par. (26) as (29) and, in subpar. (B)(ii), substituted "nonpartnership" and "(A)" for "separate" and "(A)(ii)", respectively, wherever appearing. Former par. (29) redesignated (32).

Pars. (30) to (32). Pub. L. 98–353, §421(j)(2), redesignated former pars. (27) to (29) as (30) to (32), respectively. Former pars. (30) to (32) redesignated (33) to (35), respectively.

Par. (33). Pub. L. 98–353, §421(g), (j)(2), redesignated former par. (30) as (33) and amended definition of "person" generally, thereby inserting proviso relating to consideration of certain governmental units as persons for purposes of section 1102 of this title. Former par. (33) redesignated (36).

Par. (34). Pub. L. 98–353, §421(j)(2), redesignated former par. (31) as (34). Former par. (34) redesignated (37).

Pars. (35), (36). Pub. L. 98–353, §421(j)(2), redesignated former pars. (32) and (33) as (35) and (36), respectively. Former pars. (35) and (36), as added by Pub. L. 98–353, §391(2), redesignated (38) and (39), respectively.

Pub. L. 98–353, §391, added pars. (35) and (36), and redesignated former pars. (35) and (36) as (37) and (38) which were again redesignated as (40) and (41), respectively.

Par. (37). Pub. L. 98–353, §421(j)(2), redesignated former par. (34) as (37). Former par. (37) redesignated successively as (39) and again as (42).

Par. (38). Pub. L. 98–353, §§391(2), 421(j)(2), added par. (35) and redesignated such par. (35) as (38). Former par. (38) redesignated successively as (40) and again as (43).

Par. (39). Pub. L. 98–353, §§391(2), 421(j)(2), added par. (36) and redesignated such par. (36) as (39). Former par. (39) redesignated successively as (41) and again as (45).

Par. (40). Pub. L. 98–353, §§391(1), 421(j)(2), redesignated successively former par. (35) as (37) and again as (40). Former par. (40) redesignated successively as (42) and again as (46).

Par. (41). Pub. L. 98–353, §§391(1), 401(1), 421(h), (j)(2), redesignated successively former par. (36) as (38) and again as (41), and, in subpar. (B)(vi), substituted "certificate of a kind specified in subparagraph (A)(xii)" for "certificate specified in clause (xii) of subparagraph (A)" and substituted "required to be the subject of a registration statement" for "the subject of such registration statement". Former par. (41) redesignated successively as (43), again as (44), and again as (48).

Par. (42). Pub. L. 98–353, §§391(1), 421(j)(2), redesignated successively former par. (37) as (39) and again as (42).

Par. (43). Pub. L. 98–353, §§391(1), 421(j)(2), redesignated successively former par. (38) as (40) and again as (43).

Pub. L. 98–353, §401, redesignated former par. (43), originally par. (41), as (44), and added another par. (43) which was redesignated (47).

Par. (44). Pub. L. 98–353, §421(j)(6), added par. (44). Former par. (44) originally was par. (41) and was redesignated successively as (43), again as (44), and again as (48).

Pars. (45), (46). Pub. L. 98–353, §§391(1), 421(j)(1), redesignated successively former pars. (39) and (40) as (41) and (42), and again as (45) and (46), respectively.

Par. (47). Pub. L. 98–353, §§401(2), 421(j)(1), added par. (43) and redesignated such par. (43) as (47).

Par. (48). Pub. L. 98–353, §§391(1), 401(1), 421(i), (j)(1), redesignated successively former par. (41) as (43), again as (44), and again as (48), and substituted "and foreclosure of the debtor's equity of redemption; and" for the period at the end.

Par. (49). Pub. L. 98–353, §421(j)(7), added par. (49).

1982—Par. (35). Pub. L. 97–222, §1(a)(2), added par. (35). Former par. (35) redesignated (36).

Par. (36). Pub. L. 97–222, §1(a)(1), (b), (c), redesignated par. (35) as (36) and substituted "is required to be the subject of a registration statement" for "is the subject of a registration statement" in subpar. (A)(xii) and substituted "forward contract" for "forward commodity contract" in subpar. (B)(iii). Former par. (36) redesignated (37).

Pars. (37) to (39). Pub. L. 97–222, §1(a)(1), redesignated pars. (36) to (38) as (37) to (39), respectively. Former par. (39) redesignated (40).

Pars. (40), (41). Pub. L. 97–222, §1(a)(1), (d), redesignated former par. (39) as (40) and restructured its provisions by dividing the former introductory provisions into subpars. (A) and (B) and by redesignating former subpars. (A) and (B) as cls. (i) and (ii), respectively, of subpar. (B). Former par. (40) redesignated (41).

Effective Date of 2006 Amendment

Pub. L. 109–390, §7, Dec. 12, 2006, 120 Stat. 2700, provided that: "The amendments made by this Act [see Short Title of 2006 Amendment note set out under this section] shall not apply to any cases commenced under title 11, United States Code, or appointments made under any Federal or State law, before the date of the enactment of this Act [Dec. 12, 2006]."

Effective Date of 2005 Amendment

Pub. L. 109–8, title XV, §1501, Apr. 20, 2005, 119 Stat. 216, provided that:

"(a) Effective Date.—Except as otherwise provided in this Act, this Act [see Tables for classification] and the amendments made by this Act shall take effect 180 days after the date of enactment of this Act [Apr. 20, 2005].

"(b) Application of Amendments.—

"(1) In general.—Except as otherwise provided in this Act and paragraph (2), the amendments made by this Act shall not apply with respect to cases commenced under title 11, United States Code, before the effective date of this Act.

"(2) Certain limitations applicable to debtors.—The amendments made by sections 308, 322, and 330 [amending sections 104, 522, 727, 1141, 1228, and 1328 of this title] shall apply with respect to cases commenced under title 11, United States Code, on or after the date of the enactment of this Act [Apr. 20, 2005]."

Effective Date of 1994 Amendment

Pub. L. 103–394, title VII, §702, Oct. 22, 1994, 108 Stat. 4150, provided that:

"(a) Effective Date.—Except as provided in subsection (b), this Act [see Tables for classification] shall take effect on the date of the enactment of this Act [Oct. 22, 1994].

"(b) Application of Amendments.—(1) Except as provided in paragraph (2), the amendments made by this Act shall not apply with respect to cases commenced under title 11 of the United States Code before the date of the enactment of this Act.

"(2)(A) Paragraph (1) shall not apply with respect to the amendment made by section 111 [amending section 524 of this title].

"(B) The amendments made by sections 113 and 117 [amending sections 106 and 330 of this title] shall apply with respect to cases commenced under title 11 of the United States Code before, on, and after the date of the enactment of this Act.

"(C) Section 1110 of title 11, United States Code, as amended by section 201 of this Act, shall apply with respect to any lease, as defined in such section 1110(c) as so amended, entered into in connection with a settlement of any proceeding in any case pending under title 11 of the United States Code on the date of the enactment of this Act.

"(D) The amendments made by section 305 [amending sections 1123, 1222, and 1322 of this title] shall apply only to agreements entered into after the date of enactment of this Act."

Effective Date of 1992 Amendment

Pub. L. 102–486, title XXX, §3017(c), Oct. 24, 1992, 106 Stat. 3131, provided that:

"(1) Except as provided in paragraph (2), the amendments made by this section [amending this section and section 541 of this title] shall take effect on the date of the enactment of this Act [Oct. 24, 1992].

"(2) The amendments made by this section shall not apply with respect to cases commenced under title 11 of the United States Code before the date of the enactment of this Act."

Effective Date of 1988 Amendment

Pub. L. 100–597, §12, Nov. 3, 1988, 102 Stat. 3030, provided that:

"(a) Effective Date.—Except as provided in subsection (b), this Act and the amendments made by this Act [enacting sections 927 to 929 of this title, amending this section and sections 109, 901, 902, 922, 926, and 943 of this title, and renumbering section 927 of this title as 930] shall take effect on the date of the enactment of this Act [Nov. 3, 1988].

"(b) Application of Amendments.—The amendments made by this Act shall not apply with respect to cases commenced under title 11 of the United States Code before the date of the enactment of this Act [Nov. 3, 1988]."

Pub. L. 100–506, §2, Oct. 18, 1988, 102 Stat. 2539, provided that:

"(a) Effective Date.—Except as provided in subsection (b), this Act and the amendments made by this Act [amending this section and section 365 of this title] shall take effect on the date of the enactment of this Act [Oct. 18, 1988].

"(b) Application of Amendments.—The amendments made by this Act shall not apply with respect to any case commenced under title 11 of the United States Code before the date of the enactment of this Act [Oct. 18, 1988]."

Effective Date of 1986 Amendment

Effective date and applicability of amendment by section 201 of Pub. L. 99–554 dependent upon the judicial district involved, see section 302(d), (e) of Pub. L. 99–554, set out as a note under section 581 of Title 28, Judiciary and Judicial Procedure.

Amendment by section 251 of Pub. L. 99–554 effective 30 days after Oct. 27, 1986, but not applicable to cases commenced under this title before that date, see section 302(a), (c)(1) of Pub. L. 99–554.

Amendment by section 283 of Pub. L. 99–554 effective 30 days after Oct. 27, 1986, see section 302(a) of Pub. L. 99–554.

Effective Date of 1984 Amendment

Pub. L. 98–353, title III, §552, formerly §553, July 10, 1984, 98 Stat. 392, as renumbered by Pub. L. 98–531, §1(2), Oct. 19, 1984, 98 Stat. 2704, provided that:

"(a) Except as otherwise provided in this section the amendments made by this title [see Tables for classification] shall become effective to cases filed 90 days after the date of enactment of this Act [July 10, 1984].

"(b) The amendments made by section 426(b) [amending section 303 of this title] shall become effective upon the date of enactment of this Act.

"(c) The amendments made by subtitle J [enacting section 1113 of this title], shall become effective as provided in section 541(c) [set out as an Effective Date note under section 1113 of this title]."

Short Title of 2015 Amendment

Pub. L. 114–107, §1, Dec. 18, 2015, 129 Stat. 2223, provided that: "This Act [amending provisions set out as a note under section 707 of this title] may be cited as the 'National Guard and Reservist Debt Relief Extension Act of 2015'."

Short Title of 2011 Amendment

Pub. L. 112–64, §1, Dec. 13, 2011, 125 Stat. 766, provided that: "This Act [amending provisions set out as a note under section 707 of this title] may be cited as the 'National Guard and Reservist Debt Relief Extension Act of 2011'."

Short Title of 2010 Amendment

Pub. L. 111–327, §1, Dec. 22, 2010, 124 Stat. 3557, provided that: "This Act [amending this section, sections 103, 105 to 107, 109 to 111, 303, 308, 348, 362, 363, 505, 507, 521 to 524, 526, 527, 541, 554, 704, 707, 723, 724, 726, 901, 1104, 1106, 1111, 1112, 1127, 1129, 1141, 1145, 1202, 1302, 1304, 1307, 1308, 1322, 1325, 1511, 1519, 1521, and 1529 of this title, section 157 of Title 18, Crimes and Criminal Procedure, sections 158, 159, and 586 of Title 28, Judiciary and Judicial Procedure, and provisions set out as a note under section 507 of this title] may be cited as the 'Bankruptcy Technical Corrections Act of 2010'."

Short Title of 2009 Amendment

Pub. L. 111–16, §1, May 7, 2009, 123 Stat. 1607, provided that: "This Act [amending sections 109, 322, 332, 342, 521, 704, 749, and 764 of this title, sections 983, 1514, 1963, 2252A, 2339B, 3060, 3432, 3509, and 3771 of Title 18, Crimes and Criminal Procedure, section 7 of the Classified Information Procedures Act set out in the Appendix to Title 18, section 853 of Title 21, Food and Drugs, and sections 636, 1453, and 2107 of Title 28, Judiciary and Judicial Procedure, and enacting provisions set out as a note under section 109 of this title] may be cited as the 'Statutory Time-Periods Technical Amendments Act of 2009'."

Short Title of 2008 Amendment

Pub. L. 110–438, §1, Oct. 20, 2008, 122 Stat. 5000, provided that: "This Act [amending section 707 of this title and enacting provisions set out as a note under section 707 of this title] may be cited as the 'National Guard and Reservists Debt Relief Act of 2008'."

Short Title of 2006 Amendment

Pub. L. 109–439, §1, Dec. 20, 2006, 120 Stat. 3285, provided that: "This Act [amending section 1325 of this title] may be cited as the 'Religious Liberty and Charitable Donation Clarification Act of 2006'."

Pub. L. 109–390, §1, Dec. 12, 2006, 120 Stat. 2692, provided that: "This Act [amending this section, sections 362, 546, and 741 of this title, sections 1787, 1821, 4403, and 4404 of Title 12, Banks and Banking, and section 78eee of Title 15, Commerce and Trade, and enacting provisions set out as notes under this section] may be cited as the 'Financial Netting Improvements Act of 2006'."

Short Title of 2005 Amendment

Pub. L. 109–8, §1(a), Apr. 20, 2005, 119 Stat. 23, provided that: "This Act [see Tables for classification] may be cited as the 'Bankruptcy Abuse Prevention and Consumer Protection Act of 2005'."

Pub. L. 109–8, title III, §332(a), Apr. 20, 2005, 119 Stat. 103, provided that: "This section [amending section 303 of this title and section 157 of Title 18, Crimes and Criminal Procedure] may be cited as the 'Involuntary Bankruptcy Improvement Act of 2005'."

Short Title of 2004 Amendment

Pub. L. 108–369, §1, Oct. 25, 2004, 118 Stat. 1749, provided that: "This Act [amending sections 1201 to 1208 and 1221 to 1231 of this title and enacting and amending provisions set out as notes under section 1201 of this title] may be cited as the 'Family Farmer Bankruptcy Relief Act of 2004'."

Short Title of 2003 Amendment

Pub. L. 108–73, §1, Aug. 15, 2003, 117 Stat. 891, provided that: "This Act [amending sections 1201 to 1208 and 1221 to 1231 of this title and enacting and amending provisions set out as notes under section 1201 of this title] may be cited as the 'Family Farmer Bankruptcy Relief Act of 2003'."

Short Title of 2002 Amendment

Pub. L. 107–377, §1, Dec. 19, 2002, 116 Stat. 3115, provided that: "This Act [amending sections 1201 to 1208 and 1221 to 1231 of this title, and enacting and amending provisions set out as notes under section 1201 of this title] may be cited as the 'Protection of Family Farmers Act of 2002'."

Short Title of 1998 Amendment

Pub. L. 105–183, §1, June 19, 1998, 112 Stat. 517, provided that: "This Act [amending sections 544, 546, 548, 707, and 1325 of this title and enacting provisions set out as notes under section 544 of this title] may be cited as the 'Religious Liberty and Charitable Donation Protection Act of 1998'."

Short Title of 1994 Amendment

Pub. L. 103–394, §1(a), Oct. 22, 1994, 108 Stat. 4106, provided that: "This Act [see Tables for classification] may be cited as the 'Bankruptcy Reform Act of 1994'."

Short Title of 1990 Amendment

Pub. L. 101–581, §1, Nov. 15, 1990, 104 Stat. 2865, and Pub. L. 101–647, title XXXI, §3101, Nov. 29, 1990, 104 Stat. 4916, provided respectively that such Act and such title [amending sections 523 and 1328 of this title and enacting provisions set out as a note under section 523 of this title] may be cited as the "Criminal Victims Protection Act of 1990".

Short Title of 1988 Amendment

Pub. L. 100–334, §1, June 16, 1988, 102 Stat. 610, provided that: "This Act [enacting section 1114 of this title, amending section 1129 of this title, enacting provisions set out as a note under section 1114 of this title, and amending and repealing provisions set out as notes under section 1106 of this title] may be cited as the 'Retiree Benefits Bankruptcy Protection Act of 1988'."

Short Title of 1984 Amendment

Pub. L. 98–353, title III, §361, July 10, 1984, 98 Stat. 361, provided that: "This subtitle [subtitle C (§§361–363) of title III of Pub. L. 98–353, amending sections 362, 365, and 541 of this title] may be cited as the 'Leasehold Management Bankruptcy Amendments Act of 1983'."

Savings Provision

Pub. L. 109–8, title IX, §912, as added Pub. L. 109–390, §5(d), Dec. 12, 2006, 120 Stat. 2698, provided that: "The meanings of terms used in this title [see Tables for classification] are applicable for the purposes of this title only, and shall not be construed or applied so as to challenge or affect the characterization, definition, or treatment of any similar terms under any other statute, regulation, or rule, including the Gramm-Leach-Bliley Act [Pub. L. 106–102, see Short Title of 1999 Amendment note set out under section 1811 of Title 12, Banks and Banking], the Legal Certainty for Bank Products Act of 2000 [7 U.S.C. 27 to 27f], the securities laws (as such term is defined in section 3(a)(47) of the Securities Exchange Act of 1934 [15 U.S.C. 78c(a)(47)]), and the Commodity Exchange Act [7 U.S.C. 1 et seq.]."

Separability

Pub. L. 103–394, title VII, §701, Oct. 22, 1994, 108 Stat. 4150, provided that: "If any provision of this Act [see Tables for classification] or amendment made by this Act or the application of such provision or amendment to any person or circumstance is held to be unconstitutional, the remaining provisions of and amendments made by this Act and the application of such other provisions and amendments to any person or circumstance shall not be affected thereby."

Pub. L. 98–353, title III, §551, July 10, 1984, 98 Stat. 391, provided that: "If any provision of this title [title III (§§301–553) of Pub. L. 98–353, see Tables for classification] or any amendment made by this title, or the application thereof to any person or circumstance is held invalid, the provisions of every other part, and their application shall not be affected thereby."

Construction

Pub. L. 109–8, title X, §1007(e), Apr. 20, 2005, 119 Stat. 188, provided that: "Nothing in this section [amending this section and sections 109, 1203, and 1206 of this title] shall change, affect, or amend the Fishery Conservation and Management Act of 1976 (16 U.S.C. 1801 et seq.)."

Pub. L. 109–8, title XI, §1101(c), Apr. 20, 2005, 119 Stat. 189, provided that: "The amendments made by subsection (a) of this section [amending this section] shall not affect the interpretation of section 109(b) of title 11, United States Code."

Nonlimitation of Information

Pub. L. 109–8, title I, §102(e), Apr. 20, 2005, 119 Stat. 33, provided that: "Nothing in this title [see Tables for classification] shall limit the ability of a creditor to provide information to a judge (except for information communicated ex parte, unless otherwise permitted by applicable law), United States trustee (or bankruptcy administrator, if any), or trustee."

Judicial Education

Pub. L. 109–8, title XII, §1226, Apr. 20, 2005, 119 Stat. 199, provided that: "The Director of the Federal Judicial Center, in consultation with the Director of the Executive Office for United States Trustees, shall develop materials and conduct such training as may be useful to courts in implementing this Act [see Short Title of 2005 Amendment note above] and the amendments made by this Act, including the requirements relating to the means test under section 707(b), and reaffirmation agreements under section 524, of title 11 of the United States Code, as amended by this Act."

Adjustment of Dollar Amounts

The dollar amounts specified in this section were adjusted by notices of the Judicial Conference of the United States pursuant to section 104 of this title as follows:

By notice dated Feb. 16, 2016, 81 F.R. 8748, effective Apr. 1, 2016, in par. (3), dollar amount "186,825" was adjusted to "192,450"; in par. (18), dollar amount "4,031,575" was adjusted to "4,153,150" each time it appeared; in par. (19A), dollar amount "1,868,200" was adjusted to "1,924,550" each time it appeared; and, in par. (51D), dollar amount "2,490,925" was adjusted to "2,566,050" each time it appeared. See notice of the Judicial Conference of the United States set out as a note under section 104 of this title.

By notice dated Feb. 12, 2013, 78 F.R. 12089, effective Apr. 1, 2013, in par. (3), dollar amount "175,750" was adjusted to "186,825"; in par. (18), dollar amount "3,792,650" was adjusted to "4,031,575" each time it appeared; in par. (19A), dollar amount "1,757,475" was adjusted to "1,868,200" each time it appeared; and, in par. (51D), dollar amount "2,343,300" was adjusted to "2,490,925" each time it appeared.

By notice dated Feb. 19, 2010, 75 F.R. 8747, effective Apr. 1, 2010, in par. (3), dollar amount "164,250" was adjusted to "175,750"; in par. (18)(A), (B)(ii), dollar amount "3,544,525" was adjusted to "3,792,650" each time it appeared; in par. (19A)(A)(i), (B)(ii)(II), dollar amount "1,642,500" was adjusted to "1,757,475" each time it appeared; and, in par. (51D)(A), (B), dollar amount "2,190,000" was adjusted to "2,343,300" each time it appeared.

By notice dated Feb. 7, 2007, 72 F.R. 7082, effective Apr. 1, 2007, in par. (3), dollar amount "150,000" was adjusted to "164,250"; in par. (18), dollar amount "3,237,000" was adjusted to "3,544,525" each time it appeared; in par. (19A), dollar amount "1,500,000" was adjusted to "1,642,500" each time it appeared; and, in par. (51D), dollar amount "2,000,000" was adjusted to "2,190,000" each time it appeared.

[1] See Adjustment of Dollar Amounts notes below.

[2] So in original. Probably should be followed by a comma.

[3] So in original. Probably should be "or". See 2010 Amendment note below.

[4] So in original.

§102. Rules of construction

In this title—

(1) "after notice and a hearing", or a similar phrase—

(A) means after such notice as is appropriate in the particular circumstances, and such opportunity for a hearing as is appropriate in the particular circumstances; but

(B) authorizes an act without an actual hearing if such notice is given properly and if—

(i) such a hearing is not requested timely by a party in interest; or

(ii) there is insufficient time for a hearing to be commenced before such act must be done, and the court authorizes such act;

(2) "claim against the debtor" includes claim against property of the debtor;

(3) "includes" and "including" are not limiting;

(4) "may not" is prohibitive, and not permissive;

(5) "or" is not exclusive;

(6) "order for relief" means entry of an order for relief;

(7) the singular includes the plural;

(8) a definition, contained in a section of this title that refers to another section of this title, does not, for the purpose of such reference, affect the meaning of a term used in such other section; and

(9) "United States trustee" includes a designee of the United States trustee.

(Pub. L. 95–598, Nov. 6, 1978, 92 Stat. 2554; Pub. L. 98–353, title III, §422, July 10, 1984, 98 Stat. 369; Pub. L. 99–554, title II, §202, Oct. 27, 1986, 100 Stat. 3097.)

Historical and Revision Notes

legislative statements

Section 102 specifies various rules of construction but is not exclusive. Other rules of construction that are not set out in title 11 are nevertheless intended to be followed in construing the bankruptcy code. For example, the phrase "on request of a party in interest" or a similar phrase, is used in connection with an action that the court may take in various sections of the Code. The phrase is intended to restrict the court from acting sua sponte. Rules of bankruptcy procedure or court decisions will determine who is a party in interest for the particular purposes of the provision in question, but the court will not be permitted to act on its own.

Although "property" is not construed in this section, it is used consistently throughout the code in its broadest sense, including cash, all interests in property, such as liens, and every kind of consideration including promises to act or forbear to act as in section 548(d).

Section 102(1) expands on a rule of construction contained in H.R. 8200 as passed by the House and in the Senate amendment. The phrase "after notice and a hearing", or a similar phrase, is intended to be construed according to the particular proceeding to mean after such notice as is appropriate in the particular circumstances, and such opportunity, if any, for a hearing as is appropriate in the particular circumstances. If a provision of title 11 authorizes an act to be taken "after notice and a hearing" this means that if appropriate notice is given and no party to whom such notice is sent timely requests a hearing, then the act sought to be taken may be taken without an actual hearing.

In very limited emergency circumstances, there will be insufficient time for a hearing to be commenced before an action must be taken. The action sought to be taken may be taken if authorized by the court at an ex parte hearing of which a record is made in open court. A full hearing after the fact will be available in such an instance.

In some circumstances, such as under section 1128, the bill requires a hearing and the court may act only after a hearing is held. In those circumstances the judge will receive evidence before ruling. In other circumstances, the court may take action "after notice and a hearing," if no party in interest requests a hearing. In that event a court order authorizing the action to be taken is not necessary as the ultimate action taken by the court implies such an authorization.

Section 102(8) is new. It contains a rule of construction indicating that a definition contained in a section in title 11 that refers to another section of title 11 does not, for the purposes of such reference, take the meaning of a term used in the other section. For example, section 522(a)(2) defines "value" for the purposes of section 522. Section 548(d)(2) defines "value" for purposes of section 548. When section 548 is incorporated by reference in section 522, this rule of construction makes clear that the definition of "value" in section 548 governs its meaning in section 522 notwithstanding a different definition of "value" in section 522(a)(2).

senate report no. 95–989

Section 102 provides seven rules of construction. Some are derived from current law; others are derived from 1 U.S.C. 1; a few are new. They apply generally throughout proposed title 11. These are terms that are not appropriate for definition, but that require an explanation.

Paragraph (1) defines the concept of "after notice and a hearing." The concept is central to the bill and to the separation of the administrative and judicial functions of bankruptcy judges. The phrase means after such notice as is appropriate in the particular circumstances (to be prescribed by either the Rules of Bankruptcy Procedure or by the court in individual circumstances that the Rules do not cover. In many cases, the Rules will provide for combined notice of several proceedings), and such opportunity for a hearing as is appropriate in the particular circumstances. Thus, a hearing will not be necessary in every instance. If there is no objection to the proposed action, the action may go ahead without court action. This is a significant change from present law, which requires the affirmative approval of the bankruptcy judge for almost every action. The change will permit the bankruptcy judge to stay removed from the administration of the bankruptcy or reorganization case, and to become involved only when there is a dispute about a proposed action, that is, only when there is an objection. The phrase "such opportunity for a hearing as is appropriate in the particular circumstances" is designed to permit the Rules and the courts to expedite or dispense with hearings when speed is essential. The language "or similar phrase" is intended to cover the few instances in the bill where "after notice and a hearing" is interrupted by another phrase, such as "after notice to the debtor and a hearing."

Paragraph (2) specifies that "claim against the debtor" includes claim against property of the debtor. This paragraph is intended to cover nonrecourse loan agreements where the creditor's only rights are against property of the debtor, and not against the debtor personally. Thus, such an agreement would give rise to a claim that would be treated as a claim against the debtor personally, for the purposes of the bankruptcy code.

Paragraph (3) is a codification of *American Surety Co. v. Marotta*, 287 U.S. 513 (1933). It specifies that "includes" and "including" are not limiting.

Paragraph (4) specifies that "may not" is prohibitive and not permissive (such as in "might not").

Paragraph (5) specifies that "or" is not exclusive. Thus, if a party "may do (a) or (b)", then the party may do either or both. The party is not limited to a mutually exclusive choice between the two alternatives.

Paragraph (6) makes clear that "order for relief" means entry of an order for relief. If the court orally orders relief, but the order is not entered until a later time, then any time measurements in the bill are from entry, not from the oral order. In a voluntary case, the entry of the order for relief is the filing of the petition commencing the voluntary case.

Paragraph (7) specifies that the singular includes the plural. The plural, however, generally does not include the singular. The bill uses only the singular, even when the item in question most often is found in plural quantities, in order to avoid the confusion possible if both rules of construction applied. When an item is specified in the plural, the plural is intended.

Amendments

1986—Par. (9). Pub. L. 99–554 added par. (9).

1984—Par. (8). Pub. L. 98–353 substituted "contained" for "continued".

Effective Date of 1986 Amendment

Effective date and applicability of amendment by Pub. L. 99–554 dependent upon the judicial district involved, see section 302(d), (e) of Pub. L. 99–554, set out as a note under section 581 of Title 28, Judiciary and Judicial Procedure.

Effective Date of 1984 Amendment

Amendment by Pub. L. 98–353 effective with respect to cases filed 90 days after July 10, 1984, see section 552(a) of Pub. L. 98–353, set out as a note under section 101 of this title.

§103. Applicability of chapters

(a) Except as provided in section 1161 of this title, chapters 1, 3, and 5 of this title apply in a case under chapter 7, 11, 12, or 13 of this title, and this chapter, sections 307, 362(o), 555 through 557, and 559 through 562 apply in a case under chapter 15.

(b) Subchapters I and II of chapter 7 of this title apply only in a case under such chapter.

(c) Subchapter III of chapter 7 of this title applies only in a case under such chapter concerning a stockbroker.

(d) Subchapter IV of chapter 7 of this title applies only in a case under such chapter concerning a commodity broker.

(e) Scope of Application.—Subchapter V of chapter 7 of this title shall apply only in a case under such chapter concerning the liquidation of an uninsured State member bank, or a corporation organized under section 25A of the Federal Reserve Act, which operates, or operates as, a multilateral clearing organization pursuant to section 409 [1] of the Federal Deposit Insurance Corporation Improvement Act of 1991.

(f) Except as provided in section 901 of this title, only chapters 1 and 9 of this title apply in a case under such chapter 9.

(g) Except as provided in section 901 of this title, subchapters I, II, and III of chapter 11 of this title apply only in a case under such chapter.

(h) Subchapter IV of chapter 11 of this title applies only in a case under such chapter concerning a railroad.

(i) Chapter 13 of this title applies only in a case under such chapter.

(j) Chapter 12 of this title applies only in a case under such chapter.

(k) Chapter 15 applies only in a case under such chapter, except that—

(1) sections 1505, 1513, and 1514 apply in all cases under this title; and

(2) section 1509 applies whether or not a case under this title is pending.

(Pub. L. 95–598, Nov. 6, 1978, 92 Stat. 2555; Pub. L. 97–222, §2, July 27, 1982, 96 Stat. 235; Pub. L. 98–353, title III, §423, July 10, 1984, 98 Stat. 369; Pub. L. 99–554, title II, §252, Oct. 27, 1986, 100 Stat. 3104; Pub. L. 106–554, §1(a)(5) [title I, §112(c)(5)(A)], Dec. 21, 2000, 114 Stat. 2763, 2763A-394; Pub. L. 109–8, title VIII, §802(a), Apr. 20, 2005, 119 Stat. 145; Pub. L. 111–327, §2(a)(2), Dec. 22, 2010, 124 Stat. 3557.)

Historical and Revision Notes

senate report no. 95–989

Section 103 prescribes which chapters of the proposed bankruptcy code apply in various cases. All cases, other than cases ancillary to foreign proceedings, are filed under chapter 7, 9, 11, or 13, the operative chapters of the proposed bankruptcy code. The general provisions that apply no matter which chapter a case is filed under are found in chapters 1, 3, and 5. Subsection (a) makes this explicit, with an exception for chapter 9. The other provisions, which are self-explanatory, provide the special rules for Stockbroker Liquidations, Commodity Broker Liquidations, Municipal Debt Adjustments, and Railroad Reorganizations.

References in Text

Section 25A of the Federal Reserve Act, referred to in subsec. (e), popularly known as the Edge Act, is classified to subchapter II (§611 et seq.) of chapter 6 of Title 12, Banks and Banking. For complete classification of this Act to the Code, see Short Title note set out under section 611 of Title 12 and Tables.

Section 409 of the Federal Deposit Insurance Corporation Improvement Act of 1991, referred to in subsec. (e), was classified to section 4422 of Title 12, Banks and Banking, prior to repeal by Pub. L. 111–203, title VII, §740, July 21, 2010, 124 Stat. 1729.

Amendments

2010—Subsec. (a). Pub. L. 111–327 substituted "362(o)" for "362(n)".

2005—Subsec. (a). Pub. L. 109–8, §802(a)(1), inserted ", and this chapter, sections 307, 362(n), 555 through 557, and 559 through 562 apply in a case under chapter 15" before period.

Subsec. (k). Pub. L. 109–8, §802(a)(2), added subsec. (k).

2000—Subsecs. (e) to (j). Pub. L. 106–554 added subsec. (e) and redesignated former subsecs. (e) to (i) as (f) to (j), respectively.

1986—Subsec. (a). Pub. L. 99–554, §252(1), inserted reference to chapter 12.

Subsec. (i). Pub. L. 99–554, §252(2), added subsec. (i).

1984—Subsec. (c). Pub. L. 98–353 substituted "stockbroker" for "stockholder".

1982—Subsec. (d). Pub. L. 97–222 struck out "except with respect to section 746(c) which applies to margin payments made by any debtor to a commodity broker or forward contract merchant" after "concerning a commodity broker".

Effective Date of 2005 Amendment

Amendment by Pub. L. 109–8 effective 180 days after Apr. 20, 2005, and not applicable with respect to cases commenced under this title before such effective date, except as otherwise provided, see section 1501 of Pub. L. 109–8, set out as a note under section 101 of this title.

Effective Date of 1986 Amendment

Amendment by Pub. L. 99–554 effective 30 days after Oct. 27, 1986, but not applicable to cases commenced under this title before that date, see section 302(a), (c)(1) of Pub. L. 99–554, set out as a note under section 581 of Title 28, Judiciary and Judicial Procedure.

Effective Date of 1984 Amendment

Amendment by Pub. L. 98–353 effective with respect to cases filed 90 days after July 10, 1984, see section 552(a) of Pub. L. 98–353, set out as a note under section 101 of this title.

[1] See References in Text note below.

§104. Adjustment of dollar amounts

(a) On April 1, 1998, and at each 3-year interval ending on April 1 thereafter, each dollar amount in effect under sections 101(3), 101(18), 101(19A), 101(51D), 109(e), 303(b), 507(a), 522(d), 522(f)(3) and 522(f)(4), 522(n), 522(p), 522(q), 523(a)(2)(C), 541(b), 547(c)(9), 707(b), 1322(d), 1325(b), and 1326(b)(3) of this title and section 1409(b) of title 28 immediately before such April 1 shall be adjusted—

(1) to reflect the change in the Consumer Price Index for All Urban Consumers, published by the Department of Labor, for the most recent 3-year period ending immediately before January 1 preceding such April 1, and

(2) to round to the nearest $25 the dollar amount that represents such change.

(b) Not later than March 1, 1998, and at each 3-year interval ending on March 1 thereafter, the Judicial Conference of the United States shall publish in the Federal Register the dollar amounts that will become effective on such April 1 under sections 101(3), 101(18), 101(19A), 101(51D), 109(e), 303(b), 507(a), 522(d), 522(f)(3) and 522(f)(4), 522(n), 522(p), 522(q), 523(a)(2)(C), 541(b), 547(c)(9), 707(b), 1322(d), 1325(b), and 1326(b)(3) of this title and section 1409(b) of title 28.

(c) Adjustments made in accordance with subsection (a) shall not apply with respect to cases commenced before the date of such adjustments.

(Pub. L. 95–598, Nov. 6, 1978, 92 Stat. 2555; Pub. L. 103–394, title I, §108(e), Oct. 22, 1994, 108 Stat. 4112; Pub. L. 109–8, title I, §102(j), title II, §§224(e)(2), 226(b), title III, §322(b), title IV, §432(c), title X, §1002, title XII, §1202, Apr. 20, 2005, 119 Stat. 35, 65, 67, 97, 110, 186, 193; Pub. L. 110–406, §7, Oct. 13, 2008, 122 Stat. 4293.)

Historical and Revision Notes

legislative statements

Section 104 represents a compromise between the House bill and the Senate amendment with respect to the adjustment of dollar amounts in title 11. The House amendment authorizes the Judicial Conference of the United States to transmit a recommendation for the uniform percentage of adjustment for each dollar amount in title 11 and in 28 U.S.C. 1930 to the Congress and to the President before May 1, 1985, and before May 1 of every sixth year thereafter. The requirement in the House bill that each such recommendation be based only on any change in the cost-of-living increase during the period immediately preceding the recommendation is deleted.

senate report no. 95–989

This section requires that the Director of the Administrative Office of the U. S. Courts report to Congress and the President before Oct. 1, 1985, and before May 1 every 6 years thereafter a recommendation for adjustment in dollar amounts found in this title. The Committee feels that regular adjustment of the dollar amounts by the Director will conserve congressional time and yet assure that the relative dollar amounts used in the bill are maintained. Changes in the cost of living should be a significant, but not necessarily the only, factor considered by the Director. The fact that there has been an increase in the cost of living does not necessarily mean that an adjustment of dollar amounts would be needed or warranted.

house report no. 95–595

This section requires the Judicial Conference to report to the Congress every four years after the effective date of the bankruptcy code any changes that have occurred in the cost of living during the preceding four years, and the appropriate adjustments to the dollar amounts in the bill. The dollar amounts are found primarily in the exemption section (11 U.S.C. 522), the wage priority (11 U.S.C. 507), and the eligibility for chapter 13 (11 U.S.C. 109). This section requires that the Conference recommend uniform percentage changes in these amounts based solely on cost of living changes. The dollar amounts in the bill would not change on that recommendation, absent Congressional veto. Instead, Congress is required to take affirmative action, by passing a law amending the appropriate section, if it wishes to accomplish the change.

If the Judicial Conference has policy recommendations concerning the appropriate dollar amounts in the bankruptcy code based other than on cost of living considerations there are adequate channels through which it may communicate its views. This section is solely for the housekeeping function of maintaining the dollar amounts in the code at fairly constant real dollar levels.

Amendments

2008—Pub. L. 110–406 redesignated subsec. (b)(1) as (a), subpars. (A) and (B) of subsec. (b)(1) as pars. (1) and (2), respectively, of subsec. (a), and pars. (2) and (3) of subsec. (b) as subsecs. (b) and (c), respectively, substituted "subsection (a)" for "paragraph (1)" in subsec. (c), and struck out former subsec. (a) which read as follows: "The Judicial Conference of the United States shall transmit to the Congress and to the President before May 1, 1985, and before May 1 of every sixth year after May 1, 1985, a recommendation for the uniform percentage adjustment of each dollar amount in this title and in section 1930 of title 28."

2005—Subsec. (b)(1). Pub. L. 109–8, §1202(1)–(4), in introductory provisions, inserted "101(19A)," after "101(18),", "522(f)(3) and 522(f)(4)," after "522(d),", and "541(b), 547(c)(9)," after "523(a)(2)(C)," and substituted "1322(d), 1325(b), and 1326(b)(3) of this title and section 1409(b) of title 28" for "and 1325(b)(3)".

Pub. L. 109–8, §1002, inserted "101(18)," after "101(3)," in introductory provisions.

Pub. L. 109–8, §432(c), inserted "101(51D)," after "101(3)," in introductory provisions.

Pub. L. 109–8, §322(b), inserted "522(p), 522(q)," after "522(n)," in introductory provisions.

Pub. L. 109–8, §226(b), inserted "101(3)," after "sections" in introductory provisions.

Pub. L. 109–8, §224(e)(2), inserted "522(n)," after "522(d)," in introductory provisions.

Pub. L. 109–8, §102(j), substituted "523(a)(2)(C), 707(b), and 1325(b)(3)" for "and 523(a)(2)(C)" in introductory provisions.

Subsec. (b)(2). Pub. L. 109–8, §1202(1)–(3), (5), inserted "101(19A)," after "101(18),", "522(f)(3) and 522(f)(4)," after "522(d),", and "541(b), 547(c)(9)," after "523(a)(2)(C)," and substituted "1322(d), 1325(b), and 1326(b)(3) of this title and section 1409(b) of title 28" for "and 1325(b)(3) of this title".

Pub. L. 109–8, §1002, inserted "101(18)," after "101(3),".

Pub. L. 109–8, §432(c), inserted "101(51D)," after "101(3),".

Pub. L. 109–8, §322(b), inserted "522(p), 522(q)," after "522(n),".

Pub. L. 109–8, §226(b), inserted "101(3)," after "sections".

Pub. L. 109–8, §224(e)(2), inserted "522(n)," after "522(d),".

Pub. L. 109–8, §102(j), substituted "523(a)(2)(C), 707(b), and 1325(b)(3)" for "and 523(a)(2)(C)".

1994—Pub. L. 103–394 designated existing provisions as subsec. (a) and added subsec. (b).

Effective Date of 2005 Amendment

Amendment by Pub. L. 109–8 effective 180 days after Apr. 20, 2005, with amendments by sections 102(j), 224(e)(2), 226(b), 432(c), 1002, and 1202 of Pub. L. 109–8 not applicable with respect to cases commenced under this title before such effective date, except as otherwise provided, and amendment by section 322(b) of Pub. L. 109–8 applicable with respect to cases commenced under this title on or after Apr. 20, 2005, see section 1501 of Pub. L. 109–8, set out as a note under section 101 of this title.

Effective Date of 1994 Amendment

Amendment by Pub. L. 103–394 effective Oct. 22, 1994, and not applicable with respect to cases commenced under this title before Oct. 22, 1994, see section 702 of Pub. L. 103–394, set out as a note under section 101 of this title.

Adjustment of Dollar Amounts

By notice dated Feb. 16, 2016, 81 F.R. 8748, the Judicial Conference of the United States adjusted the dollar amounts in provisions specified in subsec. (a) of this section, effective Apr. 1, 2016, as follows:

28 U.S.C.	Dollar amount to be adjusted	New (adjusted) dollar amount [1]
Section 1409(b)—a trustee may commence a proceeding arising in or related to a case to recover		
(1)—money judgment of or property worth less than	$1,250	$1,300.
(2)—a consumer debt less than	$18,675	$19,250.
(3)—a non consumer debt against a non insider less than	$12,475	$12,850.

11 U.S.C.	Dollar amount to be adjusted	New (adjusted) dollar amount [1]
Section 101(3)—definition of assisted person	$186,825	$192,450.
Section 101(18)—definition of family farmer	$4,031,575 (each time it appears)	$4,153,150 (each time it appears).
Section 101(19A)—definition of family fisherman	$1,868,200 (each time it appears)	$1,924,550 (each time it appears).
Section 101(51D)—definition of small business debtor	$2,490,925 (each time it appears)	$2,566,050 (each time it appears).
Section 109(e)—debt limits for individual filing bankruptcy under chapter 13	$383,175 (each time it appears) $1,149,525 (each time it appears)	$394,725 (each time it appears)[.] $1,184,200 (each time it appears).
Section 303(b)—minimum aggregate claims needed for the commencement of an involuntary chapter 7 or 11 petition		
(1)—in paragraph (1)	$15,325	$15,775.
(2)—in paragraph (2)	$15,325	$15,775.
Section 507(a)—priority expenses and claims		
(1)—in paragraph (4)	$12,475	$12,850.
(2)—in paragraph (5)(B)(i)	$12,475	$12,850.
(3)—in paragraph (6)(B)	$6,150	$6,325.
(4)—in paragraph (7)	$2,775	$2,850.
Section 522(d)—value of property exemptions allowed to the debtor		
(1)—in paragraph (1)	$22,975	$23,675.

(2)—in paragraph (2)		$3,675	$3,775.
(3)—in paragraph (3)		$575 $12,250	$600. $12,625.
(4)—in paragraph (4)		$1,550	$1,600.
(5)—in paragraph (5)		$1,225 $11,500	$1,250. $11,850.
(6)—in paragraph (6)		$2,300	$2,375.
(7)—in paragraph (8)		$12,250	$12,625.
(8)—in paragraph (11)(D)		$22,975	$23,675.
Section 522(f)(3)—exception to lien avoidance under certain state laws		$6,225	$6,425.
Section 522(f)(4)—items excluded from definition of household goods for lien avoidance purposes		$650 (each time it appears)	$675 (each time it appears).
Section 522(n)—maximum aggregate value of assets in individual retirement accounts exempted		$1,245,475	$1,283,025.
Section 522(p)—qualified homestead exemption		$155,675	$160,375.
Section 522(q)—state homestead exemption		$155,675	$160,375.
Section 523(a)(2)(C)—exceptions to discharge			
(1)—in paragraph (i)(I)—consumer debts for luxury goods or services incurred < 90 days before filing owed to a single creditor in the aggregate		$650	$675.
(2)—in paragraph (i)(II)—cash advances incurred < 70 days before filing in the aggregate		$925	$950.
Section 541(b)—property of the estate exclusions			
(1)—in paragraph (5)(C)—education IRA funds in the aggregate		$6,225	$6,425.
(2)—in paragraph (6)(C)—pre-purchased tuition credits in the aggregate		$6,225	$6,425.
Section 547(c)(9)—preferences, trustee may not avoid a transfer if, in a case filed by a debtor whose debts are not primarily consumer debts, the aggregate value of property is less than		$6,225	$6,425.
Section 707(b)—dismissal of a chapter 7 case or conversion to chapter 11 or 13 (means test)			
(1)—in paragraph (2)(A)(i)(I)		$7,475	$7,700.
(2)—in paragraph (2)(A)(i)(II)		$12,475	$12,850.
(3)—in paragraph (2)(A)(ii)(IV)		$1,875	$1,925.
(4)—in paragraph (2)(B)(iv)(I)		$7,475	$7,700.
(5)—in paragraph (2)(B)(iv)(II)		$12,475	$12,850.
(6)—in paragraph (5)(B)		$1,250	$1,300.
(7)—in paragraph (6)(C)		$675	$700.
(8)—in paragraph (7)(A)(iii)		$675	$700.
Section 1322(d)—contents of chapter 13 plan, monthly income		$675 (each time it appears)	$700 (each time it appears).
Section 1325(b)—chapter 13 confirmation of plan, disposable income		$675 (each time it appears)	$700 (each time it appears).
Section 1326(b)(3)—payments to former chapter 7 trustee		$25	$25.

¹ The New (Adjusted) Dollar Amounts reflect a 3.016 percent increase, rounded to the nearest $25.

Similar notices by the Judicial Conference of the United States adjusting the dollar amounts in provisions specified in subsec. (a) of this section were contained in the following:

Feb. 12, 2013, 78 F.R. 12089, effective Apr. 1, 2013.
Feb. 19, 2010, 75 F.R. 8747, effective Apr. 1, 2010.
Feb. 7, 2007, 72 F.R. 7082, effective Apr. 1, 2007.
Feb. 18, 2004, 69 F.R. 8482, effective Apr. 1, 2004.
Feb. 13, 2001, 66 F.R. 10910, effective Apr. 1, 2001.
Feb. 3, 1998, 63 F.R. 7179, effective Apr. 1, 1998.

§105. Power of court

(a) The court may issue any order, process, or judgment that is necessary or appropriate to carry out the provisions of this title. No provision of this title providing for the raising of an issue by a party in interest shall be construed to preclude the court from, sua sponte, taking any action or making any determination necessary or appropriate to enforce or implement court orders or rules, or to prevent an abuse of process.

(b) Notwithstanding subsection (a) of this section, a court may not appoint a receiver in a case under this title.

(c) The ability of any district judge or other officer or employee of a district court to exercise any of the authority or responsibilities conferred upon the court under this title shall be determined by reference to the provisions relating to such judge, officer, or employee set forth in title 28. This subsection shall not be interpreted to exclude bankruptcy judges and other officers or employees appointed pursuant to chapter 6 of title 28 from its operation.

(d) The court, on its own motion or on the request of a party in interest—

(1) shall hold such status conferences as are necessary to further the expeditious and economical resolution of the case; and

(2) unless inconsistent with another provision of this title or with applicable Federal Rules of Bankruptcy Procedure, may issue an order at any such conference prescribing such limitations and conditions as the court deems appropriate to ensure that the case is handled expeditiously and economically, including an order that—

(A) sets the date by which the trustee must assume or reject an executory contract or unexpired lease; or

(B) in a case under chapter 11 of this title—

(i) sets a date by which the debtor, or trustee if one has been appointed, shall file a disclosure statement and plan;

(ii) sets a date by which the debtor, or trustee if one has been appointed, shall solicit acceptances of a plan;

(iii) sets the date by which a party in interest other than a debtor may file a plan;

(iv) sets a date by which a proponent of a plan, other than the debtor, shall solicit acceptances of such plan;

(v) fixes the scope and format of the notice to be provided regarding the hearing on approval of the disclosure statement; or

(vi) provides that the hearing on approval of the disclosure statement may be combined with the hearing on confirmation of the plan.

(Pub. L. 95–598, Nov. 6, 1978, 92 Stat. 2555; Pub. L. 98–353, title I, §118, July 10, 1984, 98 Stat. 344; Pub. L. 99–554, title II, §203, Oct. 27, 1986, 100 Stat. 3097; Pub. L. 103–394, title I, §104(a), Oct. 22, 1994, 108 Stat. 4108; Pub. L. 109–8, title IV, §440, Apr. 20, 2005, 119 Stat. 114; Pub. L. 111–327, §2(a)(3), Dec. 22, 2010, 124 Stat. 3557.)

Historical and Revision Notes

senate report no. 95–989

Section 105 is derived from section 2a (15) of present law [section 11(a)(15) of former title 11], with two changes. First, the limitation on the power of a bankruptcy judge (the power to enjoin a court being reserved to the district judge) is removed as inconsistent with the increased powers and jurisdiction of the new bankruptcy court. Second, the bankruptcy judge is prohibited from appointing a receiver in a case under title 11 under any circumstances. The bankruptcy code has ample provision for the appointment of a trustee when needed. Appointment of a receiver would simply circumvent the established procedures.

This section is also an authorization, as required under 28 U.S.C. 2283, for a court of the United States to stay the action of a State court. As such, *Toucey v. New York Life Insurance Company*, 314 U.S. 118 (1941), is overruled.

References in Text

The Federal Rules of Bankruptcy Procedure, referred to in subsec. (d)(2), are set out in the Appendix to this title.

Amendments

2010—Subsec. (d)(2). Pub. L. 111–327 inserted "may" after "Procedure," in introductory provisions.

2005—Subsec. (d). Pub. L. 109–8, §440(1), struck out ", may" after "party in interest" in introductory provisions.

Subsec. (d)(1). Pub. L. 109–8, §440(2), added par. (1) and struck out former par. (1) which read as follows: "hold a status conference regarding any case or proceeding under this title after notice to the parties in interest; and".

1994—Subsec. (d). Pub. L. 103–394 added subsec. (d).

1986—Subsec. (a). Pub. L. 99–554 inserted at end "No provision of this title providing for the raising of an issue by a party in interest shall be construed to preclude the court from, sua sponte, taking any action or making any determination necessary or appropriate to enforce or implement court orders or rules, or to prevent an abuse of process."

1984—Subsecs. (a), (b). Pub. L. 98–353, §118(1), struck out "bankruptcy" before "court".

Subsec. (c). Pub. L. 98–353, §118(2), added subsec. (c).

Effective Date of 2005 Amendment

Amendment by Pub. L. 109–8 effective 180 days after Apr. 20, 2005, and not applicable with respect to cases commenced under this title before such effective date, except as otherwise provided, see section 1501 of Pub. L. 109–8, set out as a note under section 101 of this title.

Effective Date of 1994 Amendment

Amendment by Pub. L. 103–394 effective Oct. 22, 1994, and not applicable with respect to cases commenced under this title before Oct. 22, 1994, see section 702 of Pub. L. 103–394, set out as a note under section 101 of this title.

Effective Date of 1986 Amendment

Effective date and applicability of amendment by Pub. L. 99–554 dependent upon the judicial district involved, see section 302(d), (e) of Pub. L. 99–554, set out as a note under section 581 of Title 28, Judiciary and Judicial Procedure.

Effective Date of 1984 Amendment

Amendment by Pub. L. 98–353 effective July 10, 1984, see section 122(a) of Pub. L. 98–353, set out as an Effective Date note under section 151 of Title 28, Judiciary and Judicial Procedure.

§106. Waiver of sovereign immunity

(a) Notwithstanding an assertion of sovereign immunity, sovereign immunity is abrogated as to a governmental unit to the extent set forth in this section with respect to the following:

(1) Sections 105, 106, 107, 108, 303, 346, 362, 363, 364, 365, 366, 502, 503, 505, 506, 510, 522, 523, 524, 525, 542, 543, 544, 545, 546, 547, 548, 549, 550, 551, 552, 553, 722, 724, 726, 744, 749, 764, 901, 922, 926, 928, 929, 944, 1107, 1141, 1142, 1143, 1146, 1201, 1203, 1205, 1206, 1227, 1231, 1301, 1303, 1305, and 1327 of this title.

(2) The court may hear and determine any issue arising with respect to the application of such sections to governmental units.

(3) The court may issue against a governmental unit an order, process, or judgment under such sections or the Federal Rules of Bankruptcy Procedure, including an order or judgment awarding a money recovery, but not including an award of punitive damages. Such order or judgment for costs or fees under this title or the Federal Rules of Bankruptcy Procedure against any governmental unit shall be consistent with the provisions and limitations of section 2412(d)(2)(A) of title 28.

(4) The enforcement of any such order, process, or judgment against any governmental unit shall be consistent with appropriate nonbankruptcy law applicable to such governmental unit and, in the case of a money judgment against the United States, shall be paid as if it is a judgment rendered by a district court of the United States.

(5) Nothing in this section shall create any substantive claim for relief or cause of action not otherwise existing under this title, the Federal Rules of Bankruptcy Procedure, or nonbankruptcy law.

(b) A governmental unit that has filed a proof of claim in the case is deemed to have waived sovereign immunity with respect to a claim against such governmental unit that is property of the estate and that arose out of the same transaction or occurrence out of which the claim of such governmental unit arose.

(c) Notwithstanding any assertion of sovereign immunity by a governmental unit, there shall be offset against a claim or interest of a governmental unit any claim against such governmental unit that is property of the estate.

(Pub. L. 95–598, Nov. 6, 1978, 92 Stat. 2555; Pub. L. 103–394, title I, §113, Oct. 22, 1994, 108 Stat. 4117; Pub. L. 111–327, §2(a)(4), Dec. 22, 2010, 124 Stat. 3557.)

Historical and Revision Notes
legislative statements

Section 106(c) relating to sovereign immunity is new. The provision indicates that the use of the term "creditor," "entity," or "governmental unit" in title 11 applies to governmental units notwithstanding any assertion of sovereign immunity and that an order of the court binds governmental units. The provision is included to comply with the requirement in case law that an express waiver of sovereign immunity is required in order to be effective. Section 106(c) codifies *In re Gwilliam*, 519 F.2d 407 (9th Cir., 1975), and *In re Dolard*, 519 F.2d 282 (9th Cir., 1975), permitting the bankruptcy court to determine the amount and dischargeability of tax liabilities owing by the debtor or the estate prior to or during a bankruptcy case whether or not the governmental unit to which such taxes are owed files a proof of claim. Except as provided in sections 106(a) and (b), subsection (c) is not limited to those issues, but permits the bankruptcy court to bind governmental units on other matters as well. For example, section 106(c) permits a trustee or debtor in possession to assert avoiding powers under title 11 against a governmental unit; contrary language in the House report to H.R. 8200 is thereby overruled.

senate report no. 95–989

Section 106 provides for a limited waiver of sovereign immunity in bankruptcy cases. Though Congress has the power to waive sovereign immunity for the Federal government completely in bankruptcy cases, the policy followed here is designed to achieve approximately the same result that would prevail outside of bankruptcy. Congress does not, however, have the power to waive sovereign immunity completely with respect to claims of a bankrupt estate against a State, though it may exercise its bankruptcy power through the supremacy clause to prevent or prohibit State action that is contrary to bankruptcy policy.

There is, however, a limited change from the result that would prevail in the absence of bankruptcy; the change is two-fold and is within Congress' power vis-a-vis both the Federal Government and the States. First, the filing of a proof of claim against the estate by a governmental unit is a waiver by that governmental unit of sovereign immunity with respect to compulsory counterclaims, as defined in the Federal Rules of Civil Procedure [title 28, appendix], that is, counterclaims arising out of the same transaction or occurrence. The governmental unit cannot receive a distribution from the estate without subjecting itself to any liability it has to the estate within the confines of a compulsory counterclaim rule. Any other result would be one-sided. The counterclaim by the estate against the governmental unit is without limit.

Second, the estate may offset against the allowed claim of a governmental unit, up to the amount of the governmental unit's claim, any claim that the debtor, and thus the estate, has against the governmental unit, without regard to whether the estate's claim arose out of the same transaction or occurrence as the government's claim. Under this provision, the setoff permitted is only to the extent of the governmental unit's claim. No affirmative recovery is permitted. Subsection (a) governs affirmative recovery.

Though this subsection creates a partial waiver of immunity when the governmental unit files a proof of claim, it does not waive immunity if the debtor or trustee, and not the governmental unit, files proof of a governmental unit's claim under proposed 11 U.S.C. 501(c).

This section does not confer sovereign immunity on any governmental unit that does not already have immunity. It simply recognizes any immunity that exists and prescribes the proper treatment of claims by and against that sovereign.

References in Text

The Federal Rules of Bankruptcy Procedure, referred to in subsec. (a)(3), (5), are set out in the Appendix to this title.

Amendments

2010—Subsec. (a)(1). Pub. L. 111–327 struck out "728," after "726,".

1994—Pub. L. 103–394 amended section generally. Prior to amendment, section read as follows:

"(a) A governmental unit is deemed to have waived sovereign immunity with respect to any claim against such governmental unit that is property of the estate and that arose out of the same transaction or occurrence out of which such governmental unit's claim arose.

"(b) There shall be offset against an allowed claim or interest of a governmental unit any claim against such governmental unit that is property of the estate.

"(c) Except as provided in subsections (a) and (b) of this section and notwithstanding any assertion of sovereign immunity—

"(1) a provision of this title that contains 'creditor', 'entity', or 'governmental unit' applies to governmental units; and

"(2) a determination by the court of an issue arising under such a provision binds governmental units."

Effective Date of 1994 Amendment

Amendment by Pub. L. 103–394 effective Oct. 22, 1994, and applicable with respect to cases commenced under this title before, on, and after Oct. 22, 1994, see section 702(a), (b)(2)(B) of Pub. L. 103–394, set out as a note under section 101 of this title.

§107. Public access to papers

(a) Except as provided in subsections (b) and (c) and subject to section 112, a paper filed in a case under this title and the dockets of a bankruptcy court are public records and open to examination by an entity at reasonable times without charge.

(b) On request of a party in interest, the bankruptcy court shall, and on the bankruptcy court's own motion, the bankruptcy court may—

(1) protect an entity with respect to a trade secret or confidential research, development, or commercial information; or

(2) protect a person with respect to scandalous or defamatory matter contained in a paper filed in a case under this title.

(c)(1) The bankruptcy court, for cause, may protect an individual, with respect to the following types of information to the extent the court finds that disclosure of such information would create undue risk of identity theft or other unlawful injury to the individual or the individual's property:

(A) Any means of identification (as defined in section 1028(d) of title 18) contained in a paper filed, or to be filed, in a case under this title.

(B) Other information contained in a paper described in subparagraph (A).

(2) Upon ex parte application demonstrating cause, the court shall provide access to information protected pursuant to paragraph (1) to an entity acting pursuant to the police or regulatory power of a domestic governmental unit.

(3) The United States trustee, bankruptcy administrator, trustee, and any auditor serving under section 586(f) of title 28—

(A) shall have full access to all information contained in any paper filed or submitted in a case under this title; and

(B) shall not disclose information specifically protected by the court under this title.

(Pub. L. 95–598, Nov. 6, 1978, 92 Stat. 2556; Pub. L. 109–8, title II, §§233(c), 234(a), (c), Apr. 20, 2005, 119 Stat. 74, 75; Pub. L. 111–327, §2(a)(5), Dec. 22, 2010, 124 Stat. 3557.)

Historical and Revision Notes
senate report no. 95–989

Subsection (a) of this section makes all papers filed in a bankruptcy case and the dockets of the bankruptcy court public and open to examination at reasonable times without charge. "Docket" includes the claims docket, the proceedings docket, and all papers filed in a case.

Subsection (b) permits the court, on its own motion, and requires the court, on the request of a party in interest, to protect trade secrets, confidential research, development, or commercial information, and to protect persons against scandalous or defamatory matter.

Amendments

2010—Subsec. (a). Pub. L. 111–327 substituted "subsections (b) and (c)" for "subsection (b) of this section".

2005—Subsec. (a). Pub. L. 109–8, §234(c), which directed the substitution of "subsections (b) and (c)," for "subsection (b),", could not be executed because "subsection (b)," did not appear in text.

Pub. L. 109–8, §233(c), inserted "and subject to section 112" after "section".

Subsec. (c). Pub. L. 109–8, §234(a), added subsec. (c).

Effective Date of 2005 Amendment

Amendment by Pub. L. 109–8 effective 180 days after Apr. 20, 2005, and not applicable with respect to cases commenced under this title before such effective date, except as otherwise provided, see section 1501 of Pub. L. 109–8, set out as a note under section 101 of this title.

§108. Extension of time

(a) If applicable nonbankruptcy law, an order entered in a nonbankruptcy proceeding, or an agreement fixes a period within which the debtor may commence an action, and such period has not expired before the date of the filing of the petition, the trustee may commence such action only before the later of—

(1) the end of such period, including any suspension of such period occurring on or after the commencement of the case; or

(2) two years after the order for relief.

(b) Except as provided in subsection (a) of this section, if applicable nonbankruptcy law, an order entered in a nonbankruptcy proceeding, or an agreement fixes a period within which the debtor or an individual protected under section 1201 or 1301 of this title may file any pleading, demand, notice, or proof of claim or loss, cure a default, or perform any other similar act, and such period has not expired before the date of the filing of the petition, the trustee may only file, cure, or perform, as the case may be, before the later of—

(1) the end of such period, including any suspension of such period occurring on or after the commencement of the case; or

(2) 60 days after the order for relief.

(c) Except as provided in section 524 of this title, if applicable nonbankruptcy law, an order entered in a nonbankruptcy proceeding, or an agreement fixes a period for commencing or continuing a civil action in a court other than a bankruptcy court on a claim against the debtor, or against an individual with respect to which such individual is protected under section 1201 or 1301 of this title, and such period has not expired before the date of the filing of the petition, then such period does not expire until the later of—

(1) the end of such period, including any suspension of such period occurring on or after the commencement of the case; or

(2) 30 days after notice of the termination or expiration of the stay under section 362, 922, 1201, or 1301 of this title, as the case may be, with respect to such claim.

(Pub. L. 95–598, Nov. 6, 1978, 92 Stat. 2556; Pub. L. 98–353, title III, §424, July 10, 1984, 98 Stat. 369; Pub. L. 99–554, title II, §257(b), Oct. 27, 1986, 100 Stat. 3114; Pub. L. 109–8, title XII, §1203, Apr. 20, 2005, 119 Stat. 193.)

Historical and Revision Notes
legislative statements

Extension of time: The House amendment adopts section 108(c)(1) of the Senate amendment which expressly includes any special suspensions of statutes of limitation periods on collection outside bankruptcy when assets are under the authority of a court. For example, section 6503(b) of the Internal Revenue Code [title 26] suspends collection of tax liabilities while the debtor's assets are in the control or custody of a court, and for 6 months thereafter. By adopting the language of the Senate amendment, the House amendment insures not only that the period for collection of the taxes outside bankruptcy will not expire during the title 11 proceedings, but also that such period will not expire until at least 6 months thereafter, which is the minimum suspension period provided by the Internal Revenue Code [title 26].

senate report no. 95–989

Subsections (a) and (b), derived from Bankruptcy Act section 11 [section 29 of former title 11], permit the trustee, when he steps into the shoes of the debtor, an extension of time for filing an action or doing some other act that is required to preserve the debtor's rights. Subsection (a) extends any statute of limitation for commencing or continuing an action by the debtor for two years after the date of the order for relief, unless it would expire later. Subsection (b) gives the trustee 60 days to take other actions not covered under subsection (a), such as filing a pleading, demand, notice, or proof of claim or loss (such as an insurance claim), unless the period for doing the relevant act expires later than 60 days after the date of the order for relief.

Subsection (c) extends the statute of limitations for creditors. Thus, if a creditor is stayed from commencing or continuing an action against the debtor because of the bankruptcy case, then the creditor is permitted an additional 30 days after notice of the event by which the stay is terminated, whether that event be relief from the automatic stay under proposed 11 U.S.C. 362 or 1301, the closing of the bankruptcy case (which terminates the stay), or the exception from discharge of the debts on which the creditor claims.

In the case of Federal tax liabilities, the Internal Revenue Code [title 26] suspends the statute of limitations on a tax liability of a taxpayer from running while his assets are in the control or custody of a court and for 6 months thereafter (sec. 6503(b) of the Code [title 26]). The amendment applies this rule in a title 11 proceeding. Accordingly, the statute of limitations on collection of a nondischargeable Federal tax liability of a debtor will resume running after 6 months following the end of the period during which the debtor's assets are in the control or custody of the bankruptcy court. This rule will provide the Internal Revenue Service adequate time to collect nondischargeable taxes following the end of the title 11 proceedings.

Amendments

2005—Subsec. (c)(2). Pub. L. 109–8 substituted "922, 1201, or" for "922, or".

1986—Subsec. (b). Pub. L. 99–554, §257(b)(1), inserted reference to section 1201 of this title.

Subsec. (c). Pub. L. 99–554, §257(b)(2)(A), inserted reference to section 1201 of this title in provisions preceding par. (1).

Subsec. (c)(2). Pub. L. 99–554, §257(b)(2)(B), which directed the amendment of subsec. (c) by inserting "1201," after "722," could not be executed because "722," did not appear in text.

1984—Subsec. (a). Pub. L. 98–353, §424(b), inserted "nonbankruptcy" after "applicable" and "entered in a" in provisions preceding par. (1).

Subsec. (a)(1). Pub. L. 98–353, §424(a), substituted "or" for "and" after the semicolon.

Subsec. (b). Pub. L. 98–353, §424(b), inserted "nonbankruptcy" after "applicable" and "entered in a" in provisions preceding par. (1).

Subsec. (b)(1). Pub. L. 98–353, §424(a), substituted "or" for "and" after the semicolon.

Subsec. (c). Pub. L. 98–353, §424(b), inserted "nonbankruptcy" after "applicable" and "entered in a" in provisions preceding par. (1).

Subsec. (c)(1). Pub. L. 98–353, §424(a), substituted "or" for "and" after the semicolon.

Effective Date of 2005 Amendment

Amendment by Pub. L. 109–8 effective 180 days after Apr. 20, 2005, and not applicable with respect to cases commenced under this title before such effective date, except as otherwise provided, see section 1501 of Pub. L. 109–8, set out as a note under section 101 of this title.

Effective Date of 1986 Amendment

Amendment by Pub. L. 99–554 effective 30 days after Oct. 27, 1986, but not applicable to cases commenced under this title before that date, see section 302(a), (c)(1) of Pub. L. 99–554, set out as a note under section 581 of Title 28, Judiciary and Judicial Procedure.

Effective Date of 1984 Amendment

Amendment by Pub. L. 98–353 effective with respect to cases filed 90 days after July 10, 1984, see section 552(a) of Pub. L. 98–353, set out as a note under section 101 of this title.

§109. Who may be a debtor

(a) Notwithstanding any other provision of this section, only a person that resides or has a domicile, a place of business, or property in the United States, or a municipality, may be a debtor under this title.

(b) A person may be a debtor under chapter 7 of this title only if such person is not—

(1) a railroad;

(2) a domestic insurance company, bank, savings bank, cooperative bank, savings and loan association, building and loan association, homestead association, a New Markets Venture Capital company as defined in section 351 of the Small Business Investment Act of 1958, a small business investment company licensed by the Small Business Administration under section 301 of the Small Business Investment Act of 1958, credit union, or industrial bank or similar institution which is an insured bank as defined in section 3(h) of the Federal Deposit Insurance Act, except that an uninsured State member bank, or a corporation organized under section 25A of the Federal Reserve Act, which operates, or operates as, a multilateral clearing organization pursuant to section 409¹ of the Federal Deposit Insurance Corporation Improvement Act of 1991 may be a debtor if a petition is filed at the direction of the Board of Governors of the Federal Reserve System; or

(3)(A) a foreign insurance company, engaged in such business in the United States; or

(B) a foreign bank, savings bank, cooperative bank, savings and loan association, building and loan association, or credit union, that has a branch or agency (as defined in section 1(b) of the International Banking Act of 1978) in the United States.

(c) An entity may be a debtor under chapter 9 of this title if and only if such entity—

(1) is a municipality;

(2) is specifically authorized, in its capacity as a municipality or by name, to be a debtor under such chapter by State law, or by a governmental officer or organization empowered by State law to authorize such entity to be a debtor under such chapter;

(3) is insolvent;

(4) desires to effect a plan to adjust such debts; and

(5)(A) has obtained the agreement of creditors holding at least a majority in amount of the claims of each class that such entity intends to impair under a plan in a case under such chapter;

(B) has negotiated in good faith with creditors and has failed to obtain the agreement of creditors holding at least a majority in amount of the claims of each class that such entity intends to impair under a plan in a case under such chapter;

(C) is unable to negotiate with creditors because such negotiation is impracticable; or

(D) reasonably believes that a creditor may attempt to obtain a transfer that is avoidable under section 547 of this title.

(d) Only a railroad, a person that may be a debtor under chapter 7 of this title (except a stockbroker or a commodity broker), and an uninsured State member bank, or a corporation organized under section 25A of the Federal Reserve Act, which operates, or operates as, a multilateral clearing organization pursuant to section 409¹ of the Federal Deposit Insurance Corporation Improvement Act of 1991 may be a debtor under chapter 11 of this title.

(e) Only an individual with regular income that owes, on the date of the filing of the petition, noncontingent, liquidated, unsecured debts of less than $250,000² and noncontingent, liquidated, secured debts of less than $750,000,² or an individual with regular income and such individual's spouse, except a stockbroker or a commodity broker, that owe, on the date of the filing of the petition, noncontingent, liquidated, unsecured debts that aggregate less than $250,000² and noncontingent, liquidated, secured debts of less than $750,000² may be a debtor under chapter 13 of this title.

(f) Only a family farmer or family fisherman with regular annual income may be a debtor under chapter 12 of this title.

(g) Notwithstanding any other provision of this section, no individual or family farmer may be a debtor under this title who has been a debtor in a case pending under this title at any time in the preceding 180 days if—

(1) the case was dismissed by the court for willful failure of the debtor to abide by orders of the court, or to appear before the court in proper prosecution of the case; or

(2) the debtor requested and obtained the voluntary dismissal of the case following the filing of a request for relief from the automatic stay provided by section 362 of this title.

(h)(1) Subject to paragraphs (2) and (3), and notwithstanding any other provision of this section other than paragraph (4) of this subsection, an individual may not be a debtor under this title unless such individual has, during the 180-day period ending on the date of filing of the petition by such individual, received from an approved nonprofit budget and credit counseling agency described in section 111(a) an individual or group briefing (including a briefing conducted by telephone or on the Internet) that outlined the opportunities for available credit counseling and assisted such individual in performing a related budget analysis.

(2)(A) Paragraph (1) shall not apply with respect to a debtor who resides in a district for which the United States trustee (or the bankruptcy administrator, if any) determines that the approved nonprofit budget and credit counseling agencies for such district are not reasonably able to provide adequate services to the additional individuals who would otherwise seek credit counseling from such agencies by reason of the requirements of paragraph (1).

(B) The United States trustee (or the bankruptcy administrator, if any) who makes a determination described in subparagraph (A) shall review such determination not later than 1 year after the date of such determination, and not less frequently than annually thereafter. Notwithstanding the preceding sentence, a nonprofit budget and credit counseling agency may be disapproved by the United States trustee (or the bankruptcy administrator, if any) at any time.

(3)(A) Subject to subparagraph (B), the requirements of paragraph (1) shall not apply with respect to a debtor who submits to the court a certification that—

(i) describes exigent circumstances that merit a waiver of the requirements of paragraph (1);

(ii) states that the debtor requested credit counseling services from an approved nonprofit budget and credit counseling agency, but was unable to obtain the services referred to in paragraph (1) during the 7-day period beginning on the date on which the debtor made that request; and

(iii) is satisfactory to the court.

(B) With respect to a debtor, an exemption under subparagraph (A) shall cease to apply to that debtor on the date on which the debtor meets the requirements of paragraph (1), but in no case may the exemption apply to that debtor after the date that is 30 days after the debtor files a petition, except that the court, for cause, may order an additional 15 days.

(4) The requirements of paragraph (1) shall not apply with respect to a debtor whom the court determines, after notice and hearing, is unable to complete those requirements because of incapacity, disability, or active military duty in a military combat zone. For the purposes of this paragraph, incapacity means that the debtor is impaired by reason of mental illness or mental deficiency so that he is incapable of realizing and making rational decisions with respect to his financial responsibilities; and "disability" means that the debtor is so physically impaired as to be unable, after reasonable effort, to participate in an in person, telephone, or Internet briefing required under paragraph (1).

(Pub. L. 95–598, Nov. 6, 1978, 92 Stat. 2557; Pub. L. 97–320, title VII, §703(d), Oct. 15, 1982, 96 Stat. 1539; Pub. L. 98–353, title III, §§301, 425, July 10, 1984, 98 Stat. 352, 369; Pub. L. 99–554, title II, §253, Oct. 27, 1986, 100 Stat. 3105; Pub. L. 100–597, §2, Nov. 3, 1988, 102 Stat. 3028; Pub. L. 103–394, title I, §108(a), title II, §220, title IV, §402, title V, §501(d)(2), Oct. 22, 1994, 108 Stat. 4111, 4129, 4141, 4143; Pub. L. 106–554, §1(a)(5) [title I, §112(c)(1), (2)], §1(a)(8) [§1(e)], Dec. 21, 2000, 114 Stat. 2763, 2763A-393, 2763A-665; Pub. L. 109–8, title I, §106(a), title VIII, §802(d)(1), title X, §1007(b), title XII, §1204(1), Apr. 20, 2005, 119 Stat. 37, 146, 188, 193; Pub. L. 111–16, §2(1), May 7, 2009, 123 Stat. 1607; Pub. L. 111–327, §2(a)(6), Dec. 22, 2010, 124 Stat. 3557.)

Historical and Revision Notes

legislative statements

Section 109(b) of the House amendment adopts a provision contained in H.R. 8200 as passed by the House. Railroad liquidations will occur under chapter 11, not chapter 7.

Section 109(c) contains a provision which tracks the Senate amendment as to when a municipality may be a debtor under chapter 11 of title 11. As under the Bankruptcy Act [former title 11], State law authorization and prepetition negotiation efforts are required.

Section 109(e) represents a compromise between H.R. 8200 as passed by the House and the Senate amendment relating to the dollar amounts restricting eligibility to be a debtor under chapter 13 of title 11. The House amendment adheres to the limit of $100,000 placed on unsecured debts in H.R. 8200 as passed by the House. It adopts a midpoint of $350,000 as a limit on secured claims, a compromise between the level of $500,000 in H.R. 8200 as passed by the House and $200,000 as contained in the Senate amendment.

senate report no. 95–989

This section specifies eligibility to be a debtor under the bankruptcy laws. The first criterion, found in the current Bankruptcy Act section 2a(1) [section 11(a)(1) of former title 11] requires that the debtor reside or have a domicile, a place of business, or property in the United States.

Subsection (b) defines eligibility for liquidation under chapter 7. All persons are eligible except insurance companies, and certain banking institutions. These exclusions are contained in current law. However, the banking institution exception is expanded in light of changes in various banking laws since the current law was last amended on this point. A change is also made to clarify that the bankruptcy laws cover foreign banks and insurance companies not engaged in the banking or insurance business in the United States but having assets in the United States. Banking institutions and insurance companies engaged in business in this country are excluded from liquidation under the bankruptcy laws because they are bodies for which alternate provision is made for their liquidation under various State or Federal regulatory laws. Conversely, when a foreign bank or insurance company is not engaged in the banking or insurance business in the United States, then those regulatory laws do not apply, and the bankruptcy laws are the only ones available for administration of any assets found in United States.

The first clause of subsection (b) provides that a railroad is not a debtor except where the requirements of section 1174 are met.

Subsection (c) [enacted as (d)] provides that only a person who may be a debtor under chapter 7 and a railroad may also be a debtor under chapter 11, but a stockbroker or commodity broker is eligible for relief only under chapter 7. Subsection (d) [enacted as (e)] establishes dollar limitations on the amount of indebtedness that an individual with regular income can incur and yet file under chapter 13.

house report no. 95–595

Subsection (c) defines eligibility for chapter 9. Only a municipality that is unable to pay its debts as they mature, and that is not prohibited by State law from proceeding under chapter 9, is permitted to be a chapter 9 debtor. The subsection is derived from Bankruptcy Act §84 [section 404 of former title 11], with two changes. First, section 84 requires that the municipality be "generally authorized to file a petition under this chapter by the legislature, or by a governmental officer or organization empowered by State law to authorize the filing of a petition." The "generally authorized" language is unclear, and has generated a problem for a Colorado Metropolitan District that attempted to use chapter IX [chapter 9 of former title 11] in 1976. The "not prohibited" language provides flexibility for both the States and the municipalities involved, while protecting State sovereignty as required by Ashton v. Cameron County Water District No. 1, 298 U.S. 513 (1936) [56 S.Ct. 892, 80 L.Ed. 1309, 31 Am.Bankr.Rep.N.S. 96, rehearing denied 57 S.Ct. 5, 299 U.S. 619, 81 L.Ed. 457] and Bekins v. United States, 304 U.S. 27 (1938) [58 S.Ct. 811, 82 L.Ed. 1137, 36 Am.Bankr.Rep.N.S. 187, rehearing denied 58 S.Ct. 1043, 1044, 304 U.S. 589, 82 L.Ed. 1549].

The second change deletes the four prerequisites to filing found in section 84 [section 404 of former title 11]. The prerequisites require the municipality to have worked out a plan in advance, to have attempted to work out a plan without success, to fear that a creditor will attempt to obtain a preference, or to allege that prior negotiation is impracticable. The loopholes in those prerequisites are larger than the requirement itself. It was a compromise from pre-1976 chapter IX [chapter 9 of former title 11] under which a municipality could file only if it had worked out an adjustment plan in advance. In the meantime, chapter IX protection was unavailable. There was some controversy at the time of the enactment of current chapter IX concerning deletion of the pre-negotiation requirement. It was argued that deletion would lead to a rash of municipal bankruptcies. The prerequisites now contained in section 84 were inserted to assuage that fear. They are largely cosmetic and precatory, however, and do not offer any significant deterrent to use of chapter IX. Instead, other factors, such as a general reluctance on the part of any debtor, especially a municipality, to use the bankruptcy laws, operates as a much more effective deterrent against capricious use.

Subsection (d) permits a person that may proceed under chapter 7 to be a debtor under chapter 11, Reorganization, with two exceptions. Railroads, which are excluded from chapter 7, are permitted to proceed under chapter 11. Stockbrokers and commodity brokers, which are permitted to be debtors under chapter 7, are excluded from chapter 11. The special rules for treatment of customer accounts that are the essence of stockbroker and commodity broker liquidations are available only in chapter 7. Customers would be unprotected under chapter 11. The special protective rules are unavailable in chapter 11 because their complexity would make reorganization very difficult at best, and unintelligible at worst. The variety of options available in reorganization cases make it extremely difficult to reorganize and continue to provide the special customer protection necessary in these cases.

Subsection (e) specifies eligibility for chapter 13, Adjustment of Debts of an Individual with Regular Income. An individual with regular income, or an individual with regular income and the individual's spouse, may proceed under chapter 13. As noted in connection with the definition of the term "individual with regular income", this represents a significant departure from current law. The change might have been too great, however, without some limitation. Thus, the debtor (or the debtor and spouse) must have unsecured debts that aggregate less than $100,000, and secured debts that aggregate less than $500,000. These figures will permit the small sole proprietor, for whom a chapter 11 reorganization is too cumbersome a procedure, to proceed under chapter 13. It does not create a presumption that any sole proprietor within that range is better off in chapter 13 than chapter 11. The conversion rules found in section 1307 will govern the appropriateness of the two chapters for any particular individual. The figures merely set maximum limits.

Whether a small business operated by a husband and wife, the so-called "mom and pop grocery store," will be a partnership and thus excluded from chapter 13, or a business owned by an individual, will have to be determined on the facts of each case. Even if partnership papers have not been filed, for example, the issue will be whether the assets of the grocery store are for the benefit of all creditors of the debtor or only for business creditors, and whether such assets may be the subject of a chapter 13 proceeding. The intent of the section is to follow current law that a partnership by estoppel may be adjudicated in bankruptcy and therefore would not prevent a chapter 13 debtor from subjecting assets in such a partnership to the reach of all creditors in a chapter 13 case. However, if the partnership is found to be a partnership by agreement, even informal agreement, than a separate entity exists and the assets of that entity would be exempt from a case under chapter 13.

References in Text

Section 351 of the Small Business Investment Act of 1958, referred to in subsec. (b)(2), is classified to section 689 of Title 15, Commerce and Trade.

Section 301 of the Small Business Investment Act of 1958, referred to in subsec. (b)(2), is classified to section 681 of Title 15, Commerce and Trade.

Section 3(h) of the Federal Deposit Insurance Act, referred to in subsec. (b)(2), is classified to section 1813(h) of Title 12, Banks and Banking.

Section 25A of the Federal Reserve Act, referred to in subsecs. (b)(2) and (d), popularly known as the Edge Act, is classified to subchapter II (§611 et seq.) of chapter 6 of Title 12, Banks and Banking. For complete classification of this Act to the Code, see Short Title note set out under section 611 of Title 12 and Tables.

Section 409 of the Federal Deposit Insurance Corporation Improvement Act of 1991, referred to in subsecs. (b)(2) and (d), was classified to section 4422 of Title 12, Banks and Banking, prior to repeal by Pub. L. 111–203, title VII, §740, July 21, 2010, 124 Stat. 1729.

Section 1(b) of the International Banking Act of 1978, referred to in subsec. (b)(3)(B), is classified to section 3101 of Title 12, Banks and Banking.

Amendments

2010—Subsec. (b)(3)(B). Pub. L. 111–327, §2(a)(6)(A), inserted closing parenthesis after "1978".

Subsec. (h)(1). Pub. L. 111–327, §2(a)(6)(B), inserted "other than paragraph (4) of this subsection" after "this section" and substituted "ending on" for "preceding".

2009—Subsec. (h)(3)(A)(ii). Pub. L. 111–16 substituted "7-day" for "5-day".

2005—Subsec. (b)(2). Pub. L. 109–8, §1204(1), struck out "subsection (c) or (d) of" before "section 301".

Subsec. (b)(3). Pub. L. 109–8, §802(d)(1), added par. (3) and struck out former par. (3) which read as follows: "a foreign insurance company, bank, savings bank, cooperative bank, savings and loan association, building and loan association, homestead association, or credit union, engaged in such business in the United States."

Subsec. (f). Pub. L. 109–8, §1007(b), inserted "or family fisherman" after "family farmer".

Subsec. (h). Pub. L. 109–8, §106(a), added subsec. (h).

2000—Subsec. (b)(2). Pub. L. 106–554, §1(a)(8) [§1(e)], inserted "a New Markets Venture Capital company as defined in section 351 of the Small Business Investment Act of 1958," after "homestead association,".

Pub. L. 106–554, §1(a)(5) [title I, §112(c)(1)], substituted ", except that an uninsured State member bank, or a corporation organized under section 25A of the Federal Reserve Act, which operates, or operates as, a multilateral clearing organization pursuant to section 409 of the Federal Deposit Insurance Corporation Improvement Act of 1991 may be a debtor if a petition is filed at the direction of the Board of Governors of the Federal Reserve System; or" for "; or".

Subsec. (d). Pub. L. 106–554, §1(a)(5) [title I, §112(c)(2)], amended subsec. (d) generally. Prior to amendment, subsec. (d) read as follows: "Only a person that may be a debtor under chapter 7 of this title, except a stockbroker or a commodity broker, and a railroad may be a debtor under chapter 11 of this title."

1994—Subsec. (b)(2). Pub. L. 103–394, §§220, 501(d)(2), inserted "a small business investment company licensed by the Small Business Administration under subsection (c) or (d) of section 301 of the Small Business Investment Act of 1958," after "homestead association," and struck out "(12 U.S.C. 1813(h))" after "Insurance Act".

Subsec. (c)(2). Pub. L. 103–394, §402, substituted "specifically authorized, in its capacity as a municipality or by name," for "generally authorized".

Subsec. (e). Pub. L. 103–394, §108(a), substituted "$250,000" and "$750,000" for "$100,000" and "$350,000", respectively, in two places.

1988—Subsec. (c)(3). Pub. L. 100–597 struck out "or unable to meet such entity's debts as such debts mature" after "insolvent".

1986—Subsec. (f). Pub. L. 99–554, §253(1)(B), (2), added subsec. (f) and redesignated former subsec. (f) as (g).

Subsec. (g). Pub. L. 99–554, §253(1), redesignated former subsec. (f) as (g) and inserted reference to family farmer.

1984—Subsec. (a). Pub. L. 98–353, §425(a), struck out "in the United States," after "only a person that resides".

Subsec. (c)(5)(D). Pub. L. 98–353, §425(b), substituted "transfer that is avoidable under section 547 of this title" for "preference".

Subsec. (d). Pub. L. 98–353, §425(c), substituted "stockbroker" for "stockholder".

Subsec. (f). Pub. L. 98–353, §301, added subsec. (f).

1982—Subsec. (b)(2). Pub. L. 97–320 inserted reference to industrial banks or similar institutions which are insured banks as defined in section 3(h) of the Federal Deposit Insurance Act (12 U.S.C. 1813(h)).

Effective Date of 2009 Amendment

Pub. L. 111–16, §7, May 7, 2009, 123 Stat. 1609, provided that: "The amendments made by this Act [amending this section, sections 322, 332, 342, 521, 704, 749, and 764 of this title, sections 983, 1514, 1963, 2252A, 2339B, 3060, 3432, 3509, and 3771 of Title 18, Crimes and Criminal Procedure, section 7 of the Classified Information Procedures Act set out in the Appendix to Title 18, section 853 of Title 21, Food and Drugs, and sections 636, 1453, and 2107 of Title 28, Judiciary and Judicial Procedure] shall take effect on December 1, 2009."

Effective Date of 2005 Amendment

Amendment by Pub. L. 109–8 effective 180 days after Apr. 20, 2005, and not applicable with respect to cases commenced under this title before such effective date, except as otherwise provided, see section 1501 of Pub. L. 109–8, set out as a note under section 101 of this title.

Effective Date of 1994 Amendment

Amendment by Pub. L. 103–394 effective Oct. 22, 1994, and not applicable with respect to cases commenced under this title before Oct. 22, 1994, see section 702 of Pub. L. 103–394, set out as a note under section 101 of this title.

Effective Date of 1988 Amendment

Amendment by Pub. L. 100–597 effective Nov. 3, 1988, but not applicable to any case commenced under this title before that date, see section 12 of Pub. L. 100–597, set out as a note under section 101 of this title.

Effective Date of 1986 Amendment

Amendment by Pub. L. 99–554 effective 30 days after Oct. 27, 1986, but not applicable to cases commenced under this title before that date, see section 302(a), (c)(1) of Pub. L. 99–554, set out as a note under section 581 of Title 28, Judiciary and Judicial Procedure.

Effective Date of 1984 Amendment

Amendment by Pub. L. 98–353 effective with respect to cases filed 90 days after July 10, 1984, see section 552(a) of Pub. L. 98–353, set out as a note under section 101 of this title.

Adjustment of Dollar Amounts

The dollar amounts specified in this section were adjusted by notices of the Judicial Conference of the United States pursuant to section 104 of this title as follows:

By notice dated Feb. 16, 2016, 81 F.R. 8748, effective Apr. 1, 2016, in subsec. (e), dollar amounts "383,175" and "1,149,525" were adjusted to "394,725" and "1,184,200", respectively, each time they appeared. See notice of the Judicial Conference of the United States set out as a note under section 104 of this title.

By notice dated Feb. 12, 2013, 78 F.R. 12089, effective Apr. 1, 2013, in subsec. (e), dollar amounts "360,475" and "1,081,400" were adjusted to "383,175" and "1,149,525", respectively, each time they appeared.

By notice dated Feb. 19, 2010, 75 F.R. 8747, effective Apr. 1, 2010, in subsec. (e), dollar amounts "336,900" and "1,010,650" were adjusted to "360,475" and "1,081,400", respectively, each time they appeared.

By notice dated Feb. 7, 2007, 72 F.R. 7082, effective Apr. 1, 2007, in subsec. (e), dollar amounts "307,675" and "922,975" were adjusted to "336,900" and "1,010,650", respectively, each time they appeared.

By notice dated Feb. 18, 2004, 69 F.R. 8482, effective Apr. 1, 2004, in subsec. (e), dollar amounts "290,525" and "871,550" were adjusted to "307,675" and "922,975", respectively, each time they appeared.

By notice dated Feb. 13, 2001, 66 F.R. 10910, effective Apr. 1, 2001, in subsec. (e), dollar amounts "269,250" and "807,750" were adjusted to "290,525" and "871,550", respectively, each time they appeared.

By notice dated Feb. 3, 1998, 63 F.R. 7179, effective Apr. 1, 1998, in subsec. (e), dollar amounts "250,000" and "750,000" were adjusted to "269,250" and "807,750", respectively, each time they appeared.

[1] See References in Text note below.
[2] See Adjustment of Dollar Amounts notes below.

§110. Penalty for persons who negligently or fraudulently prepare bankruptcy petitions

(a) In this section—

(1) "bankruptcy petition preparer" means a person, other than an attorney for the debtor or an employee of such attorney under the direct supervision of such attorney, who prepares for compensation a document for filing; and

(2) "document for filing" means a petition or any other document prepared for filing by a debtor in a United States bankruptcy court or a United States district court in connection with a case under this title.

(b)(1) A bankruptcy petition preparer who prepares a document for filing shall sign the document and print on the document the preparer's name and address. If a bankruptcy petition preparer is not an individual, then an officer, principal, responsible person, or partner of the bankruptcy petition preparer shall be required to—

(A) sign the document for filing; and

(B) print on the document the name and address of that officer, principal, responsible person, or partner.

(2)(A) Before preparing any document for filing or accepting any fees from or on behalf of a debtor, the bankruptcy petition preparer shall provide to the debtor a written notice which shall be on an official form prescribed by the Judicial Conference of the United States in accordance with rule 9009 of the Federal Rules of Bankruptcy Procedure.

(B) The notice under subparagraph (A)—

(i) shall inform the debtor in simple language that a bankruptcy petition preparer is not an attorney and may not practice law or give legal advice;

(ii) may contain a description of examples of legal advice that a bankruptcy petition preparer is not authorized to give, in addition to any advice that the preparer may not give by reason of subsection (e)(2); and

(iii) shall—

(I) be signed by the debtor and, under penalty of perjury, by the bankruptcy petition preparer; and

(II) be filed with any document for filing.

(c)(1) A bankruptcy petition preparer who prepares a document for filing shall place on the document, after the preparer's signature, an identifying number that identifies individuals who prepared the document.

(2)(A) Subject to subparagraph (B), for purposes of this section, the identifying number of a bankruptcy petition preparer shall be the Social Security account number of each individual who prepared the document or assisted in its preparation.

(B) If a bankruptcy petition preparer is not an individual, the identifying number of the bankruptcy petition preparer shall be the Social Security account number of the officer, principal, responsible person, or partner of the bankruptcy petition preparer.

(d) A bankruptcy petition preparer shall, not later than the time at which a document for filing is presented for the debtor's signature, furnish to the debtor a copy of the document.

(e)(1) A bankruptcy petition preparer shall not execute any document on behalf of a debtor.

(2)(A) A bankruptcy petition preparer may not offer a potential bankruptcy debtor any legal advice, including any legal advice described in subparagraph (B).

(B) The legal advice referred to in subparagraph (A) includes advising the debtor—

(i) whether—

(I) to file a petition under this title; or

(II) commencing a case under chapter 7, 11, 12, or 13 is appropriate;

(ii) whether the debtor's debts will be discharged in a case under this title;

(iii) whether the debtor will be able to retain the debtor's home, car, or other property after commencing a case under this title;

(iv) concerning—

(I) the tax consequences of a case brought under this title; or

(II) the dischargeability of tax claims;

(v) whether the debtor may or should promise to repay debts to a creditor or enter into a reaffirmation agreement with a creditor to reaffirm a debt;

(vi) concerning how to characterize the nature of the debtor's interests in property or the debtor's debts; or

(vii) concerning bankruptcy procedures and rights.

(f) A bankruptcy petition preparer shall not use the word "legal" or any similar term in any advertisements, or advertise under any category that includes the word "legal" or any similar term.

(g) A bankruptcy petition preparer shall not collect or receive any payment from the debtor or on behalf of the debtor for the court fees in connection with filing the petition.

(h)(1) The Supreme Court may promulgate rules under section 2075 of title 28, or the Judicial Conference of the United States may prescribe guidelines, for setting a maximum allowable fee chargeable by a bankruptcy petition preparer. A bankruptcy petition preparer shall notify the debtor of any such maximum amount before preparing any document for filing for the debtor or accepting any fee from or on behalf of the debtor.

(2) A declaration under penalty of perjury by the bankruptcy petition preparer shall be filed together with the petition, disclosing any fee received from or on behalf of the debtor within 12 months immediately prior to the filing of the case, and any unpaid fee charged to the debtor. If rules or guidelines setting a maximum fee for services have been promulgated or prescribed under paragraph (1), the declaration under this paragraph shall include a certification that the bankruptcy petition preparer complied with the notification requirement under paragraph (1).

(3)(A) The court shall disallow and order the immediate turnover to the bankruptcy trustee any fee referred to in paragraph (2)—

(i) found to be in excess of the value of any services rendered by the bankruptcy petition preparer during the 12-month period immediately preceding the date of the filing of the petition; or

(ii) found to be in violation of any rule or guideline promulgated or prescribed under paragraph (1).

(B) All fees charged by a bankruptcy petition preparer may be forfeited in any case in which the bankruptcy petition preparer fails to comply with this subsection or subsection (b), (c), (d), (e), (f), or (g).

(C) An individual may exempt any funds recovered under this paragraph under section 522(b).

(4) The debtor, the trustee, a creditor, the United States trustee (or the bankruptcy administrator, if any) or the court, on the initiative of the court, may file a motion for an order under paragraph (3).

(5) A bankruptcy petition preparer shall be fined not more than $500 for each failure to comply with a court order to turn over funds within 30 days of service of such order.

(i)(1) If a bankruptcy petition preparer violates this section or commits any act that the court finds to be fraudulent, unfair, or deceptive, on the motion of the debtor, trustee, United States trustee (or the bankruptcy administrator, if any), and after notice and a hearing, the court shall order the bankruptcy petition preparer to pay to the debtor—

(A) the debtor's actual damages;

(B) the greater of—

(i) $2,000; or

(ii) twice the amount paid by the debtor to the bankruptcy petition preparer for the preparer's services; and

(C) reasonable attorneys' fees and costs in moving for damages under this subsection.

(2) If the trustee or creditor moves for damages on behalf of the debtor under this subsection, the bankruptcy petition preparer shall be ordered to pay the movant the additional amount of $1,000 plus reasonable attorneys' fees and costs incurred.

(j)(1) A debtor for whom a bankruptcy petition preparer has prepared a document for filing, the trustee, a creditor, or the United States trustee in the district in which the bankruptcy petition preparer resides, has conducted business, or the United States trustee in any other district in which the debtor resides may bring a civil action to enjoin a bankruptcy petition preparer from engaging in any conduct in violation of this section or from further acting as a bankruptcy petition preparer.

(2)(A) In an action under paragraph (1), if the court finds that—

(i) a bankruptcy petition preparer has—

(I) engaged in conduct in violation of this section or of any provision of this title;

(II) misrepresented the preparer's experience or education as a bankruptcy petition preparer; or

(III) engaged in any other fraudulent, unfair, or deceptive conduct; and

(ii) injunctive relief is appropriate to prevent the recurrence of such conduct,

the court may enjoin the bankruptcy petition preparer from engaging in such conduct.

(B) If the court finds that a bankruptcy petition preparer has continually engaged in conduct described in subclause (I), (II), or (III) of clause (i) and that an injunction prohibiting such conduct would not be sufficient to prevent such person's interference with the proper administration of this title, has not paid a penalty imposed under this section, or failed to disgorge all fees ordered by the court the court may enjoin the person from acting as a bankruptcy petition preparer.

(3) The court, as part of its contempt power, may enjoin a bankruptcy petition preparer that has failed to comply with a previous order issued under this section. The injunction under this paragraph may be issued on the motion of the court, the trustee, or the United States trustee (or the bankruptcy administrator, if any).

(4) The court shall award to a debtor, trustee, or creditor that brings a successful action under this subsection reasonable attorneys' fees and costs of the action, to be paid by the bankruptcy petition preparer.

(k) Nothing in this section shall be construed to permit activities that are otherwise prohibited by law, including rules and laws that prohibit the unauthorized practice of law.

(l)(1) A bankruptcy petition preparer who fails to comply with any provision of subsection (b), (c), (d), (e), (f), (g), or (h) may be fined not more than $500 for each such failure.

(2) The court shall triple the amount of a fine assessed under paragraph (1) in any case in which the court finds that a bankruptcy petition preparer—

(A) advised the debtor to exclude assets or income that should have been included on applicable schedules;

(B) advised the debtor to use a false Social Security account number;

(C) failed to inform the debtor that the debtor was filing for relief under this title; or

(D) prepared a document for filing in a manner that failed to disclose the identity of the bankruptcy petition preparer.

(3) A debtor, trustee, creditor, or United States trustee (or the bankruptcy administrator, if any) may file a motion for an order imposing a fine on the bankruptcy petition preparer for any violation of this section.

(4)(A) Fines imposed under this subsection in judicial districts served by United States trustees shall be paid to the United States trustees, who shall deposit an amount equal to such fines in the United States Trustee Fund.

(B) Fines imposed under this subsection in judicial districts served by bankruptcy administrators shall be deposited as offsetting receipts to the fund established under section 1931 of title 28, and shall remain available until expended to reimburse any appropriation for the amount paid out of such appropriation for expenses of the operation and maintenance of the courts of the United States.

(Added Pub. L. 103–394, title III, §308(a), Oct. 22, 1994, 108 Stat. 4135; amended Pub. L. 109–8, title II, §221, title XII, §1205, Apr. 20, 2005, 119 Stat. 59, 194; Pub. L. 110–161, div. B, title II, §212(b), Dec. 26, 2007, 121 Stat. 1914; Pub. L. 111–327, §2(a)(7), Dec. 22, 2010, 124 Stat. 3558.)

References in Text

The Federal Rules of Bankruptcy Procedure, referred to in subsec. (b)(2)(A), are set out in the Appendix to this title.

Amendments

2010—Subsec. (b)(2)(A). Pub. L. 111–327, §2(a)(7)(A), inserted "or on behalf of" after "from".

Subsec. (h)(1). Pub. L. 111–327, §2(a)(7)(B)(i), in last sentence, substituted "filing for the debtor" for "filing for a debtor" and inserted "or on behalf of" after "from".

Subsec. (h)(3)(A). Pub. L. 111–327, §2(a)(7)(B)(ii)(I), struck out "found to be in excess of the value of any services" after "paragraph (2)" in introductory provisions.

Subsec. (h)(3)(A)(i). Pub. L. 111–327, §2(a)(7)(B)(ii)(II), inserted "found to be in excess of the value of any services" after "(i)".

Subsec. (h)(4). Pub. L. 111–327, §2(a)(7)(B)(iii), substituted "paragraph (3)" for "paragraph (2)".

2007—Subsec. (l)(4)(A). Pub. L. 110–161 amended subpar. (A) generally. Prior to amendment, subpar. (A) read as follows: "Fines imposed under this subsection in judicial districts served by United States trustees shall be paid to the United States trustee, who shall deposit an amount equal to such fines in a special account of the United States Trustee System Fund referred to in section 586(e)(2) of title 28. Amounts deposited under this subparagraph shall be available to fund the enforcement of this section on a national basis."

2005—Subsec. (a)(1). Pub. L. 109–8, §221(1), substituted "for the debtor or an employee of such attorney under the direct supervision of such attorney" for "or an employee of an attorney".

Subsec. (b)(1). Pub. L. 109–8, §221(2)(A), inserted at end "If a bankruptcy petition preparer is not an individual, then an officer, principal, responsible person, or partner of the bankruptcy petition preparer shall be required to—" and added subpars. (A) and (B).

Subsec. (b)(2). Pub. L. 109–8, §221(2)(B), added par. (2) and struck out former par. (2) which read as follows: "A bankruptcy petition preparer who fails to comply with paragraph (1) may be fined not more than $500 for each such failure unless the failure is due to reasonable cause."

Subsec. (c)(2). Pub. L. 109–8, §221(3)(A), designated existing provisions as subpar. (A), substituted "Subject to subparagraph (B), for purposes" for "For purposes", and added subpar. (B).

Subsec. (c)(3). Pub. L. 109–8, §221(3)(B), struck out par. (3) which read as follows: "A bankruptcy petition preparer who fails to comply with paragraph (1) may be fined not more than $500 for each such failure unless the failure is due to reasonable cause."

Subsec. (d). Pub. L. 109–8, §221(4), struck out par. (1) designation before "A bankruptcy petition preparer shall" and struck out par. (2) which read as follows: "A bankruptcy petition preparer who fails to comply with paragraph (1) may be fined not more than $500 for each such failure unless the failure is due to reasonable cause."

Subsec. (e)(2). Pub. L. 109–8, §221(5), added par. (2) and struck out former par. (2) which read as follows: "A bankruptcy petition preparer may be fined not more than $500 for each document executed in violation of paragraph (1)."

Subsec. (f). Pub. L. 109–8, §221(6), struck out par. (1) designation before "A bankruptcy petition preparer shall not" and struck out par. (2) which read as follows: "A bankruptcy petition preparer shall be fined not more than $500 for each violation of paragraph (1)."

Subsec. (g). Pub. L. 109–8, §221(7), struck out par. (1) designation before "A bankruptcy petition preparer shall not" and struck out par. (2) which read as follows: "A bankruptcy petition preparer shall be fined not more than $500 for each violation of paragraph (1)."

Subsec. (h)(1). Pub. L. 109–8, §221(8)(B), added par. (1). Former par. (1) redesignated (2).

Subsec. (h)(2). Pub. L. 109–8, §221(8)(A), (C), redesignated par. (1) as (2), substituted "A" for "Within 10 days after the date of the filing of a petition, a bankruptcy petition preparer shall file a", inserted "by the bankruptcy petition preparer shall be filed together with the petition," after "perjury", and inserted at end "If rules or guidelines setting a maximum fee for services have been promulgated or prescribed under paragraph (1), the declaration under this paragraph shall include a certification that the bankruptcy petition preparer complied with the notification requirement under paragraph (1)." Former par. (2) redesignated (3).

Subsec. (h)(3). Pub. L. 109–8, §221(8)(D), added par. (3) and struck out former par. (3) which read as follows: "The court shall disallow and order the immediate turnover to the bankruptcy trustee of any fee referred to in paragraph (1) found to be in excess of the value of services rendered for the documents prepared. An individual debtor may exempt any funds so recovered under section 522(b)."

Pub. L. 109–8, §221(8)(A) redesignated par. (2) as (3). Former par. (3) redesignated (4).

Subsec. (h)(4). Pub. L. 109–8, §221(8)(E), substituted "the United States trustee (or the bankruptcy administrator, if any) or the court, on the initiative of the court," for "or the United States trustee".

Pub. L. 109–8, §221(8)(A) redesignated par. (3) as (4). Former par. (4) redesignated (5).

Subsec. (h)(5). Pub. L. 109–8, §221(8)(A) redesignated par. (4) as (5).

Subsec. (i)(1). Pub. L. 109–8, §221(9), inserted introductory provisions and struck out former introductory provisions which read as follows: "If a bankruptcy case or related proceeding is dismissed because of the failure to file bankruptcy papers, including papers specified in section 521(1) of this title, the negligence or intentional disregard of this title or the Federal Rules of Bankruptcy Procedure by a bankruptcy petition preparer, or if a bankruptcy petition preparer violates this section or commits any fraudulent, unfair, or deceptive act, the bankruptcy court shall certify that fact to the district court, and the district court, on motion of the debtor, the trustee, or a creditor and after a hearing, shall order the bankruptcy petition preparer to pay to the debtor—".

Subsec. (j)(2)(A)(i)(I). Pub. L. 109–8, §221(10)(A)(i), struck out "a violation of which subjects a person to criminal penalty" after "any provision of this title".

Subsec. (j)(2)(B). Pub. L. 109–8, §221(10)(A)(ii), substituted "has not paid a penalty" for "or has not paid a penalty" and inserted "or failed to disgorge all fees ordered by the court" after "a penalty imposed under this section,".

Subsec. (j)(3). Pub. L. 109–8, §221(10)(C) added par. (3). Former par. (3) redesignated (4).

Subsec. (j)(4). Pub. L. 109–8, §1205, substituted "attorneys" for "attorney's".

Pub. L. 109–8, §221(10)(B), redesignated par. (3) as (4).

Subsec. (l). Pub. L. 109–8, §221(11), added subsec. (l).

Effective Date of 2005 Amendment

Amendment by Pub. L. 109–8 effective 180 days after Apr. 20, 2005, and not applicable with respect to cases commenced under this title before such effective date, except as otherwise provided, see section 1501 of Pub. L. 109–8, set out as a note under section 101 of this title.

Effective Date

Section effective Oct. 22, 1994, and not applicable with respect to cases commenced under this title before Oct. 22, 1994, see section 702 of Pub. L. 103–394, set out as an Effective Date of 1994 Amendment note under section 101 of this title.

§111. Nonprofit budget and credit counseling agencies; financial management instructional courses

(a) The clerk shall maintain a publicly available list of—

(1) nonprofit budget and credit counseling agencies that provide 1 or more services described in section 109(h) currently approved by the United States trustee (or the bankruptcy administrator, if any); and

(2) instructional courses concerning personal financial management currently approved by the United States trustee (or the bankruptcy administrator, if any), as applicable.

(b) The United States trustee (or bankruptcy administrator, if any) shall only approve a nonprofit budget and credit counseling agency or an instructional course concerning personal financial management as follows:

(1) The United States trustee (or bankruptcy administrator, if any) shall have thoroughly reviewed the qualifications of the nonprofit budget and credit counseling agency or of the provider of the instructional course under the standards set forth in this section, and the services or instructional courses that will be offered by such agency or such provider, and may require such agency or such provider that has sought approval to provide information with respect to such review.

(2) The United States trustee (or bankruptcy administrator, if any) shall have determined that such agency or such instructional course fully satisfies the applicable standards set forth in this section.

(3) If a nonprofit budget and credit counseling agency or instructional course did not appear on the approved list for the district under subsection (a) immediately before approval under this section, approval under this subsection of such agency or such instructional course shall be for a probationary period not to exceed 6 months.

(4) At the conclusion of the applicable probationary period under paragraph (3), the United States trustee (or bankruptcy administrator, if any) may only approve for an additional 1-year period, and for successive 1-year periods thereafter, an agency or instructional course that has demonstrated during the probationary or applicable subsequent period of approval that such agency or instructional course—

(A) has met the standards set forth under this section during such period; and

(B) can satisfy such standards in the future.

(5) Not later than 30 days after any final decision under paragraph (4), an interested person may seek judicial review of such decision in the appropriate district court of the United States.

(c)(1) The United States trustee (or the bankruptcy administrator, if any) shall only approve a nonprofit budget and credit counseling agency that demonstrates that it will provide qualified counselors, maintain adequate provision for safekeeping and payment of client funds, provide adequate counseling with respect to client credit problems, and deal responsibly and effectively with other matters relating to the quality, effectiveness, and financial security of the services it provides.

(2) To be approved by the United States trustee (or the bankruptcy administrator, if any), a nonprofit budget and credit counseling agency shall, at a minimum—

(A) have a board of directors the majority of which—

(i) are not employed by such agency; and

(ii) will not directly or indirectly benefit financially from the outcome of the counseling services provided by such agency;

(B) if a fee is charged for counseling services, charge a reasonable fee, and provide services without regard to ability to pay the fee;

(C) provide for safekeeping and payment of client funds, including an annual audit of the trust accounts and appropriate employee bonding;

(D) provide full disclosures to a client, including funding sources, counselor qualifications, possible impact on credit reports, and any costs of such program that will be paid by such client and how such costs will be paid;

(E) provide adequate counseling with respect to a client's credit problems that includes an analysis of such client's current financial condition, factors that caused such financial condition, and how such client can develop a plan to respond to the problems without incurring negative amortization of debt;

(F) provide trained counselors who receive no commissions or bonuses based on the outcome of the counseling services provided by such agency, and who have adequate experience, and have been adequately trained to provide counseling services to individuals in financial difficulty, including the matters described in subparagraph (E);

(G) demonstrate adequate experience and background in providing credit counseling; and

(H) have adequate financial resources to provide continuing support services for budgeting plans over the life of any repayment plan.

(d) The United States trustee (or the bankruptcy administrator, if any) shall only approve an instructional course concerning personal financial management—

(1) for an initial probationary period under subsection (b)(3) if the course will provide at a minimum—

(A) trained personnel with adequate experience and training in providing effective instruction and services;

(B) learning materials and teaching methodologies designed to assist debtors in understanding personal financial management and that are consistent with stated objectives directly related to the goals of such instructional course;

(C) adequate facilities situated in reasonably convenient locations at which such instructional course is offered, except that such facilities may include the provision of such instructional course by telephone or through the Internet, if such instructional course is effective;

(D) the preparation and retention of reasonable records (which shall include the debtor's bankruptcy case number) to permit evaluation of the effectiveness of such instructional course, including any evaluation of satisfaction of instructional course requirements for each debtor attending such instructional course, which shall be available for inspection and evaluation by the Executive Office for United States Trustees, the United States trustee (or the bankruptcy administrator, if any), or the chief bankruptcy judge for the district in which such instructional course is offered; and

(E) if a fee is charged for the instructional course, charge a reasonable fee, and provide services without regard to ability to pay the fee; and

(2) for any 1-year period if the provider thereof has demonstrated that the course meets the standards of paragraph (1) and, in addition—

(A) has been effective in assisting a substantial number of debtors to understand personal financial management; and

(B) is otherwise likely to increase substantially the debtor's understanding of personal financial management.

(e) The district court may, at any time, investigate the qualifications of a nonprofit budget and credit counseling agency referred to in subsection (a), and request production of documents to ensure the integrity and effectiveness of such agency. The district court may, at any time, remove from the approved list under subsection (a) a nonprofit budget and credit counseling agency upon finding such agency does not meet the qualifications of subsection (b).

(f) The United States trustee (or the bankruptcy administrator, if any) shall notify the clerk that a nonprofit budget and credit counseling agency or an instructional course is no longer approved, in which case the clerk shall remove it from the list maintained under subsection (a).

(g)(1) No nonprofit budget and credit counseling agency may provide to a credit reporting agency information concerning whether a debtor has received or sought instruction concerning personal financial management from such agency.

(2) A nonprofit budget and credit counseling agency that willfully or negligently fails to comply with any requirement under this title with respect to a debtor shall be liable for damages in an amount equal to the sum of—

(A) any actual damages sustained by the debtor as a result of the violation; and

(B) any court costs or reasonable attorneys' fees (as determined by the court) incurred in an action to recover those damages.

(Added Pub. L. 109–8, title I, §106(e)(1), Apr. 20, 2005, 119 Stat. 38; amended Pub. L. 111–327, §2(a)(8), Dec. 22, 2010, 124 Stat. 3558.)

Amendments

2010—Subsec. (d)(1)(E). Pub. L. 111–327 substituted "; and" for period at end and realigned margin.

Effective Date

Section effective 180 days after Apr. 20, 2005, and not applicable with respect to cases commenced under this title before such effective date, except as otherwise provided, see section 1501 of Pub. L. 109–8, set out as an Effective Date of 2005 Amendment note under section 101 of this title.

Debtor Financial Management Training Test Program

Pub. L. 109–8, title I, §105, Apr. 20, 2005, 119 Stat. 36, provided that:

"(a) Development of Financial Management and Training Curriculum and Materials.—The Director of the Executive Office for United States Trustees (in this section referred to as the 'Director') shall consult with a wide range of individuals who are experts in the field of debtor education, including trustees who serve in cases under chapter 13 of title 11, United States Code, and who operate financial management education programs for debtors, and shall develop a financial management training curriculum and materials that can be used to educate debtors who are individuals on how to better manage their finances.

"(b) Test.—

"(1) Selection of districts.—The Director shall select 6 judicial districts of the United States in which to test the effectiveness of the financial management training curriculum and materials developed under subsection (a).

"(2) Use.—For an 18-month period beginning not later than 270 days after the date of the enactment of this Act [Apr. 20, 2005], such curriculum and materials shall be, for the 6 judicial districts selected under paragraph (1), used as the instructional course concerning personal financial management for purposes of section 111 of title 11, United States Code.

"(c) Evaluation.—

"(1) In general.—During the 18-month period referred to in subsection (b), the Director shall evaluate the effectiveness of—

"(A) the financial management training curriculum and materials developed under subsection (a); and

"(B) a sample of existing consumer education programs such as those described in the Report of the National Bankruptcy Review Commission (October 20, 1997) that are representative of consumer education programs carried out by the credit industry, by trustees serving under chapter 13 of title 11, United States Code, and by consumer counseling groups.

"(2) Report.—Not later than 3 months after concluding such evaluation, the Director shall submit a report to the Speaker of the House of Representatives and the President pro tempore of the Senate, for referral to the appropriate committees of the Congress, containing the findings of the Director regarding the effectiveness of such curriculum, such materials, and such programs and their costs."

§112. Prohibition on disclosure of name of minor children

The debtor may be required to provide information regarding a minor child involved in matters under this title but may not be required to disclose in the public records in the case the name of such minor child. The debtor may be required to disclose the name of such minor child in a nonpublic record that is maintained by the court and made available by the court for examination by the United States trustee, the trustee, and the auditor (if any) serving under section 586(f) of title 28, in the case. The court, the United States trustee, the trustee, and such auditor shall not disclose the name of such minor child maintained in such nonpublic record.

(Added Pub. L. 109–8, title II, §233(a), Apr. 20, 2005, 119 Stat. 74.)

Effective Date

Section effective 180 days after Apr. 20, 2005, and not applicable with respect to cases commenced under this title before such effective date, except as otherwise provided, see section 1501 of Pub. L. 109–8, set out as an Effective Date of 2005 Amendment note under section 101 of this title.

CHAPTER 3—CASE ADMINISTRATION

SUBCHAPTER I—COMMENCEMENT OF A CASE

Sec.
301.
Voluntary cases.
302.
Joint cases.
303.
Involuntary cases.
[304.
Repealed.]
305.
Abstention.
306.
Limited appearance.
307.
United States trustee.
308.
Debtor reporting requirements.

SUBCHAPTER II—OFFICERS

321. Eligibility to serve as trustee.
322. Qualification of trustee.
323. Role and capacity of trustee.
324. Removal of trustee or examiner.
325. Effect of vacancy.
326. Limitation on compensation of trustee.
327. Employment of professional persons.
328. Limitation on compensation of professional persons.
329. Debtor's transactions with attorneys.
330. Compensation of officers.
331. Interim compensation.
332. Consumer privacy ombudsman.
333. Appointment of patient care ombudsman.

SUBCHAPTER III—ADMINISTRATION

341. Meetings of creditors and equity security holders.
342. Notice.
343. Examination of the debtor.
344. Self-incrimination; immunity.
345. Money of estates.
346. Special provisions related to the treatment of State and local taxes.
347. Unclaimed property.
348. Effect of conversion.
349. Effect of dismissal.
350. Closing and reopening cases.
351. Disposal of patient records.

SUBCHAPTER IV—ADMINISTRATIVE POWERS

361. Adequate protection.
362. Automatic stay.
363. Use, sale, or lease of property.
364. Obtaining credit.
365. Executory contracts and unexpired leases.
366. Utility service.

Amendments

2010—Pub. L. 111-327, §2(a)(49), Dec. 22, 2010, 124 Stat. 3562, inserted "patient care" before "ombudsman" in item 333.

2005—Pub. L. 109-8, title II, §232(c), title IV, §434(a)(2), title VII, §719(a)(2), title VIII, §802(d)(4), title XI, §§1102(b), 1104(a)(2), Apr. 20, 2005, 119 Stat. 74, 111, 133, 146, 190, 192, added items 308, 332, 333, and 351, substituted "Special provisions related to the treatment of State and local taxes" for "Special tax provisions" in item 346, and struck out item 304 "Cases ancillary to foreign proceedings".

1986—Pub. L. 99-554, title II, §205(b), Oct. 27, 1986, 100 Stat. 3098, added item 307.

SUBCHAPTER I—COMMENCEMENT OF A CASE

§301. Voluntary cases

(a) A voluntary case under a chapter of this title is commenced by the filing with the bankruptcy court of a petition under such chapter by an entity that may be a debtor under such chapter.

(b) The commencement of a voluntary case under a chapter of this title constitutes an order for relief under such chapter.

(Pub. L. 95-598, Nov. 6, 1978, 92 Stat. 2558; Pub. L. 109-8, title V, §501(b), Apr. 20, 2005, 119 Stat. 118.)

Historical and Revision Notes
legislative statements

Sections 301, 302, 303, and 304 are all modified in the House amendment to adopt an idea contained in sections 301 and 303 of the Senate amendment requiring a petition commencing a case to be filed with the bankruptcy court. The exception contained in section 301 of the Senate bill relating to cases filed under chapter 9 is deleted. Chapter 9 cases will be handled by a bankruptcy court as are other title 11 cases.

senate report no. 95-989

Section 301 specifies the manner in which a voluntary bankruptcy case is commenced. The debtor files a petition under this section under the particular operative chapter of the bankruptcy code under which he wishes to proceed. The filing of the petition constitutes an order for relief in the case under that chapter. The section contains no change from current law, except for the use of the phrase "order for relief" instead of "adjudication." The term adjudication is replaced by a less pejorative phrase in light of the clear power of Congress to permit voluntary bankruptcy without the necessity for an adjudication, as under the 1898 act [former title 11], which was adopted when voluntary bankruptcy was a concept not thoroughly tested.

Amendments

2005—Pub. L. 109-8 designated existing provisions as subsec. (a), struck out "The commencement of a voluntary case under a chapter of this title constitutes an order for relief under such chapter." at end, and added subsec. (b).

Effective Date of 2005 Amendment

Amendment by Pub. L. 109-8 effective 180 days after Apr. 20, 2005, and not applicable with respect to cases commenced under this title before such effective date, except as otherwise provided, see section 1501 of Pub. L. 109-8, set out as a note under section 101 of this title.

§302. Joint cases

(a) A joint case under a chapter of this title is commenced by the filing with the bankruptcy court of a single petition under such chapter by an individual that may be a debtor under such chapter and such individual's spouse. The commencement of a joint case under a chapter of this title constitutes an order for relief under such chapter.

(b) After the commencement of a joint case, the court shall determine the extent, if any, to which the debtors' estates shall be consolidated.

(Pub. L. 95-598, Nov. 6, 1978, 92 Stat. 2558.)

Historical and Revision Notes
senate report no. 95-989

A joint case is a voluntary bankruptcy case concerning a wife and husband. Under current law, there is no explicit provision for joint cases. Very often, however, in the consumer debtor context, a husband and wife are jointly liable on their debts, and jointly hold most of their property. A joint case will facilitate consolidation of their estates, to the benefit of both the debtors and their creditors, because the cost of administration will be reduced, and there will be only one filing fee.

Section 302 specifies that a joint case is commenced by the filing of a petition under an appropriate chapter by an individual and that individual's spouse. Thus, one spouse cannot take the other into bankruptcy without the other's knowledge or consent. The filing of the petition constitutes an order for relief under the chapter selected.

Subsection (b) requires the court to determine the extent, if any, to which the estates of the two debtors will be consolidated; that is, assets and liabilities combined in a single pool to pay creditors. Factors that will be relevant in the court's determination include the extent of jointly held property and the amount of jointly-owned debts. The section, of course, is not license to consolidate in order to avoid other provisions of the title to the detriment of either the debtors or their creditors. It is designed mainly for ease of administration.

§303. Involuntary cases

(a) An involuntary case may be commenced only under chapter 7 or 11 of this title, and only against a person, except a farmer, family farmer, or a corporation that is not a moneyed, business, or commercial corporation, that may be a debtor under the chapter under which such case is commenced.

(b) An involuntary case against a person is commenced by the filing with the bankruptcy court of a petition under chapter 7 or 11 of this title—

(1) by three or more entities, each of which is either a holder of a claim against such person that is not contingent as to liability or the subject of a bona fide dispute as to liability or amount, or an indenture trustee representing such a holder, if such noncontingent, undisputed claims aggregate at least $10,000 [1] more than the value of any lien on property of the debtor securing such claims held by the holders of such claims;

(2) if there are fewer than 12 such holders, excluding any employee or insider of such person and any transferee of a transfer that is voidable under section 544, 545, 547, 548, 549, or 724(a) of this title, by one or more of such holders that hold in the aggregate at least $10,000 [1] of such claims;

(3) if such person is a partnership—

(A) by fewer than all of the general partners in such partnership; or

(B) if relief has been ordered under this title with respect to all of the general partners in such partnership, by a general partner in such partnership, the trustee of such a general partner, or a holder of a claim against such partnership; or

(4) by a foreign representative of the estate in a foreign proceeding concerning such person.

(c) After the filing of a petition under this section but before the case is dismissed or relief is ordered, a creditor holding an unsecured claim that is not contingent, other than a creditor filing under subsection (b) of this section, may join in the petition with the same effect as if such joining creditor were a petitioning creditor under subsection (b) of this section.

(d) The debtor, or a general partner in a partnership debtor that did not join in the petition, may file an answer to a petition under this section.

(e) After notice and a hearing, and for cause, the court may require the petitioners under this section to file a bond to indemnify the debtor for such amounts as the court may later allow under subsection (i) of this section.

(f) Notwithstanding section 363 of this title, except to the extent that the court orders otherwise, and until an order for relief in the case, any business of the debtor may continue to operate, and the debtor may continue to use, acquire, or dispose of property as if an involuntary case concerning the debtor had not been commenced.

(g) At any time after the commencement of an involuntary case under chapter 7 of this title but before an order for relief in the case, the court, on request of a party in interest, after notice to the debtor and a hearing, and if necessary to preserve the property of the estate or to prevent loss to the estate, may order the United States trustee to appoint an interim trustee under section 701 of this title to take possession of the property of the estate and to operate any business of the debtor. Before an order for relief, the debtor may regain possession of property in the possession of a trustee ordered appointed under this subsection if the debtor files such bond as the court requires, conditioned on the debtor's accounting for and delivering to the trustee, if there is an order for relief in the case, such property, or the value, as of the date the debtor regains possession, of such property.

(h) If the petition is not timely controverted, the court shall order relief against the debtor in an involuntary case under the chapter under which the petition was filed. Otherwise, after trial, the court shall order relief against the debtor in an involuntary case under the chapter under which the petition was filed, only if—

(1) the debtor is generally not paying such debtor's debts as such debts become due unless such debts are the subject of a bona fide dispute as to liability or amount; or

(2) within 120 days before the date of the filing of the petition, a custodian, other than a trustee, receiver, or agent appointed or authorized to take charge of less than

substantially all of the property of the debtor for the purpose of enforcing a lien against such property, was appointed or took possession.

(i) If the court dismisses a petition under this section other than on consent of all petitioners and the debtor, and if the debtor does not waive the right to judgment under this subsection, the court may grant judgment—
(1) against the petitioners and in favor of the debtor for—
(A) costs; or
(B) a reasonable attorney's fee; or

(2) against any petitioner that filed the petition in bad faith, for—
(A) any damages proximately caused by such filing; or
(B) punitive damages.

(j) Only after notice to all creditors and a hearing may the court dismiss a petition filed under this section—
(1) on the motion of a petitioner;
(2) on consent of all petitioners and the debtor; or
(3) for want of prosecution.

(k)(1) If—
(A) the petition under this section is false or contains any materially false, fictitious, or fraudulent statement;
(B) the debtor is an individual; and
(C) the court dismisses such petition,

the court, upon the motion of the debtor, shall seal all the records of the court relating to such petition, and all references to such petition.

(2) If the debtor is an individual and the court dismisses a petition under this section, the court may enter an order prohibiting all consumer reporting agencies (as defined in section 603(f) of the Fair Credit Reporting Act (15 U.S.C. 1681a(f))) from making any consumer report (as defined in section 603(d) of that Act) that contains any information relating to such petition or to the case commenced by the filing of such petition.

(3) Upon the expiration of the statute of limitations described in section 3282 of title 18, for a violation of section 152 or 157 of such title, the court, upon the motion of the debtor and for good cause, may expunge any records relating to a petition filed under this section.

(Pub. L. 95–598, Nov. 6, 1978, 92 Stat. 2559; Pub. L. 98–353, title III, §§426, 427, July 10, 1984, 98 Stat. 369; Pub. L. 99–554, title II, §§204, 254, 283(b), Oct. 27, 1986, 100 Stat. 3097, 3105, 3116; Pub. L. 103–394, title I, §108(b), Oct. 22, 1994, 108 Stat. 4112; Pub. L. 109–8, title III, §332(b), title VIII, §802(d)(2), title XII, §1234(a), Apr. 20, 2005, 119 Stat. 103, 146, 204; Pub. L. 111–327, §2(a)(9), Dec. 22, 2010, 124 Stat. 3558.)

Historical and Revision Notes
legislative statements
Section 303(b)(1) is modified to make clear that unsecured claims against the debtor must be determined by taking into account liens securing property held by third parties.

Section 303(b)(3) adopts a provision contained in the Senate amendment indicating that an involuntary petition may be commenced against a partnership by fewer than all of the general partners in such partnership. Such action may be taken by fewer than all of the general partners notwithstanding a contrary agreement between the partners or State or local law.

Section 303(h)(1) in the House amendment is a compromise of standards found in H.R. 8200 as passed by the House and the Senate amendment pertaining to the standards that must be met in order to obtain an order for relief in an involuntary case under title 11. The language specifies that the court will order such relief only if the debtor is generally not paying debtor's debts as they become due.

Section 303(h)(2) reflects a compromise pertaining to section 543 of title 11 relating to turnover of property by a custodian. It provides an alternative test to support an order for relief in an involuntary case. If a custodian, other than a trustee, receiver, or agent appointed or authorized to take charge of less than substantially all of the property of the debtor for the purpose of enforcing a lien against such property, was appointed or took possession within 120 days before the date of the filing of the petition, then the court may order relief in the involuntary case. The test under section 303(h)(2) differs from section 3a(5) of the Bankruptcy Act [section 21(a)(5) of former title 11], which requires an involuntary case to be commenced before the earlier of time such custodian was appointed or took possession. The test in section 303(h)(2) authorizes an order for relief to be entered in an involuntary case from the later date on which the custodian was appointed or took possession.

senate report no. 95–989
Section 303 governs the commencement of involuntary cases under title 11. An involuntary case may be commenced only under chapter 7, Liquidation, or chapter 11, Reorganization. Involuntary cases are not permitted for municipalities, because to do so may constitute an invasion of State sovereignty contrary to the 10th amendment, and would constitute bad policy, by permitting the fate of a municipality, governed by officials elected by the people of the municipality, to be determined by a small number of creditors of the municipality. Involuntary chapter 13 cases are not permitted either. To do so would constitute bad policy, because chapter 13 only works when there is a willing debtor that wants to repay his creditors. Short of involuntary servitude, it is difficult to keep a debtor working for his creditors when he does not want to pay them back. See chapter 3, supra.

The exceptions contained in current law that prohibit involuntary cases against farmers, ranchers and eleemosynary institutions are continued. Farmers and ranchers are excepted because of the cyclical nature of their business. One drought year or one year of low prices, as a result of which a farmer is temporarily unable to pay his creditors, should not subject him to involuntary bankruptcy. Eleemosynary institutions, such as churches, schools, and charitable organizations and foundations, likewise are exempt from involuntary bankruptcy.

The provisions for involuntary chapter 11 cases is a slight change from present law, based on the proposed consolidation of the reorganization chapters. Currently, involuntary cases are permitted under chapters X and XII [chapters 10 and 12 of former title 11] but not under chapter XI [chapter 11 of former title 11]. The consolidation requires a single rule for all kinds of reorganization proceedings. Because the assets of an insolvent debtor belong equitably to his creditors, the bill permits involuntary cases in order that creditors may realize on their assets through reorganization as well as through liquidation.

Subsection (b) of the section specifies who may file an involuntary petition. As under current law, if the debtor has more than 12 creditors, three creditors must join in the involuntary petition. The dollar amount limitation is changed from current law to $5,000. The new amount applies both to liquidation and reorganization cases in order that there not be an artificial difference between the two chapters that would provide an incentive for one or the other. Subsection (b)(1) makes explicit the right of an indenture trustee to be one of the three petitioning creditors on behalf of the creditors the trustee represents under the indenture. If all of the general partners in a partnership are in bankruptcy, then the trustee of a single general partner may file an involuntary petition against the partnership. Finally, a foreign representative may file an involuntary case concerning the debtor in the foreign proceeding, in order to administer assets in this country. This subsection is not intended to overrule Bankruptcy Rule 104(d), which places certain restrictions on the transfer of claims for the purpose of commencing an involuntary case. That Rule will be continued under section 405(d) of this bill.

Subsection (c) permits creditors other than the original petitioning creditors to join in the petition with the same effect as if the joining creditor had been one of the original petitioning creditors. Thus, if the claim of one of the original petitioning creditors is disallowed, the case will not be dismissed for want of three creditors or want of $5,000 in petitioning claims if the joining creditor suffices to fulfill the statutory requirements.

Subsection (d) permits the debtor to file an answer to an involuntary petition. The subsection also permits a general partner in a partnership debtor to answer an involuntary petition against the partnership if he did not join in the petition. Thus, a partnership petition by less than all of the general partners is treated as an involuntary, not a voluntary, petition.

The court may, under subsection (e), require the petitioners to file a bond to indemnify the debtor for such amounts as the court may later allow under subsection (i). Subsection (i) provides for costs, attorneys fees, and damages in certain circumstances. The bonding requirement will discourage frivolous petitions as well as spiteful petitions based on a desire to embarrass the debtor (who may be a competitor of a petitioning creditor) or to put the debtor out of business without good cause. An involuntary petition may put a debtor out of business even if it is without foundation and is later dismissed.

Subsection (f) is both a clarification and a change from existing law. It permits the debtor to continue to operate any business of the debtor and to dispose of property as if the case had not been commenced. The court is permitted, however, to control the debtor's powers under this subsection by appropriate orders, such as where there is a fear that the debtor may attempt to abscond with assets, dispose of them at less than their fair value, or dismantle his business, all to the detriment of the debtor's creditors.

The court may also, under subsection (g), appoint an interim trustee to take possession of the debtor's property and to operate any business of the debtor, pending trial on the involuntary petition. The court may make such an order only on the request of a party in interest, and after notice to the debtor and a hearing. There must be a showing that a trustee is necessary to preserve the property of the estate or to prevent loss to the estate. The debtor may regain possession by posting a sufficient bond.

Subsection (h) provides the standard for an order for relief on an involuntary petition. If the petition is not timely controverted (the Rules of Bankruptcy Procedure will fix time limits), the court orders relief after a trial, only if the debtor is generally unable to pay its debts as they mature, or if the debtor has failed to pay a major portion of his debts as they become due, or if a custodian was appointed during the 90-day period preceding the filing of the petition. The first two tests are variations of the equity insolvency test. They represent the most significant departure from present law concerning the grounds for involuntary bankruptcy, which requires an act of bankruptcy. Proof of the commission of an act of bankruptcy has frequently required a showing that the debtor was insolvent on a "balance-sheet" test when the act was committed. This bill abolishes the concept of acts of bankruptcy.

The equity insolvency test has been in equity jurisprudence for hundreds of years, and though it is new in the bankruptcy context (except in chapter X [chapter 10 of former title 11]), the bankruptcy courts should have no difficulty in applying it. The third test, appointment of a custodian within ninety days before the petition, is provided for simplicity. It is not a partial re-enactment of acts of bankruptcy. If a custodian of all or substantially all of the property of the debtor has been appointed, this paragraph creates an irrebuttable presumption that the debtor is unable to pay its debts as they mature. Moreover, once a proceeding to liquidate assets has been commenced, the debtor's creditors have an absolute right to have the liquidation (or reorganization) proceed in the bankruptcy court and under the bankruptcy laws with all of the appropriate creditor and debtor protections that those laws provide. Ninety days gives creditors ample time in which to seek bankruptcy liquidation after the appointment of a custodian. If they wait beyond the ninety day period, they are not precluded from filing an involuntary petition. They are simply required to prove equity insolvency rather than the more easily provable custodian test.

Subsection (i) permits the court to award costs, reasonable attorney's fees, or damages if an involuntary petition is dismissed other than by consent of all petitioning creditors and the debtor. The damages that the court may award are those that may be caused by the taking of possession of the debtor's property under subsection (g) or section 1104 of the bankruptcy code. In addition, if a petitioning creditor filed the petition in bad faith, the court may award the debtor any damages proximately caused by the filing of the petition. These damages may include such items as loss of business during and after the pendency of the case, and so on. "Or" is not exclusive in this paragraph. The court may grant any or all of the damages provided for under the provision. Dismissal in the best interests of credits under section 305(a)(1) would not give rise to a damages claim.

Under subsection (j), the court may dismiss the petition by consent only after giving notice to all creditors. The purpose of the subsection is to prevent collusive settlements among the debtor and the petitioning creditors while other creditors, that wish to see relief ordered with respect to the debtor but that did not participate in the case, are left without sufficient protection.

Subsection (k) governs involuntary cases against foreign banks that are not engaged in business in the United States but that have assets located here. The subsection prevents a foreign bank from being placed into bankruptcy in this country unless a foreign proceeding against the bank is pending. The special protection afforded by this section is needed to prevent creditors from effectively closing down a foreign bank by the commencement of an involuntary bankruptcy case in this country unless that bank is involved in a proceeding under foreign law. An involuntary case commenced under this subsection gives the foreign representative an alternative to commencing a case ancillary to a foreign proceeding under section 304.

Amendments
2010—Subsecs. (k), (l). Pub. L. 111–327 redesignated subsec. (l) as (k).
2005—Subsec. (b)(1). Pub. L. 109–8, §1234(a)(1), inserted "as to liability or amount" after "bona fide dispute" and substituted "if such noncontingent, undisputed claims" for "if such claims".

Subsec. (h)(1). Pub. L. 109–8, §1234(a)(2), inserted "as to liability or amount" before semicolon.

Subsec. (k). Pub. L. 109–8, §802(d)(2), struck out subsec. (k) which read as follows: "Notwithstanding subsection (a) of this section, an involuntary case may be commenced against a foreign bank that is not engaged in such business in the United States only under chapter 7 of this title and only if a foreign proceeding concerning such bank is pending."

Subsec. (l). Pub. L. 109–8, §332(b), added subsec. (l).
1994—Subsec. (b). Pub. L. 103–394 substituted "$10,000" for "$5,000" in pars. (1) and (2).
1986—Subsec. (a). Pub. L. 99–554, §254, inserted reference to family farmer.
Subsec. (b). Pub. L. 99–554, §283(b)(1), substituted "subject of" for "subject on".
Subsec. (g). Pub. L. 99–554, §204(1), substituted "may order the United States trustee to appoint" for "may appoint".
Subsec. (h)(1). Pub. L. 99–554, §283(b)(2), substituted "are the" for "that are the".
Subsec. (i)(1). Pub. L. 99–554, §204(2), inserted "or" at end of subpar. (A) and struck out subpar. (C) which read as follows: "any damages proximately caused by the taking of possession of the debtor's property by a trustee appointed under subsection (g) of this section or section 1104 of this title; or".
1984—Subsec. (b). Pub. L. 98–353, §426(a), inserted "against a person" after "involuntary case".

Subsec. (b)(1). Pub. L. 98–353, §426(b)(1), inserted "or the subject on a bona fide dispute,".

Subsec. (h)(1). Pub. L. 98–353, §426(b)(2), inserted "unless such debts that are the subject of a bona fide dispute".

Subsec. (j)(2). Pub. L. 98–353, §427, substituted "debtor" for "debtors".

Effective Date of 2005 Amendment

Pub. L. 109–8, title XII, §1234(b), Apr. 20, 2005, 119 Stat. 204, provided that: "This section [amending this section] and the amendments made by this section shall take effect on the date of the enactment of this Act [Apr. 20, 2005] and shall apply with respect to cases commenced under title 11 of the United States Code before, on, and after such date."

Amendment by sections 332(b) and 802(d)(2) of Pub. L. 109–8 effective 180 days after Apr. 20, 2005, and not applicable with respect to cases commenced under this title before such effective date, except as otherwise provided, see section 1501 of Pub. L. 109–8, set out as a note under section 101 of this title.

Effective Date of 1994 Amendment

Amendment by Pub. L. 103–394 effective Oct. 22, 1994, and not applicable with respect to cases commenced under this title before Oct. 22, 1994, see section 702 of Pub. L. 103–394, set out as a note under section 101 of this title.

Effective Date of 1986 Amendment

Effective date and applicability of amendment by section 204 of Pub. L. 99–554 dependent upon the judicial district involved, see section 302(d), (e) of Pub. L. 99–554, set out as a note under section 581 of Title 28, Judiciary and Judicial Procedure.

Amendment by section 254 of Pub. L. 99–554 effective 30 days after Oct. 27, 1986, but not applicable to cases commenced under this title before that date, see section 302(a), (c)(1) of Pub. L. 99–554.

Amendment by section 283 of Pub. L. 99–554 effective 30 days after Oct. 27, 1986, see section 302(a) of Pub. L. 99–554.

Effective Date of 1984 Amendment

Amendment by sections 426(a) and 427 of Pub. L. 98–353 effective with respect to cases filed 90 days after July 10, 1984, and amendment by section 426(b) of Pub. L. 98–353 effective July 10, 1984, see section 552(a), (b) of Pub. L. 98–353, set out as a note under section 101 of this title.

Adjustment of Dollar Amounts

The dollar amounts specified in this section were adjusted by notices of the Judicial Conference of the United States pursuant to section 104 of this title as follows:

By notice dated Feb. 16, 2016, 81 F.R. 8748, effective Apr. 1, 2016, in subsec. (b)(1), (2), dollar amount "15,325" was adjusted to "15,775". See notice of the Judicial Conference of the United States set out as a note under section 104 of this title.

By notice dated Feb. 12, 2013, 78 F.R. 12089, effective Apr. 1, 2013, in subsec. (b)(1), (2), dollar amount "14,425" was adjusted to "15,325".

By notice dated Feb. 19, 2010, 75 F.R. 8747, effective Apr. 1, 2010, in subsec. (b)(1), (2), dollar amount "13,475" was adjusted to "14,425".

By notice dated Feb. 7, 2007, 72 F.R. 7082, effective Apr. 1, 2007, in subsec. (b)(1), (2), dollar amount "12,300" was adjusted to "13,475".

By notice dated Feb. 18, 2004, 69 F.R. 8482, effective Apr. 1, 2004, in subsec. (b)(1), (2), dollar amount "11,625" was adjusted to "12,300".

By notice dated Feb. 13, 2001, 66 F.R. 10910, effective Apr. 1, 2001, in subsec. (b)(1), (2), dollar amount "10,775" was adjusted to "11,625".

By notice dated Feb. 3, 1998, 63 F.R. 7179, effective Apr. 1, 1998, in subsec. (b)(1), (2), dollar amount "10,000" was adjusted to "10,775".

[1] See Adjustment of Dollar Amounts notes below.

[§304. Repealed. Pub. L. 109–8, title VIII, §802(d)(3), Apr. 20, 2005, 119 Stat. 146]

Section, Pub. L. 95–598, Nov. 6, 1978, 92 Stat. 2560, related to cases ancillary to foreign proceedings.

Effective Date of Repeal

Repeal effective 180 days after Apr. 20, 2005, and not applicable with respect to cases commenced under this title before such effective date, except as otherwise provided, see section 1501 of Pub. L. 109–8, set out as an Effective Date of 2005 Amendment note under section 101 of this title.

§305. Abstention

(a) The court, after notice and a hearing, may dismiss a case under this title, or may suspend all proceedings in a case under this title, at any time if—

(1) the interests of creditors and the debtor would be better served by such dismissal or suspension; or

(2)(A) a petition under section 1515 for recognition of a foreign proceeding has been granted; and

(B) the purposes of chapter 15 of this title would be best served by such dismissal or suspension.

(b) A foreign representative may seek dismissal or suspension under subsection (a)(2) of this section.

(c) An order under subsection (a) of this section dismissing a case or suspending all proceedings in a case, or a decision not so to dismiss or suspend, is not reviewable by appeal or otherwise by the court of appeals under section 158(d), 1291, or 1292 of title 28 or by the Supreme Court of the United States under section 1254 of title 28.

(Pub. L. 95–598, Nov. 6, 1978, 92 Stat. 2561; Pub. L. 101–650, title III, §309(a), Dec. 1, 1990, 104 Stat. 5113; Pub. L. 102–198, §5, Dec. 9, 1991, 105 Stat. 1623; Pub. L. 109–8, title VIII, §802(d)(6), Apr. 20, 2005, 119 Stat. 146.)

Historical and Revision Notes

senate report no. 95–989

A principle of the common law requires a court with jurisdiction over a particular matter to take jurisdiction. This section recognizes that there are cases in which it would be appropriate for the court to decline jurisdiction. Abstention under this section, however, is of jurisdiction over the entire case. Abstention from jurisdiction over a particular proceeding in a case is governed by proposed 28 U.S.C. 1471(c). Thus, the court is permitted, if the interests of creditors and the debtor would be better served by dismissal of the case or suspension of all proceedings in the case, to so order. The court may dismiss or suspend under the first paragraph, for example, if an arrangement is being worked out by creditors and the debtor out of court, there is no prejudice to the results of creditors in that arrangement, and an involuntary case has been commenced by a few recalcitrant creditors to provide a basis for future threats to extract full payment. The less expensive out-of-court workout may better serve the interests in the case. Likewise, if there is pending a foreign proceeding concerning the debtor and the factors specified in proposed 11 U.S.C. 304(c) warrant dismissal or suspension, the court may so act.

Subsection (b) gives a foreign representative authority to appear in the bankruptcy court to request dismissal or suspension. Subsection (c) makes the dismissal or suspension order nonreviewable by appeal or otherwise. The bankruptcy court, based on its experience and discretion is vested with the power of decision.

Amendments

2005—Subsec. (a)(2). Pub. L. 109–8 added par. (2) and struck out former par. (2) which read as follows:

"(2)(A) there is pending a foreign proceeding; and

"(B) the factors specified in section 304(c) of this title warrant such dismissal or suspension."

1991—Subsec. (c). Pub. L. 102–198 substituted "title 28" for "this title" in two places.

1990—Subsec. (c). Pub. L. 101–650 inserted before period at end "by the court of appeals under section 158(d), 1291, or 1292 of this title or by the Supreme Court of the United States under section 1254 of this title".

Effective Date of 2005 Amendment

Amendment by Pub. L. 109–8 effective 180 days after Apr. 20, 2005, and not applicable with respect to cases commenced under this title before such effective date, except as otherwise provided, see section 1501 of Pub. L. 109–8, set out as a note under section 101 of this title.

§306. Limited appearance

An appearance in a bankruptcy court by a foreign representative in connection with a petition or request under section 303 or 305 of this title does not submit such foreign representative to the jurisdiction of any court in the United States for any other purpose, but the bankruptcy court may condition any order under section 303 or 305 of this title on compliance by such foreign representative with the orders of such bankruptcy court.

(Pub. L. 95–598, Nov. 6, 1978, 92 Stat. 2561; Pub. L. 109–8, title VIII, §802(d)(5), Apr. 20, 2005, 119 Stat. 146.)

Historical and Revision Notes

senate report no. 95–989

Section 306 permits a foreign representative that is seeking dismissal or suspension under section 305 of an ancillary case or that is appearing in connection with a petition under section 303 or 304 to appear without subjecting himself to the jurisdiction of any other court in the United States, including State courts. The protection is necessary to allow the foreign representative to present his case and the case of the foreign estate, without waiving the normal jurisdictional rules of the foreign country. That is, creditors in this country will still have to seek redress against the foreign estate according to the host country's jurisdictional rules. Any other result would permit local creditors to obtain unfair advantage by filing an involuntary case, thus requiring the foreign representative to appear, and then obtaining local jurisdiction over the representative in connection with his appearance in this country. That kind of bankruptcy law would legalize an ambush technique that has frequently been rejected by the common law in other contexts.

However, the bankruptcy court is permitted under section 306 to condition any relief under section 303, 304, or 305 on the compliance by the foreign representative with the orders of the bankruptcy court. The last provision is not carte blanche to the bankruptcy court to require the foreign representative to submit to jurisdiction in other courts contrary to the general policy of the section. It is designed to enable the bankruptcy court to enforce its own orders that are necessary to the appropriate relief granted under section 303, 304, or 305.

Amendments

2005—Pub. L. 109–8 struck out ", 304," after "section 303" in two places.

Effective Date of 2005 Amendment

Amendment by Pub. L. 109–8 effective 180 days after Apr. 20, 2005, and not applicable with respect to cases commenced under this title before such effective date, except as otherwise provided, see section 1501 of Pub. L. 109–8, set out as a note under section 101 of this title.

§307. United States trustee

The United States trustee may raise and may appear and be heard on any issue in any case or proceeding under this title but may not file a plan pursuant to section 1121(c) of this title.

(Added Pub. L. 99–554, title II, §205(a), Oct. 27, 1986, 100 Stat. 3098.)

Effective Date

Effective date and applicability of section dependent upon the judicial district involved, see section 302(d), (e) of Pub. L. 99–554, set out as a note under section 581 of Title 28, Judiciary and Judicial Procedure.

Standing and Authority of Bankruptcy Administrator

Pub. L. 101–650, title III, §317(b), Dec. 1, 1990, 104 Stat. 5115, provided that: "A bankruptcy administrator may raise and may appear and be heard on any issue in any case under title 11, United States Code, but may not file a plan pursuant to section 1121(c) of such title."

§308. Debtor reporting requirements

(a) For purposes of this section, the term "profitability" means, with respect to a debtor, the amount of money that the debtor has earned or lost during current and recent fiscal periods.

(b) A debtor in a small business case shall file periodic financial and other reports containing information including—

(1) the debtor's profitability;

(2) reasonable approximations of the debtor's projected cash receipts and cash disbursements over a reasonable period;

(3) comparisons of actual cash receipts and disbursements with projections in prior reports;

(4) whether the debtor is—

(A) in compliance in all material respects with postpetition requirements imposed by this title and the Federal Rules of Bankruptcy Procedure; and

(B) timely filing tax returns and other required government filings and paying taxes and other administrative expenses when due;

(5) if the debtor is not in compliance with the requirements referred to in paragraph (4)(A) or filing tax returns and other required government filings and making the payments referred to in paragraph (4)(B), what the failures are and how, at what cost, and when the debtor intends to remedy such failures; and

(6) such other matters as are in the best interests of the debtor and creditors, and in the public interest in fair and efficient procedures under chapter 11 of this title.

(Added Pub. L. 109–8, title IV, §434(a)(1), Apr. 20, 2005, 119 Stat. 111; amended Pub. L. 111–327, §2(a)(10), Dec. 22, 2010, 124 Stat. 3558.)

References in Text

The Federal Rules of Bankruptcy Procedure, referred to in subsec. (b)(4)(A), are set out in the Appendix to this title.

Amendments

2010—Subsec. (b). Pub. L. 111–327, §2(a)(10)(A), substituted "debtor in a small business case" for "small business debtor" in introductory provisions.

Subsec. (b)(4) to (6). Pub. L. 111–327, §2(a)(10)(B), struck out subpar. (A) designation before "whether the debtor" in par. (4) and redesignated cls. (i) and (ii) of former subpar. (A) as subpars. (A) and (B), respectively, redesignated former subpars. (B) and (C) of par. (4) as pars. (5) and (6), respectively, and, in par. (5), substituted "paragraph (4)(A)" for "subparagraph (A)(i)" and "paragraph (4)(B)" for "subparagraph (A)(ii)".

Effective Date

Pub. L. 109–8, title IV, §434(b), Apr. 20, 2005, 119 Stat. 111, provided that: "The amendments made by subsection (a) [enacting this section] shall take effect 60 days after the date on which rules are prescribed under section 2075 of title 28, United States Code, to establish forms to be used to comply with section 308 of title 11, United States Code, as added by subsection (a) [See Bankruptcy Form No. 25C, eff. Dec. 1, 2008]."

SUBCHAPTER II—OFFICERS

§321. Eligibility to serve as trustee

(a) A person may serve as trustee in a case under this title only if such person is—

(1) an individual that is competent to perform the duties of trustee and, in a case under chapter 7, 12, or 13 of this title, resides or has an office in the judicial district within which the case is pending, or in any judicial district adjacent to such district; or

(2) a corporation authorized by such corporation's charter or bylaws to act as trustee, and, in a case under chapter 7, 12, or 13 of this title, having an office in at least one of such districts.

(b) A person that has served as an examiner in the case may not serve as trustee in the case.

(c) The United States trustee for the judicial district in which the case is pending is eligible to serve as trustee in the case if necessary.

(Pub. L. 95–598, Nov. 6, 1978, 92 Stat. 2561; Pub. L. 98–353, title III, §428, July 10, 1984, 98 Stat. 369; Pub. L. 99–554, title II, §§206, 257(c), Oct. 27, 1986, 100 Stat. 3098, 3114.)

Historical and Revision Notes

legislative statements

Section 321 indicates that an examiner may not serve as a trustee in the case.

senate report no. 95–989

Section 321 is adapted from current Bankruptcy Act §45 [section 73 of former title 11] and Bankruptcy Rule 209. Subsection (a) specifies that an individual may serve as trustee in a bankruptcy case only if he is competent to perform the duties of trustee and resides or has an office in the judicial district within which the case is pending, or in an adjacent judicial district. A corporation must be authorized by its charter or bylaws to act as trustee, and, for chapter 7 or 13 cases, must have an office in any of the above mentioned judicial districts.

Amendments

1986—Subsec. (a). Pub. L. 99–554, §257(c), inserted reference to chapter 12 in two places.

Subsec. (c). Pub. L. 99–554, §206, added subsec. (c).

1984—Subsec. (b). Pub. L. 98–353 substituted "the case" for "a case" after "an examiner in".

Effective Date of 1986 Amendment

Effective date and applicability of amendment by section 206 of Pub. L. 99–554 dependent upon the judicial district involved, see section 302(d), (e) of Pub. L. 99–554, set out as a note under section 581 of Title 28, Judiciary and Judicial Procedure.

Amendment by section 257 of Pub. L. 99–554 effective 30 days after Oct. 27, 1986, but not applicable to cases commenced under this title before that date, see section 302(a), (c)(1) of Pub. L. 99–554.

Effective Date of 1984 Amendment

Amendment by Pub. L. 98–353 effective with respect to cases filed 90 days after July 10, 1984, see section 552(a) of Pub. L. 98–353, set out as a note under section 101 of this title.

§322. Qualification of trustee

(a) Except as provided in subsection (b)(1), a person selected under section 701, 702, 703, 1104, 1163, 1202, or 1302 of this title to serve as trustee in a case under this title qualifies if before seven days after such selection, and before beginning official duties, such person has filed with the court a bond in favor of the United States conditioned on the faithful performance of such official duties.

(b)(1) The United States trustee qualifies wherever such trustee serves as trustee in a case under this title.

(2) The United States trustee shall determine—

(A) the amount of a bond required to be filed under subsection (a) of this section; and

(B) the sufficiency of the surety on such bond.

(c) A trustee is not liable personally or on such trustee's bond in favor of the United States for any penalty or forfeiture incurred by the debtor.

(d) A proceeding on a trustee's bond may not be commenced after two years after the date on which such trustee was discharged.

(Pub. L. 95–598, Nov. 6, 1978, 92 Stat. 2562; Pub. L. 98–353, title III, §429, July 10, 1984, 98 Stat. 369; Pub. L. 99–554, title II, §§207, 257(d), Oct. 27, 1986, 100 Stat. 3098, 3114; Pub. L. 103–394, title V, §501(d)(3), Oct. 22, 1994, 108 Stat. 4143; Pub. L. 111–16, §2(2), May 7, 2009, 123 Stat. 1607.)

Historical and Revision Notes

legislative statements

Section 322(a) is modified to include a trustee serving in a railroad reorganization under subchapter IV of chapter 11.

senate report no. 95–989

A trustee qualifies in a case by filing, within five days after selection, a bond in favor of the United States, conditioned on the faithful performance of his official duties. This section is derived from the Bankruptcy Act section 50b [section 78(b) of former title 11]. The court is required to determine the amount of the bond and the sufficiency of the surety on the bond. Subsection (c), derived from Bankruptcy Act section 50i [section 78(i) of former title 11], relieves the trustee from personal liability and from liability on his bond for any penalty or forfeiture incurred by the debtor. Subsection (d), derived from section 50m [section 78(m) of former title 11], fixes a two-year statute of limitations on any action on a trustee's bond. Finally, subsection (e) dispenses with the bonding requirement for the United States trustee.

Amendments

2009—Subsec. (a). Pub. L. 111–16 substituted "seven days" for "five days".

1994—Subsec. (a). Pub. L. 103–394 substituted "1202, or 1302" for "1302, or 1202".

1986—Subsec. (a). Pub. L. 99–554, §257(d), inserted reference to section 1202 of this title.

Pub. L. 99–554, §207(1), substituted "Except as provided in subsection (b)(1), a person" for "A person".

Subsec. (b). Pub. L. 99–554, §207(2), amended subsec. (b) generally, adding par. (1), designating existing provisions as par. (2), substituting "The United States trustee" for "The court", "(A) the amount" for "(1) the amount", and "(B) the sufficiency" for "(2) the sufficiency".

1984—Subsec. (b)(1). Pub. L. 98–353 inserted "required to be".

Effective Date of 2009 Amendment

Amendment by Pub. L. 111–16 effective Dec. 1, 2009, see section 7 of Pub. L. 111–16, set out as a note under section 109 of this title.

Effective Date of 1994 Amendment

Amendment by Pub. L. 103–394 effective Oct. 22, 1994, and not applicable with respect to cases commenced under this title before Oct. 22, 1994, see section 702 of Pub. L. 103–394, set out as a note under section 101 of this title.

Effective Date of 1986 Amendment

Effective date and applicability of amendment by section 207 of Pub. L. 99–554 dependent upon the judicial district involved, see section 302(d), (e) of Pub. L. 99–554, set out as a note under section 581 of Title 28, Judiciary and Judicial Procedure.

Amendment by section 257 of Pub. L. 99–554 effective 30 days after Oct. 27, 1986, but not applicable to cases commenced under this title before that date, see section 302(a), (c)(1) of Pub. L. 99–554.

Effective Date of 1984 Amendment

Amendment by Pub. L. 98–353 effective with respect to cases filed 90 days after July 10, 1984, see section 552(a) of Pub. L. 98–353, set out as a note under section 101 of this title.

§323. Role and capacity of trustee

(a) The trustee in a case under this title is the representative of the estate.

(b) The trustee in a case under this title has capacity to sue and be sued.

(Pub. L. 95–598, Nov. 6, 1978, 92 Stat. 2562.)

Historical and Revision Notes

senate report no. 95–989

Subsection (a) of this section makes the trustee the representative of the estate. Subsection (b) grants the trustee the capacity to sue and to be sued. If the debtor remains in possession in a chapter 11 case, section 1107 gives the debtor in possession these rights of the trustee: the debtor in possession becomes the representative of the estate, and may sue and be sued. The same applies in a chapter 13 case.

§324. Removal of trustee or examiner

(a) The court, after notice and a hearing, may remove a trustee, other than the United States trustee, or an examiner, for cause.

(b) Whenever the court removes a trustee or examiner under subsection (a) in a case under this title, such trustee or examiner shall thereby be removed in all other cases under this title in which such trustee or examiner is then serving unless the court orders otherwise.

(Pub. L. 95–598, Nov. 6, 1978, 92 Stat. 2562; Pub. L. 99–554, title II, §208, Oct. 27, 1986, 100 Stat. 3098.)

Historical and Revision Notes

senate report no. 95–989

This section permits the court, after notice and a hearing, to remove a trustee for cause.

Amendments

1986—Pub. L. 99–554 amended section generally, designating existing provisions as subsec. (a), substituting "a trustee, other than the United States trustee, or an examiner" for "a trustee or an examiner", and adding subsec. (b).

Effective Date of 1986 Amendment

Effective date and applicability of amendment by Pub. L. 99–554 dependent upon the judicial district involved, see section 302(d), (e) of Pub. L. 99–554, set out as a note under section 581 of Title 28, Judiciary and Judicial Procedure.

§325. Effect of vacancy

A vacancy in the office of trustee during a case does not abate any pending action or proceeding, and the successor trustee shall be substituted as a party in such action or proceeding.

(Pub. L. 95–598, Nov. 6, 1978, 92 Stat. 2562.)

Historical and Revision Notes

senate report no. 95–989

Section 325, derived from Bankruptcy Act section 46 [section 74 of former title 11] and Bankruptcy Rule 221(b), specifies that a vacancy in the office of trustee during a case does not abate any pending action or proceeding. The successor trustee, when selected and qualified, is substituted as a party in any pending action or proceeding.

§326. Limitation on compensation of trustee

(a) In a case under chapter 7 or 11, the court may allow reasonable compensation under section 330 of this title of the trustee for the trustee's services, payable after the trustee renders such services, not to exceed 25 percent on the first $5,000 or less, 10 percent on any amount in excess of $5,000 but not in excess of $50,000, 5 percent on any amount in excess of $50,000 but not in excess of $1,000,000, and reasonable compensation not to exceed 3 percent of such moneys in excess of $1,000,000, upon all moneys disbursed or turned over in the case by the trustee to parties in interest, excluding the debtor, but including holders of secured claims.

(b) In a case under chapter 12 or 13 of this title, the court may not allow compensation for services or reimbursement of expenses of the United States trustee or of a standing trustee appointed under section 586(b) of title 28, but may allow reasonable compensation under section 330 of this title of a trustee appointed under section 1202(a) or 1302(a) of this title for the trustee's services, payable after the trustee renders such services, not to exceed five percent upon all payments under the plan.

(c) If more than one person serves as trustee in the case, the aggregate compensation of such persons for such service may not exceed the maximum compensation prescribed for a single trustee by subsection (a) or (b) of this section, as the case may be.

(d) The court may deny allowance of compensation for services or reimbursement of expenses of the trustee if the trustee failed to make diligent inquiry into facts that would permit denial of allowance under section 328(c) of this title or, with knowledge of such facts, employed a professional person under section 327 of this title.

(Pub. L. 95–598, Nov. 6, 1978, 92 Stat. 2562; Pub. L. 98–353, title III, §430(a), (b), July 10, 1984, 98 Stat. 369; Pub. L. 99–554, title II, §209, Oct. 27, 1986, 100 Stat. 3098; Pub. L. 103–394, title I, §107, Oct. 22, 1994, 108 Stat. 4111.)

Historical and Revision Notes

legislative statements

Section 326(a) of the House amendment modifies a provision as contained in H.R. 8200 as passed by the House. The percentage limitation on the fees of a trustee contained in the House bill is retained, but no additional percentage is specified for cases in which a trustee operates the business of the debtor. Section 326(b) of the Senate amendment is deleted as an unnecessary restatement of the limitation contained in section 326(a) as modified. The provision contained in section 326(a) of the Senate amendment authorizing a trustee to receive a maximum fee of $150 regardless of the availability of assets in the estate is deleted. It will not be necessary in view of the increase in section 326(a) and the doubling of the minimum fee as provided in section 330(b).

Section 326(b) of the House amendment derives from section 326(c) of H.R. 8200 as passed by the House. It is a conforming amendment to indicate a change with respect to the selection of a trustee in a chapter 13 case under section 1302(a) of title 11.

senate report no. 95–989

This section is derived in part from section 48c of the Bankruptcy Act [section 76(c) of former title 11]. It must be emphasized that this section does not authorize compensation of trustees. This section simply fixes the maximum compensation of a trustee. Proposed 11 U.S.C. 330 authorizes and fixes the standard of compensation. Under section 48c of current law, the maximum limits have tended to become minimums in many cases. This section is not intended to be so interpreted. The limits in this section, together with the limitations found in section 330, are to be applied as outer limits, and not as grants or entitlements to the maximum fees specified.

The maximum fee schedule is derived from section 48c(1) of the present act [section 76(c)(1) of former title 11], but with a change relating to the bases on which the percentage maxima are computed. The maximum fee schedule is based on decreasing percentages of increasing amounts. The amounts are the amounts of money distributed by the trustee to parties in interest, excluding the debtor, but including secured creditors. These amounts were last amended in 1952. Since then, the cost of living has approximately doubled. Thus, the bases were doubled.

It should be noted that the bases on which the maximum fee is computed includes moneys turned over to secured creditors, to cover the situation where the trustee liquidates property subject to a lien and distributes the proceeds. It does not cover cases in which the trustee simply turns over the property to the secured creditor, nor where the trustee abandons the property and the secured creditor is permitted to foreclose. The provision is also subject to the rights of the secured creditor generally under proposed section 506, especially 506(c). The $150 discretionary fee provision of current law is retained.

Subsection (b) of this section entitles an operating trustee to a reasonable fee, without any limitation based on the maximum provided for a liquidating trustee as in current law, Bankruptcy Act §48c(2) [section 76(c)(2) of former title 11].

Subsection (c) [enacted as (b)] permits a maximum fee of five percent on all payments to creditors under a chapter 13 plan to the trustee appointed in the case.

Subsection (d) [enacted as (c)] provides a limitation not found in current law. Even if more than one trustee serves in the case, the maximum fee payable to all trustees does not change. For example, if an interim trustee is appointed and an elected trustee replaces him, the combined total of the fees payable to the interim trustee and the permanent trustee may not exceed the amount specified in this section. Under current law, very often a receiver receives a full fee and a subsequent trustee also receives a full fee. The resultant "double-dipping", especially in cases in which the receiver and the trustee are the same individual, is detrimental to the interests of creditors, by needlessly increasing the cost of administering bankruptcy estates.

Subsection (e) [enacted as (d)] permits the court to deny compensation to a trustee if the trustee has been derelict in his duty by employing counsel, who is not disinterested.

Amendments

1994—Subsec. (a). Pub. L. 103–394 substituted "25 percent on the first $5,000 or less, 10 percent on any amount in excess of $5,000 but not in excess of $50,000, 5 percent on any amount in excess of $50,000 but not in excess of $1,000,000, and reasonable compensation not to exceed 3 percent of such moneys in excess of $1,000,000" for "fifteen percent on the first $1,000 or less, six percent on any amount in excess of $1,000 but not in excess of $3,000, and three percent on any amount in excess of $3,000".

1986—Subsec. (b). Pub. L. 99–554 amended subsec. (b) generally, substituting "under chapter 12 or 13 of this title" for "under chapter 13 of this title", "expenses of the United States trustee or of a standing trustee appointed under section 586(b) of title 28" for "expenses of a standing trustee appointed under section 1302(d) of this title", and "under section 1202(a) or 1302(a) of this title" for "under section 1302(a) of this title".

1984—Subsec. (a). Pub. L. 98–353, §430(a), substituted "and three percent on any amount in excess of $3000" for "three percent on any amount in excess of $3,000 but not in excess of $20,000, two percent on any amount in excess of $20,000 but not in excess of $50,000, and one percent on any amount in excess of $50,000".

Subsec. (d). Pub. L. 98–353, §430(b), amended subsec. (d) generally. Prior to amendment, subsec. (d) read as follows: "The court may deny allowance of compensation for services and reimbursement of expenses of the trustee if the trustee—

"(1) failed to make diligent inquiry into facts that would permit denial of allowance under section 328(c) of this title; or

"(2) with knowledge of such facts, employed a professional person under section 327 of this title."

Effective Date of 1994 Amendment

Amendment by Pub. L. 103–394 effective Oct. 22, 1994, and not applicable with respect to cases commenced under this title before Oct. 22, 1994, see section 702 of Pub. L. 103–394, set out as a note under section 101 of this title.

Effective Date of 1986 Amendment

Effective date and applicability of amendment by Pub. L. 99–554 dependent upon the judicial district involved, see section 302(d), (e) of Pub. L. 99–554, set out as a note under section 581 of Title 28, Judiciary and Judicial Procedure.

Effective Date of 1984 Amendment

Amendment by Pub. L. 98–353 effective with respect to cases filed 90 days after July 10, 1984, see section 552(a) of Pub. L. 98–353, set out as a note under section 101 of this title.

References in Subsection (b) Temporarily Deemed To Include Additional References

Until the amendments made by subtitle A (§§201 to 231) of title II of Pub. L. 99–554 become effective in a district and apply to a case, for purposes of such case any reference in subsec. (b) of this section—

(1) to chapter 13 of this title is deemed to be a reference to chapter 12 or 13 of this title,

(2) to section 1302(d) of this title is deemed to be a reference to section 1302(d) of this title or section 586(b) of Title 28, Judiciary and Judicial Procedure, and

(3) to section 1302(a) of this title is deemed to be a reference to section 1202(a) or 1302(a) of this title,

see section 302(c)(3)(A), (d), (e) of Pub. L. 99–554, set out in an Effective Date of 1986 Amendment; Transition and Administrative Provisions note under section 581 of Title 28.

§327. Employment of professional persons

(a) Except as otherwise provided in this section, the trustee, with the court's approval, may employ one or more attorneys, accountants, appraisers, auctioneers, or other professional persons, that do not hold or represent an interest adverse to the estate, and that are disinterested persons, to represent or assist the trustee in carrying out the trustee's duties under this title.

(b) If the trustee is authorized to operate the business of the debtor under section 721, 1202, or 1108 of this title, and if the debtor has regularly employed attorneys, accountants, or other professional persons on salary, the trustee may retain or replace such professional persons if necessary in the operation of such business.

(c) In a case under chapter 7, 12, or 11 of this title, a person is not disqualified for employment under this section solely because of such person's employment by or representation of a creditor, unless there is objection by another creditor or the United States trustee, in which case the court shall disapprove such employment if there is an actual conflict of interest.

(d) The court may authorize the trustee to act as attorney or accountant for the estate if such authorization is in the best interest of the estate.

(e) The trustee, with the court's approval, may employ, for a specified special purpose, other than to represent the trustee in conducting the case, an attorney that has represented the debtor, if in the best interest of the estate and if such attorney does not represent or hold any interest adverse to the debtor or to the estate with respect to the matter on which such attorney is to be employed.

(f) The trustee may not employ a person that has served as an examiner in the case.

(Pub. L. 95–598, Nov. 6, 1978, 92 Stat. 2563; Pub. L. 98–353, title III, §430(c), July 10, 1984, 98 Stat. 370; Pub. L. 99–554, title II, §§210, 257(e), Oct. 27, 1986, 100 Stat. 3099, 3114.)

Historical and Revision Notes

legislative statements

Section 327(a) of the House amendment contains a technical amendment indicating that attorneys, and perhaps other officers enumerated therein, represent, rather than assist, the trustee in carrying out the trustee's duties.

Section 327(c) represents a compromise between H.R. 8200 as passed by the House and the Senate amendment. The provision states that former representation of a creditor, whether secured or unsecured, will not automatically disqualify a person from being employed by a trustee, but if such person is employed by the trustee, the person may no longer represent the creditor in connection with the case.

Section 327(f) prevents an examiner from being employed by the trustee.

senate report no. 95–989

This section authorizes the trustee, subject to the court's approval, to employ professional persons, such as attorneys, accountants, appraisers, and auctioneers, to represent or perform services for the estate. The trustee may employ only disinterested persons that do not hold or represent an interest adverse to the estate.

Subsection (b) is an exception, and authorizes the trustee to retain or replace professional persons that the debtor has employed if necessary in the operation of the debtor's business.

Subsection (c) provides a professional person is not disqualified for employment solely because of the person's prior employment by or representation of a secured or unsecured creditor.

Subsection (d) permits the court to authorize the trustee, if qualified to act as his own counsel or accountant.

Subsection (e) permits the trustee, subject to the court's approval, to employ for a specified special purpose an attorney that has represented the debtor, if such employment is in the best interest of the estate and if the attorney does not hold or represent an interest adverse to the debtor of the estate with respect to the matter on which he is to be employed. This subsection does not authorize the employment of the debtor's attorney to represent the estate generally or to represent the trustee in the conduct of the bankruptcy case. The subsection will most likely be used when the debtor is involved in complex litigation, and changing attorneys in the middle of the case after the bankruptcy case has commenced would be detrimental to the progress of that other litigation.

house report no. 95–595

Subsection (c) is an additional exception. The trustee may employ as his counsel a nondisinterested person if the only reason that the attorney is not disinterested is because of his representation of an unsecured creditor.

Amendments

1986—Subsec. (b). Pub. L. 99–554, §257(e)(1), which directed the insertion of ", 1202," after "section 721," was executed by making the insertion after "section 721" to reflect the probable intent of Congress.

Subsec. (c). Pub. L. 99–554, §257(e)(2), which directed the insertion of ", 12," after "section 7," was executed by making the insertion after "chapter 7" to reflect the probable intent of Congress.

Pub. L. 99–554, §210, inserted "or the United States trustee" after "another creditor".

1984—Subsec. (c). Pub. L. 98–353 substituted "In a case under chapter 7 or 11 of this title, a person is not disqualified for employment under this section solely because of such person's employment by or representation of a creditor, unless there is objection by another creditor, in which case the court shall disapprove such employment if there is an actual conflict of interest." for "In a case under chapter 7 or 11 of this title, a person is not disqualified for employment under this section solely because of such person's employment by or representation of a creditor, but may not, while employed by the trustee, represent, in connection with the case, a creditor."

Effective Date of 1986 Amendment

Effective date and applicability of amendment by section 210 of Pub. L. 99–554 dependent upon the judicial district involved, see section 302(d), (e) of Pub. L. 99–554, set out as a note under section 581 of Title 28, Judiciary and Judicial Procedure.

Amendment by section 257 of Pub. L. 99–554 effective 30 days after Oct. 27, 1986, but not applicable to cases commenced under this title before that date, see section 302(a), (c)(1) of Pub. L. 99–554.

Effective Date of 1984 Amendment

Amendment by Pub. L. 98–353 effective with respect to cases filed 90 days after July 10, 1984, see section 552(a) of Pub. L. 98–353, set out as a note under section 101 of this title.

§328. Limitation on compensation of professional persons

(a) The trustee, or a committee appointed under section 1102 of this title, with the court's approval, may employ or authorize the employment of a professional person under section 327 or 1103 of this title, as the case may be, on any reasonable terms and conditions of employment, including on a retainer, on an hourly basis, on a fixed or percentage fee basis, or on a contingent fee basis. Notwithstanding such terms and conditions, the court may allow compensation different from the compensation provided under such terms and conditions after the conclusion of such employment, if such terms and conditions prove to have been improvident in light of developments not capable of being anticipated at the time of the fixing of such terms and conditions.

(b) If the court has authorized a trustee to serve as an attorney or accountant for the estate under section 327(d) of this title, the court may allow compensation for the trustee's services as such attorney or accountant only to the extent that the trustee performed services as attorney or accountant for the estate and not for performance of any of the trustee's duties that are generally performed by a trustee without the assistance of an attorney or accountant for the estate.

(c) Except as provided in section 327(c), 327(e), or 1107(b) of this title, the court may deny allowance of compensation for services and reimbursement of expenses of a professional person employed under section 327 or 1103 of this title if, at any time during such professional person's employment under section 327 or 1103 of this title, such professional person is not a disinterested person, or represents or holds an interest adverse to the interest of the estate with respect to the matter on which such professional person is employed.

(Pub. L. 95–598, Nov. 6, 1978, 92 Stat. 2563; Pub. L. 98–353, title III, §431, July 10, 1984, 98 Stat. 370; Pub. L. 109–8, title XII, §1206, Apr. 20, 2005, 119 Stat. 194.)

Historical and Revision Notes

legislative statements

Section 328(c) adopts a technical amendment contained in the Senate amendment indicating that an attorney for the debtor in possession is not disqualified for compensation for services and reimbursement of expenses simply because of prior representation of the debtor.

senate report no. 95–989

This section, which is parallel to section 326, fixes the maximum compensation allowable to a professional person employed under section 327. It authorizes the trustee, with the court's approval, to employ professional persons on any reasonable terms, including on a retainer, on an hourly or on a contingent fee basis. Subsection (a) further permits the court to allow compensation different from the compensation provided under the trustee's agreement if the prior agreement proves to have been improvident in light of development unanticipatable at the time of the agreement. The court's power includes the power to increase as well as decrease the agreed upon compensation. This provision is permissive, not mandatory, and should not be used by the court if to do so would violate the code of ethics of the professional involved.

Subsection (b) limits a trustee that has been authorized to serve as his own counsel to only one fee for each service. The purpose of permitting the trustee to serve as his own counsel is to reduce costs. It is not included to provide the trustee with a bonus by permitting him to receive two fees for the same service or to avoid the maxima fixed in section 326. Thus, this subsection requires the court to differentiate between the trustee's services as trustee, and his services as trustee's counsel, and to fix compensation accordingly. Services that a trustee normally performs for an estate without assistance of counsel are to be compensated under the limits fixed in section 326. Only services that he performs that are normally performed by trustee's counsel may be compensated under the maxima imposed by this section.

Subsection (c) permits the court to deny compensation for services and reimbursement of expenses if the professional person is not disinterested or if he represents or holds an interest adverse to the estate on the matter on which he is employed. The subsection provides a penalty for conflicts of interest.

Amendments

2005—Subsec. (a). Pub. L. 109–8 inserted "on a fixed or percentage fee basis," after "hourly basis,".

1984—Subsec. (a). Pub. L. 98–353 substituted "not capable of being anticipated" for "unanticipatable".

Effective Date of 2005 Amendment

Amendment by Pub. L. 109–8 effective 180 days after Apr. 20, 2005, and not applicable with respect to cases commenced under this title before such effective date, except as otherwise provided, see section 1501 of Pub. L. 109–8, set out as a note under section 101 of this title.

Effective Date of 1984 Amendment

Amendment by Pub. L. 98–353 effective with respect to cases filed 90 days after July 10, 1984, see section 552(a) of Pub. L. 98–353, set out as a note under section 101 of this title.

§329. Debtor's transactions with attorneys

(a) Any attorney representing a debtor in a case under this title, or in connection with such a case, whether or not such attorney applies for compensation under this title, shall file with the court a statement of the compensation paid or agreed to be paid, if such payment or agreement was made after one year before the date of the filing of the petition, for services rendered or to be rendered in contemplation of or in connection with the case by such attorney, and the source of such compensation.

(b) If such compensation exceeds the reasonable value of any such services, the court may cancel any such agreement, or order the return of any such payment, to the extent excessive, to—

(1) the estate, if the property transferred—

(A) would have been property of the estate; or

(B) was to be paid by or on behalf of the debtor under a plan under chapter 11, 12, or 13 of this title; or

(2) the entity that made such payment.

(Pub. L. 95–598, Nov. 6, 1978, 92 Stat. 2564; Pub. L. 98–353, title III, §432, July 10, 1984, 98 Stat. 370; Pub. L. 99–554, title II, §257(c), Oct. 27, 1986, 100 Stat. 3114.)

Historical and Revision Notes

senate report no. 95–989

This section, derived in large part from current Bankruptcy Act section 60d [section 96(d) of former title 11], requires the debtor's attorney to file with the court a statement of the compensation paid or agreed to be paid to the attorney for services in contemplation of and in connection with the case, and the source of the compensation. Payments to a debtor's attorney provide serious potential for evasion of creditor protection provisions of the bankruptcy laws, and serious potential for overreaching by the debtor's attorney, and should be subject to careful scrutiny.

Subsection (b) permits the court to deny compensation to the attorney, to cancel an agreement to pay compensation, or to order the return of compensation paid, if the compensation exceeds the reasonable value of the services provided. The return of payments already made are generally to the trustee for the benefit of the estate. However, if the property would not have come into the estate in any event, the court will order it returned to the entity that made the payment.

The Bankruptcy Commission recommended a provision similar to this that would have also permitted an examination of the debtor's transactions with insiders. S. 236, 94th Cong., 1st sess., sec. 4–311(b) (1975). Its exclusion here is to permit it to be dealt with by the Rules of Bankruptcy Procedure. It is not intended that the provision be deleted entirely, only that the flexibility of the rules is more appropriate for such evidentiary matters.

Amendments

1986—Subsec. (b)(1)(B). Pub. L. 99–554 inserted reference to chapter 12.

1984—Subsec. (a). Pub. L. 98–353, §432(a), substituted "or" for "and" after "in contemplation of".

Subsec. (b)(1). Pub. L. 98–353, §432(b), substituted "estate" for "trustee".

Effective Date of 1986 Amendment

Amendment by Pub. L. 99–554 effective 30 days after Oct. 27, 1986, but not applicable to cases commenced under this title before that date, see section 302(a), (c)(1) of Pub. L. 99–554, set out as a note under section 581 of Title 28, Judiciary and Judicial Procedure.

Effective Date of 1984 Amendment

Amendment by Pub. L. 98–353 effective with respect to cases filed 90 days after July 10, 1984, see section 552(a) of Pub. L. 98–353, set out as a note under section 101 of this title.

§330. Compensation of officers

(a)(1) After notice to the parties in interest and the United States Trustee and a hearing, and subject to sections 326, 328, and 329, the court may award to a trustee, a consumer privacy ombudsman appointed under section 332, an examiner, an ombudsman appointed under section 333, or a professional person employed under section 327 or 1103—

(A) reasonable compensation for actual, necessary services rendered by the trustee, examiner, ombudsman, professional person, or attorney and by any paraprofessional person employed by any such person; and

(B) reimbursement for actual, necessary expenses.

(2) The court may, on its own motion or on the motion of the United States Trustee, the United States Trustee for the District or Region, the trustee for the estate, or any other party in interest, award compensation that is less than the amount of compensation that is requested.

(3) In determining the amount of reasonable compensation to be awarded to an examiner, trustee under chapter 11, or professional person, the court shall consider the nature, the extent, and the value of such services, taking into account all relevant factors, including—

(A) the time spent on such services;

(B) the rates charged for such services;

(C) whether the services were necessary to the administration of, or beneficial at the time at which the service was rendered toward the completion of, a case under this title;

(D) whether the services were performed within a reasonable amount of time commensurate with the complexity, importance, and nature of the problem, issue, or task addressed;

(E) with respect to a professional person, whether the person is board certified or otherwise has demonstrated skill and experience in the bankruptcy field; and

(F) whether the compensation is reasonable based on the customary compensation charged by comparably skilled practitioners in cases other than cases under this title.

(4)(A) Except as provided in subparagraph (B), the court shall not allow compensation for—

(i) unnecessary duplication of services; or

(ii) services that were not—

(I) reasonably likely to benefit the debtor's estate; or

(II) necessary to the administration of the case.

(B) In a chapter 12 or chapter 13 case in which the debtor is an individual, the court may allow reasonable compensation to the debtor's attorney for representing the interests of the debtor in connection with the bankruptcy case based on a consideration of the benefit and necessity of such services to the debtor and the other factors set forth in this section.

(5) The court shall reduce the amount of compensation awarded under this section by the amount of any interim compensation awarded under section 331, and, if the amount of such interim compensation exceeds the amount of compensation awarded under this section, may order the return of the excess to the estate.

(6) Any compensation awarded for the preparation of a fee application shall be based on the level and skill reasonably required to prepare the application.

(7) In determining the amount of reasonable compensation to be awarded to a trustee, the court shall treat such compensation as a commission, based on section 326.

(b)(1) There shall be paid from the filing fee in a case under chapter 7 of this title $45 to the trustee serving in such case, after such trustee's services are rendered.

(2) The Judicial Conference of the United States—

(A) shall prescribe additional fees of the same kind as prescribed under section 1914(b) of title 28; and

(B) may prescribe notice of appearance fees and fees charged against distributions in cases under this title;

to pay $15 to trustees serving in cases after such trustees' services are rendered. Beginning 1 year after the date of the enactment of the Bankruptcy Reform Act of 1994, such $15 shall be paid in addition to the amount paid under paragraph (1).

(c) Unless the court orders otherwise, in a case under chapter 12 or 13 of this title the compensation paid to the trustee serving in the case shall not be less than $5 per month from any distribution under the plan during the administration of the plan.

(d) In a case in which the United States trustee serves as trustee, the compensation of the trustee under this section shall be paid to the clerk of the bankruptcy court and deposited by the clerk into the United States Trustee System Fund established by section 589a of title 28.

(Pub. L. 95–598, Nov. 6, 1978, 92 Stat. 2564; Pub. L. 98–353, title III, §§433, 434, July 10, 1984, 98 Stat. 370; Pub. L. 99–554, title II, §§211, 257(f), Oct. 27, 1986, 100 Stat. 3099, 3114; Pub. L. 103–394, title I, §117, title II, §224(b), Oct. 22, 1994, 108 Stat. 4119, 4130; Pub. L. 109–8, title II, §232(b), title IV, §§407, 415, title XI, §1104(b), Apr. 20, 2005, 119 Stat. 74, 106, 107, 192.)

Historical and Revision Notes

legislative statements

Section 330(a) contains the standard of compensation adopted in H.R. 8200 as passed by the House rather than the contrary standard contained in the Senate amendment. Attorneys' fees in bankruptcy cases can be quite large and should be closely examined by the court. However bankruptcy legal services are entitled to command the same competency of counsel as other cases. In that light, the policy of this section is to compensate attorneys and other professionals serving in a case under title 11 at the same rate as the attorney or other professional would be compensated for performing comparable services other than in a case under title 11. Contrary language in the Senate report accompanying S. 2266 is rejected, and *Massachusetts Mutual Life Insurance Company v. Brock*, 405 F.2d 429, 432 (5th Cir. 1968) is overruled. Notions of economy of the estate in fixing fees are outdated and have no place in a bankruptcy code.

Section 330(a)(2) of the Senate amendment is deleted although the Securities and Exchange Commission retains a right to file an advisory report under section 1109.

Section 330(b) of the Senate amendment is deleted as unnecessary, as the limitations contained therein are covered by section 328(c) of H.R. 8200 as passed by the House and contained in the House amendment.

Section 330(c) of the Senate amendment providing for a trustee to receive a fee of $20 for each estate from the filing fee paid to the clerk is retained as section 330(b) of the House amendment. The section will encourage private trustees to serve in cases under title 11 and in pilot districts will place less of a burden on the U.S. trustee to serve in no-asset cases.

Section 330(b) of H.R. 8200 as passed by the House is retained by the House amendment as section 330(c) [section 15330].

senate report no. 95–989

Section 330 authorizes the court to award compensation for services and reimbursement of expenses of officers of the estate, and other professionals. The compensation is to be reasonable, for economy in administration is the basic objective. Compensation is to be for actual necessary services, based on the time spent, the nature, the extent and the value of the services rendered, and the cost of comparable services in nonbankruptcy cases. There are the criteria that have been applied by the courts as analytic aids in defining "reasonable" compensation.

The reference to "the cost of comparable services" in a nonbankruptcy case is not intended as a change of existing law. In a bankruptcy case fees are not a matter for private agreement. There is inherent a "public interest" that "must be considered in awarding fees," *Massachusetts Mutual Life Insurance Co. v. Brock*, 405 F.2d 429, 432 (C.A.5, 1968), cert. denied, 395 U.S. 906 (1969). An allowance is the result of a balance struck between moderation in the interest of the estate and its security holders and the need to be "generous enough to encourage" lawyers and others to render the necessary and exacting services that bankruptcy cases often require. *In re Yale Express System, Inc.*, 366 F.Supp. 1376, 1381 (S.D.N.Y. 1973). The rates for similar kinds of services in private employment is one element, among others, in that balance. Compensation in private employment noted in subsection (a) is a point of reference, not a controlling determinant of what shall be allowed in bankruptcy cases.

One of the major reforms in 1938, especially for reorganization cases, was centralized control over fees in the bankruptcy courts. See *Brown v. Gerdes*, 321 U.S. 178, 182–184 (1944); *Leiman v. Guttman*, 336 U.S. 1, 4–9 (1949). It was intended to guard against a recurrence of "the many sordid chapters" in "the history of fees in corporate reorganizations." *Dickinson Industrial Site, Inc. v. Cowan*, 309 U.S. 382, 388 (1940). In the years since then the bankruptcy bar has flourished and prospered, and persons of merit and quality have not eschewed public service in bankruptcy cases merely because bankruptcy courts, in the interest of economy in administration, have not allowed them compensation that may be earned in the private economy of business or the professions. There is no reason to believe that, in generations to come, their successors will be less persuaded by the need to serve in the public interest because of stronger allures of private gain elsewhere.

Subsection (a) provides for compensation of paraprofessionals in order to reduce the cost of administering bankruptcy cases. Paraprofessionals can be employed to perform duties which do not require the full range of skills of a qualified professional. Some courts have not hesitated to recognize paraprofessional services as compensable under existing law. An explicit provision to that effect is useful and constructive.

The last sentence of subsection (a) provides that in the case of a public company—defined in section 1101(3)—the court shall refer, after a hearing, all applications to the Securities and Exchange Commission for a report, which shall be advisory only. In Chapter X cases in which the Commission has appeared, it generally filed reports on fee applications. Usually, courts have accorded the SEC's views substantial weight, as representing the opinion of a disinterested agency skilled and experienced in reorganization affairs. The last sentence intends for the advisory assistance of the Commission to be sought only in case of a public company in reorganization under chapter 11.

Subsection (b) reenacts section 249 of Chapter X of the Bankruptcy Act ([former] 11 U.S.C. 649). It is a codification of equitable principles designed to prevent fiduciaries in the case from engaging in the specified transactions since they are in a position to gain inside information or to shape or influence the course of the reorganization. *Wolf v. Weinstein*, 372 U.S. 633 (1963). The statutory bar of compensation and reimbursement is based on the principle that such transactions involve conflicts of interest. Private gain undoubtedly prompts the purchase or sale of claims or stock interests, while the fiduciary's obligation is to render loyal and disinterested service which his position of trust has imposed upon him. Subsection (b) extends to a trustee, his attorney, committees and their attorneys, or any other persons "acting in the case in a representative or fiduciary capacity." It bars compensation to any of the foregoing, who after assuming to act in such capacity has purchased or sold, directly or indirectly, claims against, or stock in the debtor. The bar is absolute. It makes no difference whether the transaction brought a gain or loss, or neither, and the court is not authorized to approve a purchase or sale, before or after the transaction. The exception is for an acquisition or transfer "otherwise" than by a voluntary purchase or sale, such as an acquisition by bequest. See *Otis & Co. v. Insurance Bldg. Corp.*, 110 F.2d 333, 335 (C.A.1, 1940).

Subsection (c) [enacted as (b)] is intended for no asset liquidation cases where minimal compensation for trustees is needed. The sum of $20 will be allowed in each case, which is double the amount provided under current law.

house report no. 95–595

Section 330 authorizes compensation for services and reimbursement of expenses of officers of the estate. It also prescribes the standards on which the amount of compensation is to be determined. As noted above, the compensation allowable under this section is subject to the maxima set out in sections 326, 328, and 329. The compensation is to be reasonable, for actual necessary services rendered, based on the time, the nature, the extent, and the value of the services rendered, and on the cost of comparable services other than in a case under the bankruptcy code. The effect of the last provision is to overrule *In re Beverly Crest Convalescent Hospital, Inc.*, 548 F.2d 817 (9th Cir. 1976, as amended 1977), which set an arbitrary limit on fees payable based on the amount of a district judge's salary, and other, similar cases that require fees to be determined based on notions of conservation of the estate and economy of administration. If that case were allowed to stand, attorneys that could earn much higher incomes in other fields would leave the bankruptcy arena. Bankruptcy specialists, who enable the system to operate smoothly, efficiently, and expeditiously, would be driven elsewhere, and the bankruptcy field would be occupied by those who could not find other work and those who practice bankruptcy law only occasionally almost as a public service. Bankruptcy fees that are lower than fees in other areas of the legal profession may operate properly when the attorneys appearing in bankruptcy cases do so intermittently, because a low fee in a small segment of a practice can be absorbed by other work. Bankruptcy specialists, however, if required to accept fees in all of their cases that are consistently lower than fees they could receive elsewhere, will not remain in the bankruptcy field.

This subsection provides for reimbursement of actual, necessary expenses. It further provides for compensation of paraprofessionals employed by professional persons employed by the estate of the debtor. The provision is included to reduce the cost of administering bankruptcy cases. In nonbankruptcy areas, attorneys are able to charge for a paraprofessional's time on an hourly basis, and not include it in overhead. If a similar practice does not pertain in bankruptcy cases then the attorney will be less inclined to use paraprofessionals even where the work involved could easily be handled by an attorney's assistant, at much lower cost to the estate. This provision is designed to encourage attorneys to use paraprofessional assistance where possible, and to insure that the estate, not the attorney, will bear the cost, to the benefit of both the estate and the attorneys involved.

References in Text

The date of the enactment of the Bankruptcy Reform Act of 1994, referred to in subsec. (b)(2), is the date of enactment of Pub. L. 103–394, which was approved Oct. 22, 1994.

Amendments

2005—Subsec. (a)(1). Pub. L. 109–8, §1104(b)(1), inserted "an ombudsman appointed under section 333, or" before "a professional person" in introductory provisions.

Pub. L. 109–8, §232(b), inserted "a consumer privacy ombudsman appointed under section 332," before "an examiner" in introductory provisions.

Subsec. (a)(1)(A). Pub. L. 109–8, §1104(b)(2), inserted "ombudsman," before "professional person".

Subsec. (a)(3). Pub. L. 109–8, §407(1), in introductory provisions, substituted "In" for "(A) In" and inserted "to an examiner, trustee under chapter 11, or professional person" after "awarded".

Subsec. (a)(3)(E), (F). Pub. L. 109–8, §415, added subpar. (E) and redesignated former subpar. (E) as (F).

Subsec. (a)(7). Pub. L. 109–8, §407(2), added par. (7).

1994—Subsec. (a). Pub. L. 103–394, §224(b), amended subsec. (a) generally. Prior to amendment, subsec. (a) read as follows: "After notice to any parties in interest and to the United States trustee and a hearing, and subject to sections 326, 328, and 329 of this title, the court may award to a trustee, to an examiner, to a professional person employed under section 327 or 1103 of this title, or to the debtor's attorney—

"(1) reasonable compensation for actual, necessary services rendered by such trustee, examiner, professional person, or attorney, as the case may be, and by any paraprofessional persons employed by such trustee, professional person, or attorney, as the case may be, based on the nature, the extent, and the value of such services, the time spent on such services, and the cost of comparable services other than in a case under this title; and

"(2) reimbursement for actual, necessary expenses."

Subsec. (b). Pub. L. 103–394, §117, designated existing provisions as par. (1) and added par. (2).

1986—Subsec. (a). Pub. L. 99–554, §211(1), inserted "to any parties in interest and to the United States trustee" after "notice".

Subsec. (c). Pub. L. 99–554, §257(f), inserted reference to chapter 12.

Subsec. (d). Pub. L. 99–554, §211(2), added subsec. (d).

1984—Subsec. (a). Pub. L. 98–353, §433(1), struck out "to any parties in interest and to the United States trustee" after "After notice".

Subsec. (a)(1). Pub. L. 98–353, §433(2), substituted "nature, the extent, and the value of such services, the time spent on such services" for "time, the nature, the extent, and the value of such services".

Subsec. (b). Pub. L. 98–353, §434(a), substituted "$45" for "$20".

Subsec. (c). Pub. L. 98–353, §434(b), added subsec. (c).

Effective Date of 2005 Amendment

Amendment by Pub. L. 109–8 effective 180 days after Apr. 20, 2005, and not applicable with respect to cases commenced under this title before such effective date, except as otherwise provided, see section 1501 of Pub. L. 109–8, set out as a note under section 101 of this title.

Effective Date of 1994 Amendment

Amendment by section 117 of Pub. L. 103–394 effective Oct. 22, 1994, and applicable with respect to cases commenced under this title before, on, and after Oct. 22, 1994, and amendment by section 224(b) of Pub. L. 103–394 effective Oct. 22, 1994, and not applicable with respect to cases commenced under this title before Oct. 22, 1994, see section 702 of Pub. L. 103–394, set out as a note under section 101 of this title.

Effective Date of 1986 Amendment

Effective date and applicability of amendment by section 211 of Pub. L. 99–554 dependent upon the judicial district involved, see section 302(d), (e) of Pub. L. 99–554, set out as a note under section 581 of Title 28, Judiciary and Judicial Procedure.

Amendment by section 257 of Pub. L. 99–554 effective 30 days after Oct. 27, 1986, but not applicable to cases commenced under this title before that date, see section 302(a), (c)(1) of Pub. L. 99–554.

Effective Date of 1984 Amendment

Amendment by Pub. L. 98–353 effective with respect to cases filed 90 days after July 10, 1984, see section 552(a) of Pub. L. 98–353, set out as a note under section 101 of this title.

§331. Interim compensation

A trustee, an examiner, a debtor's attorney, or any professional person employed under section 327 or 1103 of this title may apply to the court not more than once every 120 days after an order for relief in a case under this title, or more often if the court permits, for such compensation for services rendered before the date of such an application or reimbursement for expenses incurred before such date as is provided under section 330 of this title. After notice and a hearing, the court may allow and disburse to such applicant such compensation or reimbursement.

(Pub. L. 95–598, Nov. 6, 1978, 92 Stat. 2564.)

Historical and Revision Notes

senate report no. 95–989

Section 331 permits trustees and professional persons to apply to the court not more than once every 120 days for interim compensation and reimbursement payments. The court may permit more frequent applications if the circumstances warrant, such as in very large cases where the legal work is extensive and merits more frequent payments. The court is authorized to allow and order disbursement to the applicant of compensation and reimbursement that is otherwise allowable under section 330. The only effect of this section is to remove any doubt that officers of the estate may apply for, and the court may approve, compensation and reimbursement during the case, instead of being required to wait until the end of the case, which in some instances, may be years. The practice of interim compensation is followed in some courts today, but has been subject to some question. This section explicitly authorizes it.

This section will apply to professionals such as auctioneers and appraisers only if they are not paid on a per job basis.

§332. Consumer privacy ombudsman

(a) If a hearing is required under section 363(b)(1)(B), the court shall order the United States trustee to appoint, not later than 7 days before the commencement of the hearing, 1 disinterested person (other than the United States trustee) to serve as the consumer privacy ombudsman in the case and shall require that notice of such hearing be timely given to such ombudsman.

(b) The consumer privacy ombudsman may appear and be heard at such hearing and shall provide to the court information to assist the court in its consideration of the facts, circumstances, and conditions of the proposed sale or lease of personally identifiable information under section 363(b)(1)(B). Such information may include presentation of—

(1) the debtor's privacy policy;

(2) the potential losses or gains of privacy to consumers if such sale or such lease is approved by the court;

(3) the potential costs or benefits to consumers if such sale or such lease is approved by the court; and

(4) the potential alternatives that would mitigate potential privacy losses or potential costs to consumers.

(c) A consumer privacy ombudsman shall not disclose any personally identifiable information obtained by the ombudsman under this title.

(Added Pub. L. 109–8, title II, §232(a), Apr. 20, 2005, 119 Stat. 73; amended Pub. L. 111–16, §2(3), May 7, 2009, 123 Stat. 1607.)

Amendments

2009—Subsec. (a). Pub. L. 111–16 substituted "7 days" for "5 days".

Effective Date of 2009 Amendment

Amendment by Pub. L. 111–16 effective Dec. 1, 2009, see section 7 of Pub. L. 111–16, set out as a note under section 109 of this title.

Effective Date

Section effective 180 days after Apr. 20, 2005, and not applicable with respect to cases commenced under this title before such effective date, except as otherwise provided, see section 1501 of Pub. L. 109–8, set out as an Effective Date of 2005 Amendment note under section 101 of this title.

§333. Appointment of patient care ombudsman

(a)(1) If the debtor in a case under chapter 7, 9, or 11 is a health care business, the court shall order, not later than 30 days after the commencement of the case, the appointment of an ombudsman to monitor the quality of patient care and to represent the interests of the patients of the health care business unless the court finds that the appointment of such ombudsman is not necessary for the protection of patients under the specific facts of the case.

(2)(A) If the court orders the appointment of an ombudsman under paragraph (1), the United States trustee shall appoint 1 disinterested person (other than the United States trustee) to serve as such ombudsman.

(B) If the debtor is a health care business that provides long-term care, then the United States trustee may appoint the State Long-Term Care Ombudsman appointed under the Older Americans Act of 1965 for the State in which the case is pending to serve as the ombudsman required by paragraph (1).

(C) If the United States trustee does not appoint a State Long-Term Care Ombudsman under subparagraph (B), the court shall notify the State Long-Term Care Ombudsman appointed under the Older Americans Act of 1965 for the State in which the case is pending, of the name and address of the person who is appointed under subparagraph (A).

(b) An ombudsman appointed under subsection (a) shall—

(1) monitor the quality of patient care provided to patients of the debtor, to the extent necessary under the circumstances, including interviewing patients and physicians;

(2) not later than 60 days after the date of appointment, and not less frequently than at 60-day intervals thereafter, report to the court after notice to the parties in interest, at a hearing or in writing, regarding the quality of patient care provided to patients of the debtor; and

(3) if such ombudsman determines that the quality of patient care provided to patients of the debtor is declining significantly or is otherwise being materially compromised, file with the court a motion or a written report, with notice to the parties in interest immediately upon making such determination.

(c)(1) An ombudsman appointed under subsection (a) shall maintain any information obtained by such ombudsman under this section that relates to patients (including information relating to patient records) as confidential information. Such ombudsman may not review confidential patient records unless the court approves such review in advance and imposes restrictions on such ombudsman to protect the confidentiality of such records.

(2) An ombudsman appointed under subsection (a)(2)(B) shall have access to patient records consistent with authority of such ombudsman under the Older Americans Act of 1965 and under non-Federal laws governing the State Long-Term Care Ombudsman program.

(Added Pub. L. 109–8, title XI, §1104(a)(1), Apr. 20, 2005, 119 Stat. 191.)

References in Text

The Older Americans Act of 1965, referred to in subsecs. (a)(2)(B), (C) and (c)(2), is Pub. L. 89–73, July 14, 1965, 79 Stat. 218, as amended, which is classified generally to chapter 35 (§3001 et seq.) of Title 42, The Public Health and Welfare. For complete classification of this Act to the Code, see Short Title note set out under section 3001 of Title 42 and Tables.

Effective Date

Section effective 180 days after Apr. 20, 2005, and not applicable with respect to cases commenced under this title before such effective date, except as otherwise provided, see section 1501 of Pub. L. 109–8, set out as an Effective Date of 2005 Amendment note under section 101 of this title.

SUBCHAPTER III—ADMINISTRATION

§341. Meetings of creditors and equity security holders

(a) Within a reasonable time after the order for relief in a case under this title, the United States trustee shall convene and preside at a meeting of creditors.

(b) The United States trustee may convene a meeting of any equity security holders.

(c) The court may not preside at, and may not attend, any meeting under this section including any final meeting of creditors. Notwithstanding any local court rule, provision of a State constitution, any otherwise applicable nonbankruptcy law, or any other requirement that representation at the meeting of creditors under subsection (a) be by an attorney, a creditor holding a consumer debt or any representative of the creditor (which may include an entity or an employee of an entity and may be a representative for more than 1 creditor) shall be permitted to appear at and participate in the meeting of creditors in a case under chapter 7 or 13, either alone or in conjunction with an attorney for the creditor. Nothing in this subsection shall be construed to require any creditor to be represented by an attorney at any meeting of creditors.

(d) Prior to the conclusion of the meeting of creditors or equity security holders, the trustee shall orally examine the debtor to ensure that the debtor in a case under chapter 7 of this title is aware of—

(1) the potential consequences of seeking a discharge in bankruptcy, including the effects on credit history;

(2) the debtor's ability to file a petition under a different chapter of this title;

(3) the effect of receiving a discharge of debts under this title; and

(4) the effect of reaffirming a debt, including the debtor's knowledge of the provisions of section 524(d) of this title.

(e) Notwithstanding subsections (a) and (b), the court, on the request of a party in interest and after notice and a hearing, for cause may order that the United States trustee not convene a meeting of creditors or equity security holders if the debtor has filed a plan as to which the debtor solicited acceptances prior to the commencement of the case.

(Pub. L. 95–598, Nov. 6, 1978, 92 Stat. 2564; Pub. L. 99–554, title II, §212, Oct. 27, 1986, 100 Stat. 3099; Pub. L. 103–394, title I, §115, Oct. 22, 1994, 108 Stat. 4118; Pub. L. 109–8, title IV, §§402, 413, Apr. 20, 2005, 119 Stat. 104, 107.)

Historical and Revision Notes

legislative statements

Section 341(c) of the Senate amendment is deleted and a contrary provision is added indicating that the bankruptcy judge will not preside at or attend the first meeting of creditors or equity security holders but a discharge hearing for all individuals will be held at which the judge will preside.

senate report no. 95–989

Section [Subsection] (a) of this section requires that there be a meeting of creditors within a reasonable time after the order for relief in the case. The Bankruptcy Act [former title 11] and the current Rules of Bankruptcy Procedure provide for a meeting of creditors, and specify the time and manner of the meeting, and the business to be conducted. This bill leaves those matters to the rules. Under section 405(d) of the bill, the present rules will continue to govern until new rules are promulgated. Thus, pending the adoption of different rules, the present procedure for the meeting will continue.

Subsection (b) authorizes the court to order a meeting of equity security holders in cases where such a meeting would be beneficial or useful, for example, in a chapter 11 reorganization case where it may be necessary for the equity security holders to organize in order to be able to participate in the negotiation of a plan of reorganization.

Subsection (c) makes clear that the bankruptcy judge is to preside at the meeting of creditors.

Amendments

2005—Subsec. (c). Pub. L. 109–8, §413, inserted at end "Notwithstanding any local court rule, provision of a State constitution, any otherwise applicable nonbankruptcy law, or any other requirement that representation at the meeting of creditors under subsection (a) be by an attorney, a creditor holding a consumer debt or any representative of the creditor (which may include an entity or an employee of an entity and may be a representative for more than 1 creditor) shall be permitted to appear at and participate in the meeting of creditors in a case under chapter 7 or 13, either alone or in conjunction with an attorney for the creditor. Nothing in this subsection shall be construed to require any creditor to be represented by an attorney at any meeting of creditors."

Subsec. (e). Pub. L. 109–8, §402, added subsec. (e).

1994—Subsec. (d). Pub. L. 103–394 added subsec. (d).

1986—Subsec. (a). Pub. L. 99–554, §212(1), substituted "the United States trustee shall convene and preside at a meeting of creditors" for "there shall be a meeting of creditors".

Subsec. (b). Pub. L. 99–554, §212(2), substituted "United States trustee may convene" for "court may order".

Subsec. (c). Pub. L. 99–554, §212(3), inserted "including any final meeting of creditors".

Effective Date of 2005 Amendment

Amendment by Pub. L. 109–8 effective 180 days after Apr. 20, 2005, and not applicable with respect to cases commenced under this title before such effective date, except as otherwise provided, see section 1501 of Pub. L. 109–8, set out as a note under section 101 of this title.

Effective Date of 1994 Amendment

Amendment by Pub. L. 103–394 effective Oct. 22, 1994, and not applicable with respect to cases commenced under this title before Oct. 22, 1994, see section 702 of Pub. L. 103–394, set out as a note under section 101 of this title.

Effective Date of 1986 Amendment

Effective date and applicability of amendment by Pub. L. 99–554 dependent upon the judicial district involved, see section 302(d), (e) of Pub. L. 99–554, set out as a note under section 581 of Title 28, Judiciary and Judicial Procedure.

Participation by Bankruptcy Administrator at Meetings of Creditors and Equity Security Holders

Pub. L. 103–394, title I, §105, Oct. 22, 1994, 108 Stat. 4111, provided that:

"(a) Presiding Officer.—A bankruptcy administrator appointed under section 302(d)(3)(I) of the Bankruptcy Judges, United States Trustees, and Family Farmer Bankruptcy Act of 1986 (28 U.S.C. 581 note; Public Law 99–554; 100 Stat. 3123), as amended by section 317(a) of the Federal Courts Study Committee Implementation Act of 1990 (Public Law 101–650; 104 Stat. 5115), or the bankruptcy administrator's designee may preside at the meeting of creditors convened under section 341(a) of title 11, United States Code. The bankruptcy administrator or the bankruptcy administrator's designee may preside at any meeting of equity security holders convened under section 341(b) of title 11, United States Code.

"(b) Examination of the Debtor.—The bankruptcy administrator or the bankruptcy administrator's designee may examine the debtor at the meeting of creditors and may administer the oath required under section 343 of title 11, United States Code."

§342. Notice

(a) There shall be given such notice as is appropriate, including notice to any holder of a community claim, of an order for relief in a case under this title.

(b) Before the commencement of a case under this title by an individual whose debts are primarily consumer debts, the clerk shall give to such individual written notice containing—

(1) a brief description of—

(A) chapters 7, 11, 12, and 13 and the general purpose, benefits, and costs of proceeding under each of those chapters; and

(B) the types of services available from credit counseling agencies; and

(2) statements specifying that—

(A) a person who knowingly and fraudulently conceals assets or makes a false oath or statement under penalty of perjury in connection with a case under this title shall be subject to fine, imprisonment, or both; and

(B) all information supplied by a debtor in connection with a case under this title is subject to examination by the Attorney General.

(c)(1) If notice is required to be given by the debtor to a creditor under this title, any rule, any applicable law, or any order of the court, such notice shall contain the name, address, and last 4 digits of the taxpayer identification number of the debtor. If the notice concerns an amendment that adds a creditor to the schedules of assets and liabilities, the debtor shall include the full taxpayer identification number in the notice sent to that creditor, but the debtor shall include only the last 4 digits of the taxpayer identification number in the copy of the notice filed with the court.

(2)(A) If, within the 90 days before the commencement of a voluntary case, a creditor supplies the debtor in at least 2 communications sent to the debtor with the current account number of the debtor and the address at which such creditor requests to receive correspondence, then any notice required by this title to be sent by the debtor to such creditor shall be sent to such address and shall include such account number.

(B) If a creditor would be in violation of applicable nonbankruptcy law by sending any such communication within such 90-day period and if such creditor supplies the debtor in the last 2 communications with the current account number of the debtor and the address at which such creditor requests to receive correspondence, then any notice required by this title to be sent by the debtor to such creditor shall be sent to such address and shall include such account number.

(d) In a case under chapter 7 of this title in which the debtor is an individual and in which the presumption of abuse arises under section 707(b), the clerk shall give written notice to all creditors not later than 10 days after the date of the filing of the petition that the presumption of abuse has arisen.

(e)(1) In a case under chapter 7 or 13 of this title of a debtor who is an individual, a creditor at any time may both file with the court and serve on the debtor a notice of address to be used to provide notice in such case to such creditor.

(2) Any notice in such case required to be provided to such creditor by the debtor or the court later than 7 days after the court and the debtor receive such creditor's notice of address, shall be provided to such address.

(f)(1) An entity may file with any bankruptcy court a notice of address to be used by all the bankruptcy courts or by particular bankruptcy courts, as so specified by such entity at the time such notice is filed, to provide notice to such entity in all cases under chapters 7 and 13 pending in the courts with respect to which such notice is filed, in which such entity is a creditor.

(2) In any case filed under chapter 7 or 13, any notice required to be provided by a court with respect to which a notice is filed under paragraph (1), to such entity later than 30 days after the filing of such notice under paragraph (1) shall be provided to such address unless with respect to a particular case a different address is specified in a notice filed and served in accordance with subsection (e).

(3) A notice filed under paragraph (1) may be withdrawn by such entity.

(g)(1) Notice provided to a creditor by the debtor or the court other than in accordance with this section (excluding this subsection) shall not be effective notice until such notice is brought to the attention of such creditor. If such creditor designates a person or an organizational subdivision of such creditor to be responsible for receiving notices under this title and establishes reasonable procedures so that such notices receivable by such creditor are to be delivered to such person or such subdivision, then a notice provided to such creditor other than in accordance with this section (excluding this subsection) shall not be considered to have been brought to the attention of such creditor until such notice is received by such person or such subdivision.

(2) A monetary penalty may not be imposed on a creditor for a violation of a stay in effect under section 362(a) (including a monetary penalty imposed under section 362(k)) or for failure to comply with section 542 or 543 unless the conduct that is the basis of such violation or of such failure occurs after such creditor receives notice effective under this section of the order for relief.

(Pub. L. 95–598, Nov. 6, 1978, 92 Stat. 2565; Pub. L. 98–353, title III, §§302, 435, July 10, 1984, 98 Stat. 352, 370; Pub. L. 103–394, title II, §225, Oct. 22, 1994, 108 Stat. 4131; Pub. L. 109–8, title I, §§102(d), 104, title II, §234(b), title III, §315(a),

Apr. 20, 2005, 119 Stat. 33, 35, 75, 88; Pub. L. 111–16, §2(4), May 7, 2009, 123 Stat. 1607.)

Historical and Revision Notes

legislative statements

Section 342(b) and (c) of the Senate amendment are adopted in principle but moved to section 549(c), in lieu of section 342(b) of H.R. 8200 as passed by the House.

Section 342(c) of H.R. 8200 as passed by the House is deleted as a matter to be left to the Rules of Bankruptcy Procedure.

senate report no. 95–989

Subsection (a) of section 342 requires the clerk of the bankruptcy court to give notice of the order for relief. The rules will prescribe to whom the notice should be sent and in what manner notice will be given. The rules already prescribe such things, and they will continue to govern unless changed as provided in section 404(a) of the bill. Due process will certainly require notice to all creditors and equity security holders. State and Federal governmental representatives responsible for collecting taxes will also receive notice. In cases where the debtor is subject to regulation, the regulatory agency with jurisdiction will receive notice. In order to insure maximum notice to all parties in interest, the Rules will include notice by publication in appropriate cases and for appropriate issues. Other notices will be given as appropriate.

Subsections (b) and (c) [enacted as section 549(c)] are derived from section 21g of the Bankruptcy Act [section 44(g) of former title 11]. They specify that the trustee may file notice of the commencement of the case in land recording offices in order to give notice of the pendency of the case to potential transferees of the debtor's real property. Such filing is unnecessary in the county in which the bankruptcy case is commenced. If notice is properly filed, a subsequent purchaser of the property will not be a bona fide purchaser. Otherwise, a purchaser, including a purchaser at a judicial sale, that has no knowledge of the case, is not prevented from obtaining the status of a bona fide purchaser by the mere commencement of the case. "County" is defined in title 1 of the United States Code to include other political subdivisions where counties are not used.

Amendments

2009—Subsec. (e)(2). Pub. L. 111–16 substituted "7 days" for "5 days".

2005—Subsec. (b). Pub. L. 109–8, §104, amended subsec. (b) generally. Prior to amendment, subsec. (b) read as follows: "Prior to the commencement of a case under this title by an individual whose debts are primarily consumer debts, the clerk shall give written notice to such individual that indicates each chapter of this title under which such individual may proceed."

Subsec. (c). Pub. L. 109–8, §315(a)(1) designated existing provisions as par. (1), struck out ", but the failure of such notice to contain such information shall not invalidate the legal effect of such notice" after "number of the debtor", and added par. (2).

Pub. L. 109–8, §234(b), inserted "last 4 digits of the" before "taxpayer identification number" and "If the notice concerns an amendment that adds a creditor to the schedules of assets and liabilities, the debtor shall include the full taxpayer identification number in the notice sent to that creditor, but the debtor shall include only the last 4 digits of the taxpayer identification number in the copy of the notice filed with the court." at end.

Subsec. (d). Pub. L. 109–8, §102(d), added subsec. (d).

Subsecs. (e) to (g). Pub. L. 109–8, §315(a)(2), added subsecs. (e) to (g).

1994—Subsec. (c). Pub. L. 103–394 added subsec. (c).

1984—Subsec. (a). Pub. L. 98–353, §435, amended subsec. (a) generally, inserting requirement respecting notice to any holder of a community claim.

Pub. L. 98–353, §302(1), designated existing provisions as subsec. (a).

Subsec. (b). Pub. L. 98–353, §302(2), added subsec. (b).

Effective Date of 2009 Amendment

Amendment by Pub. L. 111–16 effective Dec. 1, 2009, see section 7 of Pub. L. 111–16, set out as a note under section 109 of this title.

Effective Date of 2005 Amendment

Amendment by Pub. L. 109–8 effective 180 days after Apr. 20, 2005, and not applicable with respect to cases commenced under this title before such effective date, except as otherwise provided, see section 1501 of Pub. L. 109–8, set out as a note under section 101 of this title.

Effective Date of 1994 Amendment

Amendment by Pub. L. 103–394 effective Oct. 22, 1994, and not applicable with respect to cases commenced under this title before Oct. 22, 1994, see section 702 of Pub. L. 103–394, set out as a note under section 101 of this title.

Effective Date of 1984 Amendment

Amendment by Pub. L. 98–353 effective with respect to cases filed 90 days after July 10, 1984, see section 552(a) of Pub. L. 98–353, set out as a note under section 101 of this title.

§343. Examination of the debtor

The debtor shall appear and submit to examination under oath at the meeting of creditors under section 341(a) of this title. Creditors, any indenture trustee, any trustee or examiner in the case, or the United States trustee may examine the debtor. The United States trustee may administer the oath required under this section.

(Pub. L. 95–598, Nov. 6, 1978, 92 Stat. 2565; Pub. L. 98–353, title III, §436, July 10, 1984, 98 Stat. 370; Pub. L. 99–554, title II, §213, Oct. 27, 1986, 100 Stat. 3099.)

Historical and Revision Notes

senate report no. 95–989

This section, derived from section 21a of the Bankruptcy Act [section 44(a) of former title 11], requires the debtor to appear at the meeting of creditors and submit to examination under oath. The purpose of the examination is to enable creditors and the trustee to determine if assets have improperly been disposed of or concealed or if there are grounds for objection to discharge. The scope of the examination under this section will be governed by the Rules of Bankruptcy Procedure, as it is today. See rules 205(d), 10–213(c), and 11–26. It is expected that the scope prescribed by these rules for liquidation cases, that is, "only the debtor's acts, conduct, or property, or any matter that may affect the administration of the estate, or the debtor's right to discharge" will remain substantially unchanged. In reorganization cases, the examination would be broader, including inquiry into the liabilities and financial condition of the debtor, the operation of his business, and the desirability of the continuance thereof, and other matters relevant to the case and to the formulation of the plan. Examination of other persons in connection with the bankruptcy case is left completely to the rules, just as examination of witnesses in civil cases is governed by the Federal Rules of Civil Procedure.

Amendments

1986—Pub. L. 99–554 amended section generally. Prior to amendment, section read as follows: "The debtor shall appear and submit to examination under oath at the meeting of creditors under section 341(a) of this title. Creditors, any indenture trustee, or any trustee or examiner in the case may examine the debtor."

1984—Pub. L. 98–353 substituted "examine" for "examiner".

Effective Date of 1986 Amendment

Effective date and applicability of amendment by Pub. L. 99–554 dependent upon the judicial district involved, see section 302(d), (e) of Pub. L. 99–554, set out as a note under section 581 of Title 28, Judiciary and Judicial Procedure.

Effective Date of 1984 Amendment

Amendment by Pub. L. 98–353 effective with respect to cases filed 90 days after July 10, 1984, see section 552(a) of Pub. L. 98–353, set out as a note under section 101 of this title.

Participation by Bankruptcy Administrator at Meetings of Creditors and Equity Security Holders

A bankruptcy administrator or the bankruptcy administrator's designee may examine debtor at meeting of creditors and may administer oath required by this section, see section 105 of Pub. L. 103–394, set out as a note under section 341 of this title.

§344. Self-incrimination; immunity

Immunity for persons required to submit to examination, to testify, or to provide information in a case under this title may be granted under part V of title 18.

(Pub. L. 95–598, Nov. 6, 1978, 92 Stat. 2565.)

Historical and Revision Notes

senate report no. 95–989

Part V [§6001 et seq.] of title 18 of the United States Code governs the granting of immunity to witnesses before Federal tribunals. The immunity provided under part V is only use immunity, not transactional immunity. Part V applies to all proceedings before Federal courts, before Federal grand juries, before administrative agencies, and before Congressional committees. It requires the Attorney General or the U. S. attorney to request or to approve any grant of immunity, whether before a court, grand jury, agency, or congressional committee.

This section carries part V over into bankruptcy cases. Thus, for a witness to be ordered to testify before a bankruptcy court in spite of a claim of privilege, the U. S. attorney for the district in which the court sits would have to request from the district court for that district the immunity order. The rule would apply to both debtors, creditors, and any other witnesses in a bankruptcy case. If the immunity were granted, the witness would be required to testify. If not, he could claim the privilege against self-incrimination.

Part V is a significant departure from current law. Under section 7a(10) of the Bankruptcy Act [section 25(a)(10) of former title 11], a debtor is required to testify in all circumstances, but any testimony he gives may not be used against him in any criminal proceeding, except testimony given in any hearing on objections to discharge. With that exception, section 7a(10) amounts to a blanket grant of use immunity to all debtors. Immunity for other witnesses in bankruptcy courts today is governed by part V of title 18.

The consequences of a claim of privileges by a debtor under proposed law and under current law differ as well. Under section 14c(6) of current law [section 32(c)(6) of former title 11], any refusal to answer a material question approved by the court will result in the denial of a discharge, even if the refusal is based on the privilege against self incrimination. Thus, the debtor is confronted with the choice between losing his discharge and opening himself up to possible criminal prosecution.

Under section 727(a)(6) of the proposed title 11, a debtor is only denied a discharge if he refuses to testify after having been granted immunity. If the debtor claims the privilege and the U. S. attorney does not request immunity from the district courts, then the debtor may refuse to testify and still retain his right to a discharge. It removes the Scylla and Charibdis choice for debtors that exists under the Bankruptcy Act [former title 11].

§345. Money of estates

(a) A trustee in a case under this title may make such deposit or investment of the money of the estate for which such trustee serves as will yield the maximum reasonable net return on such money, taking into account the safety of such deposit or investment.

(b) Except with respect to a deposit or investment that is insured or guaranteed by the United States or by a department, agency, or instrumentality of the United States or backed by the full faith and credit of the United States, the trustee shall require from an entity with which such money is deposited or invested—

(1) a bond—

(A) in favor of the United States;

(B) secured by the undertaking of a corporate surety approved by the United States trustee for the district in which the case is pending; and

(C) conditioned on—

(i) a proper accounting for all money so deposited or invested and for any return on such money;

(ii) prompt repayment of such money and return; and

(iii) faithful performance of duties as a depository; or

(2) the deposit of securities of the kind specified in section 9303 of title 31;

unless the court for cause orders otherwise.

(c) An entity with which such moneys are deposited or invested is authorized to deposit or invest such moneys as may be required under this section.

(Pub. L. 95–598, Nov. 6, 1978, 92 Stat. 2565; Pub. L. 97–258, §3(c), Sept. 13, 1982, 96 Stat. 1064; Pub. L. 98–353, title III, §437, July 10, 1984, 98 Stat. 370; Pub. L. 99–554, title II, §214, Oct. 27, 1986, 100 Stat. 3099; Pub. L. 103–394, title II, §210, Oct. 22, 1994, 108 Stat. 4125.)

Historical and Revision Notes

legislative statements

The House amendment moves section 345(c) of the House bill to chapter 15 as part of the pilot program for the U.S. trustees. The bond required by section 345(b) may be a blanket bond posted by the financial depository sufficient to cover deposits by trustees in several cases, as is done under current law.

senate report no. 95–989

This section is a significant departure from section 61 of the Bankruptcy Act [section 101 of former title 11]. It permits a trustee in a bankruptcy case to make such deposit of investment of the money of the estate for which he serves as will yield the maximum reasonable net return on the money, taking into account the safety of such deposit or investment. Under current law, the trustee is permitted to deposit money only with banking institutions. Thus, the trustee is generally unable to secure a high rate of return on money of estates pending distribution, to the detriment of creditors. Under this section, the trustee may make deposits in savings and loans, may purchase government bonds, or make such other deposit or investment as is appropriate. Under proposed 11 U.S.C. 541(a)(6), and except as provided in subsection (c) of this section, any interest or gain realized on the deposit or investment of funds under this section will become property of the estate, and will thus enhance the recovery of creditors.

In order to protect the creditors, subsection (b) requires certain precautions against loss of the money so deposited or invested. The trustee must require from a person with which he deposits or invests money of an estate a bond in favor of the United States secured by approved corporate surety and conditioned on a proper accounting for all money deposited or invested and for any return on such money. Alternately, the trustee may require the deposit of securities of the kind specified in section 15 of title 6 of the United States Code [31 U.S.C. 9303], which governs the posting of security by banks that receive public moneys on deposit. These bonding requirements do not apply to deposits or investments that are insured or guaranteed the United States or a department, agency, or instrumentality of the United States, or that are backed by the full faith and credit of the United States.

These provisions do not address the question of aggregation of funds by a private chapter 13 trustee and are not to be construed as excluding such possibility. The Rules of Bankruptcy Procedure may provide for aggregation under appropriate circumstances and adequate safeguards in cases where there is a significant need, such as in districts in which there is a standing chapter 13 trustee. In such case, the interest or return on the funds would help defray the cost of administering the cases in which the standing trustee serves.

Amendments

1994—Subsec. (b). Pub. L. 103–394 substituted semicolon for period at end of par. (2) and inserted concluding provisions after par. (2).

1986—Subsec. (b). Pub. L. 99–554 amended subsec. (b) generally, substituting "approved by the United States trustee for the district" for "approved by the court for the district" in par. (1)(B).

1984—Subsec. (c). Pub. L. 98–353 added subsec. (c).

1982—Subsec. (b)(2). Pub. L. 97–258 substituted "section 9303 of title 31" for "section 15 of title 6".

Effective Date of 1994 Amendment

Amendment by Pub. L. 103–394 effective Oct. 22, 1994, and not applicable with respect to cases commenced under this title before Oct. 22, 1994, see section 702 of Pub. L. 103–394, set out as a note under section 101 of this title.

Effective Date of 1986 Amendment

Effective date and applicability of amendment by Pub. L. 99–554 dependent upon the judicial district involved, see section 302(d), (e) of Pub. L. 99–554, set out as a note under section 581 of Title 28, Judiciary and Judicial Procedure.

Effective Date of 1984 Amendment

Amendment by Pub. L. 98–353 effective with respect to cases filed 90 days after July 10, 1984, see section 552(a) of Pub. L. 98–353, set out as a note under section 101 of this title.

§346. Special provisions related to the treatment of State and local taxes

(a) Whenever the Internal Revenue Code of 1986 provides that a separate taxable estate or entity is created in a case concerning a debtor under this title, and the income, gain, loss, deductions, and credits of such estate shall be taxed to or claimed by the estate, a separate taxable estate is also created for purposes of any State and local law imposing a tax on or measured by income and such income, gain, loss, deductions, and credits shall be taxed to or claimed by the estate and may not be taxed to or claimed by the debtor. The preceding sentence shall not apply if the case is dismissed. The trustee shall make tax returns of income required under any such State or local law.

(b) Whenever the Internal Revenue Code of 1986 provides that no separate taxable estate shall be created in a case concerning a debtor under this title, and the income, gain, loss, deductions, and credits of an estate shall be taxed to or claimed by the debtor, such income, gain, loss, deductions, and credits shall be taxed to or claimed by the debtor under a State or local law imposing a tax on or measured by income and may not be taxed to or claimed by the estate. The trustee shall make such tax returns of income of corporations and of partnerships as are required under any State or local law, but with respect to partnerships, shall make such returns only to the extent such returns are also required to be made under such Code. The estate shall be liable for any tax imposed on such corporation or partnership, but not for any tax imposed on partners or members.

(c) With respect to a partnership or any entity treated as a partnership under a State or local law imposing a tax on or measured by income that is a debtor in a case under this title, any gain or loss resulting from a distribution of property from such partnership, or any distributive share of any income, gain, loss, deduction, or credit of a partner or member that is distributed, or considered distributed, from such partnership, after the commencement of the case, is gain, loss, income, deduction, or credit, as the case may be, of the partner or member, and if such partner or member is a debtor in a case under this title, shall be subject to tax in accordance with subsection (a) or (b).

(d) For purposes of any State or local law imposing a tax on or measured by income, the taxable period of a debtor in a case under this title shall terminate only if and to the extent that the taxable period of such debtor terminates under the Internal Revenue Code of 1986.

(e) The estate in any case described in subsection (a) shall use the same accounting method as the debtor used immediately before the commencement of the case, if such method of accounting complies with applicable nonbankruptcy tax law.

(f) For purposes of any State or local law imposing a tax on or measured by income, a transfer of property from the debtor to the estate or from the estate to the debtor shall not be treated as a disposition for purposes of any provision assigning tax consequences to a disposition, except to the extent that such transfer is treated as a disposition under the Internal Revenue Code of 1986.

(g) Whenever a tax is imposed pursuant to a State or local law imposing a tax on or measured by income pursuant to subsection (a) or (b), such tax shall be imposed at rates generally applicable to the same types of entities under such State or local law.

(h) The trustee shall withhold from any payment of claims for wages, salaries, commissions, dividends, interest, or other payments, or collect, any amount required to be withheld or collected under applicable State or local tax law, and shall pay such withheld or collected amount to the appropriate governmental unit at the time and in the manner required by such tax law, and with the same priority as the claim from which such amount was withheld or collected was paid.

(i)(1) To the extent that any State or local law imposing a tax on or measured by income provides for the carryover of any tax attribute from one taxable period to a subsequent taxable period, the estate shall succeed to such tax attribute in any case in which such estate is subject to tax under subsection (a).

(2) After such a case is closed or dismissed, the debtor shall succeed to any tax attribute to which the estate succeeded under paragraph (1) to the extent consistent with the Internal Revenue Code of 1986.

(3) The estate may carry back any loss or tax attribute to a taxable period of the debtor that ended before the date of the order for relief under this title to the extent that—

(A) applicable State or local tax law provides for a carryback in the case of the debtor; and

(B) the same or a similar tax attribute may be carried back by the estate to such a taxable period of the debtor under the Internal Revenue Code of 1986.

(j)(1) For purposes of any State or local law imposing a tax on or measured by income, income is not realized by the estate, the debtor, or a successor to the debtor by reason of discharge of indebtedness in a case under this title, except to the extent, if any, that such income is subject to tax under the Internal Revenue Code of 1986.

(2) Whenever the Internal Revenue Code of 1986 provides that the amount excluded from gross income in respect of the discharge of indebtedness in a case under this title shall be applied to reduce the tax attributes of the debtor or the estate, a similar reduction shall be made under any State or local law imposing a tax on or measured by income to the extent such State or local law recognizes such attributes. Such State or local law may also provide for the reduction of other attributes to the extent that the full amount of income from the discharge of indebtedness has not been applied.

(k)(1) Except as provided in this section and section 505, the time and manner of filing tax returns and the items of income, gain, loss, deduction, and credit of any taxpayer shall be determined under applicable nonbankruptcy law.

(2) For Federal tax purposes, the provisions of this section are subject to the Internal Revenue Code of 1986 and other applicable Federal nonbankruptcy law.

(Pub. L. 95–598, Nov. 6, 1978, 92 Stat. 2565; Pub. L. 98–353, title III, §438, July 10, 1984, 98 Stat. 370; Pub. L. 99–554, title II, §§257(g), 283(c), Oct. 27, 1986, 100 Stat. 3114, 3116; Pub. L. 103–394, title V, §501(d)(4), Oct. 22, 1994, 108 Stat. 4143; Pub. L. 109–8, title VII, §719(a)(1), Apr. 20, 2005, 119 Stat. 131.)

Historical and Revision Notes

legislative statements

Section 346 of the House amendment, together with sections 728 and 1146, represent special tax provisions applicable in bankruptcy. The policy contained in those sections reflects the policy that should be applied in Federal, State, and local taxes in the view of the House Committee on the Judiciary. The House Ways and Means Committee and the Senate Finance Committee did not have time to process a bankruptcy tax bill during the 95th Congress. It is anticipated that early in the 96th Congress, and before the effective date of the bankruptcy code [Oct. 1, 1979], the tax committees of Congress will have an opportunity to consider action with respect to amendments to the Internal Revenue Code [title 26] and the special tax provisions in title 11. Since the special tax provisions are likely to be amended during the first part of the 96th Congress, it is anticipated that the bench and bar will also study and comment on these special tax provisions prior to their revision.

Special tax provisions: State and local rules. This section provides special tax provisions dealing with the treatment, under State or local, but not Federal, tax law, of the method of taxing bankruptcy estates of individuals, partnerships, and corporations; survival and allocation of tax attributes between the bankrupt and the estate; return filing requirements; and the tax treatment of income from discharge of indebtedness. The Senate bill removed these rules pending adoption of Federal rules on these issues in the next Congress. The House amendment returns the State and local tax rules to section 346 so that they may be studied by the bankruptcy and tax bars who may wish to submit comments to Congress.

Withholding rules: Both the House bill and Senate amendment provide that the trustee is required to comply with the normal withholding rules applicable to the payment of wages and other payments. The House amendment retains this rule for State and local taxes only. The treatment of withholding of Federal taxes will be considered in the next Congress.

Section 726 of the Senate amendment provides that the rule requiring pro rata payment of all expenses within a priority category does not apply to the payment of amounts withheld by a bankruptcy trustee. The purpose of this rule was to insure that the trustee pay the full amount of the withheld taxes to the appropriate governmental tax authority. The House amendment deletes this rule as unnecessary because the existing practice conforms essentially to that rule. If the trustee fails to pay over in full amounts that he withheld, it is a violation of his trustee's duties which would permit the taxing authority to sue the trustee on his bond.

When taxes considered "incurred": The Senate amendment contained rules of general application dealing with when a tax is "incurred" for purposes of the various tax collection rules affecting the debtor and the estate. The House amendment adopts the substance of these rules and transfers them to section 507 of title 11.

Penalty for failure to pay tax: The Senate amendment contains a rule which relieves the debtor and the trustee from certain tax penalties for failure to make timely payment of a tax to the extent that the bankruptcy rules prevent the trustee or the debtor from paying the tax on time. Since most of these penalties relate to Federal taxes, the House amendment deletes these rules pending consideration of Federal tax rules affecting bankruptcy in the next Congress.

senate report no. 95–989

Subsection (a) indicates that subsections (b), (c), (d), (e), (g), (h), (i), and (j) apply notwithstanding any State or local tax law, but are subject to Federal tax law.

Subsection (b)(1) provides that in a case concerning an individual under chapter 7 or 11 of title 11, income of the estate is taxable only to the estate and not to the debtor. The second sentence of the paragraph provides that if such individual is a partner, the tax attributes of the partnership are distributable to the partner's estate rather than to the partner, except to the extent that section 728 of title 11 provides otherwise.

Subsection (b)(2) states a general rule that the estate of an individual is to be taxed as an estate. The paragraph is made subject to the remainder of section 346 and section 728 of title 11.

Subsection (b)(3) requires the accounting method, but not necessarily the accounting period, of the estate to be the same as the method used by the individual debtor.

Subsection (c)(1) states a general rule that the estate of a partnership or a corporated debtor is not a separate entity for tax purposes. The income of the debtor is to be taxed as if the case were not commenced, except as provided in the remainder of section 346 and section 728.

Subsection (c)(2) requires the trustee, except as provided in section 728 of title 11, to file all tax returns on behalf of the partnership or corporation during the case.

Subsection (d) indicates that the estate in a chapter 13 case is not a separate taxable entity and that all income of the estate is to be taxed to the debtor.

Subsection (e) establishes a business deduction consisting of allowed expenses of administration except for tax or capital expenses that are not otherwise deductible. The deduction may be used by the estate when it is a separate taxable entity or by the entity to which the income of the estate is taxed when it is not.

Subsection (f) imposes a duty on the trustee to comply with any Federal, State, or local tax law requiring withholding or collection of taxes from any payment of wages, salaries, commissions, dividends, interest, or other payments. Any amount withheld is to be paid to the taxing authority at the same time and with the same priority as the claim from which such amount withheld was paid.

Subsection (g)(1)(A) indicates that neither gain nor loss is recognized on the transfer by law of property from the debtor or a creditor to the estate. Subparagraph (B) provides a similar policy if the property of the estate is returned from the estate to the debtor other than by a sale of property to debtor. Subparagraph (C) also provides for nonrecognition of gain or loss in a case under chapter 11 if a corporate debtor transfers property to a successor corporation or to an affiliate under a joint plan. An exception is made to enable a taxing authority to cause recognition of gain or loss to the extent provided in IRC [title 26] section 371 (as amended by section 109 of this bill).

Subsection (g)(2) provides that any of the three kinds of transferees specified in paragraph (1) take the property with the same character, holding period, and basis in the hands of the transferor at the time of such transfer. The transferor's basis may be adjusted under section 346(j)(5) even if the discharge of indebtedness occurs after the transfer of property. Of course, no adjustment will occur if the transfer is from the debtor to the estate or if the transfer is from an entity that is not discharged.

Subsection (h) provides that the creation of the estate of an individual under chapter 7 or 11 of title 11 as a separate taxable entity does not affect the number of taxable years for purposes of computing loss carryovers or carrybacks. The section applies with respect to carryovers or carrybacks of the debtor transferred into the estate under section 346(i)(1) of title 11 or back to the debtor under section 346(i)(2) of title 11.

Subsection (i)(1) states a general rule that an estate that is a separate taxable entity nevertheless succeeds to all tax attributes of the debtor. The six enumerated attributes are illustrative and not exhaustive.

Subsection (i)(2) indicates that attributes passing from the debtor into an estate that is a separate taxable entity will return to the debtor if unused by the estate. The debtor is permitted to use any such attribute as though the case had not been commenced.

Subsection (i)(3) permits an estate that is a separate taxable entity to carryback losses of the estate to a taxable period of the debtor that ended before the case was filed. The estate is treated as if it were the debtor with respect to time limitations and other restrictions. The section makes clear that the debtor may not carryback any loss of his own from a tax year during the pendency of the case to such a period until the case is closed. No tolling of any period of limitation is provided with respect to carrybacks by the debtor of post-petition losses.

Subsection (j) sets forth seven special rules treating with the tax effects of forgiveness or discharge of indebtedness. The terms "forgiveness" and "discharge" are redundant, but are used to clarify that "discharge" in the context of a special tax provision in title 11 includes forgiveness of indebtedness whether or not such indebtedness is "discharged" in the bankruptcy sense.

Paragraph (1) states the general rule that forgiveness of indebtedness is not taxable except as otherwise provided in paragraphs (2)–(7). The paragraph is patterned after sections 268, 395, and 520 of the Bankruptcy Act [sections 668, 795, and 920 of former title 11].

Paragraph (2) disallows deductions for liabilities of a deductible nature in any year during or after the year of cancellation of such liabilities. For the purposes of this paragraph, "a deduction with respect to a liability" includes a capital loss incurred on the disposition of a capital asset with respect to a liability that was incurred in connection with the acquisition of such asset.

Paragraph (3) causes any net operating loss of a debtor that is an individual or corporation to be reduced by any discharge of indebtedness except as provided in paragraphs (2) or (4). If a deduction is disallowed under paragraph (2), then no double counting occurs. Thus, paragraph (3) will reflect the reduction of losses by liabilities that have been forgiven, including deductible liabilities or nondeductible liabilities such as repayment of principal on borrowed funds.

Paragraph (4) specifically excludes two kinds of indebtedness from reduction of net operating losses under paragraph (3) or from reduction of basis under paragraph (5). Subparagraph (A) excludes items of a deductible nature that were not deducted or that could not be deducted such as gambling losses or liabilities for interest owed to a relative of the debtor. Subparagraph (B) excludes indebtedness of a debtor that is an individual or corporation that resulted in deductions which did not offset income and that did not contribute to an unexpired net operating loss or loss carryover. In these situations, the debtor has derived no tax benefit so there is no need to incur an offsetting reduction.

Paragraph (5) provides a two-point test for reduction of basis. The paragraph replaces sections 270, 396, and 522 of the Bankruptcy Act [sections 670, 796, and 922 of former title 11]. Subparagraph (A) sets out the maximum amount by which basis may be reduced—the total indebtedness forgiven less adjustments made under paragraphs (2) and (3). This avoids double counting. If a deduction is disallowed under paragraph (2) or a carryover is reduced under paragraph (3) then the tax benefit is neutralized, and there is no need to reduce basis. Subparagraph (B) reduces basis to the extent the debtor's total basis of assets before the discharge exceeds total preexisting liabilities still remaining after discharge of indebtedness. This is a "basis solvency" limitation which differs from the usual test of solvency because it measures against the remaining liabilities the benefit aspect of assets, their basis, rather than their value. Paragraph (5) applies so that any transferee of the debtor's property who is required to use the debtor's basis takes the debtor's basis reduced by the lesser of (A) and (B). Thus, basis will be reduced, but never below a level equal to undischarged liabilities.

Paragraph (6) specifies that basis need not be reduced under paragraph (5) to the extent the debtor treats discharged indebtedness as taxable income. This permits the debtor to elect whether to recognize income, which may be advantageous if the debtor anticipates subsequent net operating losses, rather than to reduce basis.

Paragraph (7) establishes two rules excluding from the category of discharged indebtedness certain indebtedness that is exchanged for an equity security issued under a plan or that is forgiven as a contribution to capital by an equity security holder. Subparagraph (A) creates the first exclusion to the extent indebtedness consisting of items not of a deductible nature is exchanged for an equity security, other than the interests of a limited partner in a limited partnership, issued by the debtor or is forgiven as a contribution to capital by an equity security holder. Subparagraph (B) excludes indebtedness consisting of items of a deductible nature, if the exchange of stock for debts has the same effect as a cash payment equal to the value of the equity security, in the amount of the fair market value of the equity security or, if less, the extent to which such exchange has such effect. The two provisions treat the debtor as if it had originally issued stock instead of debt. Subparagraph (B) rectifies the inequity under current law between a cash basis and accrual basis debtor concerning the issuance of stock in exchange for previous services rendered that were of a greater value than the stock. Subparagraph (B) also changes current law by taxing forgiveness of indebtedness to the extent that stock is exchanged for the accrued interest component of a security, because the recipient of such stock would not be regarded as having received money under the *Carman* doctrine.

References in Text

The Internal Revenue Code of 1986, referred to in text, is classified generally to Title 26, Internal Revenue Code.

Amendments

2005—Pub. L. 109–8 amended section catchline and text generally. Prior to amendment, text consisted of subsecs. (a) to (j) relating to special tax provisions.

1994—Subsec. (a). Pub. L. 103–394, §504(d)(4)(A), substituted "Internal Revenue Code of 1986" for "Internal Revenue Code of 1954 (26 U.S.C. 1 et seq.)".

Subsec. (g)(1)(C). Pub. L. 103–394, §501(d)(4)(B), substituted "Internal Revenue Code of 1986" for "Internal Revenue Code of 1954 (26 U.S.C. 371)".

1986—Subsec. (b)(1). Pub. L. 99–554, §257(g)(1), inserted reference to chapter 12.

Subsec. (g)(1)(C). Pub. L. 99–554, §257(g)(2), inserted reference to chapter 12.
Subsec. (i)(1). Pub. L. 99–554, §257(g)(3), inserted reference to chapter 12.
Subsec. (j)(7). Pub. L. 99–554, §283(c), substituted "owed" for "owned".

1984—Subsec. (c)(2). Pub. L. 98–353 substituted "corporation" for "operation".

Effective Date of 2005 Amendment

Amendment by Pub. L. 109–8 effective 180 days after Apr. 20, 2005, and not applicable with respect to cases commenced under this title before such effective date, except as otherwise provided, see section 1501 of Pub. L. 109–8, set out as a note under section 101 of this title.

Effective Date of 1994 Amendment

Amendment by Pub. L. 103–394 effective Oct. 22, 1994, and not applicable with respect to cases commenced under this title before Oct. 22, 1994, see section 702 of Pub. L. 103–394, set out as a note under section 101 of this title.

Effective Date of 1986 Amendment

Amendment by section 257 of Pub. L. 99–554 effective 30 days after Oct. 27, 1986, but not applicable to cases commenced under this title before that date, see section 302(a), (c)(1) of Pub. L. 99–554, set out as a note under section 581 of Title 28, Judiciary and Judicial Procedure.

Amendment by section 283 of Pub. L. 99–554 effective 30 days after Oct. 27, 1986, see section 302(a) of Pub. L. 99–554.

Effective Date of 1984 Amendment

Amendment by Pub. L. 98–353 effective with respect to cases filed 90 days after July 10, 1984, see section 552(a) of Pub. L. 98–353, set out as a note under section 101 of this title.

§347. Unclaimed property

(a) Ninety days after the final distribution under section 726, 1226, or 1326 of this title in a case under chapter 7, 12, or 13 of this title, as the case may be, the trustee shall stop payment on any check remaining unpaid, and any remaining property of the estate shall be paid into the court and disposed of under chapter 129 of title 28.

(b) Any security, money, or other property remaining unclaimed at the expiration of the time allowed in a case under chapter 9, 11, or 12 of this title for the presentation of a security or the performance of any other act as a condition to participation in the distribution under any plan confirmed under section 943(b), 1129, 1173, or 1225 of this title, as the case may be, becomes the property of the debtor or of the entity acquiring the assets of the debtor under the plan, as the case may be.

(Pub. L. 95–598, Nov. 6, 1978, 92 Stat. 2568; Pub. L. 99–554, title II, §257(h), Oct. 27, 1986, 100 Stat. 3114.)

Historical and Revision Notes
legislative statements

Section 347(a) of the House amendment adopts a comparable provision contained in the Senate amendment instructing the trustee to stop payment on any check remaining unpaid more than 90 days after the final distribution in a case under Chapter 7 or 13. Technical changes are made in section 347(b) to cover distributions in a railroad reorganization.

senate report no. 95–989

Section 347 is derived from Bankruptcy Act §66 [section 106 of former title 11]. Subsection (a) requires the trustee to stop payment on any distribution check that is unpaid 90 days after the final distribution in a case under chapter 7 or 13. The unclaimed funds, and any other property of the estate are paid into the court and disposed of under chapter 129 [§2041 et seq.] of title 28, which requires the clerk of court to hold the funds for their owner for 5 years, after which they escheat to the Treasury.

Subsection (b) specifies that any property remaining unclaimed at the expiration of the time allowed in a chapter 9 or 11 case for presentation (exchange) of securities or the performance of any other act as a condition to participation in the plan reverts to the debtor or the entity acquiring the assets of the debtor under the plan. Conditions to participation under a plan include such acts as cashing a check, surrendering securities for cancellation, and so on. Similar provisions are found in sections 96(d) and 205 of current law [sections 416(d) and 605 of former title 11].

Amendments

1986—Subsec. (a). Pub. L. 99–554, §257(h)(1), inserted references to section 1226 and chapter 12 of this title.

Subsec. (b). Pub. L. 99–554, §257(h)(2), inserted references to chapter 12 and section 1225 of this title.

Effective Date of 1986 Amendment

Amendment by Pub. L. 99–554 effective 30 days after Oct. 27, 1986, but not applicable to cases commenced under this title before that date, see section 302(a), (c)(1) of Pub. L. 99–554, set out as a note under section 581 of Title 28, Judiciary and Judicial Procedure.

§348. Effect of conversion

(a) Conversion of a case from a case under one chapter of this title to a case under another chapter of this title constitutes an order for relief under the chapter to which the case is converted, but, except as provided in subsections (b) and (c) of this section, does not effect a change in the date of the filing of the petition, the commencement of the case, or the order for relief.

(b) Unless the court for cause orders otherwise, in sections 701(a), 727(a)(10), 727(b), 1102(a), 1110(a)(1), 1121(b), 1121(c), 1141(d)(4), 1201(a), 1221, 1228(a), 1301(a), and 1305(a) of this title, "the order for relief under this chapter" in a chapter to which a case has been converted under section 706, 1112, 1208, or 1307 of this title means the conversion of such case to such chapter.

(c) Sections 342 and 365(d) of this title apply in a case that has been converted under section 706, 1112, 1208, or 1307 of this title, as if the conversion order were the order for relief.

(d) A claim against the estate or the debtor that arises after the order for relief but before conversion in a case that is converted under section 1112, 1208, or 1307 of this title, other than a claim specified in section 503(b) of this title, shall be treated for all purposes as if such claim had arisen immediately before the date of the filing of the petition.

(e) Conversion of a case under section 706, 1112, 1208, or 1307 of this title terminates the service of any trustee or examiner that is serving in the case before such conversion.

(f)(1) Except as provided in paragraph (2), when a case under chapter 13 of this title is converted to a case under another chapter under this title—

(A) property of the estate in the converted case shall consist of property of the estate, as of the date of filing of the petition, that remains in the possession of or is under the control of the debtor on the date of conversion;

(B) valuations of property and of allowed secured claims in the chapter 13 case shall apply only in a case converted to a case under chapter 11 or 12, but not in a case converted to a case under chapter 7, with allowed secured claims in cases under chapters 11 and 12 reduced to the extent that they have been paid in accordance with the chapter 13 plan; and

(C) with respect to cases converted from chapter 13—

(i) the claim of any creditor holding security as of the date of the filing of the petition shall continue to be secured by that security unless the full amount of such claim determined under applicable nonbankruptcy law has been paid in full as of the date of conversion, notwithstanding any valuation or determination of the amount of an allowed secured claim made for the purposes of the case under chapter 13; and

(ii) unless a prebankruptcy default has been fully cured under the plan at the time of conversion, in any proceeding under this title or otherwise, the default shall have the effect given under applicable nonbankruptcy law.

(2) If the debtor converts a case under chapter 13 of this title to a case under another chapter under this title in bad faith, the property of the estate in the converted case shall consist of the property of the estate as of the date of conversion.

(Pub. L. 95–598, Nov. 6, 1978, 92 Stat. 2568; Pub. L. 99–554, title II, §257(i), Oct. 27, 1986, 100 Stat. 3115; Pub. L. 103–394, title III, §311, title V, §501(d)(5), Oct. 22, 1994, 108 Stat. 4138, 4144; Pub. L. 109–8, title III, §309(a), title XII, §1207, Apr. 20, 2005, 119 Stat. 82, 194; Pub. L. 111–327, §2(a)(11), Dec. 22, 2010, 124 Stat. 3558.)

Historical and Revision Notes
legislative statements

The House amendment adopts section 348(b) of the Senate amendment with slight modifications, as more accurately reflecting sections to which this particular effect of conversion should apply.

Section 348(e) of the House amendment is a stylistic revision of similar provisions contained in H.R. 8200 as passed by the House and in the Senate amendment. Termination of services is expanded to cover any examiner serving in the case before conversion, as done in H.R. 8200 as passed by the House.

senate report no. 95–989

This section governs the effect of the conversion of a case from one chapter of the bankruptcy code to another chapter. Subsection (a) specifies that the date of the filing of the petition, the commencement of the case, or the order for relief are unaffected by conversion, with some exceptions specified in subsections (b) and (c).

Subsection (b) lists certain sections in the operative chapters of the bankruptcy code in which there is a reference to "the order for relief under this chapter." In those sections, the reference is to be read as a reference to the conversion order if the case has been converted into the particular chapter. Subsection (c) specifies that notice is to be given of the conversion order the same as notice was given of the order for relief, and that the time the trustee (or debtor in possession) has for assuming or rejecting executory contracts recommences, thus giving an opportunity for a newly appointed trustee to familiarize himself with the case.

Subsection (d) provides for special treatment of claims that arise during chapter 11 or 13 cases before the case is converted to a liquidation case. With the exception of claims specified in proposed 11 U.S.C. 503(b) (administrative expenses), preconversion claims are treated the same as prepetition claims.

Subsection (e) provides that conversion of a case terminates the service of any trustee serving in the case prior to conversion.

Amendments

2010—Subsec. (b). Pub. L. 111–327, §2(a)(11)(A), struck out "728(a), 728(b)," after "727(b)," and "1146(a), 1146(b)," after "1141(d)(4),".

Subsec. (f)(1)(C)(i). Pub. L. 111–327, §2(a)(11)(B), which directed insertion of "of the filing" after "date", was executed by making the insertion after "date" the first time appearing to reflect the probable intent of Congress.

2005—Subsec. (f)(1)(B). Pub. L. 109–8, §309(a)(2)(A), substituted "only in a case converted to a case under chapter 11 or 12, but not in a case converted to a case under chapter 7, with allowed secured claims in cases under chapters 11 and 12" for "in the converted case, with allowed secured claims".

Subsec. (f)(1)(C). Pub. L. 109–8, §309(a)(1), (2)(B), (3), added subpar. (C).

Subsec. (f)(2). Pub. L. 109–8, §1207, inserted "of the estate" after "bad faith, the property".

1994—Subsec. (b). Pub. L. 103–394, §501(d)(5), substituted "1201(a), 1221, 1228(a), 1301(a), and 1305(a)" for "1301(a), 1305(a), 1201(a), 1221, and 1228(a)" and "1208, or 1307" for "1307, or 1208".

Subsecs. (c) to (e). Pub. L. 103–394, §501(d)(5)(B), substituted "1208, or 1307" for "1307, or 1208".

Subsec. (f). Pub. L. 103–394, §311, added subsec. (f).

1986—Subsec. (b). Pub. L. 99–554, §257(i)(1), substituted references to sections 1201(a), 1221, and 1228(a) of this title for reference to section 1328(a) of this title, and inserted reference to section 1208 of this title.

Subsecs. (c) to (e). Pub. L. 99–554, §257(i)(2), (3), inserted reference to section 1208 of this title.

Effective Date of 2005 Amendment

Amendment by Pub. L. 109–8 effective 180 days after Apr. 20, 2005, and not applicable with respect to cases commenced under this title before such effective date, except as otherwise provided, see section 1501 of Pub. L. 109–8, set out as a note under section 101 of this title.

Effective Date of 1994 Amendment

Amendment by Pub. L. 103–394 effective Oct. 22, 1994, and not applicable with respect to cases commenced under this title before Oct. 22, 1994, see section 702 of Pub. L. 103–394, set out as a note under section 101 of this title.

Effective Date of 1986 Amendment

Amendment by Pub. L. 99–554 effective 30 days after Oct. 27, 1986, but not applicable to cases commenced under this title before that date, see section 302(a), (c)(1) of Pub. L. 99–554, set out as a note under section 581 of Title 28, Judiciary and Judicial Procedure.

§349. Effect of dismissal

(a) Unless the court, for cause, orders otherwise, the dismissal of a case under this title does not bar the discharge, in a later case under this title, of debts that were dischargeable in the case dismissed; nor does the dismissal of a case under this title prejudice the debtor with regard to the filing of a subsequent petition under this title, except as provided in section 109(g) of this title.

(b) Unless the court, for cause, orders otherwise, a dismissal of a case other than under section 742 of this title—

(1) reinstates—

(A) any proceeding or custodianship superseded under section 543 of this title;

(B) any transfer avoided under section 522, 544, 545, 547, 548, 549, or 724(a) of this title, or preserved under section 510(c)(2), 522(i)(2), or 551 of this title; and

(C) any lien voided under section 506(d) of this title;

(2) vacates any order, judgment, or transfer ordered, under section 522(i)(1), 542, 550, or 553 of this title; and

(3) revests the property of the estate in the entity in which such property was vested immediately before the commencement of the case under this title.

(Pub. L. 95–598, Nov. 6, 1978, 92 Stat. 2569; Pub. L. 98–353, title III, §303, July 10, 1984, 98 Stat. 352; Pub. L. 103–394, title V, §501(d)(6), Oct. 22, 1994, 108 Stat. 4144.)

Historical and Revision Notes

legislative statements

Section 349(b)(2) of the House amendment adds a cross reference to section 553 to reflect the new right of recovery of setoffs created under that section. Corresponding changes are made throughout the House amendment.

senate report no. 95–989

Subsection (a) specifies that unless the court for cause orders otherwise, the dismissal of a case is without prejudice. The debtor is not barred from receiving a discharge in a later case of debts that were dischargeable in the case dismissed. Of course, this subsection refers only to pre-discharge dismissals. If the debtor has already received a discharge and it is not revoked, then the debtor would be barred under section 727(a) from receiving a discharge in a subsequent liquidation case for six years. Dismissal of an involuntary on the merits will generally not give rise to adequate cause so as to bar the debtor from further relief.

Subsection (b) specifies that the dismissal reinstates proceedings or custodianships that were superseded by the bankruptcy case, reinstates avoided transfers, reinstates voided liens, vacates any order, judgment, or transfer ordered as a result of the avoidance of a transfer, and revests the property of the estate in the entity in which the property was vested at the commencement of the case. The court is permitted to order a different result for cause. The basic purpose of the subsection is to undo the bankruptcy case, as far as practicable, and to restore all property rights to the position in which they were found at the commencement of the case. This does not necessarily encompass undoing sales of property from the estate to a good faith purchaser. Where there is a question over the scope of the subsection, the court will make the appropriate orders to protect rights acquired in reliance on the bankruptcy case.

Amendments

1994—Subsec. (a). Pub. L. 103–394 substituted "109(g)" for "109(f)".

1984—Subsec. (a). Pub. L. 98–353 inserted "; nor does the dismissal of a case under this title prejudice the debtor with regard to the filing of a subsequent petition under this title, except as provided in section 109(f) of this title".

Effective Date of 1994 Amendment

Amendment by Pub. L. 103–394 effective Oct. 22, 1994, and not applicable with respect to cases commenced under this title before Oct. 22, 1994, see section 702 of Pub. L. 103–394, set out as a note under section 101 of this title.

Effective Date of 1984 Amendment

Amendment by Pub. L. 98–353 effective with respect to cases filed 90 days after July 10, 1984, see section 552(a) of Pub. L. 98–353, set out as a note under section 101 of this title.

§350. Closing and reopening cases

(a) After an estate is fully administered and the court has discharged the trustee, the court shall close the case.

(b) A case may be reopened in the court in which such case was closed to administer assets, to accord relief to the debtor, or for other cause.

(Pub. L. 95–598, Nov. 6, 1978, 92 Stat. 2569; Pub. L. 98–353, title III, §439, July 10, 1984, 98 Stat. 370.)

Historical and Revision Notes

senate report no. 95–989

Subsection (a) requires the court to close a bankruptcy case after the estate is fully administered and the trustee discharged. The Rules of Bankruptcy Procedure will provide the procedure for case closing. Subsection (b) permits reopening of the case to administer assets, to accord relief to the debtor, or for other cause. Though the court may permit reopening of a case so that the trustee may exercise an avoiding power, laches may constitute a bar to an action that has been delayed too long. The case may be reopened in the court in which it was closed. The rules will prescribe the procedure by which a case is reopened and how it will be conducted after reopening.

Amendments

1984—Subsec. (b). Pub. L. 98–353 substituted "A" for "a".

Effective Date of 1984 Amendment

Amendment by Pub. L. 98–353 effective with respect to cases filed 90 days after July 10, 1984, see section 552(a) of Pub. L. 98–353, set out as a note under section 101 of this title.

§351. Disposal of patient records

If a health care business commences a case under chapter 7, 9, or 11, and the trustee does not have a sufficient amount of funds to pay for the storage of patient records in the manner required under applicable Federal or State law, the following requirements shall apply:

(1) The trustee shall—

(A) promptly publish notice, in 1 or more appropriate newspapers, that if patient records are not claimed by the patient or an insurance provider (if applicable law permits the insurance provider to make that claim) by the date that is 365 days after the date of that notification, the trustee will destroy the patient records; and

(B) during the first 180 days of the 365-day period described in subparagraph (A), promptly attempt to notify directly each patient that is the subject of the patient records and appropriate insurance carrier concerning the patient records by mailing to the most recent known address of that patient, or a family member or contact person for that patient, and to the appropriate insurance carrier an appropriate notice regarding the claiming or disposing of patient records.

(2) If, after providing the notification under paragraph (1), patient records are not claimed during the 365-day period described under that paragraph, the trustee shall mail, by certified mail, at the end of such 365-day period a written request to each appropriate Federal agency to request permission from that agency to deposit the patient records with that agency, except that no Federal agency is required to accept patient records under this paragraph.

(3) If, following the 365-day period described in paragraph (2) and after providing the notification under paragraph (1), patient records are not claimed by a patient or insurance provider, or request is not granted by a Federal agency to deposit such records with that agency, the trustee shall destroy those records by—

(A) if the records are written, shredding or burning the records; or

(B) if the records are magnetic, optical, or other electronic records, by otherwise destroying those records so that those records cannot be retrieved.

(Added Pub. L. 109–8, title XI, §1102(a), Apr. 20, 2005, 119 Stat. 189.)

Effective Date

Section effective 180 days after Apr. 20, 2005, and not applicable with respect to cases commenced under this title before such effective date, except as otherwise provided, see section 1501 of Pub. L. 109–8, set out as an Effective Date of 2005 Amendment note under section 101 of this title.

SUBCHAPTER IV—ADMINISTRATIVE POWERS

§361. Adequate protection

When adequate protection is required under section 362, 363, or 364 of this title of an interest of an entity in property, such adequate protection may be provided by—

(1) requiring the trustee to make a cash payment or periodic cash payments to such entity, to the extent that the stay under section 362 of this title, use, sale, or lease under section 363 of this title, or any grant of a lien under section 364 of this title results in a decrease in the value of such entity's interest in such property;

(2) providing to such entity an additional or replacement lien to the extent that such stay, use, sale, lease, or grant results in a decrease in the value of such entity's interest in such property; or

(3) granting such other relief, other than entitling such entity to compensation allowable under section 503(b)(1) of this title as an administrative expense, as will result in the realization by such entity of the indubitable equivalent of such entity's interest in such property.

(Pub. L. 95–598, Nov. 6, 1978, 92 Stat. 2569; Pub. L. 98–353, title III, §440, July 10, 1984, 98 Stat. 370.)

Historical and Revision Notes

legislative statements

Section 361 of the House amendment represents a compromise between H.R. 8200 as passed by the House and the Senate amendment regarding the issue of "adequate protection" of a secured party. The House amendment deletes the provision found in section 361(3) of H.R. 8200 as passed by the House. It would have permitted adequate protection to be provided by giving the secured party an administrative expense regarding any decrease in the value of such party's collateral. In every case there is the uncertainty that the estate will have sufficient property to pay administrative expenses in full.

Section 361(4) of H.R. 8200 as passed by the House is modified in section 361(3) of the House amendment to indicate that the court may grant other forms of adequate protection, other than an administrative expense, which will result in the realization by the secured creditor of the indubitable equivalent of the creditor's interest in property. In the special instance where there is a reserve fund maintained under the security agreement, such as in the typical bondholder case, indubitable equivalent means that the bondholders would be entitled to be protected as to the reserve fund, in addition to the regular payments needed to service the debt. Adequate protection of an interest of an entity in property is intended to protect a creditor's allowed secured claim. To the extent the protection proves to be inadequate after the fact, the creditor is entitled to a first priority administrative expense under section 503(b).

In the special case of a creditor who has elected application of creditor making an election under section 1111(b)(2), that creditor is entitled to adequate protection of the creditor's interest in property to the extent of the value of the collateral not to the extent of the creditor's allowed secured claim, which is inflated to cover a deficiency as a result of such election.

senate report no. 95–989

Sections 362, 363, and 364 require, in certain circumstances, that the court determine in noticed hearings whether the interest of a secured creditor or co-owner of property with the debtor is adequately protected in connection with the sale or use of property. The interests of which the court may provide protection in the ways described in this section include equitable as well as legal interests. For example, a right to enforce a pledge and a right to recover property delivered to a debtor under a consignment agreement or an agreement of sale or return are interests that may be entitled to protection. This section specifies means by which adequate protection may be provided but, to avoid placing the court in an administrative role, does not require the court to provide it. Instead, the trustee or debtor in possession or the creditor will provide or propose a protection method. If the party that is affected by the proposed action objects, the court will determine whether the protection provided is adequate. The purpose of this section is to illustrate means by which it may be provided and to define the limits of the concept.

The concept of adequate protection is derived from the fifth amendment protection of property interests as enunciated by the Supreme Court. See *Wright v. Union Central Life Ins. Co.*, 311 U.S. 273 (1940); *Louisville Joint Stock Land Bank v. Radford*, 295 U.S. 555 (1935).

The automatic stay also provides creditor protection. Without it, certain creditors would be able to pursue their own remedies against the debtor's property. Those who acted first would obtain payment of the claims in preference to and to the detriment of other creditors. Bankruptcy is designed to provide an orderly liquidation procedure under which all creditors are treated equally. A race of diligence by creditors for the debtor's assets prevents that.

Subsection (a) defines the scope of the automatic stay, by listing the acts that are stayed by the commencement of the case. The commencement or continuation, including the issuance of process, of a judicial, administrative or other proceeding against the debtor that was or could have been commenced before the commencement of the bankruptcy case is stayed under paragraph (1). The scope of this paragraph is broad. All proceedings are stayed, including arbitration, administrative, and judicial proceedings. Proceeding in this sense encompasses civil actions and all proceedings even if they are not before governmental tribunals.

The stay is not permanent. There is adequate provision for relief from the stay elsewhere in the section. However, it is important that the trustee have an opportunity to inventory the debtor's position before proceeding with the administration of the case. Undoubtedly the court will lift the stay for proceedings before specialized or nongovernmental tribunals to allow those proceedings to come to a conclusion. Any party desiring to enforce an order in such a proceeding would thereafter have to come before the bankruptcy court to collect assets. Nevertheless, it will often be more appropriate to permit proceedings to continue in their place of origin, when no great prejudice to the bankruptcy estate would result, in order to leave the parties to their chosen forum and to relieve the bankruptcy court from many duties that may be handled elsewhere.

Paragraph (2) stays the enforcement, against the debtor or against property of the estate, of a judgment obtained before the commencement of the bankruptcy case. Thus, execution and levy against the debtors' prepetition property are stayed, and attempts to collect a judgment from the debtor personally are stayed.

Paragraph (3) stays any act to obtain possession of property of the estate (that is, property of the debtor as of the date of the filing of the petition) or property from the estate (property over which the estate has control or possession). The purpose of this provision is to prevent dismemberment of the estate. Liquidation must proceed in an orderly fashion. Any distribution of property must be by the trustee after he has had an opportunity to familiarize himself with the various rights and interests involved and with the property available for distribution.

Paragraph (4) stays lien creation against property of the estate. Thus, taking possession to perfect a lien or obtaining court process is prohibited. To permit lien creation after bankruptcy would give certain creditors preferential treatment by making them secured instead of unsecured.

Paragraph (5) stays any act to create or enforce a lien against property of the debtor, that is, most property that is acquired after the date of the filing of the petition, property that is exempted, or property that does not pass to the estate, to the extent that the lien secures a prepetition claim. Again, to permit postbankruptcy lien creation or enforcement would permit certain creditors to receive preferential treatment. It may also circumvent the debtors' discharge.

Paragraph (6) prevents creditors from attempting in any way to collect a prepetition debt. Creditors in consumer cases occasionally telephone debtors to encourage repayment in spite of bankruptcy. Inexperienced, frightened, or ill-counseled debtors may succumb to suggestions to repay notwithstanding their bankruptcy. This provision prevents evasion of the purpose of the bankruptcy laws by sophisticated creditors.

Paragraph (7) stays setoffs of mutual debts and credits between the debtor and creditors. As with all other paragraphs of subsection (a), this paragraph does not affect the right of creditors. It simply stays its enforcement pending an orderly examination of the debtor's and creditors' rights.

Subsection (b) lists seven exceptions to the automatic stay. The effect of an exception is not to make the action immune from injunction.

The court has ample other powers to stay actions not covered by the automatic stay. Section 105, of proposed title 11, derived from Bankruptcy Act §2a(15) [section 11(a)(15) of former title 11], grants the power to issue orders necessary or appropriate to carry out the provisions of title 11. The district court and the bankruptcy court as its adjunct have all the traditional injunctive powers of a court of equity, 28 U.S.C. §§151 and 164 as proposed in S. 2266, §201, and 28 U.S.C. §1334, as proposed in S. 2266, §216. Stays or injunctions issued under these other sections will not be automatic upon the commencement of the case, but will be granted or issued under the usual rules for the issuance of injunctions. By excepting an act or action from the automatic stay, the bill simply requires that the trustee move the court into action, rather than requiring the stayed party to request relief from the stay. There are some actions, enumerated in the exceptions, that generally should not be stayed automatically upon the commencement of the case, for reasons of either policy or practicality. Thus, the court will have to determine on a case-by-case basis whether a particular action which may be harming the estate should be stayed.

With respect to stays issued under other powers, or the application of the automatic stay, to governmental actions, this section and the other sections mentioned are intended to be an express waiver of sovereign immunity of the Federal Government, and an assertion of the bankruptcy power over State governments under the supremacy clause notwithstanding a State's sovereign immunity.

The first exception is of criminal proceedings against the debtor. The bankruptcy laws are not a haven for criminal offenders, but are designed to give relief from financial overextension. Thus, criminal actions and proceedings may proceed in spite of bankruptcy.

Paragraph (2) excepts from the stay the collection of alimony, maintenance or support from property that is not property of the estate. This will include property acquired after the commencement of the case, exempted property, and property that does not pass to the estate. The automatic stay is one means of protecting the debtor's discharge. Alimony, maintenance and support obligations are excepted from discharge. Staying collection of them, when not to the detriment of other creditors (because the collection effort is against property that is not property of the estate) does not further that goal. Moreover, it could lead to hardship on the part of the protected spouse or children.

Paragraph (3) excepts any act to perfect an interest in property to the extent that the trustee's rights and powers are limited under section 546(a) of the bankruptcy code. That section permits postpetition perfection of certain liens to be effective against the trustee. If the act of perfection, such as filing, were stayed, the section would be nullified.

Paragraph (4) excepts commencement or continuation of actions and proceedings by governmental units to enforce police or regulatory powers. Thus, where a governmental unit is suing a debtor to prevent or stop violation of fraud, environmental protection, consumer protection, safety, or similar police or regulatory laws, or attempting to fix damages for violation of such a law, the action or proceeding is not stayed under the automatic stay.

Paragraph (5) makes clear that the exception extends to permit an injunction and enforcement of an injunction, and to permit the entry of a money judgment, but does not extend to permit enforcement of a money judgment. Since the assets of the debtor are in the possession and control of the bankruptcy court, and since they constitute a fund out of which all creditors are entitled to share, enforcement by a governmental unit of a money judgment would give it preferential treatment to the detriment of all other creditors.

Paragraph (6) excepts the setoff of any mutual debt and claim for commodity transactions.

Paragraph (7) excepts actions by the Secretary of Housing and Urban Development to foreclose or take possession in a case of a loan insured under the National Housing Act [12 U.S.C. 1701 et seq.]. A general exception for such loans is found in current sections 263 and 517 [sections 663 and 917 of former title 11], the exception allowed by this paragraph is much more limited.

Subsection (c) of section 362 specifies the duration of the automatic stay. Paragraph (1) terminates a stay of an act against property of the estate when the property ceases to be property of the estate, such as by sale, abandonment, or exemption. It does not terminate the stay against property of the debtor if the property leaves the estate and goes to the debtor. Paragraph (2) terminates the stay of any other act on the earliest of the time the case is closed, the time the case is dismissed, or the time a discharge is granted or denied (unless the debtor is a corporation or partnership in a chapter 7 case).

Subsection (c) governs automatic termination of the stay. Subsections (d) through (g) govern termination of the stay by the court on the request of a party in interest.

Subsection (d) requires the court, upon motion of a party in interest, to grant relief from the stay for cause, such as by terminating, annulling, modifying, or conditioning the stay. The lack of adequate protection of an interest in property is one cause for relief, but is not the only cause. Other causes might include the lack of any connection with or interference with the pending bankruptcy case. Generally, proceedings in which the debtor is a fiduciary, or involving postpetition activities of the debtor, need not be stayed because they bear no relationship to the purpose of the automatic stay, which is protection of the debtor and his estate from his creditors.

Upon the court's finding that the debtor has no equity in the property subject to the stay and that the property is not necessary to an effective reorganization of the debtor, the subsection requires the court grant relief from the stay. To aid in this determination, guidelines are established where the property subject to the stay is real property. An exception to "the necessary to an effective reorganization" requirement is made for real property on which no business is being conducted other than operating the real property and activities incident thereto. The intent of this exception is to reach the single-asset apartment type cases which involve primarily tax-shelter investments and for which the bankruptcy laws have provided a too facile method to relay conditions, but not the operating shopping center and hotel cases where attempts at reorganization should be permitted. Property in which the debtor has equity but which is not necessary to an effective reorganization of the debtor should be sold under section 363. Hearings under this subsection are given calendar priority to ensure that court congestion will not unduly prejudice the rights of creditors who may be obviously entitled to relief from the operation of the automatic stay.

Subsection (e) provides protection that is not always available under present law. The subsection sets a time certain within which the bankruptcy court must rule on the adequacy of protection provided for the secured creditor's interest. If the court does not rule within 30 days from a request by motion for relief from the stay, the stay is automatically terminated with respect to the property in question. To accommodate more complex cases, the subsection permits the court to make a preliminary ruling after a preliminary hearing. After a preliminary hearing, the court may continue the stay only if there is a reasonable likelihood that the party opposing relief from the stay will prevail at the final hearing. Because the stay is essentially an injunction, the three stages of the stay may be analogized to the three stages of an injunction. The filing of the petition which gives rise to the automatic stay is similar to a temporary restraining order. The preliminary hearing is similar to the hearing on a preliminary injunction, and the final hearing and order are similar to the hearing and issuance or denial of a permanent injunction. The main difference lies in which party must bring the issue before the court. While in the injunction setting, the party seeking the injunction must prosecute the action, in proceeding for relief from the automatic stay, the enjoined party must move. The difference does not, however, shift the burden of proof. Subsection (g) leaves that burden on the party opposing relief from the stay (that is, on the party seeking continuance of the injunction) on the issue of adequate protection and existence of an equity. It is not, however, intended to be confined strictly to the constitutional requirement. This section and the concept of adequate protection are based as much on policy grounds as on constitutional grounds. Secured creditors should not be deprived of the benefit of their bargain. There may be situations in bankruptcy where giving a secured creditor an absolute right to his bargain may be impossible or seriously detrimental to the policy of the bankruptcy laws. Thus, this section recognizes the availability of alternate means of protecting a secured creditor's interest where such steps are a necessary part of the rehabilitative process. Though the creditor might not be able to retain his lien upon the specific collateral held at the time of filing, the purpose of the section is to insure that the secured creditor receives the value for which he bargained.

The section specifies two exclusive means of providing adequate protection, both of which may require an approximate determination of the value of the protected entity's interest in the property involved. The section does not specify how value is to be determined, nor does it specify when it is to be determined. These matters are left to case-by-case interpretation and development. In light of the restrictive approach of the section to the availability of means of providing adequate protection, this flexibility is important to permit the courts to adapt to varying circumstances and changing modes of financing.

Neither is it expected that the courts will construe the term value to mean, in every case, forced sale liquidation value or full going concern value. There is wide latitude between those two extremes although forced sale liquidation value will be a minimum.

In any particular case, especially a reorganization case, the determination of which entity should be entitled to the difference between the going concern value and the liquidation value must be based on equitable considerations arising from the facts of the case. Finally, the determination of value is binding only for the purposes of the specific hearing and is not to have a res judicata effect.

The first method of adequate protection outlined is the making of cash payments to compensate for the expected decrease in value of the opposing entity's interest. This provision is derived from *In re Bermec Corporation*, 445 F.2d 367 (2d Cir. 1971), though in that case it is not clear whether the payments offered were adequate to compensate the secured creditors for their loss. The use of periodic payments may be appropriate where, for example, the property in question is depreciating at a relatively fixed rate. The periodic payments would be to compensate for the depreciation and might, but need not necessarily, be in the same amount as payments due on the secured obligation.

The second method is the fixing of an additional or replacement lien on other property of the debtor to the extent of the decrease in value or actual consumption of the property involved. The purpose of this method is to provide the protected entity with an alternative means of realizing the value of the original property, if it should decline during the case, by granting an interest in additional property from whose value the entity may realize its loss. This is consistent with the view expressed in *Wright v. Union Central Life Ins. Co.*, 311 U.S. 273 (1940), where the Court suggested that it was the value of the secured creditor's collateral, and not necessarily his rights in specific collateral, that was entitled to protection.

The section makes no provision for the granting of an administrative priority as a method of providing adequate protection to an entity as was suggested in *In re Yale Express System, Inc.*, 384 F.2d 990 (2d Cir. 1967), because such protection is too uncertain to be meaningful.

house report no. 95–595

The section specifies four means of providing adequate protection. They are neither exclusive nor exhaustive. They all rely, however, on the value of the protected entity's interest in the property involved. The section does not specify how value is to be determined, nor does it specify when it is to be determined. These matters are left to case-by-case interpretation and development. It is expected that the courts will apply the concept in light of facts of each case and general equitable principles. It is not intended that the courts will develop a hard and fast rule that will apply in every case. The time and method of valuation is not specified precisely, in order to avoid that result. There are an infinite number of variations possible in dealings between debtors and creditors, the law is continually developing, and new ideas are continually being implemented in this field. The flexibility is important to permit the courts to adapt to varying circumstances and changing modes of financing.

Neither is it expected that the courts will construe the term value to mean, in every case, forced sale liquidation value or full going concern value. There is wide latitude between those two extremes. In any particular case, especially a reorganization case, the determination of which entity should be entitled to the difference between the going concern value and the liquidation value must be based on equitable considerations based on the facts of the case. It will frequently be based on negotiation between the parties. Only if they cannot agree will the court become involved.

The first method of adequate protection specified is periodic cash payments by the estate, to the extent of a decrease in value of the opposing entity's interest in the property involved. This provision is derived from *In re Yale Express, Inc.*, 384 F.2d 990 (2d Cir. 1967) (though in that case it is not clear whether the payments required were adequate to compensate the secured creditors for their loss). The use of periodic payments may be appropriate, where for example, the property in question is depreciating at a relatively fixed rate. The periodic payments would be to compensate for the depreciation.

The second method is the provision of an additional or replacement lien on other property to the extent of the decrease in value of the property involved. The purpose of this method is to provide the protected entity with a means of realizing the value of the original property, if it should decline during the case, by granting an interest in additional property from whose value the entity may realize its loss.

The third method is the granting of an administrative expense priority to the protected entity to the extent of his loss. This method, more than the others, requires a prediction as to whether the unencumbered assets that will remain if the case if converted from reorganization to liquidation will be sufficient to pay the protected entity in full. It is clearly the most risky, from the entity's perspective, and should be used only when there is relative certainty that administrative expenses will be able to be paid in full in the event of liquidation.

The fourth [enacted as third] method gives the parties and the courts flexibility by allowing such other relief as will result in the realization by the protected entity of the value of its interest in the property involved. Under this provision, the courts will be able to adapt to new methods of financing and to formulate protection that is appropriate to the circumstances of the case if none of the other methods would accomplish the desired result. For example, another form of adequate protection might be the guarantee by a third party outside the judicial process of compensation for any loss incurred in the case. Adequate protection might also, in some circumstances, be provided by permitting a secured creditor to bid in his claim at the sale of the property and to offset the claim against the price bid in.

The paragraph also defines, more clearly than the others, the general concept of adequate protection, by requiring such relief as will result in the realization of value. It is the general category, and as such, is defined by the concept involved rather than any particular method of adequate protection.

Amendments

1984—Par. (1). Pub. L. 98–353 inserted "a cash payment or" after "make".

Effective Date of 1984 Amendment

Amendment by Pub. L. 98–353 effective with respect to cases filed 90 days after July 10, 1984, see section 552(a) of Pub. L. 98–353, set out as a note under section 101 of this title.

§362. Automatic stay

(a) Except as provided in subsection (b) of this section, a petition filed under section 301, 302, or 303 of this title, or an application filed under section 5(a)(3) of the Securities Investor Protection Act of 1970, operates as a stay, applicable to all entities, of—

(1) the commencement or continuation, including the issuance or employment of process, of a judicial, administrative, or other action or proceeding against the debtor that was or could have been commenced before the commencement of the case under this title, or to recover a claim against the debtor that arose before the commencement of the case under this title;

(2) the enforcement, against the debtor or against property of the estate, of a judgment obtained before the commencement of the case under this title;

(3) any act to obtain possession of property of the estate or of property from the estate or to exercise control over property of the estate;

(4) any act to create, perfect, or enforce any lien against property of the estate;

(5) any act to create, perfect, or enforce against property of the debtor any lien to the extent that such lien secures a claim that arose before the commencement of the case under this title;

(6) any act to collect, assess, or recover a claim against the debtor that arose before the commencement of the case under this title;

(7) the setoff of any debt owing to the debtor that arose before the commencement of the case under this title against any claim against the debtor; and

(8) the commencement or continuation of a proceeding before the United States Tax Court concerning a tax liability of a debtor that is a corporation for a taxable period the bankruptcy court may determine or concerning the tax liability of a debtor who is an individual for a taxable period ending before the date of the order for relief under this title.

(b) The filing of a petition under section 301, 302, or 303 of this title, or of an application under section 5(a)(3) of the Securities Investor Protection Act of 1970, does not operate as a stay—

(1) under subsection (a) of this section, of the commencement or continuation of a criminal action or proceeding against the debtor;

(2) under subsection (a)—

(A) of the commencement or continuation of a civil action or proceeding—

(i) for the establishment of paternity;

(ii) for the establishment or modification of an order for domestic support obligations;

(iii) concerning child custody or visitation;

(iv) for the dissolution of a marriage, except to the extent that such proceeding seeks to determine the division of property that is property of the estate; or

(v) regarding domestic violence;

(B) of the collection of a domestic support obligation from property that is not property of the estate;

(C) with respect to the withholding of income that is property of the estate or property of the debtor for payment of a domestic support obligation under a judicial or administrative order or a statute;

(D) of the withholding, suspension, or restriction of a driver's license, a professional or occupational license, or a recreational license, under State law, as specified in section 466(a)(16) of the Social Security Act;

(E) of the reporting of overdue support owed by a parent to any consumer reporting agency as specified in section 466(a)(7) of the Social Security Act;

(F) of the interception of a tax refund, as specified in sections 464 and 466(a)(3) of the Social Security Act or under an analogous State law; or

(G) of the enforcement of a medical obligation, as specified under title IV of the Social Security Act;

(3) under subsection (a) of this section, of any act to perfect, or to maintain or continue the perfection of, an interest in property to the extent that the trustee's rights and powers are subject to such perfection under section 546(b) of this title or to the extent that such act is accomplished within the period provided under section 547(e)(2)(A) of this title;

(4) under paragraph (1), (2), (3), or (6) of subsection (a) of this section, of the commencement or continuation of an action or proceeding by a governmental unit or any organization exercising authority under the Convention on the Prohibition of the Development, Production, Stockpiling and Use of Chemical Weapons and on Their Destruction, opened for signature on January 13, 1993, to enforce such governmental unit's or organization's police and regulatory power, including the enforcement of a judgment other than a money judgment, obtained in an action or proceeding by the governmental unit to enforce such governmental unit's or organization's police or regulatory power;

[(5) Repealed. Pub. L. 105–277, div. I, title VI, §603(1), Oct. 21, 1998, 112 Stat. 2681–866;]

(6) under subsection (a) of this section, of the exercise by a commodity broker, forward contract merchant, stockbroker, financial institution, financial participant, or securities clearing agency of any contractual right (as defined in section 555 or 556) under any security agreement or arrangement or other credit enhancement forming a part of or related to any commodity contract, forward contract or securities contract, or of any contractual right (as defined in section 555 or 556) to offset or net out any termination value, payment amount, or other transfer obligation arising under or in connection with 1 or more such contracts, including any master agreement for such contracts;

(7) under subsection (a) of this section, of the exercise by a repo participant or financial participant of any contractual right (as defined in section 559) under any security agreement or arrangement or other credit enhancement forming a part of or related to any repurchase agreement, or of any contractual right (as defined in section 559) to offset or net out any termination value, payment amount, or other transfer obligation arising under or in connection with 1 or more such agreements, including any master agreement for such agreements;

(8) under subsection (a) of this section, of the commencement of any action by the Secretary of Housing and Urban Development to foreclose a mortgage or deed of trust in any case in which the mortgage or deed of trust held by the Secretary is insured or was formerly insured under the National Housing Act and covers property, or combinations of property, consisting of five or more living units;

(9) under subsection (a), of—

(A) an audit by a governmental unit to determine tax liability;

(B) the issuance to the debtor by a governmental unit of a notice of tax deficiency;

(C) a demand for tax returns; or

(D) the making of an assessment for any tax and issuance of a notice and demand for payment of such an assessment (but any tax lien that would otherwise attach to property of the estate by reason of such an assessment shall not take effect unless such tax is a debt of the debtor that will not be discharged in the case and such property or its proceeds are transferred out of the estate to, or otherwise revested in, the debtor).

(10) under subsection (a) of this section, of any act by a lessor to the debtor under a lease of nonresidential real property that has terminated by the expiration of the stated term of the lease before the commencement of or during a case under this title to obtain possession of such property;

(11) under subsection (a) of this section, of the presentment of a negotiable instrument and the giving of notice of and protesting dishonor of such an instrument;

(12) under subsection (a) of this section, after the date which is 90 days after the filing of such petition, of the commencement or continuation, and conclusion to the entry of final judgment, of an action which involves a debtor subject to reorganization pursuant to chapter 11 of this title and which was brought by the Secretary of Transportation under section 31325 of title 46 (including distribution of any proceeds of sale) to foreclose a preferred ship or fleet mortgage, or a security interest in or relating to a vessel or vessel under construction, held by the Secretary of Transportation under chapter 537 of title 46 or section 109(h) of title 49, or under applicable State law;

(13) under subsection (a) of this section, after the date which is 90 days after the filing of such petition, of the commencement or continuation, and conclusion to the entry of final judgment, of an action which involves a debtor subject to reorganization pursuant to chapter 11 of this title and which was brought by the Secretary of Commerce under section 31325 of title 46 (including distribution of any proceeds of sale) to foreclose a preferred ship or fleet mortgage in a vessel or a mortgage, deed of trust, or other security interest in a fishing facility held by the Secretary of Commerce under chapter 537 of title 46;

(14) under subsection (a) of this section, of any action by an accrediting agency regarding the accreditation status of the debtor as an educational institution;

(15) under subsection (a) of this section, of any action by a State licensing body regarding the licensure of the debtor as an educational institution;

(16) under subsection (a) of this section, of any action by a guaranty agency, as defined in section 435(j) of the Higher Education Act of 1965 or the Secretary of Education regarding the eligibility of the debtor to participate in programs authorized under such Act;

(17) under subsection (a) of this section, of the exercise by a swap participant or financial participant of any contractual right (as defined in section 560) under any security agreement or arrangement or other credit enhancement forming a part of or related to any swap agreement, or of any contractual right (as defined in section 560) to offset or net out any termination value, payment amount, or other transfer obligation arising under or in connection with 1 or more such agreements, including any master agreement for such agreements;

(18) under subsection (a) of the creation or perfection of a statutory lien for an ad valorem property tax, or a special tax or special assessment on real property whether or not ad valorem, imposed by a governmental unit, if such tax or assessment comes due after the date of the filing of the petition;

(19) under subsection (a), of withholding of income from a debtor's wages and collection of amounts withheld, under the debtor's agreement authorizing that withholding and collection for the benefit of a pension, profit-sharing, stock bonus, or other plan established under section 401, 403, 408, 408A, 414, 457, or 501(c) of the Internal Revenue Code of 1986, that is sponsored by the employer of the debtor, or an affiliate, successor, or predecessor of such employer—

(A) to the extent that the amounts withheld and collected are used solely for payments relating to a loan from a plan under section 408(b)(1) of the Employee Retirement Income Security Act of 1974 or is subject to section 72(p) of the Internal Revenue Code of 1986; or

(B) a loan from a thrift savings plan permitted under subchapter III of chapter 84 of title 5, that satisfies the requirements of section 8433(g) of such title;

but nothing in this paragraph may be construed to provide that any loan made under a governmental plan under section 414(d), or a contract or account under section 403(b), of the Internal Revenue Code of 1986 constitutes a claim or a debt under this title;

(20) under subsection (a), of any act to enforce any lien against or security interest in real property following entry of the order under subsection (d)(4) as to such real property in any prior case under this title, for a period of 2 years after the date of the entry of such an order, except that the debtor, in a subsequent case under this title, may move for relief from such order based upon changed circumstances or for other good cause shown, after notice and a hearing;

(21) under subsection (a), of any act to enforce any lien against or security interest in real property—

(A) if the debtor is ineligible under section 109(g) to be a debtor in a case under this title; or

(B) if the case under this title was filed in violation of a bankruptcy court order in a prior case under this title prohibiting the debtor from being a debtor in another case under this title;

(22) subject to subsection (l), under subsection (a)(3), of the continuation of any eviction, unlawful detainer action, or similar proceeding by a lessor against a debtor involving residential property in which the debtor resides as a tenant under a lease or rental agreement and with respect to which the lessor has obtained before the date of the filing of the bankruptcy petition, a judgment for possession of such property against the debtor;

(23) subject to subsection (m), under subsection (a)(3), of an eviction action that seeks possession of the residential property in which the debtor resides as a tenant under a lease or rental agreement based on endangerment of such property or the illegal use of controlled substances on such property, but only if the lessor files with the court, and serves upon the debtor, a certification under penalty of perjury that such an eviction action has been filed, or that the debtor, during the 30-day period preceding the date of the filing of the certification, has endangered property or illegally used or allowed to be used a controlled substance on the property;

(24) under subsection (a), of any transfer that is not avoidable under section 544 and that is not avoidable under section 549;

(25) under subsection (a), of—

(A) the commencement or continuation of an investigation or action by a securities self regulatory organization to enforce such organization's regulatory power;

(B) the enforcement of an order or decision, other than for monetary sanctions, obtained in an action by such securities self regulatory organization to enforce such organization's regulatory power; or

(C) any act taken by such securities self regulatory organization to delist, delete, or refuse to permit quotation of any stock that does not meet applicable regulatory requirements;

(26) under subsection (a), of the setoff under applicable nonbankruptcy law of an income tax refund, by a governmental unit, with respect to a taxable period that ended before the date of the order for relief against an income tax liability for a taxable period that also ended before the date of the order for relief, except that in any case in which the setoff of an income tax refund is not permitted under applicable nonbankruptcy law because of a pending action to determine the amount or legality of a tax liability, the governmental unit may hold the refund pending the resolution of the action, unless the court, on the motion of the trustee and after notice and a hearing, grants the taxing authority adequate protection (within the meaning of section 361) for the secured claim of such authority in the setoff under section 506(a);

(27) under subsection (a) of this section, of the exercise by a master netting agreement participant of any contractual right (as defined in section 555, 556, 559, or 560) under any security agreement or arrangement or other credit enhancement forming a part of or related to any master netting agreement, or of any contractual right (as defined in section 555, 556, 559, or 560) to offset or net out any termination value, payment amount, or other transfer obligation arising under or in connection with 1 or more such master netting agreements to the extent that such participant is eligible to exercise such rights under paragraph (6), (7), or (17) for each individual contract covered by the master netting agreement in issue; and

(28) under subsection (a), of the exclusion by the Secretary of Health and Human Services of the debtor from participation in the medicare program or any other Federal health care program (as defined in section 1128B(f) of the Social Security Act pursuant to title XI or XVIII of such Act).

The provisions of paragraphs (12) and (13) of this subsection shall apply with respect to any such petition filed on or before December 31, 1989.

(c) Except as provided in subsections (d), (e), (f), and (h) of this section—

(1) the stay of an act against property of the estate under subsection (a) of this section continues until such property is no longer property of the estate;

(2) the stay of any other act under subsection (a) of this section continues until the earliest of—

(A) the time the case is closed;

(B) the time the case is dismissed; or

(C) if the case is a case under chapter 7 of this title concerning an individual or a case under chapter 9, 11, 12, or 13 of this title, the time a discharge is granted or denied;

(3) if a single or joint case is filed by or against a debtor who is an individual in a case under chapter 7, 11, or 13, and if a single or joint case of the debtor was pending within the preceding 1-year period but was dismissed, other than a case refiled under a chapter other than chapter 7 after dismissal under section 707(b)—

(A) the stay under subsection (a) with respect to any action taken with respect to a debt or property securing such debt or with respect to any lease shall terminate with respect to the debtor on the 30th day after the filing of the later case;

(B) on the motion of a party in interest for continuation of the automatic stay and upon notice and a hearing, the court may extend the stay in particular cases as to any or all creditors (subject to such conditions or limitations as the court may then impose) after notice and a hearing completed before the expiration of the 30-day period only if the party in interest demonstrates that the filing of the later case is in good faith as to the creditors to be stayed; and

(C) for purposes of subparagraph (B), a case is presumptively filed not in good faith (but such presumption may be rebutted by clear and convincing evidence to the contrary)—

(i) as to all creditors, if—

(I) more than 1 previous case under any of chapters 7, 11, and 13 in which the individual was a debtor was pending within the preceding 1-year period;

(II) a previous case under any of chapters 7, 11, and 13 in which the individual was a debtor was dismissed within such 1-year period, after the debtor failed to—

(aa) file or amend the petition or other documents as required by this title or the court without substantial excuse (but mere inadvertence or negligence shall not be a substantial excuse unless the dismissal was caused by the negligence of the debtor's attorney);

(bb) provide adequate protection as ordered by the court; or

(cc) perform the terms of a plan confirmed by the court; or

(III) there has not been a substantial change in the financial or personal affairs of the debtor since the dismissal of the next most previous case under chapter 7, 11, or 13 or any other reason to conclude that the later case will be concluded—

(aa) if a case under chapter 7, with a discharge; or

(bb) if a case under chapter 11 or 13, with a confirmed plan that will be fully performed; and

(ii) as to any creditor that commenced an action under subsection (d) in a previous case in which the individual was a debtor if, as of the date of dismissal of such case, that action was still pending or had been resolved by terminating, conditioning, or limiting the stay as to actions of such creditor; and

(4)(A)(i) if a single or joint case is filed by or against a debtor who is an individual under this title, and if 2 or more single or joint cases of the debtor were pending within the previous year but were dismissed, other than a case refiled under a chapter other than chapter 7 after dismissal under section 707(b), the stay under subsection (a) shall not go into effect upon the filing of the later case; and

(ii) on request of a party in interest, the court shall promptly enter an order confirming that no stay is in effect;

(B) if, within 30 days after the filing of the later case, a party in interest requests the court may order the stay to take effect in the case as to any or all creditors (subject to such conditions or limitations as the court may impose), after notice and a hearing, only if the party in interest demonstrates that the filing of the later case is in good faith as to the creditors to be stayed;

(C) a stay imposed under subparagraph (B) shall be effective on the date of the entry of the order allowing the stay to go into effect; and

(D) for purposes of subparagraph (B), a case is presumptively filed not in good faith (but such presumption may be rebutted by clear and convincing evidence to the contrary)—

(i) as to all creditors if—

(I) 2 or more previous cases under this title in which the individual was a debtor were pending within the 1-year period;

(II) a previous case under this title in which the individual was a debtor was dismissed within the time period stated in this paragraph after the debtor failed to file or amend the petition or other documents as required by this title or the court without substantial excuse (but mere inadvertence or negligence shall not be substantial excuse unless the dismissal was caused by the negligence of the debtor's attorney), failed to provide adequate protection as ordered by the court, or failed to perform the terms of a plan confirmed by the court; or

(III) there has not been a substantial change in the financial or personal affairs of the debtor since the dismissal of the next most previous case under this title, or any other reason to conclude that the later case will not be concluded, if a case under chapter 7, with a discharge, and if a case under chapter 11 or 13, with a confirmed plan that will be fully performed; or

(ii) as to any creditor that commenced an action under subsection (d) in a previous case in which the individual was a debtor if, as of the date of dismissal of such case, such action was still pending or had been resolved by terminating, conditioning, or limiting the stay as to such action of such creditor.

(d) On request of a party in interest and after notice and a hearing, the court shall grant relief from the stay provided under subsection (a) of this section, such as by terminating, annulling, modifying, or conditioning such stay—

(1) for cause, including the lack of adequate protection of an interest in property of such party in interest;

(2) with respect to a stay of an act against property under subsection (a) of this section, if—

(A) the debtor does not have an equity in such property; and

(B) such property is not necessary to an effective reorganization;

(3) with respect to a stay of an act against single asset real estate under subsection (a), by a creditor whose claim is secured by an interest in such real estate, unless, not later than the date that is 90 days after the entry of the order for relief (or such later date as the court may determine for cause by order entered within that 90-day period) or 30 days after the court determines that the debtor is subject to this paragraph, whichever is later—

(A) the debtor has filed a plan of reorganization that has a reasonable possibility of being confirmed within a reasonable time; or

(B) the debtor has commenced monthly payments that—

(i) may, in the debtor's sole discretion, notwithstanding section 363(c)(2), be made from rents or other income generated before, on, or after the date of the commencement of the case by or from the property to each creditor whose claim is secured by such real estate (other than a claim secured by a judgment lien or by an unmatured statutory lien); and

(ii) are in an amount equal to interest at the then applicable nondefault contract rate of interest on the value of the creditor's interest in the real estate; or

(4) with respect to a stay of an act against real property under subsection (a), by a creditor whose claim is secured by an interest in such real property, if the court finds that the filing of the petition was part of a scheme to delay, hinder, or defraud creditors that involved either—

(A) transfer of all or part ownership of, or other interest in, such real property without the consent of the secured creditor or court approval; or

(B) multiple bankruptcy filings affecting such real property.

If recorded in compliance with applicable State laws governing notices of interests or liens in real property, an order entered under paragraph (4) shall be binding in any other case under this title purporting to affect such real property filed not later than 2 years after the date of the entry of such order by the court, except that a debtor in a subsequent case under this title may move for relief from such order based upon changed circumstances or for good cause shown, after notice and a hearing. Any Federal, State, or local governmental unit that accepts notices of interests or liens in real property shall accept any certified copy of an order described in this subsection for indexing and recording.

(e)(1) Thirty days after a request under subsection (d) of this section for relief from the stay of any act against property of the estate under subsection (a) of this section, such stay is terminated with respect to the party in interest making such request, unless the court, after notice and a hearing, orders such stay continued in effect pending the conclusion of, or as a result of, a final hearing and determination under subsection (d) of this section. A hearing under this subsection may be a preliminary hearing, or may be consolidated with the final hearing under subsection (d) of this section. The court shall order such stay continued in effect pending the conclusion of the final hearing under subsection (d) of this section if there is a reasonable likelihood that the party opposing relief from such stay will prevail at the conclusion of such final hearing. If the hearing under this subsection is a preliminary hearing, then such final hearing shall be concluded not later than thirty days after the conclusion of such preliminary hearing, unless the 30-day period is extended with the consent of the parties in interest or for a specific time which the court finds is required by compelling circumstances.

(2) Notwithstanding paragraph (1), in a case under chapter 7, 11, or 13 in which the debtor is an individual, the stay under subsection (a) shall terminate on the date that is 60 days after a request is made by a party in interest under subsection (d), unless—

(A) a final decision is rendered by the court during the 60-day period beginning on the date of the request; or

(B) such 60-day period is extended—
(i) by agreement of all parties in interest; or
(ii) by the court for such specific period of time as the court finds is required for good cause, as described in findings made by the court.

(f) Upon request of a party in interest, the court, with or without a hearing, shall grant such relief from the stay provided under subsection (a) of this section as is necessary to prevent irreparable damage to the interest of an entity in property, if such interest will suffer such damage before there is an opportunity for notice and a hearing under subsection (d) or (e) of this section.

(g) In any hearing under subsection (d) or (e) of this section concerning relief from the stay of any act under subsection (a) of this section—
(1) the party requesting such relief has the burden of proof on the issue of the debtor's equity in property; and
(2) the party opposing such relief has the burden of proof on all other issues.

(h)(1) In a case in which the debtor is an individual, the stay provided by subsection (a) is terminated with respect to personal property of the estate or of the debtor securing in whole or in part a claim, or subject to an unexpired lease, and such personal property shall no longer be property of the estate if the debtor fails within the applicable time set by section 521(a)(2)—
(A) to file timely any statement of intention required under section 521(a)(2) with respect to such personal property or to indicate in such statement that the debtor will either surrender such personal property or retain it and, if retaining such personal property, either redeem such personal property pursuant to section 722, enter into an agreement of the kind specified in section 524(c) applicable to the debt secured by such personal property, or assume such unexpired lease pursuant to section 365(p) if the trustee does not do so, as applicable; and
(B) to take timely the action specified in such statement, as it may be amended before expiration of the period for taking action, unless such statement specifies the debtor's intention to reaffirm such debt on the original contract terms and the creditor refuses to agree to the reaffirmation on such terms.

(2) Paragraph (1) does not apply if the court determines, on the motion of the trustee filed before the expiration of the applicable time set by section 521(a)(2), after notice and a hearing, that such personal property is of consequential value or benefit to the estate, and orders appropriate adequate protection of the creditor's interest, and orders the debtor to deliver any collateral in the debtor's possession to the trustee. If the court does not so determine, the stay provided by subsection (a) shall terminate upon the conclusion of the hearing on the motion.

(i) If a case commenced under chapter 7, 11, or 13 is dismissed due to the creation of a debt repayment plan, for purposes of subsection (c)(3), any subsequent case commenced by the debtor under any such chapter shall not be presumed to be filed not in good faith.

(j) On request of a party in interest, the court shall issue an order under subsection (c) confirming that the automatic stay has been terminated.

(k)(1) Except as provided in paragraph (2), an individual injured by any willful violation of a stay provided by this section shall recover actual damages, including costs and attorneys' fees, and, in appropriate circumstances, may recover punitive damages.
(2) If such violation is based on an action taken by an entity in the good faith belief that subsection (h) applies to the debtor, the recovery under paragraph (1) of this subsection against such entity shall be limited to actual damages.

(l)(1) Except as otherwise provided in this subsection, subsection (b)(22) shall apply on the date that is 30 days after the date on which the bankruptcy petition is filed, if the debtor files with the petition and serves upon the lessor a certification under penalty of perjury that—
(A) under nonbankruptcy law applicable in the jurisdiction, there are circumstances under which the debtor would be permitted to cure the entire monetary default that gave rise to the judgment for possession, after that judgment for possession was entered; and
(B) the debtor (or an adult dependent of the debtor) has deposited with the clerk of the court, any rent that would become due during the 30-day period after the filing of the bankruptcy petition.

(2) If, within the 30-day period after the filing of the bankruptcy petition, the debtor (or an adult dependent of the debtor) complies with paragraph (1) and files with the court and serves upon the lessor a further certification under penalty of perjury that the debtor (or an adult dependent of the debtor) has cured, under nonbankruptcy law applicable in the jurisdiction, the entire monetary default that gave rise to the judgment under which possession is sought by the lessor, subsection (b)(22) shall not apply, unless ordered to apply by the court under paragraph (3).

(3)(A) If the lessor files an objection to any certification filed by the debtor under paragraph (1) or (2), and serves such objection upon the debtor, the court shall hold a hearing within 10 days after the filing and service of such objection to determine if the certification filed by the debtor under paragraph (1) or (2) is true.
(B) If the court upholds the objection of the lessor filed under subparagraph (A)—
(i) subsection (b)(22) shall apply immediately and relief from the stay provided under subsection (a)(3) shall not be required to enable the lessor to complete the process to recover full possession of the property; and
(ii) the clerk of the court shall immediately serve upon the lessor and the debtor a certified copy of the court's order upholding the lessor's objection.

(4) If a debtor, in accordance with paragraph (5), indicates on the petition that there was a judgment for possession of the residential rental property in which the debtor resides and does not file a certification under paragraph (1) or (2)—
(A) subsection (b)(22) shall apply immediately upon failure to file such certification, and relief from the stay provided under subsection (a)(3) shall not be required to enable the lessor to complete the process to recover full possession of the property; and
(B) the clerk of the court shall immediately serve upon the lessor and the debtor a certified copy of the docket indicating the absence of a filed certification and the applicability of the exception to the stay under subsection (b)(22).

(5)(A) Where a judgment for possession of residential property in which the debtor resides as a tenant under a lease or rental agreement has been obtained by the lessor, the debtor shall so indicate on the bankruptcy petition and shall provide the name and address of the lessor that obtained that pre-petition judgment on the petition and on any certification filed under this subsection.
(B) The form of certification filed with the petition, as specified in this subsection, shall provide for the debtor to certify, and the debtor shall certify—
(i) whether a judgment for possession of residential rental housing in which the debtor resides has been obtained against the debtor before the date of the filing of the petition; and
(ii) whether the debtor is claiming under paragraph (1) that under nonbankruptcy law applicable in the jurisdiction, there are circumstances under which the debtor would be permitted to cure the entire monetary default that gave rise to the judgment for possession, after that judgment of possession was entered, and has made the appropriate deposit with the court.

(C) The standard forms (electronic and otherwise) used in a bankruptcy proceeding shall be amended to reflect the requirements of this subsection.
(D) The clerk of the court shall arrange for the prompt transmittal of the rent deposited in accordance with paragraph (1)(B) to the lessor.

(m)(1) Except as otherwise provided in this subsection, subsection (b)(23) shall apply on the date that is 15 days after the date on which the lessor files and serves a certification described in subsection (b)(23).
(2)(A) If the debtor files with the court an objection to the truth or legal sufficiency of the certification described in subsection (b)(23) and serves such objection upon the lessor, subsection (b)(23) shall not apply, unless ordered to apply by the court under this subsection.
(B) If the debtor files and serves the objection under subparagraph (A), the court shall hold a hearing within 10 days after the filing and service of such objection to determine if the situation giving rise to the lessor's certification under paragraph (1) existed or has been remedied.
(C) If the debtor can demonstrate to the satisfaction of the court that the situation giving rise to the lessor's certification under paragraph (1) did not exist or has been remedied, the stay provided under subsection (a)(3) shall remain in effect until the termination of the stay under this section.
(D) If the debtor cannot demonstrate to the satisfaction of the court that the situation giving rise to the lessor's certification under paragraph (1) did not exist or has been remedied—
(i) relief from the stay provided under subsection (a)(3) shall not be required to enable the lessor to proceed with the eviction; and
(ii) the clerk of the court shall immediately serve upon the lessor and the debtor a certified copy of the court's order upholding the lessor's certification.

(3) If the debtor fails to file, within 15 days, an objection under paragraph (2)(A)—
(A) subsection (b)(23) shall apply immediately upon such failure and relief from the stay provided under subsection (a)(3) shall not be required to enable the lessor to complete the process to recover full possession of the property; and
(B) the clerk of the court shall immediately serve upon the lessor and the debtor a certified copy of the docket indicating such failure.

(n)(1) Except as provided in paragraph (2), subsection (a) does not apply in a case in which the debtor—
(A) is a debtor in a small business case pending at the time the petition is filed;
(B) was a debtor in a small business case that was dismissed for any reason by an order that became final in the 2-year period ending on the date of the order for relief entered with respect to the petition;
(C) was a debtor in a small business case in which a plan was confirmed in the 2-year period ending on the date of the order for relief entered with respect to the petition; or
(D) is an entity that has acquired substantially all of the assets or business of a small business debtor described in subparagraph (A), (B), or (C), unless such entity establishes by a preponderance of the evidence that such entity acquired substantially all of the assets or business of such small business debtor in good faith and not for the purpose of evading this paragraph.

(2) Paragraph (1) does not apply—
(A) to an involuntary case involving no collusion by the debtor with creditors; or
(B) to the filing of a petition if—
(i) the debtor proves by a preponderance of the evidence that the filing of the petition resulted from circumstances beyond the control of the debtor not foreseeable at the time the case then pending was filed; and
(ii) it is more likely than not that the court will confirm a feasible plan, but not a liquidating plan, within a reasonable period of time.

(o) The exercise of rights not subject to the stay arising under subsection (a) pursuant to paragraph (6), (7), (17), or (27) of subsection (b) shall not be stayed by any order of a court or administrative agency in any proceeding under this title.

(Pub. L. 95–598, Nov. 6, 1978, 92 Stat. 2570; Pub. L. 97–222, §3, July 27, 1982, 96 Stat. 235; Pub. L. 98–353, title III, §§304, 363(b), 392, 441, July 10, 1984, 98 Stat. 352, 363, 365, 371; Pub. L. 99–509, title V, §5001(a), Oct. 21, 1986, 100 Stat. 1911; Pub. L. 99–554, title II, §§257(j), 283(d), Oct. 27, 1986, 100 Stat. 3115, 3116; Pub. L. 101–311, title I, §102, title II, §202, June 25, 1990, 104 Stat. 267, 269; Pub. L. 101–508, title III, §3007(a)(1), Nov. 5, 1990, 104 Stat. 1388–28; Pub. L. 103–394, title I, §§101, 116, title II, §§204(a), 218(b), title III, §304(b), title IV, §401, title V, §501(b)(2), (d)(7), Oct. 22, 1994, 108 Stat. 4107, 4119, 4122, 4128, 4132, 4141, 4142, 4144; Pub. L. 105–277, div. I, title VI, §603, Oct. 21, 1998, 112 Stat. 2681–886; Pub. L. 109–8, title I, §106(f), title II, §§214, 224(b), title III, §§302, 303, 305(1), 311, 320, title IV, §§401(b), 441, 444, title VII, §§709, 718, title IX, §907(d), (o)(1), (2), title XI, §1106, title XII, §1225, Apr. 20, 2005, 119 Stat. 41, 54, 64, 75, 77, 79, 84, 94, 104, 114, 117, 127, 131, 176, 181, 182, 192, 199; Pub. L. 109–304, §17(b)(1), Oct. 6, 2006, 120 Stat. 1706; Pub. L. 109–390, §5(a)(2), Dec. 12, 2006, 120 Stat. 2696; Pub. L. 111–327, §2(a)(12), Dec. 22, 2010, 124 Stat. 3558.)

Historical and Revision Notes
legislative statements
Section 362(a)(1) of the House amendment adopts the provision contained in the Senate amendment enjoining the commencement or continuation of a judicial, administrative, or other proceeding to recover a claim against the debtor that arose before the commencement of the case. The provision is beneficial and interacts with section 362(a)(6), which also covers assessment, to prevent harassment of the debtor with respect to pre-petition claims.

Section 362(a)(7) contains a provision contained in H.R. 8200 as passed by the House. The differing provision in the Senate amendment was rejected. It is not possible that a debt owing to the debtor may be offset against an interest in the debtor.

Section 362(a)(8) is new. The provision stays the commencement or continuation of any proceeding concerning the debtor before the U.S. Tax Court.

Section 362(b)(4) indicates that the stay under section 362(a)(1) does not apply to affect the commencement or continuation of an action or proceeding by a governmental unit to enforce the governmental unit's police or regulatory power. This section is intended to be given a narrow construction in order to permit governmental units to pursue actions to protect the public health and safety and not to apply to actions by a governmental unit to protect a pecuniary interest in property of the debtor or property of the estate.

Section 362(b)(6) of the House amendment adopts a provision contained in the Senate amendment restricting the exception to the automatic stay with respect to setoffs to permit only the setoff of mutual debts and claims. Traditionally, the right of setoff has been limited to mutual debts and claims and the lack of the clarifying term "mutual" in H.R. 8200 as passed by the House created an unintentional ambiguity. Section 362(b)(7) of the House amendment permits the issuance of a notice of tax deficiency. The House amendment rejects section 362(b)(7) in the Senate amendment. It would have permitted a particular governmental unit to obtain a pecuniary advantage without a hearing on the merits contrary to the exceptions contained in sections 362(b)(4) and (5).

Section 362(d) of the House amendment represents a compromise between comparable provisions in the House bill and Senate amendment. Under section

362(d)(1) of the House amendment, the court may terminate, annul, modify, or condition the automatic stay for cause, including lack of adequate protection of an interest in property of a secured party. It is anticipated that the Rules of Bankruptcy Procedure will provide that those hearings will receive priority on the calendar. Under section 362(d)(2) the court may alternatively terminate, annul, modify, or condition the automatic stay for cause including inadequate protection for the creditor. The court shall grant relief from the stay if there is no equity and it is not necessary to an effective reorganization of the debtor.

The latter requirement is contained in section 362(d)(2). This section is intended to solve the problem of real property mortgage foreclosures of property where the bankruptcy petition is filed on the eve of foreclosure. The section is not intended to apply if the business of the debtor is managing or leasing real property, such as a hotel operation, even though the debtor has no equity if the property is necessary to an effective reorganization of the debtor. Similarly, if the debtor does have an equity in the property, there is no requirement that the property be sold under section 363 of title 11 as would have been required by the Senate amendment.

Section 362(e) of the House amendment represents a modification of provisions in H.R. 8200 as passed by the House and the Senate amendment to make clear that a final hearing must be commenced within 30 days after a preliminary hearing is held to determine whether a creditor will be entitled to relief from the automatic stay. In order to insure that those hearings will in fact occur within such 30-day period, it is anticipated that the rules of bankruptcy procedure provide that such final hearings receive priority on the court calendar.

Section 362(g) places the burden of proof on the issue of the debtor's equity in collateral on the party requesting relief from the automatic stay and the burden on other issues on the debtor.

An amendment has been made to section 362(b) to permit the Secretary of the Department of Housing and Urban Development to commence an action to foreclose a mortgage or deed of trust. The commencement of such an action is necessary for tax purposes. The section is not intended to permit the continuation of such an action after it is commenced nor is the section to be construed to entitle the Secretary to take possession in lieu of foreclosure.

Automatic stay: Sections 362(b)(8) and (9) contained in the Senate amendment are largely deleted in the House amendment. Those provisions add to the list of actions not stayed (a) jeopardy assessments, (b) other assessments, and (c) the issuance of deficiency notices. In the House amendment, jeopardy assessments against property which ceases to be property of the estate is already authorized by section 362(c)(1). Other assessments are specifically stayed under section 362(a)(6), while the issuance of a deficiency notice is specifically permitted. Stay of the assessment and the permission to issue a statutory notice of a tax deficiency will permit the debtor to take his personal tax case to the Tax Court, if the bankruptcy judge authorizes him to do so (as explained more fully in the discussion of section 505).

senate report no. 95–989

The automatic stay is one of the fundamental debtor protections provided by the bankruptcy laws. It gives the debtor a breathing spell from his creditors. It stops all collection efforts, all harassment, and all foreclosure actions. It permits the debtor to attempt a repayment or reorganization plan, or simply to be relieved of the financial pressures that drove him into bankruptcy.

The action commenced by the party seeking relief from the stay is referred to as a motion to make it clear that at the expedited hearing under subsection (e), and at hearings on relief from the stay, the only issue will be the lack of adequate protection, the debtor's equity in the property, and the necessity of the property to an effective reorganization of the debtor, or the existence of other cause for relief from the stay. This hearing will not be the appropriate time at which to bring in other issues, such as counterclaims against the creditor, which, although relevant to the question of the amount of the debt, concern largely collateral or unrelated matters. This approach is consistent with that taken in cases such as *In re Essex Properties, Ltd.*, 430 F.Supp. 1112 (N.D.Cal.1977), that an action seeking relief from the stay is not the assertion of a claim which would give rise to the right or obligation to assert counterclaims. Those counterclaims are not to be handled in the summary fashion that the preliminary hearing under this provision will be. Rather, they will be the subject of more complete proceedings by the trustee to recover property of the estate or to object to the allowance of a claim. However, this would not preclude the party seeking continuance of the stay from presenting evidence on the existence of claims which the court may consider in exercising its discretion. What is precluded is a determination of such collateral claims on the merits at the hearing.

house report no. 95–595

Paragraph (7) [of subsec. (a)] stays setoffs of mutual debts and credits between the debtor and creditors. As with all other paragraphs of subsection (a), this paragraph does not affect the right of creditors. It simply stays its enforcement pending an orderly examination of the debtor's and creditors' rights.

Subsection (c) governs automatic termination of the stay. Subsections (d) through (g) govern termination of the stay by the court on the request of a party in interest. Subsection (d) requires the court, on request of a party in interest, to grant relief from the stay, such as by terminating, annulling, modifying, or conditioning the stay, for cause. The lack of adequate protection of an interest in property of the party requesting relief from the stay is one cause for relief, but is not the only cause. As noted above, a desire to permit an action to proceed to completion in another tribunal may provide another cause. Other causes might include the lack of any connection with or interference with the pending bankruptcy case. For example, a divorce or child custody proceeding involving the debtor may bear no relation to the bankruptcy case. In that case, it should not be stayed. A probate proceeding in which the debtor is the executor or administrator of another's estate usually will not be related to the bankruptcy case, and should not be stayed. Generally, proceedings in which the debtor is a fiduciary, or involving postpetition activities of the debtor, need not be stayed because they bear no relationship to the purpose of the automatic stay, which is debtor protection from his creditors. The facts of each request will determine whether relief is appropriate under the circumstances.

Subsection (e) provides a protection for secured creditors that is not available under present law. The subsection sets a time certain within which the bankruptcy court must rule on the adequacy of protection provided of the secured creditor's interest. If the court does not rule within 30 days from a request for relief from the stay, the stay is automatically terminated with respect to the property in question. In order to accommodate more complex cases, the subsection permits the court to make a preliminary ruling after a preliminary hearing. After a preliminary hearing, the court may continue the stay only if there is a reasonable likelihood that the party opposing relief from the stay will prevail at the final hearing. Because the stay is essentially an injunction, the three stages of the stay may be analogized to the three stages of an injunction. The filing of the petition which gives rise to the automatic stay is similar to a temporary restraining order. The preliminary hearing is similar to the hearing on a preliminary injunction, and the final hearing and order is similar to a permanent injunction. The main difference lies in which party must bring the issue before the court. While in the injunction setting, the party seeking the injunction must prosecute the action, in proceedings for relief from the automatic stay, the enjoined party must move. The difference does not, however, shift the burden of proof. Subsection (g) leaves that burden on the party opposing relief from the stay (that is, on the party seeking continuance of the injunction) on the issue of adequate protection.

At the expedited hearing under subsection (e), and at all hearings on relief from the stay, the only issue will be the claim of the creditor and the lack of adequate protection or existence of other cause for relief from the stay. This hearing will not be the appropriate time at which to bring in other issues, such as counterclaims against the creditor on largely unrelated matters. Those counterclaims are not to be handled in the summary fashion that the preliminary hearing under this provision will be. Rather, they will be the subject of more complete proceedings by the trustees to recover property of the estate or to object to the allowance of a claim.

References in Text

Section 5(a)(3) of the Securities Investor Protection Act of 1970, referred to in subsecs. (a) and (b), is classified to section 78eee(a)(3) of Title 15, Commerce and Trade.

The Social Security Act, referred to in subsec. (b)(2)(D) to (G), (28), is act Aug. 14, 1935, ch. 531, 49 Stat. 620. Titles IV, XI, and XVIII of the Act are classified generally to subchapters IV (§601 et seq.), XI (§1301 et seq.), and XVIII (§1395 et seq.), respectively, of chapter 7 of Title 42, The Public Health and Welfare. Sections 464, 466, and 1128B of the Act are classified to sections 664, 666, and 1320a–7b, respectively, of Title 42. For complete classification of this Act to the Code, see section 1305 of Title 42 and Tables.

The National Housing Act, referred in subsec. (b)(8), is act June 27, 1934, ch. 847, 48 Stat. 1246, which is classified principally to chapter 13 (§1701 et seq.) of Title 12, Banks and Banking. For complete classification of this Act to the Code, see section 1701 of Title 12 and Tables.

The Higher Education Act of 1965, referred to in subsec. (b)(16), is Pub. L. 89–329, Nov. 8, 1965, 79 Stat. 1219, which is classified generally to chapter 28 (§1001 et seq.) of Title 20, Education. Section 435(j) of the Act is classified to section 1085(j) of Title 20. For complete classification of this Act to the Code, see Short Title note set out under section 1001 of Title 20 and Tables.

The Internal Revenue Code of 1986, referred to in subsec. (b)(19), is classified generally to Title 26, Internal Revenue Code.

Section 408(b)(1) of the Employee Retirement Income Security Act of 1974, referred to in subsec. (b)(19)(A), is classified to section 1108(b)(1) of Title 29, Labor.

Amendments

2010—Subsec. (a)(8). Pub. L. 111–327, §2(a)(12)(A), substituted "tax liability of a debtor that is a corporation" for "corporate debtor's tax liability".

Subsec. (c)(3). Pub. L. 111–327, §2(a)(12)(B)(i), inserted "a" after "against" in introductory provisions.

Subsec. (c)(4)(A)(i). Pub. L. 111–327, §2(a)(12)(B)(ii), inserted "under a chapter other than chapter 7 after dismissal" after "refiled".

Subsec. (d)(4). Pub. L. 111–327, §2(a)(12)(C), substituted "hinder, or" for "hinder, and" in introductory provisions.

Subsec. (l)(2). Pub. L. 111–327, §2(a)(12)(D), substituted "nonbankruptcy" for "nonbankrupcty".

2006—Subsec. (b)(6), (7). Pub. L. 109–390, §5(a)(2)(A), added pars. (6) and (7) and struck out former pars. (6) and (7) which read as follows:

"(6) under subsection (a) of this section, of the setoff by a commodity broker, forward contract merchant, stockbroker, financial institution, financial participant, or securities clearing agency of any mutual debt and claim under or in connection with commodity contracts, as defined in section 761 of this title, forward contracts, or securities contracts, as defined in section 741 of this title, that constitutes the setoff of a claim against the debtor for a margin payment, as defined in section 101, 741, or 761 of this title, or settlement payment, as defined in section 101 or 741 of this title, arising out of commodity contracts, forward contracts, or securities contracts against cash, securities, or other property held by, pledged to, under the control of, or due from such commodity broker, forward contract merchant, stockbroker, financial institution, financial participant, or securities clearing agency to margin, guarantee, secure, or settle commodity contracts, forward contracts, or securities contracts;

"(7) under subsection (a) of this section, of the setoff by a repo participant or financial participant, of any mutual debt and claim under or in connection with repurchase agreements that constitutes the setoff of a claim against the debtor for a margin payment, as defined in section 741 or 761 of this title, or settlement payment, as defined in section 741 of this title, arising out of repurchase agreements against cash, securities, or other property held by, pledged to, under the control of, or due from such repo participant or financial participant to margin, guarantee, secure or settle repurchase agreements;".

Subsec. (b)(12). Pub. L. 109–304, §17(b)(1)(A), substituted "chapter 537 of title 46 or section 109(h) of title 49" for "section 207 or title XI of the Merchant Marine Act, 1936".

Subsec. (b)(13). Pub. L. 109–304, §17(b)(1)(B), substituted "chapter 537 of title 46" for "section 207 or title XI of the Merchant Marine Act, 1936".

Subsec. (b)(17). Pub. L. 109–390, §5(a)(2)(B), added par. (17) and struck out former par. (17) which read as follows: "under subsection (a), of the setoff by a swap participant or financial participant of a mutual debt and claim under or in connection with one or more swap agreements that constitutes the setoff of a claim against the debtor for any payment or other transfer of property due from the debtor under or in connection with any swap agreement against any payment due to the debtor from the swap participant or financial participant under or in connection with any swap agreement or against cash, securities, or other property held by, pledged to, under the control of, or due from such swap participant or financial participant to margin, guarantee, secure, or settle any swap agreement;".

Subsec. (b)(27). Pub. L. 109–390, §5(a)(2)(C), added par. (27) and struck out former par. (27) which read as follows: "under subsection (a), of the setoff by a master netting agreement participant of a mutual debt and claim under or in connection with one or more master netting agreements or any contract or agreement subject to such agreements that constitutes the setoff of a claim against the debtor for any payment or other transfer of property due from the debtor under or in connection with such agreements or any contract or agreement subject to such agreements against any payment due to the debtor from such master netting agreement participant under or in connection with such agreements or any contract or agreement subject to such agreements or against cash, securities, or other property held by, pledged to, under the control of, or due from such master netting agreement participant to margin, guarantee, secure, or settle such agreements or any contract or agreement subject to such agreements, to the extent that such participant is eligible to exercise such offset rights under paragraph (6), (7), or (17) for each individual contract covered by the master netting agreement in issue; and".

2005—Subsec. (a)(8). Pub. L. 109–8, §709, substituted "a corporate debtor's tax liability for a taxable period the bankruptcy court may determine or concerning the tax liability of a debtor who is an individual for a taxable period ending before the date of the order for relief under this title" for "the debtor".

Subsec. (b)(2). Pub. L. 109–8, §214, added par. (2) and struck out former par. (2) which read as follows: "under subsection (a) of this section—

"(A) of the commencement or continuation of an action or proceeding for—

"(i) the establishment of paternity; or

"(ii) the establishment or modification of an order for alimony, maintenance, or support; or

"(B) of the collection of alimony, maintenance, or support from property that is not property of the estate;".

Subsec. (b)(6). Pub. L. 109–8, §907(d)(1)(A), (o)(1), substituted "financial institution, financial participant," for "financial institutions," in two places and inserted ", pledged to, under the control of," after "held by".

Subsec. (b)(7). Pub. L. 109–8, §907(d)(1)(B), (o)(2), inserted "or financial participant" after "repo participant" in two places and ", pledged to, under the control of," after "held by".

Subsec. (b)(17). Pub. L. 109–8, §907(d)(1)(C), added par. (17) and struck out former par. (17) which read as follows: "under subsection (a) of this section, of the setoff by a swap participant, of any mutual debt and claim under or in connection with any swap agreement that constitutes the setoff of a claim against the debtor for any payment due from the debtor under or in connection with any swap agreement against any payment due to the debtor from the swap participant under or in connection with any swap agreement or against cash, securities, or other property of the debtor held by or due from such swap participant to guarantee, secure or settle any swap agreement;".

Subsec. (b)(18). Pub. L. 109–8, §1225, amended par. (18) generally. Prior to amendment, par. (18) read as follows: "under subsection (a) of the creation or perfection of a statutory lien for an ad valorem property tax imposed by the District of Columbia, or a political subdivision of a State, if such tax comes due after the filing of the petition;".

Subsec. (b)(19). Pub. L. 109–8, §224(b), added par. (19).

Subsec. (b)(20), (21). Pub. L. 109–8, §303(b), added pars. (20) and (21).

Subsec. (b)(22) to (24). Pub. L. 109–8, §311(a), added pars. (22) to (24).

Subsec. (b)(25). Pub. L. 109–8, §401(b), added par. (25).

Subsec. (b)(26). Pub. L. 109–8, §718, added par. (26).

Subsec. (b)(27). Pub. L. 109–8, §907(d)(1)(D), added par. (27).

Subsec. (b)(28). Pub. L. 109–8, §1106, added par. (28).

Subsec. (c). Pub. L. 109–8, §305(1)(A), substituted "(e), (f), and (h)" for "(e), and (f)" in introductory provisions.

Subsec. (c)(3), (4). Pub. L. 109–8, §302, added pars. (3) and (4).

Subsec. (d). Pub. L. 109–8, §303(a), added par. (4) and concluding provisions.

Subsec. (d)(3). Pub. L. 109–8, §444(1), inserted "or 30 days after the court determines that the debtor is subject to this paragraph, whichever is later" after "90-day period)" in introductory provisions.

Subsec. (d)(3)(B). Pub. L. 109–8, §444(2), added subpar. (B) and struck out former subpar. (B) which read as follows: "the debtor has commenced monthly payments to each creditor whose claim is secured by such real estate (other than a claim secured by a judgment lien or by an unmatured statutory lien), which payments are in an amount equal to interest at a current fair market rate on the value of the creditor's interest in the real estate; or".

Subsec. (e). Pub. L. 109–8, §320, designated existing provisions as par. (1) and added par. (2).

Subsec. (h). Pub. L. 109–8, §305(1)(C), added subsec. (h). Former subsec. (h) redesignated (k).

Subsecs. (i), (j). Pub. L. 109–8, §106(f), added subsecs. (i) and (j).

Subsec. (k). Pub. L. 109–8, §441(1), designated existing provisions as par. (1), substituted "Except as provided in paragraph (2), an" for "An", and added par. (2).

Pub. L. 109–8, §305(1)(B), redesignated subsec. (h) as (k).

Subsecs. (l), (m). Pub. L. 109–8, §311(b), added subsecs. (l) and (m).

Subsec. (n). Pub. L. 109–8, §441(2), added subsec. (n).

Subsec. (o). Pub. L. 109–8, §907(d)(2), added subsec. (o).

1998—Subsec. (b)(4), (5). Pub. L. 105–277 added par. (4) and struck out former pars. (4) and (5) which read as follows:

"(4) under subsection (a)(1) of this section, of the commencement or continuation of an action or proceeding by a governmental unit to enforce such governmental unit's police or regulatory power;

"(5) under subsection (a)(2) of this section, of the enforcement of a judgment, other than a money judgment, obtained in an action or proceeding by a governmental unit to enforce such governmental unit's police or regulatory power;".

1994—Subsecs. (a), (b). Pub. L. 103–394, §501(d)(7)(A), (B)(i), struck out "(15 U.S.C. 78eee(a)(3))" after "Act of 1970" in introductory provisions.

Subsec. (b)(2). Pub. L. 103–394, §304(b), amended par. (2) generally. Prior to amendment, par. (2) read as follows: "under subsection (a) of this section, of the collection of alimony, maintenance, or support from property that is not property of the estate;".

Subsec. (b)(3). Pub. L. 103–394, §204(a), inserted ", or to maintain or continue the perfection of," after "to perfect".

Subsec. (b)(6). Pub. L. 103–394, §501(b)(2)(A), substituted "section 761" for "section 761(4)", "section 741" for "section 741(7)", "section 101, 741, or 761" for "section 101(34), 741(5), or 761(15)", and "section 101 or 741" for "section 101(35) or 741(8)".

Subsec. (b)(7). Pub. L. 103–394, §501(b)(2)(B), substituted "section 741 or 761" for "section 741(5) or 761(15)" and "section 741" for "section 741(8)".

Subsec. (b)(9). Pub. L. 103–394, §116, amended par. (9) generally. Prior to amendment, par. (9) read as follows: "under subsection (a) of this section, of the issuance to the debtor by a governmental unit of a notice of tax deficiency;".

Subsec. (b)(10). Pub. L. 103–394, §501(d)(7)(B)(ii), struck out "or" at end.

Subsec. (b)(12). Pub. L. 103–394, §501(d)(7)(B)(iii), substituted "section 31325 of title 46" for "the Ship Mortgage Act, 1920 (46 App. U.S.C. 911 et seq.)" and struck out "(46 App. U.S.C. 1117 and 1271 et seq., respectively)" after "Act, 1936".

Subsec. (b)(13). Pub. L. 103–394, §501(d)(7)(B)(iv), substituted "section 31325 of title 46" for "the Ship Mortgage Act, 1920 (46 App. U.S.C. 911 et seq.)" and struck out "(46 App. U.S.C. 1117 and 1271 et seq., respectively)" after "Act, 1936" and "or" at end.

Subsec. (b)(14). Pub. L. 103–394, §501(d)(7)(B)(vii), amended par. (14) relating to the setoff by a swap participant of any mutual debt and claim under or in connection with a swap agreement by substituting "; or" for period at end, redesignating par. (14) as (17), and inserting it after par. (16).

Subsec. (b)(15). Pub. L. 103–394, §501(d)(7)(B)(v), struck out "or" at end.

Subsec. (b)(16). Pub. L. 103–394, §501(d)(7)(B)(vi), struck out "(20 U.S.C. 1001 et seq.)" after "Act of 1965" and substituted semicolon for period at end.

Subsec. (b)(17). Pub. L. 103–394, §501(d)(7)(B)(vii)(II), (III), redesignated par. (14) relating to the setoff by a swap participant of any mutual debt and claim under or in connection with a swap agreement as (17) and inserted it after par. (16).

Subsec. (b)(18). Pub. L. 103–394, §401, added par. (18).

Subsec. (d)(3). Pub. L. 103–394, §218(b), added par. (3).

Subsec. (e). Pub. L. 103–394, §101, in last sentence substituted "concluded" for "commenced" and inserted before period at end ", unless the 30-day period is extended with the consent of the parties in interest or for a specific time which the court finds is required by compelling circumstances".

1990—Subsec. (b)(6). Pub. L. 101–311, §202, inserted reference to sections 101(34) and 101(35) of this title.

Subsec. (b)(12). Pub. L. 101–508, §3007(a)(1)(A), which directed the striking of "or" after "State law;", could not be executed because of a prior amendment by Pub. L. 101–311. See below.

Pub. L. 101–311, §102(1), struck out "or" after "State law;".

Subsec. (b)(13). Pub. L. 101–508, §3007(a)(1)(B), which directed the substitution of a semicolon for period at end, could not be executed because of a prior amendment by Pub. L. 101–311. See below.

Pub. L. 101–311, §102(2), substituted "; or" for period at end.

Subsec. (b)(14) to (16). Pub. L. 101–508, §3007(a)(1)(C), added pars. (14) to (16). Notwithstanding directory language adding pars. (14) to (16) immediately following par. (13), pars. (14) to (16) were added after par. (14), as added by Pub. L. 101–311, to reflect the probable intent of Congress.

Pub. L. 101–311, §102(3), added par. (14) relating to the setoff by a swap participant of any mutual debt and claim under or in connection with a swap agreement. Notwithstanding directory language adding par. (14) at end of subsec. (b), par. (14) was added after par. (13) to reflect the probable intent of Congress.

1986—Subsec. (b). Pub. L. 99–509 inserted sentence at end.

Subsec. (b)(6). Pub. L. 99–554, §283(d)(1), substituted ", financial institutions" for "financial institution," in two places.

Subsec. (b)(9). Pub. L. 99–554, §283(d)(2), (3), struck out "or" at end of first par. (9) and redesignated as par. (10) the second par. (9) relating to leases of nonresidential property, which was added by section 363(b) of Pub. L. 98–353.

Subsec. (b)(10). Pub. L. 99–554, §283(d)(3), (4), redesignated as par. (10) the second par. (9) relating to leases of nonresidential property, added by section 363(b) of Pub. L. 99–353, and substituted "property; or" for "property.". Former par. (10) redesignated (11).

Subsec. (b)(11). Pub. L. 99–554, §283(d)(3), redesignated former par. (10) as (11).

Subsec. (b)(12), (13). Pub. L. 99–509 added pars. (12) and (13).

Subsec. (c)(2)(C). Pub. L. 99–554, §257(j), inserted reference to chapter 12 of this title.

1984—Subsec. (a)(1). Pub. L. 98–353, §441(a)(1), inserted "action or" after "other".

Subsec. (a)(3). Pub. L. 98–353, §441(a)(2), inserted "or to exercise control over property of the estate".

Subsec. (b)(3). Pub. L. 98–353, §441(b)(1), inserted "or to the extent that such act is accomplished within the period provided under section 547(e)(2)(A) of this title".

Subsec. (b)(6). Pub. L. 98–353, §441(b)(2), inserted "or due from" after "held by" and "financial institution," after "stockbroker" in two places, and substituted "secure, or settle commodity contracts" for "or secure commodity contracts".

Subsec. (b)(7) to (9). Pub. L. 98–353, §441(b)(3), (4), in par. (8) as redesignated by Pub. L. 98–353, §392, substituted "the" for "said" and struck out "or" the last place it appeared which probably meant "or" after "units;" that was struck out by Pub. L. 98–353, §363(b)(1); and, in par. (9), relating to notices of deficiencies, as redesignated by Pub. L. 98–353, §392, substituted a semicolon for the period.

Pub. L. 98–353, §392, added par. (7) and redesignated former pars. (7) and (8) as (8) and (9), respectively.

Pub. L. 98–353, §363(b), struck out "or" at end of par. (7), substituted "; or" for the period at end of par. (8), and added par. (9) relating to leases of nonresidential property.

Subsec. (b)(10). Pub. L. 98–353, §441(b)(5), added par. (10).

Subsec. (c)(2)(B). Pub. L. 98–353, §441(c), substituted "or" for "and".

Subsec. (d)(2). Pub. L. 98–353, §441(d), inserted "under subsection (a) of this section" after "property".

Subsec. (e). Pub. L. 98–353, §441(e), inserted "the conclusion of" after "pending" and substituted "The court shall order such stay continued in effect pending the conclusion of the final hearing under subsection (d) of this section if there is a reasonable likelihood that the party opposing relief from such stay will prevail at the conclusion of such final hearing. If the hearing under this subsection is a preliminary hearing, then such final hearing shall be commenced not later than thirty days after the conclusion of such preliminary hearing." for "If the hearing under this subsection is a preliminary hearing—

"(1) the court shall order such stay so continued if there is a reasonable likelihood that the party opposing relief from such stay will prevail at the final hearing under subsection (d) of this section; and

"(2) such final hearing shall be commenced within thirty days after such preliminary hearing."

Subsec. (f). Pub. L. 98–353, §441(f), substituted "Upon request of a party in interest, the court, with or" for "The court,".

Subsec. (h). Pub. L. 98–353, §304, added subsec. (h).

1982—Subsec. (a). Pub. L. 97–222, §3(a), inserted ", or an application filed under section 5(a)(3) of the Securities Investor Protection Act of 1970 (15 U.S.C. 78eee(a)(3))," after "this title" in provisions preceding par. (1).

Subsec. (b). Pub. L. 97–222, §3(b), inserted ", or of an application under section 5(a)(3) of the Securities Investor Protection Act of 1970 (15 U.S.C. 78eee(a)(3))," after "this title" in provisions preceding par. (1).

Subsec. (b)(6). Pub. L. 97–222, §3(c), substituted provisions that the filing of a bankruptcy petition would not operate as a stay, under subsec. (a) of this section, of the setoff by a commodity broker, forward contract merchant, stockbroker, or securities clearing agency of any mutual debt and claim under or in connection with commodity, forward, or securities contracts that constitutes the setoff of a claim against the debtor for a margin or settlement payment arising out of commodity, forward, or securities contracts against cash, securities, or other property held by any of the above agents to margin, guarantee, or secure commodity, forward, or securities contracts, for provisions that such filing would not operate as a stay under subsection (a)(7) of this section, of the setoff of any mutual debt and claim that are commodity futures contracts, forward commodity contracts, leverage transactions, options, warrants, rights to purchase or sell commodity futures contracts or securities, or options to purchase or sell commodities or securities.

Effective Date of 2006 Amendment

Amendment by Pub. L. 109–390 not applicable to any cases commenced under this title or to appointments made under any Federal or State law, before Dec. 12, 2006, see section 7 of Pub. L. 109–390, set out as a note under section 101 of this title.

Effective Date of 2005 Amendment

Amendment by Pub. L. 109–8 effective 180 days after Apr. 20, 2005, and not applicable with respect to cases commenced under this title before such effective date, except as otherwise provided, see section 1501 of Pub. L. 109–8, set out as a note under section 101 of this title.

Effective Date of 1994 Amendment

Amendment by Pub. L. 103–394 effective Oct. 22, 1994, and not applicable with respect to cases commenced under this title before Oct. 22, 1994, see section 702 of Pub. L. 103–394, set out as a note under section 101 of this title.

Effective Date of 1990 Amendment

Pub. L. 101–508, title III, §3007(a)(3), Nov. 5, 1990, 104 Stat. 1388–28, provided that: "The amendments made by this subsection [amending this section and section 541 of this title] shall be effective upon date of enactment of this Act [Nov. 5, 1990]."

Pub. L. 101–508, title III, §3008, Nov. 5, 1990, 104 Stat. 1388–29, provided that the amendments made by subtitle A (§§3001–3008) of title III of Pub. L. 101–508, amending this section, sections 541 and 1328 of this title, and sections 1078, 1078–1, 1078–7, 1085, 1088, and 1091 of Title 20, Education, and provisions set out as a note under section 1078–1 of Title 20, were to cease to be effective Oct. 1, 1996, prior to repeal by Pub. L. 102–325, title XV, §1558, July 23, 1992, 106 Stat. 841.

Effective Date of 1986 Amendment

Amendment by section 257 of Pub. L. 99–554 effective 30 days after Oct. 27, 1986, but not applicable to cases commenced under this title before that date, see section 302(a), (c)(1) of Pub. L. 99–554, set out as a note under section 581 of Title 28, Judiciary and Judicial Procedure.

Amendment by section 283 of Pub. L. 99–554 effective 30 days after Oct. 27, 1986, see section 302(a) of Pub. L. 99–554.

Pub. L. 99–509, title V, §5001(b), Oct. 21, 1986, 100 Stat. 1912, provided that: "The amendments made by subsection (a) of this section [amending this section] shall apply only to petitions filed under section 362 of title 11, United States Code, which are made after August 1, 1986."

Effective Date of 1984 Amendment

Amendment by Pub. L. 98–353 effective with respect to cases filed 90 days after July 10, 1984, see section 552(a) of Pub. L. 98–353, set out as a note under section 101 of this title.

Report to Congressional Committees

Pub. L. 99–509, title V, §5001(a), Oct. 21, 1986, 100 Stat. 1911, directed Secretary of Transportation and Secretary of Commerce, before July 1, 1989, to submit reports to Congress on the effects of amendments to 11 U.S.C. 362 by this subsection.

§363. Use, sale, or lease of property

(a) In this section, "cash collateral" means cash, negotiable instruments, documents of title, securities, deposit accounts, or other cash equivalents whenever acquired in which the estate and an entity other than the estate have an interest and includes the proceeds, products, offspring, rents, or profits of property and the fees, charges, accounts or other payments for the use or occupancy of rooms and other public facilities in hotels, motels, or other lodging properties subject to a security interest as provided in section 552(b) of this title, whether existing before or after the commencement of a case under this title.

(b)(1) The trustee, after notice and a hearing, may use, sell, or lease, other than in the ordinary course of business, property of the estate, except that if the debtor in connection with offering a product or a service discloses to an individual a policy prohibiting the transfer of personally identifiable information about individuals to persons that are not affiliated with the debtor and if such policy is in effect on the date of the commencement of the case, then the trustee may not sell or lease personally identifiable information to any person unless—

(A) such sale or such lease is consistent with such policy; or

(B) after appointment of a consumer privacy ombudsman in accordance with section 332, and after notice and a hearing, the court approves such sale or such lease—

(i) giving due consideration to the facts, circumstances, and conditions of such sale or such lease; and

(ii) finding that no showing was made that such sale or such lease would violate applicable nonbankruptcy law.

(2) If notification is required under subsection (a) of section 7A of the Clayton Act in the case of a transaction under this subsection, then—

(A) notwithstanding subsection (a) of such section, the notification required by such subsection to be given by the debtor shall be given by the trustee; and

(B) notwithstanding subsection (b) of such section, the required waiting period shall end on the 15th day after the date of the receipt, by the Federal Trade Commission and the Assistant Attorney General in charge of the Antitrust Division of the Department of Justice, of the notification required under such subsection (a), unless such waiting period is extended—

(i) pursuant to subsection (e)(2) of such section, in the same manner as such subsection (e)(2) applies to a cash tender offer;

(ii) pursuant to subsection (g)(2) of such section; or

(iii) by the court after notice and a hearing.

(c)(1) If the business of the debtor is authorized to be operated under section 721, 1108, 1203, 1204, or 1304 of this title and unless the court orders otherwise, the trustee may enter into transactions, including the sale or lease of property of the estate, in the ordinary course of business, without notice or a hearing, and may use property of the estate in the ordinary course of business without notice or a hearing.

(2) The trustee may not use, sell, or lease cash collateral under paragraph (1) of this subsection unless—

(A) each entity that has an interest in such cash collateral consents; or

(B) the court, after notice and a hearing, authorizes such use, sale, or lease in accordance with the provisions of this section.

(3) Any hearing under paragraph (2)(B) of this subsection may be a preliminary hearing or may be consolidated with a hearing under subsection (e) of this section, but shall be scheduled in accordance with the needs of the debtor. If the hearing under paragraph (2)(B) of this subsection is a preliminary hearing, the court may authorize such use, sale, or lease only if there is a reasonable likelihood that the trustee will prevail at the final hearing under subsection (e) of this section. The court shall act promptly on any request for authorization under paragraph (2)(B) of this subsection.

(4) Except as provided in paragraph (2) of this subsection, the trustee shall segregate and account for any cash collateral in the trustee's possession, custody, or control.

(d) The trustee may use, sell, or lease property under subsection (b) or (c) of this section—

(1) in the case of a debtor that is a corporation or trust that is not a moneyed business, commercial corporation, or trust, only in accordance with nonbankruptcy law applicable to the transfer of property by a debtor that is such a corporation or trust; and

(2) only to the extent not inconsistent with any relief granted under subsection (c), (d), (e), or (f) of section 362.

(e) Notwithstanding any other provision of this section, at any time, on request of an entity that has an interest in property used, sold, or leased, or proposed to be used, sold, or leased, by the trustee, the court, with or without a hearing, shall prohibit or condition such use, sale, or lease as is necessary to provide adequate protection of such interest. This subsection also applies to property that is subject to any unexpired lease of personal property (to the exclusion of such property being subject to an order to grant relief from the stay under section 362).

(f) The trustee may sell property under subsection (b) or (c) of this section free and clear of any interest in such property of an entity other than the estate, only if—

(1) applicable nonbankruptcy law permits sale of such property free and clear of such interest;

(2) such entity consents;

(3) such interest is a lien and the price at which such property is to be sold is greater than the aggregate value of all liens on such property;

(4) such interest is in bona fide dispute; or

(5) such entity could be compelled, in a legal or equitable proceeding, to accept a money satisfaction of such interest.

(g) Notwithstanding subsection (f) of this section, the trustee may sell property under subsection (b) or (c) of this section free and clear of any vested or contingent right in the nature of dower or curtesy.

(h) Notwithstanding subsection (f) of this section, the trustee may sell both the estate's interest, under subsection (b) or (c) of this section, and the interest of any co-owner in property in which the debtor had, at the time of the commencement of the case, an undivided interest as a tenant in common, joint tenant, or tenant by the entirety, only if—

(1) partition in kind of such property among the estate and such co-owners is impracticable;

(2) sale of the estate's undivided interest in such property would realize significantly less for the estate than sale of such property free of the interests of such co-owners;

(3) the benefit to the estate of a sale of such property free of the interests of co-owners outweighs the detriment, if any, to such co-owners; and

(4) such property is not used in the production, transmission, or distribution, for sale, of electric energy or of natural or synthetic gas for heat, light, or power.

(i) Before the consummation of a sale of property to which subsection (g) or (h) of this section applies, or of property of the estate that was community property of the debtor and the debtor's spouse immediately before the commencement of the case, the debtor's spouse, or a co-owner of such property, as the case may be, may purchase such property at the price at which such sale is to be consummated.

(j) After a sale of property to which subsection (g) or (h) of this section applies, the trustee shall distribute to the debtor's spouse or the co-owners of such property, as the case may be, and to the estate, the proceeds of such sale, less the costs and expenses, not including any compensation of the trustee, of such sale, according to the interests of such spouse or co-owners, and of the estate.

(k) At a sale under subsection (b) of this section of property that is subject to a lien that secures an allowed claim, unless the court for cause orders otherwise the holder of such claim may bid at such sale, and, if the holder of such claim purchases such property, such holder may offset such claim against the purchase price of such property.

(l) Subject to the provisions of section 365, the trustee may use, sell, or lease property under subsection (b) or (c) of this section, or a plan under chapter 11, 12, or 13 of this title may provide for the use, sale, or lease of property, notwithstanding any provision in a contract, a lease, or applicable law that is conditioned on the insolvency or financial condition of the debtor, on the commencement of a case under this title concerning the debtor, or on the appointment of or the taking possession by a trustee in a case under this title or a custodian, and that effects, or gives an option to effect, a forfeiture, modification, or termination of the debtor's interest in such property.

(m) The reversal or modification on appeal of an authorization under subsection (b) or (c) of this section of a sale or lease of property does not affect the validity of a sale or lease under such authorization to an entity that purchased or leased such property in good faith, whether or not such entity knew of the pendency of the appeal, unless such authorization and such sale or lease were stayed pending appeal.

(n) The trustee may avoid a sale under this section if the sale price was controlled by an agreement among potential bidders at such sale, or may recover from a party to such agreement any amount by which the value of the property sold exceeds the price at which such sale was consummated, and may recover any costs, attorneys' fees, or expenses incurred in avoiding such sale or recovering such amount. In addition to any recovery under the preceding sentence, the court may grant judgment for punitive damages in favor of the estate and against any such party that entered into such an agreement in willful disregard of this subsection.

(o) Notwithstanding subsection (f), if a person purchases any interest in a consumer credit transaction that is subject to the Truth in Lending Act or any interest in a consumer credit contract (as defined in section 433.1 of title 16 of the Code of Federal Regulations (January 1, 2004), as amended from time to time), and if such interest is purchased through a sale under this section, then such person shall remain subject to all claims and defenses that are related to such consumer credit transaction or such consumer credit contract, to the same extent as such person would be subject to such claims and defenses of the consumer had such interest been purchased at a sale not under this section.

(p) In any hearing under this section—

(1) the trustee has the burden of proof on the issue of adequate protection; and

(2) the entity asserting an interest in property has the burden of proof on the issue of the validity, priority, or extent of such interest.

(Pub. L. 95–598, Nov. 6, 1978, 92 Stat. 2572; Pub. L. 98–353, title III, §442, July 10, 1984, 98 Stat. 371; Pub. L. 99–554, title II, §257(k), Oct. 27, 1986, 100 Stat. 3115; Pub. L. 103–394, title I, §109, title II, §§214(b), 219(c), title V, §501(d)(8), Oct. 22, 1994, 108 Stat. 4113, 4126, 4129, 4144; Pub. L. 109–8, title II, §§204, 231(a), title XII, §1221(a), Apr. 20, 2005, 119 Stat. 49, 72, 195; Pub. L. 111–327, §2(a)(13), Dec. 22, 2010, 124 Stat. 3559.)

Historical and Revision Notes

legislative statements

Section 363(a) of the House amendment defines "cash collateral" as defined in the Senate amendment. The broader definition of "soft collateral" contained in H.R. 8200 as passed by the House is deleted to remove limitations that were placed on the use, lease, or sale of inventory, accounts, contract rights, general intangibles, and chattel paper by the trustee or debtor in possession.

Section 363(c)(2) of the House amendment is derived from the Senate amendment. Similarly, sections 363(c)(3) and (4) are derived from comparable provisions in the Senate amendment in lieu of the contrary procedure contained in section 363(c) as passed by the House. The policy of the House amendment will generally require the court to schedule a preliminary hearing in accordance with the needs of the debtor to authorize the trustee or debtor in possession to use, sell, or lease cash collateral. The trustee or debtor in possession may use, sell, or lease cash collateral in the ordinary course of business only "after notice and a hearing."

Section 363(f) of the House amendment adopts an identical provision contained in the House bill, as opposed to an alternative provision contained in the Senate amendment.

Section 363(h) of the House amendment adopts a new paragraph (4) representing a compromise between the House bill and Senate amendment. The provision adds a limitation indicating that a trustee or debtor in possession sell jointly owned property only if the property is not used in the production, transmission, or distribution for sale, of electric energy or of natural or synthetic gas for heat, light, or power. This limitation is intended to protect public utilities from being deprived of power sources because of the bankruptcy of a joint owner.

Section 363(k) of the House amendment is derived from the third sentence of section 363(e) of the Senate amendment. The provision indicates that a secured creditor may bid in the full amount of the creditor's allowed claim, including the secured portion and any unsecured portion thereof in the event the creditor is undersecured, with respect to property that is subject to a lien that secures the allowed claim of the sale of the property.

senate report no. 95–989

This section defines the right and powers of the trustee with respect to the use, sale or lease of property and the rights of other parties that have interests in the property involved. It applies in both liquidation and reorganization cases.

Subsection (a) defines "cash collateral" as cash, negotiable instruments, documents of title, securities, deposit accounts, or other cash equivalents in which the estate and an entity other than the estate have an interest, such as a lien or a co-ownership interest. The definition is not restricted to property of the estate that is cash collateral on the date of the filing of the petition. Thus, if "non-cash" collateral is disposed of and the proceeds come within the definition of "cash collateral" as set forth in this subsection, the proceeds would be cash collateral as long as they remain subject to the original lien on the "non-cash" collateral under section 552(b). To illustrate, rents received from real property before or after the commencement of the case would be cash collateral to the extent that they are subject to a lien.

Subsection (b) permits the trustees to use, sell, or lease, other than in the ordinary course of business, property of the estate upon notice and opportunity for objections and hearing thereon.

Subsection (c) governs use, sale, or lease in the ordinary course of business. If the business of the debtor is authorized to be operated under §721, 1108, or 1304 of the bankruptcy code, then the trustee may use, sell, or lease property in the ordinary course of business or enter into ordinary course transactions without need for notice and hearing. This power is subject to several limitations. First, the court may restrict the trustee's powers in the order authorizing operation of the business. Second, with respect to cash collateral, the trustee may not use, sell, or lease cash collateral except upon court authorization after notice and a hearing, or with the consent of each entity that has an interest in such cash collateral. The same preliminary hearing procedure in the automatic stay section applies to a hearing under this subsection. In addition, the trustee is required to segregate and account for any cash collateral in the trustee's possession, custody, or control.

Under subsections (d) and (e), the use, sale, or lease of property is further limited by the concept of adequate protection. Sale, use, or lease of property in which an entity other than the estate has an interest may be effected only to the extent not inconsistent with any relief from the stay granted to that interest's holder. Moreover, the court may prohibit or condition the use, sale, or lease as is necessary to provide adequate protection of that interest. Again, the trustee has the burden of proof on the issue of adequate protection. Subsection (e) also provides that where a sale of the property is proposed, an entity that has an interest in such property may bid at the sale thereof and set off against the purchase price up to the amount of such entity's claim. No prior valuation under section 506(a) would limit this bidding right, since the bid at the sale would be determinative of value.

Subsection (f) permits sale of property free and clear of any interest in the property of an entity other than the estate. The trustee may sell free and clear if applicable nonbankruptcy law permits it, if the other entity consents, if the interest is a lien and the sale price of the property is greater than the amount secured by the lien, if the interest is in bona fide dispute, or if the other entity could be compelled to accept a money satisfaction of the interest in a legal or equitable proceeding. Sale under this subsection is subject to the adequate protection requirement. Most often, adequate protection in connection with a sale free and clear of other interests will be to have those interests attach to the proceeds of the sale.

At a sale free and clear of other interests, any holder of any interest in the property being sold will be permitted to bid. If that holder is the high bidder, he will be permitted to offset the value of his interest against the purchase price of the property. Thus, in the most common situation, a holder of a lien on property being sold may bid at the sale and, if successful, may offset the amount owed to him that is secured by the lien on the property (but may not offset other amounts owed to him) against the purchase price, and be liable to the trustee for the balance of the sale price, if any.

Subsection (g) permits the trustee to sell free and clear of any vested or contingent right in the nature of dower or curtesy.

Subsection (h) permits sale of a co-owner's interest in property in which the debtor had an undivided ownership interest such as a joint tenancy, a tenancy in common, or a tenancy by the entirety. Such a sale is permissible only if partition is impracticable, if sale of the estate's interest would realize significantly less for the estate that sale of the property free of the interests of the co-owners, and if the benefit to the estate of such a sale outweighs any detriment to the co-owners. This subsection does not apply to a co-owner's interest in a public utility when a disruption of the utilities services could result.

Subsection (i) provides protections for co-owners and spouses with dower, curtesy, or community property rights. It gives a right of first refusal to the co-owner or spouse at the price at which the sale is to be consummated.

Subsection (j) requires the trustee to distribute to the spouse or co-owner the appropriate portion of the proceeds of the sale, less certain administrative expenses.

Subsection (k) [enacted as (l)] permits the trustee to use, sell, or lease property notwithstanding certain bankruptcy or ipso facto clauses that terminate the debtor's interest in the property or that work a forfeiture or modification of that interest. This subsection is not as broad as the anti-ipso facto provision in proposed 11 U.S.C. 541(c)(1).

Subsection (l) [enacted as (m)] protects good faith purchasers of property sold under this section from a reversal on appeal of the sale authorization, unless the authorization for the sale and the sale itself were stayed pending appeal. The purchaser's knowledge of the appeal is irrelevant to the issue of good faith.

Subsection (m) [enacted as (n)] is directed at collusive bidding on property sold under this section. It permits the trustee to void a sale if the price of the sale was controlled by an agreement among potential bidders. The trustees may also recover the excess of the value of the property over the purchase price, and may recover any costs, attorney's fees, or expenses incurred in voiding the sale or recovering the difference. In addition, the court is authorized to grant judgment in favor of the estate and against the collusive bidder if the agreement controlling the sale price was entered into in willful disregard of this subsection. The subsection does not specify the precise measure of damages, but simply provides for punitive damages, to be fixed in light of the circumstances.

References in Text

Section 7A of the Clayton Act, referred to in subsec. (b)(2), is classified to section 18a of Title 15, Commerce and Trade.

The Truth in Lending Act, referred to in subsec. (o), is title I of Pub. L. 90–321, May 29, 1968, 82 Stat. 146, as amended, which is classified generally to subchapter I (§1601 et seq.) of chapter 41 of Title 15, Commerce and Trade. For complete classification of this Act to the Code, see Short Title note set out under section 1601 of Title 15 and Tables.

Amendments

2010—Subsec. (d). Pub. L. 111–327, §2(a)(13)(A), struck out "only" before dash at end of introductory provisions.

Subsec. (d)(1). Pub. L. 111–327, §2(a)(13)(B), amended par. (1) generally. Prior to amendment, par. (1) read as follows: "in accordance with applicable nonbankruptcy law that governs the transfer of property by a corporation or trust that is not a moneyed, business, or commercial corporation or trust; and".

Subsec. (d)(2). Pub. L. 111–327, §2(a)(13)(C), inserted "only" before "to the extent".

2005—Subsec. (b)(1). Pub. L. 109–8, §231(a), substituted ", except that if the debtor in connection with offering a product or a service discloses to an individual a policy prohibiting the transfer of personally identifiable information about individuals to persons that are not affiliated with the debtor and if such policy is in effect on the date of the commencement of the case, then the trustee may not sell or lease personally identifiable information to any person unless—" and subpars. (A) and (B) for period at end.

Subsec. (d). Pub. L. 109–8, §1221(a), substituted "only—" and pars. (1) and (2) for "only to the extent not inconsistent with any relief granted under section 362(c), 362(d), 362(e), or 362(f) of this title."

Subsecs. (o), (p). Pub. L. 109–8, §204, added subsec. (o) and redesignated former subsec. (o) as (p).

1994—Subsec. (a). Pub. L. 103–394, §214(b), inserted "and the fees, charges, accounts or other payments for the use or occupancy of rooms and other public facilities in hotels, motels, or other lodging properties" after "property".

Subsec. (b)(2). Pub. L. 103–394, §§109, 501(d)(8)(A), struck out "(15 U.S.C. 18a)" after "Clayton Act" and amended subpars. (A) and (B) generally. Prior to amendment, subpars. (A) and (B) read as follows:

"(A) notwithstanding subsection (a) of such section, such notification shall be given by the trustee; and

"(B) notwithstanding subsection (b) of such section, the required waiting period shall end on the tenth day after the date of the receipt of such notification, unless the court, after notice and hearing, orders otherwise."

Subsec. (c)(1). Pub. L. 103–394, §501(d)(8)(B), substituted "1203, 1204, or 1304" for "1304, 1203, or 1204".

Subsec. (e). Pub. L. 103–394, §219(c), inserted at end "This subsection also applies to property that is subject to any unexpired lease of personal property (to the exclusion of such property being subject to an order to grant relief from the stay under section 362)."

1986—Subsec. (c)(1). Pub. L. 99–554, §257(k)(1), inserted reference to sections 1203 and 1204 of this title.

Subsec. (l). Pub. L. 99–554, §257(k)(2), inserted reference to chapter 12.

1984—Subsec. (a). Pub. L. 98–353, §442(a), inserted "whenever acquired" after "equivalents" and "and includes the proceeds, products, offspring, rents, or profits of property subject to a security interest as provided in section 552(b) of this title, whether existing before or after the commencement of a case under this title" after "interest".

Subsec. (b). Pub. L. 98–353, §442(b), designated existing provisions as par. (1) and added par. (2).

Subsec. (e). Pub. L. 98–353, §442(c), inserted ", with or without a hearing," after "court" and struck out "In any hearing under this section, the trustee has the burden of proof on the issue of adequate protection".

Subsec. (f)(3). Pub. L. 98–353, §442(d), substituted "all liens on such property" for "such interest".

Subsec. (h). Pub. L. 98–353, §442(e), substituted "at the time of" for "immediately before".

Subsec. (j). Pub. L. 98–353, §442(f), substituted "compensation" for "compenation".

Subsec. (k). Pub. L. 98–353, §442(g), substituted "unless the court for cause orders otherwise the holder of such claim may bid at such sale, and, if the holder" for "if the holder".

Subsec. (l). Pub. L. 98–353, §442(h), substituted "Subject to the provisions of section 365, the trustee" for "The trustee", "condition" for "conditions", "or the taking" for "a taking", and "interest" for "interests".

Subsec. (n). Pub. L. 98–353, §442(i), substituted "avoid" for "void", "avoiding" for "voiding", and "In addition to any recovery under the preceding sentence, the court may grant judgment for punitive damages in favor of the estate and against any such party that entered into such an agreement in willful disregard of this subsection" for "The court may grant judgment in favor of the estate and against any such party that entered into such agreement in willful disregard of this subsection for punitive damages in addition to any recovery under the preceding sentence".

Subsec. (o). Pub. L. 98–353, §442(j), added subsec. (o).

Effective Date of 2005 Amendment

Pub. L. 109–8, title XII, §1221(d), Apr. 20, 2005, 119 Stat. 196, provided that: "The amendments made by this section [amending this section and sections 541 and 1129 of this title and enacting provisions set out as a note under this section] shall apply to a case pending under title 11, United States Code, on the date of enactment of this Act [Apr. 20, 2005], or filed under that title on or after that date of enactment, except that the court shall not confirm a plan under chapter 11 of title 11, United States Code, without considering whether this section would substantially affect the rights of a party in interest who first acquired rights with respect to the debtor after the date of the filing of the petition. The parties who may appear and be heard in a proceeding under this section include the attorney general of the State in which the debtor is incorporated, was formed, or does business."

Amendment by sections 204 and 231(a) of Pub. L. 109–8 effective 180 days after Apr. 20, 2005, and not applicable with respect to cases commenced under this title before such effective date, except as otherwise provided, see section 1501 of Pub. L. 109–8, set out as a note under section 101 of this title.

Effective Date of 1994 Amendment

Amendment by Pub. L. 103–394 effective Oct. 22, 1994, and not applicable with respect to cases commenced under this title before Oct. 22, 1994, see section 702 of Pub. L. 103–394, set out as a note under section 101 of this title.

Effective Date of 1986 Amendment

Amendment by Pub. L. 99–554 effective 30 days after Oct. 27, 1986, but not applicable to cases commenced under this title before that date, see section 302(a), (c)(1) of Pub. L. 99–554, set out as a note under section 581 of Title 28, Judiciary and Judicial Procedure.

Effective Date of 1984 Amendment

Amendment by Pub. L. 98–353 effective with respect to cases filed 90 days after July 10, 1984, see section 552(a) of Pub. L. 98–353, set out as a note under section 101 of this title.

Construction of Section 1221 of Pub. L. 109–8

Pub. L. 109–8, title XII, §1221(e), Apr. 20, 2005, 119 Stat. 196, provided that: "Nothing in this section [see Effective Date of 2005 Amendment note above] shall be construed to require the court in which a case under chapter 11 of title 11, United States Code, is pending to remand or refer any proceeding, issue, or controversy to any other court or to require the approval of any other court for the transfer of property."

§364. Obtaining credit

(a) If the trustee is authorized to operate the business of the debtor under section 721, 1108, 1203, 1204, or 1304 of this title, unless the court orders otherwise, the trustee may obtain unsecured credit and incur unsecured debt in the ordinary course of business allowable under section 503(b)(1) of this title as an administrative expense.

(b) The court, after notice and a hearing, may authorize the trustee to obtain unsecured credit or to incur unsecured debt other than under subsection (a) of this section, allowable under section 503(b)(1) of this title as an administrative expense.

(c) If the trustee is unable to obtain unsecured credit allowable under section 503(b)(1) of this title as an administrative expense, the court, after notice and a hearing, may authorize the obtaining of credit or the incurring of debt—

(1) with priority over any or all administrative expenses of the kind specified in section 503(b) or 507(b) of this title;

(2) secured by a lien on property of the estate that is not otherwise subject to a lien; or

(3) secured by a junior lien on property of the estate that is subject to a lien.

(d)(1) The court, after notice and a hearing, may authorize the obtaining of credit or the incurring of debt secured by a senior or equal lien on property of the estate that is subject to a lien only if—

(A) the trustee is unable to obtain such credit otherwise; and

(B) there is adequate protection of the interest of the holder of the lien on the property of the estate on which such senior or equal lien is proposed to be granted.

(2) In any hearing under this subsection, the trustee has the burden of proof on the issue of adequate protection.

(e) The reversal or modification on appeal of an authorization under this section to obtain credit or incur debt, or of a grant under this section of a priority or a lien, does not affect the validity of any debt so incurred, or any priority or lien so granted, to an entity that extended such credit in good faith, whether or not such entity knew of the pendency of the appeal, unless such authorization and the incurring of such debt, or the granting of such priority or lien, were stayed pending appeal.

(f) Except with respect to an entity that is an underwriter as defined in section 1145(b) of this title, section 5 of the Securities Act of 1933, the Trust Indenture Act of 1939, and any State or local law requiring registration for offer or sale of a security or registration or licensing of an issuer of, underwriter of, or broker or dealer in, a security does not apply to the offer or sale under this section of a security that is not an equity security.

(Pub. L. 95–598, Nov. 6, 1978, 92 Stat. 2574; Pub. L. 99–554, title II, §257(l), Oct. 27, 1986, 100 Stat. 3115; Pub. L. 103–394, title V, §501(d)(9), Oct. 22, 1994, 108 Stat. 4144.)

Historical and Revision Notes

legislative statements

Section 364(f) of the House amendment is new. This provision continues the exemption found in section 3(a)(7) of the Securities Act of 1933 [15 U.S.C. 77c(a)(7)] for certificates of indebtedness issued by a trustee in bankruptcy. The exemption applies to any debt security issued under section 364 of title 11. The section does not intend to change present law which exempts such securities from the Trust Indenture Act, 15 U.S.C. 77aaa, et seq. (1976).

senate report no. 95–989

This section is derived from provisions in current law governing certificates of indebtedness, but is much broader. It governs all obtaining of credit and incurring of debt by the estate.

Subsection (a) authorizes the obtaining of unsecured credit and the incurring of unsecured debt in the ordinary course of business if the business of the debtor is authorized to be operated under section 721, 1108, or 1304. The debts so incurred are allowable as administrative expenses under section 503(b)(1). The court may limit the estate's ability to incur debt under this subsection.

Subsection (b) permits the court to authorize the trustee to obtain unsecured credit and incur unsecured debts other than in the ordinary course of business, such as in order to wind up a liquidation case, or to obtain a substantial loan in an operating case. Debt incurred under this subsection is allowable as an administrative expense under section 503(b)(1).

Subsection (c) is closer to the concept of certificates of indebtedness in current law. It authorizes the obtaining of credit and the incurring of debt with some special priority, if the trustee is unable to obtain unsecured credit under subsection (a) or (b). The various priorities are (1) with priority over any or all administrative expenses: (2) secured by a lien on unencumbered property of the estate; or (3) secured by a junior lien on encumbered property. The priorities granted under this subsection do not interfere with existing property rights.

Subsection (d) grants the court the authority to authorize the obtaining of credit and the incurring of debt with a superiority, that is a lien on encumbered property that is senior or equal to the existing lien on the property. The court may authorize such a superpriority only if the trustee is otherwise unable to obtain credit, and if there is adequate protection of the original lien holder's interest. Again, the trustee has the burden of proof on the issue of adequate protection.

Subsection (e) provides the same protection for credit extenders pending an appeal of an authorization to incur debt as is provided under section 363(l) for purchasers: the credit is not affected on appeal by reversal of the authorization and the incurring of the debt were stayed pending appeal. The protection runs to a good faith lender, whether or not he knew of the pendency of the appeal.

A claim arising as a result of lending or borrowing under this section will be a priority claim, as defined in proposed section 507(a)(1), even if the claim is granted a super-priority over administrative expenses and is to be paid in advance of other first priority claims.

References in Text

Section 5 of the Securities Act of 1933, referred to in subsec. (f), is classified to section 77e of Title 15, Commerce and Trade.

The Trust Indenture Act of 1939, referred to in subsec. (f), is title III of act May 27, 1933, ch. 38, as added Aug. 3, 1939, ch. 411, 53 Stat. 1149, as amended, which is classified generally to subchapter III (§77aaa et seq.) of chapter 2A of Title 15. For complete classification of this Act to the Code, see section 77aaa of Title 15 and Tables.

Amendments

1994—Subsec. (a). Pub. L. 103–394, §501(d)(9)(A), substituted "1203, 1204, or 1304" for "1304, 1203, or 1204".

Subsec. (f). Pub. L. 103–394, §501(d)(9)(B), struck out "(15 U.S.C. 77e)" after "Act of 1933" and "(15 U.S.C. 77aaa et seq.)" after "Act of 1939".

1986—Subsec. (a). Pub. L. 99–554 inserted reference to sections 1203 and 1204 of this title.

Effective Date of 1994 Amendment

Amendment by Pub. L. 103–394 effective Oct. 22, 1994, and not applicable with respect to cases commenced under this title before Oct. 22, 1994, see section 702 of Pub. L. 103–394, set out as a note under section 101 of this title.

Effective Date of 1986 Amendment

Amendment by Pub. L. 99–554 effective 30 days after Oct. 27, 1986, but not applicable to cases commenced under this title before that date, see section 302(a), (c)(1) of Pub. L. 99–554, set out as a note under section 581 of Title 28, Judiciary and Judicial Procedure.

§365. Executory contracts and unexpired leases

(a) Except as provided in sections 765 and 766 of this title and in subsections (b), (c), and (d) of this section, the trustee, subject to the court's approval, may assume or reject any executory contract or unexpired lease of the debtor.

(b)(1) If there has been a default in an executory contract or unexpired lease of the debtor, the trustee may not assume such contract or lease unless, at the time of assumption of such contract or lease, the trustee—

(A) cures, or provides adequate assurance that the trustee will promptly cure, such default other than a default that is a breach of a provision relating to the satisfaction of any provision (other than a penalty rate or penalty provision) relating to a default arising from any failure to perform nonmonetary obligations under an unexpired lease of real property, if it is impossible for the trustee to cure such default by performing nonmonetary acts at and after the time of assumption, except that if such default arises from a failure to operate in accordance with a nonresidential real property lease, then such default shall be cured by performance at and after the time of assumption in accordance with such lease, and pecuniary losses resulting from such default shall be compensated in accordance with the provisions of this paragraph;

(B) compensates, or provides adequate assurance that the trustee will promptly compensate, a party other than the debtor to such contract or lease, for any actual pecuniary loss to such party resulting from such default; and

(C) provides adequate assurance of future performance under such contract or lease.

(2) Paragraph (1) of this subsection does not apply to a default that is a breach of a provision relating to—

(A) the insolvency or financial condition of the debtor at any time before the closing of the case;

(B) the commencement of a case under this title;

(C) the appointment of or taking possession by a trustee in a case under this title or a custodian before such commencement; or

(D) the satisfaction of any penalty rate or penalty provision relating to a default arising from any failure by the debtor to perform nonmonetary obligations under the executory contract or unexpired lease.

(3) For the purposes of paragraph (1) of this subsection and paragraph (2)(B) of subsection (f), adequate assurance of future performance of a lease of real property in a shopping center includes adequate assurance—

(A) of the source of rent and other consideration due under such lease, and in the case of an assignment, that the financial condition and operating performance of the proposed assignee and its guarantors, if any, shall be similar to the financial condition and operating performance of the debtor and its guarantors, if any, as of the time the debtor became the lessee under the lease;

(B) that any percentage rent due under such lease will not decline substantially;

(C) that assumption or assignment of such lease is subject to all the provisions thereof, including (but not limited to) provisions such as a radius, location, use, or exclusivity provision, and will not breach any such provision contained in any other lease, financing agreement, or master agreement relating to such shopping center; and

(D) that assumption or assignment of such lease will not disrupt any tenant mix or balance in such shopping center.

(4) Notwithstanding any other provision of this section, if there has been a default in an unexpired lease of the debtor, other than a default of a kind specified in paragraph (2) of this subsection, the trustee may not require a lessor to provide services or supplies incidental to such lease before assumption of such lease unless the lessor is compensated under the terms of such lease for any services and supplies provided under such lease before assumption of such lease.

(c) The trustee may not assume or assign any executory contract or unexpired lease of the debtor, whether or not such contract or lease prohibits or restricts assignment of rights or delegation of duties, if—

(1)(A) applicable law excuses a party, other than the debtor, to such contract or lease from accepting performance from or rendering performance to an entity other than the debtor or the debtor in possession, whether or not such contract or lease prohibits or restricts assignment of rights or delegation of duties; and

(B) such party does not consent to such assumption or assignment; or

(2) such contract is a contract to make a loan, or extend other debt financing or financial accommodations, to or for the benefit of the debtor, or to issue a security of the debtor; or

(3) such lease is of nonresidential real property and has been terminated under applicable nonbankruptcy law prior to the order for relief.

(d)(1) In a case under chapter 7 of this title, if the trustee does not assume or reject an executory contract or unexpired lease of residential real property or of personal property of the debtor within 60 days after the order for relief, or within such additional time as the court, for cause, within such 60-day period, fixes, then such contract or lease is deemed rejected.

(2) In a case under chapter 9, 11, 12, or 13 of this title, the trustee may assume or reject an executory contract or unexpired lease of residential real property or of personal property of the debtor at any time before the confirmation of a plan but the court, on the request of any party to such contract or lease, may order the trustee to determine within a specified period of time whether to assume or reject such contract or lease.

(3) The trustee shall timely perform all the obligations of the debtor, except those specified in section 365(b)(2), arising from and after the order for relief under any unexpired lease of nonresidential real property, until such lease is assumed or rejected, notwithstanding section 503(b)(1) of this title. The court may extend, for cause, the time for performance of any such obligation that arises within 60 days after the date of the order for relief, but the time for performance shall not be extended beyond such 60-day period. This subsection shall not be deemed to affect the trustee's obligations under the provisions of subsection (b) or (f) of this section. Acceptance of any such performance does not constitute waiver or relinquishment of the lessor's rights under such lease or under this title.

(4)(A) Subject to subparagraph (B), an unexpired lease of nonresidential real property under which the debtor is the lessee shall be deemed rejected, and the trustee shall immediately surrender that nonresidential real property to the lessor, if the trustee does not assume or reject the unexpired lease by the earlier of—

(i) the date that is 120 days after the date of the order for relief; or

(ii) the date of the entry of an order confirming a plan.

(B)(i) The court may extend the period determined under subparagraph (A), prior to the expiration of the 120-day period, for 90 days on the motion of the trustee or lessor for cause.

(ii) If the court grants an extension under clause (i), the court may grant a subsequent extension only upon prior written consent of the lessor in each instance.

(5) The trustee shall timely perform all of the obligations of the debtor, except those specified in section 365(b)(2), first arising from or after 60 days after the order for relief in a case under chapter 11 of this title under an unexpired lease of personal property (other than personal property leased to an individual primarily for personal, family, or household purposes), until such lease is assumed or rejected notwithstanding section 503(b)(1) of this title, unless the court, after notice and a hearing and based on the equities of the case, orders otherwise with respect to the obligations or timely performance thereof. This subsection shall not be deemed to affect the trustee's obligations under the provisions of subsection (b) or (f). Acceptance of any such performance does not constitute waiver or relinquishment of the lessor's rights under such lease or under this title.

(e)(1) Notwithstanding a provision in an executory contract or unexpired lease, or in applicable law, an executory contract or unexpired lease of the debtor may not be terminated or modified, and any right or obligation under such contract or lease may not be terminated or modified, at any time after the commencement of the case solely because of a provision in such contract or lease that is conditioned on—

(A) the insolvency or financial condition of the debtor at any time before the closing of the case;

(B) the commencement of a case under this title; or

(C) the appointment of or taking possession by a trustee in a case under this title or a custodian before such commencement.

(2) Paragraph (1) of this subsection does not apply to an executory contract or unexpired lease of the debtor, whether or not such contract or lease prohibits or restricts assignment of rights or delegation of duties, if—

(A)(i) applicable law excuses a party, other than the debtor, to such contract or lease from accepting performance from or rendering performance to the trustee or to an assignee of such contract or lease, whether or not such contract or lease prohibits or restricts assignment of rights or delegation of duties; and

(ii) such party does not consent to such assumption or assignment; or

(B) such contract is a contract to make a loan, or extend other debt financing or financial accommodations, to or for the benefit of the debtor, or to issue a security of the debtor.

(f)(1) Except as provided in subsections (b) and (c) of this section, notwithstanding a provision in an executory contract or unexpired lease of the debtor, or in applicable law, that prohibits, restricts, or conditions the assignment of such contract or lease, the trustee may assign such contract or lease under paragraph (2) of this subsection.

(2) The trustee may assign an executory contract or unexpired lease of the debtor only if—

(A) the trustee assumes such contract or lease in accordance with the provisions of this section; and

(B) adequate assurance of future performance by the assignee of such contract or lease is provided, whether or not there has been a default in such contract or lease.

(3) Notwithstanding a provision in an executory contract or unexpired lease of the debtor, or in applicable law that terminates or modifies, or permits a party other than the debtor to terminate or modify, such contract or lease or a right or obligation under such contract or lease on account of an assignment of such contract or lease, such contract, lease, right, or obligation may not be terminated or modified under such provision because of the assumption or assignment of such contract or lease by the trustee.

(g) Except as provided in subsections (h)(2) and (i)(2) of this section, the rejection of an executory contract or unexpired lease of the debtor constitutes a breach of such contract or lease—

(1) if such contract or lease has not been assumed under this section or under a plan confirmed under chapter 9, 11, 12, or 13 of this title, immediately before the date of the filing of the petition; or

(2) if such contract or lease has been assumed under this section or under a plan confirmed under chapter 9, 11, 12, or 13 of this title—

(A) if before such rejection the case has not been converted under section 1112, 1208, or 1307 of this title, at the time of such rejection; or

(B) if before such rejection the case has been converted under section 1112, 1208, or 1307 of this title—

(i) immediately before the date of such conversion, if such contract or lease was assumed before such conversion; or

(ii) at the time of such rejection, if such contract or lease was assumed after such conversion.

(h)(1)(A) If the trustee rejects an unexpired lease of real property under which the debtor is the lessor and—

(i) if the rejection by the trustee amounts to such a breach as would entitle the lessee to treat such lease as terminated by virtue of its terms, applicable nonbankruptcy law, or any agreement made by the lessee, then the lessee under such lease may treat such lease as terminated by the rejection; or

(ii) if the term of such lease has commenced, the lessee may retain its rights under such lease (including rights such as those relating to the amount and timing of payment of rent and other amounts payable by the lessee and any right of use, possession, quiet enjoyment, subletting, assignment, or hypothecation) that are in or appurtenant to the real property for the balance of the term of such lease and for any renewal or extension of such rights to the extent that such rights are enforceable under applicable nonbankruptcy law.

(B) If the lessee retains its rights under subparagraph (A)(ii), the lessee may offset against the rent reserved under such lease for the balance of the term after the date of the rejection of such lease and for the term of any renewal or extension of such lease, the value of any damage caused by the nonperformance after the date of such rejection, of any obligation of the debtor under such lease, but the lessee shall not have any other right against the estate or the debtor on account of any damage occurring after such date caused by such nonperformance.

(C) The rejection of a lease of real property in a shopping center with respect to which the lessee elects to retain its rights under subparagraph (A)(ii) does not affect the enforceability under applicable nonbankruptcy law of any provision in the lease pertaining to radius, location, use, exclusivity, or tenant mix or balance.

(D) In this paragraph, "lessee" includes any successor, assign, or mortgagee permitted under the terms of such lease.

(2)(A) If the trustee rejects a timeshare interest under a timeshare plan under which the debtor is the timeshare interest seller and—

(i) if the rejection amounts to such a breach as would entitle the timeshare interest purchaser to treat the timeshare plan as terminated under its terms, applicable nonbankruptcy law, or any agreement made by timeshare interest purchaser, the timeshare interest purchaser under the timeshare plan may treat the timeshare plan as terminated by such rejection; or

(ii) if the term of such timeshare interest has commenced, then the timeshare interest purchaser may retain its rights in such timeshare interest for the balance of such term and for any term of renewal or extension of such timeshare interest to the extent that such rights are enforceable under applicable nonbankruptcy law.

(B) If the timeshare interest purchaser retains its rights under subparagraph (A), such timeshare interest purchaser may offset against the moneys due for such timeshare interest, for the balance of the term after the date of the rejection of such timeshare interest, and the term of any renewal or extension of such timeshare interest, the value of any damage caused by the nonperformance after the date of such rejection, of any obligation of the debtor under such timeshare plan, but the timeshare interest purchaser shall not have any right against the estate or the debtor on account of any damage occurring after such date caused by such nonperformance.

(i)(1) If the trustee rejects an executory contract of the debtor for the sale of real property or for the sale of a timeshare interest under a timeshare plan, under which the purchaser is in possession, such purchaser may treat such contract as terminated, or, in the alternative, may remain in possession of such real property or timeshare interest.

(2) If such purchaser remains in possession—

(A) such purchaser shall continue to make all payments due under such contract, but may, offset against such payments any damages occurring after the date of the rejection of such contract caused by the nonperformance of any obligation of the debtor after such date, but such purchaser does not have any rights against the estate on account of any damages arising after such date from such rejection, other than such offset; and

(B) the trustee shall deliver title to such purchaser in accordance with the provisions of such contract, but is relieved of all other obligations to perform under such contract.

(j) A purchaser that treats an executory contract as terminated under subsection (i) of this section, or a party whose executory contract to purchase real property from the debtor is rejected and under which such party is not in possession, has a lien on the interest of the debtor in such property for the recovery of any portion of the purchase price that such purchaser or party has paid.

(k) Assignment by the trustee to an entity of a contract or lease assumed under this section relieves the trustee and the estate from any liability for any breach of such contract or lease occurring after such assignment.

(l) If an unexpired lease under which the debtor is the lessee is assigned pursuant to this section, the lessor of the property may require a deposit or other security for the performance of the debtor's obligations under the lease substantially the same as would have been required by the landlord upon the initial leasing to a similar tenant.

(m) For purposes of this section 365 and sections 541(b)(2) and 362(b)(10), leases of real property shall include any rental agreement to use real property.

(n)(1) If the trustee rejects an executory contract under which the debtor is a licensor of a right to intellectual property, the licensee under such contract may elect—

(A) to treat such contract as terminated by such rejection if such rejection by the trustee amounts to such a breach as would entitle the licensee to treat such contract as terminated by virtue of its own terms, applicable nonbankruptcy law, or an agreement made by the licensee with another entity; or

(B) to retain its rights (including a right to enforce any exclusivity provision of such contract, but excluding any other right under applicable nonbankruptcy law to specific performance of such contract) under such contract and under any agreement supplementary to such contract, to such intellectual property (including any embodiment of such intellectual property to the extent protected by applicable nonbankruptcy law), as such rights existed immediately before the case commenced, for—

(i) the duration of such contract; and

(ii) any period for which such contract may be extended by the licensee as of right under applicable nonbankruptcy law.

(2) If the licensee elects to retain its rights, as described in paragraph (1)(B) of this subsection, under such contract—

(A) the trustee shall allow the licensee to exercise such rights;

(B) the licensee shall make all royalty payments due under such contract for the duration of such contract and for any period described in paragraph (1)(B) of this subsection for which the licensee extends such contract; and

(C) the licensee shall be deemed to waive—

(i) any right of setoff it may have with respect to such contract under this title or applicable nonbankruptcy law; and

(ii) any claim allowable under section 503(b) of this title arising from the performance of such contract.

(3) If the licensee elects to retain its rights, as described in paragraph (1)(B) of this subsection, then on the written request of the licensee the trustee shall—

(A) to the extent provided in such contract, or any agreement supplementary to such contract, provide to the licensee any intellectual property (including such embodiment) held by the trustee; and

(B) not interfere with the rights of the licensee as provided in such contract, or any agreement supplementary to such contract, to such intellectual property (including such embodiment) including any right to obtain such intellectual property (or such embodiment) from another entity.

(4) Unless and until the trustee rejects such contract, on the written request of the licensee the trustee shall—

(A) to the extent provided in such contract or any agreement supplementary to such contract—

(i) perform such contract; or

(ii) provide to the licensee such intellectual property (including any embodiment of such intellectual property to the extent protected by applicable nonbankruptcy law) held by the trustee; and

(B) not interfere with the rights of the licensee as provided in such contract, or any agreement supplementary to such contract, to such intellectual property (including such embodiment), including any right to obtain such intellectual property (or such embodiment) from another entity.

(o) In a case under chapter 11 of this title, the trustee shall be deemed to have assumed (consistent with the debtor's other obligations under section 507), and shall immediately cure any deficit under, any commitment by the debtor to a Federal depository institutions regulatory agency (or predecessor to such agency) to maintain the capital of an insured depository institution, and any claim for a subsequent breach of the obligations thereunder shall be entitled to priority under section 507. This subsection shall not extend any commitment that would otherwise be terminated by any act of such an agency.

(p)(1) If a lease of personal property is rejected or not timely assumed by the trustee under subsection (d), the leased property is no longer property of the estate and the stay under section 362(a) is automatically terminated.

(2)(A) If the debtor in a case under chapter 7 is an individual, the debtor may notify the creditor in writing that the debtor desires to assume the lease. Upon being so notified, the creditor may, at its option, notify the debtor that it is willing to have the lease assumed by the debtor and may condition such assumption on cure of any outstanding default on terms set by the contract.

(B) If, not later than 30 days after notice is provided under subparagraph (A), the debtor notifies the lessor in writing that the lease is assumed, the liability under the lease will be assumed by the debtor and not by the estate.

(C) The stay under section 362 and the injunction under section 524(a)(2) shall not be violated by notification of the debtor and negotiation of cure under this subsection.

(3) In a case under chapter 11 in which the debtor is an individual and in a case under chapter 13, if the debtor is the lessee with respect to personal property and the lease is not assumed in the plan confirmed by the court, the lease is deemed rejected as of the conclusion of the hearing on confirmation. If the lease is rejected, the stay under section 362 and any stay under section 1301 is automatically terminated with respect to the property subject to the lease.

(Pub. L. 95–598, Nov. 6, 1978, 92 Stat. 2574; Pub. L. 98–353, title III, §§362, 402–404, July 10, 1984, 98 Stat. 361, 367; Pub. L. 99–554, title II, §§257(j), (m), 283(e), Oct. 27, 1986, 100 Stat. 3115, 3117; Pub. L. 100–506, §1(b), Oct. 18, 1988, 102 Stat. 2538; Pub. L. 101–647, title XXV, §2522(c), Nov. 29, 1990, 104 Stat. 4866; Pub. L. 102–365, §19(b)–(e), Sept. 3, 1992, 106 Stat. 982–984; Pub. L. 103–394, title II, §§205(a), 219(a), (b), title V, §501(d)(10), Oct. 22, 1994, 108 Stat. 4122, 4128, 4145; Pub. L. 103–429, §1, Oct. 31, 1994, 108 Stat. 4377; Pub. L. 109–8, title III, §§309(b), 328(a), title IV, §404, Apr. 20, 2005, 119 Stat. 82, 100, 104.)

Historical and Revision Notes
legislative statements

Section 365(b)(3) represents a compromise between H.R. 8200 as passed by the House and the Senate amendment. The provision adopts standards contained in section 365(b)(5) of the Senate amendment to define adequate assurance of future performance of a lease of real property in a shopping center.

Section 365(b)(4) of the House amendment indicates that after default the trustee may not require a lessor to supply services or materials without assumption unless the lessor is compensated as provided in the lease.

Section 365(c)(2) and (3) likewise represent a compromise between H.R. 8200 as passed by the House and the Senate amendment. Section 365(c)(2) is derived from section 365(b)(4) of the Senate amendment but does not apply to a contract to deliver equipment as provided in the Senate amendment. As contained in the House amendment, the provision prohibits a trustee or debtor in possession from assuming or assigning an executory contract of the debtor to make a loan, or extend other debt financing or financial accommodations, to or for the benefit of the debtor, or the issuance of a security of the debtor.

Section 365(e) is a refinement of comparable provisions contained in the House bill and Senate amendment. Sections 365(e)(1) and (2)(A) restate section 365(e) of H.R. 8200 as passed by the House. Sections 365(e)(2)(B) expands the section to permit termination of an executory contract or unexpired lease of the debtor if such contract is a contract to make a loan, or extend other debt financing or financial accommodations, to or for the benefit of the debtor, or for the issuance of a security of the debtor.

Characterization of contracts to make a loan, or extend other debt financing or financial accommodations, is limited to the extension of cash or a line of credit and is not intended to embrace ordinary leases or contracts to provide goods or services with payments to be made over time.

Section 365(f) is derived from H.R. 8200 as passed by the House. Deletion of language in section 365(f)(3) of the Senate amendment is done as a matter of style. Restrictions with respect to assignment of an executory contract or unexpired lease are superfluous since the debtor may assign an executory contract or unexpired lease of the debtor only if such contract is first assumed under section 364(f)(2)(A) of the House amendment.

Section 363(h) of the House amendment represents a modification of section 365(h) of the Senate amendment. The House amendment makes clear that in the case of a bankrupt lessor, a lessee may remain in possession for the balance of the term of a lease and any renewal or extension of the term only to the extent that such renewal or extension may be obtained by the lessee without the permission of the landlord or some third party under applicable non-bankruptcy law.

senate report no. 95–989

Subsection (a) of this section authorizes the trustee, subject to the court's approval, to assume or reject an executory contract or unexpired lease. Though there is no precise definition of what contracts are executory, it generally includes contracts on which performance remains due to some extent on both sides. A note is not usually an executory contract if the only performance that remains is repayment. Performance on one side of the contract would have been completed and the contract is no longer executory.

Because of the volatile nature of the commodities markets and the special provisions governing commodity broker liquidations in subchapter IV of chapter 7, the provisions governing distribution in section 765(a) will govern if any conflict between those provisions and the provisions of this section arise.

Subsections (b), (c), and (d) provide limitations on the trustee's powers. Subsection (b) requires the trustee to cure any default in the contract or lease and to provide adequate assurance of future performance if there has been a default, before he may assume. This provision does not apply to defaults under ipso facto or bankruptcy clauses, which is a significant departure from present law.

Subsection (b)(3) permits termination of leases entered into prior to the effective date of this title in liquidation cases if certain other conditions are met.

Subsection (b)(4) [enacted as (c)(2)] prohibits the trustee's assumption of an executory contract requiring the other party to make a loan or deliver equipment to or to issue a security of the debtor. The purpose of this subsection is to make it clear that a party to a transaction which is based upon the financial strength of a debtor should not be required to extend new credit to the debtor whether in the form of loans, lease financing, or the purchase or discount of notes.

Subsection (b)(5) provides that in lease situations common to shopping centers, protections must be provided for the lessor if the trustee assumes the lease, including protection against decline in percentage rents, breach of agreements with other tenants, and preservation of the tenant mix. Protection for tenant mix will not be required in the office building situation.

Subsection (c) prohibits the trustee from assuming or assigning a contract or lease if applicable nonbankruptcy law excuses the other party from performance to someone other than the debtor, unless the other party consents. This prohibition applies only in the situation in which applicable law excuses the other party from performance independent of any restrictive language in the contract or lease itself.

Subsection (d) places time limits on assumption and rejection. In a liquidation case, the trustee must assume within 60 days (or within an additional 60 days, if the court, for cause, extends the time). If not assumed, the contract or lease is deemed rejected. In a rehabilitation case, the time limit is not fixed in the bill. However, if the other party to the contract or lease requests the court to fix a time, the court may specify a time within which the trustee must act. This provision will prevent parties in contractual or lease relationships with the debtor from being left in doubt concerning their status vis-a-vis the estate.

Subsection (e) invalidates ipso facto or bankruptcy clauses. These clauses, protected under present law, automatically terminate the contract or lease, or permit the other contracting party to terminate the contract or lease, in the event of bankruptcy. This frequently hampers rehabilitation efforts. If the trustee may assume or assign the contract under the limitations imposed by the remainder of the section, the contract or lease may be utilized to assist in the debtor's rehabilitation or liquidation.

The unenforcibility [sic] of ipso facto or bankruptcy clauses proposed under this section will require the courts to be sensitive to the rights of the nondebtor party to executory contracts and unexpired leases. If the trustee is to assume a contract or lease, the court will have to insure that the trustee's performance under the contract or lease gives the other contracting party the full benefit of his bargain.

This subsection does not limit the application of an ipso facto or bankruptcy clause if a new insolvency or receivership occurs after the bankruptcy case is closed. That is, the clause is not invalidated in toto, but merely made inapplicable during the case for the purposes of disposition of the executory contract or unexpired lease.

Subsection (f) partially invalidates restrictions on assignment of contracts or leases by the trustee to a third party. The subsection imposes two restrictions on the trustee: he must first assume the contract or lease, subject to all the restrictions on assumption found in the section, and adequate assurance of future performance must be provided to the other contracting party. Paragraph (3) of the subsection invalidates contractual provisions that permit termination or modification in the event of an assignment, as contrary to the policy of this subsection.

Subsection (g) defines the time as of which a rejection of an executory contract or unexpired lease constitutes a breach of the contract or lease. Generally, the breach is as of the date immediately preceding the date of the petition. The purpose is to treat rejection claims as prepetition claims. The remainder of the subsection specifies different times for cases that are converted from one chapter to another. The provisions of this subsection are not a substantive authorization to breach or reject an assumed contract. Rather, they prescribe the rules for the allowance of claims in case an assumed contract is breached, or if a case under chapter 11 in which a contract has been assumed is converted to a case under chapter 7 in which the contract is rejected.

Subsection (h) protects real property lessees of the debtor if the trustee rejects an unexpired lease under which the debtor is the lessor (or sublessor). The subsection permits the lessee to remain in possession of the leased property or to treat the lease as terminated by the rejection. The balance of the term of the lease referred to in paragraph (1) will include any renewal terms that are enforceable by the tenant, but not renewal terms if the landlord had an option to terminate. Thus, the tenant will not be deprived of his estate for the term for which he bargained. If the lessee remains in possession, he may offset the rent reserved under the lease against damages caused by the rejection, but does not have any affirmative rights against the estate for any damages after the rejection that result from the rejection.

Subsection (i) gives a purchaser of real property under a land installment sales contract similar protection. The purchaser, if the contract is rejected, may remain in possession or may treat the contract as terminated. If the purchaser remains in possession, he is required to continue to make the payments due, but may offset damages that occur after rejection. The trustee is required to deliver title, but is relieved of all other obligations to perform.

A purchaser that treats the contract as terminated is granted a lien on the property to the extent of the purchase price paid. A party with a contract to purchase land from the debtor has a lien on the property to secure the price already paid, if the contract is rejected and the purchaser is not yet in possession.

Subsection (k) relieves the trustee and the estate of liability for a breach of an assigned contract or lease that occurs after the assignment.

house report no. 95–595

Subsection (c) prohibits the trustee from assuming or assigning a contract or lease if applicable nonbankruptcy law excuses the other party from performance to someone other than the debtor, unless the other party consents. This prohibition applies only in the situation in which applicable law excuses the other party from performance independent of any restrictive language in the contract or lease itself. The purpose of this subsection, at least in part, is to prevent the trustee from requiring new advances of money or other property. The section permits the trustee to continue to use and pay for property already advanced, but is not designed to permit the trustee to demand new loans or additional transfers of property under lease commitments.

Thus, under this provision, contracts such as loan commitments and letters of credit are nonassignable, and may not be assumed by the trustee.

Subsection (e) invalidates ipso facto or bankruptcy clauses. These clauses, protected under present law, automatically terminate the contract or lease, or permit the other contracting party to terminate the contract or lease, in the event of bankruptcy. This frequently hampers rehabilitation efforts. If the trustee may assume or assign the contract under the limitations imposed by the remainder of the section, then the contract or lease may be utilized to assist in the debtor's rehabilitation or liquidation.

The unenforceability of ipso facto or bankruptcy clauses proposed under this section will require the courts to be sensitive to the rights of the nondebtor party to executory contracts and unexpired leases. If the trustee is to assume a contract or lease, the courts will have to insure that the trustee's performance under the contract or lease gives the other contracting party the full benefit of his bargain. An example of the complexity that may arise in these situations and the need for a determination of all aspects of a particular executory contract or unexpired lease is the shopping center lease under which the debtor is a tenant in a shopping center.

A shopping center is often a carefully planned enterprise, and though it consists of numerous individual tenants, the center is planned as a single unit, often subject to a master lease or financing agreement. Under these agreements, the tenant mix in a shopping center may be as important to the lessor as the actual promised rental payments, because certain mixes will attract higher patronage of the stores in the center, and thus a higher rental for the landlord from those stores that are subject to a percentage of gross receipts rental agreement. Thus, in order to assure a landlord of his bargained for exchange, the court would have to consider such factors as the nature of the business to be conducted by the trustee or his assignee, whether that business complies with the requirements of any master agreement, whether the kind of business proposed will generate gross sales in an amount such that the percentage rent specified in the lease is substantially the same as what would have been provided by the debtor, and whether the business proposed to be conducted would result in a breach of other clauses in master agreements relating, for example, to tenant mix and location.

This subsection does not limit the application of an ipso facto or bankruptcy clause to a new insolvency or receivership after the bankruptcy case is closed. That is, the clause is not invalidated in toto, but merely made inapplicable during the case for the purpose of disposition of the executory contract or unexpired lease.

Amendments

2005—Subsec. (b)(1)(A). Pub. L. 109–8, §328(a)(1)(A), inserted before semicolon at end "other than a default that is a breach of a provision relating to the satisfaction of any provision (other than a penalty rate or penalty provision) relating to a default arising from any failure to perform nonmonetary obligations under an unexpired lease of real property, if it is impossible for the trustee to cure such default by performing nonmonetary acts at and after the time of assumption, except that if such default arises from a failure to operate in accordance with a nonresidential real property lease, then such default shall be cured by performance at and after the time of assumption in accordance with such lease, and pecuniary losses resulting from such default shall be compensated in accordance with the provisions of this paragraph".

Subsec. (b)(2)(D). Pub. L. 109–8, §328(a)(1)(B), substituted "penalty rate or penalty provision" for "penalty rate or provision".

Subsec. (c)(4). Pub. L. 109–8, §328(a)(2), struck out par. (4) which read as follows: "such lease is of nonresidential real property under which the debtor is the lessee of an aircraft terminal or aircraft gate at an airport at which the debtor is the lessee under one or more additional nonresidential leases of an aircraft terminal or aircraft gate and the trustee, in connection with such assumption or assignment, does not assume all such leases or does not assume and assign all of such leases to the same person, except that the trustee may assume or assign less than all of such leases with the airport operator's written consent."

Subsec. (d)(4). Pub. L. 109–8, §404(a), amended par. (4) generally. Prior to amendment, par. (4) read as follows: "Notwithstanding paragraphs (1) and (2), in a case under any chapter of this title, if the trustee does not assume or reject an unexpired lease of nonresidential real property under which the debtor is the lessee within 60 days after the date of the order for relief, or within such additional time as the court, for cause, within such 60-day period, fixes, then such lease is deemed rejected, and the trustee shall immediately surrender such nonresidential real property to the lessor."

Subsec. (d)(5) to (10). Pub. L. 109–8, §328(a)(3), redesignated par. (10) as (5) and struck out former pars. (5) to (9) which related to rejection of leases under which the debtor is an affected air carrier that is the lessee of an aircraft terminal or aircraft gate.

Subsec. (f)(1). Pub. L. 109–8, §404(b), substituted "provided in subsections (b) and" for "provided in subsection".

Pub. L. 109–8, §328(a)(4), struck out "; except that the trustee may not assign an unexpired lease of nonresidential real property under which the debtor is an affected air carrier that is the lessee of an aircraft terminal or aircraft gate if there has occurred a termination event" before period at end.

Subsec. (p). Pub. L. 109–8, §309(b), added subsec. (p).

1994—Subsec. (b)(2)(D). Pub. L. 103–394, §219(a), added subpar. (D).

Subsec. (d)(6)(C). Pub. L. 103–429, §1(1), substituted "section 40102(a) of title 49" for "section 101 of the Federal Aviation Act of 1958 (49 App. U.S.C. 1301)".

Pub. L. 103–394, §501(d)(10)(A), which directed the substitution of "section 40102 of title 49" for "the Federal Aviation Act of 1958 (49 U.S.C. 1301)", could not be executed because the phrase "(49 U.S.C. 1301)" did not appear in text.

Subsec. (d)(10). Pub. L. 103–394, §219(b), added par. (10).

Subsec. (g)(2)(A), (B). Pub. L. 103–394, §501(d)(10)(B), substituted "1208, or 1307" for "1307, or 1208".

Subsec. (h). Pub. L. 103–394, §205(a), amended subsec. (h) generally. Prior to amendment, subsec. (h) read as follows:

"(h)(1) If the trustee rejects an unexpired lease of real property of the debtor under which the debtor is the lessor, or a timeshare interest under a timeshare plan under which the debtor is the timeshare interest seller, the lessee or timeshare interest purchaser under such lease or timeshare plan may treat such lease or timeshare plan as terminated by such rejection, where the disaffirmance by the trustee amounts to such a breach as would entitle the lessee or timeshare interest purchaser to treat such lease or timeshare plan as terminated by virtue of its own terms, applicable nonbankruptcy law, or other agreements the lessee or timeshare interest purchaser has made with other parties; or, in the alternative, the lessee or timeshare interest purchaser may remain in possession of the leasehold or timeshare interest under any lease or timeshare plan the term of which has commenced for the balance of such term and for any renewal or extension of such term that is enforceable by such lessee or timeshare interest purchaser under applicable nonbankruptcy law.

"(2) If such lessee or timeshare interest purchaser remains in possession as provided in paragraph (1) of this subsection, such lessee or timeshare interest purchaser may offset against the rent reserved under such lease or moneys due for such timeshare interest for the balance of the term after the date of the rejection of such lease or timeshare interest, and any such renewal or extension thereof, any damages occurring after such date caused by the nonperformance of any obligation of the debtor under such lease or timeshare plan after such date, but such lessee or timeshare interest purchaser does not have any rights against the estate on account of any damages arising after such date from such rejection, other than such offset."

Subsec. (n)(1)(B). Pub. L. 103–394, §501(d)(10)(C), substituted "a right to" for "a right to to".

Subsec. (o). Pub. L. 103–394, §501(d)(10)(D), substituted "a Federal depository institutions regulatory agency (or predecessor to such agency)" for "the Federal Deposit Insurance Corporation, the Resolution Trust Corporation, the Director of the Office of Thrift Supervision, the Comptroller of the Currency, or the Board of Governors of the Federal Reserve System, or its predecessors or successors,".

Subsec. (p). Pub. L. 103–429, §1(2), which directed the amendment of subsec. (p) by substituting "section 40102(a) of title 49" for "section 101(3) of the Federal

Aviation Act of 1958", could not be executed because subsec. (p) was repealed by Pub. L. 103–394, §501(d)(10)(E). See below.

Pub. L. 103–394, §501(d)(10)(E), struck out subsec. (p), which read as follows: "In this section, 'affected air carrier' means an air carrier, as defined in section 101(3) of the Federal Aviation Act of 1958, that holds 65 percent or more in number of the aircraft gates at an airport—

"(1) which is a Large Air Traffic Hub as defined by the Federal Aviation Administration in Report FAA–AP 92–1, February 1992; and

"(2) all of whose remaining aircraft gates are leased or under contract on the date of enactment of this subsection."

1992—Subsec. (c)(4). Pub. L. 102–365, §19(c), added par. (4).

Subsec. (d)(5) to (9). Pub. L. 102–365, §19(b), added pars. (5) to (9).

Subsec. (f)(1). Pub. L. 102–365, §19(d), substituted for period at end "; except that the trustee may not assign an unexpired lease of nonresidential real property under which the debtor is an affected air carrier that is the lessee of an aircraft terminal or aircraft gate if there has occurred a termination event."

Subsec. (p). Pub. L. 102–365, §19(e), added subsec. (p).

1990—Subsec. (o). Pub. L. 101–647 added subsec. (o).

1988—Subsec. (n). Pub. L. 100–506 added subsec. (n).

1986—Subsec. (c)(1)(A). Pub. L. 99–554, §283(e)(1), struck out "or an assignee of such contract or lease" after "debtor in possession".

Subsec. (c)(3). Pub. L. 99–554, §283(e)(2), inserted "is" after "lease" and "and" after "property".

Subsecs. (d)(2), (g)(1). Pub. L. 99–554, §257(j), (m)(1), inserted reference to chapter 12.

Subsec. (g)(2). Pub. L. 99–554, §257(m)(2), inserted references to chapter 12 and section 1208 of this title.

Subsec. (h)(1). Pub. L. 99–554, §283(e)(2), inserted "or timeshare plan" after "to treat such lease".

Subsec. (m). Pub. L. 99–554, §283(e)(3), substituted "362(b)(10)" for "362(b)(9)".

1984—Subsec. (a). Pub. L. 98–353, §362(a), amended subsec. (a) generally, making minor changes.

Subsec. (b). Pub. L. 98–353, §362(a), amended subsec. (b) generally, inserting in par. (3) reference to par. (2)(B) of subsec. (f) of this section, in par. (3)(A) inserting provisions relating to financial condition and operating performance in the case of an assignment, and in par. (3)(C) substituting "that assumption or assignment of such lease is subject to all the provisions thereof, including (but not limited to) provisions such as a radius, location, use, or exclusivity provision, and will not breach any such provision contained in any other lease, financing agreement, or master agreement relating to such shopping center" for "that assumption or assignment of such lease will not breach substantially any provision, such as a radius, location, use, or exclusivity provision, in any other lease, financing agreement, or master agreement relating to such shopping center".

Subsec. (c). Pub. L. 98–353, §362(a), amended subsec. (c) generally, substituting in par. (1)(A) "applicable law excuses a party, other than the debtor, to such contract or lease from accepting performance from or rendering performance to an entity other than the debtor or the debtor in possession or an assignee of such contract or lease, whether or not such contract or lease prohibits or restricts assignment of rights or delegation of duties" for "applicable law excuses a party, other than the debtor, to such contract or lease from accepting performance from or rendering performance to the trustee or an assignee of such contract or lease, whether or not such contract or lease prohibits or restricts assignment of rights or delegation of duties" and adding par. (3).

Subsec. (d). Pub. L. 98–353, §362(a), amended subsec. (d) generally, inserting in par. (1) reference to residential real property or personal property of the debtor, inserting in par. (2) reference to residential real property or personal property of the debtor, and adding pars. (3) and (4).

Subsec. (h)(1). Pub. L. 98–353, §402, amended par. (1) generally. Prior to amendment, par. (1) read as follows: "If the trustee rejects an unexpired lease of real property of the debtor under which the debtor is the lessor, the lessee under such lease may treat the lease as terminated by such rejection, or, in the alternative, may remain in possession for the balance of the term of such lease and any renewal or extension of such term that is enforceable by such lessee under applicable nonbankruptcy law."

Subsec. (h)(2). Pub. L. 98–353, §403, amended par. (2) generally. Prior to amendment, par. (2) read as follows: "If such lessee remains in possession, such lessee may offset against the rent reserved under such lease for the balance of the term after the date of the rejection of such lease, and any such renewal or extension, any damages occurring after such date caused by the nonperformance of any obligation of the debtor after such date, but such lessee does not have any rights against the estate on account of any damages arising after such date from such rejection, other than such offset."

Subsec. (i)(1). Pub. L. 98–353, §404, amended par. (1) generally, inserting provisions relating to timeshare interests under timeshare plans.

Subsecs. (l), (m). Pub. L. 98–353, §362(b), added subsecs. (l) and (m).

Effective Date of 2005 Amendment

Amendment by Pub. L. 109–8 effective 180 days after Apr. 20, 2005, and not applicable with respect to cases commenced under this title before such effective date, except as otherwise provided, see section 1501 of Pub. L. 109–8, set out as a note under section 101 of this title.

Effective Date of 1994 Amendment

Amendment by Pub. L. 103–394 effective Oct. 22, 1994, and not applicable with respect to cases commenced under this title before Oct. 22, 1994, see section 702 of Pub. L. 103–394, set out as a note under section 101 of this title.

Effective Date of 1992 Amendment

Pub. L. 102–365, §19(f), Sept. 2, 1992, 106 Stat. 984, provided that: "The amendments made by this section [amending this section] shall be in effect for the 12-month period that begins on the date of enactment of this Act [Sept. 3, 1992] and shall apply in all proceedings involving an affected air carrier (as defined in section 365(p) of title 11, United States Code, as amended by this section) that are pending during such 12-month period. Not later than 9 months after the date of enactment, the Administrator of the Federal Aviation Administration shall report to the Committee on Commerce, Science, and Transportation and Committee on the Judiciary of the Senate and the Committee on the Judiciary and Committee on Public Works and Transportation of the House of Representatives on whether this section shall apply to proceedings that are commenced after such 12-month period."

Effective Date of 1988 Amendment

Amendment by Pub. L. 100–506 effective Oct. 18, 1988, but not applicable to any case commenced under this title before such date, see section 2 of Pub. L. 100–506, set out as a note under section 101 of this title.

Effective Date of 1986 Amendment

Amendment by section 257 of Pub. L. 99–554 effective 30 days after Oct. 27, 1986, but not applicable to cases commenced under this title before that date, see section 302(a), (c)(1) of Pub. L. 99–554, set out as a note under section 581 of Title 28, Judiciary and Judicial Procedure.

Amendment by section 283 of Pub. L. 99–554 effective 30 days after Oct. 27, 1986, see section 302(a) of Pub. L. 99–554.

Effective Date of 1984 Amendment

Amendment by Pub. L. 98–353 effective with respect to cases filed 90 days after July 10, 1984, see section 552(a) of Pub. L. 98–353, set out as a note under section 101 of this title.

Airport Leases

Pub. L. 102–365, §19(a), Sept. 2, 1992, 106 Stat. 982, provided that: "Congress finds that—

"(1) there are major airports served by an air carrier that has leased a substantial majority of the airport's gates;

"(2) the commerce in the region served by such a major airport can be disrupted if the air carrier that leases most of its gates enters bankruptcy and either discontinues or materially reduces service; and

"(3) it is important that such airports be empowered to continue service in the event of such a disruption."

§366. Utility service

(a) Except as provided in subsections (b) and (c) of this section, a utility may not alter, refuse, or discontinue service to, or discriminate against, the trustee or the debtor solely on the basis of the commencement of a case under this title or that a debt owed by the debtor to such utility for service rendered before the order for relief was not paid when due.

(b) Such utility may alter, refuse, or discontinue service if neither the trustee nor the debtor, within 20 days after the date of the order for relief, furnishes adequate assurance of payment, in the form of a deposit or other security, for service after such date. On request of a party in interest and after notice and a hearing, the court may order reasonable modification of the amount of the deposit or other security necessary to provide adequate assurance of payment.

(c)(1)(A) For purposes of this subsection, the term "assurance of payment" means—

(i) a cash deposit;
(ii) a letter of credit;
(iii) a certificate of deposit;
(iv) a surety bond;
(v) a prepayment of utility consumption; or
(vi) another form of security that is mutually agreed on between the utility and the debtor or the trustee.

(B) For purposes of this subsection an administrative expense priority shall not constitute an assurance of payment.

(2) Subject to paragraphs (3) and (4), with respect to a case filed under chapter 11, a utility referred to in subsection (a) may alter, refuse, or discontinue utility service, if during the 30-day period beginning on the date of the filing of the petition, the utility does not receive from the debtor or the trustee adequate assurance of payment for utility service that is satisfactory to the utility.

(3)(A) On request of a party in interest and after notice and a hearing, the court may order modification of the amount of an assurance of payment under paragraph (2).

(B) In making a determination under this paragraph whether an assurance of payment is adequate, the court may not consider—

(i) the absence of security before the date of the filing of the petition;
(ii) the payment by the debtor of charges for utility service in a timely manner before the date of the filing of the petition; or
(iii) the availability of an administrative expense priority.

(4) Notwithstanding any other provision of law, with respect to a case subject to this subsection, a utility may recover or set off against a security deposit provided to the utility by the debtor before the date of the filing of the petition without notice or order of the court.

(Pub. L. 95–598, Nov. 6, 1978, 92 Stat. 2578; Pub. L. 98–353, title III, §443, July 10, 1984, 98 Stat. 373; Pub. L. 109–8, title IV, §417, Apr. 20, 2005, 119 Stat. 108.)

Historical and Revision Notes

legislative statements

Section 366 of the House amendment represents a compromise between comparable provisions contained in H.R. 8200 as passed by the House and the Senate amendment. Subsection (a) is modified so that the applicable date is the date of the order for relief rather than the date of the filing of the petition. Subsection (b) contains a similar change but is otherwise derived from section 366(b) of the Senate amendment, with the exception that a time period for continued service of 20 days rather than 10 days is adopted.

senate report no. 95–989

This section gives debtors protection from a cut-off of service by a utility because of the filing of a bankruptcy case. This section is intended to cover utilities that have some special position with respect to the debtor, such as an electric company, gas supplier, or telephone company that is a monopoly in the area so that the debtor cannot easily obtain comparable service from another utility. The utility may not alter, refuse, or discontinue service because of the nonpayment of a bill that would be discharged in the bankruptcy case. Subsection (b) protects the utility company by requiring the trustee or the debtor to provide, within ten days, adequate assurance of payment for service provided after the date of the petition.

Amendments

2005—Subsec. (a). Pub. L. 109–8, §417(1), substituted "subsections (b) and (c)" for "subsection (b)".

Subsec. (c). Pub. L. 109–8, §417(2), added subsec. (c).

1984—Subsec. (a). Pub. L. 98–353 inserted "of the commencement of a case under this title or" after "basis".

Effective Date of 2005 Amendment

Amendment by Pub. L. 109–8 effective 180 days after Apr. 20, 2005, and not applicable with respect to cases commenced under this title before such effective date, except as otherwise provided, see section 1501 of Pub. L. 109–8, set out as a note under section 101 of this title.

Effective Date of 1984 Amendment

Amendment by Pub. L. 98–353 effective with respect to cases filed 90 days after July 10, 1984, see section 552(a) of Pub. L. 98–353, set out as a note under section 101 of this title.

CHAPTER 5—CREDITORS, THE DEBTOR, AND THE ESTATE

SUBCHAPTER I—CREDITORS AND CLAIMS

Sec.
501.
Filing of proofs of claims or interests.

502. Allowance of claims or interests.
503. Allowance of administrative expenses.
504. Sharing of compensation.
505. Determination of tax liability.
506. Determination of secured status.
507. Priorities.
508. Effect of distribution other than under this title.
509. Claims of codebtors.
510. Subordination.
511. Rate of interest on tax claims.

SUBCHAPTER II—DEBTOR'S DUTIES AND BENEFITS

521. Debtor's duties.
522. Exemptions.
523. Exceptions to discharge.
524. Effect of discharge.
525. Protection against discriminatory treatment.
526. Restrictions on debt relief agencies.
527. Disclosures.
528. Requirements for debt relief agencies.

SUBCHAPTER III—THE ESTATE

541. Property of the estate.
542. Turnover of property to the estate.
543. Turnover of property by a custodian.
544. Trustee as lien creditor and as successor to certain creditors and purchasers.
545. Statutory liens.
546. Limitations on avoiding powers.
547. Preferences.
548. Fraudulent transfers and obligations.
549. Postpetition transactions.
550. Liability of transferee of avoided transfer.
551. Automatic preservation of avoided transfer.
552. Postpetition effect of security interest.
553. Setoff.
554. Abandonment of property of the estate.
555. Contractual right to liquidate, terminate, or accelerate a securities contract.
556. Contractual right to liquidate, terminate, or accelerate a commodities contract or forward contract.
557. Expedited determination of interests in, and abandonment or other disposition of grain assets.
558. Defenses of the estate.
559. Contractual right to liquidate, terminate, or accelerate a repurchase agreement.
560. Contractual right to liquidate, terminate, or accelerate a swap agreement.
561. Contractual right to terminate, liquidate, accelerate, or offset under a master netting agreement and across contracts; proceedings under chapter 15.
562. Timing of damage measure in connection with swap agreements, securities contracts, forward contracts, commodity contracts, repurchase agreements, and master netting agreements.

Amendments

2010—Pub. L. 111–327, §2(a)(50), Dec. 22, 2010, 124 Stat. 3562, substituted "and master netting agreements" for "or master netting agreements" in item 562.

2005—Pub. L. 109–8, title II, §§227(b), 228(b), 229(b), title VII, §704(b), title IX, §§907(k)(2), (p)(1), 910(a)(2), Apr. 20, 2005, 119 Stat. 69, 71, 72, 126, 181, 182, 184, added items 511, 526 to 528, 561 and 562 and substituted "Contractual right to liquidate, terminate, or accelerate a securities contract" for "Contractual right to liquidate a securities contract" in item 555, "Contractual right to liquidate, terminate, or accelerate a commodities contract or forward contract" for "Contractual right to liquidate a commodity contract or forward contract" in item 556, "Contractual right to liquidate, terminate, or accelerate a repurchase agreement" for "Contractual right to liquidate a repurchase agreement" in item 559, and "Contractual right to liquidate, terminate, or accelerate a swap agreement" for "Contractual right to terminate a swap agreement" in item 560.

1990—Pub. L. 101–311, title I, §106(b), June 25, 1990, 104 Stat. 268, added item 560.

1986—Pub. L. 99–554, title II, §283(g), Oct. 27, 1986, 100 Stat. 3118, amended items 557 to 559 generally, substituting "interests in, and abandonment or other disposition of grain assets" for "in and disposition of grain" in item 557.

1984—Pub. L. 98–353, title III, §§352(b), 396(b), 470(b), July 10, 1984, 98 Stat. 361, 366, 380, added items 557, 558, and 559.

1982—Pub. L. 97–222, §6(b), July 27, 1982, 96 Stat. 237, added items 555 and 556.

SUBCHAPTER I—CREDITORS AND CLAIMS

§501. Filing of proofs of claims or interests

(a) A creditor or an indenture trustee may file a proof of claim. An equity security holder may file a proof of interest.

(b) If a creditor does not timely file a proof of such creditor's claim, an entity that is liable to such creditor with the debtor, or that has secured such creditor, may file a proof of such claim.

(c) If a creditor does not timely file a proof of such creditor's claim, the debtor or the trustee may file a proof of such claim.

(d) A claim of a kind specified in section 502(e)(2), 502(f), 502(g), 502(h) or 502(i) of this title may be filed under subsection (a), (b), or (c) of this section the same as if such claim were a claim against the debtor and had arisen before the date of the filing of the petition.

(e) A claim arising from the liability of a debtor for fuel use tax assessed consistent with the requirements of section 31705 of title 49 may be filed by the base jurisdiction designated pursuant to the International Fuel Tax Agreement (as defined in section 31701 of title 49) and, if so filed, shall be allowed as a single claim.

(Pub. L. 95–598, Nov. 6, 1978, 92 Stat. 2578; Pub. L. 98–353, title III, §444, July 10, 1984, 98 Stat. 373; Pub. L. 109–8, title VII, §702, Apr. 20, 2005, 119 Stat. 125.)

Historical and Revision Notes
legislative statements

The House amendment adopts section 501(b) of the Senate amendment leaving the Rules of Bankruptcy Procedure free to determine where a proof of claim must be filed.

Section 501(c) expands language contained in section 501(c) of the House bill and Senate amendment to permit the debtor to file a proof of claim if a creditor does not timely file a proof of the creditor's claim in a case under title 11.

The House amendment deletes section 501(e) of the Senate amendment as a matter to be left to the rules of bankruptcy procedure. It is anticipated that the rules will enable governmental units, like other creditors, to have a reasonable time to file proofs of claim in bankruptcy cases.

For purposes of section 501, a proof of "interest" includes the interest of a general or limited partner in a partnership, the interest of a proprietor in a sole proprietorship, or the interest of a common or preferred stockholder in a corporation.

senate report no. 95–989

This section governs the means by which creditors and equity security holders present their claims or interests to the court. Subsection (a) permits a creditor to file a proof of claim or interest. An indenture trustee representing creditors may file a proof of claim on behalf of the creditors he represents.

This subsection is permissive only, and does not require filing of a proof of claim by any creditor. It permits filing where some purpose would be served, such as where a claim that appears on a list filed under proposed 11 U.S.C. 924 or 1111 was incorrectly stated or listed as disputed, contingent, or unliquidated, where a creditor with a lien is undersecured and asserts a claim for the balance of the debt owed him (his unsecured claim, as determined under proposed 11 U.S.C. 506(a)), or in a liquidation case where there will be a distribution of assets to the holders of allowed claims. In other instances, such as in no-asset liquidation cases, in situations where a secured creditor does not assert any claim against the estate and a determination of his claim is not made under proposed 11 U.S.C. 506, or in situations where the claim asserted would be subordinated and the creditor would not recover from the estate in any event, filing of a proof of claim may simply not be necessary. The Rules of Bankruptcy Procedure and practice under the law will guide creditors as to when filing is necessary and when it may be dispensed with. In general, however, unless a claim is listed in a chapter 9 or chapter 11 case and allowed as a result of the list, a proof of claim will be a prerequisite to allowance for unsecured claims, including priority claims and the unsecured portion of a claim asserted by the holder of a lien.

The Rules of Bankruptcy Procedure will set the time limits, the form, and the procedure for filing, which will determine whether claims are timely or tardily filed. The rules governing time limits for filing proofs of claims will continue to apply under section 405(d) of the bill. These provide a 6-month-bar date for the filing of tax claims.

Subsection (b) permits a codebtor, surety, or guarantor to file a proof of claim on behalf of the creditor to which he is liable if the creditor does not timely file a proof of claim.

In liquidation and individual repayment plan cases, the trustee or the debtor may file a proof of claim under subsection (c) if the creditor does not timely file. The purpose of this subsection is mainly to protect the debtor if the creditor's claim is nondischargeable. If the creditor does not file, there would be no distribution on the claim, and the debtor would have a greater debt to repay after the case is closed than if the claim were paid in part or in full in the case or under the plan.

Subsection (d) governs the filing of claims of the kind specified in subsections (f), (g), (h), (i), or (j) of proposed 11 U.S.C. 502. The separation of this provision from the other claim-filing provisions in this section is intended to indicate that claims of the kind specified, which do not become fixed or do not arise until after the commencement of the case, must be treated differently for filing purposes such as the bar date for filing claims. The rules will provide for later filing of claims of these kinds.

Subsection (e) gives governmental units (including tax authorities) at least six months following the date for the first meeting of creditors in a chapter 7 or chapter 13 case within which to file proof of claims.

Amendments

2005—Subsec. (e). Pub. L. 109–8 added subsec. (e).

1984—Subsec. (d). Pub. L. 98–353 inserted "502(e)(2),".

Effective Date of 2005 Amendment

Amendment by Pub. L. 109–8 effective 180 days after Apr. 20, 2005, and not applicable with respect to cases commenced under this title before such effective date, except as otherwise provided, see section 1501 of Pub. L. 109–8, set out as a note under section 101 of this title.

Effective Date of 1984 Amendment

Amendment by Pub. L. 98–353 effective with respect to cases filed 90 days after July 10, 1984, see section 552(a) of Pub. L. 98–353, set out as a note under section 101 of this title.

Child Support Creditors or Their Representatives; Appearance Before Court

Pub. L. 103–394, title III, §304(g), Oct. 22, 1994, 108 Stat. 4134, provided that: "Child support creditors or their representatives shall be permitted to appear and intervene without charge, and without meeting any special local court rule requirement for attorney appearances, in any bankruptcy case or proceeding in any bankruptcy court or district court of the United States if such creditors or representatives file a form in such court that contains information detailing the child support debt, its status, and other characteristics."

§502. Allowance of claims or interests

(a) A claim or interest, proof of which is filed under section 501 of this title, is deemed allowed, unless a party in interest, including a creditor of a general partner in a partnership that is a debtor in a case under chapter 7 of this title, objects.

(b) Except as provided in subsections (e)(2), (f), (g), (h) and (i) of this section, if such objection to a claim is made, the court, after notice and a hearing, shall determine the amount of such claim in lawful currency of the United States as of the date of the filing of the petition, and shall allow such claim in such amount, except to the extent that—

(1) such claim is unenforceable against the debtor and property of the debtor, under any agreement or applicable law for a reason other than because such claim is contingent or unmatured;

(2) such claim is for unmatured interest;

(3) if such claim is for a tax assessed against property of the estate, such claim exceeds the value of the interest of the estate in such property;

(4) if such claim is for services of an insider or attorney of the debtor, such claim exceeds the reasonable value of such services;

(5) such claim is for a debt that is unmatured on the date of the filing of the petition and that is excepted from discharge under section 523(a)(5) of this title;

(6) if such claim is the claim of a lessor for damages resulting from the termination of a lease of real property, such claim exceeds—

(A) the rent reserved by such lease, without acceleration, for the greater of one year, or 15 percent, not to exceed three years, of the remaining term of such lease, following the earlier of—

(i) the date of the filing of the petition; and

(ii) the date on which such lessor repossessed, or the lessee surrendered, the leased property; plus

(B) any unpaid rent due under such lease, without acceleration, on the earlier of such dates;

(7) if such claim is the claim of an employee for damages resulting from the termination of an employment contract, such claim exceeds—

(A) the compensation provided by such contract, without acceleration, for one year following the earlier of—

(i) the date of the filing of the petition; or

(ii) the date on which the employer directed the employee to terminate, or such employee terminated, performance under such contract; plus

(B) any unpaid compensation due under such contract, without acceleration, on the earlier of such dates;

(8) such claim results from a reduction, due to late payment, in the amount of an otherwise applicable credit available to the debtor in connection with an employment tax on wages, salaries, or commissions earned from the debtor; or

(9) proof of such claim is not timely filed, except to the extent tardily filed as permitted under paragraph (1), (2), or (3) of section 726(a) of this title or under the Federal Rules of Bankruptcy Procedure, except that a claim of a governmental unit shall be timely filed if it is filed before 180 days after the date of the order for relief or such later time as the Federal Rules of Bankruptcy Procedure may provide, and except that in a case under chapter 13, a claim of a governmental unit for a tax with respect to a return filed under section 1308 shall be timely if the claim is filed on or before the date that is 60 days after the date on which such return was filed as required.

(c) There shall be estimated for purpose of allowance under this section—

(1) any contingent or unliquidated claim, the fixing or liquidation of which, as the case may be, would unduly delay the administration of the case; or

(2) any right to payment arising from a right to an equitable remedy for breach of performance.

(d) Notwithstanding subsections (a) and (b) of this section, the court shall disallow any claim of any entity from which property is recoverable under section 542, 543, 550, or 553 of this title or that is a transferee of a transfer avoidable under section 522(f), 522(h), 544, 545, 547, 548, 549, or 724(a) of this title, unless such entity or transferee has paid the amount, or turned over any such property, for which such entity or transferee is liable under section 522(i), 542, 543, 550, or 553 of this title.

(e)(1) Notwithstanding subsections (a), (b), and (c) of this section and paragraph (2) of this subsection, the court shall disallow any claim for reimbursement or contribution of an entity that is liable with the debtor on or has secured the claim of a creditor, to the extent that—

(A) such creditor's claim against the estate is disallowed;

(B) such claim for reimbursement or contribution is contingent as of the time of allowance or disallowance of such claim for reimbursement or contribution; or

(C) such entity asserts a right of subrogation to the rights of such creditor under section 509 of this title.

(2) A claim for reimbursement or contribution of such an entity that becomes fixed after the commencement of the case shall be determined, and shall be allowed under subsection (a), (b), or (c) of this section, or disallowed under subsection (d) of this section, the same as if such claim had become fixed before the date of the filing of the petition.

(f) In an involuntary case, a claim arising in the ordinary course of the debtor's business or financial affairs after the commencement of the case but before the earlier of the appointment of a trustee and the order for relief shall be determined as of the date such claim arises, and shall be allowed under subsection (a), (b), or (c) of this section or disallowed under subsection (d) or (e) of this section, the same as if such claim had arisen before the date of the filing of the petition.

(g)(1) A claim arising from the rejection, under section 365 of this title or under a plan under chapter 9, 11, 12, or 13 of this title, of an executory contract or unexpired lease of the debtor that has not been assumed shall be determined, and shall be allowed under subsection (a), (b), or (c) of this section or disallowed under subsection (d) or (e) of this section, the same as if such claim had arisen before the date of the filing of the petition.

(2) A claim for damages calculated in accordance with section 562 shall be allowed under subsection (a), (b), or (c), or disallowed under subsection (d) or (e), as if such claim had arisen before the date of the filing of the petition.

(h) A claim arising from the recovery of property under section 522, 550, or 553 of this title shall be determined, and shall be allowed under subsection (a), (b), or (c) of this section, or disallowed under subsection (d) or (e) of this section, the same as if such claim had arisen before the date of the filing of the petition.

(i) A claim that does not arise until after the commencement of the case for a tax entitled to priority under section 507(a)(8) of this title shall be determined, and shall be allowed under subsection (a), (b), or (c) of this section, or disallowed under subsection (d) or (e) of this section, the same as if such claim had arisen before the date of the filing of the petition.

(j) A claim that has been allowed or disallowed may be reconsidered for cause. A reconsidered claim may be allowed or disallowed according to the equities of the case. Reconsideration of a claim under this subsection does not affect the validity of any payment or transfer from the estate made to a holder of an allowed claim on account of such allowed claim that is not reconsidered, but if a reconsidered claim is allowed and is of the same class as such holder's claim, such holder may not receive any additional payment or transfer from the estate on account of such holder's allowed claim until the holder of such reconsidered and allowed claim receives payment on account of such claim proportionate in value to that already received by such other holder. This subsection does not alter or modify the trustee's right to recover from a creditor any excess payment or transfer made to such creditor.

(k)(1) The court, on the motion of the debtor and after a hearing, may reduce a claim filed under this section based in whole on an unsecured consumer debt by not more than 20 percent of the claim, if—

(A) the claim was filed by a creditor who unreasonably refused to negotiate a reasonable alternative repayment schedule proposed on behalf of the debtor by an approved nonprofit budget and credit counseling agency described in section 111;

(B) the offer of the debtor under subparagraph (A)—

(i) was made at least 60 days before the date of the filing of the petition; and

(ii) provided for payment of at least 60 percent of the amount of the debt over a period not to exceed the repayment period of the loan, or a reasonable extension thereof; and

(C) no part of the debt under the alternative repayment schedule is nondischargeable.

(2) The debtor shall have the burden of proving, by clear and convincing evidence, that—

(A) the creditor unreasonably refused to consider the debtor's proposal; and

(B) the proposed alternative repayment schedule was made prior to expiration of the 60-day period specified in paragraph (1)(B)(i).

(Pub. L. 95–598, Nov. 6, 1978, 92 Stat. 2579; Pub. L. 98–353, title III, §445, July 10, 1984, 98 Stat. 373; Pub. L. 99–554, title II, §§257(j), 283(f), Oct. 27, 1986, 100 Stat. 3115, 3117; Pub. L. 103–394, title II, §213(a), title III, §304(h)(1), Oct. 22, 1994, 108 Stat. 4125, 4134; Pub. L. 109–8, title II, §201(a), title VII, §716(d), title IX, §910(b), Apr. 20, 2005, 119 Stat. 42, 130, 184.)

Historical and Revision Notes

legislative statements

The House amendment adopts a compromise position in section 502(a) between H.R. 8200, as passed by the House, and the Senate amendment. Section 502(a) has been modified to make clear that a party in interest includes a creditor of a partner in a partnership that is a debtor under chapter 7. Since the trustee of the partnership is given an absolute claim against the estate of each general partner under section 723(c), creditors of the partner must have standing to object to claims against the partnership at the partnership level because no opportunity will be afforded at the partner's level for such objection.

The House amendment contains a provision in section 502(b)(1) that requires disallowance of a claim to the extent that such claim is unenforceable against the debtor and unenforceable against property of the debtor. This is intended to result in the disallowance of any claim for deficiency by an undersecured creditor on a non-recourse loan or under a State antideficiency law, special provision for which is made in section 1111, since neither the debtor personally, nor the property of the debtor is liable for such a deficiency. Similarly claims for usurious interest or which could be barred by an agreement between the creditor and the debtor would be disallowed.

Section 502(b)(7)(A) represents a compromise between the House bill and the Senate amendment. The House amendment takes the provision in H.R. 8200 as passed by the House of Representatives but increases the percentage from 10 to 15 percent.

As used in section 502(b)(7), the phrase "lease of real property" applies only to a "true" or "bona fide" lease and does not apply to financing leases of real property or interests therein, or to leases of such property which are intended as security.

Historically, the limitation on allowable claims of lessors of real property was based on two considerations. First, the amount of the lessor's damages on breach of a real estate lease was considered contingent and difficult to prove. Partly for this reason, claims of a lessor of real estate were not provable prior to the 1934 amendments, to the Bankruptcy Act [former title 11]. Second, in a true lease of real property, the lessor retains all risks and benefits as to the value of the real estate at the termination of the lease. Historically, it was, therefore, considered equitable to limit the claims of real estate lessor.

However, these considerations are not present in "lease financing" transactions where, in substance, the "lease" involves a sale of the real estate and the rental payments are in substance the payment of principal and interest on a secured loan or sale. In a financing lease the lessor is essentially a secured or unsecured creditor (depending upon whether his interest is perfected or not) of the debtor, and the lessor's claim should not be subject to the 502(b)(7) limitation. Financing "leases" are in substance installment sales or loans. The "lessors" are essentially sellers or lenders and should be treated as such for purposes of the bankruptcy law.

Whether a "lease" is true or bona fide lease or, in the alternative a financing "lease" or a lease intended as security, depends upon the circumstances of each case. The distinction between a true lease and a financing transaction is based upon the economic substance of the transaction and not, for example, upon the locus of title, the form of the transaction or the fact that the transaction is denominated as a "lease." The fact that the lessee, upon compliance with the terms of the lease, becomes or has the option to become the owner of the leased property for no additional consideration or for nominal consideration indicates that the transaction is a financing lease or lease intended as security. In such cases, the lessor has no substantial interest in the leased property at the expiration of the lease term. In addition, the fact that the lessee assumes and discharges substantially all the risks and obligations ordinarily attributed to the outright ownership of the property is more indicative of a financing transaction than of a true lease. The rental payments in such cases are in substance payments of principal and interest either on a loan secured by the leased real property or on the purchase of the leased real property. See, e.g., Financial Accounting Standards Board Statement No. 13 and SEC Reg. S–X, 17 C.F.R. sec. 210.3–16(q) (1977); *cf. First National Bank of Chicago v. Irving Trust Co.*, 74 F.2d 263 (2nd Cir. 1934); and Albenda and Lief, "Net Lease Financing Transactions Under the Proposed Bankruptcy Act of 1973," 30 Business Lawyer, 713 (1975).

Section 502(c) of the House amendment presents a compromise between similar provisions contained in the House bill and the Senate amendment. The compromise language is consistent with an amendment to the definition of "claim" in section 104(4)(B) of the House amendment and requires estimation of any right to an equitable remedy for breach of performance if such breach gives rise to a right to payment. To the extent language in the House and Senate reports indicate otherwise, such language is expressly overruled.

Section 502(e) of the House amendment contains language modifying a similar section in the House bill and Senate amendment. Section 502(e)(1) states the general rule requiring the court to disallow any claim for reimbursement or contribution of an entity that is liable with the debtor on, or that has secured, the claim of a creditor to any extent that the creditor's claim against the estate is disallowed. This adopts a policy that a surety's claim for reimbursement or contribution is entitled to no better status than the claim of the creditor assured by such surety. Section 502(e)(1)(B) alternatively disallows any claim for reimbursement or contribution by a surety to the extent such claim is contingent as of the time of allowance. Section 502(e)(2) is clear that to the extent a claim for reimbursement or contribution becomes fixed after the commencement of the case that it is to be considered a prepetition claim for purposes of allowance. The combined effect of sections 502(e)(1)(B) and 502(e)(2) is that a surety or codebtor is generally permitted a claim for reimbursement or contribution to the extent the surety or codebtor has paid the assured party at the time of allowance. Section 502(e)(1)(C) alternatively indicates that a claim for reimbursement or contribution of a surety or codebtor is disallowed to the extent the surety or codebtor requests subrogation under section 509 with respect to the rights of the assured party. Thus, the surety or codebtor has a choice; to the extent a claim for contribution or reimbursement would be advantageous, such as in the case where such a claim is secured, a surety or codebtor may opt for reimbursement or contribution under section 502(e). On the other hand, to the extent the claim for such surety or codebtor by way of subrogation is more advantageous, such as where such claim is secured, the surety may elect subrogation under section 509.

The section changes current law by making the election identical in all other respects. To the extent a creditor's claim is satisfied by a surety or codebtor, other creditors should not benefit by the surety's inability to file a claim against the estate merely because such surety or codebtor has failed to pay such creditor's claim in full. On the other hand, to the extent the creditor's claim against the estate is otherwise disallowed, the surety or codebtor should not be entitled to increased rights by way of reimbursement or contribution, to the detriment of competing claims of other unsecured creditors, than would be realized by way of subrogation.

While the foregoing scheme is equitable with respect to other unsecured creditors of the debtor, it is desirable to preserve present law to the extent that a surety or codebtor is not permitted to compete with the creditor he has assured until the assured party's claim has paid in full. Accordingly, section 509(c) of the House amendment subordinates both a claim by way of subrogation or a claim for reimbursement or contribution of a surety or codebtor to the claim of the assured party until the assured party's claim is paid in full.

Section 502(h) of the House amendment expands similar provisions contained in the House bill and the Senate amendment to indicate that any claim arising from the recovery of property under section 522(i), 550, or 553 shall be determined as though it were a prepetition claim.

Section 502(i) of the House amendment adopts a provision contained in section 502(j) of H.R. 8200 as passed by the House but that was not contained in the Senate amendment.

Section 502(i) of H.R. 8200 as passed by the House, but was not included in the Senate amendment, is deleted as a matter to be left to the bankruptcy tax bill next year.

The House amendment deletes section 502(i) of the Senate bill but adopts the policy of that section to a limited extent for confirmation of a plan of reorganization in section 1111(b) of the House amendment.

Section 502(j) of the House amendment is new. The provision codifies section 57k of the Bankruptcy Act [section 93(k) of former title 11].

Allowance of Claims or Interest: The House amendment adopts section 502(b)(9) of the House bill which disallows any tax claim resulting from a reduction of the Federal Unemployment Tax Act (FUTA) credit (sec. 3302 of the Internal Revenue Code [26 U.S.C. 3302]) on account of a tardy contribution to a State unemployment fund if the contribution is attributable to ways or other compensation paid by the debtor before bankruptcy. The Senate amendment allowed this reduction, but would have subordinated it to other claims in the distribution of the estate's assets by treating it as a punitive (nonpecuniary loss) penalty. The House amendment would also not bar reduction of the FUTA credit on account of a trustee's late payment of a contribution to a State unemployment fund if the contribution was attributable to a trustee's payment of compensation earned from the estate.

Section 511 of the Senate amendment is deleted. Its substance is adopted in section 502(b)(9) of the House amendment which reflects an identical provision contained in H.R. 8200 as passed by the House.

senate report no. 95–989

A proof of claim or interest is prima facie evidence of the claim or interest. Thus, it is allowed under subsection (a) unless a party in interest objects. The rules and case law will determine who is a party in interest for purposes of objection to allowance. The case law is well developed on this subject today. As a result of the change in the liability of a general partner's estate for the debts of this partnership, see proposed 11 U.S.C. 723, the category of persons that are parties in interest in the partnership case will be expanded to include a creditor of a partner against whose estate the trustee of the partnership estate may proceed under proposed 11 U.S.C. 723(c).

Subsection (b) prescribes the grounds on which a claim may be disallowed. The court will apply these standards if there is an objection to a proof of claim. The burden of proof on the issue of allowance is left to the Rules of Bankruptcy Procedure. Under the current chapter XIII rules, a creditor is required to prove that his claim is free from usury, rule 13–301. It is expected that the rules will make similar provision for both liquidation and individual repayment plan cases. See Bankruptcy Act §656(b) [section 1056(b) of former title 11]; H.R. 31, 94th Cong., 1st sess., sec. 6–104(a) (1975).

Paragraph (1) requires disallowance if the claim is unenforceable against the debtor for any reason (such as usury, unconscionability, or failure of consideration) other than because it is contingent or unmatured. All such contingent or unmatured claims are to be liquidated by the bankruptcy court in order to afford the debtor complete bankruptcy relief; these claims are generally not provable under present law.

Paragraph (2) requires disallowance to the extent that the claim is for unmatured interest as of the date of the petition. Whether interest is matured or unmatured on the date of bankruptcy is to be determined without reference to any ipso facto or bankruptcy clause in the agreement creating the claim. Interest disallowed under this paragraph includes postpetition interest that is not yet due and payable, and any portion of prepaid interest that represents an original discounting of the claim, yet that would not have been earned on the date of bankruptcy. For example, a claim on a $1,000 note issued the day before bankruptcy would only be allowed to the extent of the cash actually advanced. If the original discount was 10 percent so that the cash advanced was only $900, then notwithstanding the face amount of note, only $900 would be allowed. If $900 was advanced under the note some time before bankruptcy, the interest component of the note would have to be prorated and disallowed to the extent it was for interest after the commencement of the case.

Section 502(b) thus contains two principles of present law. First, interest stops accruing at the date of the filing of the petition, because any claim for unmatured interest is disallowed under this paragraph. Second, bankruptcy operates as the acceleration of the principal amount of all claims against the debtor. One unarticulated reason for this is that the discounting factor for claims after the commencement of the case is equivalent to contractual interest rate on the claim. Thus, this paragraph does not cause disallowance of claims that have not been discounted to a present value because of the irrebuttable presumption that the discounting rate and the contractual interest rate (even a zero interest rate) are equivalent.

Paragraph (3) requires disallowance of a claim to the extent that the creditor may offset the claim against a debt owing to the debtor. This will prevent double recovery, and permit the claim to be filed only for the balance due. This follows section 68 of the Bankruptcy Act [section 108 of former title 11].

Paragraph (4) requires disallowance of a property tax claim to the extent that the tax due exceeds the value of the property. This too follows current law to the extent the property tax is ad valorem.

Paragraph (5) prevents overreaching by the debtor's attorneys and concealing of assets by debtors. It permits the court to examine the claim of a debtor's attorney independently of any other provision of this subsection, and to disallow it to the extent that it exceeds the reasonable value of the attorneys' services.

Postpetition alimony, maintenance or support claims are disallowed under paragraph (6). They are to be paid from the debtor's postpetition property, because the claims are nondischargeable.

Paragraph (7), derived from current law, limits the damages allowable to a landlord of the debtor. The history of this provision is set out at length in *Oldden v. Tonto Realty Co.*, 143 F.2d 916 (2d Cir. 1944). It is designed to compensate the landlord for his loss while not permitting a claim so large (based on a long-term lease) as to prevent other general unsecured creditors from recovering a dividend from the estate. The damages a landlord may assert from termination of a lease are limited to the rent reserved for the greater of one year or ten percent of the remaining lease term, not to exceed three years, after the earlier of the date of the filing of the petition and the date of surrender or repossession in a chapter 7 case and 3 years lease payments in a chapter 9, 11, or 13 case. The sliding scale formula for chapter 7 cases is new and designed to protect the long-term lessor. This subsection does not apply to limit administrative expense claims for use of the leased premises to which the landlord is otherwise entitled.

This paragraph will not overrule *Oldden*, or the proposition for which it has been read to stand: To the extent that a landlord has a security deposit in excess of the amount of his claim allowed under this paragraph, the excess comes into the estate. Moreover, his allowed claim is for his total damages, as limited by this paragraph. By virtue of proposed 11 U.S.C. 506(a) and 506(d), the claim will be divided into a secured portion and an unsecured portion in those cases in which the deposit that the landlord holds is less than his damages. As under *Oldden*, he will not be permitted to offset his actual damages against his security deposit and then claim for the balance under this paragraph. Rather, his security deposit will be applied in satisfaction of the claim that is allowed under this paragraph.

As used in section 502(b)(7), the phrase "lease of real property" applies only to a "true" or "bona fide" lease and does not apply to financing leases of real property or interests therein, or to leases of such property which are intended as security.

Historically, the limitation on allowable claims of lessors of real property was based on two considerations. First, the amount of the lessors damages on breach of a real estate lease was considered contingent and difficult to prove. Partly for this reason, claims of a lessor of real estate were not provable prior to the 1934 amendments to the Bankruptcy Act [former title 11]. Second, in a true lease of real property, the lessor retains all risk and benefits as to the value of the real estate at the termination of the lease. Historically, it was, therefore, considered equitable to limit the claims of a real estate lessor.

However, these considerations are not present in "lease financing" transactions where, in substance, the "lease" involves a sale of the real estate and the rental payments are in substance the payment of principal and interest on a secured loan or sale. In a financing lease the lessor is essentially a secured or unsecured creditor (depending upon whether his interest is perfected or not) of the debtor, and the lessor's claim should not be subject to the 502(b)(7) limitation. Financing "leases" are in substance installment sales or loans. The "lessors" are essentially sellers or lenders and should be treated as such for purposes of the bankruptcy law.

Whether a "lease" is true or bona fide lease or, in the alternative, a financing "lease" or a lease intended as security, depends upon the circumstances of each case. The distinction between a true lease and a financing transaction is based upon the economic substance of the transaction and not, for example, upon the locus of title, the form of the transaction or the fact that the transaction is denominated as a "lease". The fact that the lessee, upon compliance with the terms of the lease, becomes or has the option to become the owner of the leased property for no additional consideration or for nominal consideration indicates that the transaction is a financing lease or lease intended as security. In such cases, the lessor has no substantial interest in the leased property at the expiration of the lease term. In addition, the fact that the lessee assumes and discharges substantially all the risks and obligations ordinarily attributed to the outright ownership of the property is more indicative of a financing transaction than of a true lease. The rental payments in such cases are in substance payments of principal and interest either on a loan secured by the leased real property or on the purchase of the leased real property. See, e. g., Financial Accounting Standards Board Statement No. 13 and SEC Reg. S–X, 17 C.F.R. sec. 210.3–16(q) (1977); cf. *First National Bank of Chicago v. Irving Trust Co.*, 74 F.2d 263 (2nd Cir. 1934); and Albenda and Lief, "Net Lease Financing Transactions Under the Proposed Bankruptcy Act of 1973," 30 Business Lawyer, 713 (1975).

Paragraph (8) is new. It tracks the landlord limitation on damages provision in paragraph (7) for damages resulting from the breach by the debtor of an employment contract, but limits the recovery to the compensation reserved under an employment contract for the year following the earlier of the date of the petition and the termination of employment.

Subsection (c) requires the estimation of any claim liquidation of which would unduly delay the closing of the estate, such as a contingent claim, or any claim for which applicable law provides only an equitable remedy, such as specific performance. This subsection requires that all claims against the debtor be converted into dollar amounts.

Subsection (d) is derived from present law. It requires disallowance of a claim of a transferee of a voidable transfer in toto if the transferee has not paid the amount or turned over the property received as required under the sections under which the transferee's liability arises.

Subsection (e) also derived from present law, requires disallowance of the claim for reimbursement or contribution of a codebtor, surety or guarantor of an obligation of the debtor, unless the claim of the creditor on such obligation has been paid in full. The provision prevents competition between a creditor and his guarantor for the limited proceeds in the estate.

Subsection (f) specifies that "involuntary gap" creditors receive the same treatment as prepetition creditors. Under the allowance provisions of this subsection, knowledge of the commencement of the case will be irrelevant. The claim is to be allowed "the same as if such claim had arisen before the date of the filing of the petition." Under voluntary petition, proposed 11 U.S.C. 303(f), creditors must be permitted to deal with the debtor and be assured that their claims will be paid. For purposes of this subsection, "creditors" include governmental units holding claims for tax liabilities incurred during the period after the petition is filed and before the earlier of the order for relief or appointment of a trustee.

Subsection (g) gives entities injured by the rejection of an executory contract or unexpired lease, either under section 365 or under a plan or reorganization, a prepetition claim for any resulting damages, and requires that the injured entity be treated as a prepetition creditor with respect to that claim.

Subsection (h) gives a transferee of a setoff that is recovered by one trustee a prepetition claim for the amount recovered.

Subsection (i) answers the nonrecourse loan problem and gives the creditor an unsecured claim for the difference between the value of the collateral and the debt in response to the decision in *Great National Life Ins. Co. v. Pine Gate Associates, Ltd.*, Bankruptcy Case No. B75–4345A (N.D.Ga. Sept. 16, 1977).

The bill, as reported, deletes a provision in the bill as originally introduced (former sec. 502(i)) requiring a tax authority to file a proof of claim for recapture of an investment credit where, during title 11 proceedings, the trustee sells or otherwise disposes of property before the title 11 case began. The tax authority should not be required to submit a formal claim for a taxable event (a sale or other disposition of the asset) of whose occurrence the trustee necessarily knows better than the taxing authority. For procedural purposes, the recapture of investment credit is to be treated as an administrative expense, as to which only a request for payment is required.

house report no. 95–595

Paragraph (9) [of subsec. (b)] requires disallowance of certain employment tax claims. These relate to a Federal tax credit for State unemployment insurance taxes which is disallowed if the State tax is paid late. This paragraph disallows the Federal claim for the tax the same as if the credit had been allowed in full on the Federal return.

References in Text

The Federal Rules of Bankruptcy Procedure, referred to in subsec. (b)(9), are set out in the Appendix to this title.

Amendments

2005—Subsec. (b)(9). Pub. L. 109–8, §716(d), inserted ", and except that in a case under chapter 13, a claim of a governmental unit for a tax with respect to a return filed under section 1308 shall be timely if the claim is filed on or before the date that is 60 days after the date on which such return was filed as required" before period at end.

Subsec. (g). Pub. L. 109–8, §910(b), designated existing provisions as par. (1) and added par. (2).

Subsec. (k). Pub. L. 109–8, §201(a), added subsec. (k).

1994—Subsec. (b)(9). Pub. L. 103–394, §213(a), added par. (9).

Subsec. (i). Pub. L. 103–394, §304(h)(1), substituted "507(a)(8)" for "507(a)(7)".

1986—Subsec. (b)(6)(A)(ii). Pub. L. 99–554, §283(f)(1), substituted "repossessed" for "reposessed".

Subsec. (g). Pub. L. 99–554, §257(j), inserted reference to chapter 12.

Subsec. (i). Pub. L. 99–554, §283(f)(2), substituted "507(a)(7)" for "507(a)(6)".

1984—Subsec. (a). Pub. L. 98–353, §445(a), inserted "general" before "partner".

Subsec. (b). Pub. L. 98–353, §445(b)(1), (2), in provisions preceding par. (1), inserted "(e)(2)," after "subsections" and "in lawful currency of the United States" after "claim".

Subsec. (b)(1). Pub. L. 98–353, §445(b)(3), substituted "and" for ", and unenforceable against".

Subsec. (b)(3). Pub. L. 98–353, §445(b)(5), inserted "the" after "exceeds".

Pub. L. 98–353, §445(b)(4), struck out par. (3) "such claim may be offset under section 553 of this title against a debt owing to the debtor;", and redesignated par. (4) as (3).

Subsec. (b)(4). Pub. L. 98–353, §445(b)(4), redesignated par. (5) as (4). Former par. (4) redesignated (3).

Subsec. (b)(5). Pub. L. 98–353, §445(b)(6), substituted "such claim" for "the claim" and struck out the comma after "petition".

Pub. L. 98–353, §445(b)(4), redesignated par. (6) as (5). Former par. (5) redesignated (4).

Subsec. (b)(6). Pub. L. 98–353, §445(b)(4), redesignated par. (7) as (6). Former par. (6) redesignated (5).

Subsec. (b)(7). Pub. L. 98–353, §445(b)(7)(A), inserted "the claim of an employee" before "for damages".

Pub. L. 98–353, §445(b)(4), redesignated par. (8) as (7). Former par. (7) redesignated (6).

Subsec. (b)(7)(A)(i). Pub. L. 98–353, §445(b)(7)(B), substituted "or" for "and".

Subsec. (b)(7)(B). Pub. L. 98–353, §445(b)(7)(C), (D), substituted "any" for "the" and inserted a comma after "such contract".

Subsec. (b)(8), (9). Pub. L. 98–353, §445(b)(4), redesignated par. (9) as (8). Former par. (8) redesignated (7).

Subsec. (c)(1). Pub. L. 98–353, §445(c)(1), inserted "the" before "fixing" and substituted "administration" for "closing".

Subsec. (c)(2). Pub. L. 98–353, §445(c)(2), inserted "right to payment arising from a" after "any" and struck out "if such breach gives rise to a right to payment" after "breach of performance".

Subsec. (e)(1). Pub. L. 98–353, §445(d)(1), (2), in provisions preceding subpar. (A) substituted ", (b), and (c)" for "and (b)" and substituted "or has secured" for ", or has secured,".

Subsec. (e)(1)(B). Pub. L. 98–353, §445(d)(3), inserted "or disallowance" after "allowance".

Subsec. (e)(1)(C). Pub. L. 98–353, §445(d)(4), substituted "asserts a right of subrogation to the rights of such creditor" for "requests subrogation" and struck out "to the rights of such creditor" after "of this title".

Subsec. (h). Pub. L. 98–353, §445(e), substituted "522" for "522(i)".

Subsec. (j). Pub. L. 98–353, §445(f), amended subsec. (j) generally, inserting provisions relating to reconsideration of a disallowed claim, and provisions relating to reconsideration of a claim under this subsection.

Effective Date of 2005 Amendment

Amendment by Pub. L. 109–8 effective 180 days after Apr. 20, 2005, and not applicable with respect to cases commenced under this title before such effective date, except as otherwise provided, see section 1501 of Pub. L. 109–8, set out as a note under section 101 of this title.

Effective Date of 1994 Amendment

Amendment by Pub. L. 103–394 effective Oct. 22, 1994, and not applicable with respect to cases commenced under this title before Oct. 22, 1994, see section 702 of Pub. L. 103–394, set out as a note under section 101 of this title.

Effective Date of 1986 Amendment

Amendment by section 257 of Pub. L. 99–554 effective 30 days after Oct. 27, 1986, but not applicable to cases commenced under this title before that date, see section 302(a), (c)(1) of Pub. L. 99–554, set out as a note under section 581 of Title 28, Judiciary and Judicial Procedure.

Amendment by section 283 of Pub. L. 99–554 effective 30 days after Oct. 27, 1986, see section 302(a) of Pub. L. 99–554.

Effective Date of 1984 Amendment

Amendment by Pub. L. 98–353 effective with respect to cases filed 90 days after July 10, 1984, see section 552(a) of Pub. L. 98–353, set out as a note under section 101 of this title.

§503. Allowance of administrative expenses

(a) An entity may timely file a request for payment of an administrative expense, or may tardily file such request if permitted by the court for cause.

(b) After notice and a hearing, there shall be allowed administrative expenses, other than claims allowed under section 502(f) of this title, including—

(1)(A) the actual, necessary costs and expenses of preserving the estate including—

(i) wages, salaries, and commissions for services rendered after the commencement of the case; and

(ii) wages and benefits awarded pursuant to a judicial proceeding or a proceeding of the National Labor Relations Board as back pay attributable to any period of time occurring after commencement of the case under this title, as a result of a violation of Federal or State law by the debtor, without regard to the time of the occurrence of unlawful conduct on which such award is based or to whether any services were rendered, if the court determines that payment of wages and benefits by reason of the operation of this clause will not substantially increase the probability of layoff or termination of current employees, or of nonpayment of domestic support obligations, during the case under this title;

(B) any tax—

(i) incurred by the estate, whether secured or unsecured, including property taxes for which liability is in rem, in personam, or both, except a tax of a kind specified in section 507(a)(8) of this title; or

(ii) attributable to an excessive allowance of a tentative carryback adjustment that the estate received, whether the taxable year to which such adjustment relates ended before or after the commencement of the case;

(C) any fine, penalty, or reduction in credit relating to a tax of a kind specified in subparagraph (B) of this paragraph; and

(D) notwithstanding the requirements of subsection (a), a governmental unit shall not be required to file a request for the payment of an expense described in subparagraph (B) or (C), as a condition of its being an allowed administrative expense;

(2) compensation and reimbursement awarded under section 330(a) of this title;

(3) the actual, necessary expenses, other than compensation and reimbursement specified in paragraph (4) of this subsection, incurred by—

(A) a creditor that files a petition under section 303 of this title;

(B) a creditor that recovers, after the court's approval, for the benefit of the estate any property transferred or concealed by the debtor;

(C) a creditor in connection with the prosecution of a criminal offense relating to the case or to the business or property of the debtor;

(D) a creditor, an indenture trustee, an equity security holder, or a committee representing creditors or equity security holders other than a committee appointed under section 1102 of this title, in making a substantial contribution in a case under chapter 9 or 11 of this title;

(E) a custodian superseded under section 543 of this title, and compensation for the services of such custodian; or

(F) a member of a committee appointed under section 1102 of this title, if such expenses are incurred in the performance of the duties of such committee;

(4) reasonable compensation for professional services rendered by an attorney or an accountant of an entity whose expense is allowable under subparagraph (A), (B), (C), (D), or (E) of paragraph (3) of this subsection, based on the time, the nature, the extent, and the value of such services, and the cost of comparable services other than in a case under this title, and reimbursement for actual, necessary expenses incurred by such attorney or accountant;

(5) reasonable compensation for services rendered by an indenture trustee in making a substantial contribution in a case under chapter 9 or 11 of this title, based on the time, the nature, the extent, and the value of such services, and the cost of comparable services other than in a case under this title;

(6) the fees and mileage payable under chapter 119 of title 28;

(7) with respect to a nonresidential real property lease previously assumed under section 365, and subsequently rejected, a sum equal to all monetary obligations due, excluding those arising from or relating to a failure to operate or a penalty provision, for the period of 2 years following the later of the rejection date or the date of actual turnover of the premises, without reduction or setoff for any reason whatsoever except for sums actually received or to be received from an entity other than the debtor, and the claim for remaining sums due for the balance of the term of the lease shall be a claim under section 502(b)(6);

(8) the actual, necessary costs and expenses of closing a health care business incurred by a trustee or by a Federal agency (as defined in section 551(1) of title 5) or a department or agency of a State or political subdivision thereof, including any cost or expense incurred—

(A) in disposing of patient records in accordance with section 351; or

(B) in connection with transferring patients from the health care business that is in the process of being closed to another health care business; and

(9) the value of any goods received by the debtor within 20 days before the date of commencement of a case under this title in which the goods have been sold to the debtor in the ordinary course of such debtor's business.

(c) Notwithstanding subsection (b), there shall neither be allowed, nor paid—

(1) a transfer made to, or an obligation incurred for the benefit of, an insider of the debtor for the purpose of inducing such person to remain with the debtor's business, absent a finding by the court based on evidence in the record that—

(A) the transfer or obligation is essential to retention of the person because the individual has a bona fide job offer from another business at the same or greater rate of compensation;

(B) the services provided by the person are essential to the survival of the business; and

(C) either—

(i) the amount of the transfer made to, or obligation incurred for the benefit of, the person is not greater than an amount equal to 10 times the amount of the mean transfer or obligation of a similar kind given to nonmanagement employees for any purpose during the calendar year in which the transfer is made or the obligation is incurred; or

(ii) if no such similar transfers were made to, or obligations were incurred for the benefit of, such nonmanagement employees during such calendar year, the amount of the transfer or obligation is not greater than an amount equal to 25 percent of the amount of any similar transfer or obligation made to or incurred for the benefit of such insider for any purpose during the calendar year before the year in which such transfer is made or obligation is incurred;

(2) a severance payment to an insider of the debtor, unless—

(A) the payment is part of a program that is generally applicable to all full-time employees; and

(B) the amount of the payment is not greater than 10 times the amount of the mean severance pay given to nonmanagement employees during the calendar year in which the payment is made; or

(3) other transfers or obligations that are outside the ordinary course of business and not justified by the facts and circumstances of the case, including transfers made to, or obligations incurred for the benefit of, officers, managers, or consultants hired after the date of the filing of the petition.

(Pub. L. 95–598, Nov. 6, 1978, 92 Stat. 2581; Pub. L. 98–353, title III, §446, July 10, 1984, 98 Stat. 374; Pub. L. 99–554, title II, §283(g), Oct. 27, 1986, 100 Stat. 3117; Pub. L. 103–394, title I, §110, title II, §213(c), title III, §304(h)(2), Oct. 22, 1994, 108 Stat. 4113, 4126, 4134; Pub. L. 109–8, title III, §§329, 331, title IV, §445, title VII, §712(b), (c), title XI, §1103, title XII, §§1208, 1227(b), Apr. 20, 2005, 119 Stat. 101, 102, 117, 128, 190, 194, 200.)

Historical and Revision Notes

legislative statements

Section 503(a) of the House amendment represents a compromise between similar provisions in the House bill and the Senate amendment by leaving to the Rules of Bankruptcy Procedure the determination of the location at which a request for payment of an administrative expense may be filed. The preamble to section 503(b) of the House bill makes a similar change with respect to the allowance of administrative expenses.

Section 503(b)(1) adopts the approach taken in the House bill as modified by some provisions contained in the Senate amendment. The preamble to section 503(b) makes clear that none of the paragraphs of section 503(b) apply to claims or expenses of the kind specified in section 502(f) that arise in the ordinary course of the debtor's business or financial affairs and that arise during the gap between the commencement of an involuntary case and the appointment of a trustee or the order for relief, whichever first occurs. The remainder of section 503(b) represents a compromise between H.R. 8200 as passed by the House and the Senate amendments. Section 503(b)(3)(E) codifies present law in cases such as *Randolph v. Scruggs*, 190 U.S. 533, which accords administrative expense status to services rendered by a prepetition custodian or other party to the extent such services actually benefit the estate. Section 503(b)(4) of the House amendment conforms to the provision contained in H.R. 8200 as passed by the House and deletes language contained in the Senate amendment providing a different standard of compensation under section 330 of that amendment.

senate report no. 95–989

Subsection (a) of this section permits administrative expense claimants to file with the court a request for payment of an administrative expense. The Rules of Bankruptcy Procedure will specify the time, the form, and the method of such a filing.

Subsection (b) specifies the kinds of administrative expenses that are allowable in a case under the bankruptcy code. The subsection is derived mainly from section 64a(1) of the Bankruptcy Act [section 104(a)(1) of former title 11], with some changes. The actual, necessary costs and expenses of preserving the estate, including wages, salaries, or commissions for services rendered after the order for relief, and any taxes on, measured by, or withheld from such wages, salaries, or commissions, are allowable as administrative expenses.

In general, administrative expenses include taxes which the trustee incurs in administering the debtor's estate, including taxes on capital gains from sales of property by the trustee and taxes on income earned by the estate during the case. Interest on tax liabilities and certain tax penalties incurred by the trustee are also included in this first priority.

Taxes which the Internal Revenue Service may find due after giving the trustee a so-called "quickie" tax refund and later doing an audit of the refund are also payable as administrative expenses. The tax code [title 26] permits the trustee of an estate which suffers a net operating loss to carry back the loss against an earlier profit year of the estate or of the debtor and to obtain a tentative refund for the earlier year, subject, however, to a later full audit of the loss which led to the refund. The bill, in effect, requires the Internal Revenue Service to issue a tentative refund to the trustee (whether the refund was applied for by the debtor or by the trustee), but if the refund later proves to have been erroneous in amount, the Service can request that the tax attributable to the erroneous refund be payable by the estate as an administrative expense.

Postpetition payments to an individual debtor for services rendered to the estate are administrative expenses, and are not property of the estate when received by the debtor. This situation would most likely arise when the individual was a sole proprietor and was employed by the estate to run the business after the commencement of the case. An individual debtor in possession would be so employed, for example. See *Local Loan v. Hunt*, 292 U.S. 234, 243 (1943).

Compensation and reimbursement awarded officers of the estate under section 330 are allowable as administrative expenses. Actual, necessary expenses, other than compensation of a professional person, incurred by a creditor that files an involuntary petition, by a creditor that recovers property for the benefit of the estate, by a creditor that acts in connection with the prosecution of a criminal offense relating to the case, by a creditor, indenture, trustee, equity security holder, or committee of creditors or equity security holders (other than official committees) that makes a substantial contribution to a reorganization or municipal debt adjustment case, or by a superseded custodian, are all allowable administrative expenses. The phrase "substantial contribution in the case" is derived from Bankruptcy Act §§242 and 243 [sections 642 and 643 of former title 11]. It does not require a contribution that leads to confirmation of a plan, for in many cases, it will be a substantial contribution if the person involved uncovers facts that would lead to a denial of confirmation, such as fraud in connection with the case.

Paragraph (4) permits reasonable compensation for professional services rendered by an attorney or an accountant of an equity whose expense is compensable under the previous paragraph. Paragraph (5) permits reasonable compensation for an indenture trustee in making a substantial contribution in a reorganization or municipal debt adjustment case. Finally, paragraph (6) permits witness fees and mileage as prescribed under chapter 119 [§2041 et seq.] of title 28.

Amendments

2005—Subsec. (b)(1)(A). Pub. L. 109–8, §329, amended subpar. (A) generally. Prior to amendment, subpar. (A) read as follows: "the actual, necessary costs and expenses of preserving the estate, including wages, salaries, or commissions for services rendered after the commencement of the case;".

Subsec. (b)(1)(B)(i). Pub. L. 109–8, §712(b), inserted "whether secured or unsecured, including property taxes for which liability is in rem, in personam, or both," before "except".

Subsec. (b)(1)(D). Pub. L. 109–8, §712(c), added subpar. (D).

Subsec. (b)(4). Pub. L. 109–8, §1208, inserted "subparagraph (A), (B), (C), (D), or (E) of" before "paragraph (3)".

Subsec. (b)(7). Pub. L. 109–8, §445, added par. (7).

Subsec. (b)(8). Pub. L. 109–8, §1103, added par. (8).

Subsec. (b)(9). Pub. L. 109–8, §1227(b), added par. (9).

Subsec. (c). Pub. L. 109–8, §331, added subsec. (c).

1994—Subsec. (a). Pub. L. 103–394, §213(c), inserted "timely" after "may" and ", or may tardily file such request if permitted by the court for cause" before period at end.

Subsec. (b)(1)(B)(i). Pub. L. 103–394, §304(h)(2), substituted "507(a)(8)" for "507(a)(7)".

Subsec. (b)(3)(F). Pub. L. 103–394, §110, added subpar. (F).

1986—Subsec. (b)(1)(B)(i). Pub. L. 99–554, §283(g)(1), substituted "507(a)(7)" for "507(a)(6)".

Subsec. (b)(5). Pub. L. 99–554, §283(g)(2), inserted "and" after "title;".

Subsec. (b)(6). Pub. L. 99–554, §283(g)(3), substituted a period for "; and".

1984—Subsec. (b). Pub. L. 98–353, §446(1), struck out the comma after "be allowed" in provisions preceding par. (1).

Subsec. (b)(1)(C). Pub. L. 98–353, §446(2), struck out the comma after "credit".

Subsec. (b)(2). Pub. L. 98–353, §446(3), inserted "(a)" after "330".

Subsec. (b)(3). Pub. L. 98–353, §446(4), inserted a comma after "paragraph (4) of this subsection".

Subsec. (b)(3)(C). Pub. L. 98–353, §446(5), struck out the comma after "case".

Subsec. (b)(5). Pub. L. 98–353, §446(6), struck out "and" after "title;".

Subsec. (b)(6). Pub. L. 98–353, §446(7), substituted "; and" for period at end.

Effective Date of 2005 Amendment

Amendment by Pub. L. 109–8 effective 180 days after Apr. 20, 2005, and not applicable with respect to cases commenced under this title before such effective date, except as otherwise provided, see section 1501 of Pub. L. 109–8, set out as a note under section 101 of this title.

Effective Date of 1994 Amendment

Amendment by Pub. L. 103–394 effective Oct. 22, 1994, and not applicable with respect to cases commenced under this title before Oct. 22, 1994, see section 702 of Pub. L. 103–394, set out as a note under section 101 of this title.

Effective Date of 1986 Amendment

Amendment by Pub. L. 99–554 effective 30 days after Oct. 27, 1986, see section 302(a) of Pub. L. 99–554, set out as a note under section 581 of Title 28, Judiciary and Judicial Procedure.

Effective Date of 1984 Amendment

Amendment by Pub. L. 98–353 effective with respect to cases filed 90 days after July 10, 1984, see section 552(a) of Pub. L. 98–353, set out as a note under section 101 of this title.

§504. Sharing of compensation

(a) Except as provided in subsection (b) of this section, a person receiving compensation or reimbursement under section 503(b)(2) or 503(b)(4) of this title may not share or agree to share—

(1) any such compensation or reimbursement with another person; or

(2) any compensation or reimbursement received by another person under such sections.

(b)(1) A member, partner, or regular associate in a professional association, corporation, or partnership may share compensation or reimbursement received under section 503(b)(2) or 503(b)(4) of this title with another member, partner, or regular associate in such association, corporation, or partnership, and may share in any compensation or reimbursement received under such sections by another member, partner, or regular associate in such association, corporation, or partnership.

(2) An attorney for a creditor that files a petition under section 303 of this title may share compensation and reimbursement received under section 503(b)(4) of this title with any other attorney contributing to the services rendered or expenses incurred by such creditor's attorney.

(c) This section shall not apply with respect to sharing, or agreeing to share, compensation with a bona fide public service attorney referral program that operates in accordance with non-Federal law regulating attorney referral services and with rules of professional responsibility applicable to attorney acceptance of referrals.

(Pub. L. 95–598, Nov. 6, 1978, 92 Stat. 2582; Pub. L. 109–8, title III, §326, Apr. 20, 2005, 119 Stat. 99.)

Historical and Revision Notes

senate report no. 95–989

Section 504 prohibits the sharing of compensation, or fee splitting, among attorneys, other professionals, or trustees. The section provides only two exceptions: partners or associates in the same professional association, partnership, or corporation may share compensation inter se; and attorneys for petitioning creditors that join in a petition commencing an involuntary case may share compensation.

Amendments

2005—Subsec. (c). Pub. L. 109–8 added subsec. (c).

Effective Date of 2005 Amendment

Amendment by Pub. L. 109–8 effective 180 days after Apr. 20, 2005, and not applicable with respect to cases commenced under this title before such effective date, except as otherwise provided, see section 1501 of Pub. L. 109–8, set out as a note under section 101 of this title.

§505. Determination of tax liability

(a)(1) Except as provided in paragraph (2) of this subsection, the court may determine the amount or legality of any tax, any fine or penalty relating to a tax, or any addition to tax, whether or not previously assessed, whether or not paid, and whether or not contested before and adjudicated by a judicial or administrative tribunal of competent jurisdiction.

(2) The court may not so determine—

(A) the amount or legality of a tax, fine, penalty, or addition to tax if such amount or legality was contested before and adjudicated by a judicial or administrative tribunal of competent jurisdiction before the commencement of the case under this title;

(B) any right of the estate to a tax refund, before the earlier of—

(i) 120 days after the trustee properly requests such refund from the governmental unit from which such refund is claimed; or

(ii) a determination by such governmental unit of such request; or

(C) the amount or legality of any amount arising in connection with an ad valorem tax on real or personal property of the estate, if the applicable period for contesting or redetermining that amount under applicable nonbankruptcy law has expired.

(b)(1)(A) The clerk shall maintain a list under which a Federal, State, or local governmental unit responsible for the collection of taxes within the district may—

(i) designate an address for service of requests under this subsection; and

(ii) describe where further information concerning additional requirements for filing such requests may be found.

(B) If such governmental unit does not designate an address and provide such address to the clerk under subparagraph (A), any request made under this subsection may be served at the address for the filing of a tax return or protest with the appropriate taxing authority of such governmental unit.

(2) A trustee may request a determination of any unpaid liability of the estate for any tax incurred during the administration of the case by submitting a tax return for such tax and a request for such a determination to the governmental unit charged with responsibility for collection or determination of such tax at the address and in the manner designated in paragraph (1). Unless such return is fraudulent, or contains a material misrepresentation, the estate, the trustee, the debtor, and any successor to the debtor are discharged from any liability for such tax—

(A) upon payment of the tax shown on such return, if—

(i) such governmental unit does not notify the trustee, within 60 days after such request, that such return has been selected for examination; or

(ii) such governmental unit does not complete such an examination and notify the trustee of any tax due, within 180 days after such request or within such additional time as the court, for cause, permits;

(B) upon payment of the tax determined by the court, after notice and a hearing, after completion by such governmental unit of such examination; or

(C) upon payment of the tax determined by such governmental unit to be due.

(c) Notwithstanding section 362 of this title, after determination by the court of a tax under this section, the governmental unit charged with responsibility for collection of such tax may assess such tax against the estate, the debtor, or a successor to the debtor, as the case may be, subject to any otherwise applicable law.

(Pub. L. 95–598, Nov. 6, 1978, 92 Stat. 2582; Pub. L. 98–353, title III, §447, July 10, 1984, 98 Stat. 374; Pub. L. 109–8, title VII, §§701(b), 703, 715, Apr. 20, 2005, 119 Stat. 124, 125, 129; Pub. L. 111–327, §2(a)(14), Dec. 22, 2010, 124 Stat. 3559.)

Historical and Revision Notes

legislative statements

Section 505 of the House amendment adopts a compromise position with respect to the determination of tax liability from the position taken in H.R. 8200 as passed by the House and in the Senate amendment.

Determinations of tax liability: Authority of bankruptcy court to rule on merits of tax claims.—The House amendment authorizes the bankruptcy court to rule on the merits of any tax claim involving an unpaid tax, fine, or penalty relating to a tax, or any addition to a tax, of the debtor or the estate. This authority applies, in general, whether or not the tax, penalty, fine, or addition to tax had been previously assessed or paid. However, the bankruptcy court will not have jurisdiction to rule on the merits of any tax claim which has been previously adjudicated, in a contested proceeding, before a court of competent jurisdiction. For this purpose, a proceeding in the U.S. Tax Court is to be considered "contested" if the debtor filed a petition in the Tax Court by the commencement of the case and the Internal Revenue Service had filed an answer to the petition. Therefore, if a petition and answer were filed in the Tax Court before the title II petition was filed, and if the debtor later defaults in the Tax Court, then, under res judicata principles, the bankruptcy court could not then rule on the debtor's or the estate's liability for the same taxes.

The House amendment adopts the rule of the Senate bill that the bankruptcy court can, under certain conditions, determine the amount of tax refund claim by the trustee. Under the House amendment, if the refund results from an offset or counterclaim to a claim or request for payment by the Internal Revenue Service, or other tax authority, the trustee would not first have to file an administrative claim for refund with the tax authority.

However, if the trustee requests a refund in other situations, he would first have to submit an administrative claim for the refund. Under the House amendment, if the Internal Revenue Service, or other tax authority does not rule on the refund claim within 120 days, then the bankruptcy court may rule on the merits of the refund claim.

Under the Internal Revenue Code [title 26], a suit for refund of Federal taxes cannot be filed until 6 months after a claim for refund is filed with the Internal Revenue Service (sec. 6532(a) [title 26]). Because of the bankruptcy aim to close the estate as expeditiously as possible, the House amendment shortens to 120 days the period for the Internal Revenue Service to decide the refund claim.

The House amendment also adopts the substance of the Senate bill rule permitting the bankruptcy court to determine the amount of any penalty, whether punitive or pecuniary in nature, relating to taxes over which it has jurisdiction.

Jurisdiction of the tax court in bankruptcy cases: The Senate amendment provided a detailed series of rules concerning the jurisdiction of the U.S. Tax Court, or similar State or local administrative tribunal to determine personal tax liabilities of an individual debtor. The House amendment deletes these specific rules and relies on procedures to be derived from broad general powers of the bankruptcy court.

Under the House amendment, as under present law, a corporation seeking reorganization under chapter 11 is considered to be personally before the bankruptcy court for purposes of giving that court jurisdiction over the debtor's personal liability for a nondischargeable tax.

The rules are more complex where the debtor is an individual under chapter 7, 11, or 13. An individual debtor or the tax authority can, as under section 17c of the present Bankruptcy Act [section 35(c) of former title 11], file a request that the bankruptcy court determine the debtor's personal liability for the balance of any nondischargeable tax not satisfied from assets of the estate. The House amendment intends to retain these procedures and also adds a rule staying commencement or continuation of any proceeding in the Tax Court after the bankruptcy petition is filed, unless and until that stay is lifted by the bankruptcy judge under section 362(a)(8). The House amendment also stays assessment as well as collection of a prepetition claim against the debtor (sec. 362(a)(6)). A tax authority would not, however, be stayed from issuing a deficiency notice during the bankruptcy case (sec. (b)(7)) [sec. 362(b)(8)]. The Senate amendment repealed the existing authority of the Internal Revenue Service to make an immediate assessment of taxes upon bankruptcy (sec. 6871(a) of the code [title 26]. See section 321 of the Senate bill. As indicated, the substance of that provision, also affecting State and local taxes, is contained in section 362(a)(6) of the House amendment. The statute of limitations is tolled under the House amendment while the bankruptcy case is pending.

Where no proceeding in the Tax Court is pending at the commencement of the bankruptcy case, the tax authority can, under the House amendment, file a claim against the estate for a prepetition tax liability and may also file a request that the bankruptcy court hear arguments and decide the merits of an individual debtor's personal liability for the balance of any nondischargeable tax liability not satisfied from assets of the estate. Bankruptcy terminology refers to the latter type of request as a creditor's complaint to determine the dischargeability of a debt. Where such a complaint is filed, the bankruptcy court will have personal jurisdiction over an individual debtor, and the debtor himself would have no access to the Tax Court, or to any other court, to determine his personal liability for nondischargeable taxes.

If a tax authority decides not to file a claim for taxes which would typically occur where there are few, if any, assets in the estate, normally the tax authority would also not request the bankruptcy court to rule on the debtor's personal liability for a nondischargeable tax. Under the House amendment, the tax authority would then have to follow normal procedures in order to collect a nondischargeable tax. For example, in the case of nondischargeable Federal income taxes, the Internal Revenue Service would be required to issue a deficiency notice to an individual debtor, and the debtor could then file a petition in the Tax Court—or a refund suit in a district court—as the forum in which to litigate his personal liability for a nondischargeable tax.

Under the House amendment, as under present law, an individual debtor can also file a complaint to determine dischargeability. Consequently, where the tax authority does not file a claim or a request that the bankruptcy court determine dischargeability of a specific tax liability, the debtor could file such a request on his own behalf, so that the bankruptcy court would then determine both the validity of the claim against assets in the estate and also the personal liability of the debtor for any nondischargeable tax.

Where a proceeding is pending in the Tax Court at the commencement of the bankruptcy case, the commencement of the bankruptcy case automatically stays further action in the Tax Court case unless and until the stay is lifted by the bankruptcy court. The Senate amendment repealed a provision of the Internal Revenue case barring a debtor from filing a petition in the Tax Court after commencement of a bankruptcy case (sec. 6871(b) of the code [26 U.S.C. 6871(b)]). See section 321 of the Senate bill. As indicated earlier, the equivalent of the code amendment is embodied in section 362(a)(8) of the House amendment, which automatically stays commencement or continuation of any proceeding in the Tax Court until the stay is lifted or the case is terminated. The stay will permit sufficient time for the bankruptcy trustee to determine if he desires to join the Tax Court proceeding on behalf of the estate. Where the trustee chooses to join the Tax Court proceeding, it is expected that he will seek permission to intervene in the Tax Court case and then request that the stay on the Tax Court proceeding be lifted. In such a case, the merits of the tax liability will be determined by the Tax Court, and its decision will bind both the individual debtor as to any taxes which are nondischargeable and the trustee as to the tax claim against the estate.

Where the trustee does not want to intervene in the Tax Court, but an individual debtor wants to have the Tax Court determine the amount of his personal liability for nondischargeable taxes, the debtor can request the bankruptcy court to lift the automatic stay on existing Tax Court proceedings. If the stay is lifted and the Tax Court reaches its decision before the bankruptcy court's decision on the tax claim against the estate, the decision of the Tax Court would bind the bankruptcy court under principles of res judicata because the decision of the Tax Court affected the personal liability of the debtor. If the trustee does not wish to subject the estate to the decision of the Tax Court if the latter court decides the issues before the bankruptcy court rules, the trustee could resist the lifting of the stay on the existing Tax Court proceeding. If the Internal Revenue Service had issued a deficiency notice to the debtor before the bankruptcy case began, but as of the filing of the bankruptcy petition the 90-day period for filing in the Tax Court was still running, the debtor would be automatically stayed from filing a petition in the Tax Court. If either the debtor or the Internal Revenue Service then files a complaint to determine dischargeability in the bankruptcy court, the decision of the bankruptcy court would bind both the debtor and the Internal Revenue Service.

The bankruptcy judge could, however, lift the stay on the debtor to allow him to petition the Tax Court, while reserving the right to rule on the tax authority's claim against assets of the estate. The bankruptcy court could also, upon request by the trustee, authorize the trustee to intervene in the Tax Court for purposes of having the estate also governed by the decision of the Tax Court.

In essence, under the House amendment, the bankruptcy judge will have authority to determine which court will determine the merits of the tax claim both as to claims against the estate and claims against the debtor concerning his personal liability for nondischargeable taxes. Thus, if the Internal Revenue Service, or a State or local tax authority, files a petition to determine dischargeability, the bankruptcy judge can either rule on the merits of the claim and continue the stay on any pending Tax Court proceeding or lift the stay on the Tax Court and hold the dischargeability complaint in abeyance. If he rules on the merits of the complaint before the decision of the Tax Court is reached, the bankruptcy court's decision would bind the debtor as to nondischargeable taxes and the Tax Court would be governed by that decision under principles of res judicata. If the bankruptcy judge does not rule on the merits of the complaint before the decision of the Tax Court is reached, the bankruptcy court will be bound by the decision of the Tax Court as it affects the amount of any claim against the debtor's estate.

If the Internal Revenue Service does not file a complaint to determine dischargeability and the automatic stay on a pending Tax Court proceeding is not lifted, the bankruptcy court could determine the merits of any tax claim against the estate. That decision will not bind the debtor personally because he would not have been personally before the bankruptcy court unless the debtor himself asks the bankruptcy court to rule on his personal liability. In any such situation where no party filed a dischargeability petition, the debtor would have access to the Tax Court to determine his personal liability for a nondischargeable tax debt. While the Tax Court in such a situation could take into account the ruling of the bankruptcy court on claims against the estate in deciding the debtor's personal liability, the bankruptcy court's ruling would not bind the Tax Court under principles of res judicata, because the debtor, in that situation, would not have been personally before the bankruptcy court.

If neither the debtor nor the Internal Revenue Service files a claim against the estate or a request to rule on the debtor's personal liability, any pending tax court proceeding would be stayed until the closing of the bankruptcy case, at which time the stay on the tax court would cease and the tax court case could continue for purposes of deciding the merits of the debtor's personal liability for nondischargeable taxes.

Audit of trustee's returns: Under both bills, the bankruptcy court could determine the amount of any administrative period taxes. The Senate amendment, however, provided for an expedited audit procedure, which was mandatory in some cases. The House amendment (sec. 505(b)), adopts the provision of the House bill allowing the trustee discretion in all cases whether to ask the Internal Revenue Service, or State or local tax authority for a prompt audit of his returns on behalf of the estate. The House amendment, however, adopts the provision of the Senate bill permitting a prompt audit only on the basis of tax returns filed by the trustee for completed taxable periods. Procedures for a prompt audit set forth in the Senate bill are also adopted in modified form.

Under the procedure, before the case can be closed, the trustee may request a tax audit by the local, State or Federal tax authority of all tax returns filed by the trustee. The taxing authority would have to notify the trustee and the bankruptcy court within 60 days whether it accepts returns or desires to audit the returns more fully. If an audit is conducted, the taxing authority would have to notify the trustee of tax deficiency within 180 days after the original request, subject to extensions of time if the bankruptcy court approves. If the trustee does not agree with the results of the audit, the trustee could ask the bankruptcy court to resolve the dispute. Once the trustee's tax liability for administration period taxes has thus been determined, the legal effect in a case under chapter 7 or 11 would be to discharge the trustee and any predecessor of the trustee, and also the debtor, from any further liability for these taxes.

The prompt audit procedure would not be available with respect to any tax liability as to which any return required to be filed on behalf of the estate is not filed with the proper tax authority. The House amendment also specifies that a discharge of the trustee or the debtor which would otherwise occur will not be granted, or will be void if the return filed on behalf of the estate reflects fraud or material misrepresentation of facts.

For purposes of the above prompt audit procedures, it is intended that the tax authority with which the request for audit is to be filed is, as the Federal taxes, the office of the District Director in the district where the bankruptcy case is pending.

Under the House amendment, if the trustee does not request a prompt audit, the debtor would not be discharged from possible transferee liability if any assets are returned to the debtor.

Assessment after decision: As indicated above, the commencement of a bankruptcy case automatically stays assessment of any tax (sec. 362(a)(6)). However, the House amendment provides (sec. 505(c)) that if the bankruptcy court renders a final judgment with regard to any tax (under the rules discussed above), the tax authority may then make an assessment (if permitted to do so under otherwise applicable tax law) without waiting for termination of the case or confirmation of a reorganization plan.

Trustee's authority to appeal tax cases: The equivalent provision in the House bill (sec. 505(b)) and in the Senate bill (sec. 362(h)) authorizing the trustee to prosecute an appeal or review of a tax case are deleted as unnecessary. Section 541(a) of the House amendment provides that property of the estate is to include all legal or equitable interests of the debtor. These interests include the debtor's causes of action, so that the specific provisions of the House and Senate bills are not needed.

senate report no. 95–989

Subsections (a) and (b) are derived, with only stylistic changes, from section 2a(2A) of the Bankruptcy Act [section 11(a)(2A) of former title 11]. They permit determination by the bankruptcy court of any unpaid tax liability of the debtor that has not been contested before or adjudicated by a judicial or administrative tribunal of competent jurisdiction before the bankruptcy case, and the prosecution by the trustee of an appeal from an order of such a body if the time for review or appeal has not expired before the commencement of the bankruptcy case. As under current Bankruptcy Act §2a (2A), *Arkansas Corporation Commissioner v. Thompson*, 313 U.S. 132 (1941), remains good law to permit abstention where uniformity of assessment is of significant importance.

Section (c) deals with procedures for obtaining a prompt audit of tax returns filed by the trustee in a liquidation or reorganization case. Under the bill as originally introduced, a trustee who is "in doubt" concerning tax liabilities of the estate incurred during a title 11 proceeding could obtain a discharge from personal liability for himself and the debtor (but not for the debtor or the debtor's successor in a reorganization), provided that certain administrative procedures were followed. The trustee could request a prompt tax audit by the local, State, or Federal governmental unit. The taxing authority would have to notify the trustee and the court within sixty days whether it accepted the return or desired to audit the returns more fully. If an audit were conducted, the tax office would have to notify the trustee of any tax deficiency within 4 months (subject to an extension of time if the court approved).

These procedures would apply only to tax years completed on or before the case was closed and for which the trustee had filed a tax return.

The committee bill eliminates the "in doubt" rule and makes mandatory (rather than optional) the trustee's request for a prompt audit of the estate's tax returns. In many cases, the trustee could not be certain that his returns raised no doubt about possible tax issues. In addition, it is desirable not to create a situation where the taxing authority asserts a tax liability against the debtor (as transferee of surplus assets, if any, return to him) after the case is over; in any such situation, the debtor would be called on to defend a tax return which he did not prepare. Under the amendment, all disputes concerning these returns are to be resolved by the bankruptcy court, and both the trustee and the debtor himself do not then face potential post-bankruptcy tax liabilities based on these returns. This result would occur as to the debtor, however, only in a liquidation case.

In a reorganization in which the debtor or a successor to the debtor continues in existence, the trustee could obtain a discharge from personal liability through the prompt audit procedure, but the Treasury could still claim a deficiency against the debtor (or his successor) for additional taxes due on returns filed during the title 11 proceedings.

house report no. 95–595

Subsection (c) is new. It codifies in part the referee's decision in *In re Statmaster Corp.*, 465 F.2d 987 (5th Cir. 1972). Its purpose is to protect the trustee from personal liability for a tax falling on the estate that is not assessed until after the case is closed. If necessary to permit expeditious closing of the case, the court, on request of the trustee, must order the governmental unit charged with the responsibility for collection or determination of the tax to audit the trustee's return or be barred from attempting later collection. The court will be required to permit sufficient time to perform an audit, if the taxing authority requests it. The final order of the court and the payment of the tax determined in that order discharges the trustee, the debtor, and any successor to the debtor from any further liability for the tax. See Plumb, The Tax Recommendations of the Commission on the Bankruptcy Laws: Tax Procedures, 88 Harv. L. Rev. 1360, 1423–42 (1975).

Amendments

2010—Subsec. (a)(2)(C). Pub. L. 111–327 substituted "applicable nonbankruptcy law" for "any law (other than a bankruptcy law)".

2005—Subsec. (a)(2)(C). Pub. L. 109–8, §701(b), added subpar. (C).

Subsec. (b). Pub. L. 109–8, §703, added par. (1), redesignated existing provisions of subsec. (b) as par. (2) and inserted "at the address and in the manner designated in paragraph (1)" after "determination of such tax" in introductory provisions, redesignated former pars. (1) to (3) of subsec. (b) as subpars. (A) to (C), respectively, of par. (2), and redesignated former subpars (A) and (B) of par. (1) as cls. (i) and (ii), respectively, of subpar. (A).

Subsec. (b)(2). Pub. L. 109–8, §715, inserted "the estate," after "misrepresentation," in introductory provisions.

1984—Subsec. (a)(2)(B)(i). Pub. L. 98–353 substituted "or" for "and".

Effective Date of 2005 Amendment

Amendment by Pub. L. 109–8 effective 180 days after Apr. 20, 2005, and not applicable with respect to cases commenced under this title before such effective date, except as otherwise provided, see section 1501 of Pub. L. 109–8, set out as a note under section 101 of this title.

Effective Date of 1984 Amendment

Amendment by Pub. L. 98–353 effective with respect to cases filed 90 days after July 10, 1984, see section 552(a) of Pub. L. 98–353, set out as a note under section 101 of this title.

§506. Determination of secured status

(a)(1) An allowed claim of a creditor secured by a lien on property in which the estate has an interest, or that is subject to setoff under section 553 of this title, is a secured claim to the extent of the value of such creditor's interest in the estate's interest in such property, or to the extent of the amount subject to setoff, as the case may be, and is an unsecured claim to the extent that the value of such creditor's interest or the amount so subject to setoff is less than the amount of such allowed claim. Such value shall be determined in light of the purpose of the valuation and of the proposed disposition or use of such property, and in conjunction with any hearing on such disposition or use or on a plan affecting such creditor's interest.

(2) If the debtor is an individual in a case under chapter 7 or 13, such value with respect to personal property securing an allowed claim shall be determined based on the replacement value of such property as of the date of the filing of the petition without deduction for costs of sale or marketing. With respect to property acquired for personal, family, or household purposes, replacement value shall mean the price a retail merchant would charge for property of that kind considering the age and condition of the property at the time value is determined.

(b) To the extent that an allowed secured claim is secured by property the value of which, after any recovery under subsection (c) of this section, is greater than the amount of such claim, there shall be allowed to the holder of such claim, interest on such claim, and any reasonable fees, costs, or charges provided for under the agreement or State statute under which such claim arose.

(c) The trustee may recover from property securing an allowed secured claim the reasonable, necessary costs and expenses of preserving, or disposing of, such property to the extent of any benefit to the holder of such claim, including the payment of all ad valorem property taxes with respect to the property.

(d) To the extent that a lien secures a claim against the debtor that is not an allowed secured claim, such lien is void, unless—

(1) such claim was disallowed only under section 502(b)(5) or 502(e) of this title; or

(2) such claim is not an allowed secured claim due only to the failure of any entity to file a proof of such claim under section 501 of this title.

(Pub. L. 95–598, Nov. 6, 1978, 92 Stat. 2583; Pub. L. 98–353, title III, §448, July 10, 1984, 98 Stat. 374; Pub. L. 109–8, title III, §327, title VII, §712(d), Apr. 20, 2005, 119 Stat. 99, 128.)

Historical and Revision Notes

legislative statements

Section 506(a) of the House amendment adopts the provision contained in the Senate amendment and rejects a contrary provision as contained in H.R. 8200 as passed by the House. The provision contained in the Senate amendment and adopted by the House amendment recognizes that an amount subject to set-off is sufficient to recognize a secured status in the holder of such right. Additionally a determination of what portion of an allowed claim is secured and what portion is unsecured is binding only for the purpose for which the determination is made. Thus determinations for purposes of adequate protection is not binding for purposes of "cram down" on confirmation in a case under chapter 11.

Section 506(b) of the House amendment adopts language contained in the Senate amendment and rejects language contained in H.R. 8200 as passed by the House. If the security agreement between the parties provides for attorneys' fees, it will be enforceable under title 11, notwithstanding contrary law, and is recoverable from the collateral after any recovery under section 506(c).

Section 506(c) of the House amendment was contained in H.R. 8200 as passed by the House and adopted, verbatim, in the Senate amendment. Any time the trustee or debtor in possession expends money to provide for the reasonable and necessary cost and expenses of preserving or disposing of a secured creditor's collateral, the trustee or debtor in possession is entitled to recover such expenses from the secured party or from the property securing an allowed secured claim held by such party.

Section 506(d) of the House amendment is derived from H.R. 8200 as passed by the House and is adopted in lieu of the alternative test provided in section 506(d) of the Senate amendment. For purposes of section 506(d) of the House amendment, the debtor is a party in interest.

Determination of Secured Status: The House amendment deletes section 506(d)(3) of the Senate amendment, which insures that a tax lien securing a nondischargeable tax claim is not voided because a tax authority with notice or knowledge of the bankruptcy case fails to file a claim for the liability (as it may elect not to do, if it is clear there are insufficient assets to pay the liability). Since the House amendment retains section 506(d) of the House bill that a lien is not voided unless a party in interest has requested that the court determine and allow or disallow the claim, provision of the Senate amendment is not necessary.

senate report no. 95–989

Subsection (a) of this section separates an undersecured creditor's claim into two parts: He has a secured claim to the extent of the value of his collateral; and he has an unsecured claim for the balance of his claim. The subsection also provides for the valuation of claims which involve setoffs under section 553. While courts will have to determine value on a case-by-case basis, the subsection makes it clear that valuation is to be determined in light of the purpose of the valuation and the proposed disposition or use of the subject property. This determination shall be made in conjunction with any hearing on such disposition or use of property or on a plan affecting the creditor's interest. To illustrate, a valuation early in the case in a proceeding under sections 361–363 would not be binding upon the debtor or creditor at the time of confirmation of the plan. Throughout the bill, references to secured claims are only to the claim determined to be secured under this subsection, and not to the full amount of the creditor's claim. This provision abolishes the use of the terms "secured creditor" and "unsecured creditor" and substitutes in their places the terms "secured claim" and "unsecured claim."

Subsection (b) codifies current law by entitling a creditor with an oversecured claim to any reasonable fees (including attorney's fees), costs, or charges provided under the agreement under which the claim arose. These fees, costs, and charges are secured claims to the extent that the value of the collateral exceeds the amount of the underlying claim.

Subsection (c) also codifies current law by permitting the trustee to recover from property the value of which is greater than the sum of the claims secured by a lien on that property the reasonable, necessary costs and expenses of preserving, or disposing of, the property. The recovery is limited to the extent of any benefit to the holder of such claim.

Subsection (d) provides that to the extent a secured claim is not allowed, its lien is void unless the holder had neither actual notice nor knowledge of the case, the lien was not listed by the debtor in a chapter 9 or 11 case or such claim was disallowed only under section 502(e).

house report no. 95–595

Subsection (d) permits liens to pass through the bankruptcy case unaffected. However, if a party in interest requests the court to determine and allow or disallow the claim secured by the lien under section 502 and the claim is not allowed, then the lien is void to the extent that the claim is not allowed. The voiding provision does not apply to claims disallowed only under section 502(e), which requires disallowance of certain claims against the debtor by a codebtor, surety, or guarantor for contribution or reimbursement.

Amendments

2005—Subsec. (a). Pub. L. 109–8, §327, designated existing provisions as par. (1) and added par. (2).

Subsec. (b). Pub. L. 109–8, §712(d)(1), inserted "or State statute" after "agreement".

Subsec. (c). Pub. L. 109–8, §712(d)(2), inserted ", including the payment of all ad valorem property taxes with respect to the property" before period at end.

1984—Subsec. (b). Pub. L. 98–353, §448(a), inserted "for" after "provided".

Subsec. (d)(1). Pub. L. 98–353, §448(b), substituted "such claim was disallowed only under section 502(b)(5) or 502(e) of this title" for "a party in interest has not requested that the court determine and allow or disallow such claim under section 502 of this title".

Subsec. (d)(2). Pub. L. 98–353, §448(b), substituted "such claim is not an allowed secured claim due only to the failure of any entity to file a proof of such claim under section 501 of this title" for "such claim was disallowed only under section 502(e) of this title".

Effective Date of 2005 Amendment

Amendment by Pub. L. 109–8 effective 180 days after Apr. 20, 2005, and not applicable with respect to cases commenced under this title before such effective date, except as otherwise provided, see section 1501 of Pub. L. 109–8, set out as a note under section 101 of this title.

Effective Date of 1984 Amendment

Amendment by Pub. L. 98–353 effective with respect to cases filed 90 days after July 10, 1984, see section 552(a) of Pub. L. 98–353, set out as a note under section 101 of this title.

§507. Priorities

(a) The following expenses and claims have priority in the following order:

(1) First:

(A) Allowed unsecured claims for domestic support obligations that, as of the date of the filing of the petition in a case under this title, are owed to or recoverable by a spouse, former spouse, or child of the debtor, or such child's parent, legal guardian, or responsible relative, without regard to whether the claim is filed by such person or is filed by a governmental unit on behalf of such person, on the condition that funds received under this paragraph by a governmental unit under this title after the date of the filing of the petition shall be applied and distributed in accordance with applicable nonbankruptcy law.

(B) Subject to claims under subparagraph (A), allowed unsecured claims for domestic support obligations that, as of the date of the filing of the petition, are assigned by a spouse, former spouse, child of the debtor, or such child's parent, legal guardian, or responsible relative to a governmental unit (unless such obligation is assigned voluntarily by the spouse, former spouse, child, parent, legal guardian, or responsible relative of the child for the purpose of collecting the debt) or are owed directly to or recoverable by a governmental unit under applicable nonbankruptcy law, on the condition that funds received under this paragraph by a governmental unit under this title after the date of the filing of the petition be applied and distributed in accordance with applicable nonbankruptcy law.

(C) If a trustee is appointed or elected under section 701, 702, 703, 1104, 1202, or 1302, the administrative expenses of the trustee allowed under paragraphs (1)(A), (2), and (6) of section 503(b) shall be paid before payment of claims under subparagraphs (A) and (B), to the extent that the trustee administers assets that are otherwise available for the payment of such claims.

(2) Second, administrative expenses allowed under section 503(b) of this title, unsecured claims of any Federal reserve bank related to loans made through programs or facilities authorized under section 13(3) of the Federal Reserve Act (12 U.S.C. 343),[1] and any fees and charges assessed against the estate under chapter 123 of title 28.

(3) Third, unsecured claims allowed under section 502(f) of this title.

(4) Fourth, allowed unsecured claims, but only to the extent of $10,000 [2] for each individual or corporation, as the case may be, earned within 180 days before the date of the filing of the petition or the date of the cessation of the debtor's business, whichever occurs first, for—

(A) wages, salaries, or commissions, including vacation, severance, and sick leave pay earned by an individual; or

(B) sales commissions earned by an individual or by a corporation with only 1 employee, acting as an independent contractor in the sale of goods or services for the debtor in the ordinary course of the debtor's business if, and only if, during the 12 months preceding that date, at least 75 percent of the amount that the individual or corporation earned by acting as an independent contractor in the sale of goods or services was earned from the debtor.

(5) Fifth, allowed unsecured claims for contributions to an employee benefit plan—

(A) arising from services rendered within 180 days before the date of the filing of the petition or the date of the cessation of the debtor's business, whichever occurs first; but only

(B) for each such plan, to the extent of—

(i) the number of employees covered by each such plan multiplied by $10,000; [2] less

(ii) the aggregate amount paid to such employees under paragraph (4) of this subsection, plus the aggregate amount paid by the estate on behalf of such employees to any other employee benefit plan.

(6) Sixth, allowed unsecured claims of persons—

(A) engaged in the production or raising of grain, as defined in section 557(b) of this title, against a debtor who owns or operates a grain storage facility, as defined in section 557(b) of this title, for grain or the proceeds of grain, or

(B) engaged as a United States fisherman against a debtor who has acquired fish or fish produce from a fisherman through a sale or conversion, and who is engaged in operating a fish produce storage or processing facility—

but only to the extent of $4,000 [2] for each such individual.

(7) Seventh, allowed unsecured claims of individuals, to the extent of $1,800 [2] for each such individual, arising from the deposit, before the commencement of the case, of money in connection with the purchase, lease, or rental of property, or the purchase of services, for the personal, family, or household use of such individuals, that were not delivered or provided.

(8) Eighth, allowed unsecured claims of governmental units, only to the extent that such claims are for—

(A) a tax on or measured by income or gross receipts for a taxable year ending on or before the date of the filing of the petition—

(i) for which a return, if required, is last due, including extensions, after three years before the date of the filing of the petition;

(ii) assessed within 240 days before the date of the filing of the petition, exclusive of—

(I) any time during which an offer in compromise with respect to that tax was pending or in effect during that 240-day period, plus 30 days; and

(II) any time during which a stay of proceedings against collections was in effect in a prior case under this title during that 240-day period, plus 90 days; or

(iii) other than a tax of a kind specified in section 523(a)(1)(B) or 523(a)(1)(C) of this title, not assessed before, but assessable, under applicable law or by agreement, after, the commencement of the case;

(B) a property tax incurred before the commencement of the case and last payable without penalty after one year before the date of the filing of the petition;

(C) a tax required to be collected or withheld and for which the debtor is liable in whatever capacity;

(D) an employment tax on a wage, salary, or commission of a kind specified in paragraph (4) of this subsection earned from the debtor before the date of the filing of the petition, whether or not actually paid before such date, for which a return is last due, under applicable law or under any extension, after three years before the date of the filing of the petition;

(E) an excise tax on—

(i) a transaction occurring before the date of the filing of the petition for which a return, if required, is last due, under applicable law or under any extension, after three years before the date of the filing of the petition; or

(ii) if a return is not required, a transaction occurring during the three years immediately preceding the date of the filing of the petition;

(F) a customs duty arising out of the importation of merchandise—

(i) entered for consumption within one year before the date of the filing of the petition;

(ii) covered by an entry liquidated or reliquidated within one year before the date of the filing of the petition; or

(iii) entered for consumption within four years before the date of the filing of the petition but unliquidated on such date, if the Secretary of the Treasury certifies that failure to liquidate such entry was due to an investigation pending on such date into assessment of antidumping or countervailing duties or fraud, or if information needed for the proper appraisement or classification of such merchandise was not available to the appropriate customs officer before such date; or

(G) a penalty related to a claim of a kind specified in this paragraph and in compensation for actual pecuniary loss.

An otherwise applicable time period specified in this paragraph shall be suspended for any period during which a governmental unit is prohibited under applicable nonbankruptcy law from collecting a tax as a result of a request by the debtor for a hearing and an appeal of any collection action taken or proposed against the debtor, plus 90 days; plus any time during which the stay of proceedings was in effect in a prior case under this title or during which collection was precluded by the existence of 1 or more confirmed plans under this title, plus 90 days.

(9) Ninth, allowed unsecured claims based upon any commitment by the debtor to a Federal depository institutions regulatory agency (or predecessor to such agency) to maintain the capital of an insured depository institution.

(10) Tenth, allowed claims for death or personal injury resulting from the operation of a motor vehicle or vessel if such operation was unlawful because the debtor was intoxicated from using alcohol, a drug, or another substance.

(b) If the trustee, under section 362, 363, or 364 of this title, provides adequate protection of the interest of a holder of a claim secured by a lien on property of the debtor and if, notwithstanding such protection, such creditor has a claim allowable under subsection (a)(2) of this section arising from the stay of action against such property under section 362 of this title, from the use, sale, or lease of such property under section 363 of this title, or from the granting of a lien under section 364(d) of this title, then such creditor's claim under such subsection shall have priority over every other claim allowable under such subsection.

(c) For the purpose of subsection (a) of this section, a claim of a governmental unit arising from an erroneous refund or credit of a tax has the same priority as a claim for the tax to which such refund or credit relates.

(d) An entity that is subrogated to the rights of a holder of a claim of a kind specified in subsection (a)(1), (a)(4), (a)(5), (a)(6), (a)(7), (a)(8), or (a)(9) of this section is not subrogated to the right of the holder of such claim to priority under such subsection.

(Pub. L. 95–598, Nov. 6, 1978, 92 Stat. 2583; Pub. L. 98–353, title III, §§350, 449, July 10, 1984, 98 Stat. 358, 374; Pub. L. 101–647, title XXV, §2522(d), Nov. 29, 1990, 104 Stat. 4867; Pub. L. 103–394, title I, §108(c), title II, §207, title III, §304(c), title V, §501(b)(3), (d)(11), Oct. 22, 1994, 108 Stat. 4112, 4123, 4132, 4142, 4145; Pub. L. 109–8, title II, §§212, 223, title VII, §§705, 706, title XIV, §1401, title XV, §1502(a)(1), Apr. 20, 2005, 119 Stat. 51, 62, 126, 214, 216; Pub. L. 111–203, title XI, §1101(b), July 21, 2010, 124 Stat. 2115; Pub. L. 111–327, §2(a)(15), Dec. 22, 2010, 124 Stat. 3559.)

Historical and Revision Notes
legislative statements

Section 507(a)(3) of the House amendment represents a compromise dollar amount and date for the priority between similar provisions contained in H.R. 8200 as passed by the House and the Senate amendments. A similar compromise is contained in section 507(a)(4).

Section 507(a)(5) represents a compromise on amount between the priority as contained in H.R. 8200 as passed by the House and the Senate amendment. The Senate provision for limiting the priority to consumers having less than a fixed gross income is deleted.

Section 507(a)(6) of the House amendment represents a compromise between similar provisions contained in H.R. 8200 as passed by the House and the Senate amendment.

Section 507(b) of the House amendment is new and is derived from the compromise contained in the House amendment with respect to adequate protection under section 361. Subsection (b) provides that to the extent adequate protection of the interest of a holder of a claim proves to be inadequate, then the creditor's claim is given priority over every other allowable claim entitled to distribution under section 507(a). Section 507(b) of the Senate amendment is deleted.

Section 507(c) of the House amendment is new. Section 507(d) of the House amendment prevents subrogation with respect to priority for certain priority claims. Subrogation with respect to priority is intended to be permitted for administrative claims and claims arising during the gap period.

Priorities: Under the House amendment, taxes receive priority as follows:

First. Administration expenses: The amendment generally follows the Senate amendment in providing expressly that taxes incurred during the administration of the estate share the first priority given to administrative expenses generally. Among the taxes which receives first priority, as defined in section 503, are the employees' and the employer's shares of employment taxes on wages earned and paid after the petition is filed. Section 503(b)(1) also includes in administration expenses a tax liability arising from an excessive allowance by a tax authority of a "quickie refund" to the estate. (In the case of Federal taxes, such refunds are allowed under special rules based on net operating loss carrybacks (sec. 6411 of the Internal Revenue Code [title 26]).

An exception is made to first priority treatment for taxes incurred by the estate with regard to the employer's share of employment taxes on wages earned from the debtor before the petition but paid from the estate after the petition has been filed. In this situation, the employer's tax receives either sixth priority or general claim treatment.

The House amendment also adopts the provisions of the Senate amendment which include in the definition of administrative expenses under section 503 any fine, penalty (including "additions to tax" under applicable tax laws) or reduction in credit imposed on the estate.

Second. "Involuntary gap" claims: "Involuntary gap" creditors are granted second priority by paragraph (2) of section 507(a). This priority includes tax claims arising in the ordinary course of the debtor's business or financial affairs after he has been placed involuntarily in bankruptcy but before a trustee is appointed or before the order for relief.

Third. Certain taxes on prepetition wages: Wage claims entitled to third priority are for compensation which does not exceed $2,000 and was earned during the 90 days before the filing of the bankruptcy petition or the cessation of the debtor's business. Certain employment taxes receive third priority in payment from the estate along with the payment of wages to which the taxes relate. In the case of wages earned before the filing of the petition, but paid by the trustee (rather than by the debtor) after the filing of the petition, claims or the employees' share of the employment taxes (withheld income taxes and the employees' share of the social security or railroad retirement tax) receive third priority to the extent the wage claims themselves are entitled to this priority.

In the case of wages earned from and paid by the debtor before the filing of the petition, the employer's share of the employment taxes on these wages paid by the debtor receives sixth priority or, if not entitled to that priority, are treated only as general claims. Under the House amendment, the employer's share of employment taxes on wages earned by employees of the debtor, but paid by the trustee after the filing of the bankruptcy petition, will also receive sixth priority to the extent that claims for the wages receive third priority. To the extent the claims for wages do not receive third priority, but instead are treated only as general claims, claims for the employer's share of the employment taxes attributable to those wages will also be treated as general claims. In calculating the amounts payable as general wage claims, the trustee must pay the employer's share of employment taxes on such wages.

Sixth priority. The House amendment modifies the provisions of both the House bill and Senate amendment in the case of sixth priority taxes. Under the amendment, the following Federal, State and local taxes are included in the sixth priority:

First. Income and gross receipts taxes incurred before the date of the petition for which the last due date of the return, including all extensions of time granted to file the return, occurred within 3 years before the date on which the petition was filed, or after the petition date. Under this rule, the due date of the return, rather than the date on which the taxes were assessed, determines the priority.

Second. Income and gross receipts taxes assessed at any time within 240 days before the petition date. Under this rule, the date on which the governmental unit assesses the tax, rather than the due date of the return, determines the priority.

If, following assessment of a tax, the debtor submits an offer in compromise to the governmental unit, the House amendment provides that the 240-day period is to be suspended for the duration of the offer and will resume running after the offer is withdrawn or rejected by the governmental unit, but the tax liability will receive priority if the title 11 petition is filed during the balance of the 240-day period or during a minimum of 30 days after the offer is withdrawn or rejected. This rule modifies a provision of the Senate amendment dealing specifically with offers in compromise. Under the modified rule, if, after the assessment, an offer in compromise is submitted by the debtor and is still pending (without having been accepted or rejected) at the date on which a title 11 petition is filed, the underlying liability will receive sixth priority. However, if an assessment of a tax liability is made but the tax is not collected within 240 days, the tax will not receive priority under section 507(a)(6)(A)(i) and the debtor cannot revive a priority for that tax by submitting an offer in compromise.

Third. Income and gross receipts taxes not assessed before the petition date but still permitted, under otherwise applicable tax laws, to be assessed. Thus, for example, a prepetition tax liability is to receive sixth priority under this rule if, under the applicable statute of limitations, the tax liability can still be assessed by the tax authority. This rule also covers situations referred to in section 507(a)(6)(B)(ii) of the Senate amendment where the assessment or collection of a tax was prohibited before the petition pending exhaustion of judicial or administrative remedies, except that the House amendment eliminates the 300-day limitation of the Senate bill. So, for example, if before the petition a debtor was engaged in litigation in the Tax Court, during which the Internal Revenue Code [title 26] bars the Internal Revenue Service from assessing or collecting the tax, and if the tax court decision is made in favor of the Service before the petition under title 11 is filed, thereby lifting the restrictions on assessment and collection, the tax liability will receive sixth priority even if the tax authority does not make an assessment within 300 days before the petition (provided, of course, that the statute of limitations on assessment has not expired by the petition date).

In light of the above categories of the sixth priority, and tax liability of the debtor (under the Internal Revenue Code [title 26] or State or local law) as a transferee of property from another person will receive sixth priority without the limitations contained in the Senate amendment so long as the transferee liability had not been assessed by the tax authority by the petition date but could still have been assessed by that date under the applicable tax statute of limitations or, if the transferee liability had been assessed before the petition, the assessment was made no more than 240 days before the petition date.

Also in light of the above categories, the treatment of prepetition tax liabilities arising from an excessive allowance to the debtor of a tentative carryback adjustment, such as a "quickie refund" under section 6411 of the Internal Revenue Code [title 26] is revised as follows: If the tax authority has assessed the additional tax before the petition, the tax liability will receive priority if the date of assessment was within 240 days before the petition date. If the tax authority had not assessed the additional tax by the petition, the tax liability will still receive priority so long as, on the petition date, assessment of the liability is not barred by the statute of limitations.

Fourth. Any property tax assessed before the commencement of the case and last payable without penalty within 1 year before the petition, or thereafter.

Fifth. Taxes which the debtor was required by law to withhold or collect from others and for which he is liable in any capacity, regardless of the age of the tax claims. This category covers the so-called "trust fund" taxes, that is, income taxes which an employer is required to withhold from the pay of his employees, and the employees' share of social security taxes.

In addition, this category includes the liability of a responsible officer under the Internal Revenue Code (sec. 6672) [title 26] for income taxes or for the employees' share of social security taxes which that officer was responsible for withholding from the wages of employees and paying to the Treasury, although he was not himself the employer. This priority will operate when a person found to be a responsible officer has himself filed in title 11, and the priority will cover the debtor's responsible officer liability regardless of the age of the tax year to which the tax relates. The U.S. Supreme Court has interpreted present law to require the same result as will be reached under this rule. *U.S. v. Sotelo*, 436 U.S. 268 (1978) [98 S.Ct. 1795, 56 L.Ed.2d 275, rehearing denied 98 S.Ct. 3126, 438 U.S. 907, 57 L.Ed.2d 1150].

This category also includes the liability under section 3505 of the Internal Revenue Code [26 U.S.C. 3505] of a taxpayer who loans money for the payment of wages or other compensation.

Sixth. The employer's share of employment taxes on wages paid before the petition and on third-priority wages paid postpetition by the estate. The priority rules under the House amendment governing employment taxes can thus be summarized as follows: Claims for the employees' shares of employment taxes attributable to wages both earned and paid before the filing of the petition are to receive sixth priority. In the case of employee wages earned, but not paid, before the filing of the bankruptcy petition, claims for the employees' share of employment taxes receive third priority to the extent the wages themselves receive third priority. Claims which relate to wages earned before the petition, but not paid before the petition (and which are not entitled to the third priority under the rule set out above), will be paid as general claims. Since the related wages will receive no priority, the related employment taxes would also be paid as nonpriority general claims.

The employer's share of the employment taxes on wages earned and paid before the bankruptcy petition will receive sixth priority to the extent the return for these taxes was last due (including extensions of time) within 3 years before the filing of the petition, or was due after the petition was filed. Older tax claims of this nature will be payable as general claims. In the case of wages earned by employees before the petition, but actually paid by the trustee (as claims against the estate) after the title 11 case commenced, the employer's share of the employment taxes on third priority wages will be payable as sixth priority claims and the employer's taxes on prepetition wages which are treated only as general claims will be payable only as general claims. In calculating the amounts payable as general wage claims, the trustee must pay the employer's share of employment taxes on such wages. The House amendment thus deletes the provision of the Senate amendment that certain employer taxes receive third priority and are to be paid immediately after payment of third priority wages and the employees' shares of employment taxes on those wages.

In the case of employment taxes relating to wages earned and paid after the petition, both the employees' shares and the employer's share will receive first priority as administration expenses of the estate.

Seventh. Excise taxes on transactions for which a return, if required, is last due, under otherwise applicable law or under any extension of time to file the return, within 3 years before the petition was filed, or thereafter. If a return is not required with regard to a particular excise tax, priority is given if the transaction or event itself occurred within 3 years before the date on which the title 11 petition was filed. All Federal, State or local taxes generally considered or expressly treated as excises are covered by this category, including sales taxes, estate and gift taxes, gasoline and special fuel taxes, and wagering and truck taxes.

Eighth. Certain unpaid customs duties. The House amendment covers in this category duties on imports entered for consumption within 1 year before the filing of the petition, but which are still unliquidated on the petition date; duties covered by an entry liquidated or reliquidated within 1 year before the petition date; and any duty on merchandise entered for consumption within 4 years before the petition but not liquidated on the petition date, if the Secretary of the Treasury or his delegate certifies that duties were not liquidated because of possible assessment of antidumping or countervailing duties or fraud penalties.

For purposes of the above priority rules, the House amendment adopts the provision of the Senate bill that any tax liability which, under otherwise applicable tax law, is collectible in the form of a "penalty," is to be treated in the same manner as a tax liability. In bankruptcy terminology, such tax liabilities are referred to as pecuniary loss penalties. Thus, any tax liability which under the Internal Revenue Code [title 26] or State or local tax law is payable as a "penalty," in addition to the liability of a responsible person under section 6672 of the Internal Revenue Code [26 U.S.C. 6672] will be entitled to the priority which the liability would receive if it were expressly labeled as a "tax" under the applicable tax law. However, a tax penalty which is punitive in nature is given subordinated treatment under section 726(a)(4).

The House amendment also adopts the provision of the Senate amendment that a claim arising from an erroneous refund or credit of tax, other than a "quickie refund," is to receive the same priority as the tax to which the refund or credit relates.

The House amendment deletes the express provision of the Senate amendment that a tax liability is to receive sixth priority if it satisfies any one of the subparagraphs of section 507(a)(6) even if the liability fails to satisfy the terms of one or more other subparagraphs. No change of substance is intended by the deletion, however, in light of section 102(5) of the House amendment, providing a rule of construction that the word "or" is not intended to be exclusive.

The House amendment deletes from the express priority categories of the Senate amendment the priority for a debtor's liability as a third party for failing to surrender property or to pay an obligation in response to a levy for taxes of another, and the priority for amounts provided for under deferred payment agreements between a debtor and the tax authority.

The House amendment also adopts the substance of the definition in section 346(a) the Senate amendment of when taxes are to be considered "incurred" except that the House amendment applies these definitions solely for purposes of determining which category of section 507 tests the priority of a particular tax liability. Thus, for example, the House amendment contains a special rule for the treatment of taxes under the 45-day exception to the preference rules under section 547 and the definitions of when a tax is incurred for priority purposes are not to apply to such preference rules. Under the House amendment, for purposes of the priority rules, a tax on income for a particular period is to be considered "incurred" on the last day of the period. A tax on or measured by some event, such as the payment of wages or a transfer by reason of death or gift, or an excise tax on a sale or other transaction, is to be considered "incurred" on the date of the transaction or event.

senate report no. 95–989

Section 507 specifies the kinds of claims that are entitled to priority in distribution, and the order of their priority. Paragraph (1) grants first priority to allowed administrative expenses and to fees and charges assessed against the estate under chapter 123 [§1911 et seq.] of title 28. Taxes included as administrative expenses under section 503(b)(1) of the bill generally receive the first priority, but the bill makes certain qualifications: Examples of these specially treated claims are the estate's liability for recapture of an investment tax credit claimed by the debtor before the title 11 case (this liability receives sixth priority) and the estate's employment tax liabilities on wages earned before, but paid after, the petition was filed (this liability generally receives the same priority as the wages).

"Involuntary gap" creditors, granted first priority under current law, are granted second priority by paragraph (2). This priority, covering claims arising in the ordinary course of the debtor's business or financial affairs after a title 11 case has begun but before a trustee is appointed or before the order for relief, includes taxes incurred during the conduct of such activities.

Paragraph (3) expands and increases the wage priority found in current section 64a(2) [section 104(a)(2) of former title 11]. The amount entitled to priority is raised from $600 to $1,800. The former figure was last adjusted in 1926. Inflation has made it nearly meaningless, and the bill brings it more than up to date. The three month limit of current law is retained, but is modified to run from the earlier of the date of the filing of the petition or the date of the cessation of the debtor's business. The priority is expanded to cover vacation, severance, and sick leave pay. The bill adds to the third priority so-called "trust fund" taxes, that is, withheld income taxes and the employees' share of the social security or railroad retirement taxes, but only to the extent that the wages on which taxes are imposed are themselves entitled to third priority.

The employer's share, the employment tax and the employer's share of the social security or railroad retirement tax on third priority compensation, is also included in the third priority category, but only if, and to the extent that the wages and related trust fund taxes have first been paid in full. Because of the claimants urgent need for their wages in the typical cases, the employer's taxes should not be paid before the wage claims entitled to priority, as well as the related trust fund taxes, are fully paid.

Paragraph (4) overrules *United States v. Embassy Restaurant*, 359 U.S. 29 (1958), which held that fringe benefits were not entitled to wage priority status. The bill recognizes the realities of labor contract negotiations, where fringe benefits may be substituted for wage demands. The priority granted is limited to claims for contributions to employee benefit plans such as pension plans, health or life insurance plans, and others, arising from services rendered within 120 days before the commencement of the case or the date of cessation of the debtor's business, whichever occurs first. The dollar limit placed on the total of all contributions payable under this paragraph is equal to the difference between the maximum allowable priority under paragraph (3), $1,800, times the number of employees covered by the plan less the actual distributions under paragraph (3) with respect to these employees.

Paragraph (5) is a new priority for consumer creditors—those who have deposited money in connection with the purchase, lease, or rental of property, or the purchase of services, for their personal, family, or household use, that were not delivered or provided. The priority amount is not to exceed $600. In order to reach only those persons most deserving of this special priority, it is limited to individuals whose adjustable gross income from all sources derived does not exceed $20,000. See Senate Hearings, testimony of Prof. Vern Countryman, at pp. 848–849. The income of the husband and wife should be aggregated for the purposes of the $20,000 limit if either or both spouses assert such a priority claim.

The sixth priority is for certain taxes. Priority is given to income taxes for a taxable year that ended on or before the date of the filing of the petition, if the last due date of the return for such year occurred not more than 3 years immediately before the date on which the petition was filed (§507(a)(6)(A)(i)). For the purposes of this rule, the last due date of the return is the last date under any extension of time to file the return which the taxing authority may have granted the debtor.

Employment taxes and transfer taxes (including gift, estate, sales, use and other excise taxes) are also given sixth priority if the transaction or event which gave rise to the tax occurred before the petition date, provided that the required return or report of such tax liabilities was last due within 3 years before the petition was filed or was last due after the petition date (§507(a)(6)(A)(ii)). The employment taxes covered under this rule are the employer's share of the social security and railroad retirement taxes and required employer payments toward unemployment insurance.

Priority is given to income taxes and other taxes of a kind described in section 507(a)(6)(A)(i) and (ii) which the Federal, State, or local tax authority had assessed within 3 years after the last due date of the return, that is, including any extension of time to file the return, if the debtor filed in title 11 within 240 days after the assessment was made (§507(a)(6)(B)(i)). This rule may bring into the sixth priority the debtor's tax liability for some taxable years which would not qualify for priority under the general three-year rule of section 507(a)(6)(A).

The sixth priority category also includes taxes which the tax authority was barred by law from assessing or collecting at any time during the 300 days before the petition under title 11 was filed (§507(a)(6)(B)(ii)). In the case of certain Federal taxes, this preserves a priority for tax liabilities for years more than three years before the filing of the petition where the debtor and the Internal Revenue Service were negotiating over an audit of the debtor's returns or were engaged in litigation in the Tax Court. In such situations, the tax law prohibits the service's right to assess a tax deficiency until ninety days after the service sends the taxpayer a deficiency letter or, if the taxpayer files a petition in the Tax Court during that 90-day period, until the outcome of the litigation. A similar priority exists in present law, except that the taxing authority is allowed no time to assess and collect the taxes after the restrictions on assessment (discussed above) are lifted. Some taxpayers have exploited this loophole by filing in bankruptcy immediately after the end of the 90-day period or immediately after the close of Tax Court proceedings. The bill remedies this defect by preserving a priority for taxes the assessment of which was barred by law by giving the tax authority 300 days within which to make the assessment after the lifting of the bar and then to collect or file public notice of its tax lien. Thus, if a taxpayer files a title 11 petition at any time during that 300-day period, the tax deficiency will be entitled to priority. If the petition is filed more than 300 days after the restriction on assessment was lifted, the taxing authority will not have priority for the tax deficiency.

Taxes for which an offer in compromise was withdrawn by the debtor, or rejected by a governmental unit, within 240 days before the petition date (§507(a)(6)(B)(iii)) will also receive sixth priority. This rule closes a loophole under present law under which, following an assessment of tax, some taxpayers have submitted a formal offer in compromise, dragged out negotiations with the taxing authority until the tax liability would lose priority under the three-year priority period of present law, and then filed in bankruptcy before the governmental unit could take collection steps.

Also included are certain taxes for which no return or report is required by law (§507(a)(6)(C)), if the taxable transaction occurred within three years before the petition was filed.

Taxes (not covered by the third priority) which the debtor was required by law to withhold or collect from others and for which he is liable in any capacity, regardless of the age of the tax claims (§507(a)(6)(D)) are included. This category covers the so-called "trust fund" taxes, that is, income taxes which an employer is required to withhold from the pay of his employees, the employees' shares of social security and railroad retirement taxes, and also Federal unemployment insurance. This category also includes excise taxes which a seller of goods or services is required to collect from a buyer and pay over to a taxing authority.

This category also covers the liability of a responsible corporate officer under the Internal Revenue Code [title 26] for income taxes or for the employees' share of employment taxes which, under the tax law, the employer was required to withhold from the wages of employees. This priority will operate where a person found to be a responsible officer has himself filed a petition under title 11, and the priority covers the debtor's liability as an officer under the Internal Revenue Code, regardless of the age of the tax year to which the tax relates.

The priority rules under the bill governing employment taxes can be summarized as follows: In the case of wages earned and actually paid before the petition under title 11 was filed, the liability for the employees' share of the employment taxes, regardless of the prepetition year in which the wages were earned and paid. The employer's share of the employment taxes on all wages earned and paid before the petition receive sixth priority; generally, these taxes will be those for which a return was due within three years before the petition. With respect to wages earned by employees before the petition but actually paid by the trustee after the title 11 case commenced, taxes required to be withheld receives the same priority as the wages themselves. Thus, the employees' share of taxes on third priority wages also receives third priority. Taxes on the balance of such wages receive no priority and are collectible only as general claims because the wages themselves are payable only as general claims and liability for the taxes arises only to the extent the wages are actually paid. The employer's share of employment taxes on third priority wages earned before the petition but paid after the petition was filed receives third priority, but only if the wages in this category have first been paid in full. Assuming there are sufficient funds to pay third priority wages and the related employer taxes in full, the employer's share of taxes on the balance of wage payments becomes a general claim (because the wages themselves are payable as general claims). Both the employees' and the employer's share of employment taxes on wages earned and paid after the petition was filed receive first priority as administrative expenses.

Also covered by this sixth priority are property taxes required to be assessed within 3 years before the filing of the petition (§507(a)(6)(E)).

Taxes attributable to a tentative carryback adjustment received by the debtor before the petition was filed, such as a "quickie refund" received under section 6411 of the Internal Revenue Code [title 26] (§507(a)(6)(F)) are included. However, the tax claim against the debtor will rein a prepetition loss year for which the tax return was last due, including extensions, within 3 years before the petition was filed.

Taxes resulting from a recapture, occasioned by a transfer during bankruptcy, of a tax credit or deduction taken during an earlier tax year (§507(a)(6)(G)) are included. A typical example occurs when there is a sale by the trustee of depreciable property during the case and depreciation deductions taken in prepetition years are subject to recapture under section 1250 of the Code [title 26].

Taxes owed by the debtor as a transferee of assets from another person who is liable for a tax, if the tax claim against the transferor would have received priority in a chapter 11 case commenced by the transferor within 1 year before the date of the petition filed by the transferee (§507(a)(6)(H)), are included.

Also included are certain tax payments required to have been made during the 1 year immediately before the petition was filed, where the debtor had previously entered into a deferred payment agreement (including an offer in compromise) to pay an agreed liability in periodic installments but had become delinquent in one or more installments before the petition was filed (§507(a)(6)(I)). This priority covers all types of deferred or part payment agreements. The priority covers only installments which first became due during the 1 year before the petition but which remained unpaid at the date of the petition. The priority does not come into play, however, if before the case began or during the case, the debtor and the taxing authority agree to a further extension of time to pay the delinquent amounts.

Certain tax-related liabilities which are not true taxes or which are not collected by regular assessment procedures (§507(a)(6)(J)) are included. One type of liability covered in this category is the liability under section 3505 of the Internal Revenue Code [title 26] of a lender who pays wages directly to employees of another employer or who supplies funds to an employer for the payment of wages. Another is the liability under section 6332 of the Internal Revenue Code [title 26], of a person who fails to turn over money or property of the taxpayer in response to a levy. Since the taxing authority must collect such a liability from the third party by suit rather than normal assessment procedures, an extra year is added to the normal 3-year priority periods. If a suit was commenced by the taxing authority within the four-year period and before the petition was filed, the priority is also preserved, provided that the suit had not terminated more than 1 year before the date of the filing of the petition.

Also included are certain unpaid customs duties which have not grown unreasonably "stale" (§507(a)(6)(K)). These include duties on imports entered for consumption with 3 years before the filing of the petition if the duties are still unliquidated on the petition date. If an import entry has been liquidated (in general, liquidation is in an administrative determination of the value and tariff rate of the item) or reliquidated, within two years of the filing of the petition the customs liability is given priority. If the Secretary of the Treasury certifies that customs duties were not liquidated because of an investigation into possible assessment of antidumping or countervailing duties, or because of fraud penalties, duties not liquidated for this reason during the five years before the importer filed under title 11 also will receive priority.

Subsection (a) of this section also provides specifically that interest on sixth priority tax claims accrued before the filing of the petition is also entitled to sixth priority.

Subsection (b) of this section provides that any fine or penalty which represents compensation for actual pecuniary loss of a governmental unit, and which involves a tax liability entitled to sixth priority, is to receive the same priority.

Subsection (b) also provides that a claim arising from an erroneous refund or credit of tax is to be given the same priority as the tax to which the refund or credit relates.

References in Text

Section 13(3) of the Federal Reserve Act, referred to in subsec. (a)(2), is classified to section 343(3) of Title 12, Banks and Banking.

Amendments

2010—Subsec. (a)(2). Pub. L. 111–203 inserted "unsecured claims of any Federal reserve bank related to loans made through programs or facilities authorized under section 13(3) of the Federal Reserve Act (12 U.S.C. 343)," after "this title,".

Subsec. (a)(8)(A)(ii)(II). Pub. L. 111–327 substituted "; or" for period at end.

2005—Subsec. (a)(1). Pub. L. 109–8, §212(9), added par. (1). Former par. (1) redesignated (2).

Subsec. (a)(2). Pub. L. 109–8, §212(2), (3), redesignated par. (1) as (2) and substituted "Second" for "First". Former par. (2) redesignated (3).

Subsec. (a)(3). Pub. L. 109–8, §212(2), (4), redesignated par. (2) as (3) and substituted "Third" for "Second". Former par. (3) redesignated (4).

Subsec. (a)(4). Pub. L. 109–8, §1401, which directed amendment of par. (4), "as amended by section 212", by substituting "$10,000" for "$4,000" and "180" for "90" in introductory provisions, effective Apr. 20, 2005, was executed to this par., which was par. (3), to reflect the probable intent of Congress, notwithstanding that the redesignation of this par. as (4) by Pub. L. 109–8, §212(2), was effective 180 days after Apr. 20, 2005. See Effective Date of 2005 Amendment notes below.

Pub. L. 109–8, §212(2), (5), redesignated par. (3) as (4) and substituted "Fourth" for "Third" in introductory provisions and a period for semicolon at end. Former par. (4) redesignated (5).

Subsec. (a)(5). Pub. L. 109–8, §212(2), (6), redesignated par. (4) as (5) and substituted "Fifth" for "Fourth" in introductory provisions. Former par. (5) redesignated (6).

Subsec. (a)(5)(B)(i). Pub. L. 109–8, §1401(2), which directed amendment of par. (5), "as amended by section 212", by substituting "$10,000" for "$4,000", effective Apr. 20, 2005, was executed to this par., which was par. (4), to reflect the probable intent of Congress, notwithstanding that the redesignation of this par. as (5) by Pub. L. 109–8, §212(2), was effective 180 days after Apr. 20, 2005. See Effective Date of 2005 Amendment notes below.

Subsec. (a)(5)(B)(ii). Pub. L. 109–8, §1502(a)(1)(A)(i), substituted "paragraph (4)" for "paragraph (3)".

Subsec. (a)(6). Pub. L. 109–8, §212(2), (7), redesignated par. (5) as (6) and substituted "Sixth" for "Fifth" in introductory provisions. Former par. (6) redesignated (7).

Subsec. (a)(7). Pub. L. 109–8, §212(1), (2), (8), redesignated par. (6) as (7), substituted "Seventh" for "Sixth", and struck out former par. (7) which read as follows: "Seventh, allowed claims for debts to a spouse, former spouse, or child of the debtor, for alimony to, maintenance for, or support of such spouse or child, in connection with a separation agreement, divorce decree or other order of a court of record, determination made in accordance with State or territorial law by a governmental unit, or property settlement agreement, but not to the extent that such debt—

"(A) is assigned to another entity, voluntarily, by operation of law, or otherwise; or

"(B) includes a liability designated as alimony, maintenance, or support, unless such liability is actually in the nature of alimony, maintenance or support."

Subsec. (a)(8). Pub. L. 109–8, §705(2), inserted at end "An otherwise applicable time period specified in this paragraph shall be suspended for any period during which a governmental unit is prohibited under applicable nonbankruptcy law from collecting a tax as a result of a request by the debtor for a hearing and an appeal of any collection action taken or proposed against the debtor, plus 90 days; plus any time during which the stay of proceedings was in effect in a prior case under this title or during which collection was precluded by the existence of 1 or more confirmed plans under this title, plus 90 days."

Subsec. (a)(8)(A). Pub. L. 109–8, §705(1)(A), inserted "for a taxable year ending on or before the date of the filing of the petition" after "gross receipts" in introductory provisions.

Subsec. (a)(8)(A)(i). Pub. L. 109–8, §705(1)(B), struck out "for a taxable year ending on or before the date of the filing of the petition" before "for which a return".

Subsec. (a)(8)(A)(ii). Pub. L. 109–8, §705(1)(C), added cl. (ii) and struck out former cl. (ii) which read as follows: "assessed within 240 days, plus any time plus 30 days during which an offer in compromise with respect to such tax that was made within 240 days after such assessment was pending, before the date of the filing of the petition; or".

Subsec. (a)(8)(B). Pub. L. 109–8, §706, substituted "incurred" for "assessed".

Subsec. (a)(8)(D). Pub. L. 109–8, §1502(a)(1)(A)(ii), substituted "paragraph (4)" for "paragraph (3)".

Subsec. (a)(10). Pub. L. 109–8, §223, added par. (10).

Subsec. (b). Pub. L. 109–8, §1502(a)(1)(B), substituted "subsection (a)(2)" for "subsection (a)(1)".

Subsec. (d). Pub. L. 109–8, §1502(a)(1)(C), substituted "subsection (a)(1)" for "subsection (a)(3)".

1994—Subsec. (a)(3). Pub. L. 103–394, §207, amended par. (3) generally. Prior to amendment, par. (3) read as follows: "Third, allowed unsecured claims for wages, salaries, or commissions, including vacation, severance, and sick leave pay—

"(A) earned by an individual within 90 days before the date of the filing of the petition or the date of the cessation of the debtor's business, whichever occurs first; but only

"(B) to the extent of $2,000 for each such individual."

Subsec. (a)(4)(B)(i). Pub. L. 103–394, §108(c)(1), substituted "$4,000" for "$2,000".

Subsec. (a)(5). Pub. L. 103–394, §§108(c)(2), 501(b)(3), substituted "section 557(b)" for "section 557(b)(1)" after "grain, as defined in" and "section 557(b)" for "section 557(b)(2)" after "facility, as defined in" in subpar. (A) and "$4,000" for "$2,000" in concluding provisions.

Subsec. (a)(6). Pub. L. 103–394, §108(c)(3), substituted "$1,800" for "$900".

Subsec. (a)(7). Pub. L. 103–394, §304(c)(3), added par. (7). Former par. (7) redesignated (8).

Subsec. (a)(8). Pub. L. 103–394, §304(c)(2), redesignated par. (7) as (8) and substituted "Eighth" for "Seventh". Former par. (8) redesignated (9).

Subsec. (a)(9). Pub. L. 103–394, §§304(c)(1), 501(d)(11)(A), redesignated par. (8) as (9) and substituted "Ninth" for "Eighth" and "a Federal depository institutions regulatory agency (or predecessor to such agency)" for "the Federal Deposit Insurance Corporation, the Resolution Trust Corporation, the Director of the Office of Thrift Supervision, the Comptroller of the Currency, or the Board of Governors of the Federal Reserve System, or their predecessors or successors,".

Subsec. (d). Pub. L. 103–394, §501(d)(11)(B), substituted "(a)(6), (a)(7), (a)(8), or (a)(9)" for "or (a)(6)".

1990—Subsec. (a)(8). Pub. L. 101–647 added par. (8).

1984—Subsec. (a)(3). Pub. L. 98–353, §449(a)(1), inserted a comma after "severance".

Subsec. (a)(4). Pub. L. 98–353, §449(a)(2), substituted "an employee benefit plan" for "employee benefit plans" in provisions preceding subpar. (A).

Subsec. (a)(4)(B)(i). Pub. L. 98–353, §449(a)(3), inserted "each" after "covered by".

Subsec. (a)(5). Pub. L. 98–353, §350(3), added par. (5). Former par. (5) redesignated (6).

Subsec. (a)(6). Pub. L. 98–353, §350(1), redesignated former par. (5) as (6) and substituted "Sixth" for "Fifth". Former par. (6) redesignated (7).

Subsec. (a)(7). Pub. L. 98–353, §§350(2), 449(a)(4), redesignated former par. (6) as (7), substituted "Seventh" for "Sixth", and inserted "only" after "units,".

Subsec. (c). Pub. L. 98–353, §449(b), substituted "has the same priority" for "shall be treated the same".

Effective Date of 2010 Amendment

Amendment by Pub. L. 111–203 effective 1 day after July 21, 2010, except as otherwise provided, see section 4 of Pub. L. 111–203, set out as an Effective Date note under section 5301 of Title 12, Banks and Banking.

Effective Date of 2005 Amendment

Pub. L. 109–8, title XIV, §1406, Apr. 20, 2005, 119 Stat. 215, as amended by Pub. L. 111–327, §3, Dec. 22, 2010, 124 Stat. 3563, provided that:

"(a) Effective Date.—Except as provided in subsection (b), this title [amending this section and sections 523, 548, 1104, and 1114 of this title and enacting provisions set out as a note under section 523 of this title] and the amendments made by this title shall take effect on the date of the enactment of this Act [Apr. 20, 2005].

"(b) Application of Amendments.—

"(1) In general.—Except as provided in paragraph (2), the amendments made by this title shall apply only with respect to cases commenced under title 11 of the United States Code on or after the date of the enactment of this Act [Apr. 20, 2005].

"(2) Avoidance period.—The amendment made by section 1402(1) [amending section 548 of this title] shall apply only with respect to cases commenced under title 11 of the United States Code more than 1 year after the date of the enactment of this Act."

Amendment by sections 212, 223, 705, 706, and 1502(a)(1) of Pub. L. 109–8 effective 180 days after Apr. 20, 2005, and not applicable with respect to cases commenced under this title before such effective date, except as otherwise provided, see section 1501 of Pub. L. 109–8, set out as a note under section 101 of this title.

Effective Date of 1994 Amendment

Amendment by Pub. L. 103–394 effective Oct. 22, 1994, and not applicable with respect to cases commenced under this title before Oct. 22, 1994, see section 702 of Pub. L. 103–394, set out as a note under section 101 of this title.

Effective Date of 1984 Amendment

Amendment by Pub. L. 98–353 effective with respect to cases filed 90 days after July 10, 1984, see section 552(a) of Pub. L. 98–353, set out as a note under section 101 of this title.

Adjustment of Dollar Amounts

The dollar amounts specified in this section were adjusted by notices of the Judicial Conference of the United States pursuant to section 104 of this title as follows:

By notice dated Feb. 16, 2016, 81 F.R. 8748, effective Apr. 1, 2016, in subsec. (a)(4), dollar amount "12,475" was adjusted to "12,850"; in subsec. (a)(5)(B)(i), dollar amount "12,475" was adjusted to "12,850"; in subsec. (a)(6)(B), dollar amount "6,150" was adjusted to "6,325"; and, in subsec. (a)(7), dollar amount "2,775" was adjusted to "2,850". See notice of the Judicial Conference of the United States set out as a note under section 104 of this title.

By notice dated Feb. 12, 2013, 78 F.R. 12089, effective Apr. 1, 2013, in subsec. (a)(4), dollar amount "11,725" was adjusted to "12,475"; in subsec. (a)(5), dollar amount "11,725" was adjusted to "12,475"; in subsec. (a)(6), dollar amount "5,775" was adjusted to "6,150"; and, in subsec. (a)(7), dollar amount "2,600" was adjusted to "2,775".

By notice dated Feb. 19, 2010, 75 F.R. 8747, effective Apr. 1, 2010, in subsec. (a)(4), dollar amount "10,950" was adjusted to "11,725"; in subsec. (a)(5), dollar amount "10,950" was adjusted to "11,725"; in subsec. (a)(6), dollar amount "5,400" was adjusted to "5,775"; and, in subsec. (a)(7), dollar amount "2,425" was adjusted to "2,600".

By notice dated Feb. 7, 2007, 72 F.R. 7082, effective Apr. 1, 2007, in subsec. (a)(4), dollar amount "10,000" was adjusted to "10,950"; in subsec. (a)(5), dollar amount "10,000" was adjusted to "10,950"; in subsec. (a)(6), dollar amount "4,925" was adjusted to "5,400"; and, in subsec. (a)(7), dollar amount "2,225" was adjusted to "2,425".

[Pub. L. 109–8 redesignated pars. (3) to (6) of subsec. (a) as pars. (4) to (7), respectively, and amended certain dollar amounts. See 2005 Amendment notes above.]

By notice dated Feb. 18, 2004, 69 F.R. 8482, effective Apr. 1, 2004, in subsec. (a)(3), dollar amount "4,650" was adjusted to "4,925"; in subsec. (a)(4)(B)(i), dollar amount "4,650" was adjusted to "4,925"; in subsec. (a)(5), dollar amount "4,650" was adjusted to "4,925"; and, in subsec. (a)(6), dollar amount "2,100" was adjusted to "2,225".

By notice dated Feb. 13, 2001, 66 F.R. 10910, effective Apr. 1, 2001, in subsec. (a)(3), dollar amount "4,300" was adjusted to "4,650"; in subsec. (a)(4)(B)(i), dollar amount "4,300" was adjusted to "4,650"; in subsec. (a)(5), dollar amount "4,300" was adjusted to "4,650"; and, in subsec. (a)(6), dollar amount "1,950" was adjusted to "2,100".

By notice dated Feb. 3, 1998, 63 F.R. 7179, effective Apr. 1, 1998, in subsec. (a)(3), dollar amount "4,000" was adjusted to "4,300"; in subsec. (a)(4)(B)(i), dollar amount "4,000" was adjusted to "4,300"; in subsec. (a)(5), dollar amount "4,000" was adjusted to "4,300"; and, in subsec. (a)(6), dollar amount "1,800" was adjusted to "1,950".

[1] See References in Text note below.
[2] See Adjustment of Dollar Amounts notes below.

§508. Effect of distribution other than under this title

If a creditor of a partnership debtor receives, from a general partner that is not a debtor in a case under chapter 7 of this title, payment of, or a transfer of property on account of, a claim that is allowed under this title and that is not secured by a lien on property of such partner, such creditor may not receive any payment under this title on account of such claim until each of the other holders of claims on account of which such holders are entitled to share equally with such creditor under this title has received payment under this title equal in value to the consideration received by such creditor from such general partner.

(Pub. L. 95–598, Nov. 6, 1978, 92 Stat. 2585; Pub. L. 109–8, title VIII, §802(d)(7), Apr. 20, 2005, 119 Stat. 146.)

Historical and Revision Notes

legislative statements

Section 508(b) of the House amendment is new and provides an identical rule with respect to a creditor of a partnership who receives payment from a partner, to that of a creditor of a debtor who receives a payment in a foreign proceeding involving the debtor.

senate report no. 95–989

This section prohibits a creditor from receiving any distribution in the bankruptcy case if he has received payment of a portion of his claim in a foreign proceeding, until the other creditors in the bankruptcy case in this country that are entitled to share equally with that creditor have received as much as he has in the foreign proceeding.

Amendments

2005—Pub. L. 109–8 designated subsec. (b) as entire section and struck out subsec. (a) which read as follows: "If a creditor receives, in a foreign proceeding, payment of, or a transfer of property on account of, a claim that is allowed under this title, such creditor may not receive any payment under this title on account of such claim until each of the other holders of claims on account of which such holders are entitled to share equally with such creditor under this title has received payment under this title equal in value to the consideration received by such creditor in such foreign proceeding."

Effective Date of 2005 Amendment

Amendment by Pub. L. 109–8 effective 180 days after Apr. 20, 2005, and not applicable with respect to cases commenced under this title before such effective date, except as otherwise provided, see section 1501 of Pub. L. 109–8, set out as a note under section 101 of this title.

§509. Claims of codebtors

(a) Except as provided in subsection (b) or (c) of this section, an entity that is liable with the debtor on, or that has secured, a claim of a creditor against the debtor, and that pays such claim, is subrogated to the rights of such creditor to the extent of such payment.

(b) Such entity is not subrogated to the rights of such creditor to the extent that—

(1) a claim of such entity for reimbursement or contribution on account of such payment of such creditor's claim is—

(A) allowed under section 502 of this title;
(B) disallowed other than under section 502(e) of this title; or
(C) subordinated under section 510 of this title; or

(2) as between the debtor and such entity, such entity received the consideration for the claim held by such creditor.

(c) The court shall subordinate to the claim of a creditor and for the benefit of such creditor an allowed claim, by way of subrogation under this section, or for reimbursement or contribution, of an entity that is liable with the debtor on, or that has secured, such creditor's claim, until such creditor's claim is paid in full, either through payments under this title or otherwise.

(Pub. L. 95–598, Nov. 6, 1978, 92 Stat. 2585; Pub. L. 98–353, title III, §450, July 10, 1984, 98 Stat. 375.)

Historical and Revision Notes

legislative statements

Section 509 of the House amendment represents a substantial revision of provisions contained in H.R. 8200 as passed by the House and in the Senate amendment. Section 509(a) states a general rule that a surety or co-debtor is subrogated to the rights of a creditor assured by the surety or co-debtor to the extent the surety or co-debtor pays such creditor. Section 509(b) states a general exception indicating that subrogation is not granted to the extent that a claim of a surety or co-debtor for reimbursement or contribution is allowed under section 502 or disallowed other than under section 502(e). Additionally, section 509(b)(1)(C) provides that such claims for subrogation are subordinated to the extent that a claim of the surety or co-debtor for reimbursement or contribution is subordinated under section 510(a)(1) or 510(b). Section 509(b)(2) reiterates the well-known rule that prevents a debtor that is ultimately liable on the debt from recovering from a surety or a co-debtor. Although the language in section 509(b)(2) focuses in terms of receipt of consideration, legislative history appearing elsewhere indicates that an agreement to share liabilities should prevail over an agreement to share profits throughout title 11. This is particularly important in the context of co-debtors who are partners. Section 509(c) subordinates the claim of a surety or co-debtor to the claim of an assured creditor until the creditor's claim is paid in full.

senate report no. 95–989

Section 509 deals with codebtors generally, and is in addition to the disallowance provision in section 502(e). This section is based on the notion that the only rights available to a surety, guarantor, or comaker are contribution, reimbursement, and subrogation. The right that applies in a particular situation will depend on the agreement between the debtor and the codebtor, and on whether and how payment was made by the codebtor to the creditor. The claim of a surety or codebtor for contribution or reimbursement is discharged even if the claim is never filed, as is any claim for subrogation even if the surety or codebtor chooses to file a claim for contribution or reimbursement instead.

Subsection (a) subrogates the codebtor (whether as a codebtor, surety, or guarantor) to the rights of the creditor, to the extent of any payment made by the codebtor to the creditor. Whether the creditor's claim was filed under section 501(a) or 501(b) is irrelevant. The right of subrogation will exist even if the primary creditor's claim is allowed by virtue of being listed under proposed 11 U.S.C. 924 or 1111, and not by reason of a proof of claim.

Subsection (b) permits a subrogated codebtor to receive payments in the bankruptcy case only if the creditor has been paid in full, either through payments under the bankruptcy code or otherwise.

Amendments

1984—Subsec. (a). Pub. L. 98–353, §450(a), substituted "subsection (b) or" for "subsections (b) and", and inserted "against the debtor" after "a creditor".

Subsec. (b)(1). Pub. L. 98–353, §450(b), substituted "of such" for "of a" after "account".

Subsec. (c). Pub. L. 98–353, §450(c), substituted "this section" for "section 509 of this title".

Effective Date of 1984 Amendment

Amendment by Pub. L. 98–353 effective with respect to cases filed 90 days after July 10, 1984, see section 552(a) of Pub. L. 98–353, set out as a note under section 101 of this title.

§510. Subordination

(a) A subordination agreement is enforceable in a case under this title to the same extent that such agreement is enforceable under applicable nonbankruptcy law.

(b) For the purpose of distribution under this title, a claim arising from rescission of a purchase or sale of a security of the debtor or of an affiliate of the debtor, for damages arising from the purchase or sale of such a security, or for reimbursement or contribution allowed under section 502 on account of such a claim, shall be subordinated to all claims or interests that are senior to or equal the claim or interest represented by such security, except that if such security is common stock, such claim has the same priority as common stock.

(c) Notwithstanding subsections (a) and (b) of this section, after notice and a hearing, the court may—

(1) under principles of equitable subordination, subordinate for purposes of distribution all or part of an allowed claim to all or part of another allowed claim or all or part of an allowed interest to all or part of another allowed interest; or

(2) order that any lien securing such a subordinated claim be transferred to the estate.

(Pub. L. 95–598, Nov. 6, 1978, 92 Stat. 2586; Pub. L. 98–353, title III, §451, July 10, 1984, 98 Stat. 375.)

Historical and Revision Notes

legislative statements

Section 510(c)(1) of the House amendment represents a compromise between similar provisions in the House bill and Senate amendment. After notice and a hearing, the court may, under principles of equitable subordination, subordinate for purposes of distribution all or part of an allowed claim to all or part of another allowed claim or all or part of an allowed interest to all or part of another allowed interest. As a matter of equity, it is reasonable that a court subordinate claims to claims and interests to interests. It is intended that the term "principles of equitable subordination" follow existing case law and leave to the courts development of this principle. To date, under existing law, a claim is generally subordinated only if holder of such claim is guilty of inequitable conduct, or the claim itself is of a status susceptible to subordination, such as a penalty or a claim for damages arising from the purchase or sale of a security of the debtor. The fact that such a claim may be secured is of no consequence to the issue of subordination. However, it is inconceivable that the status of a claim as a secured claim could ever be grounds for justifying equitable subordination.

Subordination: Since the House amendment authorizes subordination of claims only under principles of equitable subordination, and thus incorporates principles of existing case law, a tax claim would rarely be subordinated under this provision of the bill.

Section 511 of the Senate amendment is deleted. Its substance is adopted in section 502(b)(9) of the House amendment which reflects an identical provision contained in H.R. 8200 as passed by the House.

senate report no. 95–989

Subsection (a) requires the court to enforce subordination agreements. A subordination agreement will not be enforced, however, in a reorganization case in which the class that is the beneficiary of the agreement has accepted, as specified in proposed 11 U.S.C. 1126, a plan that waives their rights under the agreement. Otherwise, the agreement would prevent just what chapter 11 contemplates: that seniors may give up rights to juniors in the interest of confirmation of a plan and rehabilitation of the debtor. The subsection also requires the court to subordinate in payment any claim for rescission of a purchase or sale of a security of the debtor or of an affiliate, or for damages arising from the purchase or sale of such a security, to all claims and interests that are senior to the claim or interest represented by the security. Thus, the later subordination varies with the claim or interest involved. If the security is a debt instrument, the damages or rescission claim will be granted the status of a general unsecured claim. If the security is an equity security, the damages or rescission claim is subordinated to all creditors and treated the same as the equity security itself.

Subsection (b) authorizes the bankruptcy court, in ordering distribution of assets, to subordinate all or any part of any claim to all or any part of another claim, regardless of the priority ranking of either claim. In addition, any lien securing such a subordinated claim may be transferred to the estate. The bill provides, however, that any subordination ordered under this provision must be based on principles of equitable subordination. These principles are defined by case law, and have generally indicated that a claim may normally be subordinated only if its holder is guilty of misconduct. As originally introduced, the bill provided specifically that a tax claim may not be subordinated on equitable grounds. The bill deletes this express exception, but the effect under the amendment should be much the same in most situations since, under the judicial doctrine of equitable subordination, a tax claim would rarely be subordinated.

Amendments

1984—Subsec. (b). Pub. L. 98–353 amended subsec. (b) generally. Prior to amendment, subsec. (b) read as follows: "Any claim for recission of a purchase or sale of a security of the debtor or of an affiliate or for damages arising from the purchase or sale of such a security shall be subordinated for purposes of distribution to all claims and interests that are senior or equal to the claim or interest represented by such security."

Effective Date of 1984 Amendment

Amendment by Pub. L. 98–353 effective with respect to cases filed 90 days after July 10, 1984, see section 552(a) of Pub. L. 98–353, set out as a note under section 101 of this title.

§511. Rate of interest on tax claims

(a) If any provision of this title requires the payment of interest on a tax claim or on an administrative expense tax, or the payment of interest to enable a creditor to receive the present value of the allowed amount of a tax claim, the rate of interest shall be the rate determined under applicable nonbankruptcy law.

(b) In the case of taxes paid under a confirmed plan under this title, the rate of interest shall be determined as of the calendar month in which the plan is confirmed.

(Added Pub. L. 109–8, title VII, §704(a), Apr. 20, 2005, 119 Stat. 125.)

Effective Date

Section effective 180 days after Apr. 20, 2005, and not applicable with respect to cases commenced under this title before such effective date, except as otherwise provided, see section 1501 of Pub. L. 109–8, set out as an Effective Date of 2005 Amendment note under section 101 of this title.

SUBCHAPTER II—DEBTOR'S DUTIES AND BENEFITS

§521. Debtor's duties

(a) The debtor shall—

(1) file—

(A) a list of creditors; and

(B) unless the court orders otherwise—

(i) a schedule of assets and liabilities;

(ii) a schedule of current income and current expenditures;

(iii) a statement of the debtor's financial affairs and, if section 342(b) applies, a certificate—

(I) of an attorney whose name is indicated on the petition as the attorney for the debtor, or a bankruptcy petition preparer signing the petition under section 110(b)(1), indicating that such attorney or the bankruptcy petition preparer delivered to the debtor the notice required by section 342(b); or

(II) if no attorney is so indicated, and no bankruptcy petition preparer signed the petition, of the debtor that such notice was received and read by the debtor;

(iv) copies of all payment advices or other evidence of payment received within 60 days before the date of the filing of the petition, by the debtor from any employer of the debtor;

(v) a statement of the amount of monthly net income, itemized to show how the amount is calculated; and

(vi) a statement disclosing any reasonably anticipated increase in income or expenditures over the 12-month period following the date of the filing of the petition;

(2) if an individual debtor's schedule of assets and liabilities includes debts which are secured by property of the estate—

(A) within thirty days after the date of the filing of a petition under chapter 7 of this title or on or before the date of the meeting of creditors, whichever is earlier, or within such additional time as the court, for cause, within such period fixes, file with the clerk a statement of his intention with respect to the retention or surrender of such property and, if applicable, specifying that such property is claimed as exempt, that the debtor intends to redeem such property, or that the debtor intends to reaffirm debts secured by such property; and

(B) within 30 days after the first date set for the meeting of creditors under section 341(a), or within such additional time as the court, for cause, within such 30-day period fixes, perform his intention with respect to such property, as specified by subparagraph (A) of this paragraph;

except that nothing in subparagraphs (A) and (B) of this paragraph shall alter the debtor's or the trustee's rights with regard to such property under this title, except as provided in section 362(h);

(3) if a trustee is serving in the case or an auditor is serving under section 586(f) of title 28, cooperate with the trustee as necessary to enable the trustee to perform the trustee's duties under this title;

(4) if a trustee is serving in the case or an auditor is serving under section 586(f) of title 28, surrender to the trustee all property of the estate and any recorded information, including books, documents, records, and papers, relating to property of the estate, whether or not immunity is granted under section 344 of this title;

(5) appear at the hearing required under section 524(d) of this title;

(6) in a case under chapter 7 of this title in which the debtor is an individual, not retain possession of personal property as to which a creditor has an allowed claim for the purchase price secured in whole or in part by an interest in such personal property unless the debtor, not later than 45 days after the first meeting of creditors under section 341(a), either—

(A) enters into an agreement with the creditor pursuant to section 524(c) with respect to the claim secured by such property; or

(B) redeems such property from the security interest pursuant to section 722; and

(7) unless a trustee is serving in the case, continue to perform the obligations required of the administrator (as defined in section 3 of the Employee Retirement Income Security Act of 1974) of an employee benefit plan if at the time of the commencement of the case the debtor (or any entity designated by the debtor) served as such administrator.

If the debtor fails to so act within the 45-day period referred to in paragraph (6), the stay under section 362(a) is terminated with respect to the personal property of the estate or of the debtor which is affected, such property shall no longer be property of the estate, and the creditor may take whatever action as to such property as is permitted by applicable nonbankruptcy law, unless the court determines on the motion of the trustee filed before the expiration of such 45-day period, and after notice and a hearing, that such property is of consequential value or benefit to the estate, orders appropriate adequate protection of the creditor's interest, and orders the debtor to deliver any collateral in the debtor's possession to the trustee.

(b) In addition to the requirements under subsection (a), a debtor who is an individual shall file with the court—

(1) a certificate from the approved nonprofit budget and credit counseling agency that provided the debtor services under section 109(h) describing the services provided to the debtor; and

(2) a copy of the debt repayment plan, if any, developed under section 109(h) through the approved nonprofit budget and credit counseling agency referred to in paragraph (1).

(c) In addition to meeting the requirements under subsection (a), a debtor shall file with the court a record of any interest that a debtor has in an education individual retirement account (as defined in section 530(b)(1) of the Internal Revenue Code of 1986), an interest in an account in a qualified ABLE program (as defined in section 529A(b) of such Code,¹ or under a qualified State tuition program (as defined in section 529(b)(1) of such Code).

(d) If the debtor fails timely to take the action specified in subsection (a)(6) of this section, or in paragraphs (1) and (2) of section 362(h), with respect to property which a lessor or bailor owns and has leased, rented, or bailed to the debtor or as to which a creditor holds a security interest not otherwise voidable under section 522(f), 544, 545, 547, 548, or 549, nothing in this title shall prevent or limit the operation of a provision in the underlying lease or agreement that has the effect of placing the debtor in default under such lease or agreement by reason of the occurrence, pendency, or existence of a proceeding under this title or the insolvency of the debtor. Nothing in this subsection shall be deemed to justify limiting such a provision in any other circumstance.

(e)(1) If the debtor in a case under chapter 7 or 13 is an individual and if a creditor files with the court at any time a request to receive a copy of the petition, schedules, and statement of financial affairs filed by the debtor, then the court shall make such petition, such schedules, and such statement available to such creditor.

(2)(A) The debtor shall provide—

(i) not later than 7 days before the date first set for the first meeting of creditors, to the trustee a copy of the Federal income tax return required under applicable law (or at the election of the debtor, a transcript of such return) for the most recent tax year ending immediately before the commencement of the case and for which a Federal income tax return was filed; and

(ii) at the same time the debtor complies with clause (i), a copy of such return (or if elected under clause (i), such transcript) to any creditor that timely requests such copy.

(B) If the debtor fails to comply with clause (i) or (ii) of subparagraph (A), the court shall dismiss the case unless the debtor demonstrates that the failure to so comply is due to circumstances beyond the control of the debtor.

(C) If a creditor requests a copy of such tax return or such transcript and if the debtor fails to provide a copy of such tax return or such transcript to such creditor at the time the debtor provides such tax return or such transcript to the trustee, then the court shall dismiss the case unless the debtor demonstrates that the failure to provide a copy of such tax return or such transcript is due to circumstances beyond the control of the debtor.

(3) If a creditor in a case under chapter 13 files with the court at any time a request to receive a copy of the plan filed by the debtor, then the court shall make available to such creditor a copy of the plan—

(A) at a reasonable cost; and

(B) not later than 7 days after such request is filed.

(f) At the request of the court, the United States trustee, or any party in interest in a case under chapter 7, 11, or 13, a debtor who is an individual shall file with the court—

(1) at the same time filed with the taxing authority, a copy of each Federal income tax return required under applicable law (or at the election of the debtor, a transcript of such tax return) with respect to each tax year of the debtor ending while the case is pending under such chapter;

(2) at the same time filed with the taxing authority, each Federal income tax return required under applicable law (or at the election of the debtor, a transcript of such tax return) that had not been filed with such authority as of the date of the commencement of the case and that was subsequently filed for any tax year of the debtor ending in the 3-year period ending on the date of the commencement of the case;

(3) a copy of each amendment to any Federal income tax return or transcript filed with the court under paragraph (1) or (2); and

(4) in a case under chapter 13—

(A) on the date that is either 90 days after the end of such tax year or 1 year after the date of the commencement of the case, whichever is later, if a plan is not confirmed before such later date; and

(B) annually after the plan is confirmed and until the case is closed, not later than the date that is 45 days before the anniversary of the confirmation of the plan;

a statement, under penalty of perjury, of the income and expenditures of the debtor during the tax year of the debtor most recently concluded before such statement is filed under this paragraph, and of the monthly income of the debtor, that shows how income, expenditures, and monthly income are calculated.

(g)(1) A statement referred to in subsection (f)(4) shall disclose—

(A) the amount and sources of the income of the debtor;

(B) the identity of any person responsible with the debtor for the support of any dependent of the debtor; and

(C) the identity of any person who contributed, and the amount contributed, to the household in which the debtor resides.

(2) The tax returns, amendments, and statement of income and expenditures described in subsections (e)(2)(A) and (f) shall be available to the United States trustee (or the bankruptcy administrator, if any), the trustee, and any party in interest for inspection and copying, subject to the requirements of section 315(c) of the Bankruptcy Abuse Prevention and Consumer Protection Act of 2005.

(h) If requested by the United States trustee or by the trustee, the debtor shall provide—

(1) a document that establishes the identity of the debtor, including a driver's license, passport, or other document that contains a photograph of the debtor; or

(2) such other personal identifying information relating to the debtor that establishes the identity of the debtor.

(i)(1) Subject to paragraphs (2) and (4) and notwithstanding section 707(a), if an individual debtor in a voluntary case under chapter 7 or 13 fails to file all of the information required under subsection (a)(1) within 45 days after the date of the filing of the petition, the case shall be automatically dismissed effective on the 46th day after the date of the filing of the petition.

(2) Subject to paragraph (4) and with respect to a case described in paragraph (1), any party in interest may request the court to enter an order dismissing the case. If requested, the court shall enter an order of dismissal not later than 7 days after such request.

(3) Subject to paragraph (4) and upon request of the debtor made within 45 days after the date of the filing of the petition described in paragraph (1), the court may allow the debtor an additional period of not to exceed 45 days to file the information required under subsection (a)(1) if the court finds justification for extending the period for the filing.

(4) Notwithstanding any other provision of this subsection, on the motion of the trustee filed before the expiration of the applicable period of time specified in paragraph (1), (2), or (3), and after notice and a hearing, the court may decline to dismiss the case if the court finds that the debtor attempted in good faith to file all the information required by subsection (a)(1)(B)(iv) and that the best interests of creditors would be served by administration of the case.

(j)(1) Notwithstanding any other provision of this title, if the debtor fails to file a tax return that becomes due after the commencement of the case or to properly obtain an extension of the due date for filing such return, the taxing authority may request that the court enter an order converting or dismissing the case.

(2) If the debtor does not file the required return or obtain the extension referred to in paragraph (1) within 90 days after a request is filed by the taxing authority under that paragraph, the court shall convert or dismiss the case, whichever is in the best interests of creditors and the estate.

(Pub. L. 95–598, Nov. 6, 1978, 92 Stat. 2586; Pub. L. 98–353, title III, §§305, 452, July 10, 1984, 98 Stat. 352, 375; Pub. L. 99–554, title II, §283(h), Oct. 27, 1986, 100 Stat. 3117; Pub. L. 109–8, title I, §106(d), title II, §225(b), title III, §§304(1), 305(2), 315(b), 316, title IV, §446(a), title VI, §603(c), title VII, §720, Apr. 20, 2005, 119 Stat. 38, 66, 78, 80, 89, 92, 118, 123, 133; Pub. L. 111–16, §2(5), (6), May 7, 2009, 123 Stat. 1607; Pub. L. 111–327, §2(a)(16), Dec. 22, 2010, 124 Stat. 3559; Pub. L. 113–295, div. B, title I, §104(c), Dec. 19, 2014, 128 Stat. 4064.)

Historical and Revision Notes
legislative statements
Section 521 of the House amendment modifies a comparable provision contained in the House bill and Senate amendment. The Rules of Bankruptcy Procedure should provide where the list of creditors is to be filed. In addition, the debtor is required to attend the hearing on discharge under section 524(d).

senate report no. 95–989
This section lists three duties of the debtor in a bankruptcy case. The Rules of Bankruptcy Procedure will specify the means of carrying out these duties. The first duty is to file with the court a list of creditors, and unless the court orders otherwise, a schedule of assets and liabilities and a statement of his financial affairs. Second, the debtor is required to cooperate with the trustee as necessary to enable the trustee to perform the trustee's duties. Finally, the debtor must surrender to the trustee all property of the estate, and any recorded information, including books, documents, records, and papers, relating to property of the estate. This phrase "recorded information, including books, documents, records, and papers," has been used here and throughout the bill as a more general term, and includes such other forms of recorded information
as data in computer storage or in other machine readable forms.

The list in this section is not exhaustive of the debtor's duties. Others are listed elsewhere in proposed title 11, such as in section 343, which requires the debtor to submit to examination, or in the Rules of Bankruptcy Procedure, as continued by §404(a) of S. 2266, such as the duty to attend any hearing on discharge, Rule 402(2).

References in Text
Section 3 of the Employee Retirement Income Security Act of 1974, referred to in subsec. (a)(7), is classified to section 1002 of Title 29, Labor.

Sections 530(b)(1), 529A(b), and 529(b)(1) of the Internal Revenue Code of 1986, referred to in subsec. (c), are classified to sections 530(b)(1), 529A(b), and 529(b)(1), respectively, of Title 26, Internal Revenue Code.

Section 315(c) of the Bankruptcy Abuse Prevention and Consumer Protection Act of 2005, referred to in subsec. (g)(2), is section 315(c) of Pub. L. 109–8, which is set out as a note under this section.

Amendments
2014—Subsec. (c). Pub. L. 113–295 inserted ", an interest in an account in a qualified ABLE program (as defined in section 529A(b) of such Code," after "Internal Revenue Code of 1986)".

2010—Subsec. (a)(2). Pub. L. 111–327, §2(a)(16)(A)(iii), in subpar. (C) substituted "except that" for subpar. (C) designation.

Subsec. (a)(2)(A). Pub. L. 111–327, §2(a)(16)(A)(i), struck out "the debtor shall" after "period fixes," and inserted "and" after semicolon at end.

Subsec. (a)(2)(B). Pub. L. 111–327, §2(a)(16)(A)(ii), struck out "the debtor shall" after "period fixes," and "and" after semicolon at end.

Subsec. (a)(3), (4). Pub. L. 111–327, §2(a)(16)(B), inserted "is" after "auditor".
2009—Subsec. (e)(3)(B). Pub. L. 111–16, §2(5), substituted "7 days" for "5 days".

Subsec. (i)(2). Pub. L. 111–16, §2(6), substituted "7 days" for "5 days".
2005—Pub. L. 109–8, §106(d)(1), designated existing provisions as subsec. (a).
Subsec. (a). Pub. L. 109–8, §304(1), added concluding provisions.

Subsec. (a)(1). Pub. L. 109–8, §315(b)(1), amended par. (1) generally. Prior to amendment, par. (1) read as follows: "file a list of creditors, and unless the court orders otherwise, a schedule of assets and liabilities, a schedule of current income and current expenditures, and a statement of the debtor's financial affairs;".

Subsec. (a)(2). Pub. L. 109–8, §305(2)(A), struck out "consumer" before "debts" in introductory provisions.

Subsec. (a)(2)(B). Pub. L. 109–8, §305(2)(B), substituted "30 days after the first date set for the meeting of creditors under section 341(a)" for "forty-five days after the filing of a notice of intent under this section" and "30-day" for "forty-five day".

Subsec. (a)(2)(C). Pub. L. 109–8, §305(2)(C), inserted ", except as provided in section 362(h)" before semicolon.

Subsec. (a)(3), (4). Pub. L. 109–8, §603(c), inserted "or an auditor serving under section 586(f) of title 28" after "serving in the case".

Subsec. (a)(6). Pub. L. 109–8, §304(1), added par. (6).
Subsec. (a)(7). Pub. L. 109–8, §446(a), added par. (7).
Subsec. (b). Pub. L. 109–8, §106(d)(2), added subsec. (b).
Subsec. (c). Pub. L. 109–8, §225(b), added subsec. (c).
Subsec. (d). Pub. L. 109–8, §305(2)(D), added subsec. (d).
Subsecs. (e) to (h). Pub. L. 109–8, §315(b)(2), added subsecs. (e) to (h).
Subsec. (i). Pub. L. 109–8, §316, added subsec. (i).
Subsec. (j). Pub. L. 109–8, §720, added subsec. (j).
1986—Par. (4). Pub. L. 99–554 inserted ", whether or not immunity is granted under section 344 of this title" after second reference to "estate".

1984—Par. (1). Pub. L. 98–353, §305(2), inserted "a schedule of current income and current expenditures," after "liabilities,".

Pars. (2) to (5). Pub. L. 98–353, §305(1), (3), added par. (2), redesignated former pars. (2) to (4) as (3) to (5), respectively.

Pub. L. 98–353, §452, which directed the insertion of ", whether or not immunity is granted under section 344 of this title" after second reference to "estate" in par. (3) as redesignated above, could not be executed because such reference appeared in par. (4) rather than in par. (3).

Effective Date of 2014 Amendment
Pub. L. 113–295, div. B, title I, §104(d), Dec. 19, 2014, 128 Stat. 4064, provided that: "The amendments made by this section [amending this section and sections 541 and 707 of this title] shall apply with respect to cases commenced under title 11, United States Code, on or after the date of the enactment of this Act [Dec. 19, 2014]."

Effective Date of 2009 Amendment
Amendment by Pub. L. 111–16 effective Dec. 1, 2009, see section 7 of Pub. L. 111–16, set out as a note under section 109 of this title.

Effective Date of 2005 Amendment
Pub. L. 109–8, title VI, §603(e), Apr. 20, 2005, 119 Stat. 123, provided that: "The amendments made by this section [amending this section, section 727 of this title and section 586 of Title 28, Judiciary and Judicial Procedure, and enacting provisions set out as a note under section 586 of Title 28] shall take effect 18 months after the date of enactment of this Act [Apr. 20, 2005]."

Amendment by sections 106(d), 225(b), 304(1), 305(2), 315(b), 316, 446(a), and 720 of Pub. L. 109–8 effective 180 days after Apr. 20, 2005, and not applicable with respect to cases commenced under this title before such effective date, except as otherwise provided, see section 1501 of Pub. L. 109–8, set out as a note under section 101 of this title.

Effective Date of 1986 Amendment
Amendment by Pub. L. 99–554 effective 30 days after Oct. 27, 1986, see section 302(a) of Pub. L. 99–554, set out as a note under section 581 of Title 28, Judiciary and Judicial Procedure.

Effective Date of 1984 Amendment
Amendment by Pub. L. 98–353 effective with respect to cases filed 90 days after July 10, 1984, see section 552(a) of Pub. L. 98–353, set out as a note under section 101 of this title.

Confidentiality of Tax Information
Pub. L. 109–8, title III, §315(c), Apr. 20, 2005, 119 Stat. 91, provided that:
"(1) Not later than 180 days after the date of the enactment of this Act [Apr. 20, 2005], the Director of the Administrative Office of the United States Courts shall establish procedures for safeguarding the confidentiality of any tax information required to be provided under this section.

"(2) The procedures under paragraph (1) shall include restrictions on creditor access to tax information that is required to be provided under this section.

"(3) Not later than 540 days after the date of enactment of this Act, the Director of the Administrative Office of the United States Courts shall prepare and submit to the President pro tempore of the Senate and the Speaker of the House of Representatives a report that—

"(A) assesses the effectiveness of the procedures established under paragraph (1); and

"(B) if appropriate, includes proposed legislation to—
"(i) further protect the confidentiality of tax information; and
"(ii) provide penalties for the improper use by any person of the tax information required to be provided under this section."

Providing Requested Tax Documents to the Court
Pub. L. 109–8, title XII, §1228, Apr. 20, 2005, 119 Stat. 200, provided that:
"(a) Chapter 7 Cases.—The court shall not grant a discharge in the case of an individual who is a debtor in a case under chapter 7 of title 11, United States Code, unless requested tax documents have been provided to the court.

"(b) Chapter 11 and Chapter 13 Cases.—The court shall not confirm a plan of reorganization in the case of an individual under chapter 11 or 13 of title 11, United States Code, unless requested tax documents have been filed with the court.

"(c) Document Retention.—The court shall destroy documents submitted in support of a bankruptcy claim not sooner than 3 years after the date of the conclusion of a case filed by an individual under chapter 7, 11, or 13 of title 11, United States Code. In the event of a pending audit or enforcement action, the court may extend the time for destruction of such requested tax documents."

[1] So in original. A closing parenthesis probably should precede the comma.

§522. Exemptions
(a) In this section—
(1) "dependent" includes spouse, whether or not actually dependent; and
(2) "value" means fair market value as of the date of the filing of the petition or, with respect to property that becomes property of the estate after such date, as of the date such property becomes property of the estate.

(b)(1) Notwithstanding section 541 of this title, an individual debtor may exempt from property of the estate the property listed in either paragraph (2) or, in the alternative, paragraph (3) of this subsection. In joint cases filed under section 302 of this title and individual cases filed under section 301 or 303 of this title by or against debtors who are husband and wife, and whose estates are ordered to be jointly administered under Rule 1015(b) of the Federal Rules of Bankruptcy Procedure, one debtor may not elect to exempt property listed in paragraph (2) and the other debtor elect to exempt property listed in paragraph (3) of this subsection. If the parties cannot agree on the alternative to be elected, they shall be deemed to elect paragraph (2), where such election is permitted under the law of the jurisdiction where the case is filed.

(2) Property listed in this paragraph is property that is specified under subsection (d), unless the State law that is applicable to the debtor under paragraph (3)(A) specifically does not so authorize.

(3) Property listed in this paragraph is—
(A) subject to subsections (o) and (p), any property that is exempt under Federal law, other than subsection (d) of this section, or State or local law that is applicable on the date of the filing of the petition to the place in which the debtor's domicile has been located for the 730 days immediately preceding the date of the filing of the petition or if the debtor's domicile has not been located in a single State for such 730-day period, the place in which the debtor's domicile was located for 180 days immediately preceding the 730-day period or for a longer portion of such 180-day period than in any other place;

(B) any interest in property in which the debtor had, immediately before the commencement of the case, an interest as a tenant by the entirety or joint tenant to the extent that such interest as a tenant by the entirety or joint tenant is exempt from process under applicable nonbankruptcy law; and

(C) retirement funds to the extent that those funds are in a fund or account that is exempt from taxation under section 401, 403, 408, 408A, 414, 457, or 501(a) of the Internal Revenue Code of 1986.

If the effect of the domiciliary requirement under subparagraph (A) is to render the debtor ineligible for any exemption, the debtor may elect to exempt property that is specified under subsection (d).

(4) For purposes of paragraph (3)(C) and subsection (d)(12), the following shall apply:
(A) If the retirement funds are in a retirement fund that has received a favorable determination under section 7805 of the Internal Revenue Code of 1986, and that determination is in effect as of the date of the filing of the petition in a case under this title, those funds shall be presumed to be exempt from the estate.

(B) If the retirement funds are in a retirement fund that has not received a favorable determination under such section 7805, those funds are exempt from the estate if the debtor demonstrates that—

(i) no prior determination to the contrary has been made by a court or the Internal Revenue Service; and

(ii)(I) the retirement fund is in substantial compliance with the applicable requirements of the Internal Revenue Code of 1986; or

(II) the retirement fund fails to be in substantial compliance with the applicable requirements of the Internal Revenue Code of 1986 and the debtor is not materially responsible for that failure.

(C) A direct transfer of retirement funds from 1 fund or account that is exempt from taxation under section 401, 403, 408, 408A, 414, 457, or 501(a) of the Internal Revenue Code of 1986, under section 401(a)(31) of the Internal Revenue Code of 1986, or otherwise, shall not cease to qualify for exemption under paragraph (3)(C) or subsection (d)(12) by reason of such direct transfer.

(D)(i) Any distribution that qualifies as an eligible rollover distribution within the meaning of section 402(c) of the Internal Revenue Code of 1986 or that is described in clause (ii) shall not cease to qualify for exemption under paragraph (3)(C) or subsection (d)(12) by reason of such distribution.

(ii) A distribution described in this clause is an amount that—

(I) has been distributed from a fund or account that is exempt from taxation under section 401, 403, 408, 408A, 414, 457, or 501(a) of the Internal Revenue Code of 1986; and

(II) to the extent allowed by law, is deposited in such a fund or account not later than 60 days after the distribution of such amount.

(c) Unless the case is dismissed, property exempted under this section is not liable during or after the case for any debt of the debtor that arose, or that is determined under section 502 of this title as if such debt had arisen, before the commencement of the case, except—

(1) a debt of a kind specified in paragraph (1) or (5) of section 523(a) (in which case, notwithstanding any provision of applicable nonbankruptcy law to the contrary, such property shall be liable for a debt of a kind specified in such paragraph);

(2) a debt secured by a lien that is—

(A)(i) not avoided under subsection (f) or (g) of this section or under section 544, 545, 547, 548, 549, or 724(a) of this title; and

(ii) not void under section 506(d) of this title; or

(B) a tax lien, notice of which is properly filed;

(3) a debt of a kind specified in section 523(a)(4) or 523(a)(6) of this title owed by an institution-affiliated party of an insured depository institution to a Federal depository institutions regulatory agency acting in its capacity as conservator, receiver, or liquidating agent for such institution; or

(4) a debt in connection with fraud in the obtaining or providing of any scholarship, grant, loan, tuition, discount, award, or other financial assistance for purposes of financing an education at an institution of higher education (as that term is defined in section 101 of the Higher Education Act of 1965 (20 U.S.C. 1001)).

(d) The following property may be exempted under subsection (b)(2) of this section:

(1) The debtor's aggregate interest, not to exceed $15,000 [1] in value, in real property or personal property that the debtor or a dependent of the debtor uses as a residence, in a cooperative that owns property that the debtor or a dependent of the debtor uses as a residence, or in a burial plot for the debtor or a dependent of the debtor.

(2) The debtor's interest, not to exceed $2,400 [1] in value, in one motor vehicle.

(3) The debtor's interest, not to exceed $400 [1] in value in any particular item or $8,000 [1] in aggregate value, in household furnishings, household goods, wearing apparel, appliances, books, animals, crops, or musical instruments, that are held primarily for the personal, family, or household use of the debtor or a dependent of the debtor.

(4) The debtor's aggregate interest, not to exceed $1,000 [1] in value, in jewelry held primarily for the personal, family, or household use of the debtor or a dependent of the debtor.

(5) The debtor's aggregate interest in any property, not to exceed in value $800 [1] plus up to $7,500 [1] of any unused amount of the exemption provided under paragraph (1) of this subsection.

(6) The debtor's aggregate interest, not to exceed $1,500 [1] in value, in any implements, professional books, or tools, of the trade of the debtor or the trade of a dependent of the debtor.

(7) Any unmatured life insurance contract owned by the debtor, other than a credit life insurance contract.

(8) The debtor's aggregate interest, not to exceed in value $8,000 [1] less any amount of property of the estate transferred in the manner specified in section 542(d) of this title, in any accrued dividend or interest under, or loan value of, any unmatured life insurance contract owned by the debtor under which the insured is the debtor or an individual of whom the debtor is a dependent.

(9) Professionally prescribed health aids for the debtor or a dependent of the debtor.

(10) The debtor's right to receive—

(A) a social security benefit, unemployment compensation, or a local public assistance benefit;

(B) a veterans' benefit;

(C) a disability, illness, or unemployment benefit;

(D) alimony, support, or separate maintenance, to the extent reasonably necessary for the support of the debtor and any dependent of the debtor;

(E) a payment under a stock bonus, pension, profitsharing, annuity, or similar plan or contract on account of illness, disability, death, age, or length of service, to the extent reasonably necessary for the support of the debtor and any dependent of the debtor, unless—

(i) such plan or contract was established by or under the auspices of an insider that employed the debtor at the time the debtor's rights under such plan or contract arose;

(ii) such payment is on account of age or length of service; and

(iii) such plan or contract does not qualify under section 401(a), 403(a), 403(b), or 408 of the Internal Revenue Code of 1986.

(11) The debtor's right to receive, or property that is traceable to—

(A) an award under a crime victim's reparation law;

(B) a payment on account of the wrongful death of an individual of whom the debtor was a dependent, to the extent reasonably necessary for the support of the debtor and any dependent of the debtor;

(C) a payment under a life insurance contract that insured the life of an individual of whom the debtor was a dependent on the date of such individual's death, to the extent reasonably necessary for the support of the debtor and any dependent of the debtor;

(D) a payment, not to exceed $15,000,[1] on account of personal bodily injury, not including pain and suffering or compensation for actual pecuniary loss, of the debtor or an individual of whom the debtor is a dependent; or

(E) a payment in compensation of loss of future earnings of the debtor or an individual of whom the debtor is or was a dependent, to the extent reasonably necessary for the support of the debtor and any dependent of the debtor.

(12) Retirement funds to the extent that those funds are in a fund or account that is exempt from taxation under section 401, 403, 408, 408A, 414, 457, or 501(a) of the Internal Revenue Code of 1986.

(e) A waiver of an exemption executed in favor of a creditor that holds an unsecured claim against the debtor is unenforceable in a case under this title with respect to such claim against property that the debtor may exempt under subsection (b) of this section. A waiver by the debtor of a power under subsection (f) or (h) of this section to avoid a transfer, under subsection (g) or (i) of this section to exempt property, or under subsection (i) of this section to recover property or to preserve a transfer, is unenforceable in a case under this title.

(f)(1) Notwithstanding any waiver of exemptions but subject to paragraph (3), the debtor may avoid the fixing of a lien on an interest of the debtor in property to the extent that such lien impairs an exemption to which the debtor would have been entitled under subsection (b) of this section, if such lien is—

(A) a judicial lien, other than a judicial lien that secures a debt of a kind that is specified in section 523(a)(5); or

(B) a nonpossessory, nonpurchase-money security interest in any—

(i) household furnishings, household goods, wearing apparel, appliances, books, animals, crops, musical instruments, or jewelry that are held primarily for the personal, family, or household use of the debtor or a dependent of the debtor;

(ii) implements, professional books, or tools, of the trade of the debtor or the trade of a dependent of the debtor; or

(iii) professionally prescribed health aids for the debtor or a dependent of the debtor.

(2)(A) For the purposes of this subsection, a lien shall be considered to impair an exemption to the extent that the sum of—

(i) the lien;

(ii) all other liens on the property; and

(iii) the amount of the exemption that the debtor could claim if there were no liens on the property;

exceeds the value that the debtor's interest in the property would have in the absence of any liens.

(B) In the case of a property subject to more than 1 lien, a lien that has been avoided shall not be considered in making the calculation under subparagraph (A) with respect to other liens.

(C) This paragraph shall not apply with respect to a judgment arising out of a mortgage foreclosure.

(3) In a case in which State law that is applicable to the debtor—

(A) permits a person to voluntarily waive a right to claim exemptions under subsection (d) or prohibits a debtor from claiming exemptions under subsection (d); and

(B) either permits the debtor to claim exemptions under State law without limitation in amount, except to the extent that the debtor has permitted the fixing of a consensual lien on any property or prohibits avoidance of a consensual lien on property otherwise eligible to be claimed as exempt property;

the debtor may not avoid the fixing of a lien on an interest of the debtor or a dependent of the debtor in property if the lien is a nonpossessory, nonpurchase-money security interest in implements, professional books, or tools of the trade of the debtor or a dependent of the debtor or farm animals or crops of the debtor or a dependent of the debtor to the extent the value of such implements, professional books, tools of the trade, animals, and crops exceeds $5,000.[1]

(4)(A) Subject to subparagraph (B), for purposes of paragraph (1)(B), the term "household goods" means—

(i) clothing;

(ii) furniture;

(iii) appliances;

(iv) 1 radio;

(v) 1 television;

(vi) 1 VCR;

(vii) linens;

(viii) china;

(ix) crockery;

(x) kitchenware;

(xi) educational materials and educational equipment primarily for the use of minor dependent children of the debtor;

(xii) medical equipment and supplies;

(xiii) furniture exclusively for the use of minor children, or elderly or disabled dependents of the debtor;

(xiv) personal effects (including the toys and hobby equipment of minor dependent children and wedding rings) of the debtor and the dependents of the debtor; and

(xv) 1 personal computer and related equipment.

(B) The term "household goods" does not include—

(i) works of art (unless by or of the debtor, or any relative of the debtor);

(ii) electronic entertainment equipment with a fair market value of more than $500 [1] in the aggregate (except 1 television, 1 radio, and 1 VCR);

(iii) items acquired as antiques with a fair market value of more than $500 [1] in the aggregate;

(iv) jewelry with a fair market value of more than $500 [1] in the aggregate (except wedding rings); and

(v) a computer (except as otherwise provided for in this section), motor vehicle (including a tractor or lawn tractor), boat, or a motorized recreational device, conveyance, vehicle, watercraft, or aircraft.

(g) Notwithstanding sections 550 and 551 of this title, the debtor may exempt under subsection (b) of this section property that the trustee recovers under section 510(c)(2), 542, 543, 550, 551, or 553 of this title, to the extent that the debtor could have exempted such property under subsection (b) of this section if such property had not been transferred, if—

(1)(A) such transfer was not a voluntary transfer of such property by the debtor; and

(B) the debtor did not conceal such property; or

(2) the debtor could have avoided such transfer under subsection (f)(1)(B) of this section.

(h) The debtor may avoid a transfer of property of the debtor or recover a setoff to the extent that the debtor could have exempted such property under subsection (g)(1) of this section if the trustee had avoided such transfer, if—

(1) such transfer is avoidable by the trustee under section 544, 545, 547, 548, 549, or 724(a) of this title or recoverable by the trustee under section 553 of this title; and

(2) the trustee does not attempt to avoid such transfer.

(i)(1) If the debtor avoids a transfer or recovers a setoff under subsection (f) or (h) of this section, the debtor may recover in the manner prescribed by, and subject to the limitations of, section 550 of this title, the same as if the trustee had avoided such transfer, and may exempt any property so recovered under subsection (b) of this section.

(2) Notwithstanding section 551 of this title, a transfer avoided under section 544, 545, 547, 548, 549, or 724(a) of this title, under subsection (f) or (h) of this section, or property recovered under section 553 of this title, may be preserved for the benefit of the debtor to the extent that the debtor may exempt such property under subsection (g) of this section or paragraph (1) of this subsection.

(j) Notwithstanding subsections (g) and (i) of this section, the debtor may exempt a particular kind of property under subsections (g) and (i) of this section only to the extent that the debtor has exempted less property in value of such kind than that to which the debtor is entitled under subsection (b) of this section.

(k) Property that the debtor exempts under this section is not liable for payment of any administrative expense except—

(1) the aliquot share of the costs and expenses of avoiding a transfer of property that the debtor exempts under subsection (g) of this section, or of recovery of such property, that is attributable to the value of the portion of such property exempted in relation to the value of the property recovered; and

(2) any costs and expenses of avoiding a transfer under subsection (f) or (h) of this section, or of recovery of property under subsection (i)(1) of this section, that the debtor has not paid.

(l) The debtor shall file a list of property that the debtor claims as exempt under subsection (b) of this section. If the debtor does not file such a list, a dependent of the debtor may file such a list, or may claim property as exempt from property of the estate on behalf of the debtor. Unless a party in interest objects, the property claimed as exempt on such list is exempt.

(m) Subject to the limitation in subsection (b), this section shall apply separately with respect to each debtor in a joint case.

(n) For assets in individual retirement accounts described in section 408 or 408A of the Internal Revenue Code of 1986, other than a simplified employee pension under section 408(k) of such Code or a simple retirement account under section 408(p) of such Code, the aggregate value of such assets exempted under this section, without regard to amounts attributable to rollover contributions under section 402(c), 402(e)(6), 403(a)(4), 403(a)(5), and 403(b)(8) of the Internal Revenue Code of 1986, and earnings thereon, shall not exceed $1,000,000 [1] in a case filed by a debtor who is an individual, except that such amount may be increased if the interests of justice so require.

(o) For purposes of subsection (b)(3)(A), and notwithstanding subsection (a), the value of an interest in—

(1) real or personal property that the debtor or a dependent of the debtor uses as a residence;

(2) a cooperative that owns property that the debtor or a dependent of the debtor uses as a residence;

(3) a burial plot for the debtor or a dependent of the debtor; or

(4) real or personal property that the debtor or a dependent of the debtor claims as a homestead;

shall be reduced to the extent that such value is attributable to any portion of any property that the debtor disposed of in the 10-year period ending on the date of the filing of the petition with the intent to hinder, delay, or defraud a creditor and that the debtor could not exempt, or that portion that the debtor could not exempt, under subsection (b), if on such date the debtor had held the property so disposed of.

(p)(1) Except as provided in paragraph (2) of this subsection and sections 544 and 548, as a result of electing under subsection (b)(3)(A) to exempt property under State or local law, a debtor may not exempt any amount of interest that was acquired by the debtor during the 1215-day period preceding the date of the filing of the petition that exceeds in the aggregate $125,000 [1] in value in—

(A) real or personal property that the debtor or a dependent of the debtor uses as a residence;

(B) a cooperative that owns property that the debtor or a dependent of the debtor uses as a residence;

(C) a burial plot for the debtor or a dependent of the debtor; or

(D) real or personal property that the debtor or dependent of the debtor claims as a homestead.

(2)(A) The limitation under paragraph (1) shall not apply to an exemption claimed under subsection (b)(3)(A) by a family farmer for the principal residence of such farmer.

(B) For purposes of paragraph (1), any amount of such interest does not include any interest transferred from a debtor's previous principal residence (which was acquired prior to the beginning of such 1215-day period) into the debtor's current principal residence, if the debtor's previous and current residences are located in the same State.

(q)(1) As a result of electing under subsection (b)(3)(A) to exempt property under State or local law, a debtor may not exempt any amount of an interest in property described in subparagraphs (A), (B), (C), and (D) of subsection (p)(1) which exceeds in the aggregate $125,000 [1] if—

(A) the court determines, after notice and a hearing, that the debtor has been convicted of a felony (as defined in section 3156 of title 18), which under the circumstances, demonstrates that the filing of the case was an abuse of the provisions of this title; or

(B) the debtor owes a debt arising from—

(i) any violation of the Federal securities laws (as defined in section 3(a)(47) of the Securities Exchange Act of 1934), any State securities laws, or any regulation or order issued under Federal securities laws or State securities laws;

(ii) fraud, deceit, or manipulation in a fiduciary capacity or in connection with the purchase or sale of any security registered under section 12 or 15(d) of the Securities Exchange Act of 1934 or under section 6 of the Securities Act of 1933;

(iii) any civil remedy under section 1964 of title 18; or

(iv) any criminal act, intentional tort, or willful or reckless misconduct that caused serious physical injury or death to another individual in the preceding 5 years.

(2) Paragraph (1) shall not apply to the extent the amount of an interest in property described in subparagraphs (A), (B), (C), and (D) of subsection (p)(1) is reasonably necessary for the support of the debtor and any dependent of the debtor.

(Pub. L. 95–598, Nov. 6, 1978, 92 Stat. 2586; Pub. L. 98–353, title III, §§306, 453, July 10, 1984, 98 Stat. 353, 375; Pub. L. 99–554, title II, §283(i), Oct. 27, 1986, 100 Stat. 3117; Pub. L. 101–647, title XXV, §2522(b), Nov. 29, 1990, 104 Stat. 4866; Pub. L. 103–394, title I, §108(d), title III, §§303, 304(d), 310, title V, §501(d)(12), Oct. 22, 1994, 108 Stat. 4112, 4132, 4133, 4137, 4145; Pub. L. 106–420, §4, Nov. 1, 2000, 114 Stat. 1868; Pub. L. 109–8, title II, §§216, 224(a), (e)(1), title III, §§307, 308, 313(a), 322(a), Apr. 20, 2005, 119 Stat. 55, 62, 65, 81, 87, 96; Pub. L. 111–327, §2(a)(17), Dec. 22, 2010, 124 Stat. 3559.)

Historical and Revision Notes

legislative statements

Section 522 of the House amendment represents a compromise on the issue of exemptions between the position taken in the House bill, and that taken in the Senate amendment. Dollar amounts specified in section 522(d) of the House bill have been reduced from amounts as contained in H.R. 8200 as passed by the House. The States may, by passing a law, determine whether the Federal exemptions will apply as an alternative to State exemptions in bankruptcy cases.

Section 522(c)(1) tracks the House bill and provides that dischargeable tax claims may not be collected out of exempt property.

Section 522(f)(2) is derived from the Senate amendment restricting the debtor to avoidance of nonpossessory, nonpurchase money security interests.

Exemptions: Section 522(c)(1) of the House amendment adopts a provision contained in the House bill that dischargeable taxes cannot be collected from exempt assets. This changes present law, which allows collection of dischargeable taxes from exempt property, a rule followed in the Senate amendment. Nondischargeable taxes, however, will continue to the [be] collectable out of exempt property. It is anticipated that in the next session Congress will review the exemptions from levy currently contained in the Internal Revenue Code [title 26] with a view to increasing the exemptions to more realistic levels.

senate report no. 95–989

Subsection (a) of this section defines two terms: "dependent" includes the debtor's spouse, whether or not actually dependent; and "value" means fair market value as of the date of the filing of the petition.

Subsection (b) tracks current law. It permits a debtor the exemptions to which he is entitled under other Federal law and the law of the State of his domicile. Some of the items that may be exempted under Federal laws other than title 11 include:

Foreign Service Retirement and Disability payments, 22 U.S.C. 1104; [1]

Social security payments, 42 U.S.C. 407;

Injury or death compensation payments from war risk hazards, 42 U.S.C. 1717;

Wages of fishermen, seamen, and apprentices, 46 U.S.C. 601; [2]

Civil service retirement benefits, 5 U.S.C. 729, 2265; [3]

Longshoremen's and Harbor Workers' Compensation Act death and disability benefits, 33 U.S.C. 916;

Railroad Retirement Act annuities and pensions, 45 U.S.C. 228(L); [4]

Veterans benefits, 45 U.S.C. 352(E); [5]

Special pensions paid to winners of the Congressional Medal of Honor, 38 U.S.C. 3101; [6] and

Federal homestead lands on debts contracted before issuance of the patent, 43 U.S.C. 175.

He may also exempt an interest in property in which the debtor had an interest as a tenant by the entirety or joint tenant to the extent that interest would have been exempt from process under applicable nonbankruptcy law.

Under proposed section 541, all property of the debtor becomes property of the estate, but the debtor is permitted to exempt certain property from property of the estate under this section. Property may be exempted even if it is subject to a lien, but only the unencumbered portion of the property is to be counted in computing the "value" of the property for the purposes of exemption.

As under current law, the debtor will be permitted to convert nonexempt property into exempt property before filing a bankruptcy petition. The practice is not fraudulent as to creditors, and permits the debtor to make full use of the exemptions to which he is entitled under the law.

Subsection (c) insulates exempt property from prepetition claims other than tax claims (whether or not dischargeable), and other than alimony, maintenance, or support claims that are excepted from discharge. The bankruptcy discharge does not prevent enforcement of valid liens. The rule of *Long v. Bullard*, 117 U.S. 617 (1886), is accepted with respect to the enforcement of valid liens on nonexempt property as well as on exempt property. Cf. *Louisville Joint Stock Land Bank v. Radford*, 295 U.S. 555, 583 (1935).

Subsection (c)(3) permits the collection of dischargeable taxes from exempt assets. Only assets exempted from levy under Section 6334 of the Internal Revenue Code [title 26] or under applicable state or local tax law cannot be applied to satisfy these tax claims. This rule applies to prepetition tax claims against the debtor regardless of whether the claims do or do not receive priority and whether they are dischargeable or nondischargeable. Thus, even if a tax is dischargeable vis-a-vis the debtor's after-acquired assets, it may nevertheless be collectible from exempt property held by the estate. (Taxes incurred by the debtor's estate which are collectible as first priority administrative expenses are not collectible from the debtor's estate which are collectible as first priority administrative expenses are not collectible from the debtor's exempt assets.)

Subsection (d) protects the debtor's exemptions, either Federal or State, by making unenforceable in a bankruptcy case a waiver of exemptions or a waiver of the debtor's avoiding powers under the following subsections.

Subsection (e) protects the debtor's exemptions, his discharge, and thus his fresh start by permitting him to avoid certain liens on exempt property. The debtor may avoid a judicial lien on any property to the extent that the property could have been exempted in the absence of the lien, and may similarly avoid a nonpurchase-money security interest in certain household and personal goods. The avoiding power is independent of any waiver of exemptions.

Subsection (f) gives the debtor the ability to exempt property that the trustee recovers under one of the trustee's avoiding powers if the property was involuntarily transferred away from the debtor (such as by the fixing of a judicial lien) and if the debtor did not conceal the property. The debtor is also permitted to exempt property that the trustee recovers as the result of the avoiding of the fixing of certain security interests to the extent that the debtor could otherwise have exempted the property.

Subsection (g) provides that if the trustee does not exercise an avoiding power to recover a transfer of property that would be exempt, the debtor may exercise it and exempt the property, if the transfer was involuntary and the debtor did not conceal the property. If the debtor wishes to preserve his right to pursue any action under this provision, then he must intervene in any action brought by the trustee based on the same cause of action. It is not intended that the debtor be given an additional opportunity to avoid a transfer or that the transferee should have to defend the same action twice. Rather, the section is primarily designed to give the debtor the rights the trustee could have, but has not, pursued. The debtor is given no greater rights under this provision than the trustee, and thus, the debtor's avoiding powers under proposed sections 544, 545, 547, and 548, are subject to proposed 546, as are the trustee's powers.

These subsections are cumulative. The debtor is not required to choose which he will use to gain an exemption. Instead, he may use more than one in any particular instance, just as the trustee's avoiding powers are cumulative.

Subsection (h) permits recovery by the debtor of property transferred by an avoided transfer from either the initial or subsequent transferees. It also permits preserving a transfer for the benefit of the debtor. In either event, the debtor may exempt the property recovered or preserved.

Subsection (i) makes clear that the debtor may exempt property under the avoiding subsections (f) and (h) only to the extent he has exempted less property than allowed under subsection (b).

Subsection (j) makes clear that the liability of the debtor's exempt property is limited to the debtor's aliquot share of the costs and expenses recovery of property that the trustee recovers and the debtor later exempts, and any costs and expenses of avoiding a transfer by the debtor that the debtor has not already paid.

Subsection (k) requires the debtor to file a list of property that he claims as exempt from property of the estate. Absent an objection to the list, the property is exempted. A dependent of the debtor may file it and thus be protected if the debtor fails to file the list.

Subsection (l) provides the rule for a joint case.

house report no. 95–595

Subsection (a) of this section defines two terms: "dependent" includes the debtor's spouse, whether or not actually dependent; and "value" means fair market value as of the date of the filing of the petition.

Subsection (b), the operative subsection of this section, is a significant departure from present law. It permits an individual debtor in a bankruptcy case a choice between exemption systems. The debtor may choose the Federal exemptions prescribed in subsection (d), or he may choose the exemptions to which he is entitled under other Federal law and the law of the State of his domicile. If the debtor chooses the latter, some of the items that may be exempted under other Federal laws include:

—Foreign Service Retirement and Disability payments, 22 U.S.C. 1104; [7]

—Social security payments, 42 U.S.C. 407;

—Injury or death compensation payments from war risk hazards, 42 U.S.C. 1717;

—Wages of fishermen, seamen, and apprentices, 46 U.S.C. 601; [8]

—Civil service retirement benefits, 5 U.S.C. 729, 2265; [9]

—Longshoremen's and Harbor Workers' Compensation Act death and disability benefits, 33 U.S.C. 916;

—Railroad Retirement Act annuities and pensions, 45 U.S.C. 228(l); [10]

—Veterans benefits, 45 U.S.C. 352(E); [11]

—Special pensions paid to winners of the Congressional Medal of Honor, 38 U.S.C. 3101; [12] and

—Federal homestead lands on debts contracted before issuance of the patent, 43 U.S.C. 175.

He may also exempt an interest in property in which the debtor had an interest as a tenant by the entirety or joint tenant to the extent that interest would have been exempt from process under applicable nonbankruptcy law. The Rules will provide for the situation where the debtor's choice of exemption, Federal or State, was improvident and should be changed, for example, where the court has ruled against the debtor with respect to a major exemption.

Under proposed 11 U.S.C. 541, all property of the debtor becomes property of the estate, but the debtor is permitted to exempt certain property from property of the estate under this section. Property may be exempted even if it is subject to a lien, but only the unencumbered portion of the property is to be counted in computing the "value" of the property for the purposes of exemption. Thus, for example, a residence worth $30,000 with a mortgage of $25,000 will be exemptable [sic] to the extent of $5,000. This follows current law. The remaining value of the property will be dealt with in the bankruptcy case as is any interest in property that is subject to a lien.

As under current law, the debtor will be permitted to convert nonexempt property into exempt property before filing a bankruptcy petition. See Hearings, pt. 3, at 1355–58. The practice is not fraudulent as to creditors and permits the debtor to make full use of the exemptions to which he is entitled under the law.

Subsection (c) insulates exempt property from prepetition claims, except tax and alimony, maintenance, or support claims that are excepted from discharge. The bankruptcy discharge will not prevent enforcement of valid liens. The rule of *Long v. Bullard*, 117 U.S. 617 (1886) [6 S.Ct. 917, 29 L.Ed. 1004], is accepted with respect to the enforcement of valid liens on nonexempt property as well as on exempt property. Cf. *Louisville Joint Stock Land Bank v. Radford*, 295 U.S. 555, 583 (1935) [55 S.Ct. 854].

Subsection (d) specifies the Federal exemptions to which the debtor is entitled. They are derived in large part from the Uniform Exemptions Act, promulgated by the Commissioners of Uniform State Laws in August, 1976. Eleven categories of property are exempted. First is a homestead to the extent of $10,000, which may be claimed in real or personal property that the debtor or a dependent of the debtor uses as a residence. Second, the debtor may exempt a motor vehicle to the extent of $1500. Third, the debtor may exempt household goods, furnishings, clothing, and similar household items, held primarily for the personal, family, or household use of the debtor or a dependent of the debtor. "Animals" includes all animals, such as pets, livestock, poultry, and fish, if they are held primarily for personal, family or household use. The limitation for third category items is $300 on any particular item. The debtor may also exempt up to $750 of personal jewelry.

Paragraph (5) permits the exemption of $500, plus any unused amount of the homestead exemption, in any property, in order not to discriminate against the nonhomeowner. Paragraph (6) grants the debtor up to $1000 in implements, professional books, or tools, of the trade of the debtor or a dependent. Paragraph (7) exempts a life insurance contract, other than a credit life insurance contract, owned by the debtor. This paragraph refers to the life insurance contract itself. It does not encompass any other rights under the contract, such as the right to borrow out the loan value. Because of this provision, the trustee may not surrender a life insurance contract, which remains property of the debtor if he chooses the Federal exemptions. Paragraph (8) permits the debtor to exempt up to $5000 in loan value in a life insurance policy owned by the debtor under which the debtor or an individual of whom the debtor is a dependent is the insured. The exemption provided by this paragraph and paragraph (7) will also include the debtor's rights in a group insurance certificate under which the insured is an individual of whom the debtor is a dependent (assuming the debtor has rights in the policy that could be exempted) or the debtor. A trustee is authorized to collect the entire loan value on every life insurance policy owned by the debtor as property of the estate. First, however, the debtor will choose which policy or policies under which the loan value will be exempted. The $5000 figure is reduced by the amount of any automatic premium loan authorized after the date of the filing of the petition under section 542(d). Paragraph (9) exempts professionally prescribed health aids.

Paragraph (10) exempts certain benefits that are akin to future earnings of the debtor. These include social security, unemployment compensation, or public assistance benefits, veteran's benefits, disability, illness, or unemployment benefits, alimony, support, or separate maintenance (but only to the extent reasonably necessary for the support of the debtor and any dependents of the debtor), and benefits under a certain stock bonus, pension, profitsharing, annuity or similar plan based on illness, disability, death, age or length of service. Paragraph (11) allows the debtor to exempt certain compensation for losses. These include crime victim's reparation benefits, wrongful death benefits (with a reasonably necessary for support limitation), life insurance proceeds (same limitation), compensation for bodily injury, not including pain and suffering ($10,000 limitation), and loss of future earnings payments (support limitation). This provision in subparagraph (D)(11) is designed to cover payments in compensation of actual bodily injury, such as the loss of a limb, and is not intended to include the attendant costs that accompany such a loss, such as medical payments, pain and suffering, or loss of earnings. Those items are handled separately by the bill.

Subsection (e) protects the debtor's exemptions, either Federal or State, by making unenforceable in a bankruptcy case a waiver of exemptions or a waiver of the debtor's avoiding powers under the following subsections.

Subsection (f) protects the debtor's exemptions, his discharge, and thus his fresh start by permitting him to avoid certain liens on exempt property. The debtor may avoid a judicial lien on any property to the extent that the property could have been exempted in the absence of the lien, and may similarly avoid a nonpurchase-money security interest in certain household and personal goods. The avoiding power is independent of any waiver of exemptions.

Subsection (g) gives the debtor the ability to exempt property that the trustee recovers under one of the trustee's avoiding powers if the property was involuntarily transferred away from the debtor (such as by the fixing of a judicial lien) and if the debtor did not conceal the property. The debtor is also permitted to exempt property that the trustee recovers as the result of the avoiding of the fixing of certain security interests to the extent that the debtor could otherwise have exempted the property.

If the trustee does not pursue an avoiding power to recover a transfer of property that would be exempt, the debtor may pursue it and exempt the property, if the transfer was involuntary and the debtor did not conceal the property. If the debtor wishes to preserve his right to pursue an action under this provision, then he must intervene in any action brought by the trustee based on the same cause of action. It is not intended that the debtor be given an additional opportunity to avoid a transfer or that the transferee have to defend the same action twice. Rather, the section is primarily designed to give the debtor the rights the trustee could have pursued if the trustee chooses not to pursue them. The debtor is given no greater rights under this provision than the trustee, and thus the debtor's avoiding powers under proposed 11 U.S.C. 544, 545, 547, and 548, are subject to proposed 11 U.S.C. 546, as are the trustee's powers.

These subsections are cumulative. The debtor is not required to choose which he will use to gain an exemption. Instead, he may use more than one in any particular instance, just as the trustee's avoiding powers are cumulative.

Subsection (i) permits recovery by the debtor of property transferred in an avoided transfer from either the initial or subsequent transferees. It also permits preserving a transfer for the benefit of the debtor. Under either case the debtor may exempt the property recovered or preserved.

Subsection (k) makes clear that the debtor's aliquot share of the costs and expenses [for] recovery of property that the trustee recovers and the debtor later exempts, and any costs and expenses of avoiding a transfer by the debtor that the debtor has not already paid.

Subsection (l) requires the debtor to file a list of property that he claims as exempt from property of the estate. Absent an objection to the list, the property is exempted. A dependent of the debtor may file it and thus be protected if the debtor fails to file the list.

Subsection (m) requires the clerk of the bankruptcy court to give notice of any exemptions claimed under subsection (l), in order that parties in interest may have an opportunity to object to the claim.

Subsection (n) provides the rule for a joint case: each debtor is entitled to the Federal exemptions provided under this section or to the State exemptions, whichever the debtor chooses.

References in Text

The Federal Rules of Bankruptcy Procedure, referred to in subsec. (b)(1), are set out in the Appendix to this title.

The Internal Revenue Code of 1986, referred to in subsecs. (b)(3)(C), (4), (d)(10)(E)(iii), (12), and (n), is classified generally to Title 26, Internal Revenue Code.

Sections 3(a)(47), 12, and 15(d) of the Securities Exchange Act of 1934, referred to in subsec. (q)(1)(B)(i), (ii), are classified to sections 78c(a)(47), 78l, and 78o(d), respectively, of Title 15, Commerce and Trade.

Section 6 of the Securities Exchange Act of 1933, referred to in subsec. (q)(1)(B)(ii), is classified to section 77f of Title 15, Commerce and Trade.

Amendments

2010—Subsec. (b)(3)(A). Pub. L. 111–327, §2(a)(17)(A), substituted "petition to the place" for "petition at the place" and "located in a single State" for "located at a single State".

Subsec. (c)(1). Pub. L. 111–327, §2(a)(17)(B), substituted "such paragraph" for "section 523(a)(5)".

2005—Subsec. (b). Pub. L. 109–8, §224(a)(1)(B)–(F), designated introductory provisions of subsec. (b) as par. (1), substituted "paragraph (3)" for "paragraph (2)" in two places and "paragraph (2)" for "paragraph (1)" wherever appearing, struck out "Such property is—" after "case is filed.", and struck out former par. (1) which read: "property that is specified under subsection (d) of this section, unless the State law that is applicable to the debtor under paragraph (2)(A) of this subsection specifically does not so authorize; or, in the alternative,".

Subsec. (b)(2). Pub. L. 109–8, §224(a)(1)(B), added par. (2). Former par. (2) redesignated (3).

Subsec. (b)(2)(C). Pub. L. 109–8, §224(a)(1)(A)(i)–(iii), added subpar. (C).

Subsec. (b)(3). Pub. L. 109–8, §307(2), inserted "If the effect of the domiciliary requirement under subparagraph (A) is to render the debtor ineligible for any exemption, the debtor may elect to exempt property that is specified under subsection (d)." at end.

Pub. L. 109–8, §224(a)(1)(A)(iv), redesignated par. (2) as (3) and inserted introductory provisions.

Subsec. (b)(3)(A). Pub. L. 109–8, §308(1), inserted "subject to subsections (o) and (p)," before "any property".

Pub. L. 109–8, §307(1), substituted "730 days" for "180 days" and "or if the debtor's domicile has not been located at a single State for such 730-day period, the place in which the debtor's domicile was located for 180 days immediately preceding the 730-day period or for a longer portion of such 180-day period than in any other place" for ", or for a longer portion of such 180-day period than in any other place".

Subsec. (b)(4). Pub. L. 109–8, §224(a)(1)(G), added par. (4).

Subsec. (c)(1). Pub. L. 109–8, §216(1), added par. (1) and struck out former par. (1) which read as follows: "a debt of a kind specified in section 523(a)(1) or 523(a)(5) of this title;".

Subsec. (d). Pub. L. 109–8, §224(a)(2)(A), substituted "subsection (b)(2)" for "subsection (b)(1)" in introductory provisions.

Subsec. (d)(12). Pub. L. 109–8, §224(a)(2)(B), added par. (12).

Subsec. (f)(1)(A). Pub. L. 109–8, §216(2), substituted "a debt of a kind that is specified in section 523(a)(5); or" for "a debt—

"(i) to a spouse, former spouse, or child of the debtor, for alimony to, maintenance for, or support of such spouse or child, in connection with a separation agreement, divorce decree or other order of a court of record, determination made in accordance with State or territorial law by a governmental unit, or property settlement agreement; and

"(ii) to the extent that such debt—

"(I) is not assigned to another entity, voluntarily, by operation of law, or otherwise; and

"(II) includes a liability designated as alimony, maintenance, or support, unless such liability is actually in the nature of alimony, maintenance or support.; or".

Subsec. (f)(4). Pub. L. 109–8, §313(a), added par. (4).

Subsec. (g)(2). Pub. L. 109–8, §216(3), substituted "subsection (f)(1)(B)" for "subsection (f)(2)".

Subsec. (n). Pub. L. 109–8, §224(e)(1), added subsec. (n).

Subsec. (o). Pub. L. 109–8, §308(2), added subsec. (o).

Subsecs. (p), (q). Pub. L. 109–8, §322(a), added subsecs. (p) and (q).

2000—Subsec. (c)(4). Pub. L. 106–420 added par. (4).

1994—Subsec. (b). Pub. L. 103–394, §501(d)(12)(A), substituted "Federal Rules of Bankruptcy Procedure" for "Bankruptcy Rules".

Subsec. (d)(1) to (6). Pub. L. 103–394, §108(d)(1)–(6), substituted "$15,000" for "$7,500" in par. (1), "$2,400" for "$1,200" in par. (2), "$400" and "$8,000" for "$200" and "$4,000", respectively, in par. (3), "$1,000" for "$500" in par. (4), "$800" and "$7,500" for "$400" and "$3,750", respectively, in par. (5), and "$1,500" for "$750" in par. (6).

Subsec. (d)(8). Pub. L. 103–394, §108(d)(7), substituted "$8,000" for "$4,000".

Subsec. (d)(10)(E)(iii). Pub. L. 103–394, §501(d)(12)(B), substituted "or 408" for "408, or 409" and "Internal Revenue Code of 1986" for "Internal Revenue Code of 1954 (26 U.S.C. 401(a), 403(a), 403(b), 408, or 409)".

Subsec. (d)(11)(D). Pub. L. 103–394, §108(d)(8), substituted "$15,000" for "$7,500".

Subsec. (f)(1). Pub. L. 103–394, §§303(3), 310(1), designated existing provisions as par. (1) and inserted "but subject to paragraph (3)" after "waiver of exemptions" in introductory provisions. Former par. (1) redesignated subpar. (A) of par. (1).

Subsec. (f)(1)(A). Pub. L. 103–394, §§303(2), 304(d), redesignated par. (1) as subpar. (A) of par. (1) and inserted ", other than a judicial lien that secures a debt—

"(i) to a spouse, former spouse, or child of the debtor, for alimony to, maintenance for, or support of such spouse or child, in connection with a separation agreement, divorce decree or other order of a court of record, determination made in accordance with State or territorial law by a governmental unit, or property settlement agreement; and

"(ii) to the extent that such debt—

"(I) is not assigned to another entity, voluntarily, by operation of law, or otherwise; and

"(II) includes a liability designated as alimony, maintenance, or support, unless such liability is actually in the nature of alimony, maintenance or support."

Subsec. (f)(1)(B). Pub. L. 103–394, §303(1), redesignated par. (2) as subpar. (B) of par. (1) and subpars. (A) to (C) of par. (2) as cls. (i) to (iii), respectively, of subpar. (B) of par. (1).

Subsec. (f)(2). Pub. L. 103–394, §303(4), added par. (2). Former par. (2) redesignated subpar. (B) of par. (1).

Subsec. (f)(3). Pub. L. 103–394, §310(2), added par. (3).

1990—Subsec. (c)(3). Pub. L. 101–647 added par. (3).

1986—Subsec. (h)(1). Pub. L. 99–554, §283(i)(1), substituted "553 of this title" for "553 of this tittle".

Subsec. (i)(2). Pub. L. 99–554, §283(i)(2), substituted "this" for "his" after "subsection (g) of".

1984—Subsec. (a)(2). Pub. L. 98–353, §453(a), inserted "or, with respect to property that becomes property of an estate after such date, as of the date such property becomes property of the estate".

Subsec. (b). Pub. L. 98–353, §306(a), inserted provision that in joint cases filed under section 302 of this title and individual cases filed under section 301 or 303 of this title by or against debtors who are husband and wife, and whose estates are ordered to be jointly administered under Rule 1015(b) of the Bankruptcy Rules, one debtor may not elect to exempt property listed in paragraph (1) and the other debtor elect to exempt property listed in paragraph (2) of this subsection, but that if the parties cannot agree on the alternative to be elected, they shall be deemed to elect paragraph (1), where such election is permitted under the law of the jurisdiction where the case is filed.

Subsec. (c). Pub. L. 98–353, §453(b), amended subsec. (c) generally. Prior to amendment, subsec. (c) read as follows: "Unless the case is dismissed, property exempted under this section is not liable during or after the case for any debt of the debtor that arose, or that is determined under section 502 of this title as if such claim had arisen before the commencement of the case, except—

"(1) a debt of a kind specified in section 523(a)(1) or section 523(a)(5) of this title; or

"(2) a lien that is—

"(A) not avoided under section 544, 545, 547, 548, 549, or 724(a) of this title;

"(B) not voided under section 506(d) of this title; or

"(C)(i) a tax lien, notice of which is properly filed; and

"(ii) avoided under section 545(2) of this title."

Subsec. (d)(3). Pub. L. 98–353, §306(b), inserted "or $4,000 in aggregate value".

Subsec. (d)(5). Pub. L. 98–353, §306(c), amended par. (5) generally. Prior to amendment, par. (5) read as follows: "The debtor's aggregate interest, not to exceed in value $400 plus any unused amount of the exemption provided under paragraph (1) of this subsection, in any property."

Subsec. (e). Pub. L. 98–353, §453(c), substituted "an exemption" for "exemptions".

Subsec. (m). Pub. L. 98–353, §306(d), substituted "Subject to the limitation in subsection (b), this section shall apply separately with respect to each debtor in a joint case" for "This section shall apply separately with respect to each debtor in a joint case".

Effective Date of 2005 Amendment

Amendment by Pub. L. 109–8 effective 180 days after Apr. 20, 2005, with amendments by sections 216, 224(a), (e)(1), 307, and 313(a) of Pub. L. 109–8 not applicable with respect to cases commenced under this title before such effective date, except as otherwise provided, and amendments by sections 308 and 322(a) of Pub. L. 109–8 applicable with respect to cases commenced under this title on or after Apr. 20, 2005, see section 1501 of Pub. L. 109–8, set out as a note under section 101 of this title.

Effective Date of 1994 Amendment

Amendment by Pub. L. 103–394 effective Oct. 22, 1994, and not applicable with respect to cases commenced under this title before Oct. 22, 1994, see section 702 of Pub. L. 103–394, set out as a note under section 101 of this title.

Effective Date of 1986 Amendment

Amendment by Pub. L. 99–554 effective 30 days after Oct. 27, 1986, see section 302(a) of Pub. L. 99–554, set out as a note under section 581 of Title 28, Judiciary and Judicial Procedure.

Effective Date of 1984 Amendment

Amendment by Pub. L. 98–353 effective with respect to cases filed 90 days after July 10, 1984, see section 552(a) of Pub. L. 98–353, set out as a note under section 101 of this title.

Adjustment of Dollar Amounts

The dollar amounts specified in this section were adjusted by notices of the Judicial Conference of the United States pursuant to section 104 of this title as follows:

By notice dated Feb. 16, 2016, 81 F.R. 8748, effective Apr. 1, 2016, in subsec. (d)(1), dollar amount "22,975" was adjusted to "23,675"; in subsec. (d)(2), dollar amount "3,675" was adjusted to "3,775"; in subsec. (d)(3), dollar amounts "575" and "12,250" were adjusted to "600" and "12,625", respectively; in subsec. (d)(4), dollar amount "1,550" was adjusted to "1,600"; in subsec. (d)(5), dollar amounts "1,225" and "11,500" were adjusted to "1,250" and "11,850", respectively; in subsec. (d)(6), dollar amount "2,300" was adjusted to "2,375"; in subsec. (d)(8), dollar amount "12,250" was adjusted to "12,625"; in subsec. (d)(11)(D), dollar amount "22,975" was adjusted to "23,675"; in subsec. (f)(3), dollar amount "6,225" was adjusted to "6,425"; in subsec. (f)(4), dollar amount "650" was adjusted to "675" each time it appeared; in subsec. (n), dollar amount "1,245,475" was adjusted to "1,283,025"; in subsec. (p), dollar amount "155,675" was adjusted to "160,375"; and, in subsec. (q), dollar amount "155,675" was adjusted to "160,375". See notice of the Judicial Conference of the United States set out as a note under section 104 of this title.

By notice dated Feb. 12, 2013, 78 F.R. 12089, effective Apr. 1, 2013, in subsec. (d)(1), dollar amount "21,625" was adjusted to "22,975"; in subsec. (d)(2), dollar amount "3,450" was adjusted to "3,675"; in subsec. (d)(3), dollar amounts "550" and "11,525" were adjusted to "575" and "12,250", respectively; in subsec. (d)(4), dollar amount "1,450" was adjusted to "1,550"; in subsec. (d)(5), dollar amounts "1,150" and "10,825" were adjusted to "1,225" and "11,500", respectively; in subsec. (d)(6), dollar amount "2,175" was adjusted to "2,300"; in subsec. (d)(8), dollar amount "11,525" was adjusted to "12,250"; in subsec. (d)(11)(D), dollar amount "21,625" was adjusted to "22,975"; in subsec. (f)(3), dollar amount "5,850" was adjusted to "6,225"; in subsec. (f)(4), dollar amount "600" was adjusted to "650" each time it appeared; in subsec. (n), dollar amount "1,171,650" was adjusted to "1,245,475"; in subsec. (p), dollar amount "146,450" was adjusted to "155,675"; and, in subsec. (q), dollar amount "146,450" was adjusted to "155,675".

By notice dated Feb. 19, 2010, 75 F.R. 8747, effective Apr. 1, 2010, in subsec. (d)(1), dollar amount "20,200" was adjusted to "21,625"; in subsec. (d)(2), dollar amount "3,225" was adjusted to "3,450"; in subsec. (d)(3), dollar amounts "525" and "10,775" were adjusted to "550" and "11,525", respectively; in subsec. (d)(4), dollar amount "1,350" was adjusted to "1,450"; in subsec. (d)(5), dollar amounts "1,075" and "10,125" were adjusted to "1,150" and "10,825", respectively; in subsec. (d)(6), dollar amount "2,025" was adjusted to "2,175"; in subsec. (d)(8), dollar amount "10,775" was adjusted to "11,525"; in subsec. (d)(11)(D), dollar amount "20,200" was adjusted to "21,625"; in subsec. (f)(3)(B), dollar amount "5,475" was adjusted to "5,850"; in subsec. (f)(4)(B), dollar amount "550" was adjusted to "600" each time it appeared; in subsec. (n), dollar amount "1,095,000" was adjusted to "1,171,650"; in subsec. (p)(1), dollar amount "136,875" was adjusted to "146,450"; and, in subsec. (q)(1), dollar amount "136,875" was adjusted to "146,450".

By notice dated Feb. 7, 2007, 72 F.R. 7082, effective Apr. 1, 2007, in subsec. (d)(1), dollar amount "18,450" was adjusted to "20,200"; in subsec. (d)(2), dollar amount "2,950" was adjusted to "3,225"; in subsec. (d)(3), dollar amounts "475" and "9,850" were adjusted to "525" and "10,775", respectively; in subsec. (d)(4), dollar amount "1,225" was adjusted to "1,350"; in subsec. (d)(5), dollar amounts "975" and "9,250" were adjusted to "1,075" and "10,125", respectively; in subsec. (d)(6), dollar amount "1,850" was adjusted to "2,025"; in subsec. (d)(8), dollar amount "9,850" was adjusted to "10,775"; in subsec. (d)(11)(D), dollar amount "18,450" was adjusted to "20,200"; in subsec. (f)(3), dollar amount "5,000" was adjusted to "5,475"; in subsec. (f)(4), dollar amount "500" was adjusted to "550" each time it appeared; in subsec. (n), dollar amount "1,000,000" was adjusted to "1,095,000"; in subsec. (p), dollar amount "125,000" was adjusted to "136,875"; and, in subsec. (q), dollar amount "125,000" was adjusted to "136,875".

By notice dated Feb. 18, 2004, 69 F.R. 8482, effective Apr. 1, 2004, in subsec. (d)(1), dollar amount "17,425" was adjusted to "18,450"; in subsec. (d)(2), dollar amount "2,775" was adjusted to "2,950"; in subsec. (d)(3), dollar amounts "450" and "9,300" were adjusted to "475" and "9,850", respectively; in subsec. (d)(4), dollar amount "1,150" was adjusted to "1,225"; in subsec. (d)(5), dollar amounts "925" and "8,725" were adjusted to "975" and "9,250", respectively; in subsec. (d)(6), dollar amount "1,750" was adjusted to "1,850"; in subsec. (d)(8), dollar amount "9,300" was adjusted to "9,850"; and, in subsec. (d)(11)(D), dollar amount "17,425" was adjusted to "18,450".

By notice dated Feb. 13, 2001, 66 F.R. 10910, effective Apr. 1, 2001, in subsec. (d)(1), dollar amount "16,150" was adjusted to "17,425"; in subsec. (d)(2), dollar amount "2,575" was adjusted to "2,775"; in subsec. (d)(3), dollar amounts "425" and "8,625" were adjusted to "450" and "9,300", respectively; in subsec. (d)(4), dollar amount "1,075" was adjusted to "1,150"; in subsec. (d)(5), dollar amounts "850" and "8,075" were adjusted to "925" and "8,725", respectively; in subsec. (d)(6), dollar amount "1,625" was adjusted to "1,750"; in subsec. (d)(8), dollar amount "8,625" was adjusted to "9,300"; and, in subsec. (d)(11)(D), dollar amount "16,150" was adjusted to "17,425".

By notice dated Feb. 3, 1998, 63 F.R. 7179, effective Apr. 1, 1998, in subsec. (d)(1), dollar amount "15,000" was adjusted to "16,150"; in subsec. (d)(2), dollar amount "2,400" was adjusted to "2,575"; in subsec. (d)(3), dollar amounts "400" and "8,000" were adjusted to "425" and "8,625", respectively; in subsec. (d)(4), dollar amount "1,000" was adjusted to "1,075"; in subsec. (d)(5), dollar amounts "800" and "7,500" were adjusted to "850" and "8,075", respectively; in subsec. (d)(6), dollar amount "1,500" was adjusted to "1,625"; in subsec. (d)(8), dollar amount "8,000" was adjusted to "8,625"; and, in subsec. (d)(11)(D), dollar amount "15,000" was adjusted to "16,150".

[1] See Adjustment of Dollar Amounts notes below.
[1] Replaced by 22 U.S.C. 4060(c).
[2] Replaced by 46 U.S.C. 11108, 11109.
[3] Replaced by 5 U.S.C. 8346.
[4] Replaced by 45 U.S.C. 231m.
[5] Railroad unemployment benefits are covered by 45 U.S.C. 352(e).
[6] Veterans benefits generally are covered by 38 U.S.C. 3101 [now 5301].
[7] Replaced by 22 U.S.C. 4060(c).
[8] Replaced by 46 U.S.C. 11108, 11109.
[9] Replaced by 5 U.S.C. 8346.
[10] Replaced by 45 U.S.C. 231m.
[11] Railroad unemployment benefits are covered by 45 U.S.C. 352(e).
[12] Veterans benefits generally are covered by 38 U.S.C. 3101 [now 5301].

§523. Exceptions to discharge

(a) A discharge under section 727, 1141, 1228(a), 1228(b), or 1328(b) of this title does not discharge an individual debtor from any debt—

(1) for a tax or a customs duty—

(A) of the kind and for the periods specified in section 507(a)(3) or 507(a)(8) of this title, whether or not a claim for such tax was filed or allowed;

(B) with respect to which a return, or equivalent report or notice, if required—

(i) was not filed or given; or

(ii) was filed or given after the date on which such return, report, or notice was last due, under applicable law or under any extension, and after two years before the date of the filing of the petition; or

(C) with respect to which the debtor made a fraudulent return or willfully attempted in any manner to evade or defeat such tax;

(2) for money, property, services, or an extension, renewal, or refinancing of credit, to the extent obtained by—

(A) false pretenses, a false representation, or actual fraud, other than a statement respecting the debtor's or an insider's financial condition;

(B) use of a statement in writing—

(i) that is materially false;

(ii) respecting the debtor's or an insider's financial condition;

(iii) on which the creditor to whom the debtor is liable for such money, property, services, or credit reasonably relied; and

(iv) that the debtor caused to be made or published with intent to deceive; or

(C)(i) for purposes of subparagraph (A)—

(I) consumer debts owed to a single creditor and aggregating more than $500 [1] for luxury goods or services incurred by an individual debtor on or within 90 days before the order for relief under this title are presumed to be nondischargeable; and

(II) cash advances aggregating more than $750 [1] that are extensions of consumer credit under an open end credit plan obtained by an individual debtor on or within 70 days before the order for relief under this title, are presumed to be nondischargeable; and

(ii) for purposes of this subparagraph—

(I) the terms "consumer", "credit", and "open end credit plan" have the same meanings as in section 103 of the Truth in Lending Act; and

(II) the term "luxury goods or services" does not include goods or services reasonably necessary for the support or maintenance of the debtor or a dependent of the debtor;

(3) neither listed nor scheduled under section 521(a)(1) of this title, with the name, if known to the debtor, of the creditor to whom such debt is owed, in time to permit—

(A) if such debt is not of a kind specified in paragraph (2), (4), or (6) of this subsection, timely filing of a proof of claim, unless such creditor had notice or actual knowledge of the case in time for such timely filing; or

(B) if such debt is of a kind specified in paragraph (2), (4), or (6) of this subsection, timely filing of a proof of claim and timely request for a determination of dischargeability of such debt under one of such paragraphs, unless such creditor had notice or actual knowledge of the case in time for such timely filing and request;

(4) for fraud or defalcation while acting in a fiduciary capacity, embezzlement, or larceny;

(5) for a domestic support obligation;

(6) for willful and malicious injury by the debtor to another entity or to the property of another entity;

(7) to the extent such debt is for a fine, penalty, or forfeiture payable to and for the benefit of a governmental unit, and is not compensation for actual pecuniary loss, other than a tax penalty—

(A) relating to a tax of a kind not specified in paragraph (1) of this subsection; or

(B) imposed with respect to a transaction or event that occurred before three years before the date of the filing of the petition;

(8) unless excepting such debt from discharge under this paragraph would impose an undue hardship on the debtor and the debtor's dependents, for—

(A)(i) an educational benefit overpayment or loan made, insured, or guaranteed by a governmental unit, or made under any program funded in whole or in part by a governmental unit or nonprofit institution; or

(ii) an obligation to repay funds received as an educational benefit, scholarship, or stipend; or

(B) any other educational loan that is a qualified education loan, as defined in section 221(d)(1) of the Internal Revenue Code of 1986, incurred by a debtor who is an individual;

(9) for death or personal injury caused by the debtor's operation of a motor vehicle, vessel, or aircraft if such operation was unlawful because the debtor was intoxicated from using alcohol, a drug, or another substance;

(10) that was or could have been listed or scheduled by the debtor in a prior case concerning the debtor under this title or under the Bankruptcy Act in which the debtor waived discharge, or was denied a discharge under section 727(a)(2), (3), (4), (5), (6), or (7) of this title, or under section 14c(1), (2), (3), (4), (6), or (7) of such Act;

(11) provided in any final judgment, unreviewable order, or consent order or decree entered in any court of the United States or of any State, issued by a Federal depository institutions regulatory agency, or contained in any settlement agreement entered into by the debtor, arising from any act of fraud or defalcation while acting in a fiduciary capacity committed with respect to any depository institution or insured credit union;

(12) for malicious or reckless failure to fulfill any commitment by the debtor to a Federal depository institutions regulatory agency to maintain the capital of an insured depository institution, except that this paragraph shall not extend any such commitment which would otherwise be terminated due to any act of such agency;

(13) for any payment of an order of restitution issued under title 18, United States Code;

(14) incurred to pay a tax to the United States that would be nondischargeable pursuant to paragraph (1);

(14A) incurred to pay a tax to a governmental unit, other than the United States, that would be nondischargeable under paragraph (1);

(14B) incurred to pay fines or penalties imposed under Federal election law;

(15) to a spouse, former spouse, or child of the debtor and not of the kind described in paragraph (5) that is incurred by the debtor in the course of a divorce or separation or in connection with a separation agreement, divorce decree or other order of a court of record, or a determination made in accordance with State or territorial law by a governmental unit;

(16) for a fee or assessment that becomes due and payable after the order for relief to a membership association with respect to the debtor's interest in a unit that has condominium ownership, in a share of a cooperative corporation, or a lot in a homeowners association, for as long as the debtor or the trustee has a legal, equitable, or possessory ownership interest in such unit, such corporation, or such lot, but nothing in this paragraph shall except from discharge the debt of a debtor for a membership association fee or assessment for a period arising before entry of the order for relief in a pending or subsequent bankruptcy case;

(17) for a fee imposed on a prisoner by any court for the filing of a case, motion, complaint, or appeal, or for other costs and expenses assessed with respect to such filing, regardless of an assertion of poverty by the debtor under subsection (b) or (f)(2) of section 1915 of title 28 (or a similar non-Federal law), or the debtor's status as a prisoner, as defined in section 1915(h) of title 28 (or a similar non-Federal law);

(18) owed to a pension, profit-sharing, stock bonus, or other plan established under section 401, 403, 408, 408A, 414, 457, or 501(c) of the Internal Revenue Code of 1986, under—

(A) a loan permitted under section 408(b)(1) of the Employee Retirement Income Security Act of 1974, or subject to section 72(p) of the Internal Revenue Code of 1986; or

(B) a loan from a thrift savings plan permitted under subchapter III of chapter 84 of title 5, that satisfies the requirements of section 8433(g) of such title;

but nothing in this paragraph may be construed to provide that any loan made under a governmental plan under section 414(d), or a contract or account under section 403(b), of the Internal Revenue Code of 1986 constitutes a claim or a debt under this title; or

(19) that—

(A) is for—

(i) the violation of any of the Federal securities laws (as that term is defined in section 3(a)(47) of the Securities Exchange Act of 1934), any of the State securities laws, or any regulation or order issued under such Federal or State securities laws; or

(ii) common law fraud, deceit, or manipulation in connection with the purchase or sale of any security; and

(B) results, before, on, or after the date on which the petition was filed, from—

(i) any judgment, order, consent order, or decree entered in any Federal or State judicial or administrative proceeding;

(ii) any settlement agreement entered into by the debtor; or

(iii) any court or administrative order for any damages, fine, penalty, citation, restitutionary payment, disgorgement payment, attorney fee, cost, or other payment owed by the debtor.

For purposes of this subsection, the term "return" means a return that satisfies the requirements of applicable nonbankruptcy law (including applicable filing requirements). Such term includes a return prepared pursuant to section 6020(a) of the Internal Revenue Code of 1986, or similar State or local law, or a written stipulation to a judgment or a final order entered by a nonbankruptcy tribunal, but does not include a return made pursuant to section 6020(b) of the Internal Revenue Code of 1986, or a similar State or local law.

(b) Notwithstanding subsection (a) of this section, a debt that was excepted from discharge under subsection (a)(1), (a)(3), or (a)(8) of this section, under section 17a(1), 17a(3), or 17a(5) of the Bankruptcy Act, under section 439A [2] of the Higher Education Act of 1965, or under section 733(g) [2] of the Public Health Service Act in a prior case concerning the debtor under this title, or under the Bankruptcy Act, is dischargeable in a case under this title unless, by the terms of subsection (a) of this section, such debt is not dischargeable in the case under this title.

(c)(1) Except as provided in subsection (a)(3)(B) of this section, the debtor shall be discharged from a debt of a kind specified in paragraph (2), (4), or (6) of subsection (a) of this section, unless, on request of the creditor to whom such debt is owed, and after notice and a hearing, the court determines such debt to be excepted from discharge under paragraph (2), (4), or (6), as the case may be, of subsection (a) of this section.

(2) Paragraph (1) shall not apply in the case of a Federal depository institutions regulatory agency seeking, in its capacity as conservator, receiver, or liquidating agent for an insured depository institution, to recover a debt described in subsection (a)(2), (a)(4), (a)(6), or (a)(11) owed to such institution by an institution-affiliated party unless the receiver, conservator, or liquidating agent was appointed in time to reasonably comply, or for a Federal depository institutions regulatory agency acting in its corporate capacity as a successor to such receiver, conservator, or liquidating agent to reasonably comply, with subsection (a)(3)(B) as a creditor of such institution-affiliated party with respect to such debt.

(d) If a creditor requests a determination of dischargeability of a consumer debt under subsection (a)(2) of this section, and such debt is discharged, the court shall grant judgment in favor of the debtor for the costs of, and a reasonable attorney's fee for, the proceeding if the court finds that the position of the creditor was not substantially justified, except that the court shall not award such costs and fees if special circumstances would make the award unjust.

(e) Any institution-affiliated party of an insured depository institution shall be considered to be acting in a fiduciary capacity with respect to the purposes of subsection (a)(4) or (11).

(Pub. L. 95–598, Nov. 6, 1978, 92 Stat. 2590; Pub. L. 96–56, §3, Aug. 14, 1979, 93 Stat. 387; Pub. L. 97–35, title XXIII, §2334(b), Aug. 13, 1981, 95 Stat. 863; Pub. L. 98–353, title III, §§307, 371, 454, July 10, 1984, 98 Stat. 353, 364, 375; Pub. L. 99–554, title II, §§257(n), 281, 283(j), Oct. 27, 1986, 100 Stat. 3115–3117; Pub. L. 101–581, §2(a), Nov. 15, 1990, 104 Stat. 2865; Pub. L. 101–647, title XXV, §2522(a), title XXXI, §3102(a), title XXXVI, §3621, Nov. 29, 1990, 104 Stat. 4865, 4916, 4964; Pub. L. 103–322, title XXXII, §320934, Sept. 13, 1994, 108 Stat. 2135; Pub. L. 103–394, title II, §221, title III, §§304(e), (h)(3), 306, 309, title V, §501(d)(13), Oct. 22, 1994, 108 Stat. 4129, 4133-4135, 4137, 4145; Pub. L. 104–134, title I, §101[(a)] [title VIII, §804(b)], Apr. 26, 1996, 110 Stat. 1321, 1321-74; renumbered title I, Pub. L. 104–140, §1(a), May 2, 1996, 110 Stat. 1327; Pub. L. 104–193, title III, §374(a), Aug. 22, 1996, 110 Stat. 2255; Pub. L. 105–244, title IX, §971(a), Oct. 7, 1998, 112 Stat. 1837; Pub. L. 107–204, title VIII, §803, July 30, 2002, 116 Stat. 801; Pub. L. 109–8, title II, §§215, 220, 224(c), title III, §§301, 310, 314(a), title IV, §412, title VII, §714, title XII, §§1209, 1235, title XIV, §1404(a), title XV, §1502(a)(2), Apr. 20, 2005, 119 Stat. 54, 59, 64, 75, 84, 88, 107, 128, 194, 204, 215, 216; Pub. L. 111–327, §2(a)(18), Dec. 22, 2010, 124 Stat. 3559.)

Historical and Revision Notes

legislative statements

Section 523(a)(1) represents a compromise between the position taken in the House bill and the Senate amendment. Section 523(a)(2) likewise represents a compromise between the position taken in the House bill and the Senate amendment with respect to the false financial statement exception to discharge. In order to clarify that a "renewal of credit" includes a "refinancing of credit", explicit reference to a refinancing of credit is made in the preamble to section 523(a)(2). A renewal of credit or refinancing of credit that was obtained by a false financial statement within the terms of section 523(a)(2) is nondischargeable. However, each of the provisions of section 523(a)(2) must be proved. Thus, under section 523(a)(2)(A) a creditor must prove that the debt was obtained by false pretenses, a false representation, or actual fraud, other than a statement respecting the debtor's or an insider's financial condition. Subparagraph (A) is intended to codify current case law e.g., *Neal v. Clark*, 95 U.S. 704 (1887) [24 L. Ed. 586], which interprets "fraud" to mean actual or positive fraud rather than fraud implied in law. Subparagraph (A) is mutually exclusive from subparagraph (B). Subparagraph (B) pertains to the so-called false financial statement. In order for the debt to be nondischargeable, the creditor must prove that the debt was obtained by the use of a statement in writing (i) that is materially false; (ii) respecting the debtor's or an insider's financial condition; (iii) on which the creditor to whom the debtor is liable for obtaining money, property, services, or credit reasonably relied; (iv) that the debtor caused to be made or published with intent to deceive. Section 523(a)(2)(B)(iv) is not intended to change from present law since the statement that the debtor causes to be made or published with the intent to deceive automatically includes a statement that the debtor actually makes or publishes with an intent to deceive. Section 523(a)(2)(B) is explained in the House report. Under section 523(a)(2)(B)(i) a discharge is barred only as to that portion of a loan with respect to which a false financial statement is materially false.

In many cases, a creditor is required by state law to refinance existing credit on which there has been no default. If the creditor does not forfeit remedies or otherwise rely to his detriment on a false financial statement with respect to existing credit, then an extension, renewal, or refinancing of such credit is nondischargeable only to the extent of the new money advanced; on the other hand, if an existing loan is in default or the creditor otherwise reasonably relies to his detriment on a false financial statement with regard to an existing loan, then the entire debt is nondischargeable under section 523(a)(2)(B). This codifies the reasoning expressed by the second circuit in *In re Danns*, 558 F.2d 114 (2d Cir. 1977).

Section 523(a)(3) of the House amendment is derived from the Senate amendment. The provision is intended to overrule *Birkett v. Columbia Bank*, 195 U.S. 345 (1904) [25 S.Ct. 38, 49 L.Ed. 231, 12 Am.Bankr.Rep. 691].

Section 523(a)(4) of the House amendment represents a compromise between the House bill and the Senate amendment.

Section 523(a)(5) is a compromise between the House bill and the Senate amendment. The provision excepts from discharge a debt owed to a spouse, former spouse or child of the debtor, in connection with a separation agreement, divorce decree, or property settlement agreement, for alimony to, maintenance for, or support of such spouse or child but not to the extent that the debt is assigned to another entity. If the debtor has assumed an obligation of the debtor's spouse to a third party in connection with a separation agreement, property settlement agreement, or divorce proceeding, such debt is dischargeable to the extent that payment of the debt by the debtor is not actually in the nature of alimony, maintenance, or support of debtor's spouse, former spouse, or child.

Section 523(a)(6) adopts the position taken in the House bill and rejects the alternative suggested in the Senate amendment. The phrase "willful and malicious injury" covers a willful and malicious conversion.

Section 523(a)(7) of the House amendment adopts the position taken in the Senate amendment and rejects the position taken in the House bill. A penalty relating to a tax cannot be nondischargeable unless the tax itself is nondischargeable.

Section 523(a)(8) represents a compromise between the House bill and the Senate amendment regarding educational loans. This provision is broader than current law which is limited to federally insured loans. Only educational loans owing to a governmental unit or a nonprofit institution of higher education are made nondischargeable under this paragraph.

Section 523(b) is new. The section represents a modification of similar provisions contained in the House bill and the Senate amendment.

Section 523(c) of the House amendment adopts the position taken in the Senate amendment.

Section 523(d) represents a compromise between the position taken in the House bill and the Senate amendment on the issue of attorneys' fees in false financial statement complaints to determine dischargeability. The provision contained in the House bill permitting the court to award damages is eliminated. The court must grant the debtor judgment or a reasonable attorneys' fee unless the granting of judgment would be clearly inequitable.

Nondischargeable debts: The House amendment retains the basic categories of nondischargeable tax liabilities contained in both bills, but restricts the time limits on certain nondischargeable taxes. Under the amendment, nondischargeable taxes cover taxes entitled to priority under section 507(a)(6) of title 11 and, in the case of individual debtors under chapters 7, 11, or 13, tax liabilities with respect to which no required return had been filed or as to which a late return had been filed if the return became last due, including extensions, within 2 years before the date of the petition or became due after the petition or as to which the debtor made a fraudulent return, entry or invoice or fraudulently attempted to evade or defeat the tax.

In the case of individuals in liquidation under chapter 7 or in reorganization under chapter 11 of title 11, section 1141(d)(2) incorporates by reference the exceptions to discharge continued in section 523. Different rules concerning the discharge of taxes where a partnership or corporation reorganizes under chapter 11, apply under section 1141.

The House amendment also deletes the reduction rule contained in section 523(e) of the Senate amendment. Under that rule, the amount of an otherwise nondischargeable tax liability would be reduced by the amount which a governmental tax authority could have collected from the debtor's estate if it had filed a timely claim against the estate but which it did not collect because no such claim was filed. This provision is deleted in order not to effectively compel a tax authority to file claim against the estate in "no asset" cases, along with a dischargeability petition. In no-asset cases, therefore, if the tax authority is not potentially penalized by failing to file a claim, the debtor in such cases will have a better opportunity to choose the prepayment forum, bankruptcy court or the Tax Court, in which to litigate his personal liability for a nondischargeable tax.

The House amendment also adopts the Senate amendment provision limiting the nondischargeability of punitive tax penalties, that is, penalties other than those which represent collection of a principal amount of tax liability through the form of a "penalty." Under the House amendment, tax penalties which are basically punitive in nature are to be nondischargeable only if the penalty is computed by reference to a related tax liability which is nondischargeable or, if the amount of the penalty is not computed by reference to a tax liability, the transaction or event giving rise to the penalty occurred during the 3-year period ending on the date of the petition.

senate report no. 95–989

This section specifies which of the debtor's debts are not discharged in a bankruptcy case, and certain procedures for effectuating the section. The provision in Bankruptcy Act §17c [section 35(c) of former title 11] granting the bankruptcy courts jurisdiction to determine dischargeability is deleted as unnecessary, in view of the comprehensive grant of jurisdiction prescribed in proposed 28 U.S.C. 1334(b), which is adequate to cover the full jurisdiction that the bankruptcy courts have today over dischargeability and related issues under Bankruptcy Act §17c. The Rules of Bankruptcy Procedure will specify, as they do today, who may request determinations of dischargeability, subject, of course, to proposed 11 U.S.C. 523(c), and when such a request may be made. Proposed 11 U.S.C. 350, providing for reopening of cases, provides one possible procedure for a determination of dischargeability and related issues after a case is closed.

Subsection (a) lists nine kinds of debts excepted from discharge. Taxes that are excepted from discharge are set forth in paragraph (1). These include claims against the debtor which receive priority in the second, third and sixth categories (§507(a)(3)(B) and (c) and (6)). These categories include taxes for which the tax authority failed to file a claim against the estate or filed its claim late. Whether or not the taxing authority's claim is secured will also not affect the claim's nondischargeability if the tax liability in question is otherwise entitled to priority.

Also included in the nondischargeable debts are taxes for which the debtor had not filed a required return as of the petition date, or for which a return had been filed beyond its last permitted due date (§523(a)(1)(B)). For this purpose, the date of the tax year to which the return relates is immaterial. The late return rule applies, however, only to the late returns filed within three years before the petition was filed, and to late returns filed after the petition in title 11 was filed. For this purpose, the taxable year in question need not be one or more of the three years immediately preceding the filing of the petition.

Tax claims with respect to which the debtor filed a fraudulent return, entry or invoice, or fraudulently attempted to evade or defeat any tax (§523(a)(1)(C)) are included. The date of the taxable year with regard to which the fraud occurred is immaterial.

Also included are tax payments due under an agreement for deferred payment of taxes, which a debtor had entered into with the Internal Revenue Service (or State or local tax authority) before the filing of the petition and which relate to a prepetition tax liability (§523(a)(1)(D)) are also nondischargeable. This classification applies only to tax claims which would have received priority under section 507(a) if the taxpayer had filed a title 11 petition on the date on which the deferred payment agreement was entered into. This rule also applies only to installment payments which become due during and after the commencement of the title 11 case. Payments which had become due within one year before the filing of the petition receive sixth priority, and will be nondischargeable under the general rule of section 523(a)(1)(A).

The above categories of nondischargeability apply to customs duties as well as to taxes.

Paragraph (2) provides that as under Bankruptcy Act §17a(2) [section 35(a)(2) of former title 11], a debt for obtaining money, property, services, or a refinancing extension or renewal of credit by false pretenses, a false representation, or actual fraud, or by use of a statement in writing respecting the debtor's financial condition that is materially false, on which the creditor reasonably relied, and which the debtor made or published with intent to deceive, is excepted from discharge. This provision is modified only slightly from current section 17a(2). First, "actual fraud" is added as a ground for exception from discharge. Second, the creditor must not only have relied on a false statement in writing, but the reliance must have been reasonable. This codifies case law construing present section 17a(2). Third, the phrase "in any manner whatsoever" that appears in current law after "made or published" is deleted as unnecessary, the word "published" is used in the same sense that it is used in defamation cases.

Unscheduled debts are excepted from discharge under paragraph (3). The provision, derived from section 17a(3) [section 35(a)(3) of former title 11], follows current law, but clarifies some uncertainties generated by the case law construing 17a(3). The debt is excepted from discharge if it was not scheduled in time to permit timely action by the creditor to protect his rights, unless the creditor had notice or actual knowledge of the case.

Paragraph (4) excepts debts for fraud incurred by the debtor while acting in a fiduciary capacity or for defalcation, embezzlement, or misappropriation.

Paragraph (5) provides that debts for willful and malicious conversion or injury by the debtor to another entity or the property of another entity are nondischargeable. Under this paragraph "willful" means deliberate or intentional. To the extent that *Tinker v. Colwell*, 139 U.S. 473 (1902), held that a less strict standard is intended, and to the extent that other cases have relied on *Tinker* to apply a "reckless disregard" standard, they are overruled.

Paragraph (6) excepts from discharge debts to a spouse, former spouse, or child of the debtor for alimony to, maintenance for, or support of the spouse or child. This language, in combination with the repeal of section 456(b) of the Social Security Act (42 U.S.C. 656(b)) by section 326 of the bill, will apply to make nondischargeable only alimony, maintenance, or support owed directly to a spouse or dependent. What constitutes alimony, maintenance, or support, will be determined under the bankruptcy law, not State law. Thus, cases such as *In re Waller*, 494 F.2d 447 (6th Cir. 1974), are overruled, and the result in cases such as *Fife v. Fife*, 1 Utah 2d 281, 265 P.2d 642 (1952) is followed. The proviso, however, makes nondischargeable any debts resulting from an agreement by the debtor to hold the debtor's spouse harmless on joint debts, to the extent that the agreement is in payment of alimony, maintenance, or support of the spouse, as determined under bankruptcy law considerations as to whether a particular agreement to pay money to a spouse is actually alimony or a property settlement.

Paragraph (7) makes nondischargeable certain liabilities for penalties including tax penalties if the underlying tax with respect to which the penalty was imposed is also nondischargeable (sec. 523(a)(7)). These latter liabilities cover those which, but are penal in nature, as distinct from so-called "pecuniary loss" penalties which, in the case of taxes, involve basically the collection of a tax under the label of a "penalty." This provision differs from the bill as introduced, which did not link the nondischarge of a tax penalty with the treatment of the underlying tax. The amended provision reflects the existing position of the Internal Revenue Service as to tax penalties imposed by the Internal Revenue Code (Rev.Rul. 68–574, 1968–2 C.B. 595).

Paragraph (8) follows generally current law and excerpts from discharge student loans until such loans have been due and owing for five years. Such loans include direct student loans as well as insured and guaranteed loans. This provision is intended to be self-executing and the lender or institution is not required to file a complaint to determine the nondischargeability of any student loan.

Paragraph (9) excepts from discharge debts that the debtor owed before a previous bankruptcy case concerning the debtor in which the debtor was denied a discharge other than on the basis of the six-year bar.

Subsection (b) of this section permits discharge in a bankruptcy case of an unscheduled debt from a prior case. This provision is carried over from Bankruptcy Act §17b [section 35(b) of former title 11]. The result dictated by the subsection would probably not be different if the subsection were not included. It is included nevertheless for clarity.

Subsection (c) requires a creditor who is owed a debt that may be excepted from discharge under paragraph (2), (4), or (5), (false statements, defalcation or larceny misappropriation, or willful and malicious injury) to initiate proceedings in the bankruptcy court for an exception to discharge. If the creditor does not act, the debt is discharged. This provision does not change current law.

Subsection (d) is new. It provides protection to a consumer debtor that dealt honestly with a creditor who sought to have a debt excepted from discharge on the ground of falsity in the incurring of the debt. The debtor may be awarded costs and a reasonable attorney's fee for the proceeding to determine the dischargeability of a debt under subsection (a)(2), if the court finds that the proceeding was frivolous or not brought by its creditor in good faith.

The purpose of the provision is to discourage creditors from initiating proceedings to obtaining a false financial statement exception to discharge in the hope of obtaining a settlement from an honest debtor anxious to save attorney's fees. Such practices impair the debtor's fresh start and are contrary to the spirit of the bankruptcy laws.

house report no. 95–595

Subsection (a) lists eight kinds of debts excepted from discharge. Taxes that are entitled to priority are excepted from discharge under paragraph (1). In addition, taxes with respect to which the debtor made a fraudulent return or willfully attempted to evade or defeat, or with respect to which a return (if required) was not filed or was not filed after the due date and after one year before the bankruptcy case are excepted from discharge. If the taxing authority's claim has been disallowed, then it would be barred by the more modern rules of collateral estoppel from reasserting that claim against the debtor after the case was closed. See Plumb, The Tax Recommendations of the Commission on the Bankruptcy Laws: Tax Procedures, 88 Harv.L.Rev. 1360, 1388 (1975).

As under Bankruptcy Act §17a(2) [section 35(a)(2) of former title 11], debt for obtaining money, property, services, or an extension or renewal of credit by false pretenses, a false representation, or actual fraud, or by use of a statement in writing respecting the debtor's financial condition that is materially false, on which the creditor reasonably relied, and that the debtor made or published with intent to deceive, is excepted from discharge. This provision is modified only slightly from current section 17a(2). First, "actual fraud" is added as a grounds for exception from discharge. Second, the creditor must not only have relied on a false statement in writing, the reliance must have been reasonable. This codifies case law construing this provision. Third, the phrase "in any manner whatsoever" that appears in current law after "made or published" is deleted as unnecessary. The word "published" is used in the same sense that it is used in slander actions.

Unscheduled debts are excepted from discharge under paragraph (3). The provision, derived from section 17a(3) [section 35(a)(3) of former title 11], follows current law, but clarifies some uncertainties generated by the case law construing 17a(3). The debt is excepted from discharge if it was not scheduled in time to permit timely action by the creditor to protect his rights, unless the creditor had notice or actual knowledge of the case.

Paragraph (4) excepts debts for embezzlement or larceny. The deletion of willful and malicious conversion from §17a(2) of the Bankruptcy Act [section 35(a)(2) of former title 11] is not intended to effect a substantive change. The intent is to include in the category of non-dischargeable debts a conversion under which the debtor willfully and maliciously intends to borrow property for a short period of time with no intent to inflict injury but on which injury is in fact inflicted.

Paragraph (5) excepts from discharge debts to a spouse, former spouse, or child of the debtor for alimony to, maintenance for, or support of, the spouse or child. This language, in combination with the repeal of section 456(b) of the Social Security Act (42 U.S.C. 656(b)) by section 327 of the bill, will apply to make nondischargeable only alimony, maintenance, or support owed directly to a spouse or dependent. See Hearings, pt. 2, at 942. What constitutes alimony, maintenance, or support, will be determined under the bankruptcy laws, not State law. Thus, cases such as *In re Waller*, 494 F.2d 447 (6th Cir. 1974); Hearings, pt. 3, at 1308–10, are overruled, and the result in cases such as *Fife v. Fife*, 1 Utah 2d 281, 265 P.2d 642 (1952) is followed. This provision will, however, make nondischargeable any debts resulting from an agreement by the debtor to hold the debtor's spouse harmless on joint debts, to the extent that the agreement is in payment of alimony, maintenance, or support of the spouse, as determined under bankruptcy law considerations that are similar to considerations of whether a particular agreement to pay money to a spouse is actually alimony or a property settlement. See Hearings, pt. 3, at 1287–1290.

Paragraph (6) excepts debts for willful and malicious injury by the debtor to another person or to the property of another person. Under this paragraph, "willful" means deliberate or intentional. To the extent that *Tinker v. Colwell*, 193 U.S. 473 (1902) [24 S.Ct. 505, 48 L.Ed. 754, 11 Am.Bankr.Rep. 568], held that a looser standard is intended, and to the extent that other cases have relied on *Tinker* to apply a "reckless disregard" standard, they are overruled.

Paragraph (7) excepts from discharge a debt for a fine, penalty, or forfeiture payable to and for the benefit of a governmental unit, that is not compensation for actual pecuniary loss.

Paragraph (8) [enacted as (9)] excepts from discharge debts that the debtor owed before a previous bankruptcy case concerning the debtor in which the debtor was denied a discharge other than on the basis of the six-year bar.

Subsection (d) is new. It provides protection to a consumer debtor that dealt honestly with a creditor who sought to have a debt excepted from discharge on grounds of falsity in the incurring of the debt. The debtor is entitled to costs of and a reasonable attorney's fee for the proceeding to determine the dischargeability of a debt under subsection (a)(2), if the creditor initiated the proceeding and the debt was determined to be dischargeable. The court is permitted to award any actual pecuniary loss that the debtor may have suffered as a result of the proceeding (such as loss of a day's pay). The purpose of the provision is to discourage creditors from initiating false financial statement exception to discharge actions in the hopes of obtaining a settlement from an honest debtor anxious to save attorney's fees. Such practices impair the debtor's fresh start.

References in Text

The Internal Revenue Code of 1986, referred to in subsec. (a), is classified generally to Title 26, Internal Revenue Code.

Section 103 of the Truth in Lending Act, referred to in subsec. (a)(2)(C)(ii)(I), is classified to section 1602 of Title 15, Commerce and Trade.

The Bankruptcy Act, referred to in subsecs. (a)(10) and (b), is act July 1, 1898, ch. 541, 30 Stat. 544, as amended, which was classified generally to former Title 11. Sections 14c and 17a of the Bankruptcy Act were classified to sections 32(c) and 35(a) of former Title 11.

Section 408(b)(1) of the Employee Retirement Income Security Act of 1974, referred to in subsec. (a)(18)(A), is classified to section 1108(b)(1) of Title 29, Labor.

Section 3(a)(47) of the Securities Exchange Act of 1934, referred to in subsec. (a)(19)(A)(i), is classified to section 78c(a)(47) of Title 15, Commerce and Trade.

Section 439A of the Higher Education Act of 1965, referred to in subsec. (b), was classified to section 1087–3 of Title 20, Education, and was repealed by Pub. L. 95–598, title III, §317, Nov. 6, 1978, 92 Stat. 2678.

Section 733(g) of the Public Health Service Act, referred to in subsec. (b), was repealed by Pub. L. 95–598, title III, §327, Nov. 6, 1978, 92 Stat. 2679. A subsec. (g), containing similar provisions, was added to section 733 by Pub. L. 97–35, title XXVII, §2730, Aug. 13, 1981, 95 Stat. 919. Section 733 was subsequently omitted in the general revision of subchapter V of chapter 6A of Title 42, The Public Health and Welfare, by Pub. L. 102–408, title I, §102, Oct. 13, 1992, 106 Stat. 1994. See section 292f(g) of Title 42.

Amendments

2010—Subsec. (a)(2)(C)(ii)(II). Pub. L. 111–327, §2(a)(18)(A), substituted semicolon for period at end.

Subsec. (a)(3). Pub. L. 111–327, §2(a)(18)(B), substituted "521(a)(1)" for "521(1)" in introductory provisions.

2005—Pub. L. 109–8, §1209(1), transferred par. (15) and inserted it after subsec. (a)(14A). See 1994 Amendments note below.

Pub. L. 109–8, §215(3), in par. (15), inserted "to a spouse, former spouse, or child of the debtor and" before "not of the kind" and "or" after "court of record," and substituted a semicolon for "unless—

"(A) the debtor does not have the ability to pay such debt from income or property of the debtor not reasonably necessary to be expended for the maintenance or support of the debtor or a dependent of the debtor and, if the debtor is engaged in a business, for the payment of expenditures necessary for the continuation, preservation, and operation of such business; or

"(B) discharging such debt would result in a benefit to the debtor that outweighs the detrimental consequences to a spouse, former spouse, or child of the debtor;".

Subsec. (a). Pub. L. 109–8, §714(2), inserted at end "For purposes of this subsection, the term 'return' means a return that satisfies the requirements of applicable nonbankruptcy law (including applicable filing requirements). Such term includes a return prepared pursuant to section 6020(a) of the Internal Revenue Code of 1986, or similar State or local law, or a written stipulation to a judgment or a final order entered by a nonbankruptcy tribunal, but does not include a return made pursuant to section 6020(b) of the Internal Revenue Code of 1986, or a similar State or local law."

Subsec. (a)(1)(A). Pub. L. 109–8, §1502(a)(2), substituted "507(a)(3)" for "507(a)(2)".

Subsec. (a)(1)(B). Pub. L. 109–8, §714(1)(A), inserted "or equivalent report or notice," after "a return," in introductory provisions.

Subsec. (a)(1)(B)(i). Pub. L. 109–8, §714(1)(B), inserted "or given" after "filed".

Subsec. (a)(1)(B)(ii). Pub. L. 109–8, §714(1)(C), inserted "or given" after "filed" and ", report, or notice" after "return".

Subsec. (a)(2)(C). Pub. L. 109–8, §310, amended subpar. (C) generally. Prior to amendment, subpar. (C) read as follows: "for purposes of subparagraph (A) of this paragraph, consumer debts owed to a single creditor and aggregating more than $1,000 for 'luxury goods or services' incurred by an individual debtor on or within 60 days before the order for relief under this title, or cash advances aggregating more than $1,000 that are extensions of consumer credit under an open end credit plan obtained by an individual debtor on or within 60 days before the order for relief under this title, are presumed to be nondischargeable; 'luxury goods or services' do not include goods or services reasonably acquired for the support or maintenance of the debtor or a dependent of the debtor; an extension of consumer credit under an open end credit plan is to be defined for purposes of this subparagraph as it is defined in the Consumer Credit Protection Act;".

Subsec. (a)(5). Pub. L. 109–8, §215(1)(A), added par. (5) and struck out former par. (5) which read as follows: "to a spouse, former spouse, or child of the debtor, for alimony to, maintenance for, or support of such spouse or child, in connection with a separation agreement, divorce decree or other order of a court of record, determination made in accordance with State or territorial law by a governmental unit, or property settlement agreement, but not to the extent that—

"(A) such debt is assigned to another entity, voluntarily, by operation of law, or otherwise (other than debts assigned pursuant to section 408(a)(3) of the Social Security Act, or any such debt which has been assigned to the Federal Government or to a State or any political subdivision of such State); or

"(B) such debt includes a liability designated as alimony, maintenance, or support, unless such liability is actually in the nature of alimony, maintenance, or support;"

Subsec. (a)(8). Pub. L. 109–8, §220, added par. (8) and struck out former par. (8) which read as follows: "for an educational benefit overpayment or loan made, insured or guaranteed by a governmental unit, or made under any program funded in whole or in part by a governmental unit or nonprofit institution, or for an obligation to repay funds received as an educational benefit, scholarship or stipend, unless excepting such debt from discharge under this paragraph will impose an undue hardship on the debtor and the debtor's dependents;".

Subsec. (a)(9). Pub. L. 109–8, §1209(2), substituted "motor vehicle, vessel, or aircraft" for "motor vehicle".

Subsec. (a)(14A). Pub. L. 109–8, §314(a), added par. (14A).

Subsec. (a)(14B). Pub. L. 109–8, §1235, added par. (14B).

Subsec. (a)(16). Pub. L. 109–8, §412, struck out "dwelling" after "debtor's interest in a" and "housing" after "share of a cooperative" and substituted "ownership," for "ownership or" and "or a lot in a homeowners association, for as long as the debtor or the trustee has a legal, equitable, or possessory ownership interest in such unit, such corporation, or such lot," for "but only if such fee or assessment is payable for a period during which—

"(A) the debtor physically occupied a dwelling unit in the condominium or cooperative project; or

"(B) the debtor rented the dwelling unit to a tenant and received payments from the tenant for such period,".

Subsec. (a)(17). Pub. L. 109–8, §301, substituted "on a prisoner by any court" for "by a court" and "subsection (b) or (f)(2) of section 1915" for "section 1915(b) or (f)" and inserted "(or a similar non-Federal law)" after "title 28" in two places.

Subsec. (a)(18). Pub. L. 109–8, §224(c), added par. (18).

Pub. L. 109–8, §215(1)(B), struck out par. (18) which read as follows: "owed under State law to a State or municipality that is—

"(A) in the nature of support, and

"(B) enforceable under part D of title IV of the Social Security Act (42 U.S.C. 601 et seq.); or".

Subsec. (a)(19)(B). Pub. L. 109–8, §1404(a), inserted ", before, on, or after the date on which the petition was filed," after "results" in introductory provisions.

Subsec. (c)(1). Pub. L. 109–8, §215(2), substituted "or (6)" for "(6), or (15)" in two places.

Subsec. (e). Pub. L. 109–8, §1209(3), substituted "an insured" for "a insured".

2002—Subsec. (a)(19). Pub. L. 107–204 added par. (19).

1998—Subsec. (a)(8). Pub. L. 105–244 substituted "stipend, unless" for "stipend, unless—" and struck out "(B)" before "excepting such debt" and subpar. (A) which read as follows: "such loan, benefit, scholarship, or stipend overpayment first became due more than 7 years (exclusive of any applicable suspension of the repayment period) before the date of the filing of the petition; or".

1996—Subsec. (a)(5)(A). Pub. L. 104–193, §374(a)(4), substituted "section 408(a)(3)" for "section 402(a)(26)".

Subsec. (a)(17). Pub. L. 104–134 added par. (17).

Subsec. (a)(18). Pub. L. 104–193, §374(a)(1)–(3), added par. (18).

1994—Par. (15). Pub. L. 103–394, §304(e)[(1)], amended this section by adding par. (15) at the end. See 2005 Amendment note above.

Subsec. (a). Pub. L. 103–394, §501(d)(13)(A)(i), substituted "1141," for "1141,," in introductory provisions.

Subsec. (a)(1)(A). Pub. L. 103–394, §304(h)(3), substituted "507(a)(8)" for "507(a)(7)".

Subsec. (a)(2)(C). Pub. L. 103–394, §§306, 501(d)(13)(A)(ii), substituted "$1,000 for" for "$500 for", "60" for "forty" after "incurred by an individual debtor on or within", and "60" for "twenty" after "obtained by an individual debtor on or within", and struck out "(15 U.S.C. 1601 et seq.)" after "Protection Act".

Subsec. (a)(11). Pub. L. 103–322, §320934(1), struck out "or" after semicolon at end.

Subsec. (a)(12). Pub. L. 103–322, §320934(2), which directed the substitution of "; or" for a period at end of par. (12), could not be executed because a period did not appear at end.

Subsec. (a)(13). Pub. L. 103–394, §221(1), substituted semicolon for period at end.

Pub. L. 103–322, §320934(3), added par. (13).

Subsec. (a)(14). Pub. L. 103–394, §221(2), added par. (14).

Subsec. (a)(16). Pub. L. 103–394, §309, added par. (16).

Subsec. (b). Pub. L. 103–394, §501(d)(13)(B), struck out "(20 U.S.C. 1087–3)" after "Act of 1965" and "(42 U.S.C. 294f)" after "Service Act".

Subsec. (c)(1). Pub. L. 103–394, §304(e)(2), substituted "(6), or (15)" for "or (6)" in two places.

Subsec. (e). Pub. L. 103–394, §501(d)(13)(C), substituted "insured depository institution" for "depository institution or insured credit union".

1990—Subsec. (a)(8). Pub. L. 101–647, §3621, substituted "for an educational benefit overpayment or loan made, insured or guaranteed by a governmental unit, or made under any program funded in whole or in part by a governmental unit or nonprofit institution, or for an obligation to repay funds received as an educational benefit, scholarship or stipend, unless" for "for an educational loan made, insured, or guaranteed by a governmental unit, or made under any program funded in whole or in part by a governmental unit or a nonprofit institution, unless" in introductory provisions and amended subpar. (A) generally. Prior to amendment, subpar. (A) read as follows: "such loan first became due before five years (exclusive of any applicable suspension of the repayment period) before the date of the filing of the petition; or".

Subsec. (a)(9). Pub. L. 101–581 and Pub. L. 101–647, §3102(a), identically amended par. (9) generally. Prior to amendment, par. (9) read as follows: "to any entity, to the extent that such debt arises from a judgment or consent decree entered in a court of record against the debtor wherein liability was incurred by such debtor as a result of the debtor's operation of a motor vehicle while legally intoxicated under the laws or regulations of any jurisdiction within the United States or its territories wherein such motor vehicle was operated and within which such liability was incurred; or".

Subsec. (a)(11), (12). Pub. L. 101–647, §2522(a)(1), added pars. (11) and (12).

Subsec. (c). Pub. L. 101–647, §2522(a)(3), designated existing provisions as par. (1) and added par. (2).

Subsec. (e). Pub. L. 101–647, §2522(a)(2), added subsec. (e).

1986—Subsec. (a). Pub. L. 99–554, §257(n), inserted reference to sections 1228(a) and 1228(b) of this title.

Subsec. (a)(1)(A). Pub. L. 99–554, §283(j)(1)(A), substituted "507(a)(7)" for "507(a)(6)".

Subsec. (a)(5). Pub. L. 99–554, §281, struck out the comma after "decree" and inserted ", determination made in accordance with State or territorial law by a governmental unit," after "record".

Subsec. (a)(9), (10). Pub. L. 99–554, §283(j)(1)(B), redesignated par. (9) relating to debts incurred by persons driving while intoxicated, added by Pub. L. 98–353, as (10).

Subsec. (b). Pub. L. 99–554, §283(j)(2), substituted "Service" for "Services".

1984—Subsec. (a)(2). Pub. L. 98–353, §454(a)(1), in provisions preceding subpar. (A), struck out "obtaining" after "for", and substituted "refinancing of credit, to the extent obtained" for "refinance of credit,".

Subsec. (a)(2)(A). Pub. L. 98–353, §307(a)(1), struck out "or" at end.

Subsec. (a)(2)(B). Pub. L. 98–353, §307(a)(2), inserted "or" at end.

Subsec. (a)(2)(B)(iii). Pub. L. 98–353, §454(a)(1)(A), struck out "obtaining" before "such".

Subsec. (a)(2)(C). Pub. L. 98–353, §307(a)(3), added subpar. (C).

Subsec. (a)(5). Pub. L. 98–353, §454(b)(1), inserted "or other order of a court of record" after "divorce decree," in provisions preceding subpar. (A).

Subsec. (a)(5)(A). Pub. L. 98–353, §454(b)(2), inserted ", or any such debt which has been assigned to the Federal Government or to a State or any political subdivision of such State".

Subsec. (a)(8). Pub. L. 98–353, §§371(1), 454(a)(2), struck out "of higher education" after "a nonprofit institution of" and struck out "or" at end.

Subsec. (a)(9). Pub. L. 98–353, §371(2), added the par. (9) relating to debts incurred by persons driving while intoxicated.

Subsec. (c). Pub. L. 98–353, §454(c), inserted "of a kind" after "debt".

Subsec. (d). Pub. L. 98–353, §307(b), substituted "the court shall grant judgment in favor of the debtor for the costs of, and a reasonable attorney's fee for, the proceeding if the court finds that the position of the creditor was not substantially justified, except that the court shall not award such costs and fees if special circumstances would make the award unjust" for "the court shall grant judgment against such creditor and in favor of the debtor for the costs of, and a reasonable attorney's fee for, the proceeding to determine dischargeability, unless such granting of judgment would be clearly inequitable".

1981—Subsec. (a)(5)(A). Pub. L. 97–35 substituted "law, or otherwise (other than debts assigned pursuant to section 402(a)(26) of the Social Security Act);" for "law, or otherwise;".

1979—Subsec. (a)(8). Pub. L. 96–56 substituted "for an educational loan made, insured, or guaranteed by a governmental unit, or made under any program funded in whole or in part by a governmental unit or a nonprofit institution of higher education" for "to a governmental unit, or a nonprofit institution of higher education, for an educational loan" in the provisions preceding subpar. (A) and inserted "(exclusive of any applicable suspension of the repayment period)" after "before five years" in subpar. (A).

Effective Date of 2005 Amendment

Pub. L. 109–8, title XIV, §1404(b), Apr. 20, 2005, 119 Stat. 215, provided that: "The amendment made by subsection (a) [amending this section] is effective beginning July 30, 2002."

Amendment by sections 215, 220, 224(c), 301, 310, 314(a), 412, 714, 1209, 1235, and 1502(a)(2) of Pub. L. 109–8 effective 180 days after Apr. 20, 2005, and not applicable with respect to cases commenced under this title before such effective date, except as otherwise provided, see section 1501 of Pub. L. 109–8, set out as a note under section 101 of this title.

Effective Date of 1998 Amendment

Pub. L. 105–244, title IX, §971(b), Oct. 7, 1998, 112 Stat. 1837, provided that: "The amendment made by subsection (a) [amending this section] shall apply only with respect to cases commenced under title 11, United States Code, after the date of enactment of this Act [Oct. 7, 1998]."

Effective Date of 1996 Amendment

Pub. L. 104–193, title III, §374(c), Aug. 22, 1996, 110 Stat. 2256, provided that: "The amendments made by this section [amending this section and section 656 of Title 42, The Public Health and Welfare] shall apply only with respect to cases commenced under title 11 of the United States Code after the date of the enactment of this Act [Aug. 22, 1996]."

For provisions relating to effective date of title III of Pub. L. 104–193, see section 395(a)–(c) of Pub. L. 104–193, set out as a note under section 654 of Title 42, The Public Health and Welfare.

Effective Date of 1994 Amendment

Amendment by Pub. L. 103–394 effective Oct. 22, 1994, and not applicable with respect to cases commenced under this title before Oct. 22, 1994, see section 702 of Pub. L. 103–394, set out as a note under section 101 of this title.

Effective Date of 1990 Amendment

Pub. L. 101–647, title XXXI, §3104, Nov. 29, 1990, 104 Stat. 4916, provided that:

"(a) Effective Date.—This title and the amendments made by this title [amending this section and section 1328 of this title and enacting provisions set out as a note under section 101 of this title] shall take effect on the date of the enactment of this Act [Nov. 29, 1990].

"(b) Application of Amendments.—The amendments made by this title [amending this section and section 1328 of this title] shall not apply with respect to cases commenced under title 11 of the United States Code before the date of the enactment of this Act."

Amendment by section 3621 of Pub. L. 101–647 effective 180 days after Nov. 29, 1990, see section 3631 of Pub. L. 101–647, set out as an Effective Date note under section 3001 of Title 28, Judiciary and Judicial Procedure.

Pub. L. 101–581, §4, Nov. 15, 1990, 104 Stat. 2865, provided that:

"(a) Effective Date.—This Act and the amendments made by this Act [amending this section and section 1328 of this title and enacting provisions set out as a note under section 101 of this title] shall take effect on the date of the enactment of this Act [Nov. 15, 1990].

"(b) Application of Amendments.—The amendments made by this Act [amending this section and section 1328 of this title] shall not apply with respect to cases commenced under title 11 of the United States Code before the date of the enactment of this Act."

Effective Date of 1986 Amendment

Amendment by section 257 of Pub. L. 99–554 effective 30 days after Oct. 27, 1986, but not applicable to cases commenced under this title before that date, see section 302(a), (c)(1) of Pub. L. 99–554, set out as a note under section 581 of Title 28, Judiciary and Judicial Procedure.

Amendment by sections 281 and 283 of Pub. L. 99–554 effective 30 days after Oct. 27, 1986, see section 302(a) of Pub. L. 99–554.

Effective Date of 1984 Amendment

Amendment by Pub. L. 98–353 effective with respect to cases filed 90 days after July 10, 1984, see section 552(a) of Pub. L. 98–353, set out as a note under section 101 of this title.

Effective Date of 1981 Amendment

Amendment by Pub. L. 97–35 effective Aug. 13, 1981, see section 2334(c) of Pub. L. 97–35, set out as a note under section 656 of Title 42, The Public Health and Welfare.

Adjustment of Dollar Amounts

The dollar amounts specified in this section were adjusted by notices of the Judicial Conference of the United States pursuant to section 104 of this title as follows:

By notice dated Feb. 16, 2016, 81 F.R. 8748, effective Apr. 1, 2016, in subsec. (a)(2)(C)(i)(I), dollar amount "650" was adjusted to "675" and, in subsec. (a)(2)(C)(i)(II), dollar amount "925" was adjusted to "950". See notice of the Judicial Conference of the United States set out as a note under section 104 of this title.

By notice dated Feb. 12, 2013, 78 F.R. 12089, effective Apr. 1, 2013, in subsec. (a)(2)(C)(i)(I), dollar amount "600" was adjusted to "650" and, in subsec. (a)(2)(C)(i)(II), dollar amount "875" was adjusted to "925".

By notice dated Feb. 19, 2010, 75 F.R. 8747, effective Apr. 1, 2010, in subsec. (a)(2)(C)(i)(I), dollar amount "550" was adjusted to "600" and, in subsec. (a)(2)(C)(i)(II), dollar amount "825" was adjusted to "875".

By notice dated Feb. 7, 2007, 72 F.R. 7082, effective Apr. 1, 2007, in subsec. (a)(2)(C)(i)(I), dollar amount "500" was adjusted to "550" and, in subsec. (a)(2)(C)(i)(II), dollar amount "750" was adjusted to "825".

[Pub. L. 109–8 amended subsec. (a)(2)(C) generally. See 2005 Amendment note above.]

By notice dated Feb. 18, 2004, 69 F.R. 8482, effective Apr. 1, 2004, in subsec. (a)(2)(C), dollar amount "1,150" was adjusted to "1,225" each time it appeared.

By notice dated Feb. 13, 2001, 66 F.R. 10910, effective Apr. 1, 2001, in subsec. (a)(2)(C), dollar amount "1,075" was adjusted to "1,150" each time it appeared.

By notice dated Feb. 3, 1998, 63 F.R. 7179, effective Apr. 1, 1998, in subsec. (a)(2)(C), dollar amount "1,000" was adjusted to "1,075" each time it appeared.

[1] See Adjustment of Dollar Amounts notes below.

[2] See References in Text note below.

§524. Effect of discharge

(a) A discharge in a case under this title—

(1) voids any judgment at any time obtained, to the extent that such judgment is a determination of the personal liability of the debtor with respect to any debt discharged under section 727, 944, 1141, 1228, or 1328 of this title, whether or not discharge of such debt is waived;

(2) operates as an injunction against the commencement or continuation of an action, the employment of process, or an act, to collect, recover or offset any such debt as a personal liability of the debtor, whether or not discharge of such debt is waived; and

(3) operates as an injunction against the commencement or continuation of an action, the employment of process, or an act, to collect or recover from, or offset against, property of the debtor of the kind specified in section 541(a)(2) of this title that is acquired after the commencement of the case, on account of any allowable community claim, except a community claim that is excepted from discharge under section 523, 1228(a)(1), or 1328(a)(1), or that would be so excepted, determined in accordance with the provisions of sections 523(c) and 523(d) of this title, in a case concerning the debtor's spouse commenced on the date of the filing of the petition in the case concerning the debtor, whether or not discharge of the debt based on such community claim is waived.

(b) Subsection (a)(3) of this section does not apply if—

(1)(A) the debtor's spouse is a debtor in a case under this title, or a bankrupt or a debtor in a case under the Bankruptcy Act, commenced within six years of the date of the filing of the petition in the case concerning the debtor; and

(B) the court does not grant the debtor's spouse a discharge in such case concerning the debtor's spouse; or

(2)(A) the court would not grant the debtor's spouse a discharge in a case under chapter 7 of this title concerning such spouse commenced on the date of the filing of the petition in the case concerning the debtor; and

(B) a determination that the court would not so grant such discharge is made by the bankruptcy court within the time and in the manner provided for a determination under section 727 of this title of whether a debtor is granted a discharge.

(c) An agreement between a holder of a claim and the debtor, the consideration for which, in whole or in part, is based on a debt that is dischargeable in a case under this title is enforceable only to any extent enforceable under applicable nonbankruptcy law, whether or not discharge of such debt is waived, only if—

(1) such agreement was made before the granting of the discharge under section 727, 1141, 1228, or 1328 of this title;

(2) the debtor received the disclosures described in subsection (k) at or before the time at which the debtor signed the agreement;

(3) such agreement has been filed with the court and, if applicable, accompanied by a declaration or an affidavit of the attorney that represented the debtor during the course of negotiating an agreement under this subsection, which states that—

(A) such agreement represents a fully informed and voluntary agreement by the debtor;

(B) such agreement does not impose an undue hardship on the debtor or a dependent of the debtor; and

(C) the attorney fully advised the debtor of the legal effect and consequences of—

(i) an agreement of the kind specified in this subsection; and

(ii) any default under such an agreement;

(4) the debtor has not rescinded such agreement at any time prior to discharge or within sixty days after such agreement is filed with the court, whichever occurs later, by giving notice of rescission to the holder of such claim;

(5) the provisions of subsection (d) of this section have been complied with; and

(6)(A) in a case concerning an individual who was not represented by an attorney during the course of negotiating an agreement under this subsection, the court approves such agreement as—

(i) not imposing an undue hardship on the debtor or a dependent of the debtor; and

(ii) in the best interest of the debtor.

(B) Subparagraph (A) shall not apply to the extent that such debt is a consumer debt secured by real property.

(d) In a case concerning an individual, when the court has determined whether to grant or not to grant a discharge under section 727, 1141, 1228, or 1328 of this title, the court may hold a hearing at which the debtor shall appear in person. At any such hearing, the court shall inform the debtor that a discharge has been granted or the reason why a discharge has not been granted. If a discharge has been granted and if the debtor desires to make an agreement of the kind specified in subsection (c) of this section and was not represented by an attorney during the course of negotiating such agreement, then the court shall hold a hearing at which the debtor shall appear in person and at such hearing the court shall—

(1) inform the debtor—

(A) that such an agreement is not required under this title, under nonbankruptcy law, or under any agreement not made in accordance with the provisions of subsection (c) of this section; and

(B) of the legal effect and consequences of—

(i) an agreement of the kind specified in subsection (c) of this section; and

(ii) a default under such an agreement; and

(2) determine whether the agreement that the debtor desires to make complies with the requirements of subsection (c)(6) of this section, if the consideration for such agreement is based in whole or in part on a consumer debt that is not secured by real property of the debtor.

(e) Except as provided in subsection (a)(3) of this section, discharge of a debt of the debtor does not affect the liability of any other entity on, or the property of any other entity for, such debt.

(f) Nothing contained in subsection (c) or (d) of this section prevents a debtor from voluntarily repaying any debt.

(g)(1)(A) After notice and hearing, a court that enters an order confirming a plan of reorganization under chapter 11 may issue, in connection with such order, an injunction in accordance with this subsection to supplement the injunctive effect of a discharge under this section.

(B) An injunction may be issued under subparagraph (A) to enjoin entities from taking legal action for the purpose of directly or indirectly collecting, recovering, or receiving payment or recovery with respect to any claim or demand that, under a plan of reorganization, is to be paid in whole or in part by a trust described in paragraph (2)(B)(i), except such legal actions as are expressly allowed by the injunction, the confirmation order, or the plan of reorganization.

(2)(A) Subject to subsection (h), if the requirements of subparagraph (B) are met at the time an injunction described in paragraph (1) is entered, then after entry of such injunction, any proceeding that involves the validity, application, construction, or modification of such injunction, or of this subsection with respect to such injunction, may be commenced only in the district court in which such injunction was entered, and such court shall have exclusive jurisdiction over any such proceeding without regard to the amount in controversy.

(B) The requirements of this subparagraph are that—

(i) the injunction is to be implemented in connection with a trust that, pursuant to the plan of reorganization—

(I) is to assume the liabilities of a debtor which at the time of entry of the order for relief has been named as a defendant in personal injury, wrongful death, or property-damage actions seeking recovery for damages allegedly caused by the presence of, or exposure to, asbestos or asbestos-containing products;

(II) is to be funded in whole or in part by the securities of 1 or more debtors involved in such plan and by the obligation of such debtor or debtors to make future payments, including dividends;

(III) is to own, or by the exercise of rights granted under such plan would be entitled to own if specified contingencies occur, a majority of the voting shares of—

(aa) each such debtor;

(bb) the parent corporation of each such debtor; or

(cc) a subsidiary of each such debtor that is also a debtor; and

(IV) is to use its assets or income to pay claims and demands; and

(ii) subject to subsection (h), the court determines that—

(I) the debtor is likely to be subject to substantial future demands for payment arising out of the same or similar conduct or events that gave rise to the claims that are addressed by the injunction;

(II) the actual amounts, numbers, and timing of such future demands cannot be determined;

(III) pursuit of such demands outside the procedures prescribed by such plan is likely to threaten the plan's purpose to deal equitably with claims and future demands;

(IV) as part of the process of seeking confirmation of such plan—

(aa) the terms of the injunction proposed to be issued under paragraph (1)(A), including any provisions barring actions against third parties pursuant to paragraph (4)(A), are set out in such plan and in any disclosure statement supporting the plan; and

(bb) a separate class or classes of the claimants whose claims are to be addressed by a trust described in clause (i) is established and votes, by at least 75 percent of those voting, in favor of the plan; and

(V) subject to subsection (h), pursuant to court orders or otherwise, the trust will operate through mechanisms such as structured, periodic, or supplemental payments, pro rata distributions, matrices, or periodic review of estimates of the numbers and values of present claims and future demands, or other comparable mechanisms, that provide reasonable assurance that the trust will value, and be in a financial position to pay, present claims and future demands that involve similar claims in substantially the same manner.

(3)(A) If the requirements of paragraph (2)(B) are met and the order confirming the plan of reorganization was issued or affirmed by the district court that has jurisdiction over the reorganization case, then after the time for appeal of the order that issues or affirms the plan—

(i) the injunction shall be valid and enforceable and may not be revoked or modified by any court except through appeal in accordance with paragraph (6);

(ii) no entity that pursuant to such plan or thereafter becomes a direct or indirect transferee of, or successor to any assets of, a debtor or trust that is the subject of the injunction shall be liable with respect to any claim or demand made against such entity by reason of its becoming such a transferee or successor; and

(iii) no entity that pursuant to such plan or thereafter makes a loan to such a debtor or trust or to such a successor or transferee shall, by reason of making the loan, be liable with respect to any claim or demand made against such entity, nor shall any pledge of assets made in connection with such a loan be upset or impaired for that reason;

(B) Subparagraph (A) shall not be construed to—

(i) imply that an entity described in subparagraph (A)(ii) or (iii) would, if this paragraph were not applicable, necessarily be liable to any entity by reason of any of the acts described in subparagraph (A);

(ii) relieve any such entity of the duty to comply with, or of liability under, any Federal or State law regarding the making of a fraudulent conveyance in a transaction described in subparagraph (A)(ii) or (iii); or

(iii) relieve a debtor of the debtor's obligation to comply with the terms of the plan of reorganization, or affect the power of the court to exercise its authority under sections 1141 and 1142 to compel the debtor to do so.

(4)(A)(i) Subject to subparagraph (B), an injunction described in paragraph (1) shall be valid and enforceable against all entities that it addresses.

(ii) Notwithstanding the provisions of section 524(e), such an injunction may bar any action directed against a third party who is identifiable from the terms of such injunction (by name or as part of an identifiable group) and is alleged to be directly or indirectly liable for the conduct of, claims against, or demands on the debtor to the extent such alleged liability of such third party arises by reason of—

(I) the third party's ownership of a financial interest in the debtor, a past or present affiliate of the debtor, or a predecessor in interest of the debtor;

(II) the third party's involvement in the management of the debtor or a predecessor in interest of the debtor, or service as an officer, director or employee of the debtor or a related party;

(III) the third party's provision of insurance to the debtor or a related party; or

(IV) the third party's involvement in a transaction changing the corporate structure, or in a loan or other financial transaction affecting the financial condition, of the debtor or a related party, including but not limited to—

(aa) involvement in providing financing (debt or equity), or advice to an entity involved in such a transaction; or

(bb) acquiring or selling a financial interest in an entity as part of such a transaction.

(iii) As used in this subparagraph, the term "related party" means—

(I) a past or present affiliate of the debtor;

(II) a predecessor in interest of the debtor; or

(III) any entity that owned a financial interest in—

(aa) the debtor;

(bb) a past or present affiliate of the debtor; or

(cc) a predecessor in interest of the debtor.

(B) Subject to subsection (h), if, under a plan of reorganization, a kind of demand described in such plan is to be paid in whole or in part by a trust described in paragraph (2)(B)(i) in connection with which an injunction described in paragraph (1) is to be implemented, then such injunction shall be valid and enforceable with respect to a demand of such kind made, after such plan is confirmed, against the debtor or debtors involved, or against a third party described in subparagraph (A)(ii), if—

(i) as part of the proceedings leading to issuance of such injunction, the court appoints a legal representative for the purpose of protecting the rights of persons that might subsequently assert demands of such kind, and

(ii) the court determines, before entering the order confirming such plan, that identifying such debtor or debtors, or such third party (by name or as part of an identifiable group), in such injunction with respect to such demands for purposes of this subparagraph is fair and equitable with respect to the persons that might subsequently assert such demands, in light of the benefits provided, or to be provided, to such trust on behalf of such debtor or debtors or such third party.

(5) In this subsection, the term "demand" means a demand for payment, present or future, that—

(A) was not a claim during the proceedings leading to the confirmation of a plan of reorganization;

(B) arises out of the same or similar conduct or events that gave rise to the claims addressed by the injunction issued under paragraph (1); and

(C) pursuant to the plan, is to be paid by a trust described in paragraph (2)(B)(i).

(6) Paragraph (3)(A)(i) does not bar an action taken by or at the direction of an appellate court on appeal of an injunction issued under paragraph (1) or of the order of confirmation that relates to the injunction.

(7) This subsection does not affect the operation of section 1144 or the power of the district court to refer a proceeding under section 157 of title 28 or any reference of a proceeding made prior to the date of the enactment of this subsection.

(h) Application to Existing Injunctions.—For purposes of subsection (g)—

(1) subject to paragraph (2), if an injunction of the kind described in subsection (g)(1)(B) was issued before the date of the enactment of this Act, as part of a plan of reorganization confirmed by an order entered before such date, then the injunction shall be considered to meet the requirements of subsection (g)(2)(B) for purposes of subsection (g)(2)(A), and to satisfy subsection (g)(4)(A)(ii), if—

(A) the court determined at the time the plan was confirmed that the plan was fair and equitable in accordance with the requirements of section 1129(b);

(B) as part of the proceedings leading to issuance of such injunction and confirmation of such plan, the court had appointed a legal representative for the purpose of protecting the rights of persons that might subsequently assert demands described in subsection (g)(4)(B) with respect to such plan; and

(C) such legal representative did not object to confirmation of such plan or issuance of such injunction; and

(2) for purposes of paragraph (1), if a trust described in subsection (g)(2)(B)(i) is subject to a court order on the date of the enactment of this Act staying such trust from settling or paying further claims—

(A) the requirements of subsection (g)(2)(B)(ii)(V) shall not apply with respect to such trust until such stay is lifted or dissolved; and

(B) if such trust meets such requirements on the date such stay is lifted or dissolved, such trust shall be considered to have met such requirements continuously from the date of the enactment of this Act.

(i) The willful failure of a creditor to credit payments received under a plan confirmed under this title, unless the order confirming the plan is revoked, the plan is in default, or the creditor has not received payments required to be made under the plan in the manner required by the plan (including crediting the amounts required under the plan), shall constitute a violation of an injunction under subsection (a)(2) if the act of the creditor to collect and failure to credit payments in the manner required by the plan caused material injury to the debtor.

(j) Subsection (a)(2) does not operate as an injunction against an act by a creditor that is the holder of a secured claim, if—

(1) such creditor retains a security interest in real property that is the principal residence of the debtor;

(2) such act is in the ordinary course of business between the creditor and the debtor; and

(3) such act is limited to seeking or obtaining periodic payments associated with a valid security interest in lieu of pursuit of in rem relief to enforce the lien.

(k)(1) The disclosures required under subsection (c)(2) shall consist of the disclosure statement described in paragraph (3), completed as required in that paragraph, together with the agreement specified in subsection (c), statement, declaration, motion and order described, respectively, in paragraphs (4) through (8), and shall be the only disclosures required in connection with entering into such agreement.

(2) Disclosures made under paragraph (1) shall be made clearly and conspicuously and in writing. The terms "Amount Reaffirmed" and "Annual Percentage Rate" shall be disclosed more conspicuously than other terms, data or information provided in connection with this disclosure, except that the phrases "Before agreeing to reaffirm a debt, review these important disclosures" and "Summary of Reaffirmation Agreement" may be equally conspicuous. Disclosures may be made in a different order and may use terminology different from that set forth in paragraphs (2) through (8), except that the terms "Amount Reaffirmed" and "Annual Percentage Rate" must be used where indicated.

(3) The disclosure statement required under this paragraph shall consist of the following:

(A) The statement: "Part A: Before agreeing to reaffirm a debt, review these important disclosures:";

(B) Under the heading "Summary of Reaffirmation Agreement", the statement: "This Summary is made pursuant to the requirements of the Bankruptcy Code";

(C) The "Amount Reaffirmed", using that term, which shall be—

(i) the total amount of debt that the debtor agrees to reaffirm by entering into an agreement of the kind specified in subsection (c), and

(ii) the total of any fees and costs accrued as of the date of the disclosure statement, related to such total amount.

(D) In conjunction with the disclosure of the "Amount Reaffirmed", the statements—

(i) "The amount of debt you have agreed to reaffirm"; and

(ii) "Your credit agreement may obligate you to pay additional amounts which may come due after the date of this disclosure. Consult your credit agreement.".

(E) The "Annual Percentage Rate", using that term, which shall be disclosed as—

(i) if, at the time the petition is filed, the debt is an extension of credit under an open end credit plan, as the terms "credit" and "open end credit plan" are defined in section 103 of the Truth in Lending Act, then—

(I) the annual percentage rate determined under paragraphs (5) and (6) of section 127(b) of the Truth in Lending Act, as applicable, as disclosed to the debtor in the most recent periodic statement prior to entering into an agreement of the kind specified in subsection (c) or, if no such periodic statement has been given to the debtor during the prior 6 months, the annual percentage rate as it would have been so disclosed at the time the disclosure statement is given to the debtor, or to the extent this annual percentage rate is not readily available or not applicable, then

(II) the simple interest rate applicable to the amount reaffirmed as of the date the disclosure statement is given to the debtor, or if different simple interest rates apply to different balances, the simple interest rate applicable to each such balance, identifying the amount of each such balance included in the amount reaffirmed, or

(III) if the entity making the disclosure elects, to disclose the annual percentage rate under subclause (I) and the simple interest rate under subclause (II); or

(ii) if, at the time the petition is filed, the debt is an extension of credit other than under an open end credit plan, as the terms "credit" and "open end credit plan" are defined in section 103 of the Truth in Lending Act, then—

(I) the annual percentage rate under section 128(a)(4) of the Truth in Lending Act, as disclosed to the debtor in the most recent disclosure statement given to the debtor prior to the entering into an agreement of the kind specified in subsection (c) with respect to the debt, or, if no such disclosure statement was given to the debtor, the annual percentage rate as it would have been so disclosed at the time the disclosure statement is given to the debtor, or to the extent this annual percentage rate is not readily available or not applicable, then

(II) the simple interest rate applicable to the amount reaffirmed as of the date the disclosure statement is given to the debtor, or if different simple interest rates apply to different balances, the simple interest rate applicable to each such balance, identifying the amount of such balance included in the amount reaffirmed, or

(III) if the entity making the disclosure elects, to disclose the annual percentage rate under (I) and the simple interest rate under (II).

(F) If the underlying debt transaction was disclosed as a variable rate transaction on the most recent disclosure given under the Truth in Lending Act, by stating "The interest rate on your loan may be a variable interest rate which changes from time to time, so that the annual percentage rate disclosed here may be higher or lower.".

(G) If the debt is secured by a security interest which has not been waived in whole or in part or determined to be void by a final order of the court at the time of the disclosure, by disclosing that a security interest or lien in goods or property is asserted over some or all of the debts the debtor is reaffirming and listing the items and their original purchase price that are subject to the asserted security interest, or if not a purchase-money security interest then listing by items or types and the original amount of the loan.

(H) At the election of the creditor, a statement of the repayment schedule using 1 or a combination of the following—

(i) by making the statement: "Your first payment in the amount of $_______ is due on _______ but the future payment amount may be different. Consult your reaffirmation agreement or credit agreement, as applicable.", and stating the amount of the first payment and the due date of that payment in the places provided;

(ii) by making the statement: "Your payment schedule will be:", and describing the repayment schedule with the number, amount, and due dates or period of payments scheduled to repay the debts reaffirmed to the extent then known by the disclosing party; or

(iii) by describing the debtor's repayment obligations with reasonable specificity to the extent then known by the disclosing party.

(I) The following statement: "Note: When this disclosure refers to what a creditor 'may' do, it does not use the word 'may' to give the creditor specific permission. The word 'may' is used to tell you what might occur if the law permits the creditor to take the action. If you have questions about your reaffirming a debt or what the law requires, consult with the attorney who helped you negotiate this agreement reaffirming a debt. If you don't have an attorney helping you, the judge will explain the effect of your reaffirming a debt when the hearing on the reaffirmation agreement is held.".

(J)(i) The following additional statements:

"Reaffirming a debt is a serious financial decision. The law requires you to take certain steps to make sure the decision is in your best interest. If these steps are not completed, the reaffirmation agreement is not effective, even though you have signed it.

"1. Read the disclosures in this Part A carefully. Consider the decision to reaffirm carefully. Then, if you want to reaffirm, sign the reaffirmation agreement in Part B (or you may use a separate agreement you and your creditor agree on).

"2. Complete and sign Part D and be sure you can afford to make the payments you are agreeing to make and have received a copy of the disclosure statement and a completed and signed reaffirmation agreement.

"3. If you were represented by an attorney during the negotiation of your reaffirmation agreement, the attorney must have signed the certification in Part C.

"4. If you were not represented by an attorney during the negotiation of your reaffirmation agreement, you must have completed and signed Part E.

"5. The original of this disclosure must be filed with the court by you or your creditor. If a separate reaffirmation agreement (other than the one in Part B) has been signed, it must be attached.

"6. If you were represented by an attorney during the negotiation of your reaffirmation agreement, your reaffirmation agreement becomes effective upon filing with the court unless the reaffirmation is presumed to be an undue hardship as explained in Part D.

"7. If you were not represented by an attorney during the negotiation of your reaffirmation agreement, it will not be effective unless the court approves it. The court will notify you of the hearing on your reaffirmation agreement. You must attend this hearing in bankruptcy court where the judge will review your reaffirmation agreement. The bankruptcy court must approve your reaffirmation agreement as consistent with your best interests, except that no court approval is required if your reaffirmation agreement is for a consumer debt secured by a mortgage, deed of trust, security deed, or other lien on your real property, like your home.

"Your right to rescind (cancel) your reaffirmation agreement. You may rescind (cancel) your reaffirmation agreement at any time before the bankruptcy court enters a discharge order, or before the expiration of the 60-day period that begins on the date your reaffirmation agreement is filed with the court, whichever occurs later. To rescind (cancel) your reaffirmation agreement, you must notify the creditor that your reaffirmation agreement is rescinded (or canceled).

"What are your obligations if you reaffirm the debt? A reaffirmed debt remains your personal legal obligation. It is not discharged in your bankruptcy case. That means that if you default on your reaffirmed debt after your bankruptcy case is over, your creditor may be able to take your property or your wages. Otherwise, your obligations will be determined by the reaffirmation agreement which may have changed the terms of the original agreement. For example, if you are reaffirming an open end credit agreement, the creditor may be permitted by that agreement or applicable law to change the terms of that agreement in the future under certain conditions.

"Are you required to enter into a reaffirmation agreement by any law? No, you are not required to reaffirm a debt by any law. Only agree to reaffirm a debt if it is in your best interest. Be sure you can afford the payments you agree to make.

"What if your creditor has a security interest or lien? Your bankruptcy discharge does not eliminate any lien on your property. A 'lien' is often referred to as a security interest, deed of trust, mortgage or security deed. Even if you do not reaffirm and your personal liability on the debt is discharged, because of the lien your creditor may still have the right to take the property securing the lien if you do not pay the debt or default on it. If the lien is on an item of personal property that is exempt under your State's law or that the trustee has abandoned, you may be able to redeem the item rather than reaffirm the debt. To redeem, you must make a single payment to the creditor equal to the amount of the allowed secured claim, as agreed by the parties or determined by the court.".

(ii) In the case of a reaffirmation under subsection (m)(2), numbered paragraph 6 in the disclosures required by clause (i) of this subparagraph shall read as follows:

"6. If you were represented by an attorney during the negotiation of your reaffirmation agreement, your reaffirmation agreement becomes effective upon filing with the court.".

(4) The form of such agreement required under this paragraph shall consist of the following:

"Part B: Reaffirmation Agreement. I (we) agree to reaffirm the debts arising under the credit agreement described below.

"Brief description of credit agreement:

"Description of any changes to the credit agreement made as part of this reaffirmation agreement:

"Signature: Date:

"Borrower:

"Co-borrower, if also reaffirming these debts:

"Accepted by creditor:

"Date of creditor acceptance:".

(5) The declaration shall consist of the following:

(A) The following certification:

"Part C: Certification by Debtor's Attorney (If Any).

"I hereby certify that (1) this agreement represents a fully informed and voluntary agreement by the debtor; (2) this agreement does not impose an undue hardship on the debtor or any dependent of the debtor; and (3) I have fully advised the debtor of the legal effect and consequences of this agreement and any default under this agreement.

"Signature of Debtor's Attorney: Date:".

(B) If a presumption of undue hardship has been established with respect to such agreement, such certification shall state that, in the opinion of the attorney, the debtor is able to make the payment.

(C) In the case of a reaffirmation agreement under subsection (m)(2), subparagraph (B) is not applicable.

(6)(A) The statement in support of such agreement, which the debtor shall sign and date prior to filing with the court, shall consist of the following:

"Part D: Debtor's Statement in Support of Reaffirmation Agreement.

"1. I believe this reaffirmation agreement will not impose an undue hardship on my dependents or me. I can afford to make the payments on the reaffirmed debt because my monthly income (take home pay plus any other income received) is $_______, and my actual current monthly expenses including monthly payments on post-bankruptcy debt and other reaffirmation agreements total $_______, leaving $_______ to make the required payments on this reaffirmed debt. I understand that if my income less my monthly expenses does not leave enough to make the payments, this reaffirmation agreement is presumed to be an undue hardship on me and must be reviewed by the court. However, this presumption may be overcome if I explain to the satisfaction of the court how I can afford to make the payments here: _______.

"2. I received a copy of the Reaffirmation Disclosure Statement in Part A and a completed and signed reaffirmation agreement.".

(B) Where the debtor is represented by an attorney and is reaffirming a debt owed to a creditor defined in section 19(b)(1)(A)(iv) of the Federal Reserve Act, the statement of support of the reaffirmation agreement, which the debtor shall sign and date prior to filing with the court, shall consist of the following:

"I believe this reaffirmation agreement is in my financial interest. I can afford to make the payments on the reaffirmed debt. I received a copy of the Reaffirmation Disclosure Statement in Part A and a completed and signed reaffirmation agreement.".

(7) The motion that may be used if approval of such agreement by the court is required in order for it to be effective, shall be signed and dated by the movant and shall consist of the following:

"Part E: Motion for Court Approval (To be completed only if the debtor is not represented by an attorney.). I (we), the debtor(s), affirm the following to be true and correct:

"I am not represented by an attorney in connection with this reaffirmation agreement.

"I believe this reaffirmation agreement is in my best interest based on the income and expenses I have disclosed in my Statement in Support of this reaffirmation agreement, and because (provide any additional relevant reasons the court should consider):

"Therefore, I ask the court for an order approving this reaffirmation agreement.".

(8) The court order, which may be used to approve such agreement, shall consist of the following:

"Court Order: The court grants the debtor's motion and approves the reaffirmation agreement described above.".

(l) Notwithstanding any other provision of this title the following shall apply:

(1) A creditor may accept payments from a debtor before and after the filing of an agreement of the kind specified in subsection (c) with the court.

(2) A creditor may accept payments from a debtor under such agreement that the creditor believes in good faith to be effective.

(3) The requirements of subsections (c)(2) and (k) shall be satisfied if disclosures required under those subsections are given in good faith.

(m)(1) Until 60 days after an agreement of the kind specified in subsection (c) is filed with the court (or such additional period as the court, after notice and a hearing and for cause, orders before the expiration of such period), it shall be presumed that such agreement is an undue hardship on the debtor if the debtor's monthly income less the debtor's monthly expenses as shown on the debtor's completed and signed statement in support of such agreement required under subsection (k)(6)(A) is less than the scheduled payments on the reaffirmed debt. This presumption shall be reviewed by the court. The presumption may be rebutted in writing by the debtor if the statement includes an explanation that identifies additional sources of funds to make the payments as agreed upon under the terms of such agreement. If the presumption is not rebutted to the satisfaction of the court, the court may disapprove such agreement. No agreement shall be disapproved without notice and a hearing to the debtor and creditor, and such hearing shall be concluded before the entry of the debtor's discharge.

(2) This subsection does not apply to reaffirmation agreements where the creditor is a credit union, as defined in section 19(b)(1)(A)(iv) of the Federal Reserve Act.

(Pub. L. 95–598, Nov. 6, 1978, 92 Stat. 2592; Pub. L. 98–353, title III, §§308, 455, July 10, 1984, 98 Stat. 354, 376; Pub. L. 99–554, title II, §§257(o), 282, 283(k), Oct. 27, 1986, 100 Stat. 3115–3117; Pub. L. 103–394, title I, §§103, 111(a), title V, §501(d)(14), Oct. 22, 1994, 108 Stat. 4108, 4113, 4145; Pub. L. 109–8, title II, §§202, 203(a), title XII, §1210, Apr. 20, 2005, 119 Stat. 43, 194; Pub. L. 111–327, §2(a)(19), Dec. 22, 2010, 124 Stat. 3559.)

Historical and Revision Notes

legislative statements

Section 524(a) of the House amendment represents a compromise between the House bill and the Senate amendment. Section 524(b) of the House amendment is new, and represents standards clarifying the operation of section 524(a)(3) with respect to community property.

Sections 524(c) and (d) represent a compromise between the House bill and Senate amendment on the issue of reaffirmation of a debt discharged in bankruptcy.

Every reaffirmation to be enforceable must be approved by the court, and any debtor may rescind a reaffirmation for 30 days from the time the reaffirmation becomes enforceable. If the debtor is an individual the court must advise the debtor of various effects of reaffirmation at a hearing. In addition, to any extent the debt is a consumer debt that is not secured by real property of the debtor reaffirmation is permitted only if the court approves the reaffirmation agreement, before granting a discharge under section 727, 1141, or 1328, as not imposing a hardship on the debtor or a dependent of the debtor and in the best interest of the debtor; alternatively, the court may approve an agreement entered into in good faith that is in settlement of litigation of a complaint to determine dischargeability or that is entered into in connection with redemption under section 722. The hearing on discharge under section 524(d) will be held whether or not the debtor desires to reaffirm any debts.

senate report no. 95–989

Subsection (a) specifies that a discharge in a bankruptcy case voids any judgment to the extent that it is a determination of the personal liability of the debtor with respect to a prepetition debt, and operates as an injunction against the commencement or continuation of an action, the employment of process, or any act, including telephone calls, letters, and personal contacts, to collect, recover, or offset any discharged debt as a personal liability of the debtor, or from property of the debtor, whether or not the debtor has waived discharge of the debt involved. The injunction is to give complete effect to the discharge and to eliminate any doubt concerning the effect of the discharge as a total prohibition on debt collection efforts. This paragraph has been expanded over a comparable provision in Bankruptcy Act §14f [section 32(f) of former title 11] to cover any act to collect, such as dunning by telephone or letter, or indirectly through friends, relatives, or employers, harassment, threats of repossession, and the like. The change is consonant with the new policy forbidding binding reaffirmation agreements under proposed 11 U.S.C. 524(b), and is intended to insure that once a debt is discharged, the debtor will not be pressured in any way to repay it. In effect, the discharge extinguishes the debt, and creditors may not attempt to avoid that. The language "whether or not discharge of such debt is waived" is intended to prevent waiver of discharge of a particular debt from defeating the purposes of this section. It is directed at waiver of discharge of a particular debt, not waiver of discharge in toto as permitted under section 727(a)(9).

Subsection (a) also codifies the split discharge for debtors in community property states. If community property was in the estate and community claims were discharged, the discharge is effective against community creditors of the nondebtor spouse as well as of the debtor spouse.

Subsection (b) gives further effect to the discharge. It prohibits reaffirmation agreements after the commencement of the case with respect to any dischargeable debt. The prohibition extends to agreements the consideration for which in whole or in part is based on a dischargeable debt, and it applies whether or not discharge of the debt involved in the agreement has been waived. Thus, the prohibition on reaffirmation agreements extends to debts that are based on discharged debts. Thus, "second generation" debts, which included all or a part of a discharged debt could not be included in any new agreement for new money. This subsection will not have any effect on reaffirmations of debts discharged under the Bankruptcy Act [former title 11]. It will only apply to discharges granted if commenced under the new title 11 bankruptcy code.

Subsection (c) grants an exception to the anti-reaffirmation provision. It permits reaffirmation in connection with the settlement of a proceeding to determine the dischargeability of the debt being reaffirmed, or in connection with a redemption agreement permitted under section 722. In either case, the reaffirmation agreement must be entered into in good faith and must be approved by the court.

Subsection (d) provides the discharge of the debtor does not affect co-debtors or guarantors.

References in Text

The Bankruptcy Act, referred to in subsec. (b)(1), is act July 1, 1898, ch. 541, 30 Stat. 544, as amended, which was classified generally to former Title 11.

The date of the enactment of this subsection, referred to in subsec. (g)(7), is the date of enactment of Pub. L. 103–394, which enacted subsec. (g) and was approved Oct. 22, 1994.

The date of the enactment of this Act, referred to in subsec. (h), probably means the date of enactment of Pub. L. 103–394, which enacted subsec. (h) and was approved Oct. 22, 1994.

The Truth in Lending Act, referred to in subsec. (k), is title I of Pub. L. 90–321, May 29, 1968, 82 Stat. 146, as amended, which is classified generally to subchapter I (§1601 et seq.) of chapter 41 of Title 15, Commerce and Trade. Sections 103, 127(b), and 128(a)(4) of the Act are classified to sections 1602, 1637(b), and 1638(a)(4), respectively, of Title 15. For complete classification of this Act to the Code, see Short Title note set out under section 1601 of Title 15 and Tables.

Section 19(b)(1)(A)(iv) of the Federal Reserve Act, referred to in subsecs. (k)(6)(B) and (m)(2), is classified to section 461(b)(1)(A)(iv) of Title 12, Banks and Banking.

Amendments

2010—Subsec. (k)(3)(J)(i). Pub. L. 111–327, §2(a)(19)(A), in last undesignated par., substituted "property securing the lien" for "security property" and "amount of the allowed secured claim" for "current value of the security property" and inserted "must" before "make a single payment".

Subsec. (k)(5)(B). Pub. L. 111–327, §2(a)(19)(B), substituted "that," for "that".

2005—Subsec. (a)(3). Pub. L. 109–8, §1210, substituted "section 523, 1228(a)(1), or 1328(a)(1), or that" for "section 523, 1228(a)(1), or 1328(a)(1) of this title, or that".

Subsec. (c)(2). Pub. L. 109–8, §203(a)(1), added par. (2) and struck out former par. (2) which read as follows:

"(2)(A) such agreement contains a clear and conspicuous statement which advises the debtor that the agreement may be rescinded at any time prior to discharge or within sixty days after such agreement is filed with the court, whichever occurs later, by giving notice of rescission to the holder of such claim; and

"(B) such agreement contains a clear and conspicuous statement which advises the debtor that such agreement is not required under this title, under nonbankruptcy law, or under any agreement not in accordance with the provisions of this subsection;".

Subsecs. (i), (j). Pub. L. 109–8, §202, added subsecs. (i) and (j).

Subsecs. (k) to (m). Pub. L. 109–8, §203(a)(2), added subsecs. (k) to (m).

1994—Subsec. (a)(3). Pub. L. 103–394, §501(d)(14)(A), substituted "1328(a)(1)" for "1328(c)(1)". See 1986 Amendment note below.

Subsec. (c)(2). Pub. L. 103–394, §103(a)(1), designated existing provisions as subpar. (A), inserted "and" at end, and added subpar. (B).

Subsec. (c)(3). Pub. L. 103–394, §103(a)(2), struck out "such agreement" after "which states that" in introductory provisions, struck out "and" at end of subpar. (A), inserted "such agreement" in subpars. (A) and (B), and added subpar. (C).

Subsec. (c)(4). Pub. L. 103–394, §501(d)(14)(B), substituted "rescission" for "recission".

Subsec. (d). Pub. L. 103–394, §103(b), inserted "and was not represented by an attorney during the course of negotiating such agreement" after "this section" in introductory provisions.

Subsec. (d)(1)(B)(ii). Pub. L. 103–394, §501(d)(14)(C), inserted "and" at end.

Subsecs. (g), (h). Pub. L. 103–394, §111(a), added subsecs. (g) and (h).

1986—Subsec. (a)(1). Pub. L. 99–554, §257(o)(1), inserted reference to section 1228 of this title.

Subsec. (a)(3). Pub. L. 99–554, §257(o)(2), which directed the substitution of ", 1228(a)(1), or 1328(a)(1)" for "or 1328(a)(1)" was executed by making the substitution for "or 1328(c)(1)" to reflect the probable intent of Congress. See 1994 Amendment note above.

Subsec. (c)(1). Pub. L. 99–554, §257(o)(1), inserted reference to section 1228 of this title.

Subsec. (d). Pub. L. 99–554, §257(o)(1), inserted reference to section 1228 of this title.

Pub. L. 99–554, §282, substituted "shall" for "may" before "hold" in first sentence, inserted "any" after "At" in second sentence, and inserted "the court shall hold a hearing at which the debtor shall appear in person and" after "then" in third sentence.

Subsec. (d)(2). Pub. L. 99–554, §283(k), substituted "section" for "subsection" after "subsection (c)(6) of this".

1984—Subsec. (a)(2). Pub. L. 98–353, §§308(a), 455, struck out "or from property of the debtor," before "whether or not discharge", and substituted "an act" for "any act".

Subsec. (a)(3). Pub. L. 98–353, §455, substituted "an act" for "any act".

Subsec. (c)(2). Pub. L. 98–353, §308(b)(1), (3), added par. (2). Former par. (2), which related to situations where the debtor had not rescinded the agreement within 30 days after the agreement became enforceable, was struck out.

Subsec. (c)(3), (4). Pub. L. 98–352, §308(b)(3), added pars. (3) and (4). Former pars. (3) and (4) redesignated (5) and (6), respectively.

Subsec. (c)(5). Pub. L. 98–353, §308(b)(2), redesignated former par. (3) as (5).

Subsec. (c)(6). Pub. L. 98–353, §308(b)(2), (4), redesignated former par. (4) as (6) and generally amended par. (6), as so redesignated, thereby striking out provisions relating to court approval of such agreements as are entered into in good faith and are in settlement of litigation under section 523 of this title or provide for redemption under section 722 of this title.

Subsec. (d)(2). Pub. L. 98–353, §308(c), substituted "subsection (c)(6)" for "subsection (c)(4)".

Subsec. (f). Pub. L. 98–353, §308(d), added subsec. (f).

Effective Date of 2005 Amendment

Amendment by Pub. L. 109–8 effective 180 days after Apr. 20, 2005, and not applicable with respect to cases commenced under this title before such effective date, except as otherwise provided, see section 1501 of Pub. L. 109–8, set out as a note under section 101 of this title.

Effective Date of 1994 Amendment

Amendment by Pub. L. 103–394 effective Oct. 22, 1994, and, except with respect to amendment by section 111(a) of Pub. L. 103–394, amendment by Pub. L. 103–394 not applicable with respect to cases commenced under this title before Oct. 22, 1994, see section 702 of Pub. L. 103–394, set out as a note under section 101 of this title.

Effective Date of 1986 Amendment

Amendment by section 257 of Pub. L. 99–554 effective 30 days after Oct. 27, 1986, but not applicable to cases commenced under this title before that date, see section 302(a), (c)(1) of Pub. L. 99–554, set out as a note under section 581 of Title 28, Judiciary and Judicial Procedure.

Amendment by sections 282 and 283 of Pub. L. 99–554 effective 30 days after Oct. 27, 1986, see section 302(a) of Pub. L. 99–554.

Effective Date of 1984 Amendment

Amendment by Pub. L. 98–353 effective with respect to cases filed 90 days after July 10, 1984, see section 552(a) of Pub. L. 98–353, set out as a note under section 101 of this title.

Construction

Pub. L. 103–394, title I, §111(b), Oct. 22, 1994, 108 Stat. 4117, provided that: "Nothing in subsection (a), or in the amendments made by subsection (a) [amending this section], shall be construed to modify, impair, or supersede any other authority the court has to issue injunctions in connection with an order confirming a plan of reorganization."

§525. Protection against discriminatory treatment

(a) Except as provided in the Perishable Agricultural Commodities Act, 1930, the Packers and Stockyards Act, 1921, and section 1 of the Act entitled "An Act making appropriations for the Department of Agriculture for the fiscal year ending June 30, 1944, and for other purposes," approved July 12, 1943, a governmental unit may not deny, revoke, suspend, or refuse to renew a license, permit, charter, franchise, or other similar grant to, condition such a grant to, discriminate with respect to such a grant against, deny employment to, terminate the employment of, or discriminate with respect to employment against, a person that is or has been a debtor under this title or a bankrupt or a debtor under the Bankruptcy Act, or another person with whom such bankrupt or debtor has been associated, solely because such bankrupt or debtor is or has been a debtor under this title or a bankrupt or debtor under the Bankruptcy Act, has been insolvent before the commencement of the case under this title, or during the case but before the debtor is granted or denied a discharge, or has not paid a debt that is dischargeable in the case under this title or that was discharged under the Bankruptcy Act.

(b) No private employer may terminate the employment of, or discriminate with respect to employment against, an individual who is or has been a debtor under this title, a debtor or bankrupt under the Bankruptcy Act, or an individual associated with such debtor or bankrupt, solely because such debtor or bankrupt—

(1) is or has been a debtor under this title or a debtor or bankrupt under the Bankruptcy Act;

(2) has been insolvent before the commencement of a case under this title or during the case but before the grant or denial of a discharge; or

(3) has not paid a debt that is dischargeable in a case under this title or that was discharged under the Bankruptcy Act.

(c)(1) A governmental unit that operates a student grant or loan program and a person engaged in a business that includes the making of loans guaranteed or insured under a student loan program may not deny a student grant, loan, loan guarantee, or loan insurance to a person that is or has been a debtor under this title or a bankrupt or debtor under the Bankruptcy Act, or another person with whom the debtor or bankrupt has been associated, because the debtor or bankrupt is or has been a debtor under this title or a bankrupt or debtor under the Bankruptcy Act, has been insolvent before the commencement of a case under this title or during the pendency of the case but before the debtor is granted or denied a discharge, or has not paid a debt that is dischargeable in the case under this title or that was discharged under the Bankruptcy Act.

(2) In this section, "student loan program" means any program operated under title IV of the Higher Education Act of 1965 or a similar program operated under State or local law.

(Pub. L. 95–598, Nov. 6, 1978, 92 Stat. 2593; Pub. L. 98–353, title III, §309, July 10, 1984, 98 Stat. 354; Pub. L. 103–394, title III, §313, title V, §501(d)(15), Oct. 22, 1994, 108 Stat. 4140, 4145; Pub. L. 109–8, title XII, §1211, Apr. 20, 2005, 119 Stat. 194.)

Historical and Revision Notes

senate report no. 95–989

This section is additional debtor protection. It codifies the result of *Perez v. Campbell*, 402 U.S. 637 (1971), which held that a State would frustrate the Congressional policy of a fresh start for a debtor if it were permitted to refuse to renew a drivers license because a tort judgment resulting from an automobile accident had been unpaid as a result of a discharge in bankruptcy.

Notwithstanding any other laws, section 525 prohibits a governmental unit from denying, revoking, suspending, or refusing to renew a license, permit, charter, franchise, or other similar grant to, from conditioning such a grant to, from discrimination with respect to such a grant against, deny employment to, terminate the employment of, or discriminate with respect to employment against, a person that is or has been a debtor or that is or has been associated with a debtor. The prohibition extends only to discrimination or other action based solely on the basis of the bankruptcy, on the basis of insolvency before or during bankruptcy prior to a determination of discharge, or on the basis of nonpayment of a debt discharged in the bankruptcy case (the *Perez* situation). It does not prohibit consideration of other factors, such as future financial responsibility or ability, and does not prohibit imposition of requirements such as net capital rules, if applied nondiscriminatorily.

In addition, the section is not exhaustive. The enumeration of various forms of discrimination against former bankrupts is not intended to permit other forms of discrimination. The courts have been developing the *Perez* rule. This section permits further development to prohibit actions by governmental or quasi-governmental organizations that perform licensing functions, such as a State bar association or a medical society, or by other organizations that can seriously affect the debtors' livelihood or fresh start, such as exclusion from a union on the basis of discharge of a debt to the union's credit union.

The effect of the section, and of further interpretations of the *Perez* rule, is to strengthen the anti-reaffirmation policy found in section 524(b). Discrimination based solely on nonpayment could encourage reaffirmations, contrary to the expressed policy.

The section is not so broad as a comparable section proposed by the Bankruptcy Commission, S. 236, 94th Cong., 1st Sess. §4–508 (1975), which would have extended the prohibition to any discrimination, even by private parties. Nevertheless, it is not limiting either, as noted. The courts will continue to mark the contours of the anti-discrimination provision in pursuit of sound bankruptcy policy.

References in Text

The Perishable Agricultural Commodities Act, 1930, referred to in subsec. (a), is act June 10, 1930, ch. 436, 46 Stat. 531, which is classified generally to chapter 20A (§499a et seq.) of Title 7, Agriculture. For complete classification of this Act to the Code, see section 499a(a) of Title 7 and Tables.

The Packers and Stockyards Act, 1921, referred to in subsec. (a), is act Aug. 15, 1921, ch. 64, 42 Stat. 159, which is classified generally to chapter 9 (§181 et seq.) of Title 7. For complete classification of this Act to the Code, see section 181 of Title 7 and Tables.

Section 1 of the Act entitled "An Act making appropriations for the Department of Agriculture for the fiscal year ending June 30, 1944, and for other purposes," approved July 12, 1943, referred to in subsec. (a), is classified to section 204 of Title 7.

The Bankruptcy Act, referred to in text, is act July 1, 1898, ch. 541, 30 Stat. 544, as amended, which was classified generally to former Title 11.

The Higher Education Act of 1965, referred to in subsec. (c)(2), is Pub. L. 89–329, Nov. 8, 1965, 79 Stat. 1219. Title IV of the Act is classified generally to subchapter IV (§1070 et seq.) of chapter 28 of Title 20, Education. For complete classification of this Act to the Code, see Short Title note set out under section 1001 of Title 20 and Tables.

Amendments

2005—Subsec. (c)(1). Pub. L. 109–8, §1211(1), inserted "student" before "grant, loan,".

Subsec. (c)(2). Pub. L. 109–8, §1211(2), substituted "any program operated under" for "the program operated under part B, D, or E of".

1994—Subsec. (a). Pub. L. 103–394, §501(d)(15), struck out "(7 U.S.C. 499a–499s)" after "Act, 1930", "(7 U.S.C. 181–229)" after "Act, 1921", and "(57 Stat. 422; 7 U.S.C. 204)" after "July 12, 1943".

Subsec. (c). Pub. L. 103–394, §313, added subsec. (c).

1984—Pub. L. 98–353 designated existing provisions as subsec. (a), inserted "the" before "Perishable", and added subsec. (b).

Effective Date of 2005 Amendment

Amendment by Pub. L. 109–8 effective 180 days after Apr. 20, 2005, and not applicable with respect to cases commenced under this title before such effective date, except as otherwise provided, see section 1501 of Pub. L. 109–8, set out as a note under section 101 of this title.

Effective Date of 1994 Amendment

Amendment by Pub. L. 103–394 effective Oct. 22, 1994, and not applicable with respect to cases commenced under this title before Oct. 22, 1994, see section 702 of Pub. L. 103–394, set out as a note under section 101 of this title.

Effective Date of 1984 Amendment

Amendment by Pub. L. 98–353 effective with respect to cases filed 90 days after July 10, 1984, see section 552(a) of Pub. L. 98–353, set out as a note under section 101 of this title.

§526. Restrictions on debt relief agencies

(a) A debt relief agency shall not—

(1) fail to perform any service that such agency informed an assisted person or prospective assisted person it would provide in connection with a case or proceeding under this title;

(2) make any statement, or counsel or advise any assisted person or prospective assisted person to make a statement in a document filed in a case or proceeding under this title, that is untrue or misleading, or that upon the exercise of reasonable care, should have been known by such agency to be untrue or misleading;

(3) misrepresent to any assisted person or prospective assisted person, directly or indirectly, affirmatively or by material omission, with respect to—

(A) the services that such agency will provide to such person; or

(B) the benefits and risks that may result if such person becomes a debtor in a case under this title; or

(4) advise an assisted person or prospective assisted person to incur more debt in contemplation of such person filing a case under this title or to pay an attorney or bankruptcy petition preparer a fee or charge for services performed as part of preparing for or representing a debtor in a case under this title.

(b) Any waiver by any assisted person of any protection or right provided under this section shall not be enforceable against the debtor by any Federal or State court or any other person, but may be enforced against a debt relief agency.

(c)(1) Any contract for bankruptcy assistance between a debt relief agency and an assisted person that does not comply with the material requirements of this section, section 527, or section 528 shall be void and may not be enforced by any Federal or State court or by any other person, other than such assisted person.

(2) Any debt relief agency shall be liable to an assisted person in the amount of any fees or charges in connection with providing bankruptcy assistance to such person that such debt relief agency has received, for actual damages, and for reasonable attorneys' fees and costs if such agency is found, after notice and a hearing, to have—

(A) intentionally or negligently failed to comply with any provision of this section, section 527, or section 528 with respect to a case or proceeding under this title for such assisted person;

(B) provided bankruptcy assistance to an assisted person in a case or proceeding under this title that is dismissed or converted to a case under another chapter of this title because of such agency's intentional or negligent failure to file any required document including those specified in section 521; or

(C) intentionally or negligently disregarded the material requirements of this title or the Federal Rules of Bankruptcy Procedure applicable to such agency.

(3) In addition to such other remedies as are provided under State law, whenever the chief law enforcement officer of a State, or an official or agency designated by a State, has reason to believe that any person has violated or is violating this section, the State—

(A) may bring an action to enjoin such violation;

(B) may bring an action on behalf of its residents to recover the actual damages of assisted persons arising from such violation, including any liability under paragraph (2); and

(C) in the case of any successful action under subparagraph (A) or (B), shall be awarded the costs of the action and reasonable attorneys' fees as determined by the court.

(4) The district courts of the United States for districts located in the State shall have concurrent jurisdiction of any action under subparagraph (A) or (B) of paragraph (3).

(5) Notwithstanding any other provision of Federal law and in addition to any other remedy provided under Federal or State law, if the court, on its own motion or on the motion of the United States trustee or the debtor, finds that a person intentionally violated this section, or engaged in a clear and consistent pattern or practice of violating this section, the court may—

(A) enjoin the violation of such section; or

(B) impose an appropriate civil penalty against such person.

(d) No provision of this section, section 527, or section 528 shall—

(1) annul, alter, affect, or exempt any person subject to such sections from complying with any law of any State except to the extent that such law is inconsistent with those sections, and then only to the extent of the inconsistency; or

(2) be deemed to limit or curtail the authority or ability—

(A) of a State or subdivision or instrumentality thereof, to determine and enforce qualifications for the practice of law under the laws of that State; or

(B) of a Federal court to determine and enforce the qualifications for the practice of law before that court.

(Added Pub. L. 109–8, title II, §227(a), Apr. 20, 2005, 119 Stat. 67; amended Pub. L. 111–327, §2(a)(20), Dec. 22, 2010, 124 Stat. 3560.)

References in Text

The Federal Rules of Bankruptcy Procedure, referred to in subsec. (c)(2)(C), are set out in the Appendix to this title.

Amendments

2010—Subsec. (a)(2). Pub. L. 111–327, §2(a)(20)(A), substituted "that is untrue or" for "that is untrue and".

Subsec. (a)(4). Pub. L. 111–327, §2(a)(20)(B), inserted "a" after "preparer".

Effective Date

Section effective 180 days after Apr. 20, 2005, and not applicable with respect to cases commenced under this title before such effective date, except as otherwise provided, see section 1501 of Pub. L. 109–8, set out as an Effective Date of 2005 Amendment note under section 101 of this title.

§527. Disclosures

(a) A debt relief agency providing bankruptcy assistance to an assisted person shall provide—

(1) the written notice required under section 342(b)(1); and

(2) to the extent not covered in the written notice described in paragraph (1), and not later than 3 business days after the first date on which a debt relief agency first offers to provide any bankruptcy assistance services to an assisted person, a clear and conspicuous written notice advising assisted persons that—

(A) all information that the assisted person is required to provide with a petition and thereafter during a case under this title is required to be complete, accurate, and truthful;

(B) all assets and all liabilities are required to be completely and accurately disclosed in the documents filed to commence the case, and the replacement value of each asset as defined in section 506 must be stated in those documents where requested after reasonable inquiry to establish such value;

(C) current monthly income, the amounts specified in section 707(b)(2), and, in a case under chapter 13 of this title, disposable income (determined in accordance with section 707(b)(2)), are required to be stated after reasonable inquiry; and

(D) information that an assisted person provides during their case may be audited pursuant to this title, and that failure to provide such information may result in dismissal of the case under this title or other sanction, including a criminal sanction.

(b) A debt relief agency providing bankruptcy assistance to an assisted person shall provide each assisted person at the same time as the notices required under subsection (a)(1) the following statement, to the extent applicable, or one substantially similar. The statement shall be clear and conspicuous and shall be in a single document separate from other documents or notices provided to the assisted person:

"IMPORTANT INFORMATION ABOUT BANKRUPTCY ASSISTANCE SERVICES FROM AN ATTORNEY OR BANKRUPTCY PETITION PREPARER.

"If you decide to seek bankruptcy relief, you can represent yourself, you can hire an attorney to represent you, or you can get help in some localities from a bankruptcy petition preparer who is not an attorney. THE LAW REQUIRES AN ATTORNEY OR BANKRUPTCY PETITION PREPARER TO GIVE YOU A WRITTEN CONTRACT SPECIFYING WHAT THE ATTORNEY OR BANKRUPTCY PETITION PREPARER WILL DO FOR YOU AND HOW MUCH IT WILL COST. Ask to see the contract before you hire anyone.

"The following information helps you understand what must be done in a routine bankruptcy case to help you evaluate how much service you need. Although bankruptcy can be complex, many cases are routine.

"Before filing a bankruptcy case, either you or your attorney should analyze your eligibility for different forms of debt relief available under the Bankruptcy Code and which form of relief is most likely to be beneficial for you. Be sure you understand the relief you can obtain and its limitations. To file a bankruptcy case, documents called a Petition, Schedules, and Statement of Financial Affairs, and in some cases a Statement of Intention, need to be prepared correctly and filed with the bankruptcy court. You will have to pay a filing fee to the bankruptcy court. Once your case starts, you will have to attend the required first meeting of creditors where you may be questioned by a court official called a 'trustee' and by creditors.

"If you choose to file a chapter 7 case, you may be asked by a creditor to reaffirm a debt. You may want help deciding whether to do so. A creditor is not permitted to coerce you into reaffirming your debts.

"If you choose to file a chapter 13 case in which you repay your creditors what you can afford over 3 to 5 years, you may also want help with preparing your chapter 13 plan and with the confirmation hearing on your plan which will be before a bankruptcy judge.

"If you select another type of relief under the Bankruptcy Code other than chapter 7 or chapter 13, you will want to find out what should be done from someone familiar with that type of relief.

"Your bankruptcy case may also involve litigation. You are generally permitted to represent yourself in litigation in bankruptcy court, but only attorneys, not bankruptcy petition preparers, can give you legal advice.".

(c) Except to the extent the debt relief agency provides the required information itself after reasonably diligent inquiry of the assisted person or others so as to obtain such information reasonably accurately for inclusion on the petition, schedules or statement of financial affairs, a debt relief agency providing bankruptcy assistance to an assisted person, to the extent permitted by nonbankruptcy law, shall provide each assisted person at the time required for the notice required under subsection (a)(1) reasonably sufficient information (which shall be provided in a clear and conspicuous writing) to the assisted person on how to provide all the information the assisted person is required to provide under this title pursuant to section 521, including—

(1) how to value assets at replacement value, determine current monthly income, the amounts specified in section 707(b)(2) and, in a chapter 13 case, how to determine disposable income in accordance with section 707(b)(2) and related calculations;

(2) how to complete the list of creditors, including how to determine what amount is owed and what address for the creditor should be shown; and

(3) how to determine what property is exempt and how to value exempt property at replacement value as defined in section 506.

(d) A debt relief agency shall maintain a copy of the notices required under subsection (a) of this section for 2 years after the date on which the notice is given the assisted person.

(Added Pub. L. 109–8, title II, §228(a), Apr. 20, 2005, 119 Stat. 69; amended Pub. L. 111–327, §2(a)(21), Dec. 22, 2010, 124 Stat. 3560.)

Amendments

2010—Subsec. (b). Pub. L. 111–327 substituted "Schedules, and Statement of Financial Affairs, and in some cases a Statement of Intention," for "Schedules and Statement of Financial Affairs, as well as in some cases a Statement of Intention" in third sentence of fourth undesignated par.

Effective Date

Section effective 180 days after Apr. 20, 2005, and not applicable with respect to cases commenced under this title before such effective date, except as otherwise provided, see section 1501 of Pub. L. 109–8, set out as an Effective Date of 2005 Amendment note under section 101 of this title.

§528. Requirements for debt relief agencies

(a) A debt relief agency shall—

(1) not later than 5 business days after the first date on which such agency provides any bankruptcy assistance services to an assisted person, but prior to such assisted person's petition under this title being filed, execute a written contract with such assisted person that explains clearly and conspicuously—

(A) the services such agency will provide to such assisted person; and

(B) the fees or charges for such services, and the terms of payment;

(2) provide the assisted person with a copy of the fully executed and completed contract;

(3) clearly and conspicuously disclose in any advertisement of bankruptcy assistance services or of the benefits of bankruptcy directed to the general public (whether in general media, seminars or specific mailings, telephonic or electronic messages, or otherwise) that the services or benefits are with respect to bankruptcy relief under this title; and

(4) clearly and conspicuously use the following statement in such advertisement: "We are a debt relief agency. We help people file for bankruptcy relief under the Bankruptcy Code." or a substantially similar statement.

(b)(1) An advertisement of bankruptcy assistance services or of the benefits of bankruptcy directed to the general public includes—

(A) descriptions of bankruptcy assistance in connection with a chapter 13 plan whether or not chapter 13 is specifically mentioned in such advertisement; and

(B) statements such as "federally supervised repayment plan" or "Federal debt restructuring help" or other similar statements that could lead a reasonable consumer to believe that debt counseling was being offered when in fact the services were directed to providing bankruptcy assistance with a chapter 13 plan or other form of bankruptcy relief under this title.

(2) An advertisement, directed to the general public, indicating that the debt relief agency provides assistance with respect to credit defaults, mortgage foreclosures, eviction proceedings, excessive debt, debt collection pressure, or inability to pay any consumer debt shall—

(A) disclose clearly and conspicuously in such advertisement that the assistance may involve bankruptcy relief under this title; and

(B) include the following statement: "We are a debt relief agency. We help people file for bankruptcy relief under the Bankruptcy Code." or a substantially similar statement.

(Added Pub. L. 109–8, title II, §229(a), Apr. 20, 2005, 119 Stat. 71.)

Effective Date

Section effective 180 days after Apr. 20, 2005, and not applicable with respect to cases commenced under this title before such effective date, except as otherwise provided, see section 1501 of Pub. L. 109–8, set out as an Effective Date of 2005 Amendment note under section 101 of this title.

SUBCHAPTER III—THE ESTATE

§541. Property of the estate

(a) The commencement of a case under section 301, 302, or 303 of this title creates an estate. Such estate is comprised of all the following property, wherever located and by whomever held:

(1) Except as provided in subsections (b) and (c)(2) of this section, all legal or equitable interests of the debtor in property as of the commencement of the case.

(2) All interests of the debtor and the debtor's spouse in community property as of the commencement of the case that is—

(A) under the sole, equal, or joint management and control of the debtor; or

(B) liable for an allowable claim against the debtor, or for both an allowable claim against the debtor and an allowable claim against the debtor's spouse, to the extent that such interest is so liable.

(3) Any interest in property that the trustee recovers under section 329(b), 363(n), 543, 550, 553, or 723 of this title.

(4) Any interest in property preserved for the benefit of or ordered transferred to the estate under section 510(c) or 551 of this title.

(5) Any interest in property that would have been property of the estate if such interest had been an interest of the debtor on the date of the filing of the petition, and that the debtor acquires or becomes entitled to acquire within 180 days after such date—

(A) by bequest, devise, or inheritance;

(B) as a result of a property settlement agreement with the debtor's spouse, or of an interlocutory or final divorce decree; or

(C) as a beneficiary of a life insurance policy or of a death benefit plan.

(6) Proceeds, product, offspring, rents, or profits of or from property of the estate, except such as are earnings from services performed by an individual debtor after the commencement of the case.

(7) Any interest in property that the estate acquires after the commencement of the case.

(b) Property of the estate does not include—

(1) any power that the debtor may exercise solely for the benefit of an entity other than the debtor;

(2) any interest of the debtor as a lessee under a lease of nonresidential real property that has terminated at the expiration of the stated term of such lease before the commencement of the case under this title, and ceases to include any interest of the debtor as a lessee under a lease of nonresidential real property that has terminated at the expiration of the stated term of such lease during the case;

(3) any eligibility of the debtor to participate in programs authorized under the Higher Education Act of 1965 (20 U.S.C. 1001 et seq.; 42 U.S.C. 2751 et seq.),[1] or any accreditation status or State licensure of the debtor as an educational institution;

(4) any interest of the debtor in liquid or gaseous hydrocarbons to the extent that—

(A)(i) the debtor has transferred or has agreed to transfer such interest pursuant to a farmout agreement or any written agreement directly related to a farmout agreement; and

(ii) but for the operation of this paragraph, the estate could include the interest referred to in clause (i) only by virtue of section 365 or 544(a)(3) of this title; or

(B)(i) the debtor has transferred such interest pursuant to a written conveyance of a production payment to an entity that does not participate in the operation of the property from which such production payment is transferred; and

(ii) but for the operation of this paragraph, the estate could include the interest referred to in clause (i) only by virtue of section 365 or 542 of this title;

(5) funds placed in an education individual retirement account (as defined in section 530(b)(1) of the Internal Revenue Code of 1986) not later than 365 days before the date of the filing of the petition in a case under this title, but—

(A) only if the designated beneficiary of such account was a child, stepchild, grandchild, or stepgrandchild of the debtor for the taxable year for which funds were placed in such account;

(B) only to the extent that such funds—

(i) are not pledged or promised to any entity in connection with any extension of credit; and

(ii) are not excess contributions (as described in section 4973(e) of the Internal Revenue Code of 1986); and

(C) in the case of funds placed in all such accounts having the same designated beneficiary not earlier than 720 days nor later than 365 days before such date, only so much of such funds as does not exceed $5,000;[2]

(6) funds used to purchase a tuition credit or certificate or contributed to an account in accordance with section 529(b)(1)(A) of the Internal Revenue Code of 1986 under a qualified State tuition program (as defined in section 529(b)(1) of such Code) not later than 365 days before the date of the filing of the petition in a case under this title, but—

(A) only if the designated beneficiary of the amounts paid or contributed to such tuition program was a child, stepchild, grandchild, or stepgrandchild of the debtor for the taxable year for which funds were paid or contributed;

(B) with respect to the aggregate amount paid or contributed to such program having the same designated beneficiary, only so much of such amount as does not exceed the total contributions permitted under section 529(b)(6) of such Code with respect to such beneficiary, as adjusted beginning on the date of the filing of the petition in a case under this title by the annual increase or decrease (rounded to the nearest tenth of 1 percent) in the education expenditure category of the Consumer Price Index prepared by the Department of Labor; and

(C) in the case of funds paid or contributed to such program having the same designated beneficiary not earlier than 720 days nor later than 365 days before such date, only so much of such funds as does not exceed $5,000;[2]

(7) any amount—

(A) withheld by an employer from the wages of employees for payment as contributions—

(i) to—

(I) an employee benefit plan that is subject to title I of the Employee Retirement Income Security Act of 1974 or under an employee benefit plan which is a governmental plan under section 414(d) of the Internal Revenue Code of 1986;

(II) a deferred compensation plan under section 457 of the Internal Revenue Code of 1986; or

(III) a tax-deferred annuity under section 403(b) of the Internal Revenue Code of 1986;

except that such amount under this subparagraph shall not constitute disposable income as defined in section 1325(b)(2); or

(ii) to a health insurance plan regulated by State law whether or not subject to such title; or

(B) received by an employer from employees for payment as contributions—

(i) to—

(I) an employee benefit plan that is subject to title I of the Employee Retirement Income Security Act of 1974 or under an employee benefit plan which is a governmental plan under section 414(d) of the Internal Revenue Code of 1986;

(II) a deferred compensation plan under section 457 of the Internal Revenue Code of 1986; or

(III) a tax-deferred annuity under section 403(b) of the Internal Revenue Code of 1986;

except that such amount under this subparagraph shall not constitute disposable income, as defined in section 1325(b)(2); or

(ii) to a health insurance plan regulated by State law whether or not subject to such title;

(8) subject to subchapter III of chapter 5, any interest of the debtor in property where the debtor pledged or sold tangible personal property (other than securities or written or printed evidences of indebtedness or title) as collateral for a loan or advance of money given by a person licensed under law to make such loans or advances, where—

(A) the tangible personal property is in the possession of the pledgee or transferee;

(B) the debtor has no obligation to repay the money, redeem the collateral, or buy back the property at a stipulated price; and

(C) neither the debtor nor the trustee have exercised any right to redeem provided under the contract or State law, in a timely manner as provided under State law and section 108(b);

(9) any interest in cash or cash equivalents that constitute proceeds of a sale by the debtor of a money order that is made—

(A) on or after the date that is 14 days prior to the date on which the petition is filed; and

(B) under an agreement with a money order issuer that prohibits the commingling of such proceeds with property of the debtor (notwithstanding that, contrary to the agreement, the proceeds may have been commingled with property of the debtor),

unless the money order issuer had not taken action, prior to the filing of the petition, to require compliance with the prohibition; or

(10) funds placed in an account of a qualified ABLE program (as defined in section 529A(b) of the Internal Revenue Code of 1986) not later than 365 days before the date of the filing of the petition in a case under this title, but—

(A) only if the designated beneficiary of such account was a child, stepchild, grandchild, or stepgrandchild of the debtor for the taxable year for which funds were placed in such account;

(B) only to the extent that such funds—

(i) are not pledged or promised to any entity in connection with any extension of credit; and

(ii) are not excess contributions (as described in section 4973(h) of the Internal Revenue Code of 1986); and

(C) in the case of funds placed in all such accounts having the same designated beneficiary not earlier than 720 days nor later than 365 days before such date, only so much of such funds as does not exceed $6,225.

Paragraph (4) shall not be construed to exclude from the estate any consideration the debtor retains, receives, or is entitled to receive for transferring an interest in liquid or gaseous hydrocarbons pursuant to a farmout agreement.

(c)(1) Except as provided in paragraph (2) of this subsection, an interest of the debtor in property becomes property of the estate under subsection (a)(1), (a)(2), or (a)(5) of this section notwithstanding any provision in an agreement, transfer instrument, or applicable nonbankruptcy law—

(A) that restricts or conditions transfer of such interest by the debtor; or

(B) that is conditioned on the insolvency or financial condition of the debtor, on the commencement of a case under this title, or on the appointment of or taking possession by a trustee in a case under this title or a custodian before such commencement, and that effects or gives an option to effect a forfeiture, modification, or termination of the debtor's interest in property.

(2) A restriction on the transfer of a beneficial interest of the debtor in a trust that is enforceable under applicable nonbankruptcy law is enforceable in a case under this title.

(d) Property in which the debtor holds, as of the commencement of the case, only legal title and not an equitable interest, such as a mortgage secured by real property, or an interest in such a mortgage, sold by the debtor but as to which the debtor retains legal title to service or supervise the servicing of such mortgage or interest, becomes property of the estate under subsection (a)(1) or (2) of this section only to the extent of the debtor's legal title to such property, but not to the extent of any equitable interest in such property that the debtor does not hold.

(e) In determining whether any of the relationships specified in paragraph (5)(A) or (6)(A) of subsection (b) exists, a legally adopted child of an individual (and a child who is a member of an individual's household, if placed with such individual by an authorized placement agency for legal adoption by such individual), or a foster child of an individual (if such child has as the child's principal place of abode the home of the debtor and is a member of the debtor's household) shall be treated as a child of such individual by blood.

(f) Notwithstanding any other provision of this title, property that is held by a debtor that is a corporation described in section 501(c)(3) of the Internal Revenue Code of 1986 and exempt from tax under section 501(a) of such Code may be transferred to an entity that is not such a corporation, but only under the same conditions as would apply if the debtor had not filed a case under this title.

(Pub. L. 95–598, Nov. 6, 1978, 92 Stat. 2594; Pub. L. 98–353, title III, §§363(a), 456, July 10, 1984, 98 Stat. 363, 376; Pub. L. 101–508, title III, §3007(a)(2), Nov. 5, 1990, 104 Stat. 1388–28; Pub. L. 102–486, title XXX, §3017(b), Oct. 24, 1992, 106 Stat. 3130; Pub. L. 103–394, title II, §§208(b), 223, Oct. 22, 1994, 108 Stat. 4124, 4129; Pub. L. 109–8, title II, §225(a), title III, §323, title XII, §§1212, 1221(c), 1230, Apr. 20, 2005, 119 Stat. 65, 97, 194, 196, 201; Pub. L. 111–327, §2(a)(22), Dec. 22, 2010, 124 Stat. 3560; Pub. L. 113–295, div. B, title I, §104(a), Dec. 19, 2014, 128 Stat. 4063.)

Historical and Revision Notes

legislative statements

Section 541(a)(7) is new. The provision clarifies that any interest in property that the estate acquires after the commencement of the case is property of the estate; for example, if the estate enters into a contract, after the commencement of the case, such a contract would be property of the estate. The addition of this provision by the House amendment merely clarifies that section 541(a) is an all-embracing definition which includes charges on property, such as liens held by the debtor on property of a third party, or beneficial rights and interests that the debtor may have in property of another. However, only the debtor's interest in such property becomes property of the estate. If the debtor holds bare legal title or holds property in trust for another, only those rights which the debtor would have otherwise had emanating from such interest pass to the estate under section 541. Neither this section nor section 545 will affect various statutory provisions that give a creditor a lien that is valid both inside and outside bankruptcy against a bona fide purchaser of property from the debtor, or that creates a trust fund for the benefit of creditors meeting similar criteria. See Packers and Stockyards Act §206, 7 U.S.C. 196 (1976).

Section 541(c)(2) follows the position taken in the House bill and rejects the position taken in the Senate amendment with respect to income limitations on a spend-thrift trust.

Section 541(d) of the House amendment is derived from section 541(e) of the Senate amendment and reiterates the general principle that where the debtor holds bare legal title without any equitable interest, that the estate acquires bare legal title without any equitable interest in the property. The purpose of section 541(d) as applied to the secondary mortgage market is identical to the purpose of section 541(e) of the Senate amendment and section 541(d) will accomplish the same result as would have been accomplished by section 541(e). Even if a mortgage seller retains for purposes of servicing legal title to mortgages or interests in mortgages sold in the secondary mortgage market, the trustee would be required by section 541(d) to turn over the mortgages or interests in mortgages to the purchaser of those mortgages.

The seller of mortgages in the secondary mortgage market will often retain the original mortgage notes and related documents and the seller will not endorse the notes to reflect the sale to the purchaser. Similarly, the purchaser will often not record the purchaser's ownership of the mortgages or interests in mortgages under State recording statutes. These facts are irrelevant and the seller's retention of the mortgage documents and the purchaser's decision not to record do not change the trustee's obligation to turn the mortgages or interests in mortgages over to the purchaser. The application of section 541(d) to secondary mortgage market transactions will not be affected by the terms of the servicing agreement between the mortgage servicer and the purchaser of the mortgages. Under section 541(d), the trustee is required to recognize the purchaser's title to the mortgages or interests in mortgages and to turn this property over to the purchaser. It makes no difference whether the servicer and the purchaser characterize their relationship as one of trust, agency, or independent contractor.

The purpose of section 541(d) as applied to the secondary mortgage market is therefore to make certain that secondary mortgage market sales as they are currently structured are not subject to challenge by bankruptcy trustees and that purchasers of mortgages will be able to obtain the mortgages or interests in mortgages which they have purchased from trustees without the trustees asserting that a sale of mortgages is a loan from the purchaser to the seller.

Thus, as section 541(a)(1) clearly states, the estate is comprised of all legal or equitable interests of the debtor in property as of the commencement of the case. To the extent such an interest is limited in the hands of the debtor, it is equally limited in the hands of the estate except to the extent that defenses which are personal against the debtor are not effective against the estate.

Property of the estate: The Senate amendment provided that property of the estate does not include amounts held by the debtor as trustee and any taxes withheld or collected from others before the commencement of the case. The House amendment removes these two provisions. As to property held by the debtor as a trustee, the House amendment provides that property of the estate will include whatever interest the debtor held in the property at the commencement of the case. Thus, where the debtor held only legal title to the property and the beneficial interest in that property belongs to another, such as exists in the case of property held in trust, the property of the estate includes the legal title, but not the beneficial interest in the property.

As to withheld taxes, the House amendment deletes the rule in the Senate bill as unnecessary since property of the estate does not include the beneficial interest in property held by the debtor as a trustee. Under the Internal Revenue Code of 1954 (section 7501) [26 U.S.C. 7501], the amounts of withheld taxes are held to be a special fund in trust for the United States. Where the Internal Revenue Service can demonstrate that the amounts of taxes withheld are still in the possession of the debtor at the commencement of the case, then if a trust is created, those amounts are not property of the estate. Compare *In re Shakesteers Coffee Shops*, 546 F.2d 821 (9th Cir. 1976) with *In re Glynn Wholesale Building Materials, Inc.* (S.D. Ga. 1978) and *In re Progress Tech Colleges, Inc.*, 42 Aftr 2d 78–5573 (S.D. Ohio 1977).

Where it is not possible for the Internal Revenue Service to demonstrate that the amounts of taxes withheld are still in the possession of the debtor at the commencement of the case, present law generally includes amounts of withheld taxes as property of the estate. See, e.g., *United States v. Randall*, 401 U.S. 513 (1973) [91 S. Ct. 991, 28 L.Ed.2d 273] and *In re Tamasha Town and Country Club*, 483 F.2d 1377 (9th Cir. 1973). Nonetheless, a serious problem exists where "trust fund taxes" withheld from others are held to be property of the estate where the withheld amounts are commingled with other assets of the debtor. The courts should permit the use of reasonable assumptions under which the Internal Revenue Service, and other tax authorities, can demonstrate that amounts of withheld taxes are still in the possession of the debtor at the commencement of the case. For example, where the debtor had commingled that amount of withheld taxes in his general checking account, it might be reasonable to assume that any remaining amounts in that account on the commencement of the case are the withheld taxes. In addition, Congress may consider future amendments to the Internal Revenue Code [title 26] making clear that amounts of withheld taxes are held by the debtor in a trust relationship and, consequently, that such amounts are not property of the estate.

senate report no. 95–989

This section defines property of the estate, and specifies what property becomes property of the estate. The commencement of a bankruptcy case creates an estate. Under paragraph (1) of subsection (a), the estate is comprised of all legal or equitable interest of the debtor in property, wherever located, as of the commencement of the case. The scope of this paragraph is broad. It includes all kinds of property, including tangible or intangible property, causes of action (see Bankruptcy Act §70a(6) [section 110(a)(6) of former title 11]), and all other forms of property currently specified in section 70a of the Bankruptcy Act §70a [section 110(a) of former title 11], as well as property recovered by the trustee under section 542 of proposed title 11, if the property recovered was merely out of the possession of the debtor, yet remained "property of the debtor." The debtor's interest in property also includes "title" to property, which is an interest, just as are a possessory interest, or lease-hold interest, for example. The result of *Segal v. Rochelle*, 382 U.S. 375 (1966), is followed, and the right to a refund is property of the estate.

Though this paragraph will include choses in action and claims by the debtor against others, it is not intended to expand the debtor's rights against others more than they exist at the commencement of the case. For example, if the debtor has a claim that is barred at the time of the commencement of the case by the statute of limitations, then the trustee would not be able to pursue that claim, because he too would be barred. He could take no greater rights than the debtor himself had. But see proposed 11 U.S.C. 108, which would permit the trustee a tolling of the statute of limitations if it had not run before the date of the filing of the petition.

Paragraph (1) has the effect of overruling *Lockwood v. Exchange Bank*, 190 U.S. 294 (1903), because it includes as property of the estate all property of the debtor, even that needed for a fresh start. After the property comes into the estate, then the debtor is permitted to exempt it under proposed 11 U.S.C. 522, and the court will have jurisdiction to determine what property may be exempted and what remains as property of the estate. The broad jurisdictional grant in proposed 28 U.S.C. 1334 would have the effect of overruling *Lockwood* independently of the change made by this provision.

Paragraph (1) also has the effect of overruling *Lines v. Frederick*, 400 U.S. 18 (1970).

Situations occasionally arise where property ostensibly belonging to the debtor will actually not be property of the debtor, but will be held in trust for another. For example, if the debtor has incurred medical bills that were covered by insurance, and the insurance company had sent the payment of the bills to the debtor before the debtor had paid the bill for which the payment was reimbursement, the payment would actually be held in a constructive trust for the person to whom the bill was owed. This section and proposed 11 U.S.C. 545 also will not affect various statutory provisions that give a creditor of the debtor a lien that is valid outside as well as inside bankruptcy, or that creates a trust fund for the benefit of a creditor of the debtor. See Packers and Stockyards Act §206, 7 U.S.C. 196.

Bankruptcy Act §8 [section 26 of former title 11] has been deleted as unnecessary. Once the estate is created, no interests in property of the estate remain in the debtor. Consequently, if the debtor dies during the case, only property exempted from property of the estate or acquired by the debtor after the commencement of the case and not included as property of the estate will be available to the representative of the debtor's probate estate. The bankruptcy proceeding will continue in rem with respect to property of the state, and the discharge will apply in personam to relieve the debtor, and thus his probate representative, of liability for dischargeable debts.

The estate also includes the interests of the debtor and the debtor's spouse in community property, subject to certain limitations; property that the trustee recovers under the avoiding powers; property that the debtor acquires by bequest, devise, inheritance, a property settlement agreement with the debtor's spouse, or as the beneficiary of a life insurance policy within 180 days after the petition; and proceeds, product, offspring, rents, and profits of or from property of the estate, except such as are earning from services performed by an individual debtor after the commencement of the case. Proceeds here is not used in a confining sense, as defined in the Uniform Commercial Code, but is intended to be a broad term to encompass all proceeds of property of the estate. The conversion in form of property of the estate does not change its character as property of the estate.

Subsection (b) excludes from property of the estate any power, such as a power of appointment, that the debtor may exercise solely for the benefit of an entity other than the debtor. This changes present law which excludes powers solely benefiting other persons but not other entities.

Subsection (c) invalidates restrictions on the transfer of property of the debtor, in order that all of the interests of the debtor in property will become property of the estate. The provisions invalidated are those that restrict or condition transfer of the debtor's interest, and those that are conditioned on the insolvency or financial condition of the debtor, on the commencement of a bankruptcy case, or on the appointment of a custodian of the debtor's property. Paragraph (2) of subsection (c), however, preserves restrictions on a transfer of a spendthrift trust that the restriction is enforceable nonbankruptcy law to the extent of the income reasonably necessary for the support of a debtor and his dependents.

Subsection (d) [enacted as (e)], derived from section 70c of the Bankruptcy Act [section 110(c) of former title 11], gives the estate the benefit of all defenses available to the debtor as against an entity other than the estate, including such defenses as statutes of limitations, statutes of frauds, usury, and other personal defenses, and makes waiver by the debtor after the commencement of the case ineffective to bind the estate.

Section 541(e) [enacted as (d)] confirms the current status under the Bankruptcy Act [former title 11] of bona fide secondary mortgage market transactions as the purchase and sale of assets. Mortgages or interests in mortgages sold in the secondary market should not be considered as part of the debtor's estate. To permit the efficient servicing of mortgages or interests in mortgages the seller often retains the original mortgage notes and related documents, and the purchaser records under State recording statutes the purchaser's ownership of the mortgages or interests in mortgages purchased. Section 541(e) makes clear that the seller's retention of the mortgage documents and the purchaser's decision not to record do not impair the asset sale character of secondary mortgage market transactions. The committee notes that in secondary mortgage market transactions the parties may characterize their relationship as one of trust, agency, or independent contractor. The characterization adopted by the parties should not affect the statutes in bankruptcy on bona fide secondary mortgage market purchases and sales.

References in Text

The Higher Education Act of 1965, referred to in subsec. (b)(3), is Pub. L. 89–329, Nov. 8, 1965, 79 Stat. 1219, which is classified generally to chapter 28 (§1001 et seq.) of Title 20, Education. Part C of title IV of the Act was formerly classified to part C (§2751 et seq.) of subchapter I of chapter 34 of Title 42, The Public Health and Welfare, prior to transfer to part C (§1087–51 et seq.) of subchapter IV of chapter 28 of Title 20. For complete classification of this Act to the Code, see Short Title note set out under section 1001 of Title 20 and Tables.

The Internal Revenue Code of 1986, referred to in subsecs. (b)(5) to (7), (10) and (f), is classified generally to Title 26, Internal Revenue Code.

The Employee Retirement Income Security Act of 1974, referred to in subsec. (b)(7)(A)(i)(I), (B)(i)(I), is Pub. L. 93–406, Sept. 2, 1974, 88 Stat. 829, as amended. Title I of the Act is classified generally to subchapter I (§1001 et seq.) of chapter 18 of Title 29, Labor. For complete classification of this Act to the Code, see Short Title note set out under section 1001 of Title 29 and Tables.

Amendments

2014—Subsec. (b)(10). Pub. L. 113–295 added par. (10).

2010—Subsec. (b)(6)(B). Pub. L. 111–327 substituted "section 529(b)(6)" for "section 529(b)(7)".

2005—Subsec. (b)(4). Pub. L. 109–8, §225(a)(1)(A), struck out "or" at end.

Subsec. (b)(4)(B)(ii). Pub. L. 109–8, §1212, inserted "365 or" before "542".

Subsec. (b)(5), (6). Pub. L. 109–8, §225(a)(1)(C), added pars. (5) and (6). Former par. (5) redesignated (9).

Subsec. (b)(7). Pub. L. 109–8, §323, added par. (7).

Subsec. (b)(8). Pub. L. 109–8, §1230, added par. (8).

Subsec. (b)(9). Pub. L. 109–8, §225(a)(1)(B), redesignated par. (5) as (9).

Subsec. (e). Pub. L. 109–8, §225(a)(2), added subsec. (e).

Subsec. (f). Pub. L. 109–8, §1221(c), added subsec. (f).

1994—Subsec. (b)(4). Pub. L. 103–394, §208(b), designated existing provisions of subpar. (A) as cl. (i) of subpar. (A), redesignated subpar. (B) as cl. (ii) of subpar. (A), substituted "the interest referred to in clause (i)" for "such interest", substituted "; or" for period at end of cl. (ii), and added subpar. (B).

Pub. L. 103–394, §223(2), which directed the amendment of subsec. (b)(4) by striking out period at end and inserting "; or", was executed by inserting "or" after semicolon at end of subsec. (b)(4)(B)(ii), as added by Pub. L. 103–394, §208(b)(3), to reflect the probable intent of Congress.

Subsec. (b)(5). Pub. L. 103–394, §223, added par. (5).

1992—Subsec. (b). Pub. L. 102–486 added par. (4) and closing provisions.

1990—Subsec. (b)(3). Pub. L. 101–508 added par. (3).

1984—Subsec. (a). Pub. L. 98–353, §456(a)(1), (2), struck out "under" after "under" and inserted "and by whomever held" after "located".

Subsec. (a)(3). Pub. L. 98–353, §456(a)(3), inserted "329(b), 363(n),".

Subsec. (a)(5). Pub. L. 98–353, §456(a)(4), substituted "Any" for "An".

Subsec. (a)(6). Pub. L. 98–353, §456(a)(5), substituted "or profits" for "and profits".

Subsec. (b). Pub. L. 98–353, §363(a), amended subsec. (b) generally. Prior to amendment, subsec. (b) read as follows: "Property of the estate does not include any power that the debtor may only exercise solely for the benefit of an entity other than the debtor."

Subsec. (c)(1). Pub. L. 98–353, §456(b)(1), inserted "in an agreement, transfer, instrument, or applicable nonbankruptcy law".

Subsec. (c)(1)(B). Pub. L. 98–353, §456(b)(2), substituted "taking" for "the taking", and inserted "before such commencement" after "custodian".

Subsec. (d). Pub. L. 98–353, §456(c), inserted "(1) or (2)" after "(a)".

Subsec. (e). Pub. L. 98–353, §456(d), struck out subsec. (e) which read as follows: "The estate shall have the benefit of any defense available to the debtor as against an entity other than the estate, including statutes of limitation, statutes of frauds, usury, and other personal defenses. A waiver of any such defense by the debtor after the commencement of the case does not bind the estate."

Effective Date of 2014 Amendment

Amendment by Pub. L. 113–295 applicable with respect to cases commenced under this title on or after Dec. 19, 2014, see section 104(d) of Pub. L. 113–295, set out as a note under section 521 of this title.

Effective Date of 2005 Amendment

Amendment by section 1221(c) of Pub. L. 109–8 applicable to cases pending under this title on Apr. 20, 2005, or filed under this title on or after Apr. 20, 2005, with certain exceptions, see section 1221(d) of Pub. L. 109–8, set out as a note under section 363 of this title.

Amendment by sections 225(a), 323, 1212, and 1230 of Pub. L. 109–8 effective 180 days after Apr. 20, 2005, and not applicable with respect to cases commenced under this title before such effective date, except as otherwise provided, see section 1501 of Pub. L. 109–8, set out as a note under section 101 of this title.

Effective Date of 1994 Amendment

Amendment by Pub. L. 103–394 effective Oct. 22, 1994, and not applicable with respect to cases commenced under this title before Oct. 22, 1994, see section 702 of Pub. L. 103–394, set out as a note under section 101 of this title.

Effective Date of 1992 Amendment

Amendment by Pub. L. 102–486 effective Oct. 24, 1992, but not applicable with respect to cases commenced under this title before Oct. 24, 1992, see section 3017(c) of Pub. L. 102–486, set out as a note under section 101 of this title.

Effective Date of 1984 Amendment

Amendment by Pub. L. 98–353 effective with respect to cases filed 90 days after July 10, 1984, see section 552(a) of Pub. L. 98–353, set out as a note under section 101 of this title.

Adjustment of Dollar Amounts

The dollar amounts specified in this section were adjusted by notices of the Judicial Conference of the United States pursuant to section 104 of this title as follows:

By notice dated Feb. 16, 2016, 81 F.R. 8748, effective Apr. 1, 2016, in subsec. (b)(5)(C), (6)(C), dollar amount "6,225" was adjusted to "6,425". See notice of the Judicial Conference of the United States set out as a note under section 104 of this title.

By notice dated Feb. 12, 2013, 78 F.R. 12089, effective Apr. 1, 2013, in subsec. (b)(5)(C), (6)(C), dollar amount "5,850" was adjusted to "6,225".

By notice dated Feb. 19, 2010, 75 F.R. 8747, effective Apr. 1, 2010, in subsec. (b)(5)(C), (6)(C), dollar amount "5,475" was adjusted to "5,850".

By notice dated Feb. 7, 2007, 72 F.R. 7082, effective Apr. 1, 2007, in subsec. (b)(5)(C), (6)(C), dollar amount "5,000" was adjusted to "5,475".

[1] See References in Text note below.

[2] See Adjustment of Dollar Amounts notes below.

§542. Turnover of property to the estate

(a) Except as provided in subsection (c) or (d) of this section, an entity, other than a custodian, in possession, custody, or control, during the case, of property that the trustee may use, sell, or lease under section 363 of this title, or that the debtor may exempt under section 522 of this title, shall deliver to the trustee, and account for, such property or the value of such property, unless such property is of inconsequential value or benefit to the estate.

(b) Except as provided in subsection (c) or (d) of this section, an entity that owes a debt that is property of the estate and that is matured, payable on demand, or payable on order, shall pay such debt to, or on the order of, the trustee, except to the extent that such debt may be offset under section 553 of this title against a claim against the debtor.

(c) Except as provided in section 362(a)(7) of this title, an entity that has neither actual notice nor actual knowledge of the commencement of the case concerning the debtor may transfer property of the estate, or pay a debt owing to the debtor, in good faith and other than in the manner specified in subsection (d) of this section, to an entity other than the trustee, with the same effect as to the entity making such transfer or payment as if the case under this title concerning the debtor had not been commenced.

(d) A life insurance company may transfer property of the estate or property of the debtor to such company in good faith, with the same effect with respect to such company as if the case under this title concerning the debtor had not been commenced, if such transfer is to pay a premium or to carry out a nonforfeiture insurance option, and is required to be made automatically, under a life insurance contract with such company that was entered into before the date of the filing of the petition and that is property of the estate.

(e) Subject to any applicable privilege, after notice and a hearing, the court may order an attorney, accountant, or other person that holds recorded information, including books, documents, records, and papers, relating to the debtor's property or financial affairs, to turn over or disclose such recorded information to the trustee.

(Pub. L. 95–598, Nov. 6, 1978, 92 Stat. 2595; Pub. L. 98–353, title III, §457, July 10, 1984, 98 Stat. 376; Pub. L. 103–394, title V, §501(d)(16), Oct. 22, 1994, 108 Stat. 4146.)

Historical and Revision Notes

legislative statements

Section 542(a) of the House amendment modifies similar provisions contained in the House bill and the Senate amendment treating with turnover of property to the estate. The section makes clear that any entity, other than a custodian, is required to deliver property of the estate to the trustee or debtor in possession whenever such property is acquired by the entity during the case, if the trustee or debtor in possession may use, sell, or lease the property under section 363, or if the debtor may exempt the property under section 522, unless the property is of inconsequential value or benefit to the estate. This section is not intended to require an entity to deliver property to the trustee if such entity has obtained an order of the court authorizing the entity to retain possession, custody or control of the property.

The House amendment adopts section 542(c) of the House bill in preference to a similar provision contained in section 542(c) of the Senate amendment. Protection afforded by section 542(c) applies only to the transferor or payor and not to a transferee or payee receiving a transfer or payment, as the case may be. Such transferee or payee is treated under section 549 and section 550 of title 11.

The extent to which the attorney client privilege is valid against the trustee is unclear under current law and is left to be determined by the courts on a case by case basis.

senate report no. 95–989

Subsection (a) of this section requires anyone holding property of the estate on the date of the filing of the petition, or property that the trustee may use, sell, or lease under section 363, to deliver it to the trustee. The subsection also requires an accounting. The holder of property of the estate is excused from the turnover requirement of this subsection if the property held is of inconsequential value to the estate. However, this provision must be read in conjunction with the remainder of the subsection, so that if the property is of inconsequential monetary value, yet has a significant use value for the estate, the holder of the property would not be excused from turnover.

Subsection (b) requires an entity that owes money to the debtor as of the date of the petition, or that holds money payable on demand or payable on order, to pay the money to the order of the trustee. An exception is made to the extent that the entity has a valid right of setoff, as recognized by section 553.

Subsection (c) provides an exception to subsections (a) and (b). It protects an entity that has neither actual notice nor actual knowledge of the case and that transfers, in good faith, property that is deliverable or payable to the trustee to someone other than to the estate or on order of the estate. This subsection codifies the result of *Bank of Marin v. England*, 385 U.S. 99 (1966), but does not go so far as to permit bank setoff in violation of the automatic stay, proposed 11 U.S.C. 362(a)(7), even if the bank offsetting the debtor's balance has no knowledge of the case.

Subsection (d) protects life insurance companies that are required by contract to make automatic premium loans from property that might otherwise be property of the estate.

Subsection (e) requires an attorney, accountant, or other professional that holds recorded information relating to the debtor's property or financial affairs, to surrender it to the trustee. This duty is subject to any applicable claim of privilege, such as attorney-client privilege. It is a new provision that deprives accountants and attorneys of the leverage that they have today, under State law lien provisions, to receive payment in full ahead of other creditors when the information they hold is necessary to the administration of the estate.

Amendments

1994—Subsec. (e). Pub. L. 103–394 substituted "to" for "to to" after "financial affairs,".

1984—Subsec. (e). Pub. L. 98–353 inserted "to turn over or" before "disclose".

Effective Date of 1994 Amendment

Amendment by Pub. L. 103–394 effective Oct. 22, 1994, and not applicable with respect to cases commenced under this title before Oct. 22, 1994, see section 702 of Pub. L. 103–394, set out as a note under section 101 of this title.

Effective Date of 1984 Amendment

Amendment by Pub. L. 98–353 effective with respect to cases filed 90 days after July 10, 1984, see section 552(a) of Pub. L. 98–353, set out as a note under section 101 of this title.

§543. Turnover of property by a custodian

(a) A custodian with knowledge of the commencement of a case under this title concerning the debtor may not make any disbursement from, or take any action in the administration of, property of the debtor, proceeds, product, offspring, rents, or profits of such property, or property of the estate, in the possession, custody, or control of such custodian, except such action as is necessary to preserve such property.

(b) A custodian shall—

(1) deliver to the trustee any property of the debtor held by or transferred to such custodian, or proceeds, product, offspring, rents, or profits of such property, that is in such custodian's possession, custody, or control on the date that such custodian acquires knowledge of the commencement of the case; and

(2) file an accounting of any property of the debtor, or proceeds, product, offspring, rents, or profits of such property, that, at any time, came into the possession, custody, or control of such custodian.

(c) The court, after notice and a hearing, shall—

(1) protect all entities to which a custodian has become obligated with respect to such property or proceeds, product, offspring, rents, or profits of such property;

(2) provide for the payment of reasonable compensation for services rendered and costs and expenses incurred by such custodian; and

(3) surcharge such custodian, other than an assignee for the benefit of the debtor's creditors that was appointed or took possession more than 120 days before the date of the filing of the petition, for any improper or excessive disbursement, other than a disbursement that has been made in accordance with applicable law or that has been approved, after notice and a hearing, by a court of competent jurisdiction before the commencement of the case under this title.

(d) After notice and hearing, the bankruptcy court—

(1) may excuse compliance with subsection (a), (b), or (c) of this section if the interests of creditors and, if the debtor is not insolvent, of equity security holders would be better served by permitting a custodian to continue in possession, custody, or control of such property, and

(2) shall excuse compliance with subsections (a) and (b)(1) of this section if the custodian is an assignee for the benefit of the debtor's creditors that was appointed or took possession more than 120 days before the date of the filing of the petition, unless compliance with such subsections is necessary to prevent fraud or injustice.

(Pub. L. 95–598, Nov. 6, 1978, 92 Stat. 2595; Pub. L. 98–353, title III, §458, July 10, 1984, 98 Stat. 376; Pub. L. 103–394, title V, §501(d)(17), Oct. 22, 1994, 108 Stat. 4146.)

Historical and Revision Notes

legislative statements

Section 543(a) is a modification of similar provisions contained in the House bill and the Senate amendment. The provision clarifies that a custodian may always act as is necessary to preserve property of the debtor. Section 543(c)(3) excepts from surcharge a custodian that is an assignee for the benefit of creditors, who was appointed or took possession before 120 days before the date of the filing of the petition, whichever is later. The provision also prevents a custodian from being surcharged in connection with payments made in accordance with applicable law.

senate report no. 95–989

This section requires a custodian appointed before the bankruptcy case to deliver to the trustee and to account for property that has come into his possession, custody, or control as a custodian. "Property of the debtor" in section (a) includes property that was property of the debtor at the time the custodian took the property, but the title to which passed to the custodian. The section requires the court to protect any obligations incurred by the custodian, provide for the payment of reasonable compensation for services rendered and costs and expenses incurred by the custodian, and to surcharge the custodian for any improper or excessive disbursement, unless it has been approved by a court of competent jurisdiction. Subsection (d) reinforces the general abstention policy in section 305 by permitting the bankruptcy court to authorize the custodianship to proceed notwithstanding this section.

Amendments

1994—Subsec. (d)(1). Pub. L. 103–394 struck out comma after "section".

1984—Subsec. (a). Pub. L. 98–353, §458(a), inserted ", product, offspring, rents, or profits" after "proceeds".

Subsec. (b)(1). Pub. L. 98–353, §458(b)(1), inserted "held by or" after "debtor", and ", product, offspring, rents, or profits" after "proceeds".

Subsec. (b)(2). Pub. L. 98–353, §458(b)(2), inserted ", product, offspring, rents, or profits" after "proceeds".

Subsec. (c)(1). Pub. L. 98–353, §458(c)(1), inserted "or proceeds, product, offspring, rents, or profits of such property" after "property".

Subsec. (c)(3). Pub. L. 98–353, §458(c)(2), inserted "that has been" before "approved".

Subsec. (d). Pub. L. 98–353, §458(d), designated existing provisions as par. (1) and added par. (2).

Effective Date of 1994 Amendment

Amendment by Pub. L. 103–394 effective Oct. 22, 1994, and not applicable with respect to cases commenced under this title before Oct. 22, 1994, see section 702 of Pub. L. 103–394, set out as a note under section 101 of this title.

Effective Date of 1984 Amendment

Amendment by Pub. L. 98–353 effective with respect to cases filed 90 days after July 10, 1984, see section 552(a) of Pub. L. 98–353, set out as a note under section 101 of this title.

§544. Trustee as lien creditor and as successor to certain creditors and purchasers

(a) The trustee shall have, as of the commencement of the case, and without regard to any knowledge of the trustee or of any creditor, the rights and powers of, or may avoid any transfer of property of the debtor or any obligation incurred by the debtor that is voidable by—

(1) a creditor that extends credit to the debtor at the time of the commencement of the case, and that obtains, at such time and with respect to such credit, a judicial lien on all property on which a creditor on a simple contract could have obtained such a judicial lien, whether or not such a creditor exists;

(2) a creditor that extends credit to the debtor at the time of the commencement of the case, and obtains, at such time and with respect to such credit, an execution against the debtor that is returned unsatisfied at such time, whether or not such a creditor exists; or

(3) a bona fide purchaser of real property, other than fixtures, from the debtor, against whom applicable law permits such transfer to be perfected, that obtains the status of a bona fide purchaser and has perfected such transfer at the time of the commencement of the case, whether or not such a purchaser exists.

(b)(1) Except as provided in paragraph (2), the trustee may avoid any transfer of an interest of the debtor in property or any obligation incurred by the debtor that is voidable under applicable law by a creditor holding an unsecured claim that is allowable under section 502 of this title or that is not allowable only under section 502(e) of this title.

(2) Paragraph (1) shall not apply to a transfer of a charitable contribution (as that term is defined in section 548(d)(3)) that is not covered under section 548(a)(1)(B), by reason of section 548(a)(2). Any claim by any person to recover a transferred contribution described in the preceding sentence under Federal or State law in a Federal or State court shall be preempted by the commencement of the case.

(Pub. L. 95–598, Nov. 6, 1978, 92 Stat. 2596; Pub. L. 98–353, title III, §459, July 10, 1984, 98 Stat. 377; Pub. L. 105–183, §3(b), June 19, 1998, 112 Stat. 518.)

Historical and Revision Notes

legislative statements

Section 544(a)(3) modifies similar provisions contained in the House bill and Senate amendment so as not to require a creditor to perform the impossible in order to perfect his interest. Both the lien creditor test in section 544(a)(1), and the bona fide purchaser test in section 544(a)(3) should not require a transferee to perfect a transfer against an entity with respect to which applicable law does not permit perfection. The avoiding powers under section 544(a)(1), (2), and (3) are new. In particular, section 544(a)(1) overrules *Pacific Finance Corp. v. Edwards*, 309 F.2d 224 (9th Cir. 1962), and *In re Federals, Inc.*, 553 F.2d 509 (6th Cir. 1977), insofar as those cases held that the trustee did not have the status of a creditor who extended credit immediately prior to the commencement of the case.

The House amendment deletes section 544(c) of the House bill.

senate report no. 95–989

Subsection (a) is the "strong arm clause" of current law, now found in Bankruptcy Act §70c [section 110(c) of former title 11]. It gives the trustee the rights of a creditor on a simple contract with a judicial lien on the property of the debtor as of the date of the petition; of a creditor with a writ of execution against the property of the debtor unsatisfied as of the date of the petition; and a bona fide purchaser of the real property of the debtor as of the date of the petition. "Simple contract" as used here is derived from Bankruptcy Act §60a(4) [section 96(a)(4) of former title 11]. The third status, that of a bona fide purchaser of real property, is new.

Subsection (b) is derived from current section 70e [section 110(e) of former title 11]. It gives the trustee the rights of actual unsecured creditors under applicable law to void transfers. It follows *Moore v. Bay*, 284 U.S. 4 (1931), and overrules those cases that hold section 70e gives the trustee the rights of secured creditors.

Amendments

1998—Subsec. (b). Pub. L. 105–183 designated existing provisions as par. (1), substituted "Except as provided in paragraph (2), the trustee" for "The trustee", and added par. (2).

1984—Subsec. (a)(1). Pub. L. 98–353, §459(1), inserted "such" after "obtained".

Subsec. (a)(2). Pub. L. 98–353, §459(2), substituted "; or" for "; and".

Subsec. (a)(3). Pub. L. 98–353, §459(3), inserted ", other than fixtures," after "property", and "and has perfected such transfer" after "purchaser" the second place it appeared.

Effective Date of 1998 Amendment

Pub. L. 105–183, §5, June 19, 1998, 112 Stat. 518, provided that: "This Act [amending this section and sections 546, 548, 707, and 1325 of this title and enacting provisions set out as notes under this section and section 101 of this title] and the amendments made by this Act shall apply to any case brought under an applicable provision of title 11, United States Code, that is pending or commenced on or after the date of enactment of this Act [June 19, 1998]."

Effective Date of 1984 Amendment

Amendment by Pub. L. 98–353 effective with respect to cases filed 90 days after July 10, 1984, see section 552(a) of Pub. L. 98–353, set out as a note under section 101 of this title.

Construction of 1998 Amendment

Pub. L. 105–183, §6, June 19, 1998, 112 Stat. 519, provided that: "Nothing in the amendments made by this Act [amending this section and sections 546, 548, 707, and 1325 of this title] is intended to limit the applicability of the Religious Freedom Restoration Act of 1993 (42 U.S.C. 2002bb [2000bb] et seq.)."

§545. Statutory liens

The trustee may avoid the fixing of a statutory lien on property of the debtor to the extent that such lien—

(1) first becomes effective against the debtor—

(A) when a case under this title concerning the debtor is commenced;

(B) when an insolvency proceeding other than under this title concerning the debtor is commenced;

(C) when a custodian is appointed or authorized to take or takes possession;

(D) when the debtor becomes insolvent;

(E) when the debtor's financial condition fails to meet a specified standard; or

(F) at the time of an execution against property of the debtor levied at the instance of an entity other than the holder of such statutory lien;

(2) is not perfected or enforceable at the time of the commencement of the case against a bona fide purchaser that purchases such property at the time of the commencement of the case, whether or not such a purchaser exists, except in any case in which a purchaser is a purchaser described in section 6323 of the Internal Revenue Code of 1986, or in any other similar provision of State or local law;

(3) is for rent; or

(4) is a lien of distress for rent.

(Pub. L. 95–598, Nov. 6, 1978, 92 Stat. 2597; Pub. L. 98–353, title III, §460, July 10, 1984, 98 Stat. 377; Pub. L. 109–8, title VII, §711, Apr. 20, 2005, 119 Stat. 127.)

Historical and Revision Notes

legislative statements

Section 545 of the House amendment modifies similar provisions contained in the House bill and Senate amendment to make clear that a statutory lien may be avoided under section 545 only to the extent the lien violates the perfection standards of section 545. Thus a Federal tax lien is invalid under section 545(2) with respect to property specified in sections 6323(b) and (c) of the Internal Revenue Code of 1954 [title 26]. As a result of this modification, section 545(b) of the Senate amendment is deleted as unnecessary.

Statutory liens: The House amendment retains the provision of section 545(2) of the House bill giving the trustee in a bankruptcy case the same power which a bona fide purchaser has to take over certain kinds of personal property despite the existence of a tax lien covering that property. The amendment thus retains present law, and deletes section 545(b) of the Senate amendment which would have no longer allowed the trustee to step into the shoes of a bona fide purchaser for this purpose.

senate report no. 95–989

This section permits the trustee to avoid the fixing of certain statutory liens. It is derived from subsections 67b and 67c of present law [section 107(b) and (c) of former title 11]. Liens that first become effective on the bankruptcy or insolvency of the debtor are voidable by the trustee. Liens that are not perfected or enforceable on the date of the petition against a bona fide purchaser are voidable. If a transferee is able to perfect under section 546(a) and that perfection relates back to an earlier date, then in spite of the filing of the bankruptcy petition, the trustee would not be able to defeat the lien, because the lien would be perfected and enforceable against a bona fide purchaser that purchased the property on the date of the filing of the petition. Finally, a lien for rent or of distress for rent is voidable, whether the lien is a statutory lien or a common law lien of distress for rent. See proposed 11 U.S.C. 101(37); Bankruptcy Act §67(c)(1)(C). The trustee may avoid a lien under this section even if the lien has been enforced by sale before the commencement of the case. To that extent, Bankruptcy Act §67c(5) is not followed.

Subsection (b) limits the trustee's power to avoid tax liens under Federal, state, or local law. For example, under §6323 of the Internal Revenue Code [Title 26]. Once public notice of a tax lien has been filed, the Government is generally entitled to priority over subsequent lienholders. However, certain purchasers who acquire an interest in certain specific kinds of personal property will take free of an existing filed tax lien attaching to such property. Among the specific kinds of personal property which a purchaser can acquire free of an existing tax lien (unless the buyer knows of the existence of the lien) are stocks and securities, motor vehicles, inventory, and certain household goods. Under the present Bankruptcy Act (§67(c)(1)) [section 107(c)(1) of former title 11], the trustee may be viewed as a bona fide purchaser, so that he can take over any such designated items free of tax liens even if the tax authority has perfected its lien. However, the reasons for enabling a bona fide purchaser to take these kinds of assets free of an unfiled tax lien, that is, to encourage free movement of these assets in general commerce, do not apply to a trustee in a title 11 case, who is not in the same position as an ordinary bona fide purchaser as to such property. The bill accordingly adds a new subsection (b) to sec. 545 providing, in effect, that a trustee in bankruptcy does not have the right under this section to take otherwise specially treated items of personal property free of a tax lien filed before the filing of the petition.

References in Text

Section 6323 of the Internal Revenue Code of 1986, referred to in par. (2), is classified to section 6323 of Title 26, Internal Revenue Code.

Amendments

2005—Par. (2). Pub. L. 109–8 inserted before semicolon at end ", except in any case in which a purchaser is a purchaser described in section 6323 of the Internal Revenue Code of 1986, or in any other similar provision of State or local law".

1984—Par. (1)(A). Pub. L. 98–353, §460(1), struck out "is" after "is".

Par. (1)(C). Pub. L. 98–353, §460(2), substituted "appointed or authorized to take" for "apponted".

Par. (2). Pub. L. 98–353, §460(3), substituted "at the time of the commencement of the case" for "on the date of the filing of the petition" in two places.

Effective Date of 2005 Amendment

Amendment by Pub. L. 109–8 effective 180 days after Apr. 20, 2005, and not applicable with respect to cases commenced under this title before such effective date, except as otherwise provided, see section 1501 of Pub. L. 109–8, set out as a note under section 101 of this title.

Effective Date of 1984 Amendment

Amendment by Pub. L. 98–353 effective with respect to cases filed 90 days after July 10, 1984, see section 552(a) of Pub. L. 98–353, set out as a note under section 101 of this title.

§546. Limitations on avoiding powers

(a) An action or proceeding under section 544, 545, 547, 548, or 553 of this title may not be commenced after the earlier of—

(1) the later of—

(A) 2 years after the entry of the order for relief; or

(B) 1 year after the appointment or election of the first trustee under section 702, 1104, 1163, 1202, or 1302 of this title if such appointment or such election occurs before the expiration of the period specified in subparagraph (A); or

(2) the time the case is closed or dismissed.

(b)(1) The rights and powers of a trustee under sections 544, 545, and 549 of this title are subject to any generally applicable law that—

(A) permits perfection of an interest in property to be effective against an entity that acquires rights in such property before the date of perfection; or

(B) provides for the maintenance or continuation of perfection of an interest in property to be effective against an entity that acquires rights in such property before the date on which action is taken to effect such maintenance or continuation.

(2) If—

(A) a law described in paragraph (1) requires seizure of such property or commencement of an action to accomplish such perfection, or maintenance or continuation of perfection of an interest in property; and

(B) such property has not been seized or such an action has not been commenced before the date of the filing of the petition;

such interest in such property shall be perfected, or perfection of such interest shall be maintained or continued, by giving notice within the time fixed by such law for such seizure or such commencement.

(c)(1) Except as provided in subsection (d) of this section and in section 507(c), and subject to the prior rights of a holder of a security interest in such goods or the proceeds thereof, the rights and powers of the trustee under sections 544(a), 545, 547, and 549 are subject to the right of a seller of goods that has sold goods to the debtor, in the ordinary course of such seller's business, to reclaim such goods if the debtor has received such goods while insolvent, within 45 days before the date of the commencement of a case under this title, but such seller may not reclaim such goods unless such seller demands in writing reclamation of such goods—

(A) not later than 45 days after the date of receipt of such goods by the debtor; or

(B) not later than 20 days after the date of commencement of the case, if the 45-day period expires after the commencement of the case.

(2) If a seller of goods fails to provide notice in the manner described in paragraph (1), the seller still may assert the rights contained in section 503(b)(9).

(d) In the case of a seller who is a producer of grain sold to a grain storage facility, owned or operated by the debtor, in the ordinary course of such seller's business (as such terms are defined in section 557 of this title) or in the case of a United States fisherman who has caught fish sold to a fish processing facility owned or operated by the debtor in the ordinary course of such fisherman's business, the rights and powers of the trustee under sections 544(a), 545, 547, and 549 of this title are subject to any statutory or common law right of such producer or fisherman to reclaim such grain or fish if the debtor has received such grain or fish while insolvent, but—

(1) such producer or fisherman may not reclaim any grain or fish unless such producer or fisherman demands, in writing, reclamation of such grain or fish before ten days after receipt thereof by the debtor; and

(2) the court may deny reclamation to such a producer or fisherman with a right of reclamation that has made such a demand only if the court secures such claim by a lien.

(e) Notwithstanding sections 544, 545, 547, 548(a)(1)(B), and 548(b) of this title, the trustee may not avoid a transfer that is a margin payment, as defined in section 101, 741, or 761 of this title, or settlement payment, as defined in section 101 or 741 of this title, made by or to (or for the benefit of) a commodity broker, forward contract merchant, stockbroker, financial institution, financial participant, or securities clearing agency, or that is a transfer made by or to (or for the benefit of) a commodity broker, forward contract merchant, stockbroker, financial institution, financial participant, or securities clearing agency, in connection with a securities contract, as defined in section 741(7), commodity contract, as defined in section 761(4), or forward contract, that is made before the commencement of the case, except under section 548(a)(1)(A) of this title.

(f) Notwithstanding sections 544, 545, 547, 548(a)(1)(B), and 548(b) of this title, the trustee may not avoid a transfer made by or to (or for the benefit of) a repo participant or financial participant, in connection with a repurchase agreement and that is made before the commencement of the case, except under section 548(a)(1)(A) of this title.

(g) Notwithstanding sections 544, 545, 547, 548(a)(1)(B) and 548(b) of this title, the trustee may not avoid a transfer, made by or to (or for the benefit of) a swap participant or financial participant, under or in connection with any swap agreement and that is made before the commencement of the case, except under section 548(a)(1)(A) of this title.

(h) Notwithstanding the rights and powers of a trustee under sections 544(a), 545, 547, 549, and 553, if the court determines on a motion by the trustee made not later than 120 days after the date of the order for relief in a case under chapter 11 of this title and after notice and a hearing, that a return is in the best interests of the estate, the debtor, with the consent of a creditor and subject to the prior rights of holders of security interests in such goods or the proceeds of such goods, may return goods shipped to the debtor by the creditor before the commencement of the case, and the creditor may offset the purchase price of such goods against any claim of the creditor against the debtor that arose before the commencement of the case.

(i)(1) Notwithstanding paragraphs (2) and (3) of section 545, the trustee may not avoid a warehouseman's lien for storage, transportation, or other costs incidental to the storage and handling of goods.

(2) The prohibition under paragraph (1) shall be applied in a manner consistent with any State statute applicable to such lien that is similar to section 7–209 of the Uniform Commercial Code, as in effect on the date of enactment of the Bankruptcy Abuse Prevention and Consumer Protection Act of 2005, or any successor to such section 7–209.

(j) Notwithstanding sections 544, 545, 547, 548(a)(1)(B), and 548(b) the trustee may not avoid a transfer made by or to (or for the benefit of) a master netting agreement participant under or in connection with any master netting agreement or any individual contract covered thereby that is made before the commencement of the case, except under section 548(a)(1)(A) and except to the extent that the trustee could otherwise avoid such a transfer made under an individual contract covered by such master netting agreement.

(Pub. L. 95–598, Nov. 6, 1978, 92 Stat. 2597; Pub. L. 97–222, §4, July 27, 1982, 96 Stat. 236; Pub. L. 98–353, title III, §§351, 393, 461, July 10, 1984, 98 Stat. 358, 365, 377; Pub. L. 99–554, title II, §§257(d), 283(l), Oct. 27, 1986, 100 Stat. 3114, 3117; Pub. L. 101–311, title I, §103, title II, §203, June 25, 1990, 104 Stat. 268, 269; Pub. L. 103–394, title II, §§204(b), 209, 216, 222(a), title V, §501(b)(4), Oct. 22, 1994, 108 Stat. 4122, 4125, 4126, 4129, 4142; Pub. L. 105–183, §3(c), June 19, 1998, 112 Stat. 518; Pub. L. 109–8, title IV, §406, title IX, §907(e), (o)(2), (3), title XII, §1227(a), Apr. 20, 2005, 119 Stat. 105, 177, 182, 199; Pub. L. 109–390, §5(b), Dec. 12, 2006, 120 Stat. 2697.)

Historical and Revision Notes

legislative statements

Section 546(a) of the House amendment is derived from section 546(c) of the Senate amendment. Section 546(c) of the House amendment is derived from section 546(b) of the Senate amendment. It applies to receipt of goods on credit as well as by cash sales. The section clarifies that a demand for reclamation must be made in writing anytime before 10 days after receipt of the goods by the debtor. The section also permits the court to grant the reclaiming creditor a lien or an administrative expense in lieu of turning over the property.

senate report no. 95–989

The trustee's rights and powers under certain of the avoiding powers are limited by section 546. First, if an interest holder against whom the trustee would have rights still has, under applicable nonbankruptcy law, and as of the date of the petition, the opportunity to perfect his lien against an intervening interest holder, then he may perfect his interest against the trustee. If applicable law requires seizure for perfection, then perfection is by notice to the trustee instead. The rights granted to a creditor under this subsection prevail over the trustee only if the transferee has perfected the transfer in accordance with applicable law, and that perfection relates back to a date that is before the commencement of the case.

The phrase "generally applicable law" relates to those provisions of applicable law that apply both in bankruptcy cases and outside of bankruptcy cases. For example, many State laws, under the Uniform Commercial Code, permit perfection of a purchase-money security interest to relate back to defeat an earlier levy by another creditor if the former was perfected within ten days of delivery of the property. U.C.C. §9–301(2). Such perfection would then be able to defeat an intervening hypothetical judicial lien creditor on the date of the filing of the petition. The purpose of the subsection is to protect, in spite of the surprise intervention of a bankruptcy petition, those whom State law protects by allowing them to perfect their liens or interests as of an effective date that is earlier than the date of perfection. It is not designed to give the States an opportunity to enact disguised priorities in the form of liens that apply only in bankruptcy cases.

Subsection (b) [enacted as (c)] specifies that the trustee's rights and powers under the strong arm clause, the successor to creditors provision, the preference section, and the postpetition transaction section are all subject to any statutory or common-law right of a seller, in the ordinary course of business, of goods to the debtor to reclaim the goods if the debtor received the goods on credit while insolvent. The seller must demand reclamation within ten days after receipt of the goods by the debtor. As under nonbankruptcy law, the right is subject to any superior rights of secured creditors. The purpose of the provision is to recognize, in part, the validity of section 2–702 of the Uniform Commercial Code, which has generated much litigation, confusion, and divergent decisions in different circuits. The right is subject, however, to the power of the court to deny reclamation and protect the seller by granting him a priority as an administrative expense for his claim arising out of the sale of the goods.

Subsection (c) [enacted as (a)] adds a statute of limitations to the use by the trustee of the avoiding powers. The limitation is two years after his appointment, or the time the case is closed or dismissed, whichever occurs later.

References in Text

The date of enactment of the Bankruptcy Abuse Prevention and Consumer Protection Act of 2005, referred to in subsec. (i)(2), is the date of enactment of Pub. L. 109–8, which was approved Apr. 20 2005.

Amendments

2006—Subsec. (e). Pub. L. 109–390, §5(b)(1), inserted "(or for the benefit of)" before "a commodity broker" and "or that is a transfer made by or to (or for the benefit of) a commodity broker, forward contract merchant, stockbroker, financial institution, financial participant, or securities clearing agency, in connection with a securities contract, as defined in section 741(7), commodity contract, as defined in section 761(4), or forward contract," after "securities clearing agency,".

Subsec. (f). Pub. L. 109–390, §5(b)(2), struck out "that is a margin payment, as defined in section 741 or 761 of this title, or settlement payment, as defined in section 741 of this title," after "avoid a transfer" and inserted "(or for the benefit of)" before "a repo participant".

Subsec. (g). Pub. L. 109–390, §5(b)(3), inserted "(or for the benefit of)" before "a swap participant".

Subsec. (j). Pub. L. 109–390, §5(b)(4), inserted "(or for the benefit of)" before "a master netting agreement participant".

2005—Subsec. (c). Pub. L. 109–8, §1227(a), amended subsec. (c) generally. Prior to amendment, subsec. (c) consisted of pars. (1) and (2) relating to reclamation of goods sold to an insolvent debtor.

Subsec. (e). Pub. L. 109–8, §907(o)(3), inserted "financial participant," after "financial institution,".

Subsec. (f). Pub. L. 109–8, §907(o)(2), inserted "or financial participant" after "repo participant".

Subsec. (g). Pub. L. 109–8, §907(e)(1), struck out "under a swap agreement" after "avoid a transfer", substituted "under or in connection with any swap agreement" for "in connection with a swap agreement", and inserted "or financial participant" after "swap participant".

Pub. L. 109–8, §406(1), redesignated subsec. (g) relating to return of goods as (h).

Subsec. (h). Pub. L. 109–8, §406(2), inserted "and subject to the prior rights of holders of security interests in such goods or the proceeds of such goods" after "consent of a creditor".

Pub. L. 109–8, §406(1), redesignated subsec. (g) relating to return of goods as (h).

Subsec. (i). Pub. L. 109–8, §406(3), added subsec. (i).

Subsec. (j). Pub. L. 109–8, §907(e)(2), added subsec. (j).

1998—Subsecs. (e) to (g). Pub. L. 105–183 substituted "548(a)(1)(B)" for "548(a)(2)" and "548(a)(1)(A)" for "548(a)(1)".

1994—Subsec. (a)(1). Pub. L. 103–394, §216, amended par. (1) generally. Prior to amendment, par. (1) read as follows: "two years after the appointment of a trustee under section 702, 1104, 1163, 1302, or 1202 of this title; or".

Subsec. (b). Pub. L. 103–394, §204(b), amended subsec. (b) generally. Prior to amendment, subsec. (b) read as follows: "The rights and powers of a trustee under sections 544, 545, and 549 of this title are subject to any generally applicable law that permits perfection of an interest in property to be effective against an entity that acquires rights in such property before the date of such perfection. If such law requires seizure of such property or commencement of an action to accomplish such perfection, and such property has not been seized or such action has not been commenced before the date of the filing of the petition, such interest in such property shall be perfected by notice within the time fixed by such law for such seizure or commencement."

Subsec. (c)(1). Pub. L. 103–394, §209, amended par. (1) generally. Prior to amendment, par. (1) read as follows: "such a seller may not reclaim any such goods unless such seller demands in writing reclamation of such goods before ten days after receipt of such goods by the debtor; and".

Subsec. (e). Pub. L. 103–394, §501(b)(4)(A), substituted "section 101, 741, or 761" for "section 101(34), 741(5), or 761(15)" and "section 101 or 741" for "section 101(35) or 741(8)".

Subsec. (f). Pub. L. 103–394, §501(b)(4)(B), substituted "section 741 or 761" for "section 741(5) or 761(15)" and "section 741" for "section 741(8)".

Subsec. (g). Pub. L. 103–394, §222(a), added subsec. (g) relating to return of goods.

1990—Subsec. (e). Pub. L. 101–311, §203, inserted reference to sections 101(34) and 101(35) of this title.

Subsec. (g). Pub. L. 101–311, §103, added subsec. (g) relating to trustee's authority to avoid transfer involving swap agreement.

1986—Subsec. (a)(1). Pub. L. 99–554, §257(d), inserted reference to section 1202 of this title.

Subsec. (e). Pub. L. 99–554, §283(l), inserted a comma after "stockbroker".

1984—Subsec. (a)(1). Pub. L. 98–353, §461(a), substituted "; or" for "; and".

Subsec. (b). Pub. L. 98–353, §461(b), substituted "a trustee under sections 544, 545, and" for "the trustee under sections 544, 545, or".

Subsec. (c). Pub. L. 98–353, §§351(1), 461(c)(1)–(4), substituted "Except as provided in subsection (d) of this section, the" for "The", substituted "a trustee" for "the trustee", struck out "right" before "or common-law", inserted "of goods that has sold goods to the debtor" after "seller", and struck out "of goods to the debtor" after "business,".

Subsec. (c)(2). Pub. L. 98–353, §461(c)(5)(A), inserted "the" after "if" in provisions preceding subpar. (A).

Subsec. (c)(2)(A). Pub. L. 98–353, §461(c)(5)(B), substituted "a claim of a kind specified in section 503(b) of this title" for "an administrative expense".

Subsec. (d). Pub. L. 98–353, §351(3), added subsec. (d). Former subsec. (d) redesignated (e).

Subsec. (e). Pub. L. 98–353, §§351(2), 461(d), redesignated former subsec. (d) as (e) and inserted "financial institution" after "stockbroker".

Subsec. (f). Pub. L. 98–353, §393, added subsec. (f).

1982—Subsec. (d). Pub. L. 97–222 added subsec. (d).

Effective Date of 2006 Amendment

Amendment by Pub. L. 109–390 not applicable to any cases commenced under this title or to appointments made under any Federal or State law, before Dec. 12, 2006, see section 7 of Pub. L. 109–390, set out as a note under section 101 of this title.

Effective Date of 2005 Amendment

Amendment by Pub. L. 109–8 effective 180 days after Apr. 20, 2005, and not applicable with respect to cases commenced under this title before such effective date, except as otherwise provided, see section 1501 of Pub. L. 109–8, set out as a note under section 101 of this title.

Effective Date of 1998 Amendment

Amendment by Pub. L. 105–183 applicable to any case brought under an applicable provision of this title that is pending or commenced on or after June 19, 1998, see section 5 of Pub. L. 105–183, set out as a note under section 544 of this title.

Effective Date of 1994 Amendment

Amendment by Pub. L. 103–394 effective Oct. 22, 1994, and not applicable with respect to cases commenced under this title before Oct. 22, 1994, see section 702 of Pub. L. 103–394, set out as a note under section 101 of this title.

Effective Date of 1986 Amendment

Amendment by section 257 of Pub. L. 99–554 effective 30 days after Oct. 27, 1986, but not applicable to cases commenced under this title before that date, see section 302(a), (c)(1) of Pub. L. 99–554, set out as a note under section 581 of Title 28, Judiciary and Judicial Procedure.

Amendment by section 283 of Pub. L. 99–554 effective 30 days after Oct. 27, 1986, see section 302(a) of Pub. L. 99–554.

Effective Date of 1984 Amendment

Amendment by Pub. L. 98–353 effective with respect to cases filed 90 days after July 10, 1984, see section 552(a) of Pub. L. 98–353, set out as a note under section 101 of this title.

§547. Preferences

(a) In this section—

(1) "inventory" means personal property leased or furnished, held for sale or lease, or to be furnished under a contract for service, raw materials, work in process, or materials used or consumed in a business, including farm products such as crops or livestock, held for sale or lease;

(2) "new value" means money or money's worth in goods, services, or new credit, or release by a transferee of property previously transferred to such transferee in a transaction that is neither void nor voidable by the debtor or the trustee under any applicable law, including proceeds of such property, but does not include an obligation substituted for an existing obligation;

(3) "receivable" means right to payment, whether or not such right has been earned by performance; and

(4) a debt for a tax is incurred on the day when such tax is last payable without penalty, including any extension.

(b) Except as provided in subsections (c) and (i) of this section, the trustee may avoid any transfer of an interest of the debtor in property—

(1) to or for the benefit of a creditor;

(2) for or on account of an antecedent debt owed by the debtor before such transfer was made;

(3) made while the debtor was insolvent;

(4) made—

(A) on or within 90 days before the date of the filing of the petition; or

(B) between ninety days and one year before the date of the filing of the petition, if such creditor at the time of such transfer was an insider; and

(5) that enables such creditor to receive more than such creditor would receive if—

(A) the case were a case under chapter 7 of this title;

(B) the transfer had not been made; and

(C) such creditor received payment of such debt to the extent provided by the provisions of this title.

(c) The trustee may not avoid under this section a transfer—

(1) to the extent that such transfer was—

(A) intended by the debtor and the creditor to or for whose benefit such transfer was made to be a contemporaneous exchange for new value given to the debtor; and

(B) in fact a substantially contemporaneous exchange;

(2) to the extent that such transfer was in payment of a debt incurred by the debtor in the ordinary course of business or financial affairs of the debtor and the transferee, and such transfer was—

(A) made in the ordinary course of business or financial affairs of the debtor and the transferee; or

(B) made according to ordinary business terms;

(3) that creates a security interest in property acquired by the debtor—

(A) to the extent such security interest secures new value that was—

(i) given at or after the signing of a security agreement that contains a description of such property as collateral;

(ii) given by or on behalf of the secured party under such agreement;

(iii) given to enable the debtor to acquire such property; and

(iv) in fact used by the debtor to acquire such property; and

(B) that is perfected on or before 30 days after the debtor receives possession of such property;

(4) to or for the benefit of a creditor, to the extent that, after such transfer, such creditor gave new value to or for the benefit of the debtor—

(A) not secured by an otherwise unavoidable security interest; and

(B) on account of which new value the debtor did not make an otherwise unavoidable transfer to or for the benefit of such creditor;

(5) that creates a perfected security interest in inventory or a receivable or the proceeds of either, except to the extent that the aggregate of all such transfers to the transferee caused a reduction, as of the date of the filing of the petition and to the prejudice of other creditors holding unsecured claims, of any amount by which the debt secured by such security interest exceeded the value of all security interests for such debt on the later of—

(A)(i) with respect to a transfer to which subsection (b)(4)(A) of this section applies, 90 days before the date of the filing of the petition; or

(ii) with respect to a transfer to which subsection (b)(4)(B) of this section applies, one year before the date of the filing of the petition; or

(B) the date on which new value was first given under the security agreement creating such security interest;

(6) that is the fixing of a statutory lien that is not avoidable under section 545 of this title;

(7) to the extent such transfer was a bona fide payment of a debt for a domestic support obligation;

(8) if, in a case filed by an individual debtor whose debts are primarily consumer debts, the aggregate value of all property that constitutes or is affected by such transfer is less than $600; or

(9) if, in a case filed by a debtor whose debts are not primarily consumer debts, the aggregate value of all property that constitutes or is affected by such transfer is less than $5,000.[1]

(d) The trustee may avoid a transfer of an interest in property of the debtor transferred to or for the benefit of a surety to secure reimbursement of such a surety that furnished a bond or other obligation to dissolve a judicial lien that would have been avoidable by the trustee under subsection (b) of this section. The liability of such surety under such bond or obligation shall be discharged to the extent of the value of such property recovered by the trustee or the amount paid to the trustee.

(e)(1) For the purposes of this section—

(A) a transfer of real property other than fixtures, but including the interest of a seller or purchaser under a contract for the sale of real property, is perfected when a bona fide purchaser of such property from the debtor against whom applicable law permits such transfer to be perfected cannot acquire an interest that is superior to the interest of the transferee; and

(B) a transfer of a fixture or property other than real property is perfected when a creditor on a simple contract cannot acquire a judicial lien that is superior to the interest of the transferee.

(2) For the purposes of this section, except as provided in paragraph (3) of this subsection, a transfer is made—

(A) at the time such transfer takes effect between the transferor and the transferee, if such transfer is perfected at, or within 30 days after, such time, except as provided in subsection (c)(3)(B);

(B) at the time such transfer is perfected, if such transfer is perfected after such 30 days; or

(C) immediately before the date of the filing of the petition, if such transfer is not perfected at the later of—

(i) the commencement of the case; or

(ii) 30 days after such transfer takes effect between the transferor and the transferee.

(3) For the purposes of this section, a transfer is not made until the debtor has acquired rights in the property transferred.

(f) For the purposes of this section, the debtor is presumed to have been insolvent on and during the 90 days immediately preceding the date of the filing of the petition.

(g) For the purposes of this section, the trustee has the burden of proving the avoidability of a transfer under subsection (b) of this section, and the creditor or party in interest against whom recovery or avoidance is sought has the burden of proving the nonavoidability of a transfer under subsection (c) of this section.

(h) The trustee may not avoid a transfer if such transfer was made as a part of an alternative repayment schedule between the debtor and any creditor of the debtor created by an approved nonprofit budget and credit counseling agency.

(i) If the trustee avoids under subsection (b) a transfer made between 90 days and 1 year before the date of the filing of the petition, by the debtor to an entity that is not an insider for the benefit of a creditor that is an insider, such transfer shall be considered to be avoided under this section only with respect to the creditor that is an insider.

(Pub. L. 95–598, Nov. 6, 1978, 92 Stat. 2597; Pub. L. 98–353, title III, §§310, 462, July 10, 1984, 98 Stat. 355, 377; Pub. L. 99–554, title II, §283(m), Oct. 27, 1986, 100 Stat. 3117; Pub. L. 103–394, title II, §203, title III, §304(f), Oct. 22, 1994, 108 Stat. 4121, 4133; Pub. L. 109–8, title II, §§201(b), 217, title IV, §§403, 409, title XII, §§1213(a), 1222, Apr. 20, 2005, 119 Stat. 42, 55, 104, 106, 194, 196.)

Historical and Revision Notes

legislative statements

No limitation is provided for payments to commodity brokers as in section 766 of the Senate amendment other than the amendment to section 548 of title 11. Section 547(c)(2) protects most payments.

Section 547(b)(2) of the House amendment adopts a provision contained in the House bill and rejects an alternative contained in the Senate amendment relating to the avoidance of a preferential transfer that is payment of a tax claim owing to a governmental unit. As provided, section 106(c) of the House amendment overrules contrary language in the House report with the result that the Government is subject to avoidance of preferential transfers.

Contrary to language contained in the House report, payment of a debt by means of a check is equivalent to a cash payment, unless the check is dishonored. Payment is considered to be made when the check is delivered for purposes of sections 547(c)(1) and (2).

Section 547(c)(6) of the House bill is deleted and is treated in a different fashion in section 553 of the House amendment.

Section 547(c)(6) represents a modification of a similar provision contained in the House bill and Senate amendment. The exception relating to satisfaction of a statutory lien is deleted. The exception for a lien created under title 11 is deleted since such a lien is a statutory lien that will not be avoidable in a subsequent bankruptcy.

Section 547(e)(1)(B) is adopted from the House bill and Senate amendment without change. It is intended that the simple contract test used in this section will be applied as under section 544(a)(1) not to require a creditor to perfect against a creditor on a simple contract in the event applicable law makes such perfection impossible. For example, a purchaser from a debtor at an improperly noticed bulk sale may take subject to the rights of a creditor on a simple contract of the debtor for 1 year after the bulk sale. Since the purchaser cannot perfect against such a creditor on a simple contract, he should not be held responsible for failing to do the impossible. In the event the debtor goes into bankruptcy within a short time after the bulk sale, the trustee should not be able to use the avoiding powers under section 544(a)(1) or 547 merely because State law has made some transfers of personal property subject to the rights of a creditor on a simple contract to acquire a judicial lien with no opportunity to perfect against such a creditor.

Preferences: The House amendment deletes from the category of transfers on account of antecedent debts which may be avoided under the preference rules, section 547(b)(2), the exception in the Senate amendment for taxes owed to governmental authorities. However, for purposes of the "ordinary course" exception to the preference rules contained in section 547(c)(2), the House amendment specifies that the 45-day period referred to in section 547(c)(2)(B) is to begin running, in the case of taxes from the last due date, including extensions, of the return with respect to which the tax payment was made.

senate report no. 95–989

This section is a substantial modification of present law. It modernizes the preference provisions and brings them more into conformity with commercial practice and the Uniform Commercial Code.

Subsection (a) contains three definitions. Inventory, new value, and receivable are defined in their ordinary senses, but are defined to avoid any confusion or uncertainty surrounding the terms.

Subsection (b) is the operative provision of the section. It authorizes the trustee to avoid a transfer if five conditions are met. These are the five elements of a preference action. First, the transfer must be to or for the benefit of a creditor. Second, the transfer must be for or on account of an antecedent debt owed by the debtor before the transfer was made. Third, the transfer must have been made when the debtor was insolvent. Fourth, the transfer must have been made during the 90 days immediately preceding the commencement of the case. If the transfer was to an insider, the trustee may avoid the transfer if it was made during the period that begins one year before the filing of the petition and ends 90 days before the filing, if the insider to whom the transfer was made had reasonable cause to believe the debtor was insolvent at the time the transfer was made.

Finally, the transfer must enable the creditor to whom or for whose benefit it was made to receive a greater percentage of his claim than he would receive under the distributive provisions of the bankruptcy code. Specifically, the creditor must receive more than he would if the case were a liquidation case, if the transfer had not been made, and if the creditor received payment of the debt to the extent provided by the provisions of the code.

The phrasing of the final element changes the application of the greater percentage test from that employed under current law. Under this language, the court must focus on the relative distribution between classes as well as the amount that will be received by the members of the class of which the creditor is a member. The language also requires the court to focus on the allowability of the claim for which the preference was made. If the claim would have been entirely disallowed, for example, then the test of paragraph (5) will be met, because the creditor would have received nothing under the distributive provisions of the bankruptcy code.

The trustee may avoid a transfer of a lien under this section even if the lien has been enforced by sale before the commencement of the case.

Subsection (b)(2) of this section in effect exempts from the preference rules payments by the debtor of tax liabilities, regardless of their priority status.

Subsection (c) contains exceptions to the trustee's avoiding power. If a creditor can qualify under any one of the exceptions, then he is protected to that extent. If he can qualify under several, he is protected by each to the extent that he can qualify under each.

The first exception is for a transfer that was intended by all parties to be a contemporaneous exchange for new value, and was in fact substantially contemporaneous. Normally, a check is a credit transaction. However, for the purposes of this paragraph, a transfer involving a check is considered to be "intended to be contemporaneous", and if the check is presented for payment in the normal course of affairs, which the Uniform Commercial Code specifies as 30 days, U.C.C. §3–503(2)(a), that will amount to a transfer that is "in fact substantially contemporaneous."

The second exception protects transfers in the ordinary course of business (or of financial affairs, where a business is not involved) transfers. For the case of a consumer, the paragraph uses the phrase "financial affairs" to include such nonbusiness activities as payment of monthly utility bills. If the debt on account of which the transfer was made was incurred in the ordinary course of both the debtor and the transferee, if the transfer was made not later than 45 days after the debt was incurred, if the transfer itself was made in the ordinary course of both the debtor and the transferee, and if the transfer was made according to ordinary business terms, then the transfer is protected. The purpose of this exception is to leave undisturbed normal financial relations, because it does not detract from the general policy of the preference section to discourage unusual action by either the debtor or his creditors during the debtor's slide into bankruptcy.

The third exception is for enabling loans in connection with which the debtor acquires the property that the loan enabled him to purchase after the loan is actually made.

The fourth exception codifies the net result rule in section 60c of current law [section 96(c) of former title 11]. If the creditor and the debtor have more than one exchange during the 90-day period, the exchanges are netted out according to the formula in paragraph (4). Any new value that the creditor advances must be unsecured in order for it to qualify under this exception.

Paragraph (5) codifies the improvement in position test, and thereby overrules such cases as *DuBay v. Williams*, 417 F.2d 1277 (C.A.9, 1966), and *Grain Merchants of Indiana, Inc. v. Union Bank and Savings Co.*, 408 F.2d 209 (C.A.7, 1969). A creditor with a security interest in a floating mass, such as inventory or accounts receivable, is subject to preference attack to the extent he improves his position during the 90-day period before bankruptcy. The test is a two-point test, and requires determination of the secured creditor's position 90 days before the petition and on the date of the petition. If new value was first given after 90 days before the case, the date on which it was first given substitutes for the 90-day point.

Paragraph (6) excepts statutory liens validated under section 545 from preference attack. It also protects transfers in satisfaction of such liens, and the fixing of a lien under section 365(j), which protects a vendee whose contract to purchase real property from the debtor is rejected.

Subsection (d), derived from section 67a of the Bankruptcy Act [section 107(a) of former title 11], permits the trustee to avoid a transfer to reimburse a surety that posts a bond to dissolve a judicial lien that would have been avoidable under this section. The second sentence protects the surety from double liability.

Subsection (e) determines when a transfer is made for the purposes of the preference section. Paragraph (1) defines when a transfer is perfected. For real property, a transfer is perfected when it is valid against a bona fide purchaser. For personal property and fixtures, a transfer is perfected when it is valid against a creditor on a simple contract that obtains a judicial lien after the transfer is perfected. "Simple contract" as used here is derived from Bankruptcy Act §60a(4) [section 96(a)(4) of former title 11]. Paragraph (2) specifies that a transfer is made when it takes effect between the transferor and the transferee if it is perfected at or within 10 days after that time. Otherwise, it is made when the transfer is perfected. If it is not perfected before the commencement of the case, it is made immediately before the commencement of the case. Paragraph (3) specifies that a transfer is not made until the debtor has acquired rights in the property transferred. This provision, more than any other in the section, overrules *DuBay* and *Grain Merchants*, and in combination with subsection (b)(2), overrules *In re King-Porter Co.*, 446 F.2d 722 (5th Cir. 1971).

Subsection (e) is designed to reach the different results under the 1962 version of Article 9 of the U.C.C. and under the 1972 version because different actions are required under each version in order to make a security agreement effective between the parties.

Subsection (f) creates a presumption of insolvency for the 90 days preceding the bankruptcy case. The presumption is as defined in Rule 301 of the Federal Rules of Evidence, made applicable in bankruptcy cases by sections 224 and 225 of the bill. The presumption requires the party against whom the presumption exists to come forward with some evidence to rebut the presumption, but the burden of proof remains on the party in whose favor the presumption exists.

Amendments

2005—Subsec. (b). Pub. L. 109–8, §1213(a)(1), substituted "subsections (c) and (i)" for "subsection (c)" in introductory provisions.

Subsec. (c)(2). Pub. L. 109–8, §409(1), added par. (2) and struck out former par. (2) which read as follows: "to the extent that such transfer was—

"(A) in payment of a debt incurred by the debtor in the ordinary course of business or financial affairs of the debtor and the transferee;

"(B) made in the ordinary course of business or financial affairs of the debtor and the transferee; and

"(C) made according to ordinary business terms;".

Subsec. (c)(3)(B). Pub. L. 109–8, §1222, substituted "30 days" for "20 days".

Subsec. (c)(7). Pub. L. 109–8, §217, amended par. (7) generally. Prior to amendment, par. (7) read as follows: "to the extent such transfer was a bona fide payment of a debt to a spouse, former spouse, or child of the debtor, for alimony to, maintenance for, or support of such spouse or child, in connection with a separation agreement, divorce decree or other order of a court of record, determination made in accordance with State or territorial law by a governmental unit, or property settlement agreement, but not to the extent that such debt—

"(A) is assigned to another entity, voluntarily, by operation of law, or otherwise; or

"(B) includes a liability designated as alimony, maintenance, or support, unless such liability is actually in the nature of alimony, maintenance or support; or".

Subsec. (c)(9). Pub. L. 109–8, §409(2), (3), added par. (9).

Subsec. (e)(2). Pub. L. 109–8, §403, substituted "30" for "10" wherever appearing.

Subsec. (h). Pub. L. 109–8, §201(b), added subsec. (h).

Subsec. (i). Pub. L. 109–8, §1213(a)(2), added subsec. (i).

1994—Subsec. (c)(3)(B). Pub. L. 103–394, §203(1), substituted "20" for "10".

Subsec. (c)(7), (8). Pub. L. 103–394, §304(f), added par. (7) and redesignated former par. (7) as (8).

Subsec. (e)(2)(A). Pub. L. 103–394, §203(2), inserted before semicolon at end ", except as provided in subsection (c)(3)(B)".

1986—Subsec. (b)(4)(B). Pub. L. 99–554 inserted "and" after the semicolon.

1984—Subsec. (a)(2). Pub. L. 98–353, §462(a)(1), inserted "including proceeds of such property," after "law,".

Subsec. (a)(4). Pub. L. 98–353, §462(a)(2), struck out ", without penalty" after "any extension", and inserted "without penalty" after "payable".

Subsec. (b). Pub. L. 98–353, §462(b)(1), substituted "of an interest of the debtor in property" for "of property of the debtor" in provisions preceding par. (1).

Subsec. (b)(4)(B). Pub. L. 98–353, §462(b)(2), amended subpar. (B) generally. Prior to amendment, subpar. (B) read as follows: "between 90 days and one year before the date of the filing of the petition, if such creditor, at the time of such transfer—

"(i) was an insider; and

"(ii) had reasonable cause to believe the debtor was insolvent at the time of such transfer; and".

Subsec. (c)(2)(A). Pub. L. 98–353, §462(d)(1), inserted "by the debtor" after "incurred".

Subsec. (c)(2)(B) to (D). Pub. L. 98–353, §462(c), struck out subpar. (B) which read as follows: "made not later than 45 days after such debt was incurred;" and redesignated subpars. (C) and (D) as (B) and (C), respectively.

Subsec. (c)(3). Pub. L. 98–353, §462(d)(2), substituted "that creates" for "of".

Subsec. (c)(3)(B). Pub. L. 98–353, §462(d)(3), inserted "on or" after "perfected", and substituted "the debtor receives possession of such property" for "such security interest attaches".

Subsec. (c)(5). Pub. L. 98–353, §462(d)(4), substituted "that creates" for "of", and "all security interests" for "all security interest".

Subsec. (c)(5)(A)(ii). Pub. L. 98–353, §462(d)(5), substituted "or" for "and".

Subsec. (c)(7). Pub. L. 98–353, §310(3), added par. (7).

Subsec. (d). Pub. L. 98–353, §462(e), substituted "The" for "A" before "trustee may avoid", inserted "an interest in" after "transfer of", inserted "to or for the benefit of a surety" after "transferred", and inserted "such" after "reimbursement of".

Subsec. (e)(2)(C)(i). Pub. L. 98–353, §462(f), substituted "or" for "and".

Subsec. (g). Pub. L. 98–353, §462(g), added subsec. (g).

Effective Date of 2005 Amendment

Pub. L. 109–8, title XII, §1213(b), Apr. 20, 2005, 119 Stat. 195, provided that: "The amendments made by this section [amending this section] shall apply to any case that is pending or commenced on or after the date of enactment of this Act [Apr. 20, 2005]."

Amendment by Pub. L. 109–8 effective 180 days after Apr. 20, 2005, and not applicable with respect to cases commenced under this title before such effective date, except as otherwise provided, see section 1501 of Pub. L. 109–8, set out as a note under section 101 of this title.

Effective Date of 1994 Amendment

Amendment by Pub. L. 103–394 effective Oct. 22, 1994, and not applicable with respect to cases commenced under this title before Oct. 22, 1994, see section 702 of Pub. L. 103–394, set out as a note under section 101 of this title.

Effective Date of 1986 Amendment

Amendment by Pub. L. 99–554 effective 30 days after Oct. 27, 1986, see section 302(a) of Pub. L. 99–554, set out as a note under section 581 of Title 28, Judiciary and Judicial Procedure.

Effective Date of 1984 Amendment

Amendment by Pub. L. 98–353 effective with respect to cases filed 90 days after July 10, 1984, see section 552(a) of Pub. L. 98–353, set out as a note under section 101 of this title.

Adjustment of Dollar Amounts

The dollar amounts specified in this section were adjusted by notices of the Judicial Conference of the United States pursuant to section 104 of this title as follows:

By notice dated Feb. 16, 2016, 81 F.R. 8748, effective Apr. 1, 2016, in subsec. (c)(9), dollar amount "6,225" was adjusted to "6,425". See notice of the Judicial Conference of the United States set out as a note under section 104 of this title.

By notice dated Feb. 12, 2013, 78 F.R. 12089, effective Apr. 1, 2013, in subsec. (c)(9), dollar amount "5,850" was adjusted to "6,225".

By notice dated Feb. 19, 2010, 75 F.R. 8747, effective Apr. 1, 2010, in subsec. (c)(9), dollar amount "5,475" was adjusted to "5,850".

By notice dated Feb. 7, 2007, 72 F.R. 7082, effective Apr. 1, 2007, in subsec. (c)(9), dollar amount "5,000" was adjusted to "5,475".

[1] See Adjustment of Dollar Amounts notes below.

§548. Fraudulent transfers and obligations

(a)(1) The trustee may avoid any transfer (including any transfer to or for the benefit of an insider under an employment contract) of an interest of the debtor in property, or any obligation (including any obligation to or for the benefit of an insider under an employment contract) incurred by the debtor, that was made or incurred on or within 2 years before the date of the filing of the petition, if the debtor voluntarily or involuntarily—

(A) made such transfer or incurred such obligation with actual intent to hinder, delay, or defraud any entity to which the debtor was or became, on or after the date that such transfer was made or such obligation was incurred, indebted; or

(B)(i) received less than a reasonably equivalent value in exchange for such transfer or obligation; and

(ii)(I) was insolvent on the date that such transfer was made or such obligation was incurred, or became insolvent as a result of such transfer or obligation;

(II) was engaged in business or a transaction, or was about to engage in business or a transaction, for which any property remaining with the debtor was an unreasonably small capital;

(III) intended to incur, or believed that the debtor would incur, debts that would be beyond the debtor's ability to pay as such debts matured; or

(IV) made such transfer to or for the benefit of an insider, or incurred such obligation to or for the benefit of an insider, under an employment contract and not in the ordinary course of business.

(2) A transfer of a charitable contribution to a qualified religious or charitable entity or organization shall not be considered to be a transfer covered under paragraph (1)(B) in any case in which—

(A) the amount of that contribution does not exceed 15 percent of the gross annual income of the debtor for the year in which the transfer of the contribution is made; or

(B) the contribution made by a debtor exceeded the percentage amount of gross annual income specified in subparagraph (A), if the transfer was consistent with the practices of the debtor in making charitable contributions.

(b) The trustee of a partnership debtor may avoid any transfer of an interest of the debtor in property, or any obligation incurred by the debtor, that was made or incurred on or within 2 years before the date of the filing of the petition, to a general partner in the debtor, if the debtor was insolvent on the date such transfer was made or such obligation was incurred, or became insolvent as a result of such transfer or obligation.

(c) Except to the extent that a transfer or obligation voidable under this section is voidable under section 544, 545, or 547 of this title, a transferee or obligee of such a transfer or obligation that takes for value and in good faith has a lien on or may retain any interest transferred or may enforce any obligation incurred, as the case may be, to the extent that such transferee or obligee gave value to the debtor in exchange for such transfer or obligation.

(d)(1) For the purposes of this section, a transfer is made when such transfer is so perfected that a bona fide purchaser from the debtor against whom applicable law permits such transfer to be perfected cannot acquire an interest in the property transferred that is superior to the interest in such property of the transferee, but if such transfer is not so perfected before the commencement of the case, such transfer is made immediately before the date of the filing of the petition.

(2) In this section—

(A) "value" means property, or satisfaction or securing of a present or antecedent debt of the debtor, but does not include an unperformed promise to furnish support to the debtor or to a relative of the debtor;

(B) a commodity broker, forward contract merchant, stockbroker, financial institution, financial participant, or securities clearing agency that receives a margin payment, as defined in section 101, 741, or 761 of this title, or settlement payment, as defined in section 101 or 741 of this title, takes for value to the extent of such payment;

(C) a repo participant or financial participant that receives a margin payment, as defined in section 741 or 761 of this title, or settlement payment, as defined in section 741 of this title, in connection with a repurchase agreement, takes for value to the extent of such payment;

(D) a swap participant or financial participant that receives a transfer in connection with a swap agreement takes for value to the extent of such transfer; and

(E) a master netting agreement participant that receives a transfer in connection with a master netting agreement or any individual contract covered thereby takes for value to the extent of such transfer, except that, with respect to a transfer under any individual contract covered thereby, to the extent that such master netting agreement participant otherwise did not take (or is otherwise not deemed to have taken) such transfer for value.

(3) In this section, the term "charitable contribution" means a charitable contribution, as that term is defined in section 170(c) of the Internal Revenue Code of 1986, if that contribution—

(A) is made by a natural person; and

(B) consists of—

(i) a financial instrument (as that term is defined in section 731(c)(2)(C) of the Internal Revenue Code of 1986); or

(ii) cash.

(4) In this section, the term "qualified religious or charitable entity or organization" means—

(A) an entity described in section 170(c)(1) of the Internal Revenue Code of 1986; or

(B) an entity or organization described in section 170(c)(2) of the Internal Revenue Code of 1986.

(e)(1) In addition to any transfer that the trustee may otherwise avoid, the trustee may avoid any transfer of an interest of the debtor in property that was made on or within 10 years before the date of the filing of the petition, if—

(A) such transfer was made to a self-settled trust or similar device;

(B) such transfer was by the debtor;

(C) the debtor is a beneficiary of such trust or similar device; and

(D) the debtor made such transfer with actual intent to hinder, delay, or defraud any entity to which the debtor was or became, on or after the date that such transfer was made, indebted.

(2) For the purposes of this subsection, a transfer includes a transfer made in anticipation of any money judgment, settlement, civil penalty, equitable order, or criminal fine incurred by, or which the debtor believed would be incurred by—

(A) any violation of the securities laws (as defined in section 3(a)(47) of the Securities Exchange Act of 1934 (15 U.S.C. 78c(a)(47))), any State securities laws, or any regulation or order issued under Federal securities laws or State securities laws; or

(B) fraud, deceit, or manipulation in a fiduciary capacity or in connection with the purchase or sale of any security registered under section 12 or 15(d) of the Securities Exchange Act of 1934 (15 U.S.C. 78l and 78o(d)) or under section 6 of the Securities Act of 1933 (15 U.S.C. 77f).

(Pub. L. 95–598, Nov. 6, 1978, 92 Stat. 2600; Pub. L. 97–222, §5, July 27, 1982, 96 Stat. 236; Pub. L. 98–353, title III, §§394, 463, July 10, 1984, 98 Stat. 365, 378; Pub. L. 99–554, title II, §283(n), Oct. 27, 1986, 100 Stat. 3117; Pub. L. 101–311, title I, §104, title II, §204, June 25, 1990, 104 Stat. 268, 269; Pub. L. 103–394, title V, §501(b)(5), Oct. 22, 1994, 108 Stat. 4142; Pub. L. 105–183, §§2, 3(a), June 19, 1998, 112 Stat. 517; Pub. L. 109–8, title IX, §907(f), (o)(4)–(6), title XIV, §1402, Apr. 20, 2005, 119 Stat. 177, 182, 214.)

Historical and Revision Notes

legislative statements

Section 548(d)(2) is modified to reflect general application of a provision contained in section 766 of the Senate amendment with respect to commodity brokers. In particular, section 548(d)(2)(B) of the House amendment makes clear that a commodity broker who receives a margin payment is considered to receive the margin payment in return for "value" for purposes of section 548.

senate report no. 95–989

This section is derived in large part from section 67d of the Bankruptcy Act [section 107(d) of former title 11]. It permits the trustee to avoid transfers by the debtor in fraud of his creditors. Its history dates from the statute of 13 Eliz. c. 5 (1570).

The trustee may avoid fraudulent transfers or obligations if made with actual intent to hinder, delay, or defraud a past or future creditor. Transfers made for less than a reasonably equivalent consideration are also vulnerable if the debtor was or thereby becomes insolvent, was engaged in business with an unreasonably small capital, or intended to incur debts that would be beyond his ability to repay.

The trustee of a partnership debtor may avoid any transfer of partnership property to a partner in the debtor if the debtor was or thereby became insolvent.

If a transferee's only liability to the trustee is under this section, and if he takes for value and in good faith, then subsection (c) grants him a lien on the property transferred, or other similar protection.

Subsection (d) specifies that for the purposes of fraudulent transfer section, a transfer is made when it is valid against a subsequent bona fide purchaser. If not made before the commencement of the case, it is considered made immediately before then. Subsection (d) also defines "value" to mean property, or the satisfaction or securing of a present or antecedent debt, but does not include an unperformed promise to furnish support to the debtor or a relative of the debtor.

References in Text

Sections 170(c) and 731(c)(2)(C) of the Internal Revenue Code of 1986, referred to in subsec. (d)(3), (4), are classified to sections 170(c) and 731(c)(2)(C), respectively, of Title 26, Internal Revenue Code.

Amendments

2005—Subsec. (a)(1). Pub. L. 109–8, §1402(2), in introductory provisions, inserted "(including any transfer to or for the benefit of an insider under an employment contract)" after "avoid any transfer" and "(including any obligation to or for the benefit of an insider under an employment contract)" after "or any obligation".

Pub. L. 109–8, §1402(1), substituted "2 years" for "one year" in introductory provisions.

Subsec. (a)(1)(B)(ii)(IV). Pub. L. 109–8, §1402(3), added subcl. (IV).

Subsec. (b). Pub. L. 109–8, §1402(1), substituted "2 years" for "one year".

Subsec. (d)(2)(B). Pub. L. 109–8, §907(o)(4), inserted "financial participant," after "financial institution,".

Subsec. (d)(2)(C). Pub. L. 109–8, §907(o)(5), inserted "or financial participant" after "repo participant".

Subsec. (d)(2)(D). Pub. L. 109–8, §907(o)(6), inserted "or financial participant" after "swap participant".

Subsec. (d)(2)(E). Pub. L. 109–8, §907(f), added subpar. (E).

Subsec. (e). Pub. L. 109–8, §1402(4), added subsec. (e).

1998—Subsec. (a). Pub. L. 105–183, §3(a), designated existing provisions as par. (1), redesignated former pars. (1) and (2) as par. (1)(A) and (B), respectively, redesignated former par. (2)(A) and (B) as par. (1)(B)(i) and (ii), respectively, and redesignated former par. (2)(B)(i) to (iii) as par. (1)(B)(ii)(I) to (III), respectively, and added par. (2).

Subsec. (d)(3), (4). Pub. L. 105–183, §2, added pars. (3) and (4).

1994—Subsec. (d)(2)(B). Pub. L. 103–394, §501(b)(5)(A), substituted "section 101, 741, or 761" for "section 101(34), 741(5) or 761(15)" and "section 101 or 741" for "section 101(35) or 741(8)".

Subsec. (d)(2)(C). Pub. L. 103–394, §501(b)(5)(B), substituted "section 741 or 761" for "section 741(5) or 761(15)" and "section 741" for "section 741(8)".

1990—Subsec. (d)(2)(B). Pub. L. 101–311, §204, inserted reference to sections 101(34) and 101(35) of this title.

Subsec. (d)(2)(D). Pub. L. 101–311, §104, added subpar. (D).

1986—Subsec. (d)(2)(B). Pub. L. 99–554 substituted ", financial institution" for "financial institution,".

1984—Subsec. (a). Pub. L. 98–353, §463(a)(1), substituted "if the debtor voluntarily or involuntarily" for "if the debtor" in provisions preceding par. (1).

Subsec. (a)(1). Pub. L. 98–353, §463(a)(2), substituted "was made" for "occurred".

Subsec. (a)(2)(B)(ii). Pub. L. 98–353, §463(a)(3), inserted "or a transaction" after "engaged in business".

Subsec. (c). Pub. L. 98–353, §463(b), inserted "or may retain" after "lien on" and struck out ", may retain any lien transferred," before "or may enforce any obligation incurred".

Subsec. (d)(1). Pub. L. 98–353, §463(c)(1), substituted "is so" for "becomes so far", "applicable law permits such transfer to be" for "such transfer could have been", and "is made" for "occurs".

Subsec. (d)(2)(B). Pub. L. 98–353, §463(c)(2), inserted "financial institution," after "stockbroker".

Subsec. (d)(2)(C). Pub. L. 98–353, §394(2), added subpar. (C).

1982—Subsec. (d)(2)(B). Pub. L. 97–222 substituted "a commodity broker, forward contract merchant, stockbroker, or securities clearing agency that receives a margin payment, as defined in section 741(5) or 761(15) of this title, or settlement payment, as defined in section 741(8) of this title, takes for value to extent of such payment" for "a commodity broker or forward contract merchant that receives a margin payment, as defined in section 761(15) of this title, takes for value".

Effective Date of 2005 Amendment

Amendment by section 1402 of Pub. L. 109–8 effective Apr. 20, 2005, and applicable only with respect to cases commenced under this title on or after such date, with amendment by par. (1) of such section applicable only with respect to cases commenced under this title more than 1 year after Apr. 20, 2005, see section 1406 of Pub. L. 109–8, set out as a note under section 507 of this title.

Amendment by section 907 of Pub. L. 109–8 effective 180 days after Apr. 20, 2005, and not applicable with respect to cases commenced under this title before such effective date, except as otherwise provided, see section 1501 of Pub. L. 109–8, set out as a note under section 101 of this title.

Effective Date of 1998 Amendment

Amendment by Pub. L. 105–183 applicable to any case brought under an applicable provision of this title that is pending or commenced on or after June 19, 1998, see section 5 of Pub. L. 105–183, set out as a note under section 544 of this title.

Effective Date of 1994 Amendment

Amendment by Pub. L. 103–394 effective Oct. 22, 1994, and not applicable with respect to cases commenced under this title before Oct. 22, 1994, see section 702 of Pub. L. 103–394, set out as a note under section 101 of this title.

Effective Date of 1986 Amendment

Amendment by Pub. L. 99–554 effective 30 days after Oct. 27, 1986, see section 302(a) of Pub. L. 99–554, set out as a note under section 581 of Title 28, Judiciary and Judicial Procedure.

Effective Date of 1984 Amendment

Amendment by Pub. L. 98–353 effective with respect to cases filed 90 days after July 10, 1984, see section 552(a) of Pub. L. 98–353, set out as a note under section 101 of this title.

§549. Postpetition transactions

(a) Except as provided in subsection (b) or (c) of this section, the trustee may avoid a transfer of property of the estate—

(1) that occurs after the commencement of the case; and

(2)(A) that is authorized only under section 303(f) or 542(c) of this title; or

(B) that is not authorized under this title or by the court.

(b) In an involuntary case, the trustee may not avoid under subsection (a) of this section a transfer made after the commencement of such case but before the order for relief to the extent any value, including services, but not including satisfaction or securing of a debt that arose before the commencement of the case, is given after the commencement of the case in exchange for such transfer, notwithstanding any notice or knowledge of the case that the transferee has.

(c) The trustee may not avoid under subsection (a) of this section a transfer of an interest in real property to a good faith purchaser without knowledge of the commencement of the case and for present fair equivalent value unless a copy or notice of the petition was filed, where a transfer of an interest in such real property may be recorded to perfect such transfer, before such transfer is so perfected that a bona fide purchaser of such real property, against whom applicable law permits such transfer to be perfected, could not acquire an interest that is superior to such interest of such good faith purchaser. A good faith purchaser without knowledge of the commencement of the case and for less than present fair equivalent value has a lien on the property transferred to the extent of any present value given, unless a copy or notice of the petition was so filed before such transfer was so perfected.

(d) An action or proceeding under this section may not be commenced after the earlier of—

(1) two years after the date of the transfer sought to be avoided; or

(2) the time the case is closed or dismissed.

(Pub. L. 95–598, Nov. 6, 1978, 92 Stat. 2601; Pub. L. 98–353, title III, §464, July 10, 1984, 98 Stat. 379; Pub. L. 99–554, title II, §283(o), Oct. 27, 1986, 100 Stat. 3117; Pub. L. 103–394, title V, §501(d)(18), Oct. 22, 1994, 108 Stat. 4146; Pub. L. 109–8, title XII, §1214, Apr. 20, 2005, 119 Stat. 195.)

Historical and Revision Notes

legislative statements

Section 549 of the House amendment has been redrafted in order to incorporate sections 342(b) and (c) of the Senate amendment. Those sections have been consolidated and redrafted in section 549(c) of the House amendment. Section 549(d) of the House amendment adopts a provision contained in section 549(c) of the Senate amendment.

senate report no. 95–989

This section modifies section 70d of current law [section 110(d) of former title 11]. It permits the trustee to avoid transfers of property that occur after the commencement of the case. The transfer must either have been unauthorized, or authorized under a section that protects only the transferor. Subsection (b) protects "involuntary gap" transferees to the extent of any value (including services, but not including satisfaction of a debt that arose before the commencement of the case), given after commencement in exchange for the transfer. Notice or knowledge of the transferee is irrelevant in determining whether he is protected under this provision.

Amendments

2005—Subsec. (c). Pub. L. 109–8 inserted "an interest in" after "transfer of" in two places and substituted "purchaser of such real property" for "purchaser of such property" and "such interest" for "the interest".

1994—Subsec. (b). Pub. L. 103–394 inserted "the trustee may not avoid under subsection (a) of this section" after "involuntary case,".

1986—Subsec. (b). Pub. L. 99–554 substituted "made" for "that occurs", and "to the extent" for "is valid against the trustee to the extent of", and inserted "is" before "given".

1984—Subsec. (a). Pub. L. 98–353, §464(a)(1), (2), substituted "(b) or (c)" for "(b) and (c)" in provisions preceding par. (1) and inserted "only" between "authorized" and "under" in par. (2)(A). In the original of Pub. L. 98–353, subsec. (a)(2) of section 464 thereof ended with a period but was followed by pars. (3), (4), and (5). Such pars. (3), (4), and (5) purported to amend subsec. (a) of this section in ways not susceptible of execution. In a predecessor bill [S. 445], these pars. (3), (4), and (5) formed a part of a subsec. (b) of section 361 thereof which amended subsec. (b) of this section. Such subsec. (b) of section 361 of S. 445 was not carried into Pub. L. 98–353, §464.

Subsec. (c). Pub. L. 98–353, §464(c), amended subsec. (c) generally. Prior to amendment, subsec. (c) read as follows: "The trustee may not avoid under subsection (a) of this section a transfer, to a good faith purchaser without knowledge of the commencement of the case and for present fair equivalent value or to a purchaser at a judicial sale, of real property located other than in the county in which the case is commenced, unless a copy of the petition was filed in the office where conveyances of real property in such county are recorded before such transfer was so far perfected that a bona fide purchaser of such property against whom applicable law permits such transfer to be perfected cannot acquire an interest that is superior to the interest of such good faith or judicial sale purchaser. A good faith purchaser, without knowledge of the commencement of the case and for less than present fair equivalent value, of real property located other than in the county in which the case is commenced, under a transfer that the trustee may avoid under this section, has a lien on the property transferred to the extent of any present value given, unless a copy of the petition was so filed before such transfer was so perfected."

Subsec. (d)(1). Pub. L. 98–353, §464(d), substituted "or" for "and".

Effective Date of 2005 Amendment

Amendment by Pub. L. 109–8 effective 180 days after Apr. 20, 2005, and not applicable with respect to cases commenced under this title before such effective date, except as otherwise provided, see section 1501 of Pub. L. 109–8, set out as a note under section 101 of this title.

Effective Date of 1994 Amendment

Amendment by Pub. L. 103–394 effective Oct. 22, 1994, and not applicable with respect to cases commenced under this title before Oct. 22, 1994, see section 702 of Pub. L. 103–394, set out as a note under section 101 of this title.

Effective Date of 1986 Amendment

Amendment by Pub. L. 99–554 effective 30 days after Oct. 27, 1986, see section 302(a) of Pub. L. 99–554, set out as a note under section 581 of Title 28, Judiciary and Judicial Procedure.

Effective Date of 1984 Amendment

Amendment by Pub. L. 98–353 effective with respect to cases filed 90 days after July 10, 1984, see section 552(a) of Pub. L. 98–353, set out as a note under section 101 of this title.

§550. Liability of transferee of avoided transfer

(a) Except as otherwise provided in this section, to the extent that a transfer is avoided under section 544, 545, 547, 548, 549, 553(b), or 724(a) of this title, the trustee may recover, for the benefit of the estate, the property transferred, or, if the court so orders, the value of such property, from—

(1) the initial transferee of such transfer or the entity for whose benefit such transfer was made; or

(2) any immediate or mediate transferee of such initial transferee.

(b) The trustee may not recover under section [1] (a)(2) of this section from—

(1) a transferee that takes for value, including satisfaction or securing of a present or antecedent debt, in good faith, and without knowledge of the voidability of the transfer avoided; or

(2) any immediate or mediate good faith transferee of such transferee.

(c) If a transfer made between 90 days and one year before the filing of the petition—

(1) is avoided under section 547(b) of this title; and

(2) was made for the benefit of a creditor that at the time of such transfer was an insider;

the trustee may not recover under subsection (a) from a transferee that is not an insider.

(d) The trustee is entitled to only a single satisfaction under subsection (a) of this section.

(e)(1) A good faith transferee from whom the trustee may recover under subsection (a) of this section has a lien on the property recovered to secure the lesser of—

(A) the cost, to such transferee, of any improvement made after the transfer, less the amount of any profit realized by or accruing to such transferee from such property; and

(B) any increase in the value of such property as a result of such improvement, of the property transferred.

(2) In this subsection, "improvement" includes—

(A) physical additions or changes to the property transferred;

(B) repairs to such property;

(C) payment of any tax on such property;

(D) payment of any debt secured by a lien on such property that is superior or equal to the rights of the trustee; and

(E) preservation of such property.

(f) An action or proceeding under this section may not be commenced after the earlier of—

(1) one year after the avoidance of the transfer on account of which recovery under this section is sought; or

(2) the time the case is closed or dismissed.

(Pub. L. 95–598, Nov. 6, 1978, 92 Stat. 2601; Pub. L. 98–353, title III, §465, July 10, 1984, 98 Stat. 379; Pub. L. 103–394, title II, §202, Oct. 22, 1994, 108 Stat. 4121.)

Historical and Revision Notes

legislative statements

Section 550(a)(1) of the House amendment has been modified in order to permit recovery from an entity for whose benefit an avoided transfer is made in addition to a recovery from the initial transferee of the transfer. Section 550(c) would still apply, and the trustee is entitled only to a single satisfaction. The liability of a transferee under section 550(a) applies only "to the extent that a transfer is avoided". This means that liability is not imposed on a transferee to the extent that a transferee is protected under a provision such as section 548(c) which grants a good faith transferee for value of a transfer that is avoided only as a fraudulent transfer, a lien on the property transferred to the extent of value given.

Section 550(b) of the House amendment is modified to indicate that value includes satisfaction or securing of a present antecedent debt. This means that the trustee may not recover under subsection (a)(2) from a subsequent transferee that takes for "value", provided the subsequent transferee also takes in good faith and without knowledge of the transfer avoided.

Section 550(e) of the House amendment is derived from section 550(e) of the Senate amendment.

senate report no. 95–989

Section 550 prescribes the liability of a transferee of an avoided transfer, and enunciates the separation between the concepts of avoiding a transfer and recovering from the transferee. Subsection (a) permits the trustee to recover from the initial transferee of an avoided transfer or from any immediate or mediate transferee of the initial transferee. The words "to the extent that" in the lead in to this subsection are designed to incorporate the protection of transferees found in proposed 11 U.S.C. 549(b) and 548(c). Subsection (b) limits the liability of an immediate or mediate transferee of the initial transferee if such secondary transferee takes for value, in good faith and without knowledge of the voidability of the transfer. An immediate or mediate good faith transferee of a protected secondary transferee is also shielded from liability. This subsection is limited to the trustee's right to recover from subsequent transferees under subsection (a)(2). It does not limit the trustee's rights against the initial transferee under subsection (a)(1). The phrase "good faith" in this paragraph is intended to prevent a transferee from whom the trustee could recover from transferring the recoverable property to an innocent transferee, and receiving a retransfer from him, that is, "washing" the transaction through an innocent third party. In order for the transferee to be excepted from liability under this paragraph, he himself must be a good faith transferee. Subsection (c) is a further limitation on recovery. It specifies that the trustee is entitled to only one satisfactory, under subsection (a), even if more than one transferee is liable.

Subsection (d) protects good faith transferees, either initial or subsequent, to the extent of the lesser of the cost of any improvement the transferee makes in the transferred property and the increase in value of the property as a result of the improvement. Paragraph (2) of the subsection defines improvement to include physical additions or changes to the property, repairs, payment of taxes on the property, payment of a debt secured by a lien on the property, discharge of a lien on the property, and preservation of the property.

Subsection (e) establishes a statute of limitations on avoidance by the Trustee. The limitation is one year after the avoidance of the transfer or the time the case is closed or dismissed, whichever is earlier.

Amendments

1994—Subsecs. (c) to (f). Pub. L. 103–394 added subsec. (c) and redesignated former subsecs. (c) to (e) as (d) to (f), respectively.

1984—Subsec. (a). Pub. L. 98–353, §465(a), substituted "549, 553(b), or 724(a) of this title" for "549, or 724(a) of this title".

Subsec. (d)(1)(A). Pub. L. 98–353, §465(b)(1), inserted "or accruing to" after "by".

Subsec. (d)(1)(B). Pub. L. 98–353, §465(b)(2), substituted "the value of such property" for "value".

Subsec. (d)(2)(D). Pub. L. 98–353, §465(b)(3), substituted "payment of any debt secured by a lien on such property that is superior or equal to the rights of the trustee; and" for "payment of any debt secured by a lien on such property."

Subsec. (d)(2)(E), (F). Pub. L. 98–353, §465(b)(3), (4), struck out subpar. (E) "discharge of any lien against such property that is superior or equal to the rights of the trustee; and" and redesignated subpar. (F) as (E).

Subsec. (e)(1). Pub. L. 98–353, §465(c), substituted "or" for "and".

Effective Date of 1994 Amendment

Amendment by Pub. L. 103–394 effective Oct. 22, 1994, and not applicable with respect to cases commenced under this title before Oct. 22, 1994, see section 702 of Pub. L. 103–394, set out as a note under section 101 of this title.

Effective Date of 1984 Amendment

Amendment by Pub. L. 98–353 effective with respect to cases filed 90 days after July 10, 1984, see section 552(a) of Pub. L. 98–353, set out as a note under section 101 of this title.

¹ So in original. Probably should be "subsection".

§551. Automatic preservation of avoided transfer

Any transfer avoided under section 522, 544, 545, 547, 548, 549, or 724(a) of this title, or any lien void under section 506(d) of this title, is preserved for the benefit of the estate but only with respect to property of the estate.

(Pub. L. 95–598, Nov. 6, 1978, 92 Stat. 2602.)

Historical and Revision Notes

legislative statements

Section 551 is adopted from the House bill and the alternative in the Senate amendment is rejected. The section is clarified to indicate that a transfer avoided or a lien that is void is preserved for the benefit of the estate, but only with respect to property of the estate. This prevents the trustee from asserting an avoided tax lien against after acquired property of the debtor.

senate report no. 95–989

This section is a change from present law. It specifies that any avoided transfer is automatically preserved for the benefit of the estate. Under current law, the court must determine whether or not the transfer should be preserved. The operation of the section is automatic, unlike current law, even though preservation may not benefit the estate in every instance. A preserved lien may be abandoned by the trustee under proposed 11 U.S.C. 554 if the preservation does not benefit the estate. The section as a whole prevents junior lienors from improving their position at the expense of the estate when a senior lien is avoided.

§552. Postpetition effect of security interest

(a) Except as provided in subsection (b) of this section, property acquired by the estate or by the debtor after the commencement of the case is not subject to any lien resulting from any security agreement entered into by the debtor before the commencement of the case.

(b)(1) Except as provided in sections 363, 506(c), 522, 544, 545, 547, and 548 of this title, if the debtor and an entity entered into a security agreement before the commencement of the case and if the security interest created by such security agreement extends to property of the debtor acquired before the commencement of the case and to proceeds, products, offspring, or profits of such property, then such security interest extends to such proceeds, products, offspring, or profits acquired by the estate after the commencement of the case to the extent provided by such security agreement and by applicable nonbankruptcy law, except to any extent that the court, after notice and a hearing and based on the equities of the case, orders otherwise.

(2) Except as provided in sections 363, 506(c), 522, 544, 545, 547, and 548 of this title, and notwithstanding section 546(b) of this title, if the debtor and an entity entered into a security agreement before the commencement of the case and if the security interest created by such security agreement extends to property of the debtor acquired before the commencement of the case and to amounts paid as rents of such property or the fees, charges, accounts, or other payments for the use or occupancy of rooms and other public facilities in hotels, motels, or other lodging properties, then such security interest extends to such rents and such fees, charges, accounts, or other payments acquired by the estate after the commencement of the case to the extent provided in such security agreement, except to any extent that the court, after notice and a hearing and based on the equities of the case, orders otherwise.

(Pub. L. 95–598, Nov. 6, 1978, 92 Stat. 2602; Pub. L. 98–353, title III, §466, July 10, 1984, 98 Stat. 380; Pub. L. 103–394, title II, §214(a), Oct. 22, 1994, 108 Stat. 4126; Pub. L. 109–8, title XII, §1204(2), Apr. 20, 2005, 119 Stat. 194.)

Historical and Revision Notes

legislative statements

Section 552(a) is derived from the House bill and the alternative provision in the Senate amendment is rejected. Section 552(b) represents a compromise between the House bill and the Senate amendment. Proceeds coverage, but not after acquired property clauses, are valid under title 11. The provision allows the court to consider the equities in each case. In the course of such consideration the court may evaluate any expenditures by the estate relating to proceeds and any related improvement in position of the secured party. Although this section grants a secured party a security interest in proceeds, product, offspring, rents, or profits, the section is explicitly subject to other sections of title 11. For example, the trustee or debtor in possession may use, sell, or lease proceeds, product, offspring, rents or profits under section 363.

senate report no. 95–989

Under the Uniform Commercial Code, article 9, creditors may take security interests in after-acquired property. Section 552 governs the effect of such a prepetition security interest in postpetition property. It applies to all security interests as defined in section 101(37) of the bankruptcy code, not only to U.C.C. security interests.

As a general rule, if a security agreement is entered into before the commencement of the case, then property that the estate acquires is not subject to the security interest created by a provision in the security agreement extending the security interest to after-acquired property. Subsection (b) provides an important exception consistent with the Uniform Commercial Code. If the security agreement extends to proceeds, product, offspring, rents, or profits of the property in question, then the proceeds would continue to be subject to the security interest pursuant to the terms of the security agreement and provisions of applicable law, except to the extent that where the estate acquires the proceeds at the expense of other creditors holding unsecured claims, the expenditure resulted in an improvement in the position of the secured party.

The exception covers the situation where raw materials, for example, are converted into inventory, or inventory into accounts, at some expense to the estate, thus depleting the fund available for general unsecured creditors, but is limited to the benefit inuring to the secured party thereby. Situations in which the estate incurs expense in simply protecting collateral are governed by 11 U.S.C. 506(c). In ordinary circumstances, the risk of loss in continued operations will remain with the estate.

house report no. 95–595

Under the Uniform Commercial Code, Article 9, creditors may take security interests in after-acquired property. This section governs the effect of such a prepetition security interest in postpetition property. It applies to all security interests as defined in section 101 of the bankruptcy code, not only to U.C.C. security interests.

As a general rule, if a security agreement is entered into before the case, then property that the estate acquires is not subject to the security interest created by the security agreement. Subsection (b) provides the only exception. If the security agreement extends to proceeds, product, offspring, rents, or profits of property that the debtor had before the commencement of the case, then the proceeds, etc., continue to be subject to the security interest, except to the extent that the estate acquired the proceeds to the prejudice of other creditors holding unsecured claims. "Extends to" as used here would include an automatically arising security interest in proceeds, as permitted under the 1972 version of the Uniform Commercial Code, as well as an interest in proceeds specifically designated, as required under the 1962 Code or similar statutes covering property not covered by the Code. "Prejudice" is not intended to be a broad term here, but is designed to cover the situation where the estate expends funds that result in an increase in the value of collateral. The exception is to cover the situation where raw materials, for example, are converted into inventory, or inventory into accounts, at some expense to the estate, thus depleting the fund available for general unsecured creditors. The term "proceeds" is not limited to the technical definition of that term in the U.C.C., but covers any property into which property subject to the security interest is converted.

Amendments

2005—Subsec. (b)(1). Pub. L. 109–8 substituted "products" for "product" in two places.

1994—Subsec. (b). Pub. L. 103–394 designated existing provisions as par. (1), struck out "rents," after "offspring," in two places, and added par. (2).

1984—Subsec. (b). Pub. L. 98–353 inserted "522," after "506(c)," substituted "an entity entered" for "a secured party enter", and substituted "except to any extent" for "except to the extent".

Effective Date of 2005 Amendment

Amendment by Pub. L. 109–8 effective 180 days after Apr. 20, 2005, and not applicable with respect to cases commenced under this title before such effective date, except as otherwise provided, see section 1501 of Pub. L. 109–8, set out as a note under section 101 of this title.

Effective Date of 1994 Amendment

Amendment by Pub. L. 103–394 effective Oct. 22, 1994, and not applicable with respect to cases commenced under this title before Oct. 22, 1994, see section 702 of Pub. L. 103–394, set out as a note under section 101 of this title.

Effective Date of 1984 Amendment

Amendment by Pub. L. 98–353 effective with respect to cases filed 90 days after July 10, 1984, see section 552(a) of Pub. L. 98–353, set out as a note under section 101 of this title.

§553. Setoff

(a) Except as otherwise provided in this section and in sections 362 and 363 of this title, this title does not affect any right of a creditor to offset a mutual debt owing by such creditor to the debtor that arose before the commencement of the case under this title against a claim of such creditor against the debtor that arose before the commencement of the case, except to the extent that—

(1) the claim of such creditor against the debtor is disallowed;

(2) such claim was transferred, by an entity other than the debtor, to such creditor—

(A) after the commencement of the case; or

(B)(i) after 90 days before the date of the filing of the petition; and

(ii) while the debtor was insolvent (except for a setoff of a kind described in section 362(b)(6), 362(b)(7), 362(b)(17), 362(b)(27), 555, 556, 559, 560, or 561); or

(3) the debt owed to the debtor by such creditor was incurred by such creditor—

(A) after 90 days before the date of the filing of the petition;

(B) while the debtor was insolvent; and

(C) for the purpose of obtaining a right of setoff against the debtor (except for a setoff of a kind described in section 362(b)(6), 362(b)(7), 362(b)(17), 362(b)(27), 555, 556, 559, 560, or 561).

(b)(1) Except with respect to a setoff of a kind described in section 362(b)(6), 362(b)(7), 362(b)(17), 362(b)(27), 555, 556, 559, 560, 561, 365(h), 546(h), or 365(i)(2) of this title, if a creditor offsets a mutual debt owing to the debtor against a claim against the debtor on or within 90 days before the date of the filing of the petition, then the trustee may recover from such creditor the amount so offset to the extent that any insufficiency on the date of such setoff is less than the insufficiency on the later of—

(A) 90 days before the date of the filing of the petition; and

(B) the first date during the 90 days immediately preceding the date of the filing of the petition on which there is an insufficiency.

(2) In this subsection, "insufficiency" means amount, if any, by which a claim against the debtor exceeds a mutual debt owing to the debtor by the holder of such claim.

(c) For the purposes of this section, the debtor is presumed to have been insolvent on and during the 90 days immediately preceding the date of the filing of the petition.

(Pub. L. 95–598, Nov. 6, 1978, 92 Stat. 2602; Pub. L. 98–353, title III, §§395, 467, July 10, 1984, 98 Stat. 365, 380; Pub. L. 101–311, title I, §105, June 25, 1990, 104 Stat. 268; Pub. L. 103–394, title II, §§205(b), 222(b), title V, §501(d)(19), Oct. 22, 1994, 108 Stat. 4123, 4129, 4146; Pub. L. 109–8, title IX, §907(n), Apr. 20, 2005, 119 Stat. 181.)

Historical and Revision Notes
legislative statements

Section 553 of the House amendment is derived from a similar provision contained in the Senate amendment, but is modified to clarify application of a two-point test with respect to setoffs.

senate report no. 95–989

This section preserves, with some changes, the right of setoff in bankruptcy cases now found in section 68 of the Bankruptcy Act [section 108 of former title 11]. One exception to the right is the automatic stay, discussed in connection with proposed 11 U.S.C. 362. Another is the right of the trustee to use property under section 363 that is subject to a right of setoff.

The section states that the right of setoff is unaffected by the bankruptcy code except to the extent that the creditor's claim is disallowed, the creditor acquired (other than from the debtor) the claim during the 90 days preceding the case while the debtor was insolvent, the debt being offset was incurred for the purpose of obtaining a right of setoff, while the debtor was insolvent and during the 90-day prebankruptcy period, or the creditor improved his position in the 90-day period (similar to the improvement in position test found in the preference section 547(c)(5)). Only the last exception is an addition to current law.

As under section 547(f), the debtor is presumed to have been insolvent during the 90 days before the case.

Amendments

2005—Subsec. (a)(2)(B)(ii). Pub. L. 109–8, §907(n)(1), inserted "(except for a setoff of a kind described in section 362(b)(6), 362(b)(7), 362(b)(17), 362(b)(27), 555, 556, 559, 560, or 561)" before semicolon.

Subsec. (a)(3)(C). Pub. L. 109–8, §907(n)(2), inserted "(except for a setoff of a kind described in section 362(b)(6), 362(b)(7), 362(b)(17), 362(b)(27), 555, 556, 559, 560, or 561)" before period.

Subsec. (b)(1). Pub. L. 109–8, §907(n)(3), substituted "362(b)(17), 362(b)(27), 555, 556, 559, 560, 561," for "362(b)(14)," in introductory provisions.

1994—Subsec. (a)(1). Pub. L. 103–394, §501(d)(19)(A), struck out before semicolon at end "other than under section 502(b)(3) of this title".

Subsec. (b)(1). Pub. L. 103–394, §501(d)(19)(B), substituted "section 362(b)(14)," for "section 362(b)(14),,".

Pub. L. 103–394, §222(b), which directed the amendment of section 553(b)(1) by inserting "546(h)," after "365(h),", was executed by making the insertion in section 553(b)(1) of this title to reflect the probable intent of Congress.

Pub. L. 103–394, §205(b), substituted "365(h)" for "365(h)(2)".

1990—Subsec. (b)(1). Pub. L. 101–311 substituted "362(b)(7), 362(b)(14)," for "362(b)(7),".

1984—Subsec. (b)(1). Pub. L. 98–353 inserted ", 362(b)(7)," after "362(b)(6)", and substituted ", 365(h)(2), or 365(i)(2)" for "or 365(h)(1)".

Effective Date of 2005 Amendment

Amendment by Pub. L. 109–8 effective 180 days after Apr. 20, 2005, and not applicable with respect to cases commenced under this title before such effective date, except as otherwise provided, see section 1501 of Pub. L. 109–8, set out as a note under section 101 of this title.

Effective Date of 1994 Amendment

Amendment by Pub. L. 103–394 effective Oct. 22, 1994, and not applicable with respect to cases commenced under this title before Oct. 22, 1994, see section 702 of Pub. L. 103–394, set out as a note under section 101 of this title.

Effective Date of 1984 Amendment

Amendment by Pub. L. 98–353 effective with respect to cases filed 90 days after July 10, 1984, see section 552(a) of Pub. L. 98–353, set out as a note under section 101 of this title.

§554. Abandonment of property of the estate

(a) After notice and a hearing, the trustee may abandon any property of the estate that is burdensome to the estate or that is of inconsequential value and benefit to the estate.

(b) On request of a party in interest and after notice and a hearing, the court may order the trustee to abandon any property of the estate that is burdensome to the estate or that is of inconsequential value and benefit to the estate.

(c) Unless the court orders otherwise, any property scheduled under section 521(a)(1) of this title not otherwise administered at the time of the closing of a case is abandoned to the debtor and administered for purposes of section 350 of this title.

(d) Unless the court orders otherwise, property of the estate that is not abandoned under this section and that is not administered in the case remains property of the estate.

(Pub. L. 95–598, Nov. 6, 1978, 92 Stat. 2603; Pub. L. 98–353, title III, §468, July 10, 1984, 98 Stat. 380; Pub. L. 99–554, title II, §283(p), Oct. 27, 1986, 100 Stat. 3118; Pub. L. 111–327, §2(a)(23), Dec. 22, 2010, 124 Stat. 3560.)

Historical and Revision Notes
legislative statements

Section 554(b) is new and permits a party in interest to request the court to order the trustee to abandon property of the estate that is burdensome to the estate or that is of inconsequential value to the estate.

senate report no. 95–989

Under this section the court may authorize the trustee to abandon any property of the estate that is burdensome to the estate or that is of inconsequential value to the estate. Abandonment may be to any party with a possessory interest in the property abandoned. In order to aid administration of the case, subsection (b) deems the court to have authorized abandonment of any property that is scheduled under section 521(1) and that is not administered before the case is closed. That property is deemed abandoned to the debtor. Subsection (c) specifies that if property is neither abandoned nor administered it remains property of the estate.

Amendments

2010—Subsec. (c). Pub. L. 111–327 substituted "521(a)(1)" for "521(1)".

1986—Subsec. (c). Pub. L. 99–554 substituted "521(1)" for "521(a)(1)".

1984—Subsecs. (a), (b). Pub. L. 98–353, §468(a), inserted "and benefit" after "value".

Subsec. (c). Pub. L. 98–353, §468(b), amended subsec. (c) generally. Prior to amendment, subsec. (c) read as follows: "Unless the court orders otherwise, any property that is scheduled under section 521(1) of this title and that is not administered before a case is closed under section 350 of this title is deemed abandoned."

Subsec. (d). Pub. L. 98–353, §468(c), struck out "section (a) or (b) of" after "not abandoned under".

Effective Date of 1986 Amendment

Amendment by Pub. L. 99–554 effective 30 days after Oct. 27, 1986, see section 302(a) of Pub. L. 99–554, set out as a note under section 581 of Title 28, Judiciary and Judicial Procedure.

Effective Date of 1984 Amendment

Amendment by Pub. L. 98–353 effective with respect to cases filed 90 days after July 10, 1984, see section 552(a) of Pub. L. 98–353, set out as a note under section 101 of this title.

§555. Contractual right to liquidate, terminate, or accelerate a securities contract

The exercise of a contractual right of a stockbroker, financial institution, financial participant, or securities clearing agency to cause the liquidation, termination, or acceleration of a securities contract, as defined in section 741 of this title, because of a condition of the kind specified in section 365(e)(1) of this title shall not be stayed, avoided, or otherwise limited by operation of any provision of this title or by order of a court or administrative agency in any proceeding under this title unless such order is authorized under the provisions of the Securities Investor Protection Act of 1970 or any statute administered by the Securities and Exchange Commission. As used in this section, the term "contractual right" includes a right set forth in a rule or bylaw of a derivatives clearing organization (as defined in the Commodity Exchange Act), a multilateral clearing organization (as defined in the Federal Deposit Insurance Corporation Improvement Act of 1991), a national securities exchange, a national securities association, a securities clearing agency, a contract market designated under the Commodity Exchange Act, a derivatives transaction execution facility registered under the Commodity Exchange Act, or a board of trade (as defined in the Commodity Exchange Act), or in a resolution of the governing board thereof, and a right, whether or not in writing, arising under common law, under law merchant, or by reason of normal business practice.

(Added Pub. L. 97–222, §6(a), July 27, 1982, 96 Stat. 236; amended Pub. L. 98–353, title III, §469, July 10, 1984, 98 Stat. 380; Pub. L. 103–394, title V, §501(b)(6), (d)(20), Oct. 22, 1994, 108 Stat. 4143, 4146; Pub. L. 109–8, title IX, §907(g), (o)(7), Apr. 20, 2005, 119 Stat. 177, 182.)

References in Text

The Securities Investor Protection Act of 1970, referred to in text, is Pub. L. 91–598, Dec. 30, 1970, 84 Stat. 1636, as amended, which is classified generally to chapter 2B–1 (§78aaa et seq.) of Title 15, Commerce and Trade. For complete classification of this Act to the Code, see section 78aaa of Title 15 and Tables.

The Commodity Exchange Act, referred to in text, is act Sept. 21, 1922, ch. 369, 42 Stat. 998, as amended, which is classified generally to chapter 1 (§1 et seq.) of Title 7, Agriculture. For complete classification of this Act to the Code, see section 1 of Title 7 and Tables.

The Federal Deposit Insurance Corporation Improvement Act of 1991, referred to in text, is Pub. L. 102–242, Dec. 19, 1991, 105 Stat. 2236, as amended. For complete classification of this Act to the Code, see Short Title of 1991 Amendment note set out under section 1811 of Title 12, Banks and Banking, and Tables.

Amendments

2005—Pub. L. 109–8, §907(g)(1), substituted "Contractual right to liquidate, terminate, or accelerate a securities contract" for "Contractual right to liquidate a securities contract" in section catchline.

Pub. L. 109–8, §907(g)(2), (o)(7), in first sentence, inserted "financial participant," after "financial institution," and substituted "liquidation, termination, or acceleration" for "liquidation," and substituted second sentence for former second sentence which read as follows: "As used in this section, the term 'contractual right' includes a right set forth in a rule or bylaw of a national securities exchange, a national securities association, or a securities clearing agency."

1994—Pub. L. 103–394 substituted "section 741 of this title" for "section 741(7)" and struck out "(15 U.S.C. 78aaa et seq.)" after "Act of 1970".

1984—Pub. L. 98–353 inserted ", financial institution," after "stockbroker".

Effective Date of 2005 Amendment

Amendment by Pub. L. 109–8 effective 180 days after Apr. 20, 2005, and not applicable with respect to cases commenced under this title before such effective date, except as otherwise provided, see section 1501 of Pub. L. 109–8, set out as a note under section 101 of this title.

Effective Date of 1994 Amendment

Amendment by Pub. L. 103–394 effective Oct. 22, 1994, and not applicable with respect to cases commenced under this title before Oct. 22, 1994, see section 702 of Pub. L. 103–394, set out as a note under section 101 of this title.

Effective Date of 1984 Amendment

Amendment by Pub. L. 98–353 effective with respect to cases filed 90 days after July 10, 1984, see section 552(a) of Pub. L. 98–353, set out as a note under section 101 of this title.

§556. Contractual right to liquidate, terminate, or accelerate a commodities contract or forward contract

The contractual right of a commodity broker, financial participant, or forward contract merchant to cause the liquidation, termination, or acceleration of a commodity contract, as defined in section 761 of this title, or forward contract because of a condition of the kind specified in section 365(e)(1) of this title, and the right to a variation or maintenance margin payment received from a trustee with respect to open commodity contracts or forward contracts, shall not be stayed, avoided, or otherwise limited by operation of any provision of this title or by the order of a court in any proceeding under this title. As used in this section, the term "contractual right" includes a right set forth in a rule or bylaw of a derivatives clearing organization (as defined in the Commodity Exchange Act), a multilateral clearing organization (as defined in the Federal Deposit Insurance Corporation Improvement Act of 1991), a national securities exchange, a national securities association, a securities clearing agency, a contract market designated under the Commodity Exchange Act, a derivatives transaction execution facility registered under the Commodity Exchange Act, or a board of trade (as defined in the Commodity Exchange Act) or in a resolution of the governing board thereof and a right, whether or not evidenced in writing, arising under common law, under law merchant or by reason of normal business practice.

(Added Pub. L. 97–222, §6(a), July 27, 1982, 96 Stat. 236; amended Pub. L. 101–311, title II, §205, June 25, 1990, 104 Stat. 270; Pub. L. 103–394, title V, §501(b)(7), Oct. 22, 1994, 108 Stat. 4143; Pub. L. 109–8, title IX, §§907(h), (o)(8), Apr. 20, 2005, 119 Stat. 178, 182.)

References in Text

The Commodity Exchange Act, referred to in text, is act Sept. 21, 1922, ch. 369, 42 Stat. 998, as amended, which is classified generally to chapter 1 (§1 et seq.) of Title 7, Agriculture. For complete classification of this Act to the Code, see section 1 of Title 7 and Tables.

The Federal Deposit Insurance Corporation Improvement Act of 1991, referred to in text, is Pub. L. 102–242, Dec. 19, 1991, 105 Stat. 2236, as amended. For complete classification of this Act to the Code, see Short Title of 1991 Amendment note set out under section 1811 of Title 12, Banks and Banking, and Tables.

Amendments

2005—Pub. L. 109–8, §907(o)(8), inserted ", financial participant," after "commodity broker" in first sentence.

Pub. L. 109–8, §907(h), substituted "Contractual right to liquidate, terminate, or accelerate a commodities contract or forward contract" for "Contractual right to liquidate a commodities contract or forward contract" in section catchline, "liquidation, termination, or acceleration" for "liquidation" in first sentence, and "As used in this section, the term 'contractual right' includes a right set forth in a rule or bylaw of a derivatives clearing organization (as defined in the Commodity Exchange Act), a multilateral clearing organization (as defined in the Federal Deposit Insurance Corporation Improvement Act of 1991), a national securities exchange, a national securities association, a securities clearing agency, a contract market designated under the Commodity Exchange Act, a derivatives transaction execution facility registered under the Commodity Exchange Act, or a board of trade (as defined in the Commodity Exchange Act) or in a resolution of the governing board thereof and a right," for "As used in this section, the term 'contractual right' includes a right set forth in a rule or bylaw of a clearing organization or contract market or in a resolution of the governing board thereof and a right,", in second sentence.

1994—Pub. L. 103–394 substituted "section 761 of this title" for "section 761(4)".

1990—Pub. L. 101–311 inserted before period at end "and a right, whether or not evidenced in writing, arising under common law, under law merchant or by reason of normal business practice".

Effective Date of 2005 Amendment

Amendment by Pub. L. 109–8 effective 180 days after Apr. 20, 2005, and not applicable with respect to cases commenced under this title before such effective date, except as otherwise provided, see section 1501 of Pub. L. 109–8, set out as a note under section 101 of this title.

Effective Date of 1994 Amendment

Amendment by Pub. L. 103–394 effective Oct. 22, 1994, and not applicable with respect to cases commenced under this title before Oct. 22, 1994, see section 702 of Pub. L. 103–394, set out as a note under section 101 of this title.

§557. Expedited determination of interests in, and abandonment or other disposition of grain assets

(a) This section applies only in a case concerning a debtor that owns or operates a grain storage facility and only with respect to grain and the proceeds of grain. This section does not affect the application of any other section of this title to property other than grain and proceeds of grain.

(b) In this section—

(1) "grain" means wheat, corn, flaxseed, grain sorghum, barley, oats, rye, soybeans, other dry edible beans, or rice;

(2) "grain storage facility" means a site or physical structure regularly used to store grain for producers, or to store grain acquired from producers for resale; and

(3) "producer" means an entity which engages in the growing of grain.

(c)(1) Notwithstanding sections 362, 363, 365, and 554 of this title, on the court's own motion the court may, and on the request of the trustee or an entity that claims an interest in grain or the proceeds of grain the court shall, expedite the procedures for the determination of interests in and the disposition of grain and the proceeds of grain, by shortening to the greatest extent feasible such time periods as are otherwise applicable for such procedures and by establishing, by order, a timetable having a duration of not to exceed 120 days for the completion of the applicable procedure specified in subsection (d) of this section. Such time periods and such timetable may be modified by the court, for cause, in accordance with subsection (f) of this section.

(2) The court shall determine the extent to which such time periods shall be shortened, based upon—

(A) any need of an entity claiming an interest in such grain or the proceeds of grain for a prompt determination of such interest;

(B) any need of such entity for a prompt disposition of such grain;

(C) the market for such grain;

(D) the conditions under which such grain is stored;

(E) the costs of continued storage or disposition of such grain;

(F) the orderly administration of the estate;

(G) the appropriate opportunity for an entity to assert an interest in such grain; and

(H) such other considerations as are relevant to the need to expedite such procedures in the case.

(d) The procedures that may be expedited under subsection (c) of this section include—

(1) the filing of and response to—

(A) a claim of ownership;

(B) a proof of claim;

(C) a request for abandonment;

(D) a request for relief from the stay of action against property under section 362(a) of this title;

(E) a request for determination of secured status;

(F) a request for determination of whether such grain or the proceeds of grain—

(i) is property of the estate;

(ii) must be turned over to the estate; or

(iii) may be used, sold, or leased; and

(G) any other request for determination of an interest in such grain or the proceeds of grain;

(2) the disposition of such grain or the proceeds of grain, before or after determination of interests in such grain or the proceeds of grain, by way of—

(A) sale of such grain;

(B) abandonment;

(C) distribution; or

(D) such other method as is equitable in the case;

(3) subject to sections 701, 702, 703, 1104, 1202, and 1302 of this title, the appointment of a trustee or examiner and the retention and compensation of any professional person required to assist with respect to matters relevant to the determination of interests in or disposition of such grain or the proceeds of grain; and

(4) the determination of any dispute concerning a matter specified in paragraph (1), (2), or (3) of this subsection.

(e)(1) Any governmental unit that has regulatory jurisdiction over the operation or liquidation of the debtor or the debtor's business shall be given notice of any request made or order entered under subsection (c) of this section.

(2) Any such governmental unit may raise, and may appear and be heard on, any issue relating to grain or the proceeds of grain in a case in which a request is made, or an order is entered, under subsection (c) of this section.

(3) The trustee shall consult with such governmental unit before taking any action relating to the disposition of grain in the possession, custody, or control of the debtor or the estate.

(f) The court may extend the period for final disposition of grain or the proceeds of grain under this section beyond 120 days if the court finds that—

(1) the interests of justice so require in light of the complexity of the case; and

(2) the interests of those claimants entitled to distribution of grain or the proceeds of grain will not be materially injured by such additional delay.

(g) Unless an order establishing an expedited procedure under subsection (c) of this section, or determining any interest in or approving any disposition of grain or the proceeds of grain, is stayed pending appeal—

(1) the reversal or modification of such order on appeal does not affect the validity of any procedure, determination, or disposition that occurs before such reversal or modification, whether or not any entity knew of the pendency of the appeal; and

(2) neither the court nor the trustee may delay, due to the appeal of such order, any proceeding in the case in which such order is issued.

(h)(1) The trustee may recover from grain and the proceeds of grain the reasonable and necessary costs and expenses allowable under section 503(b) of this title attributable to preserving or disposing of grain or the proceeds of grain, but may not recover from such grain or the proceeds of grain any other costs or expenses.

(2) Notwithstanding section 326(a) of this title, the dollar amounts of money specified in such section include the value, as of the date of disposition, of any grain that the trustee distributes in kind.

(i) In all cases where the quantity of a specific type of grain held by a debtor operating a grain storage facility exceeds ten thousand bushels, such grain shall be sold by the trustee and the assets thereof distributed in accordance with the provisions of this section.

(Added Pub. L. 98–353, title III, §352(a), July 10, 1984, 98 Stat. 359; amended Pub. L. 99–554, title II, §257(p), Oct. 27, 1986, 100 Stat. 3115.)

Amendments

1986—Subsec. (d)(3). Pub. L. 99–554 inserted reference to section 1202 of this title.

Effective Date of 1986 Amendment

Amendment by Pub. L. 99–554 effective 30 days after Oct. 27, 1986, but not applicable to cases commenced under this title before that date, see section 302(a), (c)(1) of Pub. L. 99–554, set out as a note under section 581 of Title 28, Judiciary and Judicial Procedure.

Effective Date

Section effective with respect to cases filed 90 days after July 10, 1984, see section 552(a) of Pub. L. 98–353, set out as an Effective Date of 1984 Amendment note under section 101 of this title.

§558. Defenses of the estate

The estate shall have the benefit of any defense available to the debtor as against any entity other than the estate, including statutes of limitation, statutes of frauds, usury, and other personal defenses. A waiver of any such defense by the debtor after the commencement of the case does not bind the estate.

(Added Pub. L. 98–353, title III, §470(a), July 10, 1984, 98 Stat. 380.)

Effective Date

Section effective with respect to cases filed 90 days after July 10, 1984, see section 552(a) of Pub. L. 98–353, set out as an Effective Date of 1984 Amendment note under section 101 of this title.

§559. Contractual right to liquidate, terminate, or accelerate a repurchase agreement

The exercise of a contractual right of a repo participant or financial participant to cause the liquidation, termination, or acceleration of a repurchase agreement because of a condition of the kind specified in section 365(e)(1) of this title shall not be stayed, avoided, or otherwise limited by operation of any provision of this title or by order of a court or administrative agency in any proceeding under this title, unless, where the debtor is a stockbroker or securities clearing agency, such order is authorized under the provisions of the Securities Investor Protection Act of 1970 or any statute administered by the Securities and Exchange Commission. In the event that a repo participant or financial participant liquidates one or more repurchase agreements with a debtor and under the terms of one or more such agreements has agreed to deliver assets subject to repurchase agreements to the debtor, any excess of the market prices received on liquidation of such assets (or if any such assets are not disposed of on the date of liquidation of such repurchase agreements, at the prices available at the time of liquidation of such repurchase agreements from a generally recognized source or the most recent closing bid quotation from such a source) over the sum of the stated repurchase prices and all expenses in connection with the liquidation of such repurchase agreements shall be deemed property of the estate, subject to the available rights of setoff. As used in this section, the term "contractual right" includes a right set forth in a rule or bylaw of a derivatives clearing organization (as defined in the Commodity Exchange Act), a multilateral clearing organization (as defined in the Federal Deposit Insurance Corporation Improvement Act of 1991), a national securities exchange, a national securities association, a securities clearing agency, a contract market designated under the Commodity Exchange Act, a derivatives transaction execution facility registered under the Commodity Exchange Act, or a board of trade (as defined in the Commodity Exchange Act) or in a resolution of the governing board thereof and a right, whether or not evidenced in writing, arising under common law, under law merchant or by reason of normal business practice.

(Added Pub. L. 98–353, title III, §396(a), July 10, 1984, 98 Stat. 366; amended Pub. L. 103–394, title V, §501(d)(21), Oct. 22, 1994, 108 Stat. 4146; Pub. L. 109–8, title IX, §907(i), (o)(9), Apr. 20, 2005, 119 Stat. 178, 182.)

References in Text

The Securities Investor Protection Act of 1970, referred to in text, is Pub. L. 91–598, Dec. 30, 1970, 84 Stat. 1636, as amended, which is classified generally to chapter 2B–1 (§78aaa et seq.) of Title 15, Commerce and Trade. For complete classification of this Act to the Code, see section 78aaa of Title 15 and Tables.

The Commodity Exchange Act, referred to in text, is act Sept. 21, 1922, ch. 369, 42 Stat. 998, as amended, which is classified generally to chapter 1 (§1 et seq.) of Title 7, Agriculture. For complete classification of this Act to the Code, see section 1 of Title 7 and Tables.

The Federal Deposit Insurance Corporation Improvement Act of 1991, referred to in text, is Pub. L. 102–242, Dec. 19, 1991, 105 Stat. 2236, as amended. For complete classification of this Act to the Code, see Short Title of 1991 Amendment note set out under section 1811 of Title 12, Banks and Banking, and Tables.

Amendments

2005—Pub. L. 109–8, §907(o)(9), inserted "or financial participant" after "repo participant" in two places.

Pub. L. 109–8, §907(i), substituted "Contractual right to liquidate, terminate, or accelerate a repurchase agreement" for "Contractual right to liquidate a repurchase agreement" in section catchline, "liquidation, termination, or acceleration" for "liquidation" in first sentence, and "As used in this section, the term 'contractual right' includes a right set forth in a rule or bylaw of a derivatives clearing organization (as defined in the Commodity Exchange Act), a multilateral clearing organization (as defined in the Federal Deposit Insurance Corporation Improvement Act of 1991), a national securities exchange, a national securities association, a securities clearing agency, a contract market designated under the Commodity Exchange Act, a derivatives transaction execution facility registered under the Commodity Exchange Act, or a board of trade (as defined in the Commodity Exchange Act) or in a resolution of the governing board thereof and a right," for "As used in this section, the term 'contractual right' includes a right set forth in a rule or bylaw, applicable to each party to the repurchase agreement, of a national securities exchange, a national securities association, or a securities clearing agency, and a right," in third sentence.

1994—Pub. L. 103–394 struck out "(15 U.S.C. 78aaa et seq.)" after "Act of 1970".

Effective Date of 2005 Amendment

Amendment by Pub. L. 109–8 effective 180 days after Apr. 20, 2005, and not applicable with respect to cases commenced under this title before such effective date, except as otherwise provided, see section 1501 of Pub. L. 109–8, set out as a note under section 101 of this title.

Effective Date of 1994 Amendment

Amendment by Pub. L. 103–394 effective Oct. 22, 1994, and not applicable with respect to cases commenced under this title before Oct. 22, 1994, see section 702 of Pub. L. 103–394, set out as a note under section 101 of this title.

Effective Date

Section effective with respect to cases filed 90 days after July 10, 1984, see section 552(a) of Pub. L. 98–353, set out as an Effective Date of 1984 Amendment note under section 101 of this title.

§560. Contractual right to liquidate, terminate, or accelerate a swap agreement

The exercise of any contractual right of any swap participant or financial participant to cause the liquidation, termination, or acceleration of one or more swap agreements because of a condition of the kind specified in section 365(e)(1) of this title or to offset or net out any termination values or payment amounts arising under or in connection with the termination, liquidation, or acceleration of one or more swap agreements shall not be stayed, avoided, or otherwise limited by operation of any provision of this title or by order of a court or administrative agency in any proceeding under this title. As used in this section, the term "contractual right" includes a right set forth in a rule or bylaw of a derivatives clearing organization (as defined in the Commodity Exchange Act), a multilateral clearing organization (as defined in the Federal Deposit Insurance Corporation Improvement Act of 1991), a national securities exchange, a national securities association, a securities clearing agency, a contract market designated under the Commodity Exchange Act, a derivatives transaction execution facility registered under the Commodity Exchange Act, or a board of trade (as defined in the Commodity Exchange Act) or in a resolution of the governing board thereof and a right, whether or not evidenced in writing, arising under common law, under law merchant, or by reason of normal business practice.

(Added Pub. L. 101–311, title I, §106(a), June 25, 1990, 104 Stat. 268; amended Pub. L. 109–8, title IX, §907(j), (o)(10), Apr. 20, 2005, 119 Stat. 178, 182.)

References in Text

The Commodity Exchange Act, referred to in text, is act Sept. 21, 1922, ch. 369, 42 Stat. 998, as amended, which is classified generally to chapter 1 (§1 et seq.) of Title 7, Agriculture. For complete classification of this Act to the Code, see section 1 of Title 7 and Tables.

The Federal Deposit Insurance Corporation Improvement Act of 1991, referred to in text, is Pub. L. 102–242, Dec. 19, 1991, 105 Stat. 2236, as amended. For complete classification of this Act to the Code, see Short Title of 1991 Amendment note set out under section 1811 of Title 12, Banks and Banking, and Tables.

Amendments

2005—Pub. L. 109–8, §907(o)(10), inserted "or financial participant" after "swap participant" in first sentence.

Pub. L. 109–8, §907(j)(1), in section catchline, substituted "Contractual right to liquidate, terminate, or accelerate a swap agreement" for "Contractual right to terminate a swap agreement", in first sentence, substituted "liquidation, termination, or acceleration of one or more swap agreements" for "termination of a swap agreement" and "in connection with the termination, liquidation, or acceleration of one or more swap agreements" for "in connection with any swap agreement", and in second sentence, substituted "As used in this section, the term 'contractual right' includes a right set forth in a rule or bylaw of a derivatives clearing organization (as defined in the Commodity Exchange Act), a multilateral clearing organization (as defined in the Federal Deposit Insurance Corporation Improvement Act of 1991), a national securities exchange, a national securities association, a securities clearing agency, a contract market designated under the Commodity Exchange Act, a derivatives transaction execution facility registered under the Commodity Exchange Act, or a board of trade (as defined in the Commodity Exchange Act) or in a resolution of the governing board thereof and a right," for "As used in this section, the term 'contractual right' includes a right,".

Effective Date of 2005 Amendment

Amendment by Pub. L. 109–8 effective 180 days after Apr. 20, 2005, and not applicable with respect to cases commenced under this title before such effective date, except as otherwise provided, see section 1501 of Pub. L. 109–8, set out as a note under section 101 of this title.

§561. Contractual right to terminate, liquidate, accelerate, or offset under a master netting agreement and across contracts; proceedings under chapter 15

(a) Subject to subsection (b), the exercise of any contractual right, because of a condition of the kind specified in section 365(e)(1), to cause the termination, liquidation, or acceleration of or to offset or net termination values, payment amounts, or other transfer obligations arising under or in connection with one or more (or the termination, liquidation, or acceleration of one or more)—

(1) securities contracts, as defined in section 741(7);
(2) commodity contracts, as defined in section 761(4);
(3) forward contracts;
(4) repurchase agreements;
(5) swap agreements; or
(6) master netting agreements,

shall not be stayed, avoided, or otherwise limited by operation of any provision of this title or by any order of a court or administrative agency in any proceeding under this title.

(b)(1) A party may exercise a contractual right described in subsection (a) to terminate, liquidate, or accelerate only to the extent that such party could exercise such a right under section 555, 556, 559, or 560 for each individual contract covered by the master netting agreement in issue.

(2) If a debtor is a commodity broker subject to subchapter IV of chapter 7—

(A) a party may not net or offset an obligation to the debtor arising under, or in connection with, a commodity contract traded on or subject to the rules of a contract market designated under the Commodity Exchange Act or a derivatives transaction execution facility registered under the Commodity Exchange Act against any claim arising under, or in connection with, other instruments, contracts, or agreements listed in subsection (a) except to the extent that the party has positive net equity in the commodity accounts at the debtor, as calculated under such subchapter; and

(B) another commodity broker may not net or offset an obligation to the debtor arising under, or in connection with, a commodity contract entered into or held on behalf of a customer of the debtor and traded on or subject to the rules of a contract market designated under the Commodity Exchange Act or a derivatives transaction execution facility registered under the Commodity Exchange Act against any claim arising under, or in connection with, other instruments, contracts, or agreements listed in subsection (a).

(3) No provision of subparagraph (A) or (B) of paragraph (2) shall prohibit the offset of claims and obligations that arise under—

(A) a cross-margining agreement or similar arrangement that has been approved by the Commodity Futures Trading Commission or submitted to the Commodity Futures Trading Commission under paragraph (1) or (2) of section 5c(c) of the Commodity Exchange Act and has not been abrogated or rendered ineffective by the Commodity Futures Trading Commission; or

(B) any other netting agreement between a clearing organization (as defined in section 761) and another entity that has been approved by the Commodity Futures Trading Commission.

(c) As used in this section, the term "contractual right" includes a right set forth in a rule or bylaw of a derivatives clearing organization (as defined in the Commodity Exchange Act), a multilateral clearing organization (as defined in the Federal Deposit Insurance Corporation Improvement Act of 1991), a national securities exchange, a national securities association, a securities clearing agency, a contract market designated under the Commodity Exchange Act, a derivatives transaction execution facility registered under the Commodity Exchange Act, or a board of trade (as defined in the Commodity Exchange Act) or in a resolution of the governing board thereof, and a right, whether or not evidenced in writing, arising under common law, under law merchant, or by reason of normal business practice.

(d) Any provisions of this title relating to securities contracts, commodity contracts, forward contracts, repurchase agreements, swap agreements, or master netting agreements shall apply in a case under chapter 15, so that enforcement of contractual provisions of such contracts and agreements in accordance with their terms will not be stayed or otherwise limited by operation of any provision of this title or by order of a court in any case under this title, and to limit avoidance powers to the same extent as in a proceeding under chapter 7 or 11 of this title (such enforcement not to be limited based on the presence or absence of assets of the debtor in the United States).

(Added Pub. L. 109–8, title IX, §907(k)(1), Apr. 20, 2005, 119 Stat. 179.)

References in Text

The Commodity Exchange Act, referred to in subsecs. (b)(2) and (c), is act Sept. 21, 1922, ch. 369, 42 Stat. 998, as amended, which is classified generally to chapter 1 (§1 et seq.) of Title 7, Agriculture. Section 5c(c) of the Act is classified to section 7a–2(c) of Title 7. For complete classification of this Act to the Code, see section 1 of Title 7 and Tables.

The Federal Deposit Insurance Corporation Improvement Act of 1991, referred to in subsec. (c), is Pub. L. 102–242, Dec. 19, 1991, 105 Stat. 2236, as amended. For complete classification of this Act to the Code, see Short Title of 1991 Amendment note set out under section 1811 of Title 12, Banks and Banking, and Tables.

Effective Date

Section effective 180 days after Apr. 20, 2005, and not applicable with respect to cases commenced under this title before such effective date, except as otherwise provided, see section 1501 of Pub. L. 109–8, set out as an Effective Date of 2005 Amendment note under section 101 of this title.

§562. Timing of damage measurement in connection with swap agreements, securities contracts, forward contracts, commodity contracts, repurchase agreements, and master netting agreements

(a) If the trustee rejects a swap agreement, securities contract (as defined in section 741), forward contract, commodity contract (as defined in section 761), repurchase agreement, or master netting agreement pursuant to section 365(a), or if a forward contract merchant, stockbroker, financial institution, securities clearing agency, repo participant, financial participant, master netting agreement participant, or swap participant liquidates, terminates, or accelerates such contract or agreement, damages shall be measured as of the earlier of—

(1) the date of such rejection; or
(2) the date or dates of such liquidation, termination, or acceleration.

(b) If there are not any commercially reasonable determinants of value as of any date referred to in paragraph (1) or (2) of subsection (a), damages shall be measured as of the earliest subsequent date or dates on which there are commercially reasonable determinants of value.

(c) For the purposes of subsection (b), if damages are not measured as of the date or dates of rejection, liquidation, termination, or acceleration, and the forward contract merchant, stockbroker, financial institution, securities clearing agency, repo participant, financial participant, master netting agreement participant, or swap participant or the trustee objects to the timing of the measurement of damages—

(1) the trustee, in the case of an objection by a forward contract merchant, stockbroker, financial institution, securities clearing agency, repo participant, financial participant, master netting agreement participant, or swap participant; or

(2) the forward contract merchant, stockbroker, financial institution, securities clearing agency, repo participant, financial participant, master netting agreement participant, or swap participant, in the case of an objection by the trustee,

has the burden of proving that there were no commercially reasonable determinants of value as of such date or dates.

(Added Pub. L. 109–8, title IX, §910(a)(1), Apr. 20, 2005, 119 Stat. 184.)

Effective Date

Section effective 180 days after Apr. 20, 2005, and not applicable with respect to cases commenced under this title before such effective date, except as otherwise provided, see section 1501 of Pub. L. 109–8, set out as an Effective Date of 2005 Amendment note under section 101 of this title.

CHAPTER 7—LIQUIDATION

SUBCHAPTER I—OFFICERS AND ADMINISTRATION

Sec.
701.
Interim trustee.
702.
Election of trustee.
703.
Successor trustee.
704.
Duties of trustee.
705.
Creditors' committee.
706.
Conversion.
707.
Dismissal of a case or conversion to a case under chapter 11 or 13.

SUBCHAPTER II—COLLECTION, LIQUIDATION, AND DISTRIBUTION OF THE ESTATE

721.
Authorization to operate business.
722.
Redemption.
723.
Rights of partnership trustee against general partners.
724.

Treatment of certain liens.
725.
Disposition of certain property.
726.
Distribution of property of the estate.
727.
Discharge.
[728.
Repealed.]

SUBCHAPTER III—STOCKBROKER LIQUIDATION
741.
Definitions for this subchapter.
742.
Effect of section 362 of this title in this subchapter.
743.
Notice.
744.
Executory contracts.
745.
Treatment of accounts.
746.
Extent of customer claims.
747.
Subordination of certain customer claims.
748.
Reduction of securities to money.
749.
Voidable transfers.
750.
Distribution of securities.
751.
Customer name securities.
752.
Customer property.
753.
Stockbroker liquidation and forward contract merchants, commodity brokers, stockbrokers, financial institutions, financial participants, securities clearing agencies, swap participants, repo participants, and master netting agreement participants.

SUBCHAPTER IV—COMMODITY BROKER LIQUIDATION
761.
Definitions for this subchapter.
762.
Notice to the Commission and right to be heard.
763.
Treatment of accounts.
764.
Voidable transfers.
765.
Customer instructions.
766.
Treatment of customer property.
767.
Commodity broker liquidation and forward contract merchants, commodity brokers, stockbrokers, financial institutions, financial participants, securities clearing agencies, swap participants, repo participants, and master netting agreement participants.

SUBCHAPTER V—CLEARING BANK LIQUIDATION
781.
Definitions.
782.
Selection of trustee.
783.
Additional powers of trustee.
784.
Right to be heard.

Amendments
2005—Pub. L. 109–8, title I, §102(k), title VII, §719(b)(2), title IX, §907(p)(2), Apr. 20, 2005, 119 Stat. 35, 133, 182, added items 753 and 767, substituted "Dismissal of a case or conversion to a case under chapter 11 or 13" for "Dismissal" in item 707, and struck out item 728 "Special tax provisions".
2000—Pub. L. 106–554, §1(a)(5) [title I, §112(d)], Dec. 21, 2000, 114 Stat. 2763, 2763A–396, added subchapter V heading and items 781 to 784.
1984—Pub. L. 98–353, title III, §471, July 10, 1984, 98 Stat. 380, substituted "Successor" for "Succesor" in item 703.

SUBCHAPTER I—OFFICERS AND ADMINISTRATION

§701. Interim trustee
(a)(1) Promptly after the order for relief under this chapter, the United States trustee shall appoint one disinterested person that is a member of the panel of private trustees established under section 586(a)(1) of title 28 or that is serving as trustee in the case immediately before the order for relief under this chapter to serve as interim trustee in the case.
(2) If none of the members of such panel is willing to serve as interim trustee in the case, then the United States trustee may serve as interim trustee in the case.
(b) The service of an interim trustee under this section terminates when a trustee elected or designated under section 702 of this title to serve as trustee in the case qualifies under section 322 of this title.

(c) An interim trustee serving under this section is a trustee in a case under this title.

(Pub. L. 95–598, Nov. 6, 1978, 92 Stat. 2604; Pub. L. 99–554, title II, §215, Oct. 27, 1986, 100 Stat. 3100.)

Historical and Revision Notes
legislative statements
The House amendment deletes section 701(d) of the Senate amendment. It is anticipated that the Rules of Bankruptcy Procedure will require the appointment of an interim trustee at the earliest practical moment in commodity broker bankruptcies, but no later than noon of the day after the date of the filing of the petition, due to the volatility of such cases.
senate report no. 95–989
This section requires the court to appoint an interim trustee. The appointment must be made from the panel of private trustees established and maintained by the Director of the Administrative Office under proposed 28 U.S.C. 604(e).
Subsection (a) requires the appointment of an interim trustee to be made promptly after the order for relief, unless a trustee is already serving in the case, such as before a conversion from a reorganization to a liquidation case.
Subsection (b) specifies that the appointment of an interim trustee expires when the permanent trustee is elected or designated under section 702.
Subsection (c) makes clear that an interim trustee is a trustee in a case under the bankruptcy code.
Subsection (d) provides that in a commodity broker case where speed is essential the interim trustee must be appointed by noon of the business day immediately following the order for relief.

Amendments
1986—Subsec. (a). Pub. L. 99–554 designated existing provisions as par. (1), substituted "the United States trustee shall appoint" for "the court shall appoint", "586(a)(1)" for "604(f)", "that is serving" for "that was serving", and added par. (2).

Effective Date of 1986 Amendment
Effective date and applicability of amendment by Pub. L. 99–554 dependent upon the judicial district involved, see section 302(d), (e) of Pub. L. 99–554, set out as a note under section 581 of Title 28, Judiciary and Judicial Procedure.

§702. Election of trustee
(a) A creditor may vote for a candidate for trustee only if such creditor—
(1) holds an allowable, undisputed, fixed, liquidated, unsecured claim of a kind entitled to distribution under section 726(a)(2), 726(a)(3), 726(a)(4), 752(a), 766(h), or 766(i) of this title;
(2) does not have an interest materially adverse, other than an equity interest that is not substantial in relation to such creditor's interest as a creditor, to the interest of creditors entitled to such distribution; and
(3) is not an insider.

(b) At the meeting of creditors held under section 341 of this title, creditors may elect one person to serve as trustee in the case if election of a trustee is requested by creditors that may vote under subsection (a) of this section, and that hold at least 20 percent in amount of the claims specified in subsection (a)(1) of this section that are held by creditors that may vote under subsection (a) of this section.

(c) A candidate for trustee is elected trustee if—
(1) creditors holding at least 20 percent in amount of the claims of a kind specified in subsection (a)(1) of this section that are held by creditors that may vote under subsection (a) of this section vote; and
(2) such candidate receives the votes of creditors holding a majority in amount of claims specified in subsection (a)(1) of this section that are held by creditors that vote for a trustee.

(d) If a trustee is not elected under this section, then the interim trustee shall serve as trustee in the case.

(Pub. L. 95–598, Nov. 6, 1978, 92 Stat. 2604; Pub. L. 97–222, §7, July 27, 1982, 96 Stat. 237; Pub. L. 98–353, title III, §472, July 10, 1984, 98 Stat. 380.)

Historical and Revision Notes
legislative statements
The House amendment adopts section 702(a)(2) of the Senate amendment. An insubstantial equity interest does not disqualify a creditor from voting for a candidate for trustee.
senate report no. 95–989
Subsection (a) of this section specifies which creditors may vote for a trustee. Only a creditor that holds an allowable, undisputed, fixed, liquidated, unsecured claim that is not entitled to priority, that does not have an interest materially adverse to the interest of general unsecured creditors, and that is not an insider may vote for a trustee. The phrase "materially adverse" is currently used in the Rules of Bankruptcy Procedure, rule 207(d). The application of the standard requires a balancing of various factors, such as the nature of the adversity. A creditor with a very small equity position would not be excluded from voting solely because he owns a small equity in the debtor. The Rules of Bankruptcy Procedure also currently provide for temporary allowance of claims, and will continue to do so for the purposes of determining who is eligible to vote under this provision.
Subsection (b) permits creditors at the meeting of creditors to elect one person to serve as trustee in the case. Creditors holding at least 20 percent in amount of the claims specified in the preceding paragraph must request election before creditors may elect a trustee. Subsection (c) specifies that a candidate for trustee is elected trustee if creditors holding at least 20 percent in amount of those claims actually vote, and if the candidate receives a majority in amount of votes actually cast.
Subsection (d) specifies that if a trustee is not elected, then the interim trustee becomes the permanent trustee and serves in the case permanently.

Amendments
1984—Subsec. (b). Pub. L. 98–353, §472(a), inserted "held" after "meeting of creditors".
Subsec. (c)(1). Pub. L. 98–353, §472(b)(1), inserted "of a kind" after "claims".
Subsec. (c)(2). Pub. L. 98–353, §472(b)(2), substituted "for a trustee" for "for trustee".
Subsec. (d). Pub. L. 98–353, §472(c), substituted "this section" for "subsection (c) of this section".
1982—Subsec. (a)(1). Pub. L. 97–222 substituted "726(a)(4), 752(a), 766(h), or 766(i)" for "or 726(a)(4)".

Effective Date of 1984 Amendment
Amendment by Pub. L. 98–353 effective with respect to cases filed 90 days after July 10, 1984, see section 552(a) of Pub. L. 98–353, set out as a note under section 101 of this title.

§703. Successor trustee
(a) If a trustee dies or resigns during a case, fails to qualify under section 322 of this title, or is removed under section 324 of this title, creditors may elect, in the manner specified in section 702 of this title, a person to fill the vacancy in the office of trustee.
(b) Pending election of a trustee under subsection (a) of this section, if necessary to preserve or prevent loss to the estate, the United States trustee may appoint an interim trustee in the manner specified in section 701(a).
(c) If creditors do not elect a successor trustee under subsection (a) of this section or if a trustee is needed in a case reopened under section 350 of this title, then the United States trustee—

(1) shall appoint one disinterested person that is a member of the panel of private trustees established under section 586(a)(1) of title 28 to serve as trustee in the case; or

(2) may, if none of the disinterested members of such panel is willing to serve as trustee, serve as trustee in the case.

(Pub. L. 95–598, Nov. 6, 1978, 92 Stat. 2605; Pub. L. 98–353, title III, §473, July 10, 1984, 98 Stat. 381; Pub. L. 99–554, title II, §216, Oct. 27, 1986, 100 Stat. 3100.)

Historical and Revision Notes

senate report no. 95–989

If the office of trustee becomes vacant during the case, this section makes provision for the selection of a successor trustee. The office might become vacant through death, resignation, removal, failure to qualify under section 322 by posting bond, or the reopening of a case. If it does, creditors may elect a successor in the same manner as they may elect a trustee under the previous section. Pending the election of a successor, the court may appoint an interim trustee in the usual manner if necessary to preserve or prevent loss to the estate. If creditors do not elect a successor, or if a trustee is needed in a reopened case, then the court appoints a disinterested member of the panel of private trustees to serve.

Amendments

1986—Subsec. (b). Pub. L. 99–554 amended subsec. (b) generally, substituting "the United States trustee may appoint" for "the court may appoint" and "manner specified in section 701(a)" for "manner and subject to the provisions of section 701 of this title".

Subsec. (c). Pub. L. 99–554 amended subsec. (c) generally, substituting "this section or" for "this section, or", "then the United States trustee" for "then the court", designating part of existing provisions as par. (1), and, as so designated, substituting "586(a)(1)" for "604(f)", "in the case; or" for "in the case.", and adding par. (2).

1984—Subsec. (b). Pub. L. 98–353 substituted "and subject to the provisions of section 701 of this title" for "specified in section 701(a) of this title. Sections 701(b) and 701(c) of this title apply to such interim trustee".

Effective Date of 1986 Amendment

Effective date and applicability of amendment by Pub. L. 99–554 dependent upon the judicial district involved, see section 302(d), (e) of Pub. L. 99–554, set out as a note under section 581 of Title 28, Judiciary and Judicial Procedure.

Effective Date of 1984 Amendment

Amendment by Pub. L. 98–353 effective with respect to cases filed 90 days after July 10, 1984, see section 552(a) of Pub. L. 98–353, set out as a note under section 101 of this title.

§704. Duties of trustee

(a) The trustee shall—

(1) collect and reduce to money the property of the estate for which such trustee serves, and close such estate as expeditiously as is compatible with the best interests of parties in interest;

(2) be accountable for all property received;

(3) ensure that the debtor shall perform his intention as specified in section 521(a)(2)(B) of this title;

(4) investigate the financial affairs of the debtor;

(5) if a purpose would be served, examine proofs of claims and object to the allowance of any claim that is improper;

(6) if advisable, oppose the discharge of the debtor;

(7) unless the court orders otherwise, furnish such information concerning the estate and the estate's administration as is requested by a party in interest;

(8) if the business of the debtor is authorized to be operated, file with the court, with the United States trustee, and with any governmental unit charged with responsibility for collection or determination of any tax arising out of such operation, periodic reports and summaries of the operation of such business, including a statement of receipts and disbursements, and such other information as the United States trustee or the court requires;

(9) make a final report and file a final account of the administration of the estate with the court and with the United States trustee;

(10) if with respect to the debtor there is a claim for a domestic support obligation, provide the applicable notice specified in subsection (c);

(11) if, at the time of the commencement of the case, the debtor (or any entity designated by the debtor) served as the administrator (as defined in section 3 of the Employee Retirement Income Security Act of 1974) of an employee benefit plan, continue to perform the obligations required of the administrator; and

(12) use all reasonable and best efforts to transfer patients from a health care business that is in the process of being closed to an appropriate health care business that—

(A) is in the vicinity of the health care business that is closing;

(B) provides the patient with services that are substantially similar to those provided by the health care business that is in the process of being closed; and

(C) maintains a reasonable quality of care.

(b)(1) With respect to a debtor who is an individual in a case under this chapter—

(A) the United States trustee (or the bankruptcy administrator, if any) shall review all materials filed by the debtor and, not later than 10 days after the date of the first meeting of creditors, file with the court a statement as to whether the debtor's case would be presumed to be an abuse under section 707(b); and

(B) not later than 7 days after receiving a statement under subparagraph (A), the court shall provide a copy of the statement to all creditors.

(2) The United States trustee (or bankruptcy administrator, if any) shall, not later than 30 days after the date of filing a statement under paragraph (1), either file a motion to dismiss or convert under section 707(b) or file a statement setting forth the reasons the United States trustee (or the bankruptcy administrator, if any) does not consider such a motion to be appropriate, if the United States trustee (or the bankruptcy administrator, if any) determines that the debtor's case should be presumed to be an abuse under section 707(b) and the product of the debtor's current monthly income, multiplied by 12 is not less than—

(A) in the case of a debtor in a household of 1 person, the median family income of the applicable State for 1 earner; or

(B) in the case of a debtor in a household of 2 or more individuals, the highest median family income of the applicable State for a family of the same number or fewer individuals.

(c)(1) In a case described in subsection (a)(10) to which subsection (a)(10) applies, the trustee shall—

(A)(i) provide written notice to the holder of the claim described in subsection (a)(10) of such claim and of the right of such holder to use the services of the State child support enforcement agency established under sections 464 and 466 of the Social Security Act for the State in which such holder resides, for assistance in collecting child support during and after the case under this title;

(ii) include in the notice provided under clause (i) the address and telephone number of such State child support enforcement agency; and

(iii) include in the notice provided under clause (i) an explanation of the rights of such holder to payment of such claim under this chapter;

(B)(i) provide written notice to such State child support enforcement agency of such claim; and

(ii) include in the notice provided under clause (i) the name, address, and telephone number of such holder; and

(C) at such time as the debtor is granted a discharge under section 727, provide written notice to such holder and to such State child support enforcement agency of—

(i) the granting of the discharge;

(ii) the last recent known address of the debtor;

(iii) the last recent known name and address of the debtor's employer; and

(iv) the name of each creditor that holds a claim that—

(I) is not discharged under paragraph (2), (4), or (14A) of section 523(a); or

(II) was reaffirmed by the debtor under section 524(c).

(2)(A) The holder of a claim described in subsection (a)(10) or the State child support enforcement agency of the State in which such holder resides may request from a creditor described in paragraph (1)(C)(iv) the last known address of the debtor.

(B) Notwithstanding any other provision of law, a creditor that makes a disclosure of a last known address of a debtor in connection with a request made under subparagraph (A) shall not be liable by reason of making such disclosure.

(Pub. L. 95–598, Nov. 6, 1978, 92 Stat. 2605; Pub. L. 98–353, title III, §§311(a), 474, July 10, 1984, 98 Stat. 355, 381; Pub. L. 99–554, title II, §217, Oct. 27, 1986, 100 Stat. 3100; Pub. L. 109–8, title I, §102(c), title II, §219(a), title IV, §446(b), title XI, §1105(a), Apr. 20, 2005, 119 Stat. 32, 55, 118, 192; Pub. L. 111–16, §2(7), May 7, 2009, 123 Stat. 1607; Pub. L. 111–327, §2(a)(24), Dec. 22, 2010, 124 Stat. 3560.)

Historical and Revision Notes

legislative statements

Section 704(8) of the Senate amendment is deleted in the House amendment. Trustees should give constructive notice of the commencement of the case in the manner specified under section 549(c) of title 11.

senate report no. 95–989

The essential duties of the trustee are enumerated in this section. Others, or elaborations on these, may be prescribed by the Rules of Bankruptcy Procedure to the extent not inconsistent with those prescribed by this section. The duties are derived from section 47a of the Bankruptcy Act [section 75(a) of former title 11].

The trustee's principal duty is to collect and reduce to money the property of the estate for which he serves, and to close up the estate as expeditiously as is compatible with the best interests of parties in interest. He must be accountable for all property received, and must investigate the financial affairs of the debtor. If a purpose would be served (such as if there are assets that will be distributed), the trustee is required to examine proofs of claims and object to the allowance of any claim that is improper. If advisable, the trustee must oppose the discharge of the debtor, which is for the benefit of general unsecured creditors whom the trustee represents.

The trustee is responsible to furnish such information concerning the estate and its administration as is requested by a party in interest. If the business of the debtor is authorized to be operated, then the trustee is required to file with governmental units charged with the responsibility for collection or determination of any tax arising out of the operation of the business periodic reports and summaries of the operation, including a statement of receipts and disbursements, and such other information as the court requires. He is required to give constructive notice of the commencement of the case in the manner specified under section 342(b).

References in Text

Section 3 of the Employee Retirement Income Security Act of 1974, referred to in subsec. (a)(11), is classified to section 1002 of Title 29, Labor.

Sections 464 and 466 of the Social Security Act, referred to in subsec. (c)(1)(A)(i), are classified to sections 664 and 666, respectively, of Title 42, The Public Health and Welfare.

Amendments

2010—Subsec. (a)(3). Pub. L. 111–327 substituted "521(a)(2)(B)" for "521(2)(B)".

2009—Subsec. (b)(1)(B). Pub. L. 111–16 substituted "7 days" for "5 days".

2005—Pub. L. 109–8, §102(c)(1), designated existing provisions as subsec. (a).

Subsec. (a)(10). Pub. L. 109–8, §219(a)(1), added par. (10).

Subsec. (a)(11). Pub. L. 109–8, §446(b), added par. (11).

Subsec. (a)(12). Pub. L. 109–8, §1105(a), added par. (12).

Subsec. (b). Pub. L. 109–8, §102(c)(2), added subsec. (b).

Subsec. (c). Pub. L. 109–8, §219(a)(2), added subsec. (c).

1986—Par. (8). Pub. L. 99–554, §217(1), inserted ", with the United States trustee," after "with the court" and "the United States trustee or" after "information as".

Par. (9). Pub. L. 99–554, §217(2), inserted "with the United States trustee" after "court".

1984—Par. (1). Pub. L. 98–353, §474, substituted "close such estate" for "close up such estate".

Pars. (3) to (9). Pub. L. 98–353, §311(a), added par. (3) and redesignated former pars. (3) to (8) as (4) to (9), respectively.

Effective Date of 2009 Amendment

Amendment by Pub. L. 111–16 effective Dec. 1, 2009, see section 7 of Pub. L. 111–16, set out as a note under section 109 of this title.

Effective Date of 2005 Amendment

Amendment by Pub. L. 109–8 effective 180 days after Apr. 20, 2005, and not applicable with respect to cases commenced under this title before such effective date, except as otherwise provided, see section 1501 of Pub. L. 109–8, set out as a note under section 101 of this title.

Effective Date of 1986 Amendment

Effective date and applicability of amendment by Pub. L. 99–554 dependent upon the judicial district involved, see section 302(d), (e) of Pub. L. 99–554, set out as a note under section 581 of Title 28, Judiciary and Judicial Procedure.

Effective Date of 1984 Amendment

Amendment by Pub. L. 98–353 effective with respect to cases filed 90 days after July 10, 1984, see section 552(a) of Pub. L. 98–353, set out as a note under section 101 of this title.

§705. Creditors' committee

(a) At the meeting under section 341(a) of this title, creditors that may vote for a trustee under section 702(a) of this title may elect a committee of not fewer than three, and not more than eleven, creditors, each of whom holds an allowable unsecured claim of a kind entitled to distribution under section 726(a)(2) of this title.

(b) A committee elected under subsection (a) of this section may consult with the trustee or the United States trustee in connection with the administration of the estate, make recommendations to the trustee or the United States trustee respecting the performance of the trustee's duties, and submit to the court or the United States trustee any question affecting the administration of the estate.

(Pub. L. 95–598, Nov. 6, 1978, 92 Stat. 2605; Pub. L. 99–554, title II, §218, Oct. 27, 1986, 100 Stat. 3100.)

Historical and Revision Notes

legislative statements

Section 705(a) of the House amendment adopts a provision contained in the Senate amendment that limits a committee of creditors to not more than 11; the House bill contained no maximum limitation.

senate report no. 95–989

This section is derived from section 44b of the Bankruptcy Act [section 72(b) of former title 11] without substantial change. It permits election by general unsecured creditors of a committee of not fewer than 3 members and not more than 11 members to consult with the trustee in connection with the administration of the estate, to make recommendations to the trustee respecting the performance of his duties, and to submit to the court any question affecting the administration of the estate. There is no provision for compensation or reimbursement of its counsel.

Amendments

1986—Subsec. (b). Pub. L. 99–554 inserted "or the United States trustee" in three places.

Effective Date of 1986 Amendment

Effective date and applicability of amendment by Pub. L. 99–554 dependent upon the judicial district involved, see section 302(d), (e) of Pub. L. 99–554, set out as a note under section 581 of Title 28, Judiciary and Judicial Procedure.

§706. Conversion

(a) The debtor may convert a case under this chapter to a case under chapter 11, 12, or 13 of this title at any time, if the case has not been converted under section 1112, 1208, or 1307 of this title. Any waiver of the right to convert a case under this subsection is unenforceable.

(b) On request of a party in interest and after notice and a hearing, the court may convert a case under this chapter to a case under chapter 11 of this title at any time.

(c) The court may not convert a case under this chapter to a case under chapter 12 or 13 of this title unless the debtor requests or consents to such conversion.

(d) Notwithstanding any other provision of this section, a case may not be converted to a case under another chapter of this title unless the debtor may be a debtor under such chapter.

(Pub. L. 95–598, Nov. 6, 1978, 92 Stat. 2606; Pub. L. 99–554, title II, §257(q), Oct. 27, 1986, 100 Stat. 3115; Pub. L. 103–394, title V, §501(d)(22), Oct. 22, 1994, 108 Stat. 4146; Pub. L. 109–8, title I, §101, Apr. 20, 2005, 119 Stat. 27.)

Historical and Revision Notes

legislative statements

Section 706(a) of the House amendment adopts a provision contained in the Senate amendment indicating that a waiver of the right to convert a case under section 706(a) is unenforceable. The explicit reference in title 11 forbidding the waiver of certain rights is not intended to imply that other rights, such as the right to file a voluntary bankruptcy case under section 301, may be waived.

Section 706 of the House amendment adopts a similar provision contained in H.R. 8200 as passed by the House. Competing proposals contained in section 706(c) and section 706(d) of the Senate amendment are rejected.

senate report no. 95–989

Subsection (a) of this section gives the debtor the one-time absolute right of conversion of a liquidation case to a reorganization or individual repayment plan case. If the case has already once been converted from chapter 11 or 13 to chapter 7, then the debtor does not have that right. The policy of the provision is that the debtor should always be given the opportunity to repay his debts, and a waiver of the right to convert a case is unenforceable.

Subsection (b) permits the court, on request of a party in interest and after notice and a hearing, to convert the case to chapter 11 at any time. The decision whether to convert is left in the sound discretion of the court, based on what will most inure to the benefit of all parties in interest.

Subsection (c) is part of the prohibition against involuntary chapter 13 cases, and prohibits the court from converting a case to chapter 13 without the debtor's consent.

Subsection (d) reinforces section 109 by prohibiting conversion to a chapter unless the debtor is eligible to be a debtor under that chapter.

Amendments

2005—Subsec. (c). Pub. L. 109–8 inserted "or consents to" after "requests".

1994—Subsec. (a). Pub. L. 103–394 substituted "1208, or 1307" for "1307, or 1208".

1986—Subsec. (a). Pub. L. 99–554, §257(q)(1), inserted references to chapter 12 and section 1208 of this title.

Subsec. (c). Pub. L. 99–554, §257(q)(2), inserted reference to chapter 12.

Effective Date of 2005 Amendment

Amendment by Pub. L. 109–8 effective 180 days after Apr. 20, 2005, and not applicable with respect to cases commenced under this title before such effective date, except as otherwise provided, see section 1501 of Pub. L. 109–8, set out as a note under section 101 of this title.

Effective Date of 1994 Amendment

Amendment by Pub. L. 103–394 effective Oct. 22, 1994, and not applicable with respect to cases commenced under this title before Oct. 22, 1994, see section 702 of Pub. L. 103–394, set out as a note under section 101 of this title.

Effective Date of 1986 Amendment

Amendment by Pub. L. 99–554 effective 30 days after Oct. 27, 1986, but not applicable to cases commenced under this title before that date, see section 302(a), (c)(1) of Pub. L. 99–554, set out as a note under section 581 of Title 28, Judiciary and Judicial Procedure.

§707. Dismissal of a case or conversion to a case under chapter 11 or 13

(a) The court may dismiss a case under this chapter only after notice and a hearing and only for cause, including—

(1) unreasonable delay by the debtor that is prejudicial to creditors;

(2) nonpayment of any fees or charges required under chapter 123 of title 28; and

(3) failure of the debtor in a voluntary case to file, within fifteen days or such additional time as the court may allow after the filing of the petition commencing such case, the information required by paragraph (1) of section 521(a), but only on a motion by the United States trustee.

(b)(1) After notice and a hearing, the court, on its own motion or on a motion by the United States trustee, trustee (or bankruptcy administrator, if any), or any party in interest, may dismiss a case filed by an individual debtor under this chapter whose debts are primarily consumer debts, or, with the debtor's consent, convert such a case to a case under chapter 11 or 13 of this title, if it finds that the granting of relief would be an abuse of the provisions of this chapter. In making a determination whether to dismiss a case under this section, the court may not take into consideration whether a debtor has made, or continues to make, charitable contributions (that meet the definition of "charitable contribution" under section 548(d)(3)) to any qualified religious or charitable entity or organization (as that term is defined in section 548(d)(4)).

(2)(A)(i) In considering under paragraph (1) whether the granting of relief would be an abuse of the provisions of this chapter, the court shall presume abuse exists if the debtor's current monthly income reduced by the amounts determined under clauses (ii), (iii), and (iv), and multiplied by 60 is not less than the lesser of—

(I) 25 percent of the debtor's nonpriority unsecured claims in the case, or $6,000,[1] whichever is greater; or

(II) $10,000.[1]

(ii)(I) The debtor's monthly expenses shall be the debtor's applicable monthly expense amounts specified under the National Standards and Local Standards, and the debtor's actual monthly expenses for the categories specified as Other Necessary Expenses issued by the Internal Revenue Service for the area in which the debtor resides, as in effect on the date of the order for relief, for the debtor, the dependents of the debtor, and the spouse of the debtor in a joint case, if the spouse is not otherwise a dependent. Such expenses shall include reasonably necessary health insurance, disability insurance, and health savings account expenses for the debtor, the spouse of the debtor, or the dependents of the debtor. Notwithstanding any other provision of this clause, the monthly expenses of the debtor shall not include any payments for debts. In addition, the debtor's monthly expenses shall include the debtor's reasonably necessary expenses incurred to maintain the safety of the debtor and the family of the debtor from family violence as identified under section 302 of the Family Violence Prevention and Services Act, or other applicable Federal law. The expenses included in the debtor's monthly expenses described in the preceding sentence shall be kept confidential by the court. In addition, if it is demonstrated that it is reasonable and necessary, the debtor's monthly expenses may also include an additional allowance for food and clothing of up to 5 percent of the food and clothing categories as specified by the National Standards issued by the Internal Revenue Service.

(II) In addition, the debtor's monthly expenses may include, if applicable, the continuation of actual expenses paid by the debtor that are reasonable and necessary for care and support of an elderly, chronically ill, or disabled household member or member of the debtor's immediate family (including parents, grandparents, siblings, children, and grandchildren of the debtor, the dependents of the debtor, and the spouse of the debtor in a joint case who is not a dependent) and who is unable to pay for such reasonable and necessary expenses. Such monthly expenses may include, if applicable, contributions to an account of a qualified ABLE program to the extent such contributions are not excess contributions (as described in section 4973(h) of the Internal Revenue Code of 1986) and if the designated beneficiary of such account is a child, stepchild, grandchild, or stepgrandchild of the debtor.

(III) In addition, for a debtor eligible for chapter 13, the debtor's monthly expenses may include the actual administrative expenses of administering a chapter 13 plan for the district in which the debtor resides, up to an amount of 10 percent of the projected plan payments, as determined under schedules issued by the Executive Office for United States Trustees.

(IV) In addition, the debtor's monthly expenses may include the actual expenses for each dependent child less than 18 years of age, not to exceed $1,500 [1] per year per child, to attend a private or public elementary or secondary school if the debtor provides documentation of such expenses and a detailed explanation of why such expenses are reasonable and necessary, and why such expenses are not already accounted for in the National Standards, Local Standards, or Other Necessary Expenses referred to in subclause (I).

(V) In addition, the debtor's monthly expenses may include an allowance for housing and utilities, in excess of the allowance specified by the Local Standards for housing and utilities issued by the Internal Revenue Service, based on the actual expenses for home energy costs if the debtor provides documentation of such actual expenses and demonstrates that such actual expenses are reasonable and necessary.

(iii) The debtor's average monthly payments on account of secured debts shall be calculated as the sum of—

(I) the total of all amounts scheduled as contractually due to secured creditors in each month of the 60 months following the date of the filing of the petition; and

(II) any additional payments to secured creditors necessary for the debtor, in filing a plan under chapter 13 of this title, to maintain possession of the debtor's primary residence, motor vehicle, or other property necessary for the support of the debtor and the debtor's dependents, that serves as collateral for secured debts;

divided by 60.

(iv) The debtor's expenses for payment of all priority claims (including priority child support and alimony claims) shall be calculated as the total amount of debts entitled to priority, divided by 60.

(B)(i) In any proceeding brought under this subsection, the presumption of abuse may only be rebutted by demonstrating special circumstances, such as a serious medical condition or a call or order to active duty in the Armed Forces, to the extent such special circumstances that justify additional expenses or adjustments of current monthly income for which there is no reasonable alternative.

(ii) In order to establish special circumstances, the debtor shall be required to itemize each additional expense or adjustment of income and to provide—

(I) documentation for such expense or adjustment to income; and

(II) a detailed explanation of the special circumstances that make such expenses or adjustment to income necessary and reasonable.

(iii) The debtor shall attest under oath to the accuracy of any information provided to demonstrate that additional expenses or adjustments to income are required.

(iv) The presumption of abuse may only be rebutted if the additional expenses or adjustments to income referred to in clause (i) cause the product of the debtor's current monthly income reduced by the amounts determined under clauses (ii), (iii), and (iv) of subparagraph (A) when multiplied by 60 to be less than the lesser of—

(I) 25 percent of the debtor's nonpriority unsecured claims, or $6,000,[1] whichever is greater; or

(II) $10,000.[1]

(C) As part of the schedule of current income and expenditures required under section 521, the debtor shall include a statement of the debtor's current monthly income, and the calculations that determine whether a presumption arises under subparagraph (A)(i), that show how each such amount is calculated.

(D) Subparagraphs (A) through (C) shall not apply, and the court may not dismiss or convert a case based on any form of means testing—

(i) if the debtor is a disabled veteran (as defined in section 3741(1) of title 38), and the indebtedness occurred primarily during a period during which he or she was—

(I) on active duty (as defined in section 101(d)(1) of title 10); or

(II) performing a homeland defense activity (as defined in section 901(1) of title 32); or

(ii) with respect to the debtor, while the debtor is—

(I) on, and during the 540-day period beginning immediately after the debtor is released from, a period of active duty (as defined in section 101(d)(1) of title 10) of not less than 90 days; or

(II) performing, and during the 540-day period beginning immediately after the debtor is no longer performing, a homeland defense activity (as defined in section 901(1) of title 32) performed for a period of not less than 90 days;

if after September 11, 2001, the debtor while a member of a reserve component of the Armed Forces or a member of the National Guard, was called to such active duty or performed such homeland defense activity.

(3) In considering under paragraph (1) whether the granting of relief would be an abuse of the provisions of this chapter in a case in which the presumption in paragraph (2)(A)(i) does not arise or is rebutted, the court shall consider—

(A) whether the debtor filed the petition in bad faith; or

(B) the totality of the circumstances (including whether the debtor seeks to reject a personal services contract and the financial need for such rejection as sought by the debtor) of the debtor's financial situation demonstrates abuse.

(4)(A) The court, on its own initiative or on the motion of a party in interest, in accordance with the procedures described in rule 9011 of the Federal Rules of Bankruptcy Procedure, may order the attorney for the debtor to reimburse the trustee for all reasonable costs in prosecuting a motion filed under section 707(b), including reasonable attorneys' fees, if—

(i) a trustee files a motion for dismissal or conversion under this subsection; and

(ii) the court—

(I) grants such motion; and

(II) finds that the action of the attorney for the debtor in filing a case under this chapter violated rule 9011 of the Federal Rules of Bankruptcy Procedure.

(B) If the court finds that the attorney for the debtor violated rule 9011 of the Federal Rules of Bankruptcy Procedure, the court, on its own initiative or on the motion of a party in interest, in accordance with such procedures, may order—

(i) the assessment of an appropriate civil penalty against the attorney for the debtor; and

(ii) the payment of such civil penalty to the trustee, the United States trustee (or the bankruptcy administrator, if any).

(C) The signature of an attorney on a petition, pleading, or written motion shall constitute a certification that the attorney has—

(i) performed a reasonable investigation into the circumstances that gave rise to the petition, pleading, or written motion; and

(ii) determined that the petition, pleading, or written motion—

(I) is well grounded in fact; and

(II) is warranted by existing law or a good faith argument for the extension, modification, or reversal of existing law and does not constitute an abuse under paragraph (1).

(D) The signature of an attorney on the petition shall constitute a certification that the attorney has no knowledge after an inquiry that the information in the schedules filed with such petition is incorrect.

(5)(A) Except as provided in subparagraph (B) and subject to paragraph (6), the court, on its own initiative or on the motion of a party in interest, in accordance with the procedures described in rule 9011 of the Federal Rules of Bankruptcy Procedure, may award a debtor all reasonable costs (including reasonable attorneys' fees) in contesting a motion filed by a party in interest (other than a trustee or United States trustee (or bankruptcy administrator, if any)) under this subsection if—

(i) the court does not grant the motion; and

(ii) the court finds that—

(I) the position of the party that filed the motion violated rule 9011 of the Federal Rules of Bankruptcy Procedure; or

(II) the attorney (if any) who filed the motion did not comply with the requirements of clauses (i) and (ii) of paragraph (4)(C), and the motion was made solely for the purpose of coercing a debtor into waiving a right guaranteed to the debtor under this title.

(B) A small business that has a claim of an aggregate amount less than $1,000 [1] shall not be subject to subparagraph (A)(ii)(I).

(C) For purposes of this paragraph—

(i) the term "small business" means an unincorporated business, partnership, corporation, association, or organization that—

(I) has fewer than 25 full-time employees as determined on the date on which the motion is filed; and

(II) is engaged in commercial or business activity; and

(ii) the number of employees of a wholly owned subsidiary of a corporation includes the employees of—

(I) a parent corporation; and

(II) any other subsidiary corporation of the parent corporation.

(6) Only the judge or United States trustee (or bankruptcy administrator, if any) may file a motion under section 707(b), if the current monthly income of the debtor, or in a joint case, the debtor and the debtor's spouse, as of the date of the order for relief, when multiplied by 12, is equal to or less than—

(A) in the case of a debtor in a household of 1 person, the median family income of the applicable State for 1 earner;

(B) in the case of a debtor in a household of 2, 3, or 4 individuals, the highest median family income of the applicable State for a family of the same number or fewer individuals; or

(C) in the case of a debtor in a household exceeding 4 individuals, the highest median family income of the applicable State for a family of 4 or fewer individuals, plus $525 [1] per month for each individual in excess of 4.

(7)(A) No judge, United States trustee (or bankruptcy administrator, if any), trustee, or other party in interest may file a motion under paragraph (2) if the current monthly income of the debtor, including a veteran (as that term is defined in section 101 of title 38), and the debtor's spouse combined, as of the date of the order for relief when multiplied by 12, is equal to or less than—

(i) in the case of a debtor in a household of 1 person, the median family income of the applicable State for 1 earner;

(ii) in the case of a debtor in a household of 2, 3, or 4 individuals, the highest median family income of the applicable State for a family of the same number or fewer individuals; or

(iii) in the case of a debtor in a household exceeding 4 individuals, the highest median family income of the applicable State for a family of 4 or fewer individuals, plus $525 [1] per month for each individual in excess of 4.

(B) In a case that is not a joint case, current monthly income of the debtor's spouse shall not be considered for purposes of subparagraph (A) if—

(i)(I) the debtor and the debtor's spouse are separated under applicable nonbankruptcy law; or

(II) the debtor and the debtor's spouse are living separate and apart, other than for the purpose of evading subparagraph (A); and

(ii) the debtor files a statement under penalty of perjury—

(I) specifying that the debtor meets the requirement of subclause (I) or (II) of clause (i); and

(II) disclosing the aggregate, or best estimate of the aggregate, amount of any cash or money payments received from the debtor's spouse attributed to the debtor's current monthly income.

(c)(1) In this subsection—

(A) the term "crime of violence" has the meaning given such term in section 16 of title 18; and

(B) the term "drug trafficking crime" has the meaning given such term in section 924(c)(2) of title 18.

(2) Except as provided in paragraph (3), after notice and a hearing, the court, on a motion by the victim of a crime of violence or a drug trafficking crime, may when it is in the best interest of the victim dismiss a voluntary case filed under this chapter by a debtor who is an individual if such individual was convicted of such crime.

(3) The court may not dismiss a case under paragraph (2) if the debtor establishes by a preponderance of the evidence that the filing of a case under this chapter is necessary to satisfy a claim for a domestic support obligation.

(Pub. L. 95–598, Nov. 6, 1978, 92 Stat. 2606; Pub. L. 98–353, title III, §§312, 475, July 10, 1984, 98 Stat. 355, 381; Pub. L. 99–554, title II, §219, Oct. 27, 1986, 100 Stat. 3100; Pub. L. 105–183, §4(b), June 19, 1998, 112 Stat. 518; Pub. L. 109–8, title I, §102(a), (f), Apr. 20, 2005, 119 Stat. 27, 33; Pub. L. 110–438, §2, Oct. 20, 2008, 122 Stat. 5000; Pub. L. 111–320, title II, §202(a), Dec. 20, 2010, 124 Stat. 3509; Pub. L. 111–327, §2(a)(25), Dec. 22, 2010, 124 Stat. 3560; Pub. L. 113–295, div. B, title I, §104(b), Dec. 19, 2014, 128 Stat. 4064.)

Historical and Revision Notes

legislative statements

Section 707 of the House amendment indicates that the court may dismiss a case only after notice and a hearing.

senate report no. 95–989

This section authorizes the court to dismiss a liquidation case only for cause, such as unreasonable delay by the debtor that is prejudicial to creditors or nonpayment of any fees and charges required under chapter 123 [§1911 et seq.] of title 28. These causes are not exhaustive, but merely illustrative. The section does not contemplate, however, that the ability of the debtor to repay his debts in whole or in part constitutes adequate cause for dismissal. To permit dismissal on that ground would be to enact a non-uniform mandatory chapter 13, in lieu of the remedy of bankruptcy.

References in Text

Section 302 of the Family Violence Prevention and Services Act, referred to in subsec. (b)(2)(A)(ii)(I), is classified to section 10402 of Title 42, The Public Health and Welfare.

The Internal Revenue Code of 1986, referred to in subsec. (b)(2)(A)(ii)(II), is classified generally to Title 26, Internal Revenue Code.

The Federal Rules of Bankruptcy Procedure, referred to in subsec. (b)(4)(A), (B), (5)(A), are set out in the Appendix to this title.

Amendments

2014—Subsec. (b)(2)(A)(ii)(II). Pub. L. 113–295 inserted at end "Such monthly expenses may include, if applicable, contributions to an account of a qualified ABLE program to the extent such contributions are not excess contributions (as described in section 4973(h) of the Internal Revenue Code of 1986) and if the designated beneficiary of such account is a child, stepchild, grandchild, or stepgrandchild of the debtor."

2010—Subsec. (a)(3). Pub. L. 111–327, §2(a)(25)(A), substituted "521(a)" for "521".

Subsec. (b)(2)(A)(ii)(I). Pub. L. 111–320 substituted "section 302 of the Family Violence Prevention and Services Act" for "section 309 of the Family Violence Prevention and Services Act".

Subsec. (b)(2)(A)(iii)(I). Pub. L. 111–327, §2(a)(25)(B)(i), inserted "of the filing" after "date".

Subsec. (b)(3). Pub. L. 111–327, §2(a)(25)(B)(ii), substituted "paragraph (2)(A)(i)" for "subparagraph (A)(i) of such paragraph" in introductory provisions.

2008—Subsec. (b)(2)(D). Pub. L. 110–438 substituted "testing—" for "testing," in introductory provisions, inserted cl. (i) designation before "if the debtor", redesignated former cls. (i) and (ii) as subcls. (I) and (II), respectively, of cl. (i) and added cl. (ii).

2005—Pub. L. 109–8, §102(a)(1), substituted "Dismissal of a case or conversion to a case under chapter 11 or 13" for "Dismissal" in section catchline.

Subsec. (b). Pub. L. 109–8, §102(a)(2), designated existing provisions as par. (1), substituted "trustee (or bankruptcy administrator, if any), or" for "but not at the request or suggestion of" and "an abuse" for "a substantial abuse", inserted ", or, with the debtor's consent, convert such a case to a case under chapter 11 or 13 of this title," after "consumer debts", struck out "There shall be a presumption in favor of granting the relief requested by the debtor." before "In making", and added pars. (2) to (7).

Subsec. (c). Pub. L. 109–8, §102(f), added subsec. (c).

1998—Subsec. (b). Pub. L. 105–183 inserted at end "In making a determination whether to dismiss a case under this section, the court may not take into consideration whether a debtor has made, or continues to make, charitable contributions (that meet the definition of 'charitable contribution' under section 548(d)(3)) to any qualified religious or charitable entity or organization (as that term is defined in section 548(d)(4))."

1986—Subsec. (a)(3). Pub. L. 99–554, §219(a), added par. (3).

Subsec. (b). Pub. L. 99–554, §219(b), substituted "motion or on a motion by the United States trustee, but" for "motion and".

1984—Pub. L. 98–353 designated existing provisions as subsec. (a) and in pars. (1) and (2) substituted "or" for "and", and added subsec. (b).

Effective Date of 2014 Amendment

Amendment by Pub. L. 113–295 applicable with respect to cases commenced under this title on or after Dec. 19, 2014, see section 104(d) of Pub. L. 113–295, set out as a note under section 521 of this title.

Effective Date of 2008 Amendment

Pub. L. 110–438, §4, Oct. 20, 2008, 122 Stat. 5002, as amended by Pub. L. 112–64, §2, Dec. 13, 2011, 125 Stat. 766; Pub. L. 114–107, §2, Dec. 18, 2015, 129 Stat. 2223, provided that:

"(a) Effective Date.—Except as provided in subsection (b), this Act [amending this section and enacting provisions set out as a note under section 101 of this title] and the amendments made by this Act shall take effect 60 days after the date of enactment of this Act [Oct. 20, 2008].

"(b) Application of Amendments.—The amendments made by this Act [amending this section] shall apply only with respect to cases commenced under title 11 of the United States Code in the 11-year period beginning on the effective date of this Act."

Effective Date of 2005 Amendment

Amendment by Pub. L. 109–8 effective 180 days after Apr. 20, 2005, and not applicable with respect to cases commenced under this title before such effective date, except as otherwise provided, see section 1501 of Pub. L. 109–8, set out as a note under section 101 of this title.

Effective Date of 1998 Amendment

Amendment by Pub. L. 105–183 applicable to any case brought under an applicable provision of this title that is pending or commenced on or after June 19, 1998, see section 5 of Pub. L. 105–183, set out as a note under section 544 of this title.

Effective Date of 1986 Amendment

Effective date and applicability of amendment by Pub. L. 99–554 dependent upon the judicial district involved, see section 302(d), (e) of Pub. L. 99–554, set out as a note under section 581 of Title 28, Judiciary and Judicial Procedure.

Effective Date of 1984 Amendment

Amendment by Pub. L. 98–353 effective with respect to cases filed 90 days after July 10, 1984, see section 552(a) of Pub. L. 98–353, set out as a note under section 101 of this title.

Schedules of Reasonable and Necessary Expenses

Pub. L. 109–8, title I, §107, Apr. 20, 2005, 119 Stat. 42, provided that: "For purposes of section 707(b) of title 11, United States Code, as amended by this Act, the Director of the Executive Office for United States Trustees shall, not later than

180 days after the date of enactment of this Act [Apr. 20, 2005], issue schedules of reasonable and necessary administrative expenses of administering a chapter 13 plan for each judicial district of the United States."

Adjustment of Dollar Amounts

The dollar amounts specified in this section were adjusted by notices of the Judicial Conference of the United States pursuant to section 104 of this title as follows:

By notice dated Feb. 16, 2016, 81 F.R. 8748, effective Apr. 1, 2016, in subsec. (b)(2)(A)(i)(I), dollar amount "7,475" was adjusted to "7,700"; in subsec. (b)(2)(A)(i)(II), dollar amount "12,475" was adjusted to "12,850"; in subsec. (b)(2)(A)(ii)(IV), dollar amount "1,875" was adjusted to "1,925"; in subsec. (b)(2)(B)(iv)(I), dollar amount "7,475" was adjusted to "7,700"; in subsec. (b)(2)(B)(iv)(II), dollar amount "12,475" was adjusted to "12,850"; in subsec. (b)(5)(B), dollar amount "1,250" was adjusted to "1,300"; in subsec. (b)(6)(C), dollar amount "675" was adjusted to "700"; and, in subsec. (b)(7)(A)(iii), dollar amount "675" was adjusted to "700". See notice of the Judicial Conference of the United States set out as a note under section 104 of this title.

By notice dated Feb. 12, 2013, 78 F.R. 12089, effective Apr. 1, 2013, in subsec. (b)(2)(A)(i)(I), dollar amount "7,025" was adjusted to "7,475"; in subsec. (b)(2)(A)(i)(II), dollar amount "11,725" was adjusted to "12,475"; in subsec. (b)(2)(A)(ii)(IV), dollar amount "1,775" was adjusted to "1,875"; in subsec. (b)(2)(B)(iv)(I), dollar amount "7,025" was adjusted to "7,475"; in subsec. (b)(2)(B)(iv)(II), dollar amount "11,725" was adjusted to "12,475"; in subsec. (b)(5)(B), dollar amount "1,175" was adjusted to "1,250"; in subsec. (b)(6)(C), dollar amount "625" was adjusted to "675"; and, in subsec. (b)(7)(A)(iii), dollar amount "625" was adjusted to "675".

By notice dated Feb. 19, 2010, 75 F.R. 8747, effective Apr. 1, 2010, in subsec. (b)(2)(A)(i)(I), dollar amount "6,575" was adjusted to "7,025"; in subsec. (b)(2)(A)(i)(II), dollar amount "10,950" was adjusted to "11,725"; in subsec. (b)(2)(A)(ii)(IV), dollar amount "1,650" was adjusted to "1,775"; in subsec. (b)(2)(B)(iv)(I), dollar amount "6,575" was adjusted to "7,025"; in subsec. (b)(2)(B)(iv)(II), dollar amount "10,950" was adjusted to "11,725"; in subsec. (b)(5)(B), dollar amount "1,100" was adjusted to "1,175"; in subsec. (b)(6)(C), dollar amount "575" was adjusted to "625"; and, in subsec. (b)(7)(A)(iii), dollar amount "575" was adjusted to "625".

By notice dated Feb. 7, 2007, 72 F.R. 7082, effective Apr. 1, 2007, as amended by notice dated Mar. 26, 2007, 72 F.R. 15162, in subsec. (b)(2)(A)(i)(I), dollar amount "6,000" was adjusted to "6,575"; in subsec. (b)(2)(A)(i)(II), dollar amount "10,000" was adjusted to "10,950"; in subsec. (b)(2)(A)(ii)(IV), dollar amount "1,500" was adjusted to "1,650"; in subsec. (b)(2)(B)(iv)(I), dollar amount "6,000" was adjusted to "6,575"; in subsec. (b)(2)(B)(iv)(II), dollar amount "10,000" was adjusted to "10,950"; in subsec. (b)(5)(B), dollar amount "1,000" was adjusted to "1,100"; in subsec. (b)(6)(C), dollar amount "525" was adjusted to "575"; and, in subsec. (b)(7)(A)(iii), dollar amount "525" was adjusted to "575".

Rules Promulgated by Supreme Court

United States Supreme Court to prescribe general rules implementing the practice and procedure to be followed under subsec. (b) of this section, with section 2075 of Title 28, Judiciary and Judicial Procedure, to apply with respect to such general rules, see section 320 of Pub. L. 98–353, set out as a note under section 2075 of Title 28.

[1] See Adjustment of Dollar Amounts notes below.

SUBCHAPTER II—COLLECTION, LIQUIDATION, AND DISTRIBUTION OF THE ESTATE

§721. Authorization to operate business

The court may authorize the trustee to operate the business of the debtor for a limited period, if such operation is in the best interest of the estate and consistent with the orderly liquidation of the estate.

(Pub. L. 95–598, Nov. 6, 1978, 92 Stat. 2606.)

Historical and Revision Notes

senate report no. 95–989

This section is derived from section 2a(5) of the Bankruptcy Act [section 11(a)(5) of former title 11]. It permits the court to authorize the operation of any business of the debtor for a limited period, if the operation is in the best interest of the estate and consistent with orderly liquidation of the estate. An example is the operation of a watch company to convert watch movements and cases into completed watches which will bring much higher prices than the component parts would have brought.

§722. Redemption

An individual debtor may, whether or not the debtor has waived the right to redeem under this section, redeem tangible personal property intended primarily for personal, family, or household use, from a lien securing a dischargeable consumer debt, if such property is exempted under section 522 of this title or has been abandoned under section 554 of this title, by paying the holder of such lien the amount of the allowed secured claim of such holder that is secured by such lien in full at the time of redemption.

(Pub. L. 95–598, Nov. 6, 1978, 92 Stat. 2606; Pub. L. 109–8, title III, §304(2), Apr. 20, 2005, 119 Stat. 79.)

Historical and Revision Notes

legislative statements

Section 722 of the House amendment adopts the position taken in H.R. 8200 as passed by the House and rejects the alternative contained in section 722 of the Senate amendment.

senate report no. 95–989

This section is new and is broader than rights of redemption under the Uniform Commercial Code. It authorizes an individual debtor to redeem tangible personal property intended primarily for personal, family, or household use, from a lien securing a nonpurchase money dischargeable consumer debt. It applies only if the debtor's interest in the property is exempt or has been abandoned.

This right to redeem is a very substantial change from current law. To prevent abuses such as may occur when the debtor deliberately allows the property to depreciate in value, the debtor will be required to pay the fair market value of the goods or the amount of the claim if the claim is less. The right is personal to the debtor and not assignable.

house report no. 95–595

This section is new and is broader than rights of redemption under the Uniform Commercial Code. It authorizes an individual debtor to redeem tangible personal property intended primarily for personal, family, or household use, from a lien securing a dischargeable consumer debt. It applies only if the debtor's interest in the property is exempt or has been abandoned.

The right to redeem extends to the whole of the property, not just the debtor's exempt interest in it. Thus, for example, if a debtor owned a $2,000 car, subject to a $1,200 lien, the debtor could exempt his $800 interest in the car. The debtor is permitted a $1,500 exemption in a car, proposed 11 U.S.C. 522(d)(2). This section permits him to pay the holder of the lien $1,200 and redeem the entire car, not just the remaining $700 of his exemption. The redemption is accomplished by paying the holder of the lien the amount of the allowed claim secured by the lien. The provision amounts to a right of first refusal for the debtor in consumer goods that might otherwise be repossessed. The right of redemption under this section is not waivable.

Amendments

2005—Pub. L. 109–8 inserted "in full at the time of redemption" before period at end.

Effective Date of 2005 Amendment

Amendment by Pub. L. 109–8 effective 180 days after Apr. 20, 2005, and not applicable with respect to cases commenced under this title before such effective date, except as otherwise provided, see section 1501 of Pub. L. 109–8, set out as a note under section 101 of this title.

§723. Rights of partnership trustee against general partners

(a) If there is a deficiency of property of the estate to pay in full all claims which are allowed in a case under this chapter concerning a partnership and with respect to which a general partner of the partnership is personally liable, the trustee shall have a claim against such general partner to the extent that under applicable nonbankruptcy law such general partner is personally liable for such deficiency.

(b) To the extent practicable, the trustee shall first seek recovery of such deficiency from any general partner in such partnership that is not a debtor in a case under this title. Pending determination of such deficiency, the court may order any such partner to provide the estate with indemnity for, or assurance of payment of, any deficiency recoverable from such partner, or not to dispose of property.

(c) The trustee has a claim against the estate of each general partner in such partnership that is a debtor in a case under this title for the full amount of all claims of creditors allowed in the case concerning such partnership. Notwithstanding section 502 of this title, there shall not be allowed in such partner's case a claim against such partner on which both such partner and such partnership are liable, except to any extent that such claim is secured only by property of such partner and not by property of such partnership. The claim of the trustee under this subsection is entitled to distribution in such partner's case under section 726(a) of this title the same as any other claim of a kind specified in such section.

(d) If the aggregate that the trustee recovers from the estates of general partners under subsection (c) of this section is greater than any deficiency not recovered under subsection (b) of this section, the court, after notice and a hearing, shall determine an equitable distribution of the surplus so recovered, and the trustee shall distribute such surplus to the estates of the general partners in such partnership according to such determination.

(Pub. L. 95–598, Nov. 6, 1978, 92 Stat. 2606; Pub. L. 98–353, title III, §476, July 10, 1984, 98 Stat. 381; Pub. L. 103–394, title II, §212, Oct. 22, 1994, 108 Stat. 4125; Pub. L. 111–327, §2(a)(26), Dec. 22, 2010, 124 Stat. 3560.)

Historical and Revision Notes

legislative statements

Section 723(c) of the House amendment is a compromise between similar provisions contained in the House bill and Senate amendment. The section makes clear that the trustee of a partnership has a claim against each general partner for the full amount of all claims of creditors allowed in the case concerning the partnership. By restricting the trustee's rights to claims of "creditors," the trustee of the partnership will not have a claim against the general partners for administrative expenses or claims allowed in the case concerning the partnership. As under present law, sections of the Bankruptcy Act [former title 11] applying to codebtors and sureties apply to the relationship of a partner with respect to a partnership debtor. See sections 501(b), 502(e), 506(d)(2), 509, 524(d), and 1301 of title 11.

senate report no. 95–989

This section is a significant departure from present law. It repeals the jingle rule, which, for ease of administration, denied partnership creditors their rights against general partners by permitting general partners' individual creditors to share in their estates first to the exclusion of partnership creditors. The result under this section more closely tracks generally applicable partnership law, without a significant administrative burden.

Subsection (a) specifies that each general partner in a partnership debtor is liable to the partnership's trustee for any deficiency of partnership property to pay in full all administrative expenses and all claims against the partnership.

Subsection (b) requires the trustee to seek recovery of the deficiency from any general partner that is not a debtor in a bankruptcy case. The court is empowered to order that partner to indemnify the estate or not to dispose of property pending a determination of the deficiency. The language of the subsection is directed to cases under the bankruptcy code. However, if, during the early stages of the transition period, a partner in a partnership is proceeding under the Bankruptcy Act [former title 11] while the partnership is proceeding under the bankruptcy code, the trustee should not first seek recovery against the Bankruptcy Act partner. Rather, the Bankruptcy Act partner should be deemed for the purposes of this section and the rights of the trustee to be proceeding under title 11.

Subsection (c) requires the partnership trustee to seek recovery of the full amount of the deficiency from the estate of each general partner that is a debtor in a bankruptcy case. The trustee will share equally with the partners' individual creditors in the assets of the partners' estates. Claims of partnership creditors who may have filed against the partner will be disallowed to avoid double counting.

Subsection (d) provides for the case where the total recovery from all of the bankrupt general partners is greater than the deficiency of which the trustee sought recovery. This case would most likely occur for a partnership with a large number of general partners. If the situation arises, the court is required to determine an equitable redistribution of the surplus to the estate of the general partners. The determination will be based on factors such as the relative liability of each of the general partners under the partnership agreement and the relative rights of each of the general partners in the profits of the enterprise under the partnership agreement.

Amendments

2010—Subsec. (c). Pub. L. 111–327 substituted "The trustee has" for "Notwithstanding section 728(c) of this title, the trustee has".

1994—Subsec. (a). Pub. L. 103–394 substituted "to the extent that under applicable nonbankruptcy law such general partner is personally liable for such deficiency" for "for the full amount of the deficiency".

1984—Subsec. (a). Pub. L. 98–353, §476, substituted provisions that the trustee shall have a claim for the full amount of the deficiency against a general partner who is personally liable with respect to claims concerning partnerships which are allowed in a case under this chapter, for provisions that each general partner in the partnership would be liable to the trustee for the full amount of such deficiency.

Subsec. (c). Pub. L. 98–353, §476(b), substituted "such partner's case" for "such case" in two places, "by property of such partnership" for "be property of such partnership", and "a kind specified in such section" for "the kind specified in such section".

Effective Date of 1994 Amendment

Amendment by Pub. L. 103–394 effective Oct. 22, 1994, and not applicable with respect to cases commenced under this title before Oct. 22, 1994, see section 702 of Pub. L. 103–394, set out as a note under section 101 of this title.

Effective Date of 1984 Amendment

Amendment by Pub. L. 98–353 effective with respect to cases filed 90 days after July 10, 1984, see section 552(a) of Pub. L. 98–353, set out as a note under section 101 of this title.

§724. Treatment of certain liens

(a) The trustee may avoid a lien that secures a claim of a kind specified in section 726(a)(4) of this title.

(b) Property in which the estate has an interest and that is subject to a lien that is not avoidable under this title (other than to the extent that there is a properly perfected unavoidable tax lien arising in connection with an ad valorem tax on real or personal property of the estate) and that secures an allowed claim for a tax, or proceeds of such property, shall be distributed—

(1) first, to any holder of an allowed claim secured by a lien on such property that is not avoidable under this title and that is senior to such tax lien;

(2) second, to any holder of a claim of a kind specified in section 507(a)(1)(C) or 507(a)(2) (except that such expenses under each such section, other than claims for wages, salaries, or commissions that arise after the date of the filing of the petition, shall be limited to expenses incurred under this chapter and shall not include expenses incurred under chapter 11 of this title), 507(a)(1)(A), 507(a)(1)(B), 507(a)(3), 507(a)(4), 507(a)(5), 507(a)(6), or 507(a)(7) of this title, to the extent of the amount of such allowed tax claim that is secured by such tax lien;

(3) third, to the holder of such tax lien, to any extent that such holder's allowed tax claim that is secured by such tax lien exceeds any amount distributed under paragraph (2) of this subsection;

(4) fourth, to any holder of an allowed claim secured by a lien on such property that is not avoidable under this title and that is junior to such tax lien;

(5) fifth, to the holder of such tax lien, to the extent that such holder's allowed claim secured by such tax lien is not paid under paragraph (3) of this subsection; and

(6) sixth, to the estate.

(c) If more than one holder of a claim is entitled to distribution under a particular paragraph of subsection (b) of this section, distribution to such holders under such paragraph shall be in the same order as distribution to such holders would have been other than under this section.

(d) A statutory lien the priority of which is determined in the same manner as the priority of a tax lien under section 6323 of the Internal Revenue Code of 1986 shall be treated under subsection (b) of this section the same as if such lien were a tax lien.

(e) Before subordinating a tax lien on real or personal property of the estate, the trustee shall—

(1) exhaust the unencumbered assets of the estate; and

(2) in a manner consistent with section 506(c), recover from property securing an allowed secured claim the reasonable, necessary costs and expenses of preserving or disposing of such property.

(f) Notwithstanding the exclusion of ad valorem tax liens under this section and subject to the requirements of subsection (e), the following may be paid from property of the estate which secures a tax lien, or the proceeds of such property:

(1) Claims for wages, salaries, and commissions that are entitled to priority under section 507(a)(4).

(2) Claims for contributions to an employee benefit plan entitled to priority under section 507(a)(5).

(Pub. L. 95–598, Nov. 6, 1978, 92 Stat. 2607; Pub. L. 98–353, title III, §477, July 10, 1984, 98 Stat. 381; Pub. L. 99–554, title II, §283(r), Oct. 27, 1986, 100 Stat. 3118; Pub. L. 103–394, title III, §304(h)(4), title V, §501(d)(23), Oct. 22, 1994, 108 Stat. 4134, 4146; Pub. L. 109–8, title VII, §701(a), Apr. 20, 2005, 119 Stat. 124; Pub. L. 111–327, §2(a)(27), Dec. 22, 2010, 124 Stat. 3560.)

Historical and Revision Notes

legislative statements

Section 724 of the House amendment adopts the provision taken in the House bill and rejects the provision taken in the Senate amendment. In effect, a tax claim secured by a lien is treated as a claim between the fifth and sixth priority in a case under chapter 7 rather than as a secured claim.

Treatment of certain liens: The House amendment modifies present law by requiring the subordination of tax liens on both real and personal property to the payment of claims having a priority. This means that assets are to be distributed from the debtor's estate to pay higher priority claims before the tax claims are paid, even though the tax claims are properly secured. Under present law and the Senate amendment only tax liens on personal property, but not on real property, are subordinated to the payment of claims having a priority above the priority for tax claims.

senate report no. 95–989

Subsection (a) of section 724 permits the trustee to avoid a lien that secures a fine, penalty, forfeiture, or multiple, punitive, or exemplary damages claim to the extent that the claim is not compensation for actual pecuniary loss. The subsection follows the policy found in section 57j of the Bankruptcy Act [section 93(j) of former title 11] of protecting unsecured creditors from the debtor's wrongdoing, but expands the protection afforded. The lien is made voidable rather than void in chapter 7, in order to permit the lien to be revived if the case is converted to chapter 11 under which penalty liens are not voidable. To make the lien void would be to permit the filing of a chapter 7, the voiding of the lien, and the conversion to a chapter 11, simply to avoid a penalty lien, which should be valid in a reorganization case.

Subsection (b) governs tax liens. This provision retains the rule of present bankruptcy law (§67(C)(3) of the Bankruptcy Act [section 107(c)(3) of former title 11]) that a tax lien on personal property, if not avoidable by the trustee, is subordinated in payment to unsecured claims having a higher priority than unsecured tax claims. Those other claims may be satisfied from the amount that would otherwise have been applied to the tax lien, and any excess of the amount of the lien is then applied to the tax. Any personal property (or sale proceeds) remaining is to be used to satisfy claims secured by liens which are junior to the tax lien. Any proceeds remaining are next applied to pay any unpaid balance of the tax lien.

Subsection (d) specifies that any statutory lien whose priority is determined in the same manner as a tax lien is to be treated as a tax lien under this section, even if the lien does not secure a claim for taxes. An example is the ERISA [29 U.S.C. 1001 et seq.] lien.

house report no. 95–595

Subsection (b) governs tax liens. It is derived from section 67c(3) of the Bankruptcy Act [section 107(c)(3) of former title 11], without substantial modification in result. It subordinates tax liens to administrative expense and wage claims, and solves certain circuity of liens problems that arise in connection with the subordination. The order of distribution of property subject to a tax lien is as follows: First, to holders of liens senior to the tax lien; second, to administrative expenses, wage claims, and consumer creditors that are granted priority, but only to the extent of the amount of the allowed tax claim secured by the lien. In other words, the priority claimants step into the shoes of the tax collector. Third, to the tax claimant, to the extent that priority claimants did not use up his entire claim. Fourth, to junior lien holders. Fifth, to the tax collector to the extent that he was not paid under paragraph (3). Finally, any remaining property goes to the estate. The result of these provisions are to leave senior and junior lienors and holders of unsecured claims undisturbed. If there are any liens that are equal in status to the tax lien, they share pari passu with the tax lien under the distribution provisions of this subsection.

References in Text

Section 6323 of the Internal Revenue Code of 1986, referred to in subsec. (d), is classified to section 6323 of Title 26, Internal Revenue Code.

Amendments

2010—Subsec. (b)(2). Pub. L. 111–327 substituted "507(a)(1)(C) or 507(a)(2)" for "507(a)(1)", "this chapter" for "chapter 7 of this title", and "507(a)(1)(A), 507(a)(1)(B)," for "507(a)(2)," and inserted "under each such section" after "such expenses".

2005—Subsec. (b). Pub. L. 109–8, §701(a)(1), inserted "(other than to the extent that there is a properly perfected unavoidable tax lien arising in connection with an ad valorem tax on real or personal property of the estate)" after "under this title" in introductory provisions.

Subsec. (b)(2). Pub. L. 109–8, §701(a)(2), inserted "(except that such expenses, other than claims for wages, salaries, or commissions that arise after the date of the filing of the petition, shall be limited to expenses incurred under chapter 7 of this title and shall not include expenses incurred under chapter 11 of this title)" after "section 507(a)(1)".

Subsecs. (e), (f). Pub. L. 109–8, §701(a)(3), added subsecs. (e) and (f).

1994—Subsec. (b)(2). Pub. L. 103–394, §304(h)(4), substituted "507(a)(6), or 507(a)(7)" for "or 507(a)(6)".

Subsec. (d). Pub. L. 103–394, §501(d)(23), substituted "Internal Revenue Code of 1986" for "Internal Revenue Code of 1954 (26 U.S.C. 6323)".

1986—Subsec. (b)(2). Pub. L. 99–554 inserted reference to section 507(a)(6) of this title.

1984—Subsec. (b). Pub. L. 98–353, §477(a)(1), substituted "a tax" for "taxes" in provisions preceding par. (1).

Subsec. (b)(2). Pub. L. 98–353, §477(a)(2), substituted "any holder of a claim of a kind specified" for "claims specified", "section 507(a)(1)" for "sections 507(a)(1)", and "or 507(a)(5) of this title" for "and 507(a)(5) of this title".

Subsec. (b)(3). Pub. L. 98–353, §477(a)(3), substituted "allowed tax claim" for "allowed claim".

Subsec. (c). Pub. L. 98–353, §477(b), substituted "holder of a claim is entitled" for "creditor is entitled" and "holders" for "creditors" in two places.

Subsec. (d). Pub. L. 98–353, §477(c), substituted "the priority of which" for "whose priority" and "the same as if such lien were a tax lien" for "the same as a tax lien".

Effective Date of 2005 Amendment

Amendment by Pub. L. 109–8 effective 180 days after Apr. 20, 2005, and not applicable with respect to cases commenced under this title before such effective date, except as otherwise provided, see section 1501 of Pub. L. 109–8, set out as a note under section 101 of this title.

Effective Date of 1994 Amendment

Amendment by Pub. L. 103–394 effective Oct. 22, 1994, and not applicable with respect to cases commenced under this title before Oct. 22, 1994, see section 702 of Pub. L. 103–394, set out as a note under section 101 of this title.

Effective Date of 1986 Amendment

Amendment by Pub. L. 99–554 effective 30 days after Oct. 27, 1986, see section 302(a) of Pub. L. 99–554, set out as a note under section 581 of Title 28, Judiciary and Judicial Procedure.

Effective Date of 1984 Amendment

Amendment by Pub. L. 98–353 effective with respect to cases filed 90 days after July 10, 1984, see section 552(a) of Pub. L. 98–353, set out as a note under section 101 of this title.

§725. Disposition of certain property

After the commencement of a case under this chapter, but before final distribution of property of the estate under section 726 of this title, the trustee, after notice and a hearing, shall dispose of any property in which an entity other than the estate has an interest, such as a lien, and that has not been disposed of under another section of this title.

(Pub. L. 95–598, Nov. 6, 1978, 92 Stat. 2607; Pub. L. 98–353, title III, §478, July 10, 1984, 98 Stat. 381.)

Historical and Revision Notes

legislative statements

Section 725 of the House amendment adopts the substance contained in both the House bill and Senate amendment but transfers an administrative function to the trustee in accordance with the general thrust of this legislation to separate the administrative and the judicial functions where appropriate.

senate report no. 95–989

This section requires the court to determine the appropriate disposition of property in which the estate and an entity other than the estate have an interest. It would apply, for example, to property subject to a lien or property co-owned by the estate and another entity. The court must make the determination with respect to property that is not disposed of under another section of the bankruptcy code, such as by abandonment under section 554, by sale or distribution under 363, or by allowing foreclosure by a secured creditor by lifting the stay under section 362. The purpose of the section is to give the court appropriate authority to ensure that collateral or its proceeds is returned to the proper secured creditor, that consigned or bailed goods are returned to the consignor or bailor and so on. Current law is curiously silent on this point, though case law has grown to fill the void. The section is in lieu of a section that would direct a certain distribution to secured creditors. It gives the court greater flexibility to meet the circumstances, and it is broader, permitting disposition of property subject to a co-ownership interest.

Amendments

1984—Pub. L. 98–353 substituted "distribution of property of the estate" for "distribution".

Effective Date of 1984 Amendment

Amendment by Pub. L. 98–353 effective with respect to cases filed 90 days after July 10, 1984, see section 552(a) of Pub. L. 98–353, set out as a note under section 101 of this title.

§726. Distribution of property of the estate

(a) Except as provided in section 510 of this title, property of the estate shall be distributed—

(1) first, in payment of claims of the kind specified in, and in the order specified in, section 507 of this title, proof of which is timely filed under section 501 of this title or tardily filed on or before the earlier of—

(A) the date that is 10 days after the mailing to creditors of the summary of the trustee's final report; or

(B) the date on which the trustee commences final distribution under this section;

(2) second, in payment of any allowed unsecured claim, other than a claim of a kind specified in paragraph (1), (3), or (4) of this subsection, proof of which is—

(A) timely filed under section 501(a) of this title;

(B) timely filed under section 501(b) or 501(c) of this title; or

(C) tardily filed under section 501(a) of this title, if—

(i) the creditor that holds such claim did not have notice or actual knowledge of the case in time for timely filing of a proof of such claim under section 501(a) of this title; and

(ii) proof of such claim is filed in time to permit payment of such claim;

(3) third, in payment of any allowed unsecured claim proof of which is tardily filed under section 501(a) of this title, other than a claim of the kind specified in paragraph (2)(C) of this subsection;

(4) fourth, in payment of any allowed claim, whether secured or unsecured, for any fine, penalty, or forfeiture, or for multiple, exemplary, or punitive damages, arising before the earlier of the order for relief or the appointment of a trustee, to the extent that such fine, penalty, forfeiture, or damages are not compensation for actual pecuniary loss suffered by the holder of such claim;

(5) fifth, in payment of interest at the legal rate from the date of the filing of the petition, on any claim paid under paragraph (1), (2), (3), or (4) of this subsection; and

(6) sixth, to the debtor.

(b) Payment on claims of a kind specified in paragraph (1), (2), (3), (4), (5), (6), (7), (8), (9), or (10) of section 507(a) of this title, or in paragraph (2), (3), (4), or (5) of subsection (a) of this section, shall be made pro rata among claims of the kind specified in each such particular paragraph, except that in a case that has been converted to this chapter under section 1112, 1208, or 1307 of this title, a claim allowed under section 503(b) of this title incurred under this chapter after such conversion has priority over a claim allowed under section 503(b) of this title incurred under any other chapter of this title or under this chapter before such conversion and over any expenses of a custodian superseded under section 543 of this title.

(c) Notwithstanding subsections (a) and (b) of this section, if there is property of the kind specified in section 541(a)(2) of this title, or proceeds of such property, in the estate, such property or proceeds shall be segregated from other property of the estate, and such property or proceeds and other property of the estate shall be distributed as follows:

(1) Claims allowed under section 503 of this title shall be paid either from property of the kind specified in section 541(a)(2) of this title, or from other property of the estate, as the interest of justice requires.

(2) Allowed claims, other than claims allowed under section 503 of this title, shall be paid in the order specified in subsection (a) of this section, and, with respect to claims of a kind specified in a particular paragraph of section 507 of this title or subsection (a) of this section, in the following order and manner:

(A) First, community claims against the debtor or the debtor's spouse shall be paid from property of the kind specified in section 541(a)(2) of this title, except to the extent that such property is solely liable for debts of the debtor.

(B) Second, to the extent that community claims against the debtor are not paid under subparagraph (A) of this paragraph, such community claims shall be paid from property of the kind specified in section 541(a)(2) of this title that is solely liable for debts of the debtor.

(C) Third, to the extent that all claims against the debtor including community claims against the debtor are not paid under subparagraph (A) or (B) of this paragraph such claims shall be paid from property of the estate other than property of the kind specified in section 541(a)(2) of this title.

(D) Fourth, to the extent that community claims against the debtor or the debtor's spouse are not paid under subparagraph (A), (B), or (C) of this paragraph, such claims shall be paid from all remaining property of the estate.

(Pub. L. 95–598, Nov. 6, 1978, 92 Stat. 2608; Pub. L. 98–353, title III, §479, July 10, 1984, 98 Stat. 381; Pub. L. 99–554, title II, §§257(r), 283(s), Oct. 27, 1986, 100 Stat. 3115, 3118; Pub. L. 103–394, title II, §213(b), title III, §304(h)(5), title V, §501(d)(24), Oct. 22, 1994, 108 Stat. 4126, 4134, 4146; Pub. L. 109–8, title VII, §713, title XII, §1215, Apr. 20, 2005, 119 Stat. 128, 195; Pub. L. 111–327, §2(a)(28), Dec. 22, 2010, 124 Stat. 3560.)

Historical and Revision Notes
legislative statements

Section 726(a)(4) adopts a provision contained in the Senate amendment subordinating prepetition penalties and penalties arising in the involuntary gap period to the extent the penalties are not compensation for actual pecuniary laws.

The House amendment deletes a provision following section 726(a)(6) of the Senate amendment providing that the term "claim" includes interest due owed before the date of the filing of the petition as unnecessary since a right to payment for interest due is a right to payment which is within the definition of "claim" in section 101(4) of the House amendment.

senate report no. 95–989

This section is the general distribution section for liquidation cases. It dictates the order in which distribution of property of the estate, which has usually been reduced to money by the trustee under the requirements of section 704(1).

First, property is distributed among priority claimants, as determined by section 507, and in the order prescribed by section 507. Second, distribution is to general unsecured creditors. This class excludes priority creditors and the two classes of subordinated creditors specified below. The provision is written to permit distribution to creditors that tardily file claims if their tardiness was due to lack of notice or knowledge of the case. Though it is in the interest of the estate to encourage timely filing, when tardy filing is not the result of a failure to act by the creditor, the normal subordination penalty should not apply. Third distribution is to general unsecured creditors who tardily file. Fourth distribution is to holders of fine, penalty, forfeiture, or multiple, punitive, or exemplary damage claims. More of these claims are disallowed entirely under present law. They are simply subordinated here.

Paragraph (4) provides that punitive penalties, including prepetition tax penalties, are subordinated to the payment of all other classes of claims, except claims for interest accruing during the case. In effect, these penalties are payable out of the estate's assets only if and to the extent that a surplus of assets would otherwise remain at the close of the case for distribution back to the debtor.

Paragraph (5) provides that postpetition interest on prepetition claims is also to be paid to the creditor in a subordinated position. Like prepetition penalties, such interest will be paid from the estate only if and to the extent that a surplus of assets would otherwise remain for return to the debtor at the close of the case.

This section also specifies that interest accrued on all claims (including priority and nonpriority tax claims) which accrued before the date of the filing of the title 11 petition is to be paid in the same order of distribution of the estate's assets as the principal amount of the related claims.

Any surplus is paid to the debtor under paragraph (6).

Subsection (b) follows current law. It specifies that claims within a particular class are to be paid pro rata. This provision will apply, of course, only when there are inadequate funds to pay the holders of claims of a particular class in full. The exception found in the section, which also follows current law, specifies that liquidation administrative expenses are to be paid ahead of reorganization administrative expenses if the case has been converted from a reorganization case to a liquidation case, or from an individual repayment plan case to a liquidation case.

Subsection (c) governs distributions in cases in which there is community property and other property of the estate. The section requires the two kinds of property to be segregated. The distribution is as follows: First, administrative expenses are to be paid, as the court determines on any reasonable equitable basis, from both kinds of property. The court will divide administrative expenses according to such factors as the amount of each kind of property in the estate, the cost of preservation and liquidation of each kind of property, and whether any particular administrative expenses are attributable to one kind of property or the other. Second, claims are to be paid as provided under subsection (a) (the normal liquidation case distribution rules) in the following order and manner: First, community claims against the debtor or the debtor's spouse are paid from community property, except such as is liable solely for the debts of the debtor.

Second, community claims against the debtor, to the extent not paid under the first provision, are paid from community property that is solely liable for the debts of the debtor. Third, community claims, to the extent they remain unpaid, and all other claims against the debtor, are paid from noncommunity property. Fourth, if any community claims against the debtor or the debtor's spouse remain unpaid, they are paid from whatever property remains in the estate. This would occur if community claims against the debtor's spouse are large in amount and most of the estate's property is property solely liable, under nonbankruptcy law, for debts of the debtor.

The marshalling rules in this section apply only to property of the estate. However, they will provide a guide to the courts in the interpretation of proposed 11 U.S.C. 725, relating to distribution of collateral, in cases in which there is community property. If a secured creditor has a lien on both community and noncommunity property, the marshalling rules here—by analogy would dictate that the creditor be satisfied first out of community property, and then out of separate property.

Amendments

2010—Subsec. (b). Pub. L. 111–327 substituted "(8), (9), or (10)" for "or (8)".

2005—Subsec. (a)(1). Pub. L. 109–8, §713, substituted "on or before the earlier of—" and subpars. (A) and (B) for "before the date on which the trustee commences distribution under this section;".

Subsec. (b). Pub. L. 109–8, §1215, struck out "1009," before "1112".

1994—Subsec. (a)(1). Pub. L. 103–394, §213(b), inserted before semicolon at end ", proof of which is timely filed under section 501 of this title or tardily filed before the date on which the trustee commences distribution under this section".

Subsec. (b). Pub. L. 103–394, §§304(h)(5), 501(d)(24), substituted ", (7), or (8)" for "or (7)" and "chapter under section 1009, 1112," for "chapter under section 1112".

1986—Subsec. (b). Pub. L. 99–554, §283(s), inserted reference to par. (7) of section 507(a) of this title.

Pub. L. 99–554, §257(r), inserted reference to section 1208 of this title.

1984—Subsec. (b). Pub. L. 98–353, §479(a), substituted "each such particular paragraph" for "a particular paragraph", "a claim allowed under section 503(b) of this title" for "administrative expenses" in two places, and "has priority over" for "have priority over".

Subsec. (c)(1). Pub. L. 98–353, §479(b)(1), substituted "Claims allowed under section 503 of this title" for "Administrative expenses".

Subsec. (c)(2). Pub. L. 98–353, §479(b)(2), substituted "Allowed claims, other than claims allowed under section 503 of this title," for "Claims other than for administrative expenses".

Effective Date of 2005 Amendment

Amendment by Pub. L. 109–8 effective 180 days after Apr. 20, 2005, and not applicable with respect to cases commenced under this title before such effective date, except as otherwise provided, see section 1501 of Pub. L. 109–8, set out as a note under section 101 of this title.

Effective Date of 1994 Amendment

Amendment by Pub. L. 103–394 effective Oct. 22, 1994, and not applicable with respect to cases commenced under this title before Oct. 22, 1994, see section 702 of Pub. L. 103–394, set out as a note under section 101 of this title.

Effective Date of 1986 Amendment

Amendment by section 257 of Pub. L. 99–554 effective 30 days after Oct. 27, 1986, but not applicable to cases commenced under this title before that date, see section 302(a), (c)(1) of Pub. L. 99–554, set out as a note under section 581 of Title 28, Judiciary and Judicial Procedure.

Amendment by section 283 of Pub. L. 99–554 effective 30 days after Oct. 27, 1986, see section 302(a) of Pub. L. 99–554.

Effective Date of 1984 Amendment

Amendment by Pub. L. 98–353 effective with respect to cases filed 90 days after July 10, 1984, see section 552(a) of Pub. L. 98–353, set out as a note under section 101 of this title.

§727. Discharge

(a) The court shall grant the debtor a discharge, unless—

(1) the debtor is not an individual;

(2) the debtor, with intent to hinder, delay, or defraud a creditor or an officer of the estate charged with custody of property under this title, has transferred, removed, destroyed, mutilated, or concealed, or has permitted to be transferred, removed, destroyed, mutilated, or concealed—

(A) property of the debtor, within one year before the date of the filing of the petition; or

(B) property of the estate, after the date of the filing of the petition;

(3) the debtor has concealed, destroyed, mutilated, falsified, or failed to keep or preserve any recorded information, including books, documents, records, and papers, from which the debtor's financial condition or business transactions might be ascertained, unless such act or failure to act was justified under all of the circumstances of the case;

(4) the debtor knowingly and fraudulently, in or in connection with the case—

(A) made a false oath or account;

(B) presented or used a false claim;

(C) gave, offered, received, or attempted to obtain money, property, or advantage, or a promise of money, property, or advantage, for acting or forbearing to act; or

(D) withheld from an officer of the estate entitled to possession under this title, any recorded information, including books, documents, records, and papers, relating to the debtor's property or financial affairs;

(5) the debtor has failed to explain satisfactorily, before determination of denial of discharge under this paragraph, any loss of assets or deficiency of assets to meet the debtor's liabilities;

(6) the debtor has refused, in the case—

(A) to obey any lawful order of the court, other than an order to respond to a material question or to testify;

(B) on the ground of privilege against self-incrimination, to respond to a material question approved by the court or to testify, after the debtor has been granted immunity with respect to the matter concerning which such privilege was invoked; or

(C) on a ground other than the properly invoked privilege against self-incrimination, to respond to a material question approved by the court or to testify;

(7) the debtor has committed any act specified in paragraph (2), (3), (4), (5), or (6) of this subsection, on or within one year before the date of the filing of the petition, or during the case, in connection with another case, under this title or under the Bankruptcy Act, concerning an insider;

(8) the debtor has been granted a discharge under this section, under section 1141 of this title, or under section 14, 371, or 476 of the Bankruptcy Act, in a case commenced within 8 years before the date of the filing of the petition;

(9) the debtor has been granted a discharge under section 1228 or 1328 of this title, or under section 660 or 661 of the Bankruptcy Act, in a case commenced within six years before the date of the filing of the petition, unless payments under the plan in such case totaled at least—

(A) 100 percent of the allowed unsecured claims in such case; or

(B)(i) 70 percent of such claims; and

(ii) the plan was proposed by the debtor in good faith, and was the debtor's best effort;

(10) the court approves a written waiver of discharge executed by the debtor after the order for relief under this chapter;

(11) after filing the petition, the debtor failed to complete an instructional course concerning personal financial management described in section 111, except that this paragraph shall not apply with respect to a debtor who is a person described in

section 109(h)(4) or who resides in a district for which the United States trustee (or the bankruptcy administrator, if any) determines that the approved instructional courses are not adequate to service the additional individuals who would otherwise be required to complete such instructional courses under this section (The United States trustee (or the bankruptcy administrator, if any) who makes a determination described in this paragraph shall review such determination not later than 1 year after the date of such determination, and not less frequently than annually thereafter.); or

(12) the court after notice and a hearing held not more than 10 days before the date of the entry of the order granting the discharge finds that there is reasonable cause to believe that—

(A) section 522(q)(1) may be applicable to the debtor; and

(B) there is pending any proceeding in which the debtor may be found guilty of a felony of the kind described in section 522(q)(1)(A) or liable for a debt of the kind described in section 522(q)(1)(B).

(b) Except as provided in section 523 of this title, a discharge under subsection (a) of this section discharges the debtor from all debts that arose before the date of the order for relief under this chapter, and any liability on a claim that is determined under section 502 of this title as if such claim had arisen before the commencement of the case, whether or not a proof of claim based on any such debt or liability is filed under section 501 of this title, and whether or not a claim based on any such debt or liability is allowed under section 502 of this title.

(c)(1) The trustee, a creditor, or the United States trustee may object to the granting of a discharge under subsection (a) of this section.

(2) On request of a party in interest, the court may order the trustee to examine the acts and conduct of the debtor to determine whether a ground exists for denial of discharge.

(d) On request of the trustee, a creditor, or the United States trustee, and after notice and a hearing, the court shall revoke a discharge granted under subsection (a) of this section if—

(1) such discharge was obtained through the fraud of the debtor, and the requesting party did not know of such fraud until after the granting of such discharge;

(2) the debtor acquired property that is property of the estate, or became entitled to acquire property that would be property of the estate, and knowingly and fraudulently failed to report the acquisition of or entitlement to such property, or to deliver or surrender such property to the trustee;

(3) the debtor committed an act specified in subsection (a)(6) of this section; or

(4) the debtor has failed to explain satisfactorily—

(A) a material misstatement in an audit referred to in section 586(f) of title 28; or

(B) a failure to make available for inspection all necessary accounts, papers, documents, financial records, files, and all other papers, things, or property belonging to the debtor that are requested for an audit referred to in section 586(f) of title 28.

(e) The trustee, a creditor, or the United States trustee may request a revocation of a discharge—

(1) under subsection (d)(1) of this section within one year after such discharge is granted; or

(2) under subsection (d)(2) or (d)(3) of this section before the later of—

(A) one year after the granting of such discharge; and

(B) the date the case is closed.

(Pub. L. 95–598, Nov. 6, 1978, 92 Stat. 2609; Pub. L. 98–353, title III, §480, July 10, 1984, 98 Stat. 382; Pub. L. 99–554, title II, §§220, 257(s), Oct. 27, 1986, 100 Stat. 3101, 3116; Pub. L. 109–8, title I, §106(b), title III, §§312(1), 330(a), title VI, §603(d), Apr. 20, 2005, 119 Stat. 38, 86, 101, 123.)

Historical and Revision Notes

legislative statements

Sections 727(a) (8) and (9) of the House amendment represent a compromise between provisions contained in section 727(a)(8) of the House bill and Senate amendment. Section 727(a)(8) of the House amendment adopts section 727(a)(8) of the House bill. However, section 727(a)(9) of the House amendment contains a compromise based on section 727(a)(8) of the Senate amendment with respect to the circumstances under which a plan by way of composition under Chapter XIII of the Bankruptcy Act [chapter 13 of former title 11] should be a bar to discharge in a subsequent proceeding under title 11. The paragraph provides that a discharge under section 660 or 661 of the Bankruptcy Act [section 1060 or 1061 of former title 11] or section 1328 of title 11 in a case commenced within 6 years before the date of the filing of the petition in a subsequent case, operates as a bar to discharge unless, first, payments under the plan totaled at least 100 percent of the allowed unsecured claims in the case; or second, payments under the plan totaled at least 70 percent of the allowed unsecured claims in the case and the plan was proposed by the debtor in good faith and was the debtor's best effort.

It is expected that the Rules of Bankruptcy Procedure will contain a provision permitting the debtor to request a determination of whether a plan is the debtor's "best effort" prior to confirmation of a plan in a case under chapter 13 of title 11. In determining whether a plan is the debtor's "best effort" the court will evaluate several factors. Different facts and circumstances in cases under chapter 13 operate to make any rule of thumb of limited usefulness. The court should balance the debtor's assets, including family income, health insurance, retirement benefits, and other wealth, a sum which is generally determinable, against the foreseeable necessary living expenses of the debtor and the debtor's dependents, which unfortunately is rarely quantifiable. In determining the expenses of the debtor and the debtor's dependents, the court should consider the stability of the debtor's employment, if any, the age of the debtor, the number of the debtor's dependents and their ages, the condition of equipment and tools necessary to the debtor's employment or to the operation of his business, and other foreseeable expenses that the debtor will be required to pay during the period of the plan, other than payments to be made to creditors under the plan.

Section 727(a)(10) of the House amendment clarifies a provision contained in section 727(a)(9) of the House bill and Senate amendment indicating that a discharge may be barred if the court approves a waiver of discharge executed in writing by the debtor after the order for relief under chapter 7.

Section 727(b) of the House amendment adopts a similar provision contained in the Senate amendment modifying the effect of discharge. The provision makes clear that the debtor is discharged from all debts that arose before the date of the order for relief under chapter 7 in addition to any debt which is determined under section 502 as if it were a prepetition claim. Thus, if a case is converted from chapter 11 or chapter 13 to a case under chapter 7, all debts prior to the time of conversion are discharged, in addition to debts determined after the date of conversion of a kind specified in section 502, that are to be determined as prepetition claims. This modification is particularly important with respect to an individual debtor who files a petition under chapter 11 or chapter 13 of title 11 if the case is converted to chapter 7. The logical result of the House amendment is to equate the result that obtains whether the case is converted from another chapter to chapter 7, or whether the other chapter proceeding is dismissed and a new case is commenced by filing a petition under chapter 7.

senate report no. 95–989

This section is the heart of the fresh start provisions of the bankruptcy law. Subsection (a) requires the court to grant a debtor a discharge unless one of nine conditions is met. The first condition is that the debtor is not an individual. This is a change from present law, under which corporations and partnerships may be discharged in liquidation cases, though they rarely are. The change in policy will avoid trafficking in corporate shells and in bankrupt partnerships. "Individual" includes a deceased individual, so that if the debtor dies during the bankruptcy case, he will nevertheless be released from his debts, and his estate will not be liable for them. Creditors will be entitled to only one satisfaction—from the bankruptcy estate and not from the probate estate.

The next three grounds for denial of discharge center on the debtor's wrongdoing in or in connection with the bankruptcy case. They are derived from Bankruptcy Act §14c [section 32(c) of former title 11]. If the debtor, with intent to hinder, delay, or defraud his creditors or an officer of the estate, has transferred, removed, destroyed, mutilated, or concealed, or has permitted any such action with respect to, property of the debtor within the year preceding the case, or property of the estate after the commencement of the case, then the debtor is denied discharge. The debtor is also denied discharge if he has concealed, destroyed, mutilated, falsified, or failed to keep or preserve any books and records from which his financial condition might be ascertained, unless the act or failure to act was justified under all the circumstances of the case. The fourth ground for denial of discharge is the commission of a bankruptcy crime, although the standard of proof is preponderance of the evidence rather than proof beyond a reasonable doubt. These crimes include the making of a false oath or account, the use or presentation of a false claim, the giving or receiving of money for acting or forbearing to act, and the withholding from an officer of the estate entitled to possession of books and records relating to the debtor's financial affairs.

The fifth ground for denial of discharge is the failure of the debtor to explain satisfactorily any loss of assets or deficiency of assets to meet the debtor's liabilities. The sixth ground concerns refusal to testify. It is a change from present law, under which the debtor may be denied discharge for legitimately exercising his right against self-incrimination. Under this provision, the debtor may be denied discharge if he refuses to obey any lawful order of the court, or if he refuses to testify after having been granted immunity or after improperly invoking the constitutional privilege against self-incrimination.

The seventh ground for denial of discharge is the commission of an act specified in grounds two through six during the year before the debtor's case in connection with another bankruptcy case concerning an insider.

The eighth ground for denial of discharge is derived from §14c(5) of the Bankruptcy Act [section 32(c)(5) of former title 11]. If the debtor has been granted a discharge in a case commenced within 6 years preceding the present bankruptcy case, he is denied discharge. This provision, which is no change from current law with respect to straight bankruptcy, is the 6-year bar to discharge. Discharge under chapter 11 will bar a discharge for 6 years. As under current law, confirmation of a composition wage earner plan under chapter 13 is a basis for invoking the 6-year bar.

The ninth ground is approval by the court of a waiver of discharge.

Subsection (b) specifies that the discharge granted under this section discharges the debtor from all debts that arose before the date of the order for relief. It is irrelevant whether or not a proof of claim was filed with respect to the debt, and whether or not the claim based on the debt was allowed.

Subsection (c) permits the trustee, or a creditor, to object to discharge. It also permits the court, on request of a party in interest, to order the trustee to examine the acts and conduct of the debtor to determine whether a ground for denial of discharge exists.

Subsection (d) requires the court to revoke a discharge already granted in certain circumstances. If the debtor obtained the discharge through fraud, if he acquired and concealed property of the estate, or if he refused to obey a court order or to testify, the discharge is to be revoked.

Subsection (e) permits the trustee or a creditor to request revocation of a discharge within 1 year after the discharge is granted, on the grounds of fraud, and within one year of discharge or the date of the closing of the case, whichever is later, on other grounds.

References in Text

The Bankruptcy Act, referred to in subsec. (a)(7), is act July 1, 1898, ch. 541, 30 Stat. 544, as amended, which was classified generally to former Title 11.

Sections 14, 371, and 476 of the Bankruptcy Act, referred to in subsec. (a)(8), are section 14 of act July 1, 1898, ch. 541, 30 Stat. 550, section 371 of act July 1, 1898, ch. 541, as added June 22, 1938, ch. 575, §1, 52 Stat. 912, and section 476 of act July 1, 1898, ch. 541, as added June 22, 1938, ch. 575, §1, 52 Stat. 924, which were classified to sections 32, 771, and 876 of former Title 11.

Sections 660 and 661 of the Bankruptcy Act, referred to in subsec. (a)(9), are sections 660 and 661 of act July 1, 1898, ch. 541, as added June 22, 1938, ch. 575, §1, 52 Stat. 935, 936, which were classified to sections 1060 and 1061 of former Title 11.

Amendments

2005—Subsec. (a)(8). Pub. L. 109–8, §312(1), substituted "8 years" for "six years".

Subsec. (a)(11). Pub. L. 109–8, §106(b), added par. (11).

Subsec. (a)(12). Pub. L. 109–8, §330(a), added par. (12).

Subsec. (d)(4). Pub. L. 109–8, §603(d), added par. (4).

1986—Subsec. (a)(9). Pub. L. 99–554, §257(s), inserted reference to section 1228 of this title.

Subsec. (c). Pub. L. 99–554, §220, amended subsec. (c) generally, substituting "The trustee, a creditor, or the United States trustee may object" for "The trustee or a creditor may object" in par. (1).

Subsec. (d). Pub. L. 99–554, §220, amended subsec. (d) generally, substituting ", a creditor, or the United States trustee," for "or a creditor," in provisions preceding par. (1) and "acquisition of or entitlement to such property" for "acquisition of, or entitlement to, such property" in par. (2).

Subsec. (e). Pub. L. 99–554, §220, amended subsec. (e) generally, substituting "The trustee, a creditor, or the United States trustee may" for "The trustee or a creditor may" in provisions preceding par. (1), "section within" for "section, within" and "discharge is granted" for "discharge was granted" in par. (1), "section before" for "section, before" in provisions of par. (2) preceding subpar. (A), and "discharge; and" for "discharge; or" in par. (2)(A).

1984—Subsec. (a)(6)(C). Pub. L. 98–353, §480(a)(1), substituted "properly" for "property".

Subsec. (a)(7). Pub. L. 98–353, §480(a)(2), inserted ", under this title or under the Bankruptcy Act," after "another case".

Subsec. (a)(8). Pub. L. 98–353, §480(a)(3), substituted "371," for "371".

Subsec. (c)(1). Pub. L. 98–353, §480(b), substituted "to the granting of a discharge" for "to discharge".

Subsec. (e)(2)(A). Pub. L. 98–353, §480(c), substituted "or" for "and".

Effective Date of 2005 Amendment

Amendment by section 603(d) of Pub. L. 109–8 effective 18 months after Apr. 20, 2005, see section 603(e) of Pub. L. 109–8, set out as a note under section 521 of this title.

Amendments by sections 106(b), 312(1), and 330(a) of Pub. L. 109–8 effective 180 days after Apr. 20, 2005, with amendments by sections 106(b) and 312(1) of Pub. L. 109–8 not applicable with respect to cases commenced under this title before such effective date, except as otherwise provided, and amendment by section 330(a) of Pub. L. 109–8 applicable with respect to cases commenced under this title on or after Apr. 20, 2005, see section 1501 of Pub. L. 109–8, set out as a note under section 101 of this title.

Effective Date of 1986 Amendment

Amendment by section 257 of Pub. L. 99–554 effective 30 days after Oct. 27, 1986, but not applicable to cases commenced under this title before that date, see section 302(a), (c)(1) of Pub. L. 99–554, set out as a note under section 581 of Title 28, Judiciary and Judicial Procedure.

Effective date and applicability of amendment by section 220 of Pub. L. 99–554 dependent upon the judicial district involved, see section 302(d), (e) of Pub. L. 99–554.

Effective Date of 1984 Amendment

Amendment by Pub. L. 98–353 effective with respect to cases filed 90 days after July 10, 1984, see section 552(a) of Pub. L. 98–353, set out as a note under section 101 of this title.

[§728. Repealed. Pub. L. 109–8, title VII, §719(b)(1), Apr. 20, 2005, 119 Stat. 133]

Section, Pub. L. 95–598, Nov. 6, 1978, 92 Stat. 2611; Pub. L. 98–353, title III, §481, July 10, 1984, 98 Stat. 382; Pub. L. 99–554, title II, §257(t), Oct. 27, 1986, 100 Stat. 3116, related to special tax provisions.

Effective Date of Repeal

Repeal effective 180 days after Apr. 20, 2005, and not applicable with respect to cases commenced under this title before such effective date, except as otherwise provided, see section 1501 of Pub. L. 109–8, set out as an Effective Date of 2005 Amendment note under section 101 of this title.

SUBCHAPTER III—STOCKBROKER LIQUIDATION

§741. Definitions for this subchapter

In this subchapter—

(1) "Commission" means Securities and Exchange Commission;

(2) "customer" includes—

(A) entity with whom a person deals as principal or agent and that has a claim against such person on account of a security received, acquired, or held by such person in the ordinary course of such person's business as a stockbroker, from or for the securities account or accounts of such entity—

(i) for safekeeping;
(ii) with a view to sale;
(iii) to cover a consummated sale;
(iv) pursuant to a purchase;
(v) as collateral under a security agreement; or
(vi) for the purpose of effecting registration of transfer; and

(B) entity that has a claim against a person arising out of—

(i) a sale or conversion of a security received, acquired, or held as specified in subparagraph (A) of this paragraph; or
(ii) a deposit of cash, a security, or other property with such person for the purpose of purchasing or selling a security;

(3) "customer name security" means security—

(A) held for the account of a customer on the date of the filing of the petition by or on behalf of the debtor;
(B) registered in such customer's name on such date or in the process of being so registered under instructions from the debtor; and
(C) not in a form transferable by delivery on such date;

(4) "customer property" means cash, security, or other property, and proceeds of such cash, security, or property, received, acquired, or held by or for the account of the debtor, from or for the securities account of a customer—

(A) including—
(i) property that was unlawfully converted from and that is the lawful property of the estate;
(ii) a security held as property of the debtor to the extent such security is necessary to meet a net equity claim of a customer based on a security of the same class and series of an issuer;
(iii) resources provided through the use or realization of a customer's debit cash balance or a debit item includible in the Formula for Determination of Reserve Requirement for Brokers and Dealers as promulgated by the Commission under the Securities Exchange Act of 1934; and
(iv) other property of the debtor that any applicable law, rule, or regulation requires to be set aside or held for the benefit of a customer, unless including such property as customer property would not significantly increase customer property; but

(B) not including—
(i) a customer name security delivered to or reclaimed by a customer under section 751 of this title; or
(ii) property to the extent that a customer does not have a claim against the debtor based on such property;

(5) "margin payment" means payment or deposit of cash, a security, or other property, that is commonly known to the securities trade as original margin, initial margin, maintenance margin, or variation margin, or as a mark-to-market payment, or that secures an obligation of a participant in a securities clearing agency;

(6) "net equity" means, with respect to all accounts of a customer that such customer has in the same capacity—

(A)(i) aggregate dollar balance that would remain in such accounts after the liquidation, by sale or purchase, at the time of the filing of the petition, of all securities positions in all such accounts, except any customer name securities of such customer; minus
(ii) any claim of the debtor against such customer in such capacity that would have been owing immediately after such liquidation; plus

(B) any payment by such customer to the trustee, within 60 days after notice under section 342 of this title, of any business related claim of the debtor against such customer in such capacity;

(7) "securities contract"—

(A) means—
(i) a contract for the purchase, sale, or loan of a security, a certificate of deposit, a mortgage loan, any interest in a mortgage loan, a group or index of securities, certificates of deposit, or mortgage loans or interests therein (including an interest therein or based on the value thereof), or option on any of the foregoing, including an option to purchase or sell any such security, certificate of deposit, mortgage loan, interest, group or index, or option, and including any repurchase or reverse repurchase transaction on any such security, certificate of deposit, mortgage loan, interest, group or index, or option (whether or not such repurchase or reverse repurchase transaction is a "repurchase agreement", as defined in section 101);

(ii) any option entered into on a national securities exchange relating to foreign currencies;

(iii) the guarantee (including by novation) by or to any securities clearing agency of a settlement of cash, securities, certificates of deposit, mortgage loans or interests therein, group or index of securities, or mortgage loans or interests therein (including any interest therein or based on the value thereof), or option on any of the foregoing, including an option to purchase or sell any such security, certificate of deposit, mortgage loan, interest, group or index, or option (whether or not such settlement is in connection with any agreement or transaction referred to in clauses (i) through (xi));

(iv) any margin loan;

(v) any extension of credit for the clearance or settlement of securities transactions;

(vi) any loan transaction coupled with a securities collar transaction, any prepaid forward securities transaction, or any total return swap transaction coupled with a securities sale transaction;

(vii) any other agreement or transaction that is similar to an agreement or transaction referred to in this subparagraph;

(viii) any combination of the agreements or transactions referred to in this subparagraph;

(ix) any option to enter into any agreement or transaction referred to in this subparagraph;

(x) a master agreement that provides for an agreement or transaction referred to in clause (i), (ii), (iii), (iv), (v), (vi), (vii), (viii), or (ix), together with all supplements to any such master agreement, without regard to whether the master agreement provides for an agreement or transaction that is not a securities contract under this subparagraph, except that such master agreement shall be considered to be a securities contract under this subparagraph only with respect to each agreement or transaction under such master agreement that is referred to in clause (i), (ii), (iii), (iv), (v), (vi), (vii), (viii), or (ix); or

(xi) any security agreement or arrangement or other credit enhancement related to any agreement or transaction referred to in this subparagraph, including any guarantee or reimbursement obligation by or to a stockbroker, securities clearing agency, financial institution, or financial participant in connection with any agreement or transaction referred to in this subparagraph, but not to exceed the damages in connection with any such agreement or transaction, measured in accordance with section 562; and

(B) does not include any purchase, sale, or repurchase obligation under a participation in a commercial mortgage loan;

(8) "settlement payment" means a preliminary settlement payment, a partial settlement payment, an interim settlement payment, a settlement payment on account, a final settlement payment, or any other similar payment commonly used in the securities trade; and

(9) "SIPC" means Securities Investor Protection Corporation.

(Pub. L. 95–598, Nov. 6, 1978, 92 Stat. 2611; Pub. L. 97–222, §8, July 27, 1982, 96 Stat. 237; Pub. L. 98–353, title III, §482, July 10, 1984, 98 Stat. 382; Pub. L. 103–394, title V, §501(d)(25), Oct. 22, 1994, 108 Stat. 4146; Pub. L. 109–8, title IX, §907(a)(2), Apr. 20, 2005, 119 Stat. 173; Pub. L. 109–390, §5(a)(3), Dec. 12, 2006, 120 Stat. 2697.)

Historical and Revision Notes

legislative statements

Section 741(6) of the House bill and Senate amendment is deleted by the House amendment since the defined term is used only in section 741(4)(A)(iii). A corresponding change is made in that section.

senate report no. 95–989

Section 741 sets forth definitions for subchapter III of chapter 7.

Paragraph (1) defines "Commission" to mean the Securities and Exchange Commission.

Paragraph (2) defines "customer" to include anybody that interacts with the debtor in a capacity that concerns securities transactions. The term embraces cash or margin customers of a broker or dealer in the broadest sense.

Paragraph (3) defines "customer name security" in a restrictive fashion to include only non-transferable securities that are registered, or in the process of being registered in a customer's own name. The securities must not be endorsed by the customer and the stockbroker must not be able to legally transfer the securities by delivery, by a power of attorney, or otherwise.

Paragraph (4) defines "customer property" to include all property of the debtor that has been segregated for customers or property that should have been segregated but was unlawfully converted. Clause (i) refers to customer property not properly segregated by the debtor or customer property converted and then recovered so as to become property of the estate. Unlawfully converted property that has been transferred to a third party is excluded until it is recovered as property of the estate by virtue of the avoiding powers. The concept excludes customer name securities that have been delivered to or reclaimed by a customer and any property properly belonging to the stockholder, such as money deposited by a customer to pay for securities that the stockholder has distributed to such customer.

Paragraph (5) [enacted as (6)] defines "net equity" to establish the extent to which a customer will be entitled to share in the single and separate fund. Accounts of a customer are aggregated and offset only to the extent the accounts are held by the customer in the same capacity. Thus, a personal account is separate from an account held as trustee. In a community property state an account held for the community is distinct from an account held as separate property.

The net equity is computed by liquidating all securities positions in the accounts and crediting the account with any amount due to the customer. Regardless of the actual dates, if any, of liquidation, the customer is only entitled to the liquidation value at the time of the filing of the petition. To avoid double counting, the liquidation value of customer name securities belonging to a customer is excluded from net equity. Thus, clause (ii) includes claims against a customer resulting from the liquidation of a security under clause (i). The value of a security on which trading has been suspended at the time of the filing of the petition will be estimated. Once the net liquidation value is computed, any amount that the customer owes to the stockbroker is subtracted including any amount that would be owing after the hypothetical liquidation, such as brokerage fees. Debts owed by the customer to the debtor, other than in a securities related transaction, will not reduce the net equity of the customer. Finally, net equity is increased by any payment by the customer to the debtor actually paid within 60 days after notice. The principal reason a customer would make such a payment is to reclaim customer name securities under §751.

Paragraph (6) defines "1934 Act" to mean the Securities Exchange Act of 1934 [15 U.S.C. 78a et seq.].

Paragraph (7) [enacted as (9)] defines "SIPC" to mean the Securities Investor Protection Corporation.

References in Text

The Securities Exchange Act of 1934, referred to in par. (4)(A)(iii), is act June 6, 1934, ch. 404, 48 Stat. 881, as amended, which is classified principally to chapter 2B (§78a et seq.) of Title 15, Commerce and Trade. For complete classification of this Act to the Code, see section 78a of Title 15 and Tables.

Amendments

2006—Par. (7)(A)(i). Pub. L. 109–390, §5(a)(3)(A), substituted "a mortgage loan," for "a mortgage loan or" and inserted "(whether or not such repurchase or reverse repurchase transaction is a 'repurchase agreement', as defined in section 101)" before semicolon at end.

Par. (7)(A)(iii). Pub. L. 109–390, §5(a)(3)(B), inserted "(including by novation)" after "the guarantee" and "(whether or not such settlement is in connection with any agreement or transaction referred to in clauses (i) through (xi))" before semicolon at end.

Par. (7)(A)(v) to (vii). Pub. L. 109–390, §5(a)(3)(D), (E), added cls. (v) and (vi) and redesignated former cl. (v) as (vii). Former cls. (vi) and (vii) redesignated (viii) and (ix), respectively.

Par. (7)(A)(viii). Pub. L. 109–390, §5(a)(3)(D), redesignated cl. (vi) as (viii). Former cl. (viii) redesignated (x).

Pub. L. 109–390, §5(a)(3)(C), substituted "(vii), (viii), or (ix)" for "or (vii)" in two places.

Par. (7)(A)(ix) to (xi). Pub. L. 109–390, §5(a)(3)(D), redesignated cls. (vii) to (ix) as (ix) to (xi), respectively.

2005—Par. (7). Pub. L. 109–8 added par. (7) and struck out former par. (7) which read as follows: " 'securities contract' means contract for the purchase, sale, or loan of a security, including an option for the purchase or sale of a security, certificate of deposit, or group or index of securities (including any interest therein or based on the value thereof), or any option entered into on a national securities exchange relating to foreign currencies, or the guarantee of any settlement of cash or securities by or to a securities clearing agency;".

1994—Par. (4)(A)(iii). Pub. L. 103–394 struck out "(15 U.S.C. 78a et seq.)" after "Act of 1934".

1984—Par. (2)(A). Pub. L. 98–353, §482(1), substituted "with whom a person deals" for "with whom the debtor deals", "that has a claim" for "that holds a claim", "against such person" for "against the debtor", "held by such person" for "held by the debtor", and "such person's business as a stockbroker," for "business as a stockbroker".

Par. (2)(B). Pub. L. 98–353, §482(2)(A), (B), substituted "has a claim" for "holds a claim" and "against a person" for "against the debtor" in provisions preceding cl. (i).

Par. (2)(B)(ii). Pub. L. 98–353, §482(2)(C), substituted "such person" for "the debtor".

Par. (4)(A)(i). Pub. L. 98–353, §482(3), substituted "from and that is the lawful" for "and that is".

Par. (6)(A)(i). Pub. L. 98–353, §482(4), inserted a comma after "petition" and "any" after "except".

Par. (7). Pub. L. 98–353, §482(5), amended par. (7) generally, inserting provisions relating to options for the purchase or sale of certificates of deposit, or a group or index of securities (including any interest therein or based on the value thereof), or any option entered into on a national securities exchange relating to foreign currencies.

Par. (8). Pub. L. 98–353, §482(6), inserted "a final settlement payment,".

1982—Par. (4). Pub. L. 97–222, §8(1), struck out "at any time" after "security, or property," in provisions preceding subpar. (A), and inserted "of a customer" after "claim" in subpar. (A)(ii).

Par. (5). Pub. L. 97–222, §8(3), added par. (5). Former par. (5) redesignated (6).

Par. (6). Pub. L. 97–222, §8(2), (4), redesignated former par. (5) as (6), in provisions preceding subpar. (A), substituted "all accounts of a customer that such customer has" for "the aggregate of all of a customer's accounts that such customer holds", in subpar. (A)(2) inserted "in such capacity", and in subpar. (B) inserted "in such capacity". Former par. (6) redesignated (9).

Pars. (7), (8). Pub. L. 97–222, §8(5), added pars. (7) and (8).

Par. (9). Pub. L. 97–222, §8(2), (6), redesignated former par. (6) as (9) and substituted "Securities" for "Security".

Effective Date of 2006 Amendment

Amendment by Pub. L. 109–390 not applicable to any cases commenced under this title or to appointments made under any Federal or State law, before Dec. 12, 2006, see section 7 of Pub. L. 109–390, set out as a note under section 101 of this title.

Effective Date of 2005 Amendment

Amendment by Pub. L. 109–8 effective 180 days after Apr. 20, 2005, and not applicable with respect to cases commenced under this title before such effective date, except as otherwise provided, see section 1501 of Pub. L. 109–8, set out as a note under section 101 of this title.

Effective Date of 1994 Amendment

Amendment by Pub. L. 103–394 effective Oct. 22, 1994, and not applicable with respect to cases commenced under this title before Oct. 22, 1994, see section 702 of Pub. L. 103–394, set out as a note under section 101 of this title.

Effective Date of 1984 Amendment

Amendment by Pub. L. 98–353 effective with respect to cases filed 90 days after July 10, 1984, see section 552(a) of Pub. L. 98–353, set out as a note under section 101 of this title.

§742. Effect of section 362 of this title in this subchapter

Notwithstanding section 362 of this title, SIPC may file an application for a protective decree under the Securities Investor Protection Act of 1970. The filing of such application stays all proceedings in the case under this title unless and until such application is dismissed. If SIPC completes the liquidation of the debtor, then the court shall dismiss the case.

(Pub. L. 95–598, Nov. 6, 1978, 92 Stat. 2613; Pub. L. 97–222, §9, July 27, 1982, 96 Stat. 237; Pub. L. 103–394, title V, §501(d)(26), Oct. 22, 1994, 108 Stat. 4146.)

Historical and Revision Notes

legislative statements

Section 742 of the House amendment deletes a sentence contained in the Senate amendment requiring the trustee in an interstate stock-brokerage liquidation to comply with the provisions of subchapter IV of chapter 7 if the debtor is also a commodity broker. The House amendment expands the requirement to require the SIPC trustee to perform such duties, if the debtor is a commodity broker, under section 7(b) of the Securities Investor Protection Act [15 U.S.C. 78ggg(b)]. The requirement is deleted from section 742 since the trustee of an intrastate stockbroker will be bound by the provisions of subchapter IV of chapter 7 if the debtor is also a commodity broker by reason of section 103 of title 11.

senate report no. 95–989

Section 742 indicates that the automatic stay does not prevent SIPC from filing an application for a protective decree under SIPA. If SIPA does file such an application, then all bankruptcy proceedings are suspended until the SIPC action is completed. If SIPC completes liquidation of the stockbroker then the bankruptcy case is dismissed.

References in Text

The Securities Investor Protection Act of 1970, referred to in text, is Pub. L. 91–598, Dec. 30, 1970, 84 Stat. 1636, as amended, which is classified generally to chapter 2B–1 (§78aaa et seq.) of Title 15, Commerce and Trade. For complete classification of this Act to the Code, see section 78aaa of Title 15 and Tables.

Amendments

1994—Pub. L. 103–394 struck out "(15 U.S.C. 78aaa et seq.)" after "Act of 1970".

1982—Pub. L. 97–222 substituted "title" for "chapter" after "all proceedings in the case under this".

Effective Date of 1994 Amendment

Amendment by Pub. L. 103–394 effective Oct. 22, 1994, and not applicable with respect to cases commenced under this title before Oct. 22, 1994, see section 702 of Pub. L. 103–394, set out as a note under section 101 of this title.

§743. Notice

The clerk shall give the notice required by section 342 of this title to SIPC and to the Commission.

(Pub. L. 95–598, Nov. 6, 1978, 92 Stat. 2613; Pub. L. 99–554, title II, §283(t), Oct. 27, 1986, 100 Stat. 3118; Pub. L. 103–394, title V, §501(d)(27), Oct. 22, 1994, 108 Stat. 4146.)

Historical and Revision Notes

senate report no. 95–989

Section 743 requires that notice of the order for relief be given to SIPC and to the SEC in every stockbroker case.

Amendments

1994—Pub. L. 103–394 substituted "342" for "342(a)".

1986—Pub. L. 99–554, which directed the amendment of this section by striking "(d)", rather than "(a)", could not be executed because "(d)" did not appear in text. See 1994 Amendment note above.

Effective Date of 1994 Amendment

Amendment by Pub. L. 103–394 effective Oct. 22, 1994, and not applicable with respect to cases commenced under this title before Oct. 22, 1994, see section 702 of Pub. L. 103–394, set out as a note under section 101 of this title.

Effective Date of 1986 Amendment

Amendment by Pub. L. 99–554 effective 30 days after Oct. 27, 1986, see section 302(a) of Pub. L. 99–554, set out as a note under section 581 of Title 28, Judiciary and Judicial Procedure.

§744. Executory contracts

Notwithstanding section 365(d)(1) of this title, the trustee shall assume or reject, under section 365 of this title, any executory contract of the debtor for the purchase or sale of a security in the ordinary course of the debtor's business, within a reasonable time after the date of the order for relief, but not to exceed 30 days. If the trustee does not assume such a contract within such time, such contract is rejected.

(Pub. L. 95–598, Nov. 6, 1978, 92 Stat. 2613; Pub. L. 97–222, §10, July 27, 1982, 96 Stat. 238.)

Historical and Revision Notes

senate report no. 95–989

Section 744 instructs the court to give the trustee a reasonable time, not to exceed 30 days, to assume or reject any executory contract of the stockbroker to buy or sell securities. Any contract not assumed within the time fixed by the court is considered to be rejected.

Amendments

1982—Pub. L. 97–222 inserted "but" after "relief,".

§745. Treatment of accounts

(a) Accounts held by the debtor for a particular customer in separate capacities shall be treated as accounts of separate customers.

(b) If a stockbroker or a bank holds a customer net equity claim against the debtor that arose out of a transaction for a customer of such stockbroker or bank, each such customer of such stockbroker or bank shall be treated as a separate customer of the debtor.

(c) Each trustee's account specified as such on the debtor's books, and supported by a trust deed filed with, and qualified as such by, the Internal Revenue Service, and under the Internal Revenue Code of 1986, shall be treated as a separate customer account for each beneficiary under such trustee account.

(Pub. L. 95–598, Nov. 6, 1978, 92 Stat. 2613; Pub. L. 97–222, §11, July 27, 1982, 96 Stat. 238; Pub. L. 98–353, title III, §483, July 10, 1984, 98 Stat. 383; Pub. L. 103–394, title V, §501(d)(28), Oct. 22, 1994, 108 Stat. 4146.)

Historical and Revision Notes

senate report no. 95–989

Section 745(a) indicates that each account held by a customer in a separate capacity is to be considered a separate account. This prevents the offset of accounts held in different capacities.

Subsection (b) indicates that a bank or another stockbroker that is a customer of a debtor is considered to hold its customers accounts in separate capacities. Thus a bank or other stockbroker is not treated as a mutual fund for purposes of bulk investment. This protects unrelated customers of a bank or other stockholder from having their accounts offset.

Subsection (c) effects the same result with respect to a trust so that each beneficiary is treated as the customer of the debtor rather than the trust itself. This eliminates any doubt whether a trustee holds a personal account in a separate capacity from his trustee's account.

References in Text

The Internal Revenue Code of 1986, referred to in subsec. (c), is classified generally to Title 26, Internal Revenue Code.

Amendments

1994—Subsec. (c). Pub. L. 103–394 substituted "Internal Revenue Code of 1986" for "Internal Revenue Code of 1954 (26 U.S.C. 1 et seq.)".

1984—Subsec. (a). Pub. L. 98–353 inserted "the debtor for" after "by".

1982—Subsec. (c). Pub. L. 97–222 substituted "Each" for "A".

Effective Date of 1994 Amendment

Amendment by Pub. L. 103–394 effective Oct. 22, 1994, and not applicable with respect to cases commenced under this title before Oct. 22, 1994, see section 702 of Pub. L. 103–394, set out as a note under section 101 of this title.

Effective Date of 1984 Amendment

Amendment by Pub. L. 98–353 effective with respect to cases filed 90 days after July 10, 1984, see section 552(a) of Pub. L. 98–353, set out as a note under section 101 of this title.

§746. Extent of customer claims

(a) If, after the date of the filing of the petition, an entity enters into a transaction with the debtor, in a manner that would have made such entity a customer had such transaction occurred before the date of the filing of the petition, and such transaction was entered into by such entity in good faith and before the qualification under section 322 of this title of a trustee, such entity shall be deemed a customer, and the date of such transaction shall be deemed to be the date of the filing of the petition for the purpose of determining such entity's net equity.

(b) An entity does not have a claim as a customer to the extent that such entity transferred to the debtor cash or a security that, by contract, agreement, understanding, or operation of law, is—

(1) part of the capital of the debtor; or

(2) subordinated to the claims of any or all creditors.

(Pub. L. 95–598, Nov. 6, 1978, 92 Stat. 2613; Pub. L. 97–222, §12, July 27, 1982, 96 Stat. 238.)

Historical and Revision Notes

senate report no. 95–989

Section 746(a) protects entities who deal in good faith with the debtor after the filing of the petition and before a trustee is appointed by deeming such entities to be customers. The principal application of this section will be in an involuntary case before the order for relief, because §701(b) requires prompt appointment of an interim trustee after the order for relief.

Subsection (b) indicates that an entity who holds securities that are either part of the capital of the debtor or that are subordinated to the claims of any creditor of the debtor is not a customer with respect to those securities. This subsection will apply when the stockbroker has sold securities in itself to the customer or when the customer has otherwise placed such securities in an account with the stockbroker.

Amendments

1982—Pub. L. 97–222, §12(c), substituted "claims" for "claim" in section catchline.

Subsec. (a). Pub. L. 97–222, §12(a), substituted "enters into" for "effects, with respect to cash or a security,", struck out "with respect to such cash or security" wherever appearing, and substituted "the date of the filing of the petition" for "such date", and "entered into" for "effected".

Subsec. (b). Pub. L. 97–222, §12(b), substituted "transferred to the debtor" for "has a claim for" in provisions preceding par. (1), and struck out "is" in par. (2).

§747. Subordination of certain customer claims

Except as provided in section 510 of this title, unless all other customer net equity claims have been paid in full, the trustee may not pay in full or pay in part, directly or indirectly, any net equity claim of a customer that was, on the date the transaction giving rise to such claim occurred—

(1) an insider;

(2) a beneficial owner of at least five percent of any class of equity securities of the debtor, other than—

(A) nonconvertible stock having fixed preferential dividend and liquidation rights; or

(B) interests of limited partners in a limited partnership;

(3) a limited partner with a participation of at least five percent in the net assets or net profits of the debtor; or

(4) an entity that, directly or indirectly, through agreement or otherwise, exercised or had the power to exercise control over the management or policies of the debtor.

(Pub. L. 95–598, Nov. 6, 1978, 92 Stat. 2613; Pub. L. 97–222, §13, July 27, 1982, 96 Stat. 238.)

Historical and Revision Notes

senate report no. 95–989

Section 747 subordinates to other customer claims, all claims of a customer who is an insider, a five percent owner of the debtor, or otherwise in control of the debtor.

Amendments

1982—Pub. L. 97–222 substituted "the transaction giving rise to such claim occurred" for "such claim arose" in provisions preceding par. (1).

§748. Reduction of securities to money

As soon as practicable after the date of the order for relief, the trustee shall reduce to money, consistent with good market practice, all securities held as property of the estate, except for customer name securities delivered or reclaimed under section 751 of this title.

(Pub. L. 95–598, Nov. 6, 1978, 92 Stat. 2614.)

Historical and Revision Notes

senate report no. 95–989

Section 748 requires the trustee to liquidate all securities, except for customer name securities, of the estate in a manner consistent with good market practice. The trustee should refrain from flooding a thin market with a large percentage of shares in any one issue. If the trustee holds restricted securities or securities in which trading has been suspended, then the trustee must arrange to liquidate such securities in accordance with the securities laws. A private placement may be the only exemption available with the customer of the debtor the best prospect for such a placement. The subsection does not permit such a customer to bid in his net equity as part of the purchase price; a contrary result would permit a customer to receive a greater percentage on his net equity claim than other customers.

§749. Voidable transfers

(a) Except as otherwise provided in this section, any transfer of property that, but for such transfer, would have been customer property, may be avoided by the trustee, and such property shall be treated as customer property, if and to the extent that the trustee avoids such transfer under section 544, 545, 547, 548, or 549 of this title. For the purpose of such sections, the property so transferred shall be deemed to have been property of the debtor and, if such transfer was made to a customer or for a customer's benefit, such customer shall be deemed, for the purposes of this section, to have been a creditor.

(b) Notwithstanding sections 544, 545, 547, 548, and 549 of this title, the trustee may not avoid a transfer made before seven days after the order for relief if such transfer is approved by the Commission by rule or order, either before or after such transfer, and if such transfer is—

(1) a transfer of a securities contract entered into or carried by or through the debtor on behalf of a customer, and of any cash, security, or other property margining or securing such securities contract; or

(2) the liquidation of a securities contract entered into or carried by or through the debtor on behalf of a customer.

(Pub. L. 95–598, Nov. 6, 1978, 92 Stat. 2614; Pub. L. 97–222, §14, July 27, 1982, 96 Stat. 238; Pub. L. 111–16, §2(8), May 7, 2009, 123 Stat. 1607.)

Historical and Revision Notes

senate report no. 95–989

Section 749 indicates that if the trustee avoids a transfer, property recovered is customer property to any extent it would have been customer property but for the transfer. The section clarifies that a customer who receives a transfer of property of the debtor is a creditor and that property in a customer's account is property of a creditor for purposes of the avoiding powers.

Amendments

2009—Subsec. (b). Pub. L. 111–16 substituted "seven days" for "five days" in introductory provisions.

1982—Pub. L. 97–222 substituted "(a) Except as otherwise provided in this section, any" for "Any", and "but" for "except", inserted "such property", substituted "or 549" for "549, or 724(a)", and added subsec. (b).

Effective Date of 2009 Amendment

Amendment by Pub. L. 111–16 effective Dec. 1, 2009, see section 7 of Pub. L. 111–16, set out as a note under section 109 of this title.

§750. Distribution of securities

The trustee may not distribute a security except under section 751 of this title.

(Pub. L. 95–598, Nov. 6, 1978, 92 Stat. 2614.)

Historical and Revision Notes

senate report no. 95–989

Section 750 forbids the trustee from distributing a security other than a customer name security. The term "distribution" refers to a distribution to customers in satisfaction of net equity claims and is not intended to preclude the trustee from liquidating securities under proposed 11 U.S.C. 748.

§751. Customer name securities

The trustee shall deliver any customer name security to or on behalf of the customer entitled to such security, unless such customer has a negative net equity. With the approval of the trustee, a customer may reclaim a customer name security after payment to the trustee, within such period as the trustee allows, of any claim of the debtor against such customer to the extent that such customer will not have a negative net equity after such payment.

(Pub. L. 95–598, Nov. 6, 1978, 92 Stat. 2614.)

Historical and Revision Notes

senate report no. 95–989

Section 751 requires the trustee to deliver a customer name security to the customer entitled to such security unless the customer has a negative net equity. The customer's net equity will be negative when the amount owed by the customer to the stockbroker exceeds the liquidation value of the non-customer name securities in the customer's account. If the customer is a net debtor of the stockbroker, then the trustee may permit the customer to repay debts to the stockbroker so that the customer will no longer be in debt to the stockbroker. If the customer refuses to pay such amount, then the court may order the customer to endorse the security in order that the trustee may liquidate such property.

§752. Customer property

(a) The trustee shall distribute customer property ratably to customers on the basis and to the extent of such customers' allowed net equity claims and in priority to all other claims, except claims of the kind specified in section 507(a)(2) of this title that are attributable to the administration of such customer property.

(b)(1) The trustee shall distribute customer property in excess of that distributed under subsection (a) of this section in accordance with section 726 of this title.

(2) Except as provided in section 510 of this title, if a customer is not paid the full amount of such customer's allowed net equity claim from customer property, the unpaid portion of such claim is a claim entitled to distribution under section 726 of this title.

(c) Any cash or security remaining after the liquidation of a security interest created under a security agreement made by the debtor, excluding property excluded under section 741(4)(B) of this title, shall be apportioned between the general estate and customer property in the same proportion as the general estate of the debtor and customer property were subject to such security interest.

(Pub. L. 95–598, Nov. 6, 1978, 92 Stat. 2614; Pub. L. 97–222, §15, July 27, 1982, 96 Stat. 238; Pub. L. 98–353, title III, §484, July 10, 1984, 98 Stat. 383; Pub. L. 109–8, title XV, §1502(a)(3), Apr. 20, 2005, 119 Stat. 216.)

Historical and Revision Notes

senate report no. 95–989

Section 752(a) requires the trustee to distribute customer property to customers based on the amount of their net equity claims. Customer property is to be distributed in priority to all claims except expenses of administration entitled to priority under §507(1). It is anticipated that the court will apportion such administrative claims on an equitable basis between the general estate and the customer property of the debtor.

Subsection (b)(1) indicates that in the event customer property exceeds customers net equity claims and administrative expenses, the excess pours over into the general estate. This event would occur if the value of securities increased dramatically after the order for relief but before liquidation by the trustee. Subsection (b)(2) indicates that the unpaid portion of a customer's net equity claim is entitled to share in the general estate as an unsecured claim unless subordinated by the court under proposed 11 U.S.C. 501. A net equity claim of a customer that is subordinated under section 747 is entitled to share in distribution under section 726(a)(2) unless subordinated under section 510 independently of the subordination under section 747.

Subsection (c) provides for apportionment between customer property and the general estate of any equity of the debtor in property remaining after a secured creditor liquidates a security interest. This might occur if a stockbroker hypothecates securities of his own and of his customers if the value of the hypothecated securities exceeds the debt owed to the secured party. The apportionment is to be made according to the ratio of customer property and general property of the debtor that comprised the collateral. The subsection refers to cash and securities of customers to include any customer property unlawfully converted by the stockbroker in the course of such a transaction. The apportionment is made subject to section 741(4)(B) to insure that property in a customer's account that is owed to the stockbroker will not be considered customer property. This recognizes the right of the stockbroker to withdraw money that has been erroneously placed in a customer's account or that is otherwise owing to the stockbroker.

Amendments

2005—Subsec. (a). Pub. L. 109–8 substituted "507(a)(2)" for "507(a)(1)".

1984—Subsec. (a). Pub. L. 98–353, §484(a), substituted "customers' allowed" for "customers allowed", "except claims of the kind" for "except claims", and "such customer property" for "customer property".

Subsec. (b)(2). Pub. L. 98–353, §484(b), substituted "section 726" for "section 726(a)".

1982—Subsec. (c). Pub. L. 97–222 substituted "Any cash or security remaining after the liquidation of a security interest created under a security agreement made by the debtor, excluding property excluded under section 741(4)(B) of this title, shall be apportioned between the general estate and customer property in the same proportion as the general estate of the debtor and customer property were subject to such security interest" for "Subject to section 741(4)(B) of this title, any cash or security remaining after the liquidation of a security interest created under a security agreement made by the debtor shall be apportioned between the general estate and customer property in the proportion that the general property of the debtor and the cash or securities of customers were subject to such security interest".

Effective Date of 2005 Amendment

Amendment by Pub. L. 109–8 effective 180 days after Apr. 20, 2005, and not applicable with respect to cases commenced under this title before such effective date, except as otherwise provided, see section 1501 of Pub. L. 109–8, set out as a note under section 101 of this title.

Effective Date of 1984 Amendment

Amendment by Pub. L. 98–353 effective with respect to cases filed 90 days after July 10, 1984, see section 552(a) of Pub. L. 98–353, set out as a note under section 101 of this title.

§753. Stockbroker liquidation and forward contract merchants, commodity brokers, stockbrokers, financial institutions, financial participants, securities clearing agencies, swap participants, repo participants, and master netting agreement participants

Notwithstanding any other provision of this title, the exercise of rights by a forward contract merchant, commodity broker, stockbroker, financial institution, financial participant, securities clearing agency, swap participant, repo participant, or master netting agreement participant under this title shall not affect the priority of any unsecured claim it may have after the exercise of such rights.

(Added Pub. L. 109–8, title IX, §907(m), Apr. 20, 2005, 119 Stat. 181.)

Effective Date

Section effective 180 days after Apr. 20, 2005, and not applicable with respect to cases commenced under this title before such effective date, except as otherwise provided, see section 1501 of Pub. L. 109–8, set out as an Effective Date of 2005 Amendment note under section 101 of this title.

SUBCHAPTER IV—COMMODITY BROKER LIQUIDATION

§761. Definitions for this subchapter

In this subchapter—

(1) "Act" means Commodity Exchange Act;

(2) "clearing organization" means a derivatives clearing organization registered under the Act;

(3) "Commission" means Commodity Futures Trading Commission;

(4) "commodity contract" means—

(A) with respect to a futures commission merchant, contract for the purchase or sale of a commodity for future delivery on, or subject to the rules of, a contract market or board of trade;

(B) with respect to a foreign futures commission merchant, foreign future;

(C) with respect to a leverage transaction merchant, leverage transaction;

(D) with respect to a clearing organization, contract for the purchase or sale of a commodity for future delivery on, or subject to the rules of, a contract market or board of trade that is cleared by such clearing organization, or commodity option traded on, or subject to the rules of, a contract market or board of trade that is cleared by such clearing organization;

(E) with respect to a commodity options dealer, commodity option;

(F)(i) any other contract, option, agreement, or transaction that is similar to a contract, option, agreement, or transaction referred to in this paragraph; and

(ii) with respect to a futures commission merchant or a clearing organization, any other contract, option, agreement, or transaction, in each case, that is cleared by a clearing organization;

(G) any combination of the agreements or transactions referred to in this paragraph;

(H) any option to enter into an agreement or transaction referred to in this paragraph;

(I) a master agreement that provides for an agreement or transaction referred to in subparagraph (A), (B), (C), (D), (E), (F), (G), or (H), together with all supplements to such master agreement, without regard to whether the master agreement provides for an agreement or transaction that is not a commodity contract under this paragraph, except that the master agreement shall be considered to be a commodity contract under this paragraph only with respect to each agreement or transaction under the master agreement that is referred to in subparagraph (A), (B), (C), (D), (E), (F), (G), or (H); or

(J) any security agreement or arrangement or other credit enhancement related to any agreement or transaction referred to in this paragraph, including any guarantee or reimbursement obligation by or to a commodity broker or financial participant in connection with any agreement or transaction referred to in this paragraph, but not to exceed the damages in connection with any such agreement or transaction, measured in accordance with section 562;

(5) "commodity option" means agreement or transaction subject to regulation under section 4c(b) of the Act;

(6) "commodity options dealer" means person that extends credit to, or that accepts cash, a security, or other property from, a customer of such person for the purchase or sale of an interest in a commodity option;

(7) "contract market" means a registered entity;

(8) "contract of sale", "commodity", "derivatives clearing organization", "future delivery", "board of trade", "registered entity", and "futures commission merchant" have the meanings assigned to those terms in the Act;

(9) "customer" means—

(A) with respect to a futures commission merchant—

(i) entity for or with whom such futures commission merchant deals and that holds a claim against such futures commission merchant on account of a commodity contract made, received, acquired, or held by or through such futures commission merchant in the ordinary course of such futures commission merchant's business as a futures commission merchant from or for a commodity contract account of such entity; or

(ii) entity that holds a claim against such futures commission merchant arising out of—

(I) the making, liquidation, or change in the value of a commodity contract of a kind specified in clause (i) of this subparagraph;

(II) a deposit or payment of cash, a security, or other property with such futures commission merchant for the purpose of making or margining such a commodity contract; or

(III) the making or taking of delivery on such a commodity contract;

(B) with respect to a foreign futures commission merchant—

(i) entity for or with whom such foreign futures commission merchant deals and that holds a claim against such foreign futures commission merchant on account of a commodity contract made, received, acquired, or held by or through such foreign futures commission merchant in the ordinary course of such foreign futures commission merchant's business as a foreign futures commission merchant from or for the foreign futures account of such entity; or

(ii) entity that holds a claim against such foreign futures commission merchant arising out of—

(I) the making, liquidation, or change in value of a commodity contract of a kind specified in clause (i) of this subparagraph;

(II) a deposit or payment of cash, a security, or other property with such foreign futures commission merchant for the purpose of making or margining such a commodity contract; or

(III) the making or taking of delivery on such a commodity contract;

(C) with respect to a leverage transaction merchant—

(i) entity for or with whom such leverage transaction merchant deals and that holds a claim against such leverage transaction merchant on account of a commodity contract engaged in by or with such leverage transaction merchant in the ordinary course of such leverage transaction merchant's business as a leverage transaction merchant from or for the leverage account of such entity; or

(ii) entity that holds a claim against such leverage transaction merchant arising out of—

(I) the making, liquidation, or change in value of a commodity contract of a kind specified in clause (i) of this subparagraph;

(II) a deposit or payment of cash, a security, or other property with such leverage transaction merchant for the purpose of entering into or margining such a commodity contract; or

(III) the making or taking of delivery on such a commodity contract;

(D) with respect to a clearing organization, clearing member of such clearing organization with whom such clearing organization deals and that holds a claim against such clearing organization on account of cash, a security, or other property received by such clearing organization to margin, guarantee, or secure a commodity contract in such clearing member's proprietary account or customers' account; or

(E) with respect to a commodity options dealer—

(i) entity for or with whom such commodity options dealer deals and that holds a claim on account of a commodity contract made, received, acquired, or held by or through such commodity options dealer in the ordinary course of such commodity options dealer's business as a commodity options dealer from or for the commodity options account of such entity; or

(ii) entity that holds a claim against such commodity options dealer arising out of—

(I) the making of, liquidation of, exercise of, or a change in value of, a commodity contract of a kind specified in clause (i) of this subparagraph; or

(II) a deposit or payment of cash, a security, or other property with such commodity options dealer for the purpose of making, exercising, or margining such a commodity contract;

(10) "customer property" means cash, a security, or other property, or proceeds of such cash, security, or property, received, acquired, or held by or for the account of the debtor, from or for the account of a customer—

(A) including—

(i) property received, acquired, or held to margin, guarantee, secure, purchase, or sell a commodity contract;

(ii) profits or contractual or other rights accruing to a customer as a result of a commodity contract;

(iii) an open commodity contract;

(iv) specifically identifiable customer property;

(v) warehouse receipt or other document held by the debtor evidencing ownership of or title to property to be delivered to fulfill a commodity contract from or for the account of a customer;

(vi) cash, a security, or other property received by the debtor as payment for a commodity to be delivered to fulfill a commodity contract from or for the account of a customer;

(vii) a security held as property of the debtor to the extent such security is necessary to meet a net equity claim based on a security of the same class and series of an issuer;

(viii) property that was unlawfully converted from and that is the lawful property of the estate; and

(ix) other property of the debtor that any applicable law, rule, or regulation requires to be set aside or held for the benefit of a customer, unless including such property as customer property would not significantly increase customer property; but

(B) not including property to the extent that a customer does not have a claim against the debtor based on such property;

(11) "foreign future" means contract for the purchase or sale of a commodity for future delivery on, or subject to the rules of, a board of trade outside the United States;

(12) "foreign futures commission merchant" means entity engaged in soliciting or accepting orders for the purchase or sale of a foreign future or that, in connection with such a solicitation or acceptance, accepts cash, a security, or other property, or extends credit to margin, guarantee, or secure any trade or contract that results from such a solicitation or acceptance;

(13) "leverage transaction" means agreement that is subject to regulation under section 19 of the Commodity Exchange Act, and that is commonly known to the commodities trade as a margin account, margin contract, leverage account, or leverage contract;

(14) "leverage transaction merchant" means person in the business of engaging in leverage transactions;

(15) "margin payment" means payment or deposit of cash, a security, or other property, that is commonly known to the commodities trade as original margin, initial margin, maintenance margin, or variation margin, including mark-to-market payments, settlement payments, variation payments, daily settlement payments, and final settlement payments made as adjustments to settlement prices;

(16) "member property" means customer property received, acquired, or held by or for the account of a debtor that is a clearing organization, from or for the proprietary account of a customer that is a clearing member of the debtor; and

(17) "net equity" means, subject to such rules and regulations as the Commission promulgates under the Act, with respect to the aggregate of all of a customer's accounts that such customer has in the same capacity—

(A) the balance remaining in such customer's accounts immediately after—

(i) all commodity contracts of such customer have been transferred, liquidated, or become identified for delivery; and

(ii) all obligations of such customer in such capacity to the debtor have been offset; plus

(B) the value, as of the date of return under section 766 of this title, of any specifically identifiable customer property actually returned to such customer before the date specified in subparagraph (A) of this paragraph; plus

(C) the value, as of the date of transfer, of—

(i) any commodity contract to which such customer is entitled that is transferred to another person under section 766 of this title; and

(ii) any cash, security, or other property of such customer transferred to such other person under section 766 of this title to margin or secure such transferred commodity contract.

(Pub. L. 95–598, Nov. 6, 1978, 92 Stat. 2615; Pub. L. 97–222, §16, July 27, 1982, 96 Stat. 238; Pub. L. 98–353, title III, §485, July 10, 1984, 98 Stat. 383; Pub. L. 103–394, title V, §501(d)(29), Oct. 22, 1994, 108 Stat. 4146; Pub. L. 106–554, §1(a)(5) [title I, §112(c)(6)], Dec. 21, 2000, 114 Stat. 2763, 2763A–395; Pub. L. 109–8, title IX, §907(a)(3), Apr. 20, 2005, 119 Stat. 174; Pub. L. 111–203, title VII, §724(b), July 21, 2010, 124 Stat. 1684.)

Historical and Revision Notes

legislative statements

SUBCHAPTER IV of chapter 7 represents a compromise between similar chapters in the House bill and Senate amendment. Section 761(2) of the House amendment defines "clearing organization" to cover an organization that clears commodity contracts on a contract market or a board of trade; the expansion of the definition is intended to include clearing organizations that clear commodity options. Section 761(4) of the House amendment adopts the term "commodity contract" as used in section 761(5) of the Senate amendment but with the more precise substantive definitions contained in section 761(8) of the House bill. The definition is modified to insert "board of trade" to cover commodity options. Section 761(5) of the House amendment adopts the definition contained in section 761(6) of the Senate amendment in preference to the definition contained in section 761(4) of the House bill which erroneously included onions. Section 761(9) of the House amendment represents a compromise between similar provisions contained in section 761(10) of the Senate amendment and section 761(9) of the House bill. The compromise adopts the substance contained in the House bill and adopts the terminology of "commodity contract" in lieu of "contractual commitment" as suggested in the Senate amendment. Section 761(10) of the House amendment represents a compromise between similar sections in the House bill and Senate amendment regarding the definition of "customer property." The definition of "distribution share" contained in section 761(12) of the Senate amendment is deleted as unnecessary. Section 761(12) of the House amendment adopts a definition of "foreign futures commission merchant" similar to the definition contained in section 761(14) of the Senate amendment. The definition is modified to cover either an entity engaged in soliciting orders or the purchase or sale of a foreign future, or an entity that accepts cash, a security, or other property for credit in connection with such a solicitation or acceptance. Section 761(13) of the House amendment adopts a definition of "leverage transaction" identical to the definition contained in section 761(15) of the Senate amendment. Section 761(15) of the House amendment adopts the definition of "margin payment" contained in section 761(17) of the Senate amendment. Section 761(17) of the House amendment adopts a definition of "net equity" derived from section 761(15) of the House bill.

senate report no. 95–989

Paragraph (1) defines "Act" to mean the Commodity Exchange Act [7 U.S.C. 1 et seq.].

Paragraph (2) defines "clearing organization" to mean an organization that clears (i.e., matches purchases and sales) commodity futures contracts made on or subject to the rules of a contract market or commodity options transactions made on or subject to the rules of a commodity option exchange. Although commodity option trading on exchanges is currently prohibited, it is anticipated that CFTC may permit such trading in the future.

Paragraphs (3) and (4) define terms "Commission" and "commodity futures contract".

Paragraph (5) [enacted as (4)] defines "commodity contract" to mean a commodity futures contract (§761(4)), a commodity option (§761(6)), or a leverage contract (§761(15)).

Paragraph (b) [probably should be "(6)" which was enacted as (5)] defines "commodity option" by reference to section 4c(b) of the Commodity Exchange Act [7 U.S.C. 6c(b)].

Paragraphs (7), (8), and (9) [enacted as (6), (7), and (8)] define "commodity options dealer," "contract market," "contract of sale," "commodity," "future delivery," "board of trade," and "futures commission merchant."

Paragraph (10) [enacted as (9)] defines the term "customer" to mean with respect to a futures commission merchant or a foreign futures commission merchant, the entity for whom the debtor carries a commodity futures contract or foreign future, or with whom such a contract is carried (such as another commodity broker), or from whom the debtor has received, acquired, or holds cash, securities, or other property arising out of or connected with specified transactions involving commodity futures contracts or foreign futures. This section also defines "customer" in the context of leverage transaction merchants, clearing organizations, and commodity options dealers. Persons associated with a commodity broker, such as its employees, officers, or partners, may be customers under this definition.

The definition of "customer" serves to isolate that class of persons entitled to the protection subchapter IV provides to customers. In addition, section 101(5) defines "commodity broker" to mean a futures commission merchant, foreign futures commission merchant, clearing organization, leverage transaction merchant, or commodity options dealer, with respect to which there is a customer. Accordingly, the definition of customer also serves to designate those entities which must utilize chapter 7 and are precluded from reorganizing under chapter 11.

Paragraph (11) [enacted as (10)] defines "customer property" to mean virtually all property or proceeds thereof, received, acquired, or held by or for the account of the debtor for a customer arising out of or in connection with a transaction involving a commodity contract.

Paragraph (12) defines "distribution share" to mean the amount to which a customer is entitled under section 765(a).

Paragraphs (13), (14), (15), and (16) [enacted as (11), (12), (13), and (14)] define "foreign future," "foreign futures commission merchant," "leverage transaction," and "leverage transaction merchant."

Paragraph (17) [enacted as (15)] defines "margin payment" to mean a payment or deposit commonly known to the commodities trade as original margin, initial margin, or variation margin.

Paragraph (18) [enacted as (16)] defines "member property."

Paragraph (19) [enacted as (17)] defines "net equity" to be the sum of (A) the value of all customer property remaining in a customer's account immediately after all commodity contracts of such customer have been transferred, liquidated, or become identified for delivery and all obligations of such customer to the debtor have been offset (such as margin payments, whether or not called, and brokerage commissions) plus (B) the value of specifically identifiable customer property previously returned to the customer by the trustee, plus (C) if the trustee has transferred any commodity contract to which the customer is entitled or any margin or security for such contract, the value of such contract and margin or security. Net equity, therefore, will be the total amount of customer property to which a customer is entitled as of the date of the filing of the bankruptcy petition, although valued at subsequent dates. The Commission is given authority to promulgate rules and regulations to further refine this definition.

house report no. 95–595

Paragraph (8) [enacted as (4)] is a dynamic definition of "contractual commitment". The definition will vary depending on the character of the debtor in each case. If the debtor is a futures commission merchant or a clearing organization, then subparagraphs (A) and (D) indicate that the definition means a contract of sale of a commodity for future delivery on a contract market. If the debtor is a foreign futures commission merchant, a leverage transaction merchant, or a commodity options dealer, then subparagraphs (B), (C), and (E) indicate that the definition means foreign future, leverage transaction, or commodity option, respectively.

Paragraph (9) defines "customer" in a similar style. It is anticipated that a debtor with multifaceted characteristics will have separate estates for each different kind of customer. Thus, a debtor that is a leverage transaction merchant and a commodity options dealer would have separate estates for the leverage transaction customers and for the options customers, and a general estate for other creditors. Customers for each kind of commodity broker, except the clearing organization, arise from either of two relationships. In subparagraphs (A), (B), (C), and (E), clause (i) treats with customers to the extent of contractual commitments with the debtor in either a broker or a dealer relationship. Clause (ii) treats with customers to the extent of proceeds from contractual commitments or deposits for the purpose of making contractual commitments. The customer of the clearing organization is a member with a proprietary or customers' account.

Paragraph (10) defines "customer property" to include all property in customer accounts and property that should have been in those accounts but was diverted through conversion or mistake. Clause (i) refers to customer property not properly segregated by the debtor or customer property converted and then recovered so as to become property of the estate. Clause (vii) is intended to exclude property that would cost more to recover from a third party than the value of the property itself. Subparagraph (B) excludes property in a customer's account that belongs to the commodity broker, such as a contract placed in the account by error, or cash due the broker for a margin payment that the broker has made.

Paragraph (15) [enacted as (17)] defines "net equity" to include the value of all contractual commitments at the time of liquidation or transfer less any obligations owed by the customer to the debtor, such as brokerage fees. In addition, the term includes the value of any specifically identifiable property as of the date of return to the customer and the value of any customer property transferred to another commodity broker as of the date of transfer. This definition places the risk of market fluctuations on the customer until commitments leave the estate.

References in Text

The Commodity Exchange Act, referred to in pars. (1), (2), (8), and (17), is act Sept. 21, 1922, ch. 369, 42 Stat. 998, as amended, which is classified generally to chapter 1 (§1 et seq.) of Title 7, Agriculture. Sections 4c(b) and 19 of the Act are classified to sections 6c(b) and 23, respectively, of Title 7. For complete classification of this Act to the Code, see section 1 of Title 7 and Tables.

Amendments

2010—Par. (4)(F). Pub. L. 111–203, §724(b)(1), added subpar. (F) and struck out former subpar. (F) which read as follows: "any other agreement or transaction that is similar to an agreement or transaction referred to in this paragraph;".

Par. (9)(A)(i). Pub. L. 111–203, §724(b)(2), substituted "a commodity contract account" for "the commodity futures account".

2005—Par. (4)(F) to (J). Pub. L. 109–8 added subpars. (F) to (J).

2000—Par. (2). Pub. L. 106–554, §1(a)(5) [title I, §112(c)(6)(A)], amended par. (2) generally. Prior to amendment, par. (2) read as follows: " 'clearing organization' means organization that clears commodity contracts made on, or subject to the rules of, a contract market or board of trade;".

Par. (7). Pub. L. 106–554, §1(a)(5) [title I, §112(c)(6)(B)], amended par. (7) generally. Prior to amendment, par. (7) read as follows: " 'contract market' means board of trade designated as a contract market by the Commission under the Act;".

Par. (8). Pub. L. 106–554, §1(a)(5) [title I, §112(c)(6)(C)], amended par. (8) generally. Prior to amendment, par. (8) read as follows: " 'contract of sale', 'commodity', 'future delivery', 'board of trade', and 'futures commission merchant' have the meanings assigned to those terms in the Act;".

1994—Par. (1). Pub. L. 103–394, §501(d)(29)(A), struck out "(7 U.S.C. 1 et seq.)" after "Act".

Par. (5). Pub. L. 103–394, §501(d)(29)(B), struck out "(7 U.S.C. 6c(b))" after "Act".

Par. (13). Pub. L. 103–394, §501(d)(29)(C), struck out "(7 U.S.C. 23)" after "Act".

1984—Par. (10)(A)(viii). Pub. L. 98–353 substituted "from and that is the lawful property" for "and that is property".

1982—Par. (2). Pub. L. 97–222, §16(1), inserted "made" after "commodity contracts".

Par. (4). Pub. L. 97–222, §16(2), substituted "with respect to" for "if the debtor is" wherever appearing, and substituted "cleared by such clearing organization, or commodity option traded on, or subject to the rules of, a contract market or board of trade that is cleared by such clearing organization" for "cleared by the debtor" in subpar. (D).

Par. (9). Pub. L. 97–222, §16(3), substituted "with respect to" for "if the debtor is" wherever appearing, in subpar. (A) substituted "such futures commission merchant" for "the debtor" wherever appearing and "such futures commission merchant's" for "the debtor's", in subpar. (B) substituted "such foreign futures commission merchant" for "the debtor" wherever appearing and "such foreign futures commission merchant's" for "the debtor's", in subpar. (C) substituted "such leverage transaction merchant" for "the debtor" wherever appearing and "such leverage transaction merchant's" for "the debtor's", inserted "or" after the semicolon in cl. (i), and substituted "holds" for "hold" in cl. (ii), in subpar. (D) substituted "such clearing organization" for "the debtor" wherever appearing, and in subpar. (E) substituted "such commodity options dealer" for "the debtor" wherever appearing and "such commodity options dealer's" for "the debtor's".

Par. (10). Pub. L. 97–222, §16(4), struck out "at any time" after "security, or property," in provisions preceding subpar. (A).

Par. (12). Pub. L. 97–222, §16(5), inserted a comma after "property" and struck out the comma after "credit".

Par. (13). Pub. L. 97–222, §16(6), substituted "section 19 of the Commodity Exchange Act (7 U.S.C. 23)" for "section 217 of the Commodity Futures Trading Commission Act of 1974 (7 U.S.C. 15a)".

Par. (14). Pub. L. 97–222, §16(7), struck out "that is engaged" after "means person".

Par. (15). Pub. L. 97–222, §16(8), substituted "mark-to-market payments, settlement payments, variation payments, daily settlement payments, and final settlement payments made as adjustments to settlement prices" for "a daily variation settlement payment".

Par. (16). Pub. L. 97–222, §16(9), struck out "at any time" after "customer property".

Par. (17). Pub. L. 97–222, §16(10), in provisions preceding subpar. (A) substituted "has" for "holds", in subpar. (A) inserted "the" after "(A)" in provisions preceding cl. (i), and "in such capacity" after "customer" in cl. (ii).

Effective Date of 2010 Amendment

Amendment by Pub. L. 111–203 effective on the later of 360 days after July 21, 2010, or, to the extent a provision of subtitle A (§§711–754) of title VII of Pub. L. 111–203 requires a rulemaking, not less than 60 days after publication of the final rule or regulation implementing such provision of subtitle A, see section 754 of Pub. L. 111–203, set out as a note under section 1a of Title 7, Agriculture.

Effective Date of 2005 Amendment

Amendment by Pub. L. 109–8 effective 180 days after Apr. 20, 2005, and not applicable with respect to cases commenced under this title before such effective date, except as otherwise provided, see section 1501 of Pub. L. 109–8, set out as a note under section 101 of this title.

Effective Date of 1994 Amendment

Amendment by Pub. L. 103–394 effective Oct. 22, 1994, and not applicable with respect to cases commenced under this title before Oct. 22, 1994, see section 702 of Pub. L. 103–394, set out as a note under section 101 of this title.

Effective Date of 1984 Amendment

Amendment by Pub. L. 98–353 effective with respect to cases filed 90 days after July 10, 1984, see section 552(a) of Pub. L. 98–353, set out as a note under section 101 of this title.

§762. Notice to the Commission and right to be heard

(a) The clerk shall give the notice required by section 342 of this title to the Commission.

(b) The Commission may raise and may appear and be heard on any issue in a case under this chapter.

(Pub. L. 95–598, Nov. 6, 1978, 92 Stat. 2618.)

Historical and Revision Notes

senate report no. 95–989

Section 762 provides that the Commission shall be given such notice as is appropriate of an order for relief in a bankruptcy case and that the Commission may raise and may appear and may be heard on any issue in case involving a commodity broker liquidation.

§763. Treatment of accounts

(a) Accounts held by the debtor for a particular customer in separate capacities shall be treated as accounts of separate customers.

(b) A member of a clearing organization shall be deemed to hold such member's proprietary account in a separate capacity from such member's customers' account.

(c) The net equity in a customer's account may not be offset against the net equity in the account of any other customer.

(Pub. L. 95–598, Nov. 6, 1978, 92 Stat. 2618; Pub. L. 98–353, title III, §486, July 10, 1984, 98 Stat. 383.)

Historical and Revision Notes

senate report no. 95–989

Section 763 provides for separate treatment of accounts held in separate capacities. A deficit in one account held for a customer may not be offset against the net equity in another account held by the same customer in a separate capacity or held by another customer.

Amendments

1984—Subsec. (a). Pub. L. 98–353 substituted "by the debtor for" for "by" and "treated as" for "deemed to be".

Effective Date of 1984 Amendment

Amendment by Pub. L. 98–353 effective with respect to cases filed 90 days after July 10, 1984, see section 552(a) of Pub. L. 98–353, set out as a note under section 101 of this title.

§764. Voidable transfers

(a) Except as otherwise provided in this section, any transfer by the debtor of property that, but for such transfer, would have been customer property, may be avoided by the trustee, and such property shall be treated as customer property, if and to the extent that the trustee avoids such transfer under section 544, 545, 547, 548, 549, or 724(a) of this title. For the purpose of such sections, the property so transferred shall be deemed to have been property of the debtor, and, if such transfer was made to a customer or for a customer's benefit, such customer shall be deemed, for the purposes of this section, to have been a creditor.

(b) Notwithstanding sections 544, 545, 547, 548, 549, and 724(a) of this title, the trustee may not avoid a transfer made before seven days after the order for relief, if such transfer is approved by the Commission by rule or order, either before or after such transfer, and if such transfer is—

(1) a transfer of a commodity contract entered into or carried by or through the debtor on behalf of a customer, and of any cash, securities, or other property margining or securing such commodity contract; or

(2) the liquidation of a commodity contract entered into or carried by or through the debtor on behalf of a customer.

(Pub. L. 95–598, Nov. 6, 1978, 92 Stat. 2618; Pub. L. 97–222, §17, July 27, 1982, 96 Stat. 240; Pub. L. 98–353, title III, §487, July 10, 1984, 98 Stat. 383; Pub. L. 111–16, §2(9), May 7, 2009, 123 Stat. 1607.)

Historical and Revision Notes

legislative statements

Section 764 of the House amendment is derived from the House bill.

senate report no. 95–989

Section 764 permits the trustee to void any transfer of property that, except for such transfer, would have been customer property, to the extent permitted under section 544, 545, 547, 548, 549, or 724(a).

house report no. 95–595

Section 764 indicates the extent to which the avoiding powers may be used by the trustee under subchapter IV of chapter 7. If property recovered would have been customer property if never transferred, then subsection (a) indicates that it will be so treated when recovered.

Subsection (b) prohibits avoiding any transaction that occurs before or within five days after the petition if the transaction is approved by the Commission and concerns an open contractual commitment. This enables the Commission to exercise its discretion to protect the integrity of the market by insuring that transactions cleared with other brokers will not be undone on a preference or a fraudulent transfer theory.

Subsection (c) insulates variation margin payments and other deposits from the avoiding powers except to the extent of actual fraud under section 548(a)(1). This facilitates prepetition transfers and protects the ordinary course of business in the market.

Amendments

2009—Subsec. (b). Pub. L. 111–16 substituted "seven days" for "five days" in introductory provisions.

1984—Subsec. (a). Pub. L. 98–353 substituted "any transfer by the debtor" for "any transfer".

1982—Subsec. (a). Pub. L. 97–222, §17(a), substituted "but" for "except", inserted "such property" after "trustee, and", and substituted "shall be" for "is" wherever appearing.

Subsec. (b). Pub. L. 97–222, §17(b), substituted "order for relief" for "date of the filing of the petition".

Subsec. (c). Pub. L. 97–222, §17(c), struck out subsec. (c) which provided that the trustee could not avoid a transfer that was a margin payment to or deposit with a commodity broker or forward contract merchant or was a settlement payment made by a clearing organization and that occurred before the commencement of the case.

Effective Date of 2009 Amendment

Amendment by Pub. L. 111–16 effective Dec. 1, 2009, see section 7 of Pub. L. 111–16, set out as a note under section 109 of this title.

Effective Date of 1984 Amendment

Amendment by Pub. L. 98–353 effective with respect to cases filed 90 days after July 10, 1984, see section 552(a) of Pub. L. 98–353, set out as a note under section 101 of this title.

§765. Customer instructions

(a) The notice required by section 342 of this title to customers shall instruct each customer—

(1) to file a proof of such customer's claim promptly, and to specify in such claim any specifically identifiable security, property, or commodity contract; and

(2) to instruct the trustee of such customer's desired disposition, including transfer under section 766 of this title or liquidation, of any commodity contract specifically identified to such customer.

(b) The trustee shall comply, to the extent practicable, with any instruction received from a customer regarding such customer's desired disposition of any commodity contract specifically identified to such customer. If the trustee has transferred, under section 766 of this title, such a commodity contract, the trustee shall transmit any such instruction to the commodity broker to whom such commodity contract was so transferred.

(Pub. L. 95–598, Nov. 6, 1978, 92 Stat. 2619; Pub. L. 97–222, §18, July 27, 1982, 96 Stat. 240; Pub. L. 98–353, title III, §488, July 10, 1984, 98 Stat. 383.)

Historical and Revision Notes

For Historical and Revision Notes for this section, see Historical and Revision Notes set out under section 766 of this title.

Amendments

1984—Subsec. (a). Pub. L. 98–353 substituted "notice required by" for "notice under".

1982—Subsec. (b). Pub. L. 97–222 substituted "commodity contract" for "commitment".

Effective Date of 1984 Amendment

Amendment by Pub. L. 98–353 effective with respect to cases filed 90 days after July 10, 1984, see section 552(a) of Pub. L. 98–353, set out as a note under section 101 of this title.

§766. Treatment of customer property

(a) The trustee shall answer all margin calls with respect to a specifically identifiable commodity contract of a customer until such time as the trustee returns or transfers such commodity contract, but the trustee may not make a margin payment that has the effect of a distribution to such customer of more than that to which such customer is entitled under subsection (h) or (i) of this section.

(b) The trustee shall prevent any open commodity contract from remaining open after the last day of trading in such commodity contract, or into the first day on which notice of intent to deliver on such commodity contract may be tendered, whichever occurs first. With respect to any commodity contract that has remained open after the last day of trading in such commodity contract or with respect to which delivery must be made or accepted under the rules of the contract market on which such commodity contract was made, the trustee may operate the business of the debtor for the purpose of—

(1) accepting or making tender of notice of intent to deliver the physical commodity underlying such commodity contract;

(2) facilitating delivery of such commodity; or

(3) disposing of such commodity if a party to such commodity contract defaults.

(c) The trustee shall return promptly to a customer any specifically identifiable security, property, or commodity contract to which such customer is entitled, or shall transfer, on such customer's behalf, such security, property, or commodity contract to a commodity broker that is not a debtor under this title, subject to such rules or regulations as the Commission may prescribe, to the extent that the value of such security, property, or commodity contract does not exceed the amount to which such customer would be entitled under subsection (h) or (i) of this section if such security, property, or commodity contract were not returned or transferred under this subsection.

(d) If the value of a specifically identifiable security, property, or commodity contract exceeds the amount to which the customer of the debtor is entitled under subsection (h) or (i) of this section, then such customer to whom such security, property, or commodity contract is specifically identified may deposit cash with the trustee equal to the difference between the value of such security, property, or commodity contract and such amount, and the trustee then shall—

(1) return promptly such security, property, or commodity contract to such customer; or

(2) transfer, on such customer's behalf, such security, property, or commodity contract to a commodity broker that is not a debtor under this title, subject to such rules or regulations as the Commission may prescribe.

(e) Subject to subsection (b) of this section, the trustee shall liquidate any commodity contract that—

(1) is identified to a particular customer and with respect to which such customer has not timely instructed the trustee as to the desired disposition of such commodity contract;

(2) cannot be transferred under subsection (c) of this section; or

(3) cannot be identified to a particular customer.

(f) As soon as practicable after the commencement of the case, the trustee shall reduce to money, consistent with good market practice, all securities and other property, other than commodity contracts, held as property of the estate, except for specifically identifiable securities or property distributable under subsection (h) or (i) of this section.

(g) The trustee may not distribute a security or other property except under subsection (h) or (i) of this section.

(h) Except as provided in subsection (b) of this section, the trustee shall distribute customer property ratably to customers on the basis and to the extent of such customers' allowed net equity claims, and in priority to all other claims, except claims of a kind specified in section 507(a)(2) of this title that are attributable to the administration of customer property. Such distribution shall be in the form of—

(1) cash;

(2) the return or transfer, under subsection (c) or (d) of this section, of specifically identifiable customer securities, property, or commodity contracts; or

(3) payment of margin calls under subsection (a) of this section.

Notwithstanding any other provision of this subsection, a customer net equity claim based on a proprietary account, as defined by Commission rule, regulation, or order, may not be paid either in whole or in part, directly or indirectly, out of customer property unless all other customer net equity claims have been paid in full.

(i) If the debtor is a clearing organization, the trustee shall distribute—

(1) customer property, other than member property, ratably to customers on the basis and to the extent of such customers' allowed net equity claims based on such customers' accounts other than proprietary accounts, and in priority to all other claims, except claims of a kind specified in section 507(a)(2) of this title that are attributable to the administration of such customer property; and

(2) member property ratably to customers on the basis and to the extent of such customers' allowed net equity claims based on such customers' proprietary accounts, and in priority to all other claims, except claims of a kind specified in section 507(a)(2) of this title that are attributable to the administration of member property or customer property.

(j)(1) The trustee shall distribute customer property in excess of that distributed under subsection (h) or (i) of this section in accordance with section 726 of this title.

(2) Except as provided in section 510 of this title, if a customer is not paid the full amount of such customer's allowed net equity claim from customer property, the unpaid portion of such claim is a claim entitled to distribution under section 726 of this title.

(Pub. L. 95–598, Nov. 6, 1978, 92 Stat. 2619; Pub. L. 97–222, §19, July 27, 1982, 96 Stat. 240; Pub. L. 98–353, title III, §489, July 10, 1984, 98 Stat. 383; Pub. L. 109–8, title XV, §1502(a)(4), Apr. 20, 2005, 119 Stat. 216.)

Historical and Revision Notes

legislative statements

Sections 765 and 766 of the House amendment represent a consolidation and redraft of sections 765, 766, 767, and 768 of the House bill and sections 765, 766, 767, and 768 of the Senate amendment. In particular, section 765(a) of the House amendment is derived from section 765(a) of the House bill and section 767(a) of the Senate amendment. Under section 765(a) of the House amendment customers are notified of the opportunity to immediately file proofs of claim and to identify specifically identifiable securities, property, or commodity contracts. The customer is also afforded an opportunity to instruct the trustee regarding the customer's desires concerning disposition of the customer's commodity contracts. Section 767(b) [probably should be 765(b)] makes clear that the trustee must comply with instructions received to the extent practicable, but in the event the trustee has transferred commodity contracts to a commodity broker, such instructions shall be forwarded to the broker.

Section 766(a) of the House amendment is derived from section 768(c) of the House bill and section 767(f) of the Senate amendment. Section 766(b) of the House amendment is derived from section 765(d) of the House bill, and section 767(g) of the Senate amendment. Section 766(c) of the House amendment is derived from section 768(a) of the House bill and section 767(e) of the Senate amendment. Section 766(d) of the House amendment is derived from section 768(b) of the House bill and the second sentence of section 767(e) of the Senate amendment.

Section 766(e) of the House amendment is derived from section 765(c) of the House bill and sections 767(c) and (d) of the Senate amendment. The provision clarifies that the trustee may liquidate a commodity contract only if the commodity contract cannot be transferred to a commodity broker under section 766(c), cannot be identified to a particular customer, or has been identified with respect to a particular customer, but with respect to which the customer's instructions have not been received.

Section 766(f) of the House amendment is derived from section 766(b) of the House bill and section 767(h) of the Senate amendment. The term "all securities and other property" is not intended to include a commodity contract. Section 766(g) of the House amendment is derived from section 766(a) of the House bill. Section 766(h) of the House amendment is derived from section 767(a) of the House bill and section 765(a) of the Senate amendment. In order to induce private trustees to undertake the difficult and risky job of liquidating a commodity broker, the House amendment contains a provision insuring that a pro rata share of administrative claims will be paid. The provision represents a compromise between the position taken in the House bill, subordinating customer property to all expenses of administration, and the position taken in the Senate amendment requiring the distribution of customer property in advance of any expenses of administration. The position in the Senate amendment is rejected since customers, in any event, would have to pay a brokerage commission or fee in the ordinary course of business. The compromise provision requires customers to pay only those administrative expenses that are attributable to the administration of customer property.

Section 766(i) of the House amendment is derived from section 767(b) of the House bill and contains a similar compromise with respect to expenses of administration as the compromise detailed in connection with section 766(h) of the House amendment. Section 766(j) of the House amendment is derived from section 767(c) of the House bill. No counterpart is contained in the Senate amendment. The provision takes account of the rare case where the estate has customer property in excess of customer claims and administrative expenses attributable to those claims. The section also specifies that to the extent a customer is not paid in full out of customer property, that the unpaid claim will be treated the same as any other general unsecured creditor.

Section 768 of the Senate amendment was deleted from the House amendment as unwise. The provision in the Senate amendment would have permitted the trustee to distribute customer property based upon an estimate of value of the customer's account, with no provision for recapture of excessive disbursements. Moreover, the section would have exonerated the trustee from any liability for such an excessive disbursement. Furthermore, the section is unclear with respect to the customer's rights in the event the trustee makes a distribution less than the share to which the customer is entitled. The provision is deleted in the House amendment so that this difficult problem may be handled on a case-by-case basis by the courts as the facts and circumstances of each case require.

Section 769 of the Senate amendment is deleted in the House amendment as unnecessary. The provision was intended to codify *Board of Trade v. Johnson*, 264 U.S. 1 (1924) [Ill.1924, 44 S.Ct. 232]. *Board of Trade against Johnson* is codified in section 363(f) of the House amendment which indicates the only five circumstances in which property may be sold free and clear of an interest in such property of an entity other than the estate.

Section 770 of the Senate amendment is deleted in the House amendment as unnecessary. That section would have permitted commodity brokers to liquidate commodity contracts, notwithstanding any contrary order of the court. It would require an extraordinary circumstance, such as a threat to the national security, to enjoin a commodity broker from liquidating a commodity contract. However, in those circumstances, an injunction must prevail. Failure of the House amendment to incorporate section 770 of the Senate amendment does not imply that the automatic stay prevents liquidation of commodity contracts by commodity brokers. To the contrary, whenever by contract, or otherwise, a commodity broker is entitled to liquidate a position as a result of a condition specified in a contract, other than a condition or default of the kind specified in section 365(b)(2) of title 11, the commodity broker may engage in such liquidation. To this extent, the commodity broker's contract with his customer is treated no differently than any other contract under section 365 of title 11.

senate report no. 95–989

[Section 765] Subsection (a) of this section [enacted as section 766(h)] provides that with respect to liquidation of commodity brokers which are not clearing organizations, the trustee shall distribute customer property to customers on the basis and to the extent of such customers' allowed net equity claims, and in priority to all other claims. This section grants customers' claims first priority in the distribution of the estate. Subsection (b) [enacted as section 766(i)] grants the same priority to member property and other customer property in the liquidation of a clearing organization. A fundamental purpose of these provisions is to ensure that the property entrusted by customers to their brokers will not be subject to the risks of the broker's business and will be available for disbursement to customers if the broker becomes bankrupt.

As a result of section 765, a customer need not trace any funds in order to avoid treatment as a general creditor as was required by the Seventh Circuit in *In re Rosenbaum Grain Corporation*.

Section 766 lists certain transfers which are not voidable by the trustee of a commodity broker. Subsection (a) exempts transfers approved by the Commission by rule or order, either before or after the transfer. It is expected that the Commission will use this power sparingly and only when necessary to effectuate the remedial purposes of this legislation, bearing in mind that the immediate transfer of customer accounts from bankrupt commodity brokers to solvent commodity brokers is one of the primary goals of this subchapter. The committee considered and rejected a provision in subsection (b) that would have exempted payments made to a commodity broker. The Commission may not by rule exempt such transfers. The Commission's prompt attention to the promulgation of such rules and regulations is expected.

Subsection (b) [enacted as section 764(c)] provides for the nonavoidability of margin payments made by a commodity broker, other than a clearing organization. If such payments are made by or to a clearing organization, they are nonavoidable pursuant to subsection (c). All other margin payments made by a commodity broker, other than a clearing organization, are nonavoidable if they meet the conditions set forth in subsection (b). Subsections (b)(1) and (b)(2) parallel the requirements for avoidance of fraudulent transfers and obligations under section 548. Subsection (b)(3) adds a requirement that there be collusion between the transferee and transferor in order for such payments to be voidable. It would be unfair to permit recovery from an innocent commodity broker since such brokers are, for the most part, simply conduits for margin payments and do not retain margin for use in their operations. Subsection (b)(4) would permit recovery of a subsequent transferee only if it had actual knowledge at the time of that subsequent transfer of the scheme to defraud. Again it should be noted that if the transfer is a margin payment and the subsequent transferee is a clearing organization, the transfer is nonavoidable under section 766(c).

Subsection (c) [enacted as section 548(d)(2)] overrules *Seligson v. New York Produce Exchange*, and provides as a matter of law that margin payments made by or to a clearing organization are not voidable.

Section 767 sets forth the procedures to be followed by the trustee. It should be emphasized that many of the duties imposed on the trustee are required to be discharged by the trustee immediately upon his appointment. The earlier these duties are discharged the less potential market disruption can result.

The initial duty of the trustee is to endeavor to transfer to another commodity broker or brokers all identified customer accounts together with the customer property margining such accounts, to the extent the trustee deems appropriate. Although it is preferable for all such accounts to be transferred, exigencies may dictate a partial transfer. The requirement that the value of the accounts and property transferred not exceed the customer's distribution share may necessitate a slight delay until the trustee can submit to the court, for its disapproval, an estimate of each customer's distribution share pursuant to section 768.

Subsection (c) [enacted as section 766(e)] provides that contemporaneously with the estimate of the distribution share and the transfer of identified customer accounts and property, subsection (c) provides that the trustee should make arrangements for the liquidation of all commodity contracts maintained by the debtor that are not identifiable to specific customers. These contracts would, of course, include all such contracts held in the debtor's proprietory [sic] account.

At approximately the same time, the trustee should notify each customer of the debtor's bankruptcy and instruct each customer immediately to submit a claim including any claim to a specifically identifiable security or other property, and advise the trustee as to the desired disposition of commodity contracts carried by the debtor for the customer.

This requirement is placed upon the trustee to insure that producers who have hedged their production in the commodities market are allowed the opportunity to preserve their positions. The theory of the commodity market is that it exists for producers and buyers of commodities and not for the benefit of the speculators whose transactions now comprise the overwhelming majority of trades. Maintenance of positions by hedges may require them to put up additional margin payments in the hours and days following the commodity broker bankruptcy, which they may be unable or unwilling to do. In such cases, their positions will be quickly liquidated by the trustee, but they must have the opportunity to make those margin payments before they are summarily liquidated out of the market to the detriment of their growing crop. The failure of the customer to advise the trustee as to disposition of the customer's commodity contract will not delay a transfer of a contract pursuant to subsection (b) so long as the contract can otherwise be identified to the customer. Nor will the failure of the customer to submit a claim prevent the customer from recovering the net equity in that customer's account, absent a claim the customer cannot participate in the determination of the net equity in the account.

If the customer submits instructions pursuant to subsection (a) after the customer's commodity contracts are transferred to another commodity broker, the trustee must transmit the instruction to the transferee. If the customer's commodity contracts are not transferred before the customer's instructions are received, the trustee must attempt to comply with the instruction, subject to the provisions of section 767(d).

Under subsection (d) [enacted as section 766(e)], the trustee has discretion to liquidate any commodity contract carried by the debtor at any time. This discretion must be exercised with restraint in such cases, consistent with the purposes of this subchapter and good business practices. The committee intends that hedged accounts will be given special consideration before liquidation as discussed in connection with subsection (c).

Subsection (e) [enacted as section 766(c)] instructs the trustee as to the disposition of any security or other property, not disposed of pursuant to subsection (b) or (d), that is specifically identifiable to a customer and to which the customer is entitled. Such security or other property must be returned to the customer or promptly transferred to another commodity broker for the benefit of the customer. If the value of the security or other property retained or transferred, together with any other distribution made by the trustee to or on behalf of the customer, exceeds the customer's distribution share the customer must deposit cash with the trustee equal to that difference before the return or transfer of the security or other property.

Subsection (f) [enacted as section 766(a)] requires the trustee to answer margin calls on specifically identifiable customer commodity contracts, but only to the extent that the margin payment, together with any other distribution made by the trustee to or on behalf of the customer, does not exceed the customer's distribution share.

Subsection (g) [enacted as section 766(b)] requires the trustee to liquidate all commodity futures contracts prior to the close of trading in that contract, or the first day on which notice of intent to deliver on that contract may be tendered, whichever occurs first. If the customer desires that the contract be kept open for delivery, the contract should be transferred to another commodity broker pursuant to subsection (b).

If for some reason the trustee is unable to transfer a contract on which delivery must be made or accepted and is unable to close out such contract, the trustee is authorized to operate the business of the debtor for the purpose of accepting or making tender of notice of intent to deliver the physical commodity underlying the contract, facilitating delivery of the physical commodity or disposing of the physical commodity in the event of a default. Any property received, not previously held, by the trustee in connection with its operation of the business of the debtor for these purposes, is not by the terms of this subchapter specifically included in the definition of customer property.

Finally, subsection (h) [enacted as section 766(f)] requires the trustee to liquidate the debtor's estate as soon as practicable and consistent with good market practice, except for specifically identifiable securities or other property distributable under subsection (e).

Section 768 is an integral part of the commodity broker liquidation procedures outlined in section 767. Prompt action by the trustee to transfer or liquidate customer commodity contracts is necessary to protect customers, the debtor's estate, and the marketplace generally. However, transfers of customer accounts and property valued in excess of the customer's distribution share are prohibited. Since a determination of the customer's distribution share requires a determination of the customer's net equity and the total dollar value of customer property held by or for the account of the debtor, it is possible that the customer's distribution share will not be determined, and thus the customer's contracts and property will not be transferred, on a timely basis. To avoid this problem, and to expedite transfers of customer property, section 768 permits the trustee to make distributions to customers in accordance with a preliminary estimate of the debtor's customer property and each customer's distribution share.

It is acknowledged that the necessity for prompt action may not allow the trustee to assemble all relevant facts before such an estimate is made. However, the trustee is expected to develop as accurate an estimate as possible based on the available facts. Further, in order to permit expeditious action, section 768 does not require that notice be given to customers or other creditors before the court approves or disapproves the estimate. Nor does section 768 require that customer claims be received pursuant to section 767(a) before the trustee may act upon and in accordance with the estimate. If the estimate is inaccurate, the trustee is absolved of liability for a distribution which exceeds the customer's actual distribution share so long as the distribution did not exceed the customer's estimated distribution share. However, a trustee may have a claim back against a customer who received more than its actual distribution share.

house report no. 95–595

Section 765(a) indicates that a customer must file a proof of claim, including any claim to specifically identifiable property, within such time as the court fixes.

Subsection (c) [of section 765 (enacted as section 766(e))] sets forth the general rule requiring the trustee to liquidate contractual commitments that are either not specifically identifiable or with respect to which a customer has not instructed the trustee during the time fixed by the court. Subsection (d) [enacted as section 766(b)] indicates an exception to the time limits in the rule by requiring the trustee to liquidate any open contractual commitment before the last day of trading or the first day during which delivery may be demanded, whichever first occurs, if transfer cannot be effectuated.

Section 766(a) [enacted as section 766(g)] indicates that the trustee may distribute securities or other property only under section 768. This does not preclude a distribution of cash under section 767(a) or distribution of any excess customer property under section 767(c) to the general estate.

Subsection (b) [enacted as section 766(f)] indicates that the trustee shall liquidate all securities and other property that is not specifically identifiable property as soon as practicable after the commencement of the case and in accordance with good market practice. If securities are restricted or trading has been suspended, the trustee will have to make an exempt sale or file a registration statement. In the event of a private placement, a customer is not entitled to "bid in" his net equity claim. To do so would enable him to receive a greater percentage recovery than other customers.

Section 767(a) [enacted as section 766(h)] provides for the trustee to distribute customer property pro rata according to customers' net equity claims. The court will determine an equitable portion of customer property to pay administrative expenses. Paragraphs (2) and (3) indicate that the return of specifically identifiable property constitutes a distribution of net equity.

Subsection (b) [enacted as section 766(i)] indicates that if the debtor is a clearing organization, customer property is to be segregated into customers' accounts and proprietary accounts and distributed accordingly without offset. This protects a member's customers from having their claims offset against the member's proprietary account. Subsection (c)(1) [enacted as section 766(j)(1)] indicates that any excess customer property will pour over into the general estate. This unlikely event would occur only if customers fail to file proofs of claim. Subsection (c)(2) [enacted as section 766(j)(2)] indicates that to the extent customers are not paid in full, they are entitled to share in the general estate as unsecured creditors, unless subordinated by the court under proposed 11 U.S.C. 510.

Section 768(a) [enacted as section 766(c)] requires the trustee to return specifically identifiable property to the extent that such distribution will not exceed a customer's net equity claim. Thus, if the customer owes money to a commodity broker, this will be offset under section 761(15)(A)(ii). If the value of the specifically identifiable property exceeds the net equity claim, then the customer may deposit cash with the trustee to make up the difference after which the trustee may return or transfer the customer's property.

Subsection (c) [enacted as section 766(a)] permits the trustee to answer all margin calls, to the extent of the customer's net equity claim, with respect to any specifically identifiable open contractual commitment. It should be noted that any payment under subsections (a) or (c) will be considered a reduction of the net equity claim under section 767(a). Thus the customer's net equity claim is a dynamic amount that varies with distributions of specifically identifiable property or margin payments on such property. This approach differs from the priority given to specifically identifiable property under subchapter III of chapter 7 by limiting the priority effect to a right to receive specific property as part of, rather than in addition to, a ratable share of customer property. This policy is designed to protect the small customer who is unlikely to have property in specifically identifiable form as compared with the professional trader. The CFTC is authorized to make rules defining specifically identifiable property under section 302 of the bill, in title III.

Amendments

2005—Subsec. (h). Pub. L. 109–8, §1502(a)(4)(A), substituted "507(a)(2)" for "507(a)(1)" in introductory provisions.

Subsec. (i). Pub. L. 109–8, §1502(a)(4)(B), substituted "507(a)(2)" for "507(a)(1)" in pars. (1) and (2).

1984—Subsec. (j)(2). Pub. L. 98–353 substituted "section 726" for "section 726(a)".

1982—Subsec. (a). Pub. L. 97–222, §19(a), inserted "to such customer" after "distribution".

Subsec. (b). Pub. L. 97–222, §19(b), struck out "that is being actively traded as of the date of the filing of the petition" after "any open commodity contract" and inserted "the" after "rules of".

Subsec. (d). Pub. L. 97–222, §19(c), substituted "the amount to which the customer of the debtor is entitled under subsection (h) or (i) of this section, then such" for "such amount, then the" and "the trustee then shall" for "the trustee shall".

Subsec. (h). Pub. L. 97–222, §19(d), inserted provision that notwithstanding any other provision of this subsection, a customer net equity claim based on a proprietary account, as defined by Commission rule, regulation, or order, may not be paid either in whole or in part, directly or indirectly, out of customer property unless all other customer net equity claims have been paid in full.

Effective Date of 2005 Amendment

Amendment by Pub. L. 109–8 effective 180 days after Apr. 20, 2005, and not applicable with respect to cases commenced under this title before such effective date, except as otherwise provided, see section 1501 of Pub. L. 109–8, set out as a note under section 101 of this title.

Effective Date of 1984 Amendment

Amendment by Pub. L. 98–353 effective with respect to cases filed 90 days after July 10, 1984, see section 552(a) of Pub. L. 98–353, set out as a note under section 101 of this title.

§767. Commodity broker liquidation and forward contract merchants, commodity brokers, stockbrokers, financial institutions, financial participants, securities clearing agencies, swap participants, repo participants, and master netting agreement participants

Notwithstanding any other provision of this title, the exercise of rights by a forward contract merchant, commodity broker, stockbroker, financial institution, financial participant, securities clearing agency, swap participant, repo participant, or master netting agreement participant under this title shall not affect the priority of any unsecured claim it may have after the exercise of such rights.

(Added Pub. L. 109–8, title IX, §907(l), Apr. 20, 2005, 119 Stat. 181.)

Effective Date

Section effective 180 days after Apr. 20, 2005, and not applicable with respect to cases commenced under this title before such effective date, except as otherwise provided, see section 1501 of Pub. L. 109–8, set out as an Effective Date of 2005 Amendment note under section 101 of this title.

SUBCHAPTER V—CLEARING BANK LIQUIDATION

§781. Definitions

For purposes of this subchapter, the following definitions shall apply:

(1) Board.—The term "Board" means the Board of Governors of the Federal Reserve System.

(2) Depository institution.—The term "depository institution" has the same meaning as in section 3 of the Federal Deposit Insurance Act.

(3) Clearing bank.—The term "clearing bank" means an uninsured State member bank, or a corporation organized under section 25A of the Federal Reserve Act, which operates, or operates as, a multilateral clearing organization pursuant to section 409 [1] of the Federal Deposit Insurance Corporation Improvement Act of 1991.

(Added Pub. L. 106–554, §1(a)(5) [title I, §112(c)(5)(B)], Dec. 21, 2000, 114 Stat. 2763, 2763A–394.)

References in Text

Section 3 of the Federal Deposit Insurance Act, referred to in par. (2), is classified to section 1813 of Title 12, Banks and Banking.

Section 25A of the Federal Reserve Act, referred to in par. (3), popularly known as the Edge Act, is classified to subchapter II (§611 et seq.) of chapter 6 of Title 12, Banks and Banking. For complete classification of this Act to the Code, see Short Title note set out under section 611 of Title 12 and Tables.

Section 409 of the Federal Deposit Insurance Corporation Improvement Act of 1991, referred to in par. (3), which was classified to section 4422 of Title 12, Banks and Banking, was repealed by Pub. L. 111–203, title VII, §740, July 21, 2010, 124 Stat. 1729.

[1] See References in Text note below.

§782. Selection of trustee

(a) In General.—

(1) Appointment.—Notwithstanding any other provision of this title, the conservator or receiver who files the petition shall be the trustee under this chapter, unless the Board designates an alternative trustee.

(2) Successor.—The Board may designate a successor trustee if required.

(b) Authority of Trustee.—Whenever the Board appoints or designates a trustee, chapter 3 and sections 704 and 705 of this title shall apply to the Board in the same way and to the same extent that they apply to a United States trustee.

(Added Pub. L. 106–554, §1(a)(5) [title I, §112(c)(5)(B)], Dec. 21, 2000, 114 Stat. 2763, 2763A–394.)

§783. Additional powers of trustee

(a) Distribution of Property Not of the Estate.—The trustee under this subchapter has power to distribute property not of the estate, including distributions to customers that are mandated by subchapters III and IV of this chapter.

(b) Disposition of Institution.—The trustee under this subchapter may, after notice and a hearing—

(1) sell the clearing bank to a depository institution or consortium of depository institutions (which consortium may agree on the allocation of the clearing bank among the consortium);

(2) merge the clearing bank with a depository institution;

(3) transfer contracts to the same extent as could a receiver for a depository institution under paragraphs (9) and (10) of section 11(e) of the Federal Deposit Insurance Act;

(4) transfer assets or liabilities to a depository institution; and

(5) transfer assets and liabilities to a bridge depository institution as provided in paragraphs (1), (3)(A), (5), and (6) of section 11(n) of the Federal Deposit Insurance Act, paragraphs (9) through (13) of such section, and subparagraphs (A) through (H) and subparagraph (K) of paragraph (4) of such section 11(n), except that—

(A) the bridge depository institution to which such assets or liabilities are transferred shall be treated as a clearing bank for the purpose of this subsection; and

(B) any references in any such provision of law to the Federal Deposit Insurance Corporation shall be construed to be references to the appointing agency and that references to deposit insurance shall be omitted.

(c) Certain Transfers Included.—Any reference in this section to transfers of liabilities includes a ratable transfer of liabilities within a priority class.

(Added Pub. L. 106–554, §1(a)(5) [title I, §112(c)(5)(B)], Dec. 21, 2000, 114 Stat. 2763, 2763A–395; amended Pub. L. 110–289, div. A, title VI, §1604(b)(3), July 30, 2008, 122 Stat. 2829.)

References in Text

Section 11 of the Federal Deposit Insurance Act, referred to in subsec. (b)(3), (5), is classified to section 1821 of Title 12, Banks and Banking.

Amendments

2008—Subsec. (b)(5). Pub. L. 110–289, which directed amendment of this section by substituting "bridge depository institution" for "bridge bank", was executed by making the substitution in introductory provisions and subpar. (A) of subsec. (b)(5), to reflect the probable intent of Congress.

§784. Right to be heard

The Board or a Federal reserve bank (in the case of a clearing bank that is a member of that bank) may raise and may appear and be heard on any issue in a case under this subchapter.

(Added Pub. L. 106–554, §1(a)(5) [title I, §112(c)(5)(B)], Dec. 21, 2000, 114 Stat. 2763, 2763A–395.)

CHAPTER 9—ADJUSTMENT OF DEBTS OF A MUNICIPALITY

SUBCHAPTER I—GENERAL PROVISIONS

Sec.
901.
Applicability of other sections of this title.
902.
Definitions for this chapter.
903.
Reservation of State power to control municipalities.
904.
Limitation on jurisdiction and powers of court.

SUBCHAPTER II—ADMINISTRATION

921.
Petition and proceedings relating to petition.
922.
Automatic stay of enforcement of claims against the debtor.
923.
Notice.
924.
List of creditors.
925.
Effect of list of claims.
926.
Avoiding powers.
927.
Limitation on recourse.
928.
Post petition effect of security interest.
929.

Municipal leases.
930.
Dismissal.

SUBCHAPTER III—THE PLAN
941.
Filing of plan.
942.
Modification of plan.
943.
Confirmation.
944.
Effect of confirmation.
945.
Continuing jurisdiction and closing of the case.
946.
Effect of exchange of securities before the date of the filing of the petition.

Amendments
1988—Pub. L. 100–597, §11, Nov. 3, 1988, 102 Stat. 3030, added items 927 to 929 and redesignated former item 927 as 930.

SUBCHAPTER I—GENERAL PROVISIONS

§901. Applicability of other sections of this title
(a) Sections 301, 333, 344, 347(b), 349, 350(b) 351,[1] 361, 362, 364(c), 364(d), 364(e), 364(f), 365, 366, 501, 502, 503, 504, 506, 507(a)(2), 509, 510, 524(a)(1), 524(a)(2), 544, 545, 546, 547, 548, 549(a), 549(c), 549(d), 550, 551, 552, 553, 555, 556, 557, 559, 560, 561, 562, 1102, 1103, 1109, 1111(b), 1122, 1123(a)(1), 1123(a)(2), 1123(a)(3), 1123(a)(4), 1123(a)(5), 1123(b), 1123(d), 1124, 1125, 1126(a), 1126(b), 1126(c), 1126(e), 1126(f), 1126(g), 1127(d), 1128, 1129(a)(2), 1129(a)(3), 1129(a)(6), 1129(a)(8), 1129(a)(10), 1129(b)(1), 1129(b)(2)(A), 1129(b)(2)(B), 1142(b), 1143, 1144, and 1145 of this title apply in a case under this chapter.

(b) A term used in a section of this title made applicable in a case under this chapter by subsection (a) of this section or section 103(e)[2] of this title has the meaning defined for such term for the purpose of such applicable section, unless such term is otherwise defined in section 902 of this title.

(c) A section made applicable in a case under this chapter by subsection (a) of this section that is operative if the business of the debtor is authorized to be operated is operative in a case under this chapter.

(Pub. L. 95–598, Nov. 6, 1978, 92 Stat. 2621; Pub. L. 98–353, title III, §§353, 490, July 10, 1984, 98 Stat. 361, 383; Pub. L. 100–597, §3, Nov. 3, 1988, 102 Stat. 3028; Pub. L. 109–8, title V, §502, title XII, §1216, title XV, §1502(a)(5), Apr. 20, 2005, 119 Stat. 118, 195, 216; Pub. L. 111–327, §2(a)(29), Dec. 22, 2010, 124 Stat. 3560.)

Historical and Revision Notes
legislative statements

CHAPTER 9 of the House amendment represents a compromise between chapter 9 of the House bill and 9 of the Senate amendment. In most respects this chapter follows current law with respect to the adjustment of debts of a municipality. Stylistic changes and minor substantive revisions have been made in order to conform this chapter with other new chapters of the bankruptcy code. There are few major differences between the House bill and the Senate amendment on this issue. Section 901 indicates the applicability of other sections of title 11 in cases under chapter 9. Included are sections providing for creditors' committees under sections 1102 and 1103.

house report no. 95–595

Section 901 makes applicable appropriate provisions of other chapters of proposed title 11. The general rule set out in section 103(e) is that only the provisions of chapters 1 and 9 apply in a chapter 9 case. Section 901 is the exception, and specifies other provisions that do apply. They are as follows:

§301. Voluntary cases. Application of this section makes clear, as under current chapter IX [chapter 9 of former title 11], that a municipal case can be commenced only by the municipality itself. There are no involuntary chapter 9 cases.

§344. Self-incrimination; immunity. Application of this section is of no substantive effect for the administration of the case, but merely provides that the general rules in part V [§6001 et seq.] of title 18 govern immunity.

§347(b). Unclaimed property. This provision currently appears in section 96(d) of chapter IX [section 416(d) of former title 11].

§349. Effect of dismissal. This section governs the effect of a dismissal of a chapter 9 case. It provides in substance that rights that existed before the case that were disturbed by the commencement of the case are reinstated. This section does not concern grounds for dismissal, which are found in section 926.

§361. Adequate protection. Section 361 provides the general standard for the protection of secured creditors whose property is used in a case under title 11. Its importance lies in its application to sections 362 and 364.

§362. Automatic stay. The automatic stay provisions of the general portions of the title are incorporated into chapter 9. There is an automatic stay provided in current Bankruptcy Act §85(e) [section 405(e) of former title 11]. The thrust of section 362 is the same as that of section 85(e), but, of course, its application in chapter 9 is modernized and drafted to conform with the stay generally applicable under the bankruptcy code. An additional part of the automatic stay applicable only to municipal cases is included in section 922.

§§364(c), 364(d), 364(e). Obtaining credit. This section governs the borrowing of money by a municipality in reorganization. It is narrower than a comparable provision in current law, section 82(b)(2) [section 402(b)(2) of former title 11]. The difference lies mainly in the removal under the bill of the authority of the court to supervise borrowing by the municipality in instances in which none of the special bankruptcy powers are involved. That is, if a municipality could borrow money outside of the bankruptcy court, then it should have the same authority in bankruptcy court, under the doctrine of *Ashton v. Cameron Water District No. 1*, 298 U.S. 513 (1936) [Tex.1936, 56 S.Ct. 892, 80 L.Ed. 1309, 31 Am.Bankr.Rep.N.S. 96, rehearing denied 57 S.Ct. 5, 299 U.S. 619, 81 L.Ed. 457] and *National League of Cities v. Usery*, 426 U.S. 833 (1976) [Dist.Col.1976, 96 S.Ct. 2465, 49 L.Ed.2d 245, on remand 429 F. Supp. 703]. Only when the municipality needs special authority, such as subordination of existing liens, or special priority for the borrowed funds, will the court become involved in the authorization.

§365. Executory contracts and unexpired leases. The applicability of section 365 incorporates the general power of a bankruptcy court to authorize the assumption or rejection of executory contracts or unexpired leases found in other chapters of the title. This section is comparable to section 82(b)(1) of current law [section 402(b)(1) of former title 11].

§366. Utility service. This section gives a municipality the same authority as any other debtor with respect to continuation of utility service during the proceeding, provided adequate assurance of future payment is provided. No comparable explicit provision is found in current law, although the case law seems to support the same result.

§501. Filing of proofs of claims. This section permits filing of proofs of claims in a chapter 9 case. Note, however, that section 924 permits listing of creditors' claims, as under chapter 11 and under section 85(b) of chapter IX [section 405(b) of former title 11].

§502. Allowance of claims. This section applies the general allowance rules to chapter 9 cases. This is no change from current law.

§503. Administrative expenses. Administrative expenses as defined in section 503 will be paid in a chapter 9 case, as provided under section 89(1) of current law [section 409(1) of former title 11].

§504. Sharing of compensation. There is no comparable provision in current law. However, this provision applies generally throughout the proposed law, and will not affect the progress of the case, only the interrelations between attorneys and other professionals that participate in the case.

§506. Determination of secured status. Section 506 specifies that claims secured by a lien should be separated, to the extent provided, into secured and unsecured claims. It applies generally. Current law follows this result, though there is no explicit provision.

§507(1). Priorities. Paragraph (1) of section 507 requires that administrative expenses be paid first. This rule will apply in chapter 9 cases. It is presently found in section 89(1) [section 409(1) of former title 11]. The two other priorities presently found in section 89 have been deleted. The second for claims arising within 3 months before the case is commenced, is deleted from the statute, but may be within the court's equitable power to award, under the case of *Fosdick v. Schall*, 99 U.S. 235 (1878) [25 L.Ed. 339]. Leaving the provision to the courts permits greater flexibility, as under railroad cases, than an absolute three-month rule. The third priority under current law, for claims which are entitled to priority under the laws of the United States, is deleted because of the proposed amendment to section 3466 of the Revised Statutes [former 31 U.S.C. 191, see 31 U.S.C. 3713(a)] contained in section 321(a) of title III of the bill, which previously has given the United States an absolute first priority in chapter X [chapter 10 of former title 11] and section 77 [section 205 of former title 11] cases. Because the priority rules are regularized and brought together in the bankruptcy laws by this bill, the need for incorporation of priorities elsewhere specified is eliminated.

§509. Claims of codebtors. This section provides for the treatment of sureties, guarantors, and codebtors. The general rule of postponement found in the other chapters will apply in chapter 9. This section adopts current law.

§510. Subordination of claims. This section permits the court to subordinate, on equitable grounds, any claim, and requires enforcement of contractual subordination agreements, and subordination of securities rescission claims. The section recognizes the inherent equitable power of the court under current law, and the practice followed with respect to contractual provisions.

§547. Preferences. Incorporation of section 547 will permit the debtor to recover preferences. This power will be used primarily when those who gave the preferences have been replaced by new municipal officers or when creditors coerced preferential payments. Unlike Bankruptcy Act §85(h) [section 405(h) of former title 11], the section does not permit the appointment of a trustee for the purpose of pursuing preferences. Moreover, this bill does not incorporate the other avoiding powers of a trustee for chapter 9, found in current section 85(h).

§550. Liability of transfers. Incorporation of this section is made necessary by the incorporation of the preference section, and permits recovery by the debtor from a transferee of an avoided preference.

§551. Automatic preservation of avoided transfer. Application of section 551 requires preservation of any avoided preference for the benefit of the estate.

§552. Postpetition effect of security interest. This section will govern the applicability after the commencement of the case of security interests granted by the debtor before the commencement of the case.

§553. Setoff. Under current law, certain setoff is stayed. Application of this section preserves that result, though the setoffs that are permitted under section 553 are better defined than under present law. Application of this section is necessary to stay the setoff and to provide the offsetting creditor with the protection to which he is entitled under present law.

§1122. Classification of claims. This section is derived from current section 88(b) [section 408(b) of former title 11], and is substantially similar.

§1123(a)(1)–(4), (b). Contents of plan. The general provisions governing contents of a chapter 11 plan are made applicable here, with two exceptions relating to the rights of stockholders, which are not applicable in chapter 9 cases. This section expands current law by specifying the contents of a plan in some detail. Section 91 of current law [section 411 of former title 11] speaks only in general terms. The substance of the two sections is substantially the same, however.

§1124. Impairment of claims. The confirmation standards adopted in chapter 9 are the same as those of chapter 11. This changes current chapter IX [chapter 9 of former title 11], which requires compliance with the fair and equitable rule. The greater flexibility of proposed chapter 11 is carried over into chapter 9, for there appears to be no reason why the confirmation standards for the two chapters should be different, or why the elimination of the fair and equitable rule from corporate reorganizations should not be followed in municipal debt adjustments. The current chapter IX rule is based on the confirmation rules of current chapter X [chapter 10 of former title 11]. The change in the latter suggests a corresponding change in the former. Section 1124 is one part of the new confirmation standard. It defines impairment, for use in section 1129.

§1125. Postpetition disclosure and solicitation. The change in the confirmation standard necessitates a corresponding change in the disclosure requirements for solicitation of acceptances of a plan. Under current chapter IX [chapter 9 of former title 11] there is no disclosure requirement. Incorporation of section 1125 will insure that creditors receive adequate information before they are required to vote on a plan.

§1126(a), (b), (c), (e), (f), (g). Acceptance of plan. Section 1126 incorporates the current chapter IX [chapter 9 of former title 11] acceptance requirement: two-thirds in amount and a majority in number, Bankruptcy Act §92 [section 412 of former title 11]. Section 1125 permits exclusion of certain acceptances from the computation if the acceptances were obtained in bad faith or, unlike current law, if there is a conflict of interest motivating the acceptance.

§1127(d). Modification of plan. This section governs the change of a creditor's vote on the plan after a modification is proposed. It is derived from current section 92(e) [section 412(e) of former title 11].

§1128. Hearing on confirmation. This section requires a hearing on the confirmation of the plan, and permits parties in interest to object. It is the same as Bankruptcy Act §§93 and 94(a) [sections 413 and 414(a) of former title 11], though the provision, comparable to section 206 of current chapter X [section 606 of former title 11], permitting a labor organization to appear and be heard on the economic soundness of the plan, has been deleted as more appropriate for the Rules.

§1129(a)(2), (3), (8), (b)(1), (2). Confirmation of plan. This section provides the boiler-plate language that the plan be proposed in good faith and that it comply with the provisions of the chapter, and also provides the financial standard for confirmation, which replaces the fair and equitable rule. See §1124, supra.

§1142(b). *Execution of plan.* Derived from Bankruptcy Act §96(b) [section 416(b) of former title 11], this section permits the court to order execution and delivery of instruments in order to execute the plan.

§1143. *Distribution.* This section is the same in substance as section 96(d) [section 416(d) of former title 11], which requires presentment or delivery of securities within five years, and bars creditors that do not act within that time.

§1144. *Revocation of order of confirmation.* This section permits the court to revoke the order of confirmation and the discharge if the confirmation of the plan was procured by fraud. There is no comparable provision in current chapter IX [chapter 9 of former title 11].

References in Text

Section 103(e) of this title, referred to in subsec. (b), was redesignated section 103(f) and a new section 103(e) was added by Pub. L. 106–554, §1(a)(5) [title I, §112(c)(5)(A)], Dec. 21, 2000, 114 Stat. 2763, 2763A-394.

Amendments

2010—Subsec. (a). Pub. L. 111–327 inserted "333," after "301," and "351," after "350(b)".

2005—Subsec. (a). Pub. L. 109–8, §1502(a)(5), substituted "507(a)(2)" for "507(a)(1)".

Pub. L. 109–8, §1216, inserted "1123(d)," after "1123(b),".

Pub. L. 109–8, §502, inserted "555, 556," after "553," and "559, 560, 561, 562," after "557,".

1988—Subsec. (a). Pub. L. 100–597 inserted "1129(a)(6)," after "1129(a)(3),".

1984—Subsec. (a). Pub. L. 98–353 inserted "557," after "553," and substituted "1111(b)," for "1111(b)".

Effective Date of 2005 Amendment

Amendment by Pub. L. 109–8 effective 180 days after Apr. 20, 2005, and not applicable with respect to cases commenced under this title before such effective date, except as otherwise provided, see section 1501 of Pub. L. 109–8, set out as a note under section 101 of this title.

Effective Date of 1988 Amendment

Amendment by Pub. L. 100–597 effective Nov. 3, 1988, but not applicable to any case commenced under this title before that date, see section 12 of Pub. L. 100–597, set out as a note under section 101 of this title.

Effective Date of 1984 Amendment

Amendment by Pub. L. 98–353 effective with respect to cases filed 90 days after July 10, 1984, see section 552(a) of Pub. L. 98–353, set out as a note under section 101 of this title.

[1] So in original. The second comma probably should follow "350(b)".

[2] See References in Text note below.

§902. Definitions for this chapter

In this chapter—

(1) "property of the estate", when used in a section that is made applicable in a case under this chapter by section 103(e) [1] or 901 of this title, means property of the debtor;

(2) "special revenues" means—

(A) receipts derived from the ownership, operation, or disposition of projects or systems of the debtor that are primarily used or intended to be used primarily to provide transportation, utility, or other services, including the proceeds of borrowings to finance the projects or systems;

(B) special excise taxes imposed on particular activities or transactions;

(C) incremental tax receipts from the benefited area in the case of tax-increment financing;

(D) other revenues or receipts derived from particular functions of the debtor, whether or not the debtor has other functions; or

(E) taxes specifically levied to finance one or more projects or systems, excluding receipts from general property, sales, or income taxes (other than tax-increment financing) levied to finance the general purposes of the debtor;

(3) "special tax payer" means record owner or holder of legal or equitable title to real property against which a special assessment or special tax has been levied the proceeds of which are the sole source of payment of an obligation issued by the debtor to defray the cost of an improvement relating to such real property;

(4) "special tax payer affected by the plan" means special tax payer with respect to whose real property the plan proposes to increase the proportion of special assessments or special taxes referred to in paragraph (2) of this section assessed against such real property; and

(5) "trustee", when used in a section that is made applicable in a case under this chapter by section 103(e) [1] or 901 of this title, means debtor, except as provided in section 926 of this title.

(Pub. L. 95–598, Nov. 6, 1978, 92 Stat. 2622; Pub. L. 98–353, title III, §491, July 10, 1984, 98 Stat. 383; Pub. L. 100–597, §4, Nov. 3, 1988, 102 Stat. 3028.)

Historical and Revision Notes

legislative statements

Section 902(2) of the Senate amendment is deleted since the bankruptcy court will have jurisdiction over all cases under chapter 9. The concept of a claim being materially and adversely affected reflected in section 902(1) of the Senate amendment has been deleted and replaced with the new concept of "impairment" set forth in section 1124 of the House amendment and incorporated by reference into chapter 9.

senate report no. 95–989

There are six definitions for use in chapter 9. Paragraph (1) defines what claims are included in a chapter 9 case and adopts the definition now found in section 81(1) [section 401(1) of former title 11]. All claims against the petitioner generally will be included, with one significant exception. Municipalities are authorized, under section 103(c) of the Internal Revenue Code of 1954, as amended [title 26], to issue tax-exempt industrial development revenue bonds to provide for the financing of certain projects for privately owned companies. The bonds are sold on the basis of the credit of the company on whose behalf they are issued, and the principal, interest, and premium, if any, are payable solely from payments made by the company to the trustee under the bond indenture and do not constitute claims on the tax revenues or other funds of the issuing municipalities. The municipality merely acts as the vehicle to enable the bonds to be issued on a tax-exempt basis. Claims that arise by virtue of these bonds are not among the claims defined by this paragraph and amounts owed by private companies to the holders of industrial development revenue bonds are not to be included among the assets of the municipality that would be affected by the plan. See Cong. Record, 94th Cong., 1st Sess. H.R. 12073 (statement by Mr. Don Edwards, floor manager of the bill in the House). Paragraph (2) defines the court which means the federal district court or federal district judge before which the case is pending. Paragraph (3) [enacted as (1)] specifies that when the term "property of the estate" is used in a section in another chapter made applicable in chapter 9 cases, the term means "property of the debtor". Paragraphs (4) and (5) [enacted as (2) and (3)] adopt the definition of "special taxpayer affected by the plan" that appears in current sections 81(10) and 81(11) of the Bankruptcy Act [section 401(10) and (11) of former title 11]. Paragraph (6) [enacted as (4)] provides that "trustee" means "debtor" when used in conjunction with chapter 9.

house report no. 95–595

There are only four definitions for use only in chapter 9. The first specifies that when the term "property of the estate" is used in a section in another chapter made applicable in chapter 9 cases, the term will mean "property of the debtor". Paragraphs (2) and (3) adopt the definition of "special taxpayer affected by the plan" that appears in current sections 81(10) and 81(11) [section 401(10) and (11) of former title 11]. Paragraph (4) provides for "trustee" the same treatment as provided for "property of the estate", specifying that it means "debtor" when used in conjunction with chapter 9.

References in Text

Section 103(e) of this title, referred to in pars. (1) and (5), was redesignated section 103(f) and a new section 103(e) was added by Pub. L. 106–554, §1(a)(5) [title I, §112(c)(5)(A)], Dec. 21, 2000, 114 Stat. 2763, 2763A-394.

Amendments

1988—Pars. (2) to (5). Pub. L. 100–597 added par. (2) and redesignated former pars. (2) to (4) as (3) to (5), respectively.

1984—Par. (2). Pub. L. 98–353 substituted "legal or equitable title to real property against which a special assessment or special tax has been levied" for "title, legal or equitable, to real property against which has been levied a special assessment or special tax".

Effective Date of 1988 Amendment

Amendment by Pub. L. 100–597 effective Nov. 3, 1988, but not applicable to any case commenced under this title before that date, see section 12 of Pub. L. 100–597, set out as a note under section 101 of this title.

Effective Date of 1984 Amendment

Amendment by Pub. L. 98–353 effective with respect to cases filed 90 days after July 10, 1984, see section 552(a) of Pub. L. 98–353, set out as a note under section 101 of this title.

[1] See References in Text note below.

§903. Reservation of State power to control municipalities

This chapter does not limit or impair the power of a State to control, by legislation or otherwise, a municipality of or in such State in the exercise of the political or governmental powers of such municipality, including expenditures for such exercise, but—

(1) a State law prescribing a method of composition of indebtedness of such municipality may not bind any creditor that does not consent to such composition; and

(2) a judgment entered under such a law may not bind a creditor that does not consent to such composition.

(Pub. L. 95–598, Nov. 6, 1978, 92 Stat. 2622; Pub. L. 98–353, title III, §492, July 10, 1984, 98 Stat. 383.)

Historical and Revision Notes

legislative statements

Section 903 of the House amendment represents a stylistic revision of section 903 of the Senate amendment. To the extent section 903 of the House bill would have changed present law, such section is rejected.

senate report no. 95–989

Section 903 is derived, with stylistic changes, from section 83 of current Chapter IX [section 403 of former title 11]. It sets forth the primary authority of a State, through its constitution, laws, and other powers, over its municipalities. The proviso in section 83, prohibiting State composition procedures for municipalities, is retained. Deletion of the provision would "permit all States to enact their own versions of Chapter IX [chapter 9 of former title 11]", Municipal Insolvency, 50 Am.Bankr.L.J. 55, 65, which would frustrate the constitutional mandate of uniform bankruptcy laws. Constitution of the United States, Art. I, Sec. 8.

This section provides that the municipality can consent to the court's orders in regard to use of its income or property. It is contemplated that such consent will be required by the court for the issuance of certificates of indebtedness under section 364(c). Such consent could extend to enforcement of the conditions attached to the certificates or the municipal services to be provided during the proceedings.

Amendments

1984—Par. (2). Pub. L. 98–353 struck out "to" before "that does not consent".

Effective Date of 1984 Amendment

Amendment by Pub. L. 98–353 effective with respect to cases filed 90 days after July 10, 1984, see section 552(a) of Pub. L. 98–353, set out as a note under section 101 of this title.

§904. Limitation on jurisdiction and powers of court

Notwithstanding any power of the court, unless the debtor consents or the plan so provides, the court may not, by any stay, order, or decree, in the case or otherwise, interfere with—

(1) any of the political or governmental powers of the debtor;

(2) any of the property or revenues of the debtor; or

(3) the debtor's use or enjoyment of any income-producing property.

(Pub. L. 95–598, Nov. 6, 1978, 92 Stat. 2622.)

Historical and Revision Notes

senate report no. 95–989

This section adopts the policy of section 82(c) of current law [section 402(c) of former title 11]. The only change in this section from section 82(c) is to conform the section to the style and cross-references of S. 2266.

house report no. 95–595

This section adopts the policy of section 82(c) of current law [section 402(c) of former title 11]. The *Usery* case underlines the need for this limitation on the court's powers. The only change in this section from section 82(c) is to conform the section to the style and cross-references of H.R. 8200. This section makes clear that the court may not interfere with the choices a municipality makes as to what services and benefits it will provide to its inhabitants.

SUBCHAPTER II—ADMINISTRATION

Amendments

1984—Pub. L. 98–353, title III, §493, July 10, 1984, 98 Stat. 383, substituted "SUBCHAPTER" for "SUBCHAPER".

§921. Petition and proceedings relating to petition

(a) Notwithstanding sections 109(d) and 301 of this title, a case under this chapter concerning an unincorporated tax or special assessment district that does not have such district's own officials is commenced by the filing under section 301 of this title of a petition under this chapter by such district's governing authority or the board or body having authority to levy taxes or assessments to meet the obligations of such district.

(b) The chief judge of the court of appeals for the circuit embracing the district in which the case is commenced shall designate the bankruptcy judge to conduct the case.

(c) After any objection to the petition, the court, after notice and a hearing, may dismiss the petition if the debtor did not file the petition in good faith or if the petition does not meet the requirements of this title.

(d) If the petition is not dismissed under subsection (c) of this section, the court shall order relief under this chapter notwithstanding section 301(b).

(e) The court may not, on account of an appeal from an order for relief, delay any proceeding under this chapter in the case in which the appeal is being taken; nor shall any court order a stay of such proceeding pending such appeal. The reversal on appeal of a finding of jurisdiction does not affect the validity of any debt incurred that is authorized by the court under section 364(c) or 364(d) of this title.

(Pub. L. 95–598, Nov. 6, 1978, 92 Stat. 2622; Pub. L. 98–353, title III, §494, July 10, 1984, 98 Stat. 383; Pub. L. 109–8, title V, §501(a), Apr. 20, 2005, 119 Stat. 118.)

Historical and Revision Notes

legislative statements

Section 905 of the Senate amendment is incorporated as section 921(b) of the House amendment with the difference that the chief judge of the circuit embracing the district in which the case is commenced designates a bankruptcy judge to conduct the case in lieu of a district judge as under present law. It is intended that a municipality may commence a case in any district in which the municipality is located, as under present law. Section 906 of the Senate amendment has been adopted in substance in section 109(c) of the House amendment.

senate report no. 95–989

Section 905 [enacted as section 921(b)] adopts the procedures for selection of the judge for the chapter 9 case as found in current section 82(d) [section 402(d) of former title 11]. It is expected that the large chapter 9 case might take up almost all the judicial time of the presiding judge and involve very complex legal questions. Selection should not be left to chance or the luck of the draw. This provision will insure that calendar demands and levels of experience can be considered in the selection of the judge in a chapter 9 case.

house report no. 95–595

Subsection (a) is derived from section 85(a) [section 405(a) of former title 11], second sentence, of current law. There is no substantive change in the law. The subsection permits a municipality that does not have its own officers to be moved into chapter 9 by the action of the body or board that has authority to levy taxes for the municipality.

Subsection (b) permits a party in interest to object to the filing of the petition not later than 15 days after notice. This provision tracks the third sentence of section 85(a) [section 405(a) of former title 11], except that the provision for publication in section 85(a) is left to the Rules (see Rule 9–14), and therefore the determinative date is left less definite.

Subsection (c) permits the court to dismiss a petition not filed in good faith or not filed in compliance with the requirements of the chapter. This provision is the fourth sentence of section 85(a) [section 405(a) of former title 11].

Subsection (d) directs the court to order relief on the petition if it does not dismiss the case under subsection (c).

Subsection (e) contains the fifth and sixth sentences of section 85(a) [section 405(a) of former title 11].

Amendments

2005—Subsec. (d). Pub. L. 109–8 inserted "notwithstanding section 301(b)" before period at end.

1984—Subsec. (a). Pub. L. 98–353, §494(c), substituted "109(d)" for "109(c)".

Subsec. (c). Pub. L. 98–353, §494(a), substituted "any" for "an", and "petition if the debtor did not file the petition in good faith" for "petition, if the debtor did not file the petition in good faith,".

Subsec. (d). Pub. L. 98–353, §494(b), (d), redesignated subsec. (e) as (d) and substituted "subsection (c)" for "subsection (d)". No former subsec. (d) had been enacted.

Subsecs. (e), (f). Pub. L. 98–353, §494(b), redesignated subsec. (f) as (e). Former subsec. (e) redesignated (d).

Effective Date of 2005 Amendment

Amendment by Pub. L. 109–8 effective 180 days after Apr. 20, 2005, and not applicable with respect to cases commenced under this title before such effective date, except as otherwise provided, see section 1501 of Pub. L. 109–8, set out as a note under section 101 of this title.

Effective Date of 1984 Amendment

Amendment by Pub. L. 98–353 effective with respect to cases filed 90 days after July 10, 1984, see section 552(a) of Pub. L. 98–353, set out as a note under section 101 of this title.

§922. Automatic stay of enforcement of claims against the debtor

(a) A petition filed under this chapter operates as a stay, in addition to the stay provided by section 362 of this title, applicable to all entities, of—

(1) the commencement or continuation, including the issuance or employment of process, of a judicial, administrative, or other action or proceeding against an officer or inhabitant of the debtor that seeks to enforce a claim against the debtor; and

(2) the enforcement of a lien on or arising out of taxes or assessments owed to the debtor.

(b) Subsections (c), (d), (e), (f), and (g) of section 362 of this title apply to a stay under subsection (a) of this section the same as such subsections apply to a stay under section 362(a) of this title.

(c) If the debtor provides, under section 362, 364, or 922 of this title, adequate protection of the interest of the holder of a claim secured by a lien on property of the debtor and if, notwithstanding such protection such creditor has a claim arising from the stay of action against such property under section 362 or 922 of this title or from the granting of a lien under section 364(d) of this title, then such claim shall be allowable as an administrative expense under section 503(b) of this title.

(d) Notwithstanding section 362 of this title and subsection (a) of this section, a petition filed under this chapter does not operate as a stay of application of pledged special revenues in a manner consistent with section 927 of this title to payment of indebtedness secured by such revenues.

(Pub. L. 95–598, Nov. 6, 1978, 92 Stat. 2623; Pub. L. 98–353, title III, §495, July 10, 1984, 98 Stat. 384; Pub. L. 100–597, §5, Nov. 3, 1988, 102 Stat. 3029.)

Historical and Revision Notes

house report no. 95–595

The automatic stay provided under section 362 of title 11 is incomplete for a municipality, because there is the possibility of action by a creditor against an officer or inhabitant of the municipality to collect taxes due the municipality. Section 85(e)(1) of current chapter IX [section 405(e)(1) of former title 11] stays such actions. Section 922 carries over that protection into the proposed chapter 9. Subsection (b) applies the provisions for relief from the stay that apply generally in section 362 to the stay under section 922.

Amendments

1988—Subsecs. (c), (d). Pub. L. 100–597 added subsecs. (c) and (d).

1984—Subsec. (a)(1). Pub. L. 98–353 substituted "a judicial" for "judicial", and "action or proceeding" for "proceeding".

Effective Date of 1988 Amendment

Amendment by Pub. L. 100–597 effective Nov. 3, 1988, but not applicable to any case commenced under this title before that date, see section 12 of Pub. L. 100–597, set out as a note under section 101 of this title.

Effective Date of 1984 Amendment

Amendment by Pub. L. 98–353 effective with respect to cases filed 90 days after July 10, 1984, see section 552(a) of Pub. L. 98–353, set out as a note under section 101 of this title.

§923. Notice

There shall be given notice of the commencement of a case under this chapter, notice of an order for relief under this chapter, and notice of the dismissal of a case under this chapter. Such notice shall also be published at least once a week for three successive weeks in at least one newspaper of general circulation published within the district in which the case is commenced, and in such other newspaper having a general circulation among bond dealers and bondholders as the court designates.

(Pub. L. 95–598, Nov. 6, 1978, 92 Stat. 2623.)

Historical and Revision Notes

legislative statements

Section 923 of the House amendment represents a compromise with respect to the notice provisions contained in comparable provisions of the House bill and Senate amendment. As a general matter, title 11 leaves most procedural issues to be determined by the Rules of Bankruptcy Procedure. Section 923 of the House amendment contains certain important aspects of procedure that have been retained from present law. It is anticipated that the Rules of Bankruptcy Procedure will adopt rules similar to the present rules for chapter IX of the Bankruptcy Act [chapter 9 of former title 11].

house report no. 95–595

The notice provisions in section 923 are significantly more sparse than those provided under section 85(d) of chapter IX [section 405(d) of former title 11]. The exact contours of the notice to be given under chapter 9 are left to the Rules. Because the Rules deal with notice in a municipal case (Rule 9–14), and because section 405(d) of title IV of the bill continues those Rules in effect to the extent not inconsistent with the bill, the notice provisions of current law and Rules would continue to apply.

§924. List of creditors

The debtor shall file a list of creditors.

(Pub. L. 95–598, Nov. 6, 1978, 92 Stat. 2623.)

Historical and Revision Notes

legislative statements

Section 924 of the House amendment is derived from section 924 of the House bill with the location of the filing of the list of creditors to be determined by the rules of bankruptcy procedure. The detailed requirements of section 724 [probably should be "924"] of the Senate bill are anticipated to be incorporated in the rules of bankruptcy procedure.

senate report no. 95–989

This section adopts the provision presently contained in section 85(b) of Chapter IX [section 405(b) of former title 11]. A list of creditors, as complete and accurate as practicable, must be filed with the court.

house report no. 95–595

This section directs the debtor to file a list of creditors with the court. A comparable provision is presently contained in section 85(b) of chapter IX [section 405(b) of former title 11]. The Rules, in Rule 9–7, copy the provisions of section 85(b), with additional matter. As noted above, section 405(d) of title IV will continue those Rules in effect. Because the form, time of filing, and nature of the list, are procedural matters that may call for some flexibility, those details have been left to the Rules.

§925. Effect of list of claims

A proof of claim is deemed filed under section 501 of this title for any claim that appears in the list filed under section 924 of this title, except a claim that is listed as disputed, contingent, or unliquidated.

(Pub. L. 95–598, Nov. 6, 1978, 92 Stat. 2623.)

Historical and Revision Notes

legislative statements

Section 925 of the Senate amendment regarding venue and fees has been deleted.

senate report no. 95–989

Section 926 [enacted as section 925] follows the policy contained in section 88(a) of the present Act [section 408(a) of former title 11], though certain details are left to the Rules. The language of section 926 is the same as that of proposed 11 U.S.C. 1111, which applies in chapter 11 cases. The list of creditors filed under section 924 is given weight as prima facie evidence of the claims listed (except claims that are listed as disputed, contingent, or unliquidated), which are deemed filed under section 501, obviating the need for listed creditors to file proofs of claim.

§926. Avoiding powers

(a) If the debtor refuses to pursue a cause of action under section 544, 545, 547, 548, 549(a), or 550 of this title, then on request of a creditor, the court may appoint a trustee to pursue such cause of action.

(b) A transfer of property of the debtor to or for the benefit of any holder of a bond or note, on account of such bond or note, may not be avoided under section 547 of this title.

(Pub. L. 95–598, Nov. 6, 1978, 92 Stat. 2623; Pub. L. 100–597, §6, Nov. 3, 1988, 102 Stat. 3029.)

Historical and Revision Notes

legislative statements

Section 926 of the House amendment is derived from section 928 of the Senate bill. The provision enables creditors to request the court to appoint a trustee to pursue avoiding powers if the debtor refuses to exercise those powers. Section 901 of the House amendment makes a corresponding change to incorporate avoiding powers included in the Senate amendment, but excluded from the House bill.

senate report no. 95–989

This section [928 (enacted as section 926)] adopts current section 85(h) [section 405(h) of former title 11] which provides for a trustee to be appointed for the purpose of pursuing an action under an avoiding power, if the debtor refuses to do so. This section is necessary because a municipality might, by reason of political pressure or desire for future good relations with a particular creditor or class of creditors, make payments to such creditors in the days preceding the petition to the detriment of all other creditors. No change in the elected officials of such a city would automatically occur upon filing of the petition, and it might be very awkward for those same officials to turn around and demand the return of the payments following the filing of the petition. Hence, the need for a trustee for such purpose.

The general avoiding powers are incorporated by reference in section 901 and are broader than under current law. Preference, fraudulent conveyances, and other kinds of transfers will thus be voidable.

Incorporated by reference also is the power to accept or reject executory contracts and leases (section 365). Within the definition of executory contracts are collective bargaining agreements between the city and its employees. Such contracts may be rejected despite contrary State laws. Courts should readily allow the rejection of such contracts where they are burdensome, the rejection will aid in the municipality's reorganization and in consideration of the equities of each case. On the last point, "[e]quities in favor of the city in chapter 9 will be far more compelling than the equities in favor of the employer in chapter 11. Onerous employment obligations may prevent a city from balancing its budget for some time. The prospect of an unbalanced budget may preclude judicial confirmation of the plan. Unless a city can reject its labor contracts, lack of funds may force cutbacks in police, fire, sanitation, and welfare services, imposing hardships on many citizens. In addition, because cities in the past have often seemed immune to the constraint of 'profitability' faced by private businesses, their wage contracts may be relatively more onerous than those in the private sector." Executory Contracts and Municipal Bankruptcy, 85 Yale L. J. 957, 965 (1976) (footnote omitted). Rejection of the contracts may require the municipalities to renegotiate such contracts by state collective bargaining laws. It is intended that the power to reject collective bargaining agreements will pre-empt state termination provisions, but not state collective bargaining laws. Thus, a city would not be required to maintain existing employment terms during the renegotiation period.

Amendments

1988—Pub. L. 100–597 designated existing provisions as subsec. (a) and added subsec. (b).

Effective Date of 1988 Amendment

Amendment by Pub. L. 100–597 effective Nov. 3, 1988, but not applicable to any case commenced under this title before that date, see section 12 of Pub. L. 100–597, set out as a note under section 101 of this title.

§927. Limitation on recourse

The holder of a claim payable solely from special revenues of the debtor under applicable nonbankruptcy law shall not be treated as having recourse against the debtor on account of such claim pursuant to section 1111(b) of this title.

(Added Pub. L. 100–597, §7(2), Nov. 3, 1988, 102 Stat. 3029.)

Prior Provisions

A prior section 927 was renumbered section 930 of this title.

Effective Date

Section effective Nov. 3, 1988, but not applicable to any case commenced under this title before that date, see section 12 of Pub. L. 100–597, set out as an Effective Date of 1988 Amendment note under section 101 of this title.

§928. Post petition effect of security interest

(a) Notwithstanding section 552(a) of this title and subject to subsection (b) of this section, special revenues acquired by the debtor after the commencement of the case shall remain subject to any lien resulting from any security agreement entered into by the debtor before the commencement of the case.

(b) Any such lien on special revenues, other than municipal betterment assessments, derived from a project or system shall be subject to the necessary operating expenses of such project or system, as the case may be.

(Added Pub. L. 100–597, §8, Nov. 3, 1988, 102 Stat. 3029.)

Effective Date

Section effective Nov. 3, 1988, but not applicable to any case commenced under this title before that date, see section 12 of Pub. L. 100–597, set out as an Effective Date of 1988 Amendment note under section 101 of this title.

§929. Municipal leases

A lease to a municipality shall not be treated as an executory contract or unexpired lease for the purposes of section 365 or 502(b)(6) of this title solely by reason of its being subject to termination in the event the debtor fails to appropriate rent.

(Added Pub. L. 100–597, §9, Nov. 3, 1988, 102 Stat. 3030.)

Effective Date

Section effective Nov. 3, 1988, but not applicable to any case commenced under this title before that date, see section 12 of Pub. L. 100–597, set out as an Effective Date of 1988 Amendment note under section 101 of this title.

§930. Dismissal

(a) After notice and a hearing, the court may dismiss a case under this chapter for cause, including—

(1) want of prosecution;
(2) unreasonable delay by the debtor that is prejudicial to creditors;
(3) failure to propose a plan within the time fixed under section 941 of this title;
(4) if a plan is not accepted within any time fixed by the court;
(5) denial of confirmation of a plan under section 943(b) of this title and denial of additional time for filing another plan or a modification of a plan; or
(6) if the court has retained jurisdiction after confirmation of a plan—
  (A) material default by the debtor with respect to a term of such plan; or
  (B) termination of such plan by reason of the occurrence of a condition specified in such plan.

(b) The court shall dismiss a case under this chapter if confirmation of a plan under this chapter is refused.

(Pub. L. 95–598, Nov. 6, 1978, 92 Stat. 2623, §927; Pub. L. 98–353, title III, §496, July 10, 1984, 98 Stat. 384; renumbered §930, Pub. L. 100–597, §7(1), Nov. 3, 1988, 102 Stat. 3029.)

Historical and Revision Notes

legislative statements

Section 927(b) of the House amendment is derived from section 927(b) of the Senate bill. The provision requires mandatory dismissal if confirmation of a plan is refused.

The House amendment deletes section 929 of the Senate amendment as unnecessary since the bankruptcy court has original exclusive jurisdiction of all cases under chapter 9.

The House amendment deletes section 930 of the Senate amendment and incorporates section 507(a)(1) by reference.

senate report no. 95–989

Section 927 conforms to section 98 of current law [section 418 of former title 11]. The Section permits dismissal by the court for unreasonable delay by the debtor, failure to propose a plan, failure of acceptance of a plan, or default by the debtor under a conformed plan. Mandatory dismissal is required if confirmation is refused.

house report no. 95–595

Section 926 [enacted as section 927] generally conforms to section 98(a) [section 418(a) of former title 11] of current law. Stylistic changes have been made to conform the language with that used in chapter 11, section 1112. The section permits dismissal by the court for unreasonable delay by the debtor that is prejudicial to creditors, failure to propose a plan, failure of confirmation of a plan, or material default by the debtor under a confirmed plan. The only significant change from current law lies in the second ground. Currently, section 98(a)(2) provides for dismissal if a proposed plan is not accepted, and section 98(b) *requires* dismissal if an accepted plan is not confirmed. In order to provide greater flexibility to the court, the debtor, and creditors, the bill allows the court to permit the debtor to propose another plan if the first plan is not confirmed. In that event the debtor need not, as under current law, commence the case all over again. This could provide savings in time and administrative expenses if a plan is denied confirmation.

Amendments

1984—Subsec. (b). Pub. L. 98–353 substituted "confirmation of a plan under this chapter" for "confirmation".

Effective Date of 1984 Amendment

Amendment by Pub. L. 98–353 effective with respect to cases filed 90 days after July 10, 1984, see section 552(a) of Pub. L. 98–353, set out as a note under section 101 of this title.

SUBCHAPTER III—THE PLAN

§941. Filing of plan

The debtor shall file a plan for the adjustment of the debtor's debts. If such a plan is not filed with the petition, the debtor shall file such a plan at such later time as the court fixes.

(Pub. L. 95–598, Nov. 6, 1978, 92 Stat. 2624.)

Historical and Revision Notes

senate report no. 95–989

Section 941 gives the debtor the exclusive right to propose a plan, and directs that the debtor propose one either with the petition or within such time as the court directs. The section follows section 90(a) of current law [section 410(a) of former title 11].

§942. Modification of plan

The debtor may modify the plan at any time before confirmation, but may not modify the plan so that the plan as modified fails to meet the requirements of this chapter. After the debtor files a modification, the plan as modified becomes the plan.

(Pub. L. 95–598, Nov. 6, 1978, 92 Stat. 2624.)

Historical and Revision Notes

legislative statements

The House amendment deletes section 942 of the Senate amendment in favor of incorporating section 1125 by cross-reference. Similarly, the House amendment does not incorporate section 944 or 945 of the Senate amendment since incorporation of several sections in chapter 11 in section 901 is sufficient.

senate report no. 95–989

Section 942 permits the debtor to modify the plan at any time before confirmation, as does section 90(a) of current law [section 410(a) of former title 11].

§943. Confirmation

(a) A special tax payer may object to confirmation of a plan.
(b) The court shall confirm the plan if—
(1) the plan complies with the provisions of this title made applicable by sections 103(e)[1] and 901 of this title;
(2) the plan complies with the provisions of this chapter;
(3) all amounts to be paid by the debtor or by any person for services or expenses in the case or incident to the plan have been fully disclosed and are reasonable;
(4) the debtor is not prohibited by law from taking any action necessary to carry out the plan;
(5) except to the extent that the holder of a particular claim has agreed to a different treatment of such claim, the plan provides that on the effective date of the plan each holder of a claim of a kind specified in section 507(a)(2) of this title will receive on account of such claim cash equal to the allowed amount of such claim;
(6) any regulatory or electoral approval necessary under applicable nonbankruptcy law in order to carry out any provision of the plan has been obtained, or such provision is expressly conditioned on such approval; and
(7) the plan is in the best interests of creditors and is feasible.

(Pub. L. 95–598, Nov. 6, 1978, 92 Stat. 2624; Pub. L. 98–353, title III, §497, July 10, 1984, 98 Stat. 384; Pub. L. 100–597, §10, Nov. 3, 1988, 102 Stat. 3030; Pub. L. 109–8, title XV, §1502(a)(6), Apr. 20, 2005, 119 Stat. 216.)

Historical and Revision Notes

legislative statements

Section 943(a) of the House amendment makes clear that a special taxpayer may object to confirmation of a plan. Section 943(b) of the House amendment is derived from section 943 of the House bill respecting confirmation of a plan under chapter 9. It must be emphasized that these standards of confirmation are in addition to standards in section 1129 that are made applicable to chapter 9 by section 901 of the House amendment. In particular, if the requirements of sections 1129(a)(8) are not complied with, then the proponent may request application of section 1129(b). The court will then be required to confirm the plan if it complies with the "fair and equitable" test and is in the best interests of creditors. The best interests of creditors test does not mean liquidation value as under chapter XI of the Bankruptcy Act [chapter 11 of former title 11]. In making such a determination, it is expected that the court will be guided by standards set forth in *Kelley v. Everglades Drainage District*, 319 U.S. 415 (1943) [Fla.1943, 63 S.Ct. 1141, 87 L.Ed. 1485, rehearing denied 63 S.Ct. 1444, 320 U.S. 214, 87 L.Ed. 1851, motion denied 64 S.Ct 783, 321 U.S. 754, 88 L.Ed. 1054] and *Fano v. Newport Heights Irrigation Dist.*, 114 F.2d 563 (9th Cir. 1940), as under present law, the bankruptcy court should make findings as detailed as possible to support a conclusion that this test has been met. However, it must be emphasized that unlike current law, the fair and equitable test under section 1129(b) will not apply if section 1129(a)(8) has been satisfied in addition to the other confirmation standards specified in section 943 and incorporated by reference in section 901 of the House amendment. To the extent that *American United Mutual Life Insurance Co. v. City of Avon Park*, 311 U.S. 138 (1940) [Fla.1940, 61 S.Ct. 157, 85 L.Ed. 91, 136 A.L.R. 860, rehearing denied 61 S.Ct. 395, 311 U.S. 730, 85 L.Ed. 475] and other cases are to the contrary, such cases are overruled to that extent.

senate report no. 95–989

Section 946 [enacted as section 943] is adopted from current section 94 [section 414 of former title 11]. The test for confirmation is whether or not the plan is fair and equitable and feasible. The fair and equitable test tracts current chapter X [chapter 10 of former title 11] and is known as the strict priority rule. Creditors must be provided, under the plan, the going concern value of their claims. The going concern value contemplates a "comparison of revenues and expenditures taking into account the taxing power and the extent to which tax increases are both necessary and feasible" Municipal Insolvency, supra, at p. 64, and is intended to provide more of a return to creditors than the liquidation value if the city's assets could be liquidated like those of a private corporation.

house report no. 95–595

In addition to the confirmation requirements incorporated from section 1129 by section 901, this section specifies additional requirements. Paragraph (1) requires compliance with the provisions of the title made applicable in chapter 9 cases. This provision follows section 94(b)(2) [section 414(b)(2) of former title 11]. Paragraph (2) requires compliance with the provisions of chapter 9, as does section 94(b)(2). Paragraph (3) adopts section 94(b)(4), requiring disclosure and reasonableness of all payments to be made in connection with the plan or the case. Paragraph (4), copied from section 92(b)(6) [probably should be "94(b)(6)" which was section 414(b)(6) of former title 11], requires that the debtor not be prohibited by law from taking any action necessary to carry out the plan. Paragraph (5) departs from current law by requiring that administrative expenses be paid in full, but not necessarily in cash. Finally, paragraph (6) requires that the plan be in the best interest of creditors and feasible. The best interest test was deleted in section 94(b)(1) of current chapter IX from previous chapter IX [chapter 9 of former title 11] because it was redundant with the fair and equitable rule. However, this bill proposes a new confirmation standard generally for reorganization, one element of which is the best interest of creditors test; see section 1129(a)(7). In that section, the test is phrased in terms of liquidation of the debtor. Because that is not possible in a municipal case, the test here is phrased in its more traditional form, using the words of art "best interest of creditors." The best interest of creditors test here is in addition to the financial standards imposed on the plan by sections 1129(a)(8) and 1129(b), just as those provisions are in addition to the comparable best interest test in chapter 11, 11 U.S.C. 1129(a)(7). The feasibility requirement, added in the revision of chapter IX last year, is retained.

References in Text

Section 103(e) of this title, referred to in subsec. (b)(1), was redesignated section 103(f) and a new section 103(e) was added by Pub. L. 106–554, §1(a)(5) [title I, §112(c)(5)(A)], Dec. 21, 2000, 114 Stat. 2763, 2763A–394.

Amendments

2005—Subsec. (b)(5). Pub. L. 109–8 substituted "507(a)(2)" for "507(a)(1)".

1988—Subsec. (b)(6), (7). Pub. L. 100–597 added par. (6) and redesignated former par. (6) as (7).

1984—Subsec. (b)(4). Pub. L. 98–353, §497(1), struck out "to be taken" after "necessary".

Subsec. (b)(5). Pub. L. 98–353, §497(2), substituted provisions requiring the plan to provide payment of cash in an amount equal to the allowed amount of a claim except to the extent that the holder of a particular claim has agreed to different treatment of such claim, for provisions which required the plan to provide for payment of property of a value equal to the allowed amount of such claim except to the extent that the holder of a particular claim has waived such payment on such claim.

Effective Date of 2005 Amendment

Amendment by Pub. L. 109–8 effective 180 days after Apr. 20, 2005, and not applicable with respect to cases commenced under this title before such effective date, except as otherwise provided, see section 1501 of Pub. L. 109–8, set out as a note under section 101 of this title.

Effective Date of 1988 Amendment

Amendment by Pub. L. 100–597 effective Nov. 3, 1988, but not applicable to any case commenced under this title before that date, see section 12 of Pub. L. 100–597, set out as a note under section 101 of this title.

Effective Date of 1984 Amendment

Amendment by Pub. L. 98–353 effective with respect to cases filed 90 days after July 10, 1984, see section 552(a) of Pub. L. 98–353, set out as a note under section 101 of this title.

¹ See References in Text note below.

§944. Effect of confirmation

(a) The provisions of a confirmed plan bind the debtor and any creditor, whether or not—

(1) a proof of such creditor's claim is filed or deemed filed under section 501 of this title;

(2) such claim is allowed under section 502 of this title; or

(3) such creditor has accepted the plan.

(b) Except as provided in subsection (c) of this section, the debtor is discharged from all debts as of the time when—

(1) the plan is confirmed;

(2) the debtor deposits any consideration to be distributed under the plan with a disbursing agent appointed by the court; and

(3) the court has determined—

(A) that any security so deposited will constitute, after distribution, a valid legal obligation of the debtor; and

(B) that any provision made to pay or secure payment of such obligation is valid.

(c) The debtor is not discharged under subsection (b) of this section from any debt—

(1) excepted from discharge by the plan or order confirming the plan; or

(2) owed to an entity that, before confirmation of the plan, had neither notice nor actual knowledge of the case.

(Pub. L. 95–598, Nov. 6, 1978, 92 Stat. 2624.)

Historical and Revision Notes

senate report no. 95–989

[Section 947] Subsection (a) [enacted as section 944(a)] makes the provisions of a confirmed plan binding on the debtor and creditors. It is derived from section 95(a) of chapter 9 [section 415(a) of former title 11].

Subsections (b) and (c) [enacted as section 944(b) and (c)] provide for the discharge of a municipality. The discharge is essentially the same as that granted under section 95(b) of the Bankruptcy Act [section 415(b) of former title 11].

§945. Continuing jurisdiction and closing of the case

(a) The court may retain jurisdiction over the case for such period of time as is necessary for the successful implementation of the plan.

(b) Except as provided in subsection (a) of this section, the court shall close the case when administration of the case has been completed.

(Pub. L. 95–598, Nov. 6, 1978, 92 Stat. 2625; Pub. L. 98–353, title III, §498, July 10, 1984, 98 Stat. 384.)

Historical and Revision Notes

senate report no. 95–989

Section 948 [enacted as section 945] permits the court to retain jurisdiction over the case to ensure successful execution of the plan. The provision is the same as that found in section 96(e) of Chapter 9 of the present Act [section 416(e) of former title 11].

Amendments

1984—Subsec. (a). Pub. L. 98–353 substituted "implementation" for "execution".

Effective Date of 1984 Amendment

Amendment by Pub. L. 98–353 effective with respect to cases filed 90 days after July 10, 1984, see section 552(a) of Pub. L. 98–353, set out as a note under section 101 of this title.

§946. Effect of exchange of securities before the date of the filing of the petition

The exchange of a new security under the plan for a claim covered by the plan, whether such exchange occurred before or after the date of the filing of the petition, does not limit or impair the effectiveness of the plan or of any provision of this chapter. The amount and number specified in section 1126(c) of this title include the amount and number of claims formerly held by a creditor that has participated in any such exchange.

(Pub. L. 95–598, Nov. 6, 1978, 92 Stat. 2625.)

Historical and Revision Notes

legislative statements

The House amendment deletes section 950 of the Senate amendment as unnecessary. The constitutionality of chapter 9 of the House amendment is beyond doubt.

senate report no. 95–989

[Section 949] This section [enacted as section 946], which follows section 97 of current law [section 417 of former title 11], permits an exchange of a security before the case is filed to constitute an acceptance of the plan if the exchange was under a proposal that later becomes the plan.

CHAPTER 11—REORGANIZATION

SUBCHAPTER I—OFFICERS AND ADMINISTRATION

Sec.
1101. Definitions for this chapter.
1102. Creditors' and equity security holders' committees.
1103. Powers and duties of committees.
1104. Appointment of trustee or examiner.
1105. Termination of trustee's appointment.
1106. Duties of trustee and examiner.
1107. Rights, powers, and duties of debtor in possession.
1108. Authorization to operate business.
1109. Right to be heard.
1110. Aircraft equipment and vessels.
1111. Claims and interests.
1112. Conversion or dismissal.
1113. Rejection of collective bargaining agreements.
1114. Payment of insurance benefits to retired employees.
1115. Property of the estate.
1116. Duties of trustee or debtor in possession in small business cases.

SUBCHAPTER II—THE PLAN

1121. Who may file a plan.
1122. Classification of claims or interests.
1123. Contents of plan.
1124. Impairment of claims or interests.
1125. Postpetition disclosure and solicitation.
1126. Acceptance of plan.
1127. Modification of plan.
1128. Confirmation hearing.
1129. Confirmation of plan.

SUBCHAPTER III—POSTCONFIRMATION MATTERS

1141. Effect of confirmation.
1142. Implementation of plan.
1143. Distribution.
1144. Revocation of an order of confirmation.
1145. Exemption from securities laws.
1146. Special tax provisions.

SUBCHAPTER IV—RAILROAD REORGANIZATION

1161. Inapplicability of other sections.
1162. Definition.
1163. Appointment of trustee.
1164. Right to be heard.
1165. Protection of the public interest.
1166. Effect of subtitle IV of title 49 and of Federal, State, or local regulations.
1167. Collective bargaining agreements.
1168. Rolling stock equipment.
1169. Effect of rejection of lease of railroad line.
1170. Abandonment of railroad line.
1171. Priority claims.
1172. Contents of plan.
1173. Confirmation of plan.
1174.

Liquidation.

Historical and Revision Notes
legislative statements

CHAPTER 11 of the House amendment is derived in large part from chapter 11 as contained in the House bill. Unlike chapter 11 of the Senate amendment, chapter 11 of the House amendment does not represent an extension of chapter X of current law [chapter 10 of former title 11] or any other chapter of the Bankruptcy Act [former title 11]. Rather chapter 11 of the House amendment takes a new approach consolidating subjects dealt with under chapters VIII, X, XI, and XII of the Bankruptcy Act [chapters 8, 10, 11, and 12 of former title 11]. The new consolidated chapter 11 contains no special procedure for companies with public debt or equity security holders. Instead, factors such as the standard to be applied to solicitation of acceptances of a plan of reorganization are left to be determined by the court on a case-by-case basis. In order to insure that adequate investigation of the debtor is conducted to determine fraud or wrongdoing on the part of present management, an examiner is required to be appointed in all cases in which the debtor's fixed, liquidated, and unsecured debts, other than debts for goods, services, or taxes, or owing to an insider, exceed $5 million. This should adequately represent the needs of public security holders in most cases. However, in addition, section 1109 of the House amendment enables both the Securities and Exchange Commission and any party in interest who is creditor, equity security holder, indenture trustee, or any committee representing creditors or equity security holders to raise and appear and be heard on any issue in a case under chapter 11. This will enable the bankruptcy court to evaluate all sides of a position and to determine the public interest. This approach is sharply contrasted to that under chapter X of present law in which the public interest is often determined only in terms of the interest of public security holders. The advisory role of the Securities and Exchange Commission will enable the court to balance the needs of public security holders against equally important public needs relating to the economy, such as employment and production, and other factors such as the public health and safety of the people or protection of the national interest. In this context, the new chapter 11 deletes archaic rules contained in certain chapters of present law such as the requirement of an approval hearing and the prohibition of prepetition solicitation. Such requirements were written in an age before the enactment of the Trust Indenture Act [15 U.S.C. 77aaa et seq.] and the development of securities laws had occurred. The benefits of these provisions have long been outlived but the detriment of the provisions served to frustrate and delay effective reorganization in those chapters of the Bankruptcy Act in which such provisions applied. Chapter 11 thus represents a much needed revision of reorganization laws. A brief discussion of the history of this important achievement is useful to an appreciation of the monumental reform embraced in chapter 11.

Under the existing Bankruptcy Act [former title 11] debtors seeking reorganization may choose among three reorganization chapters, chapter X, chapter XI, and chapter XII [chapters 10, 11, and 12 of former title 11]. Individuals and partnerships may file under chapter XI or, if they own property encumbered by mortgage liens, they may file under chapter XII. A corporation may file under either chapter X or chapter XI, but is ineligible to file under chapter XII. Chapter X was designed to facilitate the pervasive reorganization of corporations whose creditors include holders of publicly issued debt securities. Chapter XI, on the other hand, was designed to permit smaller enterprises to negotiate composition or extension plans with their unsecured creditors. The essential differences between chapters X and XI are as follows. Chapter X mandates that, first, an independent trustee be appointed and assume management control from the officers and directors of the debtor corporation; second, the Securities and Exchange Commission must be afforded an opportunity to participate both as an adviser to the court and as a representative of the interests of public security holders; third, the court must approve any proposed plan of reorganization, and prior to such approval, acceptances of creditors and shareholders may not be solicited; fourth, the court must apply the absolute priority rule; and fifth, the court has the power to affect, and grant the debtor a discharge in respect of, all types of claims, whether secured or unsecured and whether arising by reason of fraud or breach of contract.

The Senate amendment consolidates chapters X, XI, and XII [chapters 10, 11, and 12 of former title 11], but establishes a separate and distinct reorganization procedure for "public companies." The special provisions applicable to "public companies" are tantamount to the codification of chapter X of the existing Bankruptcy Act and thus result in the creation of a "two-track system." The narrow definition of the term "public company" would require many businesses which could have been rehabilitated under chapter XI to instead use the more cumbersome procedures of chapter X, whether needed or not.

The special provisions of the Senate amendment applicable to a "public company" are as follows:

(a) Section 1101(3) defines a "public company" as a debtor who, within 12 months prior to the filing of the petition, had outstanding $5 million or more in debt and had not less than 1000 security holders;

(b) Section 1104(a) requires the appointment of a disinterested trustee irrespective of whether creditors support such appointment and whether there is cause for such appointment;

(c) Section 1125(f) prohibits the solicitation of acceptances of a plan of reorganization prior to court approval of such plan even though the solicitation complies with all applicable securities laws;

(d) Section 1128(a) requires the court to conduct a hearing on any plan of reorganization proposed by the trustee or any other party;

(e) Section 1128(b) requires the court to refer any plans "worthy of consideration" to the Securities and Exchange Commission for their examination and report, prior to court approval of a plan; and

(f) Section 1128(c) and section 1130(a)(7) requires the court to approve a plan or plans which are "fair and equitable" and comply with the other provisions of chapter 11.

The record of the Senate hearings on S. 2266 and the House hearings on H.R. 8200 is replete with evidence of the failure of the reorganization provisions of the existing Bankruptcy Act [former title 11] to meet the needs of insolvent corporations in today's business environment. Chapter X [chapter 10 of former title 11] was designed to impose rigid and formalized procedures upon the reorganization of corporations and, although designed to protect public creditors, has often worked to the detriment of such creditors. As the House report has noted:

The negative results under chapter X [chapter 10 of former title 11] have resulted from the stilted procedures, under which management is always ousted and replaced by an independent trustee, the courts and the Securities and Exchange Commission examine the plan of reorganization in great detail, no matter how long that takes, and the court values the business, a time consuming and inherently uncertain procedure.

The House amendment deletes the "public company" exception, because it would codify the well recognized infirmities of chapter X [chapter 10 of former title 11], because it would extend the chapter X approach to a large number of new cases without regard to whether the rigid and formalized procedures of chapter X are needed, and because it is predicated upon the myth that provisions similar to those contained in chapter X are necessary for the protection of public investors. Bankruptcy practice in large reorganization cases has also changed substantially in the 40 years since the Chandler Act [June 22, 1938, ch. 575, 52 Stat. 883, amending former title 11] was enacted. This change is, in large part, attributable to the pervasive effect of the Federal securities laws and the extraordinary success of the Securities and Exchange Commission in sensitizing both management and members of the bar to the need for full disclosure and fair dealing in transactions involving publicly held securities.

It is important to note that Congress passed the Chandler Act [June 22, 1938, ch. 575, 52 Stat. 883, amending former title 11] prior to enactment of the Trust Indenture Act of 1939 [15 U.S.C. section 77aaa et seq.] and prior to the definition and enforcement of the disclosure requirements of the Securities Act of 1933 [15 U.S.C. 77a et seq.] and the Securities Exchange Act of 1934 [15 U.S.C. 78a et seq.]. The judgments made by the 75th Congress in enacting the Chandler Act are not equally applicable to the financial markets of 1978. First of all, most public debenture holders are neither weak nor unsophisticated investors. In most cases, a significant portion of the holders of publicly issued debentures are sophisticated institutions, acting for their own account or as trustees for investment funds, pension funds, or private trusts. In addition, debenture holders, sophisticated, and unsophisticated alike, are represented by indenture trustees, qualified under section 77ggg of the Trust Indenture Act [probably should be "section 307" which is 15 U.S.C. 77ggg]. Given the high standard of care to which indenture trustees are bound, they are invariably active and sophisticated participants in efforts to rehabilitate corporate debtors in distress.

It is also important to note that in 1938 when the Chandler Act [June 22, 1938, ch. 575, 52 Stat. 883, amending former title 11] was enacted, public investors commonly held senior, not subordinated, debentures and corporations were very often privately owned. In this environment, the absolute priority rule protected debenture holders from an erosion of their position in favor of equity holders. Today, however, if there are public security holders in a case, they are likely to be holders of subordinated debentures and equity and thus the application of the absolute priority rule under chapter X [chapter 10 of former title 11] leads to the exclusion, rather than the protection, of the public.

The primary problem posed by chapter X [chapter 10 of former title 11] is delay. The modern corporation is a complex and multifaceted entity. Most corporations do not have a significant market share of the lines of business in which they compete. The success, and even the survival, of a corporation in contemporary markets depends on three elements: First, the ability to attract and hold skilled management; second, the ability to obtain credit; and third, the corporation's ability to project to the public an image of vitality. Over and over again, it is demonstrated that corporations which must avail themselves of the provisions of the Bankruptcy Act [former title 11] suffer appreciable deterioration if they are caught in a chapter X proceeding for any substantial period of time.

There are exceptions to this rule. For example, King Resources filed a chapter X [chapter 10 of former title 11] petition in the District of Colorado and it emerged from such proceeding as a solvent corporation. The debtor's new found solvency was not, however, so much attributable to a brilliant rehabilitation program conceived by a trustee, but rather to a substantial appreciation in the value of the debtor's oil and uranium properties during the pendency of the proceedings.

Likewise, Equity Funding is always cited as an example of a successful chapter X [chapter 10 of former title 11] case. But it should be noted that in Equity Funding there was no question about retaining existing management. Rather, Equity Funding involved fraud on a grand scale. Under the House amendment with the deletion of the mandatory appointment of a trustee in cases involving "public companies," a bankruptcy judge, in a case like Equity Funding, would presumably have little difficulty in concluding that a trustee should be appointed under section 1104(6).

While I will not undertake to list the chapter X [chapter 10 of former title 11] failures, it is important to note a number of cases involving corporations which would be "public companies" under the Senate amendment which have successfully skirted the shoals of chapter X and confirmed plans of arrangement in chapter XI [chapter 11 of former title 11]. Among these are Daylin, Inc. ("Daylin") and Colwell Mortgage Investors ("Colwell").

Daylin filed a chapter XI [chapter 11 of former title 11] petition on February 26, 1975, and confirmed its plan of arrangement on October 20, 1976. The success of its turnaround is best evidenced by the fact that it had consolidated net income of $6,473,000 for the first three quarters of the 1978 fiscal year.

Perhaps the best example of the contrast between chapter XI and chapter X [chapters 11 and 10 of former title 11] is the recent case of *In re Colwell Mortgage Investors*. Colwell negotiated a recapitalization plan with its institutional creditors, filed a proxy statement with the Securities and Exchange Commission, and solicited consents of its creditors and shareholders prior to filing its chapter XI petition. Thereafter, Colwell confirmed its plan of arrangement 41 days after filing its chapter XI petition. This result would have been impossible under the Senate amendment since Colwell would have been a "public company."

There are a number of other corporations with publicly held debt which have successfully reorganized under chapter XI [chapter 11 of former title 11]. Among these are National Mortgage Fund (NMF), which filed a chapter XI petition in the northern district of Ohio on June 30, 1976. Prior to commencement of the chapter XI proceeding, NMF filed a proxy statement with the Securities and Exchange Commission and solicited acceptances to a proposed plan of arrangement. The NMF plan was subsequently confirmed on December 14, 1976. The Securities and Exchange Commission did not file a motion under section 328 of the Bankruptcy Act [section 728 of former title 11] to transfer the case to chapter X [chapter 10 of former title 11] and a transfer motion which was filed by private parties was denied by the court.

While there are other examples of large publicly held companies which have successfully reorganized in chapter XI [chapter 11 of former title 11], including Esgrow, Inc. (C.D.Cal. 73–02510), Sherwood Diversified Services Inc. (S.D.N.Y. 73–B–213), and United Merchants and Manufacturers, Inc. (S.D.N.Y. 77–B–1513), the numerous successful chapter XI cases demonstrate two points: first, the complicated and time-consuming provisions of chapter X [chapter 10 of former title 11] are not always necessary for the successful reorganization of a company with publicly held debt, and second, the more flexible provisions in chapter XI permit a debtor to obtain relief under the Bankruptcy Act [former title 11] in significantly less time than is required to confirm a plan of reorganization under chapter X of the Bankruptcy Act.

One cannot overemphasize the advantages of speed and simplicity to both creditors and debtors. Chapter XI [chapter 11 of former title 11] allows a debtor to negotiate a plan outside of court and, having reached a settlement with a majority in number and amount of each class of creditors, permits the debtor to bind all unsecured creditors to the terms of the arrangement. From the perspective of creditors, early confirmation of a plan of arrangement: first, generally reduces administrative expenses which have priority over the claims of unsecured creditors; second, permits creditors to receive prompt distributions on their claims with respect to which interest does not accrue after the filing date; and third, increases the ultimate recovery on creditor claims by minimizing the adverse effect on the business which often accompanies efforts to operate an enterprise under the protection of the Bankruptcy Act [former title 11].

Although chapter XI [chapter 11 of former title 11] offers the corporate debtor flexibility and continuity of management, successful rehabilitation under chapter XI is often impossible for a number of reasons. First, chapter XI does not permit a debtor to "affect" secured creditors or shareholders, in the absence of their consent. Second, whereas a debtor corporation in chapter X [chapter 10 of former title 11], upon the consummation of the plan or reorganization, is discharged from all its debts and liabilities, a corporation in chapter XI may not be able to get a discharge in respect of certain kinds of claims including fraud claims, even in cases where the debtor is being operated under new management. The language of chapter 11 in the House amendment solves these problems and thus increases the utility and flexibility of the new chapter 11, as compared to chapter XI of the existing Bankruptcy Act [chapter 11 of former title 11].

Those who would urge the adoption of a two-track system have two major obstacles to meet. First, the practical experience of those involved in business rehabilitation cases, practitioners, debtors, and bankruptcy judges, has been that the more simple and expeditious procedures of chapter XI [chapter 11 of former title 11] are appropriate in the great majority of cases. While attempts have been made to convince the courts that a chapter X [chapter 10 of former title 11] proceeding is required in every case where public debt is present, the courts have categorically rejected such arguments. Second, chapter X has been far from a success. Of the 991 chapter X cases filed during the period of January 1, 1967, through December 31, 1977, only 664 have been terminated. Of those cases recorded as "terminated," only 140 resulted in consummated plans. This 21 percent success rate suggests one of the reasons for the unpopularity of chapter X.

In summary, it has been the experience of the great majority of those who have testified before the Senate and House subcommittees that a consolidated approach to business rehabilitation is warranted. Such approach is adopted in the House amendment.

Having discussed the general reasons why chapter 11 of the House amendment is sorely needed, a brief discussion of the differences between the House bill, Senate amendment, and the House amendment, is in order. Since chapter 11 of the House amendment rejects the concept of separate treatment for a public company, sections 1101(3), 1104(a), 1125(f), 1128, and 1130(a)(7) of the Senate amendment have been deleted.

Amendments

2005—Pub. L. 109–8, title III, §321(a)(2), title IV, §436(b), Apr. 20, 2005, 119 Stat. 95, 113, added items 1115 and 1116.

1988—Pub. L. 100–334, §2(c), June 16, 1988, 102 Stat. 613, added item 1114.

1984—Pub. L. 98–353, title III, §§514(b), 541(b), July 10, 1984, 98 Stat. 387, 391, added item 1113 and substituted "Implementation" for "Execution" in item 1142.

1983—Pub. L. 97–449, §5(a)(1), Jan. 12, 1983, 96 Stat. 2442, substituted "subtitle IV of title 49" for "Interstate Commerce Act" in item 1166.

SUBCHAPTER I—OFFICERS AND ADMINISTRATION

§1101. Definitions for this chapter

In this chapter—

(1) "debtor in possession" means debtor except when a person that has qualified under section 322 of this title is serving as trustee in the case;

(2) "substantial consummation" means—

(A) transfer of all or substantially all of the property proposed by the plan to be transferred;

(B) assumption by the debtor or by the successor to the debtor under the plan of the business or of the management of all or substantially all of the property dealt with by the plan; and

(C) commencement of distribution under the plan.

(Pub. L. 95–598, Nov. 6, 1978, 92 Stat. 2626.)

Historical and Revision Notes

senate report no. 95–989

This section contains definitions of three terms that are used in chapter 11. Paragraph (1) defines debtor in possession to mean the debtor, except when a trustee who has qualified in serving in the case.

Paragraph (2), derived from section 229a of current law [section 629(a) of former title 11], defines substantial consummation. Substantial consummation of a plan occurs when transfer of all or substantially all of the property proposed by the plan to be transferred is actually transferred; when the debtor (or its successor) has assumed the business of the debtor or the management of all or substantially all of the property dealt with by the plan; and when distribution under the plan has commenced.

Paragraph (3) defines for purposes of Chapter 11 a public company to mean "a debtor who, within 12 months prior to the filing of a petition for relief under this chapter, had outstanding liabilities of $5 million or more, exclusive of liabilities for goods, services, or taxes and not less than 1,000 security holders." There are, as noted, special safeguards for public investors related to the reorganization of a public company, as so defined.

Both requirements must be met: liabilities, excluding tax obligations and trade liabilities, must be $5 million or more; and (2) the number of holders of securities, debt or equity, or both, must be not less than 1,000. The amount and number are to be determined as of any time within 12 months prior to the filing of the petition for reorganization.

§1102. Creditors' and equity security holders' committees

(a)(1) Except as provided in paragraph (3), as soon as practicable after the order for relief under chapter 11 of this title, the United States trustee shall appoint a committee of creditors holding unsecured claims and may appoint additional committees of creditors or of equity security holders as the United States trustee deems appropriate.

(2) On request of a party in interest, the court may order the appointment of additional committees of creditors or of equity security holders if necessary to assure adequate representation of creditors or of equity security holders. The United States trustee shall appoint any such committee.

(3) On request of a party in interest in a case in which the debtor is a small business debtor and for cause, the court may order that a committee of creditors not be appointed.

(4) On request of a party in interest and after notice and a hearing, the court may order the United States trustee to change the membership of a committee appointed under this subsection, if the court determines that the change is necessary to ensure adequate representation of creditors or equity security holders. The court may order the United States trustee to increase the number of members of a committee to include a creditor that is a small business concern (as described in section 3(a)(1) of the Small Business Act), if the court determines that the creditor holds claims (of the kind represented by the committee) the aggregate amount of which, in comparison to the annual gross revenue of that creditor, is disproportionately large.

(b)(1) A committee of creditors appointed under subsection (a) of this section shall ordinarily consist of the persons, willing to serve, that hold the seven largest claims against the debtor of the kinds represented on such committee, or of the members of a committee organized by creditors before the commencement of the case under this chapter, if such committee was fairly chosen and is representative of the different kinds of claims to be represented.

(2) A committee of equity security holders appointed under subsection (a)(2) of this section shall ordinarily consist of the persons, willing to serve, that hold the seven largest amounts of equity securities of the debtor of the kinds represented on such committee.

(3) A committee appointed under subsection (a) shall—

(A) provide access to information for creditors who—

(i) hold claims of the kind represented by that committee; and

(ii) are not appointed to the committee;

(B) solicit and receive comments from the creditors described in subparagraph (A); and

(C) be subject to a court order that compels any additional report or disclosure to be made to the creditors described in subparagraph (A).

(Pub. L. 95–598, Nov. 6, 1978, 92 Stat. 2626; Pub. L. 98–353, title III, §499, July 10, 1984, 98 Stat. 384; Pub. L. 99–554, title II, §221, Oct. 27, 1986, 100 Stat. 3101; Pub. L. 103–394, title II, §217(b), Oct. 22, 1994, 108 Stat. 4127; Pub. L. 109–8, title IV, §§405, 432(b), Apr. 20, 2005, 119 Stat. 105, 110.)

Historical and Revision Notes

legislative statements

Section 1102(a) of the House amendment adopts a compromise between the House bill and Senate amendment requiring appointment of a committee of creditors holding unsecured claims by the court; the alternative of creditor committee election is rejected.

Section 1102(b) of the House amendment represents a compromise between the House bill and the Senate amendment by preventing the appointment of creditors who are unwilling to serve on a creditors committee.

senate report no. 95–989

This section provides for the election and appointment of committees. Subsection (c) provides that this section does not apply in case of a public company, as to which a trustee, appointed under section 1104(a) will have responsibility to administer the estate and to formulate a plan as provided in section 1106(a).

There is no need for the election or appointment of committees for which the appointment of a trustee is mandatory. In the case of a public company there are likely to be several committees, each representing a different class of security holders and seeking authority to retain accountants, lawyers, and other experts, who will expect to be paid. If in the case of a public company creditors or stockholders wish to organize committees, they may do so, as authorized under section 1109(a). Compensation and reimbursement will be allowed for contributions to the reorganization pursuant to section 503(b) (3) and (4).

house report no. 95–595

This section provides for the appointment of creditors' and equity security holders' committees, which will be the primary negotiating bodies for the formulation of the plan of reorganization. They will represent the various classes of creditors and equity security holders from which they are selected. They will also provide supervision of the debtor in possession and of the trustee, and will protect their constituents' interests.

Subsection (a) requires the court to appoint at least one committee. That committee is to be composed of creditors holding unsecured claims. The court is authorized to appoint such additional committees as are necessary to assure adequate representation of creditors and equity security holders. The provision will be relied upon in cases in which the debtor proposes to affect several classes of debt or equity holders under the plan, and in which they need representation.

Subsection (b) contains precatory language directing the court to appoint the persons holding the seven largest claims against the debtor of the kinds represented on a creditors' committee, or the members of a prepetition committee organized by creditors before the order for relief under chapter 11. The court may continue prepetition committee members only if the committee was fairly chosen and is representative of the different kinds of claims to be represented. The court is restricted to the appointment of persons in order to exclude governmental holders of claims or interests.

Paragraph (2) of subsection (b) requires similar treatment for equity security holders' committees. The seven largest holders are normally to be appointed, but the language is only precatory.

Subsection (c) authorizes the court, on request of a party in interest, to change the size or the membership of a creditors' or equity security holders' committee if the membership of the committee is not representative of the different kinds of claims or interests to be represented. This subsection is intended, along with the nonbinding nature of subsection (b), to afford the court latitude in appointing a committee that is manageable and representative in light of the circumstances of the case.

References in Text

Section 3(a)(1) of the Small Business Act, referred to in subsec. (a)(4), is classified to section 632(a)(1) of Title 15, Commerce and Trade.

Amendments

2005—Subsec. (a)(3). Pub. L. 109–8, §432(b), inserted "debtor" after "small business".

Subsec. (a)(4). Pub. L. 109–8, §405(a), added par. (4).

Subsec. (b)(3). Pub. L. 109–8, §405(b), added par. (3).

1994—Subsec. (a). Pub. L. 103–394 substituted "Except as provided in paragraph (3), as" for "As" in par. (1) and added par. (3).

1986—Subsec. (a). Pub. L. 99–554, §221(1), amended subsec. (a) generally, substituting "chapter 11 of this title, the United States trustee shall appoint a committee of creditors holding unsecured claims and may appoint additional committees of creditors or of equity security holders as the United States trustee deems appropriate" for "this chapter, the court shall appoint a committee of creditors holding unsecured claims" in par. (1) and "United States trustee" for "court" in par. (2).

Subsec. (c). Pub. L. 99–554, §221(2), struck out subsec. (c) which read as follows: "On request of a party in interest and after notice and a hearing, the court may change the membership or the size of a committee appointed under subsection (a) of this section if the membership of such committee is not representative of the different kinds of claims or interests to be represented."

1984—Subsec. (b)(1). Pub. L. 98–353 substituted "commencement of the case" for "order for relief".

Effective Date of 2005 Amendment

Amendment by Pub. L. 109–8 effective 180 days after Apr. 20, 2005, and not applicable with respect to cases commenced under this title before such effective date, except as otherwise provided, see section 1501 of Pub. L. 109–8, set out as a note under section 101 of this title.

Effective Date of 1994 Amendment

Amendment by Pub. L. 103–394 effective Oct. 22, 1994, and not applicable with respect to cases commenced under this title before Oct. 22, 1994, see section 702 of Pub. L. 103–394, set out as a note under section 101 of this title.

Effective Date of 1986 Amendment

Effective date and applicability of amendment by Pub. L. 99–554 dependent upon the judicial district involved, see section 302(d), (e) of Pub. L. 99–554, set out as a note under section 581 of Title 28, Judiciary and Judicial Procedure.

Effective Date of 1984 Amendment

Amendment by Pub. L. 98–353 effective with respect to cases filed 90 days after July 10, 1984, see section 552(a) of Pub. L. 98–353, set out as a note under section 101 of this title.

§1103. Powers and duties of committees

(a) At a scheduled meeting of a committee appointed under section 1102 of this title, at which a majority of the members of such committee are present, and with the court's approval, such committee may select and authorize the employment by such committee of one or more attorneys, accountants, or other agents, to represent or perform services for such committee.

(b) An attorney or accountant employed to represent a committee appointed under section 1102 of this title may not, while employed by such committee, represent any other entity having an adverse interest in connection with the case. Representation of one or more creditors of the same class as represented by the committee shall not per se constitute the representation of an adverse interest.

(c) A committee appointed under section 1102 of this title may—

(1) consult with the trustee or debtor in possession concerning the administration of the case;

(2) investigate the acts, conduct, assets, liabilities, and financial condition of the debtor, the operation of the debtor's business and the desirability of the continuance of such business, and any other matter relevant to the case or to the formulation of a plan;

(3) participate in the formulation of a plan, advise those represented by such committee of such committee's determinations as to any plan formulated, and collect and file with the court acceptances or rejections of a plan;

(4) request the appointment of a trustee or examiner under section 1104 of this title; and

(5) perform such other services as are in the interest of those represented.

(d) As soon as practicable after the appointment of a committee under section 1102 of this title, the trustee shall meet with such committee to transact such business as may be necessary and proper.

(Pub. L. 95–598, Nov. 6, 1978, 92 Stat. 2627; Pub. L. 98–353, title III, §§324, 500, July 10, 1984, 98 Stat. 358, 384.)

Historical and Revision Notes

senate report no. 95–989

This section defines the powers and duties of a committee elected or appointed under section 1102.

Under subsection (a) the committee may, if authorized by the court, employ one or more attorneys, accountants, or other agents to represent or perform services for the committee. Normally one attorney should suffice; more than one may be authorized for good cause. The same considerations apply to the services of others, if the need for any at all is demonstrated.

Under subsections (c) and (d) the committee, like any party in interest, may confer with the trustee or debtor regarding the administration of the estate; may advise the court on the need for a trustee under section 1104(b). The committee may investigate matters specified in paragraph (2) of subsection (c), but only if authorized by the court and if no trustee or examiner is appointed.

house report no. 95–595

Subsection (a) of this section authorizes a committee appointed under section 1102 to select and authorize the employment of counsel, accountants, or other agents, to represent or perform services for the committee. The committee's selection and authorization is subject to the court's approval, and may only be done at a meeting of the committee at which a majority of its members are present. The subsection provides for the employment of more than one attorney. However, this will be the exception, and not the rule; cause must be shown to depart from the normal standard.

Subsection (b) requires a committee's counsel to cease representation of any other entity in connection with the case after he begins to represent the committee. This will prevent the potential of severe conflicts of interest.

Subsection (c) lists a committee's functions in a chapter 11 case. The committee may consult with the trustee or debtor in possession concerning the administration of the case, may investigate the acts, conduct, assets, liabilities and financial condition of the debtor, the operation of the debtor's business, and the desirability of the continuance of the business, and any other matter relevant to the case or to the formulation of a plan. The committee may participate in the formulation of a plan, advise those it represents of the committee's recommendation with respect to any plan formulated, and collect and file acceptances. These will be its most important functions. The committee may also determine the need for the appointment of a trustee, if one has not previously been appointed, and perform such other services as are in the interest of those represented.

Subsection (d) requires the trustee and each committee to meet as soon as practicable after their appointments to transact such business as may be necessary and proper.

Amendments

1984—Subsec. (b). Pub. L. 98–353, §§324, 500(a), substituted "An attorney or accountant" for "A person", substituted "entity having an adverse interest" for "entity", and inserted provision that representation of one or more creditors of the same class as represented by the committee shall not per se constitute the representation of an adverse interest.

Subsec. (c)(3). Pub. L. 98–353, §500(b)(1), substituted "determinations" for "recommendations", and "acceptances or rejections" for "acceptances".

Subsec. (c)(4). Pub. L. 98–353, §500(b)(2), struck out "if a trustee or examiner, as the case may be, has not previously been appointed under this chapter in the case" after "section 1104 of this title".

Effective Date of 1984 Amendment

Amendment by Pub. L. 98–353 effective with respect to cases filed 90 days after July 10, 1984, see section 552(a) of Pub. L. 98–353, set out as a note under section 101 of this title.

§1104. Appointment of trustee or examiner

(a) At any time after the commencement of the case but before confirmation of a plan, on request of a party in interest or the United States trustee, and after notice and a hearing, the court shall order the appointment of a trustee—

(1) for cause, including fraud, dishonesty, incompetence, or gross mismanagement of the affairs of the debtor by current management, either before or after the commencement of the case, or similar cause, but not including the number of holders of securities of the debtor or the amount of assets or liabilities of the debtor; or

(2) if such appointment is in the interests of creditors, any equity security holders, and other interests of the estate, without regard to the number of holders of securities of the debtor or the amount of assets or liabilities of the debtor.

(b)(1) Except as provided in section 1163 of this title, on the request of a party in interest made not later than 30 days after the court orders the appointment of a trustee under subsection (a), the United States trustee shall convene a meeting of creditors for the purpose of electing one disinterested person to serve as trustee in the case. The election of a trustee shall be conducted in the manner provided in subsections (a), (b), and (c) of section 702 of this title.

(2)(A) If an eligible, disinterested trustee is elected at a meeting of creditors under paragraph (1), the United States trustee shall file a report certifying that election.

(B) Upon the filing of a report under subparagraph (A)—

(i) the trustee elected under paragraph (1) shall be considered to have been selected and appointed for purposes of this section; and

(ii) the service of any trustee appointed under subsection (a) shall terminate.

(C) The court shall resolve any dispute arising out of an election described in subparagraph (A).

(c) If the court does not order the appointment of a trustee under this section, then at any time before the confirmation of a plan, on request of a party in interest or the United States trustee, and after notice and a hearing, the court shall order the appointment of an examiner to conduct such an investigation of the debtor as is appropriate, including an investigation of any allegations of fraud, dishonesty, incompetence, misconduct, mismanagement, or irregularity in the management of the affairs of the debtor of or by current or former management of the debtor, if—

(1) such appointment is in the interests of creditors, any equity security holders, and other interests of the estate; or

(2) the debtor's fixed, liquidated, unsecured debts, other than debts for goods, services, or taxes, or owing to an insider, exceed $5,000,000.

(d) If the court orders the appointment of a trustee or an examiner, if a trustee or an examiner dies or resigns during the case or is removed under section 324 of this title, or if a trustee fails to qualify under section 322 of this title, then the United States trustee, after consultation with parties in interest, shall appoint, subject to the court's approval, one disinterested person other than the United States trustee to serve as trustee or examiner, as the case may be, in the case.

(e) The United States trustee shall move for the appointment of a trustee under subsection (a) if there are reasonable grounds to suspect that current members of the governing body of the debtor, the debtor's chief executive or chief financial officer, or members of the governing body who selected the debtor's chief executive or chief financial officer, participated in actual fraud, dishonesty, or criminal conduct in the management of the debtor or the debtor's public financial reporting.

(Pub. L. 95–598, Nov. 6, 1978, 92 Stat. 2627; Pub. L. 99–554, title II, §222, Oct. 27, 1986, 100 Stat. 3102; Pub. L. 103–394, title II, §211(a), title V, §501(d)(30), Oct. 22, 1994, 108 Stat. 4125, 4146; Pub. L. 109–8, title IV, §§416, 442(b), title XIV, §1405, Apr. 20, 2005, 119 Stat. 107, 116, 215; Pub. L. 111–327, §2(a)(30), Dec. 22, 2010, 124 Stat. 3560.)

Historical and Revision Notes

legislative statements

Section 1104 of the House amendment represents a compromise between the House bill and the Senate amendment concerning the appointment of a trustee or examiner. The method of appointment rather than election, is derived from the House bill; the two alternative standards of appointment are derived with modifications from the Senate amendment, instead of the standard stated in the House bill. For example, if the current management of the debtor gambled away rental income before the filing of the petition, a trustee should be appointed after the petition, whether or not postpetition mismanagement can be shown. However, under no circumstances will cause include the number of security holders of the debtor or the amount of assets or liabilities of the debtor. The standard also applies to the appointment of an examiner in those circumstances in which mandatory appointment, as previously detailed, is not required.

senate report no. 95–989

Subsection (a) provides for the mandatory appointment of a disinterested trustee in the case of a public company, as defined in section 1101(3), within 10 days of the order for relief, or of a successor, in the event of a vacancy, as soon as practicable.

Section 156 of chapter X ([former] 11 U.S.C. 516 [556]) requires the appointment of a disinterested trustee if the debtor's liabilities are $250,000 or over. Section 1104(a) marks a substantial change. The appointment of a trustee is mandatory only for a public company, which under section 1101(3), has $5 million in liabilities, excluding tax and trade obligations, and 1,000 security holders. In view of past experience, cases involving public companies will under normal circumstances probably be relatively few in number but of vast importance in terms of public investor interest.

In case of a nonpublic company, the appointment or election of a trustee is discretionary if the interests of the estate and its security holders would be served thereby. A test based on probable costs and benefits of a trusteeship is not practical. The appointment may be made at any time prior to confirmation of the plan.

In case of a nonpublic company, if no trustee is appointed, the court may under subsection (c) appoint an examiner, if the appointment would serve the interests of the estate and security holders. The purpose of his appointment is specified in section 1106(b).

house report no. 95–595

Subsection (a) of this section governs the appointment of trustees in reorganization cases. The court is permitted to order the appointment of one trustee at any time after the commencement of the case if a party in interest so requests. The court may order appointment only if the protection afforded by a trustee is needed and the costs and expenses of a trustee would not be disproportionately higher than the value of the protection afforded.

The protection afforded by a trustee would be needed, for example, in cases where the current management of the debtor has been fraudulent or dishonest, or has grossly mismanaged the company, or where the debtor's management has abandoned the business. A trustee would not necessarily be needed to investigate misconduct of former management of the debtor, because an examiner appointed under this section might well be able to serve that function adequately without displacing the current management. Generally, a trustee would not be needed in any case where the protection afforded by a trustee could equally be afforded by an examiner. Though the device of examiner appears in current chapter X [chapter 10 of former title 11], it is rarely used because of the nearly absolute presumption in favor of the appointment of a trustee. Its use here will give the courts, debtors, creditors, and equity security holders greater flexibility in handling the affairs of an insolvent debtor, permitting the court to tailor the remedy to the case.

The second test, relating to the costs and expenses of a trustee, is not intended to be a strict cost/benefit analysis. It is included to require the court to have due regard for any additional costs or expenses that the appointment of a trustee would impose on the estate.

Subsection (b) permits the court, at any time after the commencement of the case and on request of a party in interest, to order the appointment of an examiner, if the court has not ordered the appointment of a trustee. The examiner would be appointed to conduct such an investigation of the debtor as is appropriate under the particular circumstances of the case, including an investigation of any allegations of fraud, dishonesty, or gross mismanagement of the debtor of or by current or former management of the debtor. The standards for the appointment of an examiner are the same as those for the appointment of a trustee: the protection must be needed, and the costs and expenses must not be disproportionately high.

By virtue of proposed 11 U.S.C. 1109, an indenture trustee and the Securities and Exchange Commission will be parties in interest for the purpose of requesting the appointment of a trustee or examiner.

Subsection (c) directs that the United States trustee actually select and appoint the trustee or examiner ordered appointed under this section. The United States trustee is required to consult with various parties in interest before selecting and appointing a trustee. He is not bound to select one of the members of the panel of private trustees established under proposed 28 U.S.C. 586(a)(1) which exists only for the purpose of providing trustees for chapter 7 cases. Neither is he precluded from selecting a panel member if the member is qualified to serve as chapter 11 trustee. Appointment by the United States trustee will remove the court from the often criticized practice of appointing an officer that will appear in litigation before the court against an adverse party.

Amendments

2010—Subsec. (a). Pub. L. 111–327, §2(a)(30)(A), inserted "or" at end of par. (1), substituted a period for "; or" at end of par. (2), and struck out par. (3) which read as follows: "if grounds exist to convert or dismiss the case under section 1112, but the court determines that the appointment of a trustee or an examiner is in the best interests of creditors and the estate."

Subsec. (b)(2)(B)(ii). Pub. L. 111–327, §2(a)(30)(B), substituted "subsection (a)" for "subsection (d)".

2005—Subsec. (a)(3). Pub. L. 109–8, §442(b), added par. (3).

Subsec. (b). Pub. L. 109–8, §416, designated existing provisions as par. (1) and added par. (2).

Subsec. (e). Pub. L. 109–8, §1405, added subsec. (e).

1994—Subsec. (b). Pub. L. 103–394, §211(a)(2), added subsec. (b). Former subsec. (b) redesignated (c).

Subsec. (c). Pub. L. 103–394, §211(a)(1), redesignated subsec. (b) as (c). Former subsec. (c) redesignated (d).

Subsec. (d). Pub. L. 103–394, §§211(a)(1), 501(d)(30), redesignated subsec. (c) as (d) and inserted comma after "interest".

1986—Subsecs. (a), (b). Pub. L. 99–554, §222(1), (2), inserted "or the United States trustee" after "party in interest".

Subsec. (c). Pub. L. 99–554, §222(3), substituted "the United States trustee, after consultation with parties in interest shall appoint, subject to the court's approval, one disinterested person other than the United States trustee to serve" for "the court shall appoint one disinterested person to serve".

Effective Date of 2005 Amendment

Amendment by section 1405 of Pub. L. 109–8 effective Apr. 20, 2005, and applicable only with respect to cases commenced under this title on or after Apr. 20, 2005, see section 1406 of Pub. L. 109–8, set out as a note under section 507 of this title.

Amendment by sections 416 and 442(b) of Pub. L. 109–8 effective 180 days after Apr. 20, 2005, and not applicable with respect to cases commenced under this title before such effective date, except as otherwise provided, see section 1501 of Pub. L. 109–8, set out as a note under section 101 of this title.

Effective Date of 1994 Amendment

Amendment by Pub. L. 103–394 effective Oct. 22, 1994, and not applicable with respect to cases commenced under this title before Oct. 22, 1994, see section 702 of Pub. L. 103–394, set out as a note under section 101 of this title.

Effective Date of 1986 Amendment

Effective date and applicability of amendment by Pub. L. 99–554 dependent upon the judicial district involved, see section 302(d), (e) of Pub. L. 99–554, set out as a note under section 581 of Title 28, Judiciary and Judicial Procedure.

§1105. Termination of trustee's appointment

At any time before confirmation of a plan, on request of a party in interest or the United States trustee, and after notice and a hearing, the court may terminate the trustee's appointment and restore the debtor to possession and management of the property of the estate and of the operation of the debtor's business.

(Pub. L. 95–598, Nov. 6, 1978, 92 Stat. 2628; Pub. L. 98–353, title III, §501, July 10, 1984, 98 Stat. 384; Pub. L. 99–554, title II, §223, Oct. 27, 1986, 100 Stat. 3102.)

Historical and Revision Notes

senate report no. 95–989

This section authorizes the court to terminate the trustee's appointment and to restore the debtor to possession and management of the property of the estate and to operation of the debtor's business. Section 1104(a) provides that this section does not apply in the case of a public company, for which the appointment of a trustee is mandatory.

house report no. 95–595

This section authorizes the court to terminate the trustee's appointment and to restore the debtor to possession and management of the property of the estate, and to operation of the debtor's business. This section would permit the court to reverse its decision to order the appointment of a trustee in light of new evidence.

Amendments

1986—Pub. L. 99–554 inserted "or the United States trustee" after "party in interest".

1984—Pub. L. 98–353 substituted "estate and of the" for "estate, and".

Effective Date of 1986 Amendment

Effective date and applicability of amendment by Pub. L. 99–554 dependent upon the judicial district involved, see section 302(d), (e) of Pub. L. 99–554, set out as a note under section 581 of Title 28, Judiciary and Judicial Procedure.

Effective Date of 1984 Amendment

Amendment by Pub. L. 98–353 effective with respect to cases filed 90 days after July 10, 1984, see section 552(a) of Pub. L. 98–353, set out as a note under section 101 of this title.

§1106. Duties of trustee and examiner

(a) A trustee shall—

(1) perform the duties of the trustee, as specified in paragraphs (2), (5), (7), (8), (9), (10), (11), and (12) of section 704(a);

(2) if the debtor has not done so, file the list, schedule, and statement required under section 521(a)(1) of this title;

(3) except to the extent that the court orders otherwise, investigate the acts, conduct, assets, liabilities, and financial condition of the debtor, the operation of the debtor's business and the desirability of the continuance of such business, and any other matter relevant to the case or to the formulation of a plan;

(4) as soon as practicable—

(A) file a statement of any investigation conducted under paragraph (3) of this subsection, including any fact ascertained pertaining to fraud, dishonesty, incompetence, misconduct, mismanagement, or irregularity in the management of the affairs of the debtor, or to a cause of action available to the estate; and

(B) transmit a copy or a summary of any such statement to any creditors' committee or equity security holders' committee, to any indenture trustee, and to such other entity as the court designates;

(5) as soon as practicable, file a plan under section 1121 of this title, file a report of why the trustee will not file a plan, or recommend conversion of the case to a case under chapter 7, 12, or 13 of this title or dismissal of the case;

(6) for any year for which the debtor has not filed a tax return required by law, furnish, without personal liability, such information as may be required by the governmental unit with which such tax return was to be filed, in light of the condition of the debtor's books and records and the availability of such information;

(7) after confirmation of a plan, file such reports as are necessary or as the court orders; and

(8) if with respect to the debtor there is a claim for a domestic support obligation, provide the applicable notice specified in subsection (c).

(b) An examiner appointed under section 1104(d) of this title shall perform the duties specified in paragraphs (3) and (4) of subsection (a) of this section, and, except to the extent that the court orders otherwise, any other duties of the trustee that the court orders the debtor in possession not to perform.

(c)(1) In a case described in subsection (a)(8) to which subsection (a)(8) applies, the trustee shall—

(A)(i) provide written notice to the holder of the claim described in subsection (a)(8) of such claim and of the right of such holder to use the services of the State child support enforcement agency established under sections 464 and 466 of the Social Security Act for the State in which such holder resides, for assistance in collecting child support during and after the case under this title; and

(ii) include in the notice required by clause (i) the address and telephone number of such State child support enforcement agency;

(B)(i) provide written notice to such State child support enforcement agency of such claim; and

(ii) include in the notice required by clause (i) the name, address, and telephone number of such holder; and

(C) at such time as the debtor is granted a discharge under section 1141, provide written notice to such holder and to such State child support enforcement agency of—

(i) the granting of the discharge;

(ii) the last recent known address of the debtor;

(iii) the last recent known name and address of the debtor's employer; and

(iv) the name of each creditor that holds a claim that—

(I) is not discharged under paragraph (2), (4), or (14A) of section 523(a); or

(II) was reaffirmed by the debtor under section 524(c).

(2)(A) The holder of a claim described in subsection (a)(8) or the State child enforcement support agency of the State in which such holder resides may request from a creditor described in paragraph (1)(C)(iv) the last known address of the debtor.

(B) Notwithstanding any other provision of law, a creditor that makes a disclosure of a last known address of a debtor in connection with a request made under subparagraph (A) shall not be liable by reason of making such disclosure.

(Pub. L. 95–598, Nov. 6, 1978, 92 Stat. 2628; Pub. L. 98–353, title III, §§311(b)(1), 502, July 10, 1984, 98 Stat. 355, 384; Pub. L. 99–554, title II, §257(c), Oct. 27, 1986, 100 Stat. 3114; Pub. L. 103–394, title II, §211(b), Oct. 22, 1994, 108 Stat. 4125; Pub. L. 109–8, title II, §219(b), title IV, §446(c), title XI, §1105(b), Apr. 20, 2005, 119 Stat. 56, 118, 192; Pub. L. 111–327, §2(a)(31), Dec. 22, 2010, 124 Stat. 3560.)

Historical and Revision Notes

senate report no. 95–989

Subsection (a) of this section prescribes the trustee's duties. He is required to perform the duties of a trustee in a liquidation case specified in section 704 (2), (4), (6), (7), (8), and (9). These include reporting and informational duties, and accountability for all property received. Paragraph (2) of this subsection requires the trustee to file with the court, if the debtor has not done so, the list of creditors, schedule of assets and liabilities, and statement of affairs required under section 521(1).

Paragraph (3) of S. 1106 requires the trustee to investigate the acts, conduct, assets, liabilities, and financial condition of the debtor, the operation of the debtor's business, and the desirability of the continuance of the business, and any other matter relevant to the case or to the formulation of a plan. Paragraph (4) requires the trustee to report the results of his investigation to the court and to creditors' committees, equity security holders' committees, indenture trustees and any other entity the court designates.

Paragraph (5) requires the trustee to file a plan or to report why a plan cannot be formulated, or to recommend conversion to liquidation or to an individual repayment plan case, or dismissal. It is anticipated that the trustee will consult with creditors and other parties in interest in the formulation of a plan, just as the debtor in possession would.

Paragraph (6) [enacted as (7)] requires final reports by the trustee, as the court orders.

Subsection (b) gives the trustee's investigative duties to an examiner, if one is appointed. The court is authorized to give the examiner additional duties as the circumstances warrant.

Paragraphs (3), (4), and (5) of subsection (a) are derived from sections 165 and 169 of chapter X [sections 565 and 569 of former title 11].

References in Text

Sections 464 and 466 of the Social Security Act, referred to in subsec. (c)(1)(A)(i), are classified to sections 664 and 666, respectively, of Title 42, The Public Health and Welfare.

Amendments

2010—Subsec. (a)(1). Pub. L. 111–327, §2(a)(31)(A), substituted "704(a)" for "704".

Subsec. (a)(2). Pub. L. 111–327, §2(a)(31)(B), substituted "521(a)(1)" for "521(1)".

2005—Subsec. (a)(1). Pub. L. 109–8, §1105(b), substituted "(11), and (12)" for "and (11)".

Pub. L. 109–8, §446(c), amended par. (1) generally. Prior to amendment, par. (1) read as follows: "perform the duties of a trustee specified in sections 704(2), 704(5), 704(7), 704(8), and 704(9) of this title;".

Subsec. (a)(8). Pub. L. 109–8, §219(b)(1), added par. (8).

Subsec. (c). Pub. L. 109–8, §219(b)(2), added subsec. (c).

1994—Subsec. (b). Pub. L. 103–394 substituted "1104(d)" for "1104(c)".

1986—Subsec. (a)(5). Pub. L. 99–554 inserted reference to chapter 12.

1984—Subsec. (a)(1). Pub. L. 98–353, §311(b)(1), substituted "704(5), 704(7), 704(8), and 704(9)" for "704(4), 704(6), 704(7) and 704(8)".

Subsec. (b). Pub. L. 98–353, §502, inserted ", except to the extent that the court orders otherwise,".

Effective Date of 2005 Amendment

Amendment by Pub. L. 109–8 effective 180 days after Apr. 20, 2005, and not applicable with respect to cases commenced under this title before such effective date, except as otherwise provided, see section 1501 of Pub. L. 109–8, set out as a note under section 101 of this title.

Effective Date of 1994 Amendment

Amendment by Pub. L. 103–394 effective Oct. 22, 1994, and not applicable with respect to cases commenced under this title before Oct. 22, 1994, see section 702 of Pub. L. 103–394, set out as a note under section 101 of this title.

Effective Date of 1986 Amendment

Amendment by Pub. L. 99–554 effective 30 days after Oct. 27, 1986, but not applicable to cases commenced under this title before that date, see section 302(a), (c)(1) of Pub. L. 99–554, set out as a note under section 581 of Title 28, Judiciary and Judicial Procedure.

Effective Date of 1984 Amendment

Amendment by Pub. L. 98–353 effective with respect to cases filed 90 days after July 10, 1984, see section 552(a) of Pub. L. 98–353, set out as a note under section 101 of this title.

Payment of Certain Benefits to Retired Former Employees

Pub. L. 99–500, §101(b) [title VI, §608], Oct. 18, 1986, 100 Stat. 1783–39, 1783-74, and Pub. L. 99–591, §101(b) [title VI, §608], Oct. 30, 1986, 100 Stat. 3341–39, 3341-74, as amended by Pub. L. 100–41, May 15, 1987, 101 Stat. 309; Pub. L. 100–99, Aug. 18, 1987, 101 Stat. 716; Pub. L. 100–334, §3(a), June 16, 1988, 102 Stat. 613, provided that:

"(a)(1) Subject to paragraphs (2), (3), (4), and (5), and notwithstanding title 11 of the United States Code, the trustee shall pay benefits to retired former employees under a plan, fund, or program maintained or established by the debtor prior to filing a petition (through the purchase of insurance or otherwise) for the purpose of providing medical, surgical, or hospital care benefits, or benefits in the event of sickness, accident, disability, or death.

"(2) The level of benefits required to be paid by this subsection may be modified prior to confirmation of a plan under section 1129 of such title if—

"(A) the trustee and an authorized representative of the former employees with respect to whom such benefits are payable agree to the modification of such benefit payments; or

"(B) the court finds that a modification proposed by the trustee meets the standards of section 1113(b)(1)(A) of such title and the balance of the equities clearly favors the modification.

If such benefits are covered by a collective bargaining agreement, the authorized representative shall be the labor organization that is signatory to such collective bargaining agreement unless there is a conflict of interest.

"(3) The trustee shall pay benefits in accordance with this subsection until—

"(A) the dismissal of the case involved; or
"(B) the effective date of a plan confirmed under section 1129 of such title which provides for the continued payment after confirmation of the plan of all such benefits at the level established under paragraph (2) of this subsection, at any time prior to the confirmation of the plan, for the duration of the period the debtor (as defined in such title) has obligated itself to provide such benefits.
"(4) No such benefits paid between the filing of a petition in a case covered by this section and the time a plan confirmed under section 1129 of such title with respect to such case becomes effective shall be deducted or offset from the amount allowed as claims for any benefits which remain unpaid, or from the amount to be paid under the plan with respect to such claims for unpaid benefits, whether such claims for unpaid benefits are based upon or arise from a right to future benefits or from any benefit not paid as a result of modifications allowed pursuant to this section.
"(5) No claim for benefits covered by this section shall be limited by section 502(b)(7) of such title.
"(b)(1) Notwithstanding any provision of title 11 of the United States Code, the trustee shall pay an allowable claim of any person for a benefit paid—
"(A) before the filing of the petition under title 11 of the United States Code; and
"(B) directly or indirectly to a retired former employee under a plan, fund, or program described in subsection (a)(1);
if, as determined by the court, such person is entitled to recover from such employee, or any provider of health care to such employee, directly or indirectly, the amount of such benefit for which such person receives no payment from the debtor.
"(2) For purposes of paragraph (1), the term 'provider of health care' means a person who—
"(A) is the direct provider of health care (including a physician, dentist, nurse, podiatrist, optometrist, physician assistant, or ancillary personnel employed under the supervision of a physician); or
"(B) administers a facility or institution (including a hospital, alcohol and drug abuse treatment facility, outpatient facility, or health maintenance organization) in which health care is provided.
"(c) This section is effective with respect to cases commenced under chapter 11, of title 11, United States Code, in which a plan for reorganization has not been confirmed by the court and in which any such benefit is still being paid on October 2, 1986, and in cases that become subject to chapter 11, title 11, United States Code, after October 2, 1986 and before the date of the enactment of the Retiree Benefits Bankruptcy Protection Act of 1988 [June 16, 1988].
"(d) This section shall not apply during any period in which a case is subject to chapter 7, title 11, United States Code."
Similar provisions were contained in Pub. L. 99–656, §2, Nov. 14, 1986, 100 Stat. 3668, as amended by Pub. L. 100–41, May 15, 1987, 101 Stat. 309; Pub. L. 100–99, Aug. 18, 1987, 101 Stat. 716, and were repealed by Pub. L. 100–334, §3(b), June 16, 1988, 102 Stat. 614.

§1107. Rights, powers, and duties of debtor in possession

(a) Subject to any limitations on a trustee serving in a case under this chapter, and to such limitations or conditions as the court prescribes, a debtor in possession shall have all the rights, other than the right to compensation under section 330 of this title, and powers, and shall perform all the functions and duties, except the duties specified in sections 1106(a)(2), (3), and (4) of this title, of a trustee serving in a case under this chapter.
(b) Notwithstanding section 327(a) of this title, a person is not disqualified for employment under section 327 of this title by a debtor in possession solely because of such person's employment by or representation of the debtor before the commencement of the case.
(Pub. L. 95–598, Nov. 6, 1978, 92 Stat. 2628; Pub. L. 98–353, title III, §503, July 10, 1984, 98 Stat. 384.)

Historical and Revision Notes

legislative statements

The House amendment adopts section 1107(b) of the Senate amendment which clarifies a point not covered by the House bill.

senate report no. 95–989

This section places a debtor in possession in the shoes of a trustee in every way. The debtor is given the rights and powers of a chapter 11 trustee. He is required to perform the functions and duties of a chapter 11 trustee (except the investigative duties). He is also subject to any limitations on a chapter 11 trustee, and to such other limitations and conditions as the court prescribes cf. *Wolf v. Weinstein*, 372 U.S. 633, 649–650 (1963).

Amendments

1984—Subsec. (a). Pub. L. 98–353 substituted "on a trustee serving in a case" for "on a trustee".

Effective Date of 1984 Amendment

Amendment by Pub. L. 98–353 effective with respect to cases filed 90 days after July 10, 1984, see section 552(a) of Pub. L. 98–353, set out as a note under section 101 of this title.

§1108. Authorization to operate business

Unless the court, on request of a party in interest and after notice and a hearing, orders otherwise, the trustee may operate the debtor's business.
(Pub. L. 95–598, Nov. 6, 1978, 92 Stat. 2629; Pub. L. 98–353, title III, §504, July 10, 1984, 98 Stat. 384.)

Historical and Revision Notes

legislative statements

The House amendment adopts section 1108 of the House bill in preference to the style of an identical substantive provision contained in the Senate amendment. Throughout title 11 references to a "trustee" is read to include other parties under various sections of the bill. For example, section 1107 applies to give the debtor in possession all the rights and powers of a trustee in a case under chapter 11; this includes the power of the trustee to operate the debtor's business under section 1108.

senate report no. 95–989

This section permits the debtor's business to continue to be operated, unless the court orders otherwise. Thus, in a reorganization case, operation of the business will be the rule, and it will not be necessary to go to the court to obtain an order authorizing operation.

house report no. 95–595

This section does not presume that a trustee will be appointed to operate the business of the debtor. Rather, the power granted to trustee under this section is one of the powers that a debtor in possession acquires by virtue of proposed 11 U.S.C. 1107.

Amendments

1984—Pub. L. 98–353 inserted ", on request of a party in interest and after notice and a hearing,".

Effective Date of 1984 Amendment

Amendment by Pub. L. 98–353 effective with respect to cases filed 90 days after July 10, 1984, see section 552(a) of Pub. L. 98–353, set out as a note under section 101 of this title.

§1109. Right to be heard

(a) The Securities and Exchange Commission may raise and may appear and be heard on any issue in a case under this chapter, but the Securities and Exchange Commission may not appeal from any judgment, order, or decree entered in the case.
(b) A party in interest, including the debtor, the trustee, a creditors' committee, an equity security holders' committee, a creditor, an equity security holder, or any indenture trustee, may raise and may appear and be heard on any issue in a case under this chapter.
(Pub. L. 95–598, Nov. 6, 1978, 92 Stat. 2629.)

Historical and Revision Notes

legislative statements

Section 1109 of the House amendment represents a compromise between comparable provisions in the House bill and Senate amendment. As previously discussed the section gives the Securities and Exchange Commission the right to appear and be heard and to raise any issue in a case under chapter 11; however, the Securities and Exchange Commission is not a party in interest and the Commission may not appeal from any judgment, order, or decree entered in the case. Under section 1109(b) a party in interest, including the debtor, the trustee, creditors committee, equity securities holders committee, a creditor, an equity security holder, or an indentured trustee, may raise and may appear and be heard on any issue in a case under chapter 11. Section 1109(c) of the Senate amendment has been moved to subchapter IV pertaining to Railroad Reorganizations.

senate report no. 95–989

Subsection (a) provides, in unqualified terms, that any creditor, equity security holder, or an indenture trustee shall have the right to be heard as a party in interest under this chapter in person, by an attorney, or by a committee. It is derived from section 206 of chapter X ([former] 11 U.S.C. 606).

Subsection (b) provides that the Securities and Exchange Commission may appear by filing an appearance in a case of a public company and may appear in other cases if authorized or requested by the court. As a party in interest in either case, the Commission may raise and be heard on any issue. The Commission may not appeal from a judgment, order, or decree in a case, but may participate in any appeal by any other party in interest. This is the present law under section 208 of chapter X ([former] 11 U.S.C. 608).

house report no. 95–595

Section 1109 authorizes the Securities and Exchange Commission and any indenture trustee to intervene in the case at any time on any issue. They may raise an issue or may appear and be heard on an issue that is raised by someone else. The section, following current law, denies the right of appeal to the Securities and Exchange Commission. It does not, however, prevent the Commission from joining or participating in an appeal taken by a true party in interest. The Commission is merely prevented from initiating the appeal in any capacity.

§1110. Aircraft equipment and vessels

(a)(1) Except as provided in paragraph (2) and subject to subsection (b), the right of a secured party with a security interest in equipment described in paragraph (3), or of a lessor or conditional vendor of such equipment, to take possession of such equipment in compliance with a security agreement, lease, or conditional sale contract, and to enforce any of its other rights or remedies, under such security agreement, lease, or conditional sale contract, to sell, lease, or otherwise retain or dispose of such equipment, is not limited or otherwise affected by any other provision of this title or by any power of the court.
(2) The right to take possession and to enforce the other rights and remedies described in paragraph (1) shall be subject to section 362 if—
(A) before the date that is 60 days after the date of the order for relief under this chapter, the trustee, subject to the approval of the court, agrees to perform all obligations of the debtor under such security agreement, lease, or conditional sale contract; and
(B) any default, other than a default of a kind specified in section 365(b)(2), under such security agreement, lease, or conditional sale contract—
(i) that occurs before the date of the order is cured before the expiration of such 60-day period;
(ii) that occurs after the date of the order and before the expiration of such 60-day period is cured before the later of—
(I) the date that is 30 days after the date of the default; or
(II) the expiration of such 60-day period; and

(iii) that occurs on or after the expiration of such 60-day period is cured in compliance with the terms of such security agreement, lease, or conditional sale contract, if a cure is permitted under that agreement, lease, or contract.

(3) The equipment described in this paragraph—
(A) is—
(i) an aircraft, aircraft engine, propeller, appliance, or spare part (as defined in section 40102 of title 49) that is subject to a security interest granted by, leased to, or conditionally sold to a debtor that, at the time such transaction is entered into, holds an air carrier operating certificate issued pursuant to chapter 447 of title 49 for aircraft capable of carrying 10 or more individuals or 6,000 pounds or more of cargo; or
(ii) a vessel documented under chapter 121 of title 46 that is subject to a security interest granted by, leased to, or conditionally sold to a debtor that is a water carrier that, at the time such transaction is entered into, holds a certificate of public convenience and necessity or permit issued by the Department of Transportation; and

(B) includes all records and documents relating to such equipment that are required, under the terms of the security agreement, lease, or conditional sale contract, to be surrendered or returned by the debtor in connection with the surrender or return of such equipment.

(4) Paragraph (1) applies to a secured party, lessor, or conditional vendor acting in its own behalf or acting as trustee or otherwise in behalf of another party.
(b) The trustee and the secured party, lessor, or conditional vendor whose right to take possession is protected under subsection (a) may agree, subject to the approval of the court, to extend the 60-day period specified in subsection (a)(1).
(c)(1) In any case under this chapter, the trustee shall immediately surrender and return to a secured party, lessor, or conditional vendor, described in subsection (a)(1), equipment described in subsection (a)(3), if at any time after the date of the order for relief under this chapter such secured party, lessor, or conditional vendor is entitled pursuant to subsection (a)(1) to take possession of such equipment and makes a written demand for such possession to the trustee.
(2) At such time as the trustee is required under paragraph (1) to surrender and return equipment described in subsection (a)(3), any lease of such equipment, and any security agreement or conditional sale contract relating to such equipment, if such security agreement or conditional sale contract is an executory contract, shall be deemed rejected.
(d) With respect to equipment first placed in service on or before October 22, 1994, for purposes of this section—
(1) the term "lease" includes any written agreement with respect to which the lessor and the debtor, as lessee, have expressed in the agreement or in a substantially contemporaneous writing that the agreement is to be treated as a lease for Federal income tax purposes; and
(2) the term "security interest" means a purchase-money equipment security interest.
(Pub. L. 95–598, Nov. 6, 1978, 92 Stat. 2629; Pub. L. 103–272, §5(c), July 5, 1994, 108 Stat. 1373; Pub. L. 103–394, title II, §201(a), Oct. 22, 1994, 108 Stat.

4119; Pub. L. 106–181, title VII, §744(b), Apr. 5, 2000, 114 Stat. 177; Pub. L. 109–304, §17(b)(2), Oct. 6, 2006, 120 Stat. 1707.)

Historical and Revision Notes

legislative statements

Section 1110 of the House amendment adopts an identical provision contained in the House bill without modifications contained in the Senate amendment. This section protects a limited class of financiers of aircraft and vessels and is intended to be narrowly construed to prevent secured parties or lessors from gaining the protection of the section unless the interest of such lessor or secured party is explicitly enumerated therein. It should be emphasized that under section 1110(a) a debtor in possession or trustee is given 60 days after the order for relief in a case under chapter 11, to have an opportunity to comply with the provisions of section 1110(a).

During this time the automatic stay will apply and may not be lifted prior to the expiration of the 60-day period. Under section 1110(b), the debtor and secured party or lessor are given an opportunity to extend the 60-day period, but no right to reduce the period is intended. It should additionally be noted that under section 1110(a) the trustee or debtor in possession is not required to assume the executory contract or unexpired lease under section 1110; rather, if the trustee or debtor in possession complies with the requirements of section 1110(a), the trustee or debtor in possession is entitled to retain the aircraft or vessels subject to the normal requirements of section 365. The discussion regarding aircraft and vessels likewise applies with respect to railroad rolling stock in a railroad reorganization under section 1168.

senate report no. 95–989

This section, to a large degree, preserves the protection given lessors and conditional vendors of aircraft to a certificated air carrier or of vessels to a certificated water carrier under section 116(5) and 116(6) of present Chapter X [section 516(5) and (6) of former title 11]. It is modified to conform with the consolidation of Chapters X and XI [chapters 10 and 11 of former title 11] and with the new chapter 11 generally. It is also modified to give the trustee in a reorganization case an opportunity to continue in possession of the equipment in question by curing defaults and by making the required lease or purchase payments. This removes the absolute veto power over a reorganization that lessors and conditional vendors have under present law, while entitling them to protection of their investment.

The section overrides the automatic stay or any power of the court to enjoin taking of possession of certain leased, conditionally sold, or liened equipment, unless, the trustee agrees to perform the debtor's obligations and cures all prior defaults (other than defaults under ipso facto or bankruptcy clauses) within 60 days after the order for relief. The trustee and the equipment financer are permitted to extend the 60-day period by agreement. During the first 60 days, the automatic stay will apply to prevent foreclosure unless the creditor gets relief from the stay.

The effect of this section will be the same if the debtor has granted the security interest to the financer or if the debtor is leasing equipment from a financer that has leveraged the lease and leased the equipment subject to a security interest of a third party.

Amendments

2006—Subsec. (a)(3)(A)(ii). Pub. L. 109–304 substituted "vessel documented under chapter 121 of title 46" for "documented vessel (as defined in section 30101(1) of title 46)".

2000—Pub. L. 106–181 amended section catchline and text generally, substituting present provisions consisting of subsecs. (a) to (d) for former subsecs. (a) to (c) which contained somewhat similar provisions.

1994—Pub. L. 103–394 amended section generally. Prior to amendment, section read as follows:

"(a) The right of a secured party with a purchase-money equipment security interest in, or of a lessor or conditional vendor of, whether as trustee or otherwise, aircraft, aircraft engines, propellers, appliances, or spare parts, as defined in section 40102(a) of title 49, or vessels of the United States, as defined in section 30101 of title 46, that are subject to a purchase-money equipment security interest granted by, leased to, or conditionally sold to, a debtor that is an air carrier operating under a certificate of convenience and necessity issued by the Secretary of Transportation, or a water carrier that holds a certificate of public convenience and necessity or permit issued by the Interstate Commerce Commission, as the case may be, to take possession of such equipment in compliance with the provisions of a purchase-money equipment security agreement, lease, or conditional sale contract, as the case may be, is not affected by section 362 or 363 of this title or by any power of the court to enjoin such taking of possession, unless—

"(1) before 60 days after the date of the order for relief under this chapter, the trustee, subject to the court's approval, agrees to perform all obligations of the debtor that become due on or after such date under such security agreement, lease, or conditional sale contract, as the case may be; and

"(2) any default, other than a default of a kind specified in section 365(b)(2) of this title, under such security agreement, lease, or conditional sale contract, as the case may be—

"(A) that occurred before such date is cured before the expiration of such 60-day period; and

"(B) that occurs after such date is cured before the later of—

"(i) 30 days after the date of such default; and

"(ii) the expiration of such 60-day period.

"(b) The trustee and the secured party, lessor, or conditional vendor, as the case may be, whose right to take possession is protected under subsection (a) of this section may agree, subject to the court's approval, to extend the 60-day period specified in subsection (a)(1) of this section."

Subsec. (a). Pub. L. 103–272 substituted "section 40102(a) of title 49" for "section 101 of the Federal Aviation Act of 1958 (49 U.S.C. 1301)", "section 30101 of title 46" for "subsection B(4) of the Ship Mortgage Act, 1920 (46 U.S.C. 911(4))", and "Secretary of Transportation" for "Civil Aeronautics Board".

Effective Date of 2000 Amendment

Amendment by Pub. L. 106–181 applicable only to fiscal years beginning after Sept. 30, 1999, see section 3 of Pub. L. 106–181, set out as a note under section 106 of Title 49, Transportation.

Effective Date of 1994 Amendment

Amendment by Pub. L. 103–394 effective Oct. 22, 1994, with this section, as amended by section 201 of Pub. L. 103–394, applicable with respect to any lease, as defined by subsec. (c) of this section, entered into in connection with a settlement of any proceeding in any case pending under this title on Oct. 22, 1994, see section 702 of Pub. L. 103–394, set out as a note under section 101 of this title.

Abolition of Interstate Commerce Commission and Transfer of Functions

Interstate Commerce Commission abolished and functions of Commission transferred, except as otherwise provided in Pub. L. 104–88, to Surface Transportation Board effective Jan. 1, 1996, by section 1302 of Title 49, Transportation, and section 101 of Pub. L. 104–88, set out as a note under section 1301 of Title 49. References to Interstate Commerce Commission deemed to refer to Surface Transportation Board, a member or employee of the Board, or Secretary of Transportation, as appropriate, see section 205 of Pub. L. 104–88, set out as a note under section 1301 of Title 49.

Aircraft Equipment Settlement Leases

Pub. L. 103–7, Mar. 17, 1993, 107 Stat. 36, provided that:

"SECTION 1. SHORT TITLE.

"This Act may be cited as the 'Aircraft Equipment Settlement Leases Act of 1993'.

"SEC. 2. TREATMENT OF AIRCRAFT EQUIPMENT SETTLEMENT LEASES WITH THE PENSION BENEFIT GUARANTY CORPORATION.

"In the case of any settlement of liability under title IV of the Employee Retirement Income Security Act of 1974 [29 U.S.C. 1301 et seq.] entered into by the Pension Benefit Guaranty Corporation and one or more other parties, if—

"(1) such settlement was entered into before, on, or after the date of the enactment of this Act [Mar. 17, 1993],

"(2) at least one party to such settlement was a debtor under title 11 of the United States Code, and

"(3) an agreement that is entered into as part of such settlement provides that such agreement is to be treated as a lease,

then such agreement shall be treated as a lease for purposes of section 1110 of such title 11."

§1111. Claims and interests

(a) A proof of claim or interest is deemed filed under section 501 of this title for any claim or interest that appears in the schedules filed under section 521(a)(1) or 1106(a)(2) of this title, except a claim or interest that is scheduled as disputed, contingent, or unliquidated.

(b)(1)(A) A claim secured by a lien on property of the estate shall be allowed or disallowed under section 502 of this title the same as if the holder of such claim had recourse against the debtor on account of such claim, whether or not such holder has such recourse, unless—

(i) the class of which such claim is a part elects, by at least two-thirds in amount and more than half in number of allowed claims of such class, application of paragraph (2) of this subsection; or

(ii) such holder does not have such recourse and such property is sold under section 363 of this title or is to be sold under the plan.

(B) A class of claims may not elect application of paragraph (2) of this subsection if—

(i) the interest on account of such claims of the holders of such claims in such property is of inconsequential value; or

(ii) the holder of a claim of such class has recourse against the debtor on account of such claim and such property is sold under section 363 of this title or is to be sold under the plan.

(2) If such an election is made, then notwithstanding section 506(a) of this title, such claim is a secured claim to the extent that such claim is allowed.

(Pub. L. 95–598, Nov. 6, 1978, 92 Stat. 2630; Pub. L. 111–327, §2(a)(32), Dec. 22, 2010, 124 Stat. 3561.)

Historical and Revision Notes

legislative statements

A discussion of section 1111(b) of the House amendment is best considered in the context of confirmation and will therefore, be discussed in connection with section 1129.

senate report no. 95–989

This section dispenses with the need for every creditor and equity security holder to file a proof of claim or interest in a reorganization case. Usually the debtor's schedules are accurate enough that they will suffice to determine the claims or interests allowable in the case. Thus, the section specifies that any claim or interest included on the debtor's schedules is deemed filed under section 501. This does not apply to claims or interests that are scheduled as disputed, contingent, or unliquidated.

Amendments

2010—Subsec. (a). Pub. L. 111–327 substituted "521(a)(1)" for "521(1)".

§1112. Conversion or dismissal

(a) The debtor may convert a case under this chapter to a case under chapter 7 of this title unless—

(1) the debtor is not a debtor in possession;

(2) the case originally was commenced as an involuntary case under this chapter; or

(3) the case was converted to a case under this chapter other than on the debtor's request.

(b)(1) Except as provided in paragraph (2) and subsection (c), on request of a party in interest, and after notice and a hearing, the court shall convert a case under this chapter to a case under chapter 7 or dismiss a case under this chapter, whichever is in the best interests of creditors and the estate, for cause unless the court determines that the appointment under section 1104(a) of a trustee or an examiner is in the best interests of creditors and the estate.

(2) The court may not convert a case under this chapter to a case under chapter 7 or dismiss a case under this chapter if the court finds and specifically identifies unusual circumstances establishing that converting or dismissing the case is not in the best interests of creditors and the estate, and the debtor or any other party in interest establishes that—

(A) there is a reasonable likelihood that a plan will be confirmed within the timeframes established in sections 1121(e) and 1129(e) of this title, or if such sections do not apply, within a reasonable period of time; and

(B) the grounds for converting or dismissing the case include an act or omission of the debtor other than under paragraph (4)(A)—

(i) for which there exists a reasonable justification for the act or omission; and

(ii) that will be cured within a reasonable period of time fixed by the court.

(3) The court shall commence the hearing on a motion under this subsection not later than 30 days after filing of the motion, and shall decide the motion not later than 15 days after commencement of such hearing, unless the movant expressly consents to a continuance for a specific period of time or compelling circumstances prevent the court from meeting the time limits established by this paragraph.

(4) For purposes of this subsection, the term "cause" includes—

(A) substantial or continuing loss to or diminution of the estate and the absence of a reasonable likelihood of rehabilitation;

(B) gross mismanagement of the estate;

(C) failure to maintain appropriate insurance that poses a risk to the estate or to the public;

(D) unauthorized use of cash collateral substantially harmful to 1 or more creditors;

(E) failure to comply with an order of the court;

(F) unexcused failure to satisfy timely any filing or reporting requirement established by this title or by any rule applicable to a case under this chapter;

(G) failure to attend the meeting of creditors convened under section 341(a) or an examination ordered under rule 2004 of the Federal Rules of Bankruptcy Procedure without good cause shown by the debtor;

(H) failure timely to provide information or attend meetings reasonably requested by the United States trustee (or the bankruptcy administrator, if any);

(I) failure timely to pay taxes owed after the date of the order for relief or to file tax returns due after the date of the order for relief;

(J) failure to file a disclosure statement, or to file or confirm a plan, within the time fixed by this title or by order of the court;

(K) failure to pay any fees or charges required under chapter 123 of title 28;

(L) revocation of an order of confirmation under section 1144;

(M) inability to effectuate substantial consummation of a confirmed plan;
(N) material default by the debtor with respect to a confirmed plan;
(O) termination of a confirmed plan by reason of the occurrence of a condition specified in the plan; and
(P) failure of the debtor to pay any domestic support obligation that first becomes payable after the date of the filing of the petition.

(c) The court may not convert a case under this chapter to a case under chapter 7 of this title if the debtor is a farmer or a corporation that is not a moneyed, business, or commercial corporation, unless the debtor requests such conversion.
(d) The court may convert a case under this chapter to a case under chapter 12 or 13 of this title only if—
(1) the debtor requests such conversion;
(2) the debtor has not been discharged under section 1141(d) of this title; and
(3) if the debtor requests conversion to chapter 12 of this title, such conversion is equitable.

(e) Except as provided in subsections (c) and (f), the court, on request of the United States trustee, may convert a case under this chapter to a case under chapter 7 of this title or may dismiss a case under this chapter, whichever is in the best interest of creditors and the estate if the debtor in a voluntary case fails to file, within fifteen days after the filing of the petition commencing such case or such additional time as the court may allow, the information required by paragraph (1) of section 521(a), including a list containing the names and addresses of the holders of the twenty largest unsecured claims (or of all unsecured claims if there are fewer than twenty unsecured claims), and the approximate dollar amounts of each of such claims.
(f) Notwithstanding any other provision of this section, a case may not be converted to a case under another chapter of this title unless the debtor may be a debtor under such chapter.
(Pub. L. 95–598, Nov. 6, 1978, 92 Stat. 2630; Pub. L. 98–353, title III, §505, July 10, 1984, 98 Stat. 384; Pub. L. 99–554, title II, §§224, 256, Oct. 27, 1986, 100 Stat. 3102, 3114; Pub. L. 103–394, title II, §217(c), Oct. 22, 1994, 108 Stat. 4127; Pub. L. 109–8, title IV, §442(a), Apr. 20, 2005, 119 Stat. 115; Pub. L. 111–327, §2(a)(33), Dec. 22, 2010, 124 Stat. 3561.)
Historical and Revision Notes
legislative statements
Section 1112 of the House amendment represents a compromise between the House bill and Senate amendment with respect to the factors constituting cause for conversion of a case to chapter 7 or dismissal. The House amendment combines two separate factors contained in section 1112(b)(1) and section 1112(b)(2) of the Senate amendment. Section 1112(b)(1) of the House amendment permits the court to convert a case to a case under chapter 7 or to dismiss the case if there is both a continuing loss to or diminution of the estate and the absence of a reasonable likelihood of rehabilitation; requiring both factors to be present simultaneously represents a compromise from the House bill which eliminated both factors from the list of causes enumerated.
Sections 1112(c) and 1112(d) of the House amendment is derived from the House bill which differs from the Senate amendment only as a matter of style.
senate report no. 95–989
This section brings together all of the conversion and dismissal rules for chapter 11 cases. Subsection (a) gives the debtor an absolute right to convert a voluntarily commenced chapter 11 case in which the debtor remains in possession to a liquidation case.
Subsection (b) gives wide discretion to the court to make an appropriate disposition of the case sua sponte or upon motion of a party in interest, or the court is permitted to convert a reorganization case to a liquidation case or to dismiss the case, whichever is in the best interest of creditors and the estate, but only for cause. Cause may include the continuing loss to or dimunition [sic] of the estate of an insolvent debtor, the absence of a reasonable likelihood of rehabilitation, the inability to effectuate a plan, unreasonable delay by the debtor that is prejudicial to creditors, failure to file a plan within the appropriate time limits, denial of confirmation and any opportunity to modify or propose a new plan, revocation of confirmation and denial of confirmation of a modified plan, inability to effectuate substantial consummation of a confirmed plan, material default by the debtor under the plan, and termination of the plan by reason of the occurrence of a condition specified in the plan. This list is not exhaustive. The court will be able to consider other factors as they arise, and to use its equitable powers to reach an appropriate result in individual cases. The power of the court to act sua sponte should be used sparingly and only in emergency situations.
Subsection (c) prohibits the court from converting a case concerning a farmer or an eleemosynary institution to a liquidation case unless the debtor consents.
Subsection (d) prohibits conversion of a reorganization case to a chapter 13 case unless the debtor requests conversion and his discharge has not been granted or has been revoked.
Subsection (e) reinforces section 109 by prohibiting conversion of a chapter 11 case to a case under another chapter proceedings under which the debtor is not permitted to proceed.
References in Text
The Federal Rules of Bankruptcy Procedure, referred to in subsec. (b)(4)(G), are set out in the Appendix to this title.
Amendments
2010—Subsec. (b)(1). Pub. L. 111–327, §2(a)(33)(A)(i), amended par. (1) generally. Prior to amendment, par. (1) read as follows: "Except as provided in paragraph (2) of this subsection, subsection (c) of this section, and section 1104(a)(3), on request of a party in interest, and after notice and a hearing, absent unusual circumstances specifically identified by the court that establish that the requested conversion or dismissal is not in the best interests of creditors and the estate, the court shall convert a case under this chapter to a case under chapter 7 or dismiss a case under this chapter, whichever is in the best interests of creditors and the estate, if the movant establishes cause."
Subsec. (b)(2). Pub. L. 111–327, §2(a)(33)(A)(ii)(I), inserted introductory provisions and struck out former introductory provisions which read as follows: "The relief provided in paragraph (1) shall not be granted absent unusual circumstances specifically identified by the court that establish that such relief is not in the best interests of creditors and the estate, if the debtor or another party in interest objects and establishes that—".
Subsec. (b)(2)(B). Pub. L. 111–327, §2(a)(33)(A)(ii)(II), substituted "converting or dismissing the case" for "granting such relief".
Subsec. (e). Pub. L. 111–327, §2(a)(33)(B), substituted "521(a)" for "521".
2005—Subsec. (b). Pub. L. 109–8 added subsec. (b) and struck out former subsec. (b) which consisted of introductory provisions and pars. (1) to (10) relating to conversion of cases under this chapter to chapter 7 cases or dismissal for cause in the best interest of creditors and the estate.
1994—Subsec. (b). Pub. L. 103–394 inserted "or bankruptcy administrator" after "United States trustee".
1986—Subsec. (b). Pub. L. 99–554, §224(1)(A), inserted "or the United States trustee" after "party in interest".
Subsec. (b)(10). Pub. L. 99–554, §224(1)(B)–(D), added par. (10).
Subsec. (d). Pub. L. 99–554, §256, inserted reference to chapter 12 and added par. (3).
Subsecs. (e), (f). Pub. L. 99–554, §224(2), (3), added subsec. (e) and redesignated former subsec. (e) as (f).
1984—Subsec. (a)(2). Pub. L. 98–353, §505(a)(1), substituted "originally was commenced as an involuntary case" for "is an involuntary case originally commenced".
Subsec. (a)(3). Pub. L. 98–353, §505(a)(2), substituted "other than on" for "on other than".
Subsec. (b)(5). Pub. L. 98–353, §505(b)(1), inserted "a request made for" before "additional".
Subsec. (b)(8). Pub. L. 98–353, §505(b)(2), substituted "or" for "and".
Effective Date of 2005 Amendment
Amendment by Pub. L. 109–8 effective 180 days after Apr. 20, 2005, and not applicable with respect to cases commenced under this title before such effective date, except as otherwise provided, see section 1501 of Pub. L. 109–8, set out as a note under section 101 of this title.
Effective Date of 1994 Amendment
Amendment by Pub. L. 103–394 effective Oct. 22, 1994, and not applicable with respect to cases commenced under this title before Oct. 22, 1994, see section 702 of Pub. L. 103–394, set out as a note under section 101 of this title.
Effective Date of 1986 Amendment
Effective date and applicability of amendment by section 224 of Pub. L. 99–554 dependent upon the judicial district involved, see section 302(d), (e) of Pub. L. 99–554, set out as a note under section 581 of Title 28, Judiciary and Judicial Procedure.
Amendment by section 256 of Pub. L. 99–554 effective 30 days after Oct. 27, 1986, but not applicable to cases commenced under this title before that date, see section 302(a), (c)(1) of Pub. L. 99–554.
Effective Date of 1984 Amendment
Amendment by Pub. L. 98–353 effective with respect to cases filed 90 days after July 10, 1984, see section 552(a) of Pub. L. 98–353, set out as a note under section 101 of this title.
§1113. Rejection of collective bargaining agreements
(a) The debtor in possession, or the trustee if one has been appointed under the provisions of this chapter, other than a trustee in a case covered by subchapter IV of this chapter and by title I of the Railway Labor Act, may assume or reject a collective bargaining agreement only in accordance with the provisions of this section.
(b)(1) Subsequent to filing a petition and prior to filing an application seeking rejection of a collective bargaining agreement, the debtor in possession or trustee (hereinafter in this section "trustee" shall include a debtor in possession), shall—
(A) make a proposal to the authorized representative of the employees covered by such agreement, based on the most complete and reliable information available at the time of such proposal, which provides for those necessary modifications in the employees benefits and protections that are necessary to permit the reorganization of the debtor and assures that all creditors, the debtor and all of the affected parties are treated fairly and equitably; and
(B) provide, subject to subsection (d)(3), the representative of the employees with such relevant information as is necessary to evaluate the proposal.

(2) During the period beginning on the date of the making of a proposal provided for in paragraph (1) and ending on the date of the hearing provided for in subsection (d)(1), the trustee shall meet, at reasonable times, with the authorized representative to confer in good faith in attempting to reach mutually satisfactory modifications of such agreement.
(c) The court shall approve an application for rejection of a collective bargaining agreement only if the court finds that—
(1) the trustee has, prior to the hearing, made a proposal that fulfills the requirements of subsection (b)(1);
(2) the authorized representative of the employees has refused to accept such proposal without good cause; and
(3) the balance of the equities clearly favors rejection of such agreement.

(d)(1) Upon the filing of an application for rejection the court shall schedule a hearing to be held not later than fourteen days after the date of the filing of such application. All interested parties may appear and be heard at such hearing. Adequate notice shall be provided to such parties at least ten days before the date of such hearing. The court may extend the time for the commencement of such hearing for a period not exceeding seven days where the circumstances of the case, and the interests of justice require such extension, or for additional periods of time to which the trustee and representative agree.
(2) The court shall rule on such application for rejection within thirty days after the date of the commencement of the hearing. In the interests of justice, the court may extend such time for ruling for such additional period as the trustee and the employees' representative may agree to. If the court does not rule on such application within thirty days after the date of the commencement of the hearing, or within such additional time as the trustee and the employees' representative may agree to, the trustee may terminate or alter any provisions of the collective bargaining agreement pending the ruling of the court on such application.
(3) The court may enter such protective orders, consistent with the need of the authorized representative of the employee to evaluate the trustee's proposal and the application for rejection, as may be necessary to prevent disclosure of information provided to such representative where such disclosure could compromise the position of the debtor with respect to its competitors in the industry in which it is engaged.
(e) If during a period when the collective bargaining agreement continues in effect, and if essential to the continuation of the debtor's business, or in order to avoid irreparable damage to the estate, the court, after notice and a hearing, may authorize the trustee to implement interim changes in the terms, conditions, wages, benefits, or work rules provided by a collective bargaining agreement. Any hearing under this paragraph shall be scheduled in accordance with the needs of the trustee. The implementation of such interim changes shall not render the application for rejection moot.
(f) No provision of this title shall be construed to permit a trustee to unilaterally terminate or alter any provisions of a collective bargaining agreement prior to compliance with the provisions of this section.
(Added Pub. L. 98–353, title III, §541(a), July 10, 1984, 98 Stat. 390.)
References in Text
The Railway Labor Act, referred to in subsec. (a), is act May 20, 1926, ch. 347, 44 Stat. 577, as amended. Title I of the Railway Labor Act is classified principally to subchapter I (§151 et seq.) of chapter 8 of Title 45, Railroads. For complete classification of this Act to the Code, see section 151 of Title 45 and Tables.
Effective Date
Pub. L. 98–353, title III, §541(c), July 10, 1984, 98 Stat. 391, provided that: "The amendments made by this section [enacting this section] shall become effective upon the date of enactment of this Act [July 10, 1984]; provided that this section shall not apply to cases filed under title 11 of the United States Code which were commenced prior to the date of enactment of this section."
§1114. Payment of insurance benefits to retired employees
(a) For purposes of this section, the term "retiree benefits" means payments to any entity or person for the purpose of providing or reimbursing payments for retired employees and their spouses and dependents, for medical, surgical, or hospital care benefits, or benefits in the event of sickness, accident, disability, or death under any plan, fund, or program (through the purchase of insurance or otherwise) maintained

or established in whole or in part by the debtor prior to filing a petition commencing a case under this title.

(b)(1) For purposes of this section, the term "authorized representative" means the authorized representative designated pursuant to subsection (c) for persons receiving any retiree benefits covered by a collective bargaining agreement or subsection (d) in the case of persons receiving retiree benefits not covered by such an agreement.

(2) Committees of retired employees appointed by the court pursuant to this section shall have the same rights, powers, and duties as committees appointed under sections 1102 and 1103 of this title for the purpose of carrying out the purposes of sections 1114 and 1129(a)(13) and, as permitted by the court, shall have the power to enforce the rights of persons under this title as they relate to retiree benefits.

(c)(1) A labor organization shall be, for purposes of this section, the authorized representative of those persons receiving any retiree benefits covered by any collective bargaining agreement to which that labor organization is signatory, unless (A) such labor organization elects not to serve as the authorized representative of such persons, or (B) the court, upon a motion by any party in interest, after notice and hearing, determines that different representation of such persons is appropriate.

(2) In cases where the labor organization referred to in paragraph (1) elects not to serve as the authorized representative of those persons receiving any retiree benefits covered by any collective bargaining agreement to which that labor organization is signatory, or in cases where the court, pursuant to paragraph (1) finds different representation of such persons appropriate, the court, upon a motion by any party in interest, and after notice and a hearing, shall appoint a committee of retired employees if the debtor seeks to modify or not pay the retiree benefits or if the court otherwise determines that it is appropriate, from among such persons, to serve as the authorized representative of such persons under this section.

(d) The court, upon a motion by any party in interest, and after notice and a hearing, shall order the appointment of a committee of retired employees if the debtor seeks to modify or not pay the retiree benefits or if the court otherwise determines that it is appropriate, to serve as the authorized representative, under this section, of those persons receiving any retiree benefits not covered by a collective bargaining agreement. The United States trustee shall appoint any such committee.

(e)(1) Notwithstanding any other provision of this title, the debtor in possession, or the trustee if one has been appointed under the provisions of this chapter (hereinafter in this section "trustee" shall include a debtor in possession), shall timely pay and shall not modify any retiree benefits, except that—

(A) the court, on motion of the trustee or authorized representative, and after notice and a hearing, may order modification of such payments, pursuant to the provisions of subsections (g) and (h) of this section, or

(B) the trustee and the authorized representative of the recipients of those benefits may agree to modification of such payments,

after which such benefits as modified shall continue to be paid by the trustee.

(2) Any payment for retiree benefits required to be made before a plan confirmed under section 1129 of this title is effective has the status of an allowed administrative expense as provided in section 503 of this title.

(f)(1) Subsequent to filing a petition and prior to filing an application seeking modification of the retiree benefits, the trustee shall—

(A) make a proposal to the authorized representative of the retirees, based on the most complete and reliable information available at the time of such proposal, which provides for those necessary modifications in the retiree benefits that are necessary to permit the reorganization of the debtor and assures that all creditors, the debtor and all of the affected parties are treated fairly and equitably; and

(B) provide, subject to subsection (k)(3), the representative of the retirees with such relevant information as is necessary to evaluate the proposal.

(2) During the period beginning on the date of the making of a proposal provided for in paragraph (1), and ending on the date of the hearing provided for in subsection (k)(1), the trustee shall meet, at reasonable times, with the authorized representative to confer in good faith in attempting to reach mutually satisfactory modifications of such retiree benefits.

(g) The court shall enter an order providing for modification in the payment of retiree benefits if the court finds that—

(1) the trustee has, prior to the hearing, made a proposal that fulfills the requirements of subsection (f);

(2) the authorized representative of the retirees has refused to accept such proposal without good cause; and

(3) such modification is necessary to permit the reorganization of the debtor and assures that all creditors, the debtor, and all of the affected parties are treated fairly and equitably, and is clearly favored by the balance of the equities;

except that in no case shall the court enter an order providing for such modification which provides for a modification to a level lower than that proposed by the trustee in the proposal found by the court to have complied with the requirements of this subsection and subsection (f): *Provided, however*, That at any time after an order is entered providing for modification in the payment of retiree benefits, or at any time after an agreement modifying such benefits is made between the trustee and the authorized representative of the recipients of such benefits, the authorized representative may apply to the court for an order increasing those benefits which order shall be granted if the increase in retiree benefits sought is consistent with the standard set forth in paragraph (3): *Provided further*, That neither the trustee nor the authorized representative is precluded from making more than one motion for a modification order governed by this subsection.

(h)(1) Prior to a court issuing a final order under subsection (g) of this section, if essential to the continuation of the debtor's business, or in order to avoid irreparable damage to the estate, the court, after notice and a hearing, may authorize the trustee to implement interim modifications in retiree benefits.

(2) Any hearing under this subsection shall be scheduled in accordance with the needs of the trustee.

(3) The implementation of such interim changes does not render the motion for modification moot.

(i) No retiree benefits paid between the filing of the petition and the time a plan confirmed under section 1129 of this title becomes effective shall be deducted or offset from the amounts allowed as claims for any benefits which remain unpaid, or from the amounts to be paid under the plan with respect to such claims for unpaid benefits, whether such claims for unpaid benefits are based upon or arise from a right to future unpaid benefits or from any benefits not paid as a result of modifications allowed pursuant to this section.

(j) No claim for retiree benefits shall be limited by section 502(b)(7) of this title.

(k)(1) Upon the filing of an application for modifying retiree benefits, the court shall schedule a hearing to be held not later than fourteen days after the date of the filing of such application. All interested parties may appear and be heard at such hearing. Adequate notice shall be provided to such parties at least ten days before the date of such hearing. The court may extend the time for the commencement of such hearing for a period not exceeding seven days where the circumstances of the case, and the interests of justice require such extension, or for additional periods of time to which the trustee and the authorized representative agree.

(2) The court shall rule on such application for modification within ninety days after the date of the commencement of the hearing. In the interests of justice, the court may extend such time for ruling for such additional period as the trustee and the authorized representative may agree to. If the court does not rule on such application within ninety days after the date of the commencement of the hearing, or within such additional time as the trustee and the authorized representative may agree to, the trustee may implement the proposed modifications pending the ruling of the court on such application.

(3) The court may enter such protective orders, consistent with the need of the authorized representative of the retirees to evaluate the trustee's proposal and the application for modification, as may be necessary to prevent disclosure of information provided to such representative where such disclosure could compromise the position of the debtor with respect to its competitors in the industry in which it is engaged.

(l) If the debtor, during the 180-day period ending on the date of the filing of the petition—

(1) modified retiree benefits; and

(2) was insolvent on the date such benefits were modified;

the court, on motion of a party in interest, and after notice and a hearing, shall issue an order reinstating as of the date the modification was made, such benefits as in effect immediately before such date unless the court finds that the balance of the equities clearly favors such modification.

(m) This section shall not apply to any retiree, or the spouse or dependents of such retiree, if such retiree's gross income for the twelve months preceding the filing of the bankruptcy petition equals or exceeds $250,000, unless such retiree can demonstrate to the satisfaction of the court that he is unable to obtain health, medical, life, and disability coverage for himself, his spouse, and his dependents who would otherwise be covered by the employer's insurance plan, comparable to the coverage provided by the employer on the day before the filing of a petition under this title.

(Added Pub. L. 100–334, §2(a), June 16, 1988, 102 Stat. 610; amended Pub. L. 109–8, title IV, §447, title XIV, §1403, Apr. 20, 2005, 119 Stat. 118, 215.)

Amendments

2005—Subsec. (d). Pub. L. 109–8, §447, substituted "order the appointment of" for "appoint" and inserted "The United States trustee shall appoint any such committee." at end.

Subsecs. (l), (m). Pub. L. 109–8, §1403, added subsec. (l) and redesignated former subsec. (l) as (m).

Effective Date of 2005 Amendment

Amendment by section 1403 of Pub. L. 109–8 effective Apr. 20, 2005, and applicable only with respect to cases commenced under this title on or after Apr. 20, 2005, see section 1406 of Pub. L. 109–8, set out as a note under section 507 of this title.

Amendment by section 447 of Pub. L. 109–8 effective 180 days after Apr. 20, 2005, and not applicable with respect to cases commenced under this title before such effective date, except as otherwise provided, see section 1501 of Pub. L. 109–8, set out as a note under section 101 of this title.

Effective Date

Pub. L. 100–334, §4, June 16, 1988, 102 Stat. 615, provided that:

"(a) General Effective Date.—Except as provided in subsection (b), this Act and the amendments made by this Act [enacting this section, amending section 1129 of this title, enacting provisions set out as a note under section 101 of this title, and amending and repealing provisions set out as notes under section 1106 of this title] shall take effect on the date of the enactment of this Act [June 16, 1988].

"(b) Application of Amendments.—The amendments made by section 2 [enacting this section and amending section 1129 of this title] shall not apply with respect to cases commenced under title 11 of the United States Code before the date of the enactment of this Act [June 16, 1988]."

Payment of Certain Benefits to Retired Former Employees

For payment of benefits by bankruptcy trustee to retired employees in enumerated circumstances with respect to cases commenced under this chapter in which a plan for reorganization had not been confirmed by the court and in which any such benefit was still being paid on October 2, 1986, and in cases that became subject to this chapter after October 2, 1986, and before June 16, 1988, see section 101(b) [title VI, §608] of Pub. L. 99–500, and Pub. L. 99–591, as amended, set out as a note under section 1106 of this title.

§1115. Property of the estate

(a) In a case in which the debtor is an individual, property of the estate includes, in addition to the property specified in section 541—

(1) all property of the kind specified in section 541 that the debtor acquires after the commencement of the case but before the case is closed, dismissed, or converted to a case under chapter 7, 12, or 13, whichever occurs first; and

(2) earnings from services performed by the debtor after the commencement of the case but before the case is closed, dismissed, or converted to a case under chapter 7, 12, or 13, whichever occurs first.

(b) Except as provided in section 1104 or a confirmed plan or order confirming a plan, the debtor shall remain in possession of all property of the estate.

(Added Pub. L. 109–8, title III, §321(a)(1), Apr. 20, 2005, 119 Stat. 94.)

Effective Date

Section effective 180 days after Apr. 20, 2005, and not applicable with respect to cases commenced under this title before such effective date, except as otherwise provided, see section 1501 of Pub. L. 109–8, set out as an Effective Date of 2005 Amendment note under section 101 of this title.

§1116. Duties of trustee or debtor in possession in small business cases

In a small business case, a trustee or the debtor in possession, in addition to the duties provided in this title and as otherwise required by law, shall—

(1) append to the voluntary petition or, in an involuntary case, file not later than 7 days after the date of the order for relief—

(A) its most recent balance sheet, statement of operations, cash-flow statement, and Federal income tax return; or

(B) a statement made under penalty of perjury that no balance sheet, statement of operations, or cash-flow statement has been prepared and no Federal tax return has been filed;

(2) attend, through its senior management personnel and counsel, meetings scheduled by the court or the United States trustee, including initial debtor interviews, scheduling conferences, and meetings of creditors convened under section 341 unless the court, after notice and a hearing, waives that requirement upon a finding of extraordinary and compelling circumstances;

(3) timely file all schedules and statements of financial affairs, unless the court, after notice and a hearing, grants an extension, which shall not extend such time period to a date later than 30 days after the date of the order for relief, absent extraordinary and compelling circumstances;

(4) file all postpetition financial and other reports required by the Federal Rules of Bankruptcy Procedure or by local rule of the district court;

(5) subject to section 363(c)(2), maintain insurance customary and appropriate to the industry;

(6)(A) timely file tax returns and other required government filings; and

(B) subject to section 363(c)(2), timely pay all taxes entitled to administrative expense priority except those being contested by appropriate proceedings being diligently prosecuted; and

(7) allow the United States trustee, or a designated representative of the United States trustee, to inspect the debtor's business premises, books, and records at

reasonable times, after reasonable prior written notice, unless notice is waived by the debtor.

(Added Pub. L. 109–8, title IV, §436(a), Apr. 20, 2005, 119 Stat. 112.)

References in Text

The Federal Rules of Bankruptcy Procedure, referred to in par. (4), are set out in the Appendix to this title.

Effective Date

Section effective 180 days after Apr. 20, 2005, and not applicable with respect to cases commenced under this title before such effective date, except as otherwise provided, see section 1501 of Pub. L. 109–8, set out as an Effective Date of 2005 Amendment note under section 101 of this title.

SUBCHAPTER II—THE PLAN

§1121. Who may file a plan

(a) The debtor may file a plan with a petition commencing a voluntary case, or at any time in a voluntary case or an involuntary case.

(b) Except as otherwise provided in this section, only the debtor may file a plan until after 120 days after the date of the order for relief under this chapter.

(c) Any party in interest, including the debtor, the trustee, a creditors' committee, an equity security holders' committee, a creditor, an equity security holder, or any indenture trustee, may file a plan if and only if—

(1) a trustee has been appointed under this chapter;

(2) the debtor has not filed a plan before 120 days after the date of the order for relief under this chapter; or

(3) the debtor has not filed a plan that has been accepted, before 180 days after the date of the order for relief under this chapter, by each class of claims or interests that is impaired under the plan.

(d)(1) Subject to paragraph (2), on request of a party in interest made within the respective periods specified in subsections (b) and (c) of this section and after notice and a hearing, the court may for cause reduce or increase the 120-day period or the 180-day period referred to in this section.

(2)(A) The 120-day period specified in paragraph (1) may not be extended beyond a date that is 18 months after the date of the order for relief under this chapter.

(B) The 180-day period specified in paragraph (1) may not be extended beyond a date that is 20 months after the date of the order for relief under this chapter.

(e) In a small business case—

(1) only the debtor may file a plan until after 180 days after the date of the order for relief, unless that period is—

(A) extended as provided by this subsection, after notice and a hearing; or

(B) the court, for cause, orders otherwise;

(2) the plan and a disclosure statement (if any) shall be filed not later than 300 days after the date of the order for relief; and

(3) the time periods specified in paragraphs (1) and (2), and the time fixed in section 1129(e) within which the plan shall be confirmed, may be extended only if—

(A) the debtor, after providing notice to parties in interest (including the United States trustee), demonstrates by a preponderance of the evidence that it is more likely than not that the court will confirm a plan within a reasonable period of time;

(B) a new deadline is imposed at the time the extension is granted; and

(C) the order extending time is signed before the existing deadline has expired.

(Pub. L. 95–598, Nov. 6, 1978, 92 Stat. 2631; Pub. L. 98–353, title III, §506, July 10, 1984, 98 Stat. 385; Pub. L. 99–554, title II, §283(u), Oct. 27, 1986, 100 Stat. 3118; Pub. L. 103–394, title II, §217(d), Oct. 22, 1994, 108 Stat. 4127; Pub. L. 109–8, title IV, §§411, 437, Apr. 20, 2005, 119 Stat. 106, 113.)

Historical and Revision Notes

legislative statements

Section 1121 of the House amendment is derived from section 1121 of the House bill; section 1121(c)(1) will be satisfied automatically in a case under subchapter IV of title 11.

senate report no. 95–989

Subsection (a) permits the debtor to file a reorganization plan with a petition commencing a voluntary case or at any time during a voluntary or involuntary case.

Subsection (b) gives the debtor the exclusive right to file a plan during the first 120 days of the case. There are exceptions, however, enumerated in subsection (c). If a trustee has been appointed, if the debtor does not meet the 120-day deadline, or if the debtor fails to obtain the required consent within 180 days after the filing of the petition, any party in interest may propose a plan. This includes the debtor, the trustee, a creditors' committee, an equity security holders' committee, a creditor, an equity security holder, and an indenture trustee. The list is not exhaustive. In the case of a public company, a trustee is appointed within 10 days of the petition. In such a case, for all practical purposes, any party in interest may file a plan.

Subsection (d) permits the court, for cause, to increase or reduce the 120-day and 180-day periods specified. Since, the debtor has an exclusive privilege for 6 months during which others may not file a plan, the granted extension should be based on a showing of some promise of probable success. An extension should not be employed as a tactical device to put pressure on parties in interest to yield to a plan they consider unsatisfactory.

Amendments

2005—Subsec. (d). Pub. L. 109–8, §411, designated existing provisions as par. (1), substituted "Subject to paragraph (2), on" for "On", and added par. (2).

Subsec. (e). Pub. L. 109–8, §437, added subsec. (e) and struck out former subsec. (e) which read as follows: "In a case in which the debtor is a small business and elects to be considered a small business—

"(1) only the debtor may file a plan until after 100 days after the date of the order for relief under this chapter;

"(2) all plans shall be filed within 160 days after the date of the order for relief; and

"(3) on request of a party in interest made within the respective periods specified in paragraphs (1) and (2) and after notice and a hearing, the court may—

"(A) reduce the 100-day period or the 160-day period specified in paragraph (1) or (2) for cause; and

"(B) increase the 100-day period specified in paragraph (1) if the debtor shows that the need for an increase is caused by circumstances for which the debtor should not be held accountable."

1994—Subsec. (e). Pub. L. 103–394 added subsec. (e).

1986—Subsec. (d). Pub. L. 99–554 inserted reference to subsection (b) of this section.

1984—Subsec. (c)(3). Pub. L. 98–353, §506(a), substituted "of claims or interests that is" for "the claims or interests of which are".

Subsec. (d). Pub. L. 98–353, §506(b), inserted "made within the respective periods specified in subsection (c) of this section".

Effective Date of 2005 Amendment

Amendment by Pub. L. 109–8 effective 180 days after Apr. 20, 2005, and not applicable with respect to cases commenced under this title before such effective date, except as otherwise provided, see section 1501 of Pub. L. 109–8, set out as a note under section 101 of this title.

Effective Date of 1994 Amendment

Amendment by Pub. L. 103–394 effective Oct. 22, 1994, and not applicable with respect to cases commenced under this title before Oct. 22, 1994, see section 702 of Pub. L. 103–394, set out as a note under section 101 of this title.

Effective Date of 1986 Amendment

Amendment by Pub. L. 99–554 effective 30 days after Oct. 27, 1986, see section 302(a) of Pub. L. 99–554, set out as a note under section 581 of Title 28, Judiciary and Judicial Procedure.

Effective Date of 1984 Amendment

Amendment by Pub. L. 98–353 effective with respect to cases filed 90 days after July 10, 1984, see section 552(a) of Pub. L. 98–353, set out as a note under section 101 of this title.

§1122. Classification of claims or interests

(a) Except as provided in subsection (b) of this section, a plan may place a claim or an interest in a particular class only if such claim or interest is substantially similar to the other claims or interests of such class.

(b) A plan may designate a separate class of claims consisting only of every unsecured claim that is less than or reduced to an amount that the court approves as reasonable and necessary for administrative convenience.

(Pub. L. 95–598, Nov. 6, 1978, 92 Stat. 2631.)

Historical and Revision Notes

senate report no. 95–989

This section codifies current case law surrounding the classification of claims and equity securities. It requires classification based on the nature of the claims or interests classified, and permits inclusion of claims or interests in a particular class only if the claim or interest being included is substantially similar to the other claims or interests of the class.

Subsection (b), also a codification of existing practice, contains an exception. The plan may designate a separate class of claims consisting only of every unsecured claim that is less than or reduced to an amount that the court approves as reasonable and necessary for administrative convenience.

§1123. Contents of plan

(a) Notwithstanding any otherwise applicable nonbankruptcy law, a plan shall—

(1) designate, subject to section 1122 of this title, classes of claims, other than claims of a kind specified in section 507(a)(2), 507(a)(3), or 507(a)(8) of this title, and classes of interests;

(2) specify any class of claims or interests that is not impaired under the plan;

(3) specify the treatment of any class of claims or interests that is impaired under the plan;

(4) provide the same treatment for each claim or interest of a particular class, unless the holder of a particular claim or interest agrees to a less favorable treatment of such particular claim or interest;

(5) provide adequate means for the plan's implementation, such as—

(A) retention by the debtor of all or any part of the property of the estate;

(B) transfer of all or any part of the property of the estate to one or more entities, whether organized before or after the confirmation of such plan;

(C) merger or consolidation of the debtor with one or more persons;

(D) sale of all or any part of the property of the estate, either subject to or free of any lien, or the distribution of all or any part of the property of the estate among those having an interest in such property of the estate;

(E) satisfaction or modification of any lien;

(F) cancellation or modification of any indenture or similar instrument;

(G) curing or waiving of any default;

(H) extension of a maturity date or a change in an interest rate or other term of outstanding securities;

(I) amendment of the debtor's charter; or

(J) issuance of securities of the debtor, or of any entity referred to in subparagraph (B) or (C) of this paragraph, for cash, for property, for existing securities, or in exchange for claims or interests, or for any other appropriate purpose;

(6) provide for the inclusion in the charter of the debtor, if the debtor is a corporation, or of any corporation referred to in paragraph (5)(B) or (5)(C) of this subsection, of a provision prohibiting the issuance of nonvoting equity securities, and providing, as to the several classes of securities possessing voting power, an appropriate distribution of such power among such classes, including, in the case of any class of equity securities having a preference over another class of equity securities with respect to dividends, adequate provisions for the election of directors representing such preferred class in the event of default in the payment of such dividends;

(7) contain only provisions that are consistent with the interests of creditors and equity security holders and with public policy with respect to the manner of selection of any officer, director, or trustee under the plan and any successor to such officer, director, or trustee; and

(8) in a case in which the debtor is an individual, provide for the payment to creditors under the plan of all or such portion of earnings from personal services performed by the debtor after the commencement of the case or other future income of the debtor as is necessary for the execution of the plan.

(b) Subject to subsection (a) of this section, a plan may—

(1) impair or leave unimpaired any class of claims, secured or unsecured, or of interests;

(2) subject to section 365 of this title, provide for the assumption, rejection, or assignment of any executory contract or unexpired lease of the debtor not previously rejected under such section;

(3) provide for—

(A) the settlement or adjustment of any claim or interest belonging to the debtor or to the estate; or

(B) the retention and enforcement by the debtor, by the trustee, or by a representative of the estate appointed for such purpose, of any such claim or interest;

(4) provide for the sale of all or substantially all of the property of the estate, and the distribution of the proceeds of such sale among holders of claims or interests;

(5) modify the rights of holders of secured claims, other than a claim secured only by a security interest in real property that is the debtor's principal residence, or of holders of unsecured claims, or leave unaffected the rights of holders of any class of claims; and

(6) include any other appropriate provision not inconsistent with the applicable provisions of this title.

(c) In a case concerning an individual, a plan proposed by an entity other than the debtor may not provide for the use, sale, or lease of property exempted under section 522 of this title, unless the debtor consents to such use, sale, or lease.

(d) Notwithstanding subsection (a) of this section and sections 506(b), 1129(a)(7), and 1129(b) of this title, if it is proposed in a plan to cure a default the amount necessary to cure the default shall be determined in accordance with the underlying agreement and applicable nonbankruptcy law.

(Pub. L. 95–598, Nov. 6, 1978, 92 Stat. 2631; Pub. L. 98–353, title III, §507, July 10, 1984, 98 Stat. 385; Pub. L. 103–394, title II, §206, title III, §§304(h)(6), 305(a), title V, §501(d)(31), Oct. 22, 1994, 108 Stat. 4123, 4134, 4146; Pub. L. 109–8, title III, §321(b), title XV, §1502(a)(7), Apr. 20, 2005, 119 Stat. 95, 216.)

Historical and Revision Notes
legislative statements

Section 1123 of the House amendment represents a compromise between similar provisions in the House bill and Senate amendment. The section has been clarified to clearly indicate that both secured and unsecured claims, or either of them, may be impaired in a case under title 11. In addition assumption or rejection of an executory contract under a plan must comply with section 365 of title 11. Moreover, section 1123(a)(1) has been substantively modified to permit classification of certain kinds of priority claims. This is important for purposes of confirmation under section 1129(a)(9).

Section 1123(a)(5) of the House amendment is derived from a similar provision in the House bill and Senate amendment but deletes the language pertaining to "fair upset price" as an unnecessary restriction. Section 1123 is also intended to indicate that a plan may provide for any action specified in section 1123 in the case of a corporation without a resolution of the board of directors. If the plan is confirmed, then any action proposed in the plan may be taken notwithstanding any otherwise applicable nonbankruptcy law in accordance with section 1142(a) of title 11.

senate report no. 95–989

Subsection (a) specifies what a plan of reorganization must contain. The plan must designate classes of claims and interests, and specify, by class, the claims or interests that are unimpaired under the plan. Priority claims are not required to be classified because they may not have arisen when the plan is filed. The plan must provide the same treatment for each claim or interest of a particular class, unless the holder of a particular claim or interest agrees to a different, but not better, treatment of his claim or interest.

Paragraph (3) applies to claims, not creditors. Thus, if a creditor is undersecured, and thus has a secured claim and an unsecured claim, this paragraph will be applied independently to each of his claims.

Paragraph (4) of subsection (a) is derived from section 216 of chapter X [section 616 of former title 11] with some modifications. It requires the plan to provide adequate means for the plans execution. These means may include retention by the debtor of all or any part of the property of the estate, transfer of all or any part of the property of the estate to one or more entities, whether organized pre- or postconfirmation, merger or consolidation of the debtor with one or more persons, sale and distribution of all or any part of the property of the estate, satisfaction or modification of any lien, cancellation or modification of any indenture or similar instrument, curing or waiving of any default, extension of maturity dates or change in interest rates of securities, amendment of the debtor's charter, and issuance of securities.

Subparagraph (C), as it applies in railroad cases, has the effect of overruling St. Joe Paper Co. v. Atlantic Coast Line R. R., 347 U.S. 298 (1954). It will allow the trustee or creditors to propose a plan of merger with another railroad without the consent of the debtor, and the debtor will be bound under proposed 11 U.S.C. 1141(a). See Hearings, pt. 3, at 1616. "Similar instrument" referred to in subparagraph (F) might include a deposit with an agent for distribution, other than an indenture trustee, such as an agent under an agreement in a railroad conditional sale or lease financing agreement.

Paragraphs (5) and (6) and subsection (b) are derived substantially from Section 216 of Chapter X ([former] 11 U.S.C. 616). Paragraph (5) requires the plan to prohibit the issuance of nonvoting equity securities, and to provide for an appropriate distribution of voting power among the various classes of equity securities. Paragraph (6) requires that the plan contain only provisions that are consistent with the interests of creditors and equity security holders, and with public policy with respect to the selection of officers, directors, and trustees, and their successors.

Subsection (b) specifies the matters that the plan may propose. The plan may impair or leave unimpaired any claim or interest. The plan may provide for the assumption or rejection of executory contracts or unexpired leases not previously rejected under section 365. The plan may also provide for the treatment of claims by the debtor against other entities that are not settled before the confirmation of the plan. The plan may propose settlement or adjustment of any claim or equity security belonging to the estate, or may propose retention and enforcement of such claim or interest by the debtor or by an agent appointed for that purpose.

The plan may also propose the sale of all or substantially all of the property of the estate, and the distribution of the proceeds of the sale among creditors and equity security holders. This would be a liquidating plan. The subsection permits the plan to include any other appropriate provision not inconsistent with the applicable provisions of the bankruptcy code.

Subsection (c) protects an individual debtor's exempt property by prohibiting its use, sale, or lease under a plan proposed by someone other than the debtor, unless the debtor consents.

Amendments

2005—Subsec. (a)(1). Pub. L. 109–8, §1502(a)(7), substituted "507(a)(2), 507(a)(3)" for "507(a)(1), 507(a)(2)".

Subsec. (a)(8). Pub. L. 109–8, §321(b), added par. (8).

1994—Subsec. (a)(1). Pub. L. 103–394, §§304(h)(6), 501(d)(31), substituted "507(a)(8) of this title," for "507(a)(7) of this title".

Subsec. (b)(5), (6). Pub. L. 103–394, §206, added par. (5) and redesignated former par. (5) as (6).

Subsec. (d). Pub. L. 103–394, §305(a), added subsec. (d).

1984—Subsec. (a). Pub. L. 98–353, §507(a)(1), in provisions preceding par. (1) substituted "Notwithstanding any otherwise applicable nonbankruptcy law, a" for "A".

Subsec. (a)(1). Pub. L. 98–353, §507(a)(2), inserted a comma after "classes of claims" and substituted "507(a)(7) of this title," for "507(a)(6) of this title".

Subsec. (a)(3). Pub. L. 98–353, §507(a)(3), struck out "shall" before "specify the treatment".

Subsec. (a)(5). Pub. L. 98–353, §507(a)(4), substituted "implementation" for "execution".

Subsec. (a)(5)(G). Pub. L. 98–353, §507(a)(5), inserted "of" after "waiving".

Subsec. (b)(2). Pub. L. 98–353, §507(b), substituted "rejection, or assignment" for "or rejection", and "under such section" for "under section 365 of this title".

Effective Date of 2005 Amendment

Amendment by Pub. L. 109–8 effective 180 days after Apr. 20, 2005, and not applicable with respect to cases commenced under this title before such effective date, except as otherwise provided, see section 1501 of Pub. L. 109–8, set out as a note under section 101 of this title.

Effective Date of 1994 Amendment

Amendment by sections 206, 304(h)(6), and 501(d)(31) of Pub. L. 103–394 effective Oct. 22, 1994, and not applicable with respect to cases commenced under this title before Oct. 22, 1994, and amendment by section 305(a) of Pub. L. 103–394 effective Oct. 22, 1994, and applicable only to agreements entered into after Oct. 22, 1994, see section 702 of Pub. L. 103–394, set out as a note under section 101 of this title.

Effective Date of 1984 Amendment

Amendment by Pub. L. 98–353 effective with respect to cases filed 90 days after July 10, 1984, see section 552(a) of Pub. L. 98–353, set out as a note under section 101 of this title.

§1124. Impairment of claims or interests

Except as provided in section 1123(a)(4) of this title, a class of claims or interests is impaired under a plan unless, with respect to each claim or interest of such class, the plan—

(1) leaves unaltered the legal, equitable, and contractual rights to which such claim or interest entitles the holder of such claim or interest; or

(2) notwithstanding any contractual provision or applicable law that entitles the holder of such claim or interest to demand or receive accelerated payment of such claim or interest after the occurrence of a default—

(A) cures any such default that occurred before or after the commencement of the case under this title, other than a default of a kind specified in section 365(b)(2) of this title or of a kind that section 365(b)(2) expressly does not require to be cured;

(B) reinstates the maturity of such claim or interest as such maturity existed before such default;

(C) compensates the holder of such claim or interest for any damages incurred as a result of any reasonable reliance by such holder on such contractual provision or such applicable law;

(D) if such claim or such interest arises from any failure to perform a nonmonetary obligation, other than a default arising from failure to operate a nonresidential real property lease subject to section 365(b)(1)(A), compensates the holder of such claim or such interest (other than the debtor or an insider) for any actual pecuniary loss incurred by such holder as a result of such failure; and

(E) does not otherwise alter the legal, equitable, or contractual rights to which such claim or interest entitles the holder of such claim or interest.

(Pub. L. 95–598, Nov. 6, 1978, 92 Stat. 2633; Pub. L. 98–353, title III, §508, July 10, 1984, 98 Stat. 385; Pub. L. 103–394, title II, §213(d), Oct. 22, 1994, 108 Stat. 4126; Pub. L. 109–8, title III, §328(b), Apr. 20, 2005, 119 Stat. 100.)

Historical and Revision Notes
legislative statements

Section 1124 of the House amendment is derived from a similar provision in the House bill and Senate amendment. The section defines the new concept of "impairment" of claims or interests; the concept differs significantly from the concept of "materially and adversely affected" under the Bankruptcy Act [former title 11]. Section 1124(3) of the House amendment provides that a holder of a claim or interest is not impaired, if the plan provides that the holder will receive the allowed amount of the holder's claim, or in the case of an interest with a fixed liquidation preference or redemption price, the greater of such price. This adopts the position contained in the House bill and rejects the contrary standard contained in the Senate amendment.

Section 1124(3) of the House amendment rejects a provision contained in section 1124(3)(B)(iii) of the House bill which would have considered a class of interest not to be impaired by virtue of the fact that the plan provided cash or property for the value of the holder's interest in the debtor.

The effect of the House amendment is to permit an interest not to be impaired only if the interest has a fixed liquidation preference or redemption price. Therefore, a class of interests such as common stock, must either accept a plan under section 1129(a)(8), or the plan must satisfy the requirements of section 1129(b)(2)(C) in order for a plan to be confirmed.

A compromise reflected in section 1124(2)(C) of the House amendment indicates that a class of claims is not impaired under the circumstances of section 1124(2) if damages are paid to rectify reasonable reliance engaged in by the holder of a claim or interest arising from the prepetition breach of a contractual provision, such as an ipso facto or bankruptcy clause, or law. Where the rights of third parties are concerned, such as in the case of lease premises which have been rerented to a third party, it is not intended that there will be adequate damages to compensate the third party.

senate report no. 95–989

The basic concept underlying this section is not new. It rests essentially on Section 107 of Chapter X ([former] 11 U.S.C. 507), which states that creditors or stockholders or any class thereof "shall be deemed to be 'affected' by a plan only if their or its interest shall be materially and adversely affected thereby."

This section is designated to indicate when contractual rights of creditors or interest holders are not materially affected. It specifies three ways in which the plan may leave a claim or interest unimpaired.

First, the plan may propose not to alter the legal, equitable, or contractual rights to which the claim or interest entitled its holder.

Second, a claim or interest is unimpaired by curing the effect of a default and reinstating the original terms of an obligation when maturity was brought on or accelerated by the default. The intervention of bankruptcy and the defaults represent a temporary crisis which the plan of reorganization is intended to clear away. The holder of a claim or interest who under the plan is restored to his original position, when others receive less or get nothing at all, is fortunate indeed and has no cause to complain. Curing of the default and the assumption of the debt in accordance with its terms is an important reorganization technique for dealing with a particular class of claims, especially secured claims.

Third, a claim or interest is unimpaired if the plan provides for their payment in cash. In the case of a debt liability, the cash payment is for the allowed amount of the claim, which does not include a redemption premium. If it is an equity security with a fixed liquidation preference, such as a preferred stock, the allowed amount is such liquidation preference, with no redemption premium. With respect to any other equity security, such as a common stock, cash payment must be equal to the "value of such holder's interest in the debtor."

Section 1124 does not include payment "in property" other than cash. Except for a rare case, claims or interests are not by their terms payable in property, but a plan may so provide and those affected thereby may accept or reject the proposed plan. They may not be forced to accept a plan declaring the holders' claims or interests to be "unimpaired."

house report no. 95–595

This section is new. It is designed to indicate when contractual rights of creditors or interest holders are not materially affected. The section specifies three ways in which the plan may leave a claim or interest unimpaired.

First, the plan may propose not to alter the legal, equitable, or contractual rights to which the claim or interest entitled its holder.

Second, the plan is permitted to reinstate a claim or interest and thus leave it unimpaired. Reinstatement consists of curing any default (other than a default under an ipso facto or bankruptcy clause) and reinstatement of the maturity of the claim or interest. Further, the plan may not otherwise alter any legal, equitable, or contractual right to which the claim or interest entitles its holder.

Third, the plan may leave a claim or interest unimpaired by paying its amount in full other than in securities of the debtor, an affiliate of the debtor participating in a joint plan, or a successor to the debtor. These securities are excluded because determination of their value would require a valuation of the business being reorganized. Use of them to pay a creditor or equity security holder without his consent may be done only under section 1129(b) and only after a valuation of the debtor. Under this paragraph, the plan must pay the allowed amount of the claim in full, in cash or other property, or, in the case of an equity security, must pay the greatest of any fixed liquidation preference to which the terms of the equity security entitle its holder, any fixed price at which the debtor, under the terms of the equity security may redeem such equity security, and the value, as of the effective date of the plan, of the holder's interest in the debtor. The value of the holder's interest need not be determined precisely by valuing the debtor's business if such value is clearly below redemption or liquidation preference values. If such value would require a full-scale valuation of the business, then such interest should be treated as impaired. But, if the debtor corporation is clearly insolvent, then the value of the common stock holder's interest in the debtor is zero, and offering them nothing under the plan of reorganization will not impair their rights.

"Value, as of the effective date of the plan," as used in paragraph (3) and in proposed 11 U.S.C. 1179(a)(7)(B), 1129(a)(9), 1129(b), 1172(2), 1325(a)(4), 1325(a)(5)(B), and 1328(b), indicates that the promised payment under the plan must be discounted to present value as of the effective date of the plan. The discounting should be based only on the unpaid balance of the amount due under the plan, until that amount, including interest, is paid in full.

Amendments

2005—Par. (2)(A). Pub. L. 109–8, §328(b)(1), inserted "or of a kind that section 365(b)(2) expressly does not require to be cured" before semicolon at end.

Par. (2)(D), (E). Pub. L. 109–8, §328(b)(2)–(4), added subpar. (D) and redesignated former subpar. (D) as (E).

1994—Par. (3). Pub. L. 103–394 struck out par. (3) which read as follows: "provides that, on the effective date of the plan, the holder of such claim or interest receives, on account of such claim or interest, cash equal to—

"(A) with respect to a claim, the allowed amount of such claim; or

"(B) with respect to an interest, if applicable, the greater of—

"(i) any fixed liquidation preference to which the terms of any security representing such interest entitle the holder of such interest; or

"(ii) any fixed price at which the debtor, under the terms of such security, may redeem such security from such holder."

1984—Par. (2)(A). Pub. L. 98–353, §508(1), amended subpar. (A) generally. Prior to amendment, subpar. (A) read as follows: "cures any such default, other than a default of a kind specified in section 365(b)(2) of this title, that occurred before or after the commencement of the case under this title;".

Par. (3)(B)(i). Pub. L. 98–353, §508(2), substituted "or" for "and".

Effective Date of 2005 Amendment

Amendment by Pub. L. 109–8 effective 180 days after Apr. 20, 2005, and not applicable with respect to cases commenced under this title before such effective date, except as otherwise provided, see section 1501 of Pub. L. 109–8, set out as a note under section 101 of this title.

Effective Date of 1994 Amendment

Amendment by Pub. L. 103–394 effective Oct. 22, 1994, and not applicable with respect to cases commenced under this title before Oct. 22, 1994, see section 702 of Pub. L. 103–394, set out as a note under section 101 of this title.

Effective Date of 1984 Amendment

Amendment by Pub. L. 98–353 effective with respect to cases filed 90 days after July 10, 1984, see section 552(a) of Pub. L. 98–353, set out as a note under section 101 of this title.

§1125. Postpetition disclosure and solicitation

(a) In this section—

(1) "adequate information" means information of a kind, and in sufficient detail, as far as is reasonably practicable in light of the nature and history of the debtor and the condition of the debtor's books and records, including a discussion of the potential material Federal tax consequences of the plan to the debtor, any successor to the debtor, and a hypothetical investor typical of the holders of claims or interests in the case, that would enable such a hypothetical investor of the relevant class to make an informed judgment about the plan, but adequate information need not include such information about any other possible or proposed plan and in determining whether a disclosure statement provides adequate information, the court shall consider the complexity of the case, the benefit of additional information to creditors and other parties in interest, and the cost of providing additional information; and

(2) "investor typical of holders of claims or interests of the relevant class" means investor having—

(A) a claim or interest of the relevant class;

(B) such a relationship with the debtor as the holders of other claims or interests of such class generally have; and

(C) such ability to obtain such information from sources other than the disclosure required by this section as holders of claims or interests in such class generally have.

(b) An acceptance or rejection of a plan may not be solicited after the commencement of the case under this title from a holder of a claim or interest with respect to such claim or interest, unless, at the time of or before such solicitation, there is transmitted to such holder the plan or a summary of the plan, and a written disclosure statement approved, after notice and a hearing, by the court as containing adequate information. The court may approve a disclosure statement without a valuation of the debtor or an appraisal of the debtor's assets.

(c) The same disclosure statement shall be transmitted to each holder of a claim or interest of a particular class, but there may be transmitted different disclosure statements, differing in amount, detail, or kind of information, as between classes.

(d) Whether a disclosure statement required under subsection (b) of this section contains adequate information is not governed by any otherwise applicable nonbankruptcy law, rule, or regulation, but an agency or official whose duty is to administer or enforce such a law, rule, or regulation may be heard on the issue of whether a disclosure statement contains adequate information. Such an agency or official may not appeal from, or otherwise seek review of, an order approving a disclosure statement.

(e) A person that solicits acceptance or rejection of a plan, in good faith and in compliance with the applicable provisions of this title, or that participates, in good faith and in compliance with the applicable provisions of this title, in the offer, issuance, sale, or purchase of a security, offered or sold under the plan, of the debtor, of an affiliate participating in a joint plan with the debtor, or of a newly organized successor to the debtor under the plan, is not liable, on account of such solicitation or participation, for violation of any applicable law, rule, or regulation governing solicitation of acceptance or rejection of a plan or the offer, issuance, sale, or purchase of securities.

(f) Notwithstanding subsection (b), in a small business case—

(1) the court may determine that the plan itself provides adequate information and that a separate disclosure statement is not necessary;

(2) the court may approve a disclosure statement submitted on standard forms approved by the court or adopted under section 2075 of title 28; and

(3)(A) the court may conditionally approve a disclosure statement subject to final approval after notice and a hearing;

(B) acceptances and rejections of a plan may be solicited based on a conditionally approved disclosure statement if the debtor provides adequate information to each holder of a claim or interest that is solicited, but a conditionally approved disclosure statement shall be mailed not later than 25 days before the date of the hearing on confirmation of the plan; and

(C) the hearing on the disclosure statement may be combined with the hearing on confirmation of a plan.

(g) Notwithstanding subsection (b), an acceptance or rejection of the plan may be solicited from a holder of a claim or interest if such solicitation complies with applicable nonbankruptcy law and if such holder was solicited before the commencement of the case in a manner complying with applicable nonbankruptcy law.

(Pub. L. 95–598, Nov. 6, 1978, 92 Stat. 2633; Pub. L. 98–353, title III, §509, July 10, 1984, 98 Stat. 385; Pub. L. 103–394, title II, §217(e), Oct. 22, 1994, 108 Stat. 4127; Pub. L. 109–8, title IV, §§408, 431, title VII, §717, Apr. 20, 2005, 119 Stat. 106, 109, 131.)

Historical and Revision Notes

legislative statements

Section 1125 of the House amendment is derived from section 1125 of the House bill and Senate amendment except with respect to section 1125(f) of the Senate amendment. It will not be necessary for the court to consider the report of the examiner prior to approval of a disclosure statement. The investigation of the examiner is to proceed on an independent basis from the procedure of the reorganization under chapter 11. In order to ensure that the examiner's report will be expeditious and fair, the examiner is precluded from serving as a trustee in the case or from representing a trustee if a trustee is appointed, whether the case remains in chapter 11 or is converted to chapter 7 or 13.

senate report no. 95–989

This section extends disclosure requirements in connection with solicitations to all cases under chapter 11. Heretofore this subject was dealt with by the Bankruptcy Act [former title 11] mainly in the special contexts of railroad reorganizations and chapter X [chapter 10 of former title 11] cases.

Subsection (a) defines (1) the subject matter of disclosure as "adequate information" and relates the standard of adequacy to an (2) "investor typical of holders or claims or interests of the relevant class." "Investor" is used broadly here, for it will almost always include a trade creditor or other creditors who originally had no investment intent or interest. It refers to the investment-type decision by those called upon to accept a plan to modify their claims or interests, which typically will involve acceptance of new securities or of a cash payment in lieu thereof.

Both the kind and form of information are left essentially to the judicial discretion of the court, guided by the specification in subparagraph (a)(1) that it be of a kind and in sufficient detail that a reasonable and typical investor can make an informed judgment about the plan. The information required will necessarily be governed by the circumstances of the case.

Reporting and audit standards devised for solvent and continuing businesses do not necessarily fit a debtor in reorganization. Subsection (a)(1) expressly incorporates consideration of the nature and history of the debtor and the condition of its books and records into the determination of what is reasonably practicable to supply. These factors are particularly pertinent to historical data and to discontinued operations of no future relevance.

A plan is necessarily predicated on knowledge of the assets and liabilities being dealt with and on factually supported expectations as to the future course of the business sufficient to meet the feasibility standard in section 1130(a)(11) of this title. It may thus be necessary to provide estimates or judgments for that purpose. Yet it remains practicable to describe, in such detail as may be relevant and needed, the basis for the plan and the data on which supporters of the plan rely.

Subsection (b) establishes the jurisdiction of the court over this subject by prohibiting solicitation of acceptance or rejection of a plan after the commencement of the case, unless the person solicited receives, before or at the time of the solicitation, a written disclosure statement approved by the court, after notice and hearing, as containing adequate information. As under present law, determinations of value, by appraisal or otherwise, are not required if not needed to accomplish the purpose specified in subsection (a)(1).

Subsection (c) requires that the same disclosure statement be transmitted to each member of a class. It recognizes that the information needed for an informed judgment about the plan may differ among classes. A class whose rights under the plan center on a particular fund or asset would have no use for an extensive description of other matters that could not affect them.

Subsection (d) relieves the court of the need to follow any otherwise applicable Federal or state law in determining the adequacy of the information contained in the disclosure statement submitted for its approval. It authorizes an agency or official, Federal or state, charged with administering cognate laws so preempted to advise the court on the adequacy of proposed disclosure statement. But they are not authorized to appeal the court's decision.

Solicitations with respect to a plan do not involve just mere requests for opinions. Acceptance of the plan vitally affects creditors and shareholders, and most frequently the solicitation involves an offering of securities in exchange for claims or interests. The present bankruptcy statute [former title 11] has exempted such offerings under each of its chapters from the registration and disclosure requirements of the Securities Act of 1933 [15 U.S.C. 77a et seq.], an exemption also continued by section 1145(a)(2) of this title. The extension of the disclosure requirements to all chapter 11 cases justifies the coordinate extension of these exemptions. By the same token, no valid purpose is served not to exempt from the requirements of similar state laws in a matter under the exclusive jurisdiction of the Federal bankruptcy laws.

Subsection (e) exonerates any person who, in good faith and in compliance with this title, solicits or participates in the offer, issuance, sale or purchase, under the plan, of a security from any liability, on account of such solicitation or participation, for violation of any law, rule, or regulation governing the offer, issuance, sale, or purchase of securities. This exoneration is coordinate with the exemption from Federal or State registration or licensing requirements provided by section 1145 of this title.

In the nonpublic case, the court, when approving the disclosure statement, has before it the texts of the plan, a proposed disclosure document, and such other information the plan proponents and other interested parties may present at the hearing. In the final analysis the exoneration which subsection (e) grants must depend on the good faith of the plan proponents and of those who participate in the preparation of the disclosure statement and in the solicitation. Subsection (e) does not affect civil or criminal liability for defects and inadequacies that are beyond the limits of the exoneration that good faith provides.

Section 1125 applies to public companies as well, subject to the qualifications of subsection (f). In case of a public company no solicitations of acceptance is permitted unless authorized by the court upon or after approval of the plan pursuant to section 1128(c). In addition to the documents specified in subsection (b), subsection (f) requires transmission of the opinion and order of the court approving the plan and, if filed, the advisory report of the Securities and Exchange Commission or a summary thereof prepared by the Commission.

house report no. 95–595

This section is new. It is the heart of the consolidation of the various reorganization chapters found in current law. It requires disclosure before solicitation of acceptances of a plan or reorganization.

Subsection (a) contains two definitions. First, "adequate information" is defined to mean information of a kind, and insufficient detail, as far as is reasonably practical in light of the nature and history of the debtor and the condition of the debtor's books and records, that would enable a hypothetical reasonable investor typical of holders of claims or interests of the relevant class to make an informed judgment about the plan. Second, "investor typical of holders of claims or interests of the relevant class" is defined to mean an investor having a claim or interest of the relevant class, having such a relationship with the debtor as the holders of other claims or interests of the relevant class have, and having such ability to obtain information from sources other than the disclosure statement as holders of claims or interests of the relevant class have, and having such ability to obtain information from sources other than the disclosure statement as holders of claims or interests of the relevant class have. That is, the hypothetical investor against which the disclosure is measured must not be an insider if other members of the class are not insiders, and so on. In other words, the adequacy of disclosure is measured against the typical investor, not an extraordinary one.

The Supreme Court's rulemaking power will not extend to rulemaking that will prescribe what constitutes adequate information. That standard is a substantive standard. Precisely what constitutes adequate information in any particular instance will develop on a case-by-case basis. Courts will take a practical approach as to what is necessary under the circumstances of each case, such as the cost of preparation of the statements, the need for relative speed in solicitation and confirmation, and, of course, the need for investor protection. There will be a balancing of interests in each case. In reorganization cases, there is frequently great uncertainty. Therefore the need for flexibility is greatest.

Subsection (b) is the operative subsection. It prohibits solicitation of acceptances or rejections of a plan after the commencement of the case unless, at the time of the solicitation or before, there is transmitted to the solicitee the plan or a summary of the plan, and a written disclosure statement approved by the court as containing adequate information. The subsection permits approval of the statement without the necessity of a valuation of the debtor or an appraisal of the debtor's assets. However, in some cases, a valuation or appraisal will be necessary to develop adequate information. The court will be able to determine what is necessary in light of the facts and circumstances of each particular case.

Subsection (c) requires that the same disclosure statement go to all members of a particular class, but permits different disclosure to different classes.

Subsection (d) excepts the disclosure statements from the requirements of the securities laws (such as section 14 of the 1934 Act [15 U.S.C. 78n] and section 5 of the 1933 Act [15 U.S.C. 77e]), and from similar State securities laws (blue sky laws, for example). The subsection permits an agency or official whose duty is to administer or enforce such laws (such as the Securities and Exchange Commission or State Corporation Commissioners) to appear and be heard on the issue of whether a disclosure statement contains adequate information, but the agencies and officials are not granted the right of appeal from an adverse determination in any capacity. They may join in an appeal by a true party in interest, however.

Subsection (e) is a safe harbor provision, and is necessary to make the exemption provided by subsection (d) effective. Without it, a creditor that solicited an acceptance or rejection in reliance on the court's approval of a disclosure statement would be potentially liable under antifraud sections designed to enforce the very sections of the securities laws from which subsection (d) excuses compliance. The subsection protects only persons that solicit in good faith and in compliance with the applicable provisions of the reorganization chapter. It provides protection from legal liability as well as from equitable liability based on an injunctive action by the SEC or other agency or official.

Amendments

2005—Subsec. (a)(1). Pub. L. 109–8, §717, inserted "including a discussion of the potential material Federal tax consequences of the plan to the debtor, any successor to the debtor, and a hypothetical investor typical of the holders of claims or interests in the case," after "records," and substituted "such a hypothetical investor" for "a hypothetical reasonable investor typical of holders of claims or interests".

Pub. L. 109–8, §431(1), inserted before semicolon "and in determining whether a disclosure statement provides adequate information, the court shall consider the complexity of the case, the benefit of additional information to creditors and other parties in interest, and the cost of providing additional information".

Subsec. (f). Pub. L. 109–8, §431(2), added subsec. (f) and struck out former subsec. (f) which read as follows: "Notwithstanding subsection (b), in a case in which the debtor has elected under section 1121(e) to be considered a small business—

"(1) the court may conditionally approve a disclosure statement subject to final approval after notice and a hearing;

"(2) acceptances and rejections of a plan may be solicited based on a conditionally approved disclosure statement as long as the debtor provides adequate information to each holder of a claim or interest that is solicited, but a conditionally approved disclosure statement shall be mailed at least 10 days prior to the date of the hearing on confirmation of the plan; and

"(3) a hearing on the disclosure statement may be combined with a hearing on confirmation of a plan."

Subsec. (g). Pub. L. 109–8, §408, added subsec. (g).

1994—Subsec. (f). Pub. L. 103–394 added subsec. (f).

1984—Subsec. (a)(1). Pub. L. 98–353, §509(a)(1), inserted ", but adequate information need not include such information about any other possible or proposed plan".

Subsec. (a)(2)(B). Pub. L. 98–353, §509(a)(2), inserted "the" after "with".

Subsec. (a)(2)(C). Pub. L. 98–353, §509(a)(3), inserted "of" after "holders".

Subsec. (d). Pub. L. 98–353, §509(b), inserted "required under subsection (b) of this section" and ", or otherwise seek review of,".

Subsec. (e). Pub. L. 98–353, §509(c), inserted "acceptance or rejection of a plan" after "solicits", and "solicitation of acceptance or rejection of a plan or" after "governing".

Effective Date of 2005 Amendment

Amendment by Pub. L. 109–8 effective 180 days after Apr. 20, 2005, and not applicable with respect to cases commenced under this title before such effective date, except as otherwise provided, see section 1501 of Pub. L. 109–8, set out as a note under section 101 of this title.

Effective Date of 1994 Amendment

Amendment by Pub. L. 103–394 effective Oct. 22, 1994, and not applicable with respect to cases commenced under this title before Oct. 22, 1994, see section 702 of Pub. L. 103–394, set out as a note under section 101 of this title.

Effective Date of 1984 Amendment

Amendment by Pub. L. 98–353 effective with respect to cases filed 90 days after July 10, 1984, see section 552(a) of Pub. L. 98–353, set out as a note under section 101 of this title.

§1126. Acceptance of plan

(a) The holder of a claim or interest allowed under section 502 of this title may accept or reject a plan. If the United States is a creditor or equity security holder, the Secretary of the Treasury may accept or reject the plan on behalf of the United States.

(b) For the purposes of subsections (c) and (d) of this section, a holder of a claim or interest that has accepted or rejected the plan before the commencement of the case under this title is deemed to have accepted or rejected such plan, as the case may be, if—

(1) the solicitation of such acceptance or rejection was in compliance with any applicable nonbankruptcy law, rule, or regulation governing the adequacy of disclosure in connection with such solicitation; or

(2) if there is not any such law, rule, or regulation, such acceptance or rejection was solicited after disclosure to such holder of adequate information, as defined in section 1125(a) of this title.

(c) A class of claims has accepted a plan if such plan has been accepted by creditors, other than any entity designated under subsection (e) of this section, that hold at least two-thirds in amount and more than one-half in number of the allowed claims of such class held by creditors, other than any entity designated under subsection (e) of this section, that have accepted or rejected such plan.

(d) A class of interests has accepted a plan if such plan has been accepted by holders of such interests, other than any entity designated under subsection (e) of this section, that hold at least two-thirds in amount of the allowed interests of such class held by holders of such interests, other than any entity designated under subsection (e) of this section, that have accepted or rejected such plan.

(e) On request of a party in interest, and after notice and a hearing, the court may designate any entity whose acceptance or rejection of such plan was not in good faith, or was not solicited or procured in good faith or in accordance with the provisions of this title.

(f) Notwithstanding any other provision of this section, a class that is not impaired under a plan, and each holder of a claim or interest of such class, are conclusively presumed to have accepted the plan, and solicitation of acceptances with respect to such class from the holders of claims or interests of such class is not required.

(g) Notwithstanding any other provision of this section, a class is deemed not to have accepted a plan if such plan provides that the claims or interests of such class do not entitle the holders of such claims or interests to receive or retain any property under the plan on account of such claims or interests.

(Pub. L. 95–598, Nov. 6, 1978, 92 Stat. 2634; Pub. L. 98–353, title III, §510, July 10, 1984, 98 Stat. 386.)

Historical and Revision Notes

legislative statements

Section 1126 of the House amendment deletes section 1126(e) as contained in the House bill. Section 105 of the bill constitutes sufficient power in the court to designate exclusion of a creditor's claim on the basis of a conflict of interest. Section 1126(f) of the House amendment adopts a provision contained in section 1127(f) of the Senate bill indicating that a class that is not impaired under a plan is deemed to have accepted a plan and solicitation of acceptances from such class is not required.

senate report no. 95–989

Subsection (a) of this section permits the holder of a claim or interest allowed under section 502 to accept or reject a proposed plan of reorganization. The subsection also incorporates a provision now found in section 199 of chapter X [section 599 of former title 11] that authorizes the Secretary of the Treasury to accept or reject a plan on behalf of the United States when the United States is a creditor or equity security holder.

Subsection (b) governs acceptances and rejections of plans obtained before commencement of a reorganization for a nonpublic company. Paragraph (3) expressly states that subsection (b) does not apply to a public company.

Prepetition solicitation is a common practice under chapter XI [chapter 11 of former title 11] today, and chapter IX [chapter 9 of former title 11] current makes explicit provision for it. Section 1126(b) counts a prepetition acceptance or rejection toward the required amounts and number of acceptances only if the solicitation of the acceptance or rejection was in compliance with any applicable nonbankruptcy law, rule, or regulation governing the adequacy of disclosure in connection with such solicitation. If there is not any such applicable law, rule, or regulation, then the acceptance or rejection is counted only if it was solicited after disclosure of adequate information, to the holder, as defined in section 1125(a)(1). This permits the court to ensure that the requirements of section 1125 are not avoided by prepetition solicitation.

Subsection (c) specifies the required amount and number of acceptances for a class of creditors. A class of creditors has accepted a plan if at least two-thirds in amount and more than one-half in number of the allowed claims of the class that are voted are cast in favor of the plan. The amount and number are computed on the basis of claims actually voted for or against the plan, not as under chapter X [chapter 10 of former title 11] on the basis of the allowed claims in the class. Subsection (f) excludes from all these calculations claims not voted in good faith, and claims procured or solicited not in good faith or not in accordance with the provisions of this title.

Subsection (c) requires that the same disclosure statement be transmitted to each member of a class. It recognizes that the information needed for an informed judgment about the plan may differ among classes. A class whose rights under the plan center on a particular fund or asset would have no use for an extensive description of other matters that could not affect them.

Subsection (d) relieves the court of the need to follow any otherwise applicable Federal or state law in determining the adequacy of the information contained in the disclosure statement submitted for its approval. It authorizes an agency or official, Federal or state, charged with administering cognate laws so pre-empted to advise the court on the adequacy of proposed disclosure statement. But they are not authorized to appeal the court's decision.

Solicitations with respect to a plan do not involve just mere requests for opinions. Acceptance of the plan vitally affects creditors and shareholders, and most frequently the solicitation involves an offering of securities in exchange for claims or interests. The present Bankruptcy Act [former title 11] has exempted such offerings under each of its chapters from the registration and disclosure requirements of the Securities Act of 1933 [15 U.S.C. 77a et seq.], an exemption also continued by section 1145 of this title. The extension of the disclosure requirements to all chapter 11 cases is justified by the integration of the separate chapters into the single chapter 11. By the same token, no valid purpose is served by failing to provide exemption from the requirements of similar state laws in a matter under the exclusive jurisdiction of the Federal bankruptcy laws.

Under subsection (d), with respect to a class of equity securities, it is sufficient for acceptance of the plan if the amount of securities voting for the plan is at least two-thirds of the total actually voted.

Subsection (e) provides that no acceptances are required from any class whose claims or interests are unimpaired under the plan or in the order confirming the plan.

Subsection (g) provides that any class denied participation under the plan is conclusively deemed to have rejected the plan. There is obviously no need to submit a plan for a vote by a class that is to receive nothing. But under subsection (g) the excluded class is like a class that has not accepted, and is a dissenting class for purposes of confirmation under section 1130.

Amendments

1984—Subsec. (b)(2). Pub. L. 98–353, §510(a), substituted "1125(a)" for "1125(a)(1)".

Subsec. (d). Pub. L. 98–353, §510(b), inserted a comma after "such interests".

Subsec. (f). Pub. L. 98–353, §510(c), substituted ", and each holder of a claim or interest of such class, are conclusively presumed" for "is deemed", "solicitation" for "solicititation", and "interests" for "interest".

Subsec. (g). Pub. L. 98–353, §510(d), substituted "receive or retain any property" for "any payment or compensation".

Effective Date of 1984 Amendment

Amendment by Pub. L. 98–353 effective with respect to cases filed 90 days after July 10, 1984, see section 552(a) of Pub. L. 98–353, set out as a note under section 101 of this title.

§1127. Modification of plan

(a) The proponent of a plan may modify such plan at any time before confirmation, but may not modify such plan so that such plan as modified fails to meet the requirements of sections 1122 and 1123 of this title. After the proponent of a plan files a modification of such plan with the court, the plan as modified becomes the plan.

(b) The proponent of a plan or the reorganized debtor may modify such plan at any time after confirmation of such plan and before substantial consummation of such plan, but may not modify such plan so that such plan as modified fails to meet the requirements of sections 1122 and 1123 of this title. Such plan as modified under this subsection becomes the plan only if circumstances warrant such modification and the court, after notice and a hearing, confirms such plan as modified, under section 1129 of this title.

(c) The proponent of a modification shall comply with section 1125 of this title with respect to the plan as modified.

(d) Any holder of a claim or interest that has accepted or rejected a plan is deemed to have accepted or rejected, as the case may be, such plan as modified, unless, within the time fixed by the court, such holder changes such holder's previous acceptance or rejection.

(e) If the debtor is an individual, the plan may be modified at any time after confirmation of the plan but before the completion of payments under the plan, whether or not the plan has been substantially consummated, upon request of the debtor, the trustee, the United States trustee, or the holder of an allowed unsecured claim, to—

(1) increase or reduce the amount of payments on claims of a particular class provided for by the plan;

(2) extend or reduce the time period for such payments; or

(3) alter the amount of the distribution to a creditor whose claim is provided for by the plan to the extent necessary to take account of any payment of such claim made other than under the plan.

(f)(1) Sections 1121 through 1128 and the requirements of section 1129 apply to any modification under subsection (e).

(2) The plan, as modified, shall become the plan only after there has been disclosure under section 1125 as the court may direct, notice and a hearing, and such modification is approved.

(Pub. L. 95–598, Nov. 6, 1978, 92 Stat. 2635; Pub. L. 98–353, title III, §511, July 10, 1984, 98 Stat. 386; Pub. L. 109–8, title III, §321(e), Apr. 20, 2005, 119 Stat. 96; Pub. L. 111–327, §2(a)(34), Dec. 22, 2010, 124 Stat. 3561.)

Historical and Revision Notes

legislative statements

Section 1127(a) of the House amendment adopts a provision contained in the House bill permitting only the proponent of a plan to modify the plan and rejecting the alternative of open modification contained in the Senate amendment.

senate report no. 95–989

Under subsection (a) the proponent may file a proposal to modify a plan prior to confirmation. In the case of a public company the modifying proposal may be filed prior to approval.

Subsection (b) provides that a party in interest eligible to file a plan may file instead of a plan a proposal to modify a plan filed by another. Under subsection (c) a party in interest objecting to some feature of a plan may submit a proposal to modify the plan to meet the objection.

After a plan has been confirmed, but before its substantial consummation, a plan may be modified by leave of court, which subsection (d) provides shall be granted for good cause. Subsection (e) provides that a proposal to modify a plan is subject to the disclosure requirements of section 1125 and as provided in subsection (f). It provides that a creditor or stockholder who voted for or against a plan is deemed to have accepted or rejected the modifying proposal. But if the modification materially and adversely affects any of their interests, they must be afforded an opportunity to change their vote in accordance with the disclosure and solicitation requirements of section 1125.

Under subsection (g) a plan, if modified prior to confirmation, shall be confirmed if it meets the requirements of section 1130.

house report no. 95–595

Subsection (a) permits the proponent of a plan to modify it at any time before confirmation, subject, of course, to the requirements of sections 1122 and 1123, governing classification and contents of a plan. After the proponent of a plan files a modification with the court, the plan as modified becomes the plan, and is to be treated the same as an original plan.

Subsection (b) permits modification of a plan after confirmation under certain circumstances. The modification must be proposed before substantial consummation of the plan. The requirements of sections 1122 and 1123 continue to apply. The plan as modified under this subsection becomes the plan only if the court confirms the plan as modified under section 1129 and the circumstances warrant the modification.

Subsection (c) requires the proponent of a modification to comply with the disclosure provisions of section 1125. Of course, if the modification were sufficiently minor, the court might determine that additional disclosure was not required under the circumstances.

Subsection (d) simplifies modification procedure by deeming any creditor or equity security holder that has already accepted or rejected the plan to have accepted or rejected the modification, unless, within the time fixed by the court, the creditor or equity security holder changes this previous acceptance or rejection.

Amendments

2010—Subsec. (f)(1). Pub. L. 111–327 substituted "subsection (e)" for "subsection (a)".

2005—Subsecs. (e), (f). Pub. L. 109–8 added subsecs. (e) and (f).

1984—Subsec. (a). Pub. L. 98–353, §511(a), inserted "of a plan" after "After the proponent", and "of such plan" after "modification".

Subsec. (b). Pub. L. 98–353, §511(b), substituted "circumstances warrant such modification and the court, after notice and a hearing, confirms such plan as modified, under section 1129 of this title" for "the court, after notice and a hearing, confirms such plan, as modified, under section 1129 of this title, and circumstances warrant such modification".

Effective Date of 2005 Amendment

Amendment by Pub. L. 109–8 effective 180 days after Apr. 20, 2005, and not applicable with respect to cases commenced under this title before such effective date, except as otherwise provided, see section 1501 of Pub. L. 109–8, set out as a note under section 101 of this title.

Effective Date of 1984 Amendment

Amendment by Pub. L. 98–353 effective with respect to cases filed 90 days after July 10, 1984, see section 552(a) of Pub. L. 98–353, set out as a note under section 101 of this title.

§1128. Confirmation hearing

(a) After notice, the court shall hold a hearing on confirmation of a plan.

(b) A party in interest may object to confirmation of a plan.

(Pub. L. 95–598, Nov. 6, 1978, 92 Stat. 2635.)

Historical and Revision Notes

senate report no. 95–989

[Section 1129 (enacted as section 1128)] Subsection (a) requires that there be a hearing in every case on the confirmation of the plan. Notice is required.

Subsection (b) permits any party in interest to object to the confirmation of the plan. The Securities and Exchange Commission and indenture trustees, as parties in interest under section 1109, may object to confirmation of the plan.

§1129. Confirmation of plan

(a) The court shall confirm a plan only if all of the following requirements are met:

(1) The plan complies with the applicable provisions of this title.

(2) The proponent of the plan complies with the applicable provisions of this title.

(3) The plan has been proposed in good faith and not by any means forbidden by law.

(4) Any payment made or to be made by the proponent, by the debtor, or by a person issuing securities or acquiring property under the plan, for services or for costs and expenses in or in connection with the case, or in connection with the plan and incident to the case, has been approved by, or is subject to the approval of, the court as reasonable.

(5)(A)(i) The proponent of the plan has disclosed the identity and affiliations of any individual proposed to serve, after confirmation of the plan, as a director, officer, or voting trustee of the debtor, an affiliate of the debtor participating in a joint plan with the debtor, or a successor to the debtor under the plan; and

(ii) the appointment to, or continuance in, such office of such individual, is consistent with the interests of creditors and equity security holders and with public policy; and

(B) the proponent of the plan has disclosed the identity of any insider that will be employed or retained by the reorganized debtor, and the nature of any compensation for such insider.

(6) Any governmental regulatory commission with jurisdiction, after confirmation of the plan, over the rates of the debtor has approved any rate change provided for in the plan, or such rate change is expressly conditioned on such approval.

(7) With respect to each impaired class of claims or interests—

(A) each holder of a claim or interest of such class—

(i) has accepted the plan; or

(ii) will receive or retain under the plan on account of such claim or interest property of a value, as of the effective date of the plan, that is not less than the amount that such holder would so receive or retain if the debtor were liquidated under chapter 7 of this title on such date; or

(B) if section 1111(b)(2) of this title applies to the claims of such class, each holder of a claim of such class will receive or retain under the plan on account of such claim property of a value, as of the effective date of the plan, that is not less than the value of such holder's interest in the estate's interest in the property that secures such claims.

(8) With respect to each class of claims or interests—

(A) such class has accepted the plan; or

(B) such class is not impaired under the plan.

(9) Except to the extent that the holder of a particular claim has agreed to a different treatment of such claim, the plan provides that—

(A) with respect to a claim of a kind specified in section 507(a)(2) or 507(a)(3) of this title, on the effective date of the plan, the holder of such claim will receive on account of such claim cash equal to the allowed amount of such claim;

(B) with respect to a class of claims of a kind specified in section 507(a)(1), 507(a)(4), 507(a)(5), 507(a)(6), or 507(a)(7) of this title, each holder of a claim of such class will receive—

(i) if such class has accepted the plan, deferred cash payments of a value, as of the effective date of the plan, equal to the allowed amount of such claim; or

(ii) if such class has not accepted the plan, cash on the effective date of the plan equal to the allowed amount of such claim;

(C) with respect to a claim of a kind specified in section 507(a)(8) of this title, the holder of such claim will receive on account of such claim regular installment payments in cash—

(i) of a total value, as of the effective date of the plan, equal to the allowed amount of such claim;

(ii) over a period ending not later than 5 years after the date of the order for relief under section 301, 302, or 303; and

(iii) in a manner not less favorable than the most favored nonpriority unsecured claim provided for by the plan (other than cash payments made to a class of creditors under section 1122(b)); and

(D) with respect to a secured claim which would otherwise meet the description of an unsecured claim of a governmental unit under section 507(a)(8), but for the secured status of that claim, the holder of that claim will receive on account of that claim, cash payments, in the same manner and over the same period, as prescribed in subparagraph (C).

(10) If a class of claims is impaired under the plan, at least one class of claims that is impaired under the plan has accepted the plan, determined without including any acceptance of the plan by any insider.

(11) Confirmation of the plan is not likely to be followed by the liquidation, or the need for further financial reorganization, of the debtor or any successor to the debtor under the plan, unless such liquidation or reorganization is proposed in the plan.

(12) All fees payable under section 1930 of title 28, as determined by the court at the hearing on confirmation of the plan, have been paid or the plan provides for the payment of all such fees on the effective date of the plan.

(13) The plan provides for the continuation after its effective date of payment of all retiree benefits, as that term is defined in section 1114 of this title, at the level established pursuant to subsection (e)(1)(B) or (g) of section 1114 of this title, at any time prior to confirmation of the plan, for the duration of the period the debtor has obligated itself to provide such benefits.

(14) If the debtor is required by a judicial or administrative order, or by statute, to pay a domestic support obligation, the debtor has paid all amounts payable under such order or such statute for such obligation that first become payable after the date of the filing of the petition.

(15) In a case in which the debtor is an individual and in which the holder of an allowed unsecured claim objects to the confirmation of the plan—

(A) the value, as of the effective date of the plan, of the property to be distributed under the plan on account of such claim is not less than the amount of such claim; or

(B) the value of the property to be distributed under the plan is not less than the projected disposable income of the debtor (as defined in section 1325(b)(2)) to be received during the 5-year period beginning on the date that the first payment is due under the plan, or during the period for which the plan provides payments, whichever is longer.

(16) All transfers of property under the plan shall be made in accordance with any applicable provisions of nonbankruptcy law that govern the transfer of property by a corporation or trust that is not a moneyed, business, or commercial corporation or trust.

(b)(1) Notwithstanding section 510(a) of this title, if all of the applicable requirements of subsection (a) of this section other than paragraph (8) are met with respect to a plan, the court, on request of the proponent of the plan, shall confirm the plan notwithstanding the requirements of such paragraph if the plan does not discriminate unfairly, and is fair and equitable, with respect to each class of claims or interests that is impaired under, and has not accepted, the plan.

(2) For the purpose of this subsection, the condition that a plan be fair and equitable with respect to a class includes the following requirements:

(A) With respect to a class of secured claims, the plan provides—

(i)(I) that the holders of such claims retain the liens securing such claims, whether the property subject to such liens is retained by the debtor or transferred to another entity, to the extent of the allowed amount of such claims; and

(II) that each holder of a claim of such class receive on account of such claim deferred cash payments totaling at least the allowed amount of such claim, of a value, as of the effective date of the plan, of at least the value of such holder's interest in the estate's interest in such property;

(ii) for the sale, subject to section 363(k) of this title, of any property that is subject to the liens securing such claims, free and clear of such liens, with such liens to attach to the proceeds of such sale, and the treatment of such liens on proceeds under clause (i) or (iii) of this subparagraph; or

(iii) for the realization by such holders of the indubitable equivalent of such claims.

(B) With respect to a class of unsecured claims—

(i) the plan provides that each holder of a claim of such class receive or retain on account of such claim property of a value, as of the effective date of the plan, equal to the allowed amount of such claim; or

(ii) the holder of any claim or interest that is junior to the claims of such class will not receive or retain under the plan on account of such junior claim or interest any property, except that in a case in which the debtor is an individual, the debtor may retain property included in the estate under section 1115, subject to the requirements of subsection (a)(14) of this section.

(C) With respect to a class of interests—

(i) the plan provides that each holder of an interest of such class receive or retain on account of such interest property of a value, as of the effective date of the plan, equal to the greatest of the allowed amount of any fixed liquidation preference to which such holder is entitled, any fixed redemption price to which such holder is entitled, or the value of such interest; or

(ii) the holder of any interest that is junior to the interests of such class will not receive or retain under the plan on account of such junior interest any property.

(c) Notwithstanding subsections (a) and (b) of this section and except as provided in section 1127(b) of this title, the court may confirm only one plan, unless the order of confirmation in the case has been revoked under section 1144 of this title. If the requirements of subsections (a) and (b) of this section are met with respect to more than one plan, the court shall consider the preferences of creditors and equity security holders in determining which plan to confirm.

(d) Notwithstanding any other provision of this section, on request of a party in interest that is a governmental unit, the court may not confirm a plan if the principal purpose of the plan is the avoidance of taxes or the avoidance of the application of section 5 of the Securities Act of 1933. In any hearing under this subsection, the governmental unit has the burden of proof on the issue of avoidance.

(e) In a small business case, the court shall confirm a plan that complies with the applicable provisions of this title and that is filed in accordance with section 1121(e) not later than 45 days after the plan is filed unless the time for confirmation is extended in accordance with section 1121(e)(3).

(Pub. L. 95–598, Nov. 6, 1978, 92 Stat. 2635; Pub. L. 98–353, title III, §512, July 10, 1984, 98 Stat. 386; Pub. L. 99–554, title II, §§225, 283(v), Oct. 27, 1986, 100 Stat. 3102, 3118; Pub. L. 100–334, §2(b), June 16, 1988, 102 Stat. 613; Pub. L. 103–394, title III, §304(h)(7), title V, §501(d)(32), Oct. 22, 1994, 108 Stat. 4134, 4146; Pub. L. 109–8, title II, §213(1), title III, §321(c), title IV, §438, title VII, §710, title XII, §1221(b), title XV, §1502(a)(8), Apr. 20, 2005, 119 Stat. 52, 95, 113, 127, 196, 216; Pub. L. 111–327, §2(a)(35), Dec. 22, 2010, 124 Stat. 3561.)

Historical and Revision Notes

legislative statements

Section 1129 of the House amendment relates to confirmation of a plan in a case under chapter 11. Section 1129(a)(3) of the House amendment adopts the position taken in the Senate amendment and section 1129(a)(5) takes the position adopted in the House bill. Section 1129(a)(7) adopts the position taken in the House bill in order to insure that the dissenting members of an accepting class will receive at least what they would otherwise receive under the best interest of creditors test; it also requires that even the members of a class that has rejected the plan be protected by the best interest of creditors test for those rare cramdown cases where a class of creditors would receive more on liquidation than under reorganization of the debtor. Section 1129(a)(7)(C) is discussed in connection with section 1129(b) and section 1111(b). Section 1129(a)(8) of the House amendment adopts the provision taken in the House bill which permits confirmation of a plan as to a particular class without resort to the fair and equitable test if the class has accepted a plan or is unimpaired under the plan.

Section 1129(a)(9) represents a compromise between a similar provision contained in the House bill and the Senate amendment. Under subparagraph (A) claims entitled to priority under section 507(a)(1) or (2) are entitled to receive cash on the effective date of the plan equal to the amount of the claim. Under subparagraph (B) claims entitled to priority under section 507(a)(3), (4), or (5), are entitled to receive deferred cash payments of a present value as of the effective date of the plan equal to the amount of the claims if the class has accepted the plan or cash payments on the effective date of the plan otherwise. Tax claims entitled to priority under section 507(a)(6) of different governmental units may not be contained in one class although all claims of one such unit may be combined and such unit may be required to take deferred cash payments over a period not to exceed 6 years after the date of assessment of the tax with the present value equal to the amount of the claim.

Section 1129(a)(10) is derived from section 1130(a)(12) of the Senate amendment.

Section 1129(b) is new. Together with section 1111(b) and section 1129(a)(7)(C), this section provides when a plan may be confirmed, notwithstanding the failure of an impaired class to accept the plan under section 1129(a)(8). Before discussing section 1129(b) an understanding of section 1111(b) is necessary. Section 1111(b)(1), the general rule that a secured claim is to be treated as a recourse claim in chapter 11 whether or not the claim is nonrecourse by agreement or applicable law. This preferred status for a nonrecourse loan terminates if the property securing the loan is sold under section 363 or is to be sold under the plan.

The preferred status also terminates if the class of which the secured claim is a part elects application of section 1111(b)(2). Section 1111(b)(2) provides that an allowed claim is a secured claim to the full extent the claim is allowed rather than to the extent of the collateral as under section 506(a). A class may elect application of paragraph (2) only if the security is not of inconsequential value and, if the creditor is a recourse creditor, the collateral is not sold under section 363 or to be sold under the plan. Sale of property under section 363 or under the plan is excluded from treatment under section 1111(b) because of the secured party's right to bid in the full amount of his allowed claim at any sale of collateral under section 363(k) of the House amendment.

As previously noted, section 1129(b) sets forth a standard by which a plan may be confirmed notwithstanding the failure of an impaired class to accept the plan.

Paragraph (1) makes clear that this alternative confirmation standard, referred to as "cram down," will be called into play only on the request of the proponent of the plan. Under this cramdown test, the court must confirm the plan if the plan does not discriminate unfairly, and is "fair and equitable," with respect to each class of claims or interests that is impaired under, and has not accepted, the plan. The requirement of the House bill that a plan not "discrimlnate unfairly" with respect to a class is included for clarity; the language in the House report interpreting that requirement, in the context of subordinated debentures, applies equally under the requirements of section 1129(b)(1) of the House amendment.

Although many of the factors interpreting "fair and equitable" are specified in paragraph (2), others, which were explicated in the description of section 1129(b) in the House report, were omitted from the House amendment to avoid statutory complexity and because they would undoubtedly be found by a court to be fundamental to "fair and equitable" treatment of a dissenting class. For example, a dissenting class should be assured that no senior class receives more than 100 percent of the amount of its claims. While that requirement was explicitly included in the House bill, the deletion is intended to be one of style and not one of substance.

Paragraph (2) provides guidelines for a court to determine whether a plan is fair and equitable with respect to a dissenting class. It must be emphasized that the fair and equitable requirement applies only with respect to dissenting classes. Therefore, unlike the fair and equitable rule contained in chapter X [chapter 10 of former title 11] and section 77 of the Bankruptcy Act [section 205 of former title 11] under section 1129(b)(2), senior accepting classes are permitted to give up value to junior classes as long as no dissenting intervening class receives less than the amount of its claims in full. If there is no dissenting intervening class and the only dissent is from a class junior to the class to which value have been given up, then the plan may still be fair and equitable with respect to the dissenting class, as long as no class senior to the dissenting class has received more than 100 percent of the amount of its claims.

Paragraph (2) contains three subparagraphs, each of which applies to a particular kind of class of claims or interests that is impaired and has not accepted the plan. Subparagraph (A) applies when a class of secured claims is impaired and has not accepted the plan. The provision applies whether or not section 1111(b) applies. The plan may be crammed down notwithstanding the dissent of a secured class only if the plan complies with clause (i), (ii), or (iii).

Clause (i) permits cramdown if the dissenting class of secured claims will retain its lien on the property whether the property is retained by the debtor or transferred. It should be noted that the lien secures the allowed secured claim held by such holder. The meaning of "allowed secured claim" will vary depending on whether section 1111(b)(2) applies to such class.

If section 1111(b)(2) applies then the "electing" class is entitled to have the entire allowed amount of the debt related to such property secured by a lien even if the value of the collateral is less than the amount of the debt. In addition, the plan must provide for the holder to receive, on account of the allowed secured claims, payments, either present or deferred, of a principal face amount equal to the amount of the debt and of a present value equal to the value of the collateral.

For example, if a creditor loaned $15,000,000 to a debtor secured by real property worth $18,000,000 and the value of the real property had dropped to $12,000,000 by the date when the debtor commenced a proceeding under chapter 11, the plan could be confirmed notwithstanding the dissent of the creditor as long as the lien remains on the collateral to secure a $15,000,000 debt, the face amount of present or extended payments to be made to the creditor under the plan is at least $15,000,000, and the present value of the present or deferred payments is not less than $12,000,000. The House report accompanying the House bill described what is meant by "present value".

Clause (ii) is self explanatory. Clause (iii) requires the court to confirm the plan notwithstanding the dissent of the electing secured class if the plan provides for the realization by the secured class of the indubitable equivalents of the secured claims. The standard of "indubitable equivalents" is taken from *In re Murel Holding Corp.*, 75 F.2d 941 (2d Cir. 1935) (Learned Hand, Jr.).

Abandonment of the collateral to the creditor would clearly satisfy indubitable equivalence, as would a lien on similar collateral. However, present cash payments less than the secured claim would not satisfy the standard because the creditor is deprived of an opportunity to gain from a future increase in value of the collateral. Unsecured notes as to the secured claim or equity securities of the debtor would not be the indubitable equivalent. With respect to an oversecured creditor, the secured claim will never exceed the allowed claim.

Although the same language applies, a different result pertains with respect to a class of secured claims to which section 1111(b)(2) does not apply. This will apply to all claims secured by a right of setoff. The court must confirm the plan notwithstanding the dissent of such a class of secured claims if any of three alternative requirements is met. Under clause (i) the plan may be confirmed if the class retains a right of setoff or a lien securing the allowed secured claims of the class and the holders will receive payments of a present value equal to the allowed amount of their secured claims. Contrary to electing classes of secured creditors who retain a lien under subparagraph (A)(i)(I) to the extent of the entire claims secured by such lien, nonelecting creditors retain a lien on collateral only to the extent of their allowed secured claims and not to the extent of any deficiency, and such secured creditors must receive present or deferred payments with a present value equal to the allowed secured claim, which in turn is only the equivalent of the value of the collateral under section 506(a).

Any deficiency claim of a nonelecting class of secured claims is treated as an unsecured claim and is not provided for under subparagraph (A). The plan may be confirmed under clause (ii) if the plan proposes to sell the property free and clear of the secured party's lien as long as the lien will attach to the proceeds and will receive treatment under clause (i) or (iii). Clause (iii) permits confirmation if the plan provides for the realization by the dissenting nonelecting class of secured claims of the indubitable equivalent of the secured claims of such class.

Contrary to an "electing" class to which section 1111(b)(2) applies, the nonelecting class need not be protected with respect to any future appreciation in value of the collateral since the secured claim of such a class is never undersecured by reason of section 506(a). Thus the lien secures only the value of interest of such creditor in the collateral. To the extent deferred payments exceed that amount, they represent interest. In the event of a subsequent default, the portion of the face amount of deferred payments representing unaccrued interest will not be secured by the lien.

Subparagraph (B) applies to a dissenting class of unsecured claims. The court must confirm the plan notwithstanding the dissent of a class of impaired unsecured claims if the plan provides for such claims to receive property with a present value equal to the allowed amount of the claims. Unsecured claims may receive any kind of "property," which is used in its broadest sense, as long as the present value of the property given to the holders of unsecured claims is equal to the allowed amount of the claims. Some kinds of property, such as securities, may require difficult valuations by the court; in such circumstances the court need only determine that there is a reasonable likelihood that the property given the dissenting class of impaired unsecured claims equals the present value of such allowed claims.

Alternatively, under clause (ii), the court must confirm the plan if the plan provides that holders of any claims or interests junior to the interests of the dissenting class of impaired unsecured claims will not receive any property under the plan on account of such junior claims or interests. As long as senior creditors have not been paid more than in full, and classes of equal claims are being treated so that the dissenting class of impaired unsecured claims is not being discriminated against unfairly, the plan may be confirmed if the impaired class of unsecured claims receives less than 100 cents on the dollar (or nothing at all) as long as no class junior to the dissenting class receives anything at all. Such an impaired dissenting class may not prevent confirmation of a plan by objection merely because a senior class has elected to give up value to a junior class that is higher in priority than the impaired dissenting class of unsecured claims as long as the above safeguards are met.

Subparagraph (C) applies to a dissenting class of impaired interests. Such interests may include the interests of general or limited partners in a partnership, the interests of a sole proprietor in a proprietorship, or the interest of common or preferred stockholders in a corporation. If the holders of such interests are entitled to a fixed liquidation preference or fixed redemption price on account of such interests then the plan may be confirmed notwithstanding the dissent of such class of interests as long as it provides the holders property of a present value equal to the greatest of the fixed redemption price, or the value of such interests. In the event there is no fixed liquidation preference or redemption price, then the plan may be confirmed as long as it provides the holders of such interests property of a present value equal to the value of such interests. If the interests are "under water" then they will be valueless and the plan may be confirmed notwithstanding the dissent of that class of interests even if the plan provides that the holders of such interests will not receive any property on account of such interests.

Alternatively, under clause (ii), the court must confirm the plan notwithstanding the dissent of a class of interests if the plan provides that holders of any interests junior to the dissenting class of interests will not receive or retain any property on account of such junior interests. Clearly, if there are no junior interests junior to the class of dissenting interests, then the condition of clause (ii) is satisfied. The safeguards that no claim or interest receive more than 100 percent of the allowed amount of such claim or interest and that no class be discriminated against unfairly will insure that the plan is fair and equitable with respect to the dissenting class of interests.

Except to the extent of the treatment of secured claims under subparagraph (A) of this statement, the House report remains an accurate description of confirmation of section 1129(b). Contrary to the example contained in the Senate report, a senior class will not be able to give up value to a junior class over the dissent of an intervening class unless the intervening class receives the full amount, as opposed to value, of its claims or interests.

One last point deserves explanation with respect to the admittedly complex subject of confirmation. Section 1129(a)(7)(C) in effect exempts secured creditors making an election under section 1111(b)(2) from application of the best interest of creditors test. In the absence of an election the amount such creditors receive in a plan of liquidation would be the value of their collateral plus any amount recovered on the deficiency in the case of a recourse loan. However, under section 1111(b)(2), the creditors are given an allowed secured claim to the full extent the claim is allowed and have no unsecured deficiency. Since section 1129(b)(2)(A) makes clear that an electing class need receive payments of a present value only equal to the value of the collateral, it is conceivable that under such a "cram down" the electing creditors would receive nothing with respect to their deficiency. The advantage to the electing creditors is that they have a lien securing the full amount of the allowed claim so that if the value of the collateral increases after the case is closed, the deferred payments will be secured claims. Thus it is both reasonable and necessary to exempt such electing class from application of section 1129(a)(7) as a logical consequence of permitting election under section 1111(b)(2).

Section 1131 of the Senate amendment is deleted as unnecessary in light of the protection given a secured creditor under section 1129(b) of the House amendment.

Payment of taxes in reorganizations: Under the provisions of section 1141 as revised by the House amendment, an individual in reorganization under chapter 11 will not be discharged from any debt, including prepetition tax liabilities, which are nondischargeable under section 523. Thus, an individual debtor whose plan of reorganization is confirmed under chapter 11 will remain liable for prepetition priority taxes, as defined in section 507, and for tax liabilities which receive no priority but are nondischargeable under section 523, including no return, late return, and fraud liabilities.

In the case of a partnership or a corporation in reorganization under chapter 11 of title 11, section 1141(d)(1) of the House amendment adopts a provision limiting the taxes that must be provided for in a plan before a plan can be confirmed to taxes which receive priority under section 507. In addition, the House amendment makes dischargeable, in effect, tax liabilities attributable to no return, late return, or fraud situations. The amendment thus does not adopt a shareholder continuity test such as was contained in section 1141(d)(2)(A)(iii) of the Senate amendment. However, the House amendment amends section 1106, relating to duties of the trustee, to require the trustee to furnish, on request of a tax authority and without personal liability, information available to the trustee concerning potential prepetition tax liabilities for unfiled returns of the debtor. Depending on the condition of the debtor's books and records, this information may include schedules and files available to the business. The House amendment also does not prohibit a tax authority from disallowing any tax benefit claimed after the reorganization if the item originated in a deduction, credit, or other item improperly reported before the reorganization occurred. It may also be appropriate for the Congress to consider in the future imposing civil or criminal liability on corporate officers for preparing a false or fraudulent tax return. The House amendment also contemplates that the Internal Revenue Service will monitor the relief from liabilities under this provision and advise the Congress if, and to the extent, any significant tax abuse may be resulting from the provision.

Medium of payment of taxes: Federal, State, and local taxes incurred during the administration period of the estate, and during the "gap" period in an involuntary case, are to be paid solely in cash. Taxes relating to third priority wages are to be paid, under the general rules, in cash on the effective date of the plan, if the class has not accepted the plan, in an amount equal to the allowed amount of the claim. If the class has accepted the plan, the taxes must be paid in cash but the payments must be made at the time the wages are paid which may be paid in deferred periodic installments having a value, on the effective date of the plan, equal to the allowed amount of the tax claims. Prepetition taxes entitled to sixth priority under section 507(a)(6) also must be paid in cash, but the plan may also permit the debtor whether a corporation, partnership, or an individual, to pay the allowed taxes in installments over a period not to exceed 6 years following the date on which the tax authority assesses the tax liability, provided the value of the deferred payments representing principal and interest, as of the effective date of the plan, equals the allowed amount of the tax claim.

The House amendment also modifies the provisions of both bills dealing with the time when tax liabilities of a debtor in reorganization may be assessed by the tax authority. The House amendment follows the Senate amendment in deleting the limitation in present law under which a priority tax assessed after a reorganization plan is confirmed must be assessed within 1 year after the date of the filing of the petition. The House amendment specifies broadly that after the bankruptcy court determines the liability of the estate for a prepetition tax or for an administration period tax, the governmental unit may thereafter assess the tax against the estate, debtor, or successor to the debtor. The party to be assessed will, of course, depend on whether the case is under chapter 7, 11, or 13, whether the debtor is an individual, partnership, or a corporation, and whether the court is determining an individual debtor's personal liability for a nondischargeable tax. Assessment of the tax may only be made, however, within the limits of otherwise applicable law, such as the statute of limitations under the tax law.

Tax avoidance purpose: The House bill provided that no reorganization plan may be approved if the principal purpose of the plan is the avoidance of taxes. The Senate amendment modified the rule so that the bankruptcy court need make a determination of tax avoidance purpose only if it is asked to do so by the appropriate tax authority. Under the Senate amendment, if the tax authority does not request the bankruptcy court to rule on the purpose of the plan, the tax authority would not be barred from later asserting a tax avoidance motive with respect to allowance of a deduction or other tax benefit claimed after the reorganization. The House amendment adopts the substance of the Senate amendment, but does not provide a basis by which a tax authority may collaterally attack confirmation of a plan of reorganization other than under section 1144.

senate report no. 95–989

[Section 1130 (enacted as section 1129)] Subsection (a) enumerates the requirement governing confirmation of a plan. The court is required to confirm a plan if and only if all of the requirements are met.

Paragraph (1) requires that the plan comply with the applicable provisions of chapter 11, such as sections 1122 and 1123, governing classification and contents of plan.

Paragraph (2) requires that the proponent of the plan comply with the applicable provisions of chapter 11, such as section 1125 regarding disclosure.

Paragraph (3) requires that the plan have been proposed in good faith, and not by any means forbidden by law.

Paragraph (4) is derived from section 221 of chapter X [section 621 of former title 11]. It requires that any payment made or promised by the proponent, the debtor, or person issuing securities or acquiring property under the plan, for services or for costs and expenses in, or in connection with the case, or in connection with the plan and incident to the case, be disclosed to the court. In addition, any payment made before confirmation must have been reasonable, and any payment to be fixed after confirmation must be subject to the approval of the court as reasonable.

Paragraph (5) is also derived from section 221 of chapter X [section 621 of former title 11]. It requires the plan to disclose the identity and affiliations of any individual proposed to serve, after confirmation, as a director, officer, or voting trustee of the reorganized debtor. The appointment to or continuance in one of these offices by the individual must be consistent with the interests of creditors and equity security holders and with public policy. The plan must also disclose the identity of any insider that will be employed or retained by the reorganized debtor, and the nature of any compensation to be paid to the insider.

Paragraph (6) permits confirmation only if any regulatory commission that will have jurisdiction over the debtor after confirmation of the plan has approved any rate change provided for in the plan. As an alternative, the rate change may be conditioned on such approval.

Paragraph (7) provides that in the case of a public company the court shall confirm the plan if it finds the plan to be fair and equitable and the plan either (1) has been accepted by classes of claims or interests as provided in section 1126, or (2), if not so accepted, satisfies the requirements of subsection (b) of this section.

Paragraphs (8) and (9) apply only in nonpublic cases. Paragraph (8) does not apply the fair and equitable standards in two situations. The first occurs if there is unanimous consent of all affected holders of claims and interests. It is also sufficient for purposes of confirmation if each holder of a claim or interest receives or retains consideration of a value, as of the effective date of the plan, that is not less than each would have or receive if the debtor were liquidated under chapter 7 of this title. This standard adapts the test of "best interest of creditors" as interpreted by the courts under chapter XI [chapter 11 of former title 11]. It is given broader application in chapter 11 of this title since a plan under chapter 11 may affect not only unsecured claims but secured claims and stock as well.

Under paragraph (9)(A), if a class of claims or interests has not accepted the plan, the court will confirm the plan if, for the dissenting class and any class of equal rank, the negotiated plan provides in value no less than under a plan that is fair and equitable. Such review and determination are not required for any other classes that accepted the plan.

Paragraph (9)(A) would permit a senior creditor to adjust his participation for the benefit of stockholders. In such a case, junior creditors, who have not been satisfied in full, may not object if, absent the "give-up," they are receiving all that a fair and equitable plan would give them. To illustrate, suppose the estate is valued at $1.5 million and claims and stock are:

	Claims and stock (millions)	Equity (millions)
(1) Senior debt	$1.2	$1.2
(2) Junior debt	.5	.3
(3) Stock	(¹)	–
Total	1.7	1.5

¹ No value.

Under the plan, the senior creditor gives up $100,000 in value for the benefit of stockholders as follows:

	Millions
(1) Senior debt	$1.1
(2) Junior debt	.3
(3) Stock	.1
Total	1.5

If the junior creditors dissent, the court may nevertheless confirm the plan since under the fair and equitable standard they had an equity of only $300,000 and the allocation to equity security holders did not affect them.

Paragraph (9)(A) provides a special alternative with respect to secured claims. A plan may be confirmed against a dissenting class of secured claims if the plan or order of confirmation provides for the realization of their security (1) by the retention of the property subject to such security; (2) by a sale of the property and transfer of the claim to the proceeds of sale if the secured creditors were permitted to bid at the sale and set off against the purchase price up to the allowed amount of their claims; or (3) by such other method that will assure them the realization of the indubitable equivalent of the allowed amount of their secured claims. The indubitable equivalent language is intended to follow the strict approach taken by Judge Learned Hand in *In Re Murel Holding Corp.* 75, F.2d 941 (2nd Cir. 1935).

Paragraph (9)(B) provides that, if a class of claims or interests is excluded from participation under the plan, the court may nevertheless confirm the plan if it determines that no class on a parity with or junior to such participates under the plan. In the previous illustration, no confirmation would be permitted if the negotiated plan would grant a participation to stockholders but nothing for junior creditors. As noted elsewhere, by reason of section 1126(g), an excluded class is a dissenting class under section 1130.

Paragraph (10) states that, to be confirmed, the plan must provide that each holder of a claim under section 507 will receive property, as therein noted, of a value equal to the allowed amount of the claim. There are two exceptions: (A) The holder thereof may agree to a different settlement in part or in whole; (B) where a debtor's business is reorganized under chapter 11, this provision requires that taxes entitled to priority (including administrative claims or taxes) must be paid in cash not later than 120 days after the plan is confirmed, unless the Secretary of the Treasury agrees to other terms or kinds of payment. The bill, as introduced, required full payment in cash within 60 days after the plan is confirmed.

Paragraph (11) requires a determination regarding feasibility of the plan. It is a slight elaboration of the law that has developed in the application of the word "feasible" in Chapter X of the present Act [chapter 10 of former title 11].

Paragraph (12) requires that at least one class must accept the plan, but any claims or interests held by insiders are not to be included for purposes of determining the number and amount of acceptances.

Subsection (b) provides that if, in the case of a public company, the plan meets the requirements of subsection (a) (except paragraphs (8) and (9) which do not apply to such a company), the court is to confirm the plan if the plan or the order of confirmation provides adequate protection for the realization of the value of the claims or interests of each class not accepting the plan. The intent is to incorporate inclusively, as a guide to the meaning of subsection (a) the provisions of section 216(7) ([former] 11 U.S.C. 616(7)) with respect to claims and section 216(8) ([former] 11 U.S.C. 616(8)) with respect to equity security interests.

Under subsection (c) the court may confirm only one plan, unless the order of confirmation has been revoked under section 1144. If the requirements for confirmation are met with respect to more than one plan, the court shall consider the preferences of creditors and stockholders in deciding which plan to confirm.

Subsection (d) provides that the bankruptcy court may not confirm a plan of reorganization if its principal purpose is the avoidance of taxes or the avoidance of section 5 of the Securities Act of 1933 (15 U.S.C. 77e). This rules modifies a similar provision of present law (section 269 of the Bankruptcy Act [section 669 of former title 11]).

house report no. 95-595

Paragraph (7) [of subsec. (a)] incorporates the former "best interest of creditors" test found in chapter 11, but spells out precisely what is intended. With respect to each class, the holders of the claims or interests of that class must receive or retain under the plan on account of those claims or interest property of a value, as of the effective date of the plan, that is not less than the amount that they would so receive or retain if the debtor were liquidated under chapter 7 on the effective date of the plan.

In order to determine the hypothetical distribution in a liquidation, the court will have to consider the various subordination provisions of proposed 11 U.S.C. 510, 726(a)(3), 726(a)(4), and the postponement provisions of proposed 11 U.S.C. 724. Also applicable in appropriate cases will be the rules governing partnership distributions under proposed 11 U.S.C. 723, and distributions of community property under proposed 11 U.S.C. 726(c). Under subparagraph (A), a particular holder is permitted to accept less than liquidation value, but his acceptance does not bind the class.

Property under subparagraph (B) may include securities of the debtor. Thus, the provision will apply in cases in which the plan is confirmed under proposed 11 U.S.C. 1129(b).

Paragraph (8) is central to the confirmation standards. It requires that each class either have accepted the plan or be unimpaired.

Paragraph (9) augments the requirements of paragraph (8) by requiring payment of each priority claim in full. It permits payments over time and payment other than in cash, but payment in securities is not intended to be permitted without consent of the priority claimant even if the class has consented. It also permits a particular claimant to accept less than full payment.

Subsection (b) permits the court to confirm a plan notwithstanding failure of compliance with paragraph (8) of subsection (a). The plan must comply with all other paragraphs of subsection (a), including paragraph (9). This subsection contains the so-called cramdown. It requires simply that the plan meet certain standards of fairness to dissenting creditors or equity security holders. The general principle of the subsection permits confirmation notwithstanding nonacceptance by an impaired class if that class and all below it in priority are treated according to the absolute priority rule. The dissenting class must be paid in full before any junior class may share under the plan. If it is paid in full, then junior classes may share. Treatment of classes of secured creditors is slightly different because they do not fall in the priority ladder, but the principle is the same.

Specifically, the court may confirm a plan over the objection of a class of secured claims if the members of that class are unimpaired or if they are to receive under the plan property of a value equal to the allowed amount of their secured claims, as determined under proposed 11 U.S.C. 506(a). The property is to be valued as of the effective date of the plan, thus recognizing the time-value of money. As used throughout this subsection, "property" includes both tangible and intangible property, such as a security of the debtor or a successor to the debtor under a reorganization plan.

The court may confirm over the dissent of a class of unsecured claims, including priority claims, only if the members of the class are unimpaired, if they will receive under the plan property of a value equal to the allowed amount of their unsecured claims, or if no class junior will share under the plan. That is, if the class is impaired, then they must be paid in full or, if paid less than in full, then no class junior may receive anything under the plan. This codifies the absolute priority rule from the dissenting class on down.

With respect to classes of equity, the court may confirm over a dissent if the members of the class are unimpaired, if they receive their liquidation preference or redemption rights, if any, or if no class junior shares under the plan. This, too, is a codification of the absolute priority rule with respect to equity. If a partnership agreement subordinates limited partners to general partners to any degree, then the general principles of paragraph (3) of this subsection would apply to prevent the general partners from being squeezed out.

One requirement applies generally to all classes before the court may confirm under this subsection. No class may be paid more than in full.

The partial codification of the absolute priority rule here is not intended to deprive senior creditor of compensation for being required to take securities in the reorganized debtor that are of an equal priority with the securities offered to a junior class. Under current law, seniors are entitled to compensation for their loss of priority, and the increased risk put upon them by being required to give up their priority will be reflected in a lower value of the securities given to them than the value of comparable securities given to juniors that have not lost a priority position.

Finally, the proponent must request use of this subsection. The court may not confirm notwithstanding nonacceptance unless the proponent requests and the court may then confirm only if subsection (b) is complied with. The court may not rewrite the plan.

A more detailed explanation follows:

The test to be applied by the court is set forth in the various paragraphs of section 1129(b). The elements of the test are new[,] departing from both the absolute priority rule and the best interests of creditors tests found under the Bankruptcy Act [former title 11]. The court is not permitted to alter the terms of the plan. It must merely decide whether the plan complies with the requirements of section 1129(b). If so, the plan is confirmed, if not the plan is denied confirmation.

The procedure followed is simple. The court examines each class of claims or interests designated under section 1123(a)(1) to see if the requirements of section 1129(b) are met. If the class is a class of secured claims, then paragraph (1) contains two tests that must be complied with in order for confirmation to occur. First, under subparagraph (A), the court must be able to find that the consideration given under the plan on account of the secured claim does not exceed the allowed amount of the claim. This condition is not prescribed as a matter of law under section 1129(a), because if the secured claim is compensated in securities of the debtor, a valuation of the business would be necessary to determine the value of the consideration. While section 1129(a) does not contemplate a valuation of the debtor's business, such a valuation will almost always be required under section 1129(b) in order to determine the value of the consideration to be distributed under the plan. Once the valuation is performed, it becomes a simple matter to impose the criterion that no claim will be paid more than in full.

Application of the test under subparagraph (A) also requires a valuation of the consideration "as of the effective date of the plan". This contemplates a present value analysis that will discount value to be received in the future; of course, if the interest rate paid is equivalent to the discount rate used, the present value and face future value will be identical. On the other hand, if no interest is proposed to be paid, the present value will be less than the face future value. For example, consider an allowed secured claim of $1,000 in a class by itself. One plan could propose to pay $1,000 on account of this claim as of the effective date of the plan. Another plan could propose to give a note with a $1,000 face amount due five years after the effective date of the plan on account of this claim. A third plan could propose to give a note in a face amount of $1,000 due five years from the effective date of the plan plus six percent annual interest commencing on the effective date of the plan on account of this claim. The first plan clearly meets the requirements of subparagraph (A) because the amount received on account of the second claim has an equivalent present value as of the effective date of the plan equal to the allowed amount of such claim.

The second plan also meets the requirements of subparagraph (A) because the present value of the five years note as of the effective date of the plan will never exceed the allowed amount of the secured claim; the higher the discount rate, the less present value the note will have. Whether the third plan complies with subparagraph (A) depends on whether the discount rate is less than six percent. Normally, the interest rate used in the plan will be prima facie evidence of the discount rate because the interest rate will reflect an arms length determination of the risk of the security involved and feasibility considerations will tend to understate interest payments. If the court found the discount rate to be greater than or equal to the interest rate used in the plan, then subparagraph (A) would be complied with because the value of the note as of the effective date of the plan would not exceed the allowed amount of the second claim. If, however, the court found the discount rate to be less than the interest rate proposed under the plan, then the present value of the note would exceed $1,000 and the plan would fail of confirmation. On the other hand, it is important to recognize that the future principal amount of a note in excess of the allowed amount of a secured claim may have a present value less than such allowed amount, if the interest rate under the plan is correspondingly less than the discount rate.

Even if the requirements of subparagraph (A) are complied with, the class of secured claims must satisfy one of the three clauses in paragraph (B) in order to pass muster. It is sufficient for confirmation if the class has accepted the plan, or if the claims of the class are unimpaired, or if each holder of a secured claim in the class will receive property of a value as of the effective date of the plan equal to the allowed amount of such claim (unless he has agreed to accept less). It is important to note that under section 506(a), the allowed amount of the secured claim will not include any extent to which the amount of such claim exceeds the value of the property securing such claim. Thus, instead of focusing on secured creditors or unsecured creditors, the statute focuses on secured claims and unsecured claims.

After the court has applied paragraph (1) to each class of secured claims, it then applies paragraph (2) to each class of unsecured claims. Again two separate components must be tested. Subparagraph (A) is identical with the test under section 1129(b)(1)(A) insofar as the holder of an unsecured claim is not permitted to receive property of a value as of the effective date of the plan on account of such claim that is greater than the allowed amount of such claim. In addition, subparagraph (B) requires compliance with one of four conditions. The conditions in clauses (i)–(iii) mirror the conditions of acceptance unimpairment, or full value found in connection with secured claims in section 1129(b)(1)(B).

The condition contained in section 1129(b)(2)(B)(iv) provides another basis for confirming the plan with respect to a class of unsecured claims. It will be of greatest use when an impaired class that has not accepted the plan is to receive less than full value under the plan. The plan may be confirmed under clause (iv) in those circumstances if the class is not unfairly discriminated against with respect to equal classes and if junior classes will receive nothing under the plan. The second criterion is the easier to understand. It is designed to prevent a senior class from giving up consideration to a junior class unless every intermediate class consents, is paid in full, or is unimpaired. This gives intermediate creditors a great deal of leverage in negotiating with senior or secured creditors who wish to have a plan that gives value to equity. One aspect of this test that is not obvious is that whether one class is senior, equal, or junior to another class is relative and not absolute. Thus from the perspective of trade creditors holding unsecured claims, claims of senior and subordinated debentures may be entitled to share on an equal basis with the trade claims. However, from the perspective of the senior unsecured debt, the subordinated debentures are junior.

This point illustrates the lack of precision in the first criterion which demands that a class not be unfairly discriminated against with respect to equal classes. From the perspective of unsecured trade claims, there is no unfair discrimination as long as the total consideration given all other classes of equal rank does not exceed the amount that would result from an exact aliquot distribution. Thus if trade creditors, senior debt, and subordinate debt are each owed $100 and the plan proposes to pay the trade debt $15, the senior debt $30, and the junior debt $0, the plan would not unfairly discriminate against the trade debt nor would any other allocation of consideration under the plan between the senior and junior debt be unfair as to the trade debt as long as the aggregate consideration is less than $30. The senior debt could take $25 and give up $5 to the junior debt and the trade debt would have no cause to complain because as far as it is concerned the junior debt is an equal class.

However, in this latter case the senior debt would have been unfairly discriminated against because the trade debt was being unfairly over-compensated; of course the plan would also fail unless the senior debt was unimpaired, received full value, or accepted the plan, because from its perspective a junior class received property under the plan. Application of the test from the perspective of senior debt is best illustrated by the plan that proposes to pay trade debt $15, senior debt $25, and junior debt $0. Here the senior debt is being unfairly discriminated against with respect to the equal trade debt even though the trade debt receives less than the senior debt. The discrimination arises from the fact that the senior debt is entitled to the rights of the junior debt which in this example entitle the senior debt to share on a 2:1 basis with the trade debt.

Finally, it is necessary to interpret the first criterion from the perspective of subordinated debt. The junior debt is subrogated to the rights of senior debt once the senior debt is paid in full. Thus, while the plan that pays trade debt $15, senior debt $25, and junior debt $0 is not unfairly discriminatory against the junior debt, a plan that proposes to pay trade debt $55, senior debt $100, and junior debt $1, would be unfairly discriminatory. In order to avoid discriminatory treatment against the junior debt, at least $10 would have to be received by such debt under those facts.

The criterion of unfair discrimination is not derived from the fair and equitable rule or from the best interests of creditors test. Rather it preserves just treatment of a dissenting class from the class's own perspective.

If each class of secured claims satisfies the requirements of section 1129(b)(1) and each class of unsecured claims satisfies the requirements of section 1129(b)(2), then the court must still see if each class of interests satisfies section 1129(b)(3) before the plan may be confirmed. Again, two separate criteria must be met. Under subparagraph (A) if the interest entitles the holder thereof to a fixed liquidation preference or if such interest may be redeemed at a fixed price, then the holder of such interest must not receive under the plan on account of such interest property of a value as of the effective date of the plan greater than the greater of these two values of the interest. Preferred stock would be an example of an interest likely to have liquidation preference or redemption price.

If an interest such as most common stock or the interest of a general partnership has neither a fixed liquidation preference nor a fixed redemption price, then the criterion in subparagraph (A) is automatically fulfilled. In addition subparagraph (B) contains five clauses that impose alternative conditions of which at least one must be satisfied in order to warrant confirmation. The first two clauses contain requirements of acceptance or unimpairment similar to the first two clauses in paragraphs (1)(B) and (2)(B). Clause (iii) is similar to the unimpairment test contained in section 1124(3)(B), except that it will apply to cover the issuance securities of the debtor of a value as of the effective date of the plan equal to the greater of any fixed liquidation preference or redemption price. The fourth clause allows confirmation if junior interests are not compensated under the plan and the fifth clause allows confirmation if there are no junior interests. These clauses recognized that as long as senior classes receive no more than full payment, the objection of a junior class will not defeat confirmation unless a class junior to it is receiving value under the plan and the objecting class is impaired. While a determination of impairment may be made under section 1124(3)(B)(iii) without a precise valuation of the business when common stock is clearly under water, once section 1129(b) is used, a more detailed valuation is a necessary byproduct. Thus, if no property is given to a holder of an interest under the plan, the interest should be clearly worthless in order to find unimpairment under section 1124(3)(B)(iii) and section 1129(a)(8); otherwise, since a class of interests receiving no property is deemed to object under section 1126(g), the more precise valuation of section 1129(b) should be used.

If all of the requirements of section 1129(b) are complied with, then the court may confirm the plan subject to other limitations such as those found in section 1129(a) and (d).

Subsection (c) of section 1129 governs confirmation when more than one plan meets the requirements of the section. The court must consider the preferences of creditors and equity security holders in determining which plan to confirm.

Subsection (d) requires the court to deny confirmation if the principal purpose of the plan is the avoidance of taxes (through use of sections 346 and 1146, and applicable provisions of State law or the Internal Revenue Code [title 26] governing bankruptcy reorganizations) or the avoidance of section 5 of the Securities Act of 1933 [15 U.S.C. 77e] (through use of section 1145).

References in Text

Section 5 of the Securities Act of 1933, referred to in subsec. (d), is classified to section 77e of Title 15, Commerce and Trade.

Amendments

2010—Subsec. (a)(16). Pub. L. 111–327 substituted "under the plan" for "of the plan".

2005—Subsec. (a)(9)(A). Pub. L. 109–8, §1502(a)(8)(A), substituted "507(a)(2) or 507(a)(3)" for "507(a)(1) or 507(a)(2)".

Subsec. (a)(9)(B). Pub. L. 109–8, §1502(a)(8)(B), substituted "507(a)(1)" for "507(a)(3)".

Subsec. (a)(9)(C). Pub. L. 109–8, §710(2), substituted "regular installment payments in cash—" and cls. (i) to (iii) for "deferred cash payments, over a period not exceeding six years after the date of assessment of such claim, of a value, as of the effective date of the plan, equal to the allowed amount of such claim."

Subsec. (a)(9)(D). Pub. L. 109–8, §710(1), (3), added subpar. (D).

Subsec. (a)(14). Pub. L. 109–8, §213(1), added par. (14).

Subsec. (a)(15). Pub. L. 109–8, §321(c)(1), added par. (15).

Subsec. (a)(16). Pub. L. 109–8, §1221(b), added par. (16).

Subsec. (b)(2)(B)(ii). Pub. L. 109–8, §321(c)(2), inserted before period at end ", except that in a case in which the debtor is an individual, the debtor may retain property included in the estate under section 1115, subject to the requirements of subsection (a)(14) of this section".

Subsec. (e). Pub. L. 109–8, §438, added subsec. (e).

1994—Subsec. (a)(4). Pub. L. 103–394, §501(d)(32)(A)(i), substituted period for semicolon at end.

Subsec. (a)(9)(B). Pub. L. 103–394, §304(h)(7)(i), substituted ", 507(a)(6), or 507(a)(7)" for "or 507(a)(6)".

Subsec. (a)(9)(C). Pub. L. 103–394, §304(h)(7)(ii), substituted "507(a)(8)" for "507(a)(7)".

Subsec. (a)(12). Pub. L. 103–394, §501(d)(32)(A)(ii), inserted "of title 28" after "section 1930".

Subsec. (d). Pub. L. 103–394, §501(d)(32)(B), struck out "(15 U.S.C. 77e)" after "Act of 1933".

1988—Subsec. (a)(13). Pub. L. 100–334 added par. (13).

1986—Subsec. (a)(7). Pub. L. 99–554, §283(v)(1), struck out "of" after "to".

Subsec. (a)(9)(B). Pub. L. 99–554, §283(v)(2), inserted reference to section 507(a)(6).

Subsec. (a)(9)(C). Pub. L. 99–554, §283(v)(3), substituted "507(a)(7)" for "507(a)(6)".

Subsec. (a)(12). Pub. L. 99–554, §225, added par. (12).

1984—Subsec. (a)(1), (2). Pub. L. 98–353, §512(a)(1), (2), substituted "title" for "chapter".

Subsec. (a)(4). Pub. L. 98–353, §512(a)(3), amended par. (4) generally. Prior to amendment, par. (4) read as follows: "(A) Any payment made or promised by the proponent, by the debtor, or by a person issuing securities or acquiring property under the plan, for services or for costs and expenses in, or in connection with, the case, or in connection with the plan and incident to the case, has been disclosed to the court; and (B)(i) any such payment made before confirmation of the plan is reasonable; or (ii) if such payment is to be fixed after confirmation of the plan, such payment is subject to the approval of the court as reasonable."

Subsec. (a)(5)(A)(ii). Pub. L. 98–353, §512(a)(4), substituted "; and" for the period at the end.

Subsec. (a)(5)(B). Pub. L. 98–353, §512(a)(5), substituted "the" for "The".

Subsec. (a)(6). Pub. L. 98–353, §512(a)(6), inserted "governmental" after "Any".

Subsec. (a)(7). Pub. L. 98–353, §512(a)(7)(A), substituted "of each impaired class of claims or interests" for "each class".

Subsec. (a)(7)(B). Pub. L. 98–353, §512(a)(7)(B), substituted "holder's" for "creditor's".

Subsec. (a)(8). Pub. L. 98–353, §512(a)(8), inserted "of claims or interests" after "each class".

Subsec. (a)(10). Pub. L. 98–353, §512(a)(9), substituted "If a class of claims is impaired under the plan, at least one class of claims that is impaired under the plan has accepted the plan, determined without including any acceptance of the plan by any insider" for "At least one class of claims has accepted the plan, determined without including any acceptance of the plan by any insider holding a claim of such class".

Subsec. (b)(2)(A)(i)(I), (ii). Pub. L. 98–353, §512(b)(1), substituted "liens" for "lien" wherever appearing.

Subsec. (b)(2)(B)(ii). Pub. L. 98–353, §512(b)(2), inserted "under the plan" after "retain".

Subsec. (b)(2)(C)(i). Pub. L. 98–353, §512(b)(3), substituted "interest" for "claim", and "or the value" for "and the value".

Subsec. (d). Pub. L. 98–353, §512(c), inserted "the application of" and provisions requiring that in any hearing under this subsection, the governmental unit has the burden of proof on the issue of avoidance.

Effective Date of 2005 Amendment

Amendment by section 1221(b) of Pub. L. 109–8 applicable to cases pending under this title on Apr. 20, 2005, or filed under this title on or after Apr. 20, 2005, with certain exceptions, see section 1221(d) of Pub. L. 109–8, set out as a note under section 363 of this title.

Amendment by sections 213(1), 321(c), 438, 710, and 1502(a)(8) of Pub. L. 109–8 effective 180 days after Apr. 20, 2005, and not applicable with respect to cases commenced under this title before such effective date, except as otherwise provided, see section 1501 of Pub. L. 109–8, set out as a note under section 101 of this title.

Effective Date of 1994 Amendment

Amendment by Pub. L. 103–394 effective Oct. 22, 1994, and not applicable with respect to cases commenced under this title before Oct. 22, 1994, see section 702 of Pub. L. 103–394, set out as a note under section 101 of this title.

Effective Date of 1988 Amendment

Amendment by Pub. L. 100–334 effective June 16, 1988, but not applicable to cases commenced under this title before that date, see section 4 of Pub. L. 100–334, set out as an Effective Date note under section 1114 of this title.

Effective Date of 1986 Amendment

Effective date and applicability of amendment by section 225 of Pub. L. 99–554 dependent upon the judicial district involved, see section 302(d), (e) of Pub. L. 99–554, set out as a note under section 581 of Title 28, Judiciary and Judicial Procedure.

Amendment by section 283 of Pub. L. 99–554 effective 30 days after Oct. 27, 1986, see section 302(a) of Pub. L. 99–554.

Effective Date of 1984 Amendment

Amendment by Pub. L. 98–353 effective with respect to cases filed 90 days after July 10, 1984, see section 552(a) of Pub. L. 98–353, set out as a note under section 101 of this title.

SUBCHAPTER III—POSTCONFIRMATION MATTERS

§1141. Effect of confirmation

(a) Except as provided in subsections (d)(2) and (d)(3) of this section, the provisions of a confirmed plan bind the debtor, any entity issuing securities under the plan, any entity acquiring property under the plan, and any creditor, equity security holder, or general partner in the debtor, whether or not the claim or interest of such creditor, equity security holder, or general partner is impaired under the plan and whether or not such creditor, equity security holder, or general partner has accepted the plan.

(b) Except as otherwise provided in the plan or the order confirming the plan, the confirmation of a plan vests all of the property of the estate in the debtor.

(c) Except as provided in subsections (d)(2) and (d)(3) of this section and except as otherwise provided in the plan or in the order confirming the plan, after confirmation of a plan, the property dealt with by the plan is free and clear of all claims and interests of creditors, equity security holders, and of general partners in the debtor.

(d)(1) Except as otherwise provided in this subsection, in the plan, or in the order confirming the plan, the confirmation of a plan—

(A) discharges the debtor from any debt that arose before the date of such confirmation, and any debt of a kind specified in section 502(g), 502(h), or 502(i) of this title, whether or not—

(i) a proof of the claim based on such debt is filed or deemed filed under section 501 of this title;

(ii) such claim is allowed under section 502 of this title; or

(iii) the holder of such claim has accepted the plan; and

(B) terminates all rights and interests of equity security holders and general partners provided for by the plan.

(2) A discharge under this chapter does not discharge a debtor who is an individual from any debt excepted from discharge under section 523 of this title.

(3) The confirmation of a plan does not discharge a debtor if—

(A) the plan provides for the liquidation of all or substantially all of the property of the estate;

(B) the debtor does not engage in business after consummation of the plan; and

(C) the debtor would be denied a discharge under section 727(a) of this title if the case were a case under chapter 7 of this title.

(4) The court may approve a written waiver of discharge executed by the debtor after the order for relief under this chapter.

(5) In a case in which the debtor is an individual—

(A) unless after notice and a hearing the court orders otherwise for cause, confirmation of the plan does not discharge any debt provided for in the plan until the court grants a discharge on completion of all payments under the plan;

(B) at any time after the confirmation of the plan, and after notice and a hearing, the court may grant a discharge to the debtor who has not completed payments under the plan if—

(i) the value, as of the effective date of the plan, of property actually distributed under the plan on account of each allowed unsecured claim is not less than the amount that would have been paid on such claim if the estate of the debtor had been liquidated under chapter 7 on such date;

(ii) modification of the plan under section 1127 is not practicable; and

(iii) subparagraph (C) permits the court to grant a discharge; and

(C) the court may grant a discharge if, after notice and a hearing held not more than 10 days before the date of the entry of the order granting the discharge, the court finds that there is no reasonable cause to believe that—

(i) section 522(q)(1) may be applicable to the debtor; and

(ii) there is pending any proceeding in which the debtor may be found guilty of a felony of the kind described in section 522(q)(1)(A) or liable for a debt of the kind described in section 522(q)(1)(B);

and if the requirements of subparagraph (A) or (B) are met.

(6) Notwithstanding paragraph (1), the confirmation of a plan does not discharge a debtor that is a corporation from any debt—

(A) of a kind specified in paragraph (2)(A) or (2)(B) of section 523(a) that is owed to a domestic governmental unit, or owed to a person as the result of an action filed under subchapter III of chapter 37 of title 31 or any similar State statute; or

(B) for a tax or customs duty with respect to which the debtor—

(i) made a fraudulent return; or

(ii) willfully attempted in any manner to evade or to defeat such tax or such customs duty.

(Pub. L. 95–598, Nov. 6, 1978, 92 Stat. 2638; Pub. L. 98–353, title III, §513, July 10, 1984, 98 Stat. 387; Pub. L. 109–8, title III, §§321(d), 330(b), title VII, §708, Apr. 20, 2005, 119 Stat. 95, 101, 126; Pub. L. 111–327, §2(a)(36), Dec. 22, 2010, 124 Stat. 3561.)

Historical and Revision Notes

legislative statements

Section 1141(d) of the House amendment is derived from a comparable provision contained in the Senate amendment. However, section 1141(d)(2) of the House amendment is derived from the House bill as preferable to the Senate amendment. It is necessary for a corporation or partnership undergoing reorganization to be able to present its creditors with a fixed list of liabilities upon which the creditors or third parties can make intelligent decisions. Retaining an exception for discharge with respect to nondischargeable taxes would leave an undesirable uncertainty surrounding reorganizations that is unacceptable. Section 1141(d)(3) is derived from the Senate amendment. Section 1141(d)(4) is likewise derived from the Senate amendment.

senate report no. 95–989

Subsection (a) of this section makes the provisions of a confirmed plan binding on the debtor, any entity issuing securities under the plan, any entity acquiring property under the plan, and any creditor, equity security holder, or general partner in the debtor, whether or not the claim or interest of the creditor, equity security holder, or partner is impaired under the plan and whether or not he has accepted the plan. There are two exceptions, enumerated in paragraph (2) and (3) of subsection (d).

Unless the plan or the order confirming the plan provides otherwise, the confirmation of a plan vests all of the property of the estate in the debtor and releases it from all claims and interests of creditors, equity security holders and general partners.

Subsection (d) contains the discharge for a reorganized debtor. Paragraph (1) specifies that the confirmation of a plan discharges the debtor from any debt that arose before the date of the order for relief unless the plan or the order confirming the plan provides otherwise. The discharge is effective against those claims whether or not proof of the claim is filed (or deemed filed), and whether or not the claim is allowed. The discharge also terminates all rights and interests of equity security holders and general partners provided for by the plan. The paragraph permits the plan or the order confirming the plan to provide otherwise, and excepts certain debts from the discharge as provided in paragraphs (2) and (3).

Paragraph (2) of subsection (d) makes clear what taxes remain nondischargeable in the case of a corporate debtor emerging from a reorganization under chapter 11. Nondischargeable taxes in such a reorganization are the priority taxes (under section 507) and tax payments which come due during and after the proceeding under a deferred or part-payment agreement which the debtor had entered into with the tax authority before the bankruptcy proceedings began. On the other hand, a corporation which is taken over by its creditors through a plan of reorganization will not continue to be liable for nonpriority taxes arising from the corporation's prepetition fraud, failure to file a return, or failure to file a timely return, since the creditors who take over the reorganized company should not bear the burden of acts for which the creditors were not at fault.

Paragraph (3) specifies that the debtor is not discharged by the confirmation of a plan if the plan is a liquidating plan and if the debtor would be denied discharge in a liquidation case under section 727. Specifically, if all or substantially all of the distribution under the plan is of all or substantially all of the property of the estate or the proceeds of it, if the business, if any, of the debtor does not continue, and if the debtor would be denied a discharge under section 727 (such as if the debtor were not an individual or if he had committed an act that would lead to a denial of discharge), the chapter 11 discharge is not granted.

Paragraph (4) authorizes the court to approve a waiver of discharge by the debtor.

house report no. 95–595

Paragraph (2) [of subsec. (d)] makes applicable to an individual debtor the general exceptions to discharge that are enumerated in section 523(a) of the bankruptcy code.

Amendments

2010—Subsec. (d)(5)(B)(iii). Pub. L. 111–327, §2(a)(36)(A), added cl. (iii).

Subsec. (d)(5)(C). Pub. L. 111–327, §2(a)(36)(B), substituted "the court may grant a discharge if," for "unless" in introductory provisions and inserted concluding provisions.

2005—Subsec. (d)(2). Pub. L. 109–8, §321(d)(1), substituted "A discharge under this chapter does not discharge a debtor who is an individual" for "The confirmation of a plan does not discharge an individual debtor".

Subsec. (d)(5). Pub. L. 109–8, §321(d)(2), added par. (5).

Subsec. (d)(5)(C). Pub. L. 109–8, §330(b), added subpar. (C).

Subsec. (d)(6). Pub. L. 109–8, §708, added par. (6).

1984—Subsec. (a). Pub. L. 98–353, §513(a), substituted "any creditor, equity security holder, or general partner in" for "any creditor or equity security holder of, or general partner in,".

Subsec. (c). Pub. L. 98–353, §513(b), amended subsec. (c) generally. Prior to amendment, subsec. (c) read as follows: "After confirmation of a plan, the property dealt with by the plan is free and clear of all claims and interests of creditors, of equity security holders, and of general partners in the debtor, except as otherwise provided in the plan or in the order confirming the plan."

Effective Date of 2005 Amendment

Amendments by Pub. L. 109–8 effective 180 days after Apr. 20, 2005, with amendments by sections 321(d) and 708 of Pub. L. 109–8 not applicable with respect to cases commenced under this title before such effective date, except as otherwise provided, and amendment by section 330(b) of Pub. L. 109–8 applicable with respect to cases commenced under this title on or after Apr. 20, 2005, see section 1501 of Pub. L. 109–8, set out as a note under section 101 of this title.

Effective Date of 1984 Amendment

Amendment by Pub. L. 98–353 effective with respect to cases filed 90 days after July 10, 1984, see section 552(a) of Pub. L. 98–353, set out as a note under section 101 of this title.

§1142. Implementation of plan

(a) Notwithstanding any otherwise applicable nonbankruptcy law, rule, or regulation relating to financial condition, the debtor and any entity organized or to be organized for the purpose of carrying out the plan shall carry out the plan and shall comply with any orders of the court.

(b) The court may direct the debtor and any other necessary party to execute or deliver or to join in the execution or delivery of any instrument required to effect a transfer of property dealt with by a confirmed plan, and to perform any other act, including the satisfaction of any lien, that is necessary for the consummation of the plan.

(Pub. L. 95–598, Nov. 6, 1978, 92 Stat. 2639; Pub. L. 98–353, title III, §514(a), (c), (d), July 10, 1984, 98 Stat. 387.)

Amendments

1984—Pub. L. 98–353, §514(a), substituted "Implementation" for "Execution" in section catchline.

Subsec. (a). Pub. L. 98–353, §514(c), struck out the comma after "shall carry out the plan".

Subsec. (b). Pub. L. 98–353, §514(d), inserted "a" after "by".

Effective Date of 1984 Amendment

Amendment by Pub. L. 98–353 effective with respect to cases filed 90 days after July 10, 1984, see section 552(a) of Pub. L. 98–353, set out as a note under section 101 of this title.

§1143. Distribution

If a plan requires presentment or surrender of a security or the performance of any other act as a condition to participation in distribution under the plan, such action shall be taken not later than five years after the date of the entry of the order of confirmation. Any entity that has not within such time presented or surrendered such entity's security or taken any such other action that the plan requires may not participate in distribution under the plan.

(Pub. L. 95–598, Nov. 6, 1978, 92 Stat. 2639.)

Historical and Revision Notes

senate report no. 95–989

Section 1143 fixes a 5-year limitation on presentment or surrender of securities or the performance of any other act that is a condition to participation in distribution under the plan. The 5 years runs from the date of the entry of the order of confirmation. Any entity that does not take the appropriate action with the 5-year period is barred from participation in the distribution under the plan.

§1144. Revocation of an order of confirmation

On request of a party in interest at any time before 180 days after the date of the entry of the order of confirmation, and after notice and a hearing, the court may revoke such order if and only if such order was procured by fraud. An order under this section revoking an order of confirmation shall—

(1) contain such provisions as are necessary to protect any entity acquiring rights in good faith reliance on the order of confirmation; and

(2) revoke the discharge of the debtor.

(Pub. L. 95–598, Nov. 6, 1978, 92 Stat. 2639; Pub. L. 98–353, title III, §515, July 10, 1984, 98 Stat. 387.)

Historical and Revision Notes

senate report no. 95–989

If an order of confirmation was procured by fraud, then the court may revoke the order on request of a party in interest if the request is made before 180 days after the date of the entry of the order of confirmation. The order revoking the order of confirmation must revoke the discharge of the debtor, and contain such provisions as are necessary to protect any entity acquiring rights in good faith reliance on the order of confirmation.

Amendments

1984—Pub. L. 98–353 inserted "if and only" after "revoke such order".

Effective Date of 1984 Amendment

Amendment by Pub. L. 98–353 effective with respect to cases filed 90 days after July 10, 1984, see section 552(a) of Pub. L. 98–353, set out as a note under section 101 of this title.

§1145. Exemption from securities laws

(a) Except with respect to an entity that is an underwriter as defined in subsection (b) of this section, section 5 of the Securities Act of 1933 and any State or local law requiring registration for offer or sale of a security or registration or licensing of an issuer of, underwriter of, or broker or dealer in, a security do not apply to—

(1) the offer or sale under a plan of a security of the debtor, of an affiliate participating in a joint plan with the debtor, or of a successor to the debtor under the plan—

(A) in exchange for a claim against, an interest in, or a claim for an administrative expense in the case concerning, the debtor or such affiliate; or

(B) principally in such exchange and partly for cash or property;

(2) the offer of a security through any warrant, option, right to subscribe, or conversion privilege that was sold in the manner specified in paragraph (1) of this subsection, or the sale of a security upon the exercise of such a warrant, option, right, or privilege;

(3) the offer or sale, other than under a plan, of a security of an issuer other than the debtor or an affiliate, if—

(A) such security was owned by the debtor on the date of the filing of the petition;

(B) the issuer of such security is—

(i) required to file reports under section 13 or 15(d) of the Securities Exchange Act of 1934; and

(ii) in compliance with the disclosure and reporting provision of such applicable section; and

(C) such offer or sale is of securities that do not exceed—

(i) during the two-year period immediately following the date of the filing of the petition, four percent of the securities of such class outstanding on such date; and

(ii) during any 180-day period following such two-year period, one percent of the securities outstanding at the beginning of such 180-day period; or

(4) a transaction by a stockbroker in a security that is executed after a transaction of a kind specified in paragraph (1) or (2) of this subsection in such security and before the expiration of 40 days after the first date on which such security was bona fide offered to the public by the issuer or by or through an underwriter, if such stockbroker provides, at the time of or before such transaction by such stockbroker, a disclosure statement approved under section 1125 of this title, and, if the court orders, information supplementing such disclosure statement.

(b)(1) Except as provided in paragraph (2) of this subsection and except with respect to ordinary trading transactions of an entity that is not an issuer, an entity is an underwriter under section 2(a)(11) of the Securities Act of 1933, if such entity—

(A) purchases a claim against, interest in, or claim for an administrative expense in the case concerning, the debtor, if such purchase is with a view to distribution of any security received or to be received in exchange for such a claim or interest;

(B) offers to sell securities offered or sold under the plan for the holders of such securities;

(C) offers to buy securities offered or sold under the plan from the holders of such securities, if such offer to buy is—

(i) with a view to distribution of such securities; and

(ii) under an agreement made in connection with the plan, with the consummation of the plan, or with the offer or sale of securities under the plan; or

(D) is an issuer, as used in such section 2(a)(11), with respect to such securities.

(2) An entity is not an underwriter under section 2(a)(11) of the Securities Act of 1933 or under paragraph (1) of this subsection with respect to an agreement that provides only for—

(A)(i) the matching or combining of fractional interests in securities offered or sold under the plan into whole interests; or

(ii) the purchase or sale of such fractional interests from or to entities receiving such fractional interests under the plan; or

(B) the purchase or sale for such entities of such fractional or whole interests as are necessary to adjust for any remaining fractional interests after such matching.

(3) An entity other than an entity of the kind specified in paragraph (1) of this subsection is not an underwriter under section 2(a)(11) of the Securities Act of 1933 with respect to any securities offered or sold to such entity in the manner specified in subsection (a)(1) of this section.

(c) An offer or sale of securities of the kind and in the manner specified under subsection (a)(1) of this section is deemed to be a public offering.

(d) The Trust Indenture Act of 1939 does not apply to a note issued under the plan that matures not later than one year after the effective date of the plan.

(Pub. L. 95–598, Nov. 6, 1978, 92 Stat. 2639; Pub. L. 98–353, title III, §516, July 10, 1984, 98 Stat. 387; Pub. L. 103–394, title V, §501(d)(33), Oct. 22, 1994, 108 Stat. 4146; Pub. L. 111–327, §2(a)(37), Dec. 22, 2010, 124 Stat. 3561.)

Historical and Revision Notes

legislative statements

Section 1145 of the House amendment deletes a provision contained in section 1145(a)(1) of the House bill in favor of a more adequate provision contained in section 364(f) of the House amendment. In addition, section 1145(d) has been added to indicate that the Trust Indenture Act [15 U.S.C. 77aaa et seq.] does not apply to a commercial note issued under a plan, if the note matures not later than 1 year after the effective date of the plan. Some commercial notes receive such an exemption under 304(a)(4) of the Trust Indenture Act of 1939 (15 U.S.C. §77ddd(a)(4)) and others may receive protection by incorporation by reference into the Trust Indenture

Act of securities exempt under section 3a(3), (7), (9), or (10) of the Securities Act of 1933 [15 U.S.C. 77c(a)(3), (7), (9), (10)].

In light of the amendments made to the Securities Act of 1933 [15 U.S.C. 77a et seq.] in title III of the House amendment to H.R. 8200, a specific exemption from the Trust Indenture Act [15 U.S.C. 77aaa et seq.] is required in order to create certainty regarding plans of reorganization. Section 1145(d) is not intended to imply that commercial notes issued under a plan that matures more than 1 year after the effective date of the plan are automatically covered by the Trust Indenture Act of 1939 since such notes may fall within another exemption thereto.

One other point with respect to Section 1145 deserves comment. Section 1145(a)(3) grants a debtor in possession or trustee in chapter 11 an extremely narrow portfolio security exemption from section 5 of the Securities Act of 1933 [15 U.S.C. 77e] or any comparable State law. The provision was considered by Congress and adopted after much study. The exemption is reasonable and is more restrictive than comparable provisions under the Securities Act [15 U.S.C. 77a et seq.] relating to the estates of decedents. Subsequent to passage of H.R. 8200 by the House of Representatives, the Securities and Exchange Commission promulgated Rule 148 to treat with this problem under existing law. Members of Congress received opinions from attorneys indicating dissatisfaction with the Commission's rule although the rule has been amended, the ultimate limitation of 1 percent promulgated by the Commission is wholly unacceptable.

The Commission rule would permit a trustee or debtor in possession to distribute securities at the rate of 1 percent every 6 months. Section 1145(a)(3) permits the trustee to distribute 4 percent of the securities during the 2-year period immediately following the date of the filing of the petition. In addition, the security must be of a reporting company under section 13 of the Securities and Exchange Act of 1934 [15 U.S.C. 78m], and must be in compliance with all applicable requirements for the continuing of trading in the security on the date that the trustee offers or sells the security.

With these safeguards the trustee or debtor in possession should be able to distribute 4 percent of the securities of a class at any time during the 2-year period immediately following the date of the filing of the petition in the interests of expediting bankruptcy administration. The same rationale that applies in expeditiously terminating decedents' estates applies no less to an estate under title 11.

senate report no. 95–989

This section, derived from similar provisions found in sections 264, 393, and 518 of the Bankruptcy Act [sections 664, 793, and 918 of former title 11], provides a limited exemption from the securities laws for securities issued under a plan of reorganization and for certain other securities. Subsection (a) exempts from the requirements of section 5 of the Securities Act of 1933 [15 U.S.C. 77e] and from any State or local law requiring registration or licensing of an issuer of, underwriter of, or broker or dealer in, a security, the offer or sale of certain securities.

Paragraph (1) of subsection (a) exempts the offer or sale under section 364 of any security that is not an equity security or convertible into an equity security. This paragraph is designed to facilitate the issuance of certificates of indebtedness, and should be read in light of the amendment made in section 306 of title III to section 3(a)(7) of the 1933 act [15 U.S.C. 77c(a)(7)].

Paragraph (2) of subsection (a) exempts the offer or sale of any security of the debtor, a successor to the debtor, or an affiliate in a joint plan, distributed under a plan if such security is exchanged in principal part for securities of the debtor or for allowed claims or administrative expenses. This exemption is carried over from present law, except as to administrative claims, but is limited to prevent distribution of securities to other than claim holders or equity security holders of the debtor or the estate.

Paragraph (3) of subsection (a) exempts the offer or sale of any security that arises from the exercise of a subscription right or from the exercise of a conversion privilege when such subscription right or conversion privilege was issued under a plan. This exemption is necessary in order to enhance the marketability of subscription rights or conversion privileges, including warrants, offered or sold under a plan. This is present law.

Paragraph (4) of subsection (a) exempts sales of portfolio securities, excluding securities of the debtor or its affiliate, owned by the debtor on the date of the filing of the petition. The purpose of this exemption is to allow the debtor or trustee to sell or distribute, without allowing manipulation schemes, restricted portfolio securities held or acquired by the debtor. Subparagraph (B) of section 1145(a)(4) limits the exemption to securities of a company that is required to file reports under section 13 of the Securities Act [15 U.S.C. 78m] and that is in compliance with all requirements for the continuance of trading those securities. This limitation effectively prevents selling into the market "cats and dogs" of a nonreporting company. Subparagraph (C) places a limitation on the amount of restricted securities that may be distributed. During the case, the trustee may sell up to 4 percent of each class of restricted securities at any time during the first 2 years and 1 percent during any 180-day period thereafter. This relaxation of the resale rules for debtors in holding restricted securities is similar to but less extensive than the relaxation in SEC Rule 114(c)(3)(v) for the estates of deceased holders of securities.

Paragraph (5) contains an exemption for brokers and dealers (stockbrokers, as defined in title 11) akin to the exemption provided by section 4(3)(A) of the Securities Act of 1933 [15 U.S.C. 77d(3)(A)]. Instead of being required to supply a prospectus, however, the stockbroker is required to supply the approved disclosure statement, and if the court orders, information supplementing the disclosure statement. Under present law, the stockholder is not required to supply anything.

Subsection (b) is new. The subsection should be read in light of the amendment in section 306 of title III to the 1933 act [15 U.S.C. 77c(a)(7), (9), (10)]. It specifies the standards under which a creditor, equity security holder, or other entity acquiring securities under the plan may resell them. The Securities Act places limitations on sales by underwriters. This subsection defines who is an underwriter, and thus restricted, and who is free to resell. Paragraph (1) enumerates real underwriters that participate in a classical underwriting. A person is an underwriter if he purchases a claim against, interest in, or claim for an administrative expense in the case concerning, the debtor, with a view to distribution or interest. This provision covers the purchase of a certificate of indebtedness issued under proposed 11 U.S.C. 364 and purchased from the debtor, if the purchase of the certificate was with a view to distribution.

A person is also an underwriter if he offers to sell securities offered or sold under the plan for the holders of such securities, or offers to buy securities offered or sold under the plan from the holders of such securities, if the offer to buy is with a view to distribution of the securities and under an agreement made in connection with the plan, with the consummation of the plan or with the offer or sale of securities under the plan. Finally, a person is an underwriter if he is an issuer, as used in section 2(11) of the Securities Act of 1933 [15 U.S.C. 77b(11)].

Paragraph (2) of subsection (b) exempts from the definition of underwriter any entity to the extent that any agreement that would bring the entity under the definition in paragraph (1) provides only for the matching combination of fractional interests in the covered securities or the purchase or sale of fractional interests. This paragraph and paragraph (1) are modeled after former rule 133 of the Securities and Exchange Commission.

Paragraph (3) specifies that if an entity is not an underwriter under the provisions of paragraph (1), as limited by paragraph (2), then the entity is not an underwriter for the purposes of the Securities Act of 1933 [15 U.S.C. 77a et seq.] with respect to the covered securities, that is, those offered or sold in an exempt transaction specified in subsection (a)(2). This makes clear that the current definition of underwriter in section 2(11) of the Securities Act of 1933 [15 U.S.C. 77b(11)] does not apply to such a creditor. The definition in that section technically applies to any person that purchases securities with "a view to distribution." If literally applied, it would prevent any creditor in a bankruptcy case from selling securities received without filing a registration statement or finding another exemption.

Subsection (b) is a first run transaction exemption and does not exempt a creditor that, for example, some years later becomes an underwriter by reacquiring securities originally issued under a plan.

Subsection (c) makes an offer or sale of securities under the plan in an exempt transaction (as specified in subsection (a)(2)) a public offering, in order to prevent characterization of the distribution as a "private placement" which would result in restrictions, under rule 144 of the SEC, on the resale of the securities.

References in Text

Section 5 of the Securities Act of 1933, referred to in subsec. (a), is classified to section 77e of Title 15, Commerce and Trade.

Sections 13 and 15(d) of the Securities Exchange Act of 1934, referred to in subsec. (a)(3)(B)(i), are classified to sections 78m and 78o(d), respectively, of Title 15, Commerce and Trade.

The Trust Indenture Act of 1939, referred to in subsec. (d), is title III of act May 27, 1933, ch. 38, as added Aug. 3, 1939, ch. 411, 53 Stat. 1149, as amended, which is classified generally to subchapter III (§77aaa et seq.) of chapter 2A of Title 15, Commerce and Trade. For complete classification of this Act to the Code, see section 77aaa of Title 15 and Tables.

Amendments

2010—Subsec. (b). Pub. L. 111–327 substituted "2(a)(11)" for "2(11)" wherever appearing.

1994—Subsec. (a). Pub. L. 103–394, §501(d)(33)(A), in introductory provisions struck out "(15 U.S.C. 77e)" after "Act of 1933" and substituted "do not apply" for "does not apply" and in par. (3)(B)(i) struck out "(15 U.S.C. 78m or 78o(d))" after "Act of 1934".

Subsec. (b)(1). Pub. L. 103–394, §501(d)(33)(B), struck out "(15 U.S.C. 77b(11))" after "Act of 1933".

Subsec. (d). Pub. L. 103–394, §501(d)(33)(C), struck out "(15 U.S.C. 77aaa et seq.)" after "Act of 1939".

1984—Subsec. (a)(3)(B)(i). Pub. L. 98–353, §516(a)(1), inserted "or 15(d)" after "13", and "or 78o(d)" after "78m".

Subsec. (a)(3)(B)(ii). Pub. L. 98–353, §516(a)(2), amended cl. (ii) generally. Prior to amendment, cl. (ii) read as follows: "in compliance with all applicable requirements for the continuance of trading in such security on the date of such offer or sale; and".

Subsec. (a)(4). Pub. L. 98–353, §516(a)(3), substituted "stockbroker" for "stockholder" in two places.

Subsec. (b)(1). Pub. L. 98–353, §516(b)(1), inserted "and except with respect to ordinary trading transactions of an entity that is not an issuer".

Subsec. (b)(1)(C). Pub. L. 98–353, §516(b)(2), substituted "from" for "for".

Subsec. (b)(2)(A)(i). Pub. L. 98–353, §516(b)(3), substituted "or combining" for "combination".

Subsec. (b)(2)(A)(ii). Pub. L. 98–353, §516(b)(4), substituted "from or to" for "among".

Subsec. (d). Pub. L. 98–353, §516(c), struck out "commercial" before "note".

Effective Date of 1994 Amendment

Amendment by Pub. L. 103–394 effective Oct. 22, 1994, and not applicable with respect to cases commenced under this title before Oct. 22, 1994, see section 702 of Pub. L. 103–394, set out as a note under section 101 of this title.

Effective Date of 1984 Amendment

Amendment by Pub. L. 98–353 effective with respect to cases filed 90 days after July 10, 1984, see section 552(a) of Pub. L. 98–353, set out as a note under section 101 of this title.

§1146. Special tax provisions

(a) The issuance, transfer, or exchange of a security, or the making or delivery of an instrument of transfer under a plan confirmed under section 1129 of this title, may not be taxed under any law imposing a stamp tax or similar tax.

(b) The court may authorize the proponent of a plan to request a determination, limited to questions of law, by a State or local governmental unit charged with responsibility for collection or determination of a tax on or measured by income, of the tax effects, under section 346 of this title and under the law imposing such tax, of the plan. In the event of an actual controversy, the court may declare such effects after the earlier of—

(1) the date on which such governmental unit responds to the request under this subsection; or

(2) 270 days after such request.

(Pub. L. 95–598, Nov. 6, 1978, 92 Stat. 2641; Pub. L. 98–353, title III, §517, July 10, 1984, 98 Stat. 388; Pub. L. 109–8, title VII, §719(b)(3), Apr. 20, 2005, 119 Stat. 133.)

Historical and Revision Notes

legislative statements

Section 1146 of the House amendment represents a compromise between the House bill and Senate amendment.

Special tax provisions: reorganization: The House bill provided rules on the effect of bankruptcy on the taxable year of the debtor and on tax return filing requirements for State and local taxes only. The House bill also exempted from State or local stamp taxes the issuance, transfer, or exchange of a security, or the making or delivery of an instrument of transfer under a plan. The House bill also authorized the bankruptcy court to declare the tax effects of a reorganization plan after the proponent of the plan had requested a ruling from State or local tax authority and either had received an unfavorable ruling or the tax authority had not issued a ruling within 270 days.

The Senate amendment deleted the rules concerning the taxable years of the debtor and tax return filing requirements since the Federal rules were to be considered in the next Congress. It broadened the rule exempting transfers of securities to include Federal stamp or similar taxes, if any. In addition, the Senate amendment deleted the provision which permitted the bankruptcy court to determine the tax effects of a plan.

The House amendment retains the State and local rules in the House bill with one modification. Under the House amendment, the power of the bankruptcy court to declare the tax effects of the plan is limited to issues of law and not to questions of fact such as the allowance of specific deductions. Thus, the bankruptcy court could declare whether the reorganization qualified for taxfree status under State or local tax rules, but it could not declare the dollar amount of any tax attributes that survive the reorganization.

senate report no. 95–989

Section 1146 provides special tax rules applicable to Title 11 reorganizations. Subsection (a) provides that the taxable period of an individual debtor terminates on the date of the order for relief, unless the case has been converted into a reorganization from a liquidation proceeding.

Subsection (b) requires the trustee of the estate of an individual debtor in a reorganization to file a tax return for each taxable period while the case is pending after the order for relief. For corporations in chapter 11, the trustee is required to file the tax returns due while the case is pending (sec. 346(c)(2)).

Subsection (c) exempts from Federal, State, or local stamp taxes the issuance, transfer, or exchange of a security, or the making or delivery of an instrument of transfer under a plan. This subsection is derived from section 267 of the present Bankruptcy Act [section 667 of former title 11].

Subsection (d) permits the court to authorize the proponent of a reorganization plan to request from the Internal Revenue Service (or State or local tax authority) an advance ruling on the tax effects of the proposed plan. If a ruling is not obtained within 270 days after the request was made, or if a ruling is obtained but the proponent of the plan disagrees with the ruling, the bankruptcy court may resolve the dispute and determine the tax effects of the proposed plan.

Subsection (e) provides that prepetition taxes which are nondischargeable in a reorganization, and all taxes arising during the administration period of the case, may be assessed and collected from the debtor or the debtor's successor in a reorganization (see sec. 505(c) of the bill).

house report no. 95–595

Section 1146 of title 11 specifies five subsections which embody special tax provisions that apply in a case under chapter 11 of title 11. Subsection (a) indicates that the tax year of an individual debtor terminates on the date of the order for relief under chapter 11. Termination of the taxable year of the debtor commences the tax period of the estate. If the case was converted from chapter 7 of title 11 then the estate is created as a separate taxable entity dating from the order for relief under chapter 7. If multiple conversion of the case occurs, then the estate is treated as a separate taxable entity on the date of the order for relief under the first chapter under which the estate is a separate taxable entity.

Subsection (d) permits the court to authorize the proponent of a plan to request a taxing authority to declare the tax effects of such plan. In the event of an actual controversy, the court may declare the tax effects of the plan of reorganization at any time after the earlier of action by such taxing authority or 270 days after the request. Such a declaration, unless appealed, becomes a final judgment and binds any tax authority that was requested by the proponent to determine the tax effects of the plan.

Amendments

2005—Pub. L. 109–8 redesignated subsecs. (c) and (d) as (a) and (b), respectively, and struck out former subsecs. (a) and (b) which read as follows:

"(a) For the purposes of any State or local law imposing a tax on or measured by income, the taxable period of a debtor that is an individual shall terminate on the date of the order for relief under this chapter, unless the case was converted under section 706 of this title.

"(b) The trustee shall make a State or local tax return of income for the estate of an individual debtor in a case under this chapter for each taxable period after the order for relief under this chapter during which the case is pending."

1984—Subsec. (c). Pub. L. 98–353, §517(a), struck out "State or local" before "law imposing a stamp tax".

Subsec. (d)(1). Pub. L. 98–353, §517(b), substituted "or" for "and".

Effective Date of 2005 Amendment

Amendment by Pub. L. 109–8 effective 180 days after Apr. 20, 2005, and not applicable with respect to cases commenced under this title before such effective date, except as otherwise provided, see section 1501 of Pub. L. 109–8, set out as a note under section 101 of this title.

Effective Date of 1984 Amendment

Amendment by Pub. L. 98–353 effective with respect to cases filed 90 days after July 10, 1984, see section 552(a) of Pub. L. 98–353, set out as a note under section 101 of this title.

SUBCHAPTER IV—RAILROAD REORGANIZATION

§1161. Inapplicability of other sections

Sections 341, 343, 1102(a)(1), 1104, 1105, 1107, 1129(a)(7), and 1129(c) of this title do not apply in a case concerning a railroad.

(Pub. L. 95–598, Nov. 6, 1978, 92 Stat. 2641.)

Historical and Revision Notes

senate report no. 95–989

This section makes inapplicable sections of the bill which are either inappropriate in railroad reorganizations, or relate to matters which are otherwise dealt with in subchapter IV.

§1162. Definition

In this subchapter, "Board" means the "Surface Transportation Board".

(Added Pub. L. 104–88, title III, §302(1), Dec. 29, 1995, 109 Stat. 943.)

Prior Provisions

A prior section 1162, Pub. L. 95–598, Nov. 6, 1978, 92 Stat. 2641, defined "Commission", prior to repeal by Pub. L. 104–88, title III, §302(1), Dec. 29, 1995, 109 Stat. 943.

Effective Date

Section effective Jan. 1, 1996, see section 2 of Pub. L. 104–88, set out as a note under section 1301 of Title 49, Transportation.

§1163. Appointment of trustee

As soon as practicable after the order for relief the Secretary of Transportation shall submit a list of five disinterested persons that are qualified and willing to serve as trustees in the case. The United States trustee shall appoint one of such persons to serve as trustee in the case.

(Pub. L. 95–598, Nov. 6, 1978, 92 Stat. 2641; Pub. L. 99–554, title II, §226, Oct. 27, 1986, 100 Stat. 3102.)

Historical and Revision Notes

legislative statements

Section 1163 of the House amendment represents a compromise between the House bill and Senate amendment with respect to the appointment of a trustee in a railroad reorganization. As soon as practicable after the order for relief, the Secretary of Transportation is required to submit a list of five disinterested persons who are qualified to serve as trustee and the court will than appoint one trustee from the list to serve as trustee in the case.

The House amendment deletes section 1163 of the Senate amendment in order to cover intrastate railroads in a case under subchapter IV of chapter 11. The bill does not confer jurisdiction on the Interstate Commerce Commission with respect to intrastate railroads.

senate report no. 95–989

[Section 1166 (enacted as section 1163)] Requires the court to appoint a trustee in every case. Since the trustee may employ whatever help he needs, multiple trusteeships are unnecessary and add to the cost of administration. The present requirement of section 77(c)(1) [section 205(c)(1) of former title 11] that the trustee be approved by the Interstate Commerce Commission is unnecessary, since the trustee will be selected either from the panel established under section 606(f) of title 28, or someone certified by the Director of the Administrative Office of the United States Courts as qualified to become a member of that panel.

house report no. 95–595

[Section 1162] This section [enacted as section 1163] requires the appointment of an independent trustee in a railroad reorganization case. The court may appoint one or more disinterested persons to serve as trustee in the case.

Amendments

1986—Pub. L. 99–554 amended section generally, substituting "relief the Secretary" for "relief, the Secretary" and "The United States trustee shall appoint" for "The court shall appoint".

Effective Date of 1986 Amendment

Effective date and applicability of amendment by Pub. L. 99–554 dependent upon the judicial district involved, see section 302(d), (e) of Pub. L. 99–554, set out as a note under section 581 of Title 28, Judiciary and Judicial Procedure.

§1164. Right to be heard

The Board, the Department of Transportation, and any State or local commission having regulatory jurisdiction over the debtor may raise and may appear and be heard on any issue in a case under this chapter, but may not appeal from any judgment, order, or decree entered in the case.

(Pub. L. 95–598, Nov. 6, 1978, 92 Stat. 2641; Pub. L. 104–88, title III, §302(2), Dec. 29, 1995, 109 Stat. 943.)

Historical and Revision Notes

legislative statements

Section 1164 of the Senate amendment is deleted as a matter to be left to the Rules of Bankruptcy Procedure. It is anticipated that the rules will require a petition in a railroad reorganization to be filed with the Interstate Commerce Commission and the Secretary of Transportation in a case concerning an interstate railroad.

Section 1164 of the House amendment is derived from section 1163 of the House bill. The section makes clear that the Interstate Commerce Commission, the Department of Transportation, and any State or local commission having regulatory jurisdiction over the debtor may raise and appear and be heard on any issue in a case under subchapter IV of chapter 11, but may not appeal from any judgment, order, or decree in the case. As under section 1109 of title 11, such intervening parties are not parties in interest.

house report no. 95–595

[Section 1163] This section [enacted as section 1164] gives the same right to raise, and appear and be heard on, any issue in a railroad reorganization case to the Interstate Commerce Commission, the Department of Transportation, and any State or local commission having regulatory jurisdiction over the debtor as is given to the SEC and indenture trustees under section 1109 in ordinary reorganization cases. The right of appeal is denied the ICC, the Department of Transportation, and State and local regulatory agencies, the same as it is denied the SEC.

Amendments

1995—Pub. L. 104–88 substituted "Board" for "Commission".

Effective Date of 1995 Amendment

Amendment by Pub. L. 104–88 effective Jan. 1, 1996, see section 2 of Pub. L. 104–88, set out as an Effective Date note under section 1301 of Title 49, Transportation.

§1165. Protection of the public interest

In applying sections 1166, 1167, 1169, 1170, 1171, 1172, 1173, and 1174 of this title, the court and the trustee shall consider the public interest in addition to the interests of the debtor, creditors, and equity security holders.

(Pub. L. 95–598, Nov. 6, 1978, 92 Stat. 2641.)

Historical and Revision Notes

legislative statements

Section 1165 of the House amendment represents a modification of sections 1165 and 1167 of the Senate amendment requiring the court and the trustee to consider the broad, general public interest in addition to the interests of the debtor, creditors, and equity security holders in applying specific sections of the subchapter.

senate report no. 95–989

Section 1165 requires the court, in consideration of the relief to be granted upon the filing of an involuntary petition, to take into account the "public interest" in the preservation of the debtor's rail service. This is an important factor in railroad reorganization, which distinguishes them from other business reorganizations. Hence, this section modifies the provisions in sections 303 and 305 that govern generally when the business of a debtor may continue to operate, when relief under the Act sought should be granted, and when the petition should be dismissed.

Section 1167 [enacted as section 1165] imposes on the trustee the obligations, in addition to his other duties and responsibilities, to take into account the "public interest" in the preservation of the debtor's rail service.

§1166. Effect of subtitle IV of title 49 and of Federal, State, or local regulations

Except with respect to abandonment under section 1170 of this title, or merger, modification of the financial structure of the debtor, or issuance or sale of securities under a plan, the trustee and the debtor are subject to the provisions of subtitle IV of title 49 that are applicable to railroads, and the trustee is subject to orders of any Federal, State, or local regulatory body to the same extent as the debtor would be if a petition commencing the case under this chapter had not been filed, but—

(1) any such order that would require the expenditure, or the incurring of an obligation for the expenditure, of money from the estate is not effective unless approved by the court; and

(2) the provisions of this chapter are subject to section 601(b) of the Regional Rail Reorganization Act of 1973.

(Pub. L. 95–598, Nov. 6, 1978, 92 Stat. 2642; Pub. L. 97–449, §5(a)(2), Jan. 12, 1983, 96 Stat. 2442; Pub. L. 98–353, title III, §518, July 10, 1984, 98 Stat. 388; Pub. L. 103–394, title V, §501(d)(34), Oct. 22, 1994, 108 Stat. 4146.)

Historical and Revision Notes

legislative statements

Section 1166 of the House amendment is derived from sections 1164 and 1165 of the House bill. An alternative proposal contained in section 1168(1) of the Senate bill is rejected as violative of the principle of equal treatment of all creditors under title 11.

senate report no. 95–989

Section 1168 [enacted as section 1166] makes the trustee subject to the Interstate Commerce Act [49 U.S.C. 10101 et seq.] and to lawful orders of the Interstate Commerce Commission, the U.S. Department of Transportation, and State and regulatory bodies. The approval of the court is required, however, if the order requires the expenditure of money or the incurring of an expenditure other than the payment of certain interline accounts. The limitation of "lawful orders" of State commissions to those involving "safety, location of tracks, and terminal facilities," which is contained in present section 77(c)(2) [section 205(c)(2) of former title 11], is eliminated.

Subsection (1) further provides that the debtor must pay in cash all amounts owed other carriers for current balances owed for interline freight, passenger and per diem, including incentive per diem, for periods both prior and subsequent to the filing of the petition, without the necessity of court approval.

Subsection (2) makes the provisions of the chapter subject to section 601(b) of the Regional Rail Reorganization Act [45 U.S.C. 791(b)], which excludes the Interstate Commerce Commission from any participation in the reorganization of certain northeast railroads that have transferred their rail properties to Consolidated Rail Corporation (Conrail).

house report no. 95–595

Section 1164 [enacted as section 1166] makes the debtor railroad subject to the provisions of the Interstate Commerce Act [49 U.S.C. 10101 et seq.] that are applicable to railroads, and the trustee subject to the orders of the Interstate Commerce Commission to the same extent as the debtor would have been if the case had not been commenced. There are several exceptions. The section does not apply with respect to abandonment of rail lines, which is provided for under section 1169, or with respect to merger under a plan, modification of the financial structure of the debtor by reason of the plan, or the issuance or sale of securities under a plan.

Further, the orders of the ICC are not effective if the order would require the expenditure or the incurring of an obligation for the expenditure of money from the estate, unless approved by the court, and the provisions of this chapter are subject to section 601(b) of the Regional Rail Reorganization Act of 1973 [45 U.S.C. 791(b)].

[Section 1165 (enacted as section 1166)] The same rules apply with respect to Federal, State, or local regulations. The trustee is subject to the orders of a Federal, State, or local regulatory body to the same extent as the debtor would be if the case had not been commenced. However, any order that would require the expenditure, or the incurring of an obligation for the expenditure, of money is not effective under [until] approved by the court.

References in Text

Section 601(b) of the Regional Rail Reorganization Act of 1973, referred to in par. (2), is classified to section 791(b) of Title 45, Railroads.

Amendments

1994—Par. (2). Pub. L. 103–394 struck out "(45 U.S.C. 791(b))" after "Act of 1973".

1984—Pub. L. 98–353 directed substitution of "subtitle IV of title 49" for "the Interstate Commerce Act (49 U.S.C. 1 et seq.)", which substitution had previously been made by Pub. L. 97–449.

1983—Pub. L. 97–449 substituted "subtitle IV of title 49" for "Interstate Commerce Act" in section catchline, and "subtitle IV of title 49" for "the Interstate Commerce Act (49 U.S.C. 1 et seq.)" in text.

Effective Date of 1994 Amendment

Amendment by Pub. L. 103–394 effective Oct. 22, 1994, and not applicable with respect to cases commenced under this title before Oct. 22, 1994, see section 702 of Pub. L. 103–394, set out as a note under section 101 of this title.

§1167. Collective bargaining agreements

Notwithstanding section 365 of this title, neither the court nor the trustee may change the wages or working conditions of employees of the debtor established by a collective bargaining agreement that is subject to the Railway Labor Act except in accordance with section 6 of such Act.

(Pub. L. 95–598, Nov. 6, 1978, 92 Stat. 2642; Pub. L. 103–394, title V, §501(d)(35), Oct. 22, 1994, 108 Stat. 4146.)

Historical and Revision Notes

senate report no. 95–989

Section 1176 [enacted as section 1167] is derived from present section 77(n) [section 205(n) of former title 11]. It provides that notwithstanding the general section governing the rejection of executory contracts (section 365), neither the court nor the trustee may change the wages or working conditions of employees of the debtor established by a collective bargaining agreement that is subject to the Railway Labor Act [45 U.S.C. 151 et seq.], except in accordance with section 6 of that Act [45 U.S.C. 156]. As reported by the subcommittee this section provided that wages and salaries of rail employees could not be affected by the trustee, but that work rules could be rejected by the trustee. The reorganization court was given the authority to review the trustee's decisions and to settle any disputes arising from the rejection. This provision was withdrawn by the full committee, and hearings will be conducted next year by the Human Resources Committee in the area of rail labor contracts and the trustee's ability to reject them in a bankruptcy situation.

house report no. 95–595

Section 1167 is derived from present section 77(n) [section 205(n) of former title 11]. It provides that notwithstanding the general section governing the rejection of executory contracts (section 365), neither the court nor the trustee may change the wages or working conditions of employees of the debtor established by a collective bargaining agreement that is subject to the Railway Labor Act [45 U.S.C. 151 et seq.], except in accordance with section 6 of that Act [45 U.S.C. 156]. The subject of railway labor is too delicate and has too long a history for this code to upset established relationships. The balance has been struck over the years. This provision continues that balance unchanged.

References in Text

The Railway Labor Act, referred to in text, is act May 20, 1926, ch. 347, 44 Stat. 577, as amended, which is classified principally to chapter 8 (§151 et seq.) of Title 45, Railroads. Section 6 of the Act is classified to section 156 of Title 45. For complete classification of this Act to the Code, see section 151 of Title 45 and Tables.

Amendments

1994—Pub. L. 103–394 struck out "(45 U.S.C. 151 et seq.)" after "Railway Labor Act" and "(45 U.S.C. 156)" after "such Act".

Effective Date of 1994 Amendment

Amendment by Pub. L. 103–394 effective Oct. 22, 1994, and not applicable with respect to cases commenced under this title before Oct. 22, 1994, see section 702 of Pub. L. 103–394, set out as a note under section 101 of this title.

§1168. Rolling stock equipment

(a)(1) The right of a secured party with a security interest in or of a lessor or conditional vendor of equipment described in paragraph (2) to take possession of such equipment in compliance with an equipment security agreement, lease, or conditional sale contract, and to enforce any of its other rights or remedies under such security agreement, lease, or conditional sale contract, to sell, lease, or otherwise retain or dispose of such equipment, is not limited or otherwise affected by any other provision of this title or by any power of the court, except that right to take possession and enforce those other rights and remedies shall be subject to section 362, if—

(A) before the date that is 60 days after the date of commencement of a case under this chapter, the trustee, subject to the court's approval, agrees to perform all obligations of the debtor under such security agreement, lease, or conditional sale contract; and

(B) any default, other than a default of a kind described in section 365(b)(2), under such security agreement, lease, or conditional sale contract—

(i) that occurs before the date of commencement of the case and is an event of default therewith is cured before the expiration of such 60-day period;

(ii) that occurs or becomes an event of default after the date of commencement of the case and before the expiration of such 60-day period is cured before the later of—

(I) the date that is 30 days after the date of the default or event of the default; or

(II) the expiration of such 60-day period; and

(iii) that occurs on or after the expiration of such 60-day period is cured in accordance with the terms of such security agreement, lease, or conditional sale contract, if cure is permitted under that agreement, lease, or conditional sale contract.

(2) The equipment described in this paragraph—

(A) is rolling stock equipment or accessories used on rolling stock equipment, including superstructures or racks, that is subject to a security interest granted by, leased to, or conditionally sold to a debtor; and

(B) includes all records and documents relating to such equipment that are required, under the terms of the security agreement, lease, or conditional sale contract, that is to be surrendered or returned by the debtor in connection with the surrender or return of such equipment.

(3) Paragraph (1) applies to a secured party, lessor, or conditional vendor acting in its own behalf or acting as trustee or otherwise in behalf of another party.

(b) The trustee and the secured party, lessor, or conditional vendor whose right to take possession is protected under subsection (a) may agree, subject to the court's approval, to extend the 60-day period specified in subsection (a)(1).

(c)(1) In any case under this chapter, the trustee shall immediately surrender and return to a secured party, lessor, or conditional vendor, described in subsection (a)(1), equipment described in subsection (a)(2), if at any time after the date of commencement of the case under this chapter such secured party, lessor, or conditional vendor is entitled pursuant to subsection (a)(1) to take possession of such equipment and makes a written demand for such possession of the trustee.

(2) At such time as the trustee is required under paragraph (1) to surrender and return equipment described in subsection (a)(2), any lease of such equipment, and any security agreement or conditional sale contract relating to such equipment, if such security agreement or conditional sale contract is an executory contract, shall be deemed rejected.

(d) With respect to equipment first placed in service on or prior to October 22, 1994, for purposes of this section—

(1) the term "lease" includes any written agreement with respect to which the lessor and the debtor, as lessee, have expressed in the agreement or in a substantially contemporaneous writing that the agreement is to be treated as a lease for Federal income tax purposes; and

(2) the term "security interest" means a purchase-money equipment security interest.

(e) With respect to equipment first placed in service after October 22, 1994, for purposes of this section, the term "rolling stock equipment" includes rolling stock equipment that is substantially rebuilt and accessories used on such equipment.

(Pub. L. 95–598, Nov. 6, 1978, 92 Stat. 2642; Pub. L. 98–353, title III, §519, July 10, 1984, 98 Stat. 388; Pub. L. 103–394, title II, §201(b), Oct. 22, 1994, 108 Stat. 4120; Pub. L. 106–181, title VII, §744(a), Apr. 5, 2000, 114 Stat. 175.)

Historical and Revision Notes

legislative statements

Section 1168 of the House amendment incorporates a provision contained in section 1166 of the House bill instead of the provision contained in section 1175 of the Senate amendment for the reasons stated in connection with the discussion of section 1110 of the House amendment.

senate report no. 95–989

Section 1175 [enacted as section 1168] continues the protection accorded in present section 77(j) [section 205(j) of former title 11] to the rights of holders of purchase-money equipment security, and of lessors or conditional vendors of railroad rolling stock, but accords to the trustee a limited period within which to assume the debtor's obligation and to cure any defaults. The rights of such lenders are not affected by the automatic stay and related provisions of sections 362 and 363, or by any power of the court, unless (1) within 60 days after the commencement of the case (or such longer period as may be agreed to by the secured party, lessor or conditional vendor) the trustees, with the approval of the court, agrees to perform all of the debtor's obligations under the security agreement, lease or conditional sale contract, and (2) all defaults are cured within the 60-day period. Defaults described in section 365(b)(2)—defaults which are breaches of provisions relating to the insolvency or financial condition of the debtor, or the commencement of a case under this title, or the appointment of a trustee—are for obvious reasons, excepted.

house report no. 95–595

[Section 1166] This section [enacted as section 1168], derived with changes from the last sentence of present section 77(j) [section 205(j) of former title 11], protects the interests of rolling stock equipment financers, while providing the trustee with some opportunity to cure defaults, agree to make payments, and retain and use the equipment. The provision is parallel to section 1110, concerning aircraft equipment and vessels.

Amendments

2000—Pub. L. 106–181 amended section catchline and text generally, substituting present provisions consisting of subsecs. (a) to (e) for former subsecs. (a) to (d) which contained somewhat similar provisions.

1994—Pub. L. 103–394 amended section generally. Prior to amendment, section read as follows:

"(a) The right of a secured party with a purchase-money equipment security interest in, or of a lessor or conditional vendor of, whether as trustee or otherwise, rolling stock equipment or accessories used on such equipment, including superstructures and racks, that are subject to a purchase-money equipment security interest granted by, leased to, or conditionally sold to, the debtor to take possession of such equipment in compliance with the provisions of a purchase-money equipment security agreement, lease, or conditional sale contract, as the case may be, is not affected by section 362 or 363 of this title or by any power of the court to enjoin such taking of possession, unless—

"(1) before 60 days after the date of the commencement of a case under this chapter, the trustee, subject to the court's approval, agrees to perform all obligations of the debtor under such security agreement, lease, or conditional sale contract, as the case may be; and

"(2) any default, other than a default of a kind specified in section 365(b)(2) of this title, under such security agreement, lease, or conditional sale contract, as the case may be—

"(A) that occurred before such date and is an event of default therewith is cured before the expiration of such 60-day period; and

"(B) that occurs or becomes an event of default after such date is cured before the later of—

"(i) 30 days after the date of such default or event of default; and

"(ii) the expiration of such 60-day period.

"(b) The trustee and the secured party, lessor, or conditional vendor, as the case may be, whose right to take possession is protected under subsection (a) of this section, may agree, subject to the court's approval, to extend the 60-day period specified in subsection (a)(1) of this section."

1984—Subsec. (b). Pub. L. 98–353 inserted a comma after "approval".

Effective Date of 2000 Amendment

Amendment by Pub. L. 106–181 applicable only to fiscal years beginning after Sept. 30, 1999, see section 3 of Pub. L. 106–181, set out as a note under section 106 of Title 49, Transportation.

Effective Date of 1994 Amendment

Amendment by Pub. L. 103–394 effective Oct. 22, 1994, and not applicable with respect to cases commenced under this title before Oct. 22, 1994, see section 702 of Pub. L. 103–394, set out as a note under section 101 of this title.

Effective Date of 1984 Amendment

Amendment by Pub. L. 98–353 effective with respect to cases filed 90 days after July 10, 1984, see section 552(a) of Pub. L. 98–353, set out as a note under section 101 of this title.

§1169. Effect of rejection of lease of railroad line

(a) Except as provided in subsection (b) of this section, if a lease of a line of railroad under which the debtor is the lessee is rejected under section 365 of this title, and if the trustee, within such time as the court fixes, and with the court's approval, elects not to operate the leased line, the lessor under such lease, after such approval, shall operate the line.

(b) If operation of such line by such lessor is impracticable or contrary to the public interest, the court, on request of such lessor, and after notice and a hearing, shall order the trustee to continue operation of such line for the account of such lessor until abandonment is ordered under section 1170 of this title, or until such operation is otherwise lawfully terminated, whichever occurs first.

(c) During any such operation, such lessor is deemed a carrier subject to the provisions of subtitle IV of title 49 that are applicable to railroads.

(Pub. L. 95–598, Nov. 6, 1978, 92 Stat. 2643; Pub. L. 97–449, §5(a)(3), Jan. 12, 1983, 96 Stat. 2442; Pub. L. 98–353, title III, §520, July 10, 1984, 98 Stat. 388.)

Historical and Revision Notes
legislative statements
Section 1169 of the Senate amendment is deleted from the House amendment as unnecessary since 28 U.S.C. 1407 treating with the judicial panel on multi-district litigation will apply by its terms to cases under title 11.

senate report no. 95–989
Section 1177 [enacted as section 1169] continues, essentially without change, the provisions relating to the rejection by the trustee of a lease of a line of railroad now contained in section 77(c)(6) [section 205(c)(6) of former title 11]. Subsection (a) requires the lessor of a line of railroad to operate it if the lease is rejected by the trustee and the trustee, with the approval of the court, elects not to operate the leased line. Subsection (b), however, further provides that if operation by the lessor is impractical or contrary to the public interest, the court shall require the trustee to operate the line for the account of the lessor until the operation is lawfully terminated. Subsection (c) provides that during such operation, the lessor is a carrier subject to the Interstate Commerce Act [49 U.S.C. 10101 et seq.].

house report no. 95–595
[Section 1168] This section [enacted as section 1169] governs the effect of the rejection by the trustee of an unexpired lease of railroad line under which the debtor is the lessee. If the trustee rejects such a lease, and if the trustee, within such time as the court allows, and with the approval of the court, elects not to operate the leased line, then the lessor under the lease must operate the line.

Subsection (b) excuses the lessor from the requirement to operate the line under certain circumstances. If operation of the line by the lessor is impracticable or contrary to the public interest, the court, on request of the lessor, must order the trustee to continue operation of the line for the account of the lessor until abandonment is ordered under section 1169, governing abandonments generally, or until the operation is otherwise lawfully terminated, such as by an order of the ICC.

Subsection (c) deems the lessor a carrier subject to the provisions of the Interstate Commerce Act [49 U.S.C. 10101 et seq.] during the operation of the line before abandonment.

Amendments
1984—Subsec. (c). Pub. L. 98–353 directed substitution of "subtitle IV of title 49" for "the Interstate Commerce Act (49 U.S.C. 1 et seq.)", which substitution had previously been made by Pub. L. 97–449.
1983—Subsec. (c). Pub. L. 97–449 substituted "subtitle IV of title 49" for "the Interstate Commerce Act (49 U.S.C. §1 et seq.)".

§1170. Abandonment of railroad line
(a) The court, after notice and a hearing, may authorize the abandonment of all or a portion of a railroad line if such abandonment is—
(1)(A) in the best interest of the estate; or
(B) essential to the formulation of a plan; and
(2) consistent with the public interest.

(b) If, except for the pendency of the case under this chapter, such abandonment would require approval by the Board under a law of the United States, the trustee shall initiate an appropriate application for such abandonment with the Board. The court may fix a time within which the Board shall report to the court on such application.

(c) After the court receives the report of the Board, or the expiration of the time fixed under subsection (b) of this section, whichever occurs first, the court may authorize such abandonment, after notice to the Board, the Secretary of Transportation, the trustee, any party in interest that has requested notice, any affected shipper or community, and any other entity prescribed by the court, and a hearing.

(d)(1) Enforcement of an order authorizing such abandonment shall be stayed until the time for taking an appeal has expired, or, if an appeal is timely taken, until such order has become final.

(2) If an order authorizing such abandonment is appealed, the court, on request of a party in interest, may authorize suspension of service on a line or a portion of a line pending the determination of such appeal, after notice to the Board, the Secretary of Transportation, the trustee, any party in interest that has requested notice, any affected shipper or community, and any other entity prescribed by the court, and a hearing. An appellant may not obtain a stay of the enforcement of an order authorizing such suspension by the giving of a supersedeas bond or otherwise, during the pendency of such appeal.

(e)(1) In authorizing any abandonment of a railroad line under this section, the court shall require the rail carrier to provide a fair arrangement at least as protective of the interests of employees as that established under section 11326(a) of title 49.

(2) Nothing in this subsection shall be deemed to affect the priorities or timing of payment of employee protection which might have existed in the absence of this subsection.

(Pub. L. 95–598, Nov. 6, 1978, 92 Stat. 2643; Pub. L. 96–448, title II, §227(a), Oct. 14, 1980, 94 Stat. 1931; Pub. L. 98–353, title III, §521, July 10, 1984, 98 Stat. 388; Pub. L. 104–88, title III, §302(2), Dec. 29, 1995, 109 Stat. 943; Pub. L. 109–8, title XII, §1217, Apr. 20, 2005, 119 Stat. 195.)

Historical and Revision Notes
senate report no. 95–989
Subsection (a) of section 1178 [enacted as section 1170] permits the court to authorize the abandonment of a railroad line if the abandonment is consistent with the public interest and either in the best interest of the estate or essential to the formulation of a plan. This avoids the normal abandonment requirements of generally applicable railroad regulatory law.

Subsection (b) permits some participation by the Interstate Commerce Commission in the abandonment process. The Commission's role, however, is only advisory. The Commission will represent the public interest, while the trustee and various creditors and equity security holders will represent the interests of those who have invested money in the enterprise. The court will balance the various interests and make an appropriate decision. The subsection specifies that if, except for the pendency of the railroad reorganization case, the proposed abandonment would require Commission approval, then the trustee, with the approval of the court, must initiate an application for the abandonment with the Commission. The court may then fix a time within which the Commission must report to the court on the application.

Subsection (c) permits the court to act after it has received the report of the Commission or the time fixed under subsection (b) has expired, whichever occurs first. The court may then authorize the abandonment after notice and a hearing. The notice must go to the Commission, the Secretary of Transportation, the trustee, and party in interest that has requested notice, any affected shipper or community, and any other entity that the court specifies.

Subsection (d) stays the enforcement of an abandonment until the time for taking an appeal has expired, or if an appeal has been taken, until the order has become final. However, the court may, and after notice and a hearing, on request of a party in interest authorize termination of service on the line or a portion of the line pending the determination of the appeal. The notice required is the same as that required under subsection (c). If the court authorizes termination of service pending determination of the appeal, an appellant may not obtain a stay of the enforcement of the order authorizing termination, either by the giving of a supersedeas bond or otherwise, during the pendency of the appeal.

Amendments
2005—Subsec. (e)(1). Pub. L. 109–8 substituted "section 11326(a)" for "section 11347".
1995—Subsecs. (b), (c), (d)(2). Pub. L. 104–88 substituted "Board" for "Commission" wherever appearing.
1984—Subsec. (a). Pub. L. 98–353, §521(a), inserted "of all or a portion" after "the abandonment".
Subsec. (c). Pub. L. 98–353, §521(b), inserted a comma after "abandonment".
Subsec. (d)(2). Pub. L. 98–353, §521(c), substituted "such abandonment" for "the abandonment of a railroad line", and "suspension" for "termination" in two places.
1980—Subsec. (e). Pub. L. 96–448 added subsec. (e).

Effective Date of 2005 Amendment
Amendment by Pub. L. 109–8 effective 180 days after Apr. 20, 2005, and not applicable with respect to cases commenced under this title before such effective date, except as otherwise provided, see section 1501 of Pub. L. 109–8, set out as a note under section 101 of this title.

Effective Date of 1995 Amendment
Amendment by Pub. L. 104–88 effective Jan. 1, 1996, see section 2 of Pub. L. 104–88, set out as an Effective Date note under section 1301 of Title 49, Transportation.

Effective Date of 1984 Amendment
Amendment by Pub. L. 98–353 effective with respect to cases filed 90 days after July 10, 1984, see section 552(a) of Pub. L. 98–353, set out as a note under section 101 of this title.

Effective Date of 1980 Amendment
Pub. L. 96–448, title VII, §710, Oct. 14, 1980, 94 Stat. 1966, provided that:
"(a) Except as provided in subsections (b), (c), and (d) of this section, the provisions of this Act and the amendments made by this Act [see Tables for classification] shall take effect on October 1, 1980.
"(b) Section 206 of this Act [enacting former section 10712 of Title 49, Transportation] shall take effect on January 1, 1981.
"(c) Section 218(b) of this Act [amending former section 10705 of Title 49] shall take effect on October 1, 1983.
"(d) Section 701 of this Act [enacting section 1018 of Title 45, Railroads, and amending sections 231f, 825, 906, 913, 914, 1002, 1005, 1007, and 1008 of Title 45] shall take effect on the date of enactment of this Act [Oct. 14, 1980]."

§1171. Priority claims
(a) There shall be paid as an administrative expense any claim of an individual or of the personal representative of a deceased individual against the debtor or the estate, for personal injury to or death of such individual arising out of the operation of the debtor or the estate, whether such claim arose before or after the commencement of the case.

(b) Any unsecured claim against the debtor that would have been entitled to priority if a receiver in equity of the property of the debtor had been appointed by a Federal court on the date of the order for relief under this title shall be entitled to the same priority in the case under this chapter.

(Pub. L. 95–598, Nov. 6, 1978, 92 Stat. 2643; Pub. L. 98–353, title III, §522, July 10, 1984, 98 Stat. 388.)

Historical and Revision Notes
legislative statements
Section 1171 of the House amendment is derived from section 1170 of the House bill in lieu of section 1173(a)(9) of the Senate amendment.

house report no. 95–595
[Section 1170] This section [enacted as section 1171] is derived from current law. Subsection (a) grants an administrative expense priority to the claim of any individual (or of the personal representative of a deceased individual) against the debtor or the estate for personal injury to or death of the individual arising out of the operation of the debtor railroad or the estate, whether the claim arose before or after commencement of the case. The priority under current law, found in section 77(n) [section 205(n) of former title 11], applies only to employees of the debtor. This subsection expands the protection provided.

Subsection (b) follows present section 77(b) of the Bankruptcy Act [section 205(b) of former title 11] by giving priority to any unsecured claims that would be entitled to priority if a receiver in equity of the property of the debtor had been appointed by a Federal court on the date of the order for relief under the bankruptcy laws. As under current law, the courts will determine the precise contours of the priority recognized by this subsection in each case.

Amendments
1984—Subsec. (b). Pub. L. 98–353 substituted "the same" for "such".

Effective Date of 1984 Amendment
Amendment by Pub. L. 98–353 effective with respect to cases filed 90 days after July 10, 1984, see section 552(a) of Pub. L. 98–353, set out as a note under section 101 of this title.

§1172. Contents of plan
(a) In addition to the provisions required or permitted under section 1123 of this title, a plan—
(1) shall specify the extent to and the means by which the debtor's rail service is proposed to be continued, and the extent to which any of the debtor's rail service is proposed to be terminated; and
(2) may include a provision for—
(A) the transfer of any or all of the operating railroad lines of the debtor to another operating railroad; or
(B) abandonment of any railroad line in accordance with section 1170 of this title.

(b) If, except for the pendency of the case under this chapter, transfer of, or operation of or over, any of the debtor's rail lines by an entity other than the debtor or a successor to the debtor under the plan would require approval by the Board under a law of the United States, then a plan may not propose such a transfer or such operation unless the proponent of the plan initiates an appropriate application for such a transfer or such operation with the Board, and within such time as the court may fix, not exceeding 180 days, the Board, with or without a hearing, as the Board may determine, and with or without modification or condition, approves such application, or does not act on such application. Any action or order of the Board approving, modifying, conditioning, or disapproving such application is subject to review by the court only under sections 706(2)(A), 706(2)(B), 706(2)(C), and 706(2)(D) of title 5.

(c)(1) In approving an application under subsection (b) of this section, the Board shall require the rail carrier to provide a fair arrangement at least as protective of the interests of employees as that established under section 11326(a) of title 49.

(2) Nothing in this subsection shall be deemed to affect the priorities or timing of payment of employee protection which might have existed in the absence of this subsection.

(Pub. L. 95–598, Nov. 6, 1978, 92 Stat. 2644; Pub. L. 96–448, title II, §227(b), Oct. 14, 1980, 94 Stat. 1931; Pub. L. 104–88, title III, §302(2), Dec. 29, 1995, 109 Stat. 943; Pub. L. 109–8, title XII, §1218, Apr. 20, 2005, 119 Stat. 195.)

Historical and Revision Notes
legislative statements

Section 1172 of the House amendment is derived from section 1171 of the House bill in preference to section 1170 of the Senate amendment with the exception that section 1170(4) of the Senate amendment is incorporated into section 1172(a)(1) of the House amendment.

Section 1172(b) of the House amendment is derived from section 1171(c) of the Senate amendment. The section gives the Interstate Commerce Commission the exclusive power to approve or disapprove the transfer of, or operation of or over, any of the debtor's rail lines over which the Commission has jurisdiction, subject to review under the Administrative Procedures Act [5 U.S.C. 551 et seq. and 701 et seq.]. The section does not apply to a transfer of railroad lines to a successor of the debtor under a plan of reorganization by merger or otherwise.

The House amendment deletes section 1171(a) of the Senate amendment as a matter to be determined by the Rules of Bankruptcy Procedure. It is anticipated that the rules will specify the period of time, such as 18 months, within which a trustee must file with the court a proposed plan of reorganization for the debtor or a report why a plan cannot be formulated. Incorporation by reference of section 1121 in section 1161 of title 11 means that a party in interest will also have a right to file a plan of reorganization. This differs from the position taken in the Senate amendment which would have permitted the Interstate Commerce Commission to file a plan of reorganization.

senate report no. 95–989

Section 1170 adds to the general provisions required or permitted in reorganization plans by section 1123. Subsection (1) requires that a reorganization plan under the railroad subchapter specify the means by which the value of the claims of creditors and the interests of equity holders which are materially and adversely affected by the plan are to be realized. Subsection (2) permits a plan to include provisions for the issuance of warrants. Subsection (3) requires that the plan provide for fixed charges by probable earnings for their payment. Subsection (4) requires that the plan specify the means by which, and the extent to which, the debtor's rail service is to be continued, and shall identify any rail service to be terminated. Subsection (5) permits other appropriate provisions not inconsistent with the chapter. With the exception of subsection (4), the requirements are comparable to those of present section 77(b) [section 205(b) of former title 11]; subsection (4) emphasizes the public interest in the preservation of rail transportation.

Section 1171 imposes on the court, rather than the Interstate Commerce Commission, as in present section 77 [section 205 of former title 11], the responsibility for the plan of reorganization. The Commission is empowered to make final decisions subject only to review by the court under the standards of the Administrative Procedure Act [5 U.S.C. 551 et seq. and 701 et seq.] as to any part of the plan which deals with transportation matters, such as the grant of operating rights of or over, or transfer of, the debtor's rail lines to other carriers.

Subsection (a) requires the trustee to file a plan of reorganization within 18 months after the petition is filed, and permits the court, for good cause shown, to extend such time limit. Subsection (b) permits a plan to be proposed by any interested person, and permits the trustee to revise his plan at any time before it is approved by the court.

Subsections (c), (d) and (e) require the court, when a plan is submitted by the trustee or, if the court deems it worthy of consideration, a plan submitted is proposed by any other person proposes the transfer of, or operation of or over, any of the debtor's lines by other carriers, to refer to such provisions of the plan to the Interstate Commerce Commission. The Commission, within 240 days, and after a hearing if the Commission so determines, is to report to the court the effects of such provisions of the plan in the light of national transportation policy and sections 5(3)(f)(A), (B), and (D), (F)–(I) of the Interstate Commerce Act [49 U.S.C. 11350(b)(1), (2), (4), (6)–(9)]. The report of the Commission is conclusive in all further hearings on the plan by the court, subject only to review pursuant to 5 U.S.C. 706(2)(A)–(D).

house report no. 95–595

[Section 1171 (enacted as section 1172)] A plan in a railroad reorganization case may include provisions in addition to those required and permitted under an ordinary reorganization plan. It may provide for the transfer of any or all of the operating railroad lines of the debtor to another operating railroad.

Paragraph (1) contemplates a liquidating plan for the debtor's rail lines, much as occurred in the Penn Central case by transfer of operating lines to ConRail. Such a liquidating plan is not per se contrary to the public interest, and the court will have to determine on a case-by-case basis, with the guidance of the Interstate Commerce Commission and of other parties in interest, whether the particular plan proposed is in the public interest, as required under proposed 11 U.S.C. 1172(3).

The plan may also provide for abandonment in accordance with section 1169, governing abandonment generally. Neither of these provisions in a plan, transfer or abandonment of lines, requires ICC approval. Confirmation of the plan by the court authorizes the debtor to comply with the plan in accordance with section 1142(a) notwithstanding any bankruptcy law to the contrary.

Amendments

2005—Subsec. (c)(1). Pub. L. 109–8 substituted "section 11326(a)" for "section 11347".

1995—Subsecs. (b), (c)(1). Pub. L. 104–88 substituted "Board" for "Commission" wherever appearing.

1980—Subsec. (c). Pub. L. 96–448 added subsec. (c).

Effective Date of 2005 Amendment

Amendment by Pub. L. 109–8 effective 180 days after Apr. 20, 2005, and not applicable with respect to cases commenced under this title before such effective date, except as otherwise provided, see section 1501 of Pub. L. 109–8, set out as a note under section 101 of this title.

Effective Date of 1995 Amendment

Amendment by Pub. L. 104–88 effective Jan. 1, 1996, see section 2 of Pub. L. 104–88, set out as an Effective Date note under section 1301 of Title 49, Transportation.

Effective Date of 1980 Amendment

Amendment by Pub. L. 96–448 effective Oct. 1, 1980, see section 710(a) of Pub. L. 96–448, set out as a note under section 1170 of this title.

Nonapplication of Subsec. (c)

For provision that subsec. (c) of this section does not apply to Amtrak and its employees, see section 142(d) of Pub. L. 105–134, set out in an Employee Protection Reforms note under section 24706 of Title 49, Transportation.

§1173. Confirmation of plan

(a) The court shall confirm a plan if—

(1) the applicable requirements of section 1129 of this title have been met;

(2) each creditor or equity security holder will receive or retain under the plan property of a value, as of the effective date of the plan, that is not less than the value of property that each such creditor or equity security holder would so receive or retain if all of the operating railroad lines of the debtor were sold, and the proceeds of such sale, and the other property of the estate, were distributed under chapter 7 of this title on such date;

(3) in light of the debtor's past earnings and the probable prospective earnings of the reorganized debtor, there will be adequate coverage by such prospective earnings of any fixed charges, such as interest on debt, amortization of funded debt, and rent for leased railroads, provided for by the plan; and

(4) the plan is consistent with the public interest.

(b) If the requirements of subsection (a) of this section are met with respect to more than one plan, the court shall confirm the plan that is most likely to maintain adequate rail service in the public interest.

(Pub. L. 95–598, Nov. 6, 1978, 92 Stat. 2644; Pub. L. 98–353, title III, §523, July 10, 1984, 98 Stat. 388.)

Historical and Revision Notes

legislative statements

Section 1173 of the House amendment concerns confirmation of a plan of railroad reorganization and is derived from section 1172 of the House bill as modified. In particular, section 1173(a)(3) of the House amendment is derived from section 1170(3) of the Senate amendment. Section 1173(b) is derived from section 1173(a)(8) of the Senate amendment.

senate report no. 95–989

Section 1173 adapts the provisions dealing with reorganization plans generally contained in section 1130 to the particular requirements of railroad reorganization plans, as set out in present section 77(e) [section 205(e) of former title 11]. Subsection (a) specifies the findings which the court must make before approving a plan: (1) The plan complies with the applicable provisions of the chapter; (2) the proponent of the plan complies with the applicable provisions of the chapter; (3) the plan has been proposed in good faith; (4) any payments for services or for costs or expenses in connection with the case or the plan are disclosed to the court and are reasonable, or, if to be paid later, are subject to the approval of the court as reasonable; (5) the proponent of the plan has disclosed the identity and affiliations of the individuals who will serve as directors, officers, or voting trustees, such appointments or continuations in office are consistent with the interests of creditors, equity security holders, and the proponent the public, and has disclosed the identity and compensation of any insider who will be employed or retained under the plan; (6) that rate changes proposed in the plan have been approved by the appropriate regulatory commission, or that the plan is contingent on such approval; (7) that confirmation of the plan is not likely to be followed by further reorganization or liquidation, unless it is contemplated by the plan; (8) that the plan, if there is more than one, is the one most likely to maintain adequate rail service and (9) that the plan provides the priority traditionally accorded by section 77(b) [section 205(b) of former title 11] to claims by rail creditors for necessary services rendered during the 6 months preceding the filing of the petition in bankruptcy.

Subsection (b) continues the present power of the court in section 77(e) [section 205(e) of former title 11] to confirm a plan over the objections of creditors or equity security holders who are materially and adversely affected. The subsection also confirms the authority of the court to approve a transfer of all or part of a debtor's property or its merger over the objections of equity security holders if it finds (1) that the "public interest" in continued rail transportation outweighs any adverse effect on creditors and equity security holders, and (2) that the plan is fair and equitable, affords due recognition to the rights of each class, and does not discriminate unfairly against any class.

Subsection (c) permits modification of a plan confirmed by a final order only for fraud.

house report no. 95–595

[Section 1172] This section [enacted as section 1173] requires the court to confirm a plan if the applicable requirements of section 1129 (relating to confirmation of reorganization plans generally) are met, if the best interest test is met, and if the plan is compatible with the public interest.

The test in this paragraph is similar to the test prescribed for ordinary corporate reorganizations. However, since a railroad cannot liquidate its assets and sell them for scrap to satisfy its creditors, the test focuses on the value of the railroad as a going concern. That is, the test is based on what the assets, sold as operating rail lines, would bring.

The public interest requirement, found in current law, will now be decided by the court, with the ICC representing the public interest before the court, rather than in the first instance by the ICC. Liquidation of the debtor is not, per se, contrary to the public interest.

Amendments

1984—Subsec. (a)(4). Pub. L. 98–353 substituted "consistent" for "compatible".

Effective Date of 1984 Amendment

Amendment by Pub. L. 98–353 effective with respect to cases filed 90 days after July 10, 1984, see section 552(a) of Pub. L. 98–353, set out as a note under section 101 of this title.

§1174. Liquidation

On request of a party in interest and after notice and a hearing, the court may, or, if a plan has not been confirmed under section 1173 of this title before five years after the date of the order for relief, the court shall, order the trustee to cease the debtor's operation and to collect and reduce to money all of the property of the estate in the same manner as if the case were a case under chapter 7 of this title.

(Pub. L. 95–598, Nov. 6, 1978, 92 Stat. 2644.)

Historical and Revision Notes

legislative statements

Section 1174 of the House amendment represents a compromise between the House bill and Senate amendment on the issue of liquidation of a railroad. The provision permits a party in interest at any time to request liquidation. In addition, if a plan has not been confirmed under section 1173 of the House amendment before 5 years after the date of order for relief, the court must order the trustee to cease the debtor's operation and to collect and reduce to money all of the property of the estate in the same manner as if the case were a case under chapter 7 of title 11. The approach differs from the conversion to chapter 7 under section 1174 of the Senate bill in order to make special provisions contained in subchapter IV of chapter 11 applicable to liquidation. However, maintaining liquidation in the context of chapter 11 is not intended to delay liquidation of the railroad to a different extent than if the case were converted to chapter 7.

Although the House amendment does not adopt provisions contained in sections 1170(1), (2), (3), or (5), of the Senate amendment such provisions are contained explicitly or implicitly in section 1123 of the House amendment.

senate report no. 95–989

Section 1174 permits the court to convert the case to a liquidation under chapter 7 if the court finds that the debtor cannot be reorganized, or if various time limits specified in the subchapter are not met. Section 77 [section 205 of former title 11] does not authorize a liquidation of a railroad under the Bankruptcy Act [former title 11]. If the railroad is not reorganizable, the only action open to the court is to dismiss the petition, which would in all likelihood be followed by a State court receivership, with all of its attendant disadvantages. If reorganization is impossible, the debtor should be liquidated under the Bankruptcy Act.

CHAPTER 12—ADJUSTMENT OF DEBTS OF A FAMILY FARMER OR FISHERMAN WITH REGULAR ANNUAL INCOME

SUBCHAPTER I—OFFICERS, ADMINISTRATION, AND THE ESTATE

Sec.
1201.
Stay of action against codebtor.
1202.
Trustee.
1203.
Rights and powers of debtor.
1204.
Removal of debtor as debtor in possession.
1205.
Adequate protection.
1206.
Sales free of interests.
1207.
Property of the estate.
1208.
Conversion or dismissal.

SUBCHAPTER II—THE PLAN

1221.
Filing of plan.
1222.
Contents of plan.
1223.
Modification of plan before confirmation.
1224.
Confirmation hearing.
1225.
Confirmation of plan.
1226.
Payments.
1227.
Effect of confirmation.
1228.
Discharge.
1229.
Modification of plan after confirmation.
1230.
Revocation of an order of confirmation.
1231.
Special tax provisions.
1232.
Claim by a governmental unit based on the disposition of property used in a farming operation.

Codification

CHAPTER repealed effective Oct. 1, 1998, by Pub. L. 99–554, title III, §302(f), Oct. 27, 1986, 100 Stat. 3124, as amended by Pub. L. 103–65, §1, Aug. 6, 1993, 107 Stat. 311. Chapter, as in effect on Sept. 30, 1998, reenacted for the period beginning on Oct. 1, 1998, and ending on Apr. 1, 1999, by Pub. L. 105–277, div. C, title I, §149(a), Oct. 21, 1998, 112 Stat. 2681–610. Chapter reenacted for successive periods running from Mar. 31, 1999, to July 1, 2005, by Pub. L. 105–277, div. C, title I, §149(a), Oct. 21, 1998, 112 Stat. 2681–610, as successively amended by Pub. L. 106–5, Mar. 30, 1999, 113 Stat. 9; Pub. L. 106–70, Oct. 9, 1999, 113 Stat. 1031; Pub. L. 107–8, May 11, 2001, 115 Stat. 10; Pub. L. 107–17, June 26, 2001, 115 Stat. 151; Pub. L. 107–170, May 7, 2002, 116 Stat. 133; Pub. L. 107–171, title X, §10814, May 13, 2002, 116 Stat. 532; Pub. L. 107–377, §2, Dec. 19, 2002, 116 Stat. 3115; Pub. L. 108–73, §2, Aug. 15, 2003, 117 Stat. 891; Pub. L. 108–369, §2, Oct. 25, 2004, 118 Stat. 1749. Chapter, as in effect on June 30, 2005, permanently reenacted effective July 1, 2005, by Pub. L. 109–8, title X, §1001(a), Apr. 20, 2005, 119 Stat. 185. See Repeal, Reenactment, and Termination of Chapter and Effective Date notes set out under section 1201 of this title.

Amendments

2017—Pub. L. 115–72, div. B, §1005(b)(2), Oct. 26, 2017, 131 Stat. 1234, added item 1232. Item was added to analysis for this chapter to reflect the probable intent of Congress, notwithstanding directory language adding item to analysis for subchapter II of this chapter.

2005—Pub. L. 109–8, title X, §1007(c)(1), Apr. 20, 2005, 119 Stat. 188, inserted "OR FISHERMAN" after "FAMILY FARMER" in chapter heading.

SUBCHAPTER I—OFFICERS, ADMINISTRATION, AND THE ESTATE

§1201. Stay of action against codebtor

(a) Except as provided in subsections (b) and (c) of this section, after the order for relief under this chapter, a creditor may not act, or commence or continue any civil action, to collect all or any part of a consumer debt of the debtor from any individual that is liable on such debt with the debtor, or that secured such debt, unless—

(1) such individual became liable on or secured such debt in the ordinary course of such individual's business; or

(2) the case is closed, dismissed, or converted to a case under chapter 7 of this title.

(b) A creditor may present a negotiable instrument, and may give notice of dishonor of such an instrument.

(c) On request of a party in interest and after notice and a hearing, the court shall grant relief from the stay provided by subsection (a) of this section with respect to a creditor, to the extent that—

(1) as between the debtor and the individual protected under subsection (a) of this section, such individual received the consideration for the claim held by such creditor;

(2) the plan filed by the debtor proposes not to pay such claim; or

(3) such creditor's interest would be irreparably harmed by continuation of such stay.

(d) Twenty days after the filing of a request under subsection (c)(2) of this section for relief from the stay provided by subsection (a) of this section, such stay is terminated with respect to the party in interest making such request, unless the debtor or any individual that is liable on such debt with the debtor files and serves upon such party in interest a written objection to the taking of the proposed action.

(Added and amended Pub. L. 99–554, title II, §255, title III, §302(f), Oct. 27, 1986, 100 Stat. 3105, 3124; Pub. L. 103–65, §1, Aug. 6, 1993, 107 Stat. 311; Pub. L. 105–277, div. C, title I, §149(a), Oct. 21, 1998, 112 Stat. 2681–610; Pub. L. 106–5, §1(1), (2), Mar. 30, 1999, 113 Stat. 9; Pub. L. 106–70, §1, Oct. 9, 1999, 113 Stat. 1031; Pub. L. 107–8, §1, May 11, 2001, 115 Stat. 10; Pub. L. 107–17, §1, June 26, 2001, 115 Stat. 151; Pub. L. 107–170, §1, May 7, 2002, 116 Stat. 133; Pub. L. 107–171, title X, §10814(a), May 13, 2002, 116 Stat. 532; Pub. L. 107–377, §2(a), Dec. 19, 2002, 116 Stat. 3115; Pub. L. 108–73, §2(a), Aug. 15, 2003, 117 Stat. 891; Pub. L. 108–369, §2(a), Oct. 25, 2004, 118 Stat. 1749; Pub. L. 109–8, title X, §1001(a)(1), (c), Apr. 20, 2005, 119 Stat. 185, 186.)

Codification

For repeal of section effective Oct. 1, 1998, and subsequent reenactment of section, see note set out preceding this section.

Effective Date of 2004 Amendment

Pub. L. 108–369, §2(b), Oct. 25, 2004, 118 Stat. 1749, provided that: "The amendments made by subsection (a) [amending this section and sections 1202 to 1208 and 1221 to 1231 of this title and amending provisions set out as a note under this section] are deemed to have taken effect on January 1, 2004."

Effective Date of 2003 Amendment

Pub. L. 108–73, §2(b), Aug. 15, 2003, 117 Stat. 891, provided that: "The amendments made by subsection (a) [amending this section and sections 1202 to 1208 and 1221 to 1231 of this title and amending provisions set out as a note under this section] take effect on July 1, 2003."

Effective Date of 2002 Amendment

Pub. L. 107–377, §2(b), Dec. 19, 2002, 116 Stat. 3115, provided that: "The amendments made by subsection (a) [amending this section and sections 1202 to 1208 and 1221 to 1231 of this title and amending provisions set out as a note under this section] shall take effect on January 1, 2003."

Pub. L. 107–171, title X, §10814(b), May 13, 2002, 116 Stat. 532, provided that: "The amendments made by subsection (a) [amending this section and sections 1202 to 1208 and 1221 to 1231 of this title and amending provisions set out as a note under this section] shall take effect on June 1, 2002."

Pub. L. 107–170, §2, May 7, 2002, 116 Stat. 133, provided that: "The amendments made by section 1 [amending this section and sections 1202 to 1208 and 1221 to 1231 of this title and amending provisions set out as a note under this section] shall take effect on October 1, 2001."

Effective Date of 2001 Amendment

Pub. L. 107–17, §2, June 26, 2001, 115 Stat. 151, provided that: "The amendments made by section 1 [amending this section and sections 1202 to 1208 and 1221 to 1231 of this title and amending provisions set out as a note under this section] shall take effect on June 1, 2001."

Pub. L. 107–8, §2, May 11, 2001, 115 Stat. 10, provided that: "The amendments made by section 1 [amending this section and sections 1202 to 1208 and 1221 to 1231 of this title and amending provisions set out as a note under this section] shall take effect on July 1, 2000."

Effective Date of 1999 Amendment

Pub. L. 106–70, §2, Oct. 9, 1999, 113 Stat. 1031, provided that: "The amendments made by section 1 [amending this section and sections 1202 to 1208 and 1221 to 1231 of this title and amending provisions set out as a note under this section] shall take effect on October 1, 1999."

Pub. L. 106–5, §2, Mar. 30, 1999, 113 Stat. 9, provided that: "The amendments made by section 1 [amending this section and sections 1202 to 1208 and 1221 to 1231 of this title and amending provisions set out as a note under this section] shall take effect on April 1, 1999."

Effective Date

CHAPTER effective 30 days after Oct. 27, 1986, but not applicable to cases commenced under this title before that date, see section 302(a), (c)(1) of Pub. L. 99–554, set out in an Effective Date of 1986 Amendment; Transition and Administrative Provisions note under section 581 of Title 28, Judiciary and Judicial Procedure.

Repeal, Reenactment, and Termination of Chapter

Pub. L. 109–8, title X, §1001(a), (b), Apr. 20, 2005, 119 Stat. 185, 186, provided that:

"(a) Reenactment.—

"(1) In general.—Chapter 12 of title 11, United States Code, as reenacted by section 149 of division C of the Omnibus Consolidated and Emergency Supplemental Appropriations Act, 1999 (Public Law 105–277) [set out as a note below], and as in effect on June 30, 2005, is hereby reenacted.

"(2) Effective date of reenactment.—Paragraph (1) shall take effect on July 1, 2005.

"(b) Amendments—Chapter 12 of title 11, United States Code, as reenacted by subsection (a), is amended by this Act [see Tables for classification]."

Pub. L. 105–277, div. C, title I, §149, Oct. 21, 1998, 112 Stat. 2681–610, as amended by Pub. L. 106–5, §1, Mar. 30, 1999, 113 Stat. 9; Pub. L. 106–70, §1, Oct. 9, 1999, 113 Stat. 1031; Pub. L. 107–8, §1, May 11, 2001, 115 Stat. 10; Pub. L. 107–17, §1, June 26, 2001, 115 Stat. 151; Pub. L. 107–170, §1, May 7, 2002, 116 Stat. 133; Pub. L. 107–171, title X, §10814(a), May 13, 2002, 116 Stat. 532; Pub. L. 107–377, §2(a), Dec. 19, 2002, 116 Stat. 3115; Pub. L. 108–73, §2(a), Aug. 15, 2003, 117 Stat. 891; Pub. L. 108–369, §2(a), Oct. 25, 2004, 118 Stat. 1749, provided that:

"(a) Chapter 12 of title 11 of the United States Code, as in effect on December 31, 2003, is hereby reenacted for the period beginning on January 1, 2004, and ending on July 1, 2005.

"(b) All cases commenced or pending under chapter 12 of title 11, United States Code, as reenacted under subsection (a), and all matters and proceedings in or relating to such cases, shall be conducted and determined under such chapter as if such chapter were continued in effect after July 1, 2005. The substantive rights of parties in connection with such cases, matters, and proceedings shall continue to be governed under the laws applicable to such cases, matters, and proceedings as if such chapter were continued in effect after July 1, 2005."

CHAPTER was repealed Oct. 1, 1998, except that cases commenced or pending under this chapter, and all matters and proceedings in or relating to such cases, were to be conducted and determined as if this chapter had not been repealed, and substantive rights of parties in connection with such cases, matters, and proceedings were to continue to be governed under the laws applicable to such cases, matters, and proceedings as if this chapter had not been repealed, see section 302(f) of Pub. L. 99–554, as amended, formerly set out in an Effective Date of 1986 Amendment note under section 581 of Title 28, Judiciary and Judicial Procedure.

§1202. Trustee

(a) If the United States trustee has appointed an individual under section 586(b) of title 28 to serve as standing trustee in cases under this chapter and if such individual qualifies as a trustee under section 322 of this title, then such individual shall serve as trustee in any case filed under this chapter. Otherwise, the United States trustee shall appoint one disinterested person to serve as trustee in the case or the United States trustee may serve as trustee in the case if necessary.

(b) The trustee shall—

(1) perform the duties specified in sections 704(a)(2), 704(a)(3), 704(a)(5), 704(a)(6), 704(a)(7), and 704(a)(9) of this title;

(2) perform the duties specified in section 1106(a)(3) and 1106(a)(4) of this title if the court, for cause and on request of a party in interest, the trustee, or the United States trustee, so orders;

(3) appear and be heard at any hearing that concerns—

(A) the value of property subject to a lien;

(B) confirmation of a plan;

(C) modification of the plan after confirmation; or

(D) the sale of property of the estate;

(4) ensure that the debtor commences making timely payments required by a confirmed plan;

(5) if the debtor ceases to be a debtor in possession, perform the duties specified in sections 704(a)(8), 1106(a)(1), 1106(a)(2), 1106(a)(6), 1106(a)(7), and 1203; and

(6) if with respect to the debtor there is a claim for a domestic support obligation, provide the applicable notice specified in subsection (c).

(c)(1) In a case described in subsection (b)(6) to which subsection (b)(6) applies, the trustee shall—

(A)(i) provide written notice to the holder of the claim described in subsection (b)(6) of such claim and of the right of such holder to use the services of the State child support enforcement agency established under sections 464 and 466 of the Social Security Act for the State in which such holder resides, for assistance in collecting child support during and after the case under this title; and

(ii) include in the notice provided under clause (i) the address and telephone number of such State child support enforcement agency;

(B)(i) provide written notice to such State child support enforcement agency of such claim; and

(ii) include in the notice provided under clause (i) the name, address, and telephone number of such holder; and

(C) at such time as the debtor is granted a discharge under section 1228, provide written notice to such holder and to such State child support enforcement agency of—

(i) the granting of the discharge;

(ii) the last recent known address of the debtor;

(iii) the last recent known name and address of the debtor's employer; and

(iv) the name of each creditor that holds a claim that—

(I) is not discharged under paragraph (2), (4), or (14A) of section 523(a); or

(II) was reaffirmed by the debtor under section 524(c).

(2)(A) The holder of a claim described in subsection (b)(6) or the State child support enforcement agency of the State in which such holder resides may request from a creditor described in paragraph (1)(C)(iv) the last known address of the debtor.

(B) Notwithstanding any other provision of law, a creditor that makes a disclosure of a last known address of a debtor in connection with a request made under subparagraph (A) shall not be liable by reason of making that disclosure.

(Added and amended Pub. L. 99–554, title II, §§227, 255, title III, §302(f), Oct. 27, 1986, 100 Stat. 3103, 3106, 3124; Pub. L. 103–65, §1, Aug. 6, 1993, 107 Stat. 311; Pub. L. 105–277, div. C, title I, §149(a), Oct. 21, 1998, 112 Stat. 2681–610; Pub. L. 106–5, §1(1), (2), Mar. 30, 1999, 113 Stat. 9; Pub. L. 106–70, §1, Oct. 9, 1999, 113 Stat. 1031; Pub. L. 107–8, §1, May 11, 2001, 115 Stat. 10; Pub. L. 107–17, §1, June 26, 2001, 115 Stat. 151; Pub. L. 107–170, §1, May 7, 2002, 116 Stat. 133; Pub. L. 107–171, title X, §10814(a), May 13, 2002, 116 Stat. 532; Pub. L. 107–377, §2(a), Dec. 19, 2002, 116 Stat. 3115; Pub. L. 108–73, §2(a), Aug. 15, 2003, 117 Stat. 891; Pub. L. 108–369, §2(a), Oct. 25, 2004, 118 Stat. 1749; Pub. L. 109–8, title II, §219(c), title X, §1001(a)(1), (c), Apr. 20, 2005, 119 Stat. 57, 185, 186; Pub. L. 111–327, §2(a)(38), Dec. 22, 2010, 124 Stat. 3561.)

References in Text

Sections 464 and 466 of the Social Security Act, referred to in subsec. (c)(1)(A)(i), are classified to sections 664 and 666, respectively, of Title 42, The Public Health and Welfare.

Codification

For repeal of section effective Oct. 1, 1998, and subsequent reenactment of section, see note set out preceding section 1201 of this title.

Amendments

2010—Subsec. (b)(1). Pub. L. 111–327, §2(a)(38)(A), substituted "704(a)(2), 704(a)(3), 704(a)(5), 704(a)(6), 704(a)(7), and 704(a)(9)" for "704(2), 704(3), 704(5), 704(6), 704(7), and 704(9)".

Subsec. (b)(5). Pub. L. 111–327, §2(a)(38)(B), substituted "704(a)(8)" for "704(8)".

2005—Subsec. (b)(6). Pub. L. 109–8, §219(c)(1), added par. (6).

Subsec. (c). Pub. L. 109–8, §219(c)(2), added subsec. (c).

1986—Subsecs. (c), (d). Pub. L. 99–554, §227, struck out subsecs. (c) and (d) which read as follows:

"(c) If the number of cases under this chapter commenced in a particular judicial district so warrants, the court may appoint one or more individuals to serve as standing trustee for such district in cases under this chapter.

"(d)(1) A court that has appointed an individual under subsection (a) of this section to serve as standing trustee in cases under this chapter shall set for such individual—

"(A) a maximum annual compensation not to exceed the lowest annual rate of basic pay in effect for grade GS–16 of the General Schedule prescribed under section 5332 of title 5; and

"(B) a percentage fee not to exceed the sum of—

"(i) not to exceed ten percent of the payments made under the plan of such debtor, with respect to payments in an aggregate amount not to exceed $450,000; and

"(ii) three percent of payments made under the plan of such debtor, with respect to payments made after the aggregate amount of payments made under the plan exceeds $450,000;

based on such maximum annual compensation and the actual, necessary expenses incurred by such individual as standing trustee.

"(2) Such individual shall collect such percentage fee from all payments under plans in the cases under this chapter for which such individual serves as standing trustee. Such individual shall pay annually to the Treasury—

"(A) any amount by which the actual compensation received by such individual exceeds five percent of all such payments made under plans in cases under this chapter for which such individual serves as standing trustee; and

"(B) any amount by which the percentage fee fixed under paragraph (1)(B) of this subsection for all such cases exceeds—

"(i) such individual's actual compensation for such cases, as adjusted under subparagraph (A) of this paragraph; plus

"(ii) the actual, necessary expenses incurred by such individual as standing trustee in such cases."

See section 586(b) and (e) of Title 28, Judiciary and Judicial Procedure.

Effective Date of 2005 Amendment

Amendment by section 219(c) of Pub. L. 109–8 effective 180 days after Apr. 20, 2005, and not applicable with respect to cases commenced under this title before such effective date, except as otherwise provided, see section 1501 of Pub. L. 109–8, set out as a note under section 101 of this title.

Effective Dates

Permanent reenactment of section effective July 1, 2005, see section 1001(a)(2) of Pub. L. 109–8, set out as a Repeal, Reenactment, and Termination of Chapter note under section 1201 of this title. For effective dates of amendments extending periods for which section was reenacted prior to permanent reenactment, see Effective Date of 1999, 2001, 2002, 2003, and 2004 Amendment notes set out under section 1201 of this title.

Section effective 30 days after Oct. 27, 1986, and before the amendment by section 227 of Pub. L. 99–554, see section 302(c)(2) of Pub. L. 99–554, set out in an Effective Date of 1986 Amendment; Transition and Administrative Provisions note under section 581 of Title 28, Judiciary and Judicial Procedure.

Effective date and applicability of amendment by section 227 of Pub. L. 99–554 dependent upon the judicial district involved, see section 302(d), (e) of Pub. L. 99–554.

References in Subsection (a) Temporarily Deemed To Be References to Other Provisions

Until the amendments made by subtitle A (§§201 to 231) of title II of Pub. L. 99–554 become effective in a district and apply to a case, in subsec. (a) of this section—

(1) the first two references to the United States trustee are deemed to be references to the court, and

(2) any reference to section 586(b) of Title 28, Judiciary and Judicial Procedure, is deemed to be a reference to subsec. (c) of this section,

see section 302(c)(3)(B), (d), (e) of Pub. L. 99–554, set out in an Effective Date of 1986 Amendment; Transition and Administrative Provisions note under section 581 of Title 28.

§1203. Rights and powers of debtor

Subject to such limitations as the court may prescribe, a debtor in possession shall have all the rights, other than the right to compensation under section 330, and powers, and shall perform all the functions and duties, except the duties specified in paragraphs (3) and (4) of section 1106(a), of a trustee serving in a case under chapter 11, including operating the debtor's farm or commercial fishing operation.

(Added and amended Pub. L. 99–554, title II, §255, title III, §302(f), Oct. 27, 1986, 100 Stat. 3107, 3124; Pub. L. 103–65, §1, Aug. 6, 1993, 107 Stat. 311; Pub. L. 105–277, div. C, title I, §149(a), Oct. 21, 1998, 112 Stat. 2681–610; Pub. L. 106–5, §1(1), (2), Mar. 30, 1999, 113 Stat. 9; Pub. L. 106–70, §1, Oct. 9, 1999, 113 Stat. 1031; Pub. L. 107–8, §1, May 11, 2001, 115 Stat. 10; Pub. L. 107–17, §1, June 26, 2001, 115 Stat. 151; Pub. L. 107–170, §1, May 7, 2002, 116 Stat. 133; Pub. L. 107–171, title X, §10814(a), May 13, 2002, 116 Stat. 532; Pub. L. 107–377, §2(a), Dec. 19, 2002, 116 Stat. 3115; Pub. L. 108–73, §2(a), Aug. 15, 2003, 117 Stat. 891; Pub. L. 108–369, §2(a), Oct. 25, 2004, 118 Stat. 1749; Pub. L. 109–8, title X, §§1001(a)(1), (c), 1007(c)(2), Apr. 20, 2005, 119 Stat. 185, 186, 188.)

Codification

For repeal of section effective Oct. 1, 1998, and subsequent reenactment of section, see note set out preceding section 1201 of this title.

Amendments

2005—Pub. L. 109–8, §1007(c)(2), inserted "or commercial fishing operation" after "farm".

Effective Date of 2005 Amendment

Amendment by section 1007(c)(2) of Pub. L. 109–8 effective 180 days after Apr. 20, 2005, and not applicable with respect to cases commenced under this title before such effective date, except as otherwise provided, see section 1501 of Pub. L. 109–8, set out as a note under section 101 of this title.

Effective Dates

Permanent reenactment of section effective July 1, 2005, see section 1001(a)(2) of Pub. L. 109–8, set out as a Repeal, Reenactment, and Termination of Chapter note under section 1201 of this title. For effective dates of section and amendments extending periods for which section was reenacted prior to permanent reenactment, see Effective Date and Effective Date of 1999, 2001, 2002, 2003, and 2004 Amendment notes set out under section 1201 of this title.

§1204. Removal of debtor as debtor in possession

(a) On request of a party in interest, and after notice and a hearing, the court shall order that the debtor shall not be a debtor in possession for cause, including fraud, dishonesty, incompetence, or gross mismanagement of the affairs of the debtor, either before or after the commencement of the case.

(b) On request of a party in interest, and after notice and a hearing, the court may reinstate the debtor in possession.

(Added and amended Pub. L. 99–554, title II, §255, title III, §302(f), Oct. 27, 1986, 100 Stat. 3107, 3124; Pub. L. 103–65, §1, Aug. 6, 1993, 107 Stat. 311; Pub. L. 105–277, div. C, title I, §149(a), Oct. 21, 1998, 112 Stat. 2681–610; Pub. L. 106–5, §1(1), (2), Mar. 30, 1999, 113 Stat. 9; Pub. L. 106–70, §1, Oct. 9, 1999, 113 Stat. 1031; Pub. L. 107–8, §1, May 11, 2001, 115 Stat. 10; Pub. L. 107–17, §1, June 26, 2001, 115 Stat. 151; Pub. L. 107–170, §1, May 7, 2002, 116 Stat. 133; Pub. L. 107–171, title X, §10814(a), May 13, 2002, 116 Stat. 532; Pub. L. 107–377, §2(a), Dec. 19, 2002, 116 Stat. 3115; Pub. L. 108–73, §2(a), Aug. 15, 2003, 117 Stat. 891; Pub. L. 108–369, §2(a), Oct. 25, 2004, 118 Stat. 1749; Pub. L. 109–8, title X, §1001(a)(1), (c), Apr. 20, 2005, 119 Stat. 185, 186.)

Codification

For repeal of section effective Oct. 1, 1998, and subsequent reenactment of section, see note set out preceding section 1201 of this title.

Effective Dates

Permanent reenactment of section effective July 1, 2005, see section 1001(a)(2) of Pub. L. 109–8, set out as a Repeal, Reenactment, and Termination of Chapter note under section 1201 of this title. For effective dates of section and amendments extending periods for which section was reenacted prior to permanent reenactment, see Effective Date and Effective Date of 1999, 2001, 2002, 2003, and 2004 Amendment notes set out under section 1201 of this title.

§1205. Adequate protection

(a) Section 361 does not apply in a case under this chapter.

(b) In a case under this chapter, when adequate protection is required under section 362, 363, or 364 of this title of an interest of an entity in property, such adequate protection may be provided by—

(1) requiring the trustee to make a cash payment or periodic cash payments to such entity, to the extent that the stay under section 362 of this title, use, sale, or lease under section 363 of this title, or any grant of a lien under section 364 of this title results in a decrease in the value of property securing a claim or of an entity's ownership interest in property;

(2) providing to such entity an additional or replacement lien to the extent that such stay, use, sale, lease, or grant results in a decrease in the value of property securing a claim or of an entity's ownership interest in property;

(3) paying to such entity for the use of farmland the reasonable rent customary in the community where the property is located, based upon the rental value, net income, and earning capacity of the property; or

(4) granting such other relief, other than entitling such entity to compensation allowable under section 503(b)(1) of this title as an administrative expense, as will adequately protect the value of property securing a claim or of such entity's ownership interest in property.

(Added and amended Pub. L. 99–554, title II, §255, title III, §302(f), Oct. 27, 1986, 100 Stat. 3107, 3124; Pub. L. 103–65, §1, Aug. 6, 1993, 107 Stat. 311; Pub. L. 105–277, div. C, title I, §149(a), Oct. 21, 1998, 112 Stat. 2681–610; Pub. L. 106–5, §1(1), (2), Mar. 30, 1999, 113 Stat. 9; Pub. L. 106–70, §1, Oct. 9, 1999, 113 Stat. 1031; Pub. L. 107–8, §1, May 11, 2001, 115 Stat. 10; Pub. L. 107–17, §1, June 26, 2001, 115 Stat. 151; Pub. L. 107–170, §1, May 7, 2002, 116 Stat. 133; Pub. L. 107–171, title X, §10814(a), May 13, 2002, 116 Stat. 532; Pub. L. 107–377, §2(a), Dec. 19, 2002, 116 Stat. 3115; Pub. L. 108–73, §2(a), Aug. 15, 2003, 117 Stat. 891; Pub. L. 108–369, §2(a), Oct. 25, 2004, 118 Stat. 1749; Pub. L. 109–8, title X, §1001(a)(1), (c), Apr. 20, 2005, 119 Stat. 185, 186.)

Codification

For repeal of section effective Oct. 1, 1998, and subsequent reenactment of section, see note set out preceding section 1201 of this title.

Effective Dates

Permanent reenactment of section effective July 1, 2005, see section 1001(a)(2) of Pub. L. 109–8, set out as a Repeal, Reenactment, and Termination of Chapter note under section 1201 of this title. For effective dates of section and amendments extending periods for which section was reenacted prior to permanent reenactment, see Effective Date and Effective Date of 1999, 2001, 2002, 2003, and 2004 Amendment notes set out under section 1201 of this title.

§1206. Sales free of interests

After notice and a hearing, in addition to the authorization contained in section 363(f), the trustee in a case under this chapter may sell property under section 363(b) and (c) free and clear of any interest in such property of an entity other than the estate if the property is farmland, farm equipment, or property used to carry out a commercial fishing operation (including a commercial fishing vessel), except that the proceeds of such sale shall be subject to such interest.

(Added and amended Pub. L. 99–554, title II, §255, title III, §302(f), Oct. 27, 1986, 100 Stat. 3108, 3124; Pub. L. 103–65, §1, Aug. 6, 1993, 107 Stat. 311; Pub. L. 105–277, div. C, title I, §149(a), Oct. 21, 1998, 112 Stat. 2681–610; Pub. L. 106–5, §1(1), (2), Mar. 30, 1999, 113 Stat. 9; Pub. L. 106–70, §1, Oct. 9, 1999, 113 Stat. 1031; Pub. L. 107–8, §1, May 11, 2001, 115 Stat. 10; Pub. L. 107–17, §1, June 26, 2001, 115 Stat. 151; Pub. L. 107–170, §1, May 7, 2002, 116 Stat. 133; Pub. L. 107–171, title X, §10814(a), May 13, 2002, 116 Stat. 532; Pub. L. 107–377, §2(a), Dec. 19, 2002, 116 Stat. 3115; Pub. L. 108–73, §2(a), Aug. 15, 2003, 117 Stat. 891; Pub. L. 108–369, §2(a), Oct. 25, 2004, 118 Stat. 1749; Pub. L. 109–8, title X, §§1001(a)(1), (c), 1007(c)(3), Apr. 20, 2005, 119 Stat. 185, 186, 188.)

Codification

For repeal of section effective Oct. 1, 1998, and subsequent reenactment of section, see note set out preceding section 1201 of this title.

Amendments

2005—Pub. L. 109–8, §1007(c)(3), substituted "if the property is farmland, farm equipment, or property used to carry out a commercial fishing operation (including a commercial fishing vessel)" for "if the property is farmland or farm equipment".

Effective Date of 2005 Amendment

Amendment by section 1007(c)(3) of Pub. L. 109–8 effective 180 days after Apr. 20, 2005, and not applicable with respect to cases commenced under this title before such effective date, except as otherwise provided, see section 1501 of Pub. L. 109–8, set out as a note under section 101 of this title.

Effective Dates

Permanent reenactment of section effective July 1, 2005, see section 1001(a)(2) of Pub. L. 109–8, set out as a Repeal, Reenactment, and Termination of Chapter note under section 1201 of this title. For effective dates of section and amendments extending periods for which section was reenacted prior to permanent reenactment, see Effective Date and Effective Date of 1999, 2001, 2002, 2003, and 2004 Amendment notes set out under section 1201 of this title.

§1207. Property of the estate

(a) Property of the estate includes, in addition to the property specified in section 541 of this title—

(1) all property of the kind specified in such section that the debtor acquires after the commencement of the case but before the case is closed, dismissed, or converted to a case under chapter 7 of this title, whichever occurs first; and

(2) earnings from services performed by the debtor after the commencement of the case but before the case is closed, dismissed, or converted to a case under chapter 7 of this title, whichever occurs first.

(b) Except as provided in section 1204, a confirmed plan, or an order confirming a plan, the debtor shall remain in possession of all property of the estate.

(Added and amended Pub. L. 99–554, title II, §255, title III, §302(f), Oct. 27, 1986, 100 Stat. 3108, 3124; Pub. L. 103–65, §1, Aug. 6, 1993, 107 Stat. 311; Pub. L. 105–277, div. C, title I, §149(a), Oct. 21, 1998, 112 Stat. 2681–610; Pub. L. 106–5, §1(1), (2), Mar. 30, 1999, 113 Stat. 9; Pub. L. 106–70, §1, Oct. 9, 1999, 113 Stat. 1031; Pub. L. 107–8, §1, May 11, 2001, 115 Stat. 10; Pub. L. 107–17, §1, June 26, 2001, 115 Stat. 151; Pub. L. 107–170, §1, May 7, 2002, 116 Stat. 133; Pub. L. 107–171, title X, §10814(a), May 13, 2002, 116 Stat. 532; Pub. L. 107–377, §2(a), Dec. 19, 2002, 116 Stat. 3115; Pub. L. 108–73, §2(a), Aug. 15, 2003, 117 Stat. 891; Pub. L. 108–369, §2(a), Oct. 25, 2004, 118 Stat. 1749; Pub. L. 109–8, title X, §1001(a)(1), (c), Apr. 20, 2005, 119 Stat. 185, 186.)

Codification

For repeal of section effective Oct. 1, 1998, and subsequent reenactment of section, see note set out preceding section 1201 of this title.

Effective Dates

Permanent reenactment of section effective July 1, 2005, see section 1001(a)(2) of Pub. L. 109–8, set out as a Repeal, Reenactment, and Termination of Chapter note under section 1201 of this title. For effective dates of section and amendments extending periods for which section was reenacted prior to permanent reenactment, see Effective Date and Effective Date of 1999, 2001, 2002, 2003, and 2004 Amendment notes set out under section 1201 of this title.

§1208. Conversion or dismissal

(a) The debtor may convert a case under this chapter to a case under chapter 7 of this title at any time. Any waiver of the right to convert under this subsection is unenforceable.

(b) On request of the debtor at any time, if the case has not been converted under section 706 or 1112 of this title, the court shall dismiss a case under this chapter. Any waiver of the right to dismiss under this subsection is unenforceable.

(c) On request of a party in interest, and after notice and a hearing, the court may dismiss a case under this chapter for cause, including—

(1) unreasonable delay, or gross mismanagement, by the debtor that is prejudicial to creditors;

(2) nonpayment of any fees and charges required under chapter 123 of title 28;

(3) failure to file a plan timely under section 1221 of this title;

(4) failure to commence making timely payments required by a confirmed plan;

(5) denial of confirmation of a plan under section 1225 of this title and denial of a request made for additional time for filing another plan or a modification of a plan;

(6) material default by the debtor with respect to a term of a confirmed plan;

(7) revocation of the order of confirmation under section 1230 of this title, and denial of confirmation of a modified plan under section 1229 of this title;

(8) termination of a confirmed plan by reason of the occurrence of a condition specified in the plan;

(9) continuing loss to or diminution of the estate and absence of a reasonable likelihood of rehabilitation; and

(10) failure of the debtor to pay any domestic support obligation that first becomes payable after the date of the filing of the petition.

(d) On request of a party in interest, and after notice and a hearing, the court may dismiss a case under this chapter or convert a case under this chapter to a case under chapter 7 of this title upon a showing that the debtor has committed fraud in connection with the case.

(e) Notwithstanding any other provision of this section, a case may not be converted to a case under another chapter of this title unless the debtor may be a debtor under such chapter.

(Added and amended Pub. L. 99–554, title II, §255, title III, §302(f), Oct. 27, 1986, 100 Stat. 3108, 3124; Pub. L. 103–65, §1, Aug. 6, 1993, 107 Stat. 311; Pub. L. 105–277, div. C, title I, §149(a), Oct. 21, 1998, 112 Stat. 2681–610; Pub. L. 106–5, §1(1), (2), Mar. 30, 1999, 113 Stat. 9; Pub. L. 106–70, §1, Oct. 9, 1999, 113 Stat. 1031; Pub. L. 107–8, §1, May 11, 2001, 115 Stat. 10; Pub. L. 107–17, §1, June 26, 2001, 115 Stat. 151; Pub. L. 107–170, §1, May 7, 2002, 116 Stat. 133; Pub. L. 107–171, title X, §10814(a), May 13, 2002, 116 Stat. 532; Pub. L. 107–377, §2(a), Dec. 19, 2002, 116 Stat. 3115; Pub. L. 108–73, §2(a), Aug. 15, 2003, 117 Stat. 891; Pub. L. 108–369, §2(a), Oct. 25, 2004, 118 Stat. 1749; Pub. L. 109–8, title II, §213(2), title X, §1001(a)(1), (c), Apr. 20, 2005, 119 Stat. 52, 185, 186.)

Codification

For repeal of section effective Oct. 1, 1998, and subsequent reenactment of section, see note set out preceding section 1201 of this title.

Amendments

2005—Subsec. (c)(10). Pub. L. 109–8, §213(2), added par. (10).

Effective Date of 2005 Amendment

Amendment by section 213(2) of Pub. L. 109–8 effective 180 days after Apr. 20, 2005, and not applicable with respect to cases commenced under this title before such effective date, except as otherwise provided, see section 1501 of Pub. L. 109–8, set out as a note under section 101 of this title.

Effective Dates

Permanent reenactment of section effective July 1, 2005, see section 1001(a)(2) of Pub. L. 109–8, set out as a Repeal, Reenactment, and Termination of Chapter note under section 1201 of this title. For effective dates of section and amendments extending periods for which section was reenacted prior to permanent reenactment, see Effective Date and Effective Date of 1999, 2001, 2002, 2003, and 2004 Amendment notes set out under section 1201 of this title.

SUBCHAPTER II—THE PLAN

§1221. Filing of plan

The debtor shall file a plan not later than 90 days after the order for relief under this chapter, except that the court may extend such period if the need for an extension is attributable to circumstances for which the debtor should not justly be held accountable.

(Added and amended Pub. L. 99–554, title II, §255, title III, §302(f), Oct. 27, 1986, 100 Stat. 3109, 3124; Pub. L. 103–65, §§1, 2, Aug. 6, 1993, 107 Stat. 311; Pub. L. 105–277, div. C, title I, §149(a), Oct. 21, 1998, 112 Stat. 2681–610; Pub. L. 106–5, §1(1), (2), Mar. 30, 1999, 113 Stat. 9; Pub. L. 106–70, §1, Oct. 9, 1999, 113 Stat. 1031; Pub. L. 107–8, §1, May 11, 2001, 115 Stat. 10; Pub. L. 107–17, §1, June 26, 2001, 115 Stat. 151; Pub. L. 107–170, §1, May 7, 2002, 116 Stat. 133; Pub. L. 107–171, title X, §10814(a), May 13, 2002, 116 Stat. 532; Pub. L. 107–377, §2(a), Dec. 19, 2002, 116 Stat. 3115; Pub. L. 108–73, §2(a), Aug. 15, 2003, 117 Stat. 891; Pub. L. 108–369, §2(a), Oct. 25, 2004, 118 Stat. 1749; Pub. L. 109–8, title X, §1001(a)(1), (c), Apr. 20, 2005, 119 Stat. 185, 186.)

Codification

For repeal of section effective Oct. 1, 1998, and subsequent reenactment of section, see note set out preceding section 1201 of this title.

Amendments

1993—Pub. L. 103–65 substituted "the need for an extension is attributable to circumstances for which the debtor should not justly be held accountable" for "an extension is substantially justified".

Effective Date of 1993 Amendment

Pub. L. 103–65, §3, Aug. 6, 1993, 107 Stat. 311, provided that:

"(a) Effective Date.—Except as provided in subsection (b), this Act [amending this section and provisions set out as a note under section 581 of Title 28, Judiciary and Judicial Procedure] and the amendments made by this Act shall take effect on the date of the enactment of this Act [Aug. 6, 1993].

"(b) Application of Amendment Made by Section 2.—The amendment made by section 2 [amending this section] shall not apply with respect to cases commenced under title 11 of the United States Code before the date of the enactment of this Act."

Effective Dates

Permanent reenactment of section effective July 1, 2005, see section 1001(a)(2) of Pub. L. 109–8, set out as a Repeal, Reenactment, and Termination of Chapter note under section 1201 of this title. For effective dates of section and amendments extending periods for which section was reenacted prior to permanent reenactment, see Effective Date and Effective Date of 1999, 2001, 2002, 2003, and 2004 Amendment notes set out under section 1201 of this title.

§1222. Contents of plan

(a) The plan shall—

(1) provide for the submission of all or such portion of future earnings or other future income of the debtor to the supervision and control of the trustee as is necessary for the execution of the plan;

(2) provide for the full payment, in deferred cash payments, of all claims entitled to priority under section 507, unless the holder of a particular claim agrees to a different treatment of that claim;

(3) if the plan classifies claims and interests, provide the same treatment for each claim or interest within a particular class unless the holder of a particular claim or interest agrees to less favorable treatment;

(4) notwithstanding any other provision of this section, a plan may provide for less than full payment of all amounts owed for a claim entitled to priority under section 507(a)(1)(B) only if the plan provides that all of the debtor's projected disposable income for a 5-year period beginning on the date that the first payment is due under the plan will be applied to make payments under the plan; and

(5) subject to section 1232, provide for the treatment of any claim by a governmental unit of a kind described in section 1232(a).

(b) Subject to subsections (a) and (c) of this section, the plan may—

(1) designate a class or classes of unsecured claims, as provided in section 1122 of this title, but may not discriminate unfairly against any class so designated; however, such plan may treat claims for a consumer debt of the debtor if an individual is liable on such consumer debt with the debtor differently than other unsecured claims;

(2) modify the rights of holders of secured claims, or of holders of unsecured claims, or leave unaffected the rights of holders of any class of claims;

(3) provide for the curing or waiving of any default;

(4) provide for payments on any unsecured claim to be made concurrently with payments on any secured claim or any other unsecured claim;

(5) provide for the curing of any default within a reasonable time and maintenance of payments while the case is pending on any unsecured claim or secured claim on which the last payment is due after the date on which the final payment under the plan is due;

(6) subject to section 365 of this title, provide for the assumption, rejection, or assignment of any executory contract or unexpired lease of the debtor not previously rejected under such section;

(7) provide for the payment of all or part of a claim against the debtor from property of the estate or property of the debtor;

(8) provide for the sale of all or any part of the property of the estate or the distribution of all or any part of the property of the estate among those having an interest in such property;

(9) provide for payment of allowed secured claims consistent with section 1225(a)(5) of this title, over a period exceeding the period permitted under section 1222(c);

(10) provide for the vesting of property of the estate, on confirmation of the plan or at a later time, in the debtor or in any other entity;

(11) provide for the payment of interest accruing after the date of the filing of the petition on unsecured claims that are nondischargeable under section 1228(a), except that such interest may be paid only to the extent that the debtor has disposable income available to pay such interest after making provision for full payment of all allowed claims; and

(12) include any other appropriate provision not inconsistent with this title.

(c) Except as provided in subsections (b)(5) and (b)(9), the plan may not provide for payments over a period that is longer than three years unless the court for cause approves a longer period, but the court may not approve a period that is longer than five years.

(d) Notwithstanding subsection (b)(2) of this section and sections 506(b) and 1225(a)(5) of this title, if it is proposed in a plan to cure a default, the amount necessary to cure the default, shall be determined in accordance with the underlying agreement and applicable nonbankruptcy law.

(Added and amended Pub. L. 99–554, title II, §255, title III, §302(f), Oct. 27, 1986, 100 Stat. 3109, 3124; Pub. L. 103–65, §1, Aug. 6, 1993, 107 Stat. 311; Pub. L. 103–394, title III, §305(b), Oct. 22, 1994, 108 Stat. 4134; Pub. L. 105–277, div. C, title I, §149(a), Oct. 21, 1998, 112 Stat. 2681–610; Pub. L. 106–5, §1(1), (2), Mar. 30, 1999, 113 Stat. 9; Pub. L. 106–70, §1, Oct. 9, 1999, 113 Stat. 1031; Pub. L. 107–8, §1, May 11, 2001, 115 Stat. 10; Pub. L. 107–17, §1, June 26, 2001, 115 Stat. 151; Pub. L. 107–170, §1, May 7, 2002, 116 Stat. 133; Pub. L. 107–171, title X, §10814(a), May 13, 2002, 116 Stat. 532; Pub. L. 107–377, §2(a), Dec. 19, 2002, 116 Stat. 3115; Pub. L. 108–73, §2(a), Aug. 15, 2003, 117 Stat. 891; Pub. L. 108–369, §2(a), Oct. 25, 2004, 118 Stat. 1749; Pub. L. 109–8, title II, §213(3), (4), title X, §§1001(a)(1), (c), 1003(a), Apr. 20, 2005, 119 Stat. 52, 185, 186; Pub. L. 115–72, div. B, §1005(b)(1)(A), Oct. 26, 2017, 131 Stat. 1233.)

Codification

For repeal of section effective Oct. 1, 1998, and subsequent reenactment of section, see note set out preceding section 1201 of this title.

Amendments

2017—Subsec. (a)(2). Pub. L. 115–72, §1005(b)(1)(A)(i), substituted "unless" for "unless—", struck out subpar. (B) designation before "the holder", and struck out subpar. (A) which read as follows: "the claim is a claim owed to a governmental unit that arises as a result of the sale, transfer, exchange, or other disposition of any farm asset used in the debtor's farming operation, in which case the claim shall be treated as an unsecured claim that is not entitled to priority under section 507, but the debt shall be treated in such manner only if the debtor receives a discharge; or".

Subsec. (a)(5). Pub. L. 115–72, §1005(b)(1)(A)(ii)–(iv), added par. (5).

2005—Subsec. (a)(2). Pub. L. 109–8, §1003(a), amended par. (2) generally. Prior to amendment, par. (2) read as follows: "provide for the full payment, in deferred cash payments, of all claims entitled to priority under section 507 of this title, unless the holder of a particular claim agrees to a different treatment of such claim;".

Subsec. (a)(4). Pub. L. 109–8, §213(3), added par. (4).

Subsec. (b)(11), (12). Pub. L. 109–8, §213(4), added par. (11) and redesignated former par. (11) as (12).

1994—Subsec. (d). Pub. L. 103–394 added subsec. (d).

Effective Date of 2017 Amendment

Pub. L. 115–72, div. B, §1005(c), Oct. 26, 2017, 131 Stat. 1234, provided that: "The amendments made by this section [enacting section 1232 of this title and amending this section and sections 1228 and 1229 of this title] shall apply to—

"(1) any bankruptcy case—

"(A) that is pending on the date of enactment of this Act [Oct. 26, 2017];

"(B) in which the plan under chapter 12 of title 11, United States Code, has not been confirmed on the date of enactment of this Act; and

"(C) relating to which an order of discharge under section 1228 of title 11, United States Code, has not been entered; and

"(2) any bankruptcy case that commences on or after the date of enactment of this Act."

Effective Date of 2005 Amendment

Pub. L. 109–8, title X, §1003(c), Apr. 20, 2005, 119 Stat. 186, provided that: "This section [amending this section and section 1231 of this title] and the amendments made by this section shall take effect on the date of the enactment of this Act [Apr. 20, 2005] and shall not apply with respect to cases commenced under title 11 of the United States Code before such date."

Amendment by section 213(3), (4) of Pub. L. 109–8 effective 180 days after Apr. 20, 2005, and not applicable with respect to cases commenced under this title before such effective date, except as otherwise provided, see section 1501 of Pub. L. 109–8, set out as a note under section 101 of this title.

Effective Date of 1994 Amendment

Amendment by Pub. L. 103–394 effective Oct. 22, 1994, and applicable only to agreements entered into after Oct. 22, 1994, see section 702 of Pub. L. 103–394, set out as a note under section 101 of this title.

Effective Dates

Permanent reenactment of section effective July 1, 2005, see section 1001(a)(2) of Pub. L. 109–8, set out as a Repeal, Reenactment, and Termination of Chapter note under section 1201 of this title. For effective dates of section and amendments extending periods for which section was reenacted prior to permanent reenactment, see Effective Date and Effective Date of 1999, 2001, 2002, 2003, and 2004 Amendment notes set out under section 1201 of this title.

§1223. Modification of plan before confirmation

(a) The debtor may modify the plan at any time before confirmation, but may not modify the plan so that the plan as modified fails to meet the requirements of section 1222 of this title.

(b) After the debtor files a modification under this section, the plan as modified becomes the plan.

(c) Any holder of a secured claim that has accepted or rejected the plan is deemed to have accepted or rejected, as the case may be, the plan as modified, unless the modification provides for a change in the rights of such holder from what such rights were under the plan before modification, and such holder changes such holder's previous acceptance or rejection.

(Added and amended Pub. L. 99–554, title II, §255, title III, §302(f), Oct. 27, 1986, 100 Stat. 3110, 3124; Pub. L. 103–65, §1, Aug. 6, 1993, 107 Stat. 311; Pub. L. 105–277, div. C, title I, §149(a), Oct. 21, 1998, 112 Stat. 2681–610; Pub. L. 106–5, §1(1), (2), Mar. 30, 1999, 113 Stat. 9; Pub. L. 106–70, §1, Oct. 9, 1999, 113 Stat. 1031; Pub. L. 107–8, §1, May 11, 2001, 115 Stat. 10; Pub. L. 107–17, §1, June 26, 2001, 115 Stat. 151; Pub. L. 107–170, §1, May 7, 2002, 116 Stat. 133; Pub. L. 107–171, title X, §10814(a), May 13, 2002, 116 Stat. 532; Pub. L. 107–377, §2(a), Dec. 19, 2002, 116 Stat. 3115; Pub. L. 108–73, §2(a), Aug. 15, 2003, 117 Stat. 891; Pub. L. 108–369, §2(a), Oct. 25, 2004, 118 Stat. 1749; Pub. L. 109–8, title X, §1001(a)(1), (c), Apr. 20, 2005, 119 Stat. 185, 186.)

Codification

For repeal of section effective Oct. 1, 1998, and subsequent reenactment of section, see note set out preceding section 1201 of this title.

Effective Dates

Permanent reenactment of section effective July 1, 2005, see section 1001(a)(2) of Pub. L. 109–8, set out as a Repeal, Reenactment, and Termination of Chapter note under section 1201 of this title. For effective dates of section and amendments extending periods for which section was reenacted prior to permanent reenactment, see Effective Date and Effective Date of 1999, 2001, 2002, 2003, and 2004 Amendment notes set out under section 1201 of this title.

§1224. Confirmation hearing

After expedited notice, the court shall hold a hearing on confirmation of the plan. A party in interest, the trustee, or the United States trustee may object to the confirmation of the plan. Except for cause, the hearing shall be concluded not later than 45 days after the filing of the plan.

(Added and amended Pub. L. 99–554, title II, §255, title III, §302(f), Oct. 27, 1986, 100 Stat. 3110, 3124; Pub. L. 103–65, §1, Aug. 6, 1993, 107 Stat. 311; Pub. L. 105–277, div. C, title I, §149(a), Oct. 21, 1998, 112 Stat. 2681–610; Pub. L. 106–5, §1(1), (2), Mar. 30, 1999, 113 Stat. 9; Pub. L. 106–70, §1, Oct. 9, 1999, 113 Stat. 1031; Pub. L. 107–8, §1, May 11, 2001, 115 Stat. 10; Pub. L. 107–17, §1, June 26, 2001, 115 Stat. 151; Pub. L. 107–170, §1, May 7, 2002, 116 Stat. 133; Pub. L. 107–171, title X, §10814(a), May 13, 2002, 116 Stat. 532; Pub. L. 107–377, §2(a), Dec. 19, 2002, 116 Stat. 3115; Pub. L. 108–73, §2(a), Aug. 15, 2003, 117 Stat. 891; Pub. L. 108–369, §2(a), Oct. 25, 2004, 118 Stat. 1749; Pub. L. 109–8, title X, §1001(a)(1), (c), Apr. 20, 2005, 119 Stat. 185, 186.)

Codification

For repeal of section effective Oct. 1, 1998, and subsequent reenactment of section, see note set out preceding section 1201 of this title.

Effective Dates

Permanent reenactment of section effective July 1, 2005, see section 1001(a)(2) of Pub. L. 109–8, set out as a Repeal, Reenactment, and Termination of Chapter note under section 1201 of this title. For effective dates of section and amendments extending periods for which section was reenacted prior to permanent reenactment, see Effective Date and Effective Date of 1999, 2001, 2002, 2003, and 2004 Amendment notes set out under section 1201 of this title.

§1225. Confirmation of plan

(a) Except as provided in subsection (b), the court shall confirm a plan if—

(1) the plan complies with the provisions of this chapter and with the other applicable provisions of this title;

(2) any fee, charge, or amount required under chapter 123 of title 28, or by the plan, to be paid before confirmation, has been paid;

(3) the plan has been proposed in good faith and not by any means forbidden by law;

(4) the value, as of the effective date of the plan, of property to be distributed under the plan on account of each allowed unsecured claim is not less than the amount that would be paid on such claim if the estate of the debtor were liquidated under chapter 7 of this title on such date;

(5) with respect to each allowed secured claim provided for by the plan—

(A) the holder of such claim has accepted the plan;

(B)(i) the plan provides that the holder of such claim retain the lien securing such claim; and

(ii) the value, as of the effective date of the plan, of property to be distributed by the trustee or the debtor under the plan on account of such claim is not less than the allowed amount of such claim; or

(C) the debtor surrenders the property securing such claim to such holder;

(6) the debtor will be able to make all payments under the plan and to comply with the plan; and

(7) the debtor has paid all amounts that are required to be paid under a domestic support obligation and that first become payable after the date of the filing of the petition if the debtor is required by a judicial or administrative order, or by statute, to pay such domestic support obligation.

(b)(1) If the trustee or the holder of an allowed unsecured claim objects to the confirmation of the plan, then the court may not approve the plan unless, as of the effective date of the plan—

(A) the value of the property to be distributed under the plan on account of such claim is not less than the amount of such claim;

(B) the plan provides that all of the debtor's projected disposable income to be received in the three-year period, or such longer period as the court may approve under section 1222(c), beginning on the date that the first payment is due under the plan will be applied to make payments under the plan; or

(C) the value of the property to be distributed under the plan in the 3-year period, or such longer period as the court may approve under section 1222(c), beginning on the date that the first distribution is due under the plan is not less than the debtor's projected disposable income for such period.

(2) For purposes of this subsection, "disposable income" means income which is received by the debtor and which is not reasonably necessary to be expended—

(A) for the maintenance or support of the debtor or a dependent of the debtor or for a domestic support obligation that first becomes payable after the date of the filing of the petition; or

(B) for the payment of expenditures necessary for the continuation, preservation, and operation of the debtor's business.

(c) After confirmation of a plan, the court may order any entity from whom the debtor receives income to pay all or any part of such income to the trustee.

(Added and amended Pub. L. 99–554, title II, §255, title III, §302(f), Oct. 27, 1986, 100 Stat. 3110, 3124; Pub. L. 103–65, §1, Aug. 6, 1993, 107 Stat. 311; Pub. L. 105–277, div. C, title I, §149(a), Oct. 21, 1998, 112 Stat. 2681–610; Pub. L. 106–5, §1(1), (2), Mar. 30, 1999, 113 Stat. 9; Pub. L. 106–70, §1, Oct. 9, 1999, 113 Stat. 1031; Pub. L. 107–8, §1, May 11, 2001, 115 Stat. 10; Pub. L. 107–17, §1, June 26, 2001, 115 Stat. 151; Pub. L. 107–170, §1, May 7, 2002, 116 Stat. 133; Pub. L. 107–171, title X, §10814(a), May 13, 2002, 116 Stat. 532; Pub. L. 107–377, §2(a), Dec. 19, 2002, 116 Stat. 3115; Pub. L. 108–73, §2(a), Aug. 15, 2003, 117 Stat. 891; Pub. L. 108–369, §2(a), Oct. 25, 2004, 118 Stat. 1749; Pub. L. 109–8, title II, §§213(5), 218, title X, §§1001(a)(1), (c), 1006(a), Apr. 20, 2005, 119 Stat. 52, 55, 185-187.)

Codification

For repeal of section effective Oct. 1, 1998, and subsequent reenactment of section, see note set out preceding section 1201 of this title.

Amendments

2005—Subsec. (a)(7). Pub. L. 109–8, §213(5), added par. (7).

Subsec. (b)(1)(C). Pub. L. 109–8, §1006(a), added subpar. (C).

Subsec. (b)(2)(A). Pub. L. 109–8, §218, inserted "or for a domestic support obligation that first becomes payable after the date of the filing of the petition" after "dependent of the debtor".

Effective Date of 2005 Amendment

Amendment by sections 213(5), 218, and 1006(a) of Pub. L. 109–8 effective 180 days after Apr. 20, 2005, and not applicable with respect to cases commenced under this title before such effective date, except as otherwise provided, see section 1501 of Pub. L. 109–8, set out as a note under section 101 of this title.

Effective Dates

Permanent reenactment of section effective July 1, 2005, see section 1001(a)(2) of Pub. L. 109–8, set out as a Repeal, Reenactment, and Termination of Chapter note under section 1201 of this title. For effective dates of section and amendments extending periods for which section was reenacted prior to permanent reenactment, see Effective Date and Effective Date of 1999, 2001, 2002, 2003, and 2004 Amendment notes set out under section 1201 of this title.

§1226. Payments

(a) Payments and funds received by the trustee shall be retained by the trustee until confirmation or denial of confirmation of a plan. If a plan is confirmed, the trustee shall distribute any such payment in accordance with the plan. If a plan is not confirmed, the trustee shall return any such payments to the debtor, after deducting—

(1) any unpaid claim allowed under section 503(b) of this title; and

(2) if a standing trustee is serving in the case, the percentage fee fixed for such standing trustee.

(b) Before or at the time of each payment to creditors under the plan, there shall be paid—

(1) any unpaid claim of the kind specified in section 507(a)(2) of this title; and

(2) if a standing trustee appointed under section 1202(c)¹ of this title is serving in the case, the percentage fee fixed for such standing trustee under section 1202(d)¹ of this title.

(c) Except as otherwise provided in the plan or in the order confirming the plan, the trustee shall make payments to creditors under the plan.

(Added and amended Pub. L. 99–554, title II, §255, title III, §302(f), Oct. 27, 1986, 100 Stat. 3111, 3124; Pub. L. 103–65, §1, Aug. 6, 1993, 107 Stat. 311; Pub. L. 103–394, title V, §501(d)(36), Oct. 22, 1994, 108 Stat. 4147; Pub. L. 105–277, div. C, title I, §149(a), Oct. 21, 1998, 112 Stat. 2681–610; Pub. L. 106–5, §1(1), (2), Mar. 30, 1999, 113 Stat. 9; Pub. L. 106–70, §1, Oct. 9, 1999, 113 Stat. 1031; Pub. L. 107–8, §1, May 11, 2001, 115 Stat. 10; Pub. L. 107–17, §1, June 26, 2001, 115 Stat. 151; Pub. L. 107–170, §1, May 7, 2002, 116 Stat. 133; Pub. L. 107–171, title X, §10814(a), May 13, 2002, 116 Stat. 532; Pub. L. 107–377, §2(a), Dec. 19, 2002, 116 Stat. 3115; Pub. L. 108–73, §2(a), Aug. 15, 2003, 117 Stat. 891; Pub. L. 108–369, §2(a), Oct. 25, 2004, 118 Stat. 1749; Pub. L. 109–8, title X, §1001(a)(1), (c), title XV, §1502(a)(9), Apr. 20, 2005, 119 Stat. 185, 186, 217.)

References in Text

Section 1202(c) and (d) of this title, referred to in subsec. (b)(2), was repealed by section 227 of Pub. L. 99–554, and provisions relating to appointment of and fixing percentage fees for standing trustees are contained in section 586(b) and (e) of Title 28, Judiciary and Judicial Procedure, as amended by section 113(b), (c) of Pub. L. 99–554.

Codification

For repeal of section effective Oct. 1, 1998, and subsequent reenactment of section, see note set out preceding section 1201 of this title.

Amendments

2005—Subsec. (b)(1). Pub. L. 109–8, §1502(a)(9), substituted "507(a)(2)" for "507(a)(1)".

1994—Subsec. (b)(2). Pub. L. 103–394 substituted "1202(c)" for "1202(d)" and "1202(d)" for "1202(e)".

Effective Date of 2005 Amendment

Amendment by section 1502(a)(9) of Pub. L. 109–8 effective 180 days after Apr. 20, 2005, and not applicable with respect to cases commenced under this title before such effective date, except as otherwise provided, see section 1501 of Pub. L. 109–8, set out as a note under section 101 of this title.

Effective Date of 1994 Amendment

Amendment by Pub. L. 103–394 effective Oct. 22, 1994, and not applicable with respect to cases commenced under this title before Oct. 22, 1994, see section 702 of Pub. L. 103–394, set out as a note under section 101 of this title.

Effective Dates

Permanent reenactment of section effective July 1, 2005, see section 1001(a)(2) of Pub. L. 109–8, set out as a Repeal, Reenactment, and Termination of Chapter note under section 1201 of this title. For effective dates of section and amendments extending periods for which section was reenacted prior to permanent reenactment, see Effective Date and Effective Date of 1999, 2001, 2002, 2003, and 2004 Amendment notes set out under section 1201 of this title.

¹ See References in Text note below.

§1227. Effect of confirmation

(a) Except as provided in section 1228(a) of this title, the provisions of a confirmed plan bind the debtor, each creditor, each equity security holder, and each general partner in the debtor, whether or not the claim of such creditor, such equity security holder, or such general partner in the debtor is provided for by the plan, and whether or not such creditor, such equity security holder, or such general partner in the debtor has objected to, has accepted, or has rejected the plan.

(b) Except as otherwise provided in the plan or the order confirming the plan, the confirmation of a plan vests all of the property of the estate in the debtor.

(c) Except as provided in section 1228(a) of this title and except as otherwise provided in the plan or in the order confirming the plan, the property vesting in the debtor under subsection (b) of this section is free and clear of any claim or interest of any creditor provided for by the plan.

(Added and amended Pub. L. 99–554, title II, §255, title III, §302(f), Oct. 27, 1986, 100 Stat. 3112, 3124; Pub. L. 103–65, §1, Aug. 6, 1993, 107 Stat. 311; Pub. L. 105–277, div. C, title I, §149(a), Oct. 21, 1998, 112 Stat. 2681–610; Pub. L. 106–5, §1(1), (2), Mar. 30, 1999, 113 Stat. 9; Pub. L. 106–70, §1, Oct. 9, 1999, 113 Stat. 1031; Pub. L. 107–8, §1, May 11, 2001, 115 Stat. 10; Pub. L. 107–17, §1, June 26, 2001, 115 Stat. 151; Pub. L. 107–170, §1, May 7, 2002, 116 Stat. 133; Pub. L. 107–171, title X, §10814(a), May 13, 2002, 116 Stat. 532; Pub. L. 107–377, §2(a), Dec. 19, 2002, 116 Stat. 3115; Pub. L. 108–73, §2(a), Aug. 15, 2003, 117 Stat. 891; Pub. L. 108–369, §2(a), Oct. 25, 2004, 118 Stat. 1749; Pub. L. 109–8, title X, §1001(a)(1), (c), Apr. 20, 2005, 119 Stat. 185, 186.)

Codification

For repeal of section effective Oct. 1, 1998, and subsequent reenactment of section, see note set out preceding section 1201 of this title.

Effective Dates

Permanent reenactment of section effective July 1, 2005, see section 1001(a)(2) of Pub. L. 109–8, set out as a Repeal, Reenactment, and Termination of Chapter note under section 1201 of this title. For effective dates of section and amendments extending periods for which section was reenacted prior to permanent reenactment, see Effective Date and Effective Date of 1999, 2001, 2002, 2003, and 2004 Amendment notes set out under section 1201 of this title.

§1228. Discharge

(a) Subject to subsection (d), as soon as practicable after completion by the debtor of all payments under the plan, and in the case of a debtor who is required by a judicial or administrative order, or by statute, to pay a domestic support obligation, after such debtor certifies that all amounts payable under such order or such statute that are due on or before the date of the certification (including amounts due before the petition was filed, but only to the extent provided for by the plan) have been paid, other than payments to holders of allowed claims provided for under section 1222(b)(5) or 1222(b)(9) of this title, unless the court approves a written waiver of discharge executed by the debtor after the order for relief under this chapter, the court shall grant the debtor a discharge of all debts provided for by the plan, allowed under section 503 of this title, or disallowed under section 502 of this title, except any debt—

(1) provided for under section 1222(b)(5) or 1222(b)(9) of this title; or

(2) of a kind specified in section 523(a) of this title, except as provided in section 1232(c).

(b) Subject to subsection (d), at any time after the confirmation of the plan and after notice and a hearing, the court may grant a discharge to a debtor that has not completed payments under the plan only if—

(1) the debtor's failure to complete such payments is due to circumstances for which the debtor should not justly be held accountable;

(2) the value, as of the effective date of the plan, of property actually distributed under the plan on account of each allowed unsecured claim is not less than the amount that would have been paid on such claim if the estate of the debtor had been liquidated under chapter 7 of this title on such date; and

(3) modification of the plan under section 1229 of this title is not practicable.

(c) A discharge granted under subsection (b) of this section discharges the debtor from all unsecured debts provided for by the plan or disallowed under section 502 of this title, except any debt—

(1) provided for under section 1222(b)(5) or 1222(b)(9) of this title; or

(2) of a kind specified in section 523(a) of this title, except as provided in section 1232(c).

(d) On request of a party in interest before one year after a discharge under this section is granted, and after notice and a hearing, the court may revoke such discharge only if—

(1) such discharge was obtained by the debtor through fraud; and

(2) the requesting party did not know of such fraud until after such discharge was granted.

(e) After the debtor is granted a discharge, the court shall terminate the services of any trustee serving in the case.

(f) The court may not grant a discharge under this chapter unless the court after notice and a hearing held not more than 10 days before the date of the entry of the order granting the discharge finds that there is no reasonable cause to believe that—

(1) section 522(q)(1) may be applicable to the debtor; and

(2) there is pending any proceeding in which the debtor may be found guilty of a felony of the kind described in section 522(q)(1)(A) or liable for a debt of the kind described in section 522(q)(1)(B).

(Added and amended Pub. L. 99–554, title II, §255, title III, §302(f), Oct. 27, 1986, 100 Stat. 3112, 3124; Pub. L. 103–65, §1, Aug. 6, 1993, 107 Stat. 311; Pub. L. 105–277, div. C, title I, §149(a), Oct. 21, 1998, 112 Stat. 2681–610; Pub. L. 106–5, §1(1), (2), Mar. 30, 1999, 113 Stat. 9; Pub. L. 106–70, §1, Oct. 9, 1999, 113 Stat. 1031; Pub. L. 106–518, title II, §208, Nov. 13, 2000, 114 Stat. 2415; Pub. L. 107–8, §1, May 11, 2001, 115 Stat. 10; Pub. L. 107–17, §1, June 26, 2001, 115 Stat. 151; Pub. L. 107–170, §1, May 7, 2002, 116 Stat. 133; Pub. L. 107–171, title X, §10814(a), May 13, 2002, 116 Stat. 532; Pub. L. 107–377, §2(a), Dec. 19, 2002, 116 Stat. 3115; Pub. L. 108–73, §2(a), Aug. 15, 2003, 117 Stat. 891; Pub. L. 108–369, §2(a), Oct. 25, 2004, 118 Stat. 1749; Pub. L. 109–8, title II, §213(6), title III, §330(c), title X, §1001(a)(1), (c), Apr. 20, 2005, 119 Stat. 53, 101, 185, 186; Pub. L. 115–72, div. B, §1005(b)(1)(B), Oct. 26, 2017, 131 Stat. 1233.)

Codification

For repeal of section effective Oct. 1, 1998, and subsequent reenactment of section, see note set out preceding section 1201 of this title.

Amendments

2017—Subsec. (a). Pub. L. 115–72, §1005(b)(1)(B)(i)(I), in introductory provisions, inserted a comma after "all debts provided for by the plan" and after "allowed under section 503 of this title".

Subsec. (a)(2). Pub. L. 115–72, §1005(b)(1)(B)(i)(II), substituted "a kind specified in section 523(a) of this title, except as provided in section 1232(c)." for "the kind specified in section 523(a) of this title."

Subsec. (c)(2). Pub. L. 115–72, §1005(b)(1)(B)(ii), inserted ", except as provided in section 1232(c)" before period at end.

2005—Subsec. (a). Pub. L. 109–8, §330(c)(1), substituted "Subject to subsection (d), as" for "As" in introductory provisions.

Pub. L. 109–8, §213(6), inserted ", and in the case of a debtor who is required by a judicial or administrative order, or by statute, to pay a domestic support obligation, after such debtor certifies that all amounts payable under such order or such statute that are due on or before the date of the certification (including amounts due before the petition was filed, but only to the extent provided for by the plan) have been paid" after "completion by the debtor of all payments under the plan" in introductory provisions.

Subsec. (b). Pub. L. 109–8, §330(c)(2), substituted "Subject to subsection (d), at" for "At" in introductory provisions.

Subsec. (f). Pub. L. 109–8, §330(c)(3), added subsec. (f).

2000—Subsecs. (a), (c)(1). Pub. L. 106–518 substituted "1222(b)(9)" for "1222(b)(10)" wherever appearing.

Effective Date of 2017 Amendment

Amendment by Pub. L. 115–72 applicable to bankruptcy cases pending on Oct. 26, 2017, in which the plan under this chapter has not been confirmed on Oct. 26, 2017, and relating to which an order of discharge under this section has not been entered, and to bankruptcy cases that commence on or after Oct. 26, 2017, see section 1005(c) of Pub. L. 115–72, set out as a note under section 1222 of this title.

Effective Date of 2005 Amendment

Amendments by sections 213(6) and 330(c) of Pub. L. 109–8 effective 180 days after Apr. 20, 2005, with amendment by section 213(6) of Pub. L. 109–8 not applicable with respect to cases commenced under this title before such effective date, except as otherwise provided, and amendment by section 330(c) of Pub. L. 109–8 applicable with respect to cases commenced under this title on or after Apr. 20, 2005, see section 1501 of Pub. L. 109–8, set out as a note under section 101 of this title.

Effective Dates

Permanent reenactment of section effective July 1, 2005, see section 1001(a)(2) of Pub. L. 109–8, set out as a Repeal, Reenactment, and Termination of Chapter note under section 1201 of this title. For effective dates of section and amendments extending periods for which section was reenacted prior to permanent reenactment, see Effective Date and Effective Date of 1999, 2001, 2002, 2003, and 2004 Amendment notes set out under section 1201 of this title.

§1229. Modification of plan after confirmation

(a) At any time after confirmation of the plan but before the completion of payments under such plan, the plan may be modified, on request of the debtor, the trustee, or the holder of an allowed unsecured claim, to—

(1) increase or reduce the amount of payments on claims of a particular class provided for by the plan;

(2) extend or reduce the time for such payments;

(3) alter the amount of the distribution to a creditor whose claim is provided for by the plan to the extent necessary to take account of any payment of such claim other than under the plan; or

(4) provide for the payment of a claim described in section 1232(a) that arose after the date on which the petition was filed.

(b)(1) Sections 1222(a), 1222(b), and 1223(c) of this title and the requirements of section 1225(a) of this title apply to any modification under subsection (a) of this section.

(2) The plan as modified becomes the plan unless, after notice and a hearing, such modification is disapproved.

(c) A plan modified under this section may not provide for payments over a period that expires after three years after the time that the first payment under the original confirmed plan was due, unless the court, for cause, approves a longer period, but the court may not approve a period that expires after five years after such time.

(d) A plan may not be modified under this section—

(1) to increase the amount of any payment due before the plan as modified becomes the plan;

(2) by anyone except the debtor, based on an increase in the debtor's disposable income, to increase the amount of payments to unsecured creditors required for a particular month so that the aggregate of such payments exceeds the debtor's disposable income for such month; or

(3) in the last year of the plan by anyone except the debtor, to require payments that would leave the debtor with insufficient funds to carry on the farming operation after the plan is completed.

(Added and amended Pub. L. 99–554, title II, §255, title III, §302(f), Oct. 27, 1986, 100 Stat. 3113, 3124; Pub. L. 103–65, §1, Aug. 6, 1993, 107 Stat. 311; Pub. L. 105–277, div. C, title I, §149(a), Oct. 21, 1998, 112 Stat. 2681–610; Pub. L. 106–5, §1(1), (2), Mar. 30, 1999, 113 Stat. 9; Pub. L. 106–70, §1, Oct. 9, 1999, 113 Stat. 1031; Pub. L. 107–8, §1, May 11, 2001, 115 Stat. 10; Pub. L. 107–17, §1, June 26, 2001, 115 Stat. 151; Pub. L. 107–170, §1, May 7, 2002, 116 Stat. 133; Pub. L. 107–171, title X, §10814(a), May 13, 2002, 116 Stat. 532; Pub. L. 107–377, §2(a), Dec. 19, 2002, 116 Stat. 3115; Pub. L. 108–73, §2(a), Aug. 15, 2003, 117 Stat. 891; Pub. L. 108–369, §2(a), Oct. 25, 2004, 118 Stat. 1749; Pub. L. 109–8, title X, §§1001(a)(1), (c), 1006(b), Apr. 20, 2005, 119 Stat. 185–187; Pub. L. 115–72, div. B, §1005(b)(1)(C), Oct. 26, 2017, 131 Stat. 1234.)

Codification

For repeal of section effective Oct. 1, 1998, and subsequent reenactment of section, see note set out preceding section 1201 of this title.

Amendments

2017—Subsec. (a)(4). Pub. L. 115–72 added par. (4).

2005—Subsec. (d). Pub. L. 109–8, §1006(b), added subsec. (d).

Effective Date of 2017 Amendment

Amendment by Pub. L. 115–72 applicable to bankruptcy cases pending on Oct. 26, 2017, in which the plan under this chapter has not been confirmed on Oct. 26, 2017, and relating to which an order of discharge under section 1228 of this title has not been entered, and to bankruptcy cases that commence on or after Oct. 26, 2017, see section 1005(c) of Pub. L. 115–72, set out as a note under section 1222 of this title.

Effective Date of 2005 Amendment

Amendment by section 1006(b) of Pub. L. 109–8 effective 180 days after Apr. 20, 2005, and not applicable with respect to cases commenced under this title before such effective date, except as otherwise provided, see section 1501 of Pub. L. 109–8, set out as a note under section 101 of this title.

Effective Dates

Permanent reenactment of section effective July 1, 2005, see section 1001(a)(2) of Pub. L. 109–8, set out as a Repeal, Reenactment, and Termination of Chapter note under section 1201 of this title. For effective dates of section and amendments extending periods for which section was reenacted prior to permanent reenactment, see Effective Date and Effective Date of 1999, 2001, 2002, 2003, and 2004 Amendment notes set out under section 1201 of this title.

§1230. Revocation of an order of confirmation

(a) On request of a party in interest at any time within 180 days after the date of the entry of an order of confirmation under section 1225 of this title, and after notice and a hearing, the court may revoke such order if such order was procured by fraud.

(b) If the court revokes an order of confirmation under subsection (a) of this section, the court shall dispose of the case under section 1207 of this title, unless, within the time fixed by the court, the debtor proposes and the court confirms a modification of the plan under section 1229 of this title.

(Added and amended Pub. L. 99–554, title II, §255, title III, §302(f), Oct. 27, 1986, 100 Stat. 3113, 3124; Pub. L. 103–65, §1, Aug. 6, 1993, 107 Stat. 311; Pub. L. 105–277, div. C, title I, §149(a), Oct. 21, 1998, 112 Stat. 2681–610; Pub. L. 106–5, §1(1), (2), Mar. 30, 1999, 113 Stat. 9; Pub. L. 106–70, §1, Oct. 9, 1999, 113 Stat. 1031; Pub. L. 107–8, §1, May 11, 2001, 115 Stat. 10; Pub. L. 107–17, §1, June 26, 2001, 115 Stat. 151; Pub. L. 107–170, §1, May 7, 2002, 116 Stat. 133; Pub. L. 107–171, title X, §10814(a), May 13, 2002, 116 Stat. 532; Pub. L. 107–377, §2(a), Dec. 19, 2002, 116 Stat. 3115; Pub. L. 108–73, §2(a), Aug. 15, 2003, 117 Stat. 891; Pub. L. 108–369, §2(a), Oct. 25, 2004, 118 Stat. 1749; Pub. L. 109–8, title X, §1001(a)(1), (c), Apr. 20, 2005, 119 Stat. 185, 186.)

Codification

For repeal of section effective Oct. 1, 1998, and subsequent reenactment of section, see note set out preceding section 1201 of this title.

Effective Dates

Permanent reenactment of section effective July 1, 2005, see section 1001(a)(2) of Pub. L. 109–8, set out as a Repeal, Reenactment, and Termination of Chapter note under section 1201 of this title. For effective dates of section and amendments extending periods for which section was reenacted prior to permanent reenactment, see Effective Date and Effective Date of 1999, 2001, 2002, 2003, and 2004 Amendment notes set out under section 1201 of this title.

§1231. Special tax provisions

(a) The issuance, transfer, or exchange of a security, or the making or delivery of an instrument of transfer under a plan confirmed under section 1225 of this title, may not be taxed under any law imposing a stamp tax or similar tax.

(b) The court may authorize the proponent of a plan to request a determination, limited to questions of law, by any governmental unit charged with responsibility for collection or determination of a tax on or measured by income, of the tax effects, under section 346 of this title and under the law imposing such tax, of the plan. In the event of an actual controversy, the court may declare such effects after the earlier of—

(1) the date on which such governmental unit responds to the request under this subsection; or

(2) 270 days after such request.

(Added and amended Pub. L. 99–554, title II, §255, title III, §302(f), Oct. 27, 1986, 100 Stat. 3113, 3124; Pub. L. 103–65, §1, Aug. 6, 1993, 107 Stat. 311; Pub. L. 105–277, div. C, title I, §149(a), Oct. 21, 1998, 112 Stat. 2681–610; Pub. L. 106–5, §1(1), (2), Mar. 30, 1999, 113 Stat. 9; Pub. L. 106–70, §1, Oct. 9, 1999, 113 Stat. 1031; Pub. L. 107–8, §1, May 11, 2001, 115 Stat. 10; Pub. L. 107–17, §1, June 26, 2001, 115 Stat. 151; Pub. L. 107–170, §1, May 7, 2002, 116 Stat. 133; Pub. L. 107–171, title X, §10814(a), May 13, 2002, 116 Stat. 532; Pub. L. 107–377, §2(a), Dec. 19, 2002, 116 Stat. 3115; Pub. L. 108–73, §2(a), Aug. 15, 2003, 117 Stat. 891; Pub. L. 108–369, §2(a), Oct. 25, 2004, 118 Stat. 1749; Pub. L. 109–8, title VII, §719(b)(4), title X, §§1001(a)(1), (c), 1003(b), Apr. 20, 2005, 119 Stat. 133, 185, 186.)

Codification

For repeal of section effective Oct. 1, 1998, and subsequent reenactment of section, see note set out preceding section 1201 of this title.

Amendments

2005—Subsec. (a). Pub. L. 109–8, §719(b)(4), redesignated subsec. (c) as (a) and struck out former subsec. (a) which read as follows: "For the purpose of any State or local law imposing a tax on or measured by income, the taxable period of a debtor that is an individual shall terminate on the date of the order for relief under this chapter, unless the case was converted under section 706 of this title."

Subsec. (b). Pub. L. 109–8, §1003(b), substituted "any governmental unit" for "a State or local governmental unit".

Pub. L. 109–8, §719(b)(4), redesignated subsec. (d) as (b) and struck out former subsec. (b) which read as follows: "The trustee shall make a State or local tax return of income for the estate of an individual debtor in a case under this chapter for each taxable period after the order for relief under this chapter during which the case is pending."

Subsecs. (c), (d). Pub. L. 109–8, §719(b)(4)(B), redesignated subsecs. (c) and (d) as (a) and (b), respectively.

Effective Date of 2005 Amendment

Amendment by section 1003(b) of Pub. L. 109–8 effective Apr. 20, 2005, and not applicable with respect to cases commenced under this title before Apr. 20, 2005, see section 1003(c) of Pub. L. 109–8, set out as a note under section 1222 of this title.

Amendment by section 719(b)(4) of Pub. L. 109–8 effective 180 days after Apr. 20, 2005, and not applicable with respect to cases commenced under this title before such effective date, except as otherwise provided, see section 1501 of Pub. L. 109–8, set out as a note under section 101 of this title.

Effective Dates

Permanent reenactment of section effective July 1, 2005, see section 1001(a)(2) of Pub. L. 109–8, set out as a Repeal, Reenactment, and Termination of Chapter note under section 1201 of this title. For effective dates of section and amendments extending periods for which section was reenacted prior to permanent reenactment, see Effective Date and Effective Date of 1999, 2001, 2002, 2003, and 2004 Amendment notes set out under section 1201 of this title.

§1232. Claim by a governmental unit based on the disposition of property used in a farming operation

(a) Any unsecured claim of a governmental unit against the debtor or the estate that arises before the filing of the petition, or that arises after the filing of the petition and before the debtor's discharge under section 1228, as a result of the sale, transfer, exchange, or other disposition of any property used in the debtor's farming operation—

(1) shall be treated as an unsecured claim arising before the date on which the petition is filed;

(2) shall not be entitled to priority under section 507;

(3) shall be provided for under a plan; and

(4) shall be discharged in accordance with section 1228.

(b) For purposes of applying sections 1225(a)(4), 1228(b)(2), and 1229(b)(1) to a claim described in subsection (a) of this section, the amount that would be paid on such claim if the estate of the debtor were liquidated in a case under chapter 7 of this title shall be the amount that would be paid by the estate in a chapter 7 case if the claim were an unsecured claim arising before the date on which the petition was filed and were not entitled to priority under section 507.

(c) For purposes of applying sections 523(a), 1228(a)(2), and 1228(c)(2) to a claim described in subsection (a) of this section, the claim shall not be treated as a claim of a kind specified in subparagraph (A) or (B) of section 523(a)(1).

(d)(1) A governmental unit may file a proof of claim for a claim described in subsection (a) that arises after the date on which the petition is filed.

(2) If a debtor files a tax return after the filing of the petition for a period in which a claim described in subsection (a) arises, and the claim relates to the tax return, the debtor shall serve notice of the claim on the governmental unit charged with the responsibility for the collection of the tax at the address and in the manner designated in section 505(b)(1). Notice under this paragraph shall state that the debtor has filed a petition under this chapter, state the name and location of the court in which the case under this chapter is pending, state the amount of the claim, and include a copy of the filed tax return and documentation supporting the calculation of the claim.

(3) If notice of a claim has been served on the governmental unit in accordance with paragraph (2), the governmental unit may file a proof of claim not later than 180 days after the date on which such notice was served. If the governmental unit has not filed a timely proof of the claim, the debtor or trustee may file proof of the claim that is consistent with the notice served under paragraph (2). If a proof of claim is filed by the debtor or trustee under this paragraph, the governmental unit may not amend the proof of claim.

(4) A claim filed under this subsection shall be determined and shall be allowed under subsection (a), (b), or (c) of section 502, or disallowed under subsection (d) or (e) of section 502, in the same manner as if the claim had arisen immediately before the date of the filing of the petition.

(Added Pub. L. 115–72, div. B, §1005(a), Oct. 26, 2017, 131 Stat. 1232.)

Effective Date

Section applicable to bankruptcy cases pending on Oct. 26, 2017, in which the plan under this chapter has not been confirmed on Oct. 26, 2017, and relating to which an order of discharge under section 1228 of this title has not been entered, and to bankruptcy cases that commence on or after Oct. 26, 2017, see section 1005(c) of Pub. L. 115–72, set out as an Effective Date of 2017 Amendment note under section 1222 of this title.

CHAPTER 13—ADJUSTMENT OF DEBTS OF AN INDIVIDUAL WITH REGULAR INCOME

SUBCHAPTER I—OFFICERS, ADMINISTRATION, AND THE ESTATE

Sec.
1301. Stay of action against codebtor.
1302. Trustee.
1303. Rights and powers of debtor.
1304. Debtor engaged in business.
1305. Filing and allowance of postpetition claims.
1306. Property of the estate.
1307. Conversion or dismissal.
1308. Filing of prepetition tax returns.

SUBCHAPTER II—THE PLAN
1321. Filing of plan.
1322. Contents of plan.
1323. Modification of plan before confirmation.
1324. Confirmation hearing.
1325. Confirmation of plan.
1326. Payments.
1327. Effect of confirmation.
1328. Discharge.
1329. Modification of plan after confirmation.
1330. Revocation of an order of confirmation.

Amendments
2005—Pub. L. 109–8, title VII, §716(b)(2), Apr. 20, 2005, 119 Stat. 130, added item 1308.

SUBCHAPTER I—OFFICERS, ADMINISTRATION, AND THE ESTATE

§1301. Stay of action against codebtor

(a) Except as provided in subsections (b) and (c) of this section, after the order for relief under this chapter, a creditor may not act, or commence or continue any civil action, to collect all or any part of a consumer debt of the debtor from any individual that is liable on such debt with the debtor, or that secured such debt, unless—

(1) such individual became liable on or secured such debt in the ordinary course of such individual's business; or

(2) the case is closed, dismissed, or converted to a case under chapter 7 or 11 of this title.

(b) A creditor may present a negotiable instrument, and may give notice of dishonor of such an instrument.

(c) On request of a party in interest and after notice and a hearing, the court shall grant relief from the stay provided by subsection (a) of this section with respect to a creditor, to the extent that—

(1) as between the debtor and the individual protected under subsection (a) of this section, such individual received the consideration for the claim held by such creditor;

(2) the plan filed by the debtor proposes not to pay such claim; or

(3) such creditor's interest would be irreparably harmed by continuation of such stay.

(d) Twenty days after the filing of a request under subsection (c)(2) of this section for relief from the stay provided by subsection (a) of this section, such stay is terminated with respect to the party in interest making such request, unless the debtor or any individual that is liable on such debt with the debtor files and serves upon such party in interest a written objection to the taking of the proposed action.

(Pub. L. 95–598, Nov. 6, 1978, 92 Stat. 2645; Pub. L. 98–353, title III, §§313, 524, July 10, 1984, 98 Stat. 355, 388.)

HISTORICAL AND REVISION NOTES
LEGISLATIVE STATEMENTS

Section 1301 of the House amendment is identical with the provision contained in section 1301 of the House bill and adopted by the Senate amendment. Section 1301(c)(1) indicates that a basis for lifting the stay is that the debtor did not receive consideration for the claim by the creditor, or in other words, the debtor is really the "codebtor." As with other sections in title 11, the standard of receiving consideration is a general rule, but where two co-debtors have agreed to share liabilities in a different manner than profits it is the individual who does not ultimately bear the liability that is protected by the stay under section 1301.

SENATE REPORT NO. 95–989

Subsection (a) automatically stays the holder of a claim based on a consumer debt of the chapter 13 debtor from acting or proceeding in any way, except as authorized pursuant to subsections (b) and (c), against an individual or the property of an individual liable with the chapter 13 debtor, unless such codebtor became liable in the ordinary course of his business, or unless the case is closed, dismissed, or converted to another chapter.

Under the terms of the agreement with the codebtor who is not in bankruptcy, the creditor has a right to collect all payments to the extent they are not made by the debtor at the time they are due. To the extent to which a chapter 13 plan does not propose to pay a creditor his claims, the creditor may obtain relief from the court from the automatic stay and collect such claims from the codebtor. Conversely, a codebtor obtains the benefit of any payments made to the creditor under the plan. If a debtor defaults on scheduled payments under the plan, then the codebtor would be liable for the remaining deficiency; otherwise, payments not made under the plan may never be made by the codebtor. The obligation of the codebtor to make the creditor whole at the time payments are due remains.

The automatic stay under this section pertains only to the collection of a consumer debt, defined by section 101(7) of this title to mean a debt incurred by an individual primarily for a personal, family, or household purpose. Therefore, not all debts owed by a chapter 13 debtor will be subject to the stay of the codebtor, particularly those business debts incurred by an individual with regular income, as defined by section 101(24) of this title, engaged in business, that is permitted by virtue of section 109(b) and section 1304 to obtain chapter 13 relief.

Subsection (b) excepts the giving of notice of dishonor of a negotiable instrument from the reach of the codebtor stay.

Under subsection (c), if the codebtor has property out of which the creditor's claim can be satisfied, the court can grant relief from the stay absent the transfer of a security interest in that property by the codebtor to the creditor. Correspondingly, if there is reasonable cause to believe that property is about to be disposed of by the codebtor which could be used to satisfy his obligation to the creditor, the court should lift the stay to allow the creditor to perfect his rights against such property. Likewise, if property is subject to rapid depreciation or decrease in value the stay should be lifted to allow the creditor to protect his rights to reach such property. Otherwise, the creditor's interest would be irreparably harmed by such stay. Property which could be used to satisfy the claim could be disposed of or encumbered and placed beyond the reach of the creditor. The creditor should be allowed to protect his rights to reach property which could satisfy his claim and prevent its erosion in value, disposal, or encumbrance.

HOUSE REPORT NO. 95–595

This section is new. It is designed to protect a debtor operating under a chapter 13 individual repayment plan case by insulating him from indirect pressures from his creditors exerted through friends or relatives that may have cosigned an obligation of the debtor. The protection is limited, however, to ensure that the creditor involved does not lose the benefit of the bargain he made for a cosigner. He is entitled to full compensation, including any interest, fees, and costs provided for by the agreement under which the debtor obtained his loan. The creditor is simply required to share with other creditors to the extent that the debtor will repay him under the chapter 13 plan. The creditor is delayed, but his substantive rights are not affected.

Subsection (a) is the operative subsection. It stays action by a creditor after an order for relief under chapter 13. The creditor may not act, or commence or continue any civil action, to collect all or any part of a consumer debt of the debtor from any individual that is liable on such debt with the debtor, or that has secured the debt, unless the individual became liable or secured the debt in the ordinary course of his business, or the case is closed, dismissed, or converted to chapter 7 or 11.

Subsection (b) permits the creditor, notwithstanding the stay, to present a negotiable instrument and to give notice of dishonor of the instrument, in order to preserve his substantive rights against the codebtor as required by applicable nonbankruptcy law.

Subsection (c) requires the court to grant relief from the stay in certain circumstances. The court must grant relief to the extent that the debtor does not propose to pay, under the plan, the amount owed to the creditor. The court must also grant relief to the extent that the debtor was really the codebtor in the transaction, that is, to the extent that the nondebtor party actually received the consideration for the claim held by the creditor. Finally, the court must grant relief to the extent that the creditor's interest would be irreparably harmed by the stay, for example, where the codebtor filed bankruptcy himself, or threatened to leave the locale, or lost his job.

Amendments
1984—Subsec. (c)(3). Pub. L. 98–353, §524, inserted "continuation of" after "by".

Subsec. (d). Pub. L. 98–353, §313, added subsec. (d).

EFFECTIVE DATE OF 1984 AMENDMENT

Amendment by Pub. L. 98–353 effective with respect to cases filed 90 days after July 10, 1984, see section 552(a) of Pub. L. 98–353, set out as a note under section 101 of this title.

§1302. Trustee

(a) If the United States trustee appoints an individual under section 586(b) of title 28 to serve as standing trustee in cases under this chapter and if such individual qualifies under section 322 of this title, then such individual shall serve as trustee in the case. Otherwise, the United States trustee shall appoint one disinterested person to serve as trustee in the case or the United States trustee may serve as a trustee in the case.

(b) The trustee shall—

(1) perform the duties specified in sections 704(a)(2), 704(a)(3), 704(a)(4), 704(a)(5), 704(a)(6), 704(a)(7), and 704(a)(9) of this title;

(2) appear and be heard at any hearing that concerns—
(A) the value of property subject to a lien;
(B) confirmation of a plan; or
(C) modification of the plan after confirmation;

(3) dispose of, under regulations issued by the Director of the Administrative Office of the United States Courts, moneys received or to be received in a case under chapter XIII of the Bankruptcy Act;

(4) advise, other than on legal matters, and assist the debtor in performance under the plan;

(5) ensure that the debtor commences making timely payments under section 1326 of this title; and

(6) if with respect to the debtor there is a claim for a domestic support obligation, provide the applicable notice specified in subsection (d).

(c) If the debtor is engaged in business, then in addition to the duties specified in subsection (b) of this section, the trustee shall perform the duties specified in sections 1106(a)(3) and 1106(a)(4) of this title.

(d)(1) In a case described in subsection (b)(6) to which subsection (b)(6) applies, the trustee shall—

(A)(i) provide written notice to the holder of the claim described in subsection (b)(6) of such claim and of the right of such holder to use the services of the State child support enforcement agency established under sections 464 and 466 of the Social Security Act for the State in which such holder resides, for assistance in collecting child support during and after the case under this title; and

(ii) include in the notice provided under clause (i) the address and telephone number of such State child support enforcement agency;

(B)(i) provide written notice to such State child support enforcement agency of such claim; and

(ii) include in the notice provided under clause (i) the name, address, and telephone number of such holder; and

(C) at such time as the debtor is granted a discharge under section 1328, provide written notice to such holder and to such State child support enforcement agency of—

(i) the granting of the discharge;
(ii) the last recent known address of the debtor;
(iii) the last recent known name and address of the debtor's employer; and
(iv) the name of each creditor that holds a claim that—
(I) is not discharged under paragraph (2) or (4) of section 523(a); or
(II) was reaffirmed by the debtor under section 524(c).

(2)(A) The holder of a claim described in subsection (b)(6) or the State child support enforcement agency of the State in which such holder resides may request from a creditor described in paragraph (1)(C)(iv) the last known address of the debtor.

(B) Notwithstanding any other provision of law, a creditor that makes a disclosure of a last known address of a debtor in connection with a request made under subparagraph (A) shall not be liable by reason of making that disclosure.

(Pub. L. 95–598, Nov. 6, 1978, 92 Stat. 2645; Pub. L. 98–353, title III, §§314, 525, July 10, 1984, 98 Stat. 356, 388; Pub. L. 99–554, title II, §§228, 283(w), Oct. 27, 1986, 100 Stat. 3103, 3118; Pub. L. 103–394, title V, §501(d)(37), Oct. 22, 1994, 108 Stat. 4147; Pub. L. 109–8, title II, §219(d), Apr. 20, 2005, 119 Stat. 58; Pub. L. 111–327, §2(a)(39), Dec. 22, 2010, 124 Stat. 3561.)

Historical and Revision Notes
legislative statements
Section 1302 of the House amendment adopts a provision contained in the Senate amendment instead of the position taken in the House bill. Sections 1302(d) and (e) are modeled on the standing trustee system contained in the House bill with the court assuming supervisory functions in districts not under the pilot program.

senate report no. 95–989
The principal administrator in a chapter 13 case is the chapter 13 trustee. Experience under chapter XIII of the Bankruptcy Act [chapter 13 of former title 11] has shown that the more efficient and effective wage earner programs have been conducted by standing chapter XIII trustees who exercise a broad range of responsibilities in both the design and the effectuation of debtor plans.

Subsection (a) provides administrative flexibility by permitting the bankruptcy judge to appoint an individual from the panel of trustees established pursuant to 28 U.S.C. §604(f) and qualified under section 322 of title 11, either to serve as a standing trustee in all chapter 13 cases filed in the district or a portion thereof, or to serve in a single case.

Subsection (b)(1) makes it clear that the chapter 13 trustee is no mere disbursing agent of the monies paid to him by the debtor under the plan [section 1322(a)(1)], by imposing upon him certain relevant duties of a liquidation trustee prescribed by section 704 of this title.

Subsection (b)(2) requires the chapter 13 trustee to appear before and be heard by the bankruptcy court whenever the value of property secured by a lien or the confirmation or modification of a plan after confirmation as provided by sections 1323–1325 is considered by the court.

Subsection (b)(3) requires the chapter 13 trustee to advise and counsel the debtor while under chapter 13, except on matters more appropriately left to the attorney for the debtor. The chapter 13 trustee must also assist the debtor in performance under the plan by attempting to tailor the requirements of the plan to the changing needs and circumstances of the debtor during the extension period.

Subsection (c) imposes on the trustee in a chapter 13 case filed by a debtor engaged in business the investigative and reporting duties normally required of a chapter 11 debtor or trustee as prescribed by section 1106(a)(3) and (4).

house report no. 95–595
Subsection (d) gives the trustee an additional duty if the debtor is engaged in business, as defined in section 1304. The trustee must perform the duties specified in sections 1106(a)(3) and 1106(a)(4), relating to investigation of the debtor.

References in Text

CHAPTER XIII of the Bankruptcy Act, referred to in subsec. (b)(3), is chapter XIII of act July 1, 1898, ch. 541, as added June 22, 1938, ch. 575, §1, 52 Stat. 930, which was classified to chapter 13 (§1001 et seq.) of former Title 11.

Sections 464 and 466 of the Social Security Act, referred to in subsec. (d)(1)(A)(i), are classified to sections 664 and 666, respectively, of Title 42, The Public Health and Welfare.

Amendments
2010—Subsec. (b)(1). Pub. L. 111–327 substituted "704(a)(2), 704(a)(3), 704(a)(4), 704(a)(5), 704(a)(6), 704(a)(7), and 704(a)(9)" for "704(2), 704(3), 704(4), 704(5), 704(6), 704(7), and 704(9)".

2005—Subsec. (b)(6). Pub. L. 109–8, §219(d)(1), added par. (6).
Subsec. (d). Pub. L. 109–8, §219(d)(2), added subsec. (d).
1994—Subsec. (b)(3). Pub. L. 103–394 struck out "and" at end.
1986—Subsec. (a). Pub. L. 99–554, §228(1), amended subsec. (a) generally. Prior to amendment, subsec. (a) read as follows: "If the court has appointed an individual under subsection (d) of this section to serve as standing trustee in cases under this chapter and if such individual qualifies under section 322 of this title, then such individual shall serve as trustee in the case. Otherwise, the court shall appoint a person to serve as trustee in the case."

Subsec. (d). Pub. L. 99–554, §228(2), struck out subsec. (d) which read as follows: "If the number of cases under this chapter commenced in a particular judicial district so warrant, the court may appoint one or more individuals to serve as standing trustee for such district in cases under this chapter."

Subsec. (e). Pub. L. 99–554, §283(w), which directed the amendment of par. (1) by substituting "set for such individual" for "fix" could not be executed in view of the repeal of subsec. (e) by section 228(2) of Pub. L. 99–554. See 1984 Amendment note below.

Pub. L. 99–554, §228(2), struck out subsec. (e) which read as follows:
"(1) A court that has appointed an individual under subsection (d) of this section to serve as standing trustee in cases under this chapter shall set for such individual—

"(A) a maximum annual compensation, not to exceed the lowest annual rate of basic pay in effect for grade GS-16 of the General Schedule prescribed under section 5332 of title 5; and

"(B) a percentage fee, not to exceed ten percent, based on such maximum annual compensation and the actual, necessary expenses incurred by such individual as standing trustee.

"(2) Such individual shall collect such percentage fee from all payments under plans in the cases under this chapter for which such individual serves as standing trustee. Such individual shall pay annually to the Treasury—

"(A) any amount by which the actual compensation received by such individual exceeds five percent of all such payments made under plans in cases under this chapter for which such individual serves as standing trustee; and

"(B) any amount by which the percentage fee fixed under paragraph (1)(B) of this subsection for all such cases exceeds—

"(i) such individual's actual compensation for such cases, as adjusted under subparagraph (A) of this paragraph; plus

"(ii) the actual, necessary expenses incurred by such individual as standing trustee in such cases."

1984—Subsec. (b)(1). Pub. L. 98–353, §314(1), substituted "704(7), and 704(9) of this title" for "and 704(8) of this title".

Subsec. (b)(2). Pub. L. 98–353, §314(2), struck out "and" at the end.
Subsec. (b)(3) to (5). Pub. L. 98–353, §525(a), added par. (3) and redesignated former pars. (3) and (4) as (4) and (5), respectively.

Pub. L. 98–353, §314(3), (4), substituted "; and" for the period at end of par. (3) and added par. (4).

Subsec. (e)(1). Pub. L. 98–353, §525(b)(1), which directed the amendment of par. (4) by substituting "set for such individual" for "fix" was executed to par. (1) as the probable intent of Congress.

Subsec. (e)(1)(A). Pub. L. 98–353, §525(b)(2), struck out "for such individual" after "a maximum annual compensation".

Subsec. (e)(2)(A). Pub. L. 98–353, §525(b)(3), substituted "received by" for "of", and "of all such payments made" for "upon all payments".

Effective Date of 2005 Amendment
Amendment by Pub. L. 109–8 effective 180 days after Apr. 20, 2005, and not applicable with respect to cases commenced under this title before such effective date, except as otherwise provided, see section 1501 of Pub. L. 109–8, set out as a note under section 101 of this title.

Effective Date of 1994 Amendment
Amendment by Pub. L. 103–394 effective Oct. 22, 1994, and not applicable with respect to cases commenced under this title before Oct. 22, 1994, see section 702 of Pub. L. 103–394, set out as a note under section 101 of this title.

Effective Date of 1986 Amendment
Effective date and applicability of amendment by section 228 of Pub. L. 99–554 dependent upon the judicial district involved, see section 302(d), (e) of Pub. L. 99–554, set out as a note under section 581 of Title 28, Judiciary and Judicial Procedure.

Amendment by section 283 of Pub. L. 99–554 effective 30 days after Oct. 27, 1986, see section 302(a) of Pub. L. 99–554.

Effective Date of 1984 Amendment
Amendment by Pub. L. 98–353 effective with respect to cases filed 90 days after July 10, 1984, see section 552(a) of Pub. L. 98–353, set out as a note under section 101 of this title.

§1303. Rights and powers of debtor
Subject to any limitations on a trustee under this chapter, the debtor shall have, exclusive of the trustee, the rights and powers of a trustee under sections 363(b), 363(d), 363(e), 363(f), and 363(l), of this title.

(Pub. L. 95–598, Nov. 6, 1978, 92 Stat. 2646.)
Historical and Revision Notes
legislative statements
Section 1303 of the House amendment specifies rights and powers that the debtor has exclusive of the trustees. The section does not imply that the debtor does not also possess other powers concurrently with the trustee. For example, although section 1323 is not specified in section 1303, certainly it is intended that the debtor has the power to sue and be sued.

senate report no. 95–989
A chapter 13 debtor is vested with the identical rights and powers, and is subject to the same limitations in regard to their exercise, as those given a liquidation trustee by virtue of section 363(b), (d), (e), (f), and (h) of title 11, relating to the sale, use or lease of property.

§1304. Debtor engaged in business
(a) A debtor that is self-employed and incurs trade credit in the production of income from such employment is engaged in business.

(b) Unless the court orders otherwise, a debtor engaged in business may operate the business of the debtor and, subject to any limitations on a trustee under sections 363(c) and 364 of this title and to such limitations or conditions as the court prescribes, shall have, exclusive of the trustee, the rights and powers of the trustee under such sections.

(c) A debtor engaged in business shall perform the duties of the trustee specified in section 704(a)(8) of this title.

(Pub. L. 95–598, Nov. 6, 1978, 92 Stat. 2646; Pub. L. 98–353, title III, §§311(b)(2), 526, July 10, 1984, 98 Stat. 355, 389; Pub. L. 111–327, §2(a)(40), Dec. 22, 2010, 124 Stat. 3562.)

Historical and Revision Notes
legislative statements
Section 1304(b) of the House amendment adopts the approach taken in the comparable section of the Senate amendment as preferable to the position taken in the House bill.

senate report no. 95–989
Increased access to the simpler, speedier, and less expensive debtor relief provisions of chapter 13 is accomplished by permitting debtors engaged in business to proceed under chapter 13, provided their income is sufficiently stable and regular to permit compliance with a chapter 13 plan [section 101(24)] and that the debtor (or the debtor and spouse) do not owe liquidated, noncontingent unsecured debts of $50,000, or liquidated, noncontingent secured debts of $200,000 (§109(d)).

Section 1304(a) states that a self-employed individual who incurs trade credit in the production of income is a debtor engaged in business.

Subsection (b) empowers a chapter 13 debtor engaged in business to operate his business, subject to the rights, powers and limitations that pertain to a trustee under sections 363(c) and 364 of title 11, and subject to such further limitations and conditions as the court may prescribe.

Subsection (c) requires a chapter 13 debtor engaged in business to file with the court certain financial statements relating to the operation of the business.

Amendments
2010—Subsec. (c). Pub. L. 111–327 substituted "704(a)(8)" for "704(8)".
1984—Subsec. (b). Pub. L. 98–353, §526, struck out the comma after "of the debtor".

Subsec. (c). Pub. L. 98–353, §311(b)(2), substituted "section 704(8)" for "section 704(7)".

Effective Date of 1984 Amendment
Amendment by Pub. L. 98–353 effective with respect to cases filed 90 days after July 10, 1984, see section 552(a) of Pub. L. 98–353, set out as a note under section 101 of this title.

§1305. Filing and allowance of postpetition claims
(a) A proof of claim may be filed by any entity that holds a claim against the debtor—

(1) for taxes that become payable to a governmental unit while the case is pending; or

(2) that is a consumer debt, that arises after the date of the order for relief under this chapter, and that is for property or services necessary for the debtor's performance under the plan.

(b) Except as provided in subsection (c) of this section, a claim filed under subsection (a) of this section shall be allowed or disallowed under section 502 of this title, but shall be determined as of the date such claim arises, and shall be allowed under section 502(a), 502(b), or 502(c) of this title, or disallowed under section 502(d) or 502(e) of this title, the same as if such claim had arisen before the date of the filing of the petition.

(c) A claim filed under subsection (a)(2) of this section shall be disallowed if the holder of such claim knew or should have known that prior approval by the trustee of the debtor's incurring the obligation was practicable and was not obtained.

(Pub. L. 95–598, Nov. 6, 1978, 92 Stat. 2647.)

Historical and Revision Notes

legislative statements

Section 1305(a)(2) of the House amendment modifies similar provisions contained in the House and Senate bills by restricting application of the paragraph to a consumer debt. Debts of the debtor that are not consumer debts should not be subjected to section 1305(c) or section 1328(d) of the House amendment.

Section 1305(b) of the House amendment represents a technical modification of similar provisions contained in the House bill and Senate amendment.

The House amendment deletes section 1305(d) of the Senate amendment as unnecessary. Section 502(b)(1) is sufficient to disallow any claim to the extent the claim represents the usurious interest or any other charge forbidden by applicable law. It is anticipated that the Rules of Bankruptcy Procedure may require a creditor filing a proof of claim in a case under chapter 13 to include an affirmative statement as contemplated by section 1305(d) of the Senate amendment.

senate report no. 95–989

Section 1305, exclusively applicable in chapter 13 cases, supplements the provisions of sections 501–511 of title 11, dealing with the filing and allowance of claims. Sections 501–511 apply in chapter 13 cases by virtue of section 103(a) of this title. Section 1305(a) provides for the filing of a proof of claim for taxes and other obligations incurred after the filing of the chapter 13 case. Subsection (b) prescribes that section 502 of title 11 governs the allowance of section 1305(a) claims, except that its standards shall be applied as of the date of allowance of the claim, rather than the date of filing of the petition. Subsection (c) requires the disallowance of a postpetition claim for property or services necessary for the debtor's performance under the plan, if the holder of the claim knew or should have known that prior approval by the trustee of the debtor's incurring of the obligation was practicable and was not obtained.

house report no. 95–595

Subsection (a) permits the filing of a proof of a claim against the debtor that is for taxes that become payable to a governmental unit while the case is pending, or that arises after the date of the filing of the petition for property or services that are necessary for the debtor's performance under the plan, such as auto repairs in order that the debtor will be able to get to work, or medical bills. The effect of the latter provision, in paragraph (2), is to treat postpetition credit extended to a chapter 13 debtor the same as a prepetition claim for purposes of allowance, distribution, and so on.

§1306. Property of the estate

(a) Property of the estate includes, in addition to the property specified in section 541 of this title—

(1) all property of the kind specified in such section that the debtor acquires after the commencement of the case but before the case is closed, dismissed, or converted to a case under chapter 7, 11, or 12 of this title, whichever occurs first; and

(2) earnings from services performed by the debtor after the commencement of the case but before the case is closed, dismissed, or converted to a case under chapter 7, 11, or 12 of this title, whichever occurs first.

(b) Except as provided in a confirmed plan or order confirming a plan, the debtor shall remain in possession of all property of the estate.

(Pub. L. 95–598, Nov. 6, 1978, 92 Stat. 2647; Pub. L. 99–554, title II, §257(u), Oct. 27, 1986, 100 Stat. 3116.)

Historical and Revision Notes

legislative statements

Section 1306(a)(2) adopts a provision contained in the Senate amendment in preference to a similar provision contained in the House bill.

senate report no. 95–989

Section 541 is expressly made applicable to chapter 13 cases by section 103(a). Section 1306 broadens the definition of property of the estate for chapter 13 purposes to include all property acquired and all earnings from services performed by the debtor after the commencement of the case.

Subsection (b) nullifies the effect of section 521(3), otherwise applicable, by providing that a chapter 13 debtor need not surrender possession of property of the estate, unless required by the plan or order of confirmation.

Amendments

1986—Subsec. (a). Pub. L. 99–554 inserted reference to chapter 12 in pars. (1) and (2).

Effective Date of 1986 Amendment

Amendment by Pub. L. 99–554 effective 30 days after Oct. 27, 1986, but not applicable to cases commenced under this title before that date, see section 302(a), (c)(1) of Pub. L. 99–554, set out as a note under section 581 of Title 28, Judiciary and Judicial Procedure.

§1307. Conversion or dismissal

(a) The debtor may convert a case under this chapter to a case under chapter 7 of this title at any time. Any waiver of the right to convert under this subsection is unenforceable.

(b) On request of the debtor at any time, if the case has not been converted under section 706, 1112, or 1208 of this title, the court shall dismiss a case under this chapter. Any waiver of the right to dismiss under this subsection is unenforceable.

(c) Except as provided in subsection (f) of this section, on request of a party in interest or the United States trustee and after notice and a hearing, the court may convert a case under this chapter to a case under chapter 7 of this title, or may dismiss a case under this chapter, whichever is in the best interests of creditors and the estate, for cause, including—

(1) unreasonable delay by the debtor that is prejudicial to creditors;

(2) nonpayment of any fees and charges required under chapter 123 of title 28;

(3) failure to file a plan timely under section 1321 of this title;

(4) failure to commence making timely payments under section 1326 of this title;

(5) denial of confirmation of a plan under section 1325 of this title and denial of a request made for additional time for filing another plan or a modification of a plan;

(6) material default by the debtor with respect to a term of a confirmed plan;

(7) revocation of the order of confirmation under section 1330 of this title, and denial of confirmation of a modified plan under section 1329 of this title;

(8) termination of a confirmed plan by reason of the occurrence of a condition specified in the plan other than completion of payments under the plan;

(9) only on request of the United States trustee, failure of the debtor to file, within fifteen days, or such additional time as the court may allow, after the filing of the petition commencing such case, the information required by paragraph (1) of section 521(a);

(10) only on request of the United States trustee, failure to timely file the information required by paragraph (2) of section 521(a); or

(11) failure of the debtor to pay any domestic support obligation that first becomes payable after the date of the filing of the petition.

(d) Except as provided in subsection (f) of this section, at any time before the confirmation of a plan under section 1325 of this title, on request of a party in interest or the United States trustee and after notice and a hearing, the court may convert a case under this chapter to a case under chapter 11 or 12 of this title.

(e) Upon the failure of the debtor to file a tax return under section 1308, on request of a party in interest or the United States trustee and after notice and a hearing, the court shall dismiss a case or convert a case under this chapter to a case under chapter 7 of this title, whichever is in the best interest of the creditors and the estate.

(f) The court may not convert a case under this chapter to a case under chapter 7, 11, or 12 of this title if the debtor is a farmer, unless the debtor requests such conversion.

(g) Notwithstanding any other provision of this section, a case may not be converted to a case under another chapter of this title unless the debtor may be a debtor under such chapter.

(Pub. L. 95–598, Nov. 6, 1978, 92 Stat. 2647; Pub. L. 98–353, title III, §§315, 527, July 10, 1984, 98 Stat. 356, 389; Pub. L. 99–554, title II, §§229, 257(v), Oct. 27, 1986, 100 Stat. 3103, 3116; Pub. L. 109–8, title II, §213(7), title VII, §716(c), Apr. 20, 2005, 119 Stat. 53, 130; Pub. L. 111–327, §2(a)(41), Dec. 22, 2010, 124 Stat. 3562.)

Historical and Revision Notes

legislative statements

Section 1307(a) is derived from the Senate amendment in preference to a comparable provision contained in the House bill.

senate report no. 95–989

Subsections (a) and (b) confirm, without qualification, the rights of a chapter 13 debtor to convert the case to a liquidating bankruptcy case under chapter 7 of title 11, at any time, or to have the chapter 13 case dismissed. Waiver of any such right is unenforceable. Subsection (c) specifies various conditions for the exercise of the power of the court to convert a chapter 13 case to one under chapter 7 or to dismiss the case. Subsection (d) deals with the conversion of a chapter 13 case to one under chapter 11. Subsection (e) prohibits conversion of the chapter 13 case filed by a farmer to chapter 7 or 11 except at the request of the debtor. No case is to be converted from chapter 13 to any other chapter, unless the debtor is an eligible debtor under the new chapter.

house report no. 95–595

Subsection (f) reinforces section 109 by prohibiting conversion to a chapter under which the debtor is not eligible to proceed.

Amendments

2010—Subsec. (c). Pub. L. 111–327, §2(a)(41)(A)(i), substituted "subsection (f)" for "subsection (e)" in introductory provisions.

Subsec. (c)(9), (10). Pub. L. 111–327, §2(a)(41)(A)(ii), (iii), substituted "521(a)" for "521".

Subsec. (d). Pub. L. 111–327, §2(a)(41)(B), substituted "subsection (f)" for "subsection (e)".

2005—Subsec. (c)(11). Pub. L. 109–8, §213(7), added par. (11).

Subsecs. (e) to (g). Pub. L. 109–8, §716(c), added subsec. (e) and redesignated former subsecs. (e) and (f) as (f) and (g), respectively.

1986—Subsec. (b). Pub. L. 99–554, §257(v)(1), inserted reference to section 1208 of this title.

Subsec. (c). Pub. L. 99–554, §229(1)(A), inserted "or the United States trustee" after "party in interest" in provisions preceding par. (1).

Subsec. (c)(9), (10). Pub. L. 99–554, §229(1)(B)–(D), added pars. (9) and (10).

Subsec. (d). Pub. L. 99–554, §257(v)(2), inserted reference to chapter 12.

Pub. L. 99–554, §229(2), inserted "or the United States trustee" after "party in interest".

Subsec. (e). Pub. L. 99–554, §257(v)(3), inserted reference to chapter 12.

1984—Subsec. (b). Pub. L. 98–353, §527(a), inserted a comma after "time".

Subsec. (c)(4). Pub. L. 98–353, §315(2), added par. (4). Former par. (4) redesignated (5).

Subsec. (c)(5). Pub. L. 98–353, §§315(1), 527(b)(1), redesignated former par. (4) as (5) and inserted "a request made for" before "additional". Former par. (5) redesignated (6).

Subsec. (c)(6). Pub. L. 98–353, §315(1), redesignated former par. (5) as (6). Former par. (6) redesignated (7).

Subsec. (c)(7). Pub. L. 98–353, §§315(1), 527(b)(2), redesignated former par. (6) as (7) and substituted "or" for "and". Former par. (7) redesignated (8).

Subsec. (c)(8). Pub. L. 98–353, §§315(1), 527(b)(3), redesignated former par. (7) as (8) and inserted "other than completion of payments under the plan" after "in the plan".

Effective Date of 2005 Amendment

Amendment by Pub. L. 109–8 effective 180 days after Apr. 20, 2005, and not applicable with respect to cases commenced under this title before such effective date, except as otherwise provided, see section 1501 of Pub. L. 109–8, set out as a note under section 101 of this title.

Effective Date of 1986 Amendment

Effective date and applicability of amendment by section 229 of Pub. L. 99–554 dependent upon the judicial district involved, see section 302(d), (e) of Pub. L. 99–554, set out as a note under section 581 of Title 28, Judiciary and Judicial Procedure.

Amendment by section 257 of Pub. L. 99–554 effective 30 days after Oct. 27, 1986, but not applicable to cases commenced under this title before that date, see section 302(a), (c)(1) of Pub. L. 99–554.

Effective Date of 1984 Amendment

Amendment by Pub. L. 98–353 effective with respect to cases filed 90 days after July 10, 1984, see section 552(a) of Pub. L. 98–353, set out as a note under section 101 of this title.

§1308. Filing of prepetition tax returns

(a) Not later than the day before the date on which the meeting of the creditors is first scheduled to be held under section 341(a), if the debtor was required to file a tax return under applicable nonbankruptcy law, the debtor shall file with appropriate tax authorities all tax returns for all taxable periods ending during the 4-year period ending on the date of the filing of the petition.

(b)(1) Subject to paragraph (2), if the tax returns required by subsection (a) have not been filed by the date on which the meeting of creditors is first scheduled to be held under section 341(a), the trustee may hold open that meeting for a reasonable period of time to allow the debtor an additional period of time to file any unfiled returns, but such additional period of time shall not extend beyond—

(A) for any return that is past due as of the date of the filing of the petition, the date that is 120 days after the date of that meeting; or

(B) for any return that is not past due as of the date of the filing of the petition, the later of—

(i) the date that is 120 days after the date of that meeting; or

(ii) the date on which the return is due under the last automatic extension of time for filing that return to which the debtor is entitled, and for which request is timely made, in accordance with applicable nonbankruptcy law.

(2) After notice and a hearing, and order entered before the tolling of any applicable filing period determined under paragraph (1), if the debtor demonstrates by a preponderance of the evidence that the failure to file a return as required under paragraph (1) is attributable to circumstances beyond the control of the debtor, the court may extend the filing period established by the trustee under paragraph (1) for—

(A) a period of not more than 30 days for returns described in paragraph (1)(A); and

(B) a period not to extend after the applicable extended due date for a return described in paragraph (1)(B).

(c) For purposes of this section, the term "return" includes a return prepared pursuant to subsection (a) or (b) of section 6020 of the Internal Revenue Code of 1986, or a similar State or local law, or a written stipulation to a judgment or a final order entered by a nonbankruptcy tribunal.

(Added Pub. L. 109–8, title VII, §716(b)(1), Apr. 20, 2005, 119 Stat. 129; amended Pub. L. 111–327, §2(a)(42), Dec. 22, 2010, 124 Stat. 3562.)

References in Text

Section 6020 of the Internal Revenue Code of 1986, referred to in subsec. (c), is classified to section 6020 of Title 26, Internal Revenue Code.

Amendments

2010—Subsec. (b)(2). Pub. L. 111–327, §2(a)(42)(C), substituted "paragraph (1)" for "this subsection" wherever appearing in introductory provisions.

Subsec. (b)(2)(A). Pub. L. 111–327, §2(a)(42)(A), substituted "paragraph (1)(A)" for "paragraph (1)".

Subsec. (b)(2)(B). Pub. L. 111–327, §2(a)(42)(B), substituted "paragraph (1)(B)" for "paragraph (2)".

Effective Date

Section effective 180 days after Apr. 20, 2005, and not applicable with respect to cases commenced under this title before such effective date, except as otherwise provided, see section 1501 of Pub. L. 109–8, set out as an Effective Date of 2005 Amendment note under section 101 of this title.

SUBCHAPTER II—THE PLAN

§1321. Filing of plan

The debtor shall file a plan.

(Pub. L. 95–598, Nov. 6, 1978, 92 Stat. 2648.)

Historical and Revision Notes

senate report no. 95–989

CHAPTER 13 contemplates the filing of a plan only by the debtor.

§1322. Contents of plan

(a) The plan—

(1) shall provide for the submission of all or such portion of future earnings or other future income of the debtor to the supervision and control of the trustee as is necessary for the execution of the plan;

(2) shall provide for the full payment, in deferred cash payments, of all claims entitled to priority under section 507 of this title, unless the holder of a particular claim agrees to a different treatment of such claim;

(3) if the plan classifies claims, shall provide the same treatment for each claim within a particular class; and

(4) notwithstanding any other provision of this section, may provide for less than full payment of all amounts owed for a claim entitled to priority under section 507(a)(1)(B) only if the plan provides that all of the debtor's projected disposable income for a 5-year period beginning on the date that the first payment is due under the plan will be applied to make payments under the plan.

(b) Subject to subsections (a) and (c) of this section, the plan may—

(1) designate a class or classes of unsecured claims, as provided in section 1122 of this title, but may not discriminate unfairly against any class so designated; however, such plan may treat claims for a consumer debt of the debtor if an individual is liable on such consumer debt with the debtor differently than other unsecured claims;

(2) modify the rights of holders of secured claims, other than a claim secured only by a security interest in real property that is the debtor's principal residence, or of holders of unsecured claims, or leave unaffected the rights of holders of any class of claims;

(3) provide for the curing or waiving of any default;

(4) provide for payments on any unsecured claim to be made concurrently with payments on any secured claim or any other unsecured claim;

(5) notwithstanding paragraph (2) of this subsection, provide for the curing of any default within a reasonable time and maintenance of payments while the case is pending on any unsecured claim or secured claim on which the last payment is due after the date on which the final payment under the plan is due;

(6) provide for the payment of all or any part of any claim allowed under section 1305 of this title;

(7) subject to section 365 of this title, provide for the assumption, rejection, or assignment of any executory contract or unexpired lease of the debtor not previously rejected under such section;

(8) provide for the payment of all or part of a claim against the debtor from property of the estate or property of the debtor;

(9) provide for the vesting of property of the estate, on confirmation of the plan or at a later time, in the debtor or in any other entity;

(10) provide for the payment of interest accruing after the date of the filing of the petition on unsecured claims that are nondischargeable under section 1328(a), except that such interest may be paid only to the extent that the debtor has disposable income available to pay such interest after making provision for full payment of all allowed claims; and

(11) include any other appropriate provision not inconsistent with this title.

(c) Notwithstanding subsection (b)(2) and applicable nonbankruptcy law—

(1) a default with respect to, or that gave rise to, a lien on the debtor's principal residence may be cured under paragraph (3) or (5) of subsection (b) until such residence is sold at a foreclosure sale that is conducted in accordance with applicable nonbankruptcy law; and

(2) in a case in which the last payment on the original payment schedule for a claim secured only by a security interest in real property that is the debtor's principal residence is due before the date on which the final payment under the plan is due, the plan may provide for the payment of the claim as modified pursuant to section 1325(a)(5) of this title.

(d)(1) If the current monthly income of the debtor and the debtor's spouse combined, when multiplied by 12, is not less than—

(A) in the case of a debtor in a household of 1 person, the median family income of the applicable State for 1 earner;

(B) in the case of a debtor in a household of 2, 3, or 4 individuals, the highest median family income of the applicable State for a family of the same number or fewer individuals; or

(C) in the case of a debtor in a household exceeding 4 individuals, the highest median family income of the applicable State for a family of 4 or fewer individuals, plus $525 [1] per month for each individual in excess of 4,

the plan may not provide for payments over a period that is longer than 5 years.

(2) If the current monthly income of the debtor and the debtor's spouse combined, when multiplied by 12, is less than—

(A) in the case of a debtor in a household of 1 person, the median family income of the applicable State for 1 earner;

(B) in the case of a debtor in a household of 2, 3, or 4 individuals, the highest median family income of the applicable State for a family of the same number or fewer individuals; or

(C) in the case of a debtor in a household exceeding 4 individuals, the highest median family income of the applicable State for a family of 4 or fewer individuals, plus $525 [1] per month for each individual in excess of 4,

the plan may not provide for payments over a period that is longer than 3 years, unless the court, for cause, approves a longer period, but the court may not approve a period that is longer than 5 years.

(e) Notwithstanding subsection (b)(2) of this section and sections 506(b) and 1325(a)(5) of this title, if it is proposed in a plan to cure a default, the amount necessary to cure the default, shall be determined in accordance with the underlying agreement and applicable nonbankruptcy law.

(f) A plan may not materially alter the terms of a loan described in section 362(b)(19) and any amounts required to repay such loan shall not constitute "disposable income" under section 1325.

(Pub. L. 95–598, Nov. 6, 1978, 92 Stat. 2648; Pub. L. 98–353, title III, §§316, 528, July 10, 1984, 98 Stat. 356, 389; Pub. L. 103–394, title III, §§301, 305(c), Oct. 22, 1994, 108 Stat. 4131, 4134; Pub. L. 109–8, title II, §§213(8), (9), 224(d), title III, §318(1), Apr. 20, 2005, 119 Stat. 53, 65, 93; Pub. L. 111–327, §2(a)(43), Dec. 22, 2010, 124 Stat. 3562.)

Historical and Revision Notes

legislative statements

Section 1322(b)(2) of the House amendment represents a compromise agreement between similar provisions in the House bill and Senate amendment. Under the House amendment, the plan may modify the rights of holders of secured claims other than a claim secured by a security interest in real property that is the debtor's principal residence. It is intended that a claim secured by the debtor's principal residence may be treated with under section 1322(b)(5) of the House amendment.

Section 1322(c) adopts a 5-year period derived from the House bill in preference to a 4-year period contained in the Senate amendment. A conforming change is made in section 1329(c) adopting the provision in the House bill in preference to a comparable provision in the Senate amendment.

Tax payments in wage earner plans: The House bill provided that a wage earner plan had to provide that all priority claims would be paid in full. The Senate amendment contained a special rule in section 1325(c) requiring that Federal tax claims must be paid in cash, but that such tax claims can be paid in deferred cash installments under the general rules applicable to the payment of debts in a wage earner plan, unless the Internal Revenue Service negotiates with the debtor for some different medium or time for payment of the tax liability.

The House bill adopts the substance of the Senate amendment rule under section 1322(a)(2) of the House amendment. A wage earner plan must provide for full payment in deferred cash payments, of all priority claims, unless the holder of a particular claim agrees with a different treatment of such claim.

senate report no. 95–989

CHAPTER 13 is designed to serve as a flexible vehicle for the repayment of part or all of the allowed claims of the debtor. Section 1322 emphasizes that purpose by fixing a minimum of mandatory plan provisions.

Subsection (a) requires that the plan submit whatever portion of the future income of the debtor is necessary to implement the plan to the control of the trustee, mandates payment in full of all section 507 priority claims, and requires identical treatment for all claims of a particular class.

Subsection (b) permits a chapter 13 plan to (1) divide unsecured claims not entitled to priority under section 507 into classes in the manner authorized for chapter 11 claims; (2) modify the rights of holders of secured and unsecured claims, except claims wholly secured by real estate mortgages; (3) cure or waive any default; (4) propose payments on unsecured claims concurrently with payments on any secured claim or any other class of unsecured claims; (5) provide for curing any default on any secured or unsecured claim on which the final payment is due after the proposed final payment under the plan; (6) provide for payment of any allowed postpetition claim; (7) assume or reject any previously unrejected executory contract or unexpired lease of the debtor; (8) propose the payment of all or any part of any claim from property of the estate or of the debtor; (9) provide for the vesting of property of the estate; and (10) include any other provision not inconsistent with other provisions of title 11.

Subsection (c) limits the payment period under the plan to 3 years, except that a 4–year payment period may be permitted by the court.

Amendments

2010—Subsec. (a). Pub. L. 111–327, §2(a)(43)(A), struck out "shall" after "plan" in introductory provisions.

Subsec. (a)(1) to (3). Pub. L. 111–327, §2(a)(43)(B)–(D), inserted "shall" before "provide".

Subsec. (a)(4). Pub. L. 111–327, §2(a)(43)(E), struck out "a plan" before "may provide".

2005—Subsec. (a)(4). Pub. L. 109–8, §213(8), added par. (4).

Subsec. (b)(10), (11). Pub. L. 109–8, §213(9), added par. (10) and redesignated former par. (10) as (11).

Subsec. (d). Pub. L. 109–8, §318(1), amended subsec. (d) generally. Prior to amendment, subsec. (d) read as follows: "The plan may not provide for payments over a period that is longer than three years, unless the court, for cause, approves a longer period, but the court may not approve a period that is longer than five years."

Subsec. (f). Pub. L. 109–8, §224(d), added subsec. (f).

1994—Subsecs. (c), (d). Pub. L. 103–394, §301, added subsec. (c) and redesignated former subsec. (c) as (d).

Subsec. (e). Pub. L. 103–394, §305(c), added subsec. (e).

1984—Subsec. (a)(2). Pub. L. 98–353, §528(a), inserted a comma after "payments".

Subsec. (b)(1). Pub. L. 98–353, §316, inserted "; however, such plan may treat claims for a consumer debt of the debtor if an individual is liable on such consumer debt with the debtor differently than other unsecured claims".

Subsec. (b)(2). Pub. L. 98–353, §528(b)(1), inserted ", or leave unaffected the rights of the holders of any class of claims".

Subsec. (b)(4). Pub. L. 98–353, §528(b)(2), inserted "other" after "claim or any".

Subsec. (b)(7). Pub. L. 98–353, §528(b)(3), inserted "subject to section 365 of this title," before "provide", substituted ", rejection, or assignment" for "or rejection", and substituted "under such section" for "under section 365 of this title".

Subsec. (b)(8). Pub. L. 98–353, §528(b)(4), struck out "any" before "part of a claim".

Effective Date of 2005 Amendment

Amendment by Pub. L. 109–8 effective 180 days after Apr. 20, 2005, and not applicable with respect to cases commenced under this title before such effective date, except as otherwise provided, see section 1501 of Pub. L. 109–8, set out as a note under section 101 of this title.

Effective Date of 1994 Amendment

Amendment by section 301 of Pub. L. 103–394 effective Oct. 22, 1994, and not applicable with respect to cases commenced under this title before Oct. 22, 1994, and amendment by section 305(c) of Pub. L. 103–394 effective Oct. 22, 1994, and applicable only to agreements entered into after Oct. 22, 1994, see section 702 of Pub. L. 103–394, set out as a note under section 101 of this title.

Effective Date of 1984 Amendment

Amendment by Pub. L. 98–353 effective with respect to cases filed 90 days after July 10, 1984, see section 552(a) of Pub. L. 98–353, set out as a note under section 101 of this title.

Adjustment of Dollar Amounts

The dollar amounts specified in this section were adjusted by notices of the Judicial Conference of the United States pursuant to section 104 of this title as follows:

By notice dated Feb. 16, 2016, 81 F.R. 8748, effective Apr. 1, 2016, in subsec. (d), dollar amount "675" was adjusted to "700" each time it appeared. See notice of the Judicial Conference of the United States set out as a note under section 104 of this title.

By notice dated Feb. 12, 2013, 78 F.R. 12089, effective Apr. 1, 2013, in subsec. (d), dollar amount "625" was adjusted to "675" each time it appeared.

By notice dated Feb. 19, 2010, 75 F.R. 8747, effective Apr. 1, 2010, in subsec. (d)(1)(C), (2)(C), dollar amount "575" was adjusted to "625".

By notice dated Feb. 7, 2007, 72 F.R. 7082, effective Apr. 1, 2007, in subsec. (d), dollar amount "525" was adjusted to "575" each time it appeared.

[1] See Adjustment of Dollar Amounts notes below.

§1323. Modification of plan before confirmation

(a) The debtor may modify the plan at any time before confirmation, but may not modify the plan so that the plan as modified fails to meet the requirements of section 1322 of this title.

(b) After the debtor files a modification under this section, the plan as modified becomes the plan.

(c) Any holder of a secured claim that has accepted or rejected the plan is deemed to have accepted or rejected, as the case may be, the plan as modified, unless the modification provides for a change in the rights of such holder from what such rights were under the plan before modification, and such holder changes such holder's previous acceptance or rejection.

(Pub. L. 95–598, Nov. 6, 1978, 92 Stat. 2649.)

Historical and Revision Notes

senate report no. 95–989

The debtor is permitted to modify the plan before confirmation without court approval so long as the modified plan, which becomes the plan on filing, complies with the requirements of section 1322.

The original acceptance or rejection of a plan by the holder of a secured claim remains binding unless the modified plan changes the rights of the holder and the holder withdraws or alters its earlier acceptance or rejection.

§1324. Confirmation hearing

(a) Except as provided in subsection (b) and after notice, the court shall hold a hearing on confirmation of the plan. A party in interest may object to confirmation of the plan.

(b) The hearing on confirmation of the plan may be held not earlier than 20 days and not later than 45 days after the date of the meeting of creditors under section 341(a), unless the court determines that it would be in the best interests of the creditors and the estate to hold such hearing at an earlier date and there is no objection to such earlier date.

(Pub. L. 95–598, Nov. 6, 1978, 92 Stat. 2649; Pub. L. 98–353, title III, §529, July 10, 1984, 98 Stat. 389; Pub. L. 99–554, title II, §283(x), Oct. 27, 1986, 100 Stat. 3118; Pub. L. 109–8, title III, §317, Apr. 20, 2005, 119 Stat. 92.)

Historical and Revision Notes

senate report no. 95–989

Any party in interest may object to the confirmation of a plan, as distinguished from merely rejecting a plan. An objection to confirmation is predicated on failure of the plan or the procedures employed prior to confirmation to conform with the requirements of chapter 13. The bankruptcy judge is required to provide notice and an opportunity for hearing any such objection to confirmation.

Amendments

2005—Pub. L. 109–8 designated existing provisions as subsec. (a), substituted "Except as provided in subsection (b) and after" for "After", and added subsec. (b).

1986—Pub. L. 99–554 struck out "the" after "object to".

1984—Pub. L. 98–353 struck out "the" before "confirmation of the plan".

Effective Date of 2005 Amendment

Amendment by Pub. L. 109–8 effective 180 days after Apr. 20, 2005, and not applicable with respect to cases commenced under this title before such effective date, except as otherwise provided, see section 1501 of Pub. L. 109–8, set out as a note under section 101 of this title.

Effective Date of 1986 Amendment

Amendment by Pub. L. 99–554 effective 30 days after Oct. 27, 1986, see section 302(a) of Pub. L. 99–554, set out as a note under section 581 of Title 28, Judiciary and Judicial Procedure.

Effective Date of 1984 Amendment

Amendment by Pub. L. 98–353 effective with respect to cases filed 90 days after July 10, 1984, see section 552(a) of Pub. L. 98–353, set out as a note under section 101 of this title.

§1325. Confirmation of plan

(a) Except as provided in subsection (b), the court shall confirm a plan if—

(1) The plan complies with the provisions of this chapter and with the other applicable provisions of this title;

(2) any fee, charge, or amount required under chapter 123 of title 28, or by the plan, to be paid before confirmation, has been paid;

(3) the plan has been proposed in good faith and not by any means forbidden by law;

(4) the value, as of the effective date of the plan, of property to be distributed under the plan on account of each allowed unsecured claim is not less than the amount that would be paid on such claim if the estate of the debtor were liquidated under chapter 7 of this title on such date;

(5) with respect to each allowed secured claim provided for by the plan—

(A) the holder of such claim has accepted the plan;

(B)(i) the plan provides that—

(I) the holder of such claim retain the lien securing such claim until the earlier of—

(aa) the payment of the underlying debt determined under nonbankruptcy law; or

(bb) discharge under section 1328; and

(II) if the case under this chapter is dismissed or converted without completion of the plan, such lien shall also be retained by such holder to the extent recognized by applicable nonbankruptcy law;

(ii) the value, as of the effective date of the plan, of property to be distributed under the plan on account of such claim is not less than the allowed amount of such claim; and

(iii) if—

(I) property to be distributed pursuant to this subsection is in the form of periodic payments, such payments shall be in equal monthly amounts; and

(II) the holder of the claim is secured by personal property, the amount of such payments shall not be less than an amount sufficient to provide to the holder of such claim adequate protection during the period of the plan; or

(C) the debtor surrenders the property securing such claim to such holder;

(6) the debtor will be able to make all payments under the plan and to comply with the plan;

(7) the action of the debtor in filing the petition was in good faith;

(8) the debtor has paid all amounts that are required to be paid under a domestic support obligation and that first become payable after the date of the filing of the petition if the debtor is required by a judicial or administrative order, or by statute, to pay such domestic support obligation; and

(9) the debtor has filed all applicable Federal, State, and local tax returns as required by section 1308.

For purposes of paragraph (5), section 506 shall not apply to a claim described in that paragraph if the creditor has a purchase money security interest securing the debt that is the subject of the claim, the debt was incurred within the 910-day period preceding the date of the filing of the petition, and the collateral for that debt consists of a motor vehicle (as defined in section 30102 of title 49) acquired for the personal use of the debtor, or if collateral for that debt consists of any other thing of value, if the debt was incurred during the 1-year period preceding that filing.

(b)(1) If the trustee or the holder of an allowed unsecured claim objects to the confirmation of the plan, then the court may not approve the plan unless, as of the effective date of the plan—

(A) the value of the property to be distributed under the plan on account of such claim is not less than the amount of such claim; or

(B) the plan provides that all of the debtor's projected disposable income to be received in the applicable commitment period beginning on the date that the first payment is due under the plan will be applied to make payments to unsecured creditors under the plan.

(2) For purposes of this subsection, the term "disposable income" means current monthly income received by the debtor (other than child support payments, foster care payments, or disability payments for a dependent child made in accordance with applicable nonbankruptcy law to the extent reasonably necessary to be expended for such child) less amounts reasonably necessary to be expended—

(A)(i) for the maintenance or support of the debtor or a dependent of the debtor, or for a domestic support obligation, that first becomes payable after the date the petition is filed; and

(ii) for charitable contributions (that meet the definition of "charitable contribution" under section 548(d)(3)) to a qualified religious or charitable entity or organization (as defined in section 548(d)(4)) in an amount not to exceed 15 percent of gross income of the debtor for the year in which the contributions are made; and

(B) if the debtor is engaged in business, for the payment of expenditures necessary for the continuation, preservation, and operation of such business.

(3) Amounts reasonably necessary to be expended under paragraph (2), other than subparagraph (A)(ii) of paragraph (2), shall be determined in accordance with subparagraphs (A) and (B) of section 707(b)(2), if the debtor has current monthly income, when multiplied by 12, greater than—

(A) in the case of a debtor in a household of 1 person, the median family income of the applicable State for 1 earner;

(B) in the case of a debtor in a household of 2, 3, or 4 individuals, the highest median family income of the applicable State for a family of the same number or fewer individuals; or

(C) in the case of a debtor in a household exceeding 4 individuals, the highest median family income of the applicable State for a family of 4 or fewer individuals, plus $525 [1] per month for each individual in excess of 4.

(4) For purposes of this subsection, the "applicable commitment period"—

(A) subject to subparagraph (B), shall be—

(i) 3 years; or

(ii) not less than 5 years, if the current monthly income of the debtor and the debtor's spouse combined, when multiplied by 12, is not less than—

(I) in the case of a debtor in a household of 1 person, the median family income of the applicable State for 1 earner;

(II) in the case of a debtor in a household of 2, 3, or 4 individuals, the highest median family income of the applicable State for a family of the same number or fewer individuals; or

(III) in the case of a debtor in a household exceeding 4 individuals, the highest median family income of the applicable State for a family of 4 or fewer individuals, plus $525 [1] per month for each individual in excess of 4; and

(B) may be less than 3 or 5 years, whichever is applicable under subparagraph (A), but only if the plan provides for payment in full of all allowed unsecured claims over a shorter period.

(c) After confirmation of a plan, the court may order any entity from whom the debtor receives income to pay all or any part of such income to the trustee.

(Pub. L. 95–598, Nov. 6, 1978, 92 Stat. 2649; Pub. L. 98–353, title III, §§317, 530, July 10, 1984, 98 Stat. 356, 389; Pub. L. 99–554, title II, §283(y), Oct. 27, 1986, 100 Stat. 3118; Pub. L. 105–183, §4(a), June 19, 1998, 112 Stat. 518; Pub. L. 109–8, title I, §102(g), (h), title II, §213(10), title III, §§306(a), (b), 309(c)(1), 318(2), (3), title VII, §716(a), Apr. 20, 2005, 119 Stat. 33, 53, 80, 83, 93, 129; Pub. L. 109–439, §2, Dec. 20, 2006, 120 Stat. 3285; Pub. L. 111–327, §2(a)(44), Dec. 22, 2010, 124 Stat. 3562.)

Historical and Revision Notes

legislative statements

Section 1325(a)(5)(B) of the House amendment modifies the House bill and Senate amendment to significantly protect secured creditors in chapter 13. Unless the secured creditor accepts the plan, the plan must provide that the secured creditor retain the lien securing the creditor's allowed secured claim in addition to receiving value, as of the effective date of the plan of property to be distributed under the plan on account of the claim not less than the allowed amount of the claim. To this extent, a secured creditor in a case under chapter 13 is treated identically with a recourse creditor under section 1111(b)(1) of the House amendment except that the secured creditor in a case under chapter 13 may receive any property of a value as of the effective date of the plan equal to the allowed amount of the creditor's secured claim rather than being restricted to receiving deferred cash payments. Of course, the secured creditors' lien only secures the value of the collateral and to the extent property is distributed of a present value equal to the allowed amount of the creditor's secured claim the creditor's lien will have been satisfied in full. Thus the lien created under section 1325(a)(5)(B)(i) is effective only to secure deferred payments to the extent of the amount of the allowed secured claim. To the extent the deferred payments exceed the value of the allowed amount of the secured claim and the debtor subsequently defaults, the lien will not secure unaccrued interest represented in such deferred payments.

senate report no. 95–989

The bankruptcy court must confirm a plan if (1) the plan satisfies the provisions of chapter 13 and other applicable provisions of title 11; (2) it is proposed in good faith; (3) it is in the best interests of creditors, and defined by subsection (a)(4) of Section 1325; (4) it has been accepted by the holder of each allowed secured claim provided for the plan or where the holder of any such secured claim is to receive value under the plan not less than the amount of the allowed secured claim, or where the debtor surrenders to the holder the collateral securing any such allowed secured claim; (5) the plan is feasible; and (6) the requisite fees and charges have been paid.

Subsection (b) authorizes the court to order an entity, as defined by Section 101(15), to pay any income of the debtor to the trustee. Any governmental unit is an entity subject to such an order.

Amendments

2010—Subsec. (a). Pub. L. 111–327, §2(a)(44)(A), inserted "period" after "910-day" in concluding provisions.

Subsec. (b)(2)(A)(ii). Pub. L. 111–327, §2(a)(44)(B), inserted closing parenthesis after "548(d)(3)".

2006—Subsec. (b)(3). Pub. L. 109–439 inserted ", other than subparagraph (A)(ii) of paragraph (2)," after "under paragraph (2)" in introductory provisions.

2005—Subsec. (a). Pub. L. 109–8, §306(b), inserted concluding provisions at end "For purposes of paragraph (5), section 506 shall not apply to a claim described in that paragraph if the creditor has a purchase money security interest securing the debt that is the subject of the claim, the debt was incurred within the 910-day preceding the date of the filing of the petition, and the collateral for that debt consists of a motor vehicle (as defined in section 30102 of title 49) acquired for the personal use of the debtor, or if collateral for that debt consists of any other thing of value, if the debt was incurred during the 1-year period preceding that filing."

Subsec. (a)(5)(B)(i). Pub. L. 109–8, §306(a), amended cl. (i) generally. Prior to amendment, cl. (i) read as follows: "the plan provides that the holder of such claim retain the lien securing such claim; and".

Subsec. (a)(5)(B)(iii). Pub. L. 109–8, §309(c)(1), added cl. (iii).

Subsec. (a)(7). Pub. L. 109–8, §102(g), added par. (7).

Subsec. (a)(8). Pub. L. 109–8, §213(10), added par. (8).

Subsec. (a)(9). Pub. L. 109–8, §716(a), added par. (9).

Subsec. (b)(1)(B). Pub. L. 109–8, §318(2), substituted "applicable commitment period" for "three-year period".

Pub. L. 109–8, §102(h)(1), inserted "to unsecured creditors" after "to make payments".

Subsec. (b)(2), (3). Pub. L. 109–8, §102(h)(2), added pars. (2) and (3) and struck out former par. (2) which read as follows: "For purposes of this subsection, 'disposable income' means income which is received by the debtor and which is not reasonably necessary to be expended—

"(A) for the maintenance or support of the debtor or a dependent of the debtor, including charitable contributions (that meet the definition of 'charitable contribution' under section 548(d)(3)) to a qualified religious or charitable entity or organization (as that term is defined in section 548(d)(4)) in an amount not to exceed 15 percent of the gross income of the debtor for the year in which the contributions are made; and

"(B) if the debtor is engaged in business, for the payment of expenditures necessary for the continuation, preservation, and operation of such business."

Subsec. (b)(4). Pub. L. 109–8, §318(3), added par. (4).

1998—Subsec. (b)(2)(A). Pub. L. 105–183 inserted before semicolon ", including charitable contributions (that meet the definition of 'charitable contribution' under section 548(d)(3)) to a qualified religious or charitable entity or organization (as that term is defined in section 548(d)(4)) in an amount not to exceed 15 percent of the gross income of the debtor for the year in which the contributions are made".

1986—Subsec. (b)(2)(A). Pub. L. 99–554 substituted "; and" for "; or".

1984—Subsec. (a). Pub. L. 98–353, §317(1), substituted "Except as provided in subsection (b), the" for "The".

Subsec. (a)(1). Pub. L. 98–353, §530, inserted "the" before "other".

Subsecs. (b), (c). Pub. L. 98–353, §317(2), (3), added subsec. (b) and redesignated former subsec. (b) as (c).

Effective Date of 2005 Amendment

Amendment by Pub. L. 109–8 effective 180 days after Apr. 20, 2005, and not applicable with respect to cases commenced under this title before such effective date, except as otherwise provided, see section 1501 of Pub. L. 109–8, set out as a note under section 101 of this title.

Effective Date of 1998 Amendment

Amendment by Pub. L. 105–183 applicable to any case brought under an applicable provision of this title that is pending or commenced on or after June 19, 1998, see section 5 of Pub. L. 105–183, set out as a note under section 544 of this title.

Effective Date of 1986 Amendment

Amendment by Pub. L. 99–554 effective 30 days after Oct. 27, 1986, see section 302(a) of Pub. L. 99–554, set out as a note under section 581 of Title 28, Judiciary and Judicial Procedure.

Effective Date of 1984 Amendment

Amendment by Pub. L. 98–353 effective with respect to cases filed 90 days after July 10, 1984, see section 552(a) of Pub. L. 98–353, set out as a note under section 101 of this title.

Adjustment of Dollar Amounts

The dollar amounts specified in this section were adjusted by notices of the Judicial Conference of the United States pursuant to section 104 of this title as follows:

By notice dated Feb. 16, 2016, 81 F.R. 8748, effective Apr. 1, 2016, in subsec. (b), dollar amount "675" was adjusted to "700" each time it appeared. See notice of the Judicial Conference of the United States set out as a note under section 104 of this title.

By notice dated Feb. 12, 2013, 78 F.R. 12089, effective Apr. 1, 2013, in subsec. (b), dollar amount "625" was adjusted to "675" each time it appeared.

By notice dated Feb. 19, 2010, 75 F.R. 8747, effective Apr. 1, 2010, in subsec. (b)(3), (4), dollar amount "575" was adjusted to "625".

By notice dated Feb. 7, 2007, 72 F.R. 7082, effective Apr. 1, 2007, in subsec. (b), dollar amount "525" was adjusted to "575" each time it appeared.

[1] See Adjustment of Dollar Amounts notes below.

§1326. Payments

(a)(1) Unless the court orders otherwise, the debtor shall commence making payments not later than 30 days after the date of the filing of the plan or the order for relief, whichever is earlier, in the amount—

(A) proposed by the plan to the trustee;

(B) scheduled in a lease of personal property directly to the lessor for that portion of the obligation that becomes due after the order for relief, reducing the payments under subparagraph (A) by the amount so paid and providing the trustee with evidence of such payment, including the amount and date of payment; and

(C) that provides adequate protection directly to a creditor holding an allowed claim secured by personal property to the extent the claim is attributable to the purchase of such property by the debtor for that portion of the obligation that becomes due after the order for relief, reducing the payments under subparagraph (A) by the amount so paid and providing the trustee with evidence of such payment, including the amount and date of payment.

(2) A payment made under paragraph (1)(A) shall be retained by the trustee until confirmation or denial of confirmation. If a plan is confirmed, the trustee shall distribute any such payment in accordance with the plan as soon as is practicable. If a plan is not confirmed, the trustee shall return any such payments not previously paid and not yet due and owing to creditors pursuant to paragraph (3) to the debtor, after deducting any unpaid claim allowed under section 503(b).

(3) Subject to section 363, the court may, upon notice and a hearing, modify, increase, or reduce the payments required under this subsection pending confirmation of a plan.

(4) Not later than 60 days after the date of filing of a case under this chapter, a debtor retaining possession of personal property subject to a lease or securing a claim attributable in whole or in part to the purchase price of such property shall provide the lessor or secured creditor reasonable evidence of the maintenance of any required insurance coverage with respect to the use or ownership of such property and continue to do so for so long as the debtor retains possession of such property.

(b) Before or at the time of each payment to creditors under the plan, there shall be paid—

(1) any unpaid claim of the kind specified in section 507(a)(2) of this title;

(2) if a standing trustee appointed under section 586(b) of title 28 is serving in the case, the percentage fee fixed for such standing trustee under section 586(e)(1)(B) of title 28; and

(3) if a chapter 7 trustee has been allowed compensation due to the conversion or dismissal of the debtor's prior case pursuant to section 707(b), and some portion of that compensation remains unpaid in a case converted to this chapter or in the case dismissed under section 707(b) and refiled under this chapter, the amount of any such unpaid compensation, which shall be paid monthly—

(A) by prorating such amount over the remaining duration of the plan; and

(B) by monthly payments not to exceed the greater of—

(i) $25; [1] or

(ii) the amount payable to unsecured nonpriority creditors, as provided by the plan, multiplied by 5 percent, and the result divided by the number of months in the plan.

(c) Except as otherwise provided in the plan or in the order confirming the plan, the trustee shall make payments to creditors under the plan.

(d) Notwithstanding any other provision of this title—

(1) compensation referred to in subsection (b)(3) is payable and may be collected by the trustee under that paragraph, even if such amount has been discharged in a prior case under this title; and

(2) such compensation is payable in a case under this chapter only to the extent permitted by subsection (b)(3).

(Pub. L. 95–598, Nov. 6, 1978, 92 Stat. 2650; Pub. L. 98–353, title III, §§318(a), 531, July 10, 1984, 98 Stat. 357, 389; Pub. L. 99–554, title II, §§230, 283(z), Oct. 27, 1986, 100 Stat. 3103, 3118; Pub. L. 103–394, title III, §307, Oct. 22, 1994, 108 Stat. 4135; Pub. L. 109–8, title III, §309(c)(2), title XII, §1224, title XV, §1502(a)(10), Apr. 20, 2005, 119 Stat. 83, 199, 217.)

Historical and Revision Notes

legislative statements

Section 1326(a)(2) of the House amendment adopts a comparable provision contained in the House bill providing for standing trustees.

senate report no. 95–989

Section 1326 supplements the priorities provisions of section 507. Subsection (a) requires accrued costs of administration and filing fees, as well as fees due the chapter 13 trustee, to be disbursed before payments to creditors under the plan. Subsection (b) makes it clear that the chapter 13 trustee is normally to make distribution to creditors of the payments made under the plan by the debtor.

house report no. 95–595

Subsection (a) requires that before or at the time of each payment any outstanding administrative expenses [and] any percentage fee due for a private standing chapter 13 trustee be paid in full.

Amendments

2005—Subsec. (a). Pub. L. 109–8, §309(c)(2), amended subsec. (a) generally. Prior to amendment subsec. (a) read as follows:

"(a)(1) Unless the court orders otherwise, the debtor shall commence making the payments proposed by a plan within 30 days after the plan is filed.

"(2) A payment made under this subsection shall be retained by the trustee until confirmation or denial of confirmation of a plan. If a plan is confirmed, the trustee shall distribute any such payment in accordance with the plan as soon as practicable. If a plan is not confirmed, the trustee shall return any such payment to the debtor, after deducting any unpaid claim allowed under section 503(b) of this title."

Subsec. (b)(1). Pub. L. 109–8, §1502(a)(10), substituted "507(a)(2)" for "507(a)(1)".

Subsec. (b)(3). Pub. L. 109–8, §1224(1), added par. (3).

Subsec. (d). Pub. L. 109–8, §1224(2), added subsec. (d).

1994—Subsec. (a)(2). Pub. L. 103–394 inserted "as soon as practicable" before period at end of second sentence.

1986—Subsec. (a)(2). Pub. L. 99–554, §283(z), substituted "payment" for "payments" in last sentence.

Subsec. (b). Pub. L. 99–554, §230, amended subsec. (b) generally, substituting "586(b) of title 28" for "1302(d) of this title" and "586(e)(1)(B) of title 28" for "1302(e) of this title" in par. (2).

1984—Subsec. (a). Pub. L. 98–353, §318(a)(2), added subsec. (a). Former subsec. (a) redesignated (b).

Subsec. (b). Pub. L. 98–353, §318(a)(1), redesignated subsec. (a) as (b). Former subsec. (b) redesignated (c).

Subsec. (b)(2). Pub. L. 98–353, §531, inserted "of this title" after "1302(d)".

Subsec. (c). Pub. L. 98–353, §318(a)(1), redesignated former subsec. (b) as (c).

Effective Date of 2005 Amendment

Amendment by Pub. L. 109–8 effective 180 days after Apr. 20, 2005, and not applicable with respect to cases commenced under this title before such effective date, except as otherwise provided, see section 1501 of Pub. L. 109–8, set out as a note under section 101 of this title.

Effective Date of 1994 Amendment

Amendment by Pub. L. 103–394 effective Oct. 22, 1994, and not applicable with respect to cases commenced under this title before Oct. 22, 1994, see section 702 of Pub. L. 103–394, set out as a note under section 101 of this title.

Effective Date of 1986 Amendment

Effective date and applicability of amendment by section 230 of Pub. L. 99–554 dependent upon the judicial district involved, see section 302(d), (e) of Pub. L. 99–554, set out as a note under section 581 of Title 28, Judiciary and Judicial Procedure.

Amendment by section 283 of Pub. L. 99–554 effective 30 days after Oct. 27, 1986, see section 302(a) of Pub. L. 99–554.

Effective Date of 1984 Amendment

Amendment by Pub. L. 98–353 effective with respect to cases filed 90 days after July 10, 1984, see section 552(a) of Pub. L. 98–353, set out as a note under section 101 of this title.

Adjustment of Dollar Amounts

The dollar amounts specified in this section were adjusted by notices of the Judicial Conference of the United States pursuant to section 104 of this title as follows:

By notice dated Feb. 16, 2016, 81 F.R. 8748, effective Apr. 1, 2016, in subsec. (b)(3), dollar amount "25" was adjusted to "25". See notice of the Judicial Conference of the United States set out as a note under section 104 of this title.

By notice dated Feb. 12, 2013, 78 F.R. 12089, effective Apr. 1, 2013, in subsec. (b)(3), dollar amount "25" was adjusted to "25".

By notice dated Feb. 19, 2010, 75 F.R. 8747, effective Apr. 1, 2010, in subsec. (b)(3)(B), dollar amount "25" was adjusted to "25".

By notice dated Feb. 7, 2007, 72 F.R. 7082, effective Apr. 1, 2007, in subsec. (b)(3), dollar amount "25" was adjusted to "25".

[1] See Adjustment of Dollar Amounts notes below.

§1327. Effect of confirmation

(a) The provisions of a confirmed plan bind the debtor and each creditor, whether or not the claim of such creditor is provided for by the plan, and whether or not such creditor has objected to, has accepted, or has rejected the plan.

(b) Except as otherwise provided in the plan or the order confirming the plan, the confirmation of a plan vests all of the property of the estate in the debtor.

(c) Except as otherwise provided in the plan or in the order confirming the plan, the property vesting in the debtor under subsection (b) of this section is free and clear of any claim or interest of any creditor provided for by the plan.

(Pub. L. 95–598, Nov. 6, 1978, 92 Stat. 2650.)

Historical and Revision Notes

senate report no. 95–989

Subsection (a) binds the debtor and each creditor to the provisions of a confirmed plan, whether or not the claim of the creditor is provided for by the plan and whether or not the creditor has accepted, rejected, or objected to the plan. Unless the plan itself or the order confirming the plan otherwise provides, confirmation is deemed to vest all property of the estate in the debtor, free and clear of any claim or interest of any creditor provided for by the plan.

§1328. Discharge

(a) Subject to subsection (d), as soon as practicable after completion by the debtor of all payments under the plan, and in the case of a debtor who is required by a judicial or administrative order, or by statute, to pay a domestic support obligation, after such debtor certifies that all amounts payable under such order or such statute that are due on or before the date of the certification (including amounts due before the petition was filed, but only to the extent provided for by the plan) have been paid, unless the court approves a written waiver of discharge executed by the debtor after the order for relief under this chapter, the court shall grant the debtor a discharge of all debts provided for by the plan or disallowed under section 502 of this title, except any debt—

(1) provided for under section 1322(b)(5);

(2) of the kind specified in section 507(a)(8)(C) or in paragraph (1)(B), (1)(C), (2), (3), (4), (5), (8), or (9) of section 523(a);

(3) for restitution, or a criminal fine, included in a sentence on the debtor's conviction of a crime; or

(4) for restitution, or damages, awarded in a civil action against the debtor as a result of willful or malicious injury by the debtor that caused personal injury to an individual or the death of an individual.

(b) Subject to subsection (d), at any time after the confirmation of the plan and after notice and a hearing, the court may grant a discharge to a debtor that has not completed payments under the plan only if—

(1) the debtor's failure to complete such payments is due to circumstances for which the debtor should not justly be held accountable;

(2) the value, as of the effective date of the plan, of property actually distributed under the plan on account of each allowed unsecured claim is not less than the amount that would have been paid on such claim if the estate of the debtor had been liquidated under chapter 7 of this title on such date; and

(3) modification of the plan under section 1329 of this title is not practicable.

(c) A discharge granted under subsection (b) of this section discharges the debtor from all unsecured debts provided for by the plan or disallowed under section 502 of this title, except any debt—

(1) provided for under section 1322(b)(5) of this title; or

(2) of a kind specified in section 523(a) of this title.

(d) Notwithstanding any other provision of this section, a discharge granted under this section does not discharge the debtor from any debt based on an allowed claim filed under section 1305(a)(2) of this title if prior approval by the trustee of the debtor's incurring such debt was practicable and was not obtained.

(e) On request of a party in interest before one year after a discharge under this section is granted, and after notice and a hearing, the court may revoke such discharge only if—

(1) such discharge was obtained by the debtor through fraud; and

(2) the requesting party did not know of such fraud until after such discharge was granted.

(f) Notwithstanding subsections (a) and (b), the court shall not grant a discharge of all debts provided for in the plan or disallowed under section 502, if the debtor has received a discharge—

(1) in a case filed under chapter 7, 11, or 12 of this title during the 4-year period preceding the date of the order for relief under this chapter, or

(2) in a case filed under chapter 13 of this title during the 2-year period preceding the date of such order.

(g)(1) The court shall not grant a discharge under this section to a debtor unless after filing a petition the debtor has completed an instructional course concerning personal financial management described in section 111.

(2) Paragraph (1) shall not apply with respect to a debtor who is a person described in section 109(h)(4) or who resides in a district for which the United States trustee (or the bankruptcy administrator, if any) determines that the approved instructional courses are not adequate to service the additional individuals who would otherwise be required to complete such instructional course by reason of the requirements of paragraph (1).

(3) The United States trustee (or the bankruptcy administrator, if any) who makes a determination described in paragraph (2) shall review such determination not later than 1 year after the date of such determination, and not less frequently than annually thereafter.

(h) The court may not grant a discharge under this chapter unless the court after notice and a hearing held not more than 10 days before the date of the entry of the order granting the discharge finds that there is no reasonable cause to believe that—

(1) section 522(q)(1) may be applicable to the debtor; and

(2) there is pending any proceeding in which the debtor may be found guilty of a felony of the kind described in section 522(q)(1)(A) or liable for a debt of the kind described in section 522(q)(1)(B).

(Pub. L. 95–598, Nov. 6, 1978, 92 Stat. 2650; Pub. L. 98–353, title III, §532, July 10, 1984, 98 Stat. 389; Pub. L. 101–508, title III, §3007(b)(1), Nov. 5, 1990, 104 Stat. 1388–28; Pub. L. 101–581, §§2(b), 3, Nov. 15, 1990, 104 Stat. 2865; Pub. L. 101–647, title XXXI, §§3102(b), 3103, Nov. 29, 1990, 104 Stat. 4916; Pub. L. 103–394, title III, §302, title V, §501(d)(38), Oct. 22, 1994, 108 Stat. 4132, 4147; Pub. L. 109–8, title I, §106(c), title II, §213(11), title III, §§312(2), 314(b), 330(d), title VII, §707, Apr. 20, 2005, 119 Stat. 38, 53, 87, 88, 102, 126.)

Historical and Revision Notes

legislative statements

Section 1328(a) adopts a provision contained in the Senate amendment permitting the court to approve a waiver of discharge by the debtor. It is anticipated that such a waiver must be in writing executed after the order for relief in a case under chapter 13.

senate report no. 95–989

The court is to enter a discharge, unless waived, as soon as practicable after completion of payments under the plan. The debtor is to be discharged of all debts provided for by the plan or disallowed under section 502, except a debt provided for under the plan the last payment on which was not due until after the completion of the plan, or a debt incurred for willful and malicious conversion of or injury to the property or person of another.

Subsection (b) is the successor to Bankruptcy Act Section 661 [section 1061 of former title 11]. This subsection permits the bankruptcy judge to grant the debtor a discharge at any time after confirmation of a plan, if the court determines, after notice and hearing, that the failure to complete payments under the plan is due to circumstances for which the debtor should not justly be held accountable, the distributions made to each creditor under the plan equal in value the amount that would have been paid to the creditor had the estate been liquidated under chapter 7 of title 11 at the date of the hearing under this subsection, and that modification of the plan is impracticable. The discharge granted under subsection (b) relieves the debtor from all unsecured debts provided for by the plan or disallowed under section 502, except nondischargeable debts described in section 523(a) of title 11 or debts of the type covered by section 1322(b)(5).

Subsection (d) excepts from any chapter 13 discharge a debt based on an allowed section 1305(a)(2) postpetition claim, if prior trustee approval of the incurring of the debt was practicable but was not obtained.

A chapter 13 discharge obtained through fraud and before the moving party gained knowledge of the fraud may be revoked by the court under subsection (e), after notice and hearing, at the request of any party in interest made within 1 year after the discharge was granted.

Amendments

2005—Subsec. (a). Pub. L. 109–8, §330(d)(1), substituted "Subject to subsection (d), as" for "As" in introductory provisions.

Pub. L. 109–8, §314(b), added pars. (1) to (4) and struck out former pars. (1) to (3) which read as follows:

"(1) provided for under section 1322(b)(5) of this title;

"(2) of the kind specified in paragraph (5), (8), or (9) of section 523(a) of this title; or

"(3) for restitution, or a criminal fine, included in a sentence on the debtor's conviction of a crime."

Pub. L. 109–8, §213(11), inserted ", and in the case of a debtor who is required by a judicial or administrative order, or by statute, to pay a domestic support obligation, after such debtor certifies that all amounts payable under such order or such statute that are due on or before the date of the certification (including amounts due before the petition was filed, but only to the extent provided for by the plan) have been paid" after "completion by the debtor of all payments under the plan" in introductory provisions.

Subsec. (a)(2). Pub. L. 109–8, §707, substituted "section 507(a)(8)(C) or in paragraph (1)(B), (1)(C)," for "paragraph".

Subsec. (b). Pub. L. 109–8, §330(d)(2), substituted "Subject to subsection (d), at" for "At" in introductory provisions.

Subsec. (f). Pub. L. 109–8, §312(2), added subsec. (f).

Subsec. (g). Pub. L. 109–8, §106(c), added subsec. (g).

Subsec. (h). Pub. L. 109–8, §330(d)(3), added subsec. (h).

1994—Subsec. (a)(2). Pub. L. 103–394, §501(d)(38)(A), substituted "(5), (8), or (9)" for "(5) or (8)".

Subsec. (a)(3). Pub. L. 103–394, §501(d)(38)(B), struck out last par. (3). See 1990 Amendment note below.

Pub. L. 103–394, §302, inserted ", or a criminal fine," after "restitution".

1990—Subsec. (a)(1). Pub. L. 101–581, §3(1), and Pub. L. 101–647, §3103(1), made identical amendments striking "or" at end.

Subsec. (a)(2). Pub. L. 101–581, §3(2), and Pub. L. 101–647, §3103(2), made identical amendments substituting "; or" for period at end.

Pub. L. 101–581, §2(b), and Pub. L. 101–647, §3102(b), which directed identical insertions of "or 523(a)(9)" after "523(a)(5)", could not be executed because of prior amendment by Pub. L. 101–508. See below.

Pub. L. 101–508 substituted "paragraph (5) or (8) of section 523(a)" for "section 523(a)(5)".

Subsec. (a)(3). Pub. L. 101–581, §3(3), and Pub. L. 101–647, §3103(3), made identical amendments adding par. (3).

1984—Subsec. (e)(1). Pub. L. 98–353, §532(1), inserted "by the debtor" after "obtained".

Subsec. (e)(2). Pub. L. 98–353, §532(2), substituted "the requesting party did not know of such fraud until" for "knowledge of such fraud came to the requesting party".

Effective Date of 2005 Amendment

Amendments by Pub. L. 109–8 effective 180 days after Apr. 20, 2005, with amendments by sections 106(c), 213(11), 312(2), 314(b), and 707 of Pub. L. 109–8 not applicable with respect to cases commenced under this title before such effective date, except as otherwise provided, and amendment by section 330(d) of Pub. L. 109–8 applicable with respect to cases commenced under this title on or after Apr. 20, 2005, see section 1501 of Pub. L. 109–8, set out as a note under section 101 of this title.

Effective Date of 1994 Amendment

Amendment by Pub. L. 103–394 effective Oct. 22, 1994, and not applicable with respect to cases commenced under this title before Oct. 22, 1994, see section 702 of Pub. L. 103–394, set out as a note under section 101 of this title.

Effective Date of 1990 Amendment

Amendment by Pub. L. 101–647 effective Nov. 29, 1990, but not applicable with respect to cases commenced under this title before Nov. 29, 1990, see section 3104 of Pub. L. 101–647, set out as a note under section 523 of this title.

Amendment by Pub. L. 101–581 effective Nov. 15, 1990, but not applicable with respect to cases commenced under this title before Nov. 15, 1990, see section 4 of Pub. L. 101–581, set out as a note under section 523 of this title.

Pub. L. 101–508, title III, §3007(b)(2), Nov. 5, 1990, 104 Stat. 1388–29, provided that: "The amendment made by paragraph (1) [amending this section] shall not apply to any case under the provisions of title 11, United States Code, commenced before the date of the enactment of this Act [Nov. 5, 1990]."

Effective Date of 1984 Amendment

Amendment by Pub. L. 98–353 effective with respect to cases filed 90 days after July 10, 1984, see section 552(a) of Pub. L. 98–353, set out as a note under section 101 of this title.

§1329. Modification of plan after confirmation

(a) At any time after confirmation of the plan but before the completion of payments under such plan, the plan may be modified, upon request of the debtor, the trustee, or the holder of an allowed unsecured claim, to—

(1) increase or reduce the amount of payments on claims of a particular class provided for by the plan;

(2) extend or reduce the time for such payments;

(3) alter the amount of the distribution to a creditor whose claim is provided for by the plan to the extent necessary to take account of any payment of such claim other than under the plan; or

(4) reduce amounts to be paid under the plan by the actual amount expended by the debtor to purchase health insurance for the debtor (and for any dependent of the debtor if such dependent does not otherwise have health insurance coverage) if the debtor documents the cost of such insurance and demonstrates that—

(A) such expenses are reasonable and necessary;

(B)(i) if the debtor previously paid for health insurance, the amount is not materially larger than the cost the debtor previously paid or the cost necessary to maintain the lapsed policy; or

(ii) if the debtor did not have health insurance, the amount is not materially larger than the reasonable cost that would be incurred by a debtor who purchases health insurance, who has similar income, expenses, age, and health status, and who lives in the same geographical location with the same number of dependents who do not otherwise have health insurance coverage; and

(C) the amount is not otherwise allowed for purposes of determining disposable income under section 1325(b) of this title;

and upon request of any party in interest, files proof that a health insurance policy was purchased.

(b)(1) Sections 1322(a), 1322(b), and 1323(c) of this title and the requirements of section 1325(a) of this title apply to any modification under subsection (a) of this section.

(2) The plan as modified becomes the plan unless, after notice and a hearing, such modification is disapproved.

(c) A plan modified under this section may not provide for payments over a period that expires after the applicable commitment period under section 1325(b)(1)(B) after the time that the first payment under the original confirmed plan was due, unless the court, for cause, approves a longer period, but the court may not approve a period that expires after five years after such time.

(Pub. L. 95–598, Nov. 6, 1978, 92 Stat. 2651; Pub. L. 98–353, title III, §§319, 533, July 10, 1984, 98 Stat. 357, 389; Pub. L. 109–8, title I, §102(i), title III, §318(4), Apr. 20, 2005, 119 Stat. 34, 94.)

Historical and Revision Notes

senate report no. 95–989

At any time prior to the completion of payments under a confirmed plan, the plan may be modified, after notice and hearing, to change the amount of payments to creditors or a particular class of creditors and to extend or reduce the payment period. A modified plan may not contain any provision which could not be included in an original plan as prescribed by section 1322. A modified plan may not call for payments to be made beyond four years as measured from the date of the commencement of payments under the original plan.

Amendments

2005—Subsec. (a)(4). Pub. L. 109–8, §102(i), added par. (4).

Subsec. (c). Pub. L. 109–8, §318(4), substituted "the applicable commitment period under section 1325(b)(1)(B)" for "three years".

1984—Subsec. (a). Pub. L. 98–353, §§319, 533(1), (2), inserted "of the plan" after "confirmation", substituted "such plan" for "a plan", and inserted provisions respecting requests by the debtor, the trustee, or the holder of an allowed unsecured claim for modification.

Subsec. (a)(3). Pub. L. 98–353, §533(3), substituted "plan to" for "plan, to".

Effective Date of 2005 Amendment

Amendment by Pub. L. 109–8 effective 180 days after Apr. 20, 2005, and not applicable with respect to cases commenced under this title before such effective date, except as otherwise provided, see section 1501 of Pub. L. 109–8, set out as a note under section 101 of this title.

Effective Date of 1984 Amendment

Amendment by Pub. L. 98–353 effective with respect to cases filed 90 days after July 10, 1984, see section 552(a) of Pub. L. 98–353, set out as a note under section 101 of this title.

§1330. Revocation of an order of confirmation

(a) On request of a party in interest at any time within 180 days after the date of the entry of an order of confirmation under section 1325 of this title, and after notice and a hearing, the court may revoke such order if such order was procured by fraud.

(b) If the court revokes an order of confirmation under subsection (a) of this section, the court shall dispose of the case under section 1307 of this title, unless, within the time fixed by the court, the debtor proposes and the court confirms a modification of the plan under section 1329 of this title.

(Pub. L. 95–598, Nov. 6, 1978, 92 Stat. 2651.)

Historical and Revision Notes

legislative statements

Section 1331 of the House bill and Senate amendment is deleted in the House amendment.

Special tax provision: Section 1331 of title 11 of the House bill and the comparable provisions in sections 1322 and 1327(d) of the Senate amendment, pertaining to assessment and collection of taxes in wage earner plans, are deleted, and the governing rule is placed in section 505(c) of the House amendment. The provisions of both bills allowing assessment and collection of taxes after confirmation of the wage-earner plan are modified to allow assessment and collection after the court fixes the fact and amount of a tax liability, including administrative period taxes, regardless of whether this occurs before or after confirmation of the plan. The provision of the House bill limiting the collection of taxes to those assessed before one year after the filing of the petition is eliminated, thereby leaving the period of limitations on assessment of these nondischargeable tax liabilities the usual period provided by the Internal Revenue Code [Title 26].

senate report no. 95–989

The court may revoke an order of confirmation procured by fraud, after notice and hearing, on application of a party in interest filed within 180 days after the entry of the order. Thereafter, unless a modified plan is confirmed, the court is to convert or dismiss the chapter 13 case as provided in section 1307.

CHAPTER 15—ANCILLARY AND OTHER CROSS-BORDER CASES

Sec.
1501.
Purpose and scope of application.

SUBCHAPTER I—GENERAL PROVISIONS
1502.
Definitions.
1503.
International obligations of the United States.
1504.
Commencement of ancillary case.
1505.
Authorization to act in a foreign country.
1506.
Public policy exception.
1507.
Additional assistance.
1508.
Interpretation.

SUBCHAPTER II—ACCESS OF FOREIGN REPRESENTATIVES AND CREDITORS TO THE COURT
1509.
Right of direct access.
1510.
Limited jurisdiction.
1511.
Commencement of case under section 301 or 303.[1]
1512.
Participation of a foreign representative in a case under this title.
1513.
Access of foreign creditors to a case under this title.
1514.
Notification to foreign creditors concerning a case under this title.

SUBCHAPTER III—RECOGNITION OF A FOREIGN PROCEEDING AND RELIEF
1515.
Application for recognition.
1516.
Presumptions concerning recognition.
1517.
Order granting recognition.
1518.
Subsequent information.
1519.
Relief that may be granted upon filing petition for recognition.
1520.
Effects of recognition of a foreign main proceeding.
1521.
Relief that may be granted upon recognition.
1522.
Protection of creditors and other interested persons.
1523.
Actions to avoid acts detrimental to creditors.
1524.
Intervention by a foreign representative.

SUBCHAPTER IV—COOPERATION WITH FOREIGN COURTS AND FOREIGN REPRESENTATIVES
1525.
Cooperation and direct communication between the court and foreign courts or foreign representatives.
1526.

Cooperation and direct communication between the trustee and foreign courts or foreign representatives.
1527.
Forms of cooperation.

SUBCHAPTER V—CONCURRENT PROCEEDINGS
1528.
Commencement of a case under this title after recognition of a foreign main proceeding.
1529.
Coordination of a case under this title and a foreign proceeding.
1530.
Coordination of more than 1 foreign proceeding.
1531.
Presumption of insolvency based on recognition of a foreign main proceeding.
1532.
Rule of payment in concurrent proceedings.

Prior Provisions
A prior chapter 15, consisting of sections 1501 to 151326, related to a pilot program for a United States trustee system, prior to repeal by Pub. L. 99–554, title II, §231, Oct. 27, 1986, 100 Stat. 3103.

[1] So in original. Section catchline amended by Pub. L. 111–327 without corresponding amendment of chapter analysis.

§1501. Purpose and scope of application
(a) The purpose of this chapter is to incorporate the Model Law on Cross-Border Insolvency so as to provide effective mechanisms for dealing with cases of cross-border insolvency with the objectives of—
(1) cooperation between—
(A) courts of the United States, United States trustees, trustees, examiners, debtors, and debtors in possession; and
(B) the courts and other competent authorities of foreign countries involved in cross-border insolvency cases;

(2) greater legal certainty for trade and investment;
(3) fair and efficient administration of cross-border insolvencies that protects the interests of all creditors, and other interested entities, including the debtor;
(4) protection and maximization of the value of the debtor's assets; and
(5) facilitation of the rescue of financially troubled businesses, thereby protecting investment and preserving employment.

(b) This chapter applies where—
(1) assistance is sought in the United States by a foreign court or a foreign representative in connection with a foreign proceeding;
(2) assistance is sought in a foreign country in connection with a case under this title;
(3) a foreign proceeding and a case under this title with respect to the same debtor are pending concurrently; or
(4) creditors or other interested persons in a foreign country have an interest in requesting the commencement of, or participating in, a case or proceeding under this title.

(c) This chapter does not apply to—
(1) a proceeding concerning an entity, other than a foreign insurance company, identified by exclusion in section 109(b);
(2) an individual, or to an individual and such individual's spouse, who have debts within the limits specified in section 109(e) and who are citizens of the United States or aliens lawfully admitted for permanent residence in the United States; or
(3) an entity subject to a proceeding under the Securities Investor Protection Act of 1970, a stockbroker subject to subchapter III of chapter 7 of this title, or a commodity broker subject to subchapter IV of chapter 7 of this title.

(d) The court may not grant relief under this chapter with respect to any deposit, escrow, trust fund, or other security required or permitted under any applicable State insurance law or regulation for the benefit of claim holders in the United States.
(Added Pub. L. 109–8, title VIII, §801(a), Apr. 20, 2005, 119 Stat. 135.)

References in Text
The Securities Investor Protection Act of 1970, referred to in subsec. (c)(3), is Pub. L. 91–598, Dec. 30, 1970, 84 Stat. 1636, as amended, which is classified generally to chapter 2B–1 (§78aaa et seq.) of Title 15, Commerce and Trade. For complete classification of this Act to the Code, see section 78aaa of Title 15 and Tables.

Prior Provisions
A prior section 1501, Pub. L. 95–598, Nov. 6, 1978, 92 Stat. 2652, related to applicability of chapter which provided a pilot program for a United States trustee system, prior to repeal by Pub. L. 99–554, title II, §231, Oct. 27, 1986, 100 Stat. 3103.

Effective Date
Section effective 180 days after Apr. 20, 2005, and not applicable with respect to cases commenced under this title before such effective date, except as otherwise provided, see section 1501 of Pub. L. 109–8, set out as an Effective Date of 2005 Amendment note under section 101 of this title.

(6) "trustee" includes a trustee, a debtor in possession in a case under any chapter of this title, or a debtor under chapter 9 of this title;
(7) "recognition" means the entry of an order granting recognition of a foreign main proceeding or foreign nonmain proceeding under this chapter; and
(8) "within the territorial jurisdiction of the United States", when used with reference to property of a debtor, refers to tangible property located within the territory of the United States and intangible property deemed under applicable nonbankruptcy law to be located within that territory, including any property subject to attachment or garnishment that may properly be seized or garnished by an action in a Federal or State court in the United States.
(Added Pub. L. 109–8, title VIII, §801(a), Apr. 20, 2005, 119 Stat. 135.)

Effective Date
Section effective 180 days after Apr. 20, 2005, and not applicable with respect to cases commenced under this title before such effective date, except as otherwise provided, see section 1501 of Pub. L. 109–8, set out as an Effective Date of 2005 Amendment note under section 101 of this title.

§1503. International obligations of the United States
To the extent that this chapter conflicts with an obligation of the United States arising out of any treaty or other form of agreement to which it is a party with one or more other countries, the requirements of the treaty or agreement prevail.
(Added Pub. L. 109–8, title VIII, §801(a), Apr. 20, 2005, 119 Stat. 136.)

Effective Date
Section effective 180 days after Apr. 20, 2005, and not applicable with respect to cases commenced under this title before such effective date, except as otherwise provided, see section 1501 of Pub. L. 109–8, set out as an Effective Date of 2005 Amendment note under section 101 of this title.

§1504. Commencement of ancillary case
A case under this chapter is commenced by the filing of a petition for recognition of a foreign proceeding under section 1515.
(Added Pub. L. 109–8, title VIII, §801(a), Apr. 20, 2005, 119 Stat. 136.)

Effective Date
Section effective 180 days after Apr. 20, 2005, and not applicable with respect to cases commenced under this title before such effective date, except as otherwise provided, see section 1501 of Pub. L. 109–8, set out as an Effective Date of 2005 Amendment note under section 101 of this title.

§1505. Authorization to act in a foreign country
A trustee or another entity (including an examiner) may be authorized by the court to act in a foreign country on behalf of an estate created under section 541. An entity authorized to act under this section may act in any way permitted by the applicable foreign law.
(Added Pub. L. 109–8, title VIII, §801(a), Apr. 20, 2005, 119 Stat. 136.)

Effective Date
Section effective 180 days after Apr. 20, 2005, and not applicable with respect to cases commenced under this title before such effective date, except as otherwise provided, see section 1501 of Pub. L. 109–8, set out as an Effective Date of 2005 Amendment note under section 101 of this title.

§1506. Public policy exception
Nothing in this chapter prevents the court from refusing to take an action governed by this chapter if the action would be manifestly contrary to the public policy of the United States.
(Added Pub. L. 109–8, title VIII, §801(a), Apr. 20, 2005, 119 Stat. 136.)

Effective Date
Section effective 180 days after Apr. 20, 2005, and not applicable with respect to cases commenced under this title before such effective date, except as otherwise provided, see section 1501 of Pub. L. 109–8, set out as an Effective Date of 2005 Amendment note under section 101 of this title.

§1507. Additional assistance
(a) Subject to the specific limitations stated elsewhere in this chapter the court, if recognition is granted, may provide additional assistance to a foreign representative under this title or under other laws of the United States.
(b) In determining whether to provide additional assistance under this title or under other laws of the United States, the court shall consider whether such additional assistance, consistent with the principles of comity, will reasonably assure—
(1) just treatment of all holders of claims against or interests in the debtor's property;
(2) protection of claim holders in the United States against prejudice and inconvenience in the processing of claims in such foreign proceeding;
(3) prevention of preferential or fraudulent dispositions of property of the debtor;
(4) distribution of proceeds of the debtor's property substantially in accordance with the order prescribed by this title; and
(5) if appropriate, the provision of an opportunity for a fresh start for the individual that such foreign proceeding concerns.
(Added Pub. L. 109–8, title VIII, §801(a), Apr. 20, 2005, 119 Stat. 136.)

Effective Date
Section effective 180 days after Apr. 20, 2005, and not applicable with respect to cases commenced under this title before such effective date, except as otherwise provided, see section 1501 of Pub. L. 109–8, set out as an Effective Date of 2005 Amendment note under section 101 of this title.

§1508. Interpretation
In interpreting this chapter, the court shall consider its international origin, and the need to promote an application of this chapter that is consistent with the application of similar statutes adopted by foreign jurisdictions.
(Added Pub. L. 109–8, title VIII, §801(a), Apr. 20, 2005, 119 Stat. 137.)

Effective Date
Section effective 180 days after Apr. 20, 2005, and not applicable with respect to cases commenced under this title before such effective date, except as otherwise provided, see section 1501 of Pub. L. 109–8, set out as an Effective Date of 2005 Amendment note under section 101 of this title.

SUBCHAPTER I—GENERAL PROVISIONS

§1502. Definitions
For the purposes of this chapter, the term—
(1) "debtor" means an entity that is the subject of a foreign proceeding;
(2) "establishment" means any place of operations where the debtor carries out a nontransitory economic activity;
(3) "foreign court" means a judicial or other authority competent to control or supervise a foreign proceeding;
(4) "foreign main proceeding" means a foreign proceeding pending in the country where the debtor has the center of its main interests;
(5) "foreign nonmain proceeding" means a foreign proceeding, other than a foreign main proceeding, pending in a country where the debtor has an establishment;

SUBCHAPTER II—ACCESS OF FOREIGN REPRESENTATIVES AND CREDITORS TO THE COURT

§1509. Right of direct access
(a) A foreign representative may commence a case under section 1504 by filing directly with the court a petition for recognition of a foreign proceeding under section 1515.

(b) If the court grants recognition under section 1517, and subject to any limitations that the court may impose consistent with the policy of this chapter—

(1) the foreign representative has the capacity to sue and be sued in a court in the United States;

(2) the foreign representative may apply directly to a court in the United States for appropriate relief in that court; and

(3) a court in the United States shall grant comity or cooperation to the foreign representative.

(c) A request for comity or cooperation by a foreign representative in a court in the United States other than the court which granted recognition shall be accompanied by a certified copy of an order granting recognition under section 1517.

(d) If the court denies recognition under this chapter, the court may issue any appropriate order necessary to prevent the foreign representative from obtaining comity or cooperation from courts in the United States.

(e) Whether or not the court grants recognition, and subject to sections 306 and 1510, a foreign representative is subject to applicable nonbankruptcy law.

(f) Notwithstanding any other provision of this section, the failure of a foreign representative to commence a case or to obtain recognition under this chapter does not affect any right the foreign representative may have to sue in a court in the United States to collect or recover a claim which is the property of the debtor.

(Added Pub. L. 109–8, title VIII, §801(a), Apr. 20, 2005, 119 Stat. 137.)

Effective Date

Section effective 180 days after Apr. 20, 2005, and not applicable with respect to cases commenced under this title before such effective date, except as otherwise provided, see section 1501 of Pub. L. 109–8, set out as an Effective Date of 2005 Amendment note under section 101 of this title.

§1510. Limited jurisdiction

The sole fact that a foreign representative files a petition under section 1515 does not subject the foreign representative to the jurisdiction of any court in the United States for any other purpose.

(Added Pub. L. 109–8, title VIII, §801(a), Apr. 20, 2005, 119 Stat. 138.)

Effective Date

Section effective 180 days after Apr. 20, 2005, and not applicable with respect to cases commenced under this title before such effective date, except as otherwise provided, see section 1501 of Pub. L. 109–8, set out as an Effective Date of 2005 Amendment note under section 101 of this title.

§1511. Commencement of case under section 301, 302, or 303

(a) Upon recognition, a foreign representative may commence—

(1) an involuntary case under section 303; or

(2) a voluntary case under section 301 or 302, if the foreign proceeding is a foreign main proceeding.

(b) The petition commencing a case under subsection (a) must be accompanied by a certified copy of an order granting recognition. The court where the petition for recognition has been filed must be advised of the foreign representative's intent to commence a case under subsection (a) prior to such commencement.

(Added Pub. L. 109–8, title VIII, §801(a), Apr. 20, 2005, 119 Stat. 138; amended Pub. L. 111–327, §2(a)(45), Dec. 22, 2010, 124 Stat. 3562.)

Amendments

2010—Pub. L. 111–327 inserted ", 302," after "301" in section catchline.

Effective Date

Section effective 180 days after Apr. 20, 2005, and not applicable with respect to cases commenced under this title before such effective date, except as otherwise provided, see section 1501 of Pub. L. 109–8, set out as an Effective Date of 2005 Amendment note under section 101 of this title.

§1512. Participation of a foreign representative in a case under this title

Upon recognition of a foreign proceeding, the foreign representative in the recognized proceeding is entitled to participate as a party in interest in a case regarding the debtor under this title.

(Added Pub. L. 109–8, title VIII, §801(a), Apr. 20, 2005, 119 Stat. 138.)

Effective Date

Section effective 180 days after Apr. 20, 2005, and not applicable with respect to cases commenced under this title before such effective date, except as otherwise provided, see section 1501 of Pub. L. 109–8, set out as an Effective Date of 2005 Amendment note under section 101 of this title.

§1513. Access of foreign creditors to a case under this title

(a) Foreign creditors have the same rights regarding the commencement of, and participation in, a case under this title as domestic creditors.

(b)(1) Subsection (a) does not change or codify present law as to the priority of claims under section 507 or 726, except that the claim of a foreign creditor under those sections shall not be given a lower priority than that of general unsecured claims without priority solely because the holder of such claim is a foreign creditor.

(2)(A) Subsection (a) and paragraph (1) do not change or codify present law as to the allowability of foreign revenue claims or other foreign public law claims in a proceeding under this title.

(B) Allowance and priority as to a foreign tax claim or other foreign public law claim shall be governed by any applicable tax treaty of the United States, under the conditions and circumstances specified therein.

(Added Pub. L. 109–8, title VIII, §801(a), Apr. 20, 2005, 119 Stat. 138.)

Effective Date

Section effective 180 days after Apr. 20, 2005, and not applicable with respect to cases commenced under this title before such effective date, except as otherwise provided, see section 1501 of Pub. L. 109–8, set out as an Effective Date of 2005 Amendment note under section 101 of this title.

§1514. Notification to foreign creditors concerning a case under this title

(a) Whenever in a case under this title notice is to be given to creditors generally or to any class or category of creditors, such notice shall also be given to the known creditors generally, or to creditors in the notified class or category, that do not have addresses in the United States. The court may order that appropriate steps be taken with a view to notifying any creditor whose address is not yet known.

(b) Such notification to creditors with foreign addresses described in subsection (a) shall be given individually, unless the court considers that, under the circumstances, some other form of notification would be more appropriate. No letter or other formality is required.

(c) When a notification of commencement of a case is to be given to foreign creditors, such notification shall—

(1) indicate the time period for filing proofs of claim and specify the place for filing such proofs of claim;

(2) indicate whether secured creditors need to file proofs of claim; and

(3) contain any other information required to be included in such notification to creditors under this title and the orders of the court.

(d) Any rule of procedure or order of the court as to notice or the filing of a proof of claim shall provide such additional time to creditors with foreign addresses as is reasonable under the circumstances.

(Added Pub. L. 109–8, title VIII, §801(a), Apr. 20, 2005, 119 Stat. 138.)

Effective Date

Section effective 180 days after Apr. 20, 2005, and not applicable with respect to cases commenced under this title before such effective date, except as otherwise provided, see section 1501 of Pub. L. 109–8, set out as an Effective Date of 2005 Amendment note under section 101 of this title.

SUBCHAPTER III—RECOGNITION OF A FOREIGN PROCEEDING AND RELIEF

§1515. Application for recognition

(a) A foreign representative applies to the court for recognition of a foreign proceeding in which the foreign representative has been appointed by filing a petition for recognition.

(b) A petition for recognition shall be accompanied by—

(1) a certified copy of the decision commencing such foreign proceeding and appointing the foreign representative;

(2) a certificate from the foreign court affirming the existence of such foreign proceeding and of the appointment of the foreign representative; or

(3) in the absence of evidence referred to in paragraphs (1) and (2), any other evidence acceptable to the court of the existence of such foreign proceeding and of the appointment of the foreign representative.

(c) A petition for recognition shall also be accompanied by a statement identifying all foreign proceedings with respect to the debtor that are known to the foreign representative.

(d) The documents referred to in paragraphs (1) and (2) of subsection (b) shall be translated into English. The court may require a translation into English of additional documents.

(Added Pub. L. 109–8, title VIII, §801(a), Apr. 20, 2005, 119 Stat. 139.)

Effective Date

Section effective 180 days after Apr. 20, 2005, and not applicable with respect to cases commenced under this title before such effective date, except as otherwise provided, see section 1501 of Pub. L. 109–8, set out as an Effective Date of 2005 Amendment note under section 101 of this title.

§1516. Presumptions concerning recognition

(a) If the decision or certificate referred to in section 1515(b) indicates that the foreign proceeding is a foreign proceeding and that the person or body is a foreign representative, the court is entitled to so presume.

(b) The court is entitled to presume that documents submitted in support of the petition for recognition are authentic, whether or not they have been legalized.

(c) In the absence of evidence to the contrary, the debtor's registered office, or habitual residence in the case of an individual, is presumed to be the center of the debtor's main interests.

(Added Pub. L. 109–8, title VIII, §801(a), Apr. 20, 2005, 119 Stat. 139.)

Effective Date

Section effective 180 days after Apr. 20, 2005, and not applicable with respect to cases commenced under this title before such effective date, except as otherwise provided, see section 1501 of Pub. L. 109–8, set out as an Effective Date of 2005 Amendment note under section 101 of this title.

§1517. Order granting recognition

(a) Subject to section 1506, after notice and a hearing, an order recognizing a foreign proceeding shall be entered if—

(1) such foreign proceeding for which recognition is sought is a foreign main proceeding or foreign nonmain proceeding within the meaning of section 1502;

(2) the foreign representative applying for recognition is a person or body; and

(3) the petition meets the requirements of section 1515.

(b) Such foreign proceeding shall be recognized—

(1) as a foreign main proceeding if it is pending in the country where the debtor has the center of its main interests; or

(2) as a foreign nonmain proceeding if the debtor has an establishment within the meaning of section 1502 in the foreign country where the proceeding is pending.

(c) A petition for recognition of a foreign proceeding shall be decided upon at the earliest possible time. Entry of an order recognizing a foreign proceeding constitutes recognition under this chapter.

(d) The provisions of this subchapter do not prevent modification or termination of recognition if it is shown that the grounds for granting it were fully or partially lacking or have ceased to exist, but in considering such action the court shall give due weight to possible prejudice to parties that have relied upon the order granting recognition. A case under this chapter may be closed in the manner prescribed under section 350.

(Added Pub. L. 109–8, title VIII, §801(a), Apr. 20, 2005, 119 Stat. 139.)

Effective Date

Section effective 180 days after Apr. 20, 2005, and not applicable with respect to cases commenced under this title before such effective date, except as otherwise provided, see section 1501 of Pub. L. 109–8, set out as an Effective Date of 2005 Amendment note under section 101 of this title.

§1518. Subsequent information

From the time of filing the petition for recognition of a foreign proceeding, the foreign representative shall file with the court promptly a notice of change of status concerning—

(1) any substantial change in the status of such foreign proceeding or the status of the foreign representative's appointment; and

(2) any other foreign proceeding regarding the debtor that becomes known to the foreign representative.

(Added Pub. L. 109–8, title VIII, §801(a), Apr. 20, 2005, 119 Stat. 140.)

Effective Date

Section effective 180 days after Apr. 20, 2005, and not applicable with respect to cases commenced under this title before such effective date, except as otherwise provided, see section 1501 of Pub. L. 109–8, set out as an Effective Date of 2005 Amendment note under section 101 of this title.

§1519. Relief that may be granted upon filing petition for recognition

(a) From the time of filing a petition for recognition until the court rules on the petition, the court may, at the request of the foreign representative, where relief is urgently needed to protect the assets of the debtor or the interests of the creditors, grant relief of a provisional nature, including—

(1) staying execution against the debtor's assets;

(2) entrusting the administration or realization of all or part of the debtor's assets located in the United States to the foreign representative or another person

authorized by the court, including an examiner, in order to protect and preserve the value of assets that, by their nature or because of other circumstances, are perishable, susceptible to devaluation or otherwise in jeopardy; and

(3) any relief referred to in paragraph (3), (4), or (7) of section 1521(a).

(b) Unless extended under section 1521(a)(6), the relief granted under this section terminates when the petition for recognition is granted.

(c) It is a ground for denial of relief under this section that such relief would interfere with the administration of a foreign main proceeding.

(d) The court may not enjoin a police or regulatory act of a governmental unit, including a criminal action or proceeding, under this section.

(e) The standards, procedures, and limitations applicable to an injunction shall apply to relief under this section.

(f) The exercise of rights not subject to the stay arising under section 362(a) pursuant to paragraph (6), (7), (17), or (27) of section 362(b) or pursuant to section 362(o) shall not be stayed by any order of a court or administrative agency in any proceeding under this chapter.

(Added Pub. L. 109–8, title VIII, §801(a), Apr. 20, 2005, 119 Stat. 140; amended Pub. L. 111–327, §2(a)(46), Dec. 22, 2010, 124 Stat. 3562.)

Amendments

2010—Subsec. (f). Pub. L. 111–327 substituted "362(o)" for "362(n)".

Effective Date

Section effective 180 days after Apr. 20, 2005, and not applicable with respect to cases commenced under this title before such effective date, except as otherwise provided, see section 1501 of Pub. L. 109–8, set out as an Effective Date of 2005 Amendment note under section 101 of this title.

§1520. Effects of recognition of a foreign main proceeding

(a) Upon recognition of a foreign proceeding that is a foreign main proceeding—

(1) sections 361 and 362 apply with respect to the debtor and the property of the debtor that is within the territorial jurisdiction of the United States;

(2) sections 363, 549, and 552 apply to a transfer of an interest of the debtor in property that is within the territorial jurisdiction of the United States to the same extent that the sections would apply to property of an estate;

(3) unless the court orders otherwise, the foreign representative may operate the debtor's business and may exercise the rights and powers of a trustee under and to the extent provided by sections 363 and 552; and

(4) section 552 applies to property of the debtor that is within the territorial jurisdiction of the United States.

(b) Subsection (a) does not affect the right to commence an individual action or proceeding in a foreign country to the extent necessary to preserve a claim against the debtor.

(c) Subsection (a) does not affect the right of a foreign representative or an entity to file a petition commencing a case under this title or the right of any party to file claims or take other proper actions in such a case.

(Added Pub. L. 109–8, title VIII, §801(a), Apr. 20, 2005, 119 Stat. 141.)

Effective Date

Section effective 180 days after Apr. 20, 2005, and not applicable with respect to cases commenced under this title before such effective date, except as otherwise provided, see section 1501 of Pub. L. 109–8, set out as an Effective Date of 2005 Amendment note under section 101 of this title.

§1521. Relief that may be granted upon recognition

(a) Upon recognition of a foreign proceeding, whether main or nonmain, where necessary to effectuate the purpose of this chapter and to protect the assets of the debtor or the interests of the creditors, the court may, at the request of the foreign representative, grant any appropriate relief, including—

(1) staying the commencement or continuation of an individual action or proceeding concerning the debtor's assets, rights, obligations or liabilities to the extent they have not been stayed under section 1520(a);

(2) staying execution against the debtor's assets to the extent it has not been stayed under section 1520(a);

(3) suspending the right to transfer, encumber or otherwise dispose of any assets of the debtor to the extent this right has not been suspended under section 1520(a);

(4) providing for the examination of witnesses, the taking of evidence or the delivery of information concerning the debtor's assets, affairs, rights, obligations or liabilities;

(5) entrusting the administration or realization of all or part of the debtor's assets within the territorial jurisdiction of the United States to the foreign representative or another person, including an examiner, authorized by the court;

(6) extending relief granted under section 1519(a); and

(7) granting any additional relief that may be available to a trustee, except for relief available under sections 522, 544, 545, 547, 548, 550, and 724(a).

(b) Upon recognition of a foreign proceeding, whether main or nonmain, the court may, at the request of the foreign representative, entrust the distribution of all or part of the debtor's assets located in the United States to the foreign representative or another person, including an examiner, authorized by the court, provided that the court is satisfied that the interests of creditors in the United States are sufficiently protected.

(c) In granting relief under this section to a representative of a foreign nonmain proceeding, the court must be satisfied that the relief relates to assets that, under the law of the United States, should be administered in the foreign nonmain proceeding or concerns information required in that proceeding.

(d) The court may not enjoin a police or regulatory act of a governmental unit, including a criminal action or proceeding, under this section.

(e) The standards, procedures, and limitations applicable to an injunction shall apply to relief under paragraphs (1), (2), (3), and (6) of subsection (a).

(f) The exercise of rights not subject to the stay arising under section 362(a) pursuant to paragraph (6), (7), (17), or (27) of section 362(b) or pursuant to section 362(o) shall not be stayed by any order of a court or administrative agency in any proceeding under this chapter.

(Added Pub. L. 109–8, title VIII, §801(a), Apr. 20, 2005, 119 Stat. 141; amended Pub. L. 111–327, §2(a)(47), Dec. 22, 2010, 124 Stat. 3562.)

Amendments

2010—Subsec. (f). Pub. L. 111–327 substituted "362(o)" for "362(n)".

Effective Date

Section effective 180 days after Apr. 20, 2005, and not applicable with respect to cases commenced under this title before such effective date, except as otherwise provided, see section 1501 of Pub. L. 109–8, set out as an Effective Date of 2005 Amendment note under section 101 of this title.

§1522. Protection of creditors and other interested persons

(a) The court may grant relief under section 1519 or 1521, or may modify or terminate relief under subsection (c), only if the interests of the creditors and other interested entities, including the debtor, are sufficiently protected.

(b) The court may subject relief granted under section 1519 or 1521, or the operation of the debtor's business under section 1520(a)(3), to conditions it considers appropriate, including the giving of security or the filing of a bond.

(c) The court may, at the request of the foreign representative or an entity affected by relief granted under section 1519 or 1521, or at its own motion, modify or terminate such relief.

(d) Section 1104(d) shall apply to the appointment of an examiner under this chapter. Any examiner shall comply with the qualification requirements imposed on a trustee by section 322.

(Added Pub. L. 109–8, title VIII, §801(a), Apr. 20, 2005, 119 Stat. 142.)

Effective Date

Section effective 180 days after Apr. 20, 2005, and not applicable with respect to cases commenced under this title before such effective date, except as otherwise provided, see section 1501 of Pub. L. 109–8, set out as an Effective Date of 2005 Amendment note under section 101 of this title.

§1523. Actions to avoid acts detrimental to creditors

(a) Upon recognition of a foreign proceeding, the foreign representative has standing in a case concerning the debtor pending under another chapter of this title to initiate actions under sections 522, 544, 545, 547, 548, 550, 553, and 724(a).

(b) When a foreign proceeding is a foreign nonmain proceeding, the court must be satisfied that an action under subsection (a) relates to assets that, under United States law, should be administered in the foreign nonmain proceeding.

(Added Pub. L. 109–8, title VIII, §801(a), Apr. 20, 2005, 119 Stat. 142.)

Effective Date

Section effective 180 days after Apr. 20, 2005, and not applicable with respect to cases commenced under this title before such effective date, except as otherwise provided, see section 1501 of Pub. L. 109–8, set out as an Effective Date of 2005 Amendment note under section 101 of this title.

§1524. Intervention by a foreign representative

Upon recognition of a foreign proceeding, the foreign representative may intervene in any proceedings in a State or Federal court in the United States in which the debtor is a party.

(Added Pub. L. 109–8, title VIII, §801(a), Apr. 20, 2005, 119 Stat. 142.)

Effective Date

Section effective 180 days after Apr. 20, 2005, and not applicable with respect to cases commenced under this title before such effective date, except as otherwise provided, see section 1501 of Pub. L. 109–8, set out as an Effective Date of 2005 Amendment note under section 101 of this title.

SUBCHAPTER IV—COOPERATION WITH FOREIGN COURTS AND FOREIGN REPRESENTATIVES

§1525. Cooperation and direct communication between the court and foreign courts or foreign representatives

(a) Consistent with section 1501, the court shall cooperate to the maximum extent possible with a foreign court or a foreign representative, either directly or through the trustee.

(b) The court is entitled to communicate directly with, or to request information or assistance directly from, a foreign court or a foreign representative, subject to the rights of a party in interest to notice and participation.

(Added Pub. L. 109–8, title VIII, §801(a), Apr. 20, 2005, 119 Stat. 143.)

Effective Date

Section effective 180 days after Apr. 20, 2005, and not applicable with respect to cases commenced under this title before such effective date, except as otherwise provided, see section 1501 of Pub. L. 109–8, set out as an Effective Date of 2005 Amendment note under section 101 of this title.

§1526. Cooperation and direct communication between the trustee and foreign courts or foreign representatives

(a) Consistent with section 1501, the trustee or other person, including an examiner, authorized by the court, shall, subject to the supervision of the court, cooperate to the maximum extent possible with a foreign court or a foreign representative.

(b) The trustee or other person, including an examiner, authorized by the court is entitled, subject to the supervision of the court, to communicate directly with a foreign court or a foreign representative.

(Added Pub. L. 109–8, title VIII, §801(a), Apr. 20, 2005, 119 Stat. 143.)

Effective Date

Section effective 180 days after Apr. 20, 2005, and not applicable with respect to cases commenced under this title before such effective date, except as otherwise provided, see section 1501 of Pub. L. 109–8, set out as an Effective Date of 2005 Amendment note under section 101 of this title.

§1527. Forms of cooperation

Cooperation referred to in sections 1525 and 1526 may be implemented by any appropriate means, including—

(1) appointment of a person or body, including an examiner, to act at the direction of the court;

(2) communication of information by any means considered appropriate by the court;

(3) coordination of the administration and supervision of the debtor's assets and affairs;

(4) approval or implementation of agreements concerning the coordination of proceedings; and

(5) coordination of concurrent proceedings regarding the same debtor.

(Added Pub. L. 109–8, title VIII, §801(a), Apr. 20, 2005, 119 Stat. 143.)

Effective Date

Section effective 180 days after Apr. 20, 2005, and not applicable with respect to cases commenced under this title before such effective date, except as otherwise provided, see section 1501 of Pub. L. 109–8, set out as an Effective Date of 2005 Amendment note under section 101 of this title.

SUBCHAPTER V—CONCURRENT PROCEEDINGS

§1528. Commencement of a case under this title after recognition of a foreign main proceeding

After recognition of a foreign main proceeding, a case under another chapter of this title may be commenced only if the debtor has assets in the United States. The effects of such case shall be restricted to the assets of the debtor that are within the territorial jurisdiction of the United States and, to the extent necessary to implement cooperation and coordination under sections 1525, 1526, and 1527, to other assets of the debtor that are within the jurisdiction of the court under sections 541(a) of this title, and 1334(e) of title 28, to the extent that such other assets are not subject to the jurisdiction and control of a foreign proceeding that has been recognized under this chapter.

(Added Pub. L. 109–8, title VIII, §801(a), Apr. 20, 2005, 119 Stat. 143.)

Effective Date

Section effective 180 days after Apr. 20, 2005, and not applicable with respect to cases commenced under this title before such effective date, except as otherwise provided, see section 1501 of Pub. L. 109–8, set out as an Effective Date of 2005 Amendment note under section 101 of this title.

§1529. Coordination of a case under this title and a foreign proceeding

If a foreign proceeding and a case under another chapter of this title are pending concurrently regarding the same debtor, the court shall seek cooperation and coordination under sections 1525, 1526, and 1527, and the following shall apply:

(1) If the case in the United States is pending at the time the petition for recognition of such foreign proceeding is filed—

(A) any relief granted under section 1519 or 1521 must be consistent with the relief granted in the case in the United States; and

(B) section 1520 does not apply even if such foreign proceeding is recognized as a foreign main proceeding.

(2) If a case in the United States under this title commences after recognition, or after the date of the filing of the petition for recognition, of such foreign proceeding—

(A) any relief in effect under section 1519 or 1521 shall be reviewed by the court and shall be modified or terminated if inconsistent with the case in the United States; and

(B) if such foreign proceeding is a foreign main proceeding, the stay and suspension referred to in section 1520(a) shall be modified or terminated if inconsistent with the relief granted in the case in the United States.

(3) In granting, extending, or modifying relief granted to a representative of a foreign nonmain proceeding, the court must be satisfied that the relief relates to assets that, under the laws of the United States, should be administered in the foreign nonmain proceeding or concerns information required in that proceeding.

(4) In achieving cooperation and coordination under sections 1528 and 1529, the court may grant any of the relief authorized under section 305.

(Added Pub. L. 109–8, title VIII, §801(a), Apr. 20, 2005, 119 Stat. 144; amended Pub. L. 111–327, §2(a)(48), Dec. 22, 2010, 124 Stat. 3562.)

Amendments

2010—Par. (1). Pub. L. 111–327, which directed amendment of par. (1) by inserting "is" after "States", was executed by making the insertion only in introductory provisions to reflect the probable intent of Congress.

Effective Date

Section effective 180 days after Apr. 20, 2005, and not applicable with respect to cases commenced under this title before such effective date, except as otherwise provided, see section 1501 of Pub. L. 109–8, set out as an Effective Date of 2005 Amendment note under section 101 of this title.

§1530. Coordination of more than 1 foreign proceeding

In matters referred to in section 1501, with respect to more than 1 foreign proceeding regarding the debtor, the court shall seek cooperation and coordination under sections 1525, 1526, and 1527, and the following shall apply:

(1) Any relief granted under section 1519 or 1521 to a representative of a foreign nonmain proceeding after recognition of a foreign main proceeding must be consistent with the foreign main proceeding.

(2) If a foreign main proceeding is recognized after recognition, or after the filing of a petition for recognition, of a foreign nonmain proceeding, any relief in effect under section 1519 or 1521 shall be reviewed by the court and shall be modified or terminated if inconsistent with the foreign main proceeding.

(3) If, after recognition of a foreign nonmain proceeding, another foreign nonmain proceeding is recognized, the court shall grant, modify, or terminate relief for the purpose of facilitating coordination of the proceedings.

(Added Pub. L. 109–8, title VIII, §801(a), Apr. 20, 2005, 119 Stat. 144.)

Effective Date

Section effective 180 days after Apr. 20, 2005, and not applicable with respect to cases commenced under this title before such effective date, except as otherwise provided, see section 1501 of Pub. L. 109–8, set out as an Effective Date of 2005 Amendment note under section 101 of this title.

§1531. Presumption of insolvency based on recognition of a foreign main proceeding

In the absence of evidence to the contrary, recognition of a foreign main proceeding is, for the purpose of commencing a proceeding under section 303, proof that the debtor is generally not paying its debts as such debts become due.

(Added Pub. L. 109–8, title VIII, §801(a), Apr. 20, 2005, 119 Stat. 144.)

Effective Date

Section effective 180 days after Apr. 20, 2005, and not applicable with respect to cases commenced under this title before such effective date, except as otherwise provided, see section 1501 of Pub. L. 109–8, set out as an Effective Date of 2005 Amendment note under section 101 of this title.

§1532. Rule of payment in concurrent proceedings

Without prejudice to secured claims or rights in rem, a creditor who has received payment with respect to its claim in a foreign proceeding pursuant to a law relating to insolvency may not receive a payment for the same claim in a case under any other chapter of this title regarding the debtor, so long as the payment to other creditors of the same class is proportionately less than the payment the creditor has already received.

(Added Pub. L. 109–8, title VIII, §801(a), Apr. 20, 2005, 119 Stat. 145.)

Prior Provisions

Sections 15101 to 151326 of prior chapter 15 were repealed by Pub. L. 99–554, title II, §231, Oct. 27, 1986, 100 Stat. 3103.

Section 15101, Pub. L. 95–598, Nov. 6, 1978, 92 Stat. 2652, related to definitions.

Section 15102, Pub. L. 95–598, Nov. 6, 1978, 92 Stat. 2652, related to a rule of construction.

Section 15103, Pub. L. 95–598, Nov. 6, 1978, 92 Stat. 2652; Pub. L. 98–353, title III, §§311(b)(3), 318(b), July 10, 1984, 98 Stat. 355, 357, related to applicability of subchapters and sections.

Section 15303, Pub. L. 95–598, Nov. 6, 1978, 92 Stat. 2653, related to involuntary cases.

Section 15321, Pub. L. 95–598, Nov. 6, 1978, 92 Stat. 2653, related to eligibility to serve as trustee.

Section 15322, Pub. L. 95–598, Nov. 6, 1978, 92 Stat. 2653, related to qualification of trustee.

Section 15324, Pub. L. 95–598, Nov. 6, 1978, 92 Stat. 2653, related to removal of trustee or examiner.

Section 15326, Pub. L. 95–598, Nov. 6, 1978, 92 Stat. 2653, related to limitation on compensation of trustee.

Section 15330, Pub. L. 95–598, Nov. 6, 1978, 92 Stat. 2653, related to compensation of officers.

Section 15343, Pub. L. 95–598, Nov. 6, 1978, 92 Stat. 2653, related to examination of debtor.

Section 15345, Pub. L. 95–598, Nov. 6, 1978, 92 Stat. 2654; Pub. L. 97–258, §3(c), Sept. 13, 1982, 96 Stat. 1064, related to money of estates.

Section 15701, Pub. L. 95–598, Nov. 6, 1978, 92 Stat. 2654, related to interim trustee.

Section 15703, Pub. L. 95–598, Nov. 6, 1978, 92 Stat. 2654, related to successor trustee.

Section 15704, Pub. L. 95–598, Nov. 6, 1978, 92 Stat. 2655, related to duties of trustee.

Section 15727, Pub. L. 95–598, Nov. 6, 1978, 92 Stat. 2655, related to discharge.

Section 151102, Pub. L. 95–598, Nov. 6, 1978, 92 Stat. 2655, related to creditors' and equity security holders' committees.

Section 151104, Pub. L. 95–598, Nov. 6, 1978, 92 Stat. 2655, related to appointment of trustee or examiner.

Section 151105, Pub. L. 95–598, Nov. 6, 1978, 92 Stat. 2656, related to termination of trustee's appointment.

Section 151163, Pub. L. 95–598, Nov. 6, 1978, 92 Stat. 2656, related to appointment of trustee.

Section 151302, Pub. L. 95–598, Nov. 6, 1978, 92 Stat. 2656; Pub. L. 98–353, title III, §§311(b)(4), 534, July 10, 1984, 98 Stat. 355, 390, related to trustees.

Section 151326, Pub. L. 95–598, Nov. 6, 1978, 92 Stat. 2657, related to payments.

Effective date and applicability of repeal by Pub. L. 99–554 dependent upon the judicial district involved, see section 302(d), (e) of Pub. L. 99–554, set out in an Effective Date of 1986 Amendment; Transition and Administrative Provisions note under section 581 of Title 28, Judiciary and Judicial Procedure.

Pub. L. 95–598, title IV, §408(c), Nov. 6, 1978, 92 Stat. 2687, as amended by Pub. L. 98–166, title II, §200, Nov. 28, 1983, 97 Stat. 1081; Pub. L. 98–353, title III, §323, July 10, 1984, 98 Stat. 358; Pub. L. 99–429, Sept. 30, 1986, 100 Stat. 985; Pub. L. 99–500, §101(b) [title II, §200], Oct. 18, 1986, 100 Stat. 1783–39, 1783–45, and Pub. L. 99–591, §101(b) [title II, §200], Oct. 30, 1986, 100 Stat. 3341–39, 3341–45; Pub. L. 99–554, title III, §307(a), Oct. 27, 1986, 100 Stat. 3125, provided for the repeal of prior chapter 15 at a prospective date, prior to repeal by Pub. L. 99–554, title III, §307(b), Oct. 27, 1986, 100 Stat. 3125.

Effective Date

Section effective 180 days after Apr. 20, 2005, and not applicable with respect to cases commenced under this title before such effective date, except as otherwise provided, see section 1501 of Pub. L. 109–8, set out as an Effective Date of 2005 Amendment note under section 101 of this title.